1

Black Baseball, 1858–1900

ALSO BY JAMES E. BRUNSON III

The Early Image of Black Baseball: Race and Representation in the Popular Press, 1871–1890 (McFarland, 2009)

Black Baseball, 1858–1900

*A Comprehensive Record
of the Teams, Players,
Managers, Owners and Umpires*

JAMES E. BRUNSON III

Foreword by John Thorn

VOLUME 1:
Foreword; Preface; Introduction;
Black Baseball Subcultures (Essay);
Team Profiles; Club Rosters; Team Contacts

McFarland & Company, Inc., Publishers
Jefferson, North Carolina

1

LIBRARY OF CONGRESS CATALOGUING-IN-PUBLICATION DATA

Names: Brunson, James E. (James Edward), 1954– author.
Title: Black Baseball, 1858–1900 : A Comprehensive Record of the Teams,
Players, Managers, Owners and Umpires / James E. Brunson III ; Foreword by John Thorn.
Description: Jefferson, North Carolina : McFarland & Company, Inc.,
Publishers, 2019 | Includes bibliographical references and index.
Contents: Volume 1. Introduction: The Scribbling Class — "They Covered
Themselves in Glory": The Lost Baseball World of the New Negro (Essay) —
Team Profiles, 1858/1900 — Club Rosters, 1858/1900 — Directory:
Managers, Promoters, and Other Contacts, 1867/1900 — Volume 2: Brothers
and Brotherhood: Black Baseball's Family Networks (Essay) — Empire and
Pastime: The Objectification of Black Baseball (Essay) — Player Register,
A/L — Volume 3: Player Register, M/Z — A Matter of Ability, and Not
Color: Umpires and Team Contacts (Essay) — Black Umpires: A Chronology of
Games, 1858/1900 — The Politics of Performance: Music, Minstrelsy and Black Baseball (Essay).
Identifiers: LCCN 2018032704 | ISBN 9780786494170 (paperback : acid free paper) ∞
Subjects: LCSH: Baseball—United States—History—19th century. | Negro
leagues—History—19th century. | African American baseball
players—Biography. | African American baseball team owners—Biography. |
African American baseball umpires—Biography. | African American baseball
managers—Biography. | Baseball—Records—United States. | Discrimination
in sports—United States—History.
Classification: LCC GV863.A1 B7848 2019 | DDC 796.35709034—dc23
LC record available at https://lccn.loc.gov/2018032704

BRITISH LIBRARY CATALOGUING DATA ARE AVAILABLE

ISBN (print) 978-0-7864-9417-0
ISBN (ebook) 978-1-4766-1658-2

Front cover illustration by James E. Brunson III

Printed in the United States of America

*McFarland & Company, Inc., Publishers
Box 611, Jefferson, North Carolina 28640
www.mcfarlandpub.com*

To my wife, Kathleen;
my daughters, Takarra and Tamerit;
my mother, Lucille Brunson;
and the rest of my family for their patience and love

Acknowledgments

Many people helped in the making of this work. Willard Draper, as usual, listened with care and shared his thoughts. Special love and thanks to my wife Kathleen, and her continued patience and support.

The NINE and Jerry Malloy Conference remain supportive. I am thankful to John Thorn, Larry Gerlach, Trey Strecker, Geri Strecker, Larry Lester, Dick Clark, Lisa Doris Alexander, Ted Knorr, Todd Peterson, Rebecca Alpert, and Leslie Heaphy who have supported my efforts.

Research for the book has been conducted over the past 25 years and took me to all parts of the country. By the mid-2000s, electronic technology began to play a crucial role even though I have been mindful that many old newspapers recently digitized have corrupted over time have limitations. I still love the stale aroma of old libraries and printed materials. I want to thank the following institutions: Northern Illinois University, University of Texas-Austin, University of Chicago, University of Illinois at Champaign-Urbana, University of Illinois-Springfield, University of Memphis, Chicago History Museum (formerly the Chicago Historical Society), University of Maryland at College Park, University of California-Berkeley, Emory University, Du Sable Museum (Chicago), Newark Public Library, Tulane University, Library of Congress, the St. Louis Public Library, and a host of other libraries and historical societies.

Table of Contents

Foreword
by John Thorn

A feature film, titled *42*, about Jackie Robinson's breaking of Major League Baseball's color barrier in 1947, enjoyed much success in 2013. The screenwriters got the story right, largely. However, a film will take dramatic license that the written word may not. Like the newsman in the great western picture *The Man Who Shot Liberty Valance*, the director of *42* must say, "This is baseball, folks. When the legend becomes fact, print the legend."

To a greater extent than Hollywood, a historian is obliged to follow the trail of fact. It diminishes Rickey and Robinson not one bit to think about all those black players of long ago who built the bridge, as my friend Buck O'Neil said, that Jackie Robinson walked across. James Brunson knows that. The stars of the Negro Leagues are now ensconced in Baseball's Hall of Fame, but the bridge to Cooperstown was built by men who barbered and bootblacked, waited table and laundred linens, men who played baseball whenever they could.

Even in its cradle, baseball was bound up with the issue of inclusion and exclusion—whom do *we*, the entrenched class, permit to play alongside *us*? In New York City around 1840 there were those who thought the newly codified game of baseball should model cricket—as a diversion for "gentlemen," those with sufficient money and thus leisure to play an afternoon's game of ball.

Clubs of working-class origin followed soon enough, to the dismay of the white-collar crowd. A largely Irish club, the Magnolia, formed in 1843; a more celebrated and long-lived one, the Atlantic, was created in Brooklyn in 1855. The first African American clubs, three in number, were thought to have been from Brooklyn as well, beginning in 1859: the Unknowns, the Monitors, and the Uniques of Williamsburgh were in the field that season, but recently a reference in the press turned up to a St. John's "colored club" in Newark, New Jersey, going back to 1855.

In truth, young people of both colors and genders had played a game they called baseball long before men from New York took to organizing clubs and restricting membership. African Americans had played baseball near Madison Square in the 1840s, not far from the grounds of the New York and Knickerbocker clubs before they relocated to Hoboken's Elysian Fields.

Researchers had found references to ball play by antebellum slaves in the South, but no evidence was put forth that the game they played was baseball as we might understand it—a game that went by that name, or one that bore the central feature of bases run in the round. (In Massachusetts well into the 1850s, for example, the names "base ball" and "round ball" were used interchangeably to describe the same game.) Frederick Douglass, Sr., wrote in his autobiography, published in 1845, that at holiday time "by far the larger part [of slave communities] engaged in such sports and merriments as ball playing, wrestling, running foot races, fiddling, dancing, and drinking whiskey: and this latter mode of spending the time was by far the most agreeable to the feelings of our masters." But in a Kingston, New York, newspaper of August 19, 1881, an elderly barber recalled that in 1820 or so—seven years before the "peculiar institution" was abolished in New York State—he and his fellow slaves had played baseball.

> We used to have a great deal better time than that you do now," said Mr. [Henry] Rosecranse, born in 1804. "We didn't have a big city with lamps and curb stones and paved walks, and had to go round through the mud, but we had more holidays. There was the Pinkster holiday, the Great Holiday for the colored men. They used to meet at Black Horse Tavern … and shoot for turkeys. Then the colored men raced horses on Peter Sharpe's lane…. After the races they used to play ball for egg nog.

The reporter asked, "Was it base ball as now played?" "Something like it," came the reply, "only the ball wasn't near so hard, and we used to have much more fun playing."

We do not have an unbroken record of blacks playing ball into the 1860s, but in the years following Emancipation black teams began not only to play against white ones but also to seek a level of acceptance in the larger society. Philadelphia's Pythian Base Ball Club, a formidable African American aggregation of the 1860s, tried to gain admission to the all-white National Association of Base Ball Players, the regulatory and rulemaking body for all first-class clubs. *The Ball Players' Chronicle*, a sporting weekly, noted, however, that the Nominating Committee in 1867 recommended the exclusion of not only the Pythians but any other club that included even one African American player.

Reconstruction after the defeat of the Confederacy was seen by many among the upper-class as a time for healing the nation's wounds, and matters involving race were to be approached with delicacy. In seeking to keep out of the convention the discussion of any subject that might be seen to have a political bearing, they had drawn the game's first overt color line. The committee further proclaimed, "If colored clubs were admitted there would be in all probability some division of feeling, whereas, by excluding them no injury could result to anyone."

In 1870 the *New York Clipper*, another sporting weekly, made bold in declaring "that the colored clubs of New York and Philadelphia at once take measures to organize a National Association of their own." In this remark one may detect the general direction for black baseball in all the years up to Jackie Robinson's debut with the Brooklyn Dodgers; yet before blacks set about forming a league of their own, there were notable forays into the mainstream of America's game.

During the early professional period that, in the 1870s, produced the first leagues, dozens of black ballplayers sought to earn a living by playing ball. Several pioneers merit mention here, among them William Edward White, born of a Georgia slave and her white master, enrolled at Brown University and played on its celebrated baseball club. On June 21, 1879, the Providence Grays, a National League club at that time, needed a replacement for the injured first baseman Joe Start. In those less formal days, before the advent of farm clubs, the Grays invited White to play. He got a hit, scored a run, and played flawlessly in the field as Providence defeated Cleveland, 5–3. White returned to the ball field for Brown in 1880 but never played for Providence again.

Until 2004, when a study revealed White's historic role as the first African American major leaguer, nearly all fans believed that the man who had earned that distinction was Jackie Robinson, in 1947. Only a handful of history buffs knew that two brothers from Oberlin College, the Walkers, had preceded Jackie by playing with the Toledo Blues in 1884. William White was the first, but the Walker story resonates more strongly with us today.

After starring in baseball with Oberlin College's inaugural nine in 1881, Moses Fleetwood Walker was invited to play for the strong semiprofessional White Sewing Machine club, based in Cleveland. The visiting Whites ran into a problem before a scheduled game with the Eclipse club in Louisville, which would enter the major-league American Association as a charter member the following spring. As the *Louisville Courier-Journal* reported on August 22, 1881, "Players of the Eclipse Club objected to Walker playing on account of his color. In vain the Clevelands protested that he was their regular catcher, and that his withdrawal would weaken the nine." The White Sewing Machine manager held Walker out, but when his replacement catcher bruised his hand and refused to come out for the second inning, the crowd began to call for the black player to go behind the bat. Walker was "disinclined to do so, after the general ill-treatment he had received; but as the game seemed to be in danger of coming to an end, he consented, and started in the catcher's stand. Louisville's players walked off the field."

In 1883, Walker helped the Toldeo Blue Stockings win the Northwestern League championship but again had a run-in with the opposition because his race. When Toledo moved up to the big leagues in 1884, joining the American Association, Walker played in 42 games, batting a respectable .263, and was joined briefly by his brother Weldy. He was released near the end of the season after suffering a broken shoulder, however, and it would be the last time a black player took the field in the major leagues until 1947. Fleet Walker nevertheless played in integrated leagues each year from 1883 through 1889, seven consecutive seasons. Although the public liked him, he continued to suffer many indignities at the hands of opponents and teammates alike.

The light-skinned Frank Grant, described as a "Spaniard" in the *Buffalo Express* in 1887, had been a star in the Eastern League one year before joining Buffalo. His reward was to come in for unceasing attack. Ned Williamson, second baseman of the Chicago White Stockings, told *Sporting Life*:

> The Buffalos … had a Negro for second base. He was a few lines blacker than a raven, but he was one of the best players…. The players of the opposing teams made it their special business in life to "spike" this brunette Buffalo. They would tarry at second when they might have easily made third, just to toy with the sensitive shins of this second baseman. The poor man played in two games out of five perhaps; the rest of the time he was on crutches. To give the frequent spiking of the darkey an appearance of accident the "feet first" slide was practiced. The negro got wooden armor for his legs and went into the field with the appearance of a man wearing nail kegs for stockings.

After leaving the Buffalo club in 1889, Grant played for many teams, though longest and most famously for the Cuban Giants. He died on May 27, 1937, with no one in baseball knowing that for decades since his playing days he had still been alive.

And yet when Jackie Robinson made his spectacular International League debut on April 19, 1946, getting four hits in Montreal's 14–1 rout of Jersey City, the *New York Times* story concluded thus: "There have been other Negro players in the International League. [Hall of Fame historian] Ernie Lanigan supplied the information that a Frank Grant played at second base for Buffalo and a Moses Walker caught for Newark in a game between those two teams on April 30, 1887."

And there were others, countless others—before and after Grant and Walker and White—ho played the game well enough to get paid for it yet have remained invisible men. All praise to James Brunson, who revives them for a resounding hail and farewell.

Preface

Before turning to the world of early black baseball, I should comment on my history with that subject and, more briefly, on the purpose and scope of this book. I am trained academically as a studio artist and art historian. More than thirty years ago, I began researching images to create a series of paintings on what is sometimes described as the first black cultural renaissance in the United States, which ran from roughly 1888 to 1917. My fascination had to do with how emancipation and the post–Civil War era fashioned black lives. I photocopied and collected nineteenth-century texts and images that said something important about the period. They offered insight not only into the styles, hopes, and aspirations of black people then but into the ways they constructed and addressed social realities.

It wasn't long into my research, however, that I realized that the full story was not to be found in the items I'd examined. I began to notice that important facets of culture were unrepresented. What about music and sports imagery, for instance? My preconceptions about what culture was, or at least what kinds of culture it was important to track, had become an obstacle to collecting and painting them. It became clear that music and sports imagery—from blues, ragtime, jazz, football, and baseball—intersected with the era's explosive class, ethnic, racial, and gender divides. My early thinking seemed confirmed by historian Joshua Brown's contention that "the social issues of the postbellum Gilded Age, in particular the crisis of depression and class conflict, along with differentiation among readers, exerted pressure on the production of representation." I expanded my subject matter.

Sometime after that, while sitting in the Northern Illinois University library's dimly lit microfilm reading room, I came across a notice in the May 3, 1884, edition of the *Cleveland Gazette* that captured my attention. It read: "Mr. Isaac Carter was shot and killed Friday evening on Oliver Street, near Twenty-Fourth Street. It was simply a case of mistaken identity, Carter having been taken for a burglar. He was a prominent member of the St. Louis Black Stockings, and a very estimable young man." In that moment, baseball presented itself as a possible topic of study, and potentially an important one, directly related to my interest in culture. Like other young boys in the early 1960s, ball-playing, attending games—I grew up on the South Side of Chicago—and reading books about famous players such as Babe Ruth consumed much of my free time. Contextualizing Carter's baseball life with the act of collecting baseball ephemera offered something different. After all, I was searching for celebrative black images worthy of painting. Still, I had no idea of what to do with Carter's story. Why did I find it significant? While the answer remained hidden, I simply photocopied the article and filed away.

Between 1985 and 1986, listening to the music of Ellington, Fitzgerald, Holiday, Parker, Christian, Coltrane and Davis, I completed 57 watercolors and countless color-pencil drawings and sketches. "The Renaissance Series," as I named the project, romanticized black life in ways that the archival material could not. Some paintings monumentalized baseball (two paintings were 40" by 60"). These colorful, celebrative works found an audience, and somewhere along the way, I developed an insatiable hunger to research nineteenth-century black baseball history. On regular family excursions to St. Louis, I began to work in visits to the Olive Street downtown library. When I attended conferences or took vacations, my itinerary devoted time to local university and public libraries. I amassed enough photocopied material to fill some thirty three-ring binders, many averaging four inches in thickness. I filled the pages of lined notebooks and color-coded legal pads (blue, pink, gray, white, and yellow), my notes inscribed in variously colored inks (black, blue, green, red, and magenta). This journey began, of course, before personal computers and electronic media were readily available.

Baseball research began to consume more time, and I sought out ways to integrate the study of art history and the game's visual culture. As it turned out, there was no shortage of material to examine. From the daguerreotype to the illustrated press to trading cards to ephemera to fine art paintings, prints and sculpture, baseball representations have been part of the national pastime since its beginnings. And I was not alone in believing this baseball artwork meaningful. Art historian Shelly Mehlman Dinhofer, for instance, has written that it "transcends the game itself," bringing "forward in timeless imprint the artist's interpretation of the color and form, the physical interaction, and the sheer energy of the game."[1]

This book is the product of more than three decades of research into the history and culture of black baseball between 1858 and 1900, a time corresponding to the beginnings of organized black play. This era can be divided into three periods. The first, existing from 1858 to 1860, saw the antebellum rise of organized blackball, which I argue was linked to the economic and leisure-class life of the black barber (often referred to then, and at times in this book, as "tonsorial artist"). The second period, lasting from 1861 to 1872, brought the rise of the hotel industry, and specifically the hotel-waiter subculture, which was vital to the spread of black ball. The third period, which lasted until at least 1899, both overlapped with and departed from the earlier, profession-dependent decades. In it, high schools, colleges, fraternal, literary, and social organizations began to support young black men (primarily) interested in playing the national pastime. Particularly in the 1870s and 1880s, the figure of the socially ambitious, educated black baseballist gained cultural currency.

The book itself, having grown to a length even I couldn't have predicted, is divided across three volumes. The essay that leads off Volume I, "'They Covered Themselves in Glory': The Lost Base Ball World of the New Negro," explores the urban beginnings of black baseball. Barbers and hotel employees deserve credit for the formation of the earliest organized black teams, and the professional and semi-professional black baseball organizations that followed are indebted to their efforts. I present several exemplary figures to support this case. Following the essay are team profiles that include historical information on hundreds of black baseball teams of the second half of the nineteenth century. The profiles are supplemented by a listing of rosters for all teams and a directory of team-contact information.

The essay "Brothers and Brotherhood: Black Baseball's Family Networks," found at the beginning of Volume II, explores something very important to our understanding of black cultural life. Historian Michael Lomax has traced the roots of black baseball's organizational structure to the rise of mutual aid societies. Literary societies, fraternal and secret organizations can be added to the list. Novelist Herman Melville wrote about fraternal orders in nineteenth-century America, and while Melville cared little for them, his work reveals how powerful and firmly entrenched they were in American life. Secret masonic organizations played a crucial role in the formation of early black baseball, and its players, managers, promoters, and owners were, as we shall see, actively involved in a range of social organizations that supported the national pastime. Still, the brotherhood (and sisterhood) was not merely symbolic: The family of black baseball included many actual families, some of them involving multiple generations. This essay, along with another on empire and objectification that examines the representation of black players, precedes an extensive register providing all available career and biographical information for thousands of nineteenth-century baseball men. The first part of this nearly 700,000-word section closes out the main text in Volume II. An appendix appears in Volume III, following the remaining register entries, and provides additional detail, identifying the many known families of early black baseball.

Volume III also includes the essay "A Matter of Ability, and Not Color: The Rise of Black Umpires." "No one really knows," write baseball historians Joel Zoss and John Bowman, in *Diamonds in the Rough*, "the name of the first umpire of even a fairly well-organized American baseball game." The name of the first black umpire is equally obscure. Poring over newspapers, I have uncovered names for a number of these men, along with the games, dates, and locations in which matches took place. Some of these umpires worked both white and black games. Knowing who was involved in management tells us something useful about black baseball organization. Officers elected to operate teams included presidents, boards of directors, managers, treasurers, as well as recording and corresponding secretaries. The archive of the Philadelphia Pythians proved especially useful here, since it includes correspondence between the Pythians and other black clubs, providing names of players and teams that would otherwise have been lost to history. There is a cultural component to these records, involving writing and literacy. Art historian Michael Fried points to the importance of calligraphy and penmanship in the nineteenth century. Some black baseball correspondence, beautifully rendered in quill pen, says something about education. Following that piece is a related list, "Black Umpires, 1859–1900: A Chronology of Games." A final, brief essay, entitled "The Politics of Performance: Music, Minstrelsy and Black Baseball," closes out the work with my recent discovery of another black-baseball community, this one made up of musicians.

Some of the themes taken up in this book have their roots in the works of scholars who have studied nineteenth- and early twentieth-century black life. Wilson Jeremiah Moses, Henry Louis Gates, Jr., Toni Morrison, Eric Lott, Robin D. G. Kelly, A. K. Sandoval-Strausz, Douglas Walter-Bristol, Sarah Burns, and Elizabeth Young. None of them explores black baseball, but their contributions allow us to peer deeply into the social and cultural politics of the national pastime. Consider, for instance, black baseball minstrelsy: To understand the relation of "[N]egro comedy" to early black baseball requires an understanding of what Kelly calls the "hidden transcript." The hidden transcript "is a dissident political culture that manifests itself in daily conversations, folklore, jokes, songs, and other cultural practices." Black baseball minstrelsy has a hidden transcript. The mask of minstrelsy enabled the colored baseballist to wage symbolic warfare against rival teams, their employers, spectators, and, more generally, all representatives of the status quo. The mask also enabled the performance of black aesthetic style and created a peculiar niche market for black baseball within the country's burgeoning entertainment industry.

Researching this book has been a humbling experience. Documenting the lived experiences of men and women who played the game has evoked a range of human emotions: shock, sadness, disgust, humor, and jubilation. Historically, colored baseballists had belonged to an aggrieved community—enslaved and then free but disenfranchised—and expressed daily acts of resistance and survival. They strived to make a living in an often hostile and unsympathetic world. Central to individualistic acts of survival and resistance was mobility, which afforded the black players, like other black workers, "some freedom to escape oppressive living and working conditions, and power to negotiate better working conditions."[2] They traversed the country, working as hotel and restaurant employees, laboring as railroad employees, operating tonsorial parlors and grooming white patrons, bootblacking, and cleaning laundry in large-scale establishments. They played in the heat, rain, mud, and cold. They elicited hecklers, peals of laughter, and enthusiastic rounds of applause. When traveling, they never knew what to expect: sometimes they were refused at restaurant and hotels. After losing a game to a white club and being chided by a reporter, one black player responded, "Perhaps we would have played better, if we hadn't slept outside on a wagon all night." Many of them went on to have successful careers outside of the game. As young men and women, however, all they ever wanted to do was play baseball—if they could—alongside their white brethren. This book is for them.

NOTES

1. Shelly Mehlman Dinhofer, *The Art of Baseball* (New York: Harmony Books, 1990), 13.

2. Robin D.G. Kelley, "'We Are Not What We Seem': Re-Thinking Black Working-Class Opposition in the South," *Journal of American History*, 80, no. 1 (1993): 95.

Introduction:
The Scribbling Class

Sol White's Official Baseball Guide is a gem. In this slim volume, published in 1907, author Solomon "Sol" White provides the earliest known account of black baseball history, tracing the stories of the major teams and identifying selected owners, players, and managers. The book also includes nearly 60 photographs of teams, players, and club executives. According to historian Larry Hogan, White had a first-hand knowledge of the black game (he had played on more than one of the top clubs of his day) that proved a great boon to researchers: "The teams' schedules were so peripatetic, so many games were played in places with scant sports reporting sources, and the white-run press paid so little attention to Negro ball that it would almost be necessary to canvas all the newspapers published throughout the Northeastern United States to find what Sol White set down in his little work." Jerry Malloy compiled and re-introduced White's book, which he referred to as "the Dead Sea Scrolls of black professional baseball's pioneering community."[1]

On May 18, 1907, the *Indianapolis Freeman* heralded the book's initial publication:

> It is unique in that no history of the popular pastime, as played by colored men, has ever before been written. In addition to the full tale of the progress of the game there are nearly one hundred half-tone pictures of old-time and present-time colored ball players, including all of the present-day celebrities, and a number of groups of the prominent teams of this and past years.

It also included all-local advertisements, which suggests that the book's limited print run primarily targeted Philadelphia's sporting community, perhaps along with the fans of their opponents, since the *Freeman* notes that the book is "on sale wherever the Philadelphia Giants are playing." While the black press confirms the book's limited availability, purchased and complimentary copies would lead to broader circulation.[2]

White's book covers the period between 1885 and 1907. It is essentially a collection of lists, covering players, teams, managers, photographs and ads—but none of them exhaustively. It is necessarily incomplete because he could not (or would not) list "professional" teams that fell outside the narrative of his career. At first he attempts a comprehensive history ("I have endeavored to follow the mutations of colored base-ball, as accurately as possible, from the organization of the first colored professional team in 1885, to the present time"), but faced with a potentially immense and uncertain history, the author proposes a series of lists instead, leaving the reader to imagine the rest.

Nevertheless, everything that he wanted to say is in the book. There is no outside; the narrative he shares constitutes a closed world. White was able to construct a closed form because he had a clear idea of the black baseball culture of his own day. White knew his world, its racial laws and social customs—written and unwritten—its causes and effects. He lamented, "In no other profession has the color line been drawn more rigidly than in base ball." He and others like him were barred from both teams and whole leagues, saw games canceled because one player on the opposition objects to taking the field with black men, and were turned away from hotels that, on the arrival of a black team, were suddenly "filled from the cellar to the garret." White's nostalgic narrative presents a baseball landscape overpopulated with heroic figures that runs parallel to white baseball, and whose roots are immersed in the shadowy mists of time.[3]

As a historian of art history and visual culture, I am interested in how the book's images, both visual and verbal, tell a story of blackball. How, for example, did the book's photographs and advertisements help to give it form? Let's begin with the ads. Scattered throughout the book, they bring together conspicuous consumption and the sporting fraternity. According to Richard Ohmann, ads "chart social space." In the print media they have historically helped to establish and announce the social status of targeted audiences. Philadelphia's sporting fraternity found in commercial ads a range of information and interests that linked them conversationally with like-minded others of the same social circle. Hypothetically, the ads linked them with like-minded "sports" across the nation. Both photographs and advertisements represent "commodities of pleasure."[4]

Local businesses purchased advertising space in White's book to promote nostrums, saloons, cafes, barber shops, billiard halls, wine and liquor and tobacco shops, and hotels. This not only defrayed the book's costs; it also promoted the notion of business operators as baseball enthusiasts. The *Philadelphia Item's* ad announced its "[s]ixty years of continuous success." Freihoffer's Baking Company, sponsor of the International League of Colored Baseball Professionals (1906), reminded fans that "ten bread labels" promised free admission to any of the league's ball games. Saloon owner A.A. Coleman promoted himself as "One of the Fans." This list formed the core of sporting businesses within White's baseball world, and it assured the local sporting crowd that old values and social relations were still somehow present and dependable.

Photographs also fill the book, and they sell baseball players, celebrities past and present, as "commodities of pleasure." The history of baseball photographs parallels the early history of the photograph in general, and it developed along the same path of technological innovations, from the daguerreotype to cabinet cards. Photographic likenesses belong to a system of conspicuous consumption that, according to Thorstein Veblen, was designed to signify "invidious class distinctions." As commodities, they give form to the sitter's prestige, identity, and social standing. For the ballplayer, whether nattily attired or dressed in a baseball uniform, they market the "celebrity" as an image of middle-class success.[5] (Interestingly, there were talented black baseball men who made a living as visual artists, some of them even creating images of forgotten figures of baseball. Treasury Department engraver, master portraitist, and Manhattan Base Ball Club member Jacob C. Strather, for instance, created images, derived from photographs, of former ballplayers for the *Washington Bee*. His portraits of *Bee* editor and publisher William Chase, who had played for Washington's Alert Base Ball Club, and sportswriter Jesse K. Roy, of Washington's Unique and Eagle Base Ball clubs, are exemplary.) Looking back through time one can imagine how an illustrated baseball narrative enhanced White's ambitious project. The portraits he includes have managed neglect and resurrected the dead.

Henry Walter Schlichter helped to finance, and probably to inspire, White's book. Schlichter, a white businessman and sportswriter for the *Philadelphia Item*, had been a fixture on the Philadelphia sporting scene. As a youth, he excelled as a cyclist and swimmer; later, he was a boxing promoter of note. By 1891, the "pugilistic matchmaker" also refereed events, and he attained a measure of immortality as the referee in Thomas Eakins's monumental boxing painting *Taking the Count* (1898). Schlichter's business efforts included baseball. Between 1902 and 1907, White and Schlichter organized the Philadelphia Giants, the latter financing and managing the club. His role seems crucial to the production of a book that marketed the team.[6]

In 1936, White conferred with Schlichter about revising his book. White had lost his only copy and contacted Schlichter. The sportswriter had two copies and "all the cuts and photographs of the reproductions in the book." Schlichter, neither historian nor book publisher, was a businessman. Quite possibly, he couldn't imagine a return on his investment. Maybe he simply didn't have the funds to loan. But if Schlichter offered no financial support, he did provide White with a copy of the book and advised the ballplayer to "sell the history of colored baseball" to his editor at the *New York Age*. The reprint edition never materialized. In 1995, Jerry Malloy compiled and edited a new edition of the book and bolstered White's original claims with additional material. The revised and updated work in certain ways fulfills a dream that never came to fruition in White's lifetime.[7]

White's book anticipates the print media's desire to capitalize on the aura of blackball's beginnings. Between 1898 and 1931, ironically, newspapers across the country sought to elevate the status of their communities within the baseball pantheon by embracing local colored celebrities. They interviewed old timers, recounted their exploits, and eulogized them. Utica newspapers celebrated the Fearless Base Ball Club and Theodore Pell, who also played for the Cuban Giants. Norfolk's *News Journal and Guide* recounted stories of black teams, including the city's own Red Stockings. The *Chicago Defender* waxed nostalgic about Chicago's Gordon Base Ball Club, and Springfield, Illinois, papers recalled the exploits of Chicago's Uniques. Following the death of John Rose, the *Poughkeepsie (NY) Daily Eagle News* reported, "Mr. Rose was a baseball player who felt that he never lost his skill as a heavy hitter."[8]

If one of the great strengths of *Sol White's Official Baseball Guide* is the author's background in black baseball, it is also what limits it. Although he played briefly in Indiana, Illinois, and Michigan, White's experiences came primarily in the east, and he seems unaware of the early black pro ball played in the Midwest. White contends that the Cuban Giants became the first professional black team in 1885— something still accepted by many as fact—but that seems now clearly to be incorrect. In 1870, for instance, St. Louis, Missouri, had a colored professional team, and its secretary, Douglass Smith, promoted

their agenda in eastern newspapers. The *Utica (NY) Daily Observer* reported: "The St. Louis Base Ball Club, composed of men with money, has undertaken to pay the traveling expenses of a strong nine of colored baseballists to travel through the Eastern States early in 1871. They desire the addresses of the secretaries of colored clubs throughout the States North." Smith also advertised in the *New York Clipper* for "colored professionals," a "good catcher and good left hand pitcher." The St. Louis Brown Stockings Base Ball Club, colored, entered the baseball business.[9]

Chicago offers another example. Between 1871 and 1883, the Unique Base Ball Club operated as professionals (their admittance, in 1878, to Chicago's Amateur Base Ball Association notwithstanding). They received money to "measure bats" with black and white clubs of Iowa, Wisconsin, Michigan, Illinois, Indiana, and Missouri. Management needed money to bankroll business operations. To schedule games against the "Unique Club" required financial guarantees. Lucrative gambling revenues supported their baseball business as well. This was hardly a pass-the-hat operation. It functioned, at least in part, on the "cooperative plan."

In 1871, the Uniques traveled east and played baseball matches with the leading colored clubs of Washington, Pennsylvania (Philadelphia, Pittsburgh), and New York (Troy). It was a highly successful tour, and the press took note, Midwestern newspapers in particular. By 1874, white and black teams had begun to inquire about scheduling games. For Decoration Day and Independence Day, the Uniques became a draw in Minnesota, Michigan, and Iowa. By 1876, at least three players had been recruited by both white and colored competition. Winona, Minnesota's Clipper Base Ball Club hired William Fisher, as a "professional" pitcher. The Minneapolis Union Base Ball Club, a black organization, hired William Berry and William P. Johnson, much to the chagrin of their opponents.[10]

In 1882, St. Louis's Henry Bridgewater organized another professional team. The *New York Clipper* reported: "The Black Stockings claim to be the only professional colored club in the country. They intend making a tour of the country through the middle and Eastern States." Local papers carried similar stories. Bridgewater, a liquor dealer, saloonkeeper, real estate mogul, and philanthropist, had the means. He recruited the best available players from around the country. Bridgewater advertised for good pitchers, promising to pay $50 per week. William Whyte and Richmond Robinson came from Boston and Washington, DC; William Smith came from Upper Canada; William Davis, an "old professional pitcher," had graduated from Oberlin College, and his battery-mate, Joseph Harris, came from Leavenworth, Kansas. Eventually, these men drifted eastward and joined Trenton's Cuban Giants or Boston's Resolutes. Bridgewater himself was a professional. When interviewed by an Ohio newspaper in 1883, he stated: "I have been playing professional baseball for about twelve years." Chronologically, Bridgewater's reminisces dovetail neatly with the story of the St. Louis Brown Stockings.[11]

Bridgewater's star players, Bill Davis and Joseph Harris, eventually demanded more money. When the manager refused, they helped to organize Chicago's Gordon Base Ball Club (1884–1890). Harris became player-manager. Combining the best practices of the Unique Club and Black Stockings, they hyped themselves, in Barnumesque fashion, as the "Gordons of St. Louis" and "Gordons (colored) of St. Louis." *Sporting Life* added: "The players in this club will receive from $35 dollars to $50 dollars per week." Playing between three and six times per week, on the road against white and colored opponents throughout the Midwest and South, they earned every penny. The skeletal framework of these early professional teams can be, I am confident, fleshed out through diligent research.[12]

This work offers practical lists of colored clubs, managers, players, and umpires of the period 1858–1900. Apart from the team rosters, which are organized geographically by year, they are arranged alphabetically. In addition, baseball families are listed in an appendix; privileging families in this way allows me to engage another form of accumulation: genealogical ties.

Some team profiles are extensive. The Fearless Base Ball Club, of Utica, New York, is one example. Organized in 1866 and operating until 1908, the Fearless was perhaps the longest-running black baseball organization in history. But the Fearless are interesting for another reason. For nearly fifty years, fathers, sons, grandsons, nephews, and cousins formed the team's nucleus. Its members were hardcore Lincoln Republicans and a threatening presence—if we accept contemporary accounts—who fought for full citizenship both on and off the diamond. The Fearless, like other colored aggregations, are as much a historical treasure as the Cuban Giants.

Other team profiles are less complete, thanks in part to gaps in the historical record (or to its inaccessibility at the time of research). The record of the Unique Base Ball Club, of Chicago (1871–1893), includes glaring gaps, for instance. In too many articles, sportswriters relied on readers' cultural memory to fill in the blanks. In 1886, the *Inter-Ocean* reported, "The Uniques, at one time the champion colored club of the Northwest, have reorganized, and are much stronger and better than ever, and, with the following players, think they can again lay claim to the title." If some readers then could recall the birth of the Unique Club, none now can, and today we are left holding the loose end. And efforts to dig for further details end in frustration, since it seems that, unlike the Utica newspapers that faithfully covered the annual exploits of their hometown Fearless, Chicago papers treated the Uniques as a peculiar appendage to the national pastime. No published rosters and box scores, for example, document the 1887 and 1888 battle for supremacy between the Uniques and Chicago Unions. Curiously, the information we do have survives in newspapers published outside of the Windy City. I have no answer for this.[13]

In this book I hope to offer insight into the elusive early world of black baseball by providing a chronological list of teams; an alphabetical list of players; a chronological list managers and team contacts; a chronological and geographical list of rosters; and a chronological list of games covered by colored umpires. In one sense, these lists represent forms of accumulation, by which I mean that they build on a repetitive sequence of words or phrases that mean the same thing.

One example of enumeration is the dizzying number of mysterious surnames for which first names have yet to be identified—the many Browns, Johnsons, Thompsons, and Williamses that linger faceless, as it were, just within our field of vision. While their biographies yield "disconnected information"—"Brown who?"—they help to map blackball's uncharted territory. Several of these individuals have been tracked only from one club to another, and it is probable that some now listed separately are indeed the same person. It is hoped that the sources listed with these entries will prove useful for future research.

This book has a mnemonic function. When racial epithets appear in the text, for example, their inclusion emphasizes the presence of colored baseballists or clubs. They also illustrate how print culture reified a social order of domination and subordination. Illuminating, if not jarring, expressions—"colored," "lemon-colored," "Spaniard," "Octoroon," "Spaniard," "mulatto," "colored persuasion," "shade(s)," "darky," "darkies," "dusky," "negro," "Ethiopian," "café-au-lait," "slate-colored," "mauve-colored," "saddle-colored," "coffee-colored," "coal-colored," "colored gemmen," "gentlemen of color," "Sons of Ham," "Dusky Sons of Ham," "coon," "colored coon," "charcoal," "Our African Brother," "Afric," "African 'scent," "radicals," "fifteenth-amendment appendages," "snowball," "snow drops," "snowflake," "chocolate-drop," "charcoal," "nigger" and so on—capture the journalist's fascination (if not derision) within a hierarchical system of naming, with "gentlemen of color" at one end and "nigger baseballists" at the other. Ironically, these terms assist in separating the texts of journalists, correspondents, and baseballists. They also provide key or code words that assist in the search for blackball.[14]

The following section scribbles on about the subject matter framed by this volume, and proposes a theoretical framework for discussing early black baseball. "Base Ball Gothic: A Modern Frankenstein" lays out an argument for nineteenth and early twentieth century representations of the colored baseballist in narrative, theatrical performance, and visual culture. "Base Ball Gothic," as I call it, looks at baseball's "dark side." It contemplates the black player as an object of fascination and ridicule, intimately connected to the history of the United States. It is a grim, though fascinating, encounter with how discourses converge with literary and visual culture, and how they fashion black baseball stories.

Base Ball Gothic: A Modern Black Frankenstein

In dealing with the negro, we should treat him not as a brute but as an infant, of larger growth, and if we turn him loose in the maturity of his physical strength, in the manhood of his passions, but in the childhood of his morals and his intellect, we shall have before us a being not unlike that which is portrayed in a romance of recent date (Frankenstein), a man artificially compounded with the thews of a giant, with a mould more than mortal, into which is infused all the power of doing mischief, but unto which its creator, failing to inspire a moral feeling, endangers his own safety in rash experiment."—*New York Herald*, November 7, 1859

The closest symbolic descendants of Frankenstein in antebellum America are illegitimate black sons, debased from and by their white paternal foundations. Yet in real-life antebellum America, the voice of the master trumped that of the slave: Thomas Dew, a respected member of the Virginia elite, became President of the College of William and Mary, while Nat Turner was caught, tried, and executed, and his body probably given to surgeons for dissection.—Elizabeth Young, *Black Frankenstein*

I guess I'd better leave for Kentucky, for I smell something strong around here, and I begin to think, that we are completely "skunk'd."—*The National Game: Three "Outs" and One "Run"*

In *The National Game: Three "Outs" and One "Run"* (1860), a lithograph created by artist Louis Mauer and published by Currier and Ives, four beardless men square off on the ball field (**Fig. 1**). These members of the "Union Club," "Little Giants," "Disunion Club," and "Wide Awake Club"—team names inscribed on the fronts of their belts—form a semi-circle around a four-legged, furry-tailed creature. While three figures sport spiked shoes and hold bats, the figure to the far right clutches a fence railing *and* the ball. From left to right the bats read "Fusion," "Non Intervention," "Slavery Extension," and "Equal Rights and Free Territory."[15]

The National Game appeared weeks before the 1860 presidential election. It depicts a base-ball game in which Abraham Lincoln, at right, has defeated (from left) John Bell, Stephen A. Douglas and John C. Breckenridge. Political and baseball puns intermingle freely.

Figure 1. *The National Game: Three "Outs" and One "Run,"* **Currier & Ives, 1860. Illustrated by Louis Maurer. Civil rights became a baseball metaphor, signified here by the skunk. By 1867, African Americans' push for recognition of their citizenship, and with the basic rights that go with it, was sometimes conflated with things foul smelling or rotten. This is American gothic expression, a baseball world haunted by the terror and anxiety of blackness (Library of Congress).**

Bell, of the Constitutional Union Party, remarks, "It appears to me very singular that we three should strike a 'foul' and be 'put out' while old Abe made such a 'good lick.'" The diminutive regular Democratic Party nominee, Douglas, declares, "That's because he had the confounded rail, to strike with, I thought our fusion might be a 'short stop' to his career." Breckenridge, a southern Democrat, holding his nose and creeping away, says, "I guess I'd better leave for Kentucky, for I smell something strong around here, and begin to think that we are completely 'skunk'd.'" Towering above them, Lincoln declares: "Gentleman, if any of you should ever take a hand in another match at this game, remember that you must have 'a good bat' and 'strike a fair ball' to make a 'clean score' & a 'home run.'" The right leg of the future sixteenth president of the United States is firmly planted on "Home Base." The skunk's upright appendage mimics the wooden appendages clutched by the ballplayers, and signifies that the three challengers have been "skunk'd," a direct reference to the game's outcome. While there is little question about whom Lincoln "skunk'd" there is much to be said about the smell permeating the antebellum air: enslavement, abolition and, ultimately, emancipation.

The "smell" is a powerful metaphor for what Toni Morrison calls

"fear of the dark" in antebellum culture. In *Playing in the Dark: Whiteness and the Literary Imagination*, Morrison informs readers that darkness played a critical role in the literary romantic expression of North America. Black enslavement "enriched the country's creative possibilities," permitting artists to explore not only the "not-free" but also the projection of the "not-me." For Morrison, "[t]he result was a playground for the imagination."[16]

The National Game reanimates mirabilia or portents: the skunk, a phantasmagorical black body, casts its ominous shadow on the ball field. Pausing between figures of non-intervention and slavery expansion, the crouching animal looks rather meekly to the right at the Union Club player. Its upright tail, suggestive of "spraying" overlaps the right leg of the Disunion Club player. What is foul? The pole cat? Slavery? Equal rights and free territory? Non-intervention? Even as Lincoln proclaims victory, danger looms. Team captains encircling the skunk brandish clubs. As their interlocking gazes suspend potential violence, Breckenridge exposes the black presence scurrying beneath them.[17]

The National Game portrays a ball field full of mystery and terror. The triangular composition, Lincoln's baseball forming its apex, reveals a foreboding, American landscape. Its pictorial space contains no sign of trees, sky, sun, clouds, or buildings. The turf, fissured along its craggy edges, seemingly collapsible under the weight of the situation, dominates a tilted ground plane, anchored by human and animal forms. Human bodies project against a white, amorphous screen. Theatrical lighting casts dark shadows along the ground, however, framing the skunk and reinforcing a stifling sense of claustrophobia. There is a haunting taking place.

In the course of my research, it became apparent that blackball's uncharted territory might be reconstructed as a series of representations, literary and visual, of the colored baseballist as threat—a monstrous figure of horror and fear. (While this book offers celebratory narratives, I was drawn to "dark side" of terrifying and irresistible images.) In *Black Frankenstein*, for example, Elizabeth Young convincingly argues that the antebellum figure of "an African American Frankenstein monster" originates in the tension between two ideas: "a transatlantic understanding of the black slave as a Frankenstein's monster who revolts against his white master and an American model of the United States as a Frankenstein's monster that revolted against Britain." During the Civil War, the monster took on new forms, in particular, "the rhetoric of national dismemberment and amalgamation."[18]

Antebellum parallels between *Frankenstein* and racial anxieties in the face of slave rebellion changed the monster's meaning (**Fig. 2**).

Figure 2. Black Frankenstein, *Lantern* **magazine, January 31, 1852. Illustrated by Frank Bellew. A black man is depicted here as an awakened monster. In Mary Shelly's novel, the monster is constructed from a smelly assemblage of body parts stolen from dissecting rooms. Theatrical performers, graphic artists and writers imagined the black player as a monstrous, reeking form.**

In 1829, David Walker condemned the "wretched, degraded and abject" condition of black America by comparing blacks to living corpses. His antislavery manifesto, *David Walker's Appeal*, declares, "[W]hat is the use of living when in fact I am dead." The living corpse evokes "the widespread antebellum fascination with séances, ghost stories, grave-robbing and dissection." According to Alexander Nemerov, antebellum dissection offered a "new kind of deathly identification, created a form of self-representation through torment and extinction." Referring to blacks and poor whites, Nemerov explains, "[T]heir powerlessness and marginal social status afforded little protection for their dead in the face of persistent shortages of cadavers needed for medical dissections." For genteel society, they were "relative nobodies."[19]

Anatomical discourse became "a dark joke," a metaphoric form of butchery—dissected, nameless black bodies demoted to the status of slaughtered meat—hence the expression "Negro steaks." Other black bodies, like Nat Turner's cadaver, had names, as literary narratives of the rebellious slave incarnated fear about black power. Following his failed slave uprising in Virginia, in 1831, Turner was tried, executed, and his body released to surgeons for dissection. Metaphoric death permeates Shelley's novel: Frankenstein assembles the monster from corpses stolen from dissecting rooms. The monster "had no name because its identity had been systematically denied to him, and he gave eloquent voice to that denial." In popular use, the term "Frankenstein" became not a reference to the creator but to the monster.[20]

In the national imagination, the presence of the colored baseballists could conjure up the most appalling phantoms. On the one hand, in their rebellion against an injustice, free blacks in antebellum America embodied liberation. As touring ball clubs, free men of color provoked fear within the slave regime, also known as the "Slave Power." As abolitionists, they often defied federal and state laws. They supported the Underground Railroad, offered safe havens, lured "servants" away from their masters, and fought slave catchers. As blackface minstrelcy reveals, well-dressed people of color—"dandies" and "dandizettes"—challenged the antebellum status quo as well. On the other hand, the postbellum focus on dismemberment and amalgamation shows that many colored baseballists sought full U. S. citizenship. The denial of access to public spaces—barber shops, hotels, restaurants, public parks, or train cars—triggered lawsuits. An unjust law was no law at all. In certain towns, boroughs, and even regions of the country, white organizations refused to play with or against them. Small wonder that postbellum critics dubbed colored baseballists "Fifteenth Amendment Club Slingers."[21]

There is an intrinsic connection between the looming presence of the colored baseballist and the literary figure of the dead metaphor. The phrase "dead metaphor" implies that "the metaphor was once a living organism, like a human being, but died and became a corpse." According to Young, "[Dead metaphors] are phrases whose original metaphoric content has ceased to register." Still, they can be reanimated and the reanimating process is one of amalgamation; many dead metaphors involve a body part (spine of a book, arm of a chair, lip of a cup and so on).[22]

Gothic stories articulate the "horrors of history," writes art historian Sarah Burns, and are often animated by unresolved issues involving, for instance, race/gender, enslavement, emancipation, freedom, civil rights and disenfranchisement. As in those stories, the colored baseballist embodies a figure of the monster. In baseball narratives, the colored player—as monster—is a literary elaboration of the dead metaphor. He is characterized abjectly; he projects dark meanings like pollution and defilement. Take, for example, bootblacking and whitewashing. Men of color dominated these menial occupations, so much so that they nicknamed their ball clubs after their lived experiences. Bootblacking and whitewashing had metonymic functions— in this instance, racial connotations. Of course, to "whitewash," a metaphoric expression for painting, became a common baseball idiom. It meant that a team had failed to score a run. (In 1870, the success of the Chicago White Stockings added "Chicagoed" to the lexicon, and it meant the same thing.) Given the relation of race, gender, politics and economics to my project, coupled with the history of American Gothic, early blackball conjures a haunting encounter with the national pastime.

When journalists referred to whitewashed colored clubs, they often engaged in crude forms of humor. In 1870, the *Ottawa Free Trader* quipped, "Does it change the complexion of a colored baseball club to be whitewashed?" Regarding a white vs. colored match, the *New York Clipper* reported, "The Dexter Club, of Springfield, Illinois (colored) was recently whitewashed all through." Still at it, thirty years later, the *Harrisburg Telegraph* joked: "An effort in black and white—whitewashing a colored team."[23]

The print media reanimated ancient sayings such as "an Ethiopian can't change its spots" and "to wash an Ethiopian white." Romans had used the latter expression to invoke natural law and conjure the monstrous. The modern phrase "to whitewash" had many meanings and stereotypical associations: (1) people of racially mixed parentage (black and white); (2) blacks who desired whiteness; and (3) blacks as whitewashers. Visual culture exploited such images. They attacked the desire for citizenship. Meanings hinged on the social whitewash as "a veneer, a cover-up, a deception, a mode of temporary [racial] concealment." Baseball couldn't escape them.[24]

Ballplayers of visibly mixed racial parentage raised uncomfortable questions about what whiteness actually meant. When some sportswriters encountered light-complexioned players, they expressed astonishment at their physiognomy. In 1881, one New Orleans journalist, struck by one team's physical appearance, felt compelled to share what he witnessed. The *Daily Picayune* reported, "The Pickwicks are composed of young colored men, all of who have bright skins, and several are so fair they would pass for white." In Louisiana's caste system, those with light skin—"octoroons" and "mulattos"— embodied the best of black society. Teams organized and dominated by mulattos were not unusual. Among the many such teams could be found Charleston's Mutuals and Ashleys; Albany's Young Bachelors; Philadelphia's Pythians and National Excelsiors; Utica's Fearless; Washington's Alerts; Cincinnati's Black Stockings, Creoles, and Western Unions; Cleveland's Blue Stockings; Chicago's Uniques and Gordons; St. Louis's Blue Stockings and Black Stockings; and San Francisco's Logans and Unions. The phenomenon of the mulatto ballplayer, as defined by Michael Lomax, seems so common today that its relevance might be taken for granted.[25]

"Throughout the antebellum period," writes Lomax, "a system of color caste emerged in the black community." Light complexions mattered. As Lomax observed, "The Philadelphia Pythians were native-born Americans and were slightly older, an average of twenty-eight, than their white counterparts, and nearly 70 percent of them were mulattoes." Like their white counterparts, the Pythians were artisans, petty proprietors, and clerks. They were not alone: the Harrisburg Monrovians and Williamsport Independents were dominated by mulattos as well. Although a light complexion did not guarantee a black person's place in the socio-economic hierarchy, as Lomax explains, it afforded greater economic opportunities, which in turn assured higher rank in black society. There may be other reasons, too, that these individuals were often found among baseball men. Mulattos, for example, dominated the barbering profession, and this lucrative business afforded financial stability and leisure time to play ball.[26]

The mulatto presence, however, caused "chronic uneasiness." Towns knew community histories and family pedigrees. Who was free or enslaved was no secret, nor who was white or mulatto. The Dereefs, of Charleston, for example, were a distinguished antebellum mulatto family. Businessman Richard Dereef dealt in real estate, lumber, and slaves. He also founded the Brown Society, which reserved membership for light-skinned free persons of color. (Charleston's "De-Reefs" and other "aristocratic colored families" formed ball clubs. Octavius Catto belonged to the "De Reef" blood line.) "Brown," writes Daniel Biddle and Murray Dubin, "marked a negro as someone whites had to watch." For the plantation aristocracy, free persons of color represented a "growing evil in the State."[27]

The same threat could be felt in the antebellum North. The demonization of mulattos, argues Elizabeth Young, strengthened the metaphorical connection between blacks and monsters. Resistance by free people of color against the Fugitive Slave Law presents an exemplary case. Mulattos prospered in Utica, New York's small black community nicknamed "Hayti." As part of the Underground Railroad, Hayti was one of the first places authorities searched for runaways. Blacks who could not prove that they were free risked arrest and enslavement solely on the word of "Negro slave catchers." Reuben N. Lippin, a mulatto, quietly supported abolitionism; his light-complexion permitting mobility and deception. Born in Pennsylvania around 1816, Lippin had been enslaved and apprenticed as a hairdresser. By 1844, he was a successful businessman. His establishment cut, styled, and dyed hair; it also sold wigs and toupees, perfumery, and fancy articles. Many players of the Fearless Base Ball Club apprenticed in his shop, including his sons (John and Thomas), grandson (Charles), and the Freeman family (Peter and Samuel). Lippen also employed white men. He became one of the city's oldest barbers and cherished residents.[28]

Harrisburg, Pennsylvania, home of early black clubs, tells another story. Many mixed-race members of the city's colored society led resistance against slave catchers. In 1850, Joseph Pople, Sr., Samuel Burris, Thomas Earley, Frank Roberson, and John Williams (Pople, Roberson, Williams, Burris and Earley fathered organizers of the Monrovia and Active Base Ball clubs), James Denny, Henry Bradley, along with other combatants, rescued three black men, who after being released from prison were claimed as runaways. R. S. Littlejohn and Company, of Virginia, sought to commit them under the Fugitive Slave Law. The local magistrate refused to entertain the claim that the defendants were horse thieves or runaways. An armed and heated battle ensued between 200 black and 40 white men, Pople and Earley among those badly beaten. The accused runaways escaped. In an 1851 court case, Pople and others were released after paying prosecution costs. Littlejohn and Company were found not guilty. Pople, Burris, Earley, Roberson and Williams became loyalist of the Republican Party. Their sons, colored baseballists, assumed the political mantle passed from their fathers.[29]

The National Game's vision of the slaveholding South being "skunk'd" reflects the black threat looming during Reconstruction. The black player, whose pursuit of citizenship represents (in the eyes of whites) a kind of monstrosity, portends disaster. Metaphoric associations often exhibit an arresting fascination with imagery of abjection: decay, putridity, vomit, bodily disorder, and dissolution. In 1867, Springfield, Illinois's Dexter Star Base Ball Club challenged Chicago's Excelsior Base Ball Club to a series of games. The *Springfield State Register* wryly noted:

> The crack colored base-ball club, of Springfield, Illinois, is of the colored persuasion. The citizens of that place are very anxious to match their crack club against the Excelsiors of this city. We are authorized to

state that if the Springfield people will varnish the colored nine so as to keep down the smell, the Excelsiors will consent to play the Dexters.

The *State Register's* droll response to whites' refusal to play with their colored brethren or colored teams, and it reinforced middle-class pretentions of social cleanliness and purity.[30]

Harrisburg newspapers expressed similar views on interracial contests. In 1867, the *Patriot* reported,

The Monrovia Base Ball Club, composed of indolent niggers—together with the 'Deacon,' went to Wrightsville on Tuesday, and played a match game with the Anglo (Heavy) Base Ball Club of the latter place. The day being an exceedingly warm one, it is said that the overheated nigs, &c, drank the town nearly dry, and the people considered it a God send when a sudden shower put an end to the game, and drove the coons from the place. It is also said that the air became very refreshing after the 'odor' had passed away.[31]

The black Frankenstein again reared its head at Rome, New York, where a journalist protested the presence of a "Freedman" covering first base for the Useless Base Ball Club, an otherwise all-white organization:

Excuse us, from making strenuous exertion to reach the first base upon a warm day when engaged in playing ball with that club…. [Mr. S] may derive the most complete benefit from the game, contrive to play during dog days, with the gentle zephyrs playing also, and take my word for it, [he] would throw up his commission, (and dinner also), and retire from the baseball arena in disgust.

The reporter portrayed the "Freedman" as a "huge darkey" and nicknamed him "Gumbo," indicating racially mixed parentage, and "Snowball," an ironic reference to the inaccessibility of whiteness. His muscularity and light-complexion—a threat to the "ideal of legitimate manhood"—amounted to a smelly assemblage of mismatched pieces.[32]

Here the relation between monster and monster-maker is clear. Critics became monster-makers, that is, Frankensteins. White antipathy toward colored baseballists created a language that defined their presence on the diamond. The black body's metaphorical putrefaction became part of the baseball lexicon, evolving as to connote a peculiar odor associated with sweaty black bodies. The views of the journalist supported a thesis that white players claimed a higher social status on the backs of the racially reconstructed black body. Concluding, he agreed to witness the colored man play, but only under from afar: "The greater the distance however from the field, the greater the enchantment." For much of baseball, notions of fusion/ amalgamation were an impossibility: "It is advisable for the races to remain separate, until the distinction of color and social position is no longer recognized."[33]

American Gothic's theatrical performances relate the monster to blackface minstrelsy, simultaneously ridiculing and satirizing middle-class white audiences. As noted elsewhere, minstrelsy penetrated baseball and paralleled the rise of the professional. Eric Lott argues that the primary purpose of the minstrel mask may have been as much to maintain control over a potentially subversive act as to ridicule, though the performers' attempts at regulation were also capable of producing a quality of blackness. Burnt cork artists performed baseball skits on the stage, and their organizations played on the diamond. Theatrical performances produced an "aura" of the "seeming counterfeit."[34]

"Most of [minstrelsy's] political content," writes David Roediger, "was given over to attacking emancipation, civil rights, and an alleged favoritism toward the 'nigger.'" The artistic practice of "blackening up," as a mode of temporary racial concealment, had its dark side.

Roediger observes, "To black up was an act of wildness in the antebellum [and postbellum] U.S. Psychoanalytically, the smearing of soot or blacking over the body represents the height of polymorphous perversity, an infantile playing with excrement or dirt. It is the polar opposite of the anal retentiveness usually associated with accumulating capitalist Protestant cultures."[35]

While the Civil War's aftermath unleashed an outpouring of minstrelsy, its engagement with baseball merely continued, nothing new. The colored baseballist invoked the threat of citizenship and suffrage. Would black clubs seek parity with white clubs? The entertainment industry thought so. Baseball minstrelsy took on new meanings. In 1867, blackface minstrel performer Richard Hooley deployed baseball farce as an innovative way to ridicule blacks by redirecting racial hostility towards them. The addition of baseball to its image-repertoire system was hardly coincidental. Less than three weeks had separated an emancipation day match from Hooley's comedic antics

The *Brooklyn Daily Eagle* reported, "The Base Ball Mania has broken out here in a humorous eruption, and a burlesque match will be played between the long and short nines; it will be a heavy game."

The burlesque of the champion game of baseball between the Atlantics and Unions is the most amusing. All who have never seen a genuine game should witness this, and all who are familiar with the game should also take it in. The former will be greatly amused, and the latter will learn points that they never dreamed of before. Every player plays "points" and sharp ones too, to the great delight of the uninitiated. Cool White makes an exceptional umpire "in a horn." His decisions are without parallel, although the audience can't see it in the light.

Baseball minstrelsy, the rage of New York theater, entertained full houses, encouraged audience participation, and drew innumerable encores. The *Brooklyn Daily Eagle* concluded, "'The Base Ball Match' is the best thing we have seen in a long time. The fun is uproarious, and the hits very palpable. The audience insists in catching a ball occasionally, which gives them an active interest in the proceedings." Hooley's Minstrel Company helped to transform baseball minstrelsy.[36]

Given Hooley's privileged background and upbringing, his productions of blackface farce, if not his antipathy toward black people, is odd. Born in Ballina, Ireland in 1822, Hooley belonged to a prosperous merchant family and received a quality education in Manchester, England. He became a violinist. His cultured family provided him with financial resources to travel. In 1844, Holley visited New York City and "liked it so much," he decided to stay. He joined Edwin P. Christy's Minstrels and, after several profitable years, organized his own company. Between 1848 and 1852, his troupe performed in London before returning to the United States and touring the West. In 1862, the company triumphantly returned to Brooklyn and opened the Hooley Opera House. The *Syracuse Union* declared, "The name of Hooley is synonymous with good music, an excelsior minstrel organization, and a superb entertainment." Hooley, not yet a citizen, lived the American dream.[37]

Black baseball minstrelsy, which extended the politics and logic of blackface minstrelsy to an emerging national pastime (**Figs. 3 and 4**), relied on ethnic stereotyping for not only its appeal but its meaning. Caricatures of the black athlete circulated on the stage and in print: sports narratives, illustrations, and cartoons. For some journalists, black Southern dialect resonated with blackface farce or "[N]egro comedy"; they deployed the vernacular to mock the performances of colored players. Visual artists appropriated stock "darky" characters or low comedy types to mock the black player. Lott calls this aura the "seeming counterfeit." Its mimetic potential: a "signifying monster." W.J.T. Mitchell concluded that this image-

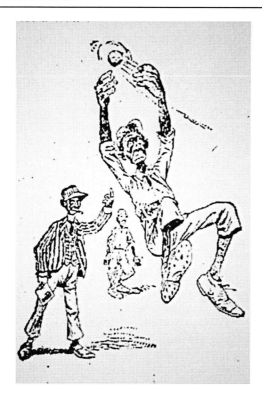

Figure 3. Caricature of Page Fence Giants Player, *Logansport (IN) Pharos-Tribune*, May 28, 1896. The theatrics of blackface minstrelsy, blackness as a surrogate skin, became something to be put on or removed. Its verbal and visual protocols (grossly exaggerated body parts, in this instance, huge hands and feet) penetrated baseball representations as early as 1858.

Figure 4. Caricature of Page Fence Giant Player, *Logansport (IN) Pharos-Tribune*, May 28, 1896. Graphic artists often portrayed black players humorously, if not derisively, with bandied legs, gargantuan feet and hands.

repertoire system is despicable and worthy of destruction, but he warned that racial and ethnic stereotypes seemed to have a life of their own. If the life of the black baseball stereotype resided in the death of its models, who does the "image-killing" and "image-resurrecting"?[38]

American Gothic pictures, according to Burns, conjure up "disturbing spectacles of grotesque bodies in which the monstrous, the animal, and the anomalous threaten the social construction of the normal." Visual representations of the black player as monster—the "not me"—emerged in the postbellum Gilded Age (literary representations in the 1850s; theatrical representations in the 1860s). Crude depictions take the form of minstrel figures: dark skin and caricatured Negroid features, bulging eyes, wide and rubbery lips, toothy grins, knotty heads, gangly and angular bodies, big hands and gargantuan feet. In 1871, the *Camden Democrat* jibed, "Base Ball is becoming quite popular among the colored youth of New York. There is on Sullivan Street a young man who gives great promise as a fielder, his feet being so large that it is impossible for a ball to pass through them" (**Figs. 5, 6 and 7**).[39]

For nineteenth-century viewers unsettled by the presence of black baseballists, these images offered a volatile mix of attraction and

Figure 5. The Raven, *Harper's Weekly*, January 1863. Illustrated by Frank Bellew. This American gothic image depicts a Negroid man-bird that embodies subhuman brutishness. Here the monstrous hybrid looms over the Confederacy. The black bird, an iconic antebellum symbol of the enslaved, became an epithet for black players of the Gilded Age.

Figure 6. The Bird of Freedom and the Black Bird, *Harper's Weekly*, January 1863. Illustrated by Frank Bellew. The Bald Eagle (pure bird form) and the Blackbird (man-bird hybrid) greet one another after President Lincoln's signing of the Emancipation Proclamation. Baseball clubs embraced bird imagery both as team names, mascots, and as emblems of male virility.

"I'VE HAD A DEAL OF TROUBLE, BUT THIS REPAYS ME FOR IT !"

Figure 7. The Centennial, *Harper's Weekly*, July 1876. Illustrated by Frank Bellew. This image represents the devolution of Bellew's blackbird, from man-bird to bird. It becomes the pure form and the eagle, the hybrid. The blackbird not only births the eaglet, but looms ominously over its well-being.

hurt themselves and others. These monstrous black bodies were disorderly and dangerous. Later, I will explore how Base Ball Gothic gave visual artists a "potent, fluid language for dealing with the darker facets of history and the psyche" that seldom intruded into the optimistic high art domains of conventional baseball paintings and sculpture. Henry Louis Stephens, Solomon Eytinge, Jr., Thomas Worth, Henry Jackson Lewis, Moses L. Tucker and James Cameron figured among those visual artists who caricatured colored baseballists through ambivalent, if not derisive, imagery.

This book's opening essay focuses on the "Lost Base Ball World of the New Negro," a topic I've explored elsewhere in print. I appropriate this apt phrase from Wilson Jeremiah Moses's groundbreaking essay "The Lost World of the Negro." When Moses published his essay, little serious work had been done on cultural impact of late nineteenth-century black life in Washington, D.C. His intriguing critique argues that black intellectuals of Washington, D.C., laid the foundations for "rebirth of the "New Negro" or New Negro Movement" (1918–1940). Moreover, they played a crucial role in training future black scholars and intellectuals who are typically associated with New York's Harlem Renaissance. These individuals embodied the "New Negro," a literary term connoting the creative possibilities that black baseball had to offer.[40]

Moses's essay doesn't cover black baseball. That's where this work comes in. My claim: Washington, D.C.'s black middle class and sporting fraternity helped to establish nineteenth-century black baseball as a viable black institution. Between 1858 and 1900, black institution-building emerged and the city's entrepreneurs came to the forefront. Their remarkable efforts paralleled antebellum black enslavement, and paralleled the rise of disenfranchisement and social segregation. Blackball, between 1858 and 1900, fits neatly into the narrative of Moses's "Lost World of the Negro." The history of blackball maps "uncharted territory," that is, until now. Part of my book's opening essay takes up the story of Henry Rosecranse Columbus, Jr. "Rosecranse," as he was known, is the prototypical figure of the antebellum colored baseballist. His story provides insights into the role of the tonsorial artist in the formation of the earliest teams. The third section zeroes in on colored baseball's hotel-waiter subculture, looking at how specific colored baseballists who excelled in the hotel industry, organized and managed strong resort teams. Finally, it revisits black baseball minstrelsy and the relation between colored baseballists and colored minstrels.

NOTES

1. Lawrence D. Hogan, *Shades of Glory* (Washington, DC: National Geographic, 2006), 45–49; Jerry Malloy, "The Strange Career of Sol White, Black Baseball's First Historian," in *Out of the Shadows: African American Baseball from the Cuban Giants to Jackie Robinson* (Lincoln: University of Nebraska Press, 2005), 63. In addition to the republished edition edited by Malloy, published in 1995 by the University

repulsion. In short, they conjured the "smell" of citizenship via an assemblage of mismatched pieces. While playing the national game, these inept creatures—an anomalous cross of human and animal— of Nebraska Press, a second republication has appeared more recently, introduced and annotated by Gary Ashwill and published by Summer Game Books in 2014.

2. "Purses I Have Fought For," *Indianapolis Freeman*, May 18, 1907.

3. *Sol White's History of Colored Base Ball* (Lincoln: University of Nebraska Press, 1995), 3.

4. James E. Brunson, *The Early Image of Black Baseball* (Jefferson, NC: McFarland, 2009).

5. Brunson, *The Early Image of Black Baseball*, 117–118; "A Picture of the Editor," *Washington Bee*, July 4, 1885; "News and Sentiment," *Huntsville (AL) Gazette*, April 10, 1886; "Our Colored Artist," *Washington Bee*, October 9, 1886; "Odds and Ends," *New York Freeman*, October 16, 1886; "The Week in Society," *Washington Bee*, June 19, 1897; "No Title," *Washington Bee*, December 4, 1897.

6. "What the Future Greats Are Doing," *Philadelphia Inquirer*, August 5, 1906; "Cubes Got Going in the 7th Inning," *Philadelphia Inquirer*, August 12, 1906.

7. *Sol White's History of Colored Base Ball*, 157.

8. "Colored Society," *Springfield (IL) Record*, June 18, 1898; "Jay Kay Talks," *Utica (NY) Globe*, May 6, 1916; "Chords and Discords," *Utica Globe*, June 12, 1920; "Unpublished History of Football and Baseball, 7," *Norfolk (VA) News Journal and Guide*, January 21, 1923; "Unpublished History of Football and Baseball, 7," *Norfolk News Journal and Guide*, January 27, 1923; "Fay Says," *Chicago Defender*, February 24, 1923; "Then and Now," *Utica (NY) Daily Press*, March 22, 1939; "Teed Pell Honored," *Utica Daily Press*, August 8, 1942; "Reminiscences From an Old-Timer's Scrap Book," *Chicago Defender*, September 2, 1933; "John W. Rose Dies," *Poughkeepsie (NY) Daily Eagle*, May 13, 1935.

9. "Base Ball," *Utica (NY) Daily Observer*, November 29, 1870; "Base Ball," *New York Clipper*, April 8, 1871; "Base Ball," *New York Clipper*, April 8, 1871.

10. "Base Ball Items," *Jackson (MI) Citizen Patriot*, May 15, 1874; "Amateur Notes," *Chicago Inter-Ocean*, September 4, 1874; "The Mutuals and Clippers," *Winona (MN) Republican*, August 14, 1875; "Base Ball," *Winona Republican*, September 13, 1875; "Base Ball," *Winona Republican*, September 15, 1875; "The Clippers," *Winona Republican*, September 16, 1875; "The Ball and Bat," *Winona Republican*, September 20, 1875; "Minnesota," *Milwaukee Sentinel*, September 20, 1875; "Red Caps and Clippers," *Winona Republican*, October 18, 1875; "The Sold Game," *Winona Republican*, October 20, 1875; "No Title," *Winona Weekly Republican*, Oct 20, 1875.

11. "Yesterday's Game Between the Colored B.B. Clubs of the Dual City," *Minneapolis Tribune*, August 31, 1876; "Base Ball Playing," *Minneapolis Tribune*, September 21, 1876; "Base Ball," *Minneapolis Tribune*, June 2, 1878; "Sporting News," *Chicago Inter-Ocean*, September 14 1878; "Base Ball," *Minneapolis Tribune*, November 10, 1878; "No Title," *New York Clipper*, April 7, 1883; "The Emerald Diamond," *St. Louis Republican*, April 7, 1883; "The Black Sox," *St. Louis Republican*, April 15, 1883; "Base Ball," *Dayton (OH) Daily Democrat*, May 7, 1883; "Diamond Dust," *St. Louis Globe-Democrat*, May 20, 1883.

12. "Base Ball," *Sporting Life*, March 5, 1884; "The Cuban Giants," *Trenton (NJ) Evening Times*, May 13, 1886.

13. "Base Ball," *Chicago Inter-Ocean*, July 19, 1886.

14. Ibid., 155.

15. Shelly Mehlman Dinoher, *The Art of Baseball* (New York: Harmony Books, 1990), 21.

16. Toni Morrison, *Playing in the Dark: Whiteness in the Literary Imagination* (New York: Random House, 1993), 38.

17. "There is a difference between a 'portent' (portentum) and 'an unnatural being' (portentuosus). Portents are beings of transformed appearance, as, for instance, is said to have happened when in Umbria a woman gave birth to a serpent. But an unnatural being strictly speaking takes the form of slight mutation, as for instance in the case of someone born with six fingers." Eco, *The Infinity of Lists*, 158.

18. Young, *Black Frankenstein*, 38–67

19. Peter P. Hinks, *David Walker's Appeal to the Colored Citizens of the World* (University Park: Penn State Press, 2000), 75; Peter P. Hinks, *To Awaken My Afflicted Brethren: David Walker and the Problem of Antebellum Slave Resistance* (University Park: Penn State Press, 1996); Harriet A. Washington, *Medical Apartheid: The Dark History of Medical Experimentation on Black Americans from Colonial Times to the Present* (New York: Random House, 2008); Todd Lee Savitt, *Race and Medicine in Nineteenth and Early Twentieth Century America* (Kent: Kent State University Press, 2007); Alexander Nemerov, *The Body of Raphaelle Peale* (Berkeley: University of California Press, 2001), 125–128

20. Young, *Black Frankenstein*, 19–43.

21. *Ibid.*, 68–71.

22. *Ibid.*

23. James E. Brunson, "James A. Smith and the Image of the Colored Sporting Fraternity of Cleveland, Ohio, 1883–1889," *Black Ball* 1, no. 2 (fall 2008): 12–40; "Base Ball," *New York Clipper*, July 23, 1870; "No Title," *Ottawa (IL) Free Trader*, August 13, 1870; "Local Brevities," *Andrew County Republicans* (Savannah, MO), August 30, 1872; "Quaker City Notes," *Harrisburg (PA) Telegraph*, July 17, 1895.

24. Sarah Burns, *Painting the Dark Side: Art and the Gothic Imagination in Nineteenth Century America* (Berkley: University of California Press, 2006), 118.

25. "Base Ball," *New Orleans Daily Picayune*, August 29, 1881.

26. Michael E. Lomax, *Black Baseball Entrepreneurs, 1860–1901* (Syracuse, NY: Syracuse University Press, 2003), 5–17.

27. *Ibid.*, 16; Daniel R. Biddle and Murray Dubin, *Tasting Freedom: Octavius Catto and the Battle for Equality in Civil War America* (Philadelphia: Temple University Press, 2010), 10–17.

28. Young, *Black Frankenstein*, 55–57; J. De Amicis, "The Search for Community: Utica's African-American," *Ethnic Utica*, 2002, 7–35; "Sesquicentennial," *Utica (NY) Observer-Dispatch*, September 7, 1882; "Base Ball," *Utica Daily Observer*, October 24, 1866; "Base Ball," *Utica Morning Herald*, November 3, 1867; "Base Ball Extraordinary," *Utica Daily Observer*, October 29, 1868; "Base-Ball Matters," *Cincinnati Commercial Tribune*, August 18, 1869; "Events of the Week," *Utica Weekly Herald*, September 14, 1869; "Fearless and Heavy Hitters," *Utica Daily Observer*, September 21, 1869; "The Fearless Base-Ball Club," *Utica Daily Observer*, May 4, 1870; "The Colored Championship," *New York Herald*, July 24, 1870; "Base Ball," *Buffalo (NY) Evening Courier and Republic*, August 26, 1876; "Grand Base Ball Tournament," *Geneva (NY) Gazette*, September 10, 1876; "Local Affair," *Buffalo Courier*, September 13, 1876; "Vicinity Items," *Geneva Gazette*, September 15, 1876; "Base Ball Tournament," *Geneva Gazette*, September 17, 1876; "Colored Ballists," *Buffalo Courier*, September 20, 1876; "Vicinity Items," *Geneva Gazette*, September 22, 1876.

29. "Corrected History," *Harrisburg (PA) Telegraph*, January 23, 1886.

30. Burns, *Painting the Dark Side*, 46–48; *Springfield (IL) State Register*, August 26, 1867; "Outdoor Sports," *New York Herald-Tribune*, May 24, 1867; "National Base Ball Convention," *Cincinnati Gazette*, December 16, 1867.

31. "A Heavy Base Ball Game," *Harrisburg Patriot*, June 20, 1867; "The National Game," *Harrisburg Patriot*, June 21, 1867.

32. "Rome Matters," *Utica (NY) Daily Observer*, August 2, 1867; "Defines His Position," *Rome (NY) Citizen*, August 9, 1867.

33. "Rome Matters," *Utica Daily Observer*, August 2, 1867; "Defines His Position," *Rome (NY) Citizen*, August 9, 1867.

34. Young, *Black Frankenstein*, 87–90; Brunson, "A Mirthful Spectacle: Race, Blackface Minstrelsy, and Baseball, 1874–1888," *Nine* 17, no. 2 (spring 2009): 13–30.

35. David Roediger, *The Wages of Whiteness: Race and the Making of the American Working Class* (London: Verso Books, 2007), 118–119.

36. "Amusements," *Brooklyn Daily Eagle*, August 30, 1867; "Amusements," *Brooklyn Daily Eagle*, November 6, 1868.

37. "Richard M. Hooley Dead," *New York Times*, September 9, 1893; "Hooley's Minstrels," *Syracuse (NY) Courier and Union*, June 30, 1869.

38. Brunson, "A Mirthful Spectacle, 13–30.

39. "Scraps of Humor," *Camden (NJ) Democrat*, August 5, 1871.

40. Brunson, *The Early Image of Black Baseball*, 161.

"They Covered Themselves in Glory": The Lost Baseball World of the New Negro

In his provocative essay "Lost World of the New Negro," historian Wilson Jeremiah Moses challenges traditional views of the origins of the New Negro Movement, also called the Negro Renaissance or Harlem Renaissance. According to such views, it was during the first period of the Great Migration, from approximately 1917–1925, that Southerners introduced black America's first cultural rebirth: country folklore and the blues aesthetic. While slumming working-class communities, upper- and middle-class whites "discovered" and patronized black creativity. Blues music, for example, had a profound impact. The blues musical genre not only references the musical scale, including "blue notes," but names "the social and psychic afflictions and aspirations" of black Americans. Blues music conjured negative associations, in particular, uninhibited sexual desires. "Sovereignty in sexual matters," writes Angela Davis, "marked an important divide between life during slavery and life after emancipation." Urban black spaces were sexualized in the minds of whites, places where social pleasure seekers imagined or participated in unabashed sexual freedom. Patrons rewarded the aesthetic practices of black musicians, dancers, literary, and visual artists who sexualized racial difference. Black urban culture came to be associated with "primitivism," and slumming was complicit in conflating black sexuality with "primitive identity."[1]

Moses offers a counterview. The District of Columbia built cultural institutions and intellectual traditions foundational to the New Negro Movement. That there was a black middle-class presence in Washington, D.C. (and other Northern cities, for that matter) before the first wave of the Great Migration is undeniable. Some of the city's black inhabitants had been freeborn, and others escaped from Southern bondage. Some possessed visibly mixed racial ancestry and could pass as whites; others had dark complexions. They came from the West Indies, Canada, Ohio, Pennsylvania, and from many Southeastern states, including Virginia, West Virginia, Kentucky, Tennessee, Alabama, Georgia, Florida, and Arkansas. Between 1845 and 1895, they built a respectable community composed of entrepreneurs, ministers, intellectuals, educators, musicians, artists, skilled workers, and athletes. Embracing class labels such as "blue-vein society," "colored aristocrats," and "aristocrats of color," they laid the foundations for the New Negro Movement.

The New Negro Movement embodied neither the birth nor rebirth of black culture. Located at the nexus of bondage and freedom, the New Negro metaphor has a complex socio-cultural history. Its earliest use was in the late 18th century and refers to newly arrived enslaved Africans in the Americas. By contrast, "Old Negroes" were enslaved Africans that had been acculturated within the North American slave regime. By 1865, however, the paradigm had been turned upside-down: black freedmen became "New Negroes"; Northern blacks and freeborn Southern blacks were "Old Negroes." The latter often described themselves as "Old Settlers," which denoted free citizens who had lived in their communities for more than 35 years. Educated and culturally refined, the Old Settlers built cultural institutions and established intellectual traditions. As Henry Louis Gates put it, the New Negro sought "to re-create the face of the race, its public face."

Blacks born before, during, and after emancipation, seeking self-empowerment and self-sufficiency through social uplift, brought about the first flowering of black intellectual and cultural creativity, soon credited to the "New Negro" and "New Negro Movement." The steady arrival of newly freed black Southern migrants, however, threatened the "colored aristocracy," viewed black peasant traditions, social customs, and the blue aesthetic as culturally backward. Anxious to protect their social status, they sought to distance themselves from their colored brethren. Among Washington's luminaries, Frederick Douglass, Alexander Crummell, William E. B. DuBois, Mary A. Hoyt, Georgia Savoy, William Marion Cook, and Paul Lawrence Dunbar figure prominently. DuBois, a baseball enthusiast and student of Crummell, was an exemplar. In 1890, the *Indianapolis Freeman* dubbed the Harvard-educated intellectual a "New Negro."[2]

But the Old Settlers cannot be dismissed simply "as toney mulatto snobs." The period saw institution-building, entrepreneurship, and baseball parallel the rise of disenfranchisement and social segregation. Commercial leisure establishments, baseball in particular, became popular. Both the colored elite and black working class embraced the national pastime, and black baseball became a form of cultural uplift and symbol of American modernism.

Moses doesn't address the relation of baseball to the New Negro. Still, blackball in the District of Columbia has a long historical tradition. Elsewhere I refer to this phenomenon as the "Lost Baseball World of the New Negro." Several 19th-century families participated in the national pastime, among them the Douglasses, Savoys, Smiths, Strathers, Roys, Cooks, Lewises, Chases, Johnsons, Colemans, Tripletts, Dorseys, Carters, Parks, and Browns. Many colored baseballists—entrepreneurs, government workers, hotel employees, educators, literary and visual artists, and musicians—belonged to the city's intelligentsia. In 1878, educated men formed the Sparta Club, a social and literary organization. Its membership included some of the city's prominent writers, musicians, visual artists, and thespians. The politician James Duncan Kennedy (Pickwick Base Ball Club), of New Orleans, belonged to the organization. In 1886, the Sparta Club organized a league, which included Howard University and the Colored High School. James H. Smith (Mutual Base Ball Club) was a trustee to the colored public schools. William Calvin Chase (Alert Base Ball Club) owned the *Washington Bee*, a colored newspaper, and Jesse Roy (Unique Base Ball Club) became its chief editor. Jacob

Figure 8. A Barber's Shop in Richmond, Virginia, *Illustrated London News*, March 3, 1861. Illustrated by Eyre Crowe. During a visit to the United States, the British artist Eyre Crowe documented the relationship of the barbering profession to enslavement. His depiction is significant because artisanal trades presented opportunities for freedom and business ownership. Before and after the Civil War, black barbers organized baseball clubs.

Strather (Manhattan Base Ball Club), a print engraver for the federal government, was a portrait artist. This is another unknown story in the history of blackball. To paraphrase Henry Louis Gates, the New Negro as baseballist re-created the face of the race, its public face.[3]

Of course, blackball contained traditional and conservative elements, non-traditional and radical elements, and baseball men who balanced their lives as devoted churchgoers and professional gamblers. Baseball's colored sporting fraternity contained writers, musicians, theatrical performers, and thinkers who were racially responsible and worthy of respect. Many of its members took politics seriously.[4]

This essay elaborates on the lost baseball world of the New Negro, specifically the roles of barbers and hotel waiters. It looks at the lived experiences of specific individuals. The colored tonsorial artist, or barber (**Fig. 8**), played an important role in the early formation of organized black baseball clubs. Colored baseball's waiter subculture provided a training ground for aspiring baseball players and steady income for veterans awaiting telegraphic dispatches to make better money and play for stronger organizations. While colored barbers could participate in an itinerate lifestyle that took them around the country, many established successful businesses that kept them in certain cities and towns (**Fig. 9**). On the other hand, colored employees of the hotel industry traveled the country, often during the summer resort season, and joined hotel teams. What colored barbers, waiters, porters, and bellhops had in common was leisure-class culture that allowed for the national growth of black baseball.

In the first section, the story of Henry Rosecranse Columbus, Jr., is examined. Enslaved at birth, Rosecranse spent his life in Kingston,

Figure 9. Robert Price, *Canonsburg (PA) Notes*, February 2, 1891. Price owned Canonsburg's Central Barber Shop and covered second base for the Barber Base Ball Club.

New York. After receiving his freedom, he went on to become a successful barber. Rosecranse's life story provides clues both to the origins of colored baseball and to the role of the barber in the formation of the earliest teams. The second section zeroes in on black baseball's hotel-waiter subculture. It looks at several baseball men who excelled in the hotel industry, attaining the management position of headwaiter, a highly sought after and esteemed status symbol. What links these men is colored baseball. Horace P. Hall, Frank P. Thompson, and Alexander Plummer organized and managed their respective hotel's baseball organizations.

Finally, black baseball minstrelsy is revisited. Black baseballist and minstrels formed a Gilded Age brotherhood. On the stage and diamond, they displayed an aesthetic style that coalesced from the vernacular rhythms and behaviors of everyday black life. Without first examining this black aesthetic, one cannot seriously discuss the problematical relationship of "negro comedy" to black baseball. Minstrel men played baseball and the players performed minstrelsy. Nineteenth-century sports journalists often misread black baseball performance as minstrelsy. It was much more complicated—and sophisticated. The players engaged in social and cultural resistance, making conscious use of what Robyn Kelly calls the "Cult of True Sambohood." This racist ideology stereotyped certain black baseball mannerisms (physical gesticulations and vernacular) as signs of laziness, ineptitude, or a childlike penchant to wander. Players understood the "Cult of True Sambohood" and used the racial contradictions to their advantage.

Tonsorial Artist as Baseballist: Henry Rosecranse Columbus, Jr.

Henry Rosecranse Columbus, Jr., is an exemplar of the black baseballist. His life is fascinating not only because it encompasses enslavement, emancipation, and the Gilded Age, but also because it sheds light on the early history of baseball among black barbers, or men of the "tonsorial arts." In 1881, a local reporter interviewed Rosecranse, and an extensive article appeared in various New York newspapers. He was born in 1804, in Ulster County, New York, at an establishment in the village of Kingston called the Coffee House. As a boy, Rosecranse and his mother worked for Levi Johnston (Rosecranse's mother was owned by the Levi Tappan family). Following the passage of laws ending slavery in New York State, he attained his freedom. He learned the barber trade from Thomas Harley, a black man and famous barber in his day. Two years later, he accepted a position as barber and waiter at the Kingston Hotel. After eleven years, he opened a barbershop, providing haircuts and shaves, hot baths, and boot blacking. He became successful, a pillar of the community who could recall the early history of Kingston and its community.[5]

Rosecranse's reminisces about Pinkster are illuminating: "There was the Pinkster holiday, the great holiday for the colored men. They used to meet at Black Hotel Tavern and shoot for turkeys. Then, the colored men raced horses on Peter Sharpe's lane. They used to come a great many of them with horses of their bosses, and run them. The bosses used to come and bet on the horses, and they had a great deal of fun. After the races, they used to *play ball* for egg nog" [italics added].[6]

At the turn of the 19th century, Ulster County had a total population of 29, 554, of whom more than 10 percent, 3,200, were of African descent. These enslaved blacks worked for Dutch farmers throughout the countryside, where as many as 30 to 60 percent of white households owned slaves. (It's possible to trace the origins of 19th-century colored players with Dutch names.) Language and culture had an impact on the black community. Historian Nell Painter

explains, "In rural counties like Ulster—in the Hudson Valley, on Long Island, and in New Jersey—the culture of local blacks was likely as not to be Afro-Dutch, although some blacks were Afro-Indian." Painter adds, "Surrounded by Dutch speakers, rural black New Yorkers grew up speaking the language of their community." The Pinkster Festival, the Dutch celebration of Pentecost (the Holy Spirit), proved significant as well. For the Afro-Dutch, Pinkster was a unique racial jubilee: by the nineteenth century, the holiday was primarily black and associated most closely with Albany, along with the Hudson Valley, on the Long Island, and in East New Jersey.[7]

Rosecranse, a master artisan, enjoyed the trappings of middle-class respectability. In newspaper advertisements, he promoted himself as a "barber and hair dresser." He operated a successful business, purchased real estate, and invested his money wisely. The reporter noted that the tonsorial artist was "an owner of lands and money in goodly quantity," and he interacted with leading political figures of his day. Physically impressive, he appeared "ten years younger" than his 67 years, and on horseback, he cut a dashing figure, being described as a "very fine specimen in the saddle." Rosecranse had the resources—leisure and money—to participate in Kingston's sporting culture.

The figure of the colored barber/baseballist is important (**Fig. 10**). It embodies verbal and visual representations of former slaves who developed artisan trades and parlayed close ties to masters and familiarity within antebellum high culture into opportunities to gain their freedom and to own barbershops. According to Douglas W. Bristol, colored men invented the first-class tonsorial parlor, their establishments combining "upscale décor and masculine conviviality." The tonsorial profession transformed colored barbers into "men of the world" and "established the basis for black middle-class identity." Like their white counterparts, colored barbers "developed a conception of respectability based on economic independence and the virtues associated with small businessmen." They had conservative

Figure 10. Negro Waiter, *Harper's Monthly Magazine*, October 1886. By the mid-1860s, black employees not only served meals but entertained hotel guests by performing theatricals and musicals, and by playing baseball matches.

goals, among which was to provide decent jobs for other black Americans and pass something on to their children. Building good reputations for thrift, community involvement, and work ethic, they would become conspicuously upstanding members of society, or at least of the black community.[8]

Descriptions of the visual objects displayed in Rosecranse's shop are illuminating: the "furniture and pictures smack of times long gone by." "Ancient pictures" of the Mexican War and revolution, "quaint" lithographs of New York City, and portraits of American generals compete for attention with a portrait of prizefighters John Morrissey and John L. Sullivan. The latter picture, displayed above the doorway, gives pause. Prizefighting images, important to certain patrons, proliferated in the visual print media. Like baseball images, they graced the walls of firehouses, saloons, and other public and private spaces. Rosecranse was an avid boxing fan. He appreciated baseball. After being asked if the sport he had played was similar to the current game, he replied, "Something like it, only the ball wasn't near so hard, and we had much more fun playing." The biographical lists of colored baseballists include men who fancied themselves prizefighters.[9]

The 1881 interview also shows that Kingston's black community engaged in ball playing during Pinkster, "the Great Holiday for the colored men." Sporting events during Pinkster can be traced to the beginning of the nineteenth century. In 1803, the *New York Spectator* reported: "Sports of various kinds commence in the different camps, where parties collect according to their different tastes, to amuse and be amused." While ball playing is not specifically mentioned here, Rosecranse's account is consistent with those that make the sport a central holiday activity. By 1859, black baseballists incorporated ballgames into their activities celebrating West Indies Emancipation Day along with other special social functions important to the community.[10]

Since the 1850s, Kingston had sponsored white and colored ballclubs, and Rosecranse probably witnessed organized antebellum contests. In 1862, Kingston's Eclipse Club and the Hudson Club of Newburgh, New York, met, with the former winning, 49–18. Rosecranse could have attended colored contests involving the towns of Brooklyn, Weeksville, Flushing, and Jamaica. He might also have seen an interracial game. Following the Civil War, Catskill's Union Base Ball Club (colored) challenged Kingston's Independent Club (white). The *Hudson Evening Register* reported: "The colored persuasion of Catskill having [been] imbued with the same spirit as the 'white trash,' had a base-ball soiree at Catskill on Tuesday. Upon this occasion they broke the friendly lance with the Independents of Ulster, and skunked them badly in five innings. The game stood Unions of Catskill 36, Independents of Kingston 7." By the 1870s, Kingston and Poughkeepsie, New York had developed a colored baseball rivalry.[11]

Included in this book are biographies of barbers involved in baseball, and they give an idea of the distribution of cities, towns, and hamlets throughout the country in which these men organized or sponsored ballclubs. In this regard, Bristol's *Knights of the Razor* is illuminating. In 1859, Baltimore hosted the Barbers' Beneficial Association picnic. More than one thousand colored barbers attended. The *Weekly Anglo-African* covered the story. While the names and hometowns of the barbers are unknown, the gathering's location makes it likely that baseball was among the festivities; in addition to host-city Baltimore, the not-so-distant towns of Flushing, Jamaica, Brooklyn, Williamsburg, and Newark also sponsored colored nines. Such antebellum activities had political consequences. By 1861, Baltimore's Board of Police had declared such events unlawful; they "violated a provision of the Code which prohibited the assembling in the State of non-resident colored people."[12]

The number of colored barbers/players covers vast territory, and the list below links the two professions throughout the country. Colored barbers organized teams throughout the country, and good ones. They were so numerous that a historical study can be made of them. One baseball writer would rightly add this topic to black baseball's "uncharted territory." It offers the story of the barber-as-baseballist as a "specimen, example, or indication" that, as Umberto Eco has said of such lists, "leav[es] the reader to imagine the rest."[13]

A cursory look at the list shows that between the 1860s and 1890s, barber-baseballists played a foundational role in the spread of the national pastime in the black community. New York, Massachusetts, Ohio, Illinois, Indiana, Minnesota, Tennessee, Georgia, and North Carolina are prominent in the biographical sketches. These men loved and promoted the game. "Rather than seeing themselves as despised menials occupying a marginal economic niche," writes Bristol, "black barbers conceived of themselves as heirs to a tradition that made them men of the world…. Their achievements in business represented only a means to an end, for they sought to establish a basis for a black middle-class identity." The "Knights of the Razor" used baseball to help define the boundaries of freedom in a post–Civil War world.[14]

Black Baseball's Hotel-Waiter Subculture

In a previous work, I explored the idea of colored baseball's hotel-waiter culture, claiming that the burgeoning hotel industry complicated the waiter's position (**Figs. 11 and 12**). Commercialization of

Figure 11. A Waiter in the Galt House, Louisville, Kentucky. From Eric King's *The Great South*, 1875. Illustrated by J. Wells Champney. "Louisville is famous for several excellent institutions," wrote King, "noteworthy among which are the Galt House, a massive stone structure in the English style, long celebrated by foreign travelers as the best hotel in the United States." The Galt House was also noted for its hotel nine. Between 1874 and 1875, the Mutuals, Socials, Fair Plays, and Globes each served as the hotel team.

Figure 12. Blackball Waiters, Danbury, Connecticut, 1880. Between 1880 and 1886, Danbury's hotel nine created a name for itself. In 1886, the hotel team played Poughkeepsie's white nine under the name Cuban Giants. At least three of the real Cuban Giants played with the Danbury men, raising the possibility that the Trenton Cuban Giants had arranged the whole affair. That same day, the Trenton Cuban Giants played a contest at Newark, New Jersey (Library of Congress).

hotel activities blurred the boundary between hospitality and entertainment. A. K. Sandoval-Strausz explains: "The operation of a hotel depended upon enormous numbers of workers doing a wide variety of tasks." Individual jobs varied greatly in their duties, income, and conditions. The desirable positions such as barber or headwaiter involved direct contact with guests. The supervisory headwaiter position brought middle-class wages, and hotels advertised openings both regionally and nationally. Experienced headwaiters could secure positions at leading hotels throughout the country. Less prestigious and well paid were the semi-skilled positions, including waiters, cooks, doormen, and bellhops. While they needed no formal education and could be trained in a matter of days or weeks, they did require a "certain amount of behavioral polish."[15]

For the hotel baseball teams listed in this work (and perhaps others unaccounted for), entertainment for guests and patrons required that colored waiters possess additional skills and talents. Many, for instance, were musicians. Hotel employees provided entertainment before, during, and after meals; they performed at indoor and outdoor events. In 1870, at the International Hotel of Niagara Falls, New York, the colored waiters organized the International Glee Club. These "colored vocalists" performed classical European works, "plantation songs," and comedic pieces that gained them a wide reputation. By 1880, headwaiter Horace H. Hall and Charles S. Butler had become celebrities throughout New York and Canada. "The concert to be given at the Prospect Park Pavilion promises to be something well worth listening to," reported the *Niagara Falls Gazette*. "A very fine program has been planned. Mr. Charles Summer Butler is the musical director and is highly spoken of by the press in different cities, where he has sung. The *Albany Press and Knickerbocker* reported: 'The rendition of the solo, 'Let all Obey,' was received with unbounded applause.' Mr. Horace H. Hall headwaiter of the International is manager."[16]

Another prerequisite was baseball ability. The International Hotel's

colored employees organized a ballclub. The team was large enough to have first and second nines. Hall, a speedy center fielder led a competitive club for years, was player-manager. Charles Butler and his brother, E. A. Butler, Hall's brother Joseph, and power hitter T. Demery played for the team as well. Between 1870 and 1871, Demery managed the International's tonsorial parlors and played for Troy, New York's Hannibal Base Ball Club. The "Internationals" (in the 1860s and 1870s, they were nicknamed "Stars" and "Rainbows") competed against white teams and top-flight black clubs such as the Mutuals of Washington, DC, and the Excelsiors of Lockport, New York. In addition, they "measured bats" with other black, New York–based hotel nines in Rochester, Elmira, Amsterdam, Schenectady, Gloversville, and Johnston. The Internationals remained a combination of "old and experienced players" and younger talents.[17]

Black baseball's relation to the hostelry is significant for at least a few reasons. First, the hotel work introduced colored players to leisure-class life. Second, it provided leisure time to play ball and intermingle with white guests, including ballplayers and members of the sporting fraternity. Finally, it offered opportunities for guests to interact with employees, enhancing the latter group's social status as ballplayers. Linked through work and play, barbers and waiters affirmed not only occupational bonds but the brotherhood of colored baseball as well. For their part, the hotels spread sporting culture through entertainment, increasing their profits through capital investments. The Cataract and International, both of Niagara Falls, served as "recreational outposts for prosperous city dwellers and did not significantly alter the region's urban geography." Moreover, these grand hotel-centered resorts had become important political symbols when violence involving black hotel staff from two of them, the Cataract and the International, captured the attention of the entire nation.[18]

The history of black hotel employees at Niagara Falls dates back to the antebellum period. In 1850, 41 free people of color resided in

250: CATARACT HOUSE FROM GREEN ISLAND, NIAGARA FALLS.

Figure 13a. Cataract House, Niagara Falls, New York, 1890s. Before and after the Civil War, wealthy Southerners patronized the hotel. Political conflicts with the black player-waiters were not unusual.

CATARACT HOUSE, NIAGARA FALLS, N.Y.

Figure 13b. Cataract House, Niagara Falls, New York, 1890s. In the 1860s, the Cataract House waiters organized a ballclub that would play white and black organizations into the 1890s.

Niagara Falls, and by 1865 the number stood at 126, more than tripling in the space of 15 years. The black population had in fact peaked at 242 in 1860, but as historian Michael Boston notes, many who lived in Niagara Falls then returned to the South to be with families and other loved ones. Two of the most prominent hotels in the tourist town were the Cataract, built in 1825, and the International, built in 1853 (**Fig. 13**). Both took on black employees. As Boston notes, "It has ever been written about the Cataract House (and probably held true for the International Hotel as well) that rich Southerners who patronized this hotel before and after the Civil War were made to feel at home by the colored help." Blacks labored as waiters, cooks, bellboys, servants, janitors, and entertainers.[19] Many of these employees supported abolition, and some were willing to act in support of it.

It was the custom of wealthy Southern planters to visit Niagara Falls and to bring with them one to three well-dressed "body servants." Colored waiters reportedly encouraged the slaves to leave their masters and cross the Canadian border to freedom. In one case, the Cataract Hotel waiters, aided by the local black community, made an unsuccessful attempt to rescue a "dusky maiden from the bonds of slavery."[20]

For proslavery and abolitionist factions, there was a political dimension to all of this. Abolitionists challenged the Fugitive Slave Law of 1850, which greatly expanded federal judicial authority and directed federal authorities to directly guarantee the security of slavery. The law made it easier to return fugitive men and women to enslavement. It allowed federal authorities to call citizens into service to aid in the law's enforcement. For the colored waiters of the Cataract and International, enforcing the rights of slaveholders at the expense of free and fugitive people of color provoked a militant response.[21]

In 1853, a warrant was issued for a colored waiter of the Cataract House, Patrick Sneed (alias "Joseph Watson"), charging him with "murder in Savannah, Georgia." "Bloodhounds," an epithet used by blacks to describe slave catchers, had targeted Sneed. To shift the discussion away from enslavement, some newspapers referred to him, oddly, as "white without any admixture of the Negro." Colored waiters fought to secure his freedom. Attempts to arrest him resulted in a "pitched battle" between waiters, law enforcement, and Irish laborers in the hotel dining room and eventually moved to the International Suspension Bridge, over which fugitive slaves often crossed into Canada. "The scene at the Falls was one of great excitement," reported the *Syracuse Journal*, "and was witnessed by hundreds on the banks of both sides of the river." Sneed's escape to Canada failed, and according to the *Syracuse Daily Standard*, he was "taken under the provisions of the Fugitive Slave Law." The press, however, later exposed a conspiracy, and a federal judge threw out the case, setting Sneed free.[22]

What do we know about the men who made up black baseball's hotel-waiter subculture, and who were they? A couple of case studies go some way toward answering such questions.

Frank P. Thompson

Between 1875 and 1879, Frank P. Thompson served as headwaiter for Savannah, Georgia's Pulaski House and caught and covered right field for Savannah's Chatham Base Ball Club, which competed against the likes of the Manhattans, of Washington, and Trenton Cuban Giants, among others. In 1879, a Philadelphia hotel

offered Thompson a headwaiter position, which he accepted. There he was introduced to another "hotel man," Stanislau Cassius Govern, "the originator of the Hotel Brotherhood."[23]

During the summer, Thompson served as headwaiter of Long Branch, New Jersey's Howland Hotel, where he came in contact with the District of Columbia's black baseball men, including Wilson Carey, Joseph Myers, Harry Cummings, Phil Smoot, and John Curry. By 1883, he had organized Philadelphia's Keystone Athletics Base Ball Club, and by 1885 the team was touring outside the Northeast: "The Athletic Base Ball Club, Mr. Thompson, manager, has gone south on a professional trip. It is said to be a strong team." When the Keystones returned to Philadelphia that fall, they stopped in Baltimore, Maryland, and played the Mutual Base Ball Club (colored), losing by a score of 19 to 3. In 1884, while playing at San Marcos Hotel in St. Augustine, Florida, one report recounted the team's exploits: "[The Keystones'] remarkable triumphs of last season have been repeated during the winter, they having lost, we are told, but one game. They will open the summer season at Babylon in June."[24]

Thompson's skills and baseball knowledge permitted cultural access (**Fig. 14**). In 1885, he organized and managed Babylon, New York's Keystone Athletics Base Ball Club, who played against hotel guests and regional competition at the Argyle Hotel: "In a series of 9 games they won 6, lost 2, and tied 1 against New York and local and white teams." The *Huntington Long Islander* reported on one of the games, which was apparently a decisive victory for Thompson's nine: "A spirited game was played on the Argyle Grounds Tuesday afternoon between the Keystone Athletics, a club composed of the black employees at the Argyle, and the Farmingdales, a white scrub club from Farmingdale. The 'cullud' boys taught the white gents from 'F' how to play base-ball, winning by a score of 29 to 1." The "Keystone" name links Thompson to the club and references Pennsylvania, the "Keystone State." Most of the players hailed from Pennsylvania.[25]

In late 1885, John L. Lang, a white Philadelphia barber and promoter, assumed control of Thompson's club and renamed it "Lang's Giants." The *Oswego Daily Times Express* reported: "The manager of Lang's Colored Giants, a Philadelphia base-ball combination of black men, who played ball in Cuba last season, has written Manager Ormabee, of the Stars, asking for a date here." This moniker didn't last; by September, the club was renamed "Cuban Giants." In 1886, Thompson and R. B. Pope co-owned and operated Boston's Coddington House, a resort that catered to the black community; it also served as headquarters for Cuban Giants, by then based in Trenton. His bond with the team remained strong: "Frank P. Thompson, the proprietor of the Coddington House, Boston, and who was formerly the manager of the Cuban Giants, offers a gold scarf pin to the mem-

Figure 14. The Argyle Hotel, Babylon, New York, undated. The Argyle Hotel had hired black waiters from Philadelphia as early as 1884. Under the supervision of headwaiter Franklin P. Thompson, they organized the Keystone Athletics, which also played winter ball in St. Augustine, Florida.

ber of the Giants making the best general average in today's game. The ornament is in the form of two bats crossed and a ball in the lower angle." By 1900, Thompson was headwaiter in chief of the Florida East Coast Hotel Company, for whom he hired 70 headwaiters and employed 700 waiters.[26]

Alexander Plummer

Originally from Boston, Massachusetts, Alexander Plummer established his reputation as an exceptional headwaiter, talented musician, and fine ballplayer. Anticipating new employment and baseball opportunities, Plummer moved to Chicago in 1883. He helped to form United Waiter's Union No. 1 of Chicago and served on the union's board of managers. He also joined the prestigious Autumn Social Club, members from which organized Chicago's Gordon and Unknown ballclubs in 1884. Plummer was at first hopeful of joining the Gordons, a professional club, but after a rift developed between him and club factions linked to the Gordons, he joined the Unknowns.[27]

By early 1885, he had moved to St. Paul, Minnesota (**Figs. 15 and 16**). There Plummer became headwaiter for Lafayette Hotel of Minnetonka Beach. Described in the *Western Appeal*, a black newspaper, as a "Boston boy," Plummer managed a young corps of black college men from throughout the East and South. He served as player-manager for the "Lafayettes," an aggregation composed of St. Louis, Chicago and Cleveland ballplayers. In the offseason, Plummer was headwaiter for St. Paul's Hotel Ryan. As in Chicago, he actively engaged with black society, with one newspaper noting that he "deserves credit for the interest he has taken in the advancement of his race, both socially and politically." He was vice president of the Excelsior Literary and Social Club. A good writer and eloquent speaker, Plummer endorsed and supported the appointment of a full company of black firemen. He was also a correspondent for the

Chicago Conservator, a black newspaper. In 1886, he briefly played (probably during the winter resort season) for Trenton, New Jersey's Cuban Giants.[28]

In 1888 Plummer became headwaiter for the Millard Hotel, in Omaha, Nebraska (**Fig. 17**). He reorganized a local black baseball nine, naming them the "Lafayettes," apparently a reference to his previous employer and team. The Lafayettes later formed the nucleus of the Lincoln Giants, and in 1889 Plummer organized the "Beacons," a collection of black players from Nebraska, Missouri, and Kansas. The Beacons would sometimes play white teams, as the *Omaha Daily Bee* reported:

> The Omahas and the Beacons, the black team, went out to the park yesterday to have a little fun with each other. They had it, and a crowd probably of one thousand people looked on with feelings of joy, regret, and remorse confusedly mingled. All three of the Omahas pitchers took a hand in the game, but Willis made the best showing of all, striking out no less than six, and not allowing Plummer's pounders a single hit. It should be explained that the black team only embraced four of the Beacons' regular men.

The Beacons lost badly, 24–6, but Plummer was undeterred. He continued to play baseball into the 1890s, covering first base for Nebraska's Lincoln Giants and Kroner Grays.[29]

Thompson and Plummer were two prominent members of black baseball's hotel-waiter subculture, but as the biographical lists in this book demonstrate, there were many others. The hotels afforded men of color places to showcase their talent and skills, both as dependable employees and baseball players. These men used the hotel industry to communicate, sending dispatches and receiving correspondence about visiting teams, scheduling, and available players. High-demand position players and pitchers might be recruited for a single contest

Figure 15. The Merchant Hotel, St. Paul, Minnesota, undated. The Merchant Hotel hired black employees from several states, including Missouri, Illinois, New York, Kentucky, and Ohio. Some of these individuals joined the hotel nine and competed against white and black organizations from the 1870s until the 1890s.

Figure 16. The Metropolitan Hotel, St. Paul, Minnesota, undated. Like the Merchant Hotel, the Metropolitan hired black employees from around the country, fielding a baseball team with some of them. Between the 1870s and 1890s, the hotel nine competed against white and black organizations.

Figure 17. The Millard Hotel, Omaha, Nebraska. From *The Omaha Illustrated*, published in 1888. Between 1888 and 1889, Walter Alexander Plummer served as headwaiter for the Millard Hotel. Plummer, a Bostonian, also managed and covered first base for the hotel's Lafayette and Beacon teams. He would later play for hotel teams in St. Paul, Chicago, and Boston, as well.

or a series of high-stakes games, with the club in need covering a player's transportation and boarding expenses and paying him handsomely. Sometimes hotel jobs were offered. The accounts follow two general patterns. In one, an itinerant player moves from one hotel to another playing ball; in the other, a principal player remains in the same town, hotel or team. "The aggregate effect of the hotel system—which combined an exuberant commercial culture with legions of mobile human participants" writes Sandoval-Strausz, "was to serve as a conduit for goods, services, behaviors, and styles in a developing and expanding market culture."[30] Black baseball both supported the system and flourished by it.

Baseball Minstrelsy and Black Aesthetic Style Revisited

Powerful minstrel men—that is, white professionals—that controlled the industry formed a brotherhood. They thrived in the "post-emancipation economy," benefitting from new forms of labor that continued to be structured by race even after enslavement had legally ended. With access to economic capital and the best theatrical talent, they collaborated with the sporting fraternity and helped to fashion the entertainment industry. Many black players—musicians, dancers, circus strong men, tumblers, and acrobats—fit the bill. The genuine colored artist embodied a black aesthetic style that coalesced from the vernacular rhythms and behaviors of everyday black life. Among the countless minstrelsy men who played baseball: Irving Sayles, William Speed, William Saunders, Horace Murray, Theodore Fry, Burrell Hawkins, Hosea Easton and Charles B. Hicks (**Fig. 18**).

In September of 1865, the "negro minstrel troupes" of Henry J. Wood and Richard M. Hooley agreed to play a ballgame at Morrisania (today the south Bronx), on the Union Grounds, near Morrisania Station. They scheduled the contest for the end of the month, at 11 a.m., "early for a base-ball match," the papers pointed out. These Brooklyn and New York troupes represented the best and perhaps most successful artists in minstrel entertainment. Curiously, the opposing nines felt compelled to express displeasure with current

Figure 18. Charles B. Hicks, owner of the Original Georgia Minstrels (1870), co-owner of the Hick-Sawyer Minstrels (1877–1879), and owner of Hicks-Georgia Minstrels. All three troupes were also baseball clubs.

race relations. The *Brooklyn Eagle* reported: "On account of the well-known opposition to colored base-ball players the [Wood and Hooley] nines will appear in white faces, returning to cork again in the early evening." The match went on as scheduled, and according to the *New York Times*, "Some very good play was shown in numerous instances, although ruffianism prevailed at times to a considerable extent. The game had not proceeded far before it became evident that the Wood's party were altogether the most skillful exponents of the game, the score at the close of the fourth inning standing 13 to 2 in favor of Wood's nine."[31]

Why this antipathy towards the colored ballplayer? How did black freedom and demands for racial equality bring blackface minstrelsy and baseball together? One answer begins by tracing the early presence of organized black baseball clubs.

By the mid-nineteenth century, black organizations throughout the country celebrated Emancipation Day, the 1834 abolition of black enslavement in the British West Indies. "The 1ˢᵗ of August is to the colored people what the Fourth is to the American nation," the *New York Evening Express* reported, "a day of thanksgiving, jubilee and praise." Between 1856 and 1887, Joseph Abraham Trower, a prominent black Republican of Brooklyn's eastern district, managed the Emancipation Day festivities at Myrtle Park, where the day would conclude with a baseball tournament. In his address, Frederick Douglass acknowledged the appropriateness of such pastimes in marking the day: "We are here to enjoy ourselves, to play ball, to dance, to make merry, to make love, and to do everything that is pleasant." That same year, Trower and Peter T. Jewell, of Brooklyn's Unique Base Ball Club, coordinated a baseball game. Trower, whom newspapers described as a "person of handsome exterior and wonderful volubility of tongue," managed Williamsburg's Van Delken (Weldenken) Base Ball Club, which was often victorious in capturing the "ball and bat."[32]

While the fight for full and equal citizenship without regard to race remained subject to federal legislation, black baseball players focused their energies on the public realm. Immediately following the Civil War, they brought a new attitude of expression, demonstrating both aesthetic style and athletic prowess. Having explored how fashion affected baseball's image elsewhere, and how sartorial display distanced teams from the appearance of poverty, here I want to zero in on aesthetic style among the earliest colored organizations. Uniformed clubs in general, and fancy baseball uniforms in particular, reinforced in the public imagination black dandyism.

Consider Jersey City's Oneida Base Ball Club, a junior club that the local press regarded as part of the colored elite. To raise money for new uniforms the "Oneidas" hosted a fancy ball, and after the uniforms were purchased, a parade was the perfect opportunity to show them off. The *Journal* reported: "[The Oneida Club] marched down State Street yesterday afternoon in their new uniform, which is of the gorgeous and tasteful colors usually indulged in by our colored friends." From the perspective of white and black players alike, sartorial expressiveness embodied self-worth and middle-class aspirations. Fancy-dressed, strutting colored baseball players disrupted the "white cultural order," as art historian Richard Powell describes it, setting themselves off as "objects of spectatorship, personifications of difference, and purveyors of visual alarm," proving blacks' fitness for citizenship.[33]

Colored baseball players also shared their white brethren's fascination with uniforms that incorporated Orientalist and masonic paraphernalia. Cincinnati's Western Union Base Ball Club (1869) had a distinctively colored uniform that, in the sports journalists' view, overshadowed their ball playing. Against Newton, Ohio's Black Stocking Base Ball Club, the Western Unions sported red shirts, green pants, black sashes, black and white checkered stockings, and yellow fez caps surmounted with long red feathers. One reporter, Millar, was also struck by their "baseball mannerisms," which caricatured the theatrics of Native American Indians. He noted, "It kept one's head in a whirl to watch the antics of the men at the bases[,] and when they swat the ball and the player broke away to first, the Cherokee, Chicopee, Comanchee Indian yells would be weak whispering compared to the present-day style of coaching." For Millar, their ball playing appeared full of "antics."[34]

Millar's description of black "baseball mannerisms," and in particular his use of the word "antics," intrigues, recalling accounts of the ludicrous behavior of blackface performers. Hooley's nine, for one, included acrobats, and the troupe's pitcher, Tony Denier, performed "double somersaults between each delivery" (**Fig. 19**), his cleverness eliciting laughter from the spectators. Colored players astounded audiences with other, similar feats, as well. During a colored match between Chicago's Blue Stockings and Rockford's Pink Stockings, for instance, reporter Louis Meacham noted a peculiarity: "It consisted in an irresistible propensity, for tumbling head over heels when in the act of running bases or going for fly catches. Somersaults, which would have permanently doubled up and disabled a White Stocking [player], were counted as nothing by they of the colored hose, and resulted in much amusement among the spectators." Meacham's comment about the audience's reaction is telling, suggesting that the players aimed to do more than vanquish the opposition; they wanted to entertain. What's less clear is whether anyone in the audience—including the reporter—recognized this secondary purpose. Meacham reported that no one he spoke with seemed to know whether the tumbles were accidental or intentional, but the players, he noted, seemed unfazed.[35]

Figure 19. Tony Denier, blackface minstrel performer and pantomimist, 1860s. In 1865, Denier pitched for the "negro minstrel troupes" of Henry J. Wood and Richard M. Hooley, performing double somersaults between each delivery.

Colored players in fact exploited acrobatic and gymnastic displays as entertainment. They also used physical and verbal displays to intimidate their opponents. Reporters and minstrel men often missed or ignored this point, colluding to transform black expressivity into a minstrel show. Interestingly, the practice emerged before Hooley's "Base-Ball Farce" appeared. In 1862, the *Brooklyn Eagle* offered this banner headline for a colored match: "A New Sensation in Base Ball Circles—Sambo as a Ball Player and Dinah as an Emulator." The journalist, reportedly in search of another game, stumbled onto a match between the Unknowns, of Weeksville, and the Monitors, of Brooklyn, "both of African descent," a fact that would have "pleased [Henry Ward] Beecher, [Horace] Greeley, or any other of the luminaries of the radical wing of the Republican Party." So might have the black umpire, C. Orphate of Newark, New Jersey's Hamilton Base Ball Club.[36]

This vivid account describes spectators encircling contestants who are "as black as an ace of spades." Among the teams "were a number of old and well-known [colored] players." This seemingly innocuous line implicates the press in media suppression by acknowledging the presence of "well-known players" and by extension an awareness of either black clubs or colored baseball play. Yet the story contradicts itself in closing, indicating that "[t]his is the first match to our knowledge that has been played in this city between players of African descent." Such contradictions framed black baseball as novelty and helped to push it to the margins.[37]

Blackface minstrelsy broaches the questions Who can be a ballplayer? and How might baseball offer social mobility? Hooley's response suggests that reconstructed blacks, no matter their status or talent, would not be permitted into amateur baseball associations. Washington, DC's Alert Base Ball Club, in fact, provides evidence of this fact. In May 1867, the *New York Herald-Tribune* reported, "The Convention of Base Ball Players of the District of Columbia will hold a meeting week. A club composed of black players has applied for admission into the convention. Their request has not been acted upon." What transpired locally occurred throughout the country, with state baseball conventions ignoring or denying black membership. These events culminated at the National Convention of Base Ball Players. Held in Philadelphia in 1867, the convention passed a resolution "to the effect no club of persons of color, or having in its membership persons of color, should be admitted in to the National Association." The Pythians applied for membership but reluctantly withdrew the application.[38]

The press, through crude jokes, expressed its ambivalence. The *Albany Evening Journal* noted that "[t]he colored boys of Cleveland have organized a base-ball—probably a 'black ball'—club." Others seemed sympathetic. The *Jersey Journal* reported: "The Oneida Base Ball Club—composed of first rate players—will not be allowed in the National Base Ball Organization, because they are composed of colored men." The National Base-Ball Association, mused one critic, took itself too seriously: "The trembling terror of 'negro equality', that has got hold of all the great lights of the Democratic party and makes them shiver with apprehension and howl with anticipatory anguish, has penetrated even the dull heads of the gentry who assume to run the base-ball clubs in this country." Another tongue-in-cheek report noted, "The colored base-ball championship of America will be decided, today, by a match between the Excelsior club of Philadelphia and the Uniques of Brooklyn. The equality of the races is proven."[39]

Blackface minstrelsy not only complicated spectators' perceptions of black baseball mannerisms but continues to confound contemporary understandings of the porous boundary between baseball minstrelsy and aesthetic style. When the press dubbed the St. Louis Black

Stockings Base Ball Club a "blackfaced team" in 1883, for example, it was doubtful that the manager, Henry Bridgewater, had this epithet in mind; many of his players, described in one newspaper account as "strawberry blondes," could pass for white. This farcical nametag exposed minstrelsy's sustained commodification of the players' black image. It was an image that Bridgewater, formerly enslaved and a Lincoln Republican, abhorred. Still, Bridgewater—whose club played "a peculiar game"—wouldn't have denied the special relationship between barbers, waiters, ballplayers, and minstrels that had existed as early as the 1860s (**Fig. 20**). They all belonged to the colored sporting fraternity, and he interacted with them all. They exchanged ideas and techniques that helped them to hone their athletic skills and polish their theatrical performances, both on stage and on the green diamond.

In 1883, when the St. Louis Black Stockings soundly defeated the white Rockford Reds in a two-game series, the journalist reporting on the game reanimated the antebellum "darky" as monstrous spectacle, "mirabilis," or "portent" of pure literary imagination: "The darkies gobbled everything that took the air; no matter how wildly it flew, 'they got there Eli!' every time, and while apparently taking things easy, they were for all that punishing the home nine." The players become figures with mouths so large that they possess an uncanny ability to consume baseballs whole (**Fig. 21**). While the sources cited elsewhere in this book tell stories equally fantastic, other accounts never mention one player's name. Intentional or otherwise, the writers of the latter stories imply that they have neither space for nor interest in supplying names, leaving readers to imagine (unless they already know) who they might be.[40]

Eric Lott's description of blackface minstrelsy and its projections of the black body's "bold swagger, irrepressible desire, and sheer bodily display" dovetails neatly with the aesthetic style of black baseball mannerisms. When the Cuban Giants played the Cincinnati Reds in

Figure 20. Henry Bridgewater, owner and manager of the St. Louis Black Stockings, *St. Louis Globe-Democrat*, 1891. Between 1882 and 1886, Bridgewater's team dominated black baseball in the Mound City. In 1883, the Black Stockings toured the country and Upper Canada, playing more than eighty games against white and black organizations.

"*Come in 'Yah.*

Figure 21. "Come in Yah," *St. Louis Republic*, August 26, 1888. In the 1880s, the *St. Louis Republic* incorporated black images into baseball accounts. When the newspaper reported a game of the New Orleans Pinchbacks and St. Louis West Ends at Sportsman's Park, a staff artist supplied cartoons. This image appropriates minstrelsy's comic mask to portray a black coacher as monstrosity.

1887, for instance, the *Rocky Mountain News* reported that they harassed or "guyed" the major leaguers: "Tebeau was a conundrum to them and when he came to bat one of the Cuban Giants players shouted to the fielders: 'Heah comes dat great playah! Get back dar to the fence! Git back!' And the smoke-colored Giants moved out of sight. Tebeau struck out as he wildly fanned the air for the fourth time, the captain shouted: 'Everybody come in! He's out.'" Such cheeky strategies were already old among colored players when the Cuban Giants applied them against the Reds. These performances were intended to rattle opponents but, like the tumbling by the Blue Stockings and Pink Stockings, also brought fans to the ballpark.[41]

By 1888, baseball observers had declared the Trenton Cuban Giants "as funny as any minstrel troupe." Clarence Williams, the team's star catcher, was called "the most comical coacher ever invented." The *Niagara Falls Gazette* reported, "This is how the Captain of the Cuban Giants [Williams] coaches: 'Hit dat ball Mr. Johnsing. There's pretty uv room in de air. Now run wid de win. Rastus—dive—dive! Cum dis way Lemuel—don't embrace dat middle cushin' hyre, third base—lemme see you sprinter. Don't linger, don't linger!' He can "roll out a string of words with the rapidity that would make an auctioneer green with envy." His abilities so impressed white opponents that teams often contracted Williams to coach for their side.[42]

Baseball farce, or "Negro comedy," however, begins with neither the Trenton Cuban Giants nor the black players recruited to that club from the Washington Manhattans, Philadelphia Orions, Philadelphia Keystones, and the Trenton Browns. The idea that it did is pure baseball mythology. Like Lott's work, this book proposes a genealogy of the aesthetic style that gave form to their "peculiar" baseball mannerisms.

In September 1885, the newly organized Cuban Giants Base Ball Club (not yet the Trenton Cuban Giants) played at Williamsport, Pennsylvania. Team captain Clarence Williams may have negotiated the contest. It was a homecoming, of sorts. In 1883, he had caught for two Williamsport teams, one black (the Lumber Citys) and one white. A local celebrity, he was adored by fans, who filled the ballpark for his return with the Cuban Giants. "Williams was the leader of all amusement," wrote the *Williamsport Daily Gazette and Bulletin*; "Always in motion he managed to keep everyone in a good humor and many and loud were the peals of laughter he provoked. To enumerate the amusing parts of the game would be *to mention all of the players and also some of the colored people of the audience whose approval or disapproval was made manifest in many ways*" [italics added]. Who mentored Williams? What inspired the Harrisburg, Pennsylvania native?[43]

Before Clarence Williams, Javan Emory had captured the local imagination. Emory's family traced its black baseball lineage back to 1866. His father, Enoch Emory, was headwaiter for Williamsport's Herdic House and both organized and managed colored hotel ballclubs. Three sons (William, Javan, and Sims) worked for him and played on the teams. In 1868, William joined Williamsport's Independents, who would play Philadelphia's Pythians and Harrisburg's Monrovians. In 1876, the brothers played for Williamsport's Enterprise Club, for whom Javan became a star catcher. Throughout the 1870s and 1880s, Javan was a popular and respected player-manager for the Lumber City Base Ball Club whose services were sought by other regional clubs when they faced must-win games. In 1879, for instance, Harrisburg's Harley Base Ball Club recruited him for a colored contest against Elmira, New York's Casino Base Ball Club. He displayed great skill and showmanship and received "many compliments for his fine catching." In 1882, John Lang, white manager of the Philadelphia Orions, paid him to catch in another colored championship game. When not playing with black clubs, Emory caught for white teams. With the Lumber Citys, Clarence Williams served as Emory's backup.[44]

Javan and Sims Emory developed relationships with blackface artists who performed in local theatrical productions, including minstrel entertainments and cakewalks.[45] In 1871, the "Georgia Original Slave Troupe" performed at an engagement in Williamsport. The troupe, guided by colored manager Charles B. Hicks, had embarked on a year-long tour of England, Ireland, Scotland, Wales, and Germany. His company claimed to be "the Only True Version of Darkey [Plantation] Life ... divested entirely of the gross burlesques resorted to by white imitators." Enoch Emory, skilled in hotel entertainments, hosted receptions for them. The minstrel men undoubtedly discussed their tour, addressed questions, exchanged theatrical ideas, and shared industry knowledge. The invited guests undoubtedly included black waiters with professional aspirations.[46]

The hidden transcript of black baseball minstrelsy, framed by the theatrics of blackface minstrel performers (who referred to themselves as "genuine colored artists"), emerges on the baseball diamond controlled by powerful business interests, though almost always in disguised forms. Black players, engaged in social and cultural resistance, exploited the racial stereotypes of whites—referred to by Kelly as the "Cult of True Sambohood"—who attributed certain physical and verbal black-baseball mannerisms to laziness, ineptitude, or a childlike penchant to wander. The players used these stereotypes to their advantage, engaging in social and cultural resistance under the guise of play.[47]

In 1888, for instance, the *St. Louis Star Sayings* called Joseph Ferrand of the New Orleans Pinchbacks "the best coacher in the baseball profession," citing as evidence Ferrand's habit of chastising his baserunners. In what the *Star Sayings* journalist imagined as a Southern "[N]egro" dialect, he reproduced one of Ferrand's harangues: "'G'will dar now sah! Git off! Yer got tar git ere secon' bag! See heah, mister baserunner, ef yer doan p'rloin dat ere bag this-a-time yo' name

am mud, and Parson Nicholson'll bein' a taken on your r'mains.'"[48] As entertaining as the journalist must have believed Ferrand to be, the professed admiration for his coaching skills surely has to do with what he believes acknowledged in the speech—that black players require a firm hand.

Black baseball deployed minstrelsy as a form of mockery. The *Star Sayings* journalist expressed particular fascination with one of the colored club's comedic sketches. Whenever a ball was hit to one player, the rest would descend on him and the ball. The *Star Sayings* reported, "They all rushed wildly toward the spot and got entangled in each other's uniforms so that the umpire had to call time, and several minutes were taken extricating them from the messes." This perceived inefficiency and penchant for not playing the game as it should be played creates havoc and chaos for both participants and spectators. A careful reading of the box scores coupled with the timing of the performance suggests that the Pinchback players strategically deployed this theatrical "worker slowdown" to both entertain and slow the game. While this chaotic display might have looked like ineptitude, it effectively brought the game—as well as any shift in momentum—to a halt and redirected the attention of the crowd from the batter-runner to the fielders, which must have had a deflating effect on the former, whose hit is either overlooked or attributed to the buffoonery of the defense.[49]

On the field or off, the idea of the shiftless or childlike black was one that many whites clung to in the late 19th century, as the threat of black mobility represented a crucial step toward empowerment and self-determination. "Central to black working-class infrapolitics was mobility," writes Kelly, "for it afforded workers some freedom to escape oppressive working and living conditions, and power to negotiate better working conditions." It is unsurprising, then, that some, including Southern newspaper editors, were quick to sound the alarm. The *Memphis Ledger* reported, for instance, that "[t]he colored base-ball brigade is one of the greatest nuisances about the suburbs of this city. Enough of lazy, thieving niggers swing a baseball bat to raise a thousand bales of cotton, if they would. They loll around in the day time and steal at night. A majority of them ought to be on the chain gang or in the penitentiary." Many black players in the region did in fact labor as field-workers or roustabouts, and for employers to give them three weeks off to play baseball might seem odd. But the response to black baseball in at least one city, New Orleans, suggests that there was strong local support to go along with the hysterics in papers such as the *Ledger*. In the Crescent City, locals celebrated the historical legacy of the Pinchbacks, many of whose players had been in the game since the 1870s. In that most Southern of major cities, even the *Times-Picayune* seemed willing to acknowledge their accomplishments: "The famous colored base-ball club, the Pinchbacks, arrived home last evening after a successful sojourn in Chicago and St. Louis, where they bore away most of the honors." Among those whites who regarded black teams and players with suspicion, black aesthetic style surely diminished the seeming threat, making it easy for them to dismiss the players and their enterprise as less than serious. Just as surely, the athletes' spirited play drew fans of all colors through the gates.[50]

Just because black players engaged in practices that contemporary critics consider demeaning, it doesn't necessarily follow that they acquiesced or accommodated to the conditions of work. In fact, the story of John M. D. Bright, manager of the Cuban Giants, makes this clear. Between 1889 and 1896, Bright's baseball operation regularly suffered defections. Work conditions and salary disputes required that he hire black scouts to search for the best available black talent. In late 1895 or early 1896, a major rift between management and labor occurred. "There is a rupture among the Cuban Giants ball team and two combinations will be in the field this season," reported the *Springfield Mercury*. "They will be known as the Cuban Giants and the Cuban X-Giants. Williams and Grant are among Manager Bright's old team, while three of the Jacksons are members of the rival organization." For black players, monkey-shining had its limits. No pay, no play.[51]

To understand the links between black baseball and minstrelsy, we need to briefly outline the history of "genuine colored artists," which amply demonstrates that the national pastime had been integrated into their theatrical repertoire. In 1865, Charles B. Hicks put together the first company of black minstrels. Hicks, a talented singer and interlocutor who claimed to have been enslaved, organized his company in Macon, Georgia. There is evidence that he had considerable experience in show business management, and as someone light enough to pass for white, he could have been employed in a circus or white minstrel company. His troupe was selected from other ex-slaves who had been performing in barber shops and other places around the city. Hicks used personal funds to purchase uniforms and musical instruments, and the troupe traveled the country under the name of the Georgia Minstrels. They used neither burnt cork nor blackface paint.[52]

In 1879, Hicks's Georgia Minstrel Company traveled across the country and the world, playing baseball in Australia and New Zealand (**Fig. 22**). The *Melbourne Argus* reported: "The deciding game between the St. Kilda Base Ball Club and Georgia Minstrels will be

Figure 23. Irving "Doc" Sayles, undated. Sayles, a minstrel artist and ballplayer, was active from the 1880s to the 1900s. He pitched for the Hicks-Sawyer Minstrels, Cleveland Colossal Minstrels, and Alhambra Theatrical Troupe.

played on St. Kilda Cricket Ground, this afternoon, at 2 o'clock sharp. As each club has won a game, an exciting contest is expected." Prior to joining the Georgia Minstrels, William Speed played for Chicago's Pytheus and Unique Base Ball Clubs. In 1888, Hicks's reorganized Hicks-Sawyer Minstrel Company again toured Australia and New Zealand: "The Hicks-Sawyer Minstrels have among them several especially expert baseball players, and before leaving San Francisco for the Colonies they played a match game against a crack club." The local press observes: "The Hicks-Sawyer Minstrels went practicing base-ball in the Gardens last Saturday. Those colored gents knew how to catch the ball. It was rather amusing to see the man with the club, and the wicket-keeper [catcher], if I might term him, immediately behind him with his face protected by a shield from the lightning deliveries of another colored gent, who was shying the ball as hard as he jolly well could."[53]

After his stint with the Hicks-Sawyer Minstrels, Irving Sayles joined another minstrel company (**Fig. 23**). Between 1890 and 1891, "Doc" Sayles hurled for the Cleveland Colossal Colored Minstrels, reported to "have some good ball talent in their club" and to have traveled to the East Coast, winning "several games" along the way. In 1892, Sayles pitched for the Alhambra Company and McAdoo's Jubilee Singers. Orpheus M. McAdoo, promoter and musician, spent ten years touring Australia, New Zealand and South Africa. McAdoo covered third base for the team.[54]

In 1872, Charles Callender, a white businessman, became the Georgia Minstrel Company's major owner. The colored troupe became the Georgia Callender Minstrels, but Hicks continued to manage the company, and he organized a competitive nine dubbed the Callender Blue Stockings Base Ball Club. In 1884, the Callender Blues toured Missouri and Texas, where they played the best black teams. While in St. Louis, they played Henry

Figure 22. Original Georgia Minstrels, between 1888 and 1889. This image portrays some of the ballplayers for Charles B. Hicks's team, whose games Australian newspapers documented in baseball accounts.

Bridgewater's Black Stockings; to the local band's rendition of "There's a New Coon in Town," the Black Stockings wiped the earth with them. In Texas, the minstrel nine had scheduled contests with the state's best black organizations. They had some success in Waco, where according to the *Galveston Daily News*, "Callender's Minstrels tackled a local colored baseball club at Waco, and with ease knocked out the Central City darkeys." But the Callender Blues also encountered the formidable Dallas Black Stockings, who beat them badly. The *Dallas Daily Herald* reported: "The game at the grounds yesterday afternoon between Callender's Minstrel Club and the Black Stockings of this city, both colored, was novel so to speak and rather entertaining. The game resulted in a score of 32 to 3 in favor of the Black Stockings."[55]

In 1900, the Williams and Walker Theatrical Company organized a baseball club (**Fig. 24**). The *Indianapolis Freeman* observed, "Now the Williams and Walker boys have organized a baseball team in which they are encouraged by the [Williams and Walker] girls, who wear their colors with much pride and never miss a game; always lending their presence as a mascot, cheering loudly as a boy, at a homerun or cry of foul ball if they think their side is being cheated." The team played other baseball clubs and theatrical companies, including Black Patti's Troubadours, formed by Sissieretta Jones, a soprano who was the first black woman to perform at Carnegie Hall. The *Philadelphia Inquirer* reported on the results of two of their games: "There is great joy in the ranks of the Black Patti Troubadours

Figure 24. In the 1890s, Bert Williams and George Walker organized the Williams and Walker Base Ball Club. The team, composed of vaudeville performers and musicians, played theatrical teams.

Figure 25. Bert Williams. In the 1890s, Bert Williams and George Walker were largely responsible for popularization of the cakewalk dance, a cultural practice that evolved from the experiences of enslaved Africans. Baseball journalists had integrated the cakewalk metaphor into their sports writing as early as 1883, when the St. Louis Black Stockings played the Rockford Reds. The black team was characterized as strutting cakewalkers. It was not uncommon for black ballplayers to participate in cakewalk performances, William Selden (of the Boston Resolutes, Cuban Giants, and Gorhams) being one example.

owing to the great victories of their representatives. The first game was between the dark-complexioned gentlemen and attaches of the People's Theatre, while the second was for blood, between the members of the Williams and Walker's aggregation and Black Patti's pets. The first game was by far more interesting, requiring a full game for the decision" (**Figs. 25 and 26**).[56]

The Twentieth Century and Clowning

In *If You Were Only White*, historian Donald Spivey characterizes Satchel Paige's trademark performance as "daring showmanship, pitching brilliance, and sheer audacity." In 1923, the young Paige hurled for Mobile, Alabama's Bay Boys. Playing for this subpar team notorious for poor fielding and blowing leads that cost the club games, Paige stood on the mound going into the bottom half of the ninth inning with a slim lead. There was a runner at first base. Fed up with the awful fielding, he ordered the outfield to come in. Reluctantly, they did so and Paige had them sit behind the pitcher's mound as he went to work. "He fired," writes Spivey, "lethal fastballs that left the hapless batters motionless as the catcher's mitt popped, followed by the umpire's repeated calls of strike. He struck out the side without anyone else getting on base, and the game ended with the Bay Boys victorious. The crowd went wild."[57]

As Spivey's introduction explains, Paige "entertained as he played to win and saw no contradiction in doing both. [He] was a master at pushing the envelope, of fooling around minstrel-like just enough to satisfy both blacks and whites in the same audience. They could laugh along with his antics rather than laughing at him as a racial caricature, while, at the same time, he demonstrated his dominance over blacks and whites from the pitcher's mound." As a form of theatrical performance, clowning combined with baseball boosted game attendance.[58]

Figure 26. Black Patti and the Troubadours, *New York Age*, February 27, 1908. In 1899, in Philadelphia, the Black Pattis swept a doubleheader by defeating the People's Theatre (white) and the Williams and Walker's club.

As familiar as clowning is to historians and fans of the Negro Leagues, its historical roots, in particular, are little understood. In *The Negro Baseball Leagues*, Phil Dixon argues that clowning begins with Trenton, New Jersey's Cuban Giants Base Ball Club. Adrian, Michigan's Page Fence Giants Base Ball Club, he adds, also relied on clowning, though usually only against weaker competition. "Teams of this ilk," he suggests, "faded out quickly."[59] Dixon continues:

> [T]here still exists the perception that Negro baseball was more of a vaudeville act than a serious sporting venture. A share of the blame for that belongs to Satchel Paige, who was renowned for his comical antics on the mound. As the most famous of the black players, his legacy as an entertainer belies his dedication and professionalism that permeated Negro baseball. In fairness to Paige, though, it should be noted that his routines were reserved for non-league exhibition games.[60]

As Dixon's apparent dismissal of the teams and tactics suggests, baseball minstrelsy perplexes and perhaps troubles some historians, invoking old antebellum stereotypes such as the plantation "darky" images that dominated the minstrel stage and circulated in "negro" dialect literature, newspaper stories, and comic strips.

Spivey, however, challenges the claim that clowning "belied … dedication and professionalism" and was "reserved for non-league exhibition games." On August 1, 1931, Paige pitched for the Pittsburg

Crawfords against the Homestead Grays, both Negro League clubs. It was the third game of their series, the scored tied at seven runs apiece. "In the fourth inning," writes Spivey, "Paige began his slow, relaxed stride to the mound. You could hear some of the fans laughing at his effortless gate and seemingly slow-motion stride. Some thought that Paige was making a mockery of the situation. He was not. Neither was he playing Stepin Fetchit." Spivey's analysis of Paige's "daring showmanship, pitching brilliance, and sheer audacity" is crucial:

> He took his time on most occasions to get to the mound, taking deliberate slow and easy strides as if in no hurry to meet his opponent. Those who knew Paige said that he did it on purpose to save his energy, while others said that the slow, methodical walk helped to throw off batters' timing. Still others said he did it to entertain the crowd with a little light vaudeville. At any rate, hitters seemed almost hypnotized by his slow pace and perhaps expected the ball to come across the plate in similar slow motion.[61]

Fans adored Paige's trademark performance, which recalled the 19th-century cultural practice melding "scientific play" and theatrical performance, was a 20th-century expression of black aesthetic style. The sporting fraternity defined "scientific play" as "pretty playing' or "simply looking good." The Buffalo Bison star, Frank Grant, elevated scientific play to another level. Grant played "with care and executed brilliant plays." He also "delighted audiences with his flashy playing" and his "antics for the benefit of the grand stand were very funny." Through black aesthetic style, the "colored second baseman" redefined the "number of plays handled" and the handling of difficult plays. However, Grant was not the first black ballplayer to make the game look easy.[62]

Paige and Grant, both Hall of Famers, shared something else—a strong interest in fashion. Spivey writes that jazz musician Jelly Roll Morton advised Paige on the "importance of wardrobe" and invited the ballplayer "to tour his personal collection of fine garments." Paige recalled the bewildering array of color, orange suits, purple and yellow shirts, lemon-colored shoes with socks and suspenders that matched them. He began to dress with considerable style, purchasing suits and ample shoes to match. Grant was also a black dandy. Newspapers published stories about his attire. The *Buffalo Courier*, for instance, noted that "Grant, the great colored second baseman of the Buffalo Club, appeared at the Long Island grounds yesterday wearing a high silk hat, purple plush coat, light colored kid gloves, very loud pantaloons and patent leather pumps." The *Cleveland Gazette* likewise took note of Grant's appearance, reporting that he had "electrified Broadway recently by appearing in a blue corduroy coat, black and white striped trousers, yellow gloves, patent leather shoes with light drab gaiters, a slate colored fedora hat and a gold headed cane."[63]

In his *Cutting a Figure: Fashioning Black Portraiture*, art historian Richard J. Powell offers an illuminating discussion of the cosmopolitan dandy. Historically, black dandies have been "objects of spectatorship, personifications of difference, and purveyors of visual alarm," bearing racial and cultural baggage that can be traced back to the antebellum period. Many white musicians, playwrights, illustrators and satirists collectively added a new urban black male figure to American popular theater, one they referred to by names such as "Dandy Jim," "Zip Coon" and "Long Tail Blue" (**Fig. 27**). "The black dandy's two greatest sins—visibility and indiscretion—made sense only in the context of a society," writes Powell, "where black people (and specifically black men) had clearly demarcated positions." The black dandy infused elegance with outrageousness. His "audacious appearance" on the urban streets "upset the white majority's assumption of racial homogeneity and cultural superiority." For Grant and Paige, wardrobe signified modernity, freedom, oppositionality, and power. In short, they claimed urban space and expressed control over the display of their bodies.[64]

Whether performed by fashionsistas or ballplayers, black aesthetic style had almost always been couched in negative, stereotypical terms. Part of it had to do with "fear of black male agency and, by inference, black enfranchisement." As Young reminds us, the figure of the American dandy was characterized by class pretentions. The black dandy became an openly ridiculed character in the minstrel show in the character of Zip Coon, a "clumsy, inept, and inappropriate translation of whites' mores into blacks' only lowly position." By 1874, the colored ballplayer had penetrated popular American periodicals. Solomon Eytinge, Jr. (illustrator of the Blackville cartoon series for *Harper's Weekly*) and Thomas Worth (illustrator of the highly popular Darktown cartoon series for Currier and Ives) situated the colored player—a form of the black dandy—in the public sphere, making him a spectacle. The humor, such as it was, hinged on the probability that the player, though resplendent in his baseball uniform, was incapable of playing the game without hurting himself. Readers who were themselves unable to master the national pastime could laugh at would-be players who were not only inept but ridiculous.[65]

Figure 27. Zip Coon, 1834. Zip Coon was an early stock character of blackface minstrelsy. Imagined as a northern urban dandy, the ostentatious figure sports a jabot, ornate vest, claw-hammer coat, stirrup pantaloons, watch fob, and jewelry. Zip Coon was invented to counter the threatening public presence of well-dressed–not to mention free, intelligent, articulate, skilled, and ambitious—black men in the North (and South).

The circus atmosphere surrounding such representations in general, and the lack of critical inquiry into black aesthetic style in particular, may not be the deepest reasons for discomfort with what some call "Negro Comedy." Because we remain caught in the grip of minstrelsy's negative stereotypical associations, we continue to gloss over players' public displays of manly strength, physical skill, aesthetic form, and social status. Paige understood this. Spivey writes, "The earlier announcement that Paige would pitch the first game [Crawford vs. Homestead Grays] accounted for, in large part, the record setting audience. During warm-ups he entertained fans with his familiar windmill windups and exaggerated high-kick pitches that spectators never seemed to tire of. The Grays fell like wheat as he mowed them down seventeen of them on his way to a no-hit performance."[66]

Gilded Age black players displayed "daring showmanship, pitching brilliance, and sheer audacity," as well. In 1882, Philadelphia's Orion Base Ball Club, a black team, played New York's Metropolitans, the white team that would join the major league American Association the next year. The *New York Times* sportswriter described the mannerisms of black pitcher, George Williams, as "one of the game's most laughable features" because he "performed with the air of a veteran."

Before each delivery, Williams calmly surveyed the field, and in every instance" found a fielder out of position. He raised his hand and "in a clear voice, called out to the player who was out of position: 'Lay in a few more feet for dis yere man.' As sure as Williams cautioned the left fielder, the batsman knocked the ball to right field, which was a signal for an uproar among spectators, who heartily applauded Williams for his display of good judgment." In short, the batter's late contact with the ball resulted in swings that sent the ball to right field. While some spectators understood William's "daring showmanship, pitching brilliance, and sheer audacity," the sportswriter misunderstood or simply ignored what had transpired. This was scientific playing and strategy at its best, meant to "rattle" and confuse the opponent. Stylistic parallels between Williams and Paige are striking. Paige inherited a long historical tradition that we struggle to appreciate.[67]

NOTES

1. Chad Heap, *Slumming: Sexual and Racial Encounters in American Nightlife, 1885–1940* (Chicago: University of Chicago Press, 2010); Angela Davis, *Blues Legacies and Black Feminism* (New York: Pantheon, 1998); Caroline Goeser, *Picturing the New Negro* (Lawrence: University Press of Kansas, 2007); Tony Martin, *Literary Garveyism* (Dover: Majority Press, 1983).

2. Henry Louis Gates, Jr., "The Trope of a New Negro and the Reconstruction of the Image of the Black," *Representations* 24.1 (Autumn 1988): 129–155; Wilson Jeremiah Moses, "The Lost World of the Negro, 1895–1917: Black Literary and Intellectual Life Before the 'Renaissance,'" *Black American Literary Forum* 21.1/2 (Spring/Summer 1987): 61–84.

3. "Local," *People's Washington Advocate*, November 8, 1879; "Sparta Club," *Washington (DC) Bee*, January 17, 1880; "The Sparta Club," *Washington People's Advocate*, January 17, 1880; "Sparta Club," *Washington National Republican*, January 26, 1880; "A Bon-Ton Colored Club," *Washington Post*, May 16, 1881; "Trustee James H. Smith Complimented," *Washington Bee*, August 11, 1883; "The Sparta Opening," *Washington Bee*, October 11, 1884; "The Ball Players," *Washington Evening Star*, May 3, 1886; "The Small Things of the Day," *Republican*, May 3, 1886; "Not At All Cast Down," *Washington Post*, May 9, 1886; "Local," *Washington Bee*, June 5, 1886; "Amateurs to Play," *Washington Times*, September 16, 1897; "Capital City Team Won," *Washington Morning Times*, September 17, 1897; "Capital City Team Won," *Washington Times*, September 17, 1897; "Capital Citys vs. Sparta," *Washington Times*, August 7, 1898.

4. Carl R. Osthaus, "The Rise and Fall of Jesse Binga," *Journal of*

Negro History 58.1 (January 1973): 39–60; Mark H. Haller, "Policy, Gambling, Entertainment, and the Emergence of Black Politics: Chicago from 1900 to 1940," *Journal of Social History*, 24 (4), Summer, 1991, 719–739; Rebecca Alpert, *Out of Left Field: Jews and Black Baseball* (New York: Oxford University Press, 2011); Larry Lester, Sammy Miller, and Dick Clark, *Black Baseball in Chicago* (Mt. Pleasant, SC: Arcadia, 2000); Michael E. Lomax, *Black Baseball Entrepreneurs, 1860–1901* (Syracuse, NY: Syracuse University Press, 2003); Davarian L. Baldwin, *Chicago's New Negroes* (Chapel Hill: University of North Carolina Press), 206.

5. Years later, Rosecranse professed abolitionist sentiments: "During the days of slavery in this State, colored folks and run away to Canada. They would hide on board sloops, and so get down to New York and there were always persons who would help them to get away from their masters. The love of freedom seemed to be strong in the breast of the slave even under the mild treatment in the North." Rosecranse probably participated in the operations of Kingston's Underground Railroad. "A Colored Resident," *Kingston (NY) Daily Freeman*, August 19, 1881; "Slavery Days in New York," *New York Evening Telegram*, May 31, 1888; "Born a Slave in Ulster County," *Fulton County Republican* (Johnston, NY), June 14, 1888.

6. "H. C. Rosecranse: Barber and Hair Dresser" (advertisement), *Kingston (NY) Daily Chronicle*, October 25, 1859; "Notes About Town," *Kingston Daily Freeman*, May 11, 1883; "A Colored Resident," *Kingston Daily Freeman*, August 19, 1881; "A Horse Drew a Log into the House," *New York Press*, January 28, 1888; "Slavery Days in New York," *New York Evening Telegram*, May 31, 1888; "Born a Slave in Ulster County," *Fulton County Republican* (Johnstown, NY), June 14, 1888; "Miller Takes Over Oldest Barber Shop," *Kingston Daily Freeman*, October 1, 1923.

7. Nell Painter, *Sojourner Truth: A Life, A Symbol* (New York: W. W. Norton, 1996).

8. Douglas Walter Bristol, *Knights of the Razor: Black Barbers in Slavery and Freedom* (Baltimore: John Hopkins University Press, 2009).

9. "A Colored Resident," *Kingston (NY) Daily Freeman*, August 19, 1881; "A Horse Drew a Log into the House," *New York Press*, January 28, 1888; "Slavery Days in New York," *New York Evening Telegram*, May 31, 1888; "Born a Slave in Ulster County," *Fulton County Republican* (Johnstown, NY), June 14, 1888.

10. "Pinkster," *New York Spectator*, July 2, 1803; "Union Emancipation Jubilee," *Brooklyn Brooklyn Daily Eagle*, August 3, 1864; "Negro Emancipation," *Brooklyn Daily Eagle*, August 2, 1865; "Local Intelligence," *New York Evening Express*, August 2, 1866; "Emancipation Day," *Brooklyn Daily Eagle*, August 2, 1866; "Emancipation Day," *Brooklyn Daily Eagle*, August 3, 1867; "Williamsburgh," *New York Daily Tribune*, December 28, 1867; "Anniversary of Negro Emancipation," *New York Herald-Tribune*, August 4, 1868; "The Celebration of Pinkster," *Paterson (NJ) Daily Press*, June 2, 1868; "The West India Anniversary," *Cleveland Plain Dealer*, August 3, 1869; "Two Centuries Ago," *Babylon (NY) Signal*, June 5, 1875; "A Colored Resident," *Kingston (NY) Daily Freeman*, August 19, 1881.

11. "Base Ball," *Rochester (NY) Evening Express*, August 19, 1867; "Base Ball at Catskill," *Hudson (NY) Evening Register*, October 28, 1869; "The Ball and Bat," *Poughkeepsie (NY) Daily Eagle*, August 4, 1874; "A Game of Ball," *Poughkeepsie Daily Eagle*, May 31, 1875; "Base Ball," *Poughkeepsie Daily Eagle*, September 13, 1875; "Base Ball," *Poughkeepsie Daily Eagle*, September 22, 1875; "Speaking of Baseballs, These Are the Ancient Ones," *Amsterdam (NY) Evening Recorder*, June 26, 1915.

12. "Colored Conference Prohibited in Baltimore," *Boston Liberator*, May 10, 1861.

13. Eco, *The Infinity of Lists*, 49.

14. Bristol, *Knights of the Razor*, 5 and 140–148.

15. A.K. Sandoval-Strausz, *Hotel: An American History* (New Haven: Yale University Press, 2007), 179.

16. "Grand Concert of Colored Vocalists," *Niagara Falls Gazette*, August 1884; "The Concert," *Niagara Falls Gazette*, August 13, 1884.

17. "A Presentation," *Niagara Falls (NY) Gazette*, August 25, 1880; "The Mystic Tie," *Niagara Falls Gazette*, July 19, 1882; "A Day at Portage," *Niagara Falls Gazette*, July 24, 1882; "Our Hotels," *Niagara Falls Gazette*, May 29, 1883; "Base Ball," *Niagara Falls Gazette*, June 20, 1883; "Base Ball," *Niagara Falls Gazette*, July 13, 1883; "Brevities," *Niagara Falls Gazette*, July 23, 1883; "An Interesting Game of Base Ball," *Niagara Falls Gazette*, August 14, 1883; "Brevities," *Niagara Falls Gazette*, July 29, 1883; "From Niagara Falls," *Ni-*

agara Falls Gazette, August 9, 1884; "Brevities," *Niagara Falls Gazette*, August 21, 1885; "Niagara Drippings," *New York Freeman*, July 24, 1886.

18. Sandoval-Strausz, *Hotel*, 247–250.

19. Michael Boston, "Blacks in Niagara Falls, NY, 1865–1965: A Survey," *Afro-Americans in New York Life and History* 28.2 (July 2004): 7–49.

20. "The Days of Slavery," *Niagara Falls (NY) Gazette*, August 25, 1883.

21. Stephen Kantrowitz, *More Than Freedom: Fighting for Black Citizenship in a White Republic, 1829–1889* (New York: Penguin, 2012), 177.

22. "Great Excitement at Niagara Falls," *Syracuse (NY) Daily Standard*, August 31, 1853; "Exciting Affair at Niagara Falls," *Syracuse (NY) Daily Journal*, August 31, 1853; "No Title," *Augusta (GA) Chronicle*, September 1, 1853; "The Affair at Niagara Falls," *Augusta Chronicle*, September 4, 1853; "Negro Impuden," *Augusta Chronicle*, September 10, 1853; "The Sneed Conspiracy Case at Niagara Falls," *Albany (NY) Evening Journal*, September 12, 1853.

23. "The Two States," *Augusta (GA) Chronicle*, Apr. 18, 1879; "An Inter-State Match Between Colored Clubs," *Augusta Chronicle*, August 23, 1879; "City Affairs," *Brunswick (GA) Advertiser*, August 23, 1879; "Georgia Victorious," *Brunswick Advertiser*, August 30, 1879; "Base Ball Tournament," *Macon (GA) Telegraph*, August 27, 1880; "Things in Georgia," *New York Globe*, March 17, 1883.

24. "Not Title," *New York Globe*, Apr. 21, 1883; "New Jersey Summer Resorts," *New York Globe*, August 4, 1883; "Howard's Letter," *Harrisburg (NY) State Journal*, May 3, 1884; "Base Ball," *Baltimore Sun*, Apr. 28, 1885; "No Title," *Sporting Life*, Apr. 29, 1885; "The Ugly Club at Dinner," *New York Freeman*, May 16, 1885.

25. "Babylon," *Huntington (NY) Long Islander*, August 21, 1885; "The Base Ballists," *Williamsport (PA) Gazette and Bulletin*, September 22, 1885; "Those Giants," *Williamsport Gazette and Bulletin*, September 23, 1885.

26. "Base Ball," *Oswego (NY) Daily Times Express*, September 4, 1885; "Philadelphia Letter," *Washington (DC) Bee*, May 8, 1886; "The Coddington House," *New York Freeman*, October 30, 1886; "Color Line Drawn Again," *New York Freeman*, September 17, 1887; "Base Ball Notes," *Trenton (NJ) Evening Times*, October 13, 1887; "Of Race Interest," *Cleveland Gazette*, August 4, 1888; "From St. Augustine," *Philadelphia Sporting Life*, February 21, 1891; "Saratoga Springs," *New York Age*, June 13, 1891; "New York State Grange Day," *Watertown (NY) Daily Times*, August 12, 1895; "The Waiter," *Indianapolis Freeman*, November 17, 1900; "The Waiter," *Indianapolis Freeman*, December 8, 1900; "F.P. Thompson Dead," *Indianapolis Freeman*, December 30, 1905.

27. "Chicago Chat," *New York Globe*, December 15, 1883; "Current Doings in Chicago," *New York Globe*, February 23, 1884; "Chicago Correspondence," *New York Globe*, March 8, 1884; "Chicago Correspondence," *New York Globe*, Apr. 12, 1884; "Gordon B.B.C.," *Cleveland Gazette*, Apr. 12, 1883; "Chicago Doings," *New York Globe*, Apr. 26, 1884; "Sports of the Season," *Chicago Sunday Herald*, June 1, 1884; "Sports of the Season," *Chicago Sunday Herald*, June 22, 1884; "Sports of the Season," *Chicago Sunday Herald*, June 29, 1884; "On the Diamond Field," *Chicago Sunday Herald*, August 17, 1884.

28. "General Notes," *St. Paul Daily Globe*, July 1, 1885; "Minnetonka," *St. Paul Daily Globe*, July 8, 1885; "Wavelots," *St. Paul Daily Globe*, July 9, 1885; "Base Ball," *St. Paul Daily Globe*, July 12, 1885; "Minneapolis," *St. Paul Western Appeal*, July 18, 1885; "General Terry Banqueted," *St. Paul Daily Globe*, Apr. 23, 1886; "E.L.S.C.," *St. Paul Western Appeal*, March 5, 1887; "Minneapolis," *St. Paul Western Appeal*, March 26, 1887; "Minneapolis," *St. Paul Western Appeal*, May 7, 1887.

29. "The Lafayettes," *Omaha (NE) Daily Bee*, May 19, 1888; "Diamond Flashes," *Omaha Daily Bee*, May 30, 1888; "Hardins vs. Lafayettes," *Omaha Daily Bee*, August 23, 1888; "Base Ball Notes," *New York Sun*, January 18, 1889; "Base Ball Notes," *New York Sun*, February 5, 1889; "Manager Plummer's Team," *Omaha Daily Bee*, March 24, 1889; "Plummer's Pounders," *Omaha Daily Bee*, March 31, 1889; "The Flour City," *St. Paul (MN) Western Appeal*, July 13, 1889; "The Flour City," *St. Paul Western Appeal*, July 20, 1889; "Grand Island Defeats the Giants," *Omaha Daily Bee*, May 6, 1895; "Grays Defeated at Wahoo," *Omaha Daily Bee*, May 6, 1895.

30. Sandoval-Strausz, *Hotel*, 247–250.

31. "A Big Thing in Cork," *New York Times*, September 18, 1865; "Richard M. Hooley Dead," *New York Times*, September 9, 1893.

32. "Emancipation Day," *New York Daily Tribune*, August 1, 1862; "Union Emancipation Jubilee," *Brooklyn Daily Eagle*, August 3, 1864; "Negro Emancipation," *Brooklyn Daily Eagle*, August 2, 1865; "The Negro Celebration," *New York Herald-Tribune*, August 2, 1865; "Local Intelli-*

gence," *New York Evening Express*, August 2, 1866; "Emancipation Day," *Brooklyn Daily Eagle*, August 2, 1866; "Emancipation Day," *Brooklyn Daily Eagle*, August 3, 1867; "Williamsburgh," *New York Herald-Tribune*, December 28, 1867; "Anniversary of Negro Emancipation," *New York Herald-Tribune*, August 4, 1868; "Colored Mass Meeting in Williamsburg," *New York Evening Telegram*, October 21, 1868; "Emancipation Day," *Brooklyn Daily Eagle*, August 3, 1869.

33. Richard J. Powell, *Cutting a Figure: Fashioning Black Portraiture* (Chicago: University of Chicago Press, 2008); "City Notes," *Jersey City (NJ) Journal*, December 20, 1867; "City Notes," *Jersey City Journal*, December 20, 1867; "Base Ball," *Jersey City Journal*, June 6, 1868; "Base Ball," *Jersey City Journal*, July 10, 1868.

34. *Cincinnati Commercial Tribune*, August 28, 1912.

35. "A Big Thing in Cork," *New York Times*, September 18, 1865; "Base Ball from a Colored Point of View," *Chicago Tribune*, August 24, 1870.

36. "A New Sensation in Base Ball Circles—Sambo as a Ball Player and Dinah as an Emulator," *Brooklyn Daily Eagle*, October 17, 1862.

37. "A New Sensation in Base Ball Circles," *Brooklyn Daily Eagle*, October 17, 1862.

38. "Out-Door Sports," *New York Herald-Tribune*, May 24, 1867; "No Title," *Trenton (NJ) State Gazette*, June 8, 1867; "Miscellaneous," *Albany (NY) Evening Journal*, August 30, 1867.

39. "Out-Door Sports," *New York Herald-Tribune*, May 24, 1867; "No Title," *Trenton (NJ) State Gazette*, June 8, 1867; "Miscellaneous," *Albany (NY) Evening Journal*, August 30, 1867; "City Notes," *Jersey City (NJ) Journal*, December 13, 1867; "Prejudice Among Small Potatoes," *Jersey City Journal*, December 16, 1867; "Late News Items," *Springfield (MA) Republican*, October 4, 1867.

40. Eric Lott, *Love and Theft: Blackface Minstrelsy and the American Working Class* (Oxford: Oxford University Press, 1993).

41. "Base Ball Gossip," *Rocky Mountain News* (Denver, CO), October 11, 1887.

42. "Brevities," *Niagara Falls (NY) Gazette*, June 22, 1887; "Sportive Pressings," *Utica (NY) Daily Press*, October 14, 1887; "Base Ball in Town," *Syracuse (NY) Standard*, April 27, 1888;

43. "Base Ball Yesterday," *Williamsport (PA) Daily Gazette and Bulletin*, August 20, 1885; "Those Giants," *Daily Gazette and Bulletin*, September 23, 1885.

44. "The Harleys Ahead," *Williamsport (PA) Daily Gazette and Bulletin*, June 21, 1879; "Base Ball Notes," *Daily Gazette and Bulletin*, September 12, 1882; "Base Ball Yesterday," *Daily Gazette and Bulletin*, September 15, 1882; "An Exciting Game," *Daily Gazette and Bulletin*, October 2, 1882.

45. "The Great Cakewalk," *Williamsport (PA) Sun Gazette*, September 11, 1900; "Vallamont Park," *Sun Gazette*, September 12, 1900.

46. "Amusements," *Williamsport (PA) Daily Gazette and Bulletin*, September 13, 1871; "Georgia Slave Troupe," *Daily Gazette and Bulletin*, September 16, 1871.

47. Robyn D. G. Kelly, *Race Rebels: Culture, Politics, and the Black Working Class* (New York; Free, Press, 1996), 21–23.

48. "The Darkies at Play," *St. Louis Sunday Star Sayings*, August 26, 1888.

49. "The Darkies at Play," *St. Louis Sunday Star Sayings*, August 26, 1888.

50. "The Pinchbacks Back," *New Orleans Daily Picayune*, August 30, 1888.

51. "The National Game," *Springfield (NY) Mercury*, March 26, 1896.

52. Herbert T. Sampson, *The Ghost Walks: A Chronological History of Blacks in Show Business, 1865–1900* (Metuchen, NJ: Scarecrow, 1988), 4–5

53. "Hick's Georgia Minstrels," *Hobart (AU) Mercury*, April 30, 1879; "Arrived," *Melbourne (AU) Argus*, June 21, 1879; "Base Ball," *Melbourne Argus*, June 21, 1879; "Base Ball," *Melbourne Argus*, June 21, 1879; "Hicks Georgia Minstrels," *Gippsland (AU) Times*, July 30, 1879; "No Title," *Gippsland Times*, August 1, 1879; "Hicks and Sawyer's Minstrels," *New York Freeman*, May 28, 1887; "The Diamond," *San Francisco Daily Alta*, July 28, 1888; "Sporting Echoes," *Brisbane (AU) Figaro and Punch*, November 8, 1888; "No Title," *Wellington (NZ) Evening Post*, November 8, 1888; "Base Ball in New Zealand," *New York Herald*, December 30, 1888; "Base Ball in Wellington," *Sydney Star*, March 6, 1889; "Base Ball," *Adelaide (AU) Advertiser*, April 11, 1889; "Base Ball Match," *Broken Hill (AU) Barrier Miner*, April 29, 1889

54. "Hicks and Sawyer's Minstrels," *New York Freeman*, May 28, 1887; "The Diamond," *San Francisco Daily Alta*, July 28, 1888; "Sporting Echoes," *Brisbane (AU) Figaro and Punch*, November 8, 1888; "No Title," *Wellington (NZ) Evening Post*, November 8, 1888; "Base Ball in New Zealand," *New York Herald*, December 30, 1888; "Base Ball in Wellington," *Sydney Star*, March 6, 1889; "Base Ball," *Adelaide (AU) Advertiser*, April 11, 1889; "Base Ball Match," *Broken Hill (AU) Barrier Miner*, April 29, 1889; "Stage," *Indianapolis Freeman*, February 1, 1890; "New Notes," *Los Angeles Herald*, February 21, 1890; "Stage," *Indianapolis Freeman*, March 22, 1890; "New Notes," *New York Herald*, October 27, 1890; "New Notes," *New York Herald*, October 28, 1890; "Base Ball," *New York Herald*, October 31, 1890; "Cleveland's Colored Minstrels," *Worcester (MA) Daily Spy*, May 12, 1891; "Base Ball," *Sydney Morning Herald*, July 5, 1892; "America vs. Australia," *New South Wales (AU) Town and Country Journal*, July 9, 1892; "Base Ball," *Sydney Mail*, July 9, 1892; "Stage," *Indianapolis Freeman*, July 27, 1895; "No Title," *Indianapolis Freeman*, July 14, 1900; "Obituary," *Washington (DC) Colored American*, September 8, 1900; "Sudden Death," *Grey River (NZ) Argus*, February 9, 1914 "Comedian Drops Dead," *Christ Church (NZ) Northern Advocate*, February 9, 1914.

55. "Base Ball," *New York Clipper*, December 30, 1882; "The Black Sox-Callender Game," *St. Louis Post-Dispatch*, September 3, 1884; "Black Sox vs. Callender's Minstrels," *St. Louis Globe-Democrat*, September 4, 1884; "Callender's Minstrels vs. Black Socks," *St. Louis Republican*, September 4, 1884; "Waco Wirings," *Galveston (TX) Daily News*, September 25, 1884; "Waco," *Galveston Daily News*, September 26, 1884; "Base Ball," *Galveston Daily News*, September 30, 1884; "No Title," *Columbus (TX) Colorado Citizen*, October 9, 1884.

56. "Hats Off to the Black Pattis," *Philadelphia Inquirer*, May 5, 1900; "Williams and Walker," *Indianpolis Freeman*, May 12, 1900.

57. Donald Spivey, *If You Were Only White* (Columbia: University of Missouri Press, 2012), 41.

58. Spivey, *If You Were Only White*, xviii.

59. Phil Dixon, *The Negro Baseball Leagues* (Mattituck: Amereron House, 1992), 18–19.

60. Dixon, *The Negro Baseball Leagues*, 18–19.

61. Spivey, *If You Were Only White*, 75.

62. "Beaten by the Buffalos," *Rochester (NY) Democrat and Chronicle*, September 9, 1886; "Buffalos vs. Hamiltons," *Buffalo (NY) Courier*, August 11, 1886.

63. "Doings of the Race," *Cleveland Gazette*, Apr. 30, 1887; "General Sporting Notes," *Buffalo (NY) Courier*, October 10, 1888; Spivey, *If You Were Only White*, 50–52.

64. Richard J. Powell, *Cutting a Figure: Fashioning Black Portraiture* (Chicago: University of Chicago Press, 2008), 59–77.

65. Powell, *Cutting a Figure*, 70.

66. *Ibid.*, 83.

67. "The Colored Orions Badly Defeated by the Metropolitan Team," *New York Times*, July 21, 1882.

Team Profiles

The profiles that follow provide at least basic information about when and where black teams played in the second half of the nineteenth century. Some are extensive, as in the case of the Fearless Base Ball Club, of Utica, New York. Organized in 1866 and operating until 1908, the Fearless was perhaps the longest-running black baseball organization in history. For nearly fifty years, fathers, sons, grandsons, nephews, and cousins formed the team's nucleus. Its members were hardcore Lincoln Republicans who—if we accept contemporary accounts—fought for full citizenship both on and off the diamond.

Other team profiles are less robust, thanks in part to gaps in the historical record, or at least to its inaccessibility at the time of research. The record of the Unique Base Ball Club, of Chicago (1871–1893), includes such gaps, for instance. In too many articles about the Uniques, sportswriters relied on readers' memory to fill in the blanks. In 1886, *Inter-Ocean* reported, "The Uniques, at one time the champion colored club of the Northwest, have reorganized, and are much stronger and better than ever, and, with the following players, think they can again lay claim to the title." If some readers then could recall the birth of the Unique Club, none now can, and today we are left holding the loose end. Efforts to dig for further details in the local papers end in frustration; it seems that, unlike the Utica newspapers that faithfully covered the annual exploits of their hometown Fearless, Chicago papers treated the Uniques as a peculiar appendage to the national pastime. No published rosters and box scores, for example, document the 1887 and 1888 battle for supremacy between the Uniques and Chicago Unions. The information we do have survives in newspapers published outside of the Windy City. I have no answer for this.

The list of profiles is arranged first by state, then by city, and finally alphabetically by team name. Each entry opens with the full or formal name of the club, its hometown, the years of its operation, and the names of the owners or founders, if known. The body of the entry then indicates where and when the team was organized and provides any unusual, interesting, or historically significant information gleaned from my research. Quotations from contemporary papers follow. In some instances, these quotations document important facts about the club (that they played white teams, for instance) or provide insight into the quality of play or public reception; in others, they amount to the entirety of our evidence that a team existed. The entry concludes with a list of the newspapers in which published mentions of these teams were made.

Alabama

Hornets Base Ball Club (Birmingham, AL; 1890s)

The Hornets B.B.C. organized in the 1890s and played black teams. *Montgomery Advertiser* (September 10, 1891): "The Hornet Base Ball Club, of Birmingham played against the Montgomery colored team at Clisby's Park. It resulted in a score of 11 to 9 in favor of the former. A purse of $20 and gate receipts were the wager. Quite a crowd saw the game." *Atlanta Constitution* (July 9, 1892): "Next Monday afternoon there will be a baseball game at Brisbane Park between two crack colored clubs, the Atlanta Grays and the Birmingham Hornets. Both clubs are in good trim and a fine game is expected. A portion of the grandstand will be reserved for white fans."

SOURCES: "Atlanta as Usual," *Atlanta (GA) Constitution*, Aug 25, 1891; "Diamond Dust," *Montgomery (AL) Advertiser*, Sep 10, 1891; "Ended in a Row," *Montgomery Advertiser*, Sep 11, 1891; "Atlanta against Birmingham" *Atlanta Constitution*, Jul 9, 1892; "Colored Base Ballists," *Tuscaloosa (AL) Weekly Times*, Sep 5, 1894; "Unions vs. Hornets," *Greensboro (AL) Alabama Beacon*, Jul 10, 1895; "Unions vs. Hornets," *Nashville (TN) Tennessean*, Jun 22, 1896; "Rock City Unions Defeated," *Nashville Tennessean*, Jun 23, 1896.

Union Base Ball Club (Birmingham, AL; 1890s). Owner(s): R. L. Jackson.

The Union B.B.C. organized in the 1890s, played black teams. *Birmingham Age-Herald* (April 25, 1897): "The Unions have secured new uniforms and are practicing daily. They expect to turn the tables on the Cliffords and retrieve the games lost to them several years ago. The team is composed of good players from the ranks of the best of the colored population, and on this account always receive the support and commendation of white lovers of the great sport." R. L. Jackson organized the team. *Age-Herald* (April 29, 1897): "R. L. Jackson, the Twelfth Street tailor, is manager of the Birmingham [Unions] and president of the [Colored] league recently organized. He is determined to have nothing, but clean sport, such any white lover of the game can see with pleasure, and for this reason certain teams in other cities have been refused admittance to the league." Jackson organized and served as president of the Southern Colored League. Its members were the Little Rock Quapaws, Memphis Cliffords, Hot Springs Arlingtons, Pensacola Acmes, Montgomery Blues and Birmingham Unions.

SOURCES: "Will Play Ball," *Birmingham (AL) Age-Herald*, Apr 25, 1897; "Tersely Told," *Birmingham Age-Herald*, Apr 29, 1897; "Games This Week," *Birmingham Age-Herald*, May 2, 1897; "Base Ball," *Birmingham Age-Herald*, May 6, 1897; "Good Local Game," *Birmingham Age-Herald*, Jun 1, 1897; "Good Local Game," *Birmingham Age-Herald*, Jun 18, 1897; "Base Ball Games," *Birmingham Age-Herald*, Jun 25, 1897; "A Hotly Contested Game," *Birmingham Age-Herald*, Jun 26, 1897; "A One-Sided Game," *Birmingham Age-Herald*, Jun 27, 1897; "Hot Springs Wins," *Birmingham Age-Herald*, Jun 30, 1897; "Base Ball at Fisk," *Nashville (TN) Tennessean*, Apr 25, 1899.

Colored Base Ball Club (Eufaula, AL; 1890s)

The Colored B.B.C. organized in the 1890s. Eufaula had a tradition of fielding strong teams that played in AL, SC, GA, and FL. *Indianapolis Freeman* (July 9, 1898): "A match game of baseball was played at the park between Eufaula nine and the Clayton nine. The score was 19 to 7 in favor of the Eufala boys."

Sources: "Among Our Neighbors," *Eufaula (AL) Times*, Aug 16, 1897; "The Ball Game," *Eufaula Times*, Jul 1, 1898; "Notes," *Indianapolis (IN) Freeman*, Jul 9, 1898; "Base Ball," *Eufaula Times*, Aug 9, 1898; "Eufala Won," *Eufaula Times*, Jul 16, 1899; "Notes," *Nashville (TN) Tennessean*, Jul 19, 1899; "Base Ball and Fighting," *Eufaula Times*, Aug 6, 1899; "The Events," *Eufaula Times*, Aug 25, 1899.

Hard Hitter Base Ball Club (Eufaula, AL; 1880s)

The Hard Hitter B.B.C. organized in the 1880s, played black nines. *Eufaula Times* (June 28, 1889): "The Rome City [Georgia] and Eufaula Hard Hitter will engage in combat at the Fair Grounds this afternoon at 3 o'clock. These clubs are composed of colored boys and some are said to be especially fine players. Admission 10 cents."

Sources: "A Game of Base Ball," *Eufaula (AL) Times*, June 28, 1889.

Modoc Base Ball Club (Eufaula, AL; 1880s)

The Modoc B.B.C. organized in the 1880s, played black nines. *Columbus Sunday Enquirer* (May 21, 1882): "The Eufaula Base Ball Club, Modocs, colored have challenged the Georgia Champions, colored, of Columbus, for a game, to be played at Eufaula. The Columbus boys will go down on the Steamer Everingham, Wednesday, and feel confident of becoming the victors in this important game."

Sources: "Base Ball Match at Eufaula," *Columbus (GA) Sunday Enquirer*, May 21, 1882.

Alabamas Base Ball Club (Greenville, AL; 1880s)

The Alabamas B.B.C., of Natchez, MS, organized in the 1870s, played black organizations. *Greenville Advocate* (July 10, 1879): "In a match game of base-ball between the Hardups and Alabamas, Greenville's colored clubs, the Hardups won, the score standing 30 for the Hardups and 29 for the Alabamas." *Advocate* (May 12, 1881): "The Alabamas, Greenville colored base-ball club, played a match game with the Evergreen club last Friday. When night came, the score stood: Alabamas 32, Evergreen 28. The Alabamas complain of unfair treatment. They have asked the Advocate to return many thanks to the citizens of Evergreen for their kind treatment." *Advocate* (June 9, 1881): "The Greenville colored base-ball club was victorious in the game with the Evergreens here last Friday. The score, we understand, stood 28 for Greenville and 15 for Evergreen."

Sources: *Greenville (AL) Advocate*, Jun 10, 1880; *Greenville (AL) Advocate*, May 12, 1881; *Greenville Advocate*, Jun 2, 1881; *Greenville Advocate*, Jun 9, 1881.

Hardups Base Ball Club (Greenville, AL; 1870s–1880s)

The Hardups B.B.C. organized in the 1870s, played black organizations. *Greenville Advocate* (July 10, 1879): "There are two colored Base Ball clubs in our city named the Hard-Ups and Metropolitans. A match game was played between them on the 4th,—resulted in a tie, each club scoring 33. Another inning was then played, giving the victory to the Hard-Ups, they making 11 to the other 1." *Advocate* (July 10, 1879): "In a match game of base-ball between the Hardups and Alabamas, Greenville's colored clubs, the Hardups won, the score standing 30 for the Hardups and 29 for the Alabamas."

Sources: *Greenville (AL) Advocate*, Jul 10, 1879; "Base Ball," *Greenville Advocate*, Aug 21, 1879; *Greenville Advocate*, Jun 10, 1880.

Metropolitan Base Ball Club (Greenville, AL; 1870s)

The Metropolitan B.B.C. organized in the 1870s, played black organizations. *Greenville Advocate* (July 10, 1879): "There are two colored Base Ball clubs in our city named the Hard-Ups and Metropolitans. A match game was played between them on the 4th,—

resulted in a tie, each club scoring 33. Another inning was then played, giving the victory to the Hard-Ups, they making 11 to the other 1."

Sources: *Greenville (AL) Advocate*. July 10, 1879.

Red Stocking Base Ball Club (Huntsville, AL; 1880s)

The Red Stocking B.B.C. organized in the 1880s. The Red Stockings played against black organizations. *Huntsville Gazette* (July 28, 1883): "Our Huntsville colored base-ball club struts around with the championship and bearing a chip aloft on its cap and gives a bold dare to any club of the sunny South." In 1881, the Reds battled and defeated Nashville's A. K. Wards for 300.00 and the black championship of the South.

Sources: "Huntsville, Alabama," *Nashville (TN) Tennessean*, Aug 11, 1881; "Huntsville vs. Nashville," *Huntsville (AL) Gazette*, Aug 11, 1881; "The A. K. Wards," *Huntsville Gazette*, Aug 20, 1881; "Huntsville," *Nashville Tennessean*, Aug 27, 1881; "Base-Ball," *Huntsville Gazette*, Jul 7, 1883; "Base-Ball," *Huntsville Gazette*, July 28, 1883.

Saucy Boys Base Ball Club (Mobile, AL; 1880s). Organizer(s): Jacob Powell.

The Saucy Boys B.B.C. organized in the 1880s. The Saucy Boys played black clubs of AL and LA. *New Orleans Times-Democrat* (May 17, 1886): "Two crack colored clubs played at Lincoln Park. Score: Alabamas, 14; Saucy Boys, 5." *Times-Democrat* (July 6, 1886): "The W.L. Cohens shut out both the Sutherland and Saucy Boy clubs by the score of 9 to 0 and 2 to 0, respectively." *Times-Democrat* (September 16, 1886): "The colored people are as much interested over baseball as others, and the champion game played yesterday between the Thompsons and Saucy Boys, two crack colored clubs, was witnessed by hundreds of people."

Sources: "Games Played Yesterday," *New Orleans (LA) Times-Democrat*, May 17, 1886; "Mobile Colored Clubs," *New Orleans Times-Democrat*, Jul 6, 1886; "Mobile Matters," *New Orleans Times-Democrat*, Jul 20, 1886; "The Colored Players," *New Orleans Times-Democrat*, Sep 16, 1886.

Spider Base Ball Club (Mobile, AL; 1890s)

The Spider B.B.C. organized in the 1890s. The team played black teams. *New Orleans Times-Democrat* (August 14, 1894): "The Paddios, of Algiers, play the Spiders, Mobile's colored club, at Frascati Park tomorrow." *New Orleans Times-Democrat* (September 25, 1894): "The Mobile colored baseball team cleaned up the Pensacola colored club at Frascati Park last evening to the tune of 11 to 6. *New Orleans Times-Picayune* (October 1, 1894): "The two crack colored baseball clubs of this city, the Alabamas and Mobiles [Spiders], played the second game of a championship series of five games at Frascati this afternoon, in the presence of an audience composed of 100 whites and 900 Negroes. The game was very exciting from start to finish, and was won by the Alabamas, who have won both games. The batteries were White and Sanders for the Alabamas, and Nicholas and Smith for the Mobiles. Randolph umpired a good game. The score was 15 to 9."

Sources: "Mobile Matters," *New Orleans (LA) Times-Democrat*, Aug 14, 1894; "Mobile Matters," *New Orleans Times-Democrat*, Sep 25, 1894; "Mobile Budget," *New Orleans (LA) Times-Picayune*, Oct 1, 1894.

Thompson Base Ball Club (Mobile, AL; 1880s). Organizer(s): Joseph Herriman.

The Thompson B.B.C. organized in the 1880s, played black clubs of AL and LA. They scheduled a five-game series with New Orleans's W. L. Cohens club. *New Orleans Picayune* (September 15, 1886): "The one game the Thompsons, of Mobile, won by from the Cohens, the crack colored local team, seems all they can get. The two nines met again at Mobile yesterday, and the Cohens won by a score of 8 to 1. This makes three straight games for the New Orleans boys and they are naturally elated. They return today and will be in the hands of their friends."

SOURCES: "Around the Bases," *New Orleans (LA) Times-Picayune*, Aug 30, 1886; "The Colored Teams," *New Orleans Times-Picayune*, Sep 6, 1886; "Base Ball," *New Orleans Times-Picayune*, Sep 8, 1886; "Around the Bases," *Times-Picayune*, Sep 13, 1886; "The Cohens Get a Creditable Victory," *New Orleans Times-Picayune*, Sep 14, 1886; "The Cohens Distance the Mobiles," *New Orleans Times-Picayune*, Sep 15, 1886.

Union Star Base Ball Club (Mobile, AL; 1860s)

The Union Star B.B.C. organized in the 1860s. The team played black teams. *Mobile Register* (July 7, 1868): "The Union Star Base Ball Club, composed of Negroes, paraded through the principal streets this morning, headed by a sheepskin band, and the captain of the first nine with the inevitable saber."

SOURCES: "The Negro Police Again," *Mobile (AL) Register*, Jun 17, 1868; "Negro Processions," *Mobile Register*, Jul 7, 1868.

Blues Base Ball Club (Montgomery, AL; 1880s–1890s). Organizer(s): Dr. C. W. Dorsett, J A. Duncan, T. Stone and E. P. Morrison; John W. Jones, John C. Alexander, Frank Lake and Frank Robinson.

The Blues B.B.C. organized in the 1880s, played black organizations. *Huntsville Gazette* (August 1, 1885): "The match game of baseball between the Florence club and the Montgomery Blues of this city played near the Fair Grounds Saturday last resulted in a victory over Florence by the score of 18 to 8." In 1886, they joined the Southern League of Colored Base Ballists. *New Orleans Times-Picayune* (June 27, 1886): "The Montgomerys will be the next of the colored league nines to play here. They will be here in time to play the [New Orleans] Unions next Sunday." *Atlanta Constitution* (August 11, 1887): "The Montgomery Colored Base Ball Club came to Atlanta yesterday accompanied by a large crowd of colored people. This afternoon the club will play the Atlanta Colored Club at Athletic Park. [John] Thompson and [Benjamin] Swift will do the battery work for the Atlantas and [Addis] Duncan and [William] Patterson for the Montgomerys." *Atlanta Constitution* (August 12, 1887): "A game of ball was played between a colored nine from Montgomery, and a colored nine composed mostly of barbers from Atlanta. A large crowd was present, good humor prevailed, and the game was greatly enjoyed. The visiting nine was victorious by a score of 17 to 4." William H. Hall, one of the club's star players, pitched and caught for New Orleans, LA's W. L. Cohen B.B.C. *Montgomery Advertiser* (September 10, 1891): "The Hornet Base Ball Club, of Birmingham played against the Montgomery colored team at Clisby's Park. It resulted in a score of 11 to 9 in favor of the former. A purse of $20 and gate receipts were the wager. Quite a crowd saw the game." The Blues played Tuskegee University's aggregation. *Greenville Advocate* (June 7, 1893): "There was a game of ball at the fairgrounds Thursday between a colored team from Montgomery and the colored team of this city, the score standing twelve to six in favor of Montgomery." *Washington Bee* (August 24, 1895): "Tuskegee's base-ball team met and defeated the Montgomery Blues, of Montgomery, Alabama recently. Tuskegee now holds the championship of the State." *Advertiser* (July 5, 1896): "At the baseball park there was a red-hot game between Montgomery and Tuskegee colored teams. Montgomery won by a score of something like 17 to 6. They outclassed the Tuskegee boys at the bat, winning out with hits; in the field the two teams were about evenly matched, though the local pitcher had the best of it in the box."

SOURCES: "Local Liners," *New Orleans (LA) Times-Picayune*, Jun 7, 1885; "A Feather for the Cap of the Montgomery Blues," *Huntsville (AL) Gazette*, Aug 1, 1885; "Base Ball," *New Orleans Times-Picayune*, Jun 27, 1886; "Colored Base Ballists," *Jacksonville (FL) Times-Union*, May 23, 1886; "Base Ball," *Montgomery (AL) Advertiser*, Jun 8, 1886; "Montgomery vs. Memphis," *Montgomery Advertiser*, Jun 15, 1886; *Prattville (AL) Southern Signal*, Jul 16, 1886; "Base Ball," *Prattville (AL) Progress*, Jun 17, 1887; "Caught on the Fly," *Atlanta (GA) Constitution*, Aug 11, 1887; "A Colored Excursion," *Atlanta Constitution*, Aug 12, 1887; "Pinchbacks and New Orleans Clubs To-Morrow," *New Orleans Picayune*, Jul 6, 1889; *Montgomery Advertiser*, Jul 31, 1890; "Base Ball and Racing," *Montgomery Advertiser*, Sep 10, 1891; "Ended in a Row," *Montgomery Advertiser*, Sep 11, 1892; "Diamond Dust," *Montgomery Advertiser*, Jun 9, 1892; "A Challenge," *Montgomery Advertiser*, Apr 28, 1893; "Little Bots of Gossip," *Montgomery Advertiser*, May 21, 1893; *Greenville (AL) Advocate*, Jun 7, 1893; "Base Ball Gossip," *Montgomery Advertiser*, Jun 28, 1894; "Negro Baseball Players," *Montgomery Advertiser*, Aug 14, 1894; "About Like a Sabbath," *Montgomery Advertiser*, Jul 5, 1895; "Alabama Notes," *Washington (DC) Bee*, Aug 24, 1895; "The Fourth of July," *Montgomery Advertiser*, Jul 4, 1896; "An Orderly Fourth," *Montgomery Advertiser*, Jul 5, 1896.

Colored Female Base Ball Club (Montgomery, AL; 1880s)

The Colored Female B.B.C. organized in the 1880s, played against black female teams. *Montgomery Advertiser* (July 4, 1889): "A match game of baseball will be played at Clisby's Park tomorrow between two colored female nines."

SOURCES: "Around Town," *Montgomery (AL) Advertiser*, Jul 4, 1889.

Red Stockings Base Ball Club (Montgomery, AL; 1890s). Organizer(s): N. E. Abercrombie, L. A. Roan, Nelson Lewis, Sam Dupree, William Swanson, Thomas Williams, I. A. Starrs and William A. Hall.

The Red Stockings B.B.C. organized in the 1880s. The Montgomery Reds played black organizations. *Montgomery Advertiser* (April 29, 1897): "The lovers of baseball in Montgomery will have an opportunity this afternoon of seeing a game between of the champion colored nines of the South—the Memphis Cliffords and the Montgomery Reds. The Reds desire to return their thanks to the merchants and business men of the city who kindly gave them their uniforms. The street parade will take place at 2:30 and the umpire will call the game at 3:20. Special seats will be kept for white people."

SOURCES: "Organized Last Night," *Montgomery (AL) Advertiser*, Apr 14, 1897; "Colored Baseball Clubs," *Montgomery Advertiser*, Apr 29, 1897; "Little Bits of Local News," *Montgomery Advertiser*, May 1, 1897; "Stolen Drink Proves Fatal," *Nashville (TN) Tennessean*, Jul 19,1899.

Dukes Base Ball Club (Selma, AL; 1880s). Organizer(s): M. W. Walker.

The Dukes B.B.C. organized in the 1880s. The Dukes played against black clubs of MS and AL. *Huntsville Gazette* (August 20, 1881): "Captan M. W. Walker, of the Selma Dukes, desires to challenge the [Huntsville] Reds, throughout the Gazette, for a game of base-ball anywhere between Huntsville and Selma. He states, in the way of warning, that his club recently defeated a Mississippi club by a score of28 to 2. The Selma Dukes and the C. R. Donegan's or Huntsville Reds, have succeeded in arranging a game of base-ball for the Championship of the State, to be played at the Fairgrounds, Thursday evening, August 25th." *Nashville Tennessean* (August 27, 1881): "A match game of base-ball was played at the Fair Grounds…

between the Selma Dukes and the Huntsville Reds, which resulted in a victory for the latter...."

SOURCES: "Base Ball," *Huntsville (AL) Gazette*, Aug 20, 1881; "Base Ball," *Huntsville Gazette*, Aug 27, 1881; "Huntsville," *Nashville (TN) Tennessean*, Aug 27, 1881.

Tuskegee University Base Ball Club (Tuskegee, AL; 1890s–1900s). Organizer(s): James B. WA.

The Tuskegee University B.B.C. organized in the 1880s. The college nine played against black clubs. James B. WA, a Hampton Institute graduate, a black school, came to Tuskegee and coached the baseball team. *Indianapolis Freeman* (December 20, 1890): "A game of baseball was played at Tuskegee College, Alabama, on the 27th of November, between a nine of students and the teachers. The teachers were defeated by a score of 16 to 10." *Montgomery Advertiser* (September 11, 1891): "The Negro baseball game at the Colored University grounds yesterday afternoon was well advertised with streamers accompanied with base and kettle drum." *Advertiser* (July 5, 1896): "At the baseball park there was a red-hot game between Montgomery and Tuskegee colored teams. Montgomery won by a score of something like 17 to 6. They outclassed the Tuskegee boys at the bat, winning out with hits; in the field the two teams were about evenly matched, though the local pitcher had the best of it in the box." *Washington Bee* (August 24, 1895): "Tuskegee's base-ball team met and defeated the Montgomery Blues, of Montgomery, Alabama recently. Tuskegee now holds the championship of the State."

SOURCES: *Indianapolis (IN) Freeman*, Dec 20, 1890; "Here and There," *Montgomery (AL) Advertiser*, Sep 11, 1891; "Alabama Notes," *Washington (DC) Bee*, Aug 24, 1895; "An Orderly Fourth," *Montgomery Advertiser*, Jul 5, 1896; *Tuskegee (AL) News*, May 25, 1899; "Tuskegee Notes," *Kansas City (KS) American Citizen*, Jul 13, 1900.

Arizona

Fort Huachuca Base Ball Club (Huachuca, AZ; 1890s)

The Fort Huachuca B.B.C. organized in the late 1890s. The nine, composed of soldiers, played white teams. *Tombstone Weekly Epitaph* (November 29, 1891): "The Huachuca club came in on two wagons and presented a natty appearance in their bright-colored suits. The game was an interesting one and resulted in a victory for Tombstone boys by a score of 25 to 5. The Huachuca nine has a splendid battery but were weak in other places." *Weekly Epitaph* (July 10, 1892): "The Huachuca nine, composed entirely of colored men, came over early Sunday afternoon. At the end of the 8th inning the score stood 18 to 17 in favor of Huachuca. Tombstone went to the bat in the 9th and scored six runs, and the Huachucas on the last half of the ninth had a lead of five runs to contend with, and lost. Two runs were all they could pull off out of it, and left our boys the victors by the score of 23 to 20."

SOURCES: "Thanksgiving," *Tombstone (AZ) Weekly Epitaph*, Nov 29, 1891; "The Day We Celebrated," *Tombstone Weekly Epitaph*, Jul 10, 1892; *Arizola (AZ) Oasis*, August 16, 1894; "The City in Brief," *Tucson (AZ) Daily Star*, August 21, 1895; *Tucson (AZ) Arizona Weekly Citizen*, August 24, 1895; "Bisbee News," *Tombstone Weekly Epitaph*, November 7, 1897; "All Over Arizona," *Phoenix (AZ) Republic*, Mar 24, 1898; "All Over Arizona," *Phoenix Republic*, Apr 14, 1898.

Barber Base Ball Club (Phoenix, AZ; 1890s). Organizer(s): Perry Polk.

The Barber B.B.C. organized in 1898. The nine played black, white, and Latino clubs of AZ and CA. *Arizona Republican* (January 12, 1894): "A match game of baseball will be played Sunday by the Fash-

ion barber shop nine and Spanish team. The Fashion barbershop nine has promised to give the Spanish team nine goose eggs or admit their inability to play ball." *Republican* (January 16, 1894): "The baseball game played by the Fashion barber shop nine and the Stars, resulted in a victory for the fashion barber shop by a score of 20 to 23. Perry Polk's great play for the Fashion nine won the game in the last inning."

SOURCES: "Sunday's Ball Game," *Phoenix (AZ) Republican*, Jan 1, 1894; "Base Ball Today," *Phoenix Republican*, Jan 14, 1894; "Base Ball Today," *Phoenix Republican*, Jan 16, 1894; "City and County in Brief," *Phoenix Republican*, Dec 1, 1897; "Today's Ball Game," *Phoenix Republican*, Jan 29, 1899; "A Tyrannical King," *Phoenix Republican*, March 7, 1899; "A Base Ball Challenge," *Phoenix Republican*, July 14, 1899.

Stearns Base Ball Club (Phoenix, AZ; 1890s–1900s). Organizer(s): Frank Shirley and Robert Stearns.

The R. B. Stearns B.B.C. organized in 1898. The club's organizer, Robert B. Stearns, black tonsorial artist and entrepreneur, originally from Oxford, MS, owned the Fashion Barber Shop. Stearns captained and managed the club. The R.B. Stearns played white and colored nines of AZ, and CA. The team roster included Robert Stevens, Theodore Thomas, Adolphus Cretil, G. W. Caldwell, Perry Polk, Frank Turner, Al Williams, Otto Williams, and Stearns. Polk also played with the Los Angeles Trilbys. *Phoenix Weekly Republican* (August 6, 1899): "A fairly good-sized crowd yesterday afternoon saw Bolton's north side Possumalas wipe up the earth and dig holes in it with Shirley's south side Bullies, defeating them by a score of 18 to 9."

SOURCES: "Shirley & Bolton's Nine," *Phoenix (AZ) Republican*, Jan 4, 1894; "Another Ball Game," *Phoenix Republican*, Jan 12, 1894; "Base Ball Today," *Phoenix Republican*, Jan 14, 1894; "Base Ball Today," *Phoenix (AZ) Arizona Republican*, Jan 14, 1894; "Sunday's Ball Game," *Phoenix Republican*, Jan 16, 1894; "A Tyrannical King," *Phoenix Republican*, Mar 7, 1899; "New of the Town," *Phoenix Republican*, July 14, 1899; "Why Captain Stearns Went to Play Ball There," *Phoenix Republican*, August 6, 1899; "Base Ball Game Off," *Phoenix Republican*, May 6, 1900; "Another Ball Game," *Phoenix Republican*, June 1, 1900.

Arkansas

Black Stocking Base Ball Club (Fort Smith, AR; 1880s–1890s). Organizer(s): Horace Haywood, Arch Turner and H. St. Clair.

The Black Stocking B.B.C. organized in the 1880s. First managed by Horace Haywood, the Black Stockings played black clubs of AR, OK, and MO. The team developed a rivalry with Springfield, MO. *Springfield Republican* (August 1, 1888): "Today at the ball park, the initial game between the Springfield Reds and Fort Smith Black Stockings will be played. The Arkansas team is composed of intelligent, hard-working men and each and every one are ball players. The Reds have wonderfully improved by practice in the last week, and a great game may be looked for." *Los Angeles Times* (August 26, 1895): "Haywood, a 25-year baseball veteran, called the Colored Anson. Adrian "Cap" Anson gave Haywood a gray uniform with the name "Chicago" stitched in big black letters across the front. According to accounts, the baseballist always wore the jersey during ball games."

SOURCES: "Base Ball Today," *Springfield (MO) Republican*, Aug 1, 1888; "Base Ball Today," *Republican*, Aug 3, 1888; "High School Graduates," *Indianapolis (IN) Freeman*, Jun 8, 1892; "A Match With Fort Smith," *Springfield Republican*, Jul 23, 1895; "Base Ball Today," *Springfield Republican*, Aug 3, 1895; "Ball Game Today," *Springfield Repub-*

lican, Aug 7, 1895; "Sporting Notes," *Los Angeles (CA) Times*, Aug 26, 1895.

Colored Base Ball Club (Fort Smith, AR; 1870s)

The Colored B.B.C. organized in the 1870s, played black teams. *St. Louis Republican* (September 4, 1875): "A game of base-ball was being played by the colored clubs of [Fort Smith and Van Buren], just outside the garrison walls. In this game, Fort Smith was victorious. I do not know the names of either of the last mentioned clubs (except black). The score was Fort Smith 48, Van Buren 21."

SOURCES: "Fort Smith, Ark.," *St. Louis (MO) Missourian*, Sep 4, 1875.

Border City Base Ball Club (Fort Smith, AR; 1880s). Organizer(s): Ellis Kidd.

The Border City B.B.C. organized in the 1880s, played black clubs. *Little Rock Democrat* (August 8, 1884): "The Fort Smith and Van Buren colored base-ball clubs played a match game last week, which closed 13 to 7 in favor of Fort Smith."

SOURCES: "State News," *Little Rock (AR) Democrat*, Jun 17, 1884; "Fort Smith," *Little Rock (AR) Gazette*, Aug 7, 1884; "Fort Smith," *Little Rock Democrat*, Aug 8, 1884; "Emancipation Anniversary," *Fort Smith (AR) Elevator*, Aug 8, 1884; "Local Paragraphs," *Little Rock (AR) Gazette*, Sep 20, 1884; "Local Brevities," *Little Rock Democrat*, Jul 15, 1886; "Van Buren," *Little Rock Gazette*, Jul 6, 1887.

A. B. C. Base Ball Club (Helena, AR; 1890s). Organizer(s): Charles Meyers.

The A. B. C. B.B.C. organized in the 1890s, played black aggregations. *Helena Weekly World* (August 19, 1896): "Last Friday the Clarendon and Helena Negro clubs played a game of ball at this place, and the score stood 16 to 1 in favor of the local team." *Weekly World* (August 19, 1896): "Newman's Anheisers and Charles Meyer's A. B. C.'s, two colored baseball teams, matched each other at South End Park yesterday. The game was highly excited and witnessed by a great crowd of the colored populace. The score stood 30 to 28 in favor of the Anheisers."

SOURCES: *Helena (AR) Weekly World*, Aug 12, 1896; "30 to 28," *Helena Weekly World*, Aug 19, 1896.

Colored Base Ball Club (Helena, AR; 1880s–1890s)

The Colored B.B.C. organized in the 1880s, played black teams. *Little Rock Gazette* (August 18, 1887): "The colored clubs of Helena and Pine Bluff mix wool at Jones' Park today." *Helena Weekly World* (June 23, 1897): "The colored baseball teams of Marianna and Helena played a match game of baseball at South End Park yesterday afternoon. The nine innings were played out resulting in a defeat for Helena, the score standing Marianna 12, Helena 11. The audience was quite large and the game was well played. Wash Amps was in the box and Will Goel caught for the Helena side. The Helenas will shortly tackle the Greenville nine." *Weekly World* (August 30, 1899): "The colored baseball teams of Marianna and Helena crossed bats at Sportsman's Park for eight innings, and Helena's excellent Negro players proceeded to knock it to the visitors in great shape, the score standing 16–5 for the home team. Wash Amps figured as the heavy twirler for Helena and William Brody officiated behind the bat. For Marianna, Al Olton and O. Lee guarded the strategic points."

SOURCES: "Pine Bluff," *Little Rock (AR) Gazette*, Aug 18, 1887; "12 to 11," *Helena (AR) Weekly World*, Jun 23, 1897; "Helena Made Big Sweep 11," *Helena (AR) Weekly World*, Aug 30, 1899.

Arlington Hotel Base Ball Club (Hot Springs, AR; 1870s–1900s)

The Arlington Hotel B.B.C. composed of waiters, played black aggregations. *Little Rock Gazette* (September 18, 1875): "The Comus Base Ball Club plays at Hot Springs [against the Arlingtons] today." *Gazette* (September 6, 1878): "The game of base-ball yesterday afternoon at the Fair Grounds between the two colored clubs, Arlingtons and Comus, resulted in a victory for the former, the score standing 32 to 12." *Gazette* (August 10, 1880): "There will be an interesting game of ball next Saturday for the state championship, between the Arlingtons, of this city, and the Red Stockings, of Pine Bluff. The Arlingtons are now the champions and will play their best to hold it." They maintained a strong team, playing rival clubs for the black championship of southeast; among them, Little Rock's Comus nine. During the winter season, northern black and white clubs went the Vapor City to enjoy the mild weather and they played the Arlingtons. William Albert Jones, of Chicago's Unions scheduled to take his club to Hot Springs. *Sporting Life* (February 11, 1899): "George Bristow, well known in the Texas and Atlantic leagues, has the matter well in hand, and secured the following players who are wintering here, to play the Arlington Club, a team composed of colored players." Between 1897 and 1900, the Arlingtons and Quapaws fought for baseball supremacy in the Southwest. In 1900, Tyler, TX's ball club, managed by Ryan Stewart, made the trip to Hot Springs, Little Rock, Pine Bluff, and other Arkansan points.

SOURCES: "The Finest Hotel in the State," *Little Rock (AR) Gazette*, Apr 20, 1875; "Base Ball Notes," *Little Rock Gazette*, Sep 14, 1875; "Capital City Brevities," *Little Rock Gazette*, Sep 18, 1875; "City and General Items," *Little Rock Gazette*, Sep 6, 1878; "Local Paragraphs," *Little Rock Gazette*, Aug 10, 1880; "Local Paragraphs," *Little Rock Gazette*, Aug 22, 1880; "Quapaws Win," *Little Rock Gazette*, May 22, 1897; "Victory for the Quapaws," *Little Rock Gazette*, May 26, 1897; "Quapaw vs. Arlingtons," *Little Rock Gazette*, August 5, 1897; "Arlington, 8; Quapaw, 4," *Little Rock Gazette*, Aug 7, 1897; "Notes of the Game," *Little Rock Gazette*, Sep 7, 1897; "Largest Crowd of the Season," *Little Rock Gazette*, Sep 7, 1897; "Best Game Yet," *Little Rock Gazette*, Sep 8, 1897; "Exciting Game Between Senators and Quapaws," *Little Rock Gazette*, Sep 9, 1897; "Hot Springs Work," *Philadelphia (PA) Sporting Life*, Feb 11, 1899; "Quapaws Won Two Games," *Little Rock (AR) Democrat*, Jul 20, 1899; "Arlingtons Defeat the Quapaws," *Little Rock Gazette*, Jul 25, 1899; *Little Rock Democrat*, Jul 26, 1899; "Local News," *Little Rock Democrat*, Jul 27, 1899; "All Over the State," *Little Rock Democrat*, Aug 2, 1899; "All Over the State," *Democrat*, Aug 3, 1899; "Arlingtons were Defeated," *Little Rock Gazette*, Aug 15, 1899; "All Over the State," *Little Rock Democrat*, Aug 17, 1899; "Sport," *Indianapolis (IN) Freeman*, Apr 20, 1900; "Tyler 9, Hot Springs 7," *Dallas (TX) Morning New*, May 25, 1900; "Sport," *Indianapolis Freeman*, Apr 20, 1900; "Palestine News," *Indianapolis Freeman*, Jul 13, 1901; "Hot Springs News," *Indianapolis Freeman*, May 16, 1903.

Active Base Ball Club (Little Rock, AR; 1870s)

The Active B.B.C. organized in the 1880s. The Actives played black nines. *Little Rock Gazette* (June 19, 1871): "The Frontier and Active (colored) base-ball clubs were to have played a match game on Saturday, but the Actives failed to appear."

SOURCES: "Base Ball Notes," *Little Rock (AR) Morning Republican*, Jun 19, 1871.

Cadet Base Ball Club (Little Rock, AR; 1880s)

The Cadet B.B.C. organized in the 1880s. The Cadets played against black nines. They fought for the championship. *Little Rock Gazette* (August 14, 1885): "There will be a game of ball at the High Street grounds this afternoon between two clubs of colored boys, the Reds and a new organized team [Cadets], for the championship." *Gazette* (August 19, 1885): "A game of ball was played yesterday afternoon on the High Street Grounds between colored clubs."

SOURCES: "Base Ball Notes," *Little Rock (AR) Gazette*, Aug 14, 1885; "Base Ball Notes," *Little Rock Gazette*, August 19, 1885.

Comus Base Ball Club (Little Rock, AR; 1870s–1880s). Organizer(s): D. S. Caldwell, John E. Bush and Chester W. Keatts.

The Comus B.B.C. organized in the 1870s. The Comus nine played against black nines. *Little Rock Gazette* (September 22, 1875): "The Comus club, of this city, bat the Dauntless, of Hot Springs, 27 to 4 in six innings. Saturday, the Dauntless were victorious 23 to 22. Third game will be played here." *Little Rock Gazette* (October 16, 1875): "The Dauntless Base Ball Club, of Hot Springs, was boiled yesterday by the Comus lads of this city." *Memphis Commercial Appeal* (October 7, 1876): "The Comus Base-Ball Club, of Little Rock, arrived in our city yesterday to play a match game with the Clippers of Memphis." *Gazette* (September 6, 1878): "The game of base-ball at the Fair Grounds, Arlingtons and Comus, resulted in a victory for the former, the score standing 32 to 12."

SOURCES: "A Card of Thanks," *Little Rock (AR) Gazette*, Aug 4, 1875; "Pick Ups," *Little Rock Gazette*, Sep 22, 1875; "Base Business," *Little Rock Gazette*, Oct 16, 1875; "The Game Today," *Memphis (TN) Commercial Appeal*, Oct 7, 1876; "City and General Items," *Little Rock Gazette*, Jun 23, 1877; "City and General Notes," *Little Rock (AR) Gazette*, Sep 6, 1878.

Lone Star Base Ball Club (Little Rock, AR; 1870s–1880s)

The Lone Star B.B.C. organized in the 1870s. The Lone Stars played against black nines. *Little Rock Republican* (July 10, 1872): "The colored baseballists played a match game, in which the Lone Stars beat the Pelicans, and at night there was a grand ball." *Little Rock Gazette* (July 6, 1880): "About 500 persons witnessed a game of base-ball between the Lone Star and Arlington clubs. Both clubs are colored. The Arlingtons defeated their opponents by a score of 13 to 12." *Little Rock Democrat* (July 23, 1880): "The Arlington and Lone Star base-ball clubs, composed of colored boys, played a match game, resulting in a victory for the former by a score of 37 to 15." *Little Rock Gazette* (July 27, 1886): "The colored barbers of this city [Hot Springs] will play a match game of base-ball some day this week with the Lone Stars, colored, of Little Rock."

SOURCES: *Little Rock (AR) Republican*, Jul 23, 1872; "Local Paragraphs," *Little Rock (AR) Gazette*, Jun 30, 1880; "Local Paragraphs," *Little Rock Gazette*, Jul 6, 1880; *Little Rock (AR) Democrat*, Jul 23, 1880; *Little Rock (AR) Gazette*, Jul 27, 1886.

Quapaw Base Ball Club (Little Rock, AR; 1880s–1890s)

The Quapaw B.B.C. organized in the 1880s. The "Quapaws" played white and black teams. They called themselves "the colored champions of the Southwest." *Arkansas Gazette* (June 15, 1897): "A large crowd was in attendance yesterday afternoon at West End Park to witness the first of a series of baseball games between the Quapaws, colored champions of Arkansas, and the strong Greenville, Mississippi Reds (colored). The game was full of ginger from the start and the boys put up as snappy a game as the present season has afforded on the local grounds." Between 1897 and 1900, the Arlington Hotel B.B.C., of Hot Springs, AR and the Quapaws fought for black baseball supremacy in the Southwest. In 1897, the Quapaws played the Little Rock professionals, white, losing in a pitcher's duel by the score of 3 to 2.

SOURCES: "Quapaws Win," *Little Rock (AR) Gazette*, May 22, 1897; "Victory for the Quapaws," *Little Rock Gazette*, May 26, 1897; "Quapaw vs. Arlingtons," *Little Rock Gazette*, August 5, 1897; "Arlington, 8; Quapaw, 4," *Little Rock Gazette*, Aug 7, 1897; "Notes of the Game," *Little Rock Gazette*, Sep 7, 1897; "Largest Crowd of the Season," *Little Rock Gazette*, Sep 7, 1897; "Best Game Yet," *Little Rock Gazette*, Sep

8, 1897; "Exciting Game Between Senators and Quapaws," *Little Rock Gazette*, Sep 9, 1897.

Red Stocking Base Ball Club (Little Rock, AR; 1880s)

The Red Stocking B.B.C. organized in the 1880s. The "Reds" played against black organizations. They fought for the local black championship. *Little Rock Gazette* (August 15, 1884): "The Little Rock Browns and the Little Rock Reds, two colored base-ball clubs of this city, played a match game of ball at the fairgrounds for silk flags offered the winning club by Elder Phillips." *Little Rock Gazette* (August 15, 1885): "There will be a game of ball at the High Street grounds this afternoon between two clubs of colored boys, the Reds and a new organized team [Cadets], for the championship." *Gazette* (August 19, 1885): "A game of ball was played yesterday afternoon on the High Street Grounds between colored clubs."

SOURCES: "Local Paragraphs," *Little Rock (AR) Gazette*, Aug 15, 1884; "Base Ball Notes," *Little Rock Gazette*, Aug 15, 1885; "Base Ball Notes," *Little Rock Gazette*, Aug 19, 1885.

Sweet Homes Base Ball Club (Little Rock, AR; 1880s)

The Sweet Homes B.B.C. organized in the 1880s. The Sweet Homes played against black nines. *Little Rock Gazette* (August 22, 1880): "A match game of base-ball was played between the Arlingtons, Sweet Homes and Athletics. The game took place near the corner of Commerce and Fifteenth, and was witnessed by quite a large crowd. The clubs are all ebony base-ballists in the state. The game was won by the Arlingtons."

SOURCES: "Local Paragraphs," *Little Rock (AR) Gazette*, Aug 22, 1880.

Browns Base Ball Club (Newport, AR; 1890s). Organizer(s): R. Edgar.

The Browns B.B.C. organized in the 1890s. The Browns played black teams. *Indianapolis Freeman* (September 9, 1893): "The Newport Browns were reorganized. They played a match game at Searcy with the Searcy Blues, which resulted in a victory for the Browns; score, 34 to 25. After dinner, both clubs were lined up in front of the Palace [Hotel], and at 2:30 the long processions of base-ball enthusiasts started for the grounds. At 3:30 the game was called by umpires Keeble and Allen. Up to the sixth inning it was a walkaway for the Browns, the score standing 21 to 1 at that time. Afterwards the Blues rallied and in the three remaining innings covered themselves with glory in batting and base-running."

SOURCES: "The Crack Base Ball Club," *Indianapolis (IN) Freeman*, Nov 19, 1892; "The Masonic Picnic," *Indianapolis Freeman*, Sep 9, 1893.

Clipper Base Ball Club (Newport, AR; 1890s). Organizer(s): R. Edgar.

The Clipper B.B.C. organized in the 1890s. The Clippers played black teams. *Indianapolis Freeman* (October 8, 1892): "[Newport's Clippers] are the best baseball club Newport has ever had. They are composed of young men about twenty years of age. We hope to reelect R. Edgar manager of the club for next season, as all of the players like his management."

SOURCES: "The Present and the Future," *Indianapolis (IN) Freeman*, Sep 17, 1892; "Newport, Arkansas," *Indianapolis Freeman*, Oct 8, 1892.

Owl Base Ball Club (Pine Bluff, AR; 1890s–1900s). Organizer(s): Wiley Jones and John Young, Jr.

The Owl B.B.C. organized in the 1890s, played against black nines. Owner Wiley Jones, considered the richest black man in the country, built a ballpark for his team. *Pine Bluff Graphic* (June 23, 1899):

"Thursday afternoon the colored people of this city were out in full force at Jones' Park to witness a game of baseball between two colored teams, the Owl Club of this city, and the Waco, Texas aggregation. The crowd from Waco numbered 150 people and they were the warmest gang of colored rooters that Pine Bluff had ever seen in her bounds. At the end of the ninth inning the game stood 12 to 8 in favor of Waco." *Graphic* (August 2, 1899): "The Owl Baseball team, colored, of Pine Bluff, went to sleep at Whittington Park in Hot Springs Tuesday, and the Arlington team of that city defeated them by a score of 12 to 4. The battery for the Owls were Taylor and Knox." *Little Rock Gazette* (August 2, 1899): "The Arlington baseball team of this city defeated the Owls, of Pine Bluff, this afternoon at Whittington Park by a score of 12 to 4. This was the second game of the series and the second victory for the Arlingtons. The batteries for the latter were: Jackson and Lewis; for the Owls, Taylor and Knox."

SOURCES: "City Items," *Pine Bluff (AR) Graphic*, Jun 14, 1899; "City Items," *Pine Bluff Graphic*, Jun 16, 1899; "Waco vs. Pine Bluff," *Pine Bluff Graphic*, Jun 23, 1899; *Pine Bluff Graphic*, Aug 2, 1899; "The Owls Were Asleep," *Little Rock (AR) Democrat*, Aug 2, 1899; *Pine Bluff Graphic*, Aug 3, 1899; "Colored Nines," *Pine Bluff Graphic*, May 26, 1901; *Pine Bluff Graphic*, May 28, 1901.

Red Stockings Base Ball Club (Pine Bluff, AR; 1880s)

The Red Stockings B.B.C. organized in the 1880s. The Red Stocking nine played against black nines. *Little Rock Gazette* (August 22, 1880): "There will be an interesting game of ball played for the state championship between the Arlingtons, of this city, and the Red Stockings, of Pine Bluff. The Arlingtons are now the champions and will play their best to hold it."

SOURCES: "Local Brevities," *Little Rock (AR) Democrat*, Aug 10, 1880; "Local Paragraphs," *Little Rock (AR) Gazette*, Aug 22, 1880.

California

Browns Base Ball Club (Bakersfield, CA; 1890s)

The Browns B.B.C. organized in the 1890s. The Browns played white and black nines. *Los Angeles Herald* (August 1, 1898): "A Bakersfield colored baseball nine, which is with the Afro-American Congress, played a match game this afternoon at the bicycle track with a local colored team and won by a score of 12 to 9. There was a good crowd and a collection was taken up to defray the expenses. It was a good game. A home run was made by catcher Pinckney of the visitors, three base-hit by Pitcher Boydston, double plays by Carr and Alexander of the home run."

SOURCES: "Bat and Ball," *Los Angeles (CA) Herald*, Aug 1, 1898; "The Championship," *Los Angeles Herald*, Aug 8, 1898; "The Colored Teams," *Bakersfield (CA) Daily Californian*, Sep 11, 1899; "Baseball Game," *Bakersfield Daily Californian*, Jun 30, 1899.

Trilby Base Ball Club (Fresno, CA; 1890s). Organizer(s): F. Ford and Walter Brown.

The Trilby B.B.C. organized in the 1890s. The "Trilbys" played white teams.

SOURCES: "Firemen vs. Trilbys," *Fresno (CA) Morning Republican*, Jan 17, 1897.

Browns Base Ball Club (Los Angeles, CA; 1890s)

The Browns B.B.C. organized in the 1890s. The "Browns" played black and white nines. *Los Angeles Herald* (April 22, 1894): "The Los Angeles Browns and the Boyle Heights Stars will play a matched game of ball at the First Street grounds today. The game promises to be an interesting one, as both clubs have a large share of victories." *Herald* (September 23, 1894): "The Los Angeles Browns defeated

the Pasadenas yesterday by a score of 19 to 17." Playing clubs in Los Angeles and Pasadena, the "Browns" established quite a reputation.

SOURCES: "Baseball," *Los Angeles (CA) Herald*, Apr 22, 1894; "Sporting Notes," *Los Angeles Herald*, May 29, 1894; "Amateur Playing," *Los Angeles Herald*, May 31, 1894; "Baseball Yesterday," *Los Angeles Herald*, Jun 4, 1894; "Baseball Today," *Los Angeles Herald*, Jun 24, 1894; "Another Game," *Los Angeles Herald*, Sep 23, 1894.

Lightweight Base Ball Club (Los Angeles, CA; 1880s–1890s). Organizer(s): James M. Alexander.

The Lightweight B.B.C. organized in the 1880s. The Lightweights, dubbed champions of Southern CA, played black and white teams. Under James M. Alexander's managerial leadership, they challenged local white aggregations. *Los Angeles Herald* (August 17, 1890): "[The game] will be an interesting one assured by the fact that, in addition to the jealousy already existing between them, a stake of $25 has already been deposited by each of the teams, to be played for."

SOURCES: "News Notes," *Los Angeles (CA) Herald*, Jun 6, 1890; "Base Ball," *Los Angeles Herald*, Aug 14, 1890; "Africa and America," *Los Angeles Herald*, Aug 17, 1890; "News Notes," *Los Angeles Herald*, April 11, 1891; "The Lightweights on Deck," *Los Angeles Herald*, Sep 26, 1891.

Quickstep Base Ball Club (Los Angeles, CA; 1880s). Organizer(s): Detrick.

The Quickstep B.B.C. organized in the 1880s. The Quicksteps played black and white nines. *Los Angeles Herald* (June 15, 1888): "Tomorrow at 2pm, at the ground corner of Ninth and Hope Streets, the Eighth Streets and the Quicksteps will again come together. A close and exciting contest in anticipated."

SOURCES: "Base Ball," *Los Angeles (CA) Herald*, Jun 10, 1888; "Two Ball Contests," *Los Angeles Herald*, Jun 15, 1888.

Star Base Ball Club (Los Angeles, CA; 1870s)

The Star B.B.C. organized in the 1870s. *Los Angeles Herald* (May 24, 1879): "The Star Club, colored, will play the Green Meadows [Athletics] Club a match game at Agricultural Park tomorrow (Sunday), for a ball, bat, and a name."

SOURCES: "Local Brevities," *Los Angeles (CA) Herald*, May 24, 1879; "Local Brevities," *Los Angeles Herald*, May 25, 1879.

Trilby Base Ball Club (Los Angeles, CA; 1890s–1900s). Organizer(s): William "Riley" Carroll.

The Trilby B.B.C. organized in 1895. The organization's players came from CA, IL, KS, NE, TX, TN, UT, and AZ. The Trilbys had two well-recognized baseballists, the battery of Robert Shaw (IL) and William Carroll (TX). They played white and black teams: professional, semiprofessional, and amateur. *Los Angeles Herald* (October 14, 1895): "One of the best games of baseball ever played in Los Angeles was witnessed yesterday afternoon at Athletic Park by a large number of people. The Francis Wilsons and the Trilbys play professional ball, and good professional ball at that.... Tyler was in the box for the Wilsons and Shaw twirled for the Trilbys, both men pitching effective ball and getting better as the game progressed." In 1896, they claimed the championship of Southern CA by defeating the Francis Wilsons. Shaw, who had pitched in Chicago, was a workhorse. He often pitched both sides of a doubleheader. Shaw defeated the Admirals by the score of 8–6 and shut out the Francis Williams by the score of 1–0. They traveled CA, NV, and AZ. *Herald* (October 25, 1897): "Five hundred people witnessed the third and fourth games of the Southern California championship series at Fiesta Park yesterday afternoon between the Trilbys and the Echoes. In the first game the Echoes put Street in the box, much to their sorrow for the Trilbys rolled up ten runs in the first inning by a combination of three hits, five bases on balls and five errors. Austin took Street's place in the second, but fared little better the other club making eleven runs off him in the eight innings that remained." The Trilbys played into the early twentieth century. *San Diego Evening Tribune* (July 31, 1899): "The Trilby colored Los Angeles ball team came down here from Los Angeles yesterday headed by their irrepressible captain "Riley" Carroll, and when they had gotten through with San Diego's new Merchant's team the score was 10 to 7 in favor of the visitors.... It was a good game up to the fifth inning, but by that time the Trilbys had commenced to connect with Park's curves and the toboggan slide began." *Evening Tribune* (April 9, 1900): "The Trilbys of Los Angeles came down here from Los Angeles yesterday and astonished their friends by the strong game of baseball they put up against the Sand Diego league team, if requiring ten innings to decide the game which stood 4 to 4 at the end of the ninth when a safe hit by Bowman followed by another beauty by Treanor brought in the winning run. San Diego played a rather loose game making six errors to only one by its opponent."

SOURCES: "Trilby in Baseball," *Los Angeles (CA) Herald*, Jun 24, 1895; "For A Good Game," *Los Angeles Herald*, Jun 26, 1895; "Baseball Today," *Los Angeles Herald*, Jul 7, 1895; "Sport, Local and General" *Los Angeles Herald*, Aug 12, 1895; "Baseball Today," *Los Angeles (CA) Times*, Oct 27, 1895; "Darktown in Gloom," *Los Angeles Times*, November 8, 1895; "In the World of Sport," *Los Angeles Herald*, Jun 14, 1896; "Baseball," *Los Angeles Herald*, Jun 16, 1896; "Brevities," *Los Angeles Herald*, Jun 18, 1896; "A Ball Game," *Los Angeles Herald*, Jun 20, 1896; "Brevities," *Los Angeles Herald*, Jun 25, 1896; "Baseball Games," *Los Angeles Herald*, Jun 27, 1896; "Baseball," *Los Angeles Times*, Jul 20, 1896; "The National Game," *Los Angeles Times*, Aug 3, 1896; Bat and Ball," *Los Angeles Herald*, Sep 10, 1896; "Baseball," *Los Angeles Times*, Dec 7, 1896; "The Chicago Unions," *St. Louis (MO) Sporting News*, Feb 6, 1897; "Los Angeles Letter," *Philadelphia (PA) Sporting Life*, Mar 20, 1897; "Los Angeles Players," *Philadelphia Sporting Life,* Jan 30, 1897; "With Ball and Bat," *Los Angeles Times*, Mar 1, 1897; "Baseball," *Los Angeles Times*, May 17, 1897; "Redondo Wins," *Los Angeles Times*, Jun 28, 1897; "Two Games of Ball," *Los Angeles Herald*, Oct 25, 1897; "Sporting," *Los Angeles Times*, Nov 8, 1897; "Today's Sports," *Los Angeles Times*. Dec. 5, 1897; "Today's Sports," *Los Angeles Times*, Dec 6, 1897; "Sunday Sports," *Los Angeles Times*, Dec 19, 1897; "Base Ball Yesterday," *San Diego (CA) Evening Tribune*, Jan 3, 1898; "Sporting," *Los Angeles Times*, Jan 17, 1898; "Good Base Ball Promised," *San Diego Evening Tribune*, Jan 18, 1898; "Base Ball," *San Diego Evening Tribune*, January 22, 1898; "Sporting," *Los Angeles Times*, Feb 14, 1898; "Baseball," *Los Angeles Herald*, Dec 19, 1898; "Was a Lively Ball Game," *Phoenix (AZ) Republican*, Jan 2, 1899; "More Base Ball," *Phoenix (AZ) Herald*, Jan 5, 1899; "Base Ball Game Today," *Phoenix Republican*, Jan 8, 1899; "Turn of the Tide," *Phoenix Republican*, Jan 23, 1899; "Today's Ball Game," *Phoenix Republican*, Jan 29, 1899; "Trilbys Defeated," *San Diego (CA) Union*, Apr 3, 1899; "Trilbys vs. W. P. Fullers," *San Diego (CA) Evening Tribune*, May 20, 1899; "League Base Ball," *San Diego Evening Tribune*, May 22, 1899; "San Diego in the Lead," *San Diego Evening Tribune*, Jun 26, 1899; "Trilbys Defeated," *San Diego Union*, Jul 17, 1899; "One Game Apiece," *San Diego Evening Tribune*, Jul 31, 1899; "Azusa Defeats Trilby," *Los Angeles (CA) Times*, Dec 4, 1899; "Athletics Are Out," *San Diego Evening Tribune*, Mar 18, 1900; "Sunday's Ball Game," *San Diego Evening Tribune*, Apr 6, 1900; "Trilbys vs. San Diegos," *San Diego Evening Tribune*, Apr 7, 1900.

Young Striker Base Ball Club (Los Angeles, CA; 1880s). Organizer(s): Detrick.

The Young Striker B.B.C. organized in the 1880s. The Young Strikers played black and white nines. *Los Angeles Herald* (September 3,

1888): "The Tribunes played against the Young Strikers at the new grounds at Prospect Park yesterday afternoon. The Los Angeles County Railroad ran excursion trains and a fair crowd was in attendance. The Tribunes led off as if to win with little effort. At the end of the fourth inning the score stood 6 to 1 in their favor. But the colored boys were on their mettle by this time and started in to retrieve themselves. They held the Tribunes down to six runs and by heavy batting and all 'round work increased their own score to nine runs by the end of the eighth inning, seven of these being made in the latter inning. The Tribunes being unable to effect anything in their half of the ninth inning, the game was given to the Young Strikers, and the crowd dispersed." Horace Wild, the great black catcher, played for the otherwise all-white Tribunes.

SOURCES: "Phoenix vs. Young Strikers," *Los Angeles (CA) Herald*, Jul 30, 1888; "Los Angeles vs Young Strikers," *Los Angeles Herald*, Aug 31, 1888; "The New Ball Grounds," *Los Angeles Herald*, Sep 2, 1888; "Base Ball," *Los Angeles Herald*, Sep 3, 1888; "On the Diamond," *Los Angeles Herald*, Sep 10, 1888; "Willow Wielders," *Los Angeles Herald*, Sep 17, 1888; "Base Ball," *Los Angeles Herald*, Sep 17, 1888; "City Briefs," *Los Angeles (CA) Times*, Nov 21, 1889.

Colored Base Ball Club (Oakland, CA; 1890s)

The Colored B.B.C. organized in the 1890s. They played black teams. *San Francisco Chronicle* (September 9, 1892): "The promise of the invitation was fulfilled; it was a heart-rending game. All the dusky belles and beaux of San Francisco were there to see their champions eat up the haughty Oaklanders, but they were broke and sad-eyed when the score—Oakland 12, San Francisco 6—was announced."

SOURCES: "Notes and Comments," *San Francisco (CA) Daily Chronicle*, Sep 9, 1892.

Logan Base Ball Club (Oakland, CA; 1870s)

The Logan B.B.C. organized in 1876. The Logans were composed of members of the Oakland Literary and Aid Society. Oakland and and Francisco developed a rivalry. *Oakland Tribune* (June 20, 1876): "According to arrangements yesterday afternoon, Logan Base Ball Club of Oakland, composed of members of the Oakland Literary and Aid Society, John R. Wilds, Captain and the Palace Hotel Base Ball Club of San Francisco, J. C. Smith, Captain, met at the Recreation grounds and played a match game of base-ball. The game was well-contested and considerable skill was shown on both sides. Time was called at 1:30 and the game ended at 4 o'clock, and resulted in a handsome victory for the Oakland boys."

SOURCES: "Colored Picnic," *Oakland (CA) Tribune*, May 22, 1876; "Oakland Boys Victorious," *Oakland Tribune*, Jun 20, 1876; "Oakland Literary Society," *Oakland Tribune*, Jul 27, 1876; "Oakland Literary Society," *Oakland Tribune*, Aug 3, 1876.

Union Base Ball Club (Oakland, CA; 1880s)

The Union B.B.C. organized in the 1880s. The "Unions" played black teams. *San Francisco Chronicle* (June 24, 1889): "The colored population of san Francisco and Oakland turned out en masse yesterday, to witness a base-ball game between two of the leading colored teams at Center-Street Grounds, Oakland. The teams competing were the Enterprise, composed of the employees of the Palace Hotel, and Unions of Oakland. The game was a great deal better than some of the championship contests, and several brilliant plays were made."

SOURCES: "Colored Ball Players," *San Francisco (CA) Chronicle*, Jun 24, 1889.

McKinley Base Ball Club (Pasadena, CA; 1890s)

The McKinley B.B.C. organized in the 1890s. The "McKinleys" played white and black nines. *Los Angeles Herald* (September 10,

1896): "The Pasadena Base Ball Club defeated the McKinley colored club by the score of 22 to 2 this afternoon on the bicycling track grounds. There were about 100 spectators. Shaw and Boston of the Los Angeles Trilbys performed the battery work for the McKinleys." *Herald* (October 27, 1896): "A game was played yesterday afternoon at the bicycle track grounds between the McKinley Guards and Rivals, two colored teams. The game was an exciting and noisy one, and was finally won by the Guards by the score of 16 to 17. The same teams will play next Sunday."

SOURCES: "Brevities," *Los Angeles (CA) Herald*, Jun 25, 1896; "Baseball Games," *Los Angeles Herald*, Jun 27, 1896; "Brevities," *Los Angeles Herald*, Jul 15, 1896; "Bat and Ball," *Los Angeles Herald*, Sep 10, 1896; "News Notes From Pasadena," *Los Angeles Herald*, Oct 27, 1896.

O. K. Base Ball Club (Sacramento, CA; 1890s)

The O. K. B.B.C. organized in the 1890s. The "O.K.s" played black nines. *San Francisco Chronicle* (August 12, 1895): "The OK Base Ball Club of Sacramento, the members of which are otherwise known as the 'Terrible Ticonderogas of the North,' came all the way from the Capital City yesterday to be defeated by the nine of the assembly Club of this city. Both teams are composed of colored gentlemen, but they can play ball. There was a great crowd present. It filled the grandstands and the top of the fences, and even the outskirts of the diamond four sturdy officers were kept busy protecting the players from the onslaught of the spectators."

SOURCES: "Colored Clubs Play Ball," *San Francisco (CA) Chronicle*, Aug 12, 1895; "Brief Notes," *Sacramento (CA) Daily Union*, May 21, 1895; "Colored Baseball Teams," *San Francisco (CA) Call*, Aug 12, 1895; "City News in Brief," *San Francisco Call*, Aug 13, 1895.

Coast Giants Base Ball Club (San Diego, CA; 1890s–1900s)

The Coast Giants B.B.C. organized in the 1890s. The Coast Giants played black and white teams. *San Diego Union* (October 5, 1899): "The baseball game at Bay View Park yesterday between the Coast Giants, colored, and the Models interested and amused the spectators, even if it wasn't a first-class exhibition of the national game. The Models won by a score of 11 to 7. There were some exciting periods, too, especially in the fourth inning, when the score was tied, each team having five runs to its credit. The colored rooters became excited and crowded from the bleachers down to the sidelines. If cheering would win a game, the Giants should have won at that juncture, but unfortunately, the rabbit root was lost, and the Models forged ahead in the next inning."

SOURCES: *San Diego (CA) Evening Tribune*, Aug 26, 1899; "Baseball Tomorrow," *San Diego Evening Tribune*, Sep 30, 1899; "Games at Bay View Park," *San Diego Evening Tribune*, Oct 14, 1899; *San Diego Evening Tribune*, Oct 27, 1899; "Coast Giants Win," *San Diego Evening Tribune*, Nov 6, 1899; "No Headline," *San Diego Evening Tribune*, Nov 13, 1899; *San Diego Evening Tribune*, Nov 18, 1899; "Base Ball Games," *San Diego (CA) Union*, Oct 5, 1899; "Base Ball Notes," *San Diego Evening Tribune*, Mar 24, 1900; "At Bay View Park," *San Diego Union*, Mar 29, 1900.

Assembly Base Ball Club (San Francisco, CA; 1890s)

The Assembly B.B.C. organized in the 1890s. The Assemblys played black teams. *San Francisco Chronicle* (August 12, 1895): "The OK Base Ball Club of Sacramento, the members of which are otherwise known as the Terrible Ticonderogas of the North, came all the way from the Capital City yesterday to be defeated by the nine of the assembly Club of this city. Both teams are composed of colored gentlemen, but they can play ball. There was a great crowd present. It filled the grandstands and the top of the fences, and even the outskirts

of the diamond four sturdy officers were kept busy protecting the players from the onslaught of the spectators."

SOURCES: "Colored Clubs Play Ball," *San Francisco (CA) Chronicle*, Aug 12, 1895; "Brief Notes," *Sacramento (CA) Daily Union*, May 21, 1895; "Colored Baseball Teams," *San Francisco (CA) Call*, Aug 12, 1895; "City News in Brief," *San Francisco Call*, Aug 13, 1895.

Enterprise Base Ball Club (San Francisco, CA; 1880s)

The Enterprise B.B.C. organized in the 1870s. The Enterprise boys played against black teams. *San Francisco Chronicle* (June 24, 1889): "The colored population of San Francisco and Oakland turned out en masse yesterday, to witness a base-ball game between two of the leading colored teams at Center-Street Grounds, Oakland. The teams competing were the Enterprise, composed of the employees of the Palace Hotel, and Unions of Oakland. The game was a great deal better than some of the championship contests, and several brilliant plays were made."

SOURCES: "Colored Ball Players," *San Francisco (CA) Chronicle*, Jun 24, 1889; "Colored Waiters Bounced From Palace Hotel," *Los Angeles (CA) Herald*, November 10, 1889; "The Profession at Oakland and San Francisco," *Indianapolis (IN) Freeman*, July 17, 1909.

Grant Base Ball Club (San Francisco, CA; 1860s). Organizer(s): J. C. Smith.

The Grant B.B.C. organized in 1868. *San Francisco Elevator* (April 24, 1868): "A match game will be played by the first and second nines of the Grant Base Ball Club on the 1st of May, at Alameda. The game will commence at 11 o'clock by order of J. C. Smith, President."

SOURCES: "Notice," *San Francisco (CA) Elevator*, Apr 24, 1868; "Notice," *San Francisco Elevator*, May 1, 1868.

Lotus Club (3rd and Stevenson Street, San Francisco, CA; 24? Third Street, San Francisco, CA.; 1880s–1890s). Organizer(s): James Jackson, E. H. Morris and Stephen Bryant.

The Lotus Club organized in the 1880s. The club represented the black aristocratic south of Market Street, its members (prizefighters, ballplayers, track and field men, jockeys, and musicians) prominent in the sporting fraternity. They indulged in all forms of gambling, and ran a gaming operations dominated by policy numbers (today's lottery). They participated in Republican politics. The press identified them as barbers and waiters. They organized a ball club and developed a rivalry with Oakland, CA.

SOURCES: "Two Sable Sloggers," *San Francisco (CA) Daily Chronicle*, Jan 11, 1889; "Around the City," *San Francisco (CA) Daily Call*, Oct 24, 1889; "Were Not Gambling," *San Francisco Daily Call*, Jun 18, 1890; "Watch and Chain Stolen," *San Francisco Daily Call*, Feb 1, 1891; "Against 'Buck' Brown," *San Francisco Daily Call*, Feb 26, 1892; "A Gambling Place Raided," *San Francisco Daily Chronicle*, Aug 4, 1892; "Notes and Comments," *San Francisco Daily Chronicle*, Sep 9, 1892; "They Fled in Terror," *San Francisco Daily Chronicle*, Oct 8, 1892; "Wild Idle Dethroned," *San Francisco Daily Chronicle*, May 14, 1893; "Notes and Comment," *San Francisco Daily Chronicle*, June 3, 1893; "The Lotus Club Raided," *San Francisco Daily Call*, Oct 18, 1893; "Policy Players," *San Francisco Daily Call*, Apr 5, 1894.

Palace Hotel (San Francisco, CA; 1870s–1890s)

Following its grand opening in 1876, the black waiters of San Francisco, CA's Palace Hotel organized baseball clubs and this tradition continued into the 1890s. The history of the hotel in particular, and blacks in general, offers additional insight. *San Francisco Chronicle* (December 8, 1884): "The Palace Hotel contains a small colony by itself, the waiters, porters, and bell boys numbering 150 people. The Baldwin Hotel employs fifty, and one effect of this congregation on Market Street has been the formation of a southern Negro quarter.

They have two musical organizations. The first is the Palace Hotel band, numbering eighteen pieces, whose music is to be heard in the courtyard of that caravansary every Monday evening in the summer. It is true the band occasionally interprets its selections by the original rules of time and tune, but generally speaking its music is quite agreeable and quite up to the average of amateur performance. The second organization is the Alpha Orchestra, a string band of some fifteen pieces, whose specialty is dance music. Most of the colored people of San Francisco are Texans or Georgians, although a great number have come from Washington, DC, and Philadelphia. Generally speaking, the Negroes of San Francisco are comparatively light-colored, although they range from the Octoroon to the blackest specimen of the Jamaican coon." In 1889, the Palace Hotel dismissed its waiters, many of them having been with the establishment since it had opened: disagreeing with their mistreatment by the hand of the new management, 123 employees refused to serve dinner. Hotel labor problems emerged throughout the country.

Sources: "Colored Picnic," *Oakland (CA) Tribune*, May 22, 1876; "Oakland Boys Victorious," *Oakland Tribune*, Jun 20, 1876; "The Negro Element," *San Francisco (CA) Chronicle*, Dec 8, 1884; "Among the Amateurs," *San Francisco Chronicle*, Apr 29, 1889; "Colored Ball Players," *San Francisco Chronicle*, Jun 24, 1889; "A Palace Lock-Out," *San Francisco Chronicle*, Nov 9, 1889; "Palace Waiters," *San Francisco Chronicle*, Nov 10, 1889; "Colored Waiters Bounced From Palace Hotel," *Los Angeles (CA) Herald*, Nov 10, 1889; "A Colored Exodus," *San Francisco (CA) Bulletin*, Nov 11, 1889.

Palace Hotel Base Ball Club (San Francisco, CA; 1870s)

The Palace Hotel B.B.C. organized in 1876. The club, composed of waiters, developed a rivalry with sister-city Oakland. The waiters played against Oakland's Logan B.B.C., composed of members of the Oakland Literary and Aid Society. *Oakland Tribune* (June 20, 1876): "According to arrangements yesterday afternoon, Logan Base Ball Club of Oakland, composed of members of the Oakland Literary and Aid Society, John R. Wilds, Captain and the Palace Hotel Base Ball Club of San Francisco, J. C. Smith, Captain, met at the Recreation grounds and played a match game of base-ball. The game was well-contested and considerable skill was shown on both sides. Time was called at 1:30 and the game ended at 4 o'clock, and resulted in a handsome victory for the Oakland boys."

Sources: "Colored Picnic," *Oakland (CA) Tribune*, May 22, 1876; "Oakland Boys Victorious," *Oakland Tribune*, June 20, 1876.

Colorado

Black Diamonds Base Ball Club (Boulder, CO; 1880s)

The Black Diamonds B.B.C. organized in the 1870s. The Black Diamonds played white and black teams. *Colorado Springs Gazette* (April 14, 1882): "Last Saturday afternoon a game of ball was played by the second nine of the Reds and the Black Diamonds (colored), resulting in a victory for the latter by a score of 23 to 23."

Sources: "Local Matters," *Colorado Springs Daily Gazette*, May 19, 1882.

Striped Stockings Base Ball Club (Boulder, CO; 1880s)

The Striped Stockings B.B.C. organized in the 1870s, played white and black teams. *Colorado Springs Gazette* (May 19, 1882): "Last Saturday afternoon the Second Nine of the Reds and the Striped Stockings (colored) played a game of ball which resulted in a score of 26 for the former to 50 for the latter. Until after the fifth inning things looked bad for the colored club, but they began to walk up on their opponents, and after the sixth inning, steadily drew ahead of them. 'Twas lots of fun for the spectators."

Sources: "Local Matters," *Colorado Springs Daily Gazette*, May 19, 1882.

Ashby Giants Base Ball Club (CO Springs, CO; 1880s)

The Ashby Giants B.B.C. organized in the 1880s, played white and black teams. *Colorado Springs Gazette* (May 23, 1888): "The game between the Ashby Giants and the Browns, advertised for Friday next, has been cancelled." *Gazette* (May 25, 1889): "The [Ashby] Giants Colored Base Ball team opened the season here on the 14th in an exciting but interesting game with the college team. The attendance was large, about 1200, score, 5 to 6, in favor of the Giants. The Giants leave on their annual tour on June 1st; will meet all clubs, white and colored."

Sources: *Colorado Springs (CO) Gazette*, May 23, 1888; "Base Ball Notes," *Leavenworth (KS) Advocate*, May 25, 1889; "Nubbins of News," *Pueblo (CO) Chieftain*, Jul 17, 1889; "Official Reports," *Pueblo Chieftain*, Sep 6, 1888; "Emancipation Day," *Pueblo Chieftain*, Aug 2, 1889.

Clipper Base Ball Club (CO Springs, CO; 1890s)

The Clipper B.B.C. organized in the 1890s, played white and black teams. *Colorado Springs Gazette* (July 11, 1896): "There will be a game of base-ball here on Thursday between the Bergen Brothers' team, of Pueblo, and the Clippers, of this city, to decide the colored championship of the State." *Gazette* (July 26, 1896): "The game of ball yesterday at Athletic Park was between the Holbrook and Perkins' nine and the Clippers, colored, and won by the Clippers by a score of 2 to 15. The P. & H. pitcher went to pieces and the colored boys had it their own way."

Sources: *Colorado Springs (CO) Gazette-Telegraph*, Jul 3, 1896; "Base Ball," *Colorado Springs Gazette-Telegraph*, July 4, 1896; "Base Ball," *Colorado Springs Gazette-Telegraph*, July 11, 1896; *Colorado Springs Gazette-Telegraph*, July 25, 1896; *Colorado Springs Gazette-Telegraph*, July 26, 1896; *Colorado Springs Gazette-Telegraph*, September 8, 1896.

Pastime Base Ball Club (CO Springs, CO; 1890s)

The Pastime B.B.C. organized in the 1890s, played white and black teams. *Colorado Springs Gazette Telegraph* (August 17, 1899): "The Pastimes are a team composed of colored men who are excellent players. They have played in this city and in other cities of the vicinity and have never failed to give a good exhibition of baseball."

Sources: "Pastimes Win," *Colorado Springs (CO) Springs Gazette-Telegraph*, Jul 24, 1899; "Ball Game," *Colorado Springs Gazette-Telegraph*, Aug 15, 1899; "Baseball," *Colorado Springs Gazette-Telegraph*, Aug 17, 1899; "Pastimes Win," *Colorado Springs Gazette-Telegraph*, Aug 18, 1899.

Rough and Ready Base Ball Club (CO Springs, CO; 1870s)

The Rough and Ready B.B.C. organized in the 1870s, played white and black teams. *Colorado Springs Gazette* (March 22, 1879): "A game of base-ball will be played today at half-past two in Alamo Park between the Colorado Springs and 'Rough and Ready' clubs. The former is composed of white people and the latter of colored. Both are of this city. The game last Saturday was wo by the colored boys by a score of 28 to 18."

Sources: *Colorado Springs (CO) Gazette*, Mar 22, 1879; *Colorado Springs Gazette*, March 23, 1879.

Stillman Giants Base Ball Club (CO Springs, CO; 1890s). Organizer(s): T. J. Manley.

The Stillman Giants B.B.C. organized in the 1890s, played white and black nines. They were led by the Hackley brothers, of MI (via OH). *Colorado Springs Gazette* (June 12, 1890): "In the afternoon the Stillman Giants, of this city, will play the Denver colored nine for the colored championship of the State." *Gazette* (July 24, 1890): "The Stillman Giants and the Stars will again cross bats at Athletic Park tomorrow afternoon. Both clubs have been recently reorganized." The Stars were defeated. *Gazette* (August 2, 1890): "The stars the ball nine whom the Giants (colored) defeated Friday, are not crushed in spirit, but have challenged their dusky rivals to another game next Thursday afternoon."

SOURCES: *Colorado Springs (CO) Gazette*, Jun 12, 1890; *Colorado Springs Gazette*, Jul 24, 1890; *Colorado Springs Gazette*, Aug 2, 1890; *Colorado Springs Gazette*, Aug 4, 1890; *Colorado Springs Gazette*, Aug 5, 1890; "Colorado City, Colorado," *St. Paul (MN) Appeal*, May 23, 1891.

Black Stockings Base Ball Club (Denver, CO; 1880s)

The Black Stockings B.B.C. organized in the 1880s, played white and black teams. *Denver Rocky Mountain News* (July 20, 1883): "The Denver Black Stockings (colored) and the Colorado Springs Pastimes (colored) will cross bats today at the old Larimer Street Grounds. Game called at 2:30 o'clock. Admission: 25 cents."

SOURCES: "The Denver Blacks," *Denver (CO) Rocky Mountain News*, Jul 20, 1883.

Lynch Base Ball Club (Pueblo, CO; 1880s). Organizer(s): B. M. Martin and B. F. Harrison.

The Lynch B.B.C. organized in the 1880s, played white and black teams. *Denver Rocky Mountain News* (June 9, 1884): "B. M. Martin, captain of the Lynch (colored) Base Ball Club, of Pueblo, desires *The News* to say that his club challenges the Denver colored club to play them a match game at any time during this or early next month." The organization adopted the nickname "Pueblo Blues."

SOURCES: *Pueblo (CO) Chieftain*, Jun 9, 1884; "Pueblo Pickings," *Denver (CO) Rocky Mountain News*, Jun 9, 1884; *Pueblo Chieftain*, Jul 3, 1884; *Pueblo Chieftain*, Jul 4, 1884; "Grand Excursion," *Pueblo Chieftain*, Jul 31, 1884.

Moonlight Base Ball Club (Pueblo, CO; 1880s)

The Moonlight B.B.C. organized in the 1880s, played black teams. *Colorado Chieftain* (June 18, 1884): "The Moonlight Base Ball Club of Pueblo (colored) will play any colored club in Colorado Springs a match game on the fourth of July either at Pueblo or Colorado Springs but prefer to play at the latter place." *Chieftain* (July 4, 1884): "A match game of the two colored base-ball clubs will take place this afternoon at the Pastimes' grounds." *Chieftain* (July 29, 1884): "The colored base-ball clubs of Pueblo and Denver have arranged for a grand match game of base-ball, and it is proposed to make the excursion one of the pleasure for all."

SOURCES: *Pueblo (CO) Colorado Chieftain*, Jun 18, 1884; *Pueblo Colorado Chieftain*, Jul 4, 1884; *Pueblo Colorado Chieftain*, Jul 29, 1884.

Connecticut

Quickstep Base Ball Club (Ansonia, CT; 1890s)

The Quickstep B.B.C. organized in the 1890s, played black teams. *New Haven Daily Morning Journal and Courier* (July 15, 1897): "The ball game at Savin Rock yesterday resulted in score of 17 to 12, in favor of the Elm Citys, who played a team from Ansonia. Both teams were composed of colored players."

SOURCES: "Elm City Defeats Ansonia," *New Haven (CT) Daily Morning Journal and Courier*, Jul 15, 1897; "Elm Citys vs. Quicksteps," *New Haven Daily Morning Journal and Courier*, Jul 29, 1897.

Volunteer Base Ball Club (Ansonia, CT; 1890s)

The Volunteer B.B.C. organized in the 1890s, played black aggregations. *New Haven Daily Morning Journal and Courier* (April 13, 1895): "The Volunteers, a colored baseball team composed of Ansonians, played the Elm Citys, another colored ball team in this city."

SOURCES: "Local News," *New Haven (CT) Daily Morning Journal and Courier*, Apr 13, 1895.

Wallace Base Ball Club (Ansonia, CT; 1880s)

The Wallace B.B.C. organized in the 1880s. The Wallace nine, composed of Wallace Hotel waiters, played black teams.

SOURCES: *Elgin (IL) Morning Frank*, October 14, 1882; "Diamond Dust," *St. Louis (MO) Globe-Democrat*, April 3, 1883; "Base Ball," *New York (NY) Clipper*, April 28, 1883.

Blue Stockings Base Ball Club (Hartford, CT; 1880s)

The Blue Stockings B.B.C. organized in the 1880s, played black and white teams. *Hartford Courant* (May 25, 1885): "The colored Blue Stocking team has purchased last year's outfits—uniforms, etc.—from the Germania guard." *Hartford Courant* (June 9, 1885): "The fun was fast and furious at the ball grounds this afternoon. The Blue Stockings batted the ball right and left in the eighth inning, and rattled their opponents [North Stars] to the tune of eight runs, and came off victors by a score of 21 to 13."

SOURCES: "Hartford News," *Hartford (CT) Courant*, Apr 17, 1885; "Notes," *Hartford Courant*, May 16, 1885; "The Ball Field," *Hartford Courant*, May 25, 1885; "Notes," *Hartford Courant*, May 27, 1885; "Notes," *Hartford Courant*, Jun 4, 1885; "Base Ball," *Hartford Courant*, Jun 6, 1885; "Base Ball," *Hartford Courant*, Jun 9, 1885; "Hartford Letter," *New York (NY) Freeman*, Sep 4, 1886.

Oceanus Base Ball Club (Hartford, CT; 1860s)

The Oceanus B.B.C. organized in the 1860s, played black nines. *Hartford Courant* (July 28, 1868): "The Oceanus (colored) base-ball club of this city, will play the Hero (colored) club of Middletown, at the latter place on Thursday. The Oceanus leave this city by the 8 o'clock boat." *Hartford Courant* (July 31, 1868): "The Oceanus (colored) base-ball club of this city played a match game on Thursday, at Douglas Park, Middletown, with the Hero, also a colored club of that city. The Hartford boys were victorious, 29 to 13. The victors were presented with a handsome silver ice pitcher, and were handsomely treated by the Middletown club, who met them at the depot, escorted them to the grounds, and gave them lunch before the game, and a substantial dinner at its termination."

SOURCES: "Brief Mention," *Hartford (CT) Courant*, Jul 24, 1868; "Base Ball," *Hartford Courant*, Jul 28, 1868; "Base Ball," *Hartford Courant*, Jul 31, 1868.

Young Pacific Base Ball Club (Hartford, CT; 1860s)

The Young Pacific B.B.C. organized in the 1860s, played black and white nines. *Hartford Courant* (August 14, 1868): "The Young Pacific Base Ball Club of this city [Hartford], and the Hero club of Middleton, both colored, are to play a match game at Middleton." *Hartford Courant* (September 17, 1868): "The Young Pacific ball club, composed of colored boys, have challenged the Young Elm club of East Hartford to a match game, but the challenge has not yet been accepted."

SOURCES: "Brief Mention," *Hartford (CT) Courant*, Aug 10, 1868; "Brief Mention," *Hartford Courant*, Aug 14, 1868; "Brief Mention," *Hartford Courant*, Sep 17, 1868.

Hero Base Ball Club (Middleton, CT; 1860s)

The Hero B.B.C. organized in the 1860s, played black nines. *Hartford Courant* (July 28, 1868): "The Oceanus (colored) base-ball club of this city, will play the Hero (colored) club of Middletown, at the latter place on Thursday. The Oceanus leave this city by the 8 o'clock boat." *Hartford Courant* (July 31, 1868): "The Oceanus (colored) base-ball club of this city played a match game on Thursday, at Douglas Park, Middletown, with the Hero, also a colored club of that city. The Hartford boys were victorious, 29 to 13. The victors were presented with a handsome silver ice pitcher, and were handsomely treated by the Middletown club, who met them at the depot, escorted them to the grounds, and gave them lunch before the game, and a substantial dinner at its termination." The Heroes played another black club. *Hartford Courant* (August 14, 1868): "The Young Pacific Base Ball Club of this city [Hartford], and the Hero club of Middleton, both colored, are to play a match game at Middleton."

SOURCES: "Brief Mention," *Hartford (CT) Courant*, Jul 24, 1868; "Base Ball," *Hartford Courant*, Jul 28, 1868; "Base Ball," *Hartford Courant*, Jul 31, 1868; "Brief Mention," *Hartford Courant*, Aug 10, 1868; "Brief Mention," *Hartford Courant*, Aug 14, 1868; "Base Ball," *Hartford Courant*, Aug 15, 1868; "Brief Mention," *Hartford Courant*, Aug 15, 1868; "Base Ball," *Hartford Courant*, Aug 20, 1868.

Athletic Base Ball Club (New Haven, CT; 1890s). Organizer(s): W. J. Murphy.

The Athletic B.B.C. organized in the 1890s, played black aggregations. *Indianapolis Freeman* (June 7, 1890): "About five hundred people assembled to see a baseball game. Men, ladies, and children of all sizes were present to see the game, for both the teams were composed of the best colored players in the city and each had defeated the Edgewoods twice. Miller, catcher, and Hall, pitcher, were the battery for the Sylvesters, and Parkens, catcher and Russell, pitcher, performed the services for the Athletics. The participants of both teams were on opposites sides of the field. After an interesting and well-contested contest, the Athletics won by a score of 23 to 22. The sharp fielding of Bush of the Athletics was fair but not up to the standard at that of James Roston of the Sylvesters."

SOURCES: "The Clubs of New Haven," *Indianapolis (IN) Freeman*, Mar 8, 1890; "The New Haven News," *Indianapolis Freeman*, May 24, 1890; "Base Ball," *Indianapolis Freeman*, Jun 7, 1890; "Tyler City Camp Meeting," *Indianapolis Freeman*, Aug 8, 1890; "More Went New Haven," *New Haven (CT) Morning Journal and Courier*, Jul 25, 1894; "Local Team Can Play Ball," *New Haven Morning Journal and Courier*, Jul 25, 1894; "Hartford 11, New Haven, 2," *New Haven Morning Journal and Courier*, Jul 26, 1894.

Barber Base Ball Club (New Haven, CT; 1880s)

The Barber B.B.C. organized in the 1880s, played white and black teams. *New Haven Register* (June 12, 1888): "The colored barbers defeated their white competitors at West Haven yesterday by a score of 24 to 15."

SOURCES: "Barbers on the Diamond," *New Haven (CT) Register*, Jun 11, 1888; "White Barbers Defeated," *New Haven Register*, Jun 12, 1888.

Edgewood Base Ball Club (New Haven, CT; 1890s)

The Edgewood B.B.C. organized in the 1890s, played black teams. *Indianapolis Freeman* (June 7, 1890): "The Edgewoods, both in the morning and afternoon gained a little honor for themselves at the Afro-American Park, formerly the Slaughter Woods. The Edgewoods have suffered about six defeats and not one victory on the base-ball field this year up to the fourth, but in the morning with Hawley, pitcher and Madison, catcher, they defeated the Sylvesters with Smith pitcher and Ralston catcher by the score of 25 to 20 in a seven-inning game."

SOURCES: "The New Haven News," *Indianapolis (IN) Freeman*, May 24, 1890; "Base Ball," *Indianapolis Freeman*, Jun 7, 1890; "Young Afro-American Sports," *Indianapolis Freeman*, Jul 12, 1890.

Elm City Base Ball Club (New Haven, CT; 1880s–1890s). Organizer(s): Frank L. Hatton.

The Elm City B.B.C. organized in the 1880s. The "Elm Citys" played white and black teams. *New Haven Daily Morning Journal and Courier* (April 13, 1895): "The Volunteers, a colored baseball team composed of Ansonians, played the Elm Citys, another colored ball team in this city." *New Haven Daily Morning Journal and Courier* (April 24, 1897): "The Elm City team (colored) of New Haven will play ball with the Wallingfords.... The New Havens are the champion colored club of the state and will put up a good game against the local team."

SOURCES: "Base Ball," *New Haven (CT) Morning Journal and Courier*, May 3, 1889; "A Colored Base Ball Nine," *New Haven (CT) Register*, Jun 6, 1889; "Another Base Ball Club," *New Haven Morning Journal and Courier*, Jun 7, 1889; "Elm City Base Ball Club," *New Haven Morning Journal and Courier*, Jun 13, 1889; "The Elm City Club's First Game," *New Haven Morning Journal and Courier*, Jun 20, 1889; "Hartford Today," *New Haven Morning Journal and Courier*, Jun 21, 1889; "Local News," *New Haven Morning Journal and Courier*, Apr 13, 1895; "Local News," *New Haven Morning Journal and Courier*, Aug 2, 1895; "Woman Badly Burned," *New Haven Morning Journal and Courier*, Aug 30, 1895; "Elm City Base Ball Team," *New Haven Register*, Feb 24, 1896; "Elm City Ball Team," *New Haven Morning Journal and Courier*, May 18, 1896; "Elm Citys Won," *New Haven Morning Journal and Courier*, Jun 11, 1897 "Elm City Defeats Ansonia," *New Haven Morning Journal and Courier*, Jul 15, 1897; "Elm City vs. Quicksteps," *New Haven Morning Journal and Courier*, Jul 29, 1897; "Edgewoods vs Elm Citys," *New Haven Morning Journal and Courier*, Jul 28, 1898; "Schuetzen Park Barbeque," *New Haven Morning Journal and Courier*, Sep 1, 1898.

Sylvester Base Ball Club (New Haven, CT; 1890s)

The Sylvester B.B.C. organized in the 1890s. The Sylvesters played black nines. They developed a rivalry with New Haven's Athletics. *Indianapolis Freeman* (June 7, 1890): "About five hundred people assembled to see a baseball game. Men, ladies, and children of all sizes were present to see the game, for both the teams were composed of the best colored players in the city and each had defeated the Edgewoods twice. Miller, catcher, and Hall, pitcher, were the battery for the Sylvesters, and Parkens, catcher and Russell, pitcher, performed the services for the Athletics. The participants of both teams were on opposites sides of the field. After an interesting and well-contested contest, the Athletics won by a score of 23 to 22."

SOURCES: "A Colored Base Ball Club," *New Haven (CT) Register*, Jun 6, 1889; "Clubs of New Haven," *Indianapolis (IN) Freeman*, Mar 8, 1890; "Base Ball," *Indianapolis Freeman*, Jun 7, 1890.

Crocker House Base Ball Club (New London, CT; 1880s–1890s). Organizer(s): DuBois Hallack.

The Crocker House B.B.C. organized in the 1870s. The Crocker House club, composed of waiters, played against white and black teams. In 1890, they played Worcester's white club. *New Age* (May 31, 1890): "The game of ball played on the Harbor Grounds Friday afternoon between the New London Base Ball Club and the City of Worcester Nine resulted in a victory for the latter by a score of 18 to 14. The team will play Thursday with the City of New York Nine. They will play three games a week all the season."

SOURCES: "New London News," *New York (NY) Freeman*, Jul 17, 1886; "New London News," *New York Freeman*, Jul 2, 1887; "New London News," *New York Freeman*, Jul 23, 1887; "Connecticut Odd Fellows," *New York Freeman*, Aug 13, 1887; "New London News," *New York (NY) Age*, Feb 1, 1890; "New London News," *New York Age*, Mar 29, 1890; "New London News," *New York Age*, Jul 19, 1890;

"New London, CONN," *New York Freeman*, Aug 9, 1890; "New London Notes," *New York Age*, Aug 16, 1890.

Night Blooming Cereus Base Ball Club (New London, CT; 1860s)

The Night Blooming Cereus B.B.C. organized in the 1860s. *Washington National Republican* (October 12, 1866): "New London has a colored baseball club." *New London Weekly Chronicle* (October 20, 1866) boasted of its "African" ball club. *Hartford Courant* (August 7, 1867): "They have a new base-ball club in New London, composed of colored gentlemen, called the Night Blooming Cereus Club. The club by any other name would smell sweet." Baseball required capital, and the players duly noted their economic hardship. *Hartford Courant* (October 13, 1866): "The organization of the club was made with great difficulty for want of funds to purchase a ball and bat but a temporary loan of 25 cents—the amount of which they fell short—was obtained, and the club went immediately into active operations." The club garnered national attention, the organization proudly representing New England. In 1867, the Phalon Night Blooming Cereus Perfume Company, of New York City sent the city a framed picture of the Night Blooming Cereus flower. The white clothier and regatta rower Charles N. Middleton prominently displayed the photograph in his store window.

Sources: *Washington (DC) National Republican*, Oct 12, 1866; *New London (CT) Weekly Chronicle*, Oct 20, 1866; "State Items," *New Haven (CT) Columbian Register*, August 24, 1867; "The National Game," *New London (CT) Courant*, July 13, 1867; "New London County," *Hartford Courant*, August 7, 1868; "Summary of the News," *New York (NY) Sabbath Recorder*, August 13, 1868.

Jackson Blues Base Ball Club (Wallingford, CT; 1870s). Organizer(s): William Smith.

The Jackson Blues B.B.C. organized in 1874. *Columbia Register* (August 8, 1874): "The great match between the Jackson Blues (colored) commanded by captain William Smith, and a picked nine came off Saturday in spite of the rain. After playing five innings, the score stood 8 for the Jackson Blues to 20 for their opponents. The game will be finished next Saturday." *Register* (August 15, 1874): "Captain William Smith, of the Colored Base Ball Club, called on us today to correct an error which we inadvertently committed. He says the name of the colored club is Jackson Blues, instead of Bald Eagles. We take great pleasure in making the correction, as the former name is much better than the latter. He also wished us to correct another mistake relative to the match game. He says there is no such club as the Boss Ankles, commanded by Captain Tyler and that the game is going to be played between the Jackson Blues and the second nine, Tyler commanding the latter."

Sources: "State Correspondence," *Columbia (CT) Register*, Aug 8, 1874; "Accident in Milford," *Columbia Register*, Aug 15, 1874; "State Correspondence," *Columbia Register*, Mar 5, 1890.

Delaware

Delaware Keystone Base Ball Club (Hamton, DE; 1880s–1890s)

The Delaware Keystone B.B.C., of Hamton [Middletown], DE organized in the 1880s, played black teams. *Wilmington Morning News* (July 2, 1889): "An exceedingly interesting game of base-ball was played on the Battery here on Saturday afternoon. The contending nines were the Delaware Keystones of Middletown and the Wide Awakes of this city [New Castle]. The two teams were evenly matched. About 300 hundred spectators, nearly all of whom were white, witnessed the contest, and were kept in convulsions of laughter by the great coaching of thee visitors which almost equaled that of the Cuban Giants. Had it not been for the costly wild throwing of the outfielders, the score would not have been more than one fourth as large. Score—Keystones, 16; Wide Awakes, 12." *Wilmington Evening Journal* (August 13, 1887): "The Delaware Keystones, a ball club composed of colored lads from Hamton, near here [Middletown], added another victory to its list when it met the Delaware City colored lads' club here yesterday afternoon. A crowd of 200 people saw the Delaware Keystones defeat their opponents by a score of 23 to 15."

Sources: "Local Base Ball," *Wilmington (DE) News Journal*, Jul 1, 1889; "Local Base Ball," *Wilmington (DE) Morning News*, Jul 16, 1889; "New Castle Notes," *Wilmington Morning News*, Jul 2, 1889; "Base Ball Matters," *Wilmington Morning News*, Jul 5, 1889; "Affairs at Middletown," *Wilmington Morning News*, Jul 10, 1889; "From Middletown," *Wilmington Morning News*, Aug 7, 1889; "Women to Judge Firemen," *Wilmington (DE) Evening Journal*, Jun 23, 1894; "Delaware City's Colored Club Beaten," *Wilmington Evening Journal*, Sep 15, 1894.

Harris Senate Base Ball Club (New Castle, DE; 1880s)

The Harris Senate B.B.C. organized in the 1880s. The Harris Senate played black nines. *Wilmington Morning News* (June 26, 1888): "The Delaware Base Ball Club, colored, yesterday afternoon defeated the Harris Senate Club, colored, of New Castle, by the following score at the Union Grounds: Delaware 29, Harris Senate 7." *Wilmington Morning News* (September 25, 1888): "The Harris Senate Base Ball Club went to Smyrna on Saturday and played the colored nine of that place. The boys were beaten by a score of 10 to 8."

Sources: "Toner is Improving," *Wilmington (DE) Evening Journal*, Jun 23, 1888; "Colored Ball Club," *Wilmington (DE) Morning News*, Jun 26, 1888; "Horribly Burned," *Wilmington Evening Journal*, Jul 28, 1888; "Local Sports," *Wilmington Morning News*, Aug 2, 1888; "New Castle Notes," *Wilmington Morning News*, Sep 7, 1888; "Swallows Homeward Fly," *Wilmington Evening Journal*, Sep 10, 1888; "Shooting Reed Birds," *Wilmington Evening Journal*, Sep 11, 1888; "New Castle Notes," *Wilmington Morning News*, Sep 15, 1888; "Democratic Enthusiasm," *Wilmington Evening Journal*, Sep 24, 1888; New Castle Notes," *Wilmington Morning News*, Sep 25, 1888;.

Wide-Awake Base Ball Club (New Castle, DE; 1880s)

The Wide-Awake B.B.C. organized in the 1880s. The Wide-Awakes played white and black nines. *Wilmington Evening Journal* (June 26, 1889): "A game of base-ball played on the Battery on Saturday between colored nines of Wilmington and New Castle, resulting in the Wilmington beating the New Castle by a score of 18 to 15." *Wilmington Morning News* (July 2, 1889): "An exceedingly interesting game of base-ball was played on the Battery here on Saturday afternoon. The contending nines were the Delaware Keystones and the Wide-Awakes of this city. The two and teams were evenly matched. About 200 spectators, nearly all of whom were whites, witnessed the contest, and were kept in convulsions of laughter by the great coaching of the visitors, which almost equally that of the Cuban Giants." *Wilmington Evening Journal* (July 3, 1889): "The Wide-Awake base ball nine of this city and the Alvas of Wilmington will play a game of ball on the battery tomorrow afternoon."

Sources: "Sunday at New Castle," *Wilmington (DE) Evening Journal*, Jun 26, 1889; "New Castle Notes," *Wilmington (DE) Morning News*, May 29, 1889; "Celebrated at New Castle," *Wilmington Morning News*, May 31, 1889; "New Castle Notes," *Wilmington Morning News*, Jul 2, 1889; "A New Castle Scandal," *Wilmington Evening Journal*, Jul 3, 1889; "Middletown," *Wilmington (DE) News Journal*, Jul 9, 1889;

"Affairs at Middletown," *Wilmington Morning News*, Jul 10, 1889; "New Castle's Budget," *Wilmington Morning News*, Aug 12, 1889; "News From New Castle," *Wilmington Evening Journal*, Aug 12, 1889.

Delaware Base Ball Club (Wilmington, DE; 1870s–1880s). Organizer(s): J. Scotland Chippey; Virgil Wright.

The Delaware B.B.C. organized in the 1870s. The Delawares played black and white nines. *Wilmington Gazette* (September 11, 1874): "The Delaware Base Ball Club defeated the Sylvan Spring club, yesterday, by a score of 33 to 8. A match game has been arranged between the Delawares and Good Will club, of Chester, to be played on the ground of the latter, tomorrow." *Gazette* (September 7, 1875): "Yesterday afternoon the Delaware club defeated the Wilmington nine by a score of 25 to 12." *Reading Times* (August 3, 1883): "The Crescent Base Ball Club (colored) left with the excursion, having made an engagement to play a match game at Wilmington with the Delaware Club." *Wilmington Republican* (August 18, 1883): "The Delaware Boys (colored) defeated the Sluggers, Jr., yesterday, by a score of 15 to 5." *New York Freeman* (June 23, 1887): "The Delaware Base Ball Club defeated the Wilmington Base Ball Club Friday afternoon, 14 to 10." *Gazette* (June 26, 1888): "The Delaware Base Ball Club, colored, yesterday afternoon, defeated the Harris Senate club, colored, of New Castle."

SOURCES: "Base Ball," *Wilmington (DE) Daily Commercial*, Sep 11, 1874; "Base Ball," *Wilmington (DE) Gazette*, Sep 7, 1875; "Base Ball Notes," *Wilmington (DE) Morning News*, Jul 26, 1882; "Base Ball," *Wilmington (DE) Republican*, Aug 8, 1882; "Yesterday's Excursion to Cape May," *Reading (PA) Times*, Aug 3, 1883; "Notes," *Wilmington Gazette*, Aug 8, 1883; "Base Ball," *Wilmington Republican*, Aug 18, 1883; "Local Points," *Wilmington Morning News*, Jul 15, 1887; "Delaware Doings," *New York Freeman*, Jul 23, 1887; "Local Base Ball," *Wilmington Morning News*, May 16, 1888; "Colored Ball Club," *Wilmington Morning News*, Jun 26, 1888.

Delaware Jr. Base Ball Club (Wilmington, DE; 1880s). Organizer(s): S. Anderson.

The Delaware Jr. B.B.C. organized in the 1880s, Delawares played black nines. *Wilmington Evening Journal* (May 21, 1888): "The Howard School, and the Young Delawares, both colored, played a game, the former winning by a score of 2 to 0."

SOURCES: "Base Ball," *Wilmington (DE) Morning News*, Jun 20, 1883; "Local Games on Saturday," *Wilmington (DE) Evening Journal*, May 21, 1888.

Delaware Grays Base Ball Club (Wilmington, DE; 1880s–1890s). Organizer(s): James Berry; S. Anderson; William Lewis.

The Delaware Grays B.B.C. organized in the 1880s, played black nines. *New York Freeman* (June 23, 1887): "The Delaware Base Ball Club defeated the Wilmington Base Ball Club Friday afternoon, 14 to 10." *Wilmington Morning News* (August 18, 1888): "At Union Street Park yesterday afternoon a game of ball was played between the Delaware Grays and Anderson Senate nine. The former won by a score of 25 to 8." *Wilmington Morning News* (August 22, 1894): "A game of base-ball will be played today at Riverview grounds between the colored barbers and Delaware Grays. The proceeds will go towards the Old Folks' Home." *Wilmington Morning News* (July 30, 1897): "The Cecilton Base Ball Club, of Cecil county, Maryland, came to Wilmington and defeated the Delaware Grays by a score of 13 to 7."

SOURCES: "Delaware M. E. Conference," *New York (NY) Freeman*, May 7, 1887; "Delaware Doings," *New York Freeman*, May 21, 1887; "Delaware Doings," *New York Freeman*, May 28, 1887; "Delaware Doings," *New York Freeman*, Jul 9, 1887; "Delaware Doings," *New York*

Freeman, Jul 23, 1887; "The Game Yesterday," *Wilmington (DE) Morning News*, Aug 18, 1888; "Local Sports," *Wilmington Morning News*, Sep 11, 1888; "Diamond Pick-Ups," *Wilmington (DE) Republican*, Apr 8, 1890; "Base Ball," *Wilmington Republican*, Jun 2, 1894; "Base Ball," *Wilmington Republican*, Jul 30, 1894; "Base Ball Yesterday," *Wilmington (DE) News Journal*, Aug 20, 1894; "Base Ball for Old Folks," *Wilmington Morning News*, Aug 22, 1894; "Base Ball," *Wilmington Republican*, Apr 30, 1895; "Colored Men to Play Ball," *Wilmington (DE) Evening Journal*, Jul 27, 1897; "To Play Champions," *Wilmington Morning News*, Jul 27, 1897; "Colored People to Play Ball," *Wilmington Morning News*, Jul 29, 1897; "Maryland Team Won," *Wilmington Morning News*, Jul 30, 1897.

Diamond State Base Ball Club (Wilmington, DE; 1880s)

The Diamond State B.B.C. organized in the 1880s, played black teams. *Wilmington Republican* (September 10, 1883): "The Diamond State and Harmony clubs of this city, both colored, will play at Front and Union Streets on Tuesday, September 11. Game will be called at 3 pm. Alonzo Ward and Horace Rhoads will be the battery for the Diamond State. This will be the first of a series of five games for the championship of the State." *Wilmington Republican* (October 22, 1883): "The Diamond State Base Ball Club will play a match game with a colored club of Chester, at the Quickstep Park on Tuesday afternoon. Admission 15 cents."

SOURCES: "Base Ball Notes," *Wilmington (DE) Republican*, Nov 2, 1882; "Dots," *Wilmington Republican*, Sep 6, 1883; "The Colored Championship," *Wilmington Republican*, Sep 10, 1883; "Base Ball," *Wilmington Republican*, Oct 22, 1883.

Fly Away Base Ball Club (Wilmington, DE; 1880s). Organizer(s): Theodore H. Gray.

The Fly Away B.B.C. organized in the 1880s, played black nines. *New York Freeman* (August 13, 1887): "The Brown's Base Ball Club defeated the Flyaway Base Ball Club on Saturday afternoon at 9th and Broome Street by a score of 24 to 17. The Flyaways are ready to receive challenges from all amateur clubs. All communications should be addressed to the captain and manager Theodore H. Gray, 819 Tatnall Street."

SOURCES: "Delaware Doings," *New York (NY) Freeman*, Aug 13, 1887.

Harmony Base Ball Club (Wilmington, DE; 1880s)

The Harmony B.B.C. organized in the 1880s. The Harmony club played black organizations. *Wilmington News Journal* (August 1, 1882): "Yesterday afternoon a very poor game of base-ball was played on the Rodney Street grounds, between Our Boys and Harmony, both colored, which resulted in an easy victory for Our Boys. The Harmony played a miserable game in the field though they did some heavy batting." *Wilmington Morning News* (September 5, 1883): "The long-postponed game between the Crescent club of Reading, and the Harmony club of this city, both colored, for the championship came off yesterday afternoon at Quickstep Park. The contest was interesting and well-fought throughout, the Wilmingtons being the victors."

SOURCES: "Base Ball Matters," *Wilmington (DE) Morning News*, Aug 1, 1882; "Notes," *Wilmington (DE) Journal*, Aug 20, 1883; "At Home and Abroad," *Wilmington Morning News*, Sep 5, 1883; "At Home and Abroad," *Wilmington Journal*, Jul 6, 1887.

Hercules Base Ball Club (Wilmington, DE; 1870s)

The Hercules B.B.C. organized in the 1870s. The Hercules club played black nines. *Wilmington News Journal* (September 17, 1875): "The Independent and Hercules nines played a match game, which resulted in favor of the former by the score of 24 to 9. The Independent is a new organization and contains very good material which is rapidly improving." *Wilmington Commercial* (October 5, 1875): "Two colored clubs had an interesting game, yesterday, on the Quickstep grounds—the Hercules, of this city, and Bostons, of Chester. The latter were too strong, even for the Hercules, winning by a score of 16 to 6."

SOURCES: "Other Notes," *Wilmington (DE) News Journal*, Sep 15, 1875; "The Ball and Bat," *Wilmington (DE) Commercial*, Sep 17, 1875; "The Ball and Bat," *Wilmington (DE) Commercial*, Sep 17, 1875; "Base Ball Notes," *Wilmington Commercial*, Oct 2, 1875; "The Ball and Bat," *Wilmington Commercial*, Oct 5, 1875; "The Ball Field," *Wilmington News Journal*, Jun 19, 1876.

Independent Base Ball Club (Wilmington, DE; 1870s). Organizer(s): Charles Smith, S. May, L. P. B. Henry, Samuel V. Carty and James A. Anderson.

The Independent B.B.C. organized in the 1870s. The Independents played against black organizations. *Wilmington News Journal* (September 17, 1875): "The Independent and Hercules nines played a match game, which resulted in favor of the former by the score of 24 to 9. The Independent is a new organization and contains very good material which is rapidly improving." *Wilmington News Journal* (August 18, 1876): "An interesting game of ball was played at the Adams Street grounds between the Independent nine of this city, and the Williams club, of Philadelphia. Both clubs played well and but few errors on either side were made. The Williams nine is considered one of the best clubs of Philadelphia, but notwithstanding, the Independents gave them considerable trouble. The score was 15 to 7 in favor of the visitors."

SOURCES: "Base Ball," *Wilmington (DE) News Journal*, Aug 22, 1874; "The City and Vicinity," *Wilmington News Journal*, Jul 2, 1875; "Base Ball," *Wilmington (DE) Daily Commercial*, Jul 19, 1875; "A New Club," *Wilmington News Journal*, Aug 19, 1875; "Other Notes," *Wilmington News Journal*, Sep 15, 1875; "The Ball and Bat," *Wilmington Daily Commercial*, Sep 17, 1875; "The Ball Field," *Wilmington News Journal*, Sep 17, 1875; "The Ball Field," *Wilmington Journal*, Sep 30, 1875; "Notes About Town," *Wilmington (DE) Journal*, Oct 1, 1875; "The Ball Field," *Wilmington News Journal*, Jul 11, 1876; "The Ball Field," *Wilmington Journal*, Jul 28, 1876; "The Ball Field," *Wilmington Journal*, Aug 7, 1876; "Local Affairs," *Wilmington Daily Commercial*, Aug 7, 1876; "Base Ball," *Wilmington (DE) Daily Gazette*, Jul 29, 1876; "The Ball Field," *Wilmington Journal*, Jul 31, 1876; "The Ball Field," *Wilmington Journal*, Aug 7, 1876; "The Diamond Field," *Wilmington Daily Gazette*, Aug 9, 1876; "The Ball Field," *Wilmington Journal*, Aug 18, 1876.

Lincoln Base Ball Club (Wilmington, DE; 1860s)

The Lincoln B.B.C. organized in the 1860s, played black nines. *Wilmington Commercial* (September 17, 1867): "The first nine of the Lincoln B.B.C. (colored), of this city, go to West Chester on Monday, the 23rf, inst., to participate in a parade there on that day, and on Tuesday, the 24th, they play the first nine of the Active B.B.C. (colored) of that place."

SOURCES: "Base Ball," *Wilmington (DE) Commercial*, Sep 17, 1867; "September 22," *Wilmington Commercial*, Sep 24, 1867; "September 22," *Wilmington (DE) State Journal and Statesman*, Sep 24, 1867.

Our Boys Base Ball Club (Wilmington, DE; 1880s). Organizer(s): Thomas Harden, Joseph Jones, Jervis A. Smith and James A. Todd.

The Our Boys B.B.C. organized in the 1880s. The Our Boys played against black organizations. *Wilmington News Journal* (August 1, 1882): "Yesterday afternoon a very poor game of base-ball was played on the Rodney Street grounds, between Our Boys and Harmony, both colored, which resulted in an easy victory for Our Boys. The Harmony played a miserable game in the field though they did some heavy batting." *Delaware County Daily Times* (August 4, 1882): "The base-ball game between the Keystone club of South Chester, and the Our Boys club of Wilmington, Delaware … stood 22 to 9 in favor of Our Boys."

SOURCES: "Reorganization," *Wilmington (DE) Morning News*, May 13, 1882; "Base Ball Notes," *Wilmington Morning News*, Jul 26, 1882; "Caught on the Fly," *Wilmington (DE) Journal*, Jul 31, 1882; "Base Ball Matters," *Wilmington Morning News*, Aug 1, 1882; "South Chester Items," *Chester (PA) Delaware County Times*, Aug 1, 1882; "South Chester Items," *Chester Delaware County Times*, Aug 4, 1882; "The Our Boys Win," *Wilmington Journal*, Jul 6, 1887.

West End Base Ball Club (Wilmington, DE; 1880s–1890s). Organizer(s): William H. Trusty and Edward L. States.

The West End B.B.C. organized in the 1880s. The "West Ends" played white and black nines. *Wilmington Evening Journal* (September 1, 1888): "The West Ends and the Delaware Giants, both colored, played two innings at Union Park yesterday, when the game was stopped by rain, the score stood 12 to 0 for the West Ends."

Philadelphia Times (January 27, 1889): "Manager Edward States claims for his team the colored championship of Delaware and stands ready to defend the title against all comers." *Reading Times* (July 18, 1889): "There will be a game of base-ball on the new agricultural grounds this afternoon between the West End Club, (colored), of Wilmington, Delaware, and the Hillsides, (white), of this city." *Reading Eagle*: "The West End colored club, of Wilmington, was defeated by the Hillsides, on the new fair grounds." *Wilmington Evening Journal* (July 16, 1889): "The West End Base Ball Club will play the Cuban Giants, Jr., of Philadelphia, on Wednesday, at the Front and Union Street Grounds. The Cuban Giants, Jr. are the champion colored club of Pennsylvania, and as the West End has signed three new players from Smyrna, a good game may be expected." *Wilmington Evening Journal* (May 12, 1890): "A nine from Bancroft's Banks defeated the West Ends, on Saturday, by a score of 25 to 16."

SOURCES: "Amateur Base Ball Gossip," *Wilmington (DE) Evening Journal*, August 9, 1888; "Brought in Late," *Wilmington Evening Journal*, Aug 30, 1888; "Base Ball Gossip," *Wilmington Evening Journal*, Sep 1, 1888; "Brought in Late," *Wilmington Evening Journal*, Sep 6, 1888; "Local Sports," *Wilmington (DE) Morning News*, Sep 11, 1888; "Among the Amateurs," *Philadelphia (PA) Times*, Jan 20, 1889; "Among the Amateurs," *Philadelphia Times*, Jan 27, 1889; "West End Wins," *Wilmington Morning News*, May 24, 1889; "Base Ball Gossip," *Reading (PA) Times*, Jul 18, 1889; "Yesterday's Ball Games," *Reading (PA) Eagle*, Jul 19, 1889; "Base Ball Notes," *Wilmington Evening Journal*, May 5, 1890; "Base Ball Notes," *Wilmington Evening Journal*, May 12, 1890; "Base Ball Notes," *Wilmington (DE) Morning Star*, Jul 11, 1890.

Wilmington Base Ball Club (Wilmington, DE; 1870s–1880s). Organizer(s): Charles H. Smith; Edward L. States and William H. Trusty.

The Wilmington B.B.C. organized in the 1870s. The Wilmingtons played against black organizations. *Wilmington Journal* (June 30, 1876): "Yesterday afternoon, at the grounds formerly used by the professional Quicksteps, the Independent nine was defeated by the Wilmington nine, both colored, by a score of 16 to 20 in eight innings. The rain stopped the game at the beginning of the ninth inning." *New York Freeman* (May 21, 1887): "Isaac Judah, business manager of the Pythian Base Ball Club of Philadelphia was in the city Friday to make arrangements for a series of games with the Wilmingtons. The Wilmington Base Ball Club will play the Pythians of Philadelphia on Saturday afternoon at Union Street Park at 4:00pm." *Freeman* (July 9, 1887): "The Wilmington Base Ball Club defeated the West Chester Base Ball Club at West Chester on the 4th, 10 to 7." *Freeman* (July 16, 1887): "E. L. States has given up the management of the Wilmington Base Ball Club. W. H. Trusty will hereafter be the manager. Owing to the Philadelphia Giants failing to appear on the Philadelphia grounds the game was forfeited to the Wilmingtons by a score of 9 to 0." *Freeman* (July 23, 1887): "The Wilmington Base Ball Club played two games last week. Thursday, they defeated the Moroccan nine of Baker's establishment 14 to 10. Friday the Delaware Grays beat the Wilmingtons 14 to 10. They will play a few more games for the championship of the city."

SOURCES: "The Ball Field," *Wilmington (DE) Journal*, Sep 29, 1875; "The Ball Field," *Wilmington Journal*, Jun 30, 1876; "The Ball Field," *Wilmington Journal*, Jul 11, 1876; "The Ball Field," *Wilmington Journal*, Jul 18, 1876; "Independents Defeat Wilmingtons," *Wilmington Journal*, Jul 18, 1876; "The Ball Field," *Wilmington Journal*, Jul 28, 1876; "The Ball Field," *Wilmington Journal*, Jul 31, 1876; "The Ball Field," *Wilmington Journal*, Aug 7, 1876; "Base Ball Notes," *Wilmington Journal*, Nov 6, 1883; "Delaware M. E. Conference," *New York (NY) Freeman*, May 7, 1887; "Base Ball Pickups," *Philadelphia (PA) Record*, May 14, 1887; "Delaware Doings," *New York Freeman*, May 21, 1887; "Delaware Doings," *New York Freeman*, May 28, 1887; "Delaware Doings," *New York Freeman*, Jul 9, 1887; "Delaware Doings," *New York Freeman*, Jul 23, 1887.

Florida

Athletic Base Ball Club (Jacksonville, FL; 1870s–1880s). Organizer(s): Thomas Baxter and M. J. Christopher.

The Athletic B.B.C. organized in the 1870s. The Athletics played black organizations. The Augusta *Chronicle* (August 23, 1879): "[The Athletics participated in] "the first grand inter-State base-ball match between colored clubs of Georgia and Florida for the championship and a valuable prize and premium ball and bat, will take place at Brunswick, Georgia." Other participants were Savannah's Chatham, Brunswick's Phoenix; Darien's Lone Star, St. Mary's Union, and Fernandina's Haymaker nines. *Brunswick Advertiser* (August 30, 1879): "A match game of base-ball was played in this city on Thursday last by the Chathams, of Savannah and the Athletics, of Jacksonville, both colored, for the championship of Georgia and Florida, and a prize of a fine bat and ball. The Chathams were victorious, as the official score will show. Captain Houston, of the Davenports, kindly umpired the game, and gave entire satisfaction to both sides." The club attained national recognition. *New Orleans Picayune* (September 12, 1883): "The Athletics, a colored base-ball club, of Jacksonville, Florida, will this week, make a tour of Savannah, Charleston, and Port Royal, playing match games at each of these places with home nines. Pitcher Brown, of this club, is one of the best in the South." The organization joined the League of Southern Colored Base Ballists in 1886.

SOURCES: "An Inter-State Match Between Colored Clubs," *Augusta (GA) Chronicle*, Aug 23, 1879; "City Affairs," *Brunswick (GA) Advertiser*, Aug 23, 1879; "Georgia Victorious," *Brunswick Advertiser*, Aug 30, 1879; "Florida Affairs," *Savannah (GA) Morning News*, Nov 18, 1879; "The Base Ball Tournament," *Savannah Morning News*, August 25, 1880; "The Chatham Base Ball Club and the Late Contest," *Savannah Morning News*, Aug 27, 1880; "Sporting," *New Orleans (LA) Daily Picayune*, Sep 12, 1883; "Colored Business Men of Jacksonville," *New York Globe*, April 26, 1884; "Colored Base Ballists," *Jacksonville (FL) Times-Union*, May 23, 1886.

Colored Base Ball Club (Palatka, FL; 1890s)

The Colored B.B.C. organized in the 1890s. The organization participated in FL's Colored Base Ball League. *Tampa Tribune* (June 21, 1895): "The first games of the colored base-ball league of the State of Florida, was called at 9:30 yesterday morning. They formed a procession on Polk Street, headed by the Jacksonville and DeLand bands, and marched in costume through the streets to the pace of a lively music. The first tilt was between the Tampa and Palatka nines. They did some excellent playing and at the close of the fifth inning the score stood: Tampa, 5; Palatka, 4. The next battle was between the DeLand and Jacksonville teams. They started out with even bats, but it was soon seen the Jacksonville boys were in the lead. At the close of the game the score stood: DeLand, 3; Jacksonville, 9."

SOURCES: *Tampa (FL) Tribune*, May 17, 1895; "State Base Ball Association," *Tampa Tribune*, May 21, 1895; *Tampa Tribune*, May 22, 1895; "Colored State League," *Tampa Tribune*, Jun 20, 1895; "Colored State League," *Tampa Tribune*, Jun 21, 1895.

Spanish Wrappers Base Ball Club (Jacksonville, FL; 1890s)

The Spanish Wrappers B.B.C., of Palatka, FL, organized in the 1890s. The Spanish Wrappers. *Thomasville Times-Enterprise*: "The Spanish Wrappers, Jacksonville's crack colored nine, will be here this morning and cross bats with the Nine Scorers, of this city [Thomasville, Georgia]. The Spanish Wrappers are the leading colored nine of Florida." In 1895, they joined FL's Southern Colored League. *Tampa Tribune* (June 21, 1895): "The first games of the colored base-ball league of the State of Florida, was called at 9:30 yesterday morning. They formed a procession on Polk Street, headed by the Jacksonville and DeLand bands, and marched in costume through the streets to the pace of a lively music. The first tilt was between the Tampa and Palatka nines. They did some excellent playing and at the close of the fifth inning the score stood: Tampa, 5; Palatka, 4. The next battle was between the DeLand and Jacksonville teams. They started out with even bats, but it was soon seen the Jacksonville boys were in the lead. At the close of the game the score stood: DeLand, 3; Jacksonville, 9."

SOURCES: *Thomasville (GA) Daily Times-Enterprise*, Jul 9, 1892; *Thomasville Daily Times-Enterprise*, Jul 17, 1892; "Yesterday With the Colored Excursionists," *Thomasville Daily Times-Enterprise*, Jul 20, 1892; "To Play This Morning," *Thomasville Daily Times-Enterprise*, Sep 7, 1892; "Base Ball Short Stops," *Thomasville Daily Times-Enterprise*, Sep 8, 1892; "Nine Scorers Win Again," *Thomasville Daily Times-Enterprise*, Sep 9, 1892; "A Large Excursion," *Thomasville Daily Times-Enterprise*, Sep 10, 1892; *Tampa (FL) Tribune*, May 17, 1895; "State Base Ball Association," *Tampa Tribune*, May 21, 1895; *Tampa Tribune*, May 22, 1895; "Colored State League," *Tampa Tribune*, Jun 20, 1895; "Colored State League," *Tampa Tribune*, Jun 21, 1895.

Acme Base Ball Club (Pensacola, FL; 1890s)

The Acme B.B.C. organized in the 1890s. The Acmes played black aggregations. *Montgomery Advertiser* (August 14, 1894): "The game of ball between the Montgomery Cracker Jack baseball club, and the Acmes resulted as follows: Montgomery, 14; Pensacola, 13." *New Orleans Times-Democrat*. September 25, 1894): "The Mobile colored baseball team cleaned up the Pensacola colored club at Frascati Park last evening to the tune of 11 to 6. The Pensacolas failed to find the ball from the Mobile pitcher's swift delivery." The organization joined the Southern Colored Base Ball League; the league included the Memphis Cliffords, Birmingham Unions, Hot Springs Arlingtons, Montgomery Blues, and Little Rock Quapaws. *Birmingham Age-Herald* (June 18, 1897): "The Birmingham Unions and Pensacola Acme Base Ball Clubs met at West End Park yesterday afternoon and put up a good exhibition of base-ball. The score resulted 7 to 5 in favor of Birmingham."

SOURCES: "Negro Baseball Players," *Montgomery (AL) Advertiser*, Jun 28, 1894; "Mobile Matters," *New Orleans (LA) Times-Democrat*, Sep 25, 1894; "Almost Like a Sabbath," *Montgomery Advertiser*, Jul 5, 1895; "The Fourth of July," *Montgomery Advertiser*, Jul 4, 1896; "At Atlanta," *Nashville (TN) Tennessean*, Apr 20, 1897; "Will Play Ball," *Birmingham (AL) Age-Herald*, Apr 25, 1897; "Tersely Told," *Birmingham Age-Herald*, Apr 29, 1897; "Games This Week," *Birmingham Age-Herald*, May 2, 1897; "Base Ball," *Birmingham Age-Herald*, May 6, 1897; "Good Local Game," *Birmingham Age-Herald*, Jun 1, 1897; "A Hotly Contested Game," *Birmingham Age-Herald*, Jun 26, 1897; "Hot Springs Wins," *Birmingham Age-Herald*, Jun 30, 1897.

Onward Base Ball Club (Pensacola, FL; 1890s). Organizer(s): John Boyle.

The Onward B.B.C. organized in the 1890s. *Indianapolis Freeman* (August 2, 1890): "Pensacola colored people are justly proud of their several base-ball clubs; prominent among them being the Onwards and 'Giants. The Onwards were organized some months since is composed of a gentlemanly lot of ball tossers, and managed by Mr. John Boyle, our most popular chef de cuisine and patron of sport generally, and now himself personally running Dunn's famous restaurant." The Onwards traveled to AL where they played the Montgomery Blues. *Montgomery Advertiser* (August 28, 1891): "On the latter excursion was the representative colored baseball team from Pensacola, the Onwards." *Montgomery Advertiser* (August 29, 1891): "The Pensacola and Montgomery base-ball clubs played a match game. The former won by a score of 17 to 10, winning $100. It was an interesting game."

SOURCES: "The Pensacola Letter," *Indianapolis (IN) Freeman*, Jul 5, 1890; "The Pensacola Letter," *Indianapolis Freeman*, Aug 2, 1890; "Big Excursions Two," *Montgomery (AL) Advertiser*, Aug 28, 1891; "Negroes at Riverside," *Montgomery Advertiser*, Aug 29, 1891.

Ponce De Leon Hotel Base Ball Club (St. Augustine, FL; 1880s–1890s). Organizer(s): Frank P. Thompson and Stanislau K. Govern.

The Ponce De Leon Hotel B.B.C. organized in 1887. *New York Age* (March 6, 1889): "The Cuban Giants defeated the Standards, in a well-played game on both sides, by a score of 12 to 8. A. G. Randolph and T. Hackett were the battery for the Standard." *Philadelphia Sporting Life*, (March 21, 1891): "The guests of Hotel Ponce De Leon organized a club composed of tennis players that are here engaged for the championship of the world to play the Ponce De Leon club as series of games, the first of which took place on Saturday, at the Ponce De Leon Hotel Base Ball and Athletic Park in which the Ponce De Leon club got the best of it."

SOURCES: "Cuban Giants Handicapped," *New York (NY) Age*, Mar 2, 1889; "Incidents at *St.* Augustine," *New York Age*, Mar 6, 1889; "Incidents at *St.* Augustine," *New York Age*, Apr 6, 1889; "From *St.* Augustine," *New York Age*, Feb 2, 1890; "Among the Amateurs," *New York Age*, May 19, 1890; "A Base Ball Game," *Richmond (VA) Planet*, Jul 19, 1890; "From *St.* Augustine," *Philadelphia (PA) Sporting Life*, Feb 2, 1891; "From *St.* Augustine," *Philadelphia Sporting Life*, Feb 7, 1891; "From *St.* Augustine," *Philadelphia Sporting Life*, Feb 21, 1891; "From *St.* Augustine," *Philadelphia Sporting Life*, Mar 21, 1891.

Georgia

Lee Street Jumpers Base Ball Club (Americus, GA; 1880s–1890s). Organizer(s): Sherman Barlow.

The Lee Street Jumpers B.B.C. organized in the 1880s. The Lee Street Jumpers played against black teams. *Americus Times-Recorder* (April 30, 1891): "The [Lee Street Jumpers] have been practicing a

great deal recently, and are in fine trim. They leave for Cuthbert tonight to play the team at that place. The game will be called tomorrow at 2 o'clock. Sherman Barlow is captain of the Jumpers." *Times-Recorder* (May 2, 1891): "The Lee Street Jumpers, Americus Negro ball team, played the Cuthbert team in that place yesterday, and defeated them by a score of seven to five."

SOURCES: "Wedding in High Colored Life," *Americus (GA) Recorder*, Mar 1, 1888; "The Lee Street Jumpers," *Americus Recorder*, Apr 30, 1891; "Shortly Stated," *Americus Recorder*, May 2, 1891.

Ranger Base Ball Club (Americus, GA; 1880s)

The Ranger B.B.C. organized in the 1880s. The Rangers played black organizations. *Americus Weekly Recorder* (July 11, 1884): "The [Rough and Ready] Colored Base Ball Club from Albany came up Friday morning and had a friendly game of ball with the Rangers, of this city. The Albany boys played well, but they were overmatched, and threw up the game in the sixth inning, the Americus club having scored 27 runs to Albany's 8. Another game will be played soon." They played Eufala, AL's nine, and defeated Montezuma, GA's Flying Squirrels. *Americus Recorder* (May 31, 1885): "Both clubs did some good playing, but [the battery of] Handy and Boss were too much for the visitors." *Americus Daily Recorder* (June 5, 1885): "Friday afternoon the Americus Rangers and Montezuma Flying Squirrels, colored clubs, had a match on McKay's Hill. A good deal of lively kicking was indulged in the Squirrels, who finally lost the game by a score of 23 to 13. The Rangers were very jubilant over their victory."

SOURCES: "Pen Points," *Americus (GA) Recorder*, May 2, 1884; "Americus vs. Albany," *Americus Recorder*, July 11, 1884; "The Rangers," *Americus Recorder*, July 25, 1884; "The Colored Boys," *Americus Recorder*, August 31, 1884; "The Colored Boys," *Americus Recorder*, September 5, 1884; "Base Ball," *Americus Recorder*, June 5, 1885; "Base Ball Matters," *Americus Recorder*, June 10, 1885; "Going to Macon," *Americus Recorder*, July 21, 1885; "Americus Annihilated," *Americus Recorder*, July 22, 1885; "Town Talk," *Americus Recorder*, July 30, 1885; "Town Talk," *Americus Recorder*, August 21, 1885.

Atlanta University Base Ball Club (Atlanta, GA; 1880s–1900s)

The Atlanta University B.B.C. organized in the 1880s, if not earlier. They played against colored organizations. *Atlanta Constitution* (April 22, 1888): "The Atlanta University Baseball Club defeated the Clark University Baseball Club yesterday afternoon in a warmly contested game by a score of 13 to 4. The game was played on the grounds of the former. Batteries—'A. U.', Young and...; 'C. U.', Sheely and Maquire. The game decides the championship for 1887–88 in favor of Atlanta University, the latter having won two out of a series of three games."

SOURCES: "Colored Students at Ball," *Atlanta (GA) Constitution*, Apr 22, 1888.

Champion Base Ball Club (Atlanta, GA; 1870s–1890s). Organizer(s): C. N. Pemberton; E. D. Mitchell and J. C. Higgins.

The Champion B.B.C. organized in the 1870s. The "Champion Club" played black nines of GA, TN, SC, AL, and GA. *Constitution* (June 23, 1876): "The Atlanta Champions and Fulton Blues had a game of baseball at the barracks yesterday. The score stood: Champions 11, Fulton 4." Atlanta and Columbus developed a rivalry. *Constitution* (August 13, 1879): "A match game of base-ball was played at the ball grounds near McPherson Barracks, between the Champions, of Atlanta, and the Fox Hunters, of Columbus, two club composed of colored boys. The game was played in the presence of a fine crowd and was quite interesting. Nine innings were played in about two hours and a half, and the game resulted in a victory for the Champions, of Atlanta, by a score of 19 to 6." *Constitution* (April 14, 1882):

"For some time considerable annoyance has been caused to citizens residing in the suburbs of the city by Negro boys who would congregate in lots, play base-ball, yell and make a general disturbance. Captain Aldridge and Captain Couch, with about a dozen members of the force, went out to the place to arrest the players. The officers succeeded in making several arrests, as follows: Robert Shields, Aleck Dawson, James Davis, Will Crockett, Emanual Gay, Thomas Green, Mack Jordan, Clarence Hurd, Thomas Ham, William Pope and Ed Walton." They played match games across the State. *Columbus Sunday Enquirer* (June 17, 1883): "A match game of base-ball was played on the east commons yesterday between the Champions, of Atlanta, and the Metropolitans, of this city, both colored clubs. At the close of the game the score stood as follows: Champions 21; Metropolitans 8." In 1886, the Georgia Champions joined the Southern League of Colored Base Ballists. *Constitution* (June 10, 1886): "About four hundred people witnessed the game of ball between the colored clubs at Athletic Park yesterday afternoon. The audience was composed largely of colored people, but quite a number of white admirers of the game went out, and were rewarded with a good game. The Georgia champions succeeded in defeating the Tennessee club, by a score of nine to six. [John] Thompson, the pitcher for the Atlantas proved to be a fine pitcher. He has a remarkable speed and great endurance." They played the black team of Selma, AL. *Constitution* (October 27, 1886): "The Atlanta colored baseball club will play the Selma, Alabama boys this morning at Athletic Park. The game will be called at 9 o'clock. Admission: 25 cents; manager E. D. Mitchell, battery, Hughes and Maddox." A rivalry with Montgomery continued. *Constitution* (August 11, 1887): "The Montgomery Colored Base Ball Club came to Atlanta yesterday accompanied by a large crowd of colored people. This afternoon the club will play the Atlanta Colored Club at Athletic Park. [John] Thompson and [Benjamin] Swift will do the battery work for the Atlantas and [Addis] Duncan and [William] Patterson for the Montgomerys." The Champions reorganized in the 1890s. *Savannah Tribune* (September 7, 1892): "The Chatham Base Ball Club and the Atlanta Champions will cross bats this afternoon at the Base Ball Park, also Monday afternoon."

Sources: "Town and Topics," *Atlanta (GA) Constitution*, May 14, 1876; "Town Topics," *Atlanta Constitution*, Jun 23, 1876; "A Match Game," *Atlanta Constitution*, Aug 13, 1879; "Arresting Ball Players," *Atlanta Constitution*, Apr 14, 1882; "City News," *Atlanta Constitution*, Apr 15, 1882; "Through the City," *Atlanta Constitution*, Jun 15, 1883; "Local Laconics," *Columbus (GA) Sunday Enquirer*, Jun 17, 1883; "Breakfast Table Chat," *Macon (GA) Telegraph*, Aug 5, 1883; "Match Game of Base Ball," *Columbus Sunday Enquirer*, Aug 11, 1883; "The Day in Macon," *Atlanta Constitution*, Jul 17, 1884; "Colored Baseballists," *Atlanta Constitution*, Aug 28, 1884; "Colored Match Game," *Atlanta Constitution*, Oct 7, 1884; "Colored Players in Macon," *Atlanta Constitution*, July 23, 1885; "Our Race's Doings," *Cleveland (OH) Gazette*, Apr 17, 1886; "Colored Base Ballists," *Jacksonville (FL) Times-Union*, May 23, 1886; "The Colored Base-Ballists," *Atlanta Constitution*, May 21, 1886; "Colored Base-Ballists," *Jacksonville Times-Union*, May 23, 1886; "Colored Baseball Players," *Atlanta Constitution*, Jun 10, 1886; "Colored Baseball Players," *Atlanta (GA) Journal*, Jun 11, 1886; "Diamond Dust," *Atlanta Constitution*, Jun 23, 1886; "Diamond Dust," *Atlanta Constitution*, Jun 25, 1886; "Our Brothers in Black," *Charleston (SC) News and Courier*, Jun 19, 1886; *Atlanta Constitution*, Aug 6, 1886; "Notes," *Atlanta Constitution*, Oct 27, 1886; "Caught on the Fly," *Atlanta Constitution*, Aug 11, 1887; *Savannah (GA) Tribune*, Sep 7, 1892.

Clipper Base Ball Club (Atlanta, GA; 1880s). Organizer(s): W. C. Dent.

The Clipper B.B.C. organized in the 1880s. The Clippers played black organizations.

Sources: "Caught on the Fly," *Atlanta (GA) Constitution*, Aug 11, 1887; "The Atlanta Base Ball Club," *Atlanta Constitution*, Sep 13, 1887.

Deppens Base Ball Club (Atlanta, GA; 1890s–1900s). Organizer(s): Thomas Morgan.

The Deppens B.B.C. organized in the 1890s, played black teams. *Indianapolis Freeman* (August 11, 1900): "Baseball was played between the Chattanooga Unions and the Atlanta Deppens, at Atlanta, Georgia. The boys met went success both financially and socially and say they had the best time they have ever witnessed on a trip of this kind. We are proud to say the Chattanooga team beat the Deppens 10 to 9 and 19 to 12."

Sources: "A Unique Fair," *Atlanta (GA) Constitution*, Oct 24, 1893; "Colored Ball Teams To Play," *Atlanta Constitution*, Jul 29, 1894; "Atlanta Crack Team Will Play Here This Afternoon," *Charlotte (NC) Observer*, Sep 4, 1897; "Charlotte Beat Atlanta," *Charlotte Observer*, Sep 5, 1897; "Locals," *Savannah (GA) Tribune*, Aug 19, 1899; "Interesting Items," *Indianapolis (IN) Freeman*, Aug 11, 1900; "Chattanooga News," *Indianapolis Freeman*, Aug 25, 1900; "Colored Baseball," *Atlanta Constitution*, Jul 12, 1901.

Grays Base Ball Club (Atlanta, GA; 1890s)

The Gray B.B.C. organized in the 1880s, played black organizations. *Atlanta Constitution* (August 25, 1891): "The Atlanta Grays and the Birmingham team, representing the colored baseball lovers of the two cities, played at the Georgia Pacific grounds yesterday afternoon. A big crowd was there, and they cheered everything. The score stood: Atlanta, 15; Birmingham, 12." *Atlanta Constitution* (July 9, 1892): "Next Monday afternoon at 3:30 o'clock there will be a baseball game at Brisbane Park between two crack colored clubs, the Atlanta Grays and the Birmingham Hornets. Both clubs are in good trim and a fine game is expected. A portion of the grandstand will be reserved, for white fans."

Sources: "The Same Old Story," *Atlanta (GA) Constitution*, Jul 21, 1891; "Atlanta, as Usual," *Atlanta Constitution*, Aug 25, 1891; "City Notes," *Atlanta Constitution*, May 27, 1892; "City Notes," *Atlanta Constitution*, Jun 20, 1892; "Atlanta vs. Birmingham," *Atlanta Constitution*, Jul 9, 1892; "A Unique Fair," *Atlanta Constitution*, Oct 4, 1893.

Augusta Hotel Base Ball Club (Augusta, GA; 1880s)

The Augusta Hotel B.B.C. organized in the 1880s, if not earlier. *Augusta Chronicle* (April 21, 1886): "The waiters of the Globe and Augusta Hotels had a game of ball yesterday on the colored base-ball grounds. The game was won by the Augusta Hotel Club by a score of 9 to 7."

Sources: "Base Ball," *Augusta (GA) Chronicle*, April 17, 1886; "Colored Base Ball," *Augusta Chronicle*, April 21, 1886.

Globe Hotel Base Ball Club (Augusta, GA; 1880s)

The Globe Hotel B.B.C. organized in the 1880s, if not earlier. *Augusta Chronicle* (April 21, 1886): "The waiters of the Globe and Augusta Hotels had a game of ball yesterday on the colored base-ball grounds. The game was won by the Augusta Hotel Club by a score of 9 to 7."

Sources: "Base Ball," *Augusta (GA) Chronicle*, Apr 17, 1886; "Colored Base Ball," *Augusta Chronicle*, April 21, 1886.

National Base Ball Club (Augusta, GA; 1870s–1880s). Organizer(s): Osborn Fullington and James E. Roberts.

The National B.B.C. organized in the 1870s. The Nationals played black organizations. *Savannah Morning News* (August 28, 1878): "The Jefferson B. B. C., of Savannah, colored, was beaten by the National

Club, of Augusta, colored, in that city by a score of 16 to 1." *Augusta Chronicle* (September 17, 1878): "The match game of base-ball between the Nationals, of Augusta, and the Chathams, of Savannah, both colored, took place yesterday in the latter city. The game was won by the Nationals by a score of 11 to 6. This is the third game played by these clubs—the first having been won by the Chathams and the second and third by the Savannahs." They developed a rivalry with Charlotte, NC's Fearless B.B.C. *Charlotte Observer* (August 21, 1888): "The game between the Augusta and Charlotte (colored) base-ball clubs yesterday afternoon, was won by the Charlottes, by a score of 11 to 6."

SOURCES: "Base Ball," *Augusta (GA) Chronicle*, Sep 8, 1874; "Local Affairs," *Aiken (SC) Courier-Journal*, Jul 8, 1876; "Base Ball," *Augusta Chronicle*, May 21, 1878; *Savannah (GA) Morning News*, Jun 1, 1878; "The City," *Augusta Chronicle*, Jun 19, 1878; "Colored Base Ball Match," *Augusta Chronicle*, Aug 27, 1878; "Base Ball Match," *Augusta Chronicle*, Sep 15, 1878; "Colored Base Ball Match," *Augusta Chronicle*, Sep 17, 1878; "Georgia News," *Columbus (GA) Enquirer*, Sep 21, 1878; "An Inter-State Match Between Colored Clubs," *Columbus Chronicle*, Aug 23, 1879; "Colored Southern Base Ball Contest," *Columbus Chronicle*, Aug 10, 1880; "Colored Base Ball Contest," *Columbus Chronicle*, Apr 5, 1881; "Minor Gleanings," *Charlotte (NC) Observer*, Aug 21, 1888.

Nine Brothers Base Ball Club (Augusta, GA; 1890s)

The Nine Brothers B.B.C. organized in the 1890s. The ball club played black teams of GA and NC. *Augusta Chronicle* (August 16, 1890): "The undersigned are members of the Nine Brothers Base Ball Club, with which Augustus Preston was connected during a recent visit to Savannah, and we wish to emphatically deny that we had him landed in the barrack, in Savannah and also deny that he misappropriated any money belonging to the club. The club plans to take immediate steps to prosecute the man who did misappropriate its funds. Respectfully Jack Jossie, Reuben Jenkins, Charles Attaway, Ryal Ware, George Taylor, John Gould, Henry Watts, Moses Ellis, Isaac Jenkins, John Jenkins, Jim Jackson."

SOURCES: "Little Locals," *Augusta (GA) Chronicle*, Aug 16, 1890; "Didn't Hold Out," *Augusta Chronicle*, August 19, 1890; "Local Ripples," *Charlotte (NC) News*, Jul 26, 1893; "Big Ball Tomorrow," *Charlotte News*, Jul 27, 1893.

Blues Base Ball Club (Columbus, GA; 1880s)

The Blues B.B.C. organized in the 1880s. *Columbus Enquirer Sun* (April 21, 1886): "The first and finest game of the season came off between colored clubs, the Columbus Blues and Girard Leapers, on the East Commons, on Friday evening last. On the ninth inning, when the game was called on account of darkness, the score stood 0 to 0. Wagner and Hicks battery for the Leapers, and Reese and Murphy for the Blues. Marshall, umpire."

SOURCES: "Base Ball," *Augusta (GA) Chronicle*, Apr 17, 1886; "Colored Base Ball," *Augusta Chronicle*, Apr 21, 1886.

Metropolitan Base Ball Club (Columbus, GA; 1880s)

The Metropolitan B.B.C. organized in the 1880s. The Metropolitans represented a merger of two teams, the Lightfoots and Stars, both of Columbus. The Lightfoot club played another local black nine, the Star club. *Enquirer-Sun* (May 31, 1883): "The Stars and Lightfoot, two colored base-ball clubs, played on the east commons yesterday afternoon. Four innings were played and resulted in victory for the Lightfoot club." They played against nines, of GA and AL. *Enquirer-Sun* (June 2, 1883): "The [N]egro boys have organized a base-ball club under the name of Metropolitans. They are now ready for the bat." The Metropolitans played against black nines, including

the Troy Foresters, Atlanta Champions, Brownville Light Runners, and Atlanta's GA Nine. *Enquirer-Sun* (June 15, 1883): "The swift pitching of Bass and the good catching of Preer, of the Metropolitans was too much for the Foresters." *Sunday Enquirer* (July 22, 1883): "A match game of base-ball was played on the east commons yesterday between the Champions, of Atlanta, and the Metropolitans, of this city, both colored clubs. At the close of the game the score stood as follows: Champions 21; Metropolitans 8."

SOURCES: "Match Game of Base Ball," *Columbus (GA) Enquirer*, May 31, 1883; "Metropolitan Base Ball Club," *Columbus Enquirer*, June 2, 1883; "Through the City," *Atlanta (GA) Constitution*, Jun 15, 1883; "Local Laconics," *Columbus (GA) Sunday Enquirer*, June 17, 1883; "Match Game of Base Ball," *Columbus Enquirer*, June 26, 1883; "Local Laconics," *Columbus Sunday Enquirer*, July 20, 1883; "Match Game of Base Ball," *Columbus Sunday Enquirer*, July 22, 1883; "Local Laconics," *Columbus Sunday Enquirer*, August 8, 1883; "Match Game of Base Ball," *Columbus Sunday Enquirer*, August 11, 1883; "Local Laconics," *Columbus Sunday Enquirer*, September 9, 1883.

Leaper Base Ball Club (Girard, GA; 1880s)

The Leaper B.B.C. organized in the 1880s. The Leapers played against black teams. *Columbus Enquirer Sun* (April 21, 1886): "The first and finest game of the season came off between colored clubs, the Columbus Blues and Girard Leapers, on the East Commons, on Friday evening last. On the ninth inning, when the game was called on account of darkness, the score stood 0 to 0. Wagner and Hicks battery for the Leapers, and Reese and Murphy for the Blues. Marshall, umpire." *Enquirer Sun* (May 8, 1888): "The Girard Leapers, a colored base-ball club, defeated the Opelika club by a score of 23 to 10 yesterday. A Georgia nine was also defeated by the Leapers by a score of 27 to 10. Hicks and Wynne were the battery for the victorious Leapers."

SOURCES: "Base Ball," *Augusta (GA) Chronicle*, Apr 17, 1886; "Colored Base Ball," *Augusta Chronicle*, Apr 21, 1886; "Local Laconics," *Columbus (GA) Enquirer-Sun*, May 27, 1887; "Local Laconics," *Columbus Enquirer-Sun*, August 16, 1887; "Whacked With a Whip, *Columbus Enquirer-Sun*, March 23, 1888; "Base Ball," *Columbus Enquirer-Sun*, April 8, 1888; "Base Ball in Opelika," *Columbus Enquirer-Sun*, May 8, 1888; "In the City," *Columbus Enquirer-Sun*, May 24, 1888; "Browneville Briefs," *Columbus Enquirer-Sun*, June 17, 1888; "Browneville Briefs," *Columbus Enquirer-Sun*, June 24, 1888.

Nine Brothers Base Ball Club (Griffin, GA; 1880s)

The Nine Brothers B.B.C. organized in the 1880s. The Nine Brothers played black nines. *Atlanta Constitution* (October 7, 1884): "A very interesting match of baseball was played between the Georgia Champions and the Nine Brothers, of Griffin, both colored nines, possessing almost professional material. A large crowd was present to witness the game. Eight innings were played when darkness interfered with further progress, and the game was called. The score, stood Georgia Champions, 25, Nine Brothers, 2. Another victory for Atlanta. The game will be repeated this afternoon when the Nine Brothers introduce a new pitcher and catcher."

SOURCES: "Base Ball Game Tomorrow," *Atlanta (GA) Constitution*, Oct 5, 1884; "Colored Match Game," *Atlanta Constitution*, Oct 7, 1884.

Athletic Base Ball Club (Macon, GA; 1880s–1890s)

The Athletic B.B.C. organized in the 1880s. The "Athletics" played against black nines of GA. In 1885, the Athletics played a match game of ball against Forsyth, GA. *Americus Recorder*: "The Wide Awakes, of Forsyth, defeated the Athletics, of Macon, by a score of 16 to 13. Report says the game was well-played at every point, and the high score was due to the roughness of the grounds." They "measured bats" with Americus's Colored Rangers B.B.C. In 1886, during the State Fair, the Athletics played against Atlanta, GA's Clipper B.B.C. In 1888, the Athletics played Atlanta's colored champions. *Macon Telegraph*: "The Athletics, of Macon, the crack colored club, played a game with the Atlanta nine, and defeated them by a score of 8 to 0. The Athletics play good ball and seldom let a visiting team get away with them."

Sources: "Going to Macon," *Americus (GA) Recorder*, Jul 21, 1885; "Colored Players in Macon," *Atlanta (GA) Constitution*, Jul 23, 1885; "Macon Matters," *Atlanta Constitution*, Aug 23, 1885; "Over the State," *Macon (GA) Telegraph*, Sep 6, 1885; "The Fair Opens Today," *Macon Telegraph*, October 27, 1886; "The Opening Day," *Macon Telegraph*, October 28, 1886; "Macon on Top Again," *Macon Telegraph*, July 15, 1888; "Another Game," *Macon Telegraph*, July 16, 1888; "Atlanta Suffers Another Defeat," *Macon Telegraph*, July 18, 1888; "The Colored Athletics," *Macon Telegraph*, August 2, 1888; "Some Colored Ball," *Macon Telegraph*, August 31, 1888; "A Turn Around the Road," *Macon Telegraph*, June 13, 1891; "The Athletics Won," *Macon Telegraph*, June 6, 1892.

Fats Base Ball Club (Macon, GA; 1890s).

The Fats B.B.C. organized in the 1890s. The "Fats" played against another local black team. *Macon Telegraph* (May 8, 1888): "The colored fats and leans will meet each other Central City Park next Monday. The game will be for the benefit of the Hospital, and much interest has been taken in it."

Sources: "Ball on the 30th," *Macon (GA) Telegraph*, Aug 15, 1897; "Fats and Leans," *Macon Telegraph*, August 23, 1897; "Fats and Leans Today," *Macon Telegraph*, August 30, 1897; "City Items," *Macon Telegraph*, August 31, 1897.

Fox Hunters Base Ball Club (Macon, GA; 1870s–1800s). Organizer(s): James Cuthbert; B. Cummings.

The Fox Hunter B.B.C. is a champion black nine of the 1870s and '80s. The Fox Hunters played black organizations. The Milledgeville and Macon developed a rivalry. *Macon Telegraph* (July 8, 1879): "The Atlantics of Milledgeville (colored) played the Fox Hunter of Macon a match game of base-ball in the latter city one day last week. The score was Atlantics, 6; Fox Hunters, 9." Macon hosted a black tournament that included the cities of Griffin, Milledgeville, Atlanta, and Macon. The Atlantics, Moonlights, and Fox Hunters –all Macon teams—figured among the nines battling for the championship. *Macon Telegraph* (September 2, 1879): "The Fox Hunters Base Ball Club, colored, leave tomorrow morning for Milledgeville, to play for a prize of thirty dollars. Captain James Cuthbert, captain, informs us that his club will play any nine in the State." The Fox Hunters and Savannah Chathams became rivals. *Macon Telegraph* (August 27, 1880): "Fully two thousand people were on the grounds, and the nines played with a will from the commencement to the end. The Chathams are a crack nine, and understand the science of handling the bat and ball. The Fox Hunters follow as the next best in the South. Their playing was excellent, and gave satisfaction to the managers of the association and the Chathams, whom they were playing." The Fox Hunters agreed to play at Griffin, GA for the championship. *Macon Telegraph* (July 18, 1882): "The Atlanta Colored Champions have challenged the Fox Hunters, of Macon, for a game, which is accepted and the match will come off at Griffin." One newspaper account printed derisive epithets. *Atlanta Constitution* (July 17, 1884): "There was a game played in this city, by the 'Fox Hunters' of Macon, and the 'Tar Baby' club" of this city—both colored clubs. The tar babies struck Br'er Fox badly—the score being 39 to 16."

Sources: "The City," *Macon (GA) Chronicle*, May 23, 1876; "Brevi-

ties," *Chronicle*, May 21, 1878; "Base Ball Jottings," *Macon Chronicle*, Aug 27, 1878; "The City," *Milledgeville (GA) Union and Recorder*, Jul 8, 1879; "A Match Game," *Atlanta (GA) Constitution*, Aug 13, 1879; "Base Ball Tournament Among Colored Clubs," *Macon (GA) Weekly Telegraph*, Sep 2, 1879; "We Hear," *Macon (GA) Telegraph*, May 29, 1880; "Base Ball Tournament," *Macon Telegraph*, Aug 27, 1880; "The City," *Macon Telegraph*, July 16, 1882; "City Items," *Macon Telegraph*, Jul 18, 1882; "City and County," *Milledgeville Union and Recorder*, Jun 19, 1883; "City Items," *Telegraph*, July 26, 1883; "Breakfast Table Chat," *Macon Telegraph*, Aug 5, 1883; "City Items," *Macon Telegraph*, May 7, 1884; "The Day in Macon," *Atlanta Constitution*, Jul 17, 1884; "A New Base Ball Club," *Macon Telegraph*, May 5, 1885; "Our Race's Doings," *Cleveland (OH) Gazette*, Apr 17, 1886; "Colored Base Ballists," *Jacksonville (FL) Times-Union*, May 23, 1886; "Notes," *Macon Weekly Telegraph*, Oct 26, 1886; "A Month of Excursions," *Atlanta Constitution*, Jul 8, 1888.

Heavyweight Base Ball Club (Macon, GA; 1890s).

The Heavyweight B.B.C. organized in the 1890s. *Macon Telegraph* (August 10, 1895): "A great game of ball, together with fun and amusement will be given the citizens of Macon by the Light-weights and heavyweights for the benefit of the City Hospital. The colored players have undertaken this game in a good spirit and desire the patronage of their friends on account of the game. The men who will participate in the game are standing all the expenses of the game and every cent taken in at the gate will be net profit to the hospital."

Sources: "Base Ball and Fun," *Macon (GA) Telegraph*, Aug 10, 1895; "Great Base Ball," *Macon Telegraph*, Aug 11, 1895; "Great Game of Ball," *Macon Telegraph*, Aug 13, 1895; "Thanks of the Players," *Macon Telegraph*, Aug 14, 1895; "Turned into Treasury," *Macon Telegraph*, Aug 17, 1895; "Colored Base Ball Club," *Macon Telegraph*, Jul 9, 1895.

Leans Base Ball Club (Macon, GA; 1890s).

The Leans B.B.C. organized in the 1890s. The Leans played against the Fats of Macon, GA. *Macon Telegraph* (May 8, 1888): "The colored fats and leans will meet each other Central City Park next Monday. The game will be for the benefit of the Hospital, and much interest has been taken in it."

Sources: "Ball on the 30th," *Macon Telegraph*, Aug 15, 1897; "Fats and Leans," *Macon Telegraph*, Aug 23, 1897; "Fats and Leans Today," *Macon Telegraph*, Aug 30, 1897; "City Items," *Macon Telegraph*, Aug 31, 1897.

Young Americans Base Ball Club (Macon, GA; 1880s)

The Young Americans B.B.C. organized in the 1880s. The Young Americans played black organizations. *Macon Telegraph* (July 23, 1882): "The colored baseballists had an interesting game at the park yesterday afternoon, despite the damp weather. The game was between the Young America's and Athletics, and resulted in a victory for the former in a score of 20 to 13." *Telegraph* (July 25, 1882): "A match game of baseball was played yesterday at the park, between two colored nines, the Young Americas and the Athletics, resulting in a victory for the former, the score being 19 to 11."

Sources: "City Items," *Macon (GA) Telegraph*, Jul 23, 1882; "Base Ball," *Macon Telegraph*, Jul 25, 1882; "The City," *Macon Telegraph*, Aug 8, 1882.

Lightweight Base Ball Club (Macon, GA; 1890s).

The Lightweight B.B.C. organized in the 1890s. *Macon Telegraph* (August 10, 1895): "A great game of ball, together with fun and amusement will be given the citizens of Macon by the Light-weights and heavyweights for the benefit of the City Hospital. The colored players have undertaken this game in a good spirit and desire the patronage of their friends on account of the game. The men who will participate in the game are standing all the expenses of the game and every cent taken in at the gate will be net profit to the hospital."

SOURCES: "Base Ball and Fun," *Macon (GA) Telegraph*, Aug 10, 1895; "Great Base Ball," *Macon Telegraph*, Aug 11, 1895; "Great Game of Ball," *Macon Telegraph*, Aug 13, 1895; "Thanks of the Players," *Macon Telegraph*, Aug 14, 1895; "Turned into Treasury," *Macon Telegraph*, Aug 17, 1895; "Colored Base Ball Club," *Macon Telegraph*, Jul 9, 1895.

Mutual Base Ball Club (Macon, GA; 1870s).

The Mutual B.B.C. organized in 1874. The Mutuals" played against black organizations. *Macon Weekly Telegraph* (September 1, 1874): "A number of colored young men met at the armory of the Lincoln Guards last night, and organized the Mutual Base Ball Club." *Atlanta Constitution* (September 10, 1874): "The Mutuals defeated the Nationals on yesterday in a game of base-ball played for the colored championship."

SOURCES: "Colored Base Ball Club," *Macon (GA) Weekly Telegraph*, Sep 1, 1874; "Summary of State News," *Atlanta (GA) Constitution*, Sep 10, 1874.

Atlantic Base Ball Club (Milledgeville, GA; 1870s–1880s). Organizer(s): L. K. Sinton.

The Atlantic B.B.C. organized in the 1870s. The "Atlantics" played against black nines. *Milledgeville Union and Recorder* (June 10, 1879): "The colored base-ball clubs of Milledgeville and Sandersville played a math game in this city Saturday. The Milledgeville club won the victory." The city of Macon hosted a base-ball tournament that included black teams from Griffin, Milledgeville, Atlanta, and Macon. *Union and Recorder* (July 8, 1879): "The Atlantics of Milledgeville (colored) played the Fox Hunter of Macon a match game of base-ball in the latter city one day last week. The score was Atlantics, 6; Fox Hunters, 9. B. Cummings was captain of the Atlantics, L. K. Sinton scorer." *Union and Recorder* (August 19, 1879): "A match game of base-ball was played at Eatonton, between the Atlantics of Milledgeville, and Tornado Club at Eatonton, both colored. The result was Atlantics 6, Tornado 4." The nine reorganized in 1884. *Union and Recorder* (August 5, 1884): "There was a game played here Thursday morning between the Sparta Red Hots and Milledgeville Atlantics, colored clubs. The latter beat the game. In the afternoon, there was a second game between other nines from the same places. Milledgeville was again victorious by large odds."

SOURCES: "Base Ball," *Milledgeville (GA) Union and Recorder*, Jun 10, 1879; "The City," *Milledgeville Union and Recorder*, Jul 8, 1879; "The 4th," *Milledgeville Union and Recorder*, Jul 8, 1879; "The City," *Milledgeville Union and Recorder*, Aug 19, 1879; "Base Ball Tournament Among Colored Clubs," *Macon (GA) Weekly Telegraph*, Sep 2, 1879; "Base Ball," *Milledgeville Union and Recorder*, Aug 5, 1884.

Flying Squirrels Base Ball Club (Montezuma, GA; 1880s)

The Flying Squirrels B.B.C., of Macon, GA, organized in the 18880s. The "Flying Squirrels" played against black organizations. *Americus Weekly Recorder* (August 29, 1884): "We understand that the Ellaville and Montezuma colored base-ball clubs will play the second nine of the home club on McKay's Hill today." *Americus Daily Recorder* (June 5, 1885): "Friday afternoon the Americus Rangers and Montezuma Flying Squirrels, colored clubs, had a match on McKay's Hill. A good deal of lively kicking was indulged in the Squirrels, who finally lost the game by a score of 23 to 13. The Rangers were very jubilant over their victory."

SOURCES: "Base Ball," *Americus (GA) Weekly Recorder*, Aug 29, 1884; "Town Talk," *Americus (GA) Daily Recorder*, May 23, 1885; "Town Talk," *Americus Recorder*, May 29, 1885; "Base Ball," *Americus Daily Recorder*, Jun 5, 1885; "Base Ball Matters," *Americus Daily Recorder*, Jun 10, 1885.

Armstrong Hotel Black Birds Base Ball Club (Rome, GA; 1890s). Organizer(s): Jerry Orr)

The Armstrong Hotel Black Bird B.B.C. organized in the 1890s, if not earlier. *Atlanta Constitution* (June 5, 1891): "A large excursion from Marietta, headed by a brass band, arrived in Rome this morning, and the Marietta baseball team (colored) played against the Rome colored nine at Printup City. A tremendous crowd was present and excitement ran high. The score was Rome 16, Marietta 18." *Constitution* (September 23, 1892): "Rome has developed a capital colored baseball team. They are known as the Georgia Black Birds and Jerry Orr, head porter at the Armstrong, is their manager. They have just returned from Birmingham and Anniston, where they beat everything that opposed them. They have played this season Chattanooga, Knoxville, Atlanta, Birmingham, and Anniston and come off victorious every time." *Constitution* (June 2, 1895): "The will be base-ball games between local clubs, and the Atlanta colored club will tackle the Rome Blackbirds at the grounds Monday."

SOURCES: "Base Ball in Rome," *Atlanta (GA) Constitution*, Jun 5, 1891; "Colored Baseball in Rome," *Atlanta Constitution*, Sep 23, 1892; "A Week of Sporting," *Atlanta Constitution*, Jun 2, 1895.

Chatham Base Ball Club (Savannah, GA; 1870s–1900s). Organizer(s): Thomas A. Simmons.

Between the 1870s and 1900s, the Chatham B.B.C. is one of champion black organizations. They played against black nines, of GA, FL, and AL. The Chathams became a powerhouse of the South. In 1879, the played in the Colored Base Ball Tournament which Savannah, GA's Chathams; Jacksonville, FL's Athletics; Brunswick, GA's Phoenixes; Darien GA's Lone Stars; St. Mary, GA's Unions; and Fernandina, FL's Haymakers. *Brunswick Advertiser* (August 30, 1879): "A match game of base-ball was played in this city on Thursday last by the Chathams, of Savannah and the Athletics, of Jacksonville, both colored, for the championship of Georgia and Florida, and a prize of a fine bat and ball. The Chathams were victorious, as the official score will show. Captain Houston, of the Davenports, kindly umpired the game, and gave entire satisfaction to both sides." By 1886, the Cuban Giants and Chathams were playing spring exhibition matches. The Chathams played Macon's Fox Hunters for the championship. *Macon Telegraph* (August 27, 1880): "Fully two thousand people were on the grounds, and the nines played with a will from the commencement to the end. The Chathams are a crack nine, and understand the science of handling the bat and ball. The Fox Hunters follow as the next best in the South. Their playing was excellent, and gave satisfaction to the managers of the association and the Chathams, whom they were playing." In 1890, they renewed a rivalry with Charleston. *Savannah Tribune* (July 8, 1899): "The Chatham Base Ball Club will leave tomorrow for Charleston where they will cross bats with the Fear Nots next week. On the following Sunday they will return accompanied by the Fear Nots and will play a series of games here next week. It will be remembered that these clubs kept up the base-ball spirit in the city last season when there were no league games." In 1900, the Chathams reorganized. *Thomasville Enterprise* (August 16, 1900): "The Chathams and Thomasville colored base-ball teams, played an interesting game at Bolton Street Park yesterday afternoon. The game resulted in a well-earned victory for the local team, which won out by a score of 9 to 0."

SOURCES: "The Two States," *Augusta (GA) Chronicle*, Apr 18, 1879; "An Inter-State Match Between Colored Clubs," *Augusta Chronicle*, Aug 23, 1879; "City Affairs," *Brunswick (GA) Advertiser*, Aug 23, 1879; "Georgia Victorious," *Brunswick Advertiser*, August 30, 1879;

"Base Ball Tournament," *Macon (GA) Telegraph*, Aug 27, 1880; "Things in Georgia," *New York (NY) Globe*, Mar 17, 1883; "Colored Baseballists," *Atlanta (GA) Constitution*, Aug 28, 1884; "Diamond Dots," *Charleston (NC) News and Courier*, Aug 12, 1891; "Struggling for the Championship," *Charleston News and Courier*, Aug 15, 1891; "Locals," *Savannah (GA) Tribune*, Jul 8, 1899; "Locals," *Savannah Tribune*, August 19, 1899; "They Laid Out Thomasville," Thomasville *(GA) Times-Enterprise*, Aug 16, 1900.

Jefferson Base Ball Club (Savannah, GA; 1870s–1880s). Organizer(s): Henry Jackson and George Jackson.

The Jefferson B.B.C. organized in the 1870s. The "Jefferson club" played against black nines. *Savannah Morning News* (June 1, 1878): "A game of base-ball was played yesterday between the Jefferson and Palmetto Base Ball Club, colored. The Jeffersons were victorious by a sore of fourteen to six." *Morning News* (August 25, 1878): "The Jefferson B. B. C., of Savannah, colored, was beaten by the National Club, of Augusta, colored, in that city by a score of 16 to 1."

SOURCES: *Savannah (GA) Morning News*, Jun 1, 1878; "Brevities," *Augusta (GA) Chronicle*, Aug 25, 1878; "Matters and Things Laconically Noted," *Savannah Morning News*, Aug 28, 1878; "Another Colored Treasurer in Trouble," *Savannah Morning News*, Oct 23, 1878; "Inter-State Base Ball Match at Brunswick," *Savannah Morning News*, Jul 26, 1880; "Grand Southern Base Ball Contest By Colored Base Ballists," *Savannah Morning News*, Aug 2, 1880.

Mutual Base Ball Club (Savannah, GA; 1890s).

The Mutual B.B.C. organized in the 1890s. The Mutuals played black aggregations. *Charleston News and Courier* (August 12, 1891): "The colored population is having some great ball. Every afternoon this week, the Fear Nots and Mutuals have played at the Base Ball Park. The Fear Nots are the unquestioned champions of South Carolina and the Mutuals are boss ball tossers from Savannah, Georgia. The Charleston club has as its crack pitcher Shavers; Brown is the catcher. The chief battery for the Savannah club is Ralston, pitcher, and Mackay catcher." The rivalry persisted. *Savannah Tribune* (June 25, 1892): "The Chatham Base Ball Club will leave tomorrow for Charleston where they will cross bats with the Fear Nots next week. On the following Sunday, they will return accompanied by the Fear Nots and will play a series of games here next week. It will be remembered that these clubs kept up the base-ball spirit in the city last season when there were no league games."

SOURCES: "Diamond Dots," *Charleston (NC) News and Courier*, Aug 12, 1891; "Struggling for the Championship," *Charleston News and Courier*, Aug 15, 1891; "Base Ball League," *Savannah (GA) Tribune*, Feb 13, 1892; *Savannah Tribune*, February 27, 1892; *Savannah Tribune*, March 5, 1892; "Chathams the Champion," *Savannah Tribune*, June 25, 1892.

National Base Ball Club (Savannah, GA; 1870s). Organizer(s): William Grant.

The National B.B.C. organized in the 1870s. The "Nationals" played against black nines. *Savannah Daily Advertiser* (June 7, 1871): "The Americas and Nationals, two colored ball clubs, met in a friendly contest yesterday, the former winning by a score of 63 to 25."

SOURCES: "Base Ball," *Savannah (GA) Advertiser*, Jun 7, 1871; "A Gan of Burglars Arrested," *Savannah Advertiser*, Aug 17, 1871.

Vigilant Base Ball Club (Thomasville, GA; 1880s–1900s). Organizer(s): William H. Reid, Jesse Daniels, Wash Jackson and Charley Key.

The Vigilant B.B.C. organized in the 1880s. The Vigilants, composed of firemen (the "Vigilant Fire Hose Company"), crossed bats black teams. *Thomasville Times-Enterprise* (August 13, 1896):

"Thomasville's colored base-ball club played against a club from Glasgow at Athletic Park yesterday and won the game in a walk, making 22 runs to the visitors 11. Quite a large crowd of people, white and black, witnessed the game, which, at times, was highly amusing."

SOURCES: "Colored Picnic," *Atlanta (GA) Constitution*, Jun 17, 1888; "Local Happenings," *Thomasville (GA) Times-Enterprise*, Aug 10, 1892; "Local Happenings," *Thomasville Times-Enterprise*, May 12, 1893; *Thomasville Times-Enterprise*, Sep 7, 1893; "Local Happenings," *Thomasville Times-Enterprise*, Sep 8, 1893; *Thomasville Times-Enterprise*, Apr 26, 1894; "Hurrah for the Vigilants," *Thomasville Times-Enterprise*, Sep 21, 1895; "The Water Fight," *Thomasville Times-Enterprise*, Mar 7, 1896; "The Fireman's Excursion," *Thomasville Times-Enterprise*, May 23, 1896; "Base Ball Today," *Thomasville Times-Enterprise*, June 17, 1896; "Local Happenings," *Thomasville Times-Enterprise*, Aug 13, 1896; "They Laid Out Thomasville," *Thomasville Times-Enterprise*, Aug 16, 1900.

Illinois

Brown Stocking Base Ball Club (Alton, IL; 1880s). Organizer(s): William Baker and William Bevenue.

The Brown Stocking B.B.C. organized in the 1880s. The Browns played white and black teams. *Alton Daily Telegraph* (September 26, 1885): "A colored base-ball club has been organized under the name of Brown Stockings." *Alton Telegraph* (July 30, 1886): "The champions of Grafton Road, the Melville Base Ball nine, were badly beaten by a colored club last Sunday. The champions feel a little sore over their defeat but hope to retrieve their laurels in a short time."

SOURCES: "City and County News," *Alton (IL) Telegraph*, Sep 26, 1885; "Local News," *Alton Telegraph*, October 1, 1885; "Reorganized," *Alton Telegraph*, April 8, 1886; "Melville," *Alton Telegraph*, July 15, 1886; "Melville," *Alton Telegraph*, July 30, 1886.

Magnolia Base Ball Club (Alton, IL; 1870s).

The Magnolia B.B.C. organized in the 1870s. The "Magnolias" played white and black nines. *Alton Weekly Telegraph* (July 12, 1872): "A match game of base-ball was played at Upper Alton on the 4th of July, between the first nine of the Magnolia, of the above place, and the first nine of the Atlantic, of this Alton, in which the latter were victorious." They played Shurtleffe College. *Alton Weekly Telegraph* (June 7, 1877): "An interesting game of base-ball was played Saturday afternoon on the college green, between a picked nine of the college boys and the Magnolia (colored club) of Upper Alton, score 22 to 9, in favor of the Shurtliffs. A return game is appointed for next Saturday." The Magnolias played Alton's Lonely Boys, another white team. *Alton Evening Telegraph* (June 28, 1877): "A coon game of base-ball was played on last Thursday at Rock Spring, between the Magnolias of Upper Alton and the Lonely Boys, of this city. Score, 7 to 4, in favor of the Magnolias." *Alton Weekly Telegraph* (August 23, 1877): "A good game of base-ball was played on last Thursday at Rock Spring, between the Magnolias of Upper Alton and the Lonely Boys, of this city. Score: 7 to 6, in favor of the Magnolias." In 1880, the Magnolia club reorganized as the Dreadnaught B.B.C.

SOURCES: "Base Ball," *Alton (IL) Weekly Telegraph*, Jul 12, 1872; "Base Ball," *Alton Weekly Telegraph*, Jun 7, 1877; *Alton Weekly Telegraph*, Jun 28, 1877; "Base Ball," *Alton Weekly Telegraph*, Aug 23, 1877; "Upper Alton," *Alton Weekly Telegraph*, May 7, 1880; "Upper Alton," *Weekly Telegraph, May 18, 1880.

Pickett Base Ball Club (Aurora, IL; 1890s)

The Pickett B.B.C. organized in the 1890s. The "Picketts" played against black teams. *Chicago Daily Inter-Ocean* (August 8, 1895): "The

Chicago Clippers will cross bats with the Aurora Picketts, at Aurora, for $25 a side and the gate receipts. Game will be played on Hurd's Island, Friday, August 9. Batteries are Somerville, Smith, and James of the Clippers; and Holland, McCann and Lane of the Pickets."

Sources: "Amateur Baseball," *Chicago (IL) Inter-Ocean*, Aug 8, 1895.

Sunset Base Ball Club (Aurora, IL; 1880s). Organizer(s): Augustus Demary.

The Sunset B.B.C. organized in the 1880s. The Sunsets played against black teams. *Rockford Gazette* (July 11, 1884): "They met upon the diamond green and bravely fought and well, but Rockford was too much for them, and just before the sable mantle of blackest night had fallen over the fairgrounds, the visitors gave up the contest, and hied themselves to the Edward House to seek a square and hearty meal. There were nine of them all told, and all colored, and they left the classic environs of Aurora to wrest the girdle of base-ball championship from their ebony hued brethren of the Forest City. The Auroraites were a well-built and gentlemanly set of players, and showed more than ordinary proficiency in playing, but they could not take as kindly to the Rockford pitcher as they desired, and the result was that they were beaten. The crowd of spectators was large, enthusiastic and good natured, and applauded the efforts of all alike. They watched with unbounded amusement the antics of the black-baseballists and roared with laughter at the droll remarks of the players."

Sources: Colored Troops," *Rockford (IL) Register*, Jul 11, 1884; *Rockford (IL) Gazette*, Jul 9, 1884; "Ethiopian Experts," *Rockford Gazette*, July 11, 1884.

Senegambian Base Ball Club (Aurora, IL; 1880s)

The Senegambian B.B.C. organized in the 1880s. The Senegambians played black organizations. Aurora and Rockford developed a rivalry. *Elgin News* (July 14, 1883): "A gentleman of sable complexion, attired in a gorgeous base-ball uniform, called on *Aurora Post* this afternoon, in the interest of the Rockford colored club, which came down to play the Aurora Senegambians. He says that the rain prevented the game today, and that the Auroras refuse to play tomorrow, assigning as a reason that they cannot leave work." *Rockford Gazette* (July 11, 1884): "They met upon the diamond green and bravely fought and well, but Rockford was too much for them, and just before the sable mantle of blackest night had fallen over the fairgrounds, the visitors gave up the contest, and hied themselves to the Edward House to seek a square and hearty meal. There were nine of them all told, and all colored, and they left the classic environs of Aurora to wrest the girdle of base-ball championship from their ebony hued brethren of the Forest City. The Auroraites were a well-built and gentlemanly set of players, and showed more than ordinary proficiency in playing, but they could not take as kindly to the Rockford pitcher as they desired, and the result was that they were beaten. The crowd of spectators was large, enthusiastic and good natured, and applauded the efforts of all alike. They watched with unbounded amusement the antics of the black-baseballists and roared with laughter at the droll remarks of the players." The rivalry remained strong. *Aurora Express* (September 19, 1889): "At the Emancipation celebration to be held here September 23, the baseball contest will be between the Black Stockings, of Elgin and the Dark Secrets, of Aurora—two first-class clubs." *Chicago Inter-Ocean*: "The Elgin Colored Base Ball Club came down Tuesday and grappled the Aurora Senegambians on the diamond. The victory perched on Aurora's standard, the score being 24 to 10."

Sources: "Base Ball," *Elgin (IL) Morning Frank*, Jul 14, 1883; "Aurora Again Beaten," *Elgin (IL) News*, Jul 17, 1883; "A Large Game,"

Elgin (IL) Advocate, Jul 17, 1883; *Rockford (IL) Gazette*, Jul 20, 1883; "Base Ball," *Elgin Morning Frank*, July 22, 1883; *Rockford (IL) Weekly Gazette*, Jul 25, 1883; *Rockford Gazette*, Aug 25, 1883; *Rockford Gazette*, Aug 29, 1883; "Colored Troops," *Rockford (IL) Register*, Jul 11, 1884; *Rockford Gazette*, Jul 9, 1884; "Ethiopian Experts," *Rockford Gazette*, Jul 11, 1884; *Aurora (IL) Express*, Sep 19, 1889; "Aurora Bulletin," *Chicago (IL) Inter-Ocean*, Sep 22, 1889.

Ashley House Base Ball Club (Bloomington, IL; 1870s). Owner(s): Henry Graham, James Holley, Henry Matthews, A. D. Scott and George Hazel.

The Ashley House B.B.C. organized in the 1870s, played black and white teams. *Bloomington Leader* (May 7, 1878): "The colored waiters of the Ashley House have organized a base-ball club, and have elected the following officers: President, Henry Graham; Vice President, James Holley; Secretary, Henry Matthews; Treasurer, A. D. Scott; Corresponding Secretary, George Hazel." *Bloomington Pantagraph* (June 22, 1878): "A match game of base-ball was played yesterday between the Ashley House nine an a picked nine. Six innings were played, resulting in a score of 8 to 3 in favor of the hotel nine."

Sources: "City Matters," *Bloomington (IL) Leader*, May 7, 1878; "Base Ball," *Bloomington (IL) Pantagraph*, Jun 22, 1878; "Personal," *Bloomington Pantagraph*, Jun 24, 1878.

Brown Stocking Base Ball Club (Bloomington, IL; 1870s)

The Brown Stocking B.B.C. organized in the 1870s, played black and white teams. *Bloomington Leader* (February 19, 1877): "The Holly Combination have reorganized their base-ball club for the season of '77, under the familiar cognomen of the Brown Sox." *Leader* (April 6, 1877): "The Holly Combination, alias Black Feet, and a picked nine, play a match game of base-ball tomorrow afternoon at the old circus ground, near the Central Depot." *Bloomington Pantagraph* (May 26, 1877): "The Brown Sox of Bloomington were defeated by a score of 19 to 9 yesterday by the Springfield Lone Stars. *Pantagraph* (June 14, 1877): "Two colored clubs named the Hard Hitters and Brown Sox, played a match game yesterday, the Hard Hitters beating the Browns by a score of 9 to 5."

Sources: "Local Matters," *Bloomington (IL) Leader*, Feb 19,1877; "City Matters," *Bloomington Leader*, Apr 6, 1877; "Base Ball," *Bloomington Leader*, May 15, 1877; "Base Ball Racket," *Bloomington Leader*, May 24, 1877; "The City," *Bloomington (IL) Pantagraph*, May 16, 1877; "Base Ball," *Bloomington Pantagraph*, May 26, 1877; "Base Ball," *Bloomington Pantagraph*, Jun 14, 1877; "Local Matters," *Springfield (IL) State Journal*, Jun 29, 1877.

Crusader Base Ball Club (Bloomington, IL; 1870s). Owner(s): M. Holly, F. Franklin, Henry Matthews, James Holly and R. Walden.

The Crusader B.B.C. organized in the 1870s, played black teams. *Bloomington Pantagraph* (May 26, 1874): Base-ball in black, this afternoon, at the Wesleyan grounds. The Crusaders of this city and the Atlantas, of Atlanta, all late of Africa will toss the bounding ball." *Bloomington Leader* (June 8, 1874): "The Crusader Base Ball Club will play a match game with the Atlantas, of Atlanta, next Wednesday. The Crusaders are requested to meet at the room of the captain tomorrow (Tuesday) morning. Our boys will go to Atlanta in a hack." *Leader* (June 12, 1874): "The Crusaders of this city beat the Atlantas last Wednesday by 10 runs at the challenge game of base-ball." *Leader* (June 25, 1874): "The Crusaders played a game of base-ball with the High School Club yesterday, beating them by 12 runs. This is the third match game the Crusaders have played and have not been beaten yet."

Sources: *Bloomington (IL) Leader*, May 13, 1874; *Bloomington (IL) Pantagraph*, May 26, 1874; "Local Matters," *Bloomington Leader*,

Jun 7, 1874; "Local Matters," *Bloomington Leader*, Jun 8, 1874; "Local Matters," *Bloomington Leader*, Jun 12, 1874; "Local Matters," *Bloomington Leader*, Jun 25, 1874.

Independent Base Ball Club (Bloomington, IL; 1860s–1870s). Owner(s): Marion Holly, George W. Holly, James Holly and George Hazel.

The Independent B.B.C. organized in the 1860s. The Independents played against white and black nines. *Bloomington Leader* (August 11, 1869): "The Union Base Ball Club, (white), and the Independent, (colored), played a friendly game of base-ball…. The colored club bore off the palm by a score of 26 to 10. Africa triumphant." Its main black rival was the Dexter Star club, of Springfield, IL. *Leader* (August 24, 1869): "The Bloomington Independents, composed of the smartest of our young colored men, has a colored club, have gone to Springfield to play a match game with the Dexter Base Ball Club, of that city. They made a very presentable appearance in their turbans and belts."

SOURCES: "Mixed Match," *Bloomington (IL) Leader*, Aug 11, 1869; "Bloomington Independents," *Bloomington Leader*, Aug 24, 1869; "Match at Springfield—Bloomington Colored Men Ahead," *Bloomington Leader*, Aug 26, 1869; "Local Notices," *Bloomington Leader*, Apr 27, 1870; "Base Ball Club," *Bloomington Daily Leader*, Apr 28, 1870; "Mixed Match," *Bloomington (IL) Pantagraph*, Apr 28, 1870; "Base Ball Match," *Bloomington Leader*, Jul 7, 1870.

Red Stocking Base Ball Club (Bloomington, IL; 1880s)

The Red Stocking B.B.C. organized in the 1880s. The Red Stockings played black teams. *Indianapolis Freeman* (June 8, 1889): "Bloomington, Illinois, has a colored club, the Bloomington 'Reds,' which challenges any colored club in the United States except the Cuban Giants, for one to five hundred dollars a side."

SOURCES: "Base Ball News," *Indianapolis (IN) Freeman*, Jun 8, 1889.

Clipper Base Ball Club (Cairo, IL; 1870s)

The Clipper B.B.C. organized in 1871, played against black nines. *Cairo Bulletin* (September 24, 1871): "A colored base-ball club of Paducah visited Cairo yesterday and played a match game with the Clipper club of this city. The Cairo boys, as expected, defeated the Paducah club without difficulty—cleaned them out with neatness and dispatch."

SOURCES: "Brevities," *Cairo (IL) Bulletin*, September 8, 1871; "Brevities," *Cairo Bulletin*, Sep 9, 1871; "Local Notes," *Cairo Bulletin*, Sep 24, 1871.

Quickstep Base Ball Club (Cairo, IL; 1870s). Organizer(s): Reuben Smith and Elias Coleman.

The Quickstep B.B.C. organized in 1874. The Quicksteps played against black organizations. The Quicksteps received a challenge from the Oziahs of Charleston, MO, an aggregation that claimed to be champions of three states. The Quicksteps defeated them, by a score of 65 to 8.

SOURCES: "Match Game of Base Ball by Colored Clubs," *Cairo (IL) Bulletin*, Oct 6, 1874; "Colored Base Ball," *Cairo Bulletin*, October 7, 1874.

Egyptian Base Ball Club (Cairo, IL; 1890s). Organizer(s): W. T. Scott; Wilson Ricks.

The Egyptian B.B.C. organized in 1890s, played against black organizations. *Indianapolis Freeman* (May 16, 1891): "The Egyptian Base Ball Club gave an entertainment last week, and an immense crowd was in attendance. On Sunday May 10th, the Paducahs and the Egyptian Base Ball Club crossed bats in a contest." *Springfield State Capital* (May 9, 1891): "W. T. Scott is making elaborate prepa-

rations for his baseball game at the fairgrounds next Sunday." *Indianapolis Freeman* (May 23, 1891): "The West End Base Ball Club, of St. Louis, will contest with the Egyptian Base Ball Club of Cairo, May 30th and 31st. Cairo has a strong club managed by W. T. Scott. *State Capital* (June 6, 1891): "The Egypt and West End baseball nines crossed bats at the fairground, Saturday, May 30th, the West Enders were too much for the Egypts, 8 to 2 in favor of the West End."

SOURCES: "Cairo Items," *Springfield (IL) State Capital*, May 9, 1891; "The Egyptian News," *Indianapolis (IN) Freeman*, May 16, 1891; "Met with an Accident," *Indianapolis Freeman*, May 23, 1891; "Doings of the Week," *Springfield State Capital*, Jun 6, 1891; "Local and Personal," *Centralia (IL) Sentinel*, Apr 26, 1895; "Acme Social Reception," *Indianapolis Freeman*, May 18, 1895.

Colored Base Ball Club (Centralia, IL; 1880s)

The Colored B.B.C. organized in the 1880s. The black nine played white and black organizations. *Centralia Sentinel* (April 22, 1886): "Our colored base-ball club have received a challenge from the colored club of DuQuoin. It is thought that these giants will attempt to knock each other out about May 1st. May the colored troops fight nobly and the best nine win."

SOURCES: "City in Abstract," *Centralia (IL) Sentinel*, Jun 20, 1885; "The City," *Centralia Sentinel*, Jul 1, 1885; *Centralia Sentinel*, Apr 1, 1886; *Centralia Sentinel*, Apr 8, 1886; *Centralia Sentinel*, Apr 19, 1886; "Local Paragraphs," *Centralia Sentinel*, Aug 8, 1886.

Lilly White Base Ball Club (Centralia, IL; 1890s). Organizer(s): Wade Duncan.

The Lilly White B.B.C. organized in the 1890s. The Lilly Whites played white and black organizations. *Centralia Sentinel* (June 1, 1893): "The Lilly Whites, the crack colored base-ball club of this city, are arranging for a series of twelve games to be played here this season, and will bloom out in a few days with a complete new outfit, uniform and all. They are open for challenges, white or colored from anywhere." *Sentinel* (June 24, 1893): "The Lilly Whites and a colored nine [Black Diamonds] from Springfield will play ball at the fairgrounds on August 3." *Sentinel* (August 4, 1893): "The ball game at the fairgrounds yesterday afternoon between the Spartan Kickers and Lilly Whites was a double headed contest. It required four hours and forty minutes to play the game, three hours of which was consumed in kicks and wrangling. The score stood 18 to 9 for the Lilly Whites." *Sentinel* (July 5, 1894): "The Lilly Whites went to Carlyle yesterday and knocked the colored club of that city out of town. The score was 40 to 7 in favor of the Lilly Whites."

SOURCES: "Emancipation Day," *Centralia (IL) Sentinel*, Aug 2, 1892; "Local and Personal," *Centralia Sentinel*, May 20, 1893; "Local and Personal," *Centralia Sentinel*, Jun 1, 1893; *Centralia Sentinel*, Aug 8, 1893; "Local and Personal," *Centralia Sentinel*, Jul 5, 1894; "Local and Personal," *Centralia Sentinel*, Aug 2, 1894.

None Such Base Ball Club (Centralia, IL; 1890s)

The None Such B.B.C. organized in the 1890s. The None Such played white and black organizations. *Centralia Sentinel* (July 29, 1897): "The colored boys have organized a ball club and have been practicing fast and furious for over a week. They have arranged for two games with the Carbondale colored club, to be played here on August 3rd and 4th and stand ready to meet all comers regardless of color or size. The boys have named the club None Such and have a challenge to all clubs in Southern Illinois and they would especially like to tackle the colored team from Sparta." *Sentinel* (August 4, 1897): "Our None Such colored base-ball went to Mt. Vernon Saturday and met a colored club from Mt. Vernon, Indiana, and mowed them down to the tune of 26 to 9."

SOURCES: *Centralia (IL) Sentinel*, Jul 29, 1897; "Local and Personal," *Centralia Sentinel*, Aug 4, 1897.

Clipper Base Ball Club (Champaign, IL; 1890s)

The Clipper B.B.C. organized in the 1890s, played black nines. *Bloomington Leader* (July 26, 1893): "The colored base-ball team went over to Champaign today to play the colored team [Clippers]of that city. They play for the gate receipts. Bob McCreary and Otis Barton are the battery for the home team. A hot game is expected."

SOURCES: "City in Abstract," *Bloomington (IL) Leader*, Jul 15, 1893; "Play Ball in Champaign," *Bloomington Leader*, Jul 26, 1893; "Personal Mention," *Bloomington Leader*, Aug 11, 1894; "Archie Too Swift," *Bloomington Leader*, Sep 1, 1894.

Acme Base Ball Club (Chicago, IL; 1880s). Organizer(s): William Albert Jones and Andrew M. Porter.

The Acme B.B.C. organized in the 1880s. The Acme club played black and white nines. *Philadelphia Sporting Life* (May 27, 1885): "The Acme Base Ball Club, colored, of Chicago, has organized for the season of 1885. Would be pleased to hear from or arrange games. Address, Andrew M. Porter, secretary, 2938 State Street." The Acmes played black and white nines. *Milwaukee Sentinels* (May 31, 1885): "The reorganized Milwaukee Whites, and the Acmes, of Chicago, cross bats this afternoon at Milwaukee's Park. The Acme club is the successor to the famous colored Gordons, and contains a number of the best players of that well-known team." *Milwaukee Journal:* "About 400 persons saw a game of ball yesterday between the reorganized Milwaukee Whites and the colored Acmes, of Chicago, played on the Wright Street Grounds. The Whites played a strong game wand won easily by a score of 15 to 4."

SOURCES: "Notes and Comments," *Philadelphia (PA) Sporting Life*, May 27, 1885; "Sunday baseball Games," *Milwaukee (WI) Sentinel*, May 31, 1885; "Sports and Sportsmen," *Milwaukee (WI) Journal*, Jun 1, 1885; "Local Sunday Games," *Milwaukee (WI) Sentinel*, Jun 1, 1885.

Artic Base Ball Club (Chicago, IL; 1890s). Organizer(s): Robert Jackson.

The Artic B.B.C. organized in the 1890s. The Artics played against local white and black teams. *Chicago Inter-Ocean* (April 21, 1890): "The Artics and Hartmans played at Sixty-Third Street and Cottage Grove Avenue yesterday. The result was a victory for the Artics by a score of 8 to 5. The features of the game were the battery work of Anderson and Starks, of the Artics, and the timely batting of Lee, Campbell, Starks, Anderson and Peterson." *Inter-Ocean* (May 5, 1890): "By the addition of Hasting Brown and James Thompson the Artics have completed their team and have arranged games with the following clubs: Crystals, Hartmans, and Jefferson Grays. They would like to hear from out-of-town clubs at once. Good games can be had by addressing Robert Jackson, Cottage Grove Postal Station."

SOURCES: "Amateur Ball Players," *Chicago (IL) Inter-Ocean*, Apr 21, 1890; "Among the Amateurs," *Chicago Inter-Ocean*, May 5, 1890; "Among the Amateurs," *Chicago Inter-Ocean*, May 26, 1890; "Coming Base Ball Stars," *Chicago Inter-Ocean*, Jun 2, 1890; "Among the Amateurs," *Chicago Inter-Ocean*, Jul 14, 1890.

Auditorium Base Ball Club (Chicago, IL; 1890s). Organizer(s): Scipio Spinks.

The Auditorium B.B.C. organized in the 1890s. The Auditoriums, composed of hotel waiters, played against similar organizations. *Chicago Inter-Ocean* (July 6, 1891): "The Uniques defeated the Auditoriums, Hotel League champions, at Grand Crossing, by the score of 11 to 1." *Chicago Tribune* (May 24, 1891): "The Auditoriums defeated the Tremonts on the Lake Front by a score of 18 to 11. The features of the game were the catching of Starks and Spinks' two home runs." They developed a rivalry with the Tremonts. *Chicago Tribune* (June 13, 1891): "The Auditoriums defeated the Black Stockings in a ten-inning game yesterday on the South Side City League grounds by a score of 8 to 5. The game was for $50 a side."

SOURCES: "Amateur Ball Notes," *Chicago (IL) Tribune*, Jul 22, 1890; "Amateur Ball Notes," *Chicago Tribune*, Aug 10, 1890; "General City News," *Chicago Tribune*, Aug 21, 1890; "Amateur Ball Notes," *Chicago Tribune*, Aug 25, 1890; "Amateur Base Ball Notes," *Chicago Tribune*, Sep 7, 1890; "Amateur Base Ball Notes," *Chicago Tribune*, Sep 10, 1890; "Amateur Ball Tossers," *Chicago Tribune*, Sep 12, 1890; "Among the Amateurs," *Chicago (IL) Times*, May 23, 1891; "Amateur Notes," *Chicago Tribune*, May 24, 1891; "Amateur Baseball Notes," *Chicago Tribune*, June 8, 1891; Amateur Baseball Notes," *Chicago Tribune*, June 13, 1891; "Among the Amateurs," *Chicago Times*, June 15, 1891; "Among the Amateurs," *Chicago Times*, June 23, 1891; "Among the Amateurs," *Chicago Times*, June 25, 1891; "Among the Local Amateurs," *Chicago (IL) Herald*, Jun 26, 1891; "Among Local Amateurs," *Chicago (IL) Herald*, June 27, 1891; "Amateur Baseball Notes," *Chicago Tribune*, June 28, 1891; "Amateur Ball," *Chicago (IL) Inter-Ocean*, Jul 6, 1891; "Amateur Base Ball," *Chicago Inter-Ocean*, Jul 27, 1891.

Australian Giants Base Ball Club (Chicago, IL. Organizer(s): Frank Leland, Edward Brown and Orange Fox; 1880s).

The Australian Giants B.B.C. is significant, no so much for its brief usage than for what the nickname implied. On July 4, 1889, Fox (a founding member of Chicago's Union club, originally from Cincinnati) announced a national search for players, and organized the "Australian Giants." The nickname cashed in on the novelty of Albert Goodwill Spalding's 1888 Australian Base Ball Tour. Edward Brown, a veteran baseballist and the club's team president, knew something about Australia well before Spalding's tour. In 1874, Brown, William Speed and R. Moody played for Chicago's Pytheus nine. In 1878, Moody and Speed had joined Hicks's GA Minstrel Company. Between 1879 and 1891, the Georgia Minstrels (and later, Cleveland's Colossal Colored Minstrels) performed in Australia and New Zealand. They also played baseball: in 1879, the Kilda B.B.C. (white), Australia's first team, organized specifically to play the Georgia Minstrels in a series of games. Brown maintained contact with Billy Speed and Moody. The exotic nature of their transatlantic experiences perhaps influenced the name choice. On July 10, 1889, Fox announced that the name would be changed to Resolutes.

SOURCES: "Amateur Base Ball," *Chicago (IL) Sunday Times*, Apr 25, 1875; "Hicks and Sawyer's Minstrels," *New York (NY) Freeman*, May 28, 1887; "The Diamond," *San Francisco (CA) Daily Alta*, Jul 28, 1888; "Sporting Echoes," Brisbane, Queensland (AUS) *Figaro and Punch*, Nov 8, 1888; *Wellington (NZ) Evening Post*, Nov 8, 1888; "Base Ball in New Zealand," *New York (NY) Herald*, Dec 30, 1888; "Base Ball in Wellington," Sydney (AUS) *Star*, Mar 6, 1889; "Base Ball," Adelaide (AUS) *Advertiser*, Apr 11, 1889; "Base Ball Match," Broken Hill, NSW (AUS) *Barrier Miner*, Apr 29, 1889; "Amateur Base Ball," *Chicago (IL) Inter-Ocean*, Jul 7, 1889; *Chicago (IL) Herald*, Jul 10, 1889; "New Notes," *Los Angeles (CA) Herald*, Feb 21, 1890; "New Notes," *Los Angeles Herald*, October 27, 1890; "New Notes," *Los Angeles Herald*, October 28, 1890; "Base Ball," *Los Angeles Herald*, October 31, 1890; "Cleveland's Colored Minstrels," *Worcester (MA) Spy*, May 12, 1891.

Avondale Base Ball Club (Chicago, IL; 1890s). Organizer(s): Andrew "Andy" Porter and James Thompson.

The Avondale B.B.C. organized in the 1890s. The Avondales, composed of waiters—including members of the Uniques and Chicago Unions—played against white and black aggregations. *Chicago Inter-Ocean* (June 15, 1895): "The Avondales defeated the Heaneys at

Avondale by a score of 9 to 2 May 24. The batteries were John Meyer, Arthur Anderson and Hastings Brown for the Avondales and Moore and Triesselman of the Heaneys."

SOURCES: "Amateur Baseball," *Chicago (IL) Inter-Ocean*, Jun 15, 1895; "Amateur Baseball," *Chicago Inter-Ocean*, August 10, 1895; "Amateur Baseball," *Chicago Inter-Ocean*, August 14, 1895; "Amateur Baseball," *Chicago Inter-Ocean*, August 26, 1895; "Amateur Base Ball," *Chicago Inter-Ocean*, May 6, 1896; "Amateur Base Ball," *Chicago Inter-Ocean*, May 29, 1896; "With the Amateurs," *Chicago Inter-Ocean*, July 2, 1896; "With the Amateurs," *Chicago Inter-Ocean*, August 8, 1896.

Beach Hotel Base Ball Club (Chicago, IL; 1900s)

The Beach Hotel B.B.C. organized in the 1900s. *Indianapolis Freeman* (August 4, 1900): "The Chicago Beach Waiters versus Windermere, was one of intense action and excitement. Not a score was made until the fourth inning by the Chicago Beach Henry Sherman, the giant first baseman, two men reached home plate but Mr. Sherman was left on third base. 'Snake, the Darktown pitcher,' did wonderful work for the Windermere. The Windermeres scored 3, the Chicago Beach 2."

SOURCES: "Gleaned From Hyde Park," *Indianapolis (IN) Freeman*, Aug 4, 1900.

Black Stocking Base Ball Club (Chicago, IL; 1880s–1890s). Organizer(s): Edward Prime.

The Black Stocking B.B.C. organized in the 1880s. The Black Stockings played white and black teams. *Chicago Inter-Ocean* (August 19, 1889): "The Models, as usual, took the Black Stockings into camp by the following score, 20 to 1. Heavy batting of the Models was a feature of the game." The Black Stockings played nines. *Inter-Ocean* (June 13, 1891): "The Auditoriums defeated the Chicago Black Stockings in a ten-inning game yesterday on the Southwest City League Grounds by a score of 8 to 5. The game was for $50 dollars a side. The batteries were Johnson and Stark; Smith and Ferguson. The batteries were: For the Auditoriums: Johnson and Stark; for the Black Stockings: Foster and Ferguson. Johnson struck out seventeen batters."

SOURCES: "Miscellaneous Games," *Chicago (IL) Inter-Ocean*, Aug 18, 1889; "Models, 20; Black Stockings 1," *Chicago Inter-Ocean*, August 19, 1889; "They Want to Play," *Chicago Inter-Ocean*, Aug 25, 1889; "Amateur Ball Players," *Chicago Inter-Ocean*, Mar 16, 1890; "Amateur Notes," *Chicago Inter-Ocean*, May 18, 1890; "Among the Amateurs," *Chicago Inter-Ocean*, May 5, 1890; *Chicago (IL) Tribune*, May 22, 1890; "Among the Amateurs," *Chicago Inter-Ocean*, May 26, 1890; "Coming Base Ball Stars," *Chicago Inter-Ocean*, Jun 2, 1890; "Among the Amateurs," *Chicago Inter-Ocean*, Jul 14, 1890; "Amateur Ball Notes," *Chicago Tribune*, Aug 25, 1890; "Amateur Baseball Notes," *Chicago Tribune*, Jun 13, 1891; "Amateur Baseball Notes," *Chicago Tribune*, Jun 15, 1891.

Chadwick Base Ball Club (Chicago, IL; 1890s)

The Chadwick B.B.C. organized in the 1890s. The Chadwicks played black and white teams. *Chicago Tribune* (June 1, 1890): "The Chadwicks defeated the Gordons at Washington Park. The features of the game were Trumbal's batting and Gill's pitching. The batteries were Gill and Gates of the Chadwicks and Starbuck and Williams of the Gordons."

SOURCES: "Amateur Notes," *Chicago (IL) Tribune*, Jun 1, 1890; "Amateur Base-Ball Notes," *Chicago Tribune*, Jul 21, 1890; "Amateur Baseball Notes," *Chicago Tribune*, Jun 24, 1891.

Clipper Base Ball Club (Chicago, IL; 1880s–1900s). Organizer(s): William James Renfroe; Edward Bowen; Frank Griggs.

The Clipper B.B.C. organized in 1889. The Clippers played black and white aggregations. *Chicago Inter-Ocean* (September 15, 1890):

"The Chicago Unions defeated the Clippers at Grand Crossing yesterday. The feature of the game was the heavy batting of the Unions." The Clippers and Eclipse nines briefly consolidated, with Edward Bowen as manager. *Inter-Ocean* (July 1, 1893): "The Chicago Clippers will play the Leaders, Of Milwaukee, next Sunday at Clippers' Park, 48th and Halsted Streets. The Clippers have consolidated with the Eclipse Baseball Club." *Inter-Ocean* (August 26, 1895): "The Chicago Clippers defeated the Avondales at Avondale. The batteries were Smith and James of the Clippers; and Meyers and Porter of the Avondales." Many of the players came from KY and TN: among them, Ewell Scales, Harry Buckner and John Mansfield. The Clippers played on the road, WI and IN. *Inter-Ocean* (September 19, 1897): "The Chicago Clippers defeated the crack Momence team of Momence, Illinois, at Morocco, Indiana, by a score of 14 to 7. The features of the game were the effective pitching of Jackson of the Clippers and the Clippers' batting and general team work."

SOURCES: "Jefferson," *Chicago (IL) Inter-Ocean*, Apr 28, 1889; "Amateur Base Ballists," *Chicago Inter-Ocean*, Sep 15, 1890; "Outside the Diamond," *Chicago Inter-Ocean*, Jul 1, 1893; "Atlas 28; Clippers, 3," *Chicago Inter-Ocean*, Jul 24, 1893; "Amateur Base Ball," *Chicago Inter-Ocean*, Jun 21, 1895; "Amateur Baseball," *Chicago Inter-Ocean*, Jul 29, 1895; "On Local Diamonds," *Chicago Inter-Ocean*, Jul 29, 1895; "Amateur Baseball," *Chicago Inter-Ocean*, Aug 8, 1895; "Amateur Baseball," *Chicago Inter-Ocean*, Aug 14, 1895; "Amateur Baseball," *Chicago Inter-Ocean*, Aug 26, 1895; "With the Amateurs," *Chicago Inter-Ocean*, Aug 27, 1896; "With the Amateurs," *Chicago Inter-Ocean*, Jun 22, 1897; "With the Amateurs," *Chicago Inter-Ocean*, May 1, 1898; With the Amateurs," *Chicago Inter-Ocean*, Jun 1, 1898; "Other Games Yesterday," *Chicago (IL) Tribune*, Jul 18, 1898; "Other Local Contests," *Chicago Tribune*, Jun 19, 1899; "Another Colored Baseball Team," *Chicago Tribune*, Mar 19, 1900.

Columbia Giants Base Ball Club (Chicago, IL; 1890s–1900s). Organizer(s): Julius Avendorph and William Cowans.

The Columbia Giants B.B.C. organized in the 1890s. The Columbia Giants played white and black aggregations. Julius N. Avendorph and William Cowans financed the team. The Kentuckian, Cowans, a real estate and insurance agent, had been involved with baseball since 1882. Avendorph, a Fisk University graduate, was player/manager for Chicago's Emergencies, of the Social League. *Des Moines Iowa Capital* (April 21, 1899): "The Columbian Giants and the local team played baseball here. It was a fine exhibition of the national game. Score 7 to 5 in favor of the Giants." *Detroit Free Press* (May 15, 1899): "The score in today's game between the Columbian Giants and the Chatham Canadian League team was 5 to 2 in favor of the Giants. It looked like a shut out up to the eighth, when the Reds managed to get a man across home plate. They tallied one more in the ninth. The game was hotly contested from start to finish." *Free Press* (August 10, 1899): "The Flint team was defeated by the Columbian Giants today in the presence of a large crowd. The Giants won the game with the stick, hitting the ball hard and often. [George] Wilson performed the feat of hitting the ball three times over the track for home runs." *Chicago Tribune* (April 15, 1900): "The Columbia Giants, the crack colored team, played an exhibition game here this afternoon with the Milwaukee American team. The Giants made some brilliant plays. Buckner made two home runs." *Chicago Tribune* (June 25, 1900): "The Columbia Giants defeated the Cuban Giants at the former's park, Thirty-ninth street and Wentworth avenue, in a close and exciting game. The Cubans tied the score in the eighth inning, and in the Columbia's half of the ninth inning Burns, the first man up, was thrown out at first from third base, and Johnson, the second man up, hit the ball over the centerfield fence, thereby winning the game."

Sources: "With the Amateurs," *Chicago (IL) Inter-Ocean*, Jun 27, 1897; "With the Amateurs," *Chicago Inter-Ocean*, Sep 25, 1897; "Voice of the People," *Chicago (IL) Tribune*, Jan 31, 1898; *Racine (WI) Daily Journal*, May 1, 1898; "The Columbia Club Picnic," *Springfield (IL) Record*, Jul 23, 1898; "William Cowans Carries the Columbia Club into Athletics," *Springfield Record*, Feb 11, 1899; "Columbian Giants Win," *Des Moines (IA) Iowa Capital*, Apr 21, 1899; "The Columbia Club's Colored Champions," *Springfield Record*, Mar 18, 1899; "Giants Keep Winning," *Detroit (MI) Free Press*, May 5, 1899; "Columbia Giants Play At Home," *Chicago Tribune*, May 13, 1899; "Columbia Giants, 12; Spaldings, 1," *Chicago Tribune*, Jun 12, 1899; "Amateur Baseball," *Detroit Free Press*, Aug 10, 1899; "Columbia Giants Win Again," *Chicago Tribune*, Aug 14, 1899; "Milwaukee, 8; Columbian Giants, 4," *Chicago Tribune*, Apr 15, 1900; "Field of Sports," *Logansport (IN) Daily Journal*, Apr 30, 1900; "Columbia Giants, 5; South Bend, 0," *Chicago Inter-Ocean*, May 7, 1900; "Columbia Giants, 10; Cuban Giants, 9," *Chicago Tribune*, Jun 25, 1900.

Cuban Giants No. 2 Base Ball Club (Chicago, IL; 1880s)

The Cuban Giants No. 2 B.B.C. organized in the 1880s. The Cuban Giants No. 2 measured bats with black teams. They played a series of games against Chicago's West Side Browns, defeating them in the opening contest by a score of 32 to 0. After agreeing to play for money, the latter club regrouped. *Chicago Tribune* (May 7, 1888): "The West Side Browns defeated the Green Cuban Giants by a score of 16 to 4 for $25. The Browns are now ready to play any club outside the fence for from $10 to $50."

Sources: "Local Base Ball Contests," *Chicago (IL) Tribune*, Apr 30, 1888; "Cuban Giants, 32; Browns, 0," *Chicago (IL) Inter-Ocean*, Apr 30, 1888; "Browns, 16; Giants, 4," *Chicago Inter-Ocean*, May 1, 1888; "Base Ball Notes," *Chicago Inter-Ocean*, May 6, 1888; "Other Games," *Chicago Tribune*, May 7, 1888.

Eclipse Base Ball Club (Chicago, IL; 1890s)

The Eclipse B.B.C. organized in the 1890s. The Eclipse played black and white organizations. The Chicago *Inter-Ocean* (June 16, 1894): "Bowen's Eclipse Baseball Club, formerly the 'South Ends,' have recently organized with Ed Bowen as manager, and are ready to meet all comers. This club was one of the strongest and most successful colored clubs in the past, and it still claims the championship, and to hold the title it issues a challenge to play any of the local teams." In 1893, Chicago's Clippers and Eclipse clubs briefly consolidated. *Indianapolis Freeman* (August 11, 1894): "The Eclipse Base-Ball Club, of Chicago, has challenged the Freeman club for a series of three games during the Pythian conclave. Manager Knox wired manager Bowen, of the Eclipse, his acceptance, and arrangements are to be made to give the Chicago boys a royal reception." *Inter-Ocean* (July 29, 1895): "The Chicago Clippers defeated the Eclipse at the Lake Front. The batteries were Somerville, Smith and Green, of the Clippers, and Rivers, Scott and Matt, of the Eclipse.

Sources: "Outside the Diamond," *Chicago (IL) Inter-Ocean*, Jul 1, 1893; "Unions vs. Eclipses," *Chicago Inter-Ocean*, Jun 16, 1894; "Champion Eclipse Club," *Chicago Inter-Ocean*, Jun 16, 1894; "Town Talk," *Indianapolis (IN) Freeman*, Aug 11, 1894; "Base Ball," *Indianapolis Freeman*, Aug 25, 1894; "Sport," *Indianapolis Freeman*, May 11, 1895; "Notes of the Club," *Indianapolis Freeman*, May 25, 1895; "On Local Diamonds," *Chicago Inter-Ocean*, Jul 29, 1895; "Amateur Baseball," *Chicago Inter-Ocean*, Aug 8, 1895; "Amateur Baseball," *Chicago Inter-Ocean*, Aug 14, 1895; "Amateur Baseball," *Chicago Inter-Ocean*, Aug 26, 1895.

Emergency Base Ball Club (Chicago, IL; 1890s–1900s). Organizer(s): Julius N. Avendorph.

The Emergency B.B.C. organized in 1894. The "Emergencies," organized by Julius N. Avendorph, belonged to the Colored Society Base Ball League. Between 1894 and 1900, they played similar organizations, semi-professionals and amateurs; white and black. They played for the benefit of Chicago's Provident Hospital, a black institution. *Chicago Inter-Ocean* (June 21, 1895): "The Provident and Emergencies, two crack colored teams, will play an amateur championship game at the Union Grounds, Thirty-Seventh and Butler Streets. The batteries will be McRoberts and Sherman, Smith and Collier." *Inter-Ocean* (August 12, 1896): "The Emergencies played and defeated the West Side Oakleys at Unions' Ball Park by a score of 11 to 10. The feature of the game was the pitching of Renfro of the Emergencies, who only allowed the Oakleys to make two safe hits. Captain Avendorph carried off the batting honors. The game was hotly contested from beginning to end. Andrews of the Oakleys covered the second base in great style." *Inter-Ocean* (August 22, 1897): "The Emergencies would like to arrange a Sunday game with the Standards of Joliet, Illinois [white team], a game to be played in Joliet. The Emergencies are composed of the best colored young men of Chicago. Address Julius N. Avendorph, No. 125 Dearborn street." *St. Paul Western Appeal* (August 25, 1900): "The Emergency Base Ball team of the South Side, under the captaincy of Mr. Julius N. Avendorph, and the Standards of the West Side [black team], under the captaincy of Mr. Ray Shelton, will play a game of ball at Columbia Park, 39th Street, near Wentworth Avenue, Saturday afternoon, August 18th. This will be a very interesting game, as the rivalry between the South and west Siders runs high. This will be the society base-ball game of the season. Emergencies' are colors, yellow and blue."

Sources: "Benefit of Provident Hospital," *Chicago (IL) Inter-Ocean*, July 16, 1894; "Amateur Baseball," *Chicago Inter-Ocean*, July 22, 1894; "Colored Charity Ball," *Chicago Inter-Ocean*, June 30, 1895; "With the Amateurs," *Chicago Inter-Ocean*, Jun 21, 1896; "With the Amateurs," *Chicago Inter-Ocean*, Aug 2, 1896; "Colored Society Folk as Minstrels," *Chicago (IL) Tribune*, Jan 6, 1897; "With the Amateurs," *Chicago Inter-Ocean*, May 19, 1897; "With the Amateurs," *Chicago Inter-Ocean*, Jun 24, 1897; *Chicago Inter-Ocean*, Aug 22, 1897; "With the Amateurs," *Chicago Inter-Ocean*, Sep 25, 1897; "Society Base Ball Game," *St. Paul (MN) Western Appeal*, Aug 4, 1900; "Chicago," *St. Paul (MN) Appeal*, Aug 18, 1900; "Capt. Avendorph's Emergencies Defeat the Standards," *St. Paul Appeal*, Aug 25, 1900.

Famous Bar Boys Base Ball Club (Chicago, IL; 1890s). Organizer(s): Joe Robertson.

The Famous Bar Boys B.B.C. organized in the 1890s. The Bar Boys played black teams. *Chicago Inter-Ocean* (August 20, 1896): "The Famous Bar Boys will play the West Side Favorites today at the Unions' Park, Thirty-Seventh and Butler Streets, for $50 a side. The Bar Boys are managed by Joe Robertson, and his team has played ten games without a defeat. The Favorites are managed by Chadwell of the West Sides." *Inter-Ocean* (September 2, 1896): "The Chicago Unions will play the Chicago Bar Boys tomorrow at Unions' ball park. The Unions will have in the box their new pitcher, [Charles] Morgan, and if he proves alright he will leave with the team Thursday night for Yorkville, where they play Friday."

Sources: "With the Amateurs," *Chicago (IL) Inter-Ocean*, Aug 20, 1896; "With the Amateurs," *Chicago Inter-Ocean*, September 2, 1896.

Favorites Base Ball Club (Chicago, IL; 1890s). Organizer(s): Chadwell.

The Favorites B.B.C. organized in the 1890s, played black teams. *Chicago Inter-Ocean* (August 20, 1896): "The Famous Bar Boys will play the West Side Favorites today at the Unions' Park, Thirty-

Seventh and Butler Streets, for $50 a side. The Bar Boys are managed by Joe Robertson, and his team has played ten games without a defeat. The Favorites are managed by Chadwell of the West Sides."

Sources: "With the Amateurs," *Chicago (IL) Inter-Ocean, Aug* 20, 1896.

Flipper Base Ball Club (Chicago, IL; 1890s)

The Flipper B.B.C. organized in the 1890s. They played against black aggregations. *Chicago Inter-Ocean* (July 6, 1897): "The Chicago Flippers (colored) have organized for the season, and would like to hear from the Racine, Joliet, Kankakee, Elgin, Dundee, Momence, and other clubs. The Chicago Flippers line up as follows: Greene, Smith, Arnett, Shaw, Bradley, Butler, Evans, Sharp, Buckner, and James."

Sources: "With the Amateurs," *Chicago (IL) Inter-Ocean,* Jul 6, 1897; "With the Amateurs," *Chicago Inter-Ocean,* Aug 17, 1897; "With the Amateurs," *Chicago Inter-Ocean,* Sep 25, 1897.

Garden City Base Ball Club (Chicago, IL; 1880s). Organizer(s): William Albert Jones ("Abe" Jones).

The Garden City B.B.C. organized in the early 1880s. The club competed against other black nines. The Garden Citys played Elgin's black team, the Adelaide club. *Elgin Morning Frank* (August 21, 1883): "The Garden Citys walked away from the Adelaides to the tune of 42 to 27. The visitors could about as easily have made the score 100 to 0." They played against Aurora's Senegambian nine. *Aurora Daily Express* (September 22, 1883): "The colored nine from Chicago who played the Jumbos of this city, at the fairgrounds yesterday, won the game by a score of 20 to 9."

Sources: "Base Ball," *Elgin (IL) Morning Frank,* Aug 13, 1883; "Base Ball," *Elgin Morning Frank,* August 15, 1883; "Base Ball," *Elgin Morning Frank,* August 16, 1883; "Base Ball," *Elgin Morning Frank,* August 21, 1883; "They Played a Picked Nine," *Elgin (IL) Daily News,* Aug 21, 1883; "About the City," *Aurora (IL) Daily Express,* Sep 22, 1883.

Garrett Base Ball Club (Chicago, IL; 1890s)

The Garrett B.B.C. organized in 1890. *Western Appeal* (April 26, 1890): "The Garrett Base Ball and Social Club meet every Tuesday evening at 8 o'clock at 215 Ferdinand Street. Anyone wishing to join may do so by addressing R. Harris, 807 Austin Avenue, or Charles Spears 215 Ferdinand Street. The following are the members: C. Thompson, B. Jackson, G. Cheatham, C. Bennett, S. French, S. Barber, F. Spears, R. Harris, C. McGowan, George Grant, A. Garrett, J. Beasley, J. Blackburn."

Sources: "Base-Ball and Social Club," *St. Paul (MN) Western Appeal,* Apr 26, 1890.

Gordon Base Ball Club (Chicago, IL) (Chicago, IL; 1880s–1890s). Organizer(s): H. N. Fisher, Harry Teenan Jones and Jack Gordon; William Albert Jones; William C. Sutliffe.

The Gordon B.B.C. organized in 1884. Between 1884 and 1893, the Gordons established a reputation in the Northwest by playing strong black and white clubs. They claimed the title colored champions of the United States. Before five thousand spectators, they played the Milwaukee Cream Citys, a white organization. The Gordons played several WI nines, including the Green Bays. *Green Bay Press Gazette* (July 5, 1884): "At the Base Ball Park was the leading feature in this line, between the Gordons, of Chicago, the champion colored club of the U. S., and the Green Bays. There were not far from 2,000 spectators to witness this game. The record of the Gordons was well known, and the confidence of the Green Bays was such that everybody expected to see some fine playing. The game was the finest ever played. It was the expressed feelings of all that they had

not witnessed a finer game by any of the league clubs." The Gordons reorganized in 1885, 1886, 1887, and 1890. *Eau Claire Leader* (September 15, 1885): "In order to wind up the season in good style the Eau Claires have at a heavy outlay secured the Gordons, of Chicago, to play today, Wednesday, and Thursday. The Gordons are undoubtedly one of the strongest clubs in the Northwest." Chicago and Louisville developed a black rivalry. *Louisville Courier-Journal* (July 18, 1886): "The Gordons, of Chicago, met the Falls Citys yesterday afternoon at the park on Sixteenth and Magnolia, and were defeated by a score of 11 to 17." *Courier-Journal* (July 19, 1886): "The crack colored club, the Gordons, of Chicago, defeated the Falls Citys yesterday afternoon at Magnolia Park, in the presence of 800 people. The Gordons batted terrifically, and won the game with ease." *Janesville Gazette* (July 5, 1887): "The morning game was won by a score of 12 to 1, but after dinner the Gordons braced up. When the ninth inning of the second game ended, the score was a tie and except for the sharp playing the Mutuals would have been left behind. As it was they took the game by a score of 15 to 13." In 1887 the team's veteran players (Abe Jones, Grant Campbell, Joseph Campbell, Darby Cottman, Albert Hackley and Frank Scott) reorganized as the Unions of Chicago. In the late–1880s William C. Sutcliffe reorganized the Gordons and they played most of their games on the road.

Sources: "Sporting Notes," *Cleveland (OH) Leader,* Feb 20, 1884; "Gordon B.B.C.," *Cleveland (OH) Gazette,* Apr 12, 1884; "9 to 1," *Terra Haute (IN) Wabash Express,* Apr 18, 1884; "Score The First," *Terra Haute (IN) Evening Gazette,* Apr 18, 1884; "Redeeming Themselves," *Terra Haute Wabash Express,* Apr 19, 1884; "Base Ball," *Terra Haute Evening Gazette,* Apr 19, 1884; "Willow Wielders," *Saginaw (MI) Morning Herald,* Apr 26, 1884; "The Gordons Left in the Vocative," *Milwaukee (WI) Journal,* May 12, 1884; "Black-Balled," *Milwaukee (WI) Sentinel,* May 12, 1884; "Gordons 19—Fostoria 3," *Cincinnati (OH) Commercial Tribune,* May 23, 1884; "Springfield 7— Gordons 2," *Cincinnati Commercial Tribune,* May 24, 1884; "The Colored Boys Defeated," *Cincinnati (OH) Enquirer,* May 30, 1884; "Gordons 1—Chillicothe 0," *Cincinnati Commercial Tribune,* Jun 1, 1884; "Piqua 15—Gordons 10," *Cincinnati Commercial Tribune,* Jun 5, 1884; "An Easy Victory," *Piqua (OH) Piqua,* Jun 5, 1884; "Colored Professionals to Play," *Chicago (IL) Tribune,* Jun 11, 1884; "In the Sporting World," *Milwaukee Sentinel,* Jul 7, 1884; "Base Ball," *Green Bay (WI) Advocate,* Jul 3, 1884; "The Celebration," *Green Bay (WI) Press-Gazette,* Jul 5, 1884; "Portsmouth," *Cleveland Gazette,* July 26, 1884; "Base Ball," *Green Bay Press-Gazette,* Jul 28, 1884; "Base Ball," *Green Bay Press-Gazette,* Jul 29, 1884; "Base Ball," *Green Bay Press-Gazette,* Aug 4, 1884; "Base Ball," *Green Bay Advocate,* Aug 7, 1884; "Base Ball," *Green Bay Advocate,* Aug 14, 1884; "Dubuques, 6; Gordons, 3," *St. Louis (MO) Globe-Democrat,* Sep 15, 1884; "Not Title," *Eau Claire (WI) Free Press,* Jun 25, 1885; "Base Ball on the 4th of July," *Eau Claire Free Press,* Jul 2, 1885; "Base Ball," *Eau Claire Free Press,* Jul 9, 1885; "Base Ball," *Chicago (IL) Inter-Ocean,* Jul 13, 1885; "The Last Game," *Eau Claire (WI) Leader,* Sep 15, 1885; "Two Out of Three," *Chicago (IL) Tribune,* Jul 4, 1886; "They Break Even," *Louisville (KY) Courier Journal,* Jul 18, 1886; "Gordons, 25—Falls Citys, 10," *Louisville Courier Journal,* Jul 19, 1886; "Politics in Louisville," *Cincinnati Commercial Tribune,* July 24, 1886; "How They Will Play," *Janesville (WI) Gazette,* Jul 2, 1887; *Janesville Gazette,* Jul 5, 1887; *Rockford (IL) Register,* Jul 7, 1887; "Colored Players Defeated," *Chicago Inter-Ocean,* Aug 8, 1890; "Amateur Notes," *Chicago Tribune,* May 18, 1890; "Amateur Notes," *Chicago Inter-Ocean,* June 1, 1890; "Amateur Base-Ball Notes," *Chicago Tribune,* July 21, 1890.

Gordon Base Ball Club Headquarters (464 State Street (Chicago, IL); (1880s–1890s)). Owner(s): Daniel Scott.

In 1884, the Gordon B.B.C. had its headquarters at 464 State Street, an old black business district. Daniel Scott, base-ballist, businessman (real estate and saloon-keeper), and entrepreneur, managed the finances for the Gordon's 1884 championship season. H. M. Fisher, Harry Teenan Jones, Gordon Jackson (for whom the team was named), Daniel Scott, and Joseph H. Harris served as the organization's management team. Fisher, Scott, Teenan and Gordon bankrolled the aggregation (see Harry Teenan and Gordon Jackson). This clubhouse (464 State Street), with saloon, barbershop, billiard and reading rooms, would play a pivotal role as a headquarters for colored ball clubs and ball players throughout the 1880s and 1890s.

Sources: "Chicago Correspondence," *New York (NY) Globe*, Apr 12, 1884; "No Title (Advertisement)," *Chicago (IL) Conservator*, Apr 12, 1886; "Chicago," *Saint Paul (MN) Appeal*, Dec 12, 1887; "The Garden City," *Saint Paul Appeal*, October 19, 1889.

Harlem Base Ball Club (Chicago, IL; 1890s). Organizer(s): Charles Morgan.

The Harlem B.B.C. organized in the 1890s. The Harlems played against white and black teams. *Chicago Inter-Ocean* (July 8, 1894): "The Harlem (colored) Base Ball Club would like to hear from the Edgars, Schrouder Brothers, Cranes, Atlas, and the Chicago Colored Unions, and any other good amateur teams in or out of the city."

Sources: "Baseball Notes," *Chicago (IL) Inter-Ocean*, May 31, 1894; "Amateur Baseball," *Chicago Inter-Ocean*, Jul 8, 1894.

Hunter Base Ball Club (Chicago, IL; 1870s)

The Hunter B.B.C. organized in the 1870s. The "Hunters" played against black and white organizations. *Chicago Tribune* (October 2, 1870): "The Hunters (colored) beat the Monitors (white), 35 to 20." *Tribune* (October 9, 1870): "The Hunters (colored) defeated the Union Turners, 29 to 0." *Tribune* (October 16, 1870): "The Protections defeated the Hunters, 8 to 2." *Chicago Times* (October 4, 1871): "The Hunters beat the Marines on yesterday by a score of 27 to 11."

Sources: "The Sporting World," *Chicago (IL) Tribune*, Oct 2, 1870; "Minor Games," *Chicago Tribune*, Oct 9, 1870; "Minor Games," *Chicago Tribune*, Oct 16, 1870; *Chicago (IL) Times*, Oct 4, 1871.

Jolly Boys Base Ball Club (Chicago, IL; 1890s). Organizer(s): G. B. Smitt.

The Jolly Boys B.B.C. organized in the 1890s. The Jolly Boys played black and white teams, inside and outside the fence. *Chicago Inter-Ocean* (May 28, 1889): "The Jolly Boys wish challenges from nines averaging 17 years." *Inter-Ocean* (June 16, 1889): "The Jolly Boys and a picked nine played at Jackson Park yesterday. The result was a victory for the Jolly Boys by a score of 18 to 8."

Sources: "Amateur Base-Ball," *Chicago (IL) Inter-Ocean*, May 26, 1889; "The Amateurs' Column," *Chicago Inter-Ocean*, May 28, 1889; "Amateur Notes," *Chicago Inter-Ocean*, May 29, 1889; "Amateur Notes," *Chicago Inter-Ocean*, May 31, 1889; "Prairie Games," *Chicago Inter-Ocean*, Jun 16, 1889; "Prairie Games," *Chicago Inter-Ocean*, Jun 24, 1889.

Letter Carrier Base Ball Club (Chicago, IL; 1890s)

The Letter Carrier B.B.C. organized in the 1890s. The Letter Carriers, a Colored Society League Club, competed against similar organizations. *Chicago Inter-Ocean* (June 26, 1896): "The Emergencies played and defeated the colored letter carriers Wednesday at City League Grounds by a score of 15 to 3. The feature of the game was the pitching of Renfro, of the Emergencies, who struck out twelve men and a running catch by Bert Anderson."

Sources: "With the Amateurs," *Chicago (IL) Inter-Ocean*, Jun 21, 1896; "With the Amateurs," *Chicago Inter-Ocean*, Jun 26, 1896.

Lone Star Base Ball Club (Chicago, IL; 1880s–1890s). Organizer(s): J. Mitchell.

The Lone Star B.B.C. organized in the 1880s. The Lone Stars, formerly the Clippers, played black and white nines. *Chicago Inter-Ocean* (August 8, 1896): "The Atlantas have lost but one game this year and will cross bats with the Lone Stars (colored) tomorrow and Twenty-First and Rockwell Streets. A good game is expected." Controversy followed; the Lone Star's manager complaining to a newspaper. *Inter-Ocean* (August 11, 1896): "To the Sporting Editor: Why did the Atlantas not deny the way they treated the Lone Stars in the ninth inning? Anyone that ever heard of the Marquettes knows that Dillon of them is over 20 years of age. The Atlantas can deny all, but the Lone Stars can get three-fourths of the three hundred spectators of Sunday's game to truly testify that they were robbed of the game and that they had three of their best bats stolen, one of them costing $1.50. They got the worst of it from start to finish. Although they were ahead of them at the end, they could not get a penny over what they put up, and the witnesses of the game say that they were lucky to get that."

Sources: "With the Amateurs," *Chicago (IL) Inter-Ocean*, Aug 8, 1896; "With the Amateurs," *Chicago Inter-Ocean*, Aug 11, 1896; "With the Amateurs," *Chicago Inter-Ocean*, Aug 12, 1896; "With the Amateurs," *Chicago Inter-Ocean*, Aug 13, 1896; "With the Amateurs," *Chicago Inter-Ocean*, Aug 19, 1896; "With the Amateurs," *Chicago Inter-Ocean*, Aug 21, 1896; "With the Amateurs," *Chicago Inter-Ocean*, Aug 27, 1896; "With the Amateurs," *Chicago Inter-Ocean*, Aug 29, 1896; "With the Amateurs," *Chicago Inter-Ocean*, Sep 1, 1896; "With the Amateurs," *Chicago Inter-Ocean*, Sep 2, 1896.

Model Base Ball Club (Chicago, IL; 1880s–1890s). Organizer(s): Robert Jackson; John Hunter and George Mead.

The Model B.B.C. organized in 1889. The Models, managed by Robert Jackson, played black and white teams. They defeated the Chicago Unions. *Chicago Inter-Ocean* (May 6, 1889): "The Models and Freedoms played at Thirty-fifth and Hanover streets yesterday. The features of the game were the battery work of Anderson and Darby, of the Models, Anderson striking out fourteen men, and the terrific batting of the Models." *Inter-Ocean* (August 7, 1889): "The Models, the junior champions, defeated the Unions, champion colored team of the West, at the barbers' picnic at Island Park, yesterday, for the gold ball and ebony bat, valued at $75, offered by the Barbers' Assembly. The Models battled [Joseph] Campbell at their will, and touched him up for four home runs. The features of the game were the battery work of Mead and Howard, the home runs of Mead (2), Williams, and Payne, and the three-baggers of Holman, Davis and Howard, of the Models." *Inter-Ocean* (September 16, 1889): "The Chicago Stars defeated the Models in a very exciting game at Athletic Park. The features of the game were the pitching of Loew and Smith." *Chicago Tribune* (June 5, 1890): "The Unions defeated the Models at Sixty-sixth street and Cottage Grove avenue. The features of the game were the numerous two-baggers of the Unions, the one-handed catch of Jackson, and the two-baggers of Mead and Parker of the Models." Several of the Model players would join the Chicago Unions.

Sources: "Amateur Base-Ball," *Chicago (IL) Inter-Ocean*, Mar 24, 1889; "Amateur Base-Ball," *Chicago Inter-Ocean*, May 23, 1889; "Players for Love," *Chicago Inter-Ocean*, May 26, 1889; "The Amateurs Play Ball," *Chicago Inter-Ocean*, Jul 14, 1889; "Models, 20; Black Stockings, 1," *Chicago Inter-Ocean*, Aug 19, 1889; "Amateurs Play Ball," *Inter-Ocean*, Jul 28, 1889; "Amateur Base Ball," *Inter-Ocean*, Sep 16, 1889; "Amateur Base-Ball Notes," *Chicago (IL) Tribune*, May 22, 1890; "Amateur Notes," *Chicago Tribune*, May 26, 1890; "Amateur Base Ball," *Chicago Tribune*, Jun 5, 1890; "Among the Local Base Ball

Amateurs," *Chicago (IL) Herald*, Jul 31, 1891; "Trio of Amateurs," *Chicago Inter-Ocean*, Jun 24, 1895.

Oakley Base Ball Club (Chicago, IL; 1890s). Organizer(s): George Andrews, R. Lee and D. McGowan.

The Oakley B.B.C. flourished in the 1890s. The Oakleys competed against black aggregations.

Sources: "With the Amateurs," *Chicago (IL) Inter-Ocean*, Aug 2, 1896; "With the Amateurs," *Chicago Inter-Ocean*, Aug 12, 1896; "With the Amateurs," *Chicago Inter-Ocean*, August 11, 1896; "With the Amateurs," *Chicago Inter-Ocean*, Aug 24, 1896.

Rapids Base Ball Club (Chicago, IL; 1870s)

The Rapids B.B.C. organized in the 1870s. The "Rapids" played against black and white organizations. *Chicago Tribune* (July 3, 1870): "The Rapids (colored) beat the Griswold Street Scrubs 34 to 7 in seven innings." *Tribune* (July 3, 1870): "The Rapids beat the Stat Juniors 9 to 0." *Tribune* (July 9, 1870): "The Rapids beat the Mohawks, 21 to 12." *Tribune* (July 4, 1870): "The Rapids beat the Star Juniors 9 to 0 in seven innings." *Tribune* (October 30, 1870): "The Rapids beat the Alpines, in a return game, 48 to 36."

Sources: "Games and Pastimes," *Chicago (IL) Tribune*, Jun 23, 1870; "The Game in Chicago," *Chicago Tribune*, Jul 3, 1870; "The National Game," *Chicago Tribune*, Jul 4, 1870; "The National Game," *Chicago Tribune*, Jul 9, 1870; "Record of Local Games," *Chicago Tribune*, Aug 5, 1870; "The Sporting World," *Chicago Tribune*, Oct 30, 1870.

Red Stockings Base Ball Club (Chicago, IL; 1870s)

The Red Stockings B.B.C. organized in the 1870s. The Red Stockings played against black and white organizations. *Chicago Tribune* (June 13, 1871): "The Red Stockings (colored) captured the Red Hands, 22 to 14." *Tribune* (June 25, 1871): "The Red Stockings beat the Blue Stars 23 to 5. The Gray Stockings beat the Red Stockings 19 to 2."

Sources: "Recent Local Games," *Chicago (IL) Tribune*, Jun 13, 1871; "Games in General," *Chicago Tribune*, Jun 23, 1871.

Resolute Base Ball Club (Chicago, IL; 1880s–1890s). Organizer(s): Frank Leland and Orange L. Fox.

In 1889 Frank C. Leland and Orange W. Fox organized Resolute B.B.C.s. Leland and Fox originally named the team, Australian Giants, perhaps capitalizing on Albert Goodwill Spalding's World Base Ball Tour. The Resolutes played white and black teams. *Chicago Daily Inter-Ocean* (August 28, 1889): "The Unions and Resolutes (colored) ball clubs played a lively game of ball at the Ball Park yesterday afternoon. The Pinchbacks, of New Orleans, were on the grandstand watching the two clubs with which they are to play today and tomorrow, and they saw a pretty stiff game, both nines playing for all there was in it. Of course, there were errors as they do not profess to be professionals, but the hitting and base-running were alright. The Unions were by far the strongest club, both in the box, in the field, and at the bat. They got the measure of Renfro's pitching, and took ten clean hits off the so-called wonder." *Inter-Ocean* (August 30, 1892): "The Resolutes defeated the Athletic Stars in one of the most exciting games of the season. The features of the game were the fine pitching of Peterson and the battery work of Peterson and Carroll."

Sources: "Amateur Base Ball," *Chicago (IL) Inter-Ocean*, Jul 7, 1889; "They desire To Play Ball," *Chicago Inter-Ocean*, Jul 14, 1889; "Amateur Base-Ball," *Chicago Inter-Ocean*, Jul 22, 1889; "Pinchbacks, 17; Resolutes, 11," *Chicago Inter-Ocean*, Aug 29, 1889; "Colored Nines on the Diamond," *Tribune* (Chicago, IL), Sep 9, 1889; "Amateur Base Ball Notes," *Chicago Tribune*, Sep 9, 1889; "Amateur Base Ball,"

Chicago Inter-Ocean, Sep 16, 1889; "Diamonds, 16; Resolutes, 7," *Chicago Tribune*, Sep 16, 1889; "Amateur Base Ball," *Chicago Inter-Ocean*, Oct 12, 1889; "Amateur Base Ball Notes," *Chicago Tribune*, Jul 19, 1890; *Chicago (IL) Times*, Aug 15, 1892; "Amateur Ball Players," *Chicago Inter-Ocean*, Aug 30, 1892.

Rhode Boys Base Ball Club (Chicago, IL; 1880s–1890s). Organizer(s): R. Rhodes.

The Rhodes Boys B.B.C. organized in the 1880s. The Rhodes Boys played white and black teams. *Chicago Tribune* (May 31, 1890): "The Rhodes defeated the State Street Stars at Sixty-First and Cottage Grove. The features of the game were the batting of the Rhodes, and the pitching of Hull and the fielding of Turner. The batteries were Hull and Woodruff of the Rhodes and Airhorn and Pretzel of the Stars." *Chicago Herald* (June 16, 1890): "The Models defeated the Rhodes at Sixty-First and Cottage Grove avenue. The features of the game were the battery work of Anderson and Darby of the Models and the batting and all-around playing of the Models."

Sources: *Chicago (IL) Tribune*, May 2, 1890; "Among the Amateurs," *Chicago (IL) Inter-Ocean*, May 5, 1890; "Amateur Ball Players," *Chicago Inter-Ocean*, May 30, 1890; "Amateur Notes," *Chicago Tribune*, May 31, 1890; "Coming Base Ball Stars," *Chicago Inter-Ocean*, Jun 2, 1890; "The Boys League," *Chicago Tribune*, Jun 9, 1890; "Among the Amateurs," *Chicago (IL) Herald*, Jun 16, 1890.

South End Athletic Base Ball Club (Chicago, IL; 1880s–1890s). Organizer(s): S. J. Chadwick; William Turner.

The South End Athletic B.B.C. organized in the 1880s. *Chicago Daily Inter-Ocean* (April 7, 1889): "The South End Athletics have organized for the season and have signed the following players: A. Cottman; Lee Starks; Wilbur Lewis; Gleaves; Charles Weekly; George Hankins; Theo Hubbard; Link Brown; Freeman. Open to play all nines outside the fence. Challenges may be addressed to the South End Athletics, No. 2790 Butterfield Street."

Sources: "The Amateur Column," *Chicago (IL) Inter-Ocean*, Apr 7, 1889; "Base Ball Gossip," *Chicago Inter-Ocean*, April 9, 1889; "Amateur Base Ball," *Chicago (IL) Tribune*. May 11, 1891.

South End Junior Base Ball Club (Chicago, IL; 1890s)

The South End Junior B.B.C. organized in the 1890s. The South Ends played black and white clubs. *Chicago Tribune* (June 5, 1890): "The South End Juniors defeated the Lafayettes at Washington Park yesterday by a score of 10 to 3. The features of the game were the battery work of the South Ends and the heavy batting of both teams."

Sources: "Amateur Base Ball Notes," *Chicago (IL) Inter-Ocean*, Apr 15, 1890; "Amateur Notes," *Chicago (IL) Tribune*, Jun 3, 1890; "Amateur Notes," *Chicago Tribune*, Jun 5, 1890.

Starlight ("Blue Stockings") Base Ball Club (Chicago, IL; 1870s). Organizer(s): Henry P. Hall, H. Beauford and William D. Berry.

The Starlight ("Blue Stockings") B.B.C. organized in 1870. The Starlight nine—nicknamed Blue Stockings—was managed by Henry P. Hall, H. Beauford, William D. Berry and George Mead. *Chicago Inter-Ocean* (August 9, 1870): "The Starlight Base Ball Club is the name of an organization composed of young colored men. They are uniformed handsomely in white with blue trimmings." The Blue Stockings developed a rivalry with Rockford's Pink Stockings club. The nines played a three-game championship. *Rockford Register* (August 6, 1870): "On Monday last, the Blue Stockings, of Chicago, played a game with the Rockfords, at the Fairgrounds and out home Club beat the visitors." The second contest took place in Chicago. *Rockford Weekly Gazette* (August 25, 1870): "At a game of base-ball in Chicago on Tuesday between the Pink Stockings, of Rockford, and Blue Stockings, of Chicago, two colored base-ball clubs, the score stood: Rockford 14; Chicago, 48. No remarks." In September, they played the final game. *Rockford Weekly Register* (October 1, 1870): "The first game was played here and won by the Rockfords; the second in Chicago by the Blues; and the third was won by the Blue Stockings, 28 to 18. The latter now claim the colored championship of the State." After the all-white Amateur League Tournament refused to admit them, the Blue Stockings defeated the amateur all-stars before a large racially-mixed crowd. They developed a local rivalry with the Uniques. *Chicago Times* (October 7, 1870): "In the first game of the series between the Blue Stockings and the Unique, for the colored championship on the grounds of the Prairie Club, corner State and twenty-Third Streets, the Unique were the winners by a score of 39 to 5." The lost two games. In 1871, the team's best players joined the Uniques, an organization that lasted for over twenty years. William P. Johnson and George Brown (e), formed the new team's nucleus. That same year, they decisively defeated the Blues for the championship of Chicago. Though the Blue Stockings continued to play in and around Chicago.

SOURCES: "Colored Clubs," *Rockford (IL) Weekly Register*, Jul 23, 1870; "The Colored Clubs," *Rockford Weekly Register*, August 6, 1870; "Miscellaneous," *Chicago (IL) Inter-Ocean*, Aug 9, 1870; "Games Played in Chicago," *Chicago (IL) Evening Journal*, Aug 23, 1870; "Colored Clubs," *Rockford Weekly Register*, Aug 20, 1870; "Blue vs. Pink," *Rockford Weekly Register*, Aug 23, 1870; "The Colored Troops," *Chicago Evening Journal*, August 23, 1870; "Base Ball from A Colored Point of View," *Chicago (IL) Tribune*, Aug 20, 1870; "On Tour," *Rockford Weekly Register*, Aug 7, 1870; "Base Ball Matters," *Chicago Evening Journal*, Sep 16, 1870; "A Denial," *Chicago Times*, Sep 20, 1870; "The Blue Stockings," *Chicago (IL) Times*, Sep 21, 1870; "The Blue Stockings," *Chicago Times*, Sep 23, 1870; "Sporting Matters," *Chicago (IL) Republican*, Sep 24, 1870; "White vs. Black," *Chicago Republican*, Sep 28, 1870; "Base Ball Gossip," *Chicago Times*, Oct 6, 1870; "Colored Clubs," *Rockford Weekly Register*, Oct 1, 1870; "Base Ball Matters," *Chicago Times*, Oct 7, 1870; "Miscellaneous," *Chicago Tribune*, Oct 7, 1870; "Base Ball," *Chicago Tribune*, Oct 10, 1870; "A Denial," *Chicago Times*, Sep 20, 1870; "The Colored Championship," *Chicago Times*, Sep 20, 1870.

Starlight ("Blue Stocking") Base Ball Club Headquarters (228 and 230 South Clark Street (Chicago, IL); 1870s). Owner(s): William P. Johnson.

The Starlight ("Blue Stockings") B.B.C. operated in the 1870s. It was organized and operated, at least initially, by the baseballist and entrepreneur, William P. Johnson. Johnson was proprietor of an establishment, a saloon, located at 228 and 230 South Clark Street. This clubhouse (228 and 230 South Clark Street), with saloon, barbershop, gambling, billiard (dubbed the African Billiard Room) and reading rooms, would play a pivotal role as a headquarters for the Blue Stockings, Uniques, and other ball clubs and ball players throughout the 1880s. In the 1870s, the headquarters provided meals for black Civil War veterans: pork, beans, hard tack and coffee. In 1875, the club also hosted the Jubilee Singers. It also served as headquarters for Chicago's Colored Republican organization; in 1875, Johnson served as president.

SOURCES: "The Blue Stockings," *Chicago (IL) Inter-Ocean*, Sep 23, 1870; "City Brevities," *Chicago Inter-Ocean*, May 26, 1874; "City Brevities," *Chicago Inter-Ocean*, May 31, 1874; "Colored Republicans," *Chicago Inter-Ocean*, December. 21, 1875; "Killed and Wounded," *Chicago Inter-Ocean*, Apr 20, 1881.

Stonewall Base Ball Club (Chicago, IL; 1890s)

The Stonewall B.B.C. organized in the 1890s. The "Stonewalls" competed against white and black organizations. *Chicago Inter-Ocean*

(June 19, 1896): "The Crack High Flyers will cross bats with the Stonewalls, the champion 18 year-old colored team of the city, for a purse of $10 at the latters' grounds, Fortieth Street and Ogden Avenue, tomorrow. The High Flyers have won fifteen out of seventeen games, while the Stonewalls have won seven and have not lost any. The game will be called at 2:30 o'clock sharp. The batteries will be Purdon and Casey of the High Flyers and Peters and Smith of the Stonewalls."

SOURCES: "With the Amateurs," And eat well, And grow strong Chicago (IL) Inter-Ocean, Jun 19, 1896; "With the Amateurs," *Chicago Inter-Ocean*, Aug 21, 1896.

South Branch Terrors Base Ball Club (Chicago, IL; 1890s). Organizer(s): H. Raven.

The South Branch Terrors B.B.C. organized in the 1890s. *Chicago Herald* (August 10, 1891): "South Branch Terrors have reorganized with these players: J. Milligan, J. Conroy, L. Thomas, Sam Edwards, B. Merrick, J. V. Brown, W. Scott, G. Shively, J. Gallagner, Henry Wilson, Bill Hennessey, and C. Wall. Will play all colored nines averaging sixteen years. Address all challenges to B. Raven, 635 Fairfield Avenue."

SOURCES: "Herald's House Ball Exchange," *Chicago (IL) Herald*, Aug 10, 1891; "Herald's Base Ball Exchange," *Chicago Herald*, Aug 17, 1891.

Thompson Base Ball Club (Chicago, IL; 1890s). Organizer(s): James L. Thompson.

The Thompson B.B.C. organized in the 1890s. *Inter-Ocean*: "The Thomsons have organized, as follows: J. L. Thomson, Lawrence, Newton, Staples, Johnson, Davis, Reidy, Hutchinson, Watkins, Anderson, Starks, Hara."

SOURCES: "Amateur Base-Ball Notes," *Chicago (IL) Tribune*, Sep 10, 1890; "Amateur Ball Tossers," *Chicago (IL) Inter-Ocean*, Sep 12, 1890; "Boy's Base Ball Boom," *Chicago (IL) Herald*, Jul 18, 1891; "Amateur Base Ball League Chat," *Chicago Herald*, Aug 9, 1891; "Herald's House Ball Exchange," *Chicago Inter-Ocean*, Aug 10, 1891; "Among the Amateurs," *Chicago (IL) Times*. Aug 22, 1891.

Tourgee Base Ball Club (Chicago, IL; 1890s)

The Tourgee B.B.C. organized in the 1890s. The Tourgees belonged to the Colored Society League; they played black teams. *Chicago Inter-Ocean* (July 16, 1894): "All lovers of baseball will be favored with a rare treat in the shape of a baseball game between the Emergencies, headed by Julius N. Avendorph, and the Tourgees, headed by A. H. Roberts, Thursday afternoon at 3 o'clock at the Unions' Base Ball Park, Thirty-Seventh and Butler Streets. The proceeds are to be given to the hospital." The Tourgees organized for a baseball benefit for Provident Hospital (here, Dr. Daniel Hale Williams, a mulatto cardiologist, performed the country's first successful open heart surgery), an institution that catered primarily to Chicago's Southside black community. The roster of the "Tourgees" (named for Albion Tourgee, the noted lawyer whom litigated for the plaintiff Homer Plessy in the case Plessy v. Ferguson in 1896) that included Jesse Binga, Harry Teenan Jones, Robert Shaw, Albert "Al" Jones, Scipio Spinks, and colored doctors.

SOURCES: "Benefit of Provident Hospital," *Chicago (IL) Inter-Ocean*, Jul 16, 1894; "Amateur Baseball," *Chicago Inter-Ocean*, Jul 22, 1894.

Tremont House Base Ball Club (Chicago, IL; 1890s). Organizer(s): Charles "Doc" Howard and Devinney Davis.

The Tremont House B.B.C. organized in the 1890s. The Tremonts, composed of waiters, played similar aggregations. The Tremonts and

Auditoriums became rivals in the Hotel League. *Chicago Tribune* (June 28, 1891): "The Auditoriums defeated the Tremons on the Lake Front by a score of 14 to 7. The feature of the game was the battery work of the Auditoriums, Spinks striking of fifteen men. Batteries—Spinks and Ware and Chandler and Sherman." *Tribune* (July 6, 1891): "The Auditoriums defeated the Tremons on the Lake Front by a score of 18 to 11. The features of the game were the catching of Starks and Spinks' two home runs." *Chicago Herald* (August 7, 1891): "The Tremons defeated the Commercials at the Lake Front by the score of 4 to 2. The feature of the game was the battery work of Chandler and Ramsey, of the Tremons, Chandler striking out twelve men in five innings."

SOURCES: "Amateur Base-Ball Notes," *Chicago (IL) Tribune*, Sep 10, 1890; "Amateur Sporting Notes," *Chicago Tribune*, May 14, 1891; "Amateur Notes," *Chicago Tribune*, May 24, 1891; "Amateur Baseball Notes," *Chicago Tribune*, Jun 14, 1891; "Among the Amateurs," *Chicago Tribune*, Jun 27, 1891; "Among Local Amateurs," *Chicago (IL) Herald*, Jun 27, 1891; "Amateur Baseball Notes," *Chicago Tribune*, Jun 28, 1891; "Amateur Ball," *Chicago (IL) Inter-Ocean*, Jul 6, 1891; "Scores of Prairie Contests," *Chicago Herald*, Aug 7, 1891.

Tybell Base Ball Club (Chicago, IL; 1890s)

The Tybell B.B.C. organized in the 1890s. The Tybells played white and black teams. *Chicago Inter-Ocean* (August 25, 1896): "The Silver Stars defeated a picked nine called the Tybells by a score of 21 to 13 in a seven-inning game. The features of the game were the batting of Farley, the fielding of Brady, the one-hand catch of a fly by Roberts. Batteries—Walker and Farley for the Stars; Condon and Pierce for the Tybells." *Chicago Inter-Ocean* (September 9, 1896): "The invincible Silver Stars again defeated the colored Tybells Sunday at California Avenue and Harrison street before a very large crowd."

SOURCES: "With the Amateurs," *Chicago (IL) Inter-Ocean*, Aug 25, 1896; "With the Amateurs," *Chicago Inter-Ocean*, Sep 9, 1896.

Union Base Ball Club (Chicago, IL; 1880s–1900s). Organizer(s): Orange W. Fox, J. R. Van Pelt, E. M. Russell, William Albert Jones ("Abe Jones"), Frank C. Leland; Frank L. Scott, Harry Teenan Jones; T. T. Farley, William Stitt Peters, H. Travis Elby, Al Donegan.

The Chicago Union B.B.C. organized in the 1880s. The Unions—later the Chicago Unions and formerly, the Gordons—played white and black organizations. *Cleveland Gazette* (May 7, 1887): "Al Jones' Union Ball Club gobbled all the gate money Sunday afternoon. Score 26 to 10 in favor of the Union Club." *St. Paul Western Appeal* (September 24, 1887): "The Union Base Ball Club under the management of W. A. [William Albert] Jones, is fast becoming the foremost nine in the West, after defeating the Dreadnaughts, white, they repeated the same to the Eckfords, white, who had picked men from several of the clubs, but that made no difference, we won just the same. They would like to hear from some good club. They will play for any amount." The Unions played three prominent black teams: the Chicago's Unique and Resolute nines, and New Orleans Pinchbacks. The Unions reorganized in 1888: they defeated the Uniques twice, claiming the championship of the Southside. The Pinchbacks traveled to Chicago to play the Unions in a three-game series for the Colored Championship. In the opener, the Unions beat the Pinchbacks, 4–1. In the second game, W. L. Cohen's club won 6–5. A third match was not played. The Unions played the Resolutes. *Inter-Ocean* (August 28, 1889): "The Unions and Resolutes (colored ball clubs) played a lively game of ball at the Ball Park yesterday afternoon. The Pinchbacks, of New Orleans, were on the grandstand watching the two clubs with which they are to play today and tomorrow, and they saw a pretty stiff game, both nines playing for all there was in it. Of course, there were errors as they do not profess to be professionals,

but the hitting and base-running were alright. The Unions were by far the strongest club, both in the box, in the field, and at the bat. They got the measure of Renfro's pitching, and took ten clean hits off the so-called wonder." The Unions continued to play white teams. *Chicago Tribune* (September 25, 1889): "The Onwards defeated the Unions (colored) on the grounds of the former. The batteries were Wall and Klose of the Onwards and [Frank] Butler and [Grant] Campbell of the Unions. The score was 12 to 8." After reorganizing in 1890, the Chicago Union spent a lot of time on the road. When in Chicago, they played competitive black teams. *Chicago Tribune* (June 5, 1890): "The Unions defeated the Models at Sixty-sixth street and Cottage Grove avenue. The features of the game were the numerous two-baggers of the Unions, the one-handed catch of Jackson, and the two-baggers of Mead and Parker of the Models." *Inter-Ocean* (September 15, 1890): "The Chicago Unions defeated the Clippers at Grand Crossing yesterday. The feature of the game was the heavy batting of the Unions. The batteries were Smith and Jones of the Unions, and Anderson, Johnson, Ferguson, and Starks, of the Clippers." In 1895, the Chicago Unions won the city championship by defeating the Edgars, a strong white aggregation. In 1897, the black team of Nashville came to Chicago to play the Unions. *Inter-Ocean*: "The Chicago Unions defeated the Rock City Unions in the first game for the colored championship by a score of 13 to 5. The southern boys started out well, but couldn't keep the pace with the locals." The NY Cuban Giants also visited Chicago several times for the next three years to play the Unions. They also continued to play strong white clubs of WI. *Janesville Gazette* (July 13, 1899): "After passing through the city a number of times and spending several nights here, the Chicago Unions tarried long enough yesterday to win a ball from Adkins, McMaster's & Company in the largest crowd of the season. Both teams were at the park early and during the warming up heats it seemed as though the colored boys had speed enough to carry weight and win in a canter." They developed a local black rivalry with Columbia Giants. *Chicago Tribune* (October 14, 1900): "The Chicago Unions defeated the Columbia Giants yesterday afternoon at the Westside National League Park in the first game of their series for the colored championship of the world by a score of 3 to 2. Wakefield's terrific home-run drive in the tenth won the game for the Unions. Both Horn and Miller pitched gilt-edged ball, keeping the hits well-scattered, but Miller especially distinguished himself by striking out eleven men."

SOURCES: "A Library Association," *Cleveland (OH) Gazette*, May 7, 1887; "Chicago, IL.," *St. Paul (MN) Western Appeal*, Sep 24, 1887; "Base Ball Items," *Chicago (IL) Tribune*, Apr 1, 1888; "Other Ball Games Yesterday," *Chicago Tribune*, Apr 16, 1888; "Ball Games Today," *Chicago Tribune*, Apr 29, 1888; "For the Colored Championship," *Chicago Tribune*, Aug 21, 1888; "Amateur Notes," *Chicago Tribune*, Sep 25, 1888; "Minor Games," *Chicago (IL) Inter-Ocean*, Oct 15, 1888; "The Amateur Column," *Chicago Inter-Ocean*, Apr 7, 1889; "Unions, 9; Rivals, 4l," *Chicago Inter-Ocean*, Apr 22, 1889; "Base Ball," *St. Paul (MN) Appeal*, Aug 17, 1889: "Amateur Base Ball," *Chicago Inter-Ocean*, August 18, 1889; "Colored Nines on the Diamond," *Chicago Tribune*, Aug 28, 1889; "Pinchbacks, 17; Resolutes, 11," *Chicago Inter-Ocean*, Aug 29, 1889; "Amateur Base Ball," *Chicago Inter-Ocean*, Sep 16, 1889; "Amateur Ball Players," *Chicago Inter-Ocean*, Mar 16, 1890; "The Union Ball Club," *Chicago Inter-Ocean*, April 2, 1890; "The National Game at Racine," *Chicago Inter-Ocean*, Jul 28, 1890; "Colored Players Defeated," *Chicago Inter-Ocean*, Aug 18, 1890; "Amateur Ball Tossers," *Chicago Inter-Ocean*, Sep 8, 1890; "Amateur Ball Tossers," *Chicago Inter-Ocean*, Sep 22, 1890; "Won by the West Ends," *Chicago Inter-Ocean*, Sep 29, 1890; "Amateur Base-Ball Notes," *Chicago Inter-Ocean*, Oct 6, 1890; "On Amateur Diamonds," *Chicago*

Inter-Ocean, May 30, 1891; "Among the Amateurs," *Chicago Tribune*, Jun 27, 1891; "Among the Local Amateurs," *Chicago (IL) Herald*, Jun 26, 1891; "Among the Local Base Ball Amateurs," *Chicago (IL) Times*, Jul 17, 1891; "Boy's Base Ball Boom," *Chicago (IL) Herald*, Jul 18, 1891; "Base Ball," *Chicago Times*, Jul 26, 1891; "Nationals, 8; Unions, 6," *Chicago Inter-Ocean*, Jul 27, 1891; "Amateur Base Ball League Chat," *Chicago Herald*, Aug 9, 1891; "Among the Amateurs," *Chicago Times*, Aug 22, 1891; "Unions Win Two Games," *Chicago Times*, Sep 7, 1891; "Record of Chicago Unions," *Chicago Herald*, Oct 10, 1891; "Manager William S. Peters," *Chicago Inter-Ocean*, Sep 19, 1891; "Amateur Ball Players," *Chicago Inter-Ocean*, May 15, 1892; "Edgars vs. Colored Champions," *Chicago Inter-Ocean*, Apr 17, 1893; "Won a Good Game," *Chicago Inter-Ocean*, Aug 28, 1893; "Goodwins vs. Unions," *Chicago Inter-Ocean*, Oct 15, 1893; "Champion Colored Team," *Chicago Inter-Ocean*, Apr 29, 1894; "Unions 15, DeKalbs 14," *DeKalb (IL) Daily Chronicle*, Aug 5, 1895; "Play for a Big Purse," *Chicago Inter-Ocean*, Sep 1, 1895; "One Game Each," *Chicago Inter-Ocean*, Sep 9, 1895; "Challenges and Announcements," *Chicago Inter-Ocean*, Sep 5, 1895; "Unions Get the Flag," *Chicago Inter-Ocean*, Nov 12, 1895; "Amateur Baseball," *Chicago Inter-Ocean*, Apr 25, 1896; "With the Amateurs," *Chicago Inter-Ocean*, Jul 7, 1896; "With the Amateurs," *Chicago Inter-Ocean*, Sep 5, 1896; Unions, 5; Illinois C.C., 4," *Chicago Tribune*, May 16, 1898; "With the Amateurs," *Chicago Inter-Ocean*, Jun 27, 1898 "Unions, 17; Spaldings, 2," *Chicago Tribune*, May 23, 1898; "Minneapolis, 8; Unions, 5," *Chicago Tribune*, May 30, 1898; "Unions Defeat Cuban Giants," *Chicago Tribune*, Jun 12, 1899; "Unions Win a Great Game," *Chicago Tribune*, May 22, 1899; "Unions Defeat Cuban Giants," *Chicago Tribune*, Jun 12, 1899; "Colored Teams Play Today," *Chicago Inter-Ocean*, Jun 18, 1899; "Colored Gentlemen Played Good Ball," *Janesville (WI) Gazette*, Jul 13, 1899; "Unions 11; Northwestern 8," *Chicago Tribune*, May 27, 1900; "Unions beat Columbia Giants," *Chicago Tribune*, Oct 14, 1900.

Union Junior Base Ball Club (Chicago, IL; 1890s). Organizer(s): John Duncan, H. H. Ash, William Harvey and Charles Parker.

The Union Junior B.B.C. organized in the 1890s. The junior played white and black organizations. *Chicago Tribune* (June 7, 1891): "Union Juniors and Spaulding Juniors will play tomorrow at Grand Crossing, Diamond No. 2, for a purse of $15." *Tribune* (September 2, 1891): "The Union Juniors have played fourteen games and only lost one, and therefore claim the championship of Chicago." *Chicago Inter-Ocean* (August 30, 1895): "The Young Sagwas defeated the Union Juniors at Washington Park yesterday. The battery was Johnson and Sandburg for the Union Juniors." *Inter-Ocean* (June 22, 1896): "The Chicago Unions Juniors defeated the Hull House at the Unions' Ball Park Sunday morning. The features of the game were Hogan's pitching and Killdorf's fielding." *Inter-Ocean* (June 29, 1896): "The Chicago Union Juniors defeated the Roseland boys at Roseland. The features of the games were the batting and all-around playing of the Juniors."

SOURCES: "Amateur Base Ball Notes," *Chicago (IL) Tribune*, Jun 6, 1891; "Amateur Base Ball Gossip," *Chicago (IL) Inter-Ocean*, Jun 7, 1891; "Amateur Base Ball Notes," *Chicago Tribune*, Jul 16, 1891; "Boy's Base Ball Boom Here," *Chicago (IL) Herald*, Jul 20, 1891; "Among the Amateurs," *Chicago Herald*, Jul 20, 1891; "Herald's Base Ball Exchange," *Chicago Herald*, Aug 31, 1891; "Amateur Base Ball Players' Parade," *Chicago Tribune*, Sep 2, 1891; "Amateur Base Ball," *Chicago Inter-Ocean*, Aug 30, 1895; "With the Amateurs," *Chicago Inter-Ocean*, Jun 22, 1896; "With the Amateurs," *Chicago Inter-Ocean*, Jun 29, 1896.

Union Reserve Base Ball Club (Chicago, IL; 1890s)

The Union Reserve B.B.C. organized in the 1890s. The Union Reserves played black and white aggregations. *Chicago Tribune* (September 6, 1896): "The Chicago Union Reserves were hardly in it with the Chicago Edgars yesterday at the Northwest City League Park and were receiving a severe drubbing when the rain ended the contest in the sixth inning."

SOURCES: *Chicago (IL) Times-Herald*, Jun 1, 1896; "With the Amateurs," *Chicago (IL) Times-Herald*, Sep 5, 1896; "Games in the Commercial League," *Chicago (IL) Tribune*, Sep 6, 1896.

Unique Base Ball Club (Chicago, IL; 1870s–1890s). Organizer(s): John Shaw, William Berry and Henry Hall; William Sutliffe; and Robert Jackson.

In 1871, the Unique B.B.C. organized under the management of John Shaw (**Fig. 28**), Henry Hall, and William Berry. The Uniques defeated the Chicago Blue Stocking club, the city's top black nine; they also played white teams. During a tour of Detroit, Upper Canada, NY, WA, MD and PA in 1871, they played Philadelphia's Pythians. The Uniques claimed to the title of colored champions of the United States. In 1874, they took second place in an amateur state tournament. In 1875, they claimed the Colored Championship of the Northwest, defeating strong nines of IL and MO. They established rivalries with St. Louis teams: Napoleons, Blue Stockings, Sunsets, White Stockings, and Black Stockings. *Chicago Inter-Ocean* (October 15, 1875): "The Chicago Uniques and the St. Louis Blue Stockings, two crack colored clubs, played for the championship on the White Stockings grounds yesterday, which resulted in favor of the home team by a score of 15to 14 in eight innings. The visitors excelled in the field, but not quite enough to counter-balance the heavy batting of the home team." The Unique and Blue Stocking rivalry last for three years. After being refused membership to Chicago's Amateur League, the Uniques were finally admitted in 1878. *Inter-Ocean* (June 19, 1879): "The Dreadnaughts and Uniques played their first game yesterday in the contest for the championship of the city." The Uniques established a regional circuit against white clubs of IL, IA, and WI; among them: the Dubuques, the Milwaukee Maple Leafs, and Janesville Mutuals. *Milwaukee News* (June 2, 1879): "This afternoon, the Uniques (colored), of Chicago, play a championship game with the Maple Leaves, of this city [Milwaukee], at the Milwaukee Ball Park. The game last Sunday resulted in a tie, after twelve hotly-contested innings, on account of darkness. A good game and large audience may be expected." The Uniques played against the Dubuque Reds, a white club that included future players of the St. Louis Browns B.B.C.: the Gleason boys (Bill and Jack), William B. Lapham, Tom Loftus and Charles Comiskey (Hall of Fame). *Dubuque Herald* (August 9, 1879): "The Uniques, the [N]egro club of Chicago, came, saw, and were con-

Figure 28. John E. Shaw, *Chicago Inter-Ocean*, January 18, 1896. Between 1871 and 1880, Shaw—a saloon owner—covered center field and captained Chicago's Unique Base Ball Club. His son, Robert A. J. Shaw, achieved fame as a pitcher for Los Angeles, California's Trilby Base Ball Club.

quered by the Dubuques [Reds]. The Uniques played a very good game except in the fifth inning when they became a little rattled and gave the Dubuques five runs on errors. At first they were unable to hit Rels [the pitcher] at all, but improved at the latter end of the game and did as well as the Chicagos did last Monday. Powell, the Uniques short stop, did some fine playing, putting out two and assisting six times." In 1886, William C. Sutcliffe (formerly of the Chicago Gordon and Unknown teams) managed the Uniques. In 1891, the Uniques reorganized under the management of Richard Hubbard and Robert P. Jackson. The Chicago Unions eclipsed the Uniques as a local black powerhouse, by decisively defeating them in a championship series in 1888. By 1890, they regularly played hotel league teams. *Inter-Ocean*: "The Uniques defeated the Auditoriums, Hotel League champions, at Grand Crossing, by the score of 11 to 1."

SOURCES: "The Colored Championship," *Chicago (IL) Times*, May 31, 1871; "Uniques vs. Alerts," *Chicago (IL) Tribune*, Jul 11, 1871; "New Items," *Lancaster (PA) Intelligencer*, Jul 19, 1871; "The Uniques," *Chicago Tribune*, Jul 11, 1871; "Condensed Locals," *Washington (DC) Evening Star*, Sep 12, 1871; "Local News," *Washington Evening Star*, Sep 13, 1871; "Condensed Locals," *Washington Evening Star*, Sep 14, 1871; "Telegraphic Brevities," *New York (NY) Times*, Sep 17, 1871; "Base Ball," *Chicago (IL) Evening Journal*, Sep 18, 1871; "Base Ball," *Pittsburgh (PA) Weekly Gazette*, Sep 19, 1871; "The Uniques," *Chicago Tribune*, Sep 19, 1871; "Base Ball," *Philadelphia (PA) Inquirer*, Sep 19, 1871; "Base Ball," *Philadelphia Inquirer*, Sep 20, 1871; "From Philadelphia," *Janesville (WI) Gazette*, Sep 20, 1871; "Base Ball," *Fort Wayne (IN) Gazette*, Sep 21, 1871; "Base Ball Items," *Chicago Tribune*, Aug 9, 1871; "Base Ball," *Brooklyn (NY) Daily Eagle*, Aug 15, 1872; *New York (NY) Clipper*, May 2, 1874; "Base Ball Items," *Jackson (MI) Citizen Patriot*, May 15, 1874; "Base Ball," *Chicago (IL) Inter-Ocean*, Jun 16, 1874; "Uniques vs. Garnets," *Chicago Inter-Ocean*, Jun 17, 1874; "The Mutuals and Clippers," *Winona (MN) Republican*, Aug 14, 1875; "The Amateurs," *Chicago (IL) Times*, Aug 16, 1874; "Sporting Notes," *Chicago Inter-Ocean*, Sep 4, 1874; "Base Ball Brevities," *St. Louis (MO) Globe*, Sep 6, 1874; "Sporting News," *Chicago Inter-Ocean*, Sep 6, 1874; "The Chicago Uniques at *St. Louis*," *Chicago Tribune*, Sep 8, 1875; "Base Ball," *Winona Republican*, Sep 13, 1875; "Base Ball," *Winona Republican*, Sep 15, 1875; "The Clippers," *Winona Republican*, Sep 16, 1875; "A Colored Game," *Chicago Times*, Oct 12, 1875; "Sporting News," *Chicago Inter-Ocean*, Oct 15, 1875; *Gloversville (NY) Intelligencer*, Feb 14, 1876; "Base Ball," *Chicago Tribune*, Jun 2, 1878; "Sporting News," *Chicago Inter-Ocean*, Sep 14 1878; "Base Ball," *Chicago Tribune*, Nov 10, 1878; "Base Ball," *Chicago Inter-Ocean*, Jun 5, 1879; "Town Talk," *Milwaukee (WI) Daily News*, Jun 2, 1879; "Brevities," *Milwaukee (WI) Sentinel*, May 19, 1879; "Town Talk," *Milwaukee Daily News*, May 31, 1879; "Uniques vs. Maple Leaves," *Milwaukee Sentinel*, Jun 2, 1879; "Base Ball," *Chicago (IL) Weekly Inter-Ocean*, Jun 5, 1879; "Short Stops," *Dubuque (IA) Herald*, Jul 25, 1879; "Base Ball," *Milwaukee Daily News*, Aug 2, 1879; "Base Ball," *Dubuque Herald*, Aug 9, 1879; "You'se Gone George," *Dubuque Herald*, Aug 10, 1879; "Base Ball," *Burlington (IA) Hawk-Eye*, Aug 10, 1879; *Waterloo (IA) Courier*, Aug 13, 1879; "Brevities," *Milwaukee Sentinel*, Aug 19, 1879; "Base Ball," *Milwaukee Daily News*, Aug 2, 1879; "Brevities," *Milwaukee Sentinel*, Aug 23, 1879; *Waterloo Courier*, Aug 13, 1879; "Base Ball," *Milwaukee Daily News*, Aug 24, 1879; "Franklins and Uniques," *Chicago Tribune*, Oct 10, 1879; "Ball Gossip," *Chicago Tribune*, Jun 27, 1880; "Around the Bases," *Chicago Tribune*, Jul 19, 1886; "Amateur Tossers," *Chicago Inter-Ocean*, Apr 24, 1887; "Around the Bases," *Chicago Tribune*, May 8, 1887; "On Many Diamonds," *Chicago Inter-Ocean*, Jun 18, 1891; "Amateur Base Ball," *Chicago Inter-Ocean*, Jul 6, 1891; "City League Base Ball," *Chicago Inter-Ocean*, Jul 17, 1891; "Herald's Base Ball Exchange," *Chicago Inter-Ocean*, Jul 27, 1891; "Scores of Prairie Contests," *Chicago Inter-Ocean*. Aug 8, 1891; "They Shine in the Prairie Clubs," *Chicago Inter-Ocean*, Aug 16, 1891; "Record of Chicago Unions," *Chicago Inter-Ocean*, Oct 19, 1891; "Base Ball Notes," *Chicago Tribune*, Jun 6, 1892; "Chicago Colored Society," *Springfield (IL) Record*, Jun 18, 1898.

Unique Base Ball Club Headquarters (228–230 South Clark Street, Chicago, IL; 1870s–1880s). Owner(s): William D. Berry.

The Unique B.B.C. operated under the auspices of baseballist William D. Berry and William Johnson. Johnson was a saloon owner, and his establishment, located at 228 and 230 South Clark Street, was the ball club's headquarters. The clubhouse a contained a saloon, barbershop, gambling, billiard ("the African Billiard Room") and reading rooms. In the 1870s, the headquarters also provided a resort for black Civil War veterans: "pork, beans, hard tack and coffee were the bill of fare." In 1875, the club hosted the Jubilee Singers.

SOURCES: "Base Ball," *Chicago (IL) Inter-Ocean*, Jun 16, 1874; "City Brevities," *Chicago Inter-Ocean*, May 26, 1874; "City Brevities," *Chicago Inter-Ocean*, May 31, 1874; "Colored Republicans," *Chicago Inter-Ocean*, Dec 21, 1875; "Killed and Wounded," *Chicago Inter-Ocean*, Apr 20, 1881.

Unknown Base Ball Club (Chicago, IL. Organizer(s): William Albert Jones and Fenton Harsh; 1883–1885).

In 1883, the Unknowns, an amateur club, played under the management of Fenton P. Harsh and William Albert Jones. The Unknowns played white and black clubs of IL, IA, MO, and WI (traveling as far North as Green Bay). They developed a rivalry with Chicago's white Pullman club. The Pullmans won the first contest, defeating the Unknowns before 1,000 spectators. Later, the Unknowns defeated their rivals before 5,000 fans.

SOURCES: "Sports of the Season," *Chicago (IL) Sunday Herald*, Jun 1, 1884; "Sporting Matters," *Chicago (IL) Times*, Jun 22, 1884; "Sports of the Season," *Chicago Sunday Herald*, Jun 22, 1884; "Chicago Doings," *New York (NY) Globe*, Jun 26, 1884; "Sports of the Season," *Chicago Sunday Herald*, Jun 29, 1884; "Chicago Doings," *New York Globe*, Aug 9, 1884; "On The Diamond Field," *Chicago Sunday Herald*, Aug 17, 1884.

Unknown Base Ball Club Headquarters (7 East Polk Street (Chicago, IL); 1880s). Organizer(s): William Abraham "Abe" Jones.

The Unknown B.B.C. operated in the 1880s. It was organized and operated under the auspices of Fenton Harsh and William Albert Jones. Jones; the team's headquarters being a saloon, located at 7 East Polk Street.

SOURCES: "Sports of the Season," *Chicago (IL) Sunday Herald*, Jun 1, 1884; "Sporting Matters," *Chicago (IL) Times*, Jun 22, 1884; "Sports of the Season," *Chicago Sunday Herald*, June 22, 1884; "Chicago Doings," *New York (NY) Globe*, Jun 26, 1884; "Sports of the Season," *Chicago Sunday Herald*, Jun 29, 1884; "Chicago Doings," *New York Globe*, Aug 9, 1884; "On the Diamond Field," *Chicago Sunday Herald*, Aug 17, 1884; "Amateurs Base Ball," *Chicago (IL) Inter-Ocean*, Jun 16, 1889; "Base Ball Items," *Chicago Inter-Ocean*, Apr 24, 1889; "The Amateurs Play Ball," *Chicago Inter-Ocean*, Aug 26, 1889.

Ward's Union Base Ball Club (Chicago, IL; 1890s). Organizer(s): R. Ward.

The Ward's Union B.B.C. organized in the 1890s. The Ward Unions, composed of Chicago Union players, played black and white nines. *Chicago Inter-Ocean* (July 21, 1894): "The Edgars and Ward Unions will play the second game of the Saturday series at the Northwest Park today. The Wards will be strengthened by Burns, Howland, Jackson, Campbell, and Brooks, of the original colored champions, the Chicago Unions." In the third game of their series, the Edgars thrashed the Ward Unions. In the third game of the series, the Edgars thrashed the Ward Unions. *Inter-Ocean* (August 12, 1894): "Lamont was in the box for the Edgars and made a record of seventeen strike-outs at the Northwest Park against the hard-hitting Unions yesterday."

Sources: "Amateur Baseball," *Chicago (IL) Inter-Ocean*, Jul 20, 1894; "Amateur Baseball," *Chicago Inter-Ocean*, Jul 21, 1894; "Amateur Baseball," *Chicago Inter-Ocean*, Aug 12, 1894; "Amateur Baseball," *Chicago Inter-Ocean*, Aug 19, 1894; "Buds of Base Ball Promise," *Chicago (IL) Times*. Aug 12, 1894.

Woods Base Ball Club (Chicago, IL; 1890s). Organizer(s): Bud Woods and Wince Dehoney.

The Woods B.B.C. organized in the 1890s. *Chicago Daily Inter-Ocean* (June 20, 1894): "Woods Base Ball Club (colored), having recently organized with Bud Woods and Wince Dehoney as managers, are ready to meet all comers. We play at our own grounds, Fortieth-Eighth and Halsted Streets."

Sources: "Amateur Baseball," *Chicago (IL) Inter-Ocean*, Jun 20, 1894.

Wrights Opera House Restaurant Base Ball Club (Chicago, IL; 1860s)

The Wrights Opera House Restaurant B.B.C. organized in the 1860s. The organization, composed of waiters, played black and white clubs. *Chicago Tribune* (August 23, 1867): "A match game of base-ball will be played on Monday at the Excelsior Grounds, between the colored waiters of Wright's Opera House restaurant and the waiters of the Sherman House."

Sources: "Base Ball," *Chicago (IL) Tribune*, Aug 23, 1867.

Plaza Hotel Union Base Ball Club (Danville, IL; 1900s). Organizer(s): William Webster.

The Plaza Hotel Union B.B.C. organized in 1900. The Unions played against black and white organizations. They played in southern IL, IN, KY, and MO. *Indianapolis Freeman* (April 28, 1900): "A new ball team has been organized in this city with William Webster as manager." *Freeman* (May 19, 1900): "The Danville Unions, the colored team from the city who have been on a southern tour, returned home last night with a record of seven games won out of eight played. They were defeated once 13 to 12 by the Paducah team but turned the tables the next day by defeating Paducah 11 to 2. Games were played with Evansville, Paducah, Mt. Vernon, Owensboro and Paris, Kentucky. The team will next make a northern trip, taking in Hoopeston, Roseville, Watseka, and other neighboring towns."

Sources: "Danville Notes," *Indianapolis (IN) Freeman*, Apr 28, 1900; "Danville News," *Indianapolis Freeman*, May 19, 1900; "Among Colored Folks," *Evansville (IN) Courier and Press*, May 26, 1900; "Among Colored Folks," *Evansville Courier and Press*, May 27, 1900; "City Notes," *Indianapolis Freeman*, Jun 2, 1900; "Interesting Items," *Indianapolis Freeman*, Jun 9, 1900; "Overcoming Obstacles," *Indianapolis Freeman*, Jun 16, 1900.

Black Diamond Base Ball Club (Decatur, IL; 1880s)

The Black Diamond B.B.C. organized in the 1880s. The Black Diamonds played black organizations. They developed a local rivalry with a black nine, the Brown Stockings. *Decatur Herald* (May 2, 1885): "The Black Diamonds defeated the Brown Stockings on the Round House Grounds yesterday by a score of 6 to 3." *Decatur Republican* (June 21, 1885): "The Black Diamonds and Brown Stockings will play a game next Tuesday at the Round House, on next Tuesday at 2:30pm. The Black Diamonds are Peter Williams, Ed Phoenix,

Ison Page, H. B. Langford, Dick Carter, Alfred Langford, Bill Short, John Caldwell and William Lucas." *Herald* (June 24, 1885): "The Black Diamonds and the Browns played a very interesting game of seven innings yesterday afternoon at the Round House Grounds. The Diamonds were badly rattled on the last inning and allowed their opponents to make five runs, thereby securing to them the game."

Sources: "About Town," *Decatur (IL) Herald*, May 2, 1885; "Local Paragraphs," *Decatur (IL) Review*, May 21, 1885; "Base Ball," *Decatur (IL) Republican*, Jun 20, 1885; "Local Paragraphs," *Decatur Review*, Jun 21, 1885; "Base Ball," *Decatur Herald*, Jun 24, 1885; "Personal Mention," *Decatur Republican*, Jul 3, 1885; "Base Ball Notes," *Decatur Review*, Jul 28, 1885; "Local Paragraphs," *Decatur Review*, Aug 8, 1885; "Diamond Dust," *Decatur Herald*, Jun 26, 1886.

Brown Stockings Base Ball Club (Decatur, IL; 1860s–1880s)

The Brown Stockings B.B.C. organized in the 1860s. The Brown Stockings played white and black teams. *Decatur Republican* (June 3, 1869): "A colored base-ball club has been organized in this city. The members practice in the fair grounds." *Daily Republican* (May 12, 1870): "The young colored men of Decatur, we are sorry to say, have taken a step backward—have organized a base-ball club!" When they defeated a local white nine, the "Browns" received national attention. *Republican* (August 13, 1875): "In a match game of base-ball yesterday afternoon, the Brown Stockings defeated the White Stockings (white) by a score of 12 to 10. A large crowd was present to witness the game, and the colored gentlemen were jubilant over the victory." A Decatur-Springfield rivalry developed. *Republican* (August 2, 1883): "The Decatur Browns tackled the Springfield Excelsiors, and were defeated by a score of 9 to 6. Bob Steward has no hesitation in declaring that the rank decisions of the umpire cost Decatur the game."

Sources: "Local Jottings," *Decatur (IL) Republican*, Jun 3, 1869; "Local Jottings," *Decatur Republican*, May 12, 1870; "Base Ball," *Decatur Republican*, Aug 13, 1875; "Match Game," *Decatur Republican*. Aug 17, 1875; "Base Ball," *Decatur Republican*, Aug 26, 1875; "Match Game of Base Ball," *Decatur Republican*, Jun 22, 1876; "City Department," *Decatur Republican*, Jun 2, 1876; "The Game of Base Ball," *Decatur Republican*, Jun 24, 1876; "City Department," *Decatur Republican*, Jul 6, 1880; "Day of Jubilee," *Decatur Republican*, August 1, 1883; "Base Ball," *Daily Republican*, Aug 2, 1883.

Black Diamond Base Ball Club (Decatur, IL; 1880s)

The Black Diamond B.B.C. organized in the 1880s. The "Black Diamonds" played black and white teams.

Sources: "Local Paragraphs," *Decatur (IL) Review*, May 21, 1885; "About Town," *Decatur (IL) Herald*, June 2, 1885; "Base Ball," *Decatur (IL) Republican*, June 20, 1885; "Local Paragraphs," *Decatur Review*, June 21, 1885; "Base Ball," *Decatur Herald*, June 24, 1885; "Diamond Dust," *Decatur Herald*, June 27, 1886.

Black Sharks Base Ball Club (Decatur, IL; 1880s)

The Black Sharks B.B.C. organized in the 1880s. The Black Sharks played black and white teams.

Sources: "Base Ball," *Decatur (IL) Daily Dispatch*, Aug 1, 1889; "A Big Score," *Decatur Daily Dispatch*, Aug 14, 1889.

Commonwealth Base Ball Club (Decatur, IL; 1880s)

The Commonwealth B.B.C. organized in the 1880s. The Commonwealth nine played black teams. *Decatur Republican* (February 19, 1886): "The colored base-ball nine 'Commonwealth' has received two challenges, and will go to Lincoln and Springfield to play as soon as the season opens, and Captain Love will play as soon as convenient." *Decatur Review* (April 28, 1886): "The colored club of this city accompanied the excursion to Jacksonville and played the colored club of that city."

SOURCES: "Base Ball," *Decatur (IL) Republican*, Feb 19, 1886; "Base Ball Yesterday," *Decatur Review*, Apr 28, 1886.

Quickstep Base Ball Club (Decatur, IL; 1880s)

The Quickstep B.B.C. organized in the 1880s. The Quicksteps played black teams. *Decatur Republican* (July 21, 1886): "The Black Diamonds and the Quicksteps played a game of base-ball yesterday afternoon at the Round House Grounds, resulting in favor of the Quicksteps by a score of 11 to 2. Both are colored clubs, and the Quicksteps composed of boys, feel very proud of their victory. The same clubs will repeat the game on Friday, at the Round House Grounds." *Decatur Herald* (July 23, 1886): "The Browns and Quicksteps, both colored clubs, played a seven inning game yesterday afternoon on the Pine Street grounds, and the former won by a score of 19 to 4."

SOURCES: "Base Ball Notes," *Decatur (IL) Review*, Jul 28, 1885; "Base Ball Notes," *Decatur (IL) Republican*, Jul 21, 1886; "The National Game," *Decatur Review*, Jul 23, 1886; "Diamond Dust," *Decatur (IL) Herald*, Jul 23, 1886.

Star Base Ball Club (Decatur, IL; 1880s). Organizer(s): Houston Singleton.

The Star B.B.C. organized in the 1880s. The Stars played black organizations. *Decatur Republican* (June 24, 1884): "The Decatur Stars, a local base-ball club of color, will go to Springfield on Tuesday next, to play the Black Diamonds [colored] of that city. Charlie Brown is captain of the Stars, and says his nine will wipe out the Diamonds." *Decatur Review* (June 27, 1884): "The Decatur Stars who went to Springfield, Illinois yesterday to down the Black Diamonds of that city, returned home last evening sore from an inglorious defeat. The club played at the League Park, the game being witnessed by a small audience. The Stars whitewashed their opponents in three innings, but when the ninth inning was played they were two tallies behind, the score standing at 27 to 25. Neither club played a good game. The Stars are in need of practice."

SOURCES: "Local and General News," *Decatur (IL) Republican*, Jun 24, 1884; "Local Paragraphs," *Decatur (IL) Review*, Jun 24, 1884; "Local Paragraphs," *Decatur Review*, Jun 27, 1884; "Local Paragraphs," *Decatur Review*, Jun 29, 1884; "Local Paragraphs," *Decatur Review*, Jul 2, 1884; *Decatur (IL) Herald*, Jul 3, 1884.

Lightfoot Base Ball Club (Du Quoin, IL; 1880s). Organizer(s): John Simmons.

The Lightfoot B.B.C. organized in the 1880s. The "Lightfoots" developed a rivalry with black clubs of MO. *St. Louis Globe-Democrat* (July 7, 1883): "The West Ends defeated the Lightfoot nine at Du Quoin, Illinois, the score standing 18 to 2." *Centralia Sentinel* (April 22, 1886): "Our colored base-ball club have received a challenge from the colored club of DuQuoin. It is thought that these giants will attempt to knock each other out about May 1st. May the colored troops fight nobly and the best nine win."

Globe-Democrat (August 19, 1886): "Jim Simmons, President of the Du Quoin Colored Ball Club has out in an authorized announcement that his club will play any colored club for ill for any amount of money. The club has lately been strengthened and is a really good one, not having been beaten in two years."

SOURCES: "Diamond Dust," *St. Louis (MO) Globe-Democrat*, Jul 7, 1883; "The City," *Centralia (IL) Sentinel*, Jul 2, 1885; "The City," *Centralia Sentinel*, Jul 24, 1885; "From Monday's Mail," *Centralia Sentinel*, Apr 22, 1886; "Colored Ball-Players of Illinois," *St. Louis Globe-Democrat*, Aug 19, 1886; "Champion Colored Players," *St. Louis*

Globe-Democrat, August 23, 1886; "Du Quoins 49, Carbondales, 19," *St. Louis Globe-Democrat*, Aug 14, 1887; "A Ball Game To-Day," *Globe-Democrat*, June 14, 1889.

Hussar Base Ball Club (Edwardsville, IL; 1890s)

The Hussar B.B.C. organized in the 1890s. The Hussars played black organizations. *Edwardsville Intelligencer* (August 13, 1895): "The Hussars, a picked nine of colored boys, went to Stanton Sunday and met defeat at the hands of the Hoosiers; score 20 to 7. Upon their return home, Charles Bradley, captain of the team, who had 'imbibed too much booze' and became unduly warm, was given a place in the cooler. Yesterday he was assessed $3 and cost by Magistrate Barraclough."

SOURCES: "Base Ball," *Edwardsville (IL) Intelligencer*, Aug 13, 1895.

Adelaide Base Ball Club (Elgin, IL; 1880s). Organizer(s): Augustus Hall and W. J. Christie.

The Adelaide B.B.C. organized in 1882. The Adelaides played against black and white clubs. Elgin and Rockford established a black rivalry. *Rockford Journal* (September 2, 1882): "The baseball game on the Fair Grounds, between the colored boys of Elgin and Rockford, resulted at the end of nine innings for Elgin and eight for Rockford in a score of 37 for Elgin and 31 for Rockford. By this time, it had become so dark that the game had to be closed, which was done by calling it a draw game." *Elgin Morning Frank* (August 14, 1883): "On Sunday the German clerks defeated the Adelaides in a score of 11 to 4." *Elgin News* (August 21, 1883): "Forty-two to 27 the Garden Citys easily best our Adelaides yesterday. In about three weeks, it is expected a return game to be played."

SOURCES: "Blue Stockings," *Elgin (IL) Frank*, Jun 19, 1882; "Local Matters," *Elgin Frank*, Jul 5, 1882; "Didn't Dare," *Elgin Frank*, Aug 3, 1882; "Local Matters," *Elgin Frank*, Aug 26, 1882; "Base Ball," *Elgin (IL) News.* Aug. 29, 1882; "Local Matters," *Elgin Frank*, Oct 14, 1882; "Aurora Again Beaten," *Elgin News*, Jul 17, 1883; "Base Ball," *Elgin Frank*, Jul 28, 1883; "Base Ball," *Elgin Frank*, Aug 14, 1883; "They Played a Picked Nine," *Elgin News*, Aug 21, 1883.

Black Stocking Base Ball Club (Elgin, IL; 1880s)

The Black Stocking B.B.C. organized in the 1880s. The "Black Stockings" played black organizations. *Aurora Express* (September 19, 1889): "At the Emancipation celebration to be held here September 23, the baseball contest will be between the Black Stockings, of Elgin and the Dark Secrets, of Aurora—two first-class clubs." *Chicago Inter-Ocean* (September 22, 1889): "The Elgin Colored Base Ball Club came down Tuesday and grappled the Aurora Senegambians on the diamond. The victory perched on Aurora's standard, the score being 24 to 10."

SOURCES: *Aurora (IL) Express*, Sep 19, 1889; "Aurora Bulletin," *Chicago (IL) Inter-Ocean*, Sep 22, 1889.

Blue Stocking Base Ball Club (Elgin, IL; 1880s). Organizer(s): Augustus Hall and W. J. Christie.

The Blue Stocking B.B.C. organized in 1882. The Blue Stockings played against black and white nines. Elgin and Aurora developed a rivalry. *Elgin Frank* (July 5, 1882): "The Blue Stockings of Elgin, wiped up the Aurora Base Ball Club, yesterday. Score, 11 to 27. Gus Hackley umpired the game and gave universal satisfaction by his decisions." *Rockford Register* (July 7, 1882): "Elgin has a club of colored men. The Elgin colored base-ball club Tuesday walloped the Auroras to the tune of 27 to 11."

SOURCES: "Blue Stockings," *Elgin (IL) Frank*, Jun 19, 1882; "Local Matters," *Elgin Frank*, Jul 5, 1882; "Base Ball," *Rockford (IL) Register*, Jul 7, 1882; "Didn't Dare," *Elgin Frank*, Aug 3, 1882; "Local Matters,"

Elgin Frank, Aug 26, 1882; "Base Ball," *Elgin (IL) News*, Aug 29, 1882; "Local Matters," *Elgin Frank*, Oct 14, 1882; "Aurora Again Beaten," *Elgin News*, Jul 17, 1883; "Base Ball," *Elgin Frank*, Jul 28, 1883.

Colored Base Ball Club (Galesburg, IL; 1890s)

The Colored B.B.C. organized in the 1890s. The ball club played black teams of IL and IA.

SOURCES: Colored Boys to Play," *Burlington (IA) Gazette*, Aug 19, 1896; "Challenged Colored Boys of Burlington," *Burlington Gazette*, Aug 19, 1896; "They Accept," *Burlington (IA) Daily Hawk-Eye*, Aug 21, 1896; "Galesburg Challenge Accepted," *Burlington Daily Hawk-Eye*, Aug 21, 1896.

Home Boys Base Ball Club (Jacksonville, IL; 1870s)

The Home Boys B.B.C. organized in 1871. The Home Boys played against similar organizations. Springfield and Jacksonville developed a rivalry. *Springfield State Journal* (July 1, 1871): "The Home Boys are fine players, and managed their cards most admirably, showing in their batting and fielding considerable skill and science; but as the result showed, they were no equal to the Dexters, who are considered one of the best—or the best-colored club in Illinois." *Chicago Pomeroy Democrat* (August 26, 1871): "Last Thursday a 'colored' match game of baseball was played in a fashion decidedly 'tall' on the Jacksonville grounds; between the 'Home Boys' and 'Dexters' of Springfield. They made a huge noise, but loud o'er the din could be heard afar, 'you niggar!—git off dat fust base dar! Ye local wer'nt there, but has heard it said that the 'Dexters' came out just forty ahead; and the reason they distanced the 'Home Boys' so far that nigger did 'git' from 'dat fust base dar!" In a two-game series, the "Dexters" were victorious both times.

SOURCES: "Local News in Lines," *Springfield (IL) Register*, Jun 28, 1871; "Base Ball," *Springfield (IL) State Journal*, Jul 1, 1871; "Base Ball at Jacksonville," *Springfield State Journal*, Jul 20, 1871; "Gropings and Groupings," *Chicago (IL) Pomeroy's Democrats*, Aug 26, 1871.

Cracker Jack Base Ball Club (Monmouth, IL; 1890s)

The Cracker Jack B.B.C. organized in the 1890s. The Cracker Jacks played black and white aggregations. *Monmouth Evening Gazette* (July 14, 1896): "The ball game at the college park yesterday between the Cracker Jacks and Maple City teams resulted in a victory for the Maple City's by a score of 5 to 3. *Monmouth Warren County Democrat* (August 19, 1897): "The Cracker Jack base-ball team drove over to Galesburg this morning in an open bus to play a game of ball this afternoon with the East End Stars of that place."

SOURCES: "Maple City Wins," *Monmouth (IL) Evening Gazette*, Jul 14, 1896; "Base Ball at Galesburg," *Monmouth (IL) Warren County Democrat*, Aug 19, 1897; "Not in the Game," *Monmouth Warren County Democrat*, Aug 19, 1897.

Pearly Blue Base Ball Club (Peoria, IL; 1880s)

The Pearly Blue B.B.C. organized in the 1880s. The Peoria Blues played black organizations. Peoria and Springfield developed a rivalry. *Springfield State Journal* (July 27, 1881): "The Pearly Blues, the Peoria House Colored Base Ball Club, and the Springfield Browns, are to play a match game at Base Ball Park, August 2. Our fellows are blue-black; the others dark brown. Trouble is to commence at 2:30, and the show of ivory will be immense. If the Blues let these Springfield coons get away with them they can make up their minds to immigrate." The competition continued into the mid–1880s. *Springfield Journal* (May 22, 1885): "Yesterday at the Base Ball Park, the Springfield Reds (colored) played against the Peoria Blues (colored), in a game of ball which resulted in a victory for the Springfields by a score of 25 to 5 in five innings. There was fair attendance, and although

the game was one-sided, and considerable interest was evinced by the spectators. The Springfield battery, Black and Williams, did effective work. The Peoria battery was very fair, but their first baseman, Cheek, was too much occupied in posing before the gaze of women to attend to business properly."

SOURCES: "Local Notes and Personals," *Springfield (IL) State Journal*, Jul 27, 1881; "Base Ball," *Springfield State Journal*, Aug 5, 1882; "The City," *Springfield State Journal*, May 20, 1885; "Base Ball," *Springfield State Journal*, May 22, 1885; "Base Ball," *Springfield State Journal*, May 23, 1885.

Black Diamond Base Ball Club (Quincy, IL; 1880s–1900s).

Organizer(s): E. Redmond.

The Black Diamond B.B.C. organized in the 1880s. The Black Diamonds played black organizations. *Quincy Journal* (October 1, 1888): "Saturday the West Ends, of St. Louis defeated the Black Diamonds here by a score of 9 to 6. Yesterday the same club defeated the Black Diamonds by a score of 13 to 2. Both clubs are composed of colored players, and the games were played at Highland." *Journal* (August 2, 1895): "They had a great game of ball out at Baldwin Park yesterday afternoon. The game was between the Quincy Black Diamonds, and the Canton, Missouri Noxalls. The game resulted in a score of 29 to 21 in favor of the Black Diamonds." *Quincy Whig* (June 11, 1899): "A colored base-ball team of Keokuk and the Quincy Black Diamonds will play a game of base-ball next Wednesday afternoon at Baldwin's. A colored excursion will come down that day." *Journal* (June 15, 1899): "The Keokuk Blues baseball club went down and played a match game with the Quincy Black Diamonds at Baldwin Park and defeated the Quincy aggregation by a score of 5 to 3." *Quincy Herald* (August 2, 1900): "There was a baseball game between the Quincy Unions and the Black Diamonds. The former won by a score of 9 to 1."

SOURCES: "West Ends vs. Black Diamonds," *Quincy (IL) Whig*, Sep 30, 1888; "Notes," *Quincy (IL) Journal*, Oct 1, 1888; "Notes," *Quincy Whig*, Oct 2, 1888; "Darktown Today," *Burlington (IA) Gazette*, Jun 28, 1894; "The City," *Burlington Gazette*, Jun 29, 1894; "Colored Teams Will Play," *Quincy Whig*, Aug 1, 1895; "The Diamond, Ring and Track," *Quincy Journal*, Aug 2, 1895; "Newsy Letter From Canton," *Quincy (IL) Herald*, Aug 8, 1895; "Gossip of the Choir," *Quincy Whig*, Jun 11, 1899; "Local and General News, *Quincy Journal*. June 15, 1899; "They Carved Much Meat," *Quincy Herald*, Aug 2, 1900.

Blues Base Ball Club (Quincy, IL; 1880s–1890s)

The Blues B.B.C. organized in the 1880s. The Quincy Blues played white and black organizations. *Quincy Herald* (June 19, 1889): "The Quincy Blues will cross bats at Louisiana with the St. Louis West Ends, another colored nine." *Quincy Journal* (October 26, 1890): "There will be a ball game tomorrow afternoon, at Sportsman's Park, between the Noxalls and the Quincy Blues. Both clubs contain good players and a close game is expected." *Quincy Whig* (June 9, 1891): "At People's Park on Sunday, the Highstanders defeated the Quincy Blues by a score of 7 to 6." *Quincy Journal* (September 22, 1891): "The Quincy Blues, the best colored team in this city, went down to Hannibal Sunday and were defeated by a colored nine of that city by a score of 10 to 0. Hannibal's team is one of the best in the country and it is said that the best feature of the game was that there was no quarreling or wrangling." *Quincy Journal* (June 27, 1893): "The Black Giants, of this city [Keokuk, Iowa], and the Quincy Blues, both colored nines, will play at Athletic Park Thursday afternoon. The Black Giants have a better team than ever and are in good trim."

SOURCES: "The Colored Clubs," *St. Louis (MO) Republic*, Jun 15, 1889; "The River and Railroads," *Quincy (IL) Herald*, Jun 19, 1889; "Brevities," *Quincy Herald*, Sep 27, 1890; "Ball Game," *Quincy (IL)*

Journal, Oct 26, 1890; "Notes," *Quincy (IL) Whig*, Jun 2, 1891; "Notes," *Quincy Whig*, Jun 9, 1891; "Badly Defeated," *Quincy Journal*, Sep 22, 1891; "City Brevities," *Quincy Herald*, Jun 27, 1893; "Local and General News," *Quincy Journal*, Jun 27, 1893.

The Tea Roses Base Ball Club (Quincy, IL; 1880s)

The Tea Roses B.B.C. organized in the 1880s. The Tea Roses played white and black teams. *Quincy Herald* (April 2, 1882): "A colored nine played what is known as the Bloom nine, (white) on Sunset Hill yesterday. The colored club won by 30 to 17." The Tea Roses challenged a prominent white organization. *Herald* (July 25, 1882): "The colored base-ball club, traveling under the euphonious name of The Tea Roses, have issued a challenge to the Pastimes for a game next Thursday afternoon, to be called after four o'clock. As yet the Pastimes [white] have not responded." The club faced prejudice. *Herald* (August 3, 1882): "The Quicksteps refused to allow the colored ball tossers to play on their grounds at Singleton Park yesterday. The players had to go to the prairie. The Herald would like to know why the colored base-ball clubs couldn't use Singleton Park last week." They measured bats with Hannibal, MO's black nine. *Herald* (September 7, 1882): "The colored base-ball club of this city played a game of base-ball with the Hannibal colored nine Tuesday resulting in the defeat of the latter club."

Sources: "Items in Brief," *Quincy (IL) Herald*, Apr 2, 1882; "Items in Brief," *Quincy Herald*, Jul 25, 1882; "Items in Brief," *Quincy Herald*, Aug 3, 1882; "Items in Brief," *Quincy Herald*, Sep 7, 1882; "Base Ball," *Quincy Herald*, Sep 10, 1882; "Items in Brief," *Quincy Herald*, Sep 19, 1882.

Union Base Ball Club (Quincy, IL; 1900s)

The Union B.B.C. organized in 1900, black teams. *Quincy Herald* (August 2, 1900): "There was a baseball game between the Quincy Unions and the Black Diamonds. The former won by a score of 9 to 1." *Herald* (August 10, 1900): "The Kansas City Unions and the Quincy Unions, both colored, crossed bats at Baldwin Park yesterday afternoon, the former winning by a score of 14 to 13. The Kansas City team is a strong one and there is some talk of their playing the Reserves."

Sources: "They Carved Much Meat," *Quincy (IL) Herald*, Aug 2, 1900; "Local and General News," *Quincy (IL) Journal*, Aug 9, 1900; "City Brevities," *Quincy (IL) Herald*, Aug 10, 1900.

Buster Base Ball Club (Rockford, IL; 1880s). Organizer(s): Henry Harris.

The Buster B.B.C. organized in the 1880s. The Busters played black organizations. Rockford, Elgin and Aurora developed a rivalry. *Elgin News* (August 23, 1883): "Rockford colored players are greatly excited over a prospective game with the Elgin coons. Henry Harris is the Rockford captain's name." *Elgin Morning Frank* (August 30, 1883): "On Tuesday, the Aurora Senegambians defeated a Rockford colored club in a score of 32 to 19, The game was played in Aurora." *Rockford Gazette* (July 11, 1884): "They met upon the diamond green and bravely fought and well, but Rockford was too much for them, and just before the sable mantle of blackest night had fallen over the fairgrounds, the visitors gave up the contest, and hied themselves to the Edward House to seek a square and hearty meal. There were nine of them all told, and all colored, and they left the classic environs of Aurora to wrest the girdle of base-ball championship from their ebony hued brethren of the Forest City. The Auroraites were a well-built and gentlemanly set of players, and showed more than ordinary proficiency in playing, but they could not take as kindly to the Rockford pitcher as they desired, and the result was that they were beaten. The crowd of spectators was large, enthusiastic and good natured, and

applauded the efforts of all alike. They watched with unbounded amusement the antics of the black-baseballists and roared with laughter at the droll remarks of the players."

Sources: "Base Ball Biz," *Rockford (IL) Weekly Gazette*, Jul 7, 1882; *Rockford (IL) Gazette*, Jul 31, 1882; *Rockford (IL) Register*, Aug 2, 1882; *Rockford Weekly Gazette*, Aug 16, 1882; "Base Ball," *Elgin (IL) News*, Aug 29, 1882; "Darkies' Day," *Rockford Gazette*, Aug 29, 1882; *Rockford Weekly Gazette*, Sep 7, 1882; *Rockford (IL) Journal*, Sep 2, 1882; *Rockford Weekly Gazette*, Sep 19, 1882; *Rockford Weekly Gazette*, Jul 25, 1883; "Base Ball Notes," *Rockford News*, Aug 25, 1883; "Base Ball Notes," *Elgin (IL) News*, Aug 25, 1883; "Base Ball," *Elgin (IL) Morning Frank*, Aug 30, 1883; *Rockford Gazette*, Jul 9, 1884; *Rockford Register*, Jul 9, 1884; "Colored Troops," *Rockford Register*, Jul 11, 1884.

Clipper Base Ball Club (Rockford, IL; 1890s)

The Clipper B.B.C. organized in the 1890s. The Clippers played black and white teams. *Rockford Morning Star* (September 11, 1891): "The second game between the Dark Secrets of Aurora and the Clippers was won by the latter by a score of 13 to 8. The locals out-batted and fielded better than their opponents. Harris the third baseman umpired the game. The Aurora boys didn't put up any money and won't have to walk home." *Morning Star* (July 7, 1892): "The Maroons and Clippers played an exciting game of ball at West End park yesterday afternoon, the former winning by as score of 5 to 4." *Rockford Republic* (May 29, 1899): "The old E & W baseball team, now known as the Grays, played a one-sided contest with the colored nine, the Clippers, at Glen Eyre Park yesterday, the former winning out by a score of 25 to 3. The battery for the Clippers was Frank Ferguson and Leo Miller."

Sources: "That Hard Aggregation," *Rockford (IL) Register*, Aug 26, 1891; "A Thing of the Past," *Rockford (IL) Morning Star*, Sep 9, 1891; "Darkness and Daylight," *Rockford Morning Star*, Sep 10, 1891; "Base Ball Chat," *Rockford Morning Star*, May 24, 1892; "Maroons vs. Clippers," *Rockford Morning Star*, Jul 7, 1892; "The City By Starlight," *Rockford Morning Star*, May 9, 1893; "From the Rosy East," *Rockford (IL) Spectator*, Jun 1, 1893; "The Season Opened," *Rockford Morning Star*, Apr 20, 1894; "Baseball at the Fairgrounds," *Rockford Morning Star*, May 9, 1894; "Other Ball Notes," *Rockford Morning Star*, Jun 17, 1894; "A Tie Game," *Rockford Morning Star*, Jun 19, 1894; "The City By Starlight," *Rockford Morning Star*, Jun 29, 1894; "At the Fair Grounds," *Rockford Morning Star*, Jul 10, 1894; "Sporting," *Rockford (IL) Register Star*, Oct 20, 1896; "Colored Base Ball Nine," *Rockford (IL) Republic*, May 22, 1899; "Colored Boys Won," *Rockford Republic*, Apr 14, 1899; "Some Diamond Dust," *Rockford Morning Star*, May 23, 1899; "Greys Beat This Time," *Rockford Republic*, May 29, 1899.

Nelson House Base Ball Club (Rockford, IL; 1880s–1890s)

The Nelson House B.B.C. flourished in the 1880s and 1890s. The Nelson House, composed of waiters, played black teams. *Rockford Register Gazette* (October 19, 1896): "There was an interesting game of base-ball scheduled at West End Park this afternoon, the Rockford ball club (colored) to play against the Nelson House team (also colored). The players are evenly matched and those who have been looking in vain for democratic money on the election without heart-breaking odds placed it even on the result of the contest."

Sources: "Close the Season," *Rockford (IL) Register Gazette*, Oct 19, 1896; "Sporting," *Rockford Register Gazette*, Oct 20, 1896.

Pink Stockings Base Ball Club (Rockford, IL; 1870s)

The Pink Stocking B.B.C. organized in 1870. The Pink Stockings played black organizations. They developed rivalries with the cities of Beloit, WI and Chicago, IL. They played a three championship games with the "Blues." Game one occurred at Rockford Fairgrounds.

Rockford Weekly Gazette (August 6, 1870): "On Monday last, the Blue Stockings, of Chicago, played a game with the Rockfords, at the Fairgrounds and out home Club beat the visitors." The second contest took place in Chicago. *Weekly Gazette* (August 25, 1870): "At a game of base-ball in Chicago on Tuesday between the Pink Stockings, of Rockford, and Blue Stockings, of Chicago, two colored base-ball clubs, the score stood: Rockford 14; Chicago, 48. No remarks." In late September, the clubs played a final game. *Rockford Register* (October 1, 1870): "The first game was played here and won by the Rockfords; the second in Chicago by the Blues; and the third was won by the Blue Stockings, 28 to 18. The latter now claim the colored championship of the State."

SOURCES: "Notings," *Rockford (IL) Weekly Gazette*, Jun 30, 1870; "The Colored Clubs," *Rockford Weekly Gazette*, Aug 6, 1870; "The Colored Clubs," *Rockford Weekly Gazette*, Aug 20, 1870; "Games to Come," *Chicago (IL) Tribune*, Aug 20, 1870; "Local Jottings," *Rockford Weekly Gazette*, Aug 20, 1870; "The Colored Troops," *Chicago (IL) Evening Journal*, Aug 23, 1870; "Base Ball From A Colored Point Of View," *Chicago Tribune*, Aug 24, 1870; "A Colored Game," *Chicago (IL) Times*, Aug 24, 1870; "On Tour," *Rockford (IL) Register*, Aug 27, 1870; "Colored Clubs," *Rockford Register*, Oct 1, 1870.

White Stocking Base Ball Club (Rockford, IL; 1870s). Organizer(s): Benjamin Davis and John Baxter.

The White Stocking B.B.C. organized in the 1870s. The White Stockings played black organizations. Beloit, WI and Rockford developed a rivalry. *Rockford Weekly Gazette*: "The colored folks of Rockford and Beloit, are going to have a gala here in Rockford, upon which occasion a game of base-ball will be played between the White Stockings of Rockford (colored) and the Base Ball Club of Beloit (colored), at the Fair Grounds." *Madison Wisconsin State Journal*: "The Beloit colored nine and Rockford, Illinois colored nine played a match game of ball at the fairgrounds. The game was well played up until the sixth inning, the game standing 20 to 13 in favor of Beloit."

SOURCES: "Local Jottings," *Rockford (IL) Weekly Gazette*. Aug. 17, 1876; *Rockford Weekly Gazette*, Aug 18, 1876; "Beloit vs. Rockford," *Rockford Weekly Gazette*, Aug 31, 1876; *Rockford Weekly Gazette*, Sep 1, 1876; "Beloit Letter," *Madison (WI) Wisconsin State Journal*, Aug 28, 1877; *Rockford Weekly Gazette*, September 6, 1877; *Rockford Weekly Gazette*, September 8, 1877; *Rockford Weekly Gazette*, September 21, 1877.

Acme Base Ball Club (Springfield, IL; 1870s). Organizer(s): A. Wright, August Knight and W. F. Wright.

The Acme B.B.C. organized in the 1870s. The Acmes played black organizations. *Springfield Illinois State Journal* (August 1, 1879): "The excursion party was accompanied by the Acme Base Ball Club, of this city, which played a match game with the Nationals of Jacksonville. The game resulted in a score of 18 to 7, in favor of the Acmes." *Illinois State Journal* (August 2, 1879): "The [excursion] party was accompanied by the Acme Base Ball Club, of this city, which played a match with the Nationals of Jacksonville. The game resulted in a score of 18 to 7, in favor of the Acmes."

SOURCES: "Organized," *Springfield (IL) State Register*, May 24, 1879; "Base Ball," *Springfield (IL) State Journal*, May 24, 1879; "Base Ball," *Springfield State Register*, May 25, 1879; "Base Ball," *Springfield State Journal*, Aug 1, 1879; "Excursion to Jacksonville," *Springfield State Journal*, Aug 2, 1879.

Black Diamond Base Ball Club (Springfield, IL; 1880s–1890s). Organizer(s): Harry Hodges.

The Black Diamond B.B.C. organized in the 1880s. The Black Diamonds played white and black organizations. In the 1880s, they devel-oped a local black rivalry with the Excelsiors. *Springfield State Journal* (May 15, 1884): "A game of base-ball was played yesterday by the Excelsiors and Black Diamond clubs. The contest was to determine the best colored club in the city. The score stood at the end of the ninth inning 13 to 11 in favor of the Excelsiors." After a hiatus, the team reorganized in the 1890s. The young Black Diamonds against the Amateur Reds, a white aggregation. *Springfield Illinois State Register* (May 23, 1893): "The Amateur Reds defeated the Black Diamonds by a score of 14 to 4 Sunday afternoon. Baker struck out fifteen men and only three safe hits were made off his delivery." *Illinois State Journal* (May 13, 1895): "The Black Diamonds received a setback yesterday from the far-famed Hub City Clothing House team. The Black Diamonds are supposed to be the strongest colored club in the state and had not been beaten in a number of years." They continued to play local white nines, including the Hustlers. *Illinois State Register* (April 11, 1897): "The Black Diamonds defeated the Hustlers yesterday in a game of base-ball at the corner of Nineteenth and Washington Streets. The battery for the Hustlers was composed of F. O'Brien and Willie Walsh. C. Reed and George King formed the battery for the Black Diamonds. Score, 1 to 0."

SOURCES: "Minor Mention," *Springfield (IL) State Register*, Apr 3, 1884; "Base Ball," *Springfield (IL) State Journal*, May 15, 1884; "The Black Diamonds Win," *Springfield State Journal*, Aug 16, 1892; "Base Ball Pick-Ups," *Springfield State Journal*, May 16, 1893; "On the Local Diamond," *Springfield State Journal*, May 22, 1893; "Brokers Pitching Was Great," *Springfield State Journal*, May 23, 1893; "Will Celebrate Today," *Springfield State Journal*, Sep 22, 1893; "On the Local Diamond," *Springfield State Journal*, May 31, 1894; "A Good Game Today," *Springfield State Journal*, Jun 17, 1894; "Local Base Ball," *Springfield State Journal*, Jun 24, 1894; "Black Diamonds Beaten," *Springfield State Journal*, May 13, 1895; "The Hubs Are Beaten," *Springfield State Journal*, May 25, 1895; "On the Local Diamond," *Springfield State Journal*, May 25, 1895; "Jacksonville Wins Again," *Springfield State Register*, May 28, 1895; "Local Ball Games," *Springfield State Register*, Jun 22, 1895; "A Warm Game," *Springfield State Journal*, Jul 5, 1896; "Juvenile Base Ball," *Springfield State Register*, Apr 11, 1897; "Black Diamonds Win Out," *Springfield State Register*, Apr 11, 1897; "Black Diamonds Win," *Springfield State Register*, May 13, 1899; "Local Ball Games," *Springfield State Register*, May 20, 1899.

Brown Stocking Base Ball Club (Springfield, IL; 1870s–1880s). Organizer(s): George McKinney and Walter Oglesby.

The Brown Stocking B.B.C. organized in 1876. The Browns played black organizations. *Springfield State Journal* (June 24, 1876): "A colored baseball club has been organized in this city, and gets in such good work on the diamond s to make its challenge to all amateur nines of some force." The Springfield club continued its colored rivalry with Jacksonville. Springfield and Peoria developed a rivalry. *State Journal* (July 27, 1881): "The Pearly Blues, the Peoria House Colored Base Ball Club, and the Springfield Browns, are to play a match game at Base Ball Park, August 2. Our fellows are blue-black; the others dark brown. Trouble is to commence at 2:30, and the show of ivory will be immense. If the Blues let these Springfield coons get away with them they can make up their minds to immigrate."

SOURCES: "Brevities," *Springfield (IL) State Journal*, Jun 24, 1876; "Base Ball," *Springfield State Journal*, Aug 30, 1876; "Ball and Bat," *Bloomington (IL) Leader*, Aug 30, 1876; "Ball and Bat," *Bloomington Leader*, Sep 11, 1876; "Base Ball," *Springfield State Journal*, Oct 4, 1876; "And Still Another," *Springfield State Journal*, May 12, 1877; "City Matters," *Bloomington Leader*, May 25, 1877; "Base Ball," *Springfield State Journal*, Aug 27, 1877; "Local Notes and Personals," *Springfield*

State Journal, Jul 27, 1881; "Local Paragraphs," *Decatur (IL) Review*, Apr 19, 1882; "Base Ball," *Springfield State Journal*, Aug 5, 1882.

Crescent Base Ball Club (Springfield, IL; 1890s–1900s)

The Crescent B.B.C. organized in the 1890s. The Crescents played black and white nines. *Springfield Illinois State Register* (May 29, 1900): "Sunday afternoon the Crescent Colored Base Ball Team defeated the Capital City Lyceum, white team, by the large score of 35 to 18 in favor of the colored team. These clubs have met twice now and another game is looked for soon. They are two strong teams, and managers Bert Barton and William Blackwell say they are willing to meet any amateur team, or would like to play the old Springfield team for once. The battery for the Crescents was Kirby and Howard, and they were well supported." *Springfield State Journal* (June 21, 1900): "The Crescent Baseball team defeated the Leland Blues yesterday by a score of 17 to 12. This was the second victory of the Crescents over the Blues. The batteries for the Crescents were Howard and Hayes; for the Blues, Burns, Outland, and Donnegan."

SOURCES: "Swell Colored Party," *Springfield (IL) State Register*, Jul 20, 1899; "Correspondence," *Springfield State Register*, Jan 8, 1898; "Birthday Party," *Springfield State Register*. Feb. 26, 1898; "X-Ray Column," *Springfield State Register*, Apr 16, 1898; "Bloomington Cake Walk," *Springfield State Register*, Jun 4, 1898; "Swell Colored Party," *Springfield State Register*, Jul 20, 1899; "Crescents Victorious," *Springfield State Register*, May 29, 1900; "Crescents' Victory," *Springfield State Register*, Jun 21, 1900; "Crescents Won Again," *Springfield (IL) State Journal*, Jun 22, 1900.

Dexter Star Base Ball Club (Springfield, IL; 1860s–1870s). Organizer(s): Charles Parker.

The Dexter Star B.B.C. organized in 1867. The Dexters challenged black and white organizations. *Springfield Illinois State Register*: "The crack colored base-ball club, of Springfield, Illinois, is of the colored persuasion. The citizens of that place are very anxious to match their crack club against the Excelsiors of this city. We are authorized to state that if the Springfield people will varnish the colored nine so as to keep down the smell, the Excelsiors will consent to play the Dexters." Between 1867 and 1870, Charles Parker (born in VA in 1842) served as team president and captained the team. They traveled the Midwest: in 1870, the Dexter club visited St. Joseph, MI, where they played a white team. Springfield and Bloomington developed a rivalry. The Dexters played Bloomington's Independent club, for the state championship. *Leader* (August 24, 1869): "The Bloomington Independents, composed of the smartest of our young colored men, has a colored club, have gone to Springfield to play a match game with the Dexter Base Ball Club, of that city. They made a very presentable appearance in their turbans and belts." *Springfield State Register* (August 25, 1869): "Yesterday afternoon a large crowd assembled at the Capitol grounds to witness the match between the Independent Club, of Bloomington, and the Dexter Club, of this city. The game resulted in favor of the Independents by 35 to 55." The Dexters also played Jacksonville's black team. *Springfield State Journal* (July 1, 1871): "The Home Boys are fine players, and managed their cards most admirably, showing in their batting and fielding considerable skill and science; but as the result showed, they were no equal to the Dexters, who are considered one of the best—or the best-colored club in Illinois." *Chicago Pomeroy Democrat* (August 26, 1871): "Last Thursday a 'colored' match game of baseball was played in a fashion decidedly tall on the Jacksonville grounds; between the Home Boys and Dexters of Springfield. They made a huge noise, but loud o'er the din could be heard afar, you niggar! —git off dat fust base dar! Ye local wer'nt there, but has heard it said that the 'Dexters' came out just forty ahead; and the reason they distanced the Home Boys so

far that nigger did git from dat fust base dar!" By 1871, what became known as comical coaching had baseball, and sportswriters incorporated real or imagined Negro dialect vernacular into their baseball narratives; this literary style, later popularized by Mark Twain, would have been familiar with the national popularity and circulation of "negro" dialect stories in genteel middle-class magazines.

SOURCES: "Base Ball," *Cincinnati (OH) Daily Gazette*, Aug 13, 1867; *Springfield (IL) State Register*, Aug 26, 1867; "Bloomington Independents," *Bloomington (IL) Leader*, Aug 24, 1869; "Base Ball," *Springfield State Register*, Aug 25, 1869; "Match at Springfield—Bloomington Colored Men Ahead," *Bloomington Leader*, Aug 26, 1869; "Talked on the Street," *St. Joseph (MI) Herald*, Jun 4, 1870; "Base Ball on the Fourth," *Bloomington (IL) Leader*, Jun 29, 1870; "Fourth of July," *Springfield State Register*, Jun 30, 1870; *Springfield (IL) State Journal*, Jul 20, 1870; "The Colored Championship," *Chicago (IL) Times*, Aug 20, 1870; "Base Ball Matters," *Cincinnati (OH) Commercial Tribune*, Sep 23, 1870; "Base Ball at Jacksonville," *Springfield State Journal*, Jul 20, 1871; "Base Ball," *Springfield State Journal*, Aug 17, 1871; "Gropings and Groupings," *Chicago (IL) Pomeroy's Democrat*, Aug 26, 1871.

Hub Base Ball Club (Springfield, IL; 1880s)

The Hub B.B.C. organized in the 1880s. The Hubs measured bats with black and white nines. *Illinois State Register* (September 22, 1889): "The Leland Blues defeated the Hubs, both colored, at the ball park before an audience of 101 people. The Hubs are sorry they 'spoke,' for the Blues made them 'tired' in one hour and forty minutes. The game was very interesting and was a tie up to the ninth inning, when the Blues made one run, winning the game by a score of 9 to 8."

SOURCES: "Local Base Ball Points," *Springfield (IL) State Journal*, Aug 21, 1889; "Leland Blues vs. Hubs," Springfield *(IL) State Register*, Sep 22, 1889.

Leland Hotel Base Ball Club (Springfield, IL; 1880s–1900s). Organizer(s): J. W. Young, Jordan Murray, J. H. Stevens and Barney Clem.

The Leland Hotel B.B.C. organized in the 1880s. In 1881, the Black Legs, composed of Leland Hotel waiters, competed against black and white organizations. *Springfield State Journal* (April 27, 1881): "Another game of baseball was played between the Leland Hotel Black Legs and the Town Scrubs yesterday afternoon resulting in 24 for each side, the Black Legs playing eight innings and the Scrubs nine." *State Journal* (April 30, 1881): "The Leland Hotel Base Ball Club played its first game under the new organization with the Machine Shop [white] club yesterday afternoon, winning an easy victory on a score of 21 to 13." The team was renamed. *State Journal* (July 28, 1881): "The name of the Leland Base Ball Club has been changed to the Fisk Base Ball Club, in honor of the Jubilee Singers." By 1889, the team had been renamed the Leland Blues. *State Journal* (September 21, 1889): "The Leland Blues, the champions of Central Illinois and the Hubs, the famous Chicago clothing house nine, will cross bats at the League Park this afternoon for the championship of the state. Proceeds [go] for the Emancipation Proclamation celebration." *Springfield Illinois State Register* (September 22, 1889): "The Leland Blues defeated the Hubs, both colored, at the ball park before an audience of 101 people. The Hubs are sorry they 'spoke,' for the Blues made them 'tired' in one hour and forty minutes. The game was very interesting and was a tie up to the ninth inning, when the Blues made one run, winning the game by a score of 9 to 8." *State Journal* (June 21, 1900): "The Crescent Baseball team defeated the Leland Blues yesterday by a score of 17 to 12. This was the second victory of the Crescents over the Blues. The batteries for the Crescents were Howard and Hayes; for the Blues, Burns, Outland, and Donnegan."

SOURCES: "Local Notes and Journal," *Springfield (IL) State Register*, Apr 24, 1881; "Local Notes and Journal," *Springfield (IL) State Journal*, Apr 27, 1881; "Local Notes and Journal," *Springfield State Register*, Apr 28, 1881; "Local Notes and Journal," *Springfield State Journal*, Apr 30, 1881; "Local Notes and Personals," *Springfield State Journal*, Jul 28, 1881; "Fun Ahead," *Decatur (IL) Weekly Republican*, Aug 15, 1889; "Defeated the Leland Blues," *Springfield State Journal*, Sep 15, 1889; "Gossip of the Game," *Springfield State Journal, Sep 21, 1889*; "Leland Blues vs. Hubs," *Springfield State Register*, Sep 22, 1889; "Defeated the Leland Blues," *Springfield State Register, Sep 5, 1891*; "Crescents' Victory," *Springfield State Register*, Jun 21, 1900; "Crescents Won Again," *Springfield State Journal*, Jun 22, 1900.

Lone Star Base Ball Club (Springfield, IL; 1870s). Organizer(s): Moses McCloud and Dennis Williams.

The Lone Star B.B.C. organized in 1877. The Lone Stars continued Springfield's black rivalry with Bloomington. *Springfield State Journal* (May 24, 1877): "The Lone Star Base Ball Club will play their first game on Friday at Bloomington, with the Brown Socks of that place." *Bloomington Pantagraph* (May 26, 1877): "The Brown Sox of Bloomington were defeated by a score of 19 to 9 by the Springfield Lone Stars."

SOURCES: "Another," *Springfield (IL) State Journal*, Apr 26, 1877; "Base Ball," *Bloomington (IL) Leader*, May 15, 1877; "The City," *Bloomington (IL) Pantagraph*, May 16, 1877; "B. B.," *Springfield State Journal, May 24, 1877*; "Base Ball Racket," *Bloomington Leader*, May 24, 1877; "Base Ball," *Bloomington Pantagraph*, May 25, 1877; "Base Ball," *Bloomington Pantagraph*, May 26, 1877.

Lowell Base Ball Club (Springfield, IL; 1870s). Organizer(s): Charles Morgan and D. Faro (Ferro).

The Lowell B.B.C. organized in the 1870s. The Lowells played white and black organizations. *Springfield State Register* (May 25, 1879): "A match of base-ball was played between the Lowells and Acmes, resulting in a victory for the former, the score standing 17 to 2." *State Register* (June 8, 1879): "The Lowell Base Ball Club, of this city, composed of colored men, went to Jacksonville, yesterday, and played a match with the Jacksonville Athletics, of the Deaf and Dumb Asylum. The score was Lowells, 20, Jacksonville, 12. The Lowells will go to St. Louis to play three games with the Napoleon Cub, of that city. The Register wishes the Lowells the best kind of luck."

SOURCES: "A Challenge," *Springfield (IL) Illinois State Journal*, May 4, 1879; "A Challenge," *Springfield Illinois State Journal*, May 14, 1879; "Base Ball," *Springfield Illinois State Journal*, May 21, 1879; "Base Ball," *Springfield (IL) Illinois State Register*, May 25, 1879; "Springfield in the Front Again," *Springfield Illinois State Register*, Jun 8, 1879; "City News," *Springfield Illinois State Journal*, Jun 11, 1879.

Record Base Ball Club (Springfield, IL; 1890s). Organizer(s): Harry Dell Hodges and Fred Wright.

The Record B.B.C. organized in the 1890s. The Records played black teams. *Springfield State Journal* (April 20, 1898): "The Illinois Record, a colored newspaper in this city, has organized a colored baseball club, composed of some of the best colored baseball talent in the state. The club at present has twelve players on its list and are negotiating with one of the Chicago Union pitchers whom they expect to land in their team before so many days. The Illinois Records challenge any team in or out of the city for games. Address all challenges to the Illinois Record office."

SOURCES: "Danville, Ill's," *Springfield (IL) Record*, Mar 5, 1898; "Amateur Base Ball," *Springfield (IL) State Journal*, Apr 20, 1898; "City News in Brief," *Springfield Record*, April 23, 1898.

Red Stocking Base Ball Club (Springfield, IL; 1880s). Owner(s): George McKinney and Walter Oglesby.

The Red Stocking B.B.C. organized in the 1880s. The Reds played black organizations. They also played St. Louis's champion club, the Eclipse. *St. Louis Republican* (August 24, 1884): "The Eclipse will play the Springfield Reds, the champion colored club of Springfield, Illinois, this afternoon. A good game can be expected, as both clubs are playing for the state championship." *Republican* (August 25, 1884): "The Eclipse club defeated the Springfield, Illinois Reds yesterday afternoon at Compton Avenue Park by a score of 14 to 4." Springfield and Peoria developed a rivalry. *Springfield Journal* (May 22, 1885): "Yesterday at the Base Ball Park, the Springfield Reds (colored) played against the Peoria Blues (colored), in a game of ball which resulted in a victory for the Springfields by a score of 25 to 5 in five innings. There was fair attendance, and although the game was one-sided, and considerable interest was evinced by the spectators. The Springfield battery, Black and Williams, did effective work. The Peoria battery was very fair, but their first baseman, Cheek, was too much occupied in posing before the gaze of women to attend to business properly."

SOURCES: "Local Notes and Personals," *Springfield (IL) State Journal*, Jul 27, 1881; "Base Ball," *Springfield State Journal*, Aug 5, 1882; "Diamond Dust," *St. Louis (MO) Republican Journal*, Aug 24, 1884; "Diamond Chips," *St. Louis Republican Journal*, Aug 25, 1884; "The City," *Springfield State Journal*, May 20, 1885; "Base Ball," *Springfield State Journal*, May 22, 1885; "Base Ball," *Springfield State Journal*, May 23, 1885; *Decatur (IL) Review*, Jun 21, 1885.

Shinie Blacks Base Ball Club (Springfield, IL; 1890s)

The Shinie Blacks B.B.C. organized in the 1890s. *Springfield State Illinois Register* (April 11, 1897): "There was a very interesting game of base-ball played yesterday evening at the corner of Eighteenth and Jefferson Street between the Shinie Blacks and the Hustlers. The score stood 11 to 7 in favor of the Hustlers."

SOURCES: "Juvenile Base Ball," *Springfield (IL) State Register*, Apr 11, 1897.

Town Scrubs Base Ball Club (Springfield, IL; 1880s). Organizer(s): Rufus Hamilton.

The Town Scrubs B.B.C. organized in the 1880s. The Town Scrubs competed against black organizations. *Springfield State Journal* (April 27, 1881): "Another game of baseball was played between the Leland Hotel Black Legs and the Town Scrubs yesterday afternoon resulting in 24 for each side, the Black Legs playing eight innings and the Scrubs nine."

SOURCES: "Local Notes and Journal," *Springfield (IL) State Register*, Apr 24, 1881; "Local Notes and Journal," *Springfield (IL) State Journal*, Apr 27, 1881; "Local Notes and Journal," *Springfield State Register*, Apr 28, 1881.

Indiana

1897 Base Ball Club (Belleville, IN; 1890s). Organizer(s): Billy Buckner.

The 1897 B.B.C. organized in the 1890s. The '97s played black teams. *Mount Vernon Democrat* (July 28, 1897): "The Belleville '97's, headed by manager Billy Buckner, and accompanied by 50 rooters, go to Mt. Vernon, IL, Saturday to play the colored club of that place." *Democrat* (August 26, 1897): "A red hot game of ball occurred at Schieber Park Tuesday between colored clubs, the 400s and the '97's. The game ended in a row. The 400 club claimed they shut the 97's out, but the little inks claim they made one run. Another game will probably be made."

SOURCES: *Mount Vernon (IN) Democrat*, Jul 28, 1897; *Mount Vernon*

Democrat, Aug 12, 1897; *Mount Vernon Democrat*, Aug 19, 1897; *Mount Vernon Democrat*, Aug 26, 1897.

Bee Hive Base Ball Club (Bloomington, IN; 1890s). Owner(s): Willis Taylor.

The Bee Hive B.B.C. organized in the 1890s. The Bee Hives played black aggregations.

SOURCES: *Greencastle (IN) Banner and Times*, Jul 17, 1897; "And the Good Die Young," *Greencastle Banner and Times*, Jul 21, 1897; *Greencastle (IN) Star Press*, Jul 24, 1897.

Black Stockings Base Ball Club (Cambridge City, IN; 1880s)

The Black Stockings B.B.C. organized in the 1880s. The Black Stockings played black teams. *Cambridge City Tribune* (August 20, 1885): "The Clippers, of Connersville, and the Black Stockings, of Cambridge City, both colored, played a very creditable game of baseball at the park, Saturday last. The attendance was not large, but those present, enjoyed the sport, as there was lots of at the Black Stockings were the victorious colored club." *City Tribune* (September 17, 1885): "The game of base-ball at the Park on Saturday afternoon, between the colored clubs (Waynes, of Richmond, and Black Stockings, of this place) was noted for a few points only—heavy batting and errors. Both clubs at times played very well, but would soon become rattle and go to pieces. The visitors were all full-grown men, while most of our club were mere boys. The score at the end of the game, which lasted three hours, stood 28 to 24 in favor of the visitors."

SOURCES: *Cambridge City (IN) City Tribune*, Aug 17, 1885; *Cambridge City Tribune*, Aug 20, 1885; *Connersville (IN) Times*, Sep 2, 1885; *Cambridge City Tribune*, Sep 3, 1885; *Times*, Sep 9, 1885; *Cambridge City Tribune*, Sep 17, 1885.

Black Diamond Base Ball Club (Columbus, IN; 1890s)

The Black Diamond B.B.C. organized in the 1890s. The Black Diamonds played against black organizations.

SOURCES: "Play Ball at Hartsville," *Columbus (IN) Republic*, Jul 17, 1900; "Colored Picnic," *Columbus Republic*, Aug 6, 1900; *Columbus (IN) Daily Herald*, Aug 7, 1900; "Base Ball News," *Columbus Republic*, Aug 9, 1900; "News From the Diamond," *Columbus Republic*, Aug 10, 1900.

Colored Base Ball Club (Columbus, IN; 1890s)

The Colored B.B.C. organized in the 1890s. The team played against black organizations.

SOURCES: "Base Ball Team," *Columbus (IN) Weekly Times*, Mar 13, 1896; "Base Ball," *Columbus (IN) Times*, Mar 13, 1896; "Colored News Notes," *Columbus Times*, May 24, 1896, "Personals," *Columbus (IN) Herald*, May 23, 1896.

Black Diamond Base Ball Club (Connellsville, IN; 1890s). Organizer(s): Frank Pierce.

The Black Diamond B.B.C. organized in the 1890s. The Black Diamonds played white and black aggregations. *Connersville Times* (August 22, 1894): "Connersville always did modestly boast of being superior to Rushville. Now the Black Diamond Base Ball Club has no reason at all to doubt it. They defeated the Rushville colored baseball team in a game there yesterday by a score of 32 to 8. The feature of the game was a home run by Tom Pierce."

SOURCES: *Connellsville (IN) Examiner*, Aug 6, 1894; *Connellsville Examiner*, Aug 14, 1894; "Base Ball," *Connellsville Examiner*, Aug 15, 1894; "Connellsville Defeats Rushville," *Connellsville (IN) Times*, Aug 22, 1894.

Colored Barbers Base Ball Club (Connellsville, IN; 1870s–1890s). Organizer(s): Eli Bass.

The Colored Barbers B.B.C. organized in the 1870s. They Colored Barbers played black organizations. *Connersville Examiner* (August 19, 1885): "Our colored boys fought nobly last Saturday with the colored base-ball club at Cambridge City, but they were defeated by a score of 14 to 8. Weeks later, the Connersville club redeemed themselves. *Connersville Examiner* (September 2, 1885): "The colored base-ball club, of Cambridge City, and the colored club, of this city, played a match game at the park last Wednesday. The home club were victors, the score standing 12 to 9." *Connersville Times* (July 20, 1894): "The clerks and barbers played a handsome game of ball at the park, yesterday afternoon, before quite a crowd of spectators. The barbers played a hard game throughout and did not take the field in the last half of their inning. The score at the close stood 22 to 15 in favor of the tonsorial artists."

SOURCES: "Local and Personal," *Connellsville (IN) Examiner*, Aug 29, 1878; "Local and Personal," *Connellsville Examiner*, September 12, 1885; "Local and Personal," *Connellsville Examiner*, Aug 19, 1885; *Connellsville (IN) Times*, Aug 19, 1885; "Local and Personal," *Connellsville Examiner*, Sep 2, 1885; "Barbers Wiped 'Em Up Nicely," *Connellsville Times*, Jul 25, 1894; "Base Ball Matters," *Connellsville (IN) News*, Jul 27, 1894.

Silver Spray Base Ball Club (Connellsville, IN; 1890s)

The Silver Spray B.B.C. organized in the 1890s. The Silver Sprays played black teams. *Connersville News* (June 9, 1896): "The Silver Sprays, a colored base-ball team of this city, will play the Rushville colored base-ball club, at this place on June 24. The names of the Silver Sprays will be given later on."

SOURCES: *Connellsville (IN) News*, Jun 9, 1896; *Connellsville News*, Jun 10, 1896.

Clipper Base Ball Club (Crawfordsville, IN; 1880s–1890s). Organizer(s): F. B. Allen and Luther Monroe.

The Clipper B.B.C. organized in the 1880s. The Clippers played white and black teams.

SOURCES: "Our Colored People," *Crawfordsville (IN) Dispatch*, Jul 18, 1887; "Our Colored People," *Crawfordsville Dispatch*, Sep 12, 1887; "Our Colored People," *Crawfordsville Dispatch*, Sep 13, 1887; "Our Colored People," *Crawfordsville Dispatch*, Sep 15, 1887; "Our Colored People," *Crawfordsville Dispatch*, Sep 16, 1887; "The Hustlers Scooped," *Crawfordsville Dispatch*, Sep 23, 1887; "About Town," *Crawfordsville Argus News*, Sep 23, 1887; "About Town," *Crawfordsville Argus News*, Sep 24, 1887; "Colored Notes," *Crawfordsville (IN) Journal*, Jun 14, 1890; "Colored Notes," *Crawfordsville Journal*, Jun 23, 1890; "Colored Notes," *Crawfordsville Journal*, Jul 17, 1890; "Colored Notes," *Crawfordsville Journal*, Jul 22, 1890; "Colored Notes," *Crawfordsville Journal*, Jul 24, 1890; "Briefs," *Crawfordsville Journal*, Sep 20, 1890.

Cyclone Base Ball Club (Evansville, IN; 1900s)

The Cyclone B.B.C. organized in the 1900s. The Cyclones played black teams. *Evansville Courier and Press* (July 11, 1900): "An interesting game of ball took place Sunday between a picked nine under the captaincy of C. McFarland and the Evansville Cyclones on the latter's diamond. The feature of the game was the sensational catch made by McFarland when the opposing team had three men on bases."

SOURCES: "Amateur Ball Game," *Evansville (IN) Courier and Press*, Jul 11, 1900; "Colored Folks," *Evansville Courier and Press*, Jul 23, 1900; "Colored Folks," *Evansville Courier and Press*, Jul 27, 1900; "Colored Folks," *Evansville Courier and Press*, Jul 30, 1900.

Delmonico Base Ball Club (Evansville, IN; 1900s)

The Delmonico B.B.C. organized in 1900, played black teams. *Evansville Courier and Press* (July 26, 1900): "There will be a championship game of base-ball at the baseball park Saturday between the Lone Stars and Delmonicos. The game will be called at 3 p.m." *Courier and Press* (May 9, 1901): "John D. Miller will accompany his base-ball team to Vincennes, Indiana, Sunday. It is highly probable that "Broad Axe" Smith will umpire the game as he is considered one of the best umpires in the State."

Sources: "Among Colored People," *Evansville (IN) Courier and Press*, Mar 21, 1900; "Among Colored Folks," *Evansville Courier and Press*, Jul 26, 1900; "Among Colored Folks," *Evansville Courier and Press*, Jul 29, 1900; "Colored Folks," *Evansville Courier and Press*, May 9, 1901; "Colored Folks," *Evansville Courier and Press*, Jul 2, 1901.

Electric Reds Base Ball Club (Evansville, IN; 1880s)

The Electric Reds B.B.C. organized in the 1880s, played black teams. *Evansville Courier and Press* (August 10, 1883): "Princeton Clarion: The colored boys of this place have organized a base-ball club, and call themselves the Eckfords. Dressed in their white uniforms, they will make a raid on the Electric Reds, of Evansville, playing on enclosed grounds for the gate money." *New Harmony Register* (August 24, 1883): "The colored base-ball club, of Princeton, was taken in by the colored Electric Reds, of Evansville, last week, 30 to 27." A return game occurred. *Princeton Democrat* (September 24, 1883): "A colored base-ball club came up from Evansville to play the colored club at this place. The Princeton boys cleaned them up badly, and they returned home pretty well satisfied that they did not amount to much as base ballists."

Sources: "Base Ball Notes," *Evansville (IN) Courier and Press*, Aug 10, 1883; "Curious Local Dirt," *New Harmony (IN) Register*, Aug 24, 1883; "Local and Miscellaneous News," *Princeton (IN) Democrat*, Sep 24, 1883.

Gold Dollar Base Ball Club (Evansville, IN; 1890s–1900s). Owner(s): Clarence McFarland; Burton Slaughter.

The Gold Dollar B.B.C. organized in the 1890s, played black teams of KY (Owensboro, Louisville, Paducah and Henderson), TN (Clarksville), and IN (Indianapolis, Crawfordsville, and Evansville), and IL (Cairo and Chicago). *Evansville Courier and Press* (May 25, 1899): "The Gold Dollars and Paducah teams tried their skill at baseball yesterday afternoon in League Park and a spirited game was played. The Gold Dollars beat the Paducah [Grays] by a score of 16 to 4." *Courier and Press* (June 10, 1899): "One of the best games played at League Park during the present season was that which occurred yesterday afternoon between the Gold Dollars and the Majors. The score was 5 to 2 in favor of the Gold Dollars." The teams briefly consolidated. *Courier and Press* (July 7, 1899): "The Majors and Gold Dollars have merged into one lean, that is, the best players of the two have united and are now said to be the world beaters on the base-ball diamond."

Sources: "Among Colored Folks," *Evansville (IN) Courier and Press*, Apr 26, 1899; "Among Colored Folks," *Evansville Courier and Press*, May 13, 1899; "Among Colored Folks," *Evansville Courier and Press*, May 14, 1899; "Among Colored Folks," *Evansville Courier and Press*, May 16, 1899; "Colored Teams to Play," *Evansville Courier and Press*, May 20, 1899; "Among Colored Folks," *Evansville Courier and Press*, Jun 3, 1899; "Among Colored Folks," *Evansville Courier and Press*, Jun 10, 1899; *Evansville Courier and Press*, Jun 25, 1899; *Evansville Courier and Press*, Jun 30, 1899; "Among Colored Folks," *Evansville Courier and Press*, Jul 7, 1899; "Among Colored Folks," *Evansville Courier and Press*, Jul 14, 1899; "Among Colored Folks," *Evansville Courier and Press*, Jul 25, 1899; "Among Colored Folks," *Evansville Courier and Press*, Aug 9, 1899; *Evansville Courier and Press*, Jul 30, 1900.

Governor Street High School Base Ball Club (Evansville, IN; 1890s)

The Governor Street High School B.B.C. organized in the 1890s, played black nines. *Evansville Courier and Press* (July 29, 1897): "The Governor Street ball club, composed of colored gentlemen with a baseball turn of mind, left the city yesterday morning on the steamer Rose Hite for Owensboro. In that city, they will meet a colored nine in a series of two games."

Sources: New Briefs," *Evansville (IN) Courier and Press*, Apr 21, 1897; "Will Try Owensboro," *Evansville Courier and Press*, Jul 29, 1897; "Start Base Ball Season With A Social," *Evansville Courier and Press*, Feb 26, 1898; *Evansville Courier and Press*, March 8, 1898.

Majors Base Ball Club (Evansville, IN; 1890s). Organizer(s): George Blakey, "Scrap" Allen, P. Williams, John Roberts, Ernest Tidrington and Ecolas K. Watson.

The Majors B.B.C. organized in the 1890s, played black teams. The club's local rival was the Gold Dollar nine. *Evansville Courier and Press* (June 10, 1899): "One of the best games played at League Park during the present season was that which occurred yesterday afternoon between the Gold Dollars and the Majors. The score was 5 to 2 in favor of the Gold Dollars." The two teams briefly merged. *Courier and Press* (July 7, 1899): "The Majors and Gold Dollars have merged into one lean, that is, the best players of the two have united and are now said to be the world beaters on the base-ball diamond." They also played the Queen City Grays and Blue Stockings of Clarksville, TN. *Courier and Press* (July 25, 1899): "The Majors of this city and the Queens Citys of Clarksville, Tennessee crossed bats yesterday afternoon. The score: Majors 14; Queen Citys 1. The Majors played an excellent game of ball and would have shut out the Queen City team had it not been for an error by Abe Jackson."

Sources: "Colored Cake Walk," *Evansville (IN) Courier and Press*, Mar 30, 1899; "Among Colored Folks," *Evansville Courier and Press*, Apr 26, 1899; "Among Colored Folks," *Evansville Courier and Press*, May 16, 1899; "Colored Teams to Play," *Evansville Courier and Press*, May 20, 1899; "Among Colored Folks," *Evansville Courier and Press*, Jun 3, 1899; "Among Colored Folks," *Evansville Courier and Press*, Jun 10, 1899; *Evansville Courier and Press*, Jun 25, 1899; *Evansville Courier and Press*, Jun 30, 1899; "Among Colored Folks," *Evansville Courier and Press*, Jul 7, 1899; "Among Colored Folks," *Evansville Courier and Press*, Jul 14, 1899; "Among Colored Folks," *Evansville Courier and Press*, Jul 25, 1899; "Among Colored Folks," *Evansville Courier and Press*, Aug 9, 1899.

Mysterious Nine Base Ball Club (Evansville, IN; 1870s). Organizer(s): Charley Dellard.

The Mysterious Nine B.B.C. organized in the 1870s played black nines. *Evansville Courier and Press* (July 2, 1878): "The Mysterious Base Ball Club, a colored organization, will play the Atlantics of Henderson, on the 4th of July at the grounds at the head of Oak Street." *Courier and Press* (August 27, 1878): "The Rag Muffins were defeated by the Mysterious Nine yesterday by a score of 13 to 10." *Courier and Press* (August 26, 1879): "Captain Charley Dellard's Mysterious Nine played Captain Sam Burn's High-Toned picked nine yesterday and defeated them. The score stood at the close of the fifth inning 2 to 1, in favor of the Mysterious. Both nines are composed of colored boys, who are number one players. The game was played on the Lincoln Reds Grounds." *Courier and Press* (August 29, 1879): "The game played by the two colored clubs, Atlantics [Henderson, Kentucky] and Mysterious Nine, on the Eckford Grounds yesterday, was very fine, indeed. The game was decided in favor of the Atlantics, by a majority of one score, the final sore standing 10 to 9."

Sources: "Base Ball," *Evansville (IN) Courier and Press*, Jul 2, 1878;

"Base Ball," *Evansville Courier and Press*, Aug 29, 1878; "Base Ball," *Evansville Courier and Press*, Aug 26, 1879; "Base Ball," *Evansville Courier and Press*, August 27, 1879; "Base Ball Notes," *Evansville Courier and Press*, Aug 29, 1879.

Red Oaks Base Ball Club (Evansville, IN; 1880s)

The Red Oaks B.B.C. organized in the 1880s, played black teams. *Evansville Courier and Press* (August 23, 1885): "At the ball park yesterday afternoon, the Red Oaks, of this city, defeated the Brown Stockings, of Owensboro, by a score of 15 to 8." *Courier and Press* (August 23, 1885): "The colored base-ball club, of Evansville, the Red Oaks, and the Henderson Dukes crossed bats at the park yesterday. The game resulted in a victory for the Evansvilles. The Hendersons expect to do the Evansville club up today. Quite a crowd will accompany the club from Henderson." *Courier and Press* (August 24, 1885): "The Evansville colored base-ball club came down to this city yesterday and were defeated by the Henderson club." They reorganized in 1886, playing an organization from TN. *Nashville Tennessean* (June 24, 1886): "The Meigs' School Greys, of Nashville, defeated the Red Oaks, of this place [Evansville, Indiana], in a game of ball, by a score of 8 to 2. Stewart and Farrow ere the battery for Nashville."

Sources: "A Local Game," *Evansville (IN) Courier and Press*, Jul 5, 1885; "Grand Athletic and Sparring Entertainment," *Evansville Courier and Press*, Aug 16, 1885; "General Notes," *Evansville Courier and Press*, Aug 23, 1885; "Henderson," *Evansville Courier and Press*, Aug 24, 1885; "The Amateurs," *Nashville (TN) Tennessean*, Jun 24, 1886.

Red Stocking Base Ball Club (Evansville, IN; 1870s)

The Red Stocking B.B.C. organized in the 1870s, played black nines. *Evansville Courier and Press* (July 13, 1876): "The 'Red Stockings' is the name of a colored base-ball organization in this city, which is preparing for a campaign in the national game this summer. It is the only club in the city, we believe, which has adopted a regular uniform. The dress consists of white shirt, white knee breeches, red and white striped stockings, red and white striped cap, and blue belt, which forms a knobby contrast. The Red Stockings go to Henderson, Kentucky next Saturday, on a challenge from the Atlantic, to contest for honors on the green diamond. On the 29th inst., the Blue Clippers, a colored baseball club, of Paducah, come to this city to play the Red Stockings. The Clippers have a neat uniform."

Sources: "Base Ball Brevities," *Evansville (IN) Courier and Press*, Jul 13, 1876.

Sheldon Blues Base Ball Club (Evansville, IN; 1880s–1890s). Organizer(s): Charles Sheldon.

The Sheldon Blues B.B.C. organized in the 1880s, played black teams. *Evansville Courier and Press* (May 23, 1889): "An amateur base-ball club, of colored extraction, has been organized in this city that will be known as the Sheldons. The team was organized by Mr. Charles Sheldon for the purpose of playing the leading colored clubs of Louisville, Cincinnati, Indianapolis, Chicago, St. Louis and other large cities." *Courier and Press* (July 14, 1889): "There will be a game of base-ball at the park today between the Sheldon Blues and Henderson Blues. Game called at 3:30. General admission: 25 cents. Ladies: 15 cents." They also played St. Louis, MO's West End B.B.C. *Courier and Press* (July 5, 1889): "Another very pleasing feature of the day's sports was the games of base-ball between two colored clubs, the Sheldon Blues and the St. Louis West Enders at the ball park. Both of the games were won by the visiting club; the score in the morning game being 7 to 9, and in the afternoon 10 to 11. These were witnessed by good audiences."

Sources: "Base Ball," *Evansville (IN) Courier and Press*, Mar 8,

1889; "Diamond Dust," *Evansville Courier and Press*, May 23, 1889; "Base Ball Notes," *Indianapolis (IN) Freeman*, Jun 1, 1889; "Today's Game," *St. Louis (MO) Republic*, Jun 1, 1889; "Base Ball News," *Indianapolis Freeman*, Jun 8, 1889; "The Fourth," *Evansville Courier and Press*, Jul 4, 1889; "The Glorious Fourth," *Evansville Courier and Press*, Jul 5, 1889; "St. Louis News," *Indianapolis Freeman*, Jul 13 1889; "Amusements," *Evansville Courier and Press*, Jul 14, 1889; *Evansville Courier and Press*, Jul 14, 1889; "About the Field," *Evansville Courier and Press*, May 22, 1892.

West Side Base Ball Club (Evansville, IN; 1890s)

The West Side B.B.C. organized in the 1890s, played black teams. *Evansville Courier and Press* (February 26, 1898): "The West Side Colored Base Ball team intend to establish a record in the coming season to be envied by all amateur trams of the city. Under the name of the Governor Street High School team they defeated every team that had the rashness to meet them last year. The boys are all good players and put their whole soul into the game."

Sources: New Briefs," *Evansville (IN) Courier and Press*, Apr 21, 1897; "Will Try Owensboro," *Evansville Courier and Press*, Jul 29, 1897; "Start Base Ball Season With A Social," *Evansville Courier and Press*, Feb 26, 1898; *Evansville Courier and Press*, Mar 8, 1898.

Black Diamond Base Ball Club (Fort Wayne, IN; 1890s). Organizer(s): Ed Black and John Rhodes.

The Black Diamond B.B.C., of Indianapolis, IN, organized in the 1890s, played white and black nines. *Fort Wayne News* (June 28, 1895): "The International College Business College team was defeated yesterday at Lakeside Park by the Black Diamonds by a score of 18 to 16." *Fort Wayne News* (June 21, 1895): "Yesterday afternoon at Lakeside the Black Diamonds and the Broadways crossed bats. The game resulted in a score of 23 to 8 in favor of the Broadways. The Diamonds were weak in the field, and handled easy ones as if they were hot irons."

Sources: "City News," *Albion (IN) County Democrat*, Dec 28, 1893; "Local News," *Fort Wayne (IN) Sentinel*, Mar 4, 1894; "News Notes," *Fort Wayne Sentinel*, May 24, 1894; "Local Lines," *Sentinel*, May 24, 1894; "The Standards Win," *Fort Wayne (IN) Gazette*, May 27, 1894; "The Darkey Sluggers," *Fort Wayne (IN) Journal-Gazette*, May 27, 1894; "Colored Base Ball," *Fort Wayne (IN) Weekly Gazette*, Jun 13, 1895; "Black and White," *Fort Wayne (IN) News*, Jun 19, 1895; "Black and White," *Fort Wayne News*, Jun 19, 1895; "Broadways Win," *Fort Wayne News*, Jun 21, 1895; "Sporting Notes," *Fort Wayne News*, Jun 28, 1895; "Notes," *Fort Wayne News*, Jun 5, 1896; "Sporting "City News," *Logansport (IN) Pharos Tribune*, Aug 24, 1898; "Speedy Players," *Logansport (IN) Reporter*, Aug 26, 1898; "Roanoke," *Huntington (IN) Weekly Herald*, Nov 10, 1899.

Colored Base Ball Club (Fort Wayne, IN; 1880s). Organizer(s): Will Cooper.

The Colored B.B.C. organized in 1881, played black and white teams. *Fort Wayne Gazette* (June 19, 1881): "A colored base-ball nine has been organized by Mr. Will Cooper. Cooper, Mart Bulgar, Charles Brackenridge, L. T. Bourie, Harry Bossler and others have been selected. They may play a game at the camp meeting now in progress, opposed by some white trash." *Fort Wayne News* (May 29, 1884): "The Fort Wayne Colored Base Ball Club beat the Van Wert Colored Base Ball Nine yesterday by a score of 32 to 21. The game was an interesting one and every brilliant play was generously applauded by a bevy of colored belles, who sat on a neighboring eminence. In the eighth inning a ball struck Gene Caldwell, the Fort Wayne catcher, in the face, and he was bundled into a hack and the game was declared over."

Sources: "City News," *Fort Wayne (IN) Gazette*, Jun 19, 1881; "City News," *Fort Wayne Gazette*, Sep 29, 1883; "News Notes," *Fort Wayne (IN) Sentinel*, May 26, 1884; "Happenings," *Fort Wayne (IN) News*, May 29, 1884; "Black and White," *Fort Wayne Gazette*, May 29, 1884; "Other Games," *Fort Wayne Gazette*, May 29, 1884; "Sheldons Abroad," *Fort Wayne Gazette*, Jun 6, 1884; "Local News," *Monroeville (IN) Weekly Breeze*, Jul 24, 1884; "City News," *Fort Wayne Gazette*, Jun 26, 1884; "City News," *Fort Wayne Gazette*, Jul 1, 1884; "Local News," *Fort Wayne Sentinel*, Jul 1, 1884; "The Railroads," *Fort Wayne Gazette*, Jul 12, 1884; "Nine to Two," *Fort Wayne Gazette*, Jul 28, 1884; "Local News," *Fort Wayne Sentinel*, Jul 28, 1884; "Local News," *Fort Wayne Sentinel*, Jun 16, 1885.

Coffee Coolers Base Ball Club (Greencastle, IN; 1890s). Organizer(s): Henry Miles and Drew Boland.

The Coffee Cooler B.B.C. organized in the 1890s, played white and black nines. *Crawfordsville Argus News* (July 5, 1895): "The Crawfordsville coons who came down here Monday expecting to play ball, were a sorry lot of hobo misfits. They like the Bloomington, Indiana mokes, are not right when they are in a base-ball game, and in the game were never warm at any stage. Seriously speaking, despite their name, are about the warmest articles on the base-ball pike. They are high born and dark, but not too shady, and when it comes to a genuine article of base-ball they will give any set of colored ball players cards and spade, a rabbit foot or two and then beat them easy with one hand on each player tied to his back."

Sources: "The Local Field," *Greencastle (IN) Banner and Times*, Sep 2, 1895; *Greencastle Banner and Times*, Jun 23, 1897; Dusky Snow Balls," *Crawfordsville (IN) Argus News*, Jul 5, 1895; "Koffee Koolers Killing," *Crawfordsville Argus News*, Sep 7, 1895; *Greencastle Banner and Times*, Jul 17, 1897; "A Confusion of Games," *Crawfordsville Argus News*, July 21, 1897; "Crawfordsville Coons," *Greencastle Banner and Times*, Jul 23, 1897; *Greencastle Banner and Times*, Aug 20, 1897.

Model Base Ball Club (Greencastle, IN; 1890s). Organizer(s): Drew Bolden.

The Model B.B.C. organized in the 1890s. The Models played white and black organizations.

Sources: "The Local Field," *Greencastle (IN) Banner and Times*, Jun 17, 1896; *Greencastle Banner and Times*, Jun 20, 1896; "Brief Local Notes," *Greencastle Banner and Times*, Sep 18, 1896; *Greencastle Banner and Times*, Aug 1, 1896; "Local Brevities," *Greencastle Banner and Times*, Aug 15, 1896.

Bates House Base Ball Club (Indianapolis, IN; 1860s–1870s). Organizer(s): R. P. Brown.

The Bates House B.B.C. organized in the 1870s, played black nines. *Indianapolis Herald* (July 27, 1867): "There are two colored clubs of fancy base-ball players in this city—the Eagles and the Mohawks. The Eagles are composed principally of Bates House attaches, while the Mohawks—so called because they are mo' hawk than eagle—are miscellaneously composed of tonsorial gentlemen from all quarters of the city." They continued to play each other into the 1870s. *Indianapolis Sentinel* (June 12, 1879): "The game between the hotel waiters and the barbers, at Southern Park, bids fair to be very close, as both clubs have been practicing daily for the past three weeks." In a closely contested game, following seven innings of play, the barbers defeated the waiters by a score of 16 to 13."

Sources: "Colored Base Ball," *Indianapolis (IN) Herald*, Jul 27, 1867; "Our Colored People," *Indianapolis (IN) The People*, Aug 19, 1876; "Base Ball Notes," *Indianapolis (IN) News*, Sep 27, 1876; "Home Notes," *Indianapolis (IN) Sentinel*, Jun 11, 1879; "The Waiters and Barbers," *Indianapolis Sentinel*, Jun 12, 1879; "Base Ball," *Indianapolis Sentinel*, June 23, 1879; "The Colored Mason's Celebration," *Indianapolis Sentinel*, Jun 25, 1879.

Black Stocking Base Ball Club (Indianapolis, IN; 1880s)

The Black Stocking B.B.C. organized in the 1880s, played black organizations. *Indianapolis Freeman* (May 18, 1889): "Indianapolis can now boast a first class colored nine which though recently organized is composed of first class players. It has been named the Hoosier Black Stockings, and it herewith challenges any amateur club in the country, white or black." *Freeman* (May 25, 1889): "The famous West End Club, of St. Louis, will pay Indianapolis a visit soon. The Black Stockings propose to make it interesting for them." *Louisville Courier-Journal* (August 4, 1889): "The colored clubs, Acorns of this city, and the Black Socks of Indianapolis, played at Daisy Park yesterday, the game resulting in a tie, each club having scored fourteen runs in the ninth inning, when the game was called on account of darkness." *Courier-Journal* (August 5, 1889): "An interesting game was played yesterday afternoon at Eclipse Park between the Acorns, the crack colored club of this city, and the Black Stockings of Indianapolis, which resulted in a victory for the former, the score being 9 to 6." *Freeman* (September 7, 1889): "The Pinchbacks, the crack colored base-ball club of New Orleans, and the Black Socks of this city will play a championship game at the ball park on Seventh Street next Wednesday." The aggregation played against the colored West Ends, of St. Louis; the latter swept two game series, to the disgust of Eric Elder Cooper, the patron and editor of the Indianapolis Freeman, who attended the contests.

Sources: "Base Ball News," *Indianapolis (IN) Freeman*, May 18, 1889; "Base Ball News," *Indianapolis Freeman*, May 25, 1889; "Base Ball," *Indianapolis Freeman*, Jun 22, 1889; "The Colored Clubs," *St. Louis (MO) Post-Dispatch*, Jun 23, 1889; "Base Ball Briefs," *St. Louis (MO) Republic*, Jun 26, 1889; "Amateur Gossip," *Louisville (KY) Courier-Journal*, Aug 4, 1889; "Resulted In A Tie," *Louisville Courier-Journal*, Aug 5, 1889; "Notes," *Louisville Courier-Journal*, Aug 4, 1889; "Notes," *Louisville Courier-Journal*, Aug 6, 1889; "Local News," *Indianapolis Freeman*, Sep 7, 1889.

Brown Stocking Base Ball Club (Indianapolis, IN; 1870s)

The Brown Stocking B.B.C. organized in the 1870s, played black organizations. *Indianapolis Sentinel* (June 20, 1877): "A goodly crowd congregated at the ball park to witness the game between the Fairplayers and Brown Stockings, two colored clubs. The game was well played from first to last, many good plays being made. The Fairplayers showed themselves to be a good lot of ball tossers and proved too much for the Browns to the tune of 15 to 9." During a match, the Brown's catcher suffered an injury. *Indianapolis News* (June 22, 1877): "Al Crumbs, catcher for the Browns, was struck on the throat by the Browns, and after walking about for a few moments fell to the ground. He was picked up, and taken away, and after a time, recovered, but was not able to take a further part in the game."

Sources: "Other Base Ball News," *Indianapolis (IN) Sentinel*, Jun 16, 1877; "Base Ball News," *Indianapolis (IN) Journal*, Jun 18, 1877; "Local Games," *Indianapolis Journal*, Jun 20, 1877; "Yesterday at the Park," *Indianapolis Sentinel*, Jun 20, 1877; "Notes," *Indianapolis Sentinel*, Jun 22, 1877; "The Colored Masons," *Indianapolis Journal*, Jun 22, 1877; "The First of the Season," *Indianapolis Sentinel*, Jun 23. 1877; "The Sons of Honor," *Indianapolis Journal*, Aug 4, 1877; "Our Colored People," *Indianapolis (IN) The People*, Aug 19, 1877; "At the Park," *Indianapolis Sentinel*, Aug 27, 1877; "A Bad Attack of the Blues," *Indianapolis Journal*, Aug 28, 1877.

Carthagenian Base Ball Club (Indianapolis, IN; 1870s). Organizer(s): Val Moss.

The Carthagenian B.B.C. organized in the 1870s, played black teams. *Indianapolis Journal* (July 7, 1877): "The Carthagenians defeated the Hotel Waiters today, by a score of 4 to 2, on the Third-Street Grounds. This club will play the champion colored club at an early date." *Indianapolis News* (August 10, 1877): "There will be a game of base-ball this afternoon at the Park between the Carthagenians and Fair Players." The Fair Plays defeated them, by a score of 14 to 4.

SOURCES: "Base Ball Notes," *Indianapolis (IN) News*, Jun 29, 1877; *Indianapolis News*, Jul 10, 1877; "City News," *Indianapolis News*, Aug 10, 1877; "Base Ball," *Indianapolis (IN) Journal*, Aug 15, 1877; "Amateur Ball Games," *Indianapolis News*, Aug 28, 1877.

Central Stars Base Ball Club (Indianapolis, IN; 1870s). Organizer(s): Bruce Singleton.

The Central Stars B.B.C. organized in the 1870s, played white and black clubs. *Indianapolis News* (May 31, 1876): "Yesterday afternoon the Western Fairplays and Central Stars, colored nines, played upon the South Street Grounds—the first winning by a score of 19 1to 11. During the game, Bruce Singleton, manager of one of the clubs, undertook to drive the crowd off the fence, and in so doing was hit by a boulder and severely bruised." *Indianapolis News* (September 1, 1876): "The Western Fairplays and Central Stars, both colored, played on the South-Street grounds, the former winning the game by a score of 19 to 12. In the game, the Fairplay's catcher, John Thomas, knocked the ball clear over the right field fence and on the roof of the I. C. and C. Freight depot. Five balls were used up before the game was finished, the batting being so terrific."

SOURCES: "Base Ball Notes," *Indianapolis (IN) News*, Aug 30, 1876; "A Row on the Ball Grounds," *Indianapolis News*, Aug 31, 1876; "Notes of the Game," *Indianapolis (IN) Journal*, Sep 1, 1876; "City News," *Indianapolis News*, Sep 4, 1876; "Base Ball Notes," *Indianapolis News*, Sep 6, 1876; "Base Ball Notes," *Indianapolis News*, Sep 7, 1876.

Barbers Base Ball Club (Indianapolis, IN; 1860s–1870s)

The Barbers B.B.C. organized in the 1860s, played black nines. *Indianapolis Daily Herald* (July 27, 1867): "There are two colored clubs of fancy base-ball players in this city—the Eagles and the Mohawks. The Eagles are composed principally of Bates House attaches, while the Mohawks—so called because they are mo' hawk than eagle—are miscellaneously composed of tonsorial gentlemen from all quarters of the city." They continued to play each other into the 1870s. In 1877, they played a benefit match game of ball. *Indianapolis News* (June 9, 1877): "A colored nine of amateur—barbers and Exchange Hotel waiters—will play ball Monday afternoon on the South Street Grounds for the benefit of colored orphans." *Indianapolis News*: "The board of managers and directors of the colored orphans' home return their thanks to the barbers and hotel waiters for the proceeds of their game of base-ball, $13.66." The two nines played at the Colored Mason's Celebration. *Indianapolis Sentinel* (June 25, 1879): "The game between the hotel waiters and the barbers, at Southern Park, bids fair to be very close, as both clubs have been practicing daily for the past three weeks." In a closely contested game, following seven innings of play, the barbers defeated the waiters by a score of 16 to 13.

SOURCES: "Colored Base Ball," *Indianapolis (IN) Herald*, Jul 27, 1867; "Base Ball Notes," *Indianapolis (IN) News*, Jun 9, 1877; "Will take Place Wednesday," *Indianapolis News*, Jun 11, 1877; "The Waiters and Barbers," *Indianapolis News*, Jun 12, 1877; "Home Notes," *Indianapolis (IN) Sentinel*, Jun 11, 1879; "The Waiters and Barbers," *Indianapolis Sentinel*, Jun 12, 1879; "Base Ball," *Indianapolis Sentinel*, Jun 23, 1879; "The Colored Mason's Celebration," *Indianapolis Sentinel*, Jun 25, 1879.

Exchange Hotel Base Ball Club (Indianapolis, IN; 1870s)

The Exchange Hotel B.B.C. organized in the 1870s, if not earlier. They competed against the black barbers of the city, and black nines visiting the city. In 1877, the barbers and waiters played a benefit match game of ball. *Indianapolis News* (June 9, 1877): "A colored nine of amateur—barbers and Exchange Hotel waiters—will play ball Monday afternoon on the South Street Grounds for the benefit of colored orphans." *Indianapolis News* (June 12, 1877): "The board of managers and directors of the colored orphans' home return their thanks to the barbers and hotel waiters for the proceeds of their game of base-ball, $13.66."

SOURCES: "Base Ball Notes," *Indianapolis (IN) News*, Jun 9, 1877; "Will Take Place Wednesday," *Indianapolis News*, Jun 11, 1877; "The Waiters and Barbers," *Indianapolis News*, Jun 12, 1877.

Grand Hotel Base Ball Club (Indianapolis, IN; 1870s–1890s)

The Grand Hotel B.B.C. organized in the 1890s, played black and white teams. *Indianapolis News* (September 27, 1896): "The Grand Hotel dining room nine defeated the Hotel Bates club yesterday 21 to 9." *Indianapolis Journal* (May 13, 1890): "The Grand Hotel team will play the Bates House nine on the Indiana Avenue grounds, at 3:30 o'clock this afternoon. Both nines are composed of waiters exclusively, with W. Jackson and Toney Thompson as captains, and Charles Jackson as umpire." *Journal* (April 17, 1891): "The Grand Hotel nine defeated the Bates House team, 23 to 10, yesterday. Batteries—Dowd and Marshall; Winslow and Bryant." *Indianapolis Sun* (July 14, 1894): "The employees of the Grand Hotel have a base-ball team that they think can be any amateur team in these parts. They are open for games." *Sun* (July 20, 1894): "The Grand Hotel ball nine played the insane asylum clerks [white], Thursday afternoon, and were beaten 29 to 12. The former paid $50 for their uniforms and have lost every game they have ever played." *Sun* (August 7, 1894): "Grand Hotel nine has busted. It had an eventful career of three weeks in which it was badly beaten in every game."

SOURCES: "Base Ball Notes," *Indianapolis (IN) News*, Sep 27, 1876; "Base Ball Notes," *Indianapolis (IN) Journal*, May 13, 1890; "The Sporting News," *Indianapolis Journal*, May 23, 1890; "Minor City Matters," *Indianapolis Journal*, Apr 17, 1891; "Features of Sporting Life," *Indianapolis (IN) Sun*, Jul 14, 1894; "City Life," *Indianapolis Sun*, Jul 20, 1894; "City Life," *Indianapolis Sun*, Aug 7, 1894; "Fight at Ball Game," *Indianapolis (IN) News*, Jul 31, 1895.

Herculean Base Ball Club (Indianapolis, IN; 1890s–1900s)

The Herculean B.B.C. organized in 1893. The Herculeans were a social, political and cultural organization. *Indianapolis News* (March 2, 1895): "The Herculeans one of the largest and best equipped Negro Republican Clubs in the State." The "Hercs" bought a two-story building and opened their club house at 139 IN Avenue. *Freeman* gave the organization positive press. The Herculeans invited Henry C. Smith (**Fig. 29**), the black proprietor of *Cleveland Gazette* to Indianapolis. Smith had succeeded in pushing through the OH State legislature an anti-lynching bill. The club honored Preston E. Eagleson, a young black orator, of IN University. They also hosted the League of Colored Republican Clubs of Marion County. They formed the Herculean Quartette. They also fielded a ball club. Between 1893 and 1904, the Herculeans played black and white teams, competing against clubs of IN, KY, MO, and IL. The Herculeans remained a positive force in Indianapolis. *Indianapolis Freeman* (May 11, 1895): "The Herculeans defeated the Daltons by a score of 17 to 4. The game was very exciting notwithstanding the one-sided score the boys going to bat in the ninth inning with the score against them. Then by some terrific batting and daring base-running, couple with some very yellow errors on the part of the Dal-

Figure 29. Henry C. Smith. Smith was the editor and publisher of the *Cleveland Gazette*, a black newspaper. Between 1877 and 1883, he pitched for Cleveland's Zulus (1879), South Stars (1882), and Blue Stockings (1883). In 1889, Smith hurled for Cleveland's newspapermen nine, an otherwise all-white aggregation.

tons, the boys turned defeat into victory." *Freeman* (May 25, 1895): "The Herculean ball team defeated the crack New Castle in two hotly contested games by the scores of 5 to 1 and 3 to 1. The Herks have not been defeated this season, and are very anxious to meet the unbeaten Unions of Chicago." That same year, they played the Chicago Unions, losing both games.

SOURCES: "Personal and Social," *Indianapolis (IN) News*, Aug 9, 1894; "Miscellaneous Comment and Resolution," *Indianapolis (IN) Freeman*, Mar 2, 1895; "Sport," *Indianapolis Freeman*, May 11, 1895; "Sport," *Indianapolis Freeman*, May 25, 1895; "The Herculean Club Picnic," *Indianapolis News*, Jun 18, 1895; "Major Taylor," *Indianapolis Freeman*, Jul 5, 1895; "Sporting Notes," *Indianapolis News*, Aug 1, 1895; "The Organization Shaky," *Indianapolis News*, Aug 5, 1895; "Amateur Games Sunday," *Indianapolis News*, Aug 26, 1895; "Herculean Club Notes," *Indianapolis Freeman*, Aug 31, 1895; "Elected Officers," *Indianapolis Freeman*, Nov 2, 1895; "Sporting News," *Indianapolis (IN) Journal*, Jul 25, 1895; "Daltons 10; Herculeans 3," *Indianapolis Journal*, Jun 15, 1896; "Herculeans 12; Brenner's Stars 2," *Indianapolis Journal*, Jun 15, 1896; "Picnic Excursions," *Indianapolis News*, Jun 22, 1897; "Herculean Club Ball," *Indianapolis News*, Jan 1, 1898; "Colored Ball Players' Tour," *Indianapolis News*, Aug 13, 1902.

Western Fairplay Base Ball Club (Indianapolis, IN; 1870s). Organizer(s): Leslie Mack.

The Western Fairplay B.B.C. organized in the mid–1870s, black nines. *Indianapolis News* (August 4, 1875): "The colored base-ball nine of Louisville [Globes] and Indianapolis [Fairplays] played this forenoon, at the head of Tennessee Street." Leslie Mack served as player/manager. Harry Lee was the team's star pitcher. *Indianapolis News* (August 30, 1876): "The Fairplays and the Central Stars, colored nines of this city, and said to be strong amateur teams, contested this afternoon on the South Street Grounds. Game was called at 3:30." A local rival was the Brown Stockings. *Indianapolis Sentinel* (June 20, 1877): "A goodly crowd congregated at the ball park to witness the game between the Fairplayers and Brown Stockings, two

colored clubs. The game was well played from first to last, many good plays being made. The Fairplayers showed themselves to be a good lot of ball tossers and proved too much for the Browns to the tune of 15 to 9." The organization posted its successful season. *Indianapolis News* (August 28, 1877): "The Browns were defeated by the Fairplays yesterday, 18 to 0. The Fairplays have met with reasonable success this season, the score being as follows: May 27, Fairplays 9, Browns 9; June 18, Fairplays 15, Browns 8; June 21, Fairplays 18, Browns 8; July 23, Optics, of Logansport 2, Fairplays, 5; July 24, Fairplays, 21, Kokomos 5; July 25, Fairplays, 11, Perus 7; August 16, Fairplays, 15, Carthagenians 4; August 16, Fairplays, 14, Carthagenians 4. The club will probably play the Vigilants at Cincinnati on Saturday."

SOURCES: "City News," *Indianapolis (IN) News*, Aug 4, 1875; "Base Ball Notes," *Indianapolis News*, Aug 30, 1876; "A Row on the Ball Grounds," *Indianapolis News*, Aug 31, 1876; "Ball and Bat," *Indianapolis News*, May 11, 1877; "Other Base Ball News," *Indianapolis (IN) Sentinel*, Jun 16, 1877; "Base Ball Notes," *Indianapolis News*, Jun 19, 1877; "Base Ball Notes," *Indianapolis News*, Jun 20, 1877; "Yesterday at the Park," *Indianapolis Sentinel*, Jun 20, 1877; "Notes," *Indianapolis Sentinel*, Jun 22, 1877; "The First of the Season," *Indianapolis Sentinel*, Jun 23, 1877; "At the Park," *Indianapolis Sentinel*, Aug 27, 1877; "Amateur Ball Games," *Indianapolis News*, Aug 28, 1877; "Base Ball Notes," *Indianapolis News*, Aug 30, 1877.

Black Stocking Base Ball Club (Lafayette, IN; 1880s)

The Black Stocking B.B.C. organized in the 1880s, played black teams. *Crawfordsville Dispatch* (September 15, 1887): "The Hustlers, the crack colored club of the Hoosier Athens played the Black Stockings at the park and were defeated by a score of 21 to 17. The game was close and exciting and witnessed by a large crowd. Huff Robinson, who caught for the home club, made the banner play of the season. He jumped over the high board fence without touching it and caught a high foul tip. It was a great play."

SOURCES: "Our Colored People," *Crawfordsville (IN) Dispatch*, Sep 12, 1887; "Our Colored People," *Crawfordsville Dispatch*, Sep 15, 1887; "Our Colored People," *Crawfordsville Dispatch*, Sep 21, 1887; "The Hustlers Scooped," *Crawfordsville Dispatch*, Sep 23, 1887.

Browns Base Ball Club (Logansport, IN; 1890s). Organizer(s): Gernie Winslow and Charles W. Hill.

The Browns B.B.C. organized in the 1890s, played white and black organizations. *Logansport Pharos-Tribune* (June 22, 1894): "A fair-sized crowd gathered at the Driving Park yesterday afternoon to witness a game of ball between the Jordan Hechts and the Browns. In the first inning, the Browns found that they had a good thing of it by bringing in eight scores."

SOURCES: "Additional Items," *Logansport (IN) Pharos*, Apr 11, 1894; "The Latest Local News," *Logansport (IN) Reporter*, Apr 10, 1894; "Local," *Reporter*, Apr 13, 1894; "City Local," *Logansport Reporter*, June 6, 1894; "Base Ball," *Logansport (IN) Pharos-Tribune*, Jun 22, 1894; "Additional Items," *Logansport Pharos*, Sep 8, 1894; "No Pie," *Logansport (IN) Journal*, Sep 26, 1894; "Base Ball," *Logansport Pharos*, Oct 17, 1894.

Logan Blues Base Ball Club (Logansport, IN; 1880s). Organizer(s): Frank Turner, Charles Brooks and Sheridan Tutt.

The Logan Blues B.B.C. organized in 1883, played white and black teams. *Logansport Chronicle* (August 18, 1883): "A colored club of Peru came to Logansport rigged out in Pigeon tailed coats and dude shoes. They came to show the colored boys here how to play ball. So confident were they in the success of the trip that they staked every cent they had on the result, going so far as to pawn their dude shoes for money to wager."

SOURCES: "Late Local Lines," *Logansport (IN) Pharos*, Aug 13, 1883; "Base Ball," *Logansport (IN) Tribune*, Aug 14, 1883; *Logansport (IN) Journal*, Aug 14, 1883; "Dizzy Dive Diversions," *Logansport (IN) Chronicle*, Aug 18, 1883; "Late Local Lines," *Logansport Tribune*, Aug 31, 1883; "Budget Briefs," *Logansport Journal*, Sep 1, 1883; *Logansport (IN) Weekly Journal*, Sep 8, 1883.

Logan Giants Base Ball Club (Logansport, IN; 1900s). Owner(s): Charles S. Jones and George Parker.

The Logan Giants B.B.C. organized in 1900, played white and black aggregations. *Logansport Journal* (June 26, 1900): "Quite a large crowd witnessed the game of base-ball between the Laurels and Logan Giants at the Driving Park Sunday afternoon. The contest was a warm one and resulted in the victory of the Laurels by a score of 12 to 5. The Giants is a colored team and with a little more practice will be able to put up a good game of ball. The Laurels put up an excellent game."

SOURCES: "City News," *Logansport (IN) Pharos*, Jun 23, 1900; "The Game Sunday," *Logansport (IN) Journal*, Jun 23, 1900; "Base Ball Sunday," *Logansport (IN) Reporter*, Jun 23, 1900; "Laurels Defeat Giants," *Logansport Journal*, Jun 26, 1900.

Optic Base Ball Club (Logansport, IN; 1870s)

The Optic B.B.C. organized in 1877, played white and black organizations. *Logansport Chronicle*: "The Optics, the colored club of this city played the colored club of Indianapolis on Monday last. When our reporter left the ground the Indianapolis club was batting the ball all around the field, as though it was the side of a barn. If the nine innings were played as they ought to the score would have stood Indianapolis 9000; Logansport 0. No scorers were needed."

SOURCES: *Logansport (IN) Journal*, May 8, 1877; "Local Summary," *Logansport (IN) Chronicle*, Jul 14, 1877; "The National Game," *Logansport Chronicle*, Jul 21, 1877; "Local Summary," *Logansport Chronicle*, Jul 21, 1877.

Slow Boys Base Ball Club (Logansport, IN; 1870s). Owner(s): James Waldron and John Parker.

The Slow Boys B.B.C. organized in 1876. The Slow Boys played against white and black organizations.

SOURCES: "A Query," *Logansport (IN) Journal*, Jun 3, 1876; "Base Ball Notes," *Logansport Journal*, Jun 6, 1876; "Base Ball Notes," *Logansport Journal*, Jun 24, 1876; "Base Ball Notes," *Logansport Journal*, Jun 28, 1876; "Base Ball Notes," *Logansport Journal*, Jun 29, 1876; "Base Ball Notes," *Logansport Journal*, Jul 11, 1876; "Personal," *Logansport Journal*, Jul 13, 1876.

Spalding Blues Base Ball Club (Logansport, IN; 1880s). Owner(s): Frank Turner and Charles Brooks.

The Spalding Blues B.B.C. organized in 1885, played white and black organizations. *Logansport Pharos* (September 8, 1885): "The two colored base-ball clubs of the city played a match game yesterday afternoon at the show grounds. The Spaulding Blues beat the hotel waiters by a score of 26 to 21." *Pharos* (September 11, 1885): "The Spaulding Blues, the crack colored nine, of the city, defeated a select nine of colored baseballists, yesterday afternoon on the Westside Grounds." *Logansport Journal* (September 12, 1885): "The Logansport Reds will play the colored base-ball club next Tuesday afternoon on the West Side grounds."

SOURCES: "City News," *Logansport (IN) Pharos*, Aug 24, 1885; "City News," *Logansport Pharos*, Sep 8, 1885; "City News," *Logansport Pharos*, Sep 11, 1885; *Logansport Pharos*, Sep 16, 1885; "City News," *Logansport Pharos*, Sep 17, 1885; "City News," *Logansport Pharos*, Jul 13, 1886; *Logansport (IN) Journal*, Aug 3, 1886; "Local News of the Week," *Logansport (IN) Chronicle*, Aug 7, 1886.

Up-To-Date Base Ball Club (Logansport, IN; 1890s). Organizer(s): Charles S. Jones.

The Up-To-Date B.B.C. organized in the 1890s, played white and black teams. *Logansport Reporter* (July 16, 1897) announces: "The Darktown Base Ball Team, under the cognomen of the Up-To-Dates, suffered defeat at the park yesterday afternoon at the hands of the Globes. The worst feature of the drubbing was that the fielding of their own players lost them the game. The contest stood 9 to 9 in the ninth inning, with two men out and two strikes on the batter, when the Casey act was performed. The wielder of the hickory connected up with the horsehide and the ball sailed out into centerfield, striking a sleepy fielder in the slats. The hit was a two-bagger, and followed by another in the same place, brought in the winning run. It was a hot game all the way through and the spectators received a long, warm run for their money. The rooting was one of the features of the game."

SOURCES: "Honors Even," *Logansport (IN) Pharos*, Jul 5, 1897; "City News," *Logansport Pharos*, Jul 13, 1897; "A Hot Game," *Logansport (IN) Reporter*, Jul 16, 1897; "Colored Boys Fought Nobly," *Logansport Pharos*, Jul 16, 1897; "City News," *Logansport Pharos*, Jul 23, 1897; "City News," *Logansport Pharos*, Jul 24, 1897; "Base Ball Championship," *Logansport Pharos*, Aug 2, 1897; "Base Ball Game," *Logansport Pharos*, Aug 26, 1897; "Manager Walked," *Logansport Pharos*, Aug 27, 1897.

French Lick Base Ball Club (Mitchell, IN; 1890s). Owner(s): Allen Clay.

The French Lick B.B.C. organized in the 1890s. The "French Licks" played against black and white teams.

SOURCES: "City News," *Bedford (IN) Mail*, Jul 17, 1896; "Diamond Dust," *Bedford Mail*, August 2, 1895; *Mitchell (IN) Commercial*, July 23, 1896.

400 Base Ball Club (Mount Vernon, IN; 1890s). Organizer(s): Ben Davis.

The 400 B.B.C. organized in the 1890s, played black aggregations. *Mount Vernon Democrat* (June 20, 1896): "The A.B.C.'s and 400, our two colored clubs, played at the Fair Grounds yesterday. The 400 won by a score of 15 to 13." *Mount Vernon Republican* (June 19, 1897): The 400 Base-Ball Club of this city defeated the Morganfield Nine at the Fair Grounds last Saturday." *Democrat* (August 26, 1897): "A red hot game of ball occurred at Schieber Park Tuesday between colored clubs, the 400s and the '97's. The game ended in a row. The 400 club claimed they shut the 97's out, but the little inks claim they made one run. Another game will probably be made."

SOURCES: "Personals," *Mount Vernon (IN) Republican*, Jun 20, 1896; *Mount Vernon Republican*, Jun 19, 1897; *Mount Vernon (IN) Democrat*, Jul 20, 1897; *Mount Vernon Democrat*, Aug 26, 1897.

Famous Base Ball Club (Muncie, IN; 1890s)

The Famous B.B.C. organized in the 1890s, played black and white teams. *Indianapolis Journal* (July 30, 1894): "At Athletic Park this afternoon nearly two-thousand people witnessed an interesting game of ball between the Famous (colored) team and the Shamrocks."

SOURCES: "Shamrocks, 11; Famous, 8," *Indianapolis (IN) Journal*, Jul 30, 1894.

London Creole Giants Base Ball Club (Muncie, IN; 1890s). Organizer(s): John W. Jackson ("Bud" Fowler).

The London Creole Giants B.B.C. organized in the 1890s, played white and black nines. James W. Jackson (Bud Fowler) (**Fig. 30**) organized the team. *Nashville Tennessean* (March 3, 1896): "Bud Fowler arrived in the city [Nashville] last week, and has made arrangements with the famous colored team, the Rock City Unions, to represent Muncie, Indiana, for the coming season." Fowler scheduled a local exhibition. *Nashville Tennessean* (April 17, 1896): "The

Figure 30. John W. Jackson, Jr., better known as Bud Fowler, unknown date. Between 1878 and 1899, Bud Fowler played for and managed white and black teams throughout the country. He began his career as a pitcher, and while he would play most often at second base, he covered other positions, as well, including catcher.

Londons, of Muncie, Indiana, will play a game today at Athletic Park with the [Bud] Fowler Blues. Both clubs are composed of good players and a good game may be expected. The players are colored." *Huntington Weekly Herald* (May 22, 1896): "Muncie has a team of colored base-ball artists who are right in line, when it comes to putting up a hot game. They made the Fort Wayne team lay down a few days ago, and of the Muncie pitcher, the Fort Wayne Journal says: Only the widespread prejudice against the colored base-ball player prevents the recognition of Buckner as a star of the first magnitude. He is without doubt one of the best pitchers in the country, and if he were white he would be in first class company. The Muncie team stands a show

against any team with Buckner in the box. The Fort Waynes simply could do nothing with him."

SOURCES: "Sporting Notes," *Nashville (TN) Tennessean*, Mar 3, 1896; "Base Ball Notes," *Nashville Tennessean*, Apr 17, 1896; "A Victory for Fort Wayne," *Indianapolis (IN) News*, Apr 28, 1896; "We Win at Muncie," *Fort Wayne (IN) News*, Apr 29, 1896; "Muncie Day," *Fort Wayne (IN) Journal Gazette*, Apr 30, 1896; "A Good Thing," *Fort Wayne Journal Gazette*, May 1, 1896; "Fowler Skipped Out," *Delphos (OH) Herald*, May 15, 1896; "Base Ball Talk," *Huntington (IN) Weekly Herald*, May 22, 1896.

Cyclone Base Ball Club (New Albany, IN; 1890s). Organizer(s): Frank Chatman, James Larue and Leonard Hawkins.

The Cyclone B.B.C. organized in the 1890s, played white and black teams. *New Albany Evening Tribune* (July 6, 1894): "The Cyclones, colored, defeated the Monons, white, yesterday in a game of base-ball by a score of 9 to 8." *Evening Tribune* (July 7, 1894): "The Cyclones, of this city, beat the Blue Suits, of Jeffersonville, yesterday in a game of base-ball by a score of 9 to 8." *Evening Tribune* (July 14, 1894): "The Cyclones defeated the Irish Hills yesterday in a game of base-ball by a score of 20 to 16." *Jeffersonville News* (May 24, 1895): "The Jeffries nine and the New Albany Cyclones, colored, baseball clubs, will play net Sunday."

SOURCES: *New Albany (IN) Evening Tribune*, Jul 6, 1894; *New Albany Evening Tribune*, Jul 7, 1894; *New Albany Evening Tribune*, Jul 14, 1894; *Jeffersonville (IN) News*, May 24, 1895.

Fair Play Base Ball Club (Peru, IN; 1880s). Organizer(s): Frederick Marsh.

The Fair Play B.B.C. organized in the 1880s, played black teams. *Logansport Pharos Tribune* (September 3, 1881): "The colored base-ball club from the wicked little village of Peru came down on Thursday, and after wrestling the home club, defeated them by a score of

21 to 7." A rivalry developed. *Pharos Tribune* (July 26, 1883): "The colored base-ball club of Peru, which was expected here this afternoon, failed to arrive for some unexplained explanation. It begins to look as if the 'Peru Muffers' were afraid to play the Logansport club." *Pharos Tribune* (August 14, 1883): "The game of base-ball played yesterday afternoon between the Logan Blues and the Peru Fair Plays, two colored clubs, resulted in an easy victory for the Logansport boys. The Peru club was shown some points in the game that it had not known before, and the boys left the city feeling that in base-ball matters, as well as other things, Logansport takes the lead."

SOURCES: *Logansport (IN) Chronicle*, Sep 3, 1881; *Logansport (IN) Journal*, Sep 10, 1881; *Logansport Journal*, Jul 12, 1883; *Logansport (IN) Pharos Tribune*, Aug 9, 1882; *Pharos Tribune*, Jul 22, 1883; "City News," *Pharos Tribune*, Jul 26, 1883; *Peru (IN) Miami County Sentinel*, Aug 9, 1883; *Logansport Pharos Tribune*, Aug 13, 1883; *Logansport Pharos Tribune*, Aug 14, 1883; *Logansport Journal*, Aug 18, 1883 *Peru Miami County Sentinel*, Aug 23, 1883; *Logansport Journal*, Aug 24, 1883.

Eckford Base Ball Club (Princeton, IN; 1880s)

The Eckford B.B.C. organized in the 1880s, played black teams. *Evansville Courier and Press* (August 10, 1883): "Princeton Clarion: The colored boys of this place have organized a base-ball club, and call themselves the Eckfords. Dressed in their white uniforms, they will make a raid on the Electric Reds, of Evansville, playing on enclosed grounds for the gate money." *New Harmony Register* (August 24, 1883): "The colored base-ball club, of Princeton, was taken in by the colored Electric Reds, of Evansville, last week, 30 to 27." A return game was played. *Princeton Democrat* (September 24, 1883): "A colored base-ball club came up from Evansville to play the colored club at this place. The Princeton boys cleaned them up badly, and they returned home pretty well satisfied that they did not amount to much as base ballists."

SOURCES: "Base Ball Notes," *Evansville (IN) Courier and Press*, Aug 10, 1883; "Curious Local Dirt," *New Harmony (IN) Register*, Aug 24, 1883; "Local and Miscellaneous News," *Princeton (IN) Democrat*, Sep 24, 1883.

Acme Base Ball Club (Richmond, IN; 1900s). Owner(s): Allen Clay.

The Acme B.B.C. organized in 1900, played black aggregations. *Richmond Item* (September 10, 1900): "The Richmond Acmes, the local colored baseball team, defeated a colored team from New Castle by a score of 15 to 13 yesterday. The game took place on the Hawkins diamond and was witnessed by 350 enthusiastic rooters. Benson and Sharp served as the battery for the local team."

SOURCES: "Base Ball," *Richmond (IN) Item*, Jul 26, 1900; *Richmond Item*, Aug 7, 1900; *Richmond Item*, Sep 7, 1900; "The Acmes Won," *Richmond Item*, Sep 10, 1900.

Colored Base Ball Club (Richmond, IN; 1890s)

The Colored B.B.C. organized in the 1890s, played black teams. *Connersville Examiner* (September 12, 1894): "The Richmond ball tossers won from our local Black Diamonds by a score of 34 to 12. The Connersville battery was alright, but it requires seven more players to make a ball nine. The Richmonds played a fairly good game throughout."

SOURCES: *Connersville (IN) Examiner*, Sep 8, 1894; *Connersville Examiner*, Sep 10, 1894; "Richmond Victorious," *Richmond (IN) Item*, Sep 12, 1894; "Base Game," *Connersville Examiner*, Sep 12, 1894; "Colored Ball Players," *Richmond Item*, Sep 6, 1895; "Grand," *Richmond Item*, Aug 7, 1896.

Wayne Base Ball Club (Richmond, IN; 1880s)

The Wayne B.B.C. organized in the 1880s, played against black teams. *Cleveland Gazette* (June 6, 1885): "The Springfield Base Ball Club played against the Richmond, Indiana boys last Thursday. The latter was defeated by a score of 24 to 8. The feature of the game was the skillful pitched of Master Yates, who succeeded in striking out nineteen visitors. He was well-supported by Mr. Edward Gant."

SOURCES: *Richmond (IN) Item*, Mar 31, 1885; *Richmond Item*, May 23, 1885; *Richmond Item*, May 27, 1885; "Our Colored Club," *Richmond Item*, May 29, 1885; *Richmond Item*, Jun 1, 1885; "The Champion City," *Cleveland (OH) Gazette*, Jun 6, 1885; *Richmond Item*, Aug 6, 1885; *Cambridge (IN) City Tribune*, Sep 17, 1885.

Colored Base Ball Club (Rushville, IN; 1890s)

The Colored B.B.C. organized in the 1890s, played black teams. *Connersville Times* (August 22, 1894): "Connersville always did modestly boast of being superior to Rushville. Now the Black Diamond Base Ball Club has no reason at all to doubt it. They defeated the Rushville colored base-ball team in a game there yesterday by a score of 32 to 8. The feature of the game was a home run by Tom Pierce."

SOURCES: *Connersville (IN) Times*, Aug 21, 1894; "Connersville Downs Rushville," *Connersville Times*, Aug 22, 1894; "Local and Personal," *Connersville Times*, Jun 10, 1896; "City News," *Connersville (IN) Daily Examiner*, Aug 12, 1897; "Dead Easy," *Connersville (IN) News*, Aug 13, 1897.

Black Diamond Base Ball Club (Shelbyville, IN; 1880s). Organizer(s): Lee "Sugar" Hill.

The Black Diamond B.B.C. organized in the 1880s, played white and black nines. *Shelbyville Democrat* (May 14, 1888): "Lee Hill will take his baseball nine to Connersville Sunday to play a colored nine of that place. Sugar says the score will stand in favor of his club, the Black Diamonds." *Democrat* (August 6, 1888): "The game of baseball between the Black Diamonds and Lyons' nine, the Eagles, yesterday afternoon at James' Park, was a regular old-fashioned slugging match. Sugar's men, as well as himself, seeming to be indifferent to the result of the game, going out and coming in from their respective positions like so many old broken-down work horses."

SOURCES: *Shelbyville (IN) Democrat*, May 14, 1888; "Fun Over the River Yesterday Afternoon," *Shelbyville Democrat*, May 21, 1888; *Shelbyville Democrat*, Aug 4, 1888; *Shelbyville Democrat*, August 6, 1888; "City News," *Connersville (IN) Examiner*, May 14, 1888.

Reds Base Ball Club (West Baden Springs, IN; 1890s–1900s). Organizer(s): Frederick Marsh.

The Reds B.B.C. organized in the 1890s. The Reds, composed of waiters of the West Baden Springs Resort, played white and black teams. *West Baden Springs Journal* (July 7, 1896): "In the game of baseball between the West Baden and Orleans nines, for a purse of $25, the score stood 7 to 1 in favor of West Baden, which would indicate that the Orlean boys were hardly in it." *Journal* (July 12, 1898): "The Olympics, a colored base-ball club from Louisville, struggled and toiled nine innings, last Tuesday, to down the mighty West Badens, but failed, the score standing 9 to 9. It was a pretty contest, and was witnessed by a large crowd." A rivalry developed. *Journal* (July 11, 1899): "There was a game of base-ball between the Louisville Olympics and the West Baden club, both colored, which was witnessed by an enormous crowd, resulting in the defeat of the Olympics."

SOURCES: *West Baden Springs (IN) Journal*, Jun 9, 1896; *West Baden Springs Journal*, Jun 30, 1896; *West Baden Springs Journal*, Jul 7, 1896; *West Baden Springs Journal*, Jul 14, 1896; *West Baden Springs Journal*, Jul 21, 1896; "That Gold Medal," *West Baden Springs Journal*, Aug 6, 1896; *West Baden Springs Journal*, Aug 11, 1896; *West Baden Springs Journal*, Sep 1, 1896; *West Baden Springs Journal*, May 25, 1897; *West Baden Springs Journal*, Jul 27, 1897; "Base Ball Notes," *West Baden Springs Journal*, Aug 24, 1897; *West Baden Springs Journal*, Jul 12, 1898; *West Baden Springs Journal*, Jul 11, 1899; *West Baden Springs Journal*, May 22, 1900; *West Baden Springs Journal*, Jul 27, 1900.

Iowa

Clipper Base Ball Club (Burlington, IA; 1870s). Organizer(s): Jim Canterberry.

The Clipper B.B.C. organized in 1875, played against black and white nines. *Burlington Hawk-Eye* (August 6, 1875): "The game yesterday afternoon between the Atlantics and Clippers resulted in the defeat of the former by a score of 19 to 11. The Atlantics had only part of their nine and played three subs, while the Clippers appeared in full force. They scored no less than ten runs on passed balls as the Atlantics were minus their catcher. The first base play of Jim Morrison, of the Clippers, being noteworthy." *Burlington Hawkeye* (September 4, 1875): "The second game of the series between the Atlantics [white] of this city and the Clippers (colored) came off yesterday on the Acme Grounds, in the presence of about three hundred spectators. Thomas Foster played well, making a clear score, and also making some splendid stops and throws; while Jim Canterberry made the best catch of the game, he jumping for it and taking it with one hand on the dead level, and also making some splendid catches behind the bat. Jim Morrison covered first with glory. Pete Palmer is also being credited with several good hits."

SOURCES: "Base Ball," *Burlington (IA) Hawk-Eye*, Aug 6, 1875; "Base Ball," *Burlington Hawk-Eye*, Aug 7, 1875; "Base Ball," *Burlington Hawk-Eye*, Aug 14, 1875; *Burlington Hawk-Eye*, Aug 19, 1875; "Base Ball," *Burlington Hawk-Eye*, Sep 4, 1875.

Lime Kiln Base Ball Club (Burlington, IA; 1890s)

The Lime Kiln B.B.C. organized in the 1890s, played black and white clubs of IA and IL.

SOURCES: "Darktown Today," *Burlington (IA) Gazette*, Jun 28, 1894; "Home News," *Burlington (IA) Daily Hawk-Eye*, Jun 28, 1894; "The City," *Burlington Gazette*, Jun 29, 1894; "Colored Boys to Play," *Burlington Gazette*, Aug 19, 1896; "Challenged Colored Boys of Burlington," *Burlington Gazette*, Aug 19, 1896; "They Accept," *Burlington Daily Hawk-Eye*, Aug 21, 1896; "Galesburg Challenge Accepted," *Burlington Daily Hawk-Eye*, Aug 21, 1896,

Sons of Enterprise Base Ball Club (Cedar Rapids, IA; 1890s)

The Sons of Enterprise B.B.C. organized in the 1890s, played black and white clubs.

SOURCES: "Young Colored Men," *Cedar Rapids (IA) Gazette*, May 22, 1894; "Colored Club," *Cedar Rapids Gazette*, May 29, 1894; "The City in Brief," *Cedar Rapids Gazette*, Jun 29, 1894; "Sons of Enterprise," *Cedar Rapids Gazette*, July 13, 1894; "The City in Brief," *Cedar Rapids Gazette*, Aug 1, 1894; "The City in Brief," *Cedar Rapids Gazette*, Aug 11, 1894; "The City in Brief," *Cedar Rapids Gazette*, Aug 17, 1894; "The City in Brief," *Cedar Rapids Gazette*, Nov 20, 1894.

Merchant Maroon Base Ball Club (Council Bluff, IA; 1890s)

The Merchant Maroon B.B.C. organized in the 1890s, played black and white aggregations.

SOURCES: "Base Ball Tomorrow," *Council Bluff (IA) Daily Nonpariel*, Jun 2, 1894; "Good Ball," *Council Bluff Daily Nonpariel*, Jun 6, 1894; "Base Ball Notes," *Council Bluff Daily Nonpariel*, Jul 8, 1894; "To Have a Good Ball Team," *Council Bluff Daily Nonpariel*, Apr 28, 1895; "Base Ball Notes," *Burlington (IA) Evening Gazette*, Jul 19, 1897.

Davenport Blues Base Ball Club (Davenport, IA; 1890s)

The Davenport Blues B.B.C. organized in 1891, played white and black aggregations. *Cedar Rapids Evening Gazette* (August 7, 1891): "The colored base-ball clubs of Dubuque and Davenport are expected to be in Marion on the 17th and 18th of this month to play with the Trestevons." *Davenport Tribune* (August 20, 1891): "The Davenport Blues went to Marion Monday and defeated the Trestevons by a score of 15 to 11 and Tuesday defeated the Dubuques by a score of 11 to 2. The Davenport Blues must certainly be a good ball team since it is victorious in nearly every game."

SOURCES: "Brevities," *Davenport (IA) Tribune*, Aug 4, 1891; "At the County Seat," *Cedar Rapids (IA) Evening Gazette*, Aug 7, 1891; "Brevities," *Davenport Tribune*, Aug 20, 1891.

Avalanche Base Ball Club (Des Moines, IA; 1890s). Organizer(s): Roger McGinness.

The Avalanche B.B.C. organized in 1894, played black teams. *Waterloo Courier* (August 8, 1894): "A letter from Des Moines states that Mr. Roger McGinness, manager of the Avalanche Base Ball Club, of Des Moines, is anxious to know if Waterloo (Iowa) people will give odds of five to one on the Waterloo team in a game against the Des Moines colored club. If our people have that amount if faith, he says he will put up $50 on the colored boys against $250 for the Waterloo team. If out sports want to accept these terms particulars may be learned at this office."

SOURCES: "Personal," *Waterloo (IA) Courier*, Aug 8, 1894; "Wants to Bat," *Waterloo Courier*, Aug 14, 1894.

Reindeer Base Ball Club (Des Moines, IA; 1880s)

The Reindeer B.B.C. organized in the 1880s, played black teams. *Des Moines Register* (July 24, 1883): "The Reindeer Base Ball Club, composed of waiters of the Kirkwood played the Independents, made up of colored waiters of the Morgan, at the ball park yesterday afternoon. There were about one hundred present to witness the game, which was quite fairly contested. The Reindeers were credited with eleven base hits, with a total of sixteen, and eight errors; while the Independents mad five hits, with a total of seven and sixteen errors." *Register* (August 6, 1885): "The crowning feature of the afternoon was the game of base-ball between the Moberly nine and the Reindeers of this city for the championship of two States. While the Moberlys played a good game they were in no sense a match for the local players who won the game by a score of 14 to 1. The Reindeers are a strong nine and their victory leaves them the champion colored club of Iowa and Missouri."

SOURCES: "The American Game," *Des Moines (IA) Register*, Jul 24, 1883; "A Successful Picnic," *Des Moines Register*, Aug 6, 1885; "Base Ball," *Des Moines Register*, Jul 21, 1886.

Olympic Base Ball Club (Dubuque, IA; 1880s–1900s). Organizer(s): Richard Shepard and William Morgan.

The Olympic B.B.C. organized in the 1880s, played black and white clubs. *Dubuque Sunday Herald* (July 7, 1885): "The Olympics, colored, defeated the Onwards at the base-ball park Sunday afternoon by a score of 7 to 2." *Sunday Herald* (July 14, 1885): "About 1,500 people witnessed the game of base-ball Saturday forenoon between the Olympics, of Dubuque, and the Blues, of Clinton. The African population was out en masse, and not a few of Clinton's sports were present, counting on a game remarkable for its numerous laughable errors rather than for good play. Both batteries were effective and would do credit to any team, while Frank Hamilton at short played a perfect game."

SOURCES: "Caught on the Fly," *Dubuque (IA) Herald*, Apr 29, 1885; "Base Ball," *Dubuque (IA) Sunday Herald*, Jul 7, 1885; "Caught on the Fly," *Dubuque Sunday Herald*, Jul 8, 1885; "Caught on the Fly," *Dubuque Sunday Herald*, Jul 9, 1885; "Caught on the Fly," *Dubuque Sunday Herald*, Jul 14, 1885; "Caught on the Fly," *Dubuque Sunday Herald*, Jul 28, 1885; "The City," *Dubuque (IA) Times*, Aug 20, 1885; "The News in Brief," *Dubuque Herald*, Jun 27, 1886; "The City," *Dubuque Times*, Aug 1, 1888; "Coon vs. Coon," *Dubuque Herald*, Aug 2, 1888; "Base Ball," *Dubuque Times*, Sep 3, 1891; "Curbstone Chronicles," *Dubuque Times*, Aug 1, 1892.

Unique Base Ball Club (Dubuque, IA; 1880s)

The Unique B.B.C. organized in the 1880s, played black and white teams. *Dubuque Herald* (August 7, 1883): "The Myrtle Leaves are a good nine, and some splendid plays. An amusing feature of the game was the work behind the bat of Drane, the catcher of the Uniques, and his numerous remarks to the pitcher and second baseman." *Herald* (August 24, 1883): "Probably the most entertaining game of the season was played at the ball park before a fair sided audience. The Laureates played the Uniques (colored) nine and throughout the game ample opportunity was offered the spectators to laugh and long. It was a closely played game and resulted in favor of the Uniques by a score of 15 to 9. The pitching and catching of Morgan and Dranes of the colored nine was good.

SOURCES: "Sports and Pastimes," *Dubuque (IA) Herald*, Aug 5, 1883; "Base Ball," *Dubuque Herald*, Aug 7, 1883; "The Game Yesterday," *Dubuque Herald*, Aug 24, 1883; "Ball and Bat," *Dubuque Herald*, Aug 26, 1883; "Diamond Dots," *Dubuque Herald*, Aug 28, 1883.

Colored Base Ball Club (Knoxville Junction, IA; 1890s)

The Colored B.B.C. organized in the 1890s, played black and white clubs. *Pella Weekly Herald* (June 9, 1893): "The base-ball game between our team and the colored boys from the Junction, played last Friday on the depot ground was not as close as had been, and it was no hard playing for our nimble sphere wrestlers. The score stood Pella 25, Visiting Club. 4. We understand the colored boys have $100 that they can defeat the Pella boys. We think a game will be arranged to accommodate the Junction boys."

SOURCES: "In and Around Pella," *Pella (IA) Weekly Herald*, Jun 9, 1893; "Easily Distanced," *Pella Weekly Herald*, Aug 11, 1893.

Mondamin Hotel Union Base Ball Club (Sioux City, IA; 1890s). Organizer(s): Roger McGinness.

The Mondamin Hotel Union B.B.C. organized in the 1890s, played black and white clubs. *Sioux City Journal* (May 30, 1895): "The Black Crooks and the Mondamin Unions, two colored base-ball teams, will play a game of ball this afternoon at the 'Y.' Both teams have been practicing hard and an interesting contest is looked for."

SOURCES: "The New Mondamin Hotel," *Sioux City (IA) Journal*, Apr 2, 1895; "Jottings about Town," *Sioux City Journal*, May 30, 1895; "Amateur Base Ball," *Sioux City Journal*, Jun 9, 1895; "Other Games," *Sioux City Journal*, Jun 17, 1895; "Jottings about Town," *Sioux City Journal*, Jul 10, 1895; "Amateur Base Ball," *Sioux City Journal*, Aug 9, 1895; "Gossip of the Sports," *Sioux City Journal*, Dec 30, 1895.

Union Base Ball Club (Sioux City, IA; 1890s). Owner(s): Lew Hall.

The Union B.B.C. organized in the 1890s. *Sioux City Journal*: "The Giants, Lew Hall's aggregation of colored baseball players, were defeated yesterday afternoon at Boyer's Park by the Tutti Fruttis in one of the best games of the season. The game was close and exciting throughout and at no stage did either team have much the best of the fight. The grandstand and bleachers were filled with a large crowd of baseball cranks and rooters, and they were on their feet with excitement most of the time. At times some intensely interesting plays were made, which called forth the yells of the cranks. Several sharp double plays were made on both sides. The battery work of the Giants was first class, but they lost mainly on account of poor support in the field."

Sources: "Good Game of Ball," *Sioux City (IA) Journal*, Jul 20, 1896; "Maroons and Giants," *Sioux City Journal*, Jul 27, 1896; "A Tame Ball Game," *Lemars (IA) Globe*, Aug 1, 1896; "The Tuttis Won," *Sioux City Journal*, Aug 3, 1896; "With the Amateurs," *Omaha (NE) World Herald*, Aug 7, 1896 "Bloomers to Play to Giants," *Sioux City Journal*, Aug 8, 1896; "Victory for the Stars," *Sioux City Journal*, Aug 10, 1896; "Jottings About Town," *Sioux City Journal*, Aug 16, 1896.

Kansas

Wide Awake Base Ball Club (Atchison, KS; 1870s)

The Wide Awake B.B.C. organized in the 1870s, played against black teams. *Atchison Champion* (June 20, 1874): "The Wide Awake Base Ball Club of Atchison, and the Rattlers of Leavenworth, both colored, play a match game of base-ball this afternoon at 2 o'clock."

Sources: "Items of All Kinds," *Atchison (KS) Champion*, Jun 19, 1874; "Items of All Kinds," *Atchison Champion*, Jun 20, 1874; *Atchison (KS) Patriot*, Jun 2, 1875.

Lone Star Base Ball Club (Atchison, KS; 1880s–1890s). Organizer(s): A. Williams, T. Lewis and J. W. Smith; Fred H. Gleason.

The Lone Star B.B.C. organized in the 1880s. The Lone Stars (also called the Atchison Reds) played black and white nines. Atchison and Leavenworth had an established black rivalry, traceable to the 1870s. *Atchison Globe* (June 16, 1884): "Yesterday morning the Atchison Lone Stars went to Leavenworth in a special coach attached to a regular freight train, and in the afternoon, were met on the diamond by the Leapers of the last-named city. The game took place on the fairgrounds, and was largely attended. Andy McSpiatten did most of the talking. The score stood 10 to 3 in favor the Lone Stars." Atchison and Kansas City developed a rivalry. *Atchison Globe* (September 12, 1887): "The Maroons, of Kansas City, defeated the Lone Stars, of this city, yesterday, by a score of 6 to 1. The game was quite interesting and drew a large crowd. The Maroons presented their crack battery William Castone and Frank Maupin, and the home team was almost powerless in their hands. Castone, the Maroons' pitcher, is the same individual that shut out so many clubs last year while pitching for Concordia." In the mid–1890s, a younger generation took over the Lone Star organization.

Sources: "Additional Local," *Atchison (KS) Patriot*, Jun 26, 1883; "Things Worth Knowing," *Atchison (KS) Patriot*, Sep 23, 1883; *Atchison (KS) Globe*, Oct 9, 1883; "The Coons' Game," *Atchison Globe*, Jun 16, 1884; "Base Ball," *Lawrence (KS) Western Recorder*, Jun 27, 1884; "Base Ball," *Lawrence Western Recorder*, Jul 4, 1884; "City Briefs," *Lawrence Western Recorder*, Jul 18, 1884; "City News," *Atchison Patriot*, Aug 19, 1884; "Street Gossip," *Atchison Patriot*, Jun 17, 1884; "Pick-Ups," *Atchison Patriot*, Jun 28, 1884; "Pick-Ups," *Atchison Patriot*, Sep 5, 1884; "City News," *Atchison Patriot*, Aug 4, 1885; "City News," *Atchison Patriot*, Apr 24, 1886; "Street Gossip," *Atchison (KS) Champion*, Jul 23, 1886; "City News," *Atchison Patriot*, Jul 29, 1886; *Atchison Globe*, Jul 29, 1886; *Atchison Globe*, Aug 27, 1887; *Atchison Globe*, Aug 29, 1887; "City Brevities," *Topeka (KS) Commonwealth*, Aug 31, 1887; "Base Ball To-Day," *Atchison Champion*, Sep 11, 1887; "City News," *Atchison Patriot*, Oct 3, 1887; *Atchison Globe*, Jun 29, 1888; *Atchison Globe*, Jul 2, 1888; *Atchison Globe*, Jun 29, 1888; *Atchison Globe*, Jul 2, 1888; "Base Ball," *Leavenworth (KS) Times*, Jul 26, 1888; "Atchison Affairs," *Atchison Globe*, May 28, 1895.

Osage Champions Base Ball Club (Burlingame, KS; 1870s)

The Osage Champions B.B.C. organized in the 1870s, played black nines. *Burlingame Osage County Chronicle*: "The colored youths of

this city have organized a base-ball club, called the Osage Champions, and propose to enter the arena the coming summer."

Sources: *Burlingame (KS) Osage County Chronicle*, May 16, 1878.

Rock Creek Valley Base Ball Club (Bloomington, KS; 1870s)

The Rock Creek Valley B.B.C. organized in the 1870s, played against black nines. *Lawrence Kansas Tribune* (August 20, 1870): "The following is the score of the game of base-ball between the Eagles, and the Rock Creek Valley Club, of [Bloomington]: Eagles, 55; Rock Valleys, 17." *Kansas Tribune* (June 17, 1871): "Yesterday a match game of base-ball was played between the Rock Creek valley club, of Bloomington, in this county, and the Eagles, of this city, on the grounds of the latter. Both are colored organizations. The game, although one-sided, was a spirited one. We append the score: Eagles, 55; Rock Valleys, 23." *Lawrence Journal* (August 10, 1871): "The Red Jackets, of Eudora, played the Rock Valleys, of Rock Creek, Saturday, and the Rock Valley club coming out victors by a score of 39 to 25."

Sources: "Base Ball," *Lawrence (KS) Kansas Tribune*, Aug 3, 1870; "Base Ball," *Lawrence Kansas Tribune*, Aug 6, 1870; *Lawrence Kansas Tribune*, Aug 19, 1870; "Base Ball," *Lawrence Kansas Tribune*, Aug 20, 1870; "Base Ball," *Lawrence Kansas Tribune*, Oct 4, 1870; "Base Ball," *Lawrence Kansas Tribune*, Oct 15, 1870; "Base Ball," *Lawrence Kansas Tribune*, Jun 17, 1871; "Bad Conduct," *Lawrence Kansas Tribune*, Jun 18, 1871; "Base Ball," *Lawrence (KS) Journal*, Aug 10, 1871; "The National Game," *Lawrence Kansas Tribune*, Aug 10, 1871.

Black Diamond Base Ball Club (Cheptopa, KS; 1890s)

The Black Diamond B.B.C. organized in the 1890s, played black and white nines of KS, MO and OK. *Coffeyville Weekly Journal* (August 17, 1894): "Chetopa's Africans played against Coffeyville's Kansas Blackman's Club a game of ball Wednesday afternoon which furnished amusement to a number of people. The Chetopa team were big, black, and gritty, and looked formidable enough, but as the sequel will show, they deceived their looks.… The excitement among the spectators was intense, as the Chetopa team had the reputation of being almost invincible.… After a two hours' wrangle, each umpire awarded the game to his team, the score being 9 to 0 in favor of Coffeyville." They played white teams. *Parsons Weekly Blade* (July 7, 1894): "The Black Diamond and Russell Creek base-ball nines crossed bats at Timber Hill celebration for a small purse, the score standing 7 to 17 in favor of the Black Diamonds." *Weekly Blade* (May 6, 1896): "The first game of base-ball between the Columbus Hot Shots and Chetopa Black Diamonds Base Ball Club was played last Saturday; quite a number of Columbus citizens came to witness the game."

Sources: "Local News," *Coffeyville (KS) Afro-American Advocate*, Jul 1, 1892; "Chetopa, Kansas," *Indianapolis (IN) Freeman*, Jul 9, 1892; "Will Play To-Day," *Wichita (KS) Daily Eagle*, Jun 15, 1894; "Chetopa Wins Again," *Parsons (KS) Weekly Blade*, Jul 7, 1894; "Pitcher's Contest," *Wichita Eagle*, Jul 11, 1894; *Parsons Weekly Blade*, Aug 18, 1894; "Cheptopa News," *Parsons Weekly Blade*, Apr 15, 1896; "Cheptopa News," *Parsons Weekly Blade*, May 2, 1896; "Cheptopa News," *Parsons Weekly Blade*, May 9, 1896; *Coffeyville (KS) Journal*, May 12, 1894; *Coffeyville (KS) Weekly Journal*, May 14, 1894; "A Great Game," *Coffeyville Weekly Journal*, May 15, 1894; "Ended in a Wrangle," *Coffeyville Weekly Journal*, Aug 17, 1894; "A Walk Away," *Coffeyville Weekly Journal*, Sep 14, 1894; *Parsons Weekly Blade*, May 23, 1896; "Cheptopa News," *Parsons Weekly Blade*, Aug 15, 1896.

Sure Shot Base Ball Club (Coffeyville, KS; 1890s). Organizer(s): Sanford Jones, James Roberts and Alfred Shobe.

The Sure Shot B.B.C. organized in the 1890s, played black nines. *Coffeyville Journal* (August 11, 1899): "The Coffeyville Hot Shot base-ball team challenges any colored team in Kansas. We really believe we are the warmest team out this season. We don't know what it is to get beaten. Sanford Jones, manager." *Journal* (August 29, 1899): "The Coffeyville and Cherryvale colored nines will play ball here Thursday afternoon at 3 p. m. at the new base-ball park in North Walnut Street. With such fellows as Sanford and Hayes Jones in the home team the game will certainly be the most interesting and amusing ever played in Coffeyville." *Journal* (September 1, 1899): "The Coffeyville colored boys defeated Cherryvale's colored team here Thursday, the score being 12 to 11. Jones and Wallace were the Coffeyville battery and Smith and Speaks, Cherryvale's.

Sources: "Coffeyville Ball Team," *Coffeyville (KS) Journal*, Apr 25, 1899; "Baseball Notes," *Coffeyville Journal*, Aug 11, 1899; "Baseball Notes," *Coffeyville Journal*, August 29, 1899; "Baseball Notes," *Coffeyville Journal*, Aug 30, 1899; "Baseball Notes," *Coffeyville Journal*, September 1, 1899.

Clipper Base Ball Club (Emporia, KS; 1890s). Organizer(s): Harry O'Dair; O. Whilhite.

The Clipper B.B.C. organized in the 1890s, played against black teams. *Council Grove Republican* (August 10, 1894): "The Council Grove ball club played three games with the Clippers of Emporia this week on the home ground, winning all three games. The score Wednesday afternoon was 24 to 10, Thursday morning 36 to 10 and Thursday afternoon 15 to 10. The home nine put up a good article of ball, the playing of the Johnson boys, Claude Kennedy and Lee Redmond being specially worthy of mention. The Emporia team were crippled by the absence of several of their best players." *Osage City Free Press* (August 8, 1895): "A large crowd of local fans gathered at the ball grounds Friday last. The attraction was a base-ball game between the Emporia Clippers and Osage City Browns, both colored. The Browns were unable to overcome the lead taken by the Clippers in the second inning, and Emporia took the game. Score 14 to 10." *Emporia Gazette* (July 9, 1896): "The Emporia Clippers and Hartford Reds, two colored ball teams, are crossing bats at Hartford today. The battery for the Emporia team is the Ray brothers who nearly won the game for the Haymakers on the Fourth."

Sources: "Local News," *Osage City (KS) Free Press*, Jun 28, 1894; *Council Grove (KS) Republican*, Aug 10, 1894; *Emporia (KS) Gazette*, May 1, 1895; "Base Ball," *Osage City Free Press*, Aug 8, 1895; *Emporia (KS) Gazette*, Jul 9, 1896; *Emporia Gazette*, Aug 3, 1899; *Emporia Gazette*, Aug 5, 1899; *Emporia Gazette*, Aug 9, 1899.

Red Jackets Base Ball Club (Eudora, KS; 1870s)

The Red Jackets B.B.C. organized in the 1870s, played against black and white teams. *Lawrence Kansas Tribune* (October 2, 1870): "The Red Jackets, of Eudora, played the Atlantics, of Lawrence, at Eudora on September 30th, and were beaten in a score, in eight innings, of 20 to 35." *Kansas Tribune* (October 9, 1870): "In a game of base-ball at Lawrence, on the Kaw Valley grounds, and the Red Jackets, of Eudora, the Lawrence boys won, by a score of 46 to 26." *Lawrence Journal* (August 10, 1871): "The Red Jackets, of Eudora, played the Rock Valleys, of Rock Creek, Saturday, and the Rock Valley club coming out victors by a score of 39 to 25." *Kansas Tribune* (September 26, 1871): "Last Saturday, a match fame of base-ball between Wakarusa Valley Club, of Eudora, a colored organization, and the Blue Mound [Tads] club, a white organization, took place, in which the colored boys won by the following score: Wakarusa, 87; Blue Mound, 53."

Sources: "Base Ball," *Lawrence (KS) Kansas Tribune*, Sep 10, 1870; "Base Ball," *Lawrence Kansas Tribune*, Oct 2, 1870; *Lawrence Kansas Tribune*, Oct 9, 1870; "Base Ball," *Lawrence (KS) Journal*, Jul 23, 1871; "Base Ball," *Lawrence (KS) Journal*, Aug 10, 1871; "National Game," *Lawrence Kansas Tribune*, Sep 26, 1871.

Olympic Base Ball Club (Fort Scott, KS; 1870s–1880s)

The Olympic B.B.C. organized in the 1870s. The nine, composed waiters of the Gulf House, played black organizations. *Fort Scott Monitor* (August 11, 1877): "The match game played yesterday between the Stars and Olympics, was won by the former in a score of 20 to 10. The Olympics were whitewashed in the first and second innings. Mortimer's left underhand throwing had no effect on the Stars, who batted him all over the field with ease. H. Hawkins, of the Stars, made a very nice double play in the sixth inning." *Parsons Weekly Sun* (August 2, 1879): "The [Fort Scott] new catcher passed under the name of Charles Brown, he being the alleged brother of Ed Brown, the crack pitcher of the Kansas and Scott nine. Our boys noticed that this morning a thick-set bullet-headed, circus-dressed young man standing in an alley-way endeavoring to catch the balls thrown to him by an ebony-hued Abyssinian. Some say he was an imported catcher. Fortunately, for us, he was the new catcher, so called." *Monitor* (September 23, 1879): "In the game of base-ball yesterday, between the Fort Scott and Parsons Clubs, (colored), the score stood 26 to 6 in favor of [Parsons]. In the last game between the Nameless, of Parsons, and the Olympics, of this city, it is quite possible the colored base-ballists of Fort Scott may be able to wipe out the record of the two defeats of our Olympics at the hands of the Nameless by pounding the conceit out of the red-capped colored ball players of Parsons."

Sources: "Base Ball," *Fort Scott (KS) Monitor*, Jun 2, 1876; "Base Ball Challenge," *Fort Scott Monitor*, Jun 6, 1876; "Base Ball," *Fort Scott Monitor*, Jun 13, 1876; "Base Ball," *Fort Scott Monitor*, Aug 11, 1877; "Base Ball," *Fort Scott Monitor*, Aug 14, 1877; "Base Ball in Fort Scott," *Fort Scott Monitor*, May 16, 1879; *Fort Scott Monitor*, Jun 28, 1879; *Fort Scott Monitor*, Jul 8, 1879; *Fort Scott Monitor*, Jul 26, 1879; *Fort Scott Monitor*, Jul 27, 1879; "Fort Scott Fallen," *Parsons (KS) Weekly Sun*, Aug 2, 1879; *Fort Scott Monitor*, Sep 23, 1879; *Parsons Weekly Sun*, Sep 27, 1879; *Fort Scott Monitor*, May 7, 1880; Jun 16, 1880.

Star Base Ball Club (Fort Scott, KS; 1870s). Organizer(s): James Eagleson, David M. Gordon and A. M. Thornton.

The Star B.B.C. organized in the 1870s. The Star club was composed of barbers from the Star Barber Shop; team organizers: James Eagleson, David M. Gordon and A. M. Thornton. They played black and white and nines. *Fort Scott* (April 4, 1874) *Monitor*: "The Colored Star Club and the Clippers [white], of this city, yesterday, played a match game for the championship ball. The game was won by the Star Club, the score standing 42 for the Stars and 38 for the Clippers." They developed a rivalry with the Olympics, a white club. *Fort Scott Monitor* (August 11, 1877): "The match game played yesterday between the Stars and Olympics, was won by the former in a score of 20 to 10. The Olympics were whitewashed in the first and second innings. Mortimer's left underhand throwing had no effect on the Stars, who batted him all over the field with ease. H. Hawkins, of the Stars, made a very nice double play in the sixth inning."

Sources: "Star Barber Shop," *Fort Scott (KS) Monitor*, Nov 22, 1873; "Base Ball," *Fort Scott Monitor*, Apr 4, 1874; "Challenge," *Fort Scott Monitor*, Jun 25, 1875; "Base Ball," *Fort Scott Monitor*, Jun 30, 1875; *Fort Scott Monitor*, Aug 31, 1875; "Emancipation," *Fort Scott Monitor*, Sep 23, 1875; "Base Ball Challenge," *Fort Scott Monitor*, Jun 6, 1876; *Fort Scott Monitor*, Sep 15, 1877; "Base Ball," *Fort Scott Monitor*, Aug 11, 1877; *Fort Scott Monitor*, Aug 14, 1877; "Challenge," *Fort Scott Monitor*, Aug 15, 1877; "Base Ball," *Fort Scott Monitor*, Sep 12, 1877; "Base Ball Notes," *Fort Scott Monitor*, Jun 19, 1879.

Liberty Base Ball Club (Fort Scott, KS; 1870s–1880s). Organizer(s): H. French; H. Curtis; Colonel Jordan.

The Liberty B.B.C. organized in the 1870s, played black nines. They developed a local rivalry. *Fort Scott Monitor* (June 3, 1879): "We, the Libertys, accept the challenge from the Westerns for two bats and the championship of the city, on Thursday, June 5, at 3 o'clock." *Monitor* (June 11, 1879): "We, the Liberty Base Ball Club do hereby challenge the Western Boys to a second game of base-ball on Thursday, June 19th, at 3 o'clock." *Monitor* (June 20, 1879): "The two leading colored clubs, the Western Boys and the Liberties, had an interesting game of ball yesterday, of which the following is the score: Western Boys, 30; Liberties, 15."

SOURCES: *Fort Scott (KS) Monitor*, Jun 3, 1879; *Fort Scott Monitor*, Jun 11, 1879; *Fort Scott Monitor*, Jun 12, 1879; *Fort Scott Monitor*, Jun 20, 1879; "Base Ball," *Fort Scott Monitor*, Jun 26, 1879; *Fort Scott Monitor*, Jul 16, 1879; *Fort Scott Monitor*, Jun 13, 1882; *Fort Scott Monitor*, Jun 14, 1882; "Base Ball," *Fort Scott Monitor*, Jul 2, 1882.

Western Base Ball Club (Fort Scott, KS; 1870s–1880s). Organizer(s): R. Downing, George C. Bryant, Henry Hawkins and N. Barker.

The Western B.B.C. organized in the 1870s, played against white and black nines. *Fort Scott Monitor* (July 14, 1877): "We, the members of the Western Base Ball Club, do hereby challenge you, the members of the Star Base Ball Club, to play a match game of base-ball, on the Mutual Grounds, Wednesday, July 18, 1877." *Monitor* (August 9, 1879): "Yesterday's game between the Western Boys (colored) and the Strangers (white) resulted in favor of the Westerns by a score of 26 to 23." *Monitor* (August 22, 1879): "To the Secretary of the Stranger Base Ball Club: We the members of the Western Boys, do not accept the challenge received from your club, because the grounds on which we play are engaged for tomorrow afternoon by Mayflower and Eastern Boys, but will receive a challenge by August 29, from any club under 18 years of age in this city."

SOURCES: *Fort Scott (KS) Monitor*, Jul 14, 1877; "Base Ball," *Fort Scott Monitor*, Aug 11, 1877; "Challenge," *Fort Scott Monitor*, Aug 15, 1877; "Base Ball," *Fort Scott Monitor*, Sep 12, 1877; *Fort Scott Monitor*, Sep 27, 1877; *Fort Scott Monitor*, Mar 26, 1878; "Base Ball," *Fort Scott Monitor*, Apr 4, 1878; *Fort Scott Monitor*, Oct 4, 1878; *Fort Scott Monitor*, Jun 20, 1879; "Base Ball," *Fort Scott Monitor*, Jun 26, 1879; *Fort Scott Monitor*, Jul 30, 1879; *Fort Scott Monitor*, May 10, 1882; *Fort Scott Monitor*, Jun 13, 1882; *Fort Scott Monitor*, Jun 14, 1882; *Fort Scott Monitor*, May 30, 1884; *Fort Scott Monitor*, Jun 22, 1884.

Girard Blues Base Ball Club (Girard, KS; 1880s–1890s)

The Girard Blues B.B.C. organized in the 1870s, played against white and black nines. *Girard Press* (May 11, 1887): "The colored nine of base-ball players had a game of ball with the white men last Saturday. The former were victorious." *Press* (April 21, 1888): "A match game of base-ball was played at Higgie's Park between the first nine of the Girard Browns (white) and the second nine of the Girard Blues (colored), the Browns being victorious, the score standing 40 to 13." *Press* (September 12, 1889): "Last Thursday a match game of base-ball was played between the Whites and the Blues, resulting in a victory for the Blues, the score standing 14 to 13 in their favor. We are told this is the first time the Blues have all been together this season. Gus Hammers and James Monroe were the battery for the Blues, and played a good game." *Press* (August 6, 1891): "The game of base-ball at Baxter Springs last Saturday between the colored club and Joplin, Missouri, resulted in a victory for the Joplin club, the score standing 5 to 2. Only six innings were played."

SOURCES: "Base Ball," *Girard (MO) Press*, Apr 21, 1888; "The Girard Blues Victorious," *Girard Press*, Aug 4, 1888; "The Blues Victorious," *Girard Press*, Aug 18, 1888; "Base Ball," *Girard Press*, Jun 20, 1889; "Base Ball," *Girard Press*, Sep 12, 1889; "Going to Baxter Springs," *Girard Press*, Jul 30, 1891; "Base Ball at Baxter," *Girard Press*, Aug 6, 1891.

Athletic Base Ball Club (Hutchinson, KS; 1880s–1890s)

The Athletic B.B.C. organized in the 1880s, played black and white teams. *Hutchinson News* (September 14, 1888): "Yesterday's game of ball between the home team and the Athletics (colored) furnished a vast amount of fun to a small but appreciative audience. The game resulted in a victory for the home team by a score of 19 to 14. The battery for the colored team was Stevens and Babe, who at times played well, Babe throwing to bases being superb, but Charlie Bean carried off the honors of the day for the colored team." *News* (June 25, 1893): "We, the third base-ball nine, of Hutchison, do hereby accept the challenge to play the second colored nine on Wednesday afternoon for a purse of $15."

SOURCES: *Hutchinson (KS) News*, Aug 17, 1886; "Base Ball," *Hutchinson News*, Sep 11, 1888; "Base Ball," *Hutchinson News*, Sep 14, 1888; "Wind Wins," *Wichita (KS) Eagle*, Aug 2, 1889; "We Accept the Challenge," *Hutchinson News*, Jun 30, 1893; "Base Ball," *Hutchinson News*, Aug 12, 1895; "An Interesting Game," *Hutchinson News*, Aug 16, 1895; "Ten Innings," *Hutchinson News*, Sep 7, 1895; "Base Ball," *Hutchinson News*, Sep 10, 1895.

Clipper Base Ball Club (Hutchinson, KS; 1890s)

The Clipper B.B.C. organized in the 1890s. The Clippers developed a rivalry with Wichita's Athletics, another black aggregation. *Wichita Eagle* (August 5, 1893): "The Wichita Athletics and the Hutchinson Clippers played a hot and interesting ball game at Riverside Park yesterday. The attendance was not extra-large, but the crowd that was there was well pleased. Both teams will play two games here again real soon, at which time the attendance will be larger."

SOURCES: "We Accept the Challenge," *Hutchinson (KS) News*, Jun 30, 1893; "Base Ball," *Wichita (KS) Eagle*. Aug 5, 1893; "Corrected Report," *Hutchinson News*, Aug 5, 1893; "Black Wins," *Hutchinson News*, Aug 7, 1893; "An Interesting Game," *Hutchinson News*, Aug 16, 1895; "Celebrate the Day," *Hutchinson News*, Jul 6, 1897.

Modoc Base Ball Club (Hutchinson, KS; 1880s)

The Modoc B.B.C. organized in the 1880s. *Hutchinson News* (August 30, 1888): "The Hutchinson Modocs, the colored base-ball club of our city, went down to Wichita and played a game with the Wichita Browns, also a colored club Tuesday afternoon. The game was called at the fifth inning on account of rain, the score standing 8 to 1 in the Modocs' favor."

SOURCES: "Base Ball," *Hutchinson (KS) News*, Aug 30, 1888; "A Close Game Anticipated," *Hutchinson News*, September 7, 1888.

Blues Base Ball Club (Independence, KS; 1890s)

The Blues B.B.C. organized in the 1890s, played black and white teams. *Independence Weekly Star and Kansan* (May 24, 1895): "There will be a practice game of base-ball next week between Captain Truby's nine and the Yellow Jackets, a colored nine of this city." *Independence Reporter* (July 12, 1894): "The Independence Blues, our colored ball team, went over to Cherryvale yesterday and showed the Cherryvale Yellow Jackets how to play ball to the tune of 14 to 4." *Independence Reporter* (August 8, 1894): "A game of ball was played at Washburn Park yesterday afternoon by the Parsons Browns and Independence Blues (though the real color of each team is black) and was won by the home team by a score of 20 to 14. The Parsons fellows came over to do up our gallant club. They brought sixteen men with them and our boys did not even know that they were coming, but although taken by surprise they rallied their forces and licked the enemy in fine style."

SOURCES: *Independence (KS) Reporter*, Jun 30, 1894; *Independence Reporter*, Jul 12, 1894; "Local News," *Independence Reporter*, Aug 8, 1894.

Yellow Jacket Base Ball Club (Independence, KS; 1890s)

The Yellow Jacket B.B.C. organized in the 1890s, played black and white teams. *Independence Weekly Star and Kansan* (May 24, 1895): "There will be a practice game of base-ball next week between Captain Truby's nine and the Yellow Jackets, a colored nine of this city." *Independence Reporter* (May 8, 1896): "The ball game between Denver Spencer's nine and the Yellow Jackets yesterday afternoon resulted in the defeat of the Spencerians by the awful score of 14 to 2."

SOURCES: *Independence (KS) Weekly Star and Kansan*, May 24, 1895; "Local News," *Independence (KS) Reporter*, May 24, 1895; *Independence Reporter*, May 25, 1895; *Independence Reporter*, Jun 14, 1896 *Independence Reporter*, Jul 10, 1895; *Independence Reporter*, May 7, 1896; *Independence Reporter*, May 8, 1896; *Independence Reporter*, May 15, 1896; *Independence Reporter*, May 17, 1896; "The Game of the Season," *Independence Weekly Star and Kansan*, Sep 25, 1896.

Eagle Base Ball Club (Lawrence, KS; 1870s–1880s). Organizer(s): T. J. Banks and Thomas Berry; Elijah Matthews; James Gross and William Gray; James W. Hoyt and William H. Fry.

The Eagle B.B.C. organized in 1866, played white and black teams. *Lawrence Republican Journal* (August 2, 1871): "The Eagle Base Ball Club of this city made a visit to Kansas City yesterday, and engaged the Union Club of that city in a friendly game of base-ball. The game was closely contested, and good playing was done on both sides. The Lawrence boys came out ahead, by a score of 31 to 17, which of itself shows the skill displayed." *Republican Journal* (July 20, 1873): "The match game of base-ball which was played at Leavenworth, between the Eagles of this city and the Unions of Leavenworth, on Tuesday, resulted in a victory for the Eagles, who can now claim the championship among the colored clubs of the state." They played the St. Louis Blue Stockings, a champion black club. *Republican Journal* (July 13, 1876): "A swarthy, sweaty, first-class assemblage witnessed the game of base-ball yesterday between the Blue Stockings of St. Louis and the Eagles of Lawrence. The crowd was very decorous, though showing some enthusiasm at the several successes of the Eagles. The Blues will not go to Topeka, but will leave this morning for Louisville, Kentucky. They were entertained last evening in Miller's Hall. The call the Eagles the best amateur club they have met with west of St. Louis, and considering the fact that they have had no practice for eight consecutive months, we guess they are." They also played local black talent. *Republican Journal* (August 22, 1876): "The Red Stockings and the Eagles had a friendly match on the old Kaw Valley Grounds commencing at three o'clock. The Eagles soared to an unusual altitude, cleaning their red-legged opponents out, by a score of 25 to 4. Watt McConnell saw that everything went fair and square to the best of his ability, and satisfactorily." The Eagles also played against Lawrence's white nine. *Lawrence Evening Tribune*: "The game of base-ball yesterday afternoon was the finest exhibition of ball playing yet seen in the park. At the end of the eighth inning the score stood Lawrence 3, Eagles 2. The last inning the white boys got 4 runs and the Eagles 2, the game resulting 7 to 4 in favor of the Lawrence Club." In 1887, they played Independence's OK B.B.C. *Evening Tribune* (August 28, 1886): "The game yesterday between the OK's of Independence, Missouri and the Lawrence Eagles was very interesting. The umpire had probably been a champion umpire during slavery days, but did not know much of the game as it is played in '87. He frequently called ball when the batter had struck at them. Several of the Lawrence players had been infused with Missouri whiskey, which loosened their tongues and caused several bolts in the game over altercations with the umpire. The Oks did very poor batting, and most of their runs were made on errors. The Eagles did some heavy batting in the forepart of the game, but after the Oks had changed pitchers did not succeed in batting so freely. Both clubs have good ball playing material, and it is to be hoped that today's game was a better one."

SOURCES: "Eagles to Bat," *Lawrence (KS) Kansas Tribune*, Jul 27, 1870; *Lawrence Kansas Tribune*, Aug 4, 1870; "Base Ball," *Lawrence Kansas Tribune*, Aug 6, 1870; "Base Ball Match," *Lawrence (KS) Republican Journal*, Aug 2, 1871; "Base Ball," *Lawrence Republican Journal*, Aug 16, 1871; "Base Ball," *Lawrence Republican Journal*, Jul 24, 1873; "Base Ball," *Lawrence Republican Journal*, Aug 19, 1873; "Local News," *Lawrence Republican Journal*, Jun 25, 1875; *Topeka (KS) Commonwealth*, Jul 22, 1875; "Base Ball," *Lawrence Kansas Tribune*, Jul 7, 1876; "Blue Stockings vs. Eagles," *Lawrence Republican Journal*, Jul 13, 1876; "The Colored Champions," *St. Louis (MO) Globe-Democrat*, Jul 13, 1876; "Base Ball Match," *Lawrence Kansas Tribune*, Jul 13, 1876; "Base Ball," *Lawrence Republican Journal*, Jul 27, 1876; *Lawrence Republican Journal*, Aug 22, 1876; "Local Notices," *Lawrence Republican Journal*, Jul 23, 1878; "Town and Country," *Lawrence Republican Journal*, Aug 20, 1878; "Base Ball," *Lawrence (KS) Journal World*, Jul 31, 1886; *Lawrence Journal World*, Aug 14, 1886; "A Kansas City Club That Wins," *Kansas City (KS) Times*, Aug 20, 1886; "Not Title," *Lawrence Journal*, Aug 26, 1886; "Base Ball," *Lawrence (KS) Evening Tribune*, Aug 28, 1886; "Base Ball," *Lawrence Evening Tribune*, Sep 4, 1886; *Lawrence (KS) Weekly Journal*, Sep 9, 1886; "Base Ball," *Lawrence Evening Tribune*, Sep 4, 1886; *Lawrence Evening Tribune*, Oct 4, 1886; *Lawrence Evening Tribune*, Oct 18, 1886; "City News in Brief," *Lawrence Evening Tribune*, Jun 1, 1887; "City News in Brief," *Lawrence Evening Tribune*, Jun 2, 1887; "Yesterday's Ball Game," *Lawrence Evening Tribune*, Jun 9, 1887.

Leaper Base Ball Club (Lawrence, KS; 1890s). Organizer(s): William H. Barker.

The Leaper B.B.C. organized in the 1890s, played black nines. *Lawrence Weekly Record* (July 10, 1891): "The Kings of the Diamond, an aggregation of alleged ballplayers from Topeka, came down to Lawrence last Monday and received their usual discipline at the hands of out crack ball team, the Leapers. The score stood 8 to 7 in favor of the Leapers. The Topekas have a high-sounding name, pretty uniforms, plenty of balls and bats, and an abundance of loud mouth. All that they need now to complete the outfit is a ball club and a gentleman on first base. The latter article is badly needed." They also played MO's Black clubs. *Kansas City Star* (July 10, 1893): "The Kansas City Blues, colored, defeated the Lawrence Leapers at Exposition Park yesterday, by a score of 21 to 6. They will play a return game at Lawrence, Kansas, on Friday next."

SOURCES: "The Leapers at Topeka," *Lawrence Weekly Record*, Jul 10, 1891; *Lawrence (KS) Historic Times*, Aug 29, 1891; "City News," *Lawrence (KS) Gazette*, Jul 10, 1891; "Amateur Base Ball Notes," *Kansas City (MO) Star*, Jul 10, 1893.

Moonlight Base Ball Club (Lawrence, KS; 1870s)

The Moonlight B.B.C. organized in the 1870s, played black teams. *Lawrence Tribune* (May 17, 1873): "The Eagle and Moonlight Base Ball Clubs (colored) had a practice game on the ball grounds yesterday afternoon. The game attracted quite a large crowd, and taking into consideration the little practice these clubs have had this season, they did some good playing. The Eagles won the game, the score being: Eagles, 44; Moonlights, 34." The played Topeka's black club. *Tribune* (August 14, 1873): "The Independents, of Topeka, and the Moonlights, of Lawrence (both colored) played a match game yesterday, resulting in a defeat of the former by a score of 37 to 41." *Trib-*

une (September 6, 1873): "The Eagles claim to be the champions of the State and also the best talkers. As far as the best talkers' part is concerned we acknowledge their claims. They challenged the Kaw Valleys and because that club would not play within fifteen days the Eagles claimed the championship. We (the Moonlights) offered them a game fifteen days ago, and they have not accepted, on the grounds they had only seven men in the nine present. This is not a sufficient excuse, according to regulations, and we claim the championship. We acknowledge nothing but their claim to good talking." *Tribune* (September 7, 1873): "On the 10th day of May the Moonlights challenged us to play them three games for the championship. We accepted and beat them. This is as much as the law requires. The Moonlights have never won a game since they have been in existence. [The Eagle captain] advises them to beat some club before they complain of the Eagles."

SOURCES: "Base Ball," *Lawrence (KS) Tribune,* May 17, 1873; "Base Ball," *Lawrence Tribune,* Jun 4, 1873; "Base Ball," *Lawrence Tribune.* Aug 14, 1873; "A Little Moonlight on the Base Ball Question," *Lawrence Tribune,* Sep 6, 1873; "The Eagle Screams Again," *Lawrence Tribune,* Sep 7, 1873.

Red Stocking Base Ball Club (Lawrence, KS; 1870s)

The Red Stocking B.B.C. organized in 1871. The Red Stockings developed a local rivalry. *Lawrence Republican Journal* (August 22, 1876): "The Red Stockings and the Eagles had a friendly match on the old Kaw Valley Grounds commencing at three o'clock. The Eagles soared to an unusual altitude, cleaning their red-legged opponents out, by a score of 25 to 4. Watt McConnell saw that everything went fair and square to the best of his ability, and satisfactorily."

SOURCES: "Local News," *Lawrence (KS) Republican Journal,* Aug 15, 1871; "Base Ball," *Lawrence Republican Journal,* Jul 27, 1876; *Lawrence Republican Journal,* Aug 22, 1876.

Union Regulator Base Ball Club (Lawrence, KS; 1860s–1870s). Organizer(s): Elijah Matthews.

The Union Regulator B.B.C. organized in the 1860s, played against black nines. *Lawrence Kansas Tribune* (March 14, 1868): "In a match game of base-ball played on Friday afternoon between the Stars and Regulators, the former won the game in a score of 51 to 19, both clubs played well, but as usual the Stars being very plucky, win the game in the above score." *Leavenworth Bulletin* (March 23, 1868): "In a match game of base-ball played on Friday afternoon between the Stars and Regulators, the former won the game in a score of 51 to 19, both clubs played well, but as usual the Stars being very plucky, won the game in the above score." *Kansas Tribune* (June 23, 1868): "The Independent Base Ball Club (colored), of Leavenworth, came over yesterday and played against the Union Club, of this city, for the purpose of redeeming, if possible, the tarnished fame of their town, but unfortunately met with no more success than their white compeers in that line. Both clubs are composed of boys of several shades of color; and they are as ambitious as young Caesars." *Kansas Tribune* (July 10, 1868): "The Union (colored) Base Ball Club of this city, went to Leavenworth on Wednesday, to play against the Independents, and were defeated. The score stood, 20 to 17. The Conservative [newspaper] argues from this, that Leavenworth is the center of activity and muscle."

SOURCES: "Base Ball," *Lawrence (KS) Kansas Tribune,* Mar 14, 1868; "General News," *Leavenworth (KS) Bulletin,* Mar 23, 1868; "Defeated Again," *Lawrence (KS) Kansas Tribune,* Jun 23, 1868; "Defeated Again," *Lawrence Kansas Tribune,* Jun 23, 1868; *Lawrence Kansas Tribune,* July 7, 1868; "Base Ball," *Leavenworth (KS) Bulletin,* Jul 9, 1868; "Base Ball," *Lawrence Kansas Tribune,* Jul 10, 1868; "Base Ball," *Lawrence Kansas Tribune,* Sep 3, 1869; "A Challenge," *Lawrence*

Kansas Tribune, May 25, 1870; *Lawrence Kansas Tribune,* Aug 19, 1870; "Base Ball," *Lawrence Kansas Tribune,* Oct 4, 1870.

Colored Browns Base Ball Club (Leavenworth, KS; 1880s–1890s)

The Colored Browns B.B.C. organized in the 1880s. *Leavenworth Advocate* (May 3, 1890): "Last Sunday, the North Leavenworth Browns—about the cleverest young base-ball club in the city—defeated before a large audience, the Cincinnati club which is composed of some very promising young ball tossers, by the score of 21 to 14. The game would have been interesting but fir the wild pitching of Robinson of the Cincinnatis off of whom the Browns scored seventeen runs in the first inning."

SOURCES: "At Exposition Park," *Kansas City (MO) Times,* Jul 15, 1888; "Base Ball," *Leavenworth (KS) Advocate,* May 3, 1890.

Independent Union Star Base Ball Club (Leavenworth, KS; 1860s–1870s)

The Independent Union Star B.B.C. organized in the 1860s. The Independents (also called the Stars or the Union Stars) played black organizations; they developed a rivalry with Lawrence's Union Regulators. *Lawrence Kansas Tribune* (March 14, 1868): "In a match game of base-ball played on Friday afternoon between the Stars and Regulators, the former won the game in a score of 51 to 19, both clubs played well, but as usual the Stars being very plucky, win the game in the above score." *Leavenworth Bulletin* (March 23, 1868): "In a match game of base-ball played on Friday afternoon between the Stars and Regulators, the former won the game in a score of 51 to 19, both clubs played well, but as usual the Stars being very plucky, won the game in the above score." *Kansas Tribune* (June 23, 1868): "The Independent Base Ball Club (colored), of Leavenworth, came over yesterday and played against the Union Club, of this city, for the purpose of redeeming, if possible, the tarnished fame of their town, but unfortunately met with no more success than their white compeers in that line. Both clubs are composed of boys of several shades of color; and they are as ambitious as young Caesars."

SOURCES: "Base Ball," *Lawrence (KS) Kansas Tribune,* Mar 14, 1868; "General News," *Leavenworth (KS) Bulletin,* Mar 23, 1868; "Defeated Again," *Lawrence Kansas Tribune,* Jun 23, 1868; *Lawrence Kansas Tribune,* Jul 7, 1868; "Base Ball," *Leavenworth Bulletin,* Jul 9, 1868; "Base Ball," *Lawrence Kansas Tribune,* Jul 10, 1868; "City Scrap," *Lawrence Kansas Tribune,* Aug 17, 1871; "The National Game," *Kansas City (MO) Journal of Daily Commerce,* Aug 22, 1871; "Base Ball," *Lawrence (KS) Republican Journal,* Jul 24, 1873.

Leaper Base Ball Club (Leavenworth, KS; 1870s–1890s). Organizer(s): Dennis A. Jones, Jr.

The Leaper B.B.C. organized in the 1870s, played against black nines. Leavenworth and Kansas City developed a rivalry. *Kansas City Journal of Commerce* (July 8, 1877): "The game of base-ball between the Brown Stockings of this city, and the Leapers of Leavenworth, played yesterday afternoon at the Eighteenth Street Grounds, resulted in the victory of the Browns by a score of 18 to 14. The game was umpired by F. Ringo." Like other black organizations, the Leapers committed their services to civic life. *Journal of Commerce* (July 11, 1877): "We understand that the Leaper Base Ball Club (colored), of this city, have tendered their services to the fire department as a hook and ladder company. They are all fine, able-bodied fellows, and we think they would do good service at a fire." Following successful years, they reorganized in the 1880s. *Leavenworth Times* (August 2, 1881): "In the ball game between the Leavenworth Leapers and the Topeka Stars, the Leapers won by a score of 40 to 15." *Times* (August 19, 1884): "The Leapers is the name of a base-ball club recently organized among the colored boys, Dennis Jones, Jr., is manager. The Club has ten games ahead of the season." *Kansas City Times* (July 19, 1888): "The Athletic Park was the scene of a thrilling contest in the shape of a match game of base-ball between two colored clubs, the Leapers and the Black Stockings. All the young colored bloods of the city were there, and with their ladies, crowded the amphitheater, while several hundred Caucasians hung on the fence and cheered wilding at every brilliant play. The Leapers were clad in pink shirts, red stockings, and white pants, while their opponents wore suits of dark blue, relieved by chaste stripes about half a foot wide. Excited men ran up and down the amphitheater flourishing real money and shouting.... The game resulted in a victory for the Leapers on a score of 10 to 9 and great was the rejoicing thereat." *Kansas City Star* (August 3, 1887): "A match game was played between the Kansas City Leapers, the colored base-ball club of this city, and the Red Stockings at Sedalia on yesterday. [A]t the conclusion of the nine innings the score stood 24 to 14 in favor of the Sedalia team. The return game will be played at Kansas City at an early date." *Atchison Globe* (July 2, 1888): "The Leavenworth Leapers, the colored baseball club, which was to have played the Lone Stars at Prospect Park yesterday, did not make their appearance. The Atchison boys had gone to the expense of advertising the game, and were greatly disappointed."

SOURCES: "Jottings," *Kansas City (MO) Journal of Commerce*, Jul 8, 1877; "Jottings," *Kansas City Journal of Commerce*, Jul 11, 1877; "Jottings," *Kansas City Journal of Commerce*, Jul 20, 1877; "Jottings," *Kansas City Journal of Commerce*, Jul 21, 1877; "Leavenworth," *Kansas City Journal of Commerce*, Aug 16, 1877; "City News," *Leavenworth (KS) Times*, Aug 2, 1881; "Colored Base Ball," *Kansas City (MO) Star*, Aug 21, 1881; "Dusky Diamond," *Kansas City (MO) Star*, Jun 4, 1883; "Late Locals," *Kansas City Star*, Aug 14, 1883; *Atchison (KS) Globe*, Jun 25, 1884; *Atchison Globe*, Jun 28, 1884; "Base Ball," *Lawrence (KS) Western Recorder*, Jun 27, 1884; "Short Stops," *Leavenworth Times*, Aug 19, 1884; "Base Ball," *Leavenworth Times*, Jul 31, 1887; "Sprays of Sport," *Kansas City Star*, Aug 3, 1887; "Base Ball," *Leavenworth Times*, Aug 2, 1887; *Atchison Globe*, Jul 2, 1888; "Colored Ball Tossers," *Kansas City (MO) Times*, Jul 19, 1888; "Base Ball," *Lawrence (KS) Republican*, Aug 1, 1888; "Base Ball Today," *Lawrence Republican*, Aug 3, 1888; "Forfeited the Game," *Lawrence Republican*, Aug 4, 1888; "Sporting Notes," *Lawrence (KS) Journal*, May 21, 1889; "Sporting Notes," *Kansas City (MO) Times*, Jul 29, 1892.

White Stocking Base Ball Club (Lyndon, KS; 1880s)

The White Stocking B.B.C. organized in the 1880s, played white and black teams. *Burlingame Osage County Chronicle* (July 21, 1881): "An exciting and hotly contested game of base-ball was played in this city on Saturday last, between the White Stockings, (colored), and the Red Stockings, (white). The white folks met their match in the colored boys. The game was closed at the last half of the sixth inning, on account of darkness, when the score stood: White Stockings, 31; Red Stockings, 34." They arranged a return match. *Osage County Chronicle* (August 4, 1881): "Quite an interesting game of base-ball was played at Lyndon on Friday last between the Red Stockings of Burlingame and the White Stockings of Lyndon, the score running as follows: Red Stockings, 16; White Stockings, 18."

SOURCES: *Burlingame (KS) Osage County Chronicle*, Jul 21, 1881; "Base Ball," *Burlingame Osage County Chronicle*, Aug 4, 1881.

Osage City Blues Base Ball Club (Osage City, KS; 1890s). Organizer(s): J. S. Hanks.

The Osage City Blues B.B.C. organized in the 1890s, played black teams. *Burlingame Osage County Chronicle* (August 2, 1899): "The colored ball team from Ottawa played a game of ball with the Osage City Brownies last Thursday on the home grounds. Osage City won,

the score being 18 to 19." *Osage City Free Press* (August 17, 1899): "The Osage City Blues played the Burlingame nine at baseball Saturday. Blues, 12; Burlingame, 7."

SOURCES: *Osage City (KS) Free Press*, Aug 12, 1897; *Osage City Free Press*, Aug 19, 1897; "City and Vicinity," *Osage City Free Press*, May 4, 1899; *Osage City Free Press*, Jun 15, 1899; "Gleanings," *Burlingame (KS) Enterprise*, Jun 22, 1899; *Osage City Free Press*, Jul 20, 1899; *Burlingame (KS) Osage County Chronicle*, Aug 2, 1899; "Burlingame Chronicles," *Osage City Free Press*, Aug 17, 1899.

Osage City Browns Base Ball Club (Osage City, KS; 1890s). Organizer(s): C. Austin.

The Osage City Browns B.B.C. organized in the 1890s, played black and white teams. *Osage City Free Press* (June 27, 1895): "C. Austin, manager of the Browns, intends to take his boys down to Emporia July 3, where they will play three games of ball with the colored nine [Clippers] of that city, two on the 3rd and one on the 5th." *Free Press* (July 8, 1895): "The Browns defeated the Jersey Creek nine in a seven-inning game. Lyons and Orendoff, of the Browns, are fine pitchers and would have shut out the Jersey Creek players but for the errors made by some of the other players. The score was 21 to 3." *Free Press* (August 8, 1895): "A large crowd of local fans gathered at the ball grounds Friday last. The attraction was a base-ball game between the Emporia Clippers and Osage City Browns, both colored. The Browns were unable to overcome the lead taken by the Clippers in the second inning, and Emporia took the game. Score 14 to 10." *Emporia Gazette* (July 9, 1896): "The Emporia Clippers and Hartford Reds, two colored ball teams, are crossing bats at Hartford today. The battery for the Emporia team is the Ray brothers who nearly won the game for the Haymakers on the Fourth." *Free Press* (August 22, 1895): "Last Friday a colored nine composed of Ottawa and Baldwin men played a game of base-ball with the Browns of this city on the Black Diamond ground. They went home sadder but wiser. The game was close until the eighth inning when the Baldwin nine went to pieces, allowing nine runs to be made."

SOURCES: "City and Vicinity," *Osage City (KS) Free Press*, Jun 6, 1895; "Base Ball Games," *Osage City Free Press*, Jun 20, 1895; *Osage City Free Press*, Jun 27, 1895; "Base Ball Games," *Osage City Free Press*, Jul 8, 1895; "Base Ball," *Osage City (KS) Free Press*, Aug 8, 1895; "Two Base Ball Games," *Osage City Free Press*, Aug 22, 1895

Browns Base Ball Club (Parsons, KS; 1890s)

The Browns B.B.C. organized in the 1890s, played black and white teams. *Parsons Sun* (July 22, 1894): "The colored club and the Parsons first nine [white] crossed bats at the fairgrounds yesterday afternoon in the presence of a fair crowd of spectators. The colored club proved to be the strongest and downed their opponents by a score of 19 to 10." *Independence Reporter* (August 8, 1894): "A game of ball was played at Washburn Park yesterday afternoon by the Parsons Browns and Independence Blues (though the real color of each team is black) and was won by the home team by a score of 20 to 14. The Parsons fellows came over to do up our gallant club. They brought sixteen men with them and our boys did not even know that they were coming, but although taken by surprise they rallied their forces and licked the enemy in fine style." *Coffeyville Journal* (July 1, 1895): "The colored base-ball team of Parsons will be pitted against the colored team of this city [Clippers], at Osborne's Park, on Tuesday afternoon."

SOURCES: "Won by Chetopa," *Parsons (KS) Sun*, Jul 1, 1894; "Local Brevities," *Parsons Sun*, Jul 4, 1894; "Chetopa Wins Again," *Parsons (KS) Weekly Blade*, Jul 7, 1894; "The Colored Boys Won," *Parsons Sun*, Jul 22, 1894; "Local News," *Independence (KS) Reporter*, Aug 8, 1894; *Coffeyville (KS) Journal*, Jul 1, 1895; "A Close Game," *Coffeyville (KS) Journal*, Jul 3, 1895.

Nameless Base Ball Club (Parsons, KS; 1870s–1880s)

The Nameless B.B.C. organized in the 1870s, played against black nines. *Parsons Weekly Sun* (August 2, 1879): "The [Fort Scott] new catcher passed under the name of Charles Brown, he being the alleged brother of Ed Brown, the crack pitcher of Kansas and Scott nine. Our boys noticed that this morning a thick-set bullet-headed, circus-dressed young man standing in an alley-way endeavoring to catch the balls thrown to him by an ebony-hued Abyssinian. Some say he was an 'imported' catcher. Fortunately, for us, he was the new catcher, so called." *Fort Scott Monitor* (September 23, 1879): "In the game of base-ball yesterday, between the Fort Scott and Parsons Clubs, (colored), the score stood 26 to 6 in favor of Fort Scott. In the last game between the Nameless, of Parsons, and the Olympics, of this city, it is quite possible the colored baseballists of Fort Scott may be able to wipe out the record of the two defeats of our Olympics at the hands of the Nameless by pounding the conceit out of the red-capped colored ball players of Parsons."

SOURCES: *Parsons (KS) Weekly Sun*, Jun 21, 1879; *Fort Scott (KS) Monitor*, Jun 28, 1879; *Fort Scott Monitor*, Jul 8, 1879; *Fort Scott Monitor*, Jul 26, 1879; *Fort Scott Monitor*, Jul 27, 1879; "Fort Scott Fallen," *Parsons Weekly Sun*, Aug 2, 1879; *Fort Scott Monitor*, Sep 23, 1879; *Parsons Weekly Sun*, September 27, 1879; *Fort Scott Monitor*, May 7, 1880; *Fort Scott Monitor*, Jun 16, 1880; *Fort Scott Monitor, Jun 18,* 1880.

Brown Stockings Base Ball Club (Topeka, KS; 1880s–1890s). Organizer(s): Henry Dillard and W. D. Donnell; James Booker.

The Brown Stockings B.B.C. organized in the 1880s. *Topeka Tribune and Western Recorder* (July 18, 1885): "This is the time at which our Base Ball Club, the Topeka Browns, defeated the former champions, the Lone Stars of Atchison, last Thursday at the Fair Ground. It was the best game ever witnessed by the Topekans. Our boys certainly played well, and covered themselves all over in victory. The Atchison boys are all good players, but they seemed to forget there was even a first base, and as for second and third bases they scarcely got far enough around to even see if there was a man there. They played well, struck hard, and fanned the air in a way that was laughable in the extreme. McLanore's pitching was entirely too much for them." *Topeka Capital* (July 31, 1885): "The Brown Stocking Club will play the Kersands nine—the Burnt Cork Club—at the Fair Grounds Saturday afternoon at 4 o'clock." *Lawrence Journal* (August 14, 1886): "The Eagle Base Ball Club of this city played a game at Topeka last week with the Topeka Brown Stockings, in which the Eagles won by a score of 27 to 13. The Brown Stockings play a return game here next week." The Browns played into the 1890s. *Tribune and Western Recorder* (August 7, 1892): "The Topeka Browns and Tennessee Reds played an interesting game at Garfield Park last Monday afternoon resulting in a victory for Browns in a score of 14 to 8."

SOURCES: "A Challenge," *Topeka (KS) Commonwealth*, Jul 10, 1885; "Challenge Accepted," *Topeka Commonwealth*, Jul 11, 1885; "Fair Grounds Today," *Topeka Commonwealth*, Jul 18, 1885; "Base Ball," *Topeka (KS) Tribune and Western Recorder*, Jul 18, 1885; "Saturday Sports," *Topeka Commonwealth*, Jul 19, 1885; "Sheard's Say," *Topeka Commonwealth*, Jul 21, 1885; *Topeka Commonwealth*, Jul 25, 1885; *Topeka Commonwealth*, Jul 26, 1885; *Topeka Commonwealth*, Jul 28, 1885; *Topeka Commonwealth*, Jul 30, 1885; "City Chat," *Topeka (KS) Capital*, Jul 31, 1885; "Topeka Browns Defeated," *Topeka Commonwealth*, Aug 2, 1885; *Topeka Commonwealth*, Aug 22, 1885; *Topeka Commonwealth*, Sep 19, 1885; "Eagles vs. Blue Stockings," *Lawrence (KS) Weekly Journal*, Aug 5, 1886; *Lawrence (KS) Journal World*, Aug 14, 1886; *Lawrence (KS) Evening Tribune*, Jun 16, 1887; "Henry Moore Reinstated," *St. Louis (MO) Sporting News*, Aug 9, 1886; *Lawrence*

(KS) Journal, Aug 14, 1886; "Base Ball," *Topeka Tribune and Western Recorder*, Aug 7, 1892.

Diamond Kings Base Ball Club (Topeka, KS; 1890s). Organizer(s): Mote Ware.

The Diamond Kings B.B.C. organized in the 1890s, played black teams. *Lawrence Weekly Record* (July 10, 1891): "The Kings of the Diamond, an aggregation of alleged ballplayers from Topeka, came down to Lawrence last Monday and received their usual discipline at the hands of out crack ball team, the Leapers. The score stood 8 to 7 in favor of the Leapers. The Topekas have a high-sounding name, pretty uniforms, plenty of balls and bats, and an abundance of loud mouth. All that they need now to complete the outfit is a ball club and a gentleman on first base. The latter article is badly needed." *Lawrence Daily Journal* (August 1, 1891): "The Leapers of this city are playing the Topeka colored nine, the 'Kings of the Diamond,' this afternoon."

SOURCES: "The Leapers at Topeka," *Lawrence (KS) Weekly Record*, Jul 10, 1891; "Base Ball," *Lawrence (KS) Journal*, Aug 1, 1891; *Lawrence (KS) Historic Times*, Aug 29, 1891; "City News," *Topeka (KS) Call*, Aug 30, 1891; "Base Ball Pick-ups," *Topeka (KS) Times-Observer*, Sep 4, 1891.

Independent Black Stockings Base Ball Club (Topeka, KS; 1870s)

The Independent Black Stockings B.B.C. organized in the 1870s, played white and black nines. *Lawrence Tribune* (August 14, 1873): "The Independents, of Topeka, and the Moonlights, of Lawrence (both colored) played a match game yesterday, resulting in a defeat of the former by a score of 37 to 41." *Topeka Commonwealth* (June 26, 1874): "The colored athletes of Topeka have organized a baseball club, and as the evening shades approach they hie to the practice grounds with sturdy feet and blistered hands, and without murmur stop red hot grounders with their swollen palms." *Topeka Commonwealth* (May 11, 1875): "The colored Independent Base Ball Club play a game next Thursday at the corner of Eleventh and Harrison Streets, with a colored club of Perryville." *Commonwealth* (June 26, 1875): "The number of young colored gentlemen who march about town with blue caps pulled down over their ears is astonishing. The Black Stockings lead all the other colors in numerousness." The Independents played the Lawrence Eagles. *Commonwealth* (June 29, 1875): "The Eagles of Lawrence arrived on the Midland at 4:30pm, yesterday, and the game with the Independents of Topeka commenced immediately, with Mr. Marks of the Westerns as umpire. Six innings were played, and the eagles declined to play longer, and the umpire declared that the score stood—Independents, 9, Eagles 0."

SOURCES: "Base Ball," *Lawrence (KS) Tribune*, Aug 14, 1873 *Topeka (KS) Commonwealth*, Jun 26, 1874; *Topeka Commonwealth*, May 11, 1875; *Topeka Commonwealth*, Jun 18, 1875; *Topeka Commonwealth*, Jun 22, 1875; *Lawrence (KS) Journal*, Jun 26, 1875; *Lawrence Journal*, Jun 25, 1875; *Lawrence Commonwealth*, Jun 26, 1875; *Lawrence Journal*, Jun 26, 1875; *Lawrence Commonwealth*, Jun 29, 1875; *Lawrence Commonwealth*, Jun 30, 1875; "A Challenge," *Lawrence Commonwealth*, Aug 10, 1875; *Lawrence Journal*, Aug 27, 1875.

Mascot Base Ball Club (Topeka, KS; 1890s). Organizer(s): Fred J. Jones and Fred W. Hedge.

The Mascot B.B.C. organized in the 1890s. The Mascots, formerly the Topeka Locals, played black aggregations.

SOURCES: "Reorganization," *Topeka (KS) State Ledger, Mar 27,* 1896; "A Word in Passing," *Topeka (KS) Capital*, Jun 16, 1896.

Modoc Base Ball Club (Topeka, KS; 1880s)

Proprietor: W. D. Donnell

The Colored Modoc Railroad B.B.C. organized in 1883, if not earlier. *Topeka State Journal* (May 31, 1882): "A number of young men of color engaged in a game of base-ball on Second Street just west of the Avenue yesterday afternoon. Will the time-honored game be revived in Topeka again?" Topeka and Kansas City developed a rivalry. *Topeka Commonwealth* (August 14, 1883): "The Topeka Modoc Base Ball Club will play the Brown Stockings of Kansas City at Hartzell Park Thursday afternoon." They reorganized, in 1884. *Topeka Tribune and Western Recorder* (July 4, 1884): "The Old Modoc Base Ball Club held a meeting last evening. W. D. Donnell was elected manager and William Blythe captain. *Tribune and Western Recorder* (July 18, 1884): "The Modocs—our Base Ball Club—covered themselves all over with glory last week by defeating another home nine, 27 to 3. They play the Atchison club, July 4, at the Fair Grounds. Everybody should go out and see the game."

SOURCES: *Topeka (KS) State Journal*, May 31, 1882; *Topeka (KS) Capital*, Aug 25, 1882; *Topeka (KS) Capital*, Aug 27, 1882; *Topeka (KS) Commonwealth*, Aug 14, 1883; *Topeka Commonwealth*, Jun 3, 1884; "Base Ball," *Topeka State Journal*, Jun 7, 1884; *Topeka Commonwealth*, Jun 12, 1884; *Topeka Commonwealth*, Jun 18, 1884; "Base Ball," *Topeka (KS) Western Recorder*, Jul 4, 1884; *Atchison (KS) Globe*, Jul 15, 1884; *Atchison Globe*, Jul 16, 1884; "City Briefs," *Topeka Western Recorder*, Jul 18, 1884; "Base Ball," *Topeka Commonwealth*, Aug 14, 1884.

National Base Ball Club (Topeka, KS; 1870s)

The National B.B.C. organized in the 1870s, played against black and white nines. *Burlingame County Chronicle* (June 11, 1875): "The National Base Ball Club of Topeka write us stating that they will play any nine in Burlingame, and ask a correspondence with their agent, Elisha Freeman. Here is a chance for our B.B.C. to show their pluck." *Burlingame County Chronicle* (July 11, 1875): "The National Base Ball Club (colored), of Topeka, played the Grasshoppers, of this place, a game on Saturday last, beating them by a score of 60 to 20."

SOURCES: *Topeka (KS) Commonwealth*, Jun 26, 1874; *Burlingame (KS) Osage County Chronicle*, Jun 11, 1875; *Burlingame Osage County Chronicle*, Jun 30, 1875; *Topeka Commonwealth*, Jul 11, 1875.

Silver Kings Base Ball Club (Topeka, KS. Organizer(s): Fred McMann; 1890s).

The Silver Kings B.B.C. organized in the 1890s, played black teams. *Topeka State Ledger* (September 16, 1892): "Silver King's vs. Topeka Browns Tuesday afternoon, 16th, the Kings were defeated by a score of 16 to 13. For a while things looked rather blue for the Browns, for the score up to the eighth inning was ten to four in favor of the Kings. Wallace came to bat in the eighth when two men were out and two men on bases, drove the ball to left for a two-bagger and Richardson followed with a home run." *Topeka Capital* (July 27, 1895): "The Topeka Locals and the Silver Kings played an interesting game of ball yesterday at Athletic Park before a rather large crowd, the game resulting in a victory for the Locals, by a score of 14 to 6."

SOURCES: "Base Ball," *Topeka (KS) State Ledger*, Sep 16, 1892; *Topeka (KS) Evening Call*, Jun 13, 1893; "Base Ball Items," *Topeka State Ledger*, Aug 17, 1894; "Live Sporting News," *Topeka (KS) Daily Capital*, Jul 27, 1895; "Silver Kings Want Games," *Topeka Capital*, May 22, 1896; "News About Town," *Topeka Capital*, May 23, 1896; "Local Mention," *Topeka (KS) Colored Citizen*, Jul 1, 1897.

Topeka Locals Base Ball Club (Topeka, KS; 1890s)

The Topeka Locals B.B.C. organized in the 1890s, played black teams. *Topeka State Ledger* (June 29, 1894): "The Lawrence Leapers and the Topeka Local team had a pleasant game of the warm sport resulting in a complete whitewashing and victory for the Topekas.

The score: Lawrence 3; Topeka, 20." *Topeka Capital* (July 2, 1895): "The Topeka Locals, colored base-ball team, want to play any amateur club in the state." *Capital* (July 26, 1895): "The colored population of Topeka is agog over the baseball game which will be played at Athletic Park between the Silver King team and the Topeka Locals. The two teams are composed of colored players and each has a lot of talent. The game will be interesting." *Capital* (July 27, 1895): "The Topeka Locals and Silver Kings played an interesting game yesterday at Athletic Park before a rather large crowd, the game resulting in a victory for the Locals, by a score of 14 to 6."

SOURCES: "Locals," *Coffeyville (KS) Kansas Blackman*, Jun 1, 1894; *Topeka (KS) State Ledger*, Jun 29, 1894; "News About Town," *Topeka (KS) Capital*, Jul 2, 1895; "News About Town," *Topeka Capital*, Jul 26, 1895; "Live Sporting News," *Topeka Capital*, July 27, 1895.

Western Clippers Base Ball Club (Topeka, KS; 1880s). Organizer(s): Charles Charles, B. F. Hatcher and William Hallum.

The Western Clippers B.B.C. organized in the 1880s, played black and white clubs of KS and MO.

SOURCES: *Topeka (KS) Capital, Jun 24, 1886; "Notes," *Topeka Capital*, Jul 4, 1886.

Boston Athletic Base Ball Club (Wichita, KS; 1890s). Organizer(s): George W. Robinson and Lake (Luke) Robinson; L. T. Brown; W. A. Betts.

The Boston Athletic B.B.C. organized in the 1890s. The Athletics (also called the Colored Athletics and Colored Champions), played white and black nines. *Wichita Eagle* (July 21, 1889): "An interesting game of ball was played yesterday between the high school and the colored nines at the Fifteenth Street grounds. The score stood 12 to 3 in favor of the colored boys." The High School boys returned the favor. *Eagle* (August 8, 1889): "The colored nine and the high school nine played an interesting game of ball yesterday afternoon at the corner of Fifteenth and Lawrence for a purse of $10. The score was 22 to 17 in favor of the high school boys, the playing on both sides being good. The battery for the colored boys was Cunningham and Anderson." They also played white rivals, the Wichita Maroons. They developed a rivalry with Hutchinson. *Eagle* (August 5, 1893): "The Wichita Athletics and the Hutchinson Clippers played a hot and interesting ball game at Riverside Park yesterday. The attendance was not extra-large, but the crowd that was there was well pleased. Both teams will play two games here again real soon, at which time the attendance will be larger." *Eagle* (October 8, 1892): "The colored champions will be on hand and cross bats with the Wichita Maroons on tomorrow at 3 o'clock at the Riverside Ball Park. The colored champions claim to be the strongest aggregation in the west. The Maroons have been strengthened and the fairs who attend this game will surely witness one of the most hotly contested games of ball ever played in Wichita as each club is confident of winning and they will play for blood." The Athletics played against the Pets, another local white nine. *Eagle* (July 24, 1894): "The rubber was played off yesterday at the Fair Grounds between the Pets and the Boston Athletics, amid much wrangling on both sides, and the umpire's life was in jeopardy until the finish. Up until the fifth inning it seemed to be a walkover for the colored boys but they went to pieces in the sixth and seventh innings, giving the Pets a lead they could not overcome. Anderson pitched his usual winning game, but his support at times was a trifle erratic. It seems to be the general impression that the colored boys are too strong for the Pets, barring out-of-town material. His boys are to have a champagne supper in consequence."

SOURCES: "Minor Mention," *Parsons (KS) Sun*, Aug 6, 1892; "That Base Ball Game," *Wichita (KS) Eagle*, Oct 8, 1892; "Base Ball," *Wichita Eagle*, August 5, 1893; "Pitcher's Contest," *Wichita Eagle*, July 11,

1894; "A Good Game," *Hutchinson (KS) News*, Aug 2, 1894; "A Hard Game," *Wichita (KS) People's Friend*, Jul 27, 1894; "Victorious," *Belle Plaine (KS) News*, Aug 23, 1894; "Local News," *Wichita People's Friend*, Aug 24, 1894.

Carey Hotel Base Ball Club (Wichita, KS; 1890s). Organizer(s): J. D. Mason.

The Carey Hotel B.B.C. organized in the 1890s, competed against black nines. *Wichita Eagle* (June 5, 1894): "The Boston store sluggers and the Carey hash slingers will cross bats on the baseball diamond of the Fair Grounds at 3 o'clock this afternoon. The sluggers claim to be the best colored team in the state and are aching to meet the Henderson pets."

SOURCES: "Will Play Today," *Wichita (KS) Eagle*, Jun 5, 1894.

Wichita Valley Base Ball Club (Wichita, KS; 1870s)

The Wichita Valley B.B.C. organized in the 1870s, played against black and white teams. *Wichita Eagle* (June 18, 1874): "The match game of base-ball played between the colored boys of our city and the avenue boys was witnessed by a large number of citizens."

SOURCES: *Wichita (KS) Eagle*, May 28, 1874; *Wichita Eagle*, Jun 18, 1874.

Brown Stocking Base Ball Club (Wyandotte, KS; 1880s–1890s)

The Brown Stocking B.B.C. organized in the 1880s, played black teams. *Kansas City Gazette* (May 27, 1889): "A game of ball between the Wyandotte Browns and the Amourdale Get There's, both colored clubs, resulted in the Browns winning by a score of 17 to 15." *Gazette* (May 29, 1893): "There was a large attendance at Vic Roy Park yesterday to witness the game of ball between the Wyandotte Browns and Kansas City Blues. The score resulted in the Blues' victory by 15 to 5." *Kansas City Star* (June 9, 1893): "The Wyandotte Browns, a colored ball team, will play the Kansas City Blues, also colored, at Vic Roy Park Sunday afternoon." *Star* (July 19, 1893): "The Kansas City Colored Blues and the Wyandotte Browns played a hot game at Vic Roy Park yesterday. The Blues won by a score of 18 to 14 but the Wyandotte team declares that it was robbed of the game and the umpire ran away." *Star* (July 19, 1893): "The Kansas City Clippers and Wyandotte Browns will play a match game at Vic Roy Park, Amourdale, next Sunday."

SOURCES: "Neighborhood News Notes," *Kansas City (MO) Gazette*, May 27, 1889; Amourdale," *Kansas City Gazette*, Apr 16, 1893; "The Blues Won," *Kansas City Gazette*, May 29, 1893; "Amourdale," *Kansas City Gazette*, May 29, 1893; "Amateur Base Ball Notes," *Kansas City (MO) Star*, Jun 7, 1893; "Amateur Base Ball Notes," *Kansas City (MO) Star*, Jun 9, 1893; "Amateur Base Ball Notes," *Kansas City Star*, Jun 19, 1893; "Amateur Base Ball Notes," *Kansas City Star*, Jul 9, 1893; "Amateur Base Ball Notes," *Kansas City Star*, Jul 19, 1893; "Amateur Base Ball Notes," *Kansas City Star*, Jul 19, 1893.

Fair Play Base Ball Club (Wyandotte, KS; 1890s)

The Fair Play B.B.C. organized in the 1890s, played black nines. *Kansas City Star* (July 18, 1893): "The Kansas City Blues (colored) were defeated at Exposition Park re will be a ball game at Exposition Park by the newly organized Fair Plays in a closely contested game by a score of 21 to 20."

SOURCES: "Amateur Base Ball Notes," *Kansas City (MO) Star*, Jun 16, 1893; "Amateur Base Ball Notes," *Kansas City Star*, Jun 9, 1894; "Amateur Base Ball Notes," *Kansas City Star*, Jul 1, 1894.

Western Drivers Base Ball Club (Wyandotte, KS; 1870s). Organizer(s): James "Baby" Fields.

The Western Drivers B.B.C. organized in the 1870s, played black teams. *Kansas City Journal and Commerce* (April 18, 1875): "A match game was played at Wyandotte, between Wyandotte and Kansas City colored base-ball clubs, in which the Wyandotte boys came off victorious." *Journal and Commerce* (June 12, 1875): "Yesterday the colored base-ball clubs, Sumner of Kansas City, and Western Drives, of Wyandotte, played match game on the grounds of the latter. The following is the score: Sumners, 25; Western Drives, 14." *Journal and Commerce* (July 20, 1875): "The following is the result of the baseball match between the colored clubs on Saturday: Western Drivers, 36; War Eagles, 18."

SOURCES: "Wyandotte, Armstrong, and Kansas City," *Kansas City (MO) Journal and Commerce*, Apr 16, 1874; "Wyandotte, Armstrong, and Kansas City," *Kansas City Journal and Commerce*, Aug 25, 1874; "Wyandotte, Armstrong, and Kansas City," *Kansas City Journal and Commerce*, Apr 18, 1875; "Wyandotte, Armstrong, and Kansas City," *Kansas City Journal and Commerce*, Jun 12, 1875; "Wyandotte, Armstrong, and Kansas City," *Kansas City Journal and Commerce*, Jul 20, 1875.

Kentucky

Colored Base Ball Club (Bowling Green, KY; 1890s)

The Colored B.B.C. organized in the 1890s, played black teams. *Louisville Courier-Journal* (September 18, 1898): "The Bowling Greens will play the Brotherhoods today at the Brotherhoods' Park, Sixteenth Street and Magnolia Avenue. The Bowling Greens are considered one of the best teams in the State. There will also be a foot race and long-distance throwing match. Batteries: Brotherhoods, Hoods, Means, or Ross, p; Haywood, c; Bowling Greens, Price or Smith, p; Proctor, c. Game called at 3 o'clock."

SOURCES: "Among the Amateurs," *Louisville (KY) Courier-Journal*, Sep 18, 1898.

Clayton Base Ball Club (Clayton, KY; 1880s)

The Clayton B.B.C. organized in the 1880, played black organizations. *Louisville Courier Journal* (August 2, 1886): "The two crack colored clubs, the Claytons and the Falls Citys, played a game yesterday afternoon at Magnolia Park. The Falls Citys held the lead until the eighth inning, when their opponents scored three runs off a double and two singles, and won the game. The contest was very close and well played."

SOURCES: "Claytons vs. Falls Citys," *Louisville (KY) Courier Journal*, Aug 1, 1886; "Victory for the Claytons," *Louisville Courier Journal*, Aug 2, 1886.

Active Base Ball Club (Covington, KY; 1870s)

The Active B.B.C. organized in the 1870s, played against black nines. *Covington Ticket* (June 27, 1876): "The Actives of Covington and the Vigilants of Cincinnati, both colored clubs, play on the Star Grounds on Saturday afternoon, for the championship of Kentucky and Ohio, as far as colored clubs go." The Vigilants defeated them. *Cincinnati Times* (July 20, 1876): "The colored base-ball boys of Cincinnati beat the colored base-ballists of Covington. Go way chile; quit yere foolin' round us." The Actives traveled to OH. *Cincinnati Times* (July 21, 1876): "The game between the Actives, of Covington, and the Vigilants, of Cincinnati, both colored clubs, which was played at the Cincinnati Base Ball Park, yesterday afternoon, resulted in favor of the latter by a score of 13 to 6."

SOURCES: "Base Ball Notes," *Cincinnati (OH) Commercial Tribune*, Aug 1, 1875; "The Active of Covington and the Vigilants of Cincinnati," *Covington (KY) Ticket*, Jun 27, 1876; "Colored Base Ball Match," *Covington Ticket*, Jul 1, 1876; "Base Ball," *Cincinnati (OH) Enquirer*, Jul 20, 1876; "Local and City Matters," *Cincinnati Times*, Jul 20, 1876;

"Covington," *Cincinnati (OH) Times*, Jul 21, 1876; "Base Ball By Midnight," *Covington Ticket*, Aug 15, 1876.

Kenton Base Ball Club (Covington, KY; 1890s)

The Kenton B.B.C. organized in 1895. *Cincinnati Enquirer* (March 11, 1895): "The Kenton Colored Base Ball Club has organized and is now ready to accept challenges. It would like to arrange the opening game with some crack club. Address S. page, Manager, 73 West Eighth Street, Covington, Kentucky."

SOURCES: "Base Ball Gossip," *Cincinnati (OH) Enquirer*, Mar 11, 1895.

Starlight Base Ball Club (Covington, KY; 1870s)

The Starlight B.B.C. organized in 1870. *Cincinnati Gazette* (August 24, 1870): "A colored base-ball club called the Starlights was organized in this city on Monday night. The following are the officers: President Isaac Black; Secretary, W. J. Hamilton; Treasurer D. G. Durgin. Captain of the First Nine [is] Fred J. Williams."

SOURCES: "Covington," *Cincinnati (OH) Enquirer*, Feb 16, 1870; *Cincinnati Enquirer*, Jun 18, 1870; "Covington," *Cincinnati Enquirer*, Jun 20, 1870; "Suburban News," *Cincinnati (OH) Gazette*, Aug 24, 1870.

Corn Cracker Base Ball Club (Danville, KY; 1900s)

The Corn Cracker B.B.C. organized in 1900, played black teams. *Danville Advocate* (July 24, 1900): "The Danville Corn Crackers went to Lexington yesterday and beat the Sluggers there in a hard game by 9 to 8. Danville can't be beaten." *Advocate* (July 24, 1900): "About the best ball game of the season was played on the Centre College grounds yesterday afternoon between the Cincinnati's and the Corn Crackers (both colored). Up to the latter part of the eighth inning the score stood a tie, 3 to 3, but both teams got on their batting clothes and at the close of the ninth the tally sheet showed Danville 12, Cincinnati 3. This same team defeated the Danville nine several times last year, so the home boys are highly elated and deserve to be, as it took good playing to win the game. A very large crowd were in attendance." *Advocate* (August 22, 1900): "The Covington Stars out-shone the Corn-crackers Monday afternoon, defeating them by a score of 11 to 10. Tuesday the Corncrackers turned the tables by a score of 13 to 9."

SOURCES: "Danville and Vicinity," *Danville (KY) Advocate*, Jun 11, 1900; "Social and Personal," *Danville Advocate*, Jul 24, 1900; "Danville and Vicinity," *Danville Advocate*, Jul 25, 1900; "Social and Personal," *Danville Advocate*, Jul 27, 1900; "Crackers vs. Stars," *Danville Advocate*, Aug 22, 1900.

L. C. Base Ball Club (Danville, KY; 1890s). Organizer(s): Shelby Bowman.

The L. C. B.B.C. organized in the 1890s. The L.C.'s played against black aggregations. *Danville Advocate* (July 16, 1894): "As predicted in the last issue of the Advocate, the Danville colored base-ball team swept the Paris club from the face of the earth on the Centre College grounds, the score being 22 to 10 in favor of Danville." *Advocate* (June 14, 1895): "There will be a game of base-ball next Wednesday between the Danville L. C.'s and the Versaille's team, both colored, on the College grounds." *Stanford Interior Journal* (July 2, 1895): "The colored boys [of Stanford, Kentucky] have organized a base-ball club known as the Black Interior Journals. They went over to Danville the other day and beat the team of that place by a score of 5 to 2." *Advocate* (August 9, 1895): "No use of Lexington, Frankfort, or Versailles trying to beat the Danville base-ball team. It can't be done. In the game here yesterday afternoon, Frankfort was defeated by a score of 18 to 15. The game was characterized by heavy batting."

SOURCES: "Cleaned 'Em Up," *Danville (KY) Advocate*, Jul 16, 1894; *Stanford (KY) Interior Journal*, Jul 2, 1895; "Base Ball," *Danville Advocate*, Aug 7, 1895; "Can't Beat 'Em," *Danville Advocate*, Aug 9, 1895.

O. K. Base Ball Club (Danville, KY; 1890s). Organizer(s): Shelby Bowman.

The O. K. B.B.C. organized in the 1890s, played against black teams. *Danville Advocate* (June 27, 1893): "The O. K. Club, a baseball team composed of members of Danville's colored population, went to Louisville Sunday and wiped up the earth with the Black Diamonds, of that city. The score was 7 to 2." *Advocate* (July 15, 1893): "There were five hundred, about four hundred and eighty-two of them colored citizens, at the College ball park, Thursday afternoon, to see the ball game between the colored boys of Danville and Frankfurt, and they saw a first-class game of base-ball, both clubs putting up a good article of ball." *Advocate* (July 22, 1893): "The Danville colored base-ball team was victorious at Paris Wednesday by a score of 16 to 5."

SOURCES: "A Good Game," *Danville (KY) Advocate*, Jun 27, 1893; "Danville and Vicinity," *Danville Advocate*, Jul 6, 1893; "Danville Won," *Danville Advocate*, Jul 15, 1893; "Danville and Vicinity," *Danville Advocate*, Jul 22, 1893.

Athletic Base Ball Club (Frankfort, KY; 1870s–1890s). Organizer(s): James Woolfolk; Robert Hampton.

The Athletic B.B.C. organized in the 1870s, played against black nines of KY, OH, and IN. *Louisville Courier-Journal* (August 25, 1875): "Some rich sport will also take place at Eagle Park this afternoon when the Globes and Athletics play. Both clubs are composed of colored players, the Globes being Louisville brunette, and the Athletics, Frankfort Browns. Twenty-five cents admission will be charged." They developed a rivalry with Louisville's Mutuals. *Frankfort Roundabout* (June 14, 1884): "A game of base-ball was played at Lake Park Wednesday between the Mutuals, of Louisville, and the Athletics of this city, both colored clubs, which resulted in a score of 14 to 11 in favor of the Louisville club. The game was close and hotly contested and required fourteen innings to decide who should be the victors." They had a rivalry with Cincinnati's Vigilant nine. They played nearby clubs, including Shelbyville's Blue Troublers. *Courier-Journal* (June 22, 1884): "The Athletics, of Frankfort, and the Blue Troublers, of this place [Shelbyville, Kentucky], both colored clubs, crossed bats upon the green diamond this afternoon. The game was well-played and interesting, resulting in favor of the Frankfort boys by a score of 28 to 21." The Mutual-Athletic rivalry continued as well. *Courier-Journal* (May 31, 1886): "The Falls Citys and the Frankforts, the two crack colored clubs, of this state, played a very good game yesterday afternoon at the park near Sixteenth-Street and Magnolia Avenue. About 900 people were present and enjoyed the contest throughout. The Falls Citys showed their superiority at every point and won easily by a score of 10 to 8. The same clubs play to-day, when Smith will pitch for the visitors." This is the second defeat Shelby has sustained at the hands of the Frankfort boys in two consecutive days." The Falls Citys and Athletics renewed their rivalry in the 1890s. *Roundabout* (June 27, 1891): "The Falls Citys, of Louisville, and the Athletics, of this city, two colored base-ball clubs, played two games, one Sunday and the other Monday afternoon, at Athletic Park, on the Owen Pike. The first resulted in a score of 9 to 10 in favor of Falls Citys and the latter in a victory for the home team, the score standing 28 to 5."

SOURCES: "Miscellaneous Items," *Louisville (KY) Courier-Journal*, Aug 25, 1874; "Other Ball and Bat Items," *Louisville Courier-Journal*, Jul 28, 1875; "Base-Ball Notes," *Cincinnati (OH) Enquirer*, Jul 30, 1875; "To-day's Sport," *Louisville Courier-Journal*, Aug 25, 1875; "Athletics vs. Globes," *Louisville Courier-Journal*, Aug 26, 1875; "General Notes," *Louisville Courier-Journal*, Aug 16, 1876; *Frankfort (KY) Roundabout*, Jun 14, 1884; *Frankfort Roundabout*, Jun 21, 1884; "A Close Contest," *Louisville Courier-Journal*, Jun 22, 1884; "Base Ball," *Frankfort Roundabout*, Aug 2, 1884; *Frankfort Roundabout*, Aug 22, 1885; "Base Ball," *Frankfort Roundabout*, Sep 5, 1885; "Fall City vs. Frankfort," *Louisville Courier-Journal*, May 30, 1886; "Fall Citys, 10; Frankforts, 8," *Louisville Courier Journal*, May 31, 1886; "Base Ball," *Frankfort Roundabout*, Jun 27, 1891; "Sport," *Indianapolis (IN) Freeman*, May 5, 1894; "Base Ball," *Jeffersonville (IN) Evening News*, Jul 1894.

Frankfort Turf Base Ball Club (Frankfort, KY; 1890s)

The Frankfort Turf B.B.C. organized in 1892. *Frankfort Roundabout* (May 28, 1892): "The Frankfort Turf, is the name of a colored base-ball club, which has been organized here, and which promises to make it interesting for any club which may accept its challenge. It is composed of young amateurs of this city."

SOURCES: *Frankfort (KY) Roundabout*, May 28, 1892.

Kentucky State University Base Ball Club (Frankfort, KY; 1890s)

The Kentucky State University B.B.C. organized in the 1890s, played black and white teams. *Indianapolis Freeman* (March 21, 1896): "The boys of the [Louisville Colored] high school have organized their baseball team, and are making preparations for a series of games with the State University team." *Danville Advocate* (May 8, 1896): "The Danville colored base-ball club will play the colored State University nine, in Danville, next Friday and Saturday. The visitors will also bring a glee club with them and give a concert while here." *Advocate* (May 8, 1896): "It is seldom that the Danville colored baseball team gets beat, but it went down yesterday before the State University nine, from Louisville, by a score of 13 to 11. The visitors gave a concert at the Opera House last night to a good audience." *Louisville Courier Journal* (May 8, 1898): "The Reccius team will play the University colored team the second game of a series at Louisville Park, Monday afternoon at 3 o'clock." *Advocate* (May 22, 1899): "The Danville Athletic Club, colored, defeated the State University baseball team, of Louisville, in a hot game, by a score of 6 to 5, in eleven innings."

SOURCES: "Brotherhood's Services," *Indianapolis (IN) Freeman*, Mar 21, 1896; "Two Games," *Danville (KY) Advocate*, Apr 24, 1896; "Base Ball," *Danville Advocate*, Apr 29, 1896; "Base Ball," *Danville Advocate*, May 6, 1896; "Louisville Won," *Danville Advocate*, May 8, 1896; "Among the Amateurs," *Louisville (KY) Courier-Journal*, Apr 24, 1898; "A Budget of Newsy Jottings," *Indianapolis (IN) Freeman*, Apr 30, 1898; "With the Amateurs," *Louisville Courier-Journal*, May 8, 1898; "Beat 'Em," *Danville Advocate*, May 22, 1899.

Atlantic Base Ball Club (Henderson, KY; 1870s)

The Atlantic B.B.C. organized in the 1870s, played black nines. *Evansville Courier and Press* (July 13, 1876): "The Red Stockings [of Evansville, Indiana] go to Henderson next Saturday on a challenge from the Atlantics of that city, to contest for the honors on the green diamond." *Courier and Press* (July 2, 1878): "The Mysterious Base Ball Club, a colored organization, will play the Atlantics of Henderson, on the 4th of July at the grounds at the head of Oak Street." *Courier and Press* (August 29, 1879): "The game played by the two-colored clubs, Atlantics [Henderson, Kentucky] and Mysterious Nine, on the Eckford Grounds yesterday, was very fine, indeed. The game was decided in favor of the Atlantics, by a majority of one score, the final sore standing 10 to 9."

SOURCES: "Base Ball Brevities," *Evansville (IN) Courier and Press*, Jul 13, 1876; "Base Ball," *Evansville Courier and Press*, Jul 2, 1878; "Base Ball," *Evansville Courier and Press*, Aug 29, 1878; "Base Ball," *Evansville Courier and Press*, Aug 26, 1879; "Base Ball," *Evansville Courier and Press*, August 27, 1879; "Base Ball Notes," *Evansville Courier and Press*, Aug 29, 1879.

Blues Base Ball Club (Henderson, KY; 1880s)

The Blues B.B.C. organized in the 1880s, played black organizations. *Evansville Courier and Press* (July 14, 1889): "There will be a game of base-ball at the park today between the Sheldon Blues and Henderson Blues. Game called at 3:30. General admission: 25 cents. Ladies: 15 cents."

SOURCES: "Amusements," *Evansville Courier and Press*, Jul 14, 1889.

Dukes Base Ball Club (Henderson, KY; 1880s–1900s). Organizer(s): George Duprey.

The Dukes B.B.C. organized in the 1880s, played black nines of KY, TN, and IN. *Evansville Courier and Press* (August 23, 1885): "The colored base-ball club, of Evansville, the Red Oaks, and the Henderson Dukes crossed bats at the park yesterday. The game resulted in a victory for the Evansvilles. The Hendersons expect to do the Evansville club up today. Quite a crowd will accompany the club from Henderson." *Courier and Press* (August 24, 1885): "The Evansville colored base-ball club came down to this city yesterday and were defeated by the Henderson club." *Hopkinsville Semi-Weekly Kentuckian* (September 16, 1887): "On September 12th and 13th the Henderson Dukes and Hopkinsville Hard Hitters, colored base-ball clubs, played two games in this city, at the Old Fair Grounds. In both games, the Hard Hitters won easy victories, though the Henderson Club was given decided advantages. The score Monday was 11 to 6 and on Tuesday 9 to 7. Duprey was manager of the Dukes and James Glass manager of the Hard Hitters" *Hopkinsville Kentuckian* (July 26, 1895): "The Hopkinsville Hamlets and Henderson Dukes, colored ball teams, played at Athletic Park in this city, Monday and Tuesday. The Hamlets won both games. Score 9 to 3, and 24 to 9. Large crowds witnessed both games." *Courier and Press* (August 13, 1900): "The May Juniors played against the Henderson Dukes Sunday and they played a close game, but the home team got the best of it. Score stood 9 to 8."

SOURCES: "General Notes," *Evansville (IN) Courier and Press*, Aug 23, 1885; "Henderson," *Evansville Courier and Press*, Aug 24, 1885; "Here and There," *Hopkinsville (KY) Kentuckian*, Sep 16, 1887; "The Field of Sports," *Indianapolis (IN) Freeman*, Aug 8, 1891; "Base Ball Today," *Nashville (TN) Tennessean*, Sep 19, 1892; "The Pacifics Win," *Nashville Tennessean*, Sep 20, 1892; "Open Trial by Jury," *Indianapolis Freeman*, Jun 15, 1895; "Here and There," *Hopkinsville Kentuckian*, July 26, 1895; *Nashville Tennessean*, Apr 20, 1897; *Mount Vernon (IN) Democrat*, Jul 24, 1897; "Colored Folks," *Evansville Courier and Press*, Aug 13, 1900; "Henderson Dukes Won," *Evansville Courier and Press*, June 9, 1902; "Gold Dollars Defeat Dukes of Henderson," *Evansville Courier and Press*, Jul 5, 1902.

Hard Hitters Base Ball Club (Hopkinsville, KY; 1880s)

The Hard Hitters B.B.C. organized in the 1880s, played black nines. *Hopkinsville Semi-Weekly South Kentuckian* (September 16, 1887): "On Sept. 12th and 13th the Henderson Dukes and Hopkinsville Hard Hitters, colored baseball clubs, played two games in this city, at the Old Fair Grounds. In both games the Hard Hitters won easy victories, though the Henderson club was given decided advantages. The score Monday was 11 to 6 and on Tuesday 9 to 7." *Semi-Weekly South Kentuckian* (May 22, 1888): "The Hard Hitters played a game of ball Thursday with the Stemwinders in which the Hard Hitters were done up by the young colored club."

SOURCES: *Hopkinsville (KY) Semi-Weekly South Kentuckian,* Jun 24, 1887; *Hopkinsville Semi-Weekly South Kentuckian,* Aug 19, 1887; "Here and There," *Hopkinsville Semi-Weekly South Kentuckian,* May 22, 1888; *Hopkinsville Semi-Weekly South Kentuckian,* Jun 28, 1888.

Sailor Boys Base Ball Club (Hopkinsville, KY; 1880s)

The Sailor Boys B.B.C. organized in the 1880s, played black nines. *Hopkinsville Semi-Weekly South Kentuckian:* "A colored base-ball club of Bowling Green will play the Hopkinsville colored club, the Sailor Boys, a match game in Sharp's Field tomorrow." *Hopkinsville New Era:* "The Sailor Boys, the crack colored baseball club of this city, met with a very sad accident Saturday. They tried to play a Bowling Green Club, but we won't publish the score on them."

SOURCES: *Hopkinsville (KY) Semi-Weekly South Kentuckian,* July 23, 1886; "Pencil Focusings," *Hopkinsville (KY) New Era,* July 23, 1886; *Hopkinsville New Era,* July 30, 1886; "Pencil Focusings," *Hopkinsville New Era,* July 30, 1886; "Pencil Focusings," *Hopkinsville New Era,* Aug. 13, 1886.

Heavy Hitters Base Ball Club (Lexington, KY; 1890s–1900s)

The Heavy Hitters B.B.C. organized in the 1890s. *Lexington Morning Herald* (May 28, 1900): "A good-sized crowd of colored spectators saw the Heavy Hitters defeat the Cinch Indians in an exciting game yesterday. At the end of the seventh inning it was hard to foretell who would be victorious, but in that terrible 'eighth' the Heavy Hitters made a mighty rally of eight runs."

SOURCES: "Hot Game is Expected," *Lexington (KY) Morning Herald,* Aug 24, 1899; "Heavy Hitters," *Lexington Morning Herald,* May 28, 1900; "Heavy Hitters," *Lexington Morning Herald,* Jul 30, 1900.

Acorn Base Ball Club (Louisville, KY; 1880s)

The Acorn B.B.C. organized in the 1880s. The Acorns played black teams. *Louisville Courier-Journal* (August 4, 1889): "The Acorns of this city and the Black-Stockings of Indianapolis, two colored clubs, play a game at Daisy Park this afternoon." *Courier-Journal* (August 5, 1889): "The colored clubs, Acorns of this city, and the Black Socks of Indianapolis, played at Daisy Park yesterday, the game resulting in a tie, each club having scored fourteen runs in the ninth inning, when the game was called on account of darkness." *Courier-Journal* (August 6, 1889): "An interesting game was played yesterday afternoon at Eclipse Park between the Acorns, the crack colored club of this city, and the Black Stockings of Indianapolis, which resulted in a victory for the former, the score being 9 to 6."

SOURCES: "Amateur Gossip," *Louisville (KY) Courier-Journal,* Aug 4, 1889; "Notes," *Louisville Courier-Journal,* Aug 4, 1889; "Resulted in a Tie," *Louisville Courier-Journal,* Aug 5, 1889; "Notes," *Louisville Courier-Journal,* Aug 6, 1889.

Black Stocking Base Ball Club (Louisville, KY; 1880s)

The Black Stocking B.B.C. organized in the 1880s. The organization played black nines. *Louisville Courier-Journal* (May 17, 1886): "The two leading colored clubs of the city, the Falls Citys and the Black Socks, played a splendid game of base-ball yesterday at Sixteenth Street and Ormsby Avenue, which resulted in a victory for the Falls Citys by a score of 19 to 12." *Courier-Journal* (July 26, 1886): "At the Falls City Park yesterday afternoon the Black Stockings defeated the Heroes by a close score of 10 to 9. In the ninth inning Brooks won the game with a timely thee-base hit."

SOURCES: "Local Amateurs," *Louisville (KY) Courier Journal,* Jul 12, 1886; "Black Stockings, 10; Heroes, 9," *Louisville Courier Journal,* Jul 26, 1886; "Falls Citys 18; Black Stockings 7," *Louisville Courier Journal,* Sep 13, 1886.

Brotherhood Base Ball Club (Louisville, KY; 1890s). Organizer(s): A. W. Stewart; Samuel Gibbs.

The Brotherhood B.B.C. organized in the 1890s, played white and black aggregations. *Indianapolis Freeman* (August 8, 1891): "The [Dukes] base-ball club, of Henderson, Kentucky, played against the Brotherhood club, of Louisville, August 2nd." The organization traveled to MO. *St. Louis Post-Dispatch* (July 25, 1892): "The West Ends defeated the Brotherhoods of Kentucky at Compton Avenue Park yesterday afternoon by a score of 16 to 6." Louisville and Nashville developed a rivalry. *Nashville Tennessean* (July 21, 1895): "There is a friendly but intense rivalry between the two teams [Rock City Unions and Brotherhoods], and the game will be well-worth seeing. The Brotherhoods beat the Rock Citys at Louisville, June 30, by a score of 4 to 2, but the Rock City boys say they can't do it again." They played local white teams. *Louisville Courier Journal* (August 2, 1897): "The Brotherhoods defeated the Senn and Ackermann Club yesterday in an exciting game by the score of 12 to 11. The feature of the game was the batting of the Brotherhoods. They made eighteen hits off McCord. Talbott made five hits out of five times at bat." They traveled to Jeffersonville, IN, and played a black team. *Jeffersonville Evening News* (August 20, 1898): "The crack colored Brotherhood Club, of Louisville, will cross bats with the home team at Athletic Park Sunday afternoon. The Brotherhoods have not lost a game this season, and have just completed a successful tour through Kentucky, defeating all clubs at home and abroad. The home club have been practicing hard for this battle, and a good warm game is expected." The Brotherhood and Old Imps (Olymps) developed a local rivalry. *Courier Journal* (August 20, 1899): "The Brotherhoods and the Olymps will cross bats at Daisy Park, Sixteenth and Magnolia Streets, this afternoon for a purse of $50.00. The Brotherhoods have engaged a battery from Chicago, and the Olymps' battery will be Smith and Welch, formerly of the West Baden Springs (Indiana). The contest promises to be the best colored game of the season. The game will be called at 3 o'clock sharp."

SOURCES: "The Field of Sport," *Indianapolis (IN) Freeman,* Aug 8, 1891; "Base Ball," *Indianapolis Freeman,* Oct 10, 1891; "Amateur Gossip," *St. Louis (MO) Post-Dispatch,* July 24, 1892; "Colored Colonels on Top," *St. Louis (MO) Globe-Democrat,* July 24, 1892; "Amateur Gossip," *St. Louis Post-Dispatch,* July 25, 1892; "Crack Colored Clubs," *Nashville (TN) Tennessean,* Jul 21, 1895; "Colored Clubs of Nashville and Louisville to Play Off the Horse," *Nashville Tennessean,* Jul 23, 1895; "Brotherhoods and Olymps," *Louisville (KY) Courier-Journal,* Aug 20, 1896; "Base Ball Gossip," *Louisville Courier-Journal,* Oct 11, 1896; *Nashville (TN) Tennessean,* Apr 20, 1897; "General Sporting Notes," *Nashville Tennessean,* Jun 6, 1897; "Play Ball Today," *Nashville Tennessean,* Jun 7, 1897; "On the Commons," *Louisville Courier-Journal,* Aug 2, 1897; "Among the Amateurs," *Louisville Courier-Journal,* Sep 12, 1897; "With the Amateurs," *Louisville Courier-Journal,* May 1, 1898; "With the Amateurs," *Louisville Courier-Journal,* Jul 3, 1898; "Colored Base Ball," *Jeffersonville (IN) Evening News,* Jul 11, 1898; "Game of the Season," *Jeffersonville Evening News,* Aug 20, 1898; "Base Ball," *Jeffersonville Evening News,* Sep 10, 1898; *Jeffersonville Evening News,* Sep 26, 1898; "Rose vs. Brotherhood," *Louisville Courier-Journal,* Sep 3, 1899; "With the Amateurs," *Louisville Courier-Journal,* Sep 17, 1899; "Rock City Unions vs. Brotherhoods," *Louisville Courier-Journal,* Jun 23, 1900; "With the Amateurs," *Louisville Courier-Journal,* Jul 1, 1900.

Brown Stocking Base Ball Club (Louisville, KY; 1870s)

The Brown Stocking B.B.C. organized in the 1870s, played against black organizations. The Brown Socks developed a local rivalry with Lucien Wagner's "Band of Brunettes," the Globe ball club.

SOURCES: "Lucien's Band of Brunettes," *Louisville (KY) Courier-Journal*, Aug 3, 1875.

Daisy Line Base Ball Park Association (Fifteenth Street and Magnolia Avenue, Louisville, KY; 1880s–1890s). Owner(s): C. W. Hines and Lafayette Condon.

The Daisy Park Association, a colored business group, purchased the grounds formerly owned by the Falls Citys Colored B.B.C. *Louisville Courier-Journal* (April 15, 1888): "A number of thinking, progressive colored men of this city have formed an association, hereafter to be known as the Daisy Pleasure Park Association, incorporated April 1888, under the General Statuettes of the State of Kentucky. This company has purchased the old base-ball park on Fifteenth Street. The Daisy road runs to the fate, and two street car lines, on Fifteenth and Eighteenth Streets, will go to the gates. The park is ready to go on May 20, with good light and water, shade, a large dancing hall, and plenty of shelter in case of rain" (The "old ball park," located at Fifteenth Street and Magnolia Avenue, had been erected by the Falls Citys baseball organization in 1886). The association transformed the ball park into a resort area, planting trees, erecting buildings and other improvements. Black clubs—the Falls Citys, Acorns, Brotherhoods, and Olymps—utilized the facility. *Courier-Journal* (August 20, 1899): "The Brotherhoods and Olymps will cross bats at Daisy Park, Sixteenth and Magnolia Streets this afternoon for a purse of $50."

SOURCES: "Amateur Organizations," *Louisville (KY) Courier-Journal*, Apr 13, 1886; *New Orleans (LA) Weekly Pelican*, Mar 12, 1887; "He was Alright," *Louisville Courier-Journal*, September 12, 1887; "Notes," *Louisville Courier-Journal*, Apr 15, 1888; "Out of the Depths," *Louisville Courier-Journal*, Sep 6, 1888; *Louisville Courier-Journal*, Jul 10, 1889; "Resulted in a Tie," *Louisville Courier-Journal*, Aug 5, 1889; "Brotherhoods and Olymps," *Louisville Courier-Journal, Aug* 20, 1899; "Olymps and Cubans," *Louisville Courier-Journal*, Aug 27, 1899.

Diamond Joe Base Ball Club (Louisville, KY; 1890s). Organizer(s): John Weaver.

The Diamond Joe B.B.C. organized in the 1890s. *Louisville Courier* (April 17, 1898): "The Colored Diamond Joe's Base-Ball Club has organized for the season, and challenges will be accepted from all clubs in the State."

SOURCES: "With the Amateurs," *Louisville (KY) Courier-Journal*, Apr 17, 1898.

Fair Play Base Ball Club (Louisville, KY; 1870s)

The Fair Play B.B.C. organized in the 1870s. They played against black clubs of KY, OH and IN. *Louisville Courier Journal* (August 24, 1876): "The Globes and Fair Plays, two of our colored nines, played an exciting ten inning game at Olympic Park yesterday afternoon … those who are anxious to know how the Dark blacks sling the sphere and swing the willow." The Fair Plays developed a rivalry with the Social B.B.C. *Journal* (September 3, 1876): "The Fair Plays and Socials, colored clubs, played a ten-inning game on the Olympic Grounds yesterday afternoon." *Indianapolis People* (August 19, 1876): "The Indianapolis Western Base Ball Club played the Fair Plays, at Louisville, and our boys were defeated by a score of 27 to 12. The Louisville club will return the visit shortly." They traveled to Indianapolis. *Indianapolis Sentinel* (August 4, 1877): "The base-ball match was played by the Fairplays, of Louisville, and the Brown Stockings, of this city, and resulted in an easy victory for the home club by a score of 14 to 10."

SOURCES: "General Notes," *Louisville (KY) Courier-Journal*, Aug 16, 1876; "Globes vs. Fair Play," *Louisville Courier-Journal*, Aug 16, 1876; "Our Colored People," *Indianapolis (IN) People*, Aug 19, 1876;

"General Notes," *Louisville Courier-Journal*, September 3, 1876; "Around Town," *Louisville Courier-Journal*, September 14, 1876; "The First of the Season," *Indianapolis (IN) Sentinel*, Aug 4. 1877.

Falls Citys Base Ball Club (Louisville, KY; 1880s–1890s)

The Falls Citys B.B.C. organized in the 1880s, played white and black organizations. The organization owned and operated Daisy Park, their home grounds. Among the regional teams to play the Falls Citys included Chicago's Gordons. In 1887, the organization joined the National Colored Base Ball League. Following the league's collapse, the nine played local and regional games. *Louisville Courier-Journal*: "The Falls City colored club defeated the Spaulding Blues at the Falls City Park by a score of 27 to 0. The battery work of Smith and Mayfield was very fine." In October, the Falls Citys played a home series against Trenton's Cuban Giants; the Cuban Giants defeating them twice, 12 to 7; 13 to 6. The nine reorganized in the 1890s. *Frankfort Roustabout* (June 27, 1891): "The Falls City of Louisville, and the Athletics, of this city, two Colored Base Ball Clubs, played two games, one Sunday and the other Monday afternoon, at Athletic Park, on the Owenton Pike. The first resulted in a score of 9 to 10 in favor of Falls Citys and the latter in victory for the home team, the score standing 28 to 5."

SOURCES: "Amateur Organizations," *Louisville (KY) Courier Journal*, Apr 13, 1886; "Notes and Comments," *Louisville Courier Journal*, Apr 25, 1886; "Green Diamond Gossip," *Louisville Courier Journal*, May 16, 1886; "Crack Colored Clubs," *Louisville Courier Journal*, Jun 7, 1886; "Major Hughes, 19; Falls City, 5," *Louisville Courier Journal*, Jun 21, 1886; "Falls City 15; Sterlings 3," *Courier Journal*, Sep 6, 1886; "Notes and Comments," *Courier Journal*, Sep 13, 1886; "Green Diamond Gossip," *Louisville Courier Journal*, Mar 13, 1887; "Base Ball in Louisville," *New York (NY) Freeman*, Apr 16, 1887; "Notes and Comments," *Louisville Courier Journal*, Mar 17, 1887; "Base Ball Notes," *Louisville Courier Journal*, Apr 24, 1887; "The Colored League," *Louisville Courier Journal*, May 1, 1887; "Colored League," *Louisville Courier Journal*, May 8, 1887; "Colored League," *Louisville Courier-Journal*, May 9, 1887; "Base Ball Notes," *Louisville Courier Journal*, May 16, 1887; "Notes of the Game," *Louisville Courier Journal*, Jun 17, 1887; "Notes of the Game," *Louisville Courier Journal*, Jul 18, 1887; "The Cuban Giants," *Louisville Courier Journal*, Oct 15, 1887; "Won By the Giants," *Louisville Courier Journal*, Oct 19, 1887; "Won By The Cuban Giants," *Louisville Courier Journal*, Oct 20, 1887; "Base Ball," *Frankfort (KY) Roustabout*, Jun 27, 1891; "Sport," *Indianapolis (IN) Freeman*, May 5, 1894.

Globe Base Ball Club (Louisville, KY; 1870s). Organizer(s): Lucien Wagner.

The Globe B.B.C. organized in the 1870s, played against black nines of KY, IN, IL, and OH. Local rivals: Fair Plays, Socials, Brown Stockings and Mutuals, and Frankfort Athletics. The team's regional competition included Cincinnati's Vigilants, Chicago's White Stockings (Uniques), St. Louis's Blue Stockings, and Covington's Actives. *Louisville Courier Journal* (July 20, 1874): "The Globe Base Ball Club, consisting of colored men, has been recently organized in the city. They will have two players from abroad in their nine, and, if suitable grounds can be obtained, they intend to rent them. If they succeed, Louisville may soon see a novelty; in a game of base-ball between some colored club from abroad and the one now in the city." The team's principal players—Lucian Wagner, George Banks and Frank Garrett—played into the 1880s. The competition was the colored Mutual Club. *Courier Journal* (August 25, 1874): "The Mutuals and Globes, two city colored clubs, played a game of ball on the Eckford Grounds yesterday afternoon. The Globes were victorious by a score of 44 to 18. The Globes have not been defeated as yet by any colored club they have played with." The team was remembered ten years later. *New York Freeman*: "The glory achieved by the Globes, a colored club that played in the east years ago, and never lost but one game … still inspires Louisvillians."

SOURCES: "Miscellaneous Items," *Louisville (KY) Courier-Journal*, Aug 25, 1874; "An Interesting Game of Base-Ball," *Louisville Courier-Journal*, Sep 16, 1874; "Other Ball and Bat Items," *Louisville Courier-Journal*, Jul 28, 1875; "Colored Players," *Cincinnati (OH) Gazette*, Jul 29, 1875; "Base-Ball Notes," *Cincinnati (OH) Enquirer, Jul 30, 1875*; "Lucien's Band of Brunettes," *Louisville Courier-Journal*, Aug 8, 1875; "Today's Sport," *Louisville Courier-Journal*, Aug 25, 1875; "Athletics vs. Globes," *Louisville Courier-Journal*, Aug 26, 1875; "Local News," *Lawrence (KS) Republican Journal*, Jul 19, 1876; "General Notes," *Louisville Courier-Journal*, Aug 16, 1876; "Globes vs. Fair Play," *Louisville Courier-Journal*, Aug 16, 1876; "Globe vs. Fair Play," *Louisville Courier-Journal*, Aug 26, 1876; "Base Ball," *Louisville Courier-Journal*, Sep 3, 1878; "Picked Nine vs. Globes," *Louisville Courier-Journal, Sep 6, 1878*; "Appeal of the Anarchists," *New York (NY) Freeman, Jan 22, 1887.*

Mutual (Blue Stockings) Base Ball Club (Louisville, KY; 1860s–1880s). Organizer(s): Lucien Wagner; John W. Jackson (Bud Fowler).

The Mutual B.B.C. organized in the 1860s, played black and white teams. In 1867, they played a home/away series against Portsmouth, OH's Independent club. *New York Clipper* (August 2, 1867): "The Mutuals, of Louisville, Kentucky, and the Independents, of Portsmouth, Ohio played in the latter city July 24. Score being 11 to 10 in favor of the Mutes. Both nines are colored. They play again on July 25." A local rivalry developed with the Globes. *Courier Journal* (August 25, 1874): "The Mutuals and Globes, two city colored clubs, played a game of ball on the Eckford Grounds yesterday afternoon. The Globes were victorious by a score of 44 to 18. The Globes have not been defeated as yet by any colored club they have played with." The rivalry continued. *Courier Journal* (September 16, 1874): "The base-ball game between the Globes and Mutuals, both of Louisville. Attracted considerable attention, and resulted in favor of the Globes by a score of 25 to 18. One of the members of the Globes met with an accident that may prove of a serious nature. His position being that of shortstop, and his attention being attracted by the golden features of a maiden dressed in a pea green dress, witnessing the game from the shady position at his right, he stopped a passed ball with his eye." In 1883 and 1884, the Mutuals toured TN, OH, MO, IL and MI. They played the St. Louis Black Stockings at home, in St. Louis, and Ann Arbor. They played the University of MI nine. *Ann Arbor Courier* (June 29, 1883): "A baseball nine composed of colored men from Louisville, Kentucky amused the university nine a while Monday afternoon. There was considerable fun for spectators and when the rain stopped the game at the close of the fifth inning, the score stood 9 to 2 in favor of the home nine." In 1884, they toured MO, IL, and OH. *Cincinnati Enquirer* (July 23, 1884): "The Mutuals (colored), of Louisville, who were badly beaten here yesterday, turned the tables on the Urbanas today, and defeated them 12 to 14. The Urbanas, judging from yesterday's game that they would have a soft snap, played their weakest nine. Shaffer, a colored amateur of the Urbana pitched for the amateurs, and they want him to go with them." They defeated the Portsmouth Independents, a black team, in a fiercely contested match. In 1885, they renamed themselves the Falls Citys.

SOURCES: "Base Hits Everywhere," *New York (NY) Clipper*, Aug 2, 1867; "Miscellaneous Items," *Louisville (KY) Courier Journal*, Aug 25, 1874; "An Interesting Game of Base-Ball," *Louisville Courier-Journal*, Sep 16, 1874; "Base Ball Notes," *New York (NY) Truth*, Dec 13, 1883; "Base Ball," *Louisville Courier Journal*, Jun 10, 1883; "Local Notes," *Louisville Courier Journal*, Jun 10, 1883; "University Items," *Ann Arbor (MI) Courier*, Jun 29, 1883; "Picked Up," *Louisville Courier-Journal*, Feb 24, 1886; *Louisville Courier-Journal*, Jun 21, 1884; *Roundabout* (Frankfort, KY), June 21, 1884; "Base Ball Notes," *Portsmouth (OH) Times*, Jul 19, 1884; "Base Ball Notes," *Portsmouth Times*, Jul 26, 1884; *Cincinnati (OH) Enquirer*, Jul 23, 1884; *Cincinnati Enquirer*, Jul 26, 1884.

Old Honestys Base Ball Club (Louisville, KY; 1880s)

The Old Honestys B.B.C. organized in the 1880s, played black teams. *Louisville Courier-Journal* (July 6, 1886): "The two crack colored base-ball teams, Falls Citys and Old Honestys, crossed bats yesterday at their park near Sixteenth Street and Magnolia Avenue. The Old Honestys had things their own way until the eighth inning, when the Falls Citys, began to bat hard and effectively, and eventually won the game."

SOURCES: "Around the Bases," *Louisville (KY) Courier Journal*, Jun 6, 1886; "Crack Colored Clubs," *Louisville Courier Journal*, Jun 7, 1886; "The Amateurs," *Louisville Courier Journal*, Jul 6, 1886; "Falls Citys vs. Old Honestys," *Louisville Courier Journal*, Oct 17, 1886.

Old Imp Base Ball Club (Olympics) (Louisville, KY; 1890s–1900s)

The Old Imp B.B.C. organized in the 1890s, played black nines. They developed a rivalry with Louisville's Brotherhood club. *Louisville Courier Journal* (August 20, 1899): "The Brotherhoods and the Olymps will cross bats at Daisy Park, Sixteenth and Magnolia Streets, this afternoon for a purse of $50.00. The Brotherhoods have engaged a battery from Chicago, and the Olymps' battery will be Smith and Welch, formerly of the West Baden Springs (Indiana). The contest promises to be the best colored game of the season. The game will be called at 3 o'clock sharp." *Courier-Journal* (June 24, 1900): "At League Park today, the colored teams, Olympics, of this city, and Nashvilles, of Nashville, Tennessee, will play for a purse of $50. The game will be called at 3 o'clock. Both are crack teams and the chances are there will be a hot game."

SOURCES: "With the Amateurs," *Louisville (KY) Courier-Journal*, May 1, 1898; "With the Amateurs," *Louisville Courier-Journal*, Jul 3, 1898; "Brotherhoods and Olymps," *Louisville Courier-Journal*, Aug 20, 1899; "Olymps and Cubans," *Louisville Courier-Journal*, Aug 27, 1899; "Amateur Ball Games," *Louisville Courier-Journal*, Jun 24, 1900. "Local and General," *West Baden (IN) Journal*, Jul 11, 1899; "Local and General," *West Baden Journal*, Jul 12, 1899;

Rose Base Ball Club (Louisville, KY; 1890s–1900s)

The Rose B.B.C. organized in the 1890s, played black teams. *Louisville Courier Journal* (September 3, 1899): "This afternoon at League Park the Rose Baseball team will play a game with the Brotherhood team to settle the colored championship of the state and a purse of $50. Both teams have been playing god ball this year, especially the Brotherhoods, who have defeated the crack colored teams of Chattanooga and Nashville. This afternoon game promises to be a very interesting match. The game will be called promptly of 3 o'clock."

SOURCES: "Amateur Gossip," *Louisville (KY) Courier-Journal*, Aug 4, 1889; "Resulted In A Tie," *Louisville Courier-Journal*, Aug 5, 1889; "Notes," *Louisville Courier-Journal*, Aug 4, 1889; "Base Ball Gossip," *Louisville Courier-Journal*, Aug 23, 1896; "Amateur Games To-Day," *Louisville Courier-Journal*, Jul 16, 1899; "Rose vs. Brotherhood," *Louisville Courier-Journal*, Sep 3, 1899; "With the Amateurs," *Louisville Courier-Journal, Sep 17, 1899*; "With the Amateurs," *Louisville Courier-Journal*, July 1, 1900.

Sterling Base Ball Club (Louisville, KY; 1880s)

The Sterling B.B.C. organized in 1886. The nine played black teams. *Louisville Courier* (September 6, 1886): "The Falls Citys champions added another victory to their lost list yesterday afternoon. This club is composed of some of the very best colored talent in and around the country and if the players could be kept together a season or two the nine could certainly develop into a formidable rival to almost any aggregation."

SOURCES: "Falls City 15; Sterlings 3," *Louisville (KY) Courier Journal*, Sep 6, 1886.

Tonic Base Ball Club (Louisville, KY; 1890s)

The Tonic B.B.C. organized in the 1890s. The Tonics played black teams of KY, MO, and IL. *St. Louis Globe Democrat* (August 24, 1890): "There will be fun at Compton Avenue Park this afternoon. The Tonics, the champion colored club of Kentucky, will arrive by special train this morning and play the local colored champions, the West Ends. The Tonics are making a tour of the country, and go from here to Chicago. Play will begin at 2:30."

SOURCES: "Among the Amateurs," *St. Louis (MO) Globe-Democrat*, Aug 24, 1890.

East End Base Ball Club (Maysville, KY; 1890s)

The East End B.B.C. organized in the 1890s, played black teams. *Maysville Public Ledger* (July 26, 1895): "What is the funniest thing that has happened in Maysville in a long time? In the baseball world, the funniest thing was the game of ball yesterday afternoon between the two colored nines at East End Park, the East Enders winning by a score of 20 to 10."

SOURCES: "Short Stops," *Maysville (KY) Public Ledger*, Jul 25, 1895; "Colored Troops Fought Nobly," *Maysville Public Ledger*, Jul 26, 1895.

West End Base Ball Club (Maysville, KY; 1890s)

The West End B.B.C. organized in the 1890s, played black teams. *Maysville Public Ledger* (July 26, 1895): "What is the funniest thing that has happened in Maysville in a long time? In the baseball world, the funniest thing was the game of ball yesterday afternoon between the two colored nines at East End Park, the East Enders winning by a score of 20 to 10." *New York Clipper*: "The colored teams adopted the double umpire system in a game played August 27, at Maysville, Kentucky. During the game the umpires Charles Yates and Charles Dimmitt got into a dispute. Yates pulled a knife and was promptly knocked down by Dimmitt with a bat, and the injuries Yates received may prove serious."

SOURCES: "Short Stops," *Maysville (KY) Public Ledger*, Jul 25, 1895; "Colored Troops Fought Nobly," *Maysville Public Ledger*, Jul 26, 1895; "Diamond Field Gossip," *New York (NY) Clipper*, Sep 7, 1896.

Union Base Ball Club (Owensboro, KY; 1890s)

The Union B.B.C. organized in the 1890s, played black teams. *Louisville Courier-Journal* (August 16, 1897): "The Brotherhoods, colored, defeated the Owensboro Unions, also colored, by the score of 13 to 7 yesterday. The feature of the game was the timely batting of the Brotherhoods and the fielding of Trimbo of the Unions. A return game will be played in Owensboro next month."

SOURCES: "Gossip of the Games," *Louisville (KY) Courier-Journal*, Aug 16, 1897.

Blue Clipper Base Ball Club (Paducah, KY; 1870s)

The Blue Clipper B.B.C. organized in the 1900s, played black aggregations. *Evansville Courier and Press* (July 13, 1876): "On the 29th inst., the Blue Clippers, a colored base-ball club of Paducah, come to this city to play the Red Stockings. The Blue Clippers also have a neat uniform."

SOURCES: "Base Ball Brevities," *Evansville (IN) Courier and Press*, Jul 13, 1876.

Colored Grays Base Ball Club (Paducah, KY; 1890s)

The Colored Grays B.B.C. organized in the 1890s, played black teams. *Indianapolis Freeman* (September 2, 1899): "Mr. Samuel Gibbs manager of the Brotherhood Base Ball Club of Louisville, Kentucky, issued a bona fide challenge to the club in this city [Clarksville, Tennessee] to play there recently. His challenge was not acceptable on reasonable grounds. Mr. and Mrs. S. G. Kivel, of Paducah, Kentucky together with the base-ball club there under the management of Ben Boyd showed great kindness to the club during their stay there." They competed against Evansville, IN's Gold Dollar B.B.C. *Evansville Courier and Press* (May 25, 1899): "The Gold Dollars and Paducah teams tried their skill at baseball yesterday afternoon in League Park and a spirited game was played. The Gold Dollars beat the Paducah [Grays] by a score of 16 to 4."

SOURCES: "Interesting Item," *Indianapolis (IN) Freeman*, Apr 1, 1899; "Among Colored Folks," *Evansville (IN) Courier and Press*, May 10, 1899; "Among Colored Folks," *Evansville Courier and Press*, May 13, 1899; "Among Colored Folks," *Evansville Courier and Press*, May 16, 1899; "News Item," *Indianapolis Freeman*, May 20, 1899; "Among Colored Folks," *Evansville Courier and Press*, May 24, 1899; "Among Colored Folks," *Evansville Courier and Press*, May 25, 1899; "General News," *Indianapolis Freeman*, Aug 19, 1899; "Clarksville, Tennessee," *Indianapolis Freeman*, Sep 2, 1899.

LO & 4 B Base Ball Club (Paducah, KY; 1900s)

The LO & 4 B B.B.C. organized in the 1900s. The LO & 4 B played black aggregations.

SOURCES: "Base Ball," *Indianapolis (IN) Freeman*, Jun 2, 1900.

R&R Base Ball Club (Paducah, KY; 1900s)

The R&R B.B.C. organized in the 1900s. The R&R played black aggregations.

SOURCES: "Base Ball," *Indianapolis (IN) Freeman*, Jun 2, 1900.

Riverside Red Stockings Base Ball Club (Paducah, KY; 1880s)

The Riverside Red Stockings B.B.C. organized in the 1880s, played black nines. Rivalries developed with Cairo and Memphis. *Cairo Bulletin* (July 6, 1882): "Two colored baseball clubs, the Riversides of Paducah, and the Cairo Gazette, of this city, played a match game up town yesterday, in which the Cairo club came out ahead as usual." *Bulletin* (July 26, 1883): "The colored base-ball club of Paducah, beat the Cairo colored club yesterday, by one score, the game stood 3 for Cairo and 4 for Paducah." *Memphis Appeal* (July 1, 1884): "The darky baseballists were much more successful than other Memphis clubs have been lately. The Poplar Lincks played a game with the Riversides at Paducah, defeating them by a score of 21 to 10." *Memphis Appeal* (July 1, 1884): "Nearly 1000 people witnessed a game of baseball at Olympic Park between a couple of colored clubs. The Poplar Lincks of Memphis defeated the Riversides, of Paducah, by a score of 8 to 3." They reorganized in 1886. *St. Louis Sporting News* (May 31, 1886): "The Cairo Black Diamonds, the champion team of Illinois, played against the Paducah Reds, champion colored team of Kentucky. About 700 people witnessed the game—Cairo, 15, Paducah 12."

SOURCES: "General Local Items," *Cairo (IL) Bulletin*, Jul 6, 1882; "General Local Items," *Cairo Bulletin*, Jul 24, 1883; "River Items," *Cairo Bulletin*, Jul 26, 1883; "General Local Items," *Cairo Bulletin*, Jul 26, 1883; "General Local Items," *Cairo Bulletin*, Jul 27, 1883; "General Local Items," *Cairo Bulletin*, Jun 27, 1884; "Local Paragraphs," *Memphis (TN) Appeal*, Jun 29, 1884; "Local Paragraphs," *Memphis Appeal*, Jul 1, 1884; "Memphis," *Nashville (TN) Tennessean*, Aug 4, 1884;

"Wonders to the Surface," *St. Louis (MO) Sporting News*, May 31, 1886.

Blue Troublers Base Ball Club (Shelbyville, KY; 1880s)

The Colored B.B.C. organized in the 1880s, played black nines. *Louisville Courier-Journal* (June 22, 1884): "The Athletics, of Frankfort, and the Blue Troublers, of this place [Shelbyville, Kentucky], both colored clubs, crossed bats upon the green diamond this afternoon. The game was well-played and interesting, resulting in favor of the Frankfort boys by a score of 28 to 21." *Cleveland Gazette*: "The following constitute a champion nine of base-ball players: Will Orphan, c; James Prentis, p; John Clairbourn, ss; John Williams, 2b; Dave Massie, 1b; George Fortune, 3b; James Bloomer, rf; Buck Robinson, cf; Harry Payne, lf. They desire to hear from any club wishing to play a match game."

SOURCES: "A Close Contest," *Louisville (KY) Courier-Journal*, Jun 22, 1884; "Base Ball," *Cleveland (OH) Gazette*, Apr 21, 1888.

Louisiana

Acid Iron Earth Base Ball Club (Algiers, LA; 1880s)

The Acid Iron Earth B.B.C. organized in the 1880s, played black teams. *New Orleans Weekly Pelican* (August 20, 1887): "The Acid Iron Earth and Robert Maker Base Ball Clubs played a very interesting game of base-ball last Sunday. The Earth's won by a score of 28 to 7."

SOURCES: "Algiers Anglings," *New Orleans (LA) Weekly Pelican*, Jul 16, 1887; "Algiers Anglings," *New Orleans Weekly Pelican*, Aug 13, 1887; "Algiers Anglings," *New Orleans Weekly Pelican, Aug 20*, 1887; "Algiers Anglings," *New Orleans Weekly Pelican*, Aug 27, 1887.

A. J. Dumont Base Ball Club (Algiers, LA; 1880s). Organizer(s): H. E. De Fuentes and Charles Watson; M. Powells, J. M. Nelson and W. Jones.

The A. J. Dumont B.B.C. organized in the 1880s, played black and white nines. The team was named after its patron, Andrew J. Dumont (1845–1885). The offspring of white-black parentage, Dumont was raised in Plaquemines Parish. Moving to Mexico City in 1856, he later served as a military officer in Emperor Maximillian's army during the French occupation, returning to New Orleans with the French withdrawal. In 1866, he served as Police Sergeant. From 1868 to 1880 he served as State Senator, State Central Executive Committee member of the Republican Party, Deputy Collector, and General Sherman's active agent and delegate to the Chicago Convention. Between 1881 and 1882, they belonged to the LA's Union Colored League. *New York Clipper* (May 20, 1881): "The opening game of the Union League of Colored Clubs was played in New Orleans on March 3, when the Dumonts defeated the Marcos by a score of 31 to 19." *New Orleans Louisianan* (May 14, 1881): "The competitive game of base-ball between the Pickwicks and A. J. Dumonts on Tuesday at Oakland Park, was warmly contested. Both sides showed dexterity, which plainly indicated that they are far above the ordinary base-ball players. The game ended in seven innings in favor of the A. J. Dumonts." *New Orleans Times-Picayune* (August 15, 1881): "The Tournament of the League Clubs at the Fair Grounds was a spirited contest. The Bostons and the Pickwicks were the first to cross bats. Bostons [won] by hand playing. Then the Aetnas and the Dumonts entered the diamond field, Dumonts coming out winners. The contest now [narrowed] down to the 'winning nines' of the first and second games. The Bostons and Dumonts played a fine game. The Dumonts won. The first prize of $25 was awarded to the Dumonts. The second prize of $15 was awarded to the Bostons." They played the Orleans nine. *Times-Picayune* (October 21, 1884): "The Orleans and A. J. Dumonts,

two leading colored nines, played at the New Orleans Base Ball Park yesterday. The crowd was enthusiastic and the game well-contested. It was called on the eighth inning on account of darkness. The Orleans won by a score of 10 to 3." In 1886, they battled New Orleans's W. L. Cohen nine for the championship. *Times-Picayune* (June 28, 1886): "Dumonts and Cohens played five innings, and the Cohens won by a score of 5 to 4. Then, the Cohens tackled the Unions and the Unions shut them out by a score of 8 to 0. Jones pitched for the Cohens, and Walker was in the box for the Unions."

SOURCES: *New Orleans (LA) Louisianan*, May 15, 1880; "On the Diamond," *New Orleans (LA) Times-Democrat*, Jul 18, 1880; *New Orleans Louisianan*, May 14, 1881; "Base Ball," *New York (NY) Clipper*, May 20, 1881; *New Orleans Louisianan*, May 21, 1881; *New Orleans Louisianian*, Jul 2, 1881; "Base Ball," *New Orleans (LA) Times-Picayune*, Aug 15, 1881; "Base Ball," *New Orleans Times-Picayune*, Sep 8, 1881; "Base Ball," *New Orleans Times-Picayune*, Sep 12, 1881; "Celebration by the Colored Masons," *New Orleans Times-Picayune*, Jun 25, 1882; "Base-Ball," *New Orleans Times-Picayune*, May 18, 1884; "Items of Local Interest," *New Orleans Times-Picayune*, Oct 9, 1884; "Items of Local Interest," *New Orleans Times-Picayune*, Oct 12, 1884; "Base Ball," *New Orleans Times-Picayune*, Oct 21, 1884; "Other Plays and Players," *New Orleans Times-Picayune*, Nov 9, 1884; "Around Home Bases," *New Orleans Picayune*, Aug 28, 1885; "Base Ball," *New Orleans Times-Picayune*, Aug 30, 1885; "Base Ball," *New Orleans Picayune*, May 16, 1886; "Around Various Bases," *New Orleans Picayune*, Jun 17, 1886; "Around Various Bases," *New Orleans Picayune*, Jun 26, 1886; "Around the Bases," *New Orleans Picayune*, Jun 28, 1886; "The Colored League," *New Orleans (LA) Times-Democrat*, Jul 18, 1886; "Around Various Bases," *New Orleans Picayune*, Aug 7, 1886.

H. Browns Base Ball Club (Algiers, LA; 1880s). Organizer(s): H. Brown and D. Noble, Jr.

The H. Browns B.B.C. organized in the 1880s, played black teams. *New Orleans Weekly Pelican* (July 16, 1887): "Last Sunday a game of base-ball was played between the Brown's and Brice's which was won by the latter, by a score of 9 to 3." They played against the nines of New Orleans and Algiers. *Weekly Pelican* (September 10, 1887): "The H. Brown Base Ball Club, the champion club of this place, defeated the Ross club last Sunday, by a score of 16 to 8. The Browns play the Acid Iron Earths tomorrow." The contest brought out a large audience. *Weekly Pelican* (September 17, 1887): "The game between the Acid Iron Earths and the H. Browns resulted in a victory for the former by a score of 21 to 11. The game was marked by magnificent playing on the part of the Acids, and poor judgment on part of the Browns. The game was witnessed by fifteen hundred spectators, and on account of darkness was called after the seventh inning."

SOURCES: "Around Various Bases," *New Orleans (LA) Picayune*, Jun 30, 1886; "The Colored League," *New Orleans (LA) Times-Democrat*, Jul 18, 1886; "The Colored League," *New Orleans Times-Democrat*, Jul 19, 1886; "Carrollton Etchings," *New Orleans (LA) Weekly Pelican*, Jul 2, 1887; "Algiers Anglings," *New Orleans Weekly Pelican*, Jul 16, 1887; "Algiers Anglings," *New Orleans Weekly Pelican*, Jul 23, 1887; "Rakings," *New Orleans Weekly Pelican*, Aug 6, 1887; "Algiers Anglings," *New Orleans Weekly Pelican*, Aug 20, 1887; "Algiers Anglings," *New Orleans Weekly Pelican*, Aug 27, 1887; "Algiers Anglings," *New Orleans Weekly Pelican*, Sep 3, 1887; "Algiers Anglings," *New Orleans Weekly Pelican*, Sep 10, 1887; "Algiers Anglings," *New Orleans Weekly Pelican*, Sep 17, 1887; "Algiers Anglings," *New Orleans Weekly Pelican*, Sep 24, 1887; "Around Various Bases," *New Orleans Picayune*, Jul 13, 1888; "Diamond Dots," *New Orleans Times-Democrat*, Jul 17, 1888; "The Colored Clubs," *New Orleans Picayune*, Oct 23, 1888.

Pacific Base Ball Club (Algiers, LA; 1880s). Organizer(s): W. Labarosiere; Edward Native.

The Pacific B.B.C. organized in the 1880s, played white and black teams. *New Orleans Times-Picayune* (July 10, 1881): "The Pacifics and Pickwick play on Pioneer Green." *Times-Picayune* (August 1, 1881): "The champion Pacifics scored another victory over the Poet Cub by a score of 21 to 15. The pitching and catching on both sides was especially noticed." *Times-Picayune* (September 11, 1881): "The Pacifics, claiming to be the champion junior colored club, play the Poets at the Racquette Green this evening." *Times-Picayune* (September 18, 1881): "The Pacifics, claiming to be the champion junior colored nine, will cross bats with the W. R. Masons on Pioneer Green today." *Times-Picayune* (October 9, 1881): "The Pacifics and the Whitmores play at the Pioneer Green today." In 1886, the organization joined New Orleans's Junior Colored Base Ball League which included the Robinsons, Blue Stockings, M. Sullivans, M. Browns, Bordels, Louisianas, Klusbys, Crainies, and Pacifics. The team traveled between Algiers, Carrollton, and New Orleans. In 1888, the club reorganized. *Times-Picayune* (April 16, 1888): "The Pacifics were reorganized yesterday with Dan Mitchell as captain." *New Orleans Times-Democrat* (June 11, 1888): "The Pacifics defeated the Bostons at the old Racquette Green yesterday by a score of 8 to 5."

Sources: "Base Ball," *New Orleans (LA) Times-Picayune*, Jul 10, 1881; "Base Ball," *New Orleans Times-Picayune*, Aug 1, 1881; "Base Ball," *New Orleans Times-Picayune*, Sep 11, 1881; "Base Ball," *New Orleans Times-Picayune*, Sep 18, 1881; "Base Ball," *New Orleans Times-Picayune*, Oct 9, 1881; "Around the Bases," *New Orleans Times-Picayune*, Jul 19, 1886; "The Junior Colored League," *New Orleans Times-Picayune*, Jul 25, 1886; "Around the Bases," *New Orleans Times-Picayune*, Apr 16, 1888; "Diamond Dots," *New Orleans (LA) Times-Democrat*, Jun 11, 1881; "The Colored League," *New Orleans Times-Democrat*, Jul 19, 1886; "Diamond Dots," *New Orleans Times-Picayune*, Jul 22, 1888; "Diamond Dots," *New Orleans Times-Picayune*, Jul 23, 1888; "Diamond Dots," *New Orleans Times-Picayune*, Aug 3, 1888.

Robert L. Browns Base Ball Club (Algiers, LA; 1880s). Organizer(s): Robert L. Brown.

The Robert L. Browns B.B.C. organized in the 1880s, played black nines. *New Orleans Times-Picayune* (August 21, 1882): "The R. L. Browns defeated the J. Pullum by a score of 31 to 10 at Loeper's Park." *Times-Picayune* (August 20, 1883): "The R. L. Browns, a rising colored team, defeated the T. B. Stamps at Carrollton by a score of 17 to 11."

Sources: "Base Ball," *New Orleans (LA) Times-Picayune*, Aug 21, 1882; "Around Different Bases," *New Orleans Times-Picayune*, Aug 20, 1883; "Base Ball," *New Orleans (LA) Times-Democrat*, May 22, 1884; "Base Ball," *New Orleans (LA) Times-Democrat*, Jun 27, 1886; "Around Various Bases," *New Orleans Times-Picayune*, Jun 30, 1886; "Base Ball," *New Orleans Times-Democrat*, Jul 17, 1886; "Around the Bases," *New Orleans Times-Picayune*, Aug 17, 1886; "Around the Bases," *New Orleans Times-Picayune*, Sep 6, 1886.

Southern University Base Ball Club (Baton Rouge, LA; 1880s)

The Southern University B.B.C. organized in the 1880s, played black nines. *New Orleans Weekly Pelican* (April 30, 1887): "Last Saturday the New Orleans Base Ball Park was crowded by the teachers, students and friends of Straight and Southern Universities to witness the contest between the base-ball nines of the respective universities. The game was a one-sided affair after the third inning. Straight University out-batted, out-fielded and outplayed their opponents in every way as the score will show. The attendance was large and intense. Straight University evidently had the call, so far as the sympathy and applause were concerned. This helped the Straight nine and had a

depressing effect on the Southern team. It is to be hoped that such friendly contests will be repeated, for we feel quite sure it will meet with popular favor, while the healthy exercise incident to this manly American game cannot fail to be of benefit to the ball tossers."

Sources: "Rakings," *New Orleans (LA) Weekly Pelican*, Apr 9, 1887; "Southern vs. Straight," *New Orleans Weekly Pelican*, Apr 30, 1887; "Notes," *New Orleans (LA) Times-Democrat*, Jun 11, 1887; "Notes," *New Orleans (LA) Times-Democrat*, Jun 11, 1887.

Allen Base Ball Club (Carrollton, LA; 1890s)

The Allen B.B.C. organized in the 1890s, played black and white nines. *New Orleans Times-Democrat* (April 11, 1892): "The Spanish Fort B. B. C. defeated the Allen Club by a score of 15 to 8." A rivalry developed between the Allens and Bramcotes, a white aggregation. *New Orleans Times-Picayune* (October 21, 1895): "There were upwards of 1000 people at Ferrand's Parks, in Carrollton, yesterday to witness the game between the Bramcotes and Allens. The latter team represent that section of the city, and it was supposed, judging from their previous work, that they would make a fair showing against any team, but the difference between amateur and professional ball tossers was never better exemplified than in this contest, and the Allens, the colored champions were ignominiously defeated."

Sources: "Notes," *New Orleans (LA) Times-Democrat*, Apr 11, 1892; "Baseball and Bullets," *New Orleans (LA) Times-Picayune*, Aug 15, 1892; "Base Ball," *New Orleans (LA) Item*, Mar 17, 1894; "At Carrollton," *New Orleans Times-Democrat*, Mar 18, 1894; "A Game Today," *New Orleans Times-Democrat*, May 28, 1894; "Colored Championship," *New Orleans (LA) Item*, Jul 14, 1894; "Allens, 11; Jeff Lewis, 0," *New Orleans Times Picayune*, Sep 3, 1894; "Base Ball," *New Orleans Times Picayune*, Oct 17, 1895; "Base Ball," *New Orleans Times Picayune*, Oct 19, 1895; "A Time Game," *New Orleans Times Picayune*, Oct 31, 1895; "Base Ball," *New Orleans Times Picayune*, Oct 21, 1895; "Blacks vs. Whites," *New Orleans Times-Democrat*, Sep 25, 1896; "Masons 9, Allens 3," *New Orleans Times Picayune*, Oct 26, 1896; "Masons Win," *New Orleans Times-Democrat*, Oct 26, 1896; "Baseball," *New Orleans Times-Democrat*, Nov 22, 1896; "Masons 12, Allens 1," *New Orleans Times Picayune*, Nov 23, 1896; "Allens vs. Professionals," *New Orleans Times-Democrat*, Sep 20, 1897; "A Game at Carrollton," *New Orleans Times Picayune*, Oct 23, 1898; "Professionals vs. Allens," *New Orleans Times Picayune*, Nov 6, 1898; "Base Ball," *New Orleans Times Picayune*, Nov 13, 1898; "Tennessee Blacks vs. Allens," *New Orleans Times Picayune*, Jun 25, 1899.

William Wilson Base Ball Club (Carrollton, LA; 1880s–1890s). Organizer(s): William Wilson; E. LK. Brown; James Brooks and Eddie Black.

The William Wilson B.B.C. organized in the 1880s, played black teams. In 1886, the organization joined the LA Junior Colored League; the league was composed of ball clubs from the cities of Carrollton, Algiers, Gretna, and New Orleans. After 1886, the Wilsons continued to schedule matches against local Clubs. *New Orleans Weekly Pelican* (July 2, 1887): "The match game between the Wilson's of Carrollton, and the Browns, of Algiers was won by the former by a score of 10 to 8. The features of the game were the fielding of Black and Joseph of the Wilson's." The Wilsons played the New Orleans Pinchbacks in 1888.

Sources: "Sporting Events," *New Orleans (LA) Times-Democrat*, Jun 28, 1886; "Around Various Bases," *New Orleans (LA) Times-Picayune*, Jul 11, 1886; "Rakings," *New Orleans (LA) Weekly Pelican*, May 21, 1887; "Rakings," *New Orleans Weekly Pelican*, May 28, 1887; "Carrollton Etchings," *New Orleans Weekly Pelican*, Jul 2, 1887; "The R. A. Foreman Base Ball Club," *New Orleans Weekly Pelican*, Sep 24, 1887; "Around Home Bases," *New Orleans Times-Picayune*, Jul 16,

1888; "Baseball and Bullets," *New Orleans Times-Picayune*, Aug 15, 1892; "Base Ball," *New Orleans (LA) Item*, Mar 17, 1894; "Base Ball," *New Orleans (LA) Times-Democrat*, Mar 18, 1894; "At Carrollton," *New Orleans Times-Democrat*, Apr 29, 1894.

Duffel Base Ball Club (Donaldsonville, LA; 1880s)

The Duffel B.B.C. organized in the 1880s, played black teams. *New Orleans Times-Picayune* (August 2, 1885): "The Duffy Base Ball Club, of Donaldsonville and the Walkers, of this place, both colored, played a game here today, which resulted in a victory for the former by a score of 15 to 3." *Donaldsonville Chief* (August 15, 1885): "The colored clubs, Duffels, of Donaldsonville and Isaacs of Port Barrow, were playing on the Nolan Square, and they were compelled by the rain to suspend their game. They stopped at the beginning of the fifth inning with the score 8 to 3 in favor of the Duffels. The Duffels visited Plaquemine on the 1st inst., and beat the Walker of that town 16 to 3."

SOURCES: "Base Ball at Plaquemine," *New Orleans (LA) Times-Picayune*, Aug 2, 1885; "Base Ball," *Donaldsonville (LA) Chief*, Aug 15, 1885.

Excelsior Base Ball Club (Donaldsonville, LA; 1870s–1880s)

The Excelsior B.B.C. organized in the 1870s, played black teams. *Donaldsonville Chief* (September 16, 1876): "Accompanying the part of excursionists who arrived here from New Orleans Saturday were nine young colored men who thought to teach their colored brethren a few things about base-ball. So they played a game with the Excelsiors of Donaldsonville on the Public Square, and were surprised to find that their anticipated easy victory developed into a close defeat, the score showing 26 runs for the Excelsiors to 25 for the city boys, in a game of seven innings. It was a well contested match, some fine playing being shown on both sides. The Donaldsonville boys are proud of their success." They reorganized in the 1880s. *Chief* (June 4, 1881): "The Old Eagles of Darrowville and the Excelsiors of Donaldsonville, both colored clubs, played at Darrowville last Sunday, the game resulting 13 to 12 in favor of the Eagles."

SOURCES: "Local Jottings," *Donaldsonville (LA) Chief*, Sep 16, 1876; "Local Jottings," *Donaldsonville Chief*, Jun 9, 1877; "Local Jottings," *Donaldsonville Chief*, Jul 28, 1877; "Local Jottings," *Donaldsonville Chief*, Aug 11, 1877; *Donaldsonville Chief*, Jun 4, 1881.

Kelly Base Ball Club (Donaldsonville, LA; 1880s)

The Kelly B.B.C. organized in the 1880s, played black nines. *Donaldsonville Chief* (August 7, 1886): "The Wilsons and Kellys, clubs of young colored men of Donaldsonville, played a game of 5 to 9 in favor of the latter." *New Orleans Times-Picayune* (September 7, 1886): "The [New Orleans] Unions will leave on the Larendon Rifles' excursion on Saturday, and meet the Kelleys, of Donaldsonville, at that place. The next day the Unions play the Wilsons."

SOURCES: "Base Ball," *Donaldsonville (LA) Chief*, Aug 7, 1886; "Around the Bases," *New Orleans (LA) Times-Picayune*, Sep 14, 1886; "At Donaldsonville," *New Orleans (LA) Times-Democrat*, Sep 14, 1886.

Kling Base Ball Club (Donaldsonville, LA; 1880s). Organizer(s): Charles W. Kling.

The Kling B.B.C. organized in the 1880s, played black teams. *New Orleans Times-Democrat* (March 18, 1887): "The Union Base Ball Club of New Orleans will leave Saturday, March 19, for Donaldsonville, to play a series of games with the Klings, of Donaldsonville, for a purse of $50 and all the gate receipts. Arnold and Moise will be the battery for the Unions. Mollers and Merrett will be the battery for the Klings." *New Orleans Weekly Pelican* (June 25, 1887): "The Klings Base Ball Club, of Donaldsonville, played two games recently with the Hop Bitters of Houma. The Kling won one game by a score

of 9 to 11, and the other game was won by the Hop Bitters by a score of 7 to 9." *Times-Picayune* (July 14, 1887): "The C. W. Klings arrived from Donaldsonville last night and will play the Pickwicks at New Orleans Park this evening. The winner of the game will play the Unions immediately afterwards. The three teams are the crack colored clubs of the South." *Times-Picayune* (July 18, 1887): "The Klings of Donaldsonville were not much in the hands of the Pickwicks who defeated them by a score of 8 to 0." *Weekly Pelican* (September 3, 1887): "The Kling Base Ball Club, of Donaldsonville, played to three games with the Hop Bitters, our local team. Honer and Brown, the Union battery of New Orleans, did splendid work for the visitors. The home town however won two out of the three games."

SOURCES: "The Colored Players," *New Orleans (LA) Times-Democrat*, Mar 18, 1887; *New Orleans (LA) Weekly Pelican*, Jun 25, 1887; "Around Various Bases," *New Orleans (LA) Times-Picayune*, Jul 14, 1887; "Around Various Bases," *New Orleans Daily Picayune*, Jul 17, 1887; "Around Various Bases," *New Orleans Times-Picayune*, Jul 18, 1887; "Houma, LA," *New Orleans Weekly Pelican*, Aug 20, 1887; "Houma, LA," *New Orleans Weekly Pelican*, Sep 3, 1887.

Wilson Base Ball Club (Donaldsonville, LA; 1880s). Organizer(s): Joe Wilson.

The Wilson B.B.C. organized in the 1880s, played black organizations. *Donaldsonville Chief* (August 7, 1886): "The Wilsons and Kellys, clubs of young colored men of Donaldsonville, played a game of 5 to 9 in favor of the latter." *New Orleans Times-Picayune* (September 7, 1886): "The [New Orleans] Unions will leave on the Larendon Rifles' excursion on Saturday, and meet the Kelleys, of Donaldsonville, at that place. The next day the Unions play the Wilsons."

SOURCES: "Base Ball," *Donaldsonville (LA) Chief*, Aug 7, 1886; "Around the Bases," *New Orleans (LA) Times-Picayune*, Sep 14, 1886; "At Donaldsonville," *New Orleans (LA) Times-Democrat*, Sep 14, 1886.

Knox Base Ball Club (Iberia, LA; 1880s). Organizer(s): Eugene Knox.

The E. Knox B.B.C. organized in the 1880s. *New Orleans Weekly Pelican* (July 23, 1887): "The E. Knox Base Ball Club and the Pride of Iberia played a game Saturday for a purse of $15. The Knox [club] won by a score of 22 to 8. The next day they defeated the 'Will Nots' of Napoleonville, by a score of 30 to 17."

SOURCES: "Thibodaux," *New Orleans (LA) Weekly Pelican*, Jul 23, 1887.

Slugger Base Ball Club (Lafourche, LA; 1880s). Organizer(s): John Purnell.

The Slugger B.B.C. organized in the 1880s. *New Orleans Weekly Pelican* (July 2, 1887): "The latest flurry in based-ball circles here is the organization of the 'Indomitable Sluggers' whose height ranges from 6 ? to 7 feet. The success of these gentlemen in the base-ball arena, judging by their boisterous predictions, is already assured."

SOURCES: "Lafourche Budget," *New Orleans (LA) Weekly Pelican*, Jul 2, 1887.

Aetna (Etna) Base Ball Club (New Orleans, LA; 1870s–1880s). Organizer(s): Henri L. Baptiste and Joseph Mitchell.

The Aetna B.B.C. organized in the 1870s, played black teams. *New Orleans Weekly Louisianan* (April 3, 1880): "The Aetna Base Ball Club will cross bats with the Bostons, at the Oakland Riding Park, April 5th, for a purse of $25." *Weekly Louisianan* (June 11, 1881): "The game of Base Ball between the Aetnas and Bostons on Sunday at Delachasie Grounds, was won by the Bostons, the score stood 13 to 3." In 1881, *New Orleans Times-Picayune* (August 15, 1881): "The Tournament of the League Clubs at the Fair Grounds was a spirited contest. The Bostons and the Pickwicks were the first to cross bats.

Bostons [won] by hand playing. Then the Aetnas and the Dumonts entered the diamond field, Dumonts coming out winners. The contest now [narrowed] down to the 'winning nines' of the first and second games. The Bostons and Dumonts played a fine game. The Dumonts won. The first prize of $25 was awarded to the Dumonts. The second prize of $15 was awarded to the Bostons."

SOURCES: "Base Ball in Colors," *New Orleans (LA) Times*, Sep 4, 1877; *New Orleans (LA) Louisianan*, Apr 3, 1880; *New Orleans Louisianan*, May 15, 1880; "On the Diamond," *New Orleans (LA) Times-Democrat*, Jul 18, 1880; "Short Stops," *New Orleans Times*, Apr 19, 1881; *New Orleans Louisianan*, May 21, 1881; *Louisianan*, Jun 11, 1881; *New Orleans Louisianian*, Jul 2, 1881; "Base Ball," *New Orleans (LA) Times-Picayune*, Aug 15, 1881; "Base Ball," *New Orleans Times-Picayune*, Sep 8, 1881; "Base Ball," *New Orleans Times-Picayune*, Sep 12, 1881; "Base Ball," *New Orleans (LA) Times-Democrat*, Jun 17, 1884; "Around Various Bases," *New Orleans Times-Picayune*, Jul 17, 1887.

Anchor Line Base Ball Club (New Orleans, LA; 1880s)

The Anchor Line B.B.C. organized in the 1880s. *St. Louis Post-Dispatch* (June 7, 1884): "The Athletic and Anchor Line colored base-ball clubs play at the Compton Avenue Park tomorrow afternoon at 3:30pm. The Anchors will arrive from the South." *St. Louis Republican* (June 9, 1884): "The Anchor Line club of New Orleans, and the Athletics of St. Louis, both colored, crossed bats yesterday at Compton Avenue Park in the presence of about 400 people. The Athletics won by a score of 17 to 16."

SOURCES: "Diamond Chips," *St. Louis (MO) Post-Dispatch*, Jun 5, 1884; "Diamond Chips," *St. Louis Post-Dispatch*, Jun 7, 1884; "Diamond Chips," *St. Louis (MO) Republican*, Jun 8, 1884; "Diamond Chips," *St. Louis Republican*, Jun 9, 1884.

Athletic Base Ball Club (New Orleans, LA; 1870s–1880s). Owner(s): Senator J. Henri Burch.

The Athletic B.B.C. organized in the 1870s, played black nines. They developed a local rivalry with the Union club. *New Orleans Times-Picayune* (July 28, 1875): "The Unions and the Athletics Base Ball Clubs played a game for the champion pennant of the State. The Unions were triumphant. Score, 18 to 10." The Athletics played a key role in the formation of a baseball association. *New Orleans Times-Democrat* (August 8, 1875): "A base-ball convention of the colored clubs of the city will be called on the 23rd inst., to form a Base Ball Association. The movement was inaugurated by the Athletic B. B. Club. Clubs who are thoroughly organized, are requested to send two delegates to the convention." *New Orleans Weekly Louisianian* (September 4, 1875): "The Athletics, a Base Ball organization, composed of young players, had a match game of Base-ball with the Union Base Ball Club at the Masonic picnic at Pass Christian [Mississippi] last Saturday. The Athletics backed by Senator Burch were the decided victors. As a consequence, a set of foul flags of heavy blue silk and fringed with silver edging, bearing the letter F in white, the centre, were awarded the Athletics." The team reorganized in 1876. *Times-Picayune* (May 31, 1876): "At the Coral Vine Social Club Centennial picnic, the Union Base Ball Club defeated the Athletic Club by a score of 5 to 2." By 1877, the Athletics, Unions, Pickwicks, Bostons, and Excelsior Reds were competing for the local black championship. *Weekly Louisianian* (October 6, 1877): "In a contested game of base-ball between the Pickwicks and Athletics at the Fair Grounds last Tuesday, the former carried away the laurels." They played at least one white nine. *Times-Democrat* (July 27, 1879): "The B. M. Club will cross bats with the Athletic (colored) on the Montegut Street, for $10, this afternoon." *Times-Picayune* (August 2, 1885): "The famous Athletics have organized and would like to hear from the Cohens and Unions at any early date."

SOURCES: "Base Ball," *New Orleans (LA) Republican*, Jul 28, 1875; "Local Brevities," *New Orleans (LA) Times-Democrat*, Aug 8, 1875; *New Orleans (LA) Weekly Louisianian*, Sep 4, 1875; "Odd Fellows' Aid Association," *New Orleans Times-Picayune*, Jul 28, 1875; "City Gossip," *New Orleans Picayune*, May 31, 1876; "City Gossip," *New Orleans Times-Picayune*, Oct 15, 1876; "Base Ball," *New Orleans (LA) Times-Picayune*, Apr 30, 1877; "Base Ball in Colors," *New Orleans (LA) Times*, Sep 4, 1877; "Base Ball," *New Orleans Times*, Oct 4, 1877; "Local," *New Orleans Weekly Louisianian*, Oct 6, 1877; "Base Ball," *New Orleans Times*, Feb 10, 1878; "Base Ball," *New Orleans (LA) Times-Democrat*, Jul 27, 1879; "Sporting," *New Orleans Times-Picayune*, Aug 2, 1885; "Around Home Bases," *New Orleans Times-Picayune*, Sep 8, 1885; "Around Home Bases," *New Orleans Times-Picayune*, Sep 13, 1885; "Around Home Bases," *New Orleans Times-Picayune*, Sep 19, 1885.

Blue Stockings Base Ball Club (New Orleans, LA; 1880s)

The Blue Stockings B.B.C. organized in the 1880s, played black nines. In 1886, the team joined the city's Junior Colored League. *New Orleans Times-Picayune* (July 25, 1886): "The Junior Colored League opened its series of game Thursday at Loeper's Park between thee Robinsons and Blue Stockings. Score 8 to 4 in favor of the Robinsons." *Times-Picayune* (July 26, 1886): "The J. Lewis, Jr., and the Blue Stockings, of the Colored Amateur League, played yesterday at Loeper's Park. The score was J. Lewis, Jr., 7; Blue Stockings, 3."

SOURCES: "Around Various Bases," *New Orleans (LA) Times-Picayune*, Jul 6, 1886; "Colored Junior League," *New Orleans (LA) Times-Democrat*, Jul 21, 1886; "Around the Bases," *New Orleans Times-Picayune*, Jul 23, 1886; "Base Ball," *New Orleans Times-Picayune*, Jul 25, 1886; "Around the Bases," *New Orleans Times-Picayune*, Jul 26, 1886; "Three Games for One Admission," *New Orleans Times-Democrat*, Aug 10, 1886.

Boston Base Ball Club (New Orleans, LA; 1870s–1880s)

The Boston B.B.C. organized in the 1870s, played black nines. *New Orleans Louisianan* (June 11, 1881): "The Aetna Base Ball Club will cross bats with the Bostons, at the Oakland Riding Park, April 5th, for a purse of $25." *Louisianan* (June 11, 1881): "The game of Base Ball between the Aetnas and Bostons on Sunday at Delachasie Grounds, was won by the Bostons, the score stood 13 to 3." *Louisianan* (July 2, 1881): "The Tournament of the League Clubs at the Fair Grounds was a spirited contest. The Bostons and the Pickwicks were the first to cross bats. Bostons [won] by hand playing. Then the Aetnas and the Dumonts entered the diamond field, Dumonts coming out winners. The contest now [narrowed] down to the 'winning nines' of the first and second games. The Bostons and Dumonts played a fine game. The Dumonts won. The first prize of $25 was awarded to the Dumonts. The second prize of $15 was awarded to the Bostons." In 1888, the Bostons and Unions fought for the championship. *New Orleans Times-Democrat* (June 11, 1888): "The Pacifics defeated the Bostons at the old Racquette Green yesterday by a score of 8 to 5." *New Orleans Times-Picayune* (October 8, 1888): "The Unions defeated the Bostons yesterday by a score of 9 to 2, in a game for the colored championship."

SOURCES: "Base Ball in Colors," *New Orleans (LA) Times*, Sep 4, 1877; "Base Ball," *New Orleans Times*, February 10, 1878; *New Orleans (LA) Louisianan*, Apr 3, 1880; "Short Stops," *New Orleans Times*, Apr 19, 1881; *New Orleans Louisianan*, May 21, 1881; *New Orleans Louisianan*, Jun 11, 1881; *New Orleans Louisianian*, Jul 2, 1881; "Base Ball," *New Orleans (LA) Times-Picayune*, Aug 15, 1881; "Base Ball," *New Orleans Times-Picayune*, Sep 8, 1881; "Base Ball," *New Orleans Times-Picayune*, Sep 12, 1881; "Diamond Dots," *New Orleans (LA) Times-Democrat*, Jun 11, 1888; "Diamond Dots," *New Orleans Times-*

Democrat, Jul 23, 1888; "Diamond Dots," *New Orleans Times-Democrat,* Oct 7, 1888; "Base Ball," *New Orleans Times-Picayune,* Oct 8, 1888; "Colored Clubs," *New Orleans Times-Picayune,* Aug 10, 1889; "Today's game," *New Orleans Times-Picayune,* Sep 29, 1889; "The Pinchback's Win," *New Orleans Times-Picayune,* Sep 30, 1889; "Notes," *New Orleans Times-Democrat,* Jun 28, 1892.

Clay Base Ball Club (New Orleans, LA; 1870s). Organizer(s): Henry Clay, Peter Joseph, Steven Johnson and William A. Barron.

The Clay B.B.C. organized in the 1870s, played black teams. *New Orleans Bulletin* (July 20, 1875): "Eleven cars of colored folks left by the Mobile Road yesterday morning at 10 ? for Bay State St. Louis. The occasion was an excursion given by the Clay Base Ball Club (colored) of this city. A brass band accompanied the party."

SOURCES: "On Dit," *New Orleans (LA) Bulletin,* Jul 20, 1875; "Local Intelligence," *New Orleans (LA) Republican,* August 26, 1875.

Cohen Base Ball Club (New Orleans, LA; 1880s–1890s). Organizer(s): James Madison Vance, Joseph Williams, George E. Mills and Walter L. Cohen.

The Cohen B.B.C. organized in 1885. Walter L. Cohen (**Fig. 31**) reorganized the Pickwicks as the W. L. Cohens. The organization played black nines from Mobile, Memphis, and St. Louis; an attempt was made to arrange a match with Chicago's Gordons. A heated local rivalry existed by the Cohen and Union teams. *New Orleans Times-Picayune* (May 18, 1885): "One of the most exciting and hotly contested games was played yesterday at New Orleans Base Ball Park between two crack colored clubs of the city. Fully 880 persons were present, a large portion being white. It was a challenge game for a purse of $50 between the Unions and W. L. Cohens, and was won by the Unions, after playing twelve innings, by a score of 9 to 8. These two clubs will play on next Sunday for an increased purse." In this hotly-contested rivalry, they recruited players as others jumped between teams. Cohen recruited Asa and David Price, a St. Louis, MO battery. In 1885, the Cohens played a professional white nine of the Southern League, from Columbus GA, for $500. In 1886, the Cohens, Unions and Dumonts battled for the championship. *Times-Picayune* (June 23, 1886): "Dumonts and Cohens played five innings, and the Cohens won by a score of 5 to 4. Then, the Cohens tackled the Unions and the Unions shut them out by a score of 8 to 0. Jones pitched for the Cohens, and Walker was in the box for the Unions." When Unions joined League of Southern Colored Base Ballists in 1886, the W. L. Cohens nine remained independent. After a hiatus, the team briefly reorganized in the 1890s. They played a series of games against the Pelz Professionals (white club). *Times-Picayune* (November 18, 1895): "The first game of the series for the local championship between the Pelz and

Figure 31. Walter L. Cohen, *New Orleans (LA) Times-Picayune,* 1890s. Between 1876 and 1895, Cohen covered first base and managed several New Orleans teams, including the Pickwicks (1876-1882), Orleans (1883-1884), W. L. Cohens (1885-1886), P. B. S. Pinchbacks (1887-1890), and Cohens (1895).

Cohen teams was played at Ferran's Park, Carrolton yesterday and was witnessed by almost 500 people. It was a very close and exciting contest until the fourth inning, when Joseph was replaced by Brooks, and the Pelzs batted him at will and scored eight runs. Which so discouraged the Cohens that they played listlessly for the rest of the game."

SOURCES: "Base Ball," *New Orleans (LA) Times-Picayune,* May 18, 1884; "Dots from Local Diamonds," *New Orleans Times-Picayune,* May 23, 1884; "Items of Local Interest," *New Orleans Times-Picayune,* Oct 12, 1884; "Items of Local Interest," *New Orleans Times-Picayune,* Oct 21, 1884; "Dots from Local Diamonds," *New Orleans Times-Picayune,* Oct 26, 1884; "Items of Local Interest," *New Orleans Times-Picayune,* Oct 9, 1884; "Base Ball," *New Orleans Times-Picayune,* May 3, 1885; "Local Liners," *New Orleans Times-Picayune,* Jun 7, 1885; "Petries Defeat the Cohens," *New Orleans Times-Picayune,* Jul 20, 1885; "The Unions Defeat the Cohens," *New Orleans Times-Picayune,* Aug 3, 1885; "Around the Bases," *New Orleans Times-Picayune,* Nov 27, 1885; "Base Ball," *New Orleans Times-Picayune,* Aug 30, 1885; "Around Home Bases," *New Orleans Times-Picayune,* Oct 1, 1885; "The Colored Champions Defeat the Daurers," *New Orleans Times-Picayune,* Oct 2, 1885; "The Columbians and the Cohens," *New Orleans Times-Picayune,* Oct 4, 1885; "The Columbians Conquer the Colored Champions," *New Orleans Times-Picayune,* Oct 4, 1885; "Base Ball," *New Orleans Times-Picayune,* Aug 30, 1885; "Base Ball," *New Orleans (LA) Times-Democrat,* May 2, 1886; "Base Ball," *New Orleans Times-Picayune,* May 16, 1886; "Sporting Events," *New Orleans Times-Democrat,* May 17, 1886; "Rakings," *New Orleans (LA) Weekly Pelican,* Jun 11, 1886; "The Cohens Defeat the Memphis Team," *New Orleans Times-Picayune,* June 23, 1886; "Base Ball," *New Orleans Times-Picayune,* Nov 9, 1895; "Base Ball," *New Orleans Daily Picayune,* Nov 10, 1895; "Base Ball," *New Orleans Times-Picayune,* Nov 17, 1895; "The Pelz Team Wins Again," *New Orleans Times-Picayune,* Nov 18, 1895.

Dan Kings Base Ball Club (New Orleans, LA; 1890s)

The Dan Kings B.B.C. organized in the 1890s, played black and white teams. *New Orleans Times-Picayune* (October 31, 1897): "Patrons will witness a great game of ball between the Professionals and Dan Kings at Ferran's Park for a purse of $50 and entire gate receipts. The Kings are worthy successors to the Cuban Giants, are good hitters, base runners, and play a systematic game. Nace Mason, the crack Eastern League umpire will officiate, and it is needless to say that there will be no kicking."

SOURCES: "Professionals and Dan Kings," *New Orleans (LA) Times-Picayune,* Oct 31, 1897; "Baseball Professionals and Dan Kings," *New Orleans Times-Picayune,* Nov 5, 1897; "Professionals and Dan Kings," *New Orleans Times-Picayune,* Nov 7, 1897; "Baseball," *New Orleans Times-Picayune,* Nov 11, 1897.

Excelsior Reds Base Ball Club (New Orleans, LA; 1870s–1880s)

The Excelsior B.B.C. organized in the 1870s, competed against black organizations. *New Orleans Times-Picayune* (March 31, 1878): "Ogden Park will be enlivened today by a game between those crack organizations, the Pickwicks and Excelsior Reds, of the Second District." *Abbeville Meridional* (July 26, 1879): "A match game of ball was played on the Burnside Grounds Saturday afternoon by the Pickwick and Excelsior clubs of New Orleans. The game was a very interesting one and attracted quite a crowd of spectators. Following is the score: Excelsior 19, Pickwick 3." In 1880, the Pickwicks and Excelsiors consolidated to become Orleans club. They played the C. T. Howards nine, a white organization. *Weekly Louisianan* (March 30, 1880): "The Howards played the Orleans Base Ball Club recently. It was the first time colored and white clubs played together. Now that the ice now has been broken, we expect the Lee and other crack clubs will cross bats with their dark-hued brethren."

SOURCES: "Base Ball," *New Orleans (LA) Times-Picayune*, Mar 31, 1878; *Abbeville (LA) Meridional*, Jul 26, 1879; "Base Ball," *New Orleans (LA) Times-Democrat*, Mar 6, 1880; *New Orleans (LA) Weekly Pelican*, Mar 30, 1880.

F. A. Johnson Base Ball Club (New Orleans, LA; 1880s). Organizer(s): F. A. Johnson.

The F. A. Johnson B.B.C. organized in the 1880s. *New Orleans Weekly Pelican* (June 11, 1887): "The Johnson Base Ball Club defeated the Foreman's club last Sunday at First Field. William Perry and Theo Harris distinguished themselves by their playing." *Weekly Pelican* (June 18, 1887): "The Johnson Base Ball Club defeated the Louisiana Club by a score of 15 to 10 last Wednesday afternoon."

SOURCES: "Rakings," *New Orleans (LA) Weekly Pelican*, May 28, 1887; "Rakings," *New Orleans Weekly Pelican*, Jun 11, 1887; "Rakings," *New Orleans Weekly Pelican*, Jul 30, 1887; "Rakings," *New Orleans Weekly Pelican*, Aug 6, 1887; "A Challenge," *New Orleans Weekly Pelican*, Sep 10, 1887.

Frank Williams Base Ball Club (New Orleans, LA; 1880s). Organizer(s): Frank Williams.

The Frank Williams B.B.C. organized in the 1880s. *New Orleans Times-Picayune* (August 30, 1881): "A game was played in Algiers between the Williams and Lorester nines, which was won by the former, by a score of 20 to 17."

SOURCES: "Local," *New Orleans (LA) Weekly Louisianan*, Jul 13, 1881; "Base Ball," *New Orleans Times-Picayune*, Aug 30, 1881.

Geddes Base Ball Club (New Orleans, LA; 1880s). Organizer(s): George D. Geddes, Sr., and George D. Geddes, Jr.

The Geddes B.B.C. organized in the 1880s. *New Orleans Weekly Pelican* (August 27, 1887): "The George D. Geddes Base-Ball Club defeated the T. J. Monaghans on the Claiborne green, last Sunday, by a score of 14 to 12."

SOURCES: "Rakings," *New Orleans (LA) Weekly Pelican*, Jul 2, 1887; "Rakings," *New Orleans Weekly Pelican*, Aug 27, 1887.

J. Bemiss Base Ball Club (New Orleans, LA; 1880s)

The J. Bemiss B.B.C. organized in the 1880s, played black nines. In 1886, the team joined the city's Junior Colored League. *New Orleans Times-Democrat* (August 4, 1886): "A contest for the junior championship between the Clifton, Dan Mitchell, Logan, and J. Bemiss colored base-ball clubs will take place today at the New Orleans Base Ball Park. Three games will be played." *New Orleans Times-Picayune* (June 28, 1886): "The game between the Clarks and the Bemisses resulted in favor of the Bemisses by a score of 10 to 8." *Times-Picayune* (October 14, 1889): "The Bemiss and Boston Nines, as they call themselves, played a good game at the New Orleans Park. The Bostons expected to win, but the Bemiss men made them play hard ball and a tie, 5 to 5, was acceptable to both sides." *Times-Picayune* (October 14, 1889): "Nearly 600 people witnessed the Pinchbacks down the Bemisses at New Orleans Base Ball Park by a score of 19 to 6."

SOURCES: "Three Games for One Admission," *New Orleans (LA) Weekly Pelican*, Aug 10, 1886; "Contest for the Junior Championship Today," *New Orleans (LA) Times-Democrat*, Aug 4, 1886; "Triumphs of Dan Mitchells," *New Orleans (LA) Times-Picayune*, Aug 12, 1889; "A Tie," *New Orleans Times-Picayune*, Sep 9, 1889; "Colored Clubs Contesting," *New Orleans Times-Picayune*, Oct 12, 1889; "Free Game Today," *New Orleans Times-Picayune*, Oct 13, 1889; "The Pinchbacks Down the Bemisses," *New Orleans Times-Picayune*, Oct 14, 1889.

James Lewis Junior Base Ball Club (New Orleans, LA; 1880s). Organizer(s): Isaac Jackson, George Moore, Theodore Rouse and Joseph Hill.

The James Lewis, Jr. B.B.C. organized in the 1880s. *New Orleans Times-Picayune* (July 30, 1885): "The James Lewis, Jrs, formerly the Ben Browns, organized last night. They would like to hear from any colored nine." In 1886, the team joined New Orleans's Junior Colored Base Ball League.

SOURCES: "Base Ball," *New Orleans (LA) Times-Picayune*, Jul 17, 1885; "Sporting," *New Orleans Times-Picayune*, Jul 30, 1885; "Around Home Bases," *New Orleans Times-Picayune*, Aug 28, 1885; "Around the Bases," *New Orleans Times-Picayune*, Jul 19, 1886; "The Junior Colored League," *New Orleans Times-Picayune*, Jul 25, 1886.

Lang Base Ball Club (New Orleans, LA; 1880s)

The Lang B.B.C. organized in the 1880s. *New Orleans Weekly Pelican* (June 4, 1887): "The Lang Boys Base Ball Club has organized with the following players: Joseph Matthews, Captain, Henry Johnson, J. Douglass, J. Goodridge, N. Green, George Stuttney, A. Davis, Albert Felix and Henry Anderson."

SOURCES: "Rakings," *New Orleans (LA) Weekly Pelican*, Jun 4, 1887.

Orlean Base Ball Club (New Orleans, LA; 1880s). Organizer(s): F. O. Boisseau, George Smith, J. Felix Jallilott, James P. Pullum and James M. Vance.

The Orlean B.B.C. organized in the 1880s. Formerly, the Pickwick nine, the Orleans team continued a local rivalry with the A. J. Dumonts. They attained notoriety in playing the Howards, a professional white nine visiting the city. *New York Clipper* (March 20, 1880): "About 2500 people assembled at the ball park in the above-named city on March 4 to witness the game between the Howards and the Orleans, the latter nine being selected from two crack colored clubs. The Orleans played pretty well, but were a little nervous, it being the first game that any colored club had ever played in New Orleans against white brethren. The crowd, comprised mostly of colored people, was very enthusiastic. Their pitcher (a white boy), has always been considered a good local pitcher, but the heavy batters of the Howards were a little too much for him." The white boy was an Octoroon, James Duncan Kennedy; Kennedy was a famed hurler who pitched for several colored clubs in the 1870 and 1880s. In 1883, the Orleans club again became the Pickwicks.

SOURCES: "No Title [Advertisement]," *New Orleans (LA) Times-Picayune*, Mar 3, 1880; "Base Ball," *New Orleans (LA) Times-Democrat*, Mar 6, 1880; *Weekly Louisianan*, March 13, 1880; "The Game in New Orleans," *New York (NY) Clipper*, Mar 20, 1880; "Sports and Pastimes," *Washington (DC) Sunday Herald*, Apr 18, 1880; "Short Stops," *New Orleans (LA) Times-Democrat*, May 26, 1884; "Items of Local Interest," *New Orleans Times-Picayune*, Oct 9, 1884; "Items of Local Interest," *New Orleans Times-Picayune*, Oct 9, 1884; "Other Plays and Players," *New Orleans Times-Picayune*, Nov 9, 1884.

P. B. S. Pinchback Orlean Base Ball Club (New Orleans, LA; 1880s). Organizer(s): Walter L. Cohen and James M. Vance.

The P. B. S. Pinchback B.B.C. (**Fig. 32**) organized in the 1880s, played black and white teams. The Galveston, TX Flyaways traveled to LA, where they played the Pinchbacks. *New Orleans Picayune* (July 15, 1888): "About 500 people witnessed the Galvestons defeat the Pinchbacks yesterday by a score of 10 to 3. Battery for the Galvestons, Runnels and Walker." Later that summer, the Pinchbacks went North to play the top black teams. A three-game series had been scheduled with the Chicago Unions. In the opener, the Unions defeated the Pinchbacks, 4–1. In the second game, Cohen's club won 6–5. They also went to St. Louis. *St. Louis Globe-Democrat* (August 24, 1888):

Figure 32. Pinckney Benton Stewart Pinchback, ca. 1870s. Pinchback was a Union Army officer (Corps d'Afrique and Second Louisiana Native Guard/74th U.S. Colored Infantry), publisher of the *Weekly Louisianian*, and the first black governor in the United States. During the Reconstruction era, he mentored Walter Lewis Cohen, a young politician and baseballist. In 1887, Cohen named the Pinchback team in his honor. During his residency in St. Louis, Pinchback boarded at the home of the young pitcher George Hopkins, whom he lured to New Orleans.

"The New Orleans, backed by the colored ex-senator, Pinchback, of New Orleans, made their first appearance at Sportsman's Park yesterday, and defeated the West Ends, of St. Louis, the champion local club. The Pinchbacks showed themselves to be a very clever team and outplayed the West Ends at every point. The battery work of Hopkins and Josephs was the best feature of the Pinchbacks. For the West Ends, Bracey, Jones, and pitcher Garig carried off the honors." The third contest was never played.

SOURCES: "The City," *New Orleans (LA) Weekly Pelican*, Oct 1, 1887; "Around Home Bases," *New Orleans (LA) Times-Picayune*, Jul 15, 1888; "Minor Games," *Chicago (IL) Inter-Ocean*, Aug 23, 1888; "Minor Games," *Chicago Inter-Ocean*, Aug 24, 1888; "Minor Games," *Chicago (IL) Times*, Aug 25, 1888; "The Great Coon Game," *St. Louis (MO) Republic*, Aug 24, 1888; "For the Colored Championship," *St. Louis (MO) Globe-Democrat*, Aug 25, 1888; "New Orleans, 6; *St. Louis*, 1," *St. Louis Globe-Democrat*, Aug 26, 1888; "Pinchbacks Won Again," *St. Louis Republic*, Aug 27, 1888; "A Great Game," *St. Louis Republic*, Aug 29, 1888; "Pinchbacks and New Orleans Clubs To-Morrow," *New Orleans (LA) Picayune*, Jul 6, 1889; "Baseball," *New Orleans Picayune*, Jul 7, 1889; Baseball," *New Orleans Picayune*, Jul 8, 1889; "Pinchbacks, 17; Resolutes, 11," *New Orleans (LA) Tribune*, Aug 29, 1889; "Downed by New Orleans Men," *New Orleans Picayune*, Aug 30, 1889.

Pickwick Base Ball Club (New Orleans, LA; 1870s–1880s). Organizer(s): William A. Halston, George Walker, Henry S. Baptiste, M. J. Simms; A. Roudez, James Cohen, Edward Cohen and Walter Lewis Cohen; William Wilson.

The Pickwick B.B.C. organized in 1876, with the following officers: President, Edward M. Cohen; Vice President, Joe Johnson; Secretary, O.F. Boisseau; Assistant Secretary, Stephen Ternoir; Treasurer, Richard Nixon and sixteen-year-old captain, Walter L. Cohen. The Pickwicks competed for the local championship. *Weekly Louisianian* (October 6, 1877): "In the contested game of base-ball between the Pickwicks and Athletics at the Fair Grounds last week, the former carried away the laurels." A rivalry also developed with the Excelsiors. *New Orleans Times-Picayune* (March 31, 1878): "Ogden Park will be enlivened today by a game between those crack organizations, the Pickwicks and Excelsior Reds, of the Second District." *Abbeville Meridional* (July 26, 1879): "A match game of ball was played on the Burnside Grounds Saturday afternoon by the Pickwick and Excelsior clubs of New Orleans. The game was a very interesting one and attracted quite a crowd of spectators. Following is the score: Excelsior 19, Pickwick 3." Under Walter Lewis Cohen's leadership, the Pickwicks emerged as a dominant force. Between 1880 and 1881, they helped to organize and participate in LA's Union Colored Base Ball League. In 1880, the Pickwicks and Excelsiors consolidated to become Orleans club. They played the C. T. Howards nine, a professional white organization. *Weekly Louisianan* (March 30, 1880): "The Howards played the Orleans Base Ball Club recently. It was the first time colored and white clubs played together. Now that the ice now has been broken, we expect the Lee and other crack clubs will cross bats with their dark-hued brethren." The Pickwicks organized a local Colored League. *New Orleans Item* (April 19, 1881): "A league has been formed by our local colored clubs embracing the Pickwicks, Bostons, Aetnas, Dumonts and one other club. Their series opens on the first of May with the Pickwicks and Dumonts. In an exhibition, yesterday at the Oakland, between the Bostons and Pickwicks, the latter were victorious by a score of 24 to 23. They played under the new rules of 1881." They also played white teams. When the Pickwicks played the Tom Brennans, the press seemed surprised by their physical appearance. *New Orleans Times-Picayune* (August 29, 1881): "The Pickwicks are composed of young colored men, all of whom have bright skins, and several are so fair that they would pass for white." That same year, Bud Fowler (John W. Jackson) joined the Pickwicks. In 1882, the Pickwicks became the Orleans Club. In 1887, Cohen reorganized the Pickwicks. *New Orleans Weekly Pelican* (May 21, 1887): "The Eclipse Base Ball Club (a white club) will play the Pickwicks tomorrow (Sunday) at New Orleans Park for a purse of $100 and all the gate receipts. A large crowd will no doubt be in attendance as this will be the first appearance of the Eclipse Club."

SOURCES: "Society as Seen by Warick," *New Orleans (LA) Weekly Louisianian*, Sep 12, 1874; *New Orleans (LA) Times-Picayune*, Feb 2, 1876; "The Pickwicks," *New Orleans (LA) Republican*, Sep 3, 1876; "City Gossip," *New Orleans Times-Picayune*, Sep 25, 1876; "Base Ball," *New Orleans Times-Picayune*, Aug 28, 1877; "Base Ball in Colors," *New Orleans (LA) Times*, Sep 4, 1877; "Base Ball," *New Orleans Times-Picayune*, Sep 16, 1877; "Local Brevities," *New Orleans Times*. October. 5, 1877; "Local," *New Orleans Weekly Louisianian*, Oct 6, 1877; "Round About Town," *New Orleans Times*, Oct 15, 1877; "Persons and Things," *New Orleans Weekly Louisianian*, Aug 28, 1875; "Base Ball," *New Orleans Times*, Feb 10, 1878; "Base Ball," *New Orleans Times-Picayune*, Mar 31, 1878; "Local Brevities," *New Orleans Times*, Apr 7, 1878; "Local Sporting Notes," *New Orleans Times*, Aug 18, 1878; "Base Ball," *New Orleans (LA) Times-Democrat*, May 26, 1879; *Abbeville (LA) Meridional*, Jul 26, 1879; "Base Ball," *New Orleans*

(LA) Times-Democrat, Aug 20, 1879; "No Title [Advertisement]," *New Orleans Daily Picayune*, Mar 3, 1880; "Base Ball," *New Orleans (LA) Times-Democrat*, Mar 6, 1880; *New Orleans Weekly Louisianan*, Mar 13, 1880; *New Orleans (LA) Weekly Pelican*, Mar 30, 1880; "The Game in New Orleans," *New York (NY) Clipper*, Mar 20, 1880; "Sports and Pastimes," *Washington (DC) Sunday Herald*, Apr 18, 1880; "Short Stops," *New Orleans (LA) Item*, Apr 19, 1881; "The Colored Clubs at Oakland Park," *New Orleans Times-Picayune*, Aug 15, 1881; "A Pickwickian Championship," *New Orleans Times-Picayune*, Aug 29, 1881; "Base Ball," *New Orleans Times-Picayune*, Sep 16, 1882; "Base Ball," *New Orleans Picayune*, May 18, 1884; "Dots from Local Diamonds," *New Orleans Picayune*, May 23, 1884; "Items of Local Interest," *New Orleans Picayune*, Oct 12, 1884; "Items of Local Interest," *New Orleans Picayune*, Oct 21, 1884; "Dots from Local Diamonds," *New Orleans Picayune*, Oct 26, 1884; "Items of Local Interest," *New Orleans Picayune*, Oct 9, 1884; "Base Ball," *New Orleans Picayune*, Mar 26, 1887; "Sporting Notes," *New Orleans Times-Democrat*, Mar 6, 1887; "Rakings," *New Orleans (LA) Weekly Pelican*, Apr 16, 1887; "Sporting Notes," *New Orleans Times-Democrat*, Apr 24, 1887; "Notes," *New Orleans Times-Democrat*, Apr 25, 1887; "Ball Notes," *New Orleans Times-Democrat*, May 4, 1887; "Base Ball," *New Orleans Times-Democrat*, May 8, 1887; *New Orleans Weekly Pelican*, May 21, 1887; "A Colored Victory," *New Orleans Times-Democrat*, May 23, 1887; "Rakings," *New Orleans Weekly Pelican*, Jul 16, 1887; "Around Various Bases," *New Orleans Picayune*, Jul 18, 1887.

R. E. Foreman Base Ball Club (New Orleans, LA; 1880s)

The R. E. Foreman B.B.C. organized in the 1880s, played black nines. *New Orleans Weekly Republican* (May 28, 1887): "The game last Sunday at the First Street Field between the R. E. Foreman and Camelia Base Ball Clubs was a fine one and was won by the Foremans by a score of 29 to 10. Mr. A. A. The Foremans are anxious to meet any club in the city." Following a challenge from the Foreman club, the F. A. Johnson nine agreed to play them. *Weekly Pelican* (June 11, 1887): "The Johnson Base Ball Club defeated the Foreman's club last Sunday at First Field. William Perry and Theo Harris distinguished themselves by their playing."

SOURCES: "Rakings," *New Orleans (LA) Weekly Pelican*, May 21, 1887; "Rakings," *New Orleans Weekly Pelican*, May 28, 1887; "The R. A. Foreman Base Ball Club," *New Orleans Weekly Pelican*, Sep 24, 1887.

Rose Bud Base Ball Club (New Orleans, LA; 1870s). Organizer(s): George M. Kenner, William Roxborough, P. N. Pinchback, Uncas Wilson, H. S. Baxter, Alexander Bailey and Joseph Wilkins.

The Rose Bud B.B.C. organized in the 1870s, played against black organizations. *New Orleans Times-Democrat* (January 22, 1876): "The Pickwicks and Rose Buds will play a game of baseball, near Fillmore Square, Sunday morning at 9 0'clock, for a keg of doughnuts."

SOURCES: "Local Brevities," *New Orleans (LA) Times-Democrat*, Jan 22, 1876; "Election of Officers," *New Orleans (LA) Republican*, Feb 11, 1876.

Straight University Base Ball Club (New Orleans, LA; 1880s)

The Straight University B.B.C. organized in the 1880s, played black teams. *New Orleans Weekly Pelican* (April 30, 1887): "Last Saturday the New Orleans Base Ball Park was crowded by the teachers, students and friends of Straight and Southern Universities to witness the contest between the base-ball nines of the respective universities. The game was a one-sided affair after the third inning. Straight University out-batted, out-fielded and outplayed their opponents in every way as the score will show. The attendance was large and intense. Straight University evidently had the call, so far as the sympathy and

applause were concerned. This helped the Straight nine and had a depressing effect on the Southern team. It is to be hoped that such friendly contests will be repeated, for we feel quite sure it will meet with popular favor, while the healthy exercise incident to this manly American game cannot fail to be of benefit to the ball tossers."

SOURCES: "Rakings," *New Orleans (LA) Weekly Pelican*, Apr 9, 1887; "Southern vs. Straight," *New Orleans Weekly Pelican*, Apr 30, 1887.

Union Base Ball Club (New Orleans, LA; 1870s–1880s). Organizer(s): Tom Walker, Isaac Walker and Joseph Mitchell; M. C. Oliver, M. Kellum and A. Walba; Benjamin Rice; R. B. Johnson, Joseph Mitchell, T. S. Butler and Lawrence Scott.

The Union B.B.C. organized in the 1870s. Captained by Joseph Mitchell, the Unions were an attaché of the Protective Union Benevolent Association. *New Orleans Republican* (August 1, 1875): "This club of colored base-ball players played with the Athletic Base Ball Club of this city at the Fair Grounds, and won by a score of 18 to 12." *New Orleans Times-Picayune* (August 1, 1875): "The Union Base Ball Club, of this city, (colored) offer to play any colored club for twenty-five dollars to a hundred. This colored club has thus far captured all the colored clubs in the State." *New Orleans Times-Picayune* (May 31, 1876): "At the Coral Vine Social Club Centennial picnic, the Union Base Ball Club defeated the Athletic Club by a score of 5 to 2." By 1877, the Unions, Pickwicks, Bostons, and Athletics were competing for the local championship. For over a decade, the Union organization put a strong nine in the field. *Times-Picayune*: "The colored clubs had the crowd yesterday. 2000 people saw the game between the Eclipse, of St. Louis and the local Unions. The Unions lost through loose playing in the field. The battery work of the visitors was again of a high order, and the catcher's throwing superb. The sensation of the game was Sullivan's home run which brought in two men and set the crowd wild." In 1886, Unions participated in the Southern League of Colored Base-Ballists. The organization continued to play into the late 1880s.

SOURCES: "Odd Fellows' Aid Association," *New Orleans (LA) Times-Picayune*, Jul 28, 1875; "The Union Base Ball Club," *New Orleans (LA) Republican*, Aug 1, 1875; "Jets," *New Orleans Times-Picayune*, Aug 1, 1875; "Flag Presentation," *New Orleans Republican*, Sep 1, 1875; *New Orleans (LA) Weekly Louisianian*, Sep 4, 1875; "City Gossip," *New Orleans Times-Picayune*, May 31, 1876; "Brief Mention," *New Orleans Republican*, Jun 10, 1876; "Base Ball," *New Orleans Times-Picayune*, Apr 30, 1877; "Base Ball," *New Orleans (LA) Times*, Oct 4, 1877; "Base Ball," *New Orleans Times*, Feb 10, 1878; Base Ball," *New Orleans (LA) Times-Democrat*, Mar 19, 1882; "Dots From Local Diamonds," *New Orleans Times-Picayune*, May 23, 1884; "Base Ball," *New Orleans Times-Picayune*, Aug 9, 1885; "The Colored Clubs," *New Orleans Times-Picayune*, Aug 30, 1885; "Base Ball," *New Orleans Daily Picayune*, Aug 31, 1885; "Called Balls," *New Orleans Times-Picayune*, Oct 19, 1885; "Base Ball," *New Orleans Times-Democrat*, Nov 10, 1885; "Base Ball," *New Orleans Democrat*, Apr 13, 1886; "The Colored Players," *New Orleans Times-Democrat*, Sep 16, 1886; "The Colored Championship," *New Orleans Times-Picayune*, Oct 11, 1886; "Rakings," *New Orleans (LA) Weekly Pelican*, Apr 16, 1887; "Rakings," *New Orleans Weekly Pelican*, Apr 23, 1887; "Around Various Bases," *New Orleans Times-Picayune*, May 8, 1887; "Rakings," *New Orleans Weekly Pelican*, Jul 16, 1887; "Around Various Bases," *New Orleans Times-Picayune*, Jul 17, 1887; "The Colored Clubs," *New Orleans Times-Picayune*, Oct 24, 1888; "The Colored Clubs," *New Orleans Times-Picayune*, Oct 26, 1888; "Base Ball," *New Orleans Times-Picayune*, Oct 28, 1888; "The Two Champions Meet To-Morrow," *New Orleans Weekly Pelican*, May 11, 1889; "Pinchbacks and Unions," *New Orleans Times-Picayune*, Jul 21, 1889; "Pinchbacks and Unions Tomorrow,"

New Orleans Weekly Pelican, Jun 22, 1889; "Notes About Town," *New Orleans Weekly Pelican*, Jun 27, 1889; "Notes About Town," *New Orleans Weekly Pelican*, Jun 29, 1889; "Baseball," *New Orleans Times-Picayune*, Jul 20, 1889.

Union Colored Base Ball League (New Orleans, LA; 1880s).

Organizer(s): Walter Lewis Cohen, H. E. De Fuentes, Joseph Fabacher and James. P. Pullum.

The Union Colored Base Ball League organized in the 1880s. The Bostons, Aetnas, A. J. Dumonts, Unions, Pickwicks, Marones and Pacifics belonged to the league. *New Orleans Item* (July 7, 1881): "The Colored League have received a handsome purple flag, made in Cincinnati, which will be awarded to the champion club.... The flag is trimmed with gold fringe, and Champion Union League painted on one of the sides. It is really a beautiful piece of work. The Pickwicks expect to fly this flay as the champion club."

SOURCES: "Base Ball," *New York (NY) Clipper*, Jun 18, 1881; "Short Stops," *New Orleans (LA) Item*, Jul 7, 1881; "Base Ball," *New Orleans (LA) Times-Picayune*, Jul 30, 1881; "Short Stops," *New Orleans Item*, Oct 26, 1881; "Colored Players of New Orleans," *New York Clipper*, May 6, 1882.

Isaac Base Ball Club (Port Barrow, LA; 1880s)

The Isaac B.B.C., of New Orleans, LA, organized in the 1880s, competed with the Duffel, Walker, and Larock clubs. *Donaldsonville Chief* (October 24, 1885): "The Isaacs of Port Barrow and the Larocks of Donaldsonville, colored clubs, played an interesting game at Cleveland Park last Sunday, which the Isaacs readily won by a score of 17 to 11. The Isaacs are exceedingly anxious to get a game with one of the white clubs, either the Fortiers or Lees."

SOURCES: *Donaldsonville (LA) Chief*, Mar 28, 1885; "Base Ball," *Donaldsonville Chief*, Aug 15, 1885; "Base Ball," *Donaldsonville Chief*, Aug 22, 1885; "Base Ball Challenge," *Donaldsonville Chief*, Oct 17, 1885; "Base Ball," *Donaldsonville Chief*, Oct 10, 1885; "Base Ball," *Donaldsonville Chief*, Oct 24, 1885.

W. J. Neams Base Ball Club (Port Barrow, LA; 1880s). Organizer(s): J. W. Jones and Alfred Williams.

The W. J. Neams B.B.C., of New Orleans, LA, organized in the 1880s. The W. J. Neams played black nines. *Donaldsonville Chief* (May 8, 1886): "A number of young colored men of Port Barrow and vicinity, formerly the Isaacs Club, have organized the W. J. Neams Base Ball Club and we propose to challenge all of the colored clubs of Ascension or adjacent parishes to try conclusions with them on the diamond field during the season. J. W. Jones is president and captain of the club and Alfred Williams is secretary." *Chief* (August 7, 1886): "The Wilsons and Kellys, clubs of young colored men of Donaldsonville, played a game of 5 to 9, in favor of the latter, on Monday. The Wilsons play the Neams, of Port Barrow, next Sunday, for purse of $20."

SOURCES: "Local Jottings," *Donaldsonville (LA) Chief*, Apr 3, 1886; "Base Ball," *Donaldsonville Chief*, May 8, 1886; "Base Ball," *Donaldsonville Chief*, Aug 7, 1886.

Bennett Base Ball Club (Shreveport, LA; 1880s). Organizer(s): R. Bennett.

The Bennett B.B.C. organized in the 1880s, played black teams. *Shreveport Times* (June 20, 1889): "A match game of base-ball will be played at Lakeside Park this evening at 4 o'clock between the Walkers and Bennetts, colored clubs. The Walkers have imported a battery from New Orleans." *Times* (August 25, 1889): "Two games will be played at Lakeside Park today between colored clubs. The first will take place between the Bennetts, of Shreveport, and the Donaldsonvilles."

SOURCES: "Base Ball," *Shreveport (LA) Times*, Jun 20, 1889; "Base Ball," *Shreveport Times*, Jul 7, 1889; "Base Ball," *Shreveport Times*, Jul 9, 1889; "Base Ball," *Shreveport Times*, Jul 24, 1889; "Base Ball," *Shreveport (LA) Times*, Aug 4, 1889; "Walkers and Bennetts," *Shreveport Times*, Aug 16, 1889; "Base Ball," *Shreveport Times*, Aug 25, 1889.

True Blues Base Ball Club (Shreveport, LA; 1890s)

The True Blues B.B.C., of New Orleans, LA, organized in the 1890s, played black aggregations. *Shreveport Times* (April 24, 1895): "A colored team from Shreveport is playing Marshall. The first game, Monday, which was a pretty one, resulted in a victory for Shreveport by a score of 16 to 9. The second game was played yesterday. Battery for Marshall: Johnson and Nixon; Shreveport: Fox and Alexander." *Times* (April 25, 1895): The Shreveport Blues and Marshall Heavy Weights, colored clubs, played their second game Tuesday with a score of 14 to 12 in favor of Shreveport." *Little Rock Gazette* (August 29, 1897): "There will be a game of baseball at the West End Park Tuesday, August 31, between the Shreveport club and the Quapaws of Little Rock. Battery for Shreveport, Rogers and Williams; for Little Rock, Keaton and Crawford."

SOURCES: "Base Ball Excursion," *Marshall (TX) Messenger*, Jul 22, 1893; "Shreveport Won," *Marshall Messenger*, Apr 23, 1893; "Base Ball at Marshall," *Shreveport (LA) Times*, May 20, 1894; "Marshall Defeated," *Shreveport Times*, May 22, 1894; "Base Ball," *Shreveport Times*, Jun 5, 1894; "Base Ball at Marshall," *Shreveport Times*, Apr 24, 1895; "Shreveport vs. Marshall," *Shreveport Times*, Apr 25, 1895; "Base Ball," *Shreveport Times*, Jul 17, 1897; "A Rooter's View," *Shreveport Times*, Aug 25, 1897; "Down They Went," *Shreveport Times*, Aug 26, 1897; "Quapaws vs. Shreveport," *Little Rock (AR) Gazette*, Aug 29, 1897.

Hudson Base Ball Club (Shreveport, LA; 1880s). Organizer(s): A. A. Hudson.

The Hudson B.B.C. organized in the 1880s, played black teams of LA, MS, and TX. They developed a local rivalry with the Sunset club. *New Orleans Weekly Pelican* (July 2, 1887): "The Hudson and Sunset Base Ball Clubs played a game Sunday. The Hudsons were victorious." *Weekly Pelican* (September 17, 1887): "The Hudson Base Ball Club, under the management of Mr. A. A. Hudson, will cross bats with the Monroe's on July 9th, at the Fair Grounds in Shreveport; and on the 15th with the Vicksburg's in Vicksburg. The Hudson's will be glad to hear from North or South Louisiana." In 1888, the team reorganized and traveled to TX. *Dallas Morning News* (June 21, 1888): "The second game between the Dallas Blues and Shreveport Hudsons, colored baseball teams, came off yesterday afternoon at Oak Cliff Park. The game was a better one on both sides yesterday than the day before, especially on the part of the Shreveport team. They played with more verve and succeeded in keeping down the score of the Dallas Blues and increasing their own although they were beaten."

SOURCES: "Shreveport Sparks," *New Orleans (LA) Weekly Pelican*, Jul 2, 1887; "Shreveport, LA.," *New Orleans Weekly Pelican*, Sep 17, 1887; "Base Ball," *Shreveport (LA) Times*, May 27, 1888; "Colored Clubs," *Galveston (TX) Daily News*, Jun 17, 1888; "Challenge Accepted," *Dallas (TX) Morning News*, Jun 17, 1888; "Colored Base Ball Game," *Dallas Morning News*, Jun 19, 1888; "Colored Clubs," *Dallas Daily News*, Jun 21, 1888; "Dallas 13, Shreveport 6," *Dallas Daily News*, Jun 21, 1888; "Base Ball," *Shreveport Times*, Jun 24, 1888.

Robert E. Lee Base Ball Club (Shreveport, LA; 1880s)

The Robert E. Lee B.B.C. organized in the 1880s, played black nines. During a tour of Northern LA, Vicksburg's F. O'Neil club met its Shreveport, LA rival. *Dallas Morning News* (July 2, 1886): "In a game of base-ball at the Fair Grounds the R. E. Lees, of Shreveport, and the Vicksburgs, of Vicksburg, Mississippi, both colored clubs, the Shreveport club won by a score of 8 to 4." *Times* (August 4, 1889): "The Walkers and Lees, colored, will play at Lakeside Park this evening at 4 o'clock."

SOURCES: "Senegambian Sluggers at Shreveport," *Dallas (TX) Morning News*, Jul 2, 1886; "Base Ball," *Shreveport (LA) Times*, Aug 4, 1889.

Walker Base Ball Club (Shreveport, LA; 1880s)

The Walker B.B.C., of Marshall, TX, organized in the 1890s, played black teams. *Shreveport Times* (July 14, 1889): "The Walkers, of Shreveport and the Jeffersons, of Jefferson, Texas, two strong colored clubs, will play three games—this evening, Monday, and Tuesday—at Lakeside Park, beginning at 4 o'clock each day." *Times* (August 20, 1889): "The Walkers, of Shreveport, and the Blues, of Baton Rouge, will play a game at the fairgrounds beginning today at 10 o'clock. These two teams are very strong. Great sport is promised. The cars will run to the fairgrounds." *Times* (August 27, 1889): "The games played between the Walkers, of Shreveport, and Prides, of Marshall, (colored clubs), resulted: Sunday—Walkers 12, Marshall, 10; Monday—Marshall 12, Walkers 6."

SOURCES: "Base Ball," *Shreveport (LA) Times*, Jun 18, 1889; "Base Ball," *Shreveport Times*, Jun 20, 1889; "Base Ball," *Shreveport Times*, Jul 14, 1889; "Base Ball," *Shreveport Times*, Jul 16, 1889; "Base Ball," *Shreveport (LA) Times*, Aug 4, 1889; *Shreveport (LA) Times*, Aug 16, 1889; "The Colored Champions," *Shreveport Times*, Aug 20, 1889; "Base Ball," *Shreveport Times*, Aug 21, 1889; "Base Ball," *Shreveport Times*, Aug 27, 1889; "Base Ball," *Shreveport Times*, Sep 1, 1889.

Maine

Rochester Base Ball Club (Portland, ME; 1870s)

The Rochester B.B.C., of Boston, MA, organized in 1871. *Portland Daily Press* (August 18, 1871): "The Rochester Base Ball Club (colored), present champions of the Bay State, have accepted the challenge of the Resolutes of this city and play them August 22nd."

SOURCES: "Brief Jottings," *Portland (ME) Daily Press*, Aug 18, 1871.

Maryland

Clifton Base Ball Club (Annapolis, MD; 1890s)

The Clifton B.B.C. organized in the 1890s, played black teams. *Washington Bee* (January 30, 1897): "The Clifton Base Ball Club, of Annapolis, organized a few days ago with the following young men who have won a wide reputation in baseball circles: H. E. Spriggs, catcher, has a reputation that is hard to beat behind the bat; J. Stepney is the famous Blue Mountain twirler of in and out curves, down and up shoots; J. Pomter is the phenomenal first base; W. Addison, the igniting second base; H. Hill is the man that stops you short; J. C. Darnell is the stuck last on third base; J. Miller, the great left fielder, and George Collins knows his business in the centerfield and pockets everything that comes his way; Thomas Gray makes them sick ion the right field; and all these fellows are hard hitters and makes these youngsters turn green when they man the stick. Wallace Parker, that man of a few words is manager; Samuel Davage, the quick-eyed man on Calvert Street, is captain. This crew means business and has made up their minds to whip the first team that comes in sight. Luck to you boys, watch that green-eyed monster."

SOURCES: "Annapolis Notes," *Washington (DC) Bee*, Jan 30, 1897.

Atlantic Base Ball Club (Baltimore, MD; 1870s–1880s)

The Atlantic B.B.C. organized in the 1870s, played black teams. *Baltimore American and Commercial Advertiser* (July 4, 1874): "At ten o'clock a very entertaining game will commence between the Oriental and Atlantic colored clubs, which promises much sport. Both nines are heavy batters, and run like thoroughbreds, and a full twenty-five cents of fun may be expected." *American and Commercial Advertiser* (July 6, 1874): "About one thousand persons attended the morning game at the Newton Grounds on the Fourth to witness the contest between two crack colored clubs—the Orientals and Atlantics—and those who expected to see hard-hitting and much 'muffing' were disappointed as the ball turned out to be a very dead one, and the fielding of the two nines were brought into requisition, and compared favorably with that displayed at many professional games played during the season." In 1884, they joined a Colored League; it included clubs from Baltimore [Mutuals and Haymakers], Harrisburg [Olympics], Pottsville, WA and several other cities [Carlisle, PA and Hagerstown, MD]. *Baltimore Herald* (July 5, 1884): "The Atlantics, a colored baseball club of Baltimore, went to Chambersburg, Pennsylvania yesterday and defeated the Alerts of that city by a score of 9 to 1." *Baltimore Sun* (August 19, 1884): "The Atlantics, colored, of Baltimore, and the Mutuals, colored, of Philadelphia, played a game yesterday at the Monumental Base Ball Park, resulting in a score of 17 to 14 in favor of the home team. The Atlantics made ten errors and the Mutuals 18. In base hits the Mutuals had the advantage, making 15 to the Atlantics 9." The Atlantics again played the Mutuals. *Baltimore Sun* (August 21, 1884): "The Atlantics, colored, of Baltimore, and the Mutuals, colored, of Philadelphia, played a game yesterday at the Monumental Base Ball Park, resulting in a score of 17 to 14 in favor of the home team. The Atlantics made ten errors and the Mutuals 18. In base hits the Mutuals had the advantage, making 15 to the Atlantics 9."

SOURCES: "Base Ball," *Baltimore (MD) Sun*, Jul 2, 1874; "Base Ball," *Baltimore Sun*, Jul 4, 1874; "Base Ball Notes," *Baltimore (MD) American and Commercial Advertiser*, Jul 4, 1874; "Base Ball Playing on the Fourth," *Baltimore (MD) Sun*, Jul 6, 1874; "The Colored Ball Tossers," *Baltimore American and Commercial Advertiser*, Jul 6, 1874; "Notes," *Baltimore American and Commercial Advertiser*, Jul 30, 1874; "Base Ball Yesterday," *Baltimore Sun*, Jul 30, 1874; "Colored Boys at the Bat," *Baltimore Sun*, Aug 7, 1874; "Local Briefs," *Baltimore Sun*, Jun 24, 1875; "Base Ball," *Baltimore Sun*, Jul 15, 1875; "Base Ball," *Baltimore Sun*, Sep 15, 1875; "Base Ball," *Baltimore Sun*, Jul 17, 1883; "One More Game Lost," *Baltimore American and Commercial Advertiser*, Jul 27, 1883; "Local Liners," *Fort Wayne (IN) Daily News*, Jan 11, 1884; "Games Elsewhere," *Baltimore Sun*, Apr 28, 1884; "The National Game," *Baltimore Sun*, Jun 24, 1884; "Base Ball Notes," *Baltimore (MD) Herald*, Jun 24, 1884; "Base Ball Notes," *Baltimore Herald, Jul 5, 1884; "Games Elsewhere," *Baltimore Sun*, Jul 19, 1884; "Base Ball Notes," *Baltimore Herald*, Aug 5, 1884; "Local Games Yesterday," *Baltimore Sun*, Aug 19, 1884; "A Stranded Base Ball Nine," *Baltimore Sun*, Aug 21, 1884; "Base Ball Players in Hard Luck," *Baltimore Herald*, Aug 21, 1884; "Base Ball Notes," *Baltimore Herald, Aug 22, 1884; "The National Games," *Baltimore Sun*, Sep 16, 1884; "Other Games," *Baltimore Sun*, Sep 24, 1884; "Colored Clubs at Union Park," *Baltimore (MD) American*, Apr 28, 1885; "Base Ball," *Baltimore Sun, Apr 28, 1885; "Base Ball Matters," *Frederick (MD) News*, Aug 25, 1885; "Local Games," *Baltimore Sun*, Jul 14, 1886.

Biddle Rangers Base Ball Club (Baltimore, MD; 1870s)

The Biddle Rangers B.B.C. organized in the 1870s, played against black teams. *Cincinnati Times* (July 6, 1874): "The Biddle Alley Rangers and the Sarah Ann Larks, two base-ball organizations, the members of which are colored youths, met upon the diamond field, Madison Avenue extended, yesterday afternoon, and enjoyed a most extraordinary game of base-ball. The members of both nines were dressed in white tights and loose fitting knit shirts. The Rangers had their muscular calves encased in blue stockings, and their heads covered with caps of rainbow colors, while their yarns sports army brogans heavily spiked. The Larks sported blue and white stockings, white caps with variegated stars in the center and shoes similar to those worn by the Rangers. Fully two-thousand colored persons, many of whom were damsels, witnessed the game, and when Clarkson, opened the game with a hot ball to left field, and made a home run, the yells of the excited Sarah Anners could be heard full a half mile away. For three hours and a half did the game thus progress, and at the conclusion of the ninth inning the score stood: Rangers, 75; Larks, 163; majority for the Larks, 88."

SOURCES: "Base Ball Delusion," *Cincinnati (OH) Times,* Jul 6, 1874; "Sloshin' the Ball," *Quincy (IL) Whig,* Jul 9, 1874.

Blues Base Ball Club (Baltimore, MD; 1890s). Organizer(s): Walter Williams.

The Blues B.B.C. organized in the 1890s, played black and white teams. *Baltimore American* (April 3, 1898): "The Baltimore Blues Baseball Club (colored) have organized, and are prepared to play any team after their return from a southern trip. Their pitcher is J. C. Feggans of the Gorham Club, of New York." *American* (September 11, 1898): "The Baltimore Blues and the Black Americans played two games at Oehm Park Thursday. The scores were as follows: First game: Blues, 16; Black Americans, 8. Second game—Black Americans, 5; Blues, 4. The Baltimore Blues and the Douglass team, of Annapolis, will play tomorrow at Oehm Park." The Blues traveled to NC, where they played the Charlotte Quicksteps.

SOURCES: "The Giants Name Dates," *Charlotte (NC) Observer,* Mar 29, 1898; "Local Amateur Sports," *Baltimore (MD) American,* Apr 3, 1898; "Colored Ball," *Charlotte Observer,* Apr 7, 1898; "Amateur Sporting Notes," *Baltimore American,* Apr 10, 1898; "Base Ball Today," *Charlotte Observer,* May 11, 1898; "The Fort Stormed," *Charlotte Observer,* May 13, 1898; "About the Burg," *Charlotte Observer,* May 14, 1898; "Amateur Base Ball," *Baltimore American,* Sep 1, 1898; "Amateur Ball Games," *Baltimore American,* Sep 11, 1898.

Colored Giants Base Ball Club (Baltimore, MD; 1890s–1900s). Organizer(s): William T. Jordan.

The Colored Giants B.B.C. organized in the 1890s, played black and white teams. *Frederick News* (August 9, 1900): "An interesting and exciting game of ball was played at Athletic Park yesterday afternoon between the Maryland Trotters and the Baltimore Club which resulted in a victory for the Baltimore Club by a score of 10 to 6. Brown and Evans did good battery work for the visitors. A good crowd witnessed the contest." *Baltimore Sun* (September 3, 1900): "At Union Park yesterday the Baltimore Giants (colored) outplayed the Yanigans by 3 runs to 1. The Giants fielded well, and their pitcher, Duvall, struck out 12 men. Reynolds, of the Giants, made a great catch, and Washington threw from deep centerfield to home plate, catching Brown." They developed a rivalry with Frederick's Maryland Trotters club.

SOURCES: "Among the Amateurs," *Baltimore (MD) American,* Apr 6, 1898; "Southern Champions," *Philadelphia (PA) Sporting Life,* Feb 11, 1899; "News and Comment," *Philadelphia Sporting Life,* Mar 4, 1899; "News and Comment," *Philadelphia Sporting Life,* Apr 3, 1899; "A Very Exciting Game," *Norfolk (VA) Virginia-Pilot,* Apr 6, 1899; "Some News," *Springfield (MA) Republican,* Apr 12, 1899; "Newark Defeats Colored Team," *Paterson (NJ) Call,* Apr 13, 1899; "Patersons vs. Baltimores," *Paterson (NJ) Call,* Apr 15, 1899; "News and Comment," *Philadelphia Sporting Life,* Apr 8, 1899; "Emancipation Day," *Frederick (MD) News,* Aug 9, 1900; "Great Game at Union Park," *Baltimore American,* Aug 21, 1900; "Combination, 6; Giants, 6," *Baltimore*

(MD) Sun, Aug 28, 1900; "Labor Day Baseball," *Baltimore American,* Aug 29, 1900; "Yanigans and Colored Giants," *Baltimore Sun,* Sep 3, 1900; "Baltimore Giants Lost Both," *Baltimore American,* Sep 4, 1900; "Baseball at Union Park," *Baltimore American,* Sep 9, 1900; "Colored Giants, 3; Yanigans, 1" *Baltimore Sun,* Sep 11, 1900.

Detroit Base Ball Club (Baltimore, MD; 1890s–1900s). Organizer(s): Walter Williams.

The Detroit B.B.C. organized in the 1890s, played black and white nines. *Baltimore American* (April 6, 1898): "The Detroit baseball Club, colored, has reorganized for the season of 1901, under the management of Walter Williams. It may be remembered that the Detroits made a great reputation for themselves in the season of 1897, 1898, and 1899. They were the famous colored team of this city, and had many rooters."

SOURCES: "Among the Amateurs," *Baltimore (MD) American,* Apr 6, 1898; "Colored Men as Ball Players," *Baltimore American,* Mar 31, 1901.

Enterprise Base Ball Club (Baltimore, MD; 1870s)

The Enterprise B.B.C. organized in 1870, played black teams. The Excelsiors were local rivals. *Baltimore American and Commercial Advertiser* (May 16, 1871): "The Excelsior (colored) Club of Baltimore think that they can fairly lay claim to the title of champion of the colored clubs of Maryland, and they are anxious to test it with any nine that will play them a game." The Enterprise reminded the sporting crowd of the previous season's contests. *American and Commercial Advertiser* (May 17, 1871): "The Excelsior Base Ball Club can hardly think that they can fairly lay claim to the title of champion of the colored clubs of Maryland when they were defeated twice last season by the same club—once to the tune of 9 to 40. But they are not satisfied they know very well *what has been done can be done again* by the Enterprise." In 1871, they defeated the Mutuals, of Washington, D.C., in a rain-suspended contest. *American and Commercial Advertiser* (May 16, 1871): "The Enterprise Base Ball Club, colored, of this city, visited Washington the 4th for the purpose of playing the Mutuals, off that city. The game began at 4 o'clock on the Olympic Grounds, but was stopped in the third inning by the rain, the score standing 9 to 2 in favor of the Enterprise." They dominated another local nine, the Alerts, who they played against on West Indies Emancipation Day. *American and Commercial Advertiser* (July 14, 1874): "A game of base-ball was played between the Enterprise and Alert Clubs. The Alert placed much confidence in their pitcher, and consequently were much surprised at the way the Enterprise handled his ball. On the part of the Enterprise, Spillman bids fair to become a crack player."

SOURCES: "Base Ball Matters," *Baltimore (MD) American and Commercial Advertiser,* May 16, 1871; "Base Ball," *Baltimore American,* May 17, 1871; "Enterprise vs. Mutuals," *Baltimore American,* Jul 6, 1871; "Local Matters," *Baltimore (MD) Sun,* Jul 6, 1871; "Base Ball," *Baltimore American,* Jul 27, 1871; "Base Ball," *Baltimore American,* Aug 3, 1871; "Enterprise vs. Orientals," *Baltimore American and Commercial Advertiser,* Jul 14, 1874.

Excelsior Base Ball Club (Baltimore, MD; 1870s)

The Excelsior B.B.C. organized in the 1870s. The "Excelsiors" played black nines of MD and WA DC; they developed a local rivalry with the Enterprise club. *Baltimore American and Commercial Advertiser* (May 17, 1871): "The Excelsior (colored) Club of Baltimore think that they can fairly lay claim to the title of champion of the colored clubs of Maryland, and they are anxious to test it with any nine that will play them a game." The Enterprise reminded the sporting crowd of the previous season's contests. *American and Commercial*

Advertiser (May 17, 1871): "The Excelsior Base Ball Club can hardly think that they can fairly lay claim to the title of champion of the colored clubs of Maryland when they were defeated twice last season by the same club—once to the tune of 9 to 40. But they are not satisfied they know very well *what has been done can be done again* by the Enterprise." They battled the Lord Hannibal B.B.C. *New York Clipper* (August 7, 1875): "On the 25th the Excelsior and Lord Hannibal colored nines were opposed to each other at Baltimore, Maryland, the latter winning by a count of 12 to 11." The colored club played against Philadelphia's colored teams. The Excelsiors played against WA's Monumental Club. *Washington National Republican* (September 4, 1873): "A match game was played between the Excelsior club, of Baltimore, and the Monumental, of this city. The score stood: Monumental, 27; Excelsior, 14." *Philadelphia Times* (August 31, 1875): "In Baltimore yesterday the Williams Club, of Philadelphia, defeated the Excelsior, of Baltimore, by 19 to 3. Both clubs are colored."

SOURCES: "Base Ball Matters," *Baltimore (MD) American and Commercial Advertiser*, May 16, 1871; "Base Ball," *Baltimore American*, May 17, 1871; "Excelsior vs. Monumental," *Washington (DC) National Republican*, Sep 3, 1873; "Excelsior vs. Monumental," *Washington National Republican*, Sep 4, 1873; "Notes," *Baltimore American and Commercial Advertiser*, Jul 30, 1874; "Fly Tips," *New York (NY) Clipper*, Aug 7, 1875; "Base Ball Notes," *Philadelphia (PA) Times*, Aug 31, 1875.

Lord Baltimore Base Ball Club (Baltimore, MD; 1880s–1890s). Organizer(s): P. Tarrer and Jesse Joseph Callis.

The Lord Baltimore B.B.C. organized in 1883, played black organizations. The Lord Baltimores joined the National Colored Base Ball League in 1887. Prior to the start of the league, they played Baltimore's Mutual club. *Baltimore Sun* (April 26, 1887): "The base-running was a special feature. The men did not care where the ball was. They ran and took chances, which kept the ball always in motion and the excitement at fever heat. The batting was terrific, especially by the Mutuals. Had the ground been dry and the sun shining, an interesting game might have been looked for, with a heavy score. The only difference noticeable between the playing of the colored clubs and that of the professional teams was that there was no attempt to make it a pitchers' game. It was go from the start. The only difference noticeable between the playing of the colored clubs and that of the professional teams was that there was no attempt to make it a pitchers' game. It was 'go' from the start." In the league season opener, the Lord Baltimores defeated the Philadelphia Pythians. *Sun* (May 7, 1887): "The game was very exciting and was thoroughly enjoyed by the 400 white and colored people present. The coaching was lively." *Baltimore American* (May 14, 1887): "The Lord Baltimore of the National league, (colored), were defeated yesterday by the Gorhams, of New York, by a score of 15 to 8." The nine reorganized in the 1890s. In 1894, the Lord Baltimores played Frederick's Maryland Trotters. *Frederick News* (July 31, 1894) reports "A crowd of not less than one thousand people assembled to witness a game of ball between the Maryland Trotters, the crack colored base-ball team of this city, and the Lord Baltimore Club, one of the best colored teams in the city of Baltimore. The game was one of the best that has been played in Frederick this season, the battery work of Stanton and Robinson above that of amateurs. The visitors also played a fine game, but the Trotters were too fast for them."

SOURCES: "Base Ball," *Baltimore (MD) Sun*, Jul 17, 1883; "The Official Roster," *St. Louis (MO) Sporting News*, Jan 29, 1887; "Orioles vs. Statesmen," *Philadelphia (PA) Sporting Life*, Mar 9, 1887; "Base Ball Notes," *Baltimore Sun*, Apr 22, 1887; "Base Ball Notes," *Baltimore Sun*, Apr. 23, 1887; "The Colored Men Play," *Baltimore Sun*, Apr. 26, 1887;

"Rain Did Not Stop Them," *Baltimore (MD) American*, Apr 26, 1887; "Lord Baltimore Wins," *Baltimore Sun*, Apr 27, 1887; "Gossip of the Diamond," *Baltimore American*, May 1, 1887; "Gossip of the Diamond," *Baltimore American*, May 4, 1887; "The Colored League," *Baltimore Sun*, May 6, 1887; "The Colored League," *Baltimore American*, May 7, 1887; "Base Ball Notes," *Baltimore Sun*, May 7, 1887; "The Pythians Get There," *Philadelphia (PA) Inquirer*, May 10, 1887; "The Colored League," *Philadelphia (PA) Times*, May 11, 1887; "Base Ball Notes," *Baltimore Sun*, May 12, 1887; "Gossip of the Diamond," *Baltimore American*, May 14, 1887; "Gossip of the Diamond," *Baltimore American*, May 15, 1887; "The Colored League," *Pittsburgh (PA) Commercial Gazette*, May 17, 1887; "The Colored League," *Pittsburgh Commercial Gazette*, May 18, 1887; "Lord Baltimores Defeated," *Baltimore American*, May 18, 1887; "Gossip of the Diamond," *Baltimore American*, May 30, 1887; "Base Ball," *Frederick (MD) News*, Jul 31, 1894; "Base Ball," *Frederick News*, Aug 4, 1894; "Diamond Flashes," *Baltimore Sun*, Aug 7, 1894; "Base Ball," *Frederick News*, Aug 8, 1894; "Trotters vs. Lords," *Baltimore Sun*, Aug 8, 1894.

Lord Hannibal Base Ball Club (Baltimore, MD; 1850s–1880s). Organizer(s): Harris Mitchell, Thomas W. Johnson, and Charles Hobbs; Charles J. Hardy and George Asking.

The Lord Hannibal B.B.C. composed of young men, organized in 1859. *Baltimore Bee* (July 13, 1876): "The Lord Hannibal Base Ball Club was formed in 1859, and expects to be admitted to the convention next fall." Black teams, including the Hannibals, marched in the Emancipation Day celebration. *Baltimore Sun* (May 19, 1870): "[The Lord Hannibal] Club officers Harris Mitchell, Thomas W. Johnson, and Charles Hobbs marched before fifty men in baseball uniform yellow shorts trimmed with blue velvet red, white and blue belts black pants and black slouched hats." The Lord Hannibals were Lincoln Republicans: in 1870, club member, William Young, was murdered in an act that augured the assassination of Octavius Catto (Philadelphia Pythians B.B.C.). During Young's funeral procession, the organization's one-hundred members followed the horse-driven hearse. Baseball life embodied sumptuary display. In 1874, before one-thousand black and white spectators, the Hannibals defeated the Orientals, which lost for the first time that season. A rivalry developed in which the Lord Hannibals took three of four games. They battled the Excelsior Club, another local team. *New York Clipper* (August 8, 1874): "On the 25th the Excelsior and Lord Hannibal colored nines were opposed to each other at Baltimore, Maryland, the latter winning by a count of 12 to 11." They played the WA Manhattans. *Baltimore Bee* (July 4, 1876): "The Lord Hannibals, of this city, will play the Manhattans, of Washington. These are two of the best colored clubs in the country, and a fine game may be expected." *Baltimore Bee* (July 7, 1876): "The Lord Hannibal Base Ball Club (colored) of South Baltimore express a willingness to play any other club." The organization challenged a white club. *Bee* (July 13, 1876): "The members of the Lord Hannibal Base Ball Club (colored) intend challenging the Lone star club to a match or a series of games at Newington Park at an early day." The Lone Stars, white, responded to Hardy's challenge. *Bee* (July 14, 1876): "The Lone Star Base Ball Club wished to inform the Lord Hannibal Base Ball Club (colored) of city that they will not accept a challenge from them or any other colored club." Hardy responded. *Bee* (July 15, 1876): "We, the Lord Hannibal Base Ball Club, do not consider the Lone Stars a base-ball club since they decline to play against any club. The Lord Hannibal Club was formed in 1859, and expects to be admitted to the convention next fall." In 1876, they played Towson's Quickstep and Richmond's Atlantic nines at Baltimore's Newington Park. In 1880, the Richmond Swans challenged the Hannibals. At Richmond's Base Ball Park, the Swans defeated them by a score of 11 to 1. In 1883, the Hannibals defeated the Lord Baltimores (black) by a score of 21 to 0; they twice defeated the New Bedfords (also black) at the Gas House Grounds.

SOURCES: "Emancipation in Maryland," *Baltimore (MD) Sun*, Nov 5, 1869; "The Colored Celebration Today," *Baltimore Sun*, May 19, 1870; "A Wanton Case of Shooting," *Baltimore Sun*, May 19, 1870; "The Funeral of William Young, Colored," *Baltimore Sun*, May 21, 1870; "Legal," *Baltimore Sun*, Jun 25, 1870; "Murder Trial," *Baltimore Sun*, Jun 28, 1870; *Baltimore Sun*, Aug 31, 1870; "Fifteenth Amendment Celebration," *Baltimore (MD) American and Commercial Advertiser*, May 26, 1871; "Base Ball," *Baltimore Sun*, Jul 4, 1874; "Base Ball," *Baltimore Sun*, Jul 5, 1874; "Base Ball," *Baltimore Sun*, July 17, 1874; "Local Matters," *Baltimore Sun*, Jul 30, 1874; "Base Ball Yesterday," *Baltimore Sun*, Jul 30, 1874; "Colored Boys at the Bat," *Baltimore Sun*, Aug 7, 1874; "Short Stops," *New York (NY) Clipper*, Aug 8, 1874; "Local Briefs," *Baltimore Sun*, Jun 15, 1875; "Local Briefs," *Baltimore Sun*, Jun 24, 1875; "Fly Tips," *New York Clipper*, Aug 7, 1875; "Base Ball," *Baltimore (MD) Bee*, Jul 7, 1876; "Local Matters," *Baltimore Sun*, Jul 4, 1876; "Base Ball," *Baltimore (MD) Bee*, Jul 7, 1876; "Base Ball," *Baltimore Bee*, Jul 13, 1876; "Base Ball," *Baltimore Bee*, Jul 14, 1876; "Base Ball," *Baltimore Bee*, Jul 15, 1876; "Base Ball," *Baltimore Bee*, Aug 3, 1876; "Base Ball," *Baltimore Bee*, Aug 9, 1876; "Hannibal Base Ball Club, of Baltimore vs. Swan, of Richmond," *Richmond (VA) Dispatch*, Jul 15, 1880; "Base Ball," *Richmond Dispatch*, Jul 17, 1880; "Base Ball [Advertisement]," *Richmond Dispatch*, Jul 17, 1880; "Base Ball," *Richmond Dispatch*, Jul 19, 1880; "Base Ball," *Baltimore Sun*, Jul 17, 1883; "Base Ball," *Sun*, Jul 18, 1883; "Base Ball Notes," *Baltimore Sun*, Aug 21, 1883; "A Disgraceful Game," *Baltimore Sun*, Sep 5, 1883; "Sporting Notes," *Baltimore Sun*, Sep 19, 1883; "Local Games," *Baltimore Sun*, Jul 14, 1886.

Mansfield Base Ball Club (Baltimore, MD; 1870s–1880s). Organizer(s): William Matthews.

The Mansfield B.B.C. organized in the 1870s, played black nines. *Baltimore Bee* (August 9, 1876): "Yesterday afternoon on the Jefferson Street grounds, Mansfield 39; Blue Cloud 21. At the Hartford Road grounds, Mansfield 43, Northeastern 23. Umpire, George Asking, of the Lord Hannibal (colored) club. All of the above are colored clubs. They battled for the black championship. *New York Clipper* (September 9, 1882): "The deciding game for thee colored championship of Baltimore and Washington was played September 1 at Newington Park, in the former city. The contestants were the Mansfields of Baltimore and the Atlantics of Washington, the former winning by a score of 18 to 14. About three thousand people, mostly colored, witnessed the game." *Baltimore American* (July 17, 1883): "The Louisville and Mansfield colored clubs played in South Baltimore yesterday—Louisville 13, Mansfield 11."

SOURCES: "Base Ball," *Baltimore* (MD) *Bee*, August 9, 1876; "Base Ball," *Baltimore Bee*, August 16, 1876; "Base Ball," *Baltimore* (MD) *Bee*, August 19, 1876; "Base Ball," *Baltimore* (MD) *Sun*, Aug 18, 1882; *New York* (NY) *Clipper*, Sep 9, 1882; "Base Ball," *Baltimore Sun*, Jul 17, 1883; "Notes of the Diamond," *Baltimore* (MD) *American*, Aug 2, 1884.

Monumental Base Ball Club (Baltimore, MD; 1880s)

The Monumental B.B.C. organized in the 1880s. Formerly the Atlantics, they played black teams. They scheduled an exhibition against the St. Augustine Cuban Giants. *Baltimore Sun* (April 27, 1886): "The Cuban Giants, of St. Augustine, Florida, defeated, at Oriole Park yesterday, the Monumentals of this city, by the overwhelming score of 14 to 1. Both clubs are composed of colored men."

SOURCES: "Gossip of the Diamond," *Baltimore* (MD) *American*, Apr 26, 1886; "Base-Ball in Baltimore," *Baltimore* (MD) *Sun*, Apr 27,

1886; "Colored Teams Playing Ball," *Baltimore American*, Apr 27, 1886.

Mutual Base Ball Club (Baltimore, MD; 1880s)

The Mutual B.B.C. organized in the 1880s, played black teams. The Mutuals developed a local rivalry with the Lord Baltimores. While the Mutuals didn't join the National Colored Base Ball League of 1887, the nine played the Lord Baltimores. *Baltimore Sun* (April 26, 1887): "The base-running was a special feature. The men did not care where the ball was. They ran and took chances, which kept the ball always in motion and the excitement at fever heat. The batting was terrific, especially by the Mutuals. Had the ground been dry and the sun shining, an interesting game might have been looked for, with a heavy score. The only difference noticeable between the playing of the colored clubs and that of the professional teams was that there was no attempt to make it a pitchers' game. It was 'go' from the start. The only difference noticeable between the playing of the colored clubs and that of the professional teams was that there was no attempt to make it a pitchers' game. It was 'go' from the start."

SOURCES: "Base Ball," *Baltimore* (MD) *Sun*, Jul 17, 1883; "Base Ball Notes," *Baltimore Sun*, May 23, 1884; "Other Games," *Baltimore Sun*, Sep 16, 1884; "The Colored Men Play," *Baltimore Sun*, Apr 26, 1887; "Lord Baltimore Wins," *Baltimore Sun*, Apr 27, 1887; "Base Ball Notes," *Baltimore Sun*, May 12, 1887.

Oriental Base Ball Club (Baltimore, MD; 1870s)

The Oriental B.B.C. organized in the 1870s, played black teams. *Baltimore American and Commercial Advertiser* (July 4, 1874): "At ten o'clock a very entertaining game will commence between the Oriental and Atlantic colored clubs, which promises much sport. Both nines are heavy batters, and run like thoroughbreds, and a full twenty-five cents of fun may be expected." *American and Commercial Advertiser* (July 6, 1874): "About one thousand persons attended the morning game at the Newton Grounds on the Fourth to witness the contest between two crack colored clubs—the Orientals and Atlantics—and those who expected to see hard-hitting and much muffing were disappointed as the ball turned out to be a very dead one, and the fielding of the two nines were brought into requisition, and compared favorably with that displayed at many professional games played during the season."

SOURCES: "Base Ball Notes," *Baltimore* (MD) *American and Commercial Advertiser*, Jul 4, 1874; "Base Ball Playing on the Fourth," *Baltimore* (MD) *Sun*, Jul 6, 1874; "The Colored Ball Tossers," *Baltimore American and Commercial Advertiser*, Jul 6, 1874; "Enterprise vs. Orientals," *Baltimore American and Commercial Advertiser*, Jul 14, 1874; "Base Ball Yesterday," *Baltimore Sun*, Jul 30, 1874; "Colored Boys at the Bat," *Baltimore Sun*, Aug 7, 1874.

Pennsylvania (Cuban Giants) Base Ball Club (Baltimore, MD; 1890s)

The PA B.B.C. organized in the 1890s. The Pennsylvanias (also called the Cuban Giants) played black and white teams. *Baltimore American* (June 20, 1897): "The Lord Baltimore Club defeated the Pennsylvania Club by a score of 18 to 14. Winning battery—Duvall and Reynolds." *Baltimore Sun* (July 17, 1897): "The Cuban Giants are Afro-American citizens, ranging in color from that of a bell which has been used to play for several innings to that of a brand new stove plate. It took two umpires, Messrs. Dorsey and Cabbage, to control the game, which resulted in a victory for the Yanigans by a score of 28 to 2."

SOURCES: "Among the Amateurs," *Baltimore* (MD) *American*, Jun 26, 1897; "Yanigans, 28; Cuban Giants, 2," *Baltimore* (MD) *Sun*, Jul 17, 1897; "Yanigans in a Walk," *Baltimore American*, Jul 17, 1897.

Pioneer Base Ball Club (Baltimore, MD; 1870s–1890s). Organizer(s): James Lucas and Joseph Lucas; Robert Pinder and Thomas Pinder.

The Pioneer B.B.C. organized in the 1870s, played black teams. In 1886, the team defeated the Lord Hannibals. *Baltimore Sun* (July 14, 1886): "The colored nines, the Pioneers and Hannibals, played a game on the Almshouse grounds. The score was 19 to 16 in favor of the Pioneers. Marfield and Pinder were the battery for the winners." *Philadelphia Sporting Life* (March 5, 1892): "The champion colored club of the State for the past four years is the Pioneer of Baltimore. The team plays a good game and draws like smoke when it exhibits." Under the management of Robert and Thomas Pinder, the Pioneers established themselves as champions. It was composed of familiar names known in MD, dominated by the Pinder (Thomas and Robert), Savoy (Charles, John and William) families; the latter were likely related to the Savoy baseballists of Washington, D.C.), the Carroll (Edward and Samuel) and Jenkins ("P.W.") families. *Baltimore Sun* (July 19, 1895): "The Pioneer Colored Base Ball Club, of Baltimore, showed the Orange Cuban Giants Colored Base Ball Club, of New Jersey, at Union Park how to play a game of base-ball and win. The score was: Pioneers, 23; Orange Cuban Giants, 3. The clubs are playing for the championship of the colored base-ball clubs of Maryland and New Jersey. Two other games will follow." *Baltimore American* (June 20, 1895): "The Pioneers defeated the Manhattans, both colored, at Union Park yesterday, by a score of 10 to 7." Many of the team's players became the foundation for the Baltimore Giants B.B.C. in 1899.

Sources: "Base Ball," *Baltimore* (MD) *Bee*, Aug 14, 1876; "Base Ball," *Baltimore Bee*, Aug 18, 1876; "Base Ball," *Baltimore Bee*, Aug 19, 1876; "Other Games," *Baltimore* (MD) *Sun*, Jul 28, 1886; "Local Games," *Baltimore Sun*, Jul 14, 1886; "Baltimore Bulletin," *Philadelphia* (PA) *Sporting Life*, Mar 5, 1892; "Among the Amateurs," *Baltimore* (MD) *American*, Jun 20, 1895; "Visiting Colored Club Badly Defeated," *Baltimore Sun*, Jul 20, 1895; "Notes," *York* (PA) *Daily*, Aug 3, 1895; "Diamond Flashes," *Baltimore Sun*, Sep 2, 1896; "Yanigans, 28; Cuban Giants, 2," *Baltimore Sun*, Jul 17, 1897; "Southern Champions," *Philadelphia Sporting Life*, Feb 11, 1899; "News and Comment," *Philadelphia Sporting Life*, Mar 4, 1899; "News and Comment," *Philadelphia Sporting Life*, Apr 3, 1899; "Some News," *Springfield* (MA) *Republican*, Apr 12, 1899; "News and Comment," *Philadelphia Sporting Life*, Apr 8, 1899; "Colored Giants, 3; Yanigans, 1," *Baltimore Sun*, Sep 11, 1900.

Quickstep Base Ball Club (Baltimore, MD; 1870s–1880s). Organizer(s): W. I. Smith.

The Quickstep B.B.C. organized in the 1880s, played black nines. *Baltimore Sun* (July 4, 1876): "Two colored nines played at Oriole Park yesterday, the Douglass, of Washington, and the Quicksteps of Baltimore. The Washington nine was successful by a score of 22 to 6." *Baltimore American and Commercial Advertiser* (June 19, 1883): "At Oriole Park yesterday afternoon, the Quicksteps of West Baltimore, and the Baltimore, of South Baltimore, played a fine game of ball. The members of both clubs are colored, and the playing was far above the average of amateurs. The score was 6 to 2 in favor of the Quicksteps." *American and Commercial Advertiser* (June 19, 1883): "The Quicksteps beat the Lord Hannibals at Newington Park by a score of 14 to 13. There were about 200 people present."

Sources: "Base Ball," *Baltimore* (MD) *Sun*, Jul 4, 1876; "Base Ball," *Baltimore* (MD) *Bee*, July 27, 1876; "Base Ball," *Baltimore Sun*, Jun 19, 1883; "Base Ball," *Baltimore Sun*, Jul 17, 1883; *Baltimore* (MD) *American Commercial and Advertiser*, Jun 19, 1883; *Baltimore American Commercial and Advertiser*, Jul 18, 1883; "Base Ball," *Baltimore Sun*, Jul 18, 1883; "Base Ball," *Baltimore Sun*, Aug 2, 1883.

Colored Base Ball Club (Cecilton, MD; 1890s)

The Colored B.B.C. organized in the 1890s, played black teams. *Elkton Cecil Whig* (April 24, 1897): "The colored people of Elkton and Cecilton joined hands in baseball in Elkton on Monday. The Cecilton ball tossers won the victory and went home with the ball. The game was played in Howards Meadow and the ball field echoed with the shouts of the Cecilton warriors." *Wilmington Morning News* (July 30, 1897): "The Cecilton Base Ball Club, of Cecil county, Maryland, came to Wilmington and defeated the Delaware Grays by a score of 13 to 7. The game was an interesting one despite the rain. The diamond was full of mud puddles and the men waddled in them like ducks." *Cecil Whig* (August 7, 1897): "The Cecilton Base Ball Club defeated the Delaware Grays in Wilmington, on Thursday, last week, score 13 to 7." *Cecil Whig* (July 23, 1898): "The colored baseball club, of Cecilton, will play a match game with the Elkton colored club, today, in West Elkton."

Sources: "Base Ball," *Elkton* (MD) *Cecil Whig*, Apr 24, 1897; "Local Baseball Game," *Wilmington* (DE) *Evening Journal*, Jun 30, 1897; "To Play Champions," *Wilmington* (DE) *Morning News*, Jul 27, 1897; "Colored People Play Ball," *Wilmington Morning News*, Jul 29, 1897; "Maryland Team Won," *Wilmington Morning News*, Jun 30, 1897; "Base Ball," *Cecil Whig*, Aug 7, 1897; "News in Brief," *Cecil Whig*, Jun 25, 1898; "Base Ball," *Cecil Whig*, Jul 23, 1898.

Colored Base Ball Club (Cumberland, MD; 1870s). Organizer(s): Elida Long.

The Colored B.B.C. organized in the 1870s, played black teams. *Cumberland News* (May 20, 1871): "A number of our fellow colored citizens have formed a base-ball club, for the purpose of entering into a contest with one of the same ilk in Baltimore for the colored championship of the State. They may be seen every afternoon industriously practicing on Thruston's field, above the railroad."

Sources: "Base Ball," *Cumberland* (MD) *News*, May 20, 1871; "Very Serious Base Ball Accident," *Cumberland News*, Jun 15, 1871.

Windsor Hotel Base Ball Club (Cumberland, MD; 1880s–1890s). Organizer(s): Charles Freeman.

The Windsor Hotel B.B.C. organized in the 1880s, played black teams. *Cumberland Times* (August 4, 1885): "The Windsors and Ionians (both colored clubs) play the second game of their series at Association Park tomorrow afternoon." *Times* (May 31, 1889): "The Windsor club, of Cumberland, gained a victory yesterday over the Bedford club. The battery for the Cumberland club was C. Washington, catcher, and A. Washington, pitcher; for the Bedfords, Griffith Marshall, catcher and Shannon Barks, pitcher. Barks struck out 9, and Washington 15." *Uniontown Evening News* (September 1, 1893): "The [Uniontown, Pennsylvania] Cuban Giants were defeated Wednesday at the hands of the Windsor's of Cumberland. The score was 6 to 1 in favor of Windsor." In 1895, the Windsors joined a Colored Baseball League, composed of teams from Cumberland, and the PA towns of Johnston, Bedford, and Uniontown. *Cumberland Evening Times* (July 18, 1895): "The game of baseball played at Uniontown yesterday between the Windsors, of this city, and the Uniontown club, was won by the former, the score being: Windsors, 7; Uniontown 1." *Pittsburgh Post* (September 4, 1895): "There was an interesting game of base-ball played here this afternoon between the Uniontown Giants and the Windsors, of this city. The game resulted in a score of 4 to 3 in favor of the Uniontown club."

Sources: "Latest Local Laconics," *Cumberland* (MD) *Times*, Jul 10, 1885; "Base Ball Notes," *Cumberland Times*, Aug 4, 1885; "Base Ball Game," *Cumberland Times*, Sep 21, 1886; "Latest Laconics," *Cumberland Times*, May 29, 1889; "They Won the Game," *Cumberland Times*, May 31, 1889; "About Town," *Uniontown* (PA) *Evening News*,

Sep 1, 1893; "Colored Baseball League," *Pittsburgh (PA) Post*, Jul 12, 1895; "Will Play Ball at Uniontown," *Cumberland Times*, Jul 16, 1895; "The Windsor Boys Win," *Cumberland Evening Times*, Jul 18, 1895; "Uniontown Wins," *Pittsburgh Post*, Sep 4, 1895.

Giants Base Ball Club (Elkton, MD; 1890s). Organizer(s): Charles H. Bowzer and William Starling.

The Giants B.B.C. organized in the 1890s, played black teams. *Elkton Cecil Whig* (August 3, 1895): "The Elkton colored base-ball team has been organized under the name of Elkton Giants, and is open for games." *Cecil Whig* (August 10, 1895): "The Elkton Giants visited Port Deposit, on Tuesday, and played the colored base-ball club of that town, the home club winning by a score of 19 to 8. The return game will be played at Elkton, on Saturday, August 17." *Cecil Whig* (August 17, 1895): "The Elkton colored base-ball team played in Havre de Grace on Tuesday and was defeated by the club of that place; score, 29 to 23."

SOURCES: "Base Ball," *Elkton (MD) Cecil Whig*, Aug 3, 1895; "Base Ball Hits," *Elkton Cecil Whig*, Aug 10, 1895; "Base Ball Hits," *Elkton Cecil Whig*, Aug 17, 1895.

Star Green Base Ball Club (Elkton, MD; 1890s)

The Star Green B.B.C. organized in the 1890s, played black teams. *Elkton Cecil Whig* (August 24, 1895): "A return game of base-ball was played on the Elkton Fair Grounds on Tuesday last between the Star Green colored club of Elkton, and the Maryland Boys, a colored club from Havre de Grace. The Elkton Stars outshone the Maryland Boys by a score of 23 to 17. Winning battery, John Hammond and Fred Holland. Exceptionally good playing was done by Hinson, Green and Simpers, of Elkton."

SOURCES: "Base Ball," *Elkton (MD) Cecil Whig*, Aug 24, 1895.

Boot Black Athletic Base Ball Club (Frederick, MD; 1880s). Organizer(s): John Mills.

The Boot Black Athletic B.B.C. organized in the 1880s. *Frederick News* (July 9, 1886): "A great many colored people of both sexes and a fair number of whites witnessed the game yesterday afternoon at Association Park, between the Boot Blacks and Excelsior Clubs of this city. The game opened well and was contested with spirit on both sides. The pitching and catching was remarkably good, and the fieldwork about equaled it. The game resulted with a score of 17 to 15 in favor of the Boot Blacks." The Boot Blacks and Valley Blues developed a rivalry. This exceptionally strong team reorganized the next year. *News* (August 12, 1887): "There will be a game of ball at Association Park on Thursday next between the Valley Blues, of Hagertown, and the Boot Blacks, of this city. The battery for the Boot Blacks will be Beatty and Miller. The game will be called at 2 p.m., and the admission will be 10 cents. Ladies free." *News* (July 14, 1887): "The Bootblack Club, of this city, colored, left here today in company with the Nazarite organization for Hagertown, where they played against the Valley Blues, of that place. The battery for the Bootblacks consisted of Frank Beatty, pitcher, and John Pye, catcher." *Hagertown Herald and Torch Light* (August 18, 1887): "On Friday last, the Valley Blues, of Hagertown, were defeated by the Bootblacks, of Frederick—both colored—in a game at Frederick. The score stood fifteen to fourteen."

SOURCES: "Another B. B. Club," *Frederick (MD) News*, Jun 12, 1886; "The Boot Blacks Play," *Frederick News*, Jun 14, 1886; "At Association Park," *Frederick News*, Jul 9, 1886; "Base Ball," *Frederick News*, Jul 15, 1886; "Base Ball at Island Park," *Frederick News*, Jul 28, 1886; "Colored Boot Blacks Fight," *Frederick News*, Feb 10, 1887; "Amateur Games," *Frederick News*, Jul 14, 1887; "Amateur Games," *Frederick News*, Aug 9, 1887; "Amateur Games," *Frederick News*, Aug 12, 1887; "Base Ball," *Hagertown (MD) Herald and Torch Light*, Aug 18, 1887.

Maryland Trotters (Frederick, MD; 1880s–1900s). Organizer(s): J. J. Tolliver.

The Maryland Trotters organized in the 1880s, played black and white nines. J. J. Tolliver managed the team. In the 1870s and 1880s Tolliver caught for clubs in Baltimore-District of Columbia. He also managed black nines in Syracuse; the Pastimes (1885) and Wide Awakes (1886–87). The Trotters and Lord Baltimores developed a rivalry. *Frederick News* (July 31, 1894) reports "A crowd of not less than one thousand people assembled to witness a game of ball between the Maryland Trotters, the crack colored base-ball team of this city, and the Lord Baltimore Club, one of the best colored teams in the city of Baltimore. The game was one of the best that has been played in Frederick this season, the battery work of Stanton and Robinson above that of amateurs. The visitors also played a fine game, but the Trotters were too fast for them." Tolliver's star pitcher, James Dorsey Robinson, signed with the Cuban Giants.

SOURCES: "Base Ball Matters," *Frederick (MD) News*, May 21, 1888; "Personal and Pertinent," *Frederick News*, Jun 11, 1889; "Personal and Pertinent," *Frederick News*, Jun 21, 1889; "Emancipation Day," *Frederick News*, Aug 1, 1889; "Base Ball," *Frederick News*, May 7, 1890; "Brief Bits," *Frederick News*, May 17, 1890; "Base Ball," *Frederick News*, May 19, 1890; "Base Ball Bits," *Frederick News*, May 20, 1890; "A Colored Base Ballist," *Frederick News*, Jun 7, 1890; "First Game of the Season," *Frederick News*, May 18, 1891; "Base Ball," *Frederick News*, May 19, 1891; "Base Ball," *Frederick News*, May 26, 1891; "Base Ball," *Frederick News*, Jul 8, 1891; "Base Ball," *Frederick News*, May 31, 1894; "Emancipation Echoes," *Frederick News*, Aug 11, 1893; "Base Ball News," *Frederick News*, Aug 16, 1893; "Base Ball News," *Frederick News*, Aug 25, 1893; "Base Ball," *Frederick News*, May 31, 1894 "Base Ball," *Frederick News*, Jul 31, 1894; "Base Ball," *Frederick Daily News*, Aug 4, 1894; "Diamond Flashes," *Baltimore (MD) Sun*, Aug 7, 1894; "Base Ball," *Frederick News*, Aug 8, 1894; "Trotters vs. Lords," *Baltimore Sun*, Aug 8, 1894; "Base Ball," *Frederick News*, Feb 15, 1895; "Emancipation Day," *Frederick News*, Aug 9, 1895; "Base Ball," *Frederick News*, May 1, 1896; "Emancipation Day," *Frederick News*, Aug 13, 1896; "Base Ball," *Frederick News*, Jul 31, 1900; "Maryland Trotters Won," *Frederick News*, Aug 3, 1900; "Emancipation Day," *Frederick News*, Aug 10, 1900.

Red Stocking Base Ball Club (Frederick, MD; 1880s). Organizer(s): James Dorsey Robinson.

The Red Stocking B.B.C. organized in the 1880s. *Frederick News* (May 15, 1884): "The Red Stockings Base Ball Club (colored), of this city, with [Dorsey] David Robinson, captain, will go to York on Friday, the 16th inst. to play the Home nine of that place. We are anxious to see the Red Stockings win and would dislike terribly to report their defeat. The York Dispatch yesterday reported: One of the most interesting games of the season, will probably be that between the colored nines at the fairgrounds between the Frederick City and the York nine. It will be the only game between colored nines this season and will doubtless attract a large crowd of visitors." One of the star players suffered an accident before the trip to York. *News* (May 15, 1884): "William Boose, one of the amateur members of one of the colored amateur ball clubs of this city, while engaged in a game at the Association Grounds met with a painful accident. A ball thrown with great force struck the index finger of his left hand, tearing it completely open from the nail to the last knuckle. He was attempting to catch a ball at the time." They travelled to York, PA, where they played a black club. *York Daily* (May 17, 1884): "More fun was developed in yesterday's game between the Hunters of York, and the Red Stockings of Frederick could not be well extracted from one game of base-ball. The audience yelled itself hoarse, and laughed until its sides ached;

and more real rollicking fun is not often in return for an investment of twenty-five cents. In point of complexion the two teams were evenly matched, but on account of the difference in costuming they were designated by the audience as blondes and brunettes.

SOURCES: [qm]Frederick Club to Play at York," *Frederick (MD) News*, May 15, 1884; "The Weekly News," *Frederick News*, May 15, 1884; "Gone to York," *Frederick News*, May 16, 1884; "Fun on the Diamond," *York (PA) Daily*, May 17, 1884.

Active Base Ball Club (Hagerstown, MD; 1880s)

The Active B.B.C. organized in the 1880s, played black nines. In 1884, they joined a Colored League. *Fort Wayne News* (January 11, 1884): "A Colored Base Ball League, with clubs at Baltimore [Mutuals and Haymakers], Harrisburg [Olympics], Pottsville, Washington and several other cities [Carlisle, Pennsylvania and Hagerstown, Maryland]." *Hagerstown Herald and Torch Light* (June 26, 1884): "The Alert Club, of Chambersburg, and the Actives, of Hagerstown, both colored, played on the grounds of the Chambersburg association, last Wednesday afternoon. The Hagerstown club was blocked out, the score being 19 to 0in favor of the Alerts." *Harrisburg State Journal* (July 12, 1884): "The Alert visited Hagerstown today, and played the Actives a return game of ball. At the end of three innings, the game was stopped on account of rain, the score standing: Alert 4; Active 3. The boys returned home on the New York Express well pleased with their visit and the gentlemanly treatment accorded them by the Actives and the citizens of Hagerstown generally." *Charleston Spirit of Jefferson* (September 25, 1888): "A colored base-ball club from this place visited Hagertown last Thursday, and beat a club there 12 to 7."

SOURCES: "Local Lines," *Fort Wayne (IN) News*, Jan 11, 1884; "Our Ballists," *Hagerstown (MD) Herald and Torch Light*, Jun 26, 1884; "Chambersburg," *Harrisburg (PA) State Journal*, Jun 28, 1884; "Gathered About Town," *Harrisburg State Journal*, Jul 12, 1884; "Local Lines," Charleston (WVA) *Spirit of Jefferson*, Sep 25, 1888.

Valley Blues Base Ball Club (Hagerstown, MD; 1880s)

The Valley Blues B.B.C. organized in the 1880s, played black organizations. *Frederick News* (July 13, 1887): "There will be a game of ball at Association Park on Thursday next between the Valley Blues, of Hagertown, and the Boot Blacks, of this city. The battery for the Boot Blacks will be Beatty and Miller. The game will be called at 2 p.m., and the admission will be 10 cents. Ladies free." *News* (July 14, 1887): "The Bootblack Club, of this city, colored, left here today in company with the Nazarite organization for Hagertown, where they played against the Valley Blues, of that place. The battery for the Bootblacks consisted of Frank Beatty, pitcher, and John Pye, catcher." *Hagertown Herald and Torch Light* (July 14, 1884): "On Friday last, the Valley Blues, of Hagertown, were defeated by the Bootblacks, of Frederick—both colored—in a game at Frederick. The score stood fifteen to fourteen."

SOURCES: "Base Ball," *Cleveland (OH) Gazette*, Jun 4, 1887; "Base Ball Matters," *Frederick (MD) News*, Jul 13, 1887; "Amateur Games," *Frederick News*, Jul 14, 1887; "Colored Base Ballists," *Hagerstown (MD) Herald and Torch Light*, Jul 14, 1884; "Base Ball," *Frederick News*, Jul 15, 1887; "Colored People Indulge in the National Pastime," *Frederick News*, Jul 21, 1887; "Amateur Games," *Frederick News*, Aug 9, 1887; "Amateur Games," *Frederick News*, Aug 12, 1887; "Base Ball," *Hagerstown Herald and Torch Light*, Aug 18, 1887.

Young Republican Base Ball Club (Havre de Grace, MD; 1880s)

The Young Republican B.B.C., of Elkton, MD, organized in the 1880s, played black teams. *Elkton Cecil Whig* (June 28, 1888): "The Elkton colored base-ball nine on Wednesday afternoon defeated the colored nine of Havre de Grace, in this town, by a score of 19 to 16. The game was hotly contested." *Wilmington Morning News* (August 7, 1888): "There will be a great game of ball tomorrow afternoon at Union Street Park between the Young Republican base-ball nine of Havre de Grace, and the West End nine of this city. Both teams are colored." *Wilmington Evening Journal* (October 8, 1888): "The West End of this city defeated the Young Republicans, of Havre de Grace, Maryland, by a score of 19 to 15. The umpires gave decisions on plays and the game was orderly throughout. Berry and Chippey were the battery for the local colored men and Taylor and Smith for the visitors." *Cecil Whig* (May 18, 1889): "The Elkton colored base-ball club played in Havre de Grace yesterday afternoon."

SOURCES: "Local Department," *Elkton (MD) Cecil Whig*, Jun 28, 1888; "Local Sports," *Wilmington (DE) Morning News*, Aug 7, 1888; "Base Ball Gossip," *Wilmington (DE) Evening Journal*, Aug 8, 1888; "Base Ball Gossip," *Wilmington Evening Journal*, Aug 9, 1888; "Sporting Notes," *Wilmington Evening Journal*, Oct 8, 1888; "Local Department," *Elkton (MD) Cecil Whig*, May 18, 1889.

Grays Base Ball Club (Westminister, MD; 1890s)

The Grays B.B.C. organized in the 1890s, played white and black teams. *Westminster Democrat Advocate* (July 7, 1894): "The McSherrytown, Pa., club, white, defeated the Westminster Grays, colored, at McSherrytown. The Grays defeated the Royal Blues by a score of 19 to 4."

SOURCES: "Local Affairs," *Westminister (MD) Democrat Advocate*, Apr 21, 1894; "Base Ball," *Westminster Democrat Advocate*, Jun 2, 1894; "Out-Door Sports," *Westminster Democrat Advocate*, Jun 2, 1894; "Base Ball," *Westminister Democrat Advocate*, Jul 7, 1894; "Local Affairs," *Westminister Democrat Advocate*, Sep 29, 1894.

Massachusetts

Albion Base Ball Club (Boston, MA; 1860s–1880s). Organizer(s): William H. Walker; Howard L. Smith and William I. Powell.

The Albion B.B.C. organized in 1868, played against black and white nines. *Boston Evening Transcript* (April 18, 1872): "A match game of base-ball was played yesterday afternoon on the Common, between the Albion (colored) and the Wyomings, both junior organizations of the West End. From the beginning of the game to the end of the fourth inning the contest was quite close. The score at this juncture stood 10 to 4 in favor of the colored youths. During the remaining five innings, the Albions had it all their own way, and won the game by a score of 40 to 28." *Boston Herald* (May 23, 1872): "A match game of base-ball was played on the Technology grounds yesterday afternoon, between the Albions (colored) and the King Phillips clubs, which resulted in favor of the King Phillips, the score being 12 to 17." By the mid–1870s, the club had become linked to another black nine. The Albions played against the "Lowells," a white organization. *Lowell Citizen and News* (September 7, 1876): "The Albions played very poorly in the first few innings and showed themselves no match for the Lowells. They made numerous changes in their field, none of which seemed to do any good. The Albion club is composed mainly of the old Resolute (colored) club, of Boston, which gained a high reputation two years ago. The players seem to be considerably out of practice."

SOURCES: "Base Ball," *Boston (MA) Journal*, May 8, 1871; "Base Ball," *New York (NY) Clipper*, Apr 27, 1872; "Base Ball," *Boston Journal*, Apr 5, 1872; "Base Ball," *Boston (MA) Daily Evening Transcript*, Apr 18, 1872; "Local Varieties," *Boston (MA) Herald*, Apr 18, 1872; "Base Ball," *Boston (MA) Traveler*, May 21, 1872; "Local Varieties,"

Boston Herald, May 23, 1872; "Base Ball," *Boston Journal,* Jun 10, 1872; "Base Ball," *Boston Herald,* Jun 11, 1872; "Local Varieties," *Boston Herald,* Jun 26, 1872; "Base Ball," *Boston (MA) Advertiser,* May 9, 1873; "Minor Games," *Boston Advertiser,* May 4, 1874; "Base Ball," *Lowell (MA) Citizen and News,* Sep 6, 1876; "Base Ball," *Lowell Citizen and News,* Sep 7, 1876; "Base Ball," *Lowell (MA) Courier,* Sep 7, 1876.

Monarch Base Ball Club (Boston, MA; 1890s). Organizer(s): Alfred Jupiter.

The Monarch B.B.C. organized in the 1890s, played black and white aggregations. *Worcester Spy* (June 12, 1893): "The Monarchs, colored, of Boston, will play the Websters on the local grounds. Seven of the Cuban Giants are on the team." *Boston Globe* (June 16, 1893): "The wonderful Monarchs (colored) succeeded for the second time in defeating the strong Milford nine after an exciting game of nine innings, the feature of which was the battle between the pitches, Woodcock and Robinson." *Boston Herald* (July 25, 1893): "The Gazettes defeated the Monarchs, formerly the Cuban Giants, this afternoon at Athletic Park, batting Selden with ease."

SOURCES: "Base Ball Notes," *Boston (MA) Globe,* Apr 29, 1893; "Amateur Mention," *Boston Globe,* May 26, 1893; "Base Ball Notes," *Boston (MA) Herald,* Jun 6, 1893; "Webster," *Worcester (MA) Spy,* Jun 12, 1893; "Monarchs 2, Milfords 1," *Boston Globe,* Jun 16, 1893; "Monarchs Defeat Websters," *Worcester Spy,* Jul 4, 1893; "Boston Monarchs 21, Milfords 3," *Boston Globe,* Jul 5, 1893; "Gazettes 13, Monarchs 4," *Boston Globe, Jul 25, 1893.

Resolute Base Ball Club (Boston, MA; 1870s–1890s). Organizer(s): William H. Walker; James Taylor; Alexander A. Selden; R. S. Church and Marshall Thompson; H. F. Hicks; Theodore L. Roberts.

The Resolute B.B.C. organized in 1870. The original members included William H. Walker, William Cruckendle, Charles Churchill, M. T. Gregory, D. E. Sheppard, William Taylor, William "Bill" Lee, James Taylor, H. B. Chapman, Emanuel Molineaux, Frank "Frenchy" Johnson, Peter Latimer and Paul Humphrey. The junior organization, played against white and black clubs. They battled a white club for rights to the Resolute nickname. *Boston Journal* (September 29, 1870): "A novel match was played on the Union Grounds yesterday afternoon, both of the contending nines (one composed of white members and the other colored), rejoining in the name of Resolute, and the game was to settle which should hold the name, the defeated club to choose another name under which to gain fame and honor in succeeding seasons. The colored boys were first at bat, and were disposed of for one run, their opponents scoring two. In the second inning the colored players added six runs, while the whites duplicated the number of the first inning. In the next three innings the whites made nine runs, allowing their opponents to make but one, and that in the third inning. From this point, the colored players, by good batting, assisted by the loose playing of the whites, gained the lead and won the game." The nine claimed the junior championship. The Mutuals, of Washington, D.C. (colored), played the Resolutes. *Boston Advertiser* (August 19, 1871): "The game yesterday at the Boston grounds, between the Resolutes, the nominal junior champions of the State, and the Mutuals of Washington (both colored), proved to be a very poor display of skill. Both nines seemed to vie with each other in muffing indiscriminately every fly offered, while the umpire [Octavius Catto, of the Philadelphia Pythians] seemed to known but little of the game. The Mute's are an amateur nine, composed principally of players in the employ of the government printing bureau at Washington, and on the whole they presented a neat and gentlemanly appearance. The Resolutes took the lead at the beginning, and retained it to the end of the game." In 1873, having lost 10 successive

games, they dropped out of the junior league. Walker, Howard L. Smith and William I. Powell reorganized the Albion club. In 1878, Walker and Cruckendle reorganized the Resolutes. By the early–1880s, the Selden brothers (Alexander and William) managed the team. Willie Selden, the Boston Red Stockings' mascot in the mid–1870s, would have a long career—it extended to the early 20th century—pitching for the Resolutes, Cuban Giants, Cuban-X Giants, Monarchs, and several white clubs in the Boston area. The Resolutes joined the National Colored Base Ball League. *Boston Globe* (January 23, 1887): "The Resolute Base Ball Club of Boston has joined the National Colored League, and is making preparations to see that the colored men of the Hub are well represented on the diamond. Marshal Thompson, who is to be manager the team, is an employee of State government, and Beacon Hill officials give him high character. With him J. W. Noon will be associated as assistant manager. Henry C. Taylor will be secretary of the club. The expenses of the team for the season will be heavy, somewhere in the neighborhood of $7000, and it is necessary for the club to raise a proportionate amount of that sum in order to place itself on a solid financial basis." In an exhibition match, the Resolutes defeated the Vendomes, a nine composed of black hotel waiters. During the Louisville trip, they team was stranded and financial difficulties forced them to withdraw from the league. The Resolutes cultivated homegrown talent, and they established reserve and junior clubs. In 1891 the team briefly merged with another nine, the Seasides. In the 1890s, the club reorganized under William Walker's leadership, who managed both the Resolutes and Resolute Juniors.

SOURCES: "Base Ball," *Boston (MA) Advertiser,* Aug 12, 1870; "White vs. Colored Resolutes," *Boston (MA) Journal,* Sep 29, 1870; "A Game For A Name," *Boston Advertiser,* Sep 29, 1870; "Local Matters," *Boston Advertiser,* Jul 3, 1871; "Base Ball," *Boston Journal,* Jun 26, 1871; "Base Ball," *Boston Journal,* Jul 27, 1871; "Base Ball," *Boston Daily Advertiser,* Aug 19, 1871; "Base Ball," *Boston Journal,* Sep 2, 1871; "Base Ball," *Boston Journal,* Apr 5, 1872; "Base Ball," *Boston Journal,* Jun 10, 1872; "Salem," *Boston Journal,* Sep 16, 1874; "Short Stops," *Boston Advertiser,* Aug 7, 1876; "Base Ball," *Boston Advertiser,* Apr 15, 1878; "Gossip Gleanings," *Boston (MA) Globe,* May 12, 1885; "Base Ball," *Springfield (MA) Republican,* May 26, 1885; "Brockton, 15; Resolutes, 3," *Boston Globe,* Jun 7, 1885; "Base Ball," *Boston Journal,* Aug 10, 1885; "Other Base Ball," *Boston Journal,* Sep 16, 1885; "Other Base Ball," *Boston Journal,* Sep 26, 1885; "Back Stops," *Boston Globe,* May 14, 1886; "Plans of the Colored Club," *Boston Globe,* Jan 23, 1887; "Honor for Massachusetts," *New York (NY) Freeman,* Mar 5, 1887; "Resolutes 9, Vendomes 8," *Boston Journal,* Apr 13, 1887; "Boston Easter Services," *New York Freeman,* Apr 16, 1887; "Providence Defeated by the Boston Resolutes," *Boston Globe,* Apr 15, 1887; "A Crack Base Ball Team," *New York Freeman,* Apr 16, 1887; "Colored League," *Louisville (KY) Courier-Journal,* May 8, 1887; "Colored Ball Players," *Boston Globe,* May 21, 1887; "True Political Manhood," *New York Freeman,* Feb 19, 1887; "Honor for Massachusetts," *New York Freeman,* Mar 5, 1887; "Baltimore Notes," *Boston Globe,* Apr 12, 1887; "Two Colored Nines," *Boston Globe, Apr 15,* 1887; "Resolutes 9, Vendomes 8," *Boston Journal,* Apr 13, 1887; "National Colored League," *Boston Globe,* May 8, 1887; "Colored League," *Louisville Courier Journal,* May 8, 1887; "Hard Lines for the Resolutes," *Boston Globe,* May 11, 1887; "Base Ball Notes," *Baltimore (MA) Sun,* May 11, 1887; "Base Ball Notes," *Baltimore Sun,* May 12, 1887; "Base Ball Notes," *Baltimore Sun,* May 13, 1887; "Colored Ball Players," *Boston Globe,* May 21, 1887; "A Ball Team Lost," *Pittsburgh (PA) Post,* May 24, 1887; "Base Ball Notes," *New York (NY) Sun,* Jun 5, 1887; "Prejudiced Republicans," *New York Freeman,* Oct 8, 1887; "Reorganize the Old Resolutes," *Boston (MA) Sunday Globe.* Jan. 27, 1889; "Fitchburgs, 19;

Resolutes, 10," *Fitchburg (MA) Sentinel*, May 25, 1891; "Embryo Kellys," *Boston Globe*, May 28, 1891; "Lebanon, 10; Resolutes, 0," *Boston Globe*, Aug 16, 1891; "Haverhill, 15; Resolute, 1," *Boston Globe*, Jul 2, 1891; "Walker Wanted $15," *Boston Globe*, Aug 15, 1897.

Resolute Junior Base Ball Club (Boston, MA; 1880s–1890s). Organizer(s): E. C. Bryant and Henry Carter; J. Bullick.

The Resolute Junior B.B.C. organized in the 1880s, played black and white teams. *Boston Globe* (May 7, 1888): "The Resolute Juniors club (colored) would like to arrange games with out-of-town clubs for June 30 and July 4. Address Henry Carter: 7 Sears Place, Boston." Between 1888 and 1890, they claimed the 14 year-old junior championship of the State.

Sources: "Boston Amateur League," *Boston (MA) Globe*, May 7, 1888; "Coming Ball Players," *Boston Globe*, Apr 2, 1888; "Amateur Ball," *Boston Globe*, Jun 25, 1888; "Amateur Ball Players," *Boston Globe*, Jul 8, 1888; "Among the Amateurs," *Boston Globe*, May 19, 1890; "Minor Games Yesterday," *Boston (MA) Herald*, Jun 21, 1890; "Amateur Mention," *Boston Globe*, Jul 17, 1893.

Resolute Reserve Base Ball Club (Boston, MA; 1880s–1890s). Organizer(s): B. F. Tate; H. F. Hicks.

The Resolute Reserve B.B.C. organized in the 1880s, played black and white nines. *Boston Globe* (April 27, 1891): "The Resolute Reserves challenge any 14 year-old club to play games on the Common or out-of-town Saturday afternoons." *Boston Herald*: "The Resolute Reserves, a colored aggregation of red-hot ball players, will cross bats with the Emmanuel Athletic Association nine at the South End Grounds afternoon. The same teams met on the common on July 9, and the Resolutes were victorious were victorious by a score of 10 to 9."

Sources: "Minor Games," *Boston (MA) Sunday Globe*, Aug 18, 1889; "Amateur Column," *Boston (MA) Globe*, Apr 27, 1891; "Amateur Column," *Boston Globe*, May 9, 1891; "Amateur Column," *Boston Globe*, Aug 3, 1891; "Amateur Column," *Boston Globe*, Aug 24, 1891; "Amateur Column," *Boston Globe*, Aug 8, 1893; "Other Games," *Boston (MA) Herald*, Jul 30, 1893; "Rising Ball Players," *Boston (MA) Post*, Jul 5, 1896; "On the Little Diamond," *Boston Post*, Jul 12, 1896; "Sprightly Young Ball Players," *Boston Herald*, Apr 19, 1897; "Coming Players," *Boston Globe*, Apr 21, 1897; "Attention, Ball Players," *Boston Herald*, Jun 28, 1897; "Liners," *Boston Herald*, Jul 30, 1897.

Riverside Base Ball Club (Malden, MA; 1890s–1900s). Organizer(s): B. F. Tate; Joseph A. Ivy.

The Riverside B.B.C. organized in the 1890s. *Boston Globe* (May 8, 1899): "The Riverside Athletic Club, champion colored team of eastern Massachusetts, would like to fill open dates. The team is made up of fast young players who will make it interesting for any team. The club would like to arrange a series of games for the colored championship with the Atlantics. Address B. F. Tate, Sanborn House, Malden, stating guarantee and expenses."

Sources: "Local Baseball Season," *Boston (MA) Globe*, May 8, 1899; "Amateurs Want Games," *Boston Globe*, Jul 3, 1899; "Coming Leaguers," *Boston Globe*, Jul 24, 1899; "Amateur Base Ball," *Boston Globe*, Jun 11, 1900.

Seaside Hotel Base Ball Club (Boston, MA; 1880s–1890s). Organizer(s): Theodore E. Roberts.

The Seaside Hotel B.B.C. organized in the 1880s, played black and white teams. *Boston Herald* (July 26, 1887): "At the grove there were lots of amusements, among them a game of ball between the Seasides and West End clubs. The contest resulted in favor of the Seasides, score 6 to 5." *Herald* (April 23, 1888): "The champion Seasides (col-

ored) will begin their season on or about May 30. The club will be made up of the same players as last season, with one or two exceptions." *Boston Globe* (July 2, 1889): "At a meeting held yesterday afternoon the Resolutes and the Seasides, two colored base-ball organizations at the West End, consolidated and will hereafter be known as the Seasides. The new club is under the management of Theodore E. Roberts, 92 Union Street, and has the best colored ball players now in New England." *Herald* (June 9, 1889): "There will be a game on the Common this afternoon between the Seasides, the new colored team, and a nine made up principally from the Sparrows."

Sources: "Fly Balls," *Boston (MA) Globe*, Jun 9, 1886; "Colored People at Picnic," *Boston (MA) Herald*, Jul 26, 1887; "Future Professionals," *Boston Herald*, Apr 23, 1888; "Miscellaneous Games," *Boston Herald*, May 31, 1888; "Minor Games," *Boston Herald*, Jun 10, 1888; "Other Games," *Boston Herald*, Jun 19, 1888; "Minor Games," *Boston Herald*, Jul 8, 1888; "Minor Games," *Boston Herald*, Aug 26, 1888; "Look Out for Their Coaching," *Boston Globe*, Mar 14, 1889; "Out at Home," *Boston Herald*, May 21, 1889; "Caught Napping," *Boston Herald*, May 24, 1889; "Around the Bases," *Boston Herald*, Jun 5, 1889; "Other Games," *Boston Herald*, Jun 9, 1889; "Thrown Out," *Boston Herald*, Jun 9, 1889; "Base Ball Notes," *Boston Globe*, Jul 2, 1889; "Local Matters," *Bangor (ME) Whig and Courier*, Jul 9, 1889; "Base Ball Notes," *Bangor Whig and Courier*, Jul 13, 1889; "Local Matters," *Bangor Whig and Courier*, Jul 23, 1889; "Local Matters," *Bangor Whig and Courier*, Jul 24, 1889; "Base Ball Notes," *Bangor Whig and Courier*, Jul 25, 1889; "Minor Games," *Boston Herald*, May 31, 1890; "Minor Games," *Boston Herald*, Jun 18, 1890.

Vendome Hotel Base Ball Club (Boston, MA; 1880s–1890s). Organizer(s): R. B. Pope and Franklin P. Thompson.

The Vendome Hotel B.B.C. organized in the 1880s, played black nines. *New York Globe* (June 2, 1883): "The U. L. C. Nine, commanded by W. J. Miner, has challenged the Vendome nine, Captain Sam Harris, to play at the Apollo Gardens June 7." *Boston Herald* (June 4, 1888): "The Resolutes played their first game of the season on the Union grounds yesterday, with the Vendomes as their opponents. The latter had the assistance of William Selden and Edward Smith, one of the Resolutes' regular batteries. Alfred Jupiter and Joseph Harris were the battery of the Resolutes, who won by a score of 9 to 8 in game of five innings." In 1888, the aggregation reorganized. *Herald* (August 23, 1888): "The Hotel Brunswick waiters defeated the Hotel Vendome waiters, 13 to 9, Friday afternoon." *Herald* (June 9, 1891): "The Hotel Oxford waiters defeated the Hotel Vendome waiters on the Back Bay yesterday afternoon, 30 to 4, for a purse of $5.00."

Sources: "Boston Letter," *New York (NY) Globe*, Feb 3, 1883; "Our Hub Letter," *New York Globe*, Jun 2, 1883; "Resolutes 9, Vendomes 8," *Boston (MA) Journal*, Apr 13, 1887; "Boston Easter Services," *New York (NY) Freeman*, Apr 16, 1887; "The Amateurs," *Boston (MA) Herald*, Jun 4, 1888; "Gathered at the Plate," *Boston Herald*, Aug 23, 1888; *Boston Herald*, Jun 9, 1891.

Atlantic Base Ball Club (Cambridge, MA; 1890s)

The Atlantic B.B.C. organized in the 1890s, played white and black teams. *Boston Herald* (June 27, 1897): "The National Athletic Club of Waltham defeated the Atlantics, a colored nine of Boston, at Waltham yesterday afternoon, 9 to 4."

Sources: "Other Ball Games Yesterday," *Boston (MA) Herald*, Jun 27, 1897; "Few Open Dates Left," *Boston Herald*, Jul 26, 1897; "Sporting Young Ball Players," *Boston Herald*, Aug 2, 1897; "Base Ball Notes," *Boston (MA) Globe*, Jul 4, 1897; "In Quest of Ball Games," *Boston Herald*, Jun 20, 1898; "National A. C. 9; Atlantic 4," *Boston Herald*,

Jun 26, 1898; "Invitation to Ball Players," *Boston Herald*, Aug 1, 1898; "Craigies, 11; Atlantics 8," *Boston Herald*, Aug 14, 1898.

Bay State Base Ball Club (Cambridge, MA; 1880s–1890s). Organizer(s): John Smith; T. W. Scott; W. C. Ward; Henry F. Hicks.

The Bay State B.B.C. organized in the 1880s, played black and white nines. *Boston Herald* (March 30, 1884): "The Bay State Club (colored), John Smith, secretary, is organized for the season, is open for challenges from all nines with enclosed grounds." *Lowell Courier* (July 6, 1886): "The game of base-ball between the Hood's Sarsaparilla nine and the champion colored team of the state, the Bay States of Boston, at the Fair Grounds yesterday afternoon, proved very one-sided but nevertheless, interesting and amusing. The colored lads could not bat Connors, who struck out five of the first six men at bat. The Hoods scored in every inning and won the game by a score of 22 to 4. The umpire was A. J. Taylor, a colored man who came with the Bay States, and he gave good satisfaction. Green, the catcher for the visitors, played for the grand stand, and by his curious comments on the game and changes of temper, caused much amusement."

SOURCES: "Around the Diamond," *Boston (MA) Herald*, Mar 30, 1884; "Base Ball Briefs," *Boston (MA) Globe*, Mar 22, 1885; "Other Games Played Saturday," *Boston Herald, May* 10, 1885; "Diamond Dust," *Boston Globe*, May 13, 1885; "Pick-Ups," *Boston Herald*, Jul 25, 1885; "Diamond Truths," *Boston Herald, Aug* 6, 1885; "Other Games Yesterday," *Boston Herald*, Aug 8, 1885; "Diamond Doings," *Boston Herald*, Aug 15, 1885; "Diamond Notes," *Boston Herald*, Aug 19, 1885; "Other Games Played Saturday," *Boston Herald*, Aug 23, 1885; "Other Games," *Boston Globe*, Sep 20, 1885; "Diamond Sayings," *Boston Herald*, Oct 2, 1885; "Other Games," *Boston Herald*, Oct 5, 1885; "Diamond Truths," *Boston Herald, Oct* 6, 1885; "Other Games," *Boston Herald*, Oct 8, 1885; "Double Plays," *Boston Globe*, May 25, 1886; "Base Ball," *Lowell (MA) Courier*, Jul 6, 1886; "Fly Balls," *Boston Herald*, Apr 22, 1887; "Among the Amateurs," *Boston Globe*, Apr 23, 1887; "With the Amateurs," *Boston Herald*, May 23, 1892; "Other Games," *Boston Herald*, Jul 23, 1893.

Colored Grays Base Ball Club (Cambridge, MA; 1880s). Organizer(s): C. Miller.

The Colored Grays B.B.C. organized in the 1880s, played white and black teams. *Boston Globe* (July 30, 1888): "The Cambridge Grays would like a game with the sergeants of Mt. Hope, Old Dominions of West Newton, of West Quincys, old Dominions preferred. Address, C. Miller." The Colored Grays challenged Boston's Resolutes. *Globe* (March 25, 1889): "The Cambridge Grays (colored) have organized for the season under the management of William Dunn. The club is in good financial condition, and [they] are ready to go on the field at once. They are anxious to meet the Resolutes of Boston. Where is Marshall Thompson?"

SOURCES: "Amateur Baseballists," *Boston (MA) Daily Globe*, Jul 30, 1888; "Rising Ball Players," *Boston Globe*, Aug 6, 1888; "Among the Amateurs," *Boston Globe*, Mar 25, 1889; "Among the Amateurs," *Boston Globe*, Apr 22, 1889.

Franklin Base Ball Club (Boston, MA; 1880s). Organizer(s): A. W. Bright.

The Franklin B.B.C. organized in the 1880s, played black and white nines. *Boston Globe* (April 15, 1889): "The Franklins have reorganized for the season, with the following players: Battles, Currier, Gage, Sheppard, Bright, Gill, Folsom, Black, Wilson. A. W. Bright, manager, of Franklin Street. They would like to hear from strong amateur nines."

SOURCES: "Among the Amateurs," *Boston Globe*, Apr 15, 1889; "Minor Games," *Boston Globe*, May 17, 1889; "Base Ball Notes," *Boston Globe*, Jun 13, 1889; "Base Ball Notes," *Boston Globe*, Jul 9, 1889.

Franklin Base Ball Club (Cambridge, MA; 1880s–1890s)

The Franklin B.B.C. organized in the 1880s, played black and white nines. *Boston Herald* (August 23, 1885): "A game that has occasioned a great deal of local interest in Cambridge was played on the Boston league grounds, yesterday afternoon, between the Cambridges and Franklins of that city, the prize being the gate receipts and the championship of the city. Each club had a large number of its friends present, who clapped and applauded every error made by their favorites' opponents, though, after the third inning, the franklin element had the field to themselves, the Cambridge contingent finding but little comfort from the contest. Each club by mutual agreement, imported players especially for the occasion, the Franklins having several of the members of the colored club, including the latter's fine amateur battery—William Selden and Edward Smith."

SOURCES: "Other Games," *Boston (MA) Herald*, Aug 23, 1885; "Diamond Jottings," *Boston Herald*, Aug 27, 1885; "Fair Hit Balls," *Boston Herald*, Aug 30, 1885; "Base Ball Notes," *Boston Herald, Sep* 26, 1885; "Other Base Ball," *Boston (MA) Journal*, Sep 26, 1885; "Cambridge Champions," *Boston Herald*, Sep 26, 1885; "Other Games," *Boston Herald*, Jun 1, 1886; "Out Shoots," *Boston Herald, Aug* 26, 1886; "Among the Amateurs," *Boston (MA) Globe*, Jul 4, 1887.

Memorial Hall Base Ball Club (Cambridge, MA; 1870s–1900s). Organizer(s): E. H. Johnson; Joseph Carrington.

The Memorial Hall B.B.C. organized in the 1870s. The Memorial Halls, composed of dining waiters of Harvard University, played black and white clubs. *Boston Post* (May 18, 1876): "On Tuesday last, a picked nine of Memorial Hall waiters played a nine from the Port. The waiters came off victorious." *Boston Herald* (April 26, 1879): "Memorial Hall waiters sent out a nine, and in their first game defeated their opponents by a score of 14 to 6." *Boston Globe* (April 6, 1884): "The Memorial Hall waiters have recently formed a base-ball nine, with E. H. Johnson as captain, and as there are some fine players among them, they expect to have a good team." The club had first and second nines, many of the players having been members of the Vendomes and Resolutes. The second nine, called the Lead Heels, beat the Memorials (first nine), two games out of three, for the Memorial Hall championship. The Memorials also played white university teams. *Cambridge Harvard Crimson* (April 21, 1885): "In a game last Saturday the Memorial waiters beat the University Press nine, 11 to 10. The Memorial nine plays Wednesday with the Cambridge High School, and Saturday with the University Press again." *Harvard Crimson* (May 2, 1888): "In a baseball match between the Athletics and Memorials, each composed of waiters in Memorial Hall, the former nine was victorious by a score of 10 to 8. The battery of the Athletics was Stewart and Crawford; of the Memorials Pidgeon and Carrington."

SOURCES: "Harvard Items," *Boston (MA) Post*, May 18, 1876; "Harvard Notes," *Boston (MA) Herald*, Apr 26, 1879; "Fact and Rumor," *Cambridge (MA) Crimson*, Apr 4, 1884; "Base Ball Notes," *Boston (MA) Globe*, Apr 6, 1884; "Base Ball Notes," *Boston Herald*, Apr 11, 1884; "Other Games," *Boston Globe*, Apr 30, 1884; "Other Games," *Boston Globe*, Jun 5, 1884; "Fact and Rumor," *Cambridge Crimson*, Apr 21, 1885; "Diamond Sparks," *Boston Herald*, Apr 22, 1885; "Fact and Rumor," *Cambridge Crimson*, Apr 30, 1885; "Other Games Played Saturday," *Boston Herald*, May 31, 1885; "Fact and Rumor," *Cambridge Crimson*, Apr 25, 1888; "Fact and Rumor," *Cambridge Crimson*, May 2, 1888; "Baseball," *Cambridge (MA) Chronicle*, May 12, 1900.

City Hotel Base Ball Club (Chelsea, MA; 1890s). Organizer(s): William A. Tarby.

The City Hotel B.B.C. organized in the 1890s, if not earlier. The team, composed of hotel barbers, played black and white teams. *Boston Globe* (August 19, 1892): "A very exciting game of base-ball took place on the Everett Avenue Grounds yesterday afternoon between the white and colored barbers of the city. William F. Nute of the City Hotel was captain of the whites and William A. Tarby of the colored. The game was a tie up to the fifth inning, standing 7 runs each. In the sixth inning the colored barbers seemed to get demoralized, and from that to the close made only 4 runs, while the white boys scored 14, making a total in their favor of 21 runs against 14 for the colored boys."

Sources: "Three Call Five," *Boston (MA) Herald*, Mar 1, 1886; "Chelsea," *Boston (MA) Globe*, Aug 19, 1892; "Meeting of Colored Men," *Boston Daily Globe*, Apr 25, 1893; "Custom House Changes," *Boston (MA) Journal*, Nov 2, 1894.

Puritan Base Ball Club (Worcester, MA; 1880s)

The Puritan B.B.C. organized in the 1880s. *New York Freeman* (May 21, 1887): "The Puritan Social Club has organized a base-ball nine with F. Gimby, manager, and Benjamin Walker, captain, have order their uniforms of Mr. Alex Clapp. The uniforms will be gray pants, blue jerseys, gray cap, and blue stockings." The Puritans played against black teams. *Freeman* (September 3, 1887): The Puritan B.B.C. defeated the Hackmen of Worcester with a score of 41 to 10."

Sources: "Worcester Whispers," *New York (NY) Freeman*, May 21, 1887; "Worcester Whispers," *New York Freeman*, Sep 3, 1887.

Michigan

Page Fence Giants Base Ball Club (Adrian, MI; 1890s). Organizer(s): Bud Fowler & Gus Parsons.

The Page Fence B.B.C. organized in the 1890s, played black and white teams. *Philadelphia Sporting Life* (October 20, 1894): "Bud Fowler, an old colored league player," who played second base for the Findlay B.B.C. the past season, has organized a colored ball team for next season. It will be backed by a wire-fence company of Adrian, MI, and a bicycle company of MA, and will be used as an advertising card for their wares. A bicycle parade will be given prior to each game. Fowler says his team will be the strongest colored aggregation ever organized." While playing the Cincinnati Reds, a sportswriter noted a remarkable, if not old-style, feature of the team. *Cincinnati Enquirer* (April 12, 1895): "The big glove rule has no terrors for the Page Fence Giants. Every man on the team except the catcher and first baseman plays bare-handed." *St. Paul Globe* (April 28, 1896): "The Mankato Maroons opened the base-ball season here today with the Page Fence Giants in a game which resulted five to nothing in favor of the Giants. The members of the team are all colored and travel in a palace car." *Logansport Reporter* (May 25, 1896): "Out of 150 games played by the Page Fence Giants last season, they won 120. Some of the National League teams went down before them." *Muskegon Chronicle* (June 28, 1897): "If it hadn't been for Johnson and Johnson, Jr., and seven other colored gentlemen playing such fast ball and the Muskegon Reds playing ball that was as yellow as a Bay Hill sunset the latter might have won Sunday's game. They might have. They had the crowd and it was a good crowd too—the largest of the season. Every inch of the bleachers and grandstand was filled and many spectators roosted on the fence or knelt on the ground. The crowd was ready to root for Muskegon too but it seldom got the chance. Sometimes it groaned. But it was the outside contingent that did this. The local crowd was more charitable." *Green Bay Press Gazette* (July 22, 1898): "The Green Bay baseball team was defeated by the Page Fence Giants again in yesterday's game at Washington Park baseball grounds. The score was 12 to 0."

Sources: "More Giants," *Philadelphia (PA) Sporting Life*, Oct 20, 1894; "Come Seven," *Cincinnati (OH) Enquirer*, Apr 12, 1895; "Pounded

at Haha," *Minneapolis (MN) Journal*, Apr 22, 1895; "Ham's Sons Fanned the Air," *Minneapolis Journal*, Apr 23, 1895; "White vs. Black," *Fort Wayne (IN) Journal-Gazette*, May 23, 1895; "Another Easy Victory for the Giants," *Detroit (MI) Free Press*, Jun 29, 1895; "An Interesting Game," *Saginaw (MI) News*, Aug 16, 1895; "The Giants Beat Kalkaska," *Detroit Free Press*, Aug 22, 1895; "Base Ball," *Lima (OH) Times Democrat*, Sep 14, 1895; "Neighborhood Notes," *Jackson (MI) Patriot Citizen*, Mar 28, 1896; "Shut Out the Maroons," *St. Paul (MN) Globe*, Apr 28, 1896; "Second Shut Out," *Logansport (IN) Reporter*, May 25, 1896; "Page Fence Giants," *Logansport Reporter*, May 26, 1896; "The Fence Giants Won Again," *Detroit Free Press*, Jun 20, 1896; "Other Games," *Detroit Free Press*, Jul 2, 1896; "Page Fence Giants," *Saginaw News*, Jul 20, 1896; "P.F.G.'s Made Hits," *Saginaw News*, Aug 31, 1896; "P.F.G.'s Made Hits," *Saginaw News*, Aug 31, 1896; "Giants vs. Giants," *Detroit Free Press*, Sep 21, 1896; "Giants Win," *Adrian (MI) Evening Telegram*, Apr 8, 1897; "Giants Win," *Cedar Rapids (IA) Evening Gazette*, Apr 23, 1897; "News and Notes," *Adrian Evening Telegram*, May 17, 1897; "News and Notes," *Adrian Evening Telegram*, Jun 28, 1897; "Page Fence Giants Beat Battle Creek," *Detroit Free Press*, Aug 30, 1897; "Too Much Johnson," *Muskegon (MI) Chronicle*, Jun 28, 1897; "Giants vs. Colts," *Oshkosh (WI) Daily Northwestern*, Sep 10, 1897; "A Close Game," *Canton (OH) Repository*, May 9, 1898; "Other Games," *Cleveland (OH) Plain Dealer*, May 9, 1898; "The Giants Again," *Adrian Telegram*, May 16, 1898; "Page Fence Giants," *Saginaw News*, May 16, 1898; "Page Fence Giants Shut Green Bay Out," *Green Bay (WI) Press Gazette*, Jul 22, 1898; "Amateur Baseball," *Detroit Free Press*, Sep 30, 1898.

Powers Base Ball Club (Adrian, MI; 1890s)

The Powers B.B.C. organized in the 1890s. *Adrian Evening Telegraph* (June 19, 1895): "A colored base-ball team has been organized. They are between the ages of 16 and 18 years, have ordered suit and will play teams in the neighboring towns. They will be known as Powers Clothing Company, Club, and hope to be able to tackle the Giants when they visit Adrian again." The nine played white and black teams. *Evening Telegraph* (August 19, 1895): "The Powers Clothing Co. Ball Club defeated the Adrian Center Pumpkin Huskers on Saturday by a score of 17 to 8. The Giants played all around and mopped the earth with the visitors."

Sources: "New and Notes," *Adrian (MI) Evening Telegram*, Jun 19, 1895; "New and Notes," *Adrian Evening Telegram*, Jun 29, 1895; "New and Notes," *Adrian Evening Telegram*, Jul 8, 1895; "New and Notes," *Adrian Evening Telegram*, Aug 19, 1895.

Colored Base Ball Club (Battle Creek, MI; 1880s). Organizer(s): Elijah Walker.

The Colored B.B.C. organized in the 1880s. The nine competed against black clubs of Battle Creek, Grand Rapids, and Kalamazoo. Contests often took place during Emancipation Day celebrations. *Kalamazoo Gazette* (August 7, 1879): "The Red Stockings of this city played a game of baseball with a Grand Rapids nine, resulting in a victory for the Kalamazoo boys in a score of 4 to 2." *Kalamazoo Telegraph* (October 20, 1886): "The colored nine of this city [Battle Creek] and the colored nine of Kalamazoo will play a match game of ball next week at the Driving Park and a dance will be held in the evening at Centennial Hall." *Kalamazoo Gazette* (October 27, 1886): "The colored nine of ball players went to Battle Creek and played a colored nine of would-be players of that village. They returned loaded with glory ad victory."

Sources: *Kalamazoo (MI) Gazette*, Aug 7, 1879; "The Fallen Shackles," *Kalamazoo Gazette*, Aug 4, 1886; "Kalamazoo Again Victorious," *Kalamazoo (MI) Telegraph*, Sep 3, 1886; "Not Title," *Kalamazoo Telegraph*, Oct 20, 1886; "A Victory Scored," *Kalamazoo

Gazette, Oct 27, 1886; "Kalamazoo Still at the Front," *Kalamazoo Telegraph*, Oct 27, 1886; "A Victory Scored," *Kalamazoo Gazette*, Oct 27, 1886.

Mascot Base Ball Club (Detroit, MI; 1880s–1890s)

The Mascot B.B.C. organized in the 1880s, played black and white aggregations. They regularly played in Canada. *Windsor Evening Record* (May 25, 1893): "A base-ball game between Mascots, a famous colored nine and a crack nine from Toledo, did not take place owing to the non-appearance of the latter, but nine were scratched up on the grounds to be slaughtered by a score of 16 to 5." That year, 5000 spectators witnessed the Detroit News defeat the Windsor News. *Windsor Evening Record* (August 7, 1893): "The news aggregation was composed of eight chocolate colored tossers and one white."

SOURCES: "The Amateurs," *Detroit (MI) Free Press*, May 12, 1889; "Sporting Notes," *Detroit Free Press*, July 17, 1889; *Detroit (MI) Plaindealer*, Sep 27, 1889; "Annexation," *Windsor Evening Record*, May 20, 1893; "Broke the Record," *Windsor Evening Record*, May 25, 1893; "Ball Game," *Windsor Evening Record*, Jul 11, 1893; "The Ball Game," *Windsor Evening Record*, Aug 3, 1893; "Did 'Em Up," *Windsor Evening Record*, Aug 7, 1893; "August the First," *Windsor Evening Record*, Aug 2, 1894.

Red Stocking Base Ball Club (Detroit, MI; 1870s)

The Red Stocking B.B.C. organized in the 1870s, played black teams. *Ann Arbor Argus* (July 23, 1875): "A match game of baseball between the Red Stockings, of Detroit, and Sweepstakes, of this city—both colored clubs—will be played in this city next Monday afternoon." *Ypsilanti Commercial* (August 28, 1875): "On Monday the colored club of Detroit [Red Stockings] played the Aetnas (colored) of Ypsilanti. Score: Detroits, 4; Aetnas, 19."

SOURCES: "Local Affairs," *Ypsilanti (MI) Commercial*, Aug 28, 1875; "Local Affairs," *Ann Arbor (MI) Argus*, Jul 23, 1875; "Local Affairs," *Ann Arbor Argus*, Jul 30, 1875.

Rialto Base Ball Club (Detroit, MI; 1860s)

The Rialto B.B.C. organized in the 1860s. The Tecumseh Club, of London, Ontario hosted a grand base-ball tournament. *New York Wilkes Spirit of the Times* (August 1869): "[The tournament included] a special class composed of colored citizens of the United States and Dominion of Canada." The press derided the black participants. *Detroit Free Press* (August 26, 1869): "One of the Negro Base-Ball Clubs of Detroit is to compete for a prize at the London, Ontario base-ball tournament. They can show the Londoners some big feet." The Rialtos and Goodwills, of London, Ontario, met in the black championship match. *Charlotte Eaton County Republican* (September 3, 1869): The Rialtos, of Detroit, won a first prize of $50 in gold at the London base-ball tournament."

SOURCES: "Base Ball," *New York (NY) Wilkes Spirit of the Times*. Aug 1869; "Saying and Doings," *Detroit (MI) Free Press*, Aug 26, 1869; "Saying and Doings," *Detroit Free Press*, Aug 27, 1869; "A Colored Base Ball Club," *Charlotte (MI) Eaton County Republican*, Sep 3, 1869; "The Base Ball Field," *New York Wilkes Spirit of the Times*, Sep 4, 1869.

Union Base Ball Club (Detroit, MI; 1880s–1890s). Organizer(s): Fred Slaughter.

The Union B.B.C. organized in the 1880s, played black and white organizations. *Detroit Plaindealer* (May 12, 1889): "The Union ball club is ready to ready to contest with any seventeen year-old club in the city." The aggregation challenged the Natural Gas, Russell House, and Hotel Wayne nines to play on any grounds selected. *Free Press* (July 17, 1889): "The Unions Beat the Clovers 10 to 5" (The Clover's colored catcher, William Jackson, later joined the Cuban Giants). *Free Press* (July 21, 1889): "The Unions defeated a picked nine yes-terday 19 to 1. Features of the game, [Ed] Smith's catch of a high fly and [Fred] Slaughter's catching."

SOURCES: "The Amateurs," *Detroit (MI) Free Press*, May 12, 1889; "The Amateurs," *Detroit Free Press*, Jun 25, 1889; "Sporting Notes," *Detroit Free Pres*, Jul 17, 1889; "The Amateurs," *Detroit Free Press*, Jul 21, 1889; "The Amateurs," *Detroit Free Press*, Aug 7, 1889; *Detroit (MI) Plaindealer*, Sep 27, 1889; "Mere Mention" *Detroit Plaindealer*, May 23, 1890; *Detroit Plaindealer*, Jul 4, 1890; *Detroit Plaindealer*, Jul 11, 1890; "Mere Mention," *Detroit Plaindealer*, Nov 28, 1890.

Waving Lilies Base Ball Club (Detroit, MI; 1870s)

The Waving Lilies B.B.C. organized in the 1870s, played black organizations. *Millersburg Free Press* (May 20, 1871): "Detroit has a colored base-ball club called the Waving Lilies." The black players of Detroit and Windsor, Ontario continued a rivalry traceable to the 1860s. Social interaction could lead to violence. *Detroit Free Press* (May 20, 1871): "A selected three of a Negro base-ball club entitled: The Waving Lilies, yesterday proceeded to Windsor and played a game on the forepart of the head of an opposing club named B. H. Phillips, bulging his eyes and battering his nose in a bad way, claiming that he had insulted the sister of one of the assailants. The club got back to this side just in time to evade a warrant for assault and battery." *Free Press* (July 22, 1871): "Three Negro base-ball clubs were playing each other in Windsor yesterday." During an eastern tour, the Chicago Uniques visited MI and Upper Canada. *Free Press* (July 28, 1871): "The Negro Base Ball Club of this city has been notified that the Negro club of Chicago will arrive here in a day or two, en route to the east, intending to match themselves against any club, white or black, which desires to play." *Free Press* (August 24, 1871): "The Detroit Negro Base Ball Club is going on a tour inland."

SOURCES: "Base Ball," *Detroit (MI) Free Press*, May 20, 1871; "New Items," *Millersburg (OH) Free Press*, May 20, 1871; "Sayings and Doings," *Detroit Free Press*, Jul 22, 1871; "Expected," *Detroit Free Press*, Jul 28, 1871; "Sayings and Doings," *Detroit Free Press*, Aug 24, 1871.

Wayne Hotel Base Ball Club (Detroit, MI; 1880s–1890s)

The Wayne Hotel B.B.C. organized in the 1880s, played black and white teams. *Detroit Plaindealer* (July 3, 1891): "Wednesday the waiters of the Wayne paralyzed the Cadillac waiters by a score of 19 to1." *Detroit Free Press* (July 2, 1892): "The [Hotel] Normandie, Jr., team has challenged the Wayne Hotel team to play a game July 8, or any other date."

SOURCES: "Notes," *Detroit (MI) Free Press*, Apr 29, 1888; *Detroit (MI) Plaindealer*, Sep 27, 1889; "Meer Mention," *Detroit Plaindealer*, Jan 24, 1890; "Windsor and Vicinity," *Detroit Plaindealer*, Jul 3, 1891; "Base Ball Notes," *Detroit Free Press*, Jul 2, 1892.

Colored Base Ball Club (Grand Rapids, MI; 1870s–1880s)

The Colored B.B.C. organized in the 1870s. The nines of Battle Creek, Grand Rapids, and Kalamazoo established a rivalry. Contests often took place during Emancipation Day celebrations. *Kalamazoo Gazette* (August 7, 1879): "The Red Stockings of this city played a game of baseball with a Grand Rapids nine, resulting in a victory for the Kalamazoo boys in a score of 4 to 2." On Emancipation Day in 1886, Battle Creek and Grand Rapids measured bats. *Kalamazoo Gazette* (August 4, 1886): "Battle Creek and Grand Rapids both sent colored nines."

SOURCES: *Kalamazoo (MI) Gazette*, Aug 7, 1879; "The Fallen Shackles," *Kalamazoo Gazette*, Aug 4, 1886.

Central City Base Ball Club (Jackson, MI; 1880s). Organizer(s): Fred Harper.

The Colored B.B.C. organized in the 1880s. Manager Fred Harper claimed (*Jackson Citizen Patriot.* March 17, 1888) that his "sturdy and active young men will be able to play good ball and perhaps afford the league club opportunities of practice requiring their full strength to knock out the colored boys in blue." *Citizen Patriot* (June 28, 1888): "In the base-ball game Fred Harper's nine won over the visitor's picked nine by a score of 12 to 1. Batteries: Harper and Thomas, and Bunberry and Kingsbury."

SOURCES: "Central City Colored Club," *Jackson (MI) Citizen Patriot,* Mar 17, 1888; "Little Pop-Ups," *Jackson Citizen Patriot,* Jun 28, 1888; "Emancipation Day," *Jackson Citizen Patriot,* Aug 2, 1888.

Bootblack Base Ball Club (Kalamazoo, MI; 1890s)

The Bootblack B.B.C. organized in the 1890s. *Kalamazoo Gazette* (August 1, 1895) report: "A large number of Kalamazoo's colored citizens will go to Battle Creek today to celebrate Emancipation Day. This morning a game of ball will be played between teams from Battle Creek and Niles. This afternoon the winner of the morning game will play the Unions, the colored team of Kalamazoo. The Kalamazoo boys have showed that they play good ball." *Gazette* (July 13, 1899): "The East Side Sliders defeated the Bootblacks in a slugging match on the East Side campus Saturday afternoon by a score of 32 to 28." *Gazette* (July 19, 1899): "The East Side Sliders defeated the Bootblacks in a slugging match on the East Side campus Saturday afternoon by a score of 32 to 28."

SOURCES: *Kalamazoo (MI) Gazette,* Jun 25, 1895; "Sporting Notes," *Kalamazoo (MI) Telegraph,* Jun 25, 1895; "A Challenge," *Telegraph,* June 26, 1895; "To Celebrate Emancipation Day" *Kalamazoo Gazette,* Aug 1, 1895; "A Challenge," *Kalamazoo Gazette,* Sep 18, 1898; "Victory for Sugar Beets," *Kalamazoo Gazette,* Jul 13, 1899; "Another Leader Fallen," *Kalamazoo Gazette,* Jul 19, 1899; "Gain Favor with Ladies," *Kalamazoo Gazette,* Aug 6, 1899.

Colored Stars Base Ball Club (Kalamazoo, MI; 1890s). Organizer(s): William Stewart.

The Colored Stars B.B.C. organized in the 1890s. *Kalamazoo Gazette* (August 6, 1898): "The Colored stars defeated the Oshtemo team by a score of 27 to 10. The features of the game were the Stars heavy batting. Hackley secured a home run, a three base hit and two singles." *Gazette* (September 8, 1898): "The Kalamazoo Colored Unions challenge the Stars for a game of ball on Campus October 5, or earlier for $5 a side and a league baseball." The Colored Stars reorganized in 1899. *Gazette* (April 12, 1899): "A number of Kalamazoo's colored baseball enthusiasts met Tuesday evening and organized a baseball team. William Stewart was elected captain and manager and will be pleased to accept challenges from any team in this part of Michigan. The name of the team will the Colored Stars."

SOURCES: Will Come Together," *Kalamazoo (MI) Gazette,* May 31, 1898; "Stopped the Fight," *Kalamazoo Gazette,* Jun 10, 1898; "Notes," *Kalamazoo Gazette,* Jun 12, 1898; "Base Ball," *Kalamazoo Gazette,* Jul 26, 1898; "Jottings," *Kalamazoo Gazette,* Aug 6, 1898; "Base Ball," *Kalamazoo Gazette,* Aug 17, 1898; "Base Ball," *Kalamazoo Gazette,* Aug 18, 1898; "A Great Success," *Kalamazoo Gazette,* Dec 15, 1898; "The Colored Stars," *Kalamazoo Gazette,* Apr 12, 1899; "Lose the First Game," *Kalamazoo Gazette,* Jun 7, 1898; "Snowed Under," *Kalamazoo Gazette,* Jun 30, 1899; "Sporting Notes," *Kalamazoo Gazette,* Jul 4, 1899.

Excelsior Base Ball Club (Kalamazoo, MI; 1880s). Organizer(s): Ed McKay and W. H. Robbins.

The Excelsior B.B.C. organized in the 1890s, played black and white teams.

SOURCES: "Sporting Matters," *Kalamazoo (MI) Gazette,* Apr 16, 1889; "The Oxford Selected," *Kalamazoo Gazette,* Apr 24, 1889.

Union Base Ball Club (Kalamazoo, MI; 1890s).

The Union B.B.C. organized in the 1890s. *Kalamazoo Gazette* (August 1, 1895) report: "A large number of Kalamazoo's colored citizens will go to Battle Creek today to celebrate Emancipation Day. This morning a game of ball will be played between teams from Battle Creek and Niles. This afternoon the winner of the morning game will play the Unions, the colored team of Kalamazoo. The Kalamazoo boys have showed that they play good ball."

SOURCES: "To Celebrate Emancipation Day," *Kalamazoo (MI) Gazette,* Aug 1, 1895; "Strikes," *Kalamazoo Gazette,* Jun 16, 1897; "A Challenge," *Kalamazoo Gazette,* Sep 18, 1898.

Minnesota

Mutual Base Ball Club (Minneapolis, MN; 1880s)

The Mutual B.B.C. organized in the 1880s, played white and black teams. *Minneapolis Star Tribune* (August 19, 1880): "The Minneapolis Browns will play a practice game on their grounds in South Minneapolis with the colored nine of this city." The Mutuals and St. Paul Clippers played for the black championship of the State. *Star Tribune* (August 31, 1880): "The Mutual, colored base-ball club of this city, played with the Clippers of St. Paul, and made the boys pass over the purse of $25. The score stood 23 to 3 in favor of Minneapolis. The St. Paul boys are to play a return game in this city sometime this week."

SOURCES: "About People," *Minneapolis (MN) Star Tribune,* Aug 19, 1880; "Gossip About Town," *Minneapolis Star Tribune,* Aug 31, 1880; "Base Ball," *Minneapolis Star Tribune,* Sep 21, 1880; "Gossip About Town," *Minneapolis Star Tribune,* Sep 22, 1880; "Gossip About Town," *Minneapolis Star Tribune,* Oct 1, 1880; "Minneapolis Globules," *St. Paul (MN) Globe.* Oct. 3, 1880; "Minneapolis Globules," *St. Paul Globe,* Oct 4, 1880.

Union Base Ball Club (Minneapolis, MN; 1870s–1880s). Organizer(s): James Cheatum, James Cunningham and L. Mason.

The Union B.B.C. organized in the 1870s. The members of the Unions—originally composed of barbers, named the Minnehaha Hotel B.B.C.—belonged to baseball's hotel-waiter subculture. In 1876, the Unions and Saint Paul Blue Stars played a series of matches for the championship: in game one, the Unions won by a score of 37 to 28; in the second game, the Blue Stars defeated the Unions by a score of 27 to 0. The Unions claimed that the Stars had recruited black professionals from Chicago. They also played the white barber nine. *Minneapolis Star Tribune* (August 25, 1876): "The Union (colored) base-ball club beat the white barbers by a score of 19 to 38."

SOURCES: "Colored Club," *Minneapolis (MN) Star Tribune,* Aug 19, 1876; "Brevities," *Minneapolis Star Tribune,* Aug 21, 1876; "Brevities," *Minneapolis Star Tribune,* Aug 24, 1876; "Brevities," *Minneapolis Star Tribune,* Aug 25, 1876; "Yesterday's Game Between the Colored B. B. Clubs of the Dual City," *Minneapolis Star Tribune,* Aug 31, 1876; "Westerns vs. Unions," *Minneapolis Star Tribune,* Sep 2, 1876; "Brevities," *Minneapolis Star Tribune,* Sep 4, 1876; "Gossip About Town," *Minneapolis Star Tribune,* Sep 7, 1876; "Black Base Ballists," *Minneapolis Star Tribune,* Sep 21, 1876; "The Sports," *Minneapolis Star Tribune,* Sep 25, 1876; "Gossip About Town," *Minneapolis Star Tribune,* Oct 3, 1876; "Base Hits," *Minneapolis Star Tribune,* Oct 14, 1876.

Mascott Base Ball Club (St. Paul, MN; 1880s). Organizer(s): H. J. Edwards and F. R. Lanier.

The Mascott B.B.C. organized in the 1880s, played black and white organizations. *St. Paul Globe* (June 6, 1887): "The Mascotts and Western Avenue nines played a well-contested game Sunday afternoon on the Grand Avenue grounds, the former winning by a score of 11 to 7. The feature of the game was the errorless playing of the Mascotts." *St. Paul Western Appeal* (August 13, 1887): "The Mascott and Lafayette clubs crossed bats last Tuesday. Good playing was done by both clubs. Score: Mascott, 12; Lafayette 11. Manager Harbora says he will give a prize to the player making the greatest number of home runs. The St. Louis Reserves will play the Lafayettes next week."

SOURCES: "Scraps of Sports," *St. Paul (MN) Globe*, Jun 6, 1887; "Minnetonka Beach," *St. Paul (MN) Western Appeal*, Jul 2, 1887; "Lake Breezes," *Minneapolis (MN) Star Tribune*, Jul 17, 1887; "Base Ball Chatter," *Cleveland (OH) Gazette*, Jul 23, 1887; "Minnetonka Beach," *St. Paul Western Appeal*, Jun 18, 1887; "Minnetonka Beach," *St. Paul Western Appeal*, Jul 30, 1887; "Minnetonka Beach," *St. Paul Western Appeal*, Aug 13, 1887.

Barber Merchant Hotel Base Ball Club (St. Paul, MN; 1870s–1880s). Organizer(s): Benjamin Underwood and Lloyd Wheeler.

The Barber Merchant Hotel B.B.C. organized in the 1870s. The Merchants (originally Bass Tavern, circa 1867) Hotel, of Saint Paul, and Metropolitan Hotel, of Minneapolis (circa 1869–1870) employed both white and black hotel staff; significantly, both groups made clear racial distinctions in the press when hosting social events. *St. Paul Globe* (September 28, 1884): "The waiters of the Metropolitan Hotel and the barbers of the Merchants will play a game of baseball at the Seventh Street Park this afternoon at 2:30 for the colored championship of the northwest. Admission is free." *Globe* (October 12, 1884): "The waiters of the Metropolitan Hotel gave the Merchants Hotel barbers a clean shave this afternoon by a score of 15 to 0. The Merchants were strengthened by four men from the Fort (Snelling) and two from Minneapolis; they were no match, and gave up before the game was over. (This was the second time they have been beaten.) The Metropolitans will play any colored nine in the northwest for fun, money, marbles or chalk." They also played against the Hall's barber nine. *Globe* (October 13, 1884): "The barbers from the Merchants and Hall's shops had a game on West Seventh Park yesterday evening. There was a good crowd in attendance, and from the score, there must have been some pretty lively playing."

SOURCES: "For the Colored Championship," *St. Paul (MN) Globe*, Sep 28, 1884; "Barbers at Base Ball," *St. Paul Globe*, Oct 12, 1884; "City Globules," *St. Paul Globe*, Oct 13, 1884.

Blue Stars Base Ball Club (St. Paul, MN; 1870s)

The Blue Stars B.B.C. organized in the 1870s, played black and white nines. In 1876, the Unions and Saint Paul Blue Stars played a series for the black championship. The Unions won by a score of 37 to 28; and the Blue Stars defeated the Unions, by a score of 27 to 0. Hostility resulted from the latter contest, the Unions claiming that the Stars had recruited black professionals from the Chicago Unique club. *Minneapolis Star Tribune* (September 21, 1876): "The colored base-ball clubs of this city and St. Paul, Unions and Blue Stars, played three innings of a game at Blue Stocking Park yesterday afternoon. The Unions state that the Blue Stars numbered in their playing nine yesterday three professionals from the best colored nine in the west— that of Chicago—and that wool was very much pulled over their eyes, to the tune of 23 to nothing. Colored base-ball ardor in this city has cooled."

SOURCES: "Yesterday's Game Between the Colored B. B. Clubs of the Dual City," *Minneapolis (MN) Star Tribune*, Aug 31, 1876; "Westerns vs. Unions," *Minneapolis Star Tribune*, Sep 2, 1876; "Brevities," *Minneapolis Star Tribune*, Sep 4, 1876; "Gossip About Town," *Minneapolis Star Tribune*, Sep 7, 1876; "Black Base Ballists," *Minneapolis Star Tribune*, Sep 21, 1876; "The Sports," *Minneapolis Star Tribune*,

Sep 25, 1876; "Gossip About Town," *Minneapolis Star Tribune*, Oct 3, 1876; "Base Hits," *Minneapolis Star Tribune*, Oct 14, 1876.

Douglass Base Ball Club (Minneapolis, MN; 1890s)

The Douglass B.B.C. organized in 1897, played black and white teams. *St. Paul Western Appeal* (June 12, 1897): "The Douglass Base Ball Club has been reorganized and would like a game for every Saturday during the summer. The first game will be played Saturday with the Adler Kids at Aurora Park." *Minneapolis Journal* (August 10, 1897): "The Quicksteps and Douglass clubs will play Sunday afternoon at the old ball park on Twenty-Fourth Street. The Douglass club is composed of colored men of Minneapolis and St. Paul. Howard, late of the Nashville Southern [Colored] League team will pitch for the Douglass team."

SOURCES: *St. Paul (MN) Appeal*, Jun 12, 1897; "Base Ball," *Minneapolis (MN) Journal*, Aug 7, 1897; "Amateur Notes," *Minneapolis Journal*, Aug 10, 1897; "With the Amateurs," *Minneapolis (MN) Star Tribune*, Aug 10, 1897.

Hall's Barber Base Ball Club (St. Paul, MN; 1880s). Organizer(s): O. C. Hall.

The Hall's Barber B.B.C. organized in the 1880s, played black teams. *St. Paul Globe* (August 14, 1884): "The barbers from the Merchants and Hall's shops had a game on West Seventh Park yesterday evening. There was a good crowd in attendance, and from the score, there must have been some pretty lively playing."

SOURCES: "Barber Ball Tossers," *St. Paul (MN) Globe*, Aug 14, 1884.

Lafayette Hotel Quickstep Base Ball Club (St. Paul, MN; 1880s). Organizer(s): Harbora and Walter Alexander Plummer.

The Lafayette Hotel Quickstep B.B.C. organized in the 1880s, played white and black nines. *St. Paul Globe* (July 8, 1885): "The waiters of the Lafayette played a game of base-ball with the Fronts yesterday afternoon and received a crushing defeat. Al Plummer, head waiter of the Lafayette, umpired the game successfully and there was considerable sport during the progress. A number of the best players among the waiters did not materialize on the diamond and to this fact they attribute their defeat. At the close of the game the scorer footed the tallies and found the score, Bell Boys, 20, Waiters, 6." They also played the Mascott nine. *Globe* (August 13, 1887): "The Mascott and Lafayette clubs crossed bats last Tuesday. Good playing was done by both clubs. Manager Harbora says he will give a prize to the player making the greatest number of home runs. The St. Louis Reserves will play the Lafayettes next week." *St. Paul Western Appeal* (August 13, 1887): "The Quicksteps by winning the game with the Minneapolis club became the champion of the Northwest. They have accepted a challenge from the Fort Snelling Club and will play the game on Monday the 15 inst. The game will take place on the Fort Snelling Grounds." *Globe* (August 16, 1887): "An interesting game of baseball was played at Fort Snelling yesterday afternoon between the St. Paul Quicksteps and the Fort Snelling nine. The game also abounded in fine plays and resulted in a victory for the home club by a score of 14 to 8." The Quicksteps also played the Shakopee Reserve nine.

SOURCES: "Minnetonka," *St. Paul (MN) Globe*, Jul 2, 1885; "Minnetonka," *St. Paul Globe*, Jul 8, 1885; "Minnetonka," *St. Paul Globe*, Jul 19, 1885; "Minnetonka Gossip," *St. Paul Globe*, Aug 1, 1885; "At Minnetonka," *St. Paul Globe*, Jul 10, 1887; "Fort Snelling," *St. Paul (MN) Western Appeal*, Jul 30, 1887; "Minnetonka Beach," *St. Paul Western Appeal*, Aug 13, 1887; "Scraps of Sports," *St. Paul Globe*, Aug 16, 1887; "Scraps of Sports," *St. Paul Globe*, Aug 20, 1887; *St. Paul Western Appeal*, Aug 27, 1887; *St. Paul Western Appeal*, Aug 20, 1887; *Cleveland (OH) Gazette*, Aug 27, 1887; "Pretty Badly Walloped," *St. Paul Globe*, Aug 29, 1887.

Metropolitan Hotel Base Ball Club (St. Paul, MN; 1870s–1880s)

The Metropolitan Hotel B.B.C. organized in the 1870s, played black nines. They developed a rivalry with the Merchant Hotel. *St. Paul Globe* (August 15, 1878): "The game of base-ball between the Merchants and Metropolitan Hotel waiters resulted in a score of seven to two in favor of Allen's Club." *Globe* (September 28, 1884): "The waiters of the Metropolitan Hotel and the barbers of the Merchants will play a game of base-ball at the Seventh Street Park this afternoon at 2:30 for the colored championship of the northwest. Admission is free." *Globe* (October 13, 1884): "The waiters of the Metropolitan Hotel gave the Merchants Hotel barbers a clean shave this afternoon by a score of 15 to 0. Although the Merchants nine was strengthened by four men from the Fort (Snelling) and two from Minneapolis they were no match for the hash slingers, and gave up before the game was over. The Metropolitans will play any colored nine in the northwest for fun, money, marbles or chalk."

SOURCES: "City Globules," *St. Paul (MN) Daily Globe*, Aug 15, 1878; "City Globules," *St. Paul Globe*, Aug 18, 1879; "Minneapolis Globules," *St. Paul Globe*, Oct 3, 1880; "Minneapolis Globules," *St. Paul Globe*, Oct 4, 1880; "Barber Ball Tossers," *St. Paul Globe*, Aug 14, 1884; "For the Colored Championship," *St. Paul Globe*, Sep 28, 1884; "Barbers at Base Ball," *St. Paul Globe*, Oct 12, 1884; "City Globules," *St. Paul Globe*, Oct 13, 1884.

Ryan Hotel Base Ball Club (St. Paul, MN; 1880s–1900s)

The Ryan Hotel B.B.C. organized in the 1880s, played against similar teams. *St. Paul Globe* (May 29, 1894): "At 2:30 yesterday afternoon a match game of base-ball was played near the Irving School on Grand Avenue, between picked nines from colored employees of the Ryan and Aberdeen Hotels. The game closed at about 5:15 p.m., at which time the score stood 10 to 5 in favor of the Ryan nine. The Ryan team was uniformed in gray pantaloons and shirts, black stockings and black caps, and the Aberdeen team were attired in blue caps, white shirts, blue pantaloons and black stockings. The Ryan team were very successful last summer, losing only one game—that to the Nonpareils."

SOURCES: *St. Paul (MN) Appeal*, Jul 13, 1889; *St. Paul Appeal*, Aug 17, 1889; "Colored Ball Game," *St. Paul (MN) Globe*, May 29, 1894; *St. Paul (MN) Broad Axe*, Aug 15, 1895; "Saint Paul," *St. Paul Appeal*, Aug 15, 1914.

St. Peter Base Ball Club (St. Paul, MN; 1890s). Organizer(s): Fred J. McGhee.

The St. Peter B.B.C. organized in 1895, played black nines. *St. Paul Globe* (June 30, 1895): "The St. Peters, newly organized base-ball team, will cross bats with the Strike Outs, at the picnic to be held at Fetsch's Grove, Como Park, on the Fourth of July."

SOURCES: "Champions of Color," *St. Paul (MN) Globe*, Jun 30, 1895.

Strike Out Base Ball Club (St. Paul, MN; 1890s)

The Strike Outs B.B.C. organized in 1895, played black teams. *St. Paul Globe* (June 30, 1895): "The St. peters, newly organized base-ball team, will cross bats with the Strike Outs, at the picnic to be held at Fetsch's Grove, Como Park, on the Fourth of July."

SOURCES: "Champions of Color," *St. Paul (MN) Daily Globe*, Jun 30, 1895.

Mississippi

MIssissippi Grays Base Ball Club (Biloxi, MS; 1890s)

The MIssissippi Grays B.B.C. organized in the 1880s, played black nines. *Vicksburg Evening Post* (April 20, 1895): "The Mississippi Grays

won the first game of the series to be played for the colored championship of this city from the Crackhards. The Grays would like to get a game from the Bay St. Louis Team."

SOURCES: "Local Happenings," *Biloxi (MS) Herald*, Apr 20, 1895.

Black Stockings Base Ball Club (Natchez, MS; 1880s)

The Black Stockings B.B.C. organized in the 1880s, played black organizations. *Natchez Weekly Democrat* (September 8, 1886): "It is said that the way in which one of the colored nines of our city—the Black Stockings—play base-ball, would do credit even to the crack nines that belong to the base-ball leagues of the country. Each member of the nine works like clock-work in his place on the diamond, and there are no nines about here that can down them."

SOURCES: "Good Ball Players," *Natchez (MS) Weekly Democrat*, Sep 1, 1886; "For the Championship of Natchez," *Natchez Weekly Democrat*, Sep 8, 1886.

G. F. Bowles Base Ball Club (Natchez, MS; 1880s)

The G. F. Bowles B.B.C. organized in the 1880s, played black teams. *New Orleans Times-Picayune* (June 13, 1886): "The [New Orleans] Pinchbacks returned Natchez yesterday morning, having defeated the G. H. [G. F.] Bowles Baseball Club on Tuesday by a score of 9 to 6."

SOURCES: "Good Ball Players," *New Orleans (LA) Times-Picayune*, Jun 13, 1889; "News Item," *Vicksburg (MS) Commercial Herald*, Jun 21, 1893.

Home Boys Base Ball Club (Natchez, MS; 1880s). Organizer(s): Sam Johnson, Miller Maguire and George Weir.

The Home Boys B.B.C. organized in the 1880s, played black organizations. *Natchez Weekly Democrat* (September 16, 1885): "The game of base-ball that took place in Vidalia on Sunday last between the Home Boys, of Natchez, and the Vidalia nine, resulted in a victory for the first named nine by a score of thirty-six to thirteen." *Natchez Weekly Democrat* (September 8, 1886): "There has been considerable rivalry between those two colored base-ball nines—the Black Stockings and the Home Boys—and as each of them have defeated the others twice in the four games played, they are going to play the fifth game for the championship of Natchez."

SOURCES: "Local Brevities," *Natchez (MS) Weekly Democrat*, Jul 8, 1885; "Base Ball Matters," *Natchez Weekly Democrat*, Sep 16, 1885; "Local Brevities," *Natchez Weekly Democrat*, Sep 23, 1885; "The Gauntlet Throws Down to the State," *Natchez Weekly Democrat*, Mar 24, 1886; "Local Brevities," *Natchez Weekly Democrat*, May 5, 1886; "Home Boys and Blue Stockings," *Natchez Weekly Democrat*, Aug 25, 1886; "Good Ball Players," *Natchez Weekly Democrat*, Sep 1, 1886; "For the Championship of Natchez," *Natchez Weekly Democrat*, Sep 8, 1886.

Red Stocking Base Ball Club (Greenville, MS; 1890s)

The Red Stocking B.B.C. organized in the 1890s, played black organizations. The Reds developed a rivalry with Little Rock's Quapaws. *Little Rock Gazette* (June 15, 1897): "A large crowd was in attendance yesterday afternoon at West End Park to witness the first of a series of games between the Quapaws, colored champions of Arkansas, and the strong Greenville Mississippi Reds. The game was full of ginger from the start and the boys put up as snappy a game as the present season has afforded on the local grounds."

SOURCES: "Quapaws Still Champions," *Little Rock (AR) Gazette*, Jun 15, 1897; "Quapaws Win Again," *Little Rock Gazette*, Jun 16, 1897.

Crayton Base Ball Club (Vicksburg, MS; 1880s). Organizer(s): Fred Buckner.

The Crayton B.B.C. organized in the 1880s, played against black teams. *Vicksburg Evening Post* (August 3, 1886): "The Illegal Base

Ball Club (a new colored organization) has challenged the Alderman Clayton Club, to play a match game for the championship. The game will take place at the Fairgrounds next Saturday evening. F. Foote is Captain of the Illegals, and Fred Buckner, Captain of the Craytons. The Clubs are made up from the ranks of the best young colored men in the city." *Evening Post* (September 4, 1886): "The Alderman Crayton and Home Run Base Ball Clubs will play a match game in Flood's Bottom tomorrow afternoon at 3 ? o'clock." *Evening Post* (September 6, 1886): "The Alderman Crayton Base Ball Club defeated the Home Runs yesterday by a score 11 to 8, the latter club playing 7 innings and the Crayton's 6. Fred Buckner is captain and pitcher of the Crayton's; Tobe Morton is captain and pitcher of the Home Runs. The clubs will play another game next Sunday. The colored clubs of Vicksburg think that they can defeat the celebrated colored club of Natchez."

SOURCES: "Local Line," *Vicksburg (MS) Evening Post*, Aug 3, 1886; "Base Ball," *Vicksburg Evening Post*, Sep 4, 1886; "New Items," *Vicksburg (MS) Herald*, Sep 5, 1886; "Local Lines," *Vicksburg Evening Post*, Sep 6, 1886; "New Items," *Vicksburg Herald*, Sep 12, 1886; "New Items," *Vicksburg Herald*, Sep 19, 1886.

E. M. Snowden Base Ball Club (Vicksburg, MS; 1880s). Organizer(s): Edward M. Snowden.

The E. M. Snowden B.B.C. organized in the 1880s, played black teams. *Vicksburg Evening Post* (June 25, 1886): "The E. M. Snowdens and the Greenville Blues, the crack colored base-ball clubs of the State, will play two match games for $100 a side, at the Greenville Fair Grounds." *Vicksburg Evening Post* (July 5, 1886): "The E. M. Snowden, Jr., Base Ball Club, of Vicksburg, defeated the Greenville Blues last Saturday and Sunday. There were 300 people present on Saturday and 700 on Sunday."

SOURCES: "Local Lines," *Vicksburg (MS) Evening Post*, Jun 25, 1886; "Vicksburg Ahead," *Vicksburg Evening Post*, Jul 5, 1886.

Frank O'Neil Base Ball Club (Vicksburg, MS; 1880s). Organizer(s): Frank O'Neil and Ed Smith.

The Frank O'Neil B.B.C. organized in the 1880s, played black teams. The team was named in honor of Frank O'Neil, a local white businessman. *Vicksburg Evening Post* (July 1, 1884): "There was a match game of base-ball played in the American Bottom Sunday afternoon, between the Pastimes and F. O'Neils, resulting in a victory for the latter. It is claimed that the Pastimes had a picked nine, while the O'Neils played their regular club, all very young players. The Pastimes made 7 score, the O'Neils 24. Each club played seven innings. Another game will be played on July 4th. *Evening Post* (August 26, 1886): "A colored base-ball club of this city organized last season in honor of Frank O'Neil, claims the championship of Vicksburg. The club has an open challenge for any colored base-ball club in this city or State for the championship and any stake agreed upon." The Vicksburgs played Shreveport's Hudson club. *Vicksburg Herald* (August 26, 1886): "The J. M. Blow Base Ball Club defeated the F. O'N's third nine in a match game yesterday evening in Flood's Bottom—score 11 to 8. Both are juvenile colored clubs." *New Orleans Weekly Pelican* (July 2, 1887): "In a game of base-ball at the Fair Grounds the R. E. Lees, of Shreveport, and the Vicksburgs, of Vicksburg, Mississippi, both colored clubs, the Shreveport club won by a score of 8 to 4."

SOURCES: "O'Neil's and Pastimes," *Vicksburg Evening Post*, Jun 23, 1884; "Base Ball Items," *Vicksburg Evening Post*, Jul 1, 1884; "F. O'Neil Base Ball Club," *Vicksburg Evening Post*, Aug 26, 1886; "Local Lines," *Vicksburg Evening Post*, Aug 26, 1886; "News Items," *Vicksburg (MS) Herald*, Aug 26, 1886; "Senegambian Sluggers at Shreveport," *Dallas (TX) Morning News*, July 2, 1886; "News Item," *Vicksburg (MS) Herald*, October 16, 1886; "Shreveport Sparks," *New Orleans (LA) Weekly Pelican*, Jul 2, 1887; "Shreveport, LA.," *New Orleans Weekly Pelican*, Sep 17, 1887.

J. M. Blowe Base Ball Club (Vicksburg, MS; 1880s). Organizer(s): J. M. Blowe.

The J. M. Blowe B.B.C. organized in the 1880s, played black nines. *Vicksburg Evening Post* (August 26, 1886): "The J. M. Blow Base Ball Club defeated the F. O'N.'s third nine in a match game yesterday evening in Flood's Bottom—score 11 to 8. Both are juvenile colored clubs." *Vicksburg Herald* (August 26, 1886): "The J. M. Blowe Base Ball Club met and defeated the F. ON.'s at Flood's Bottom in a score of 11 to 8. Some good playing was done, especially by Peter Forbes, captain of the Blowe's, who made a home run and brought three men home on one stroke."

SOURCES: "News Items," *Vicksburg (MS) Herald*, Aug 24, 1886; "Local Lines," *Vicksburg (MS) Evening Post*, Aug 26, 1886; "News Items," *Vicksburg Herald*, Aug 26, 1886.

J. M. Doyle Base Ball Club (Vicksburg, MS; 1880s). Organizer(s): J. M. Doyle.

The J. M. Doyle B.B.C. organized in the 1880s, played black organizations. *Vicksburg Evening Post* (August 25, 1886): "The club is ready to play and colored club in the State for the championship and stakes that may be agreed upon."

SOURCES: "The J. M. Doyle Base Ball Club," *Vicksburg (MS) Evening Post*, Aug 25, 1886.

Lazy Boys Base Ball Club (Vicksburg, MS; 1880s)

The Lazy Boys B.B.C. organized in the 1880s, played black teams. *Vicksburg Herald* (August 1, 1886): "The Jackson Road Eclipse and the Lazy Boys, two colored baseball clubs, were to have played a game at Parisot's Bottom last evening for $2.50, but the Jackson Road Eclipse could raise but twenty-five cents, and they got into a squabble over the matter; the club went to pieces and the game did not come off. The Lazy Boys have each ordered another gallus to be attached to their uniforms in honor of their victory." *Herald* (August 15, 1886): "The Lazy Boys defeated the Cowengtons yesterday in a game of 16 to 7, at Sam Allens Bottom, on Belmont Street. Both are crack colored baseball clubs."

SOURCES: "News Items," *Vicksburg (MS) Herald*, Aug 1, 1886; "News Items," *Vicksburg Herald*, Aug 15, 1886.

W. P. B. Base Ball Club (Vicksburg, MS; 1870s)

The W. P. B. B.B.C. organized in the 1870s, played against black teams. *Vicksburg Herald* (May 28, 1878): "The Young Men's Base Ball Club and the W.P.B. Base Ball Club, both colored, of this city had a contest at Bedford's Grove, in which the former gained victory by a score of 46 to 16. The Y.M.B's will be presented with a ball and bat today by Mr. F. G. Pierce."

SOURCES: "Base Ball," *Vicksburg (MS) Herald*, May 28, 1878.

Young Men's Base Ball Club (Vicksburg, MS; 1870s)

The Young Men's B.B.C. organized in the 1870s, played against black organizations. *Vicksburg Herald* (May 28, 1878): "The Young Men's Base Ball Club and the W.P.B. Base Ball Club, both colored, of this city had a contest at Bedford's Grove, in which the former gained victory by a score of 46 to 16. The Y.M.B's will be presented with a ball and bat today by Mr. F. G. Pierce."

SOURCES: "Base Ball," *Vicksburg (MS) Herald*, May 28, 1878.

Rough and Ready Base Ball Club (Woodville, MS; 1880s)

The Rough and Ready B.B.C., of Vicksburg, MS, organized in the 1880s, played black nines of MS and LA. *Woodville Republican* (November 3, 1888): "The match game of ball between the celebrated colored clubs, the Rough & Readys and Willnots for a purse of $25 won by the Willnots. Score 15 to 2." *Republican* (August 10, 1889): "Quite an interesting game of baseball was played in Woodville on Thursday evening, by two colored clubs, the Willnots and the Woodville club, which resulted in a score of 21 to 10 in favor of the Willnots." *New Orleans Times-Democrat* (August 1, 1888): "A match game today for $50 a side and the gate receipts, between the Unions, of Orleans, and the Rough and Readys, of Woodville, resulted in favor of the Unions by a score of 15 to 9."

SOURCES: "Game at Bayou Sara," *New Orleans (LA) Times-Democrat*, Aug 1, 1888; *Woodville (MS) Republican*, Oct 27, 1888; *Woodville Republican*, Nov 3, 1888; *Woodville Republican*, Aug 10, 1889.

Missouri

Grays Base Ball Club (Carthage, MO; 1890s)

The Grays B.B.C., of Springfield, MO, organized in the 1890s, played black nines. *Springfield Democrat* (June 18, 1895): "Tomorrow and Wednesday the Carthage Grays, a strong team of colored players, will meet the D. R. C. club of Springfield at the old fairgrounds." *Springfield Republican* (June 19, 1895): "The Springfield colored baseball club defeated the Carthage team at the old fairgrounds yesterday by a score of 31 to 17, and now claim the colored championship of the southwest." *Springfield Republican* (June 20, 1895): "The Springfield colored base-ball club defeated the Carthage team again yesterday. Quite a fair-sized audience witnessed, which was characterized by brilliant fumbles and numerous errors. The score was 26 to 21. The Carthage team is anxious for another game, which no doubt will be arranged soon, because the motto of the Springfield team is Carthago delendo est."

SOURCES: "Local Glances," *Springfield (MO) Democrat*, Jun 18, 1895; "Colored Baseball," *Springfield (MO) Republican*, Jun 19, 1895; "Springfield Won Again," *Springfield Republican*, Jun 20, 1895.

Colored Base Ball Club (DeSoto, MO; 1900s). Owner(s): W. L. Smith.

The Colored B.B.C. organized in the 1900s. *Indianapolis Freeman* (May 12, 1900) announces: "Our young men of the baseball fraternity, met at their club house and organized last week, for the season with W. L. Smith manager, and George Bozier captain. They are open for challenges from any amateur club with a radius of 150 miles. All communications concerning games and dates should be addressed to the manager. The team is registered as the De Soto Colored Base Ball Club, and they are not playing for their health alone."

SOURCES: "DeSoto Letter," *Indianapolis (IN) Freeman*, May 12, 1900; "Interesting Points," *Indianapolis Freeman*, May 19, 1900.

OK Base Ball Club (Independence, Missouri; 1880s)

The OK B.B.C. organized in the 1880s, played black teams. *Lawrence Journal* (May 25, 1887): "The Lawrence Eagles have accepted a challenge from a colored ball club, of Independence, Missouri, to play a game at Lawrence next month." *Lawrence Evening Tribune* (June 9, 1887): "The game yesterday between the OK's of Independence, Missouri and the Lawrence Eagles was very interesting. The umpire had probably been a champion umpire during slavery days, but did not know much of the game as it is played in '87. He frequently called ball when the batter had struck at them. Several of the Lawrence players had been infused with Missouri whiskey, which loosened their tongues and caused several bolts in the game over altercations with the umpire. The OKs did very poor batting, and most of their runs were made on errors. The Eagles did some heavy

batting in the forepart of the game, but after the Oks had changed pitchers did not succeed in batting so freely. Both clubs have good ball playing material, and it is to be hoped that today's game was a better one." They club reorganized in 1888. *Kansas City Times* (April 17, 1888): "The OK's, a colored ball club of Independence, beat the Pastimes of Kansas City, colored, yesterday by a score of 10 to 9."

SOURCES: *Lawrence (KS) Evening Tribune*, May 24, 1887; "News Around Town," *Lawrence (KS) Journal*, May 25, 1887; "City News in Brief," *Lawrence Evening Tribune*, Jun 1, 1887; "City News in Brief," *Lawrence Evening Tribune*, Jun 2, 1887; *Lawrence (KS) Daily Journal*, Jun 8, 1887; "Base Ball Notes," *Lawrence Daily Journal*, Jun 10, 1887; "Yesterday's Ball Game," *Lawrence Evening Tribune*, Jun 9, 1887; "Independence," *Kansas City (MO) Times*, Apr 17, 1888.

Black Stockings Base Ball Club (Kansas City, MO; 1880s). Organizer(s): Sam Thomas and James Logan.

The Black Stocking B.B.C. organized in the 1880s, played black nines. *Kansas City Star* (June 4, 1883): "The Athletic Park was the scene of a thrilling contest in the shape of a match game of base-ball between two colored clubs, the Leapers and the Black Stockings. All the young colored bloods of the city were there, and with their ladies, crowded the amphitheater, while several hundred Caucasians hung on the fence and cheered wilding at every brilliant play. The Leapers were clad in pink shirts, red stockings, and white pants, while their opponents wore suits of dark blue, relieved by chaste stripes about half a foot wide. Excited men ran up and down the amphitheater flourishing real money and shouting…. The game resulted in a victory for the Leapers on a score of 10 to 9 and great was the rejoicing thereat." The Black Stockings went on the road. *Atchison Globe* (June 7, 1883): "The Black Stockings, colored base-ball club from Kansas City, passed through the city today for St. Joe, where they will play a match game today." Kansas City and St. Joseph developed a rivalry. *St. Joseph Gazette-Herald* (May 31, 1883): "The Eclipse Base Ball Club of this city, will go to Kansas City to meet the Black Stockings upon the diamond patch. These clubs are colored and lively tossers." *Gazette-Herald* (June 8, 1883): "Yesterday afternoon, at College Hill, the Black Stockings, of Kansas City, played the Eclipse nine of this city. The Kansas City nine was victorious, the score standing seven to two. The series consists of three games for the championship, and the return game will be played at Kansas City on the 20th."

SOURCES: "Mere Mention," *St. Joseph (MO) Gazette-Herald*, May 31, 1883; "The City," *Kansas City (MO) Star*, Jun 4, 1883; "A Base Ball Game," *St. Joseph (MO) Herald*, Jun 8, 1883; "Base Ball," *St. Joseph Gazette-Herald*, Jun 8, 1883; "Dusky Diamond," *Kansas City Star*, Jun 4, 1883; *Atchison (KS) Globe*, Jun 7, 1883; *Atchison Daily Globe*, July 19, 1883; "Successful Coons," *Sedalia (MO) Weekly Bazoo*, Jul 24, 1883.

Blue Stocking Base Ball Club (Kansas City, MO; 1890s). Organizer(s): S. Grear; A. L. Thomas and T. Woodson; Patterson.

The Blue Stocking B.B.C. organized in the 1890s, played black teams. *Kansas City Star* (July 30, 1892): "The Kansas City Blues (colored) will play the crack colored team of Leavenworth, the Pastimes, at Exposition Park tomorrow afternoon." *Kansas City Times* (April 11, 1893): "An amateur base-ball team of colored players, to be known as the Kansas City Blues, has been organized for the season. The manager is F. Woodson of 566 Oak Street." *Kansas City Star* (May 18, 1893): "The Kansas City Colored Blues and the Wyandotte Browns [colored] played a hot game yesterday, at Vic Roy Park. The Blues won by a score of 18 to 14 but the Wyandotte team declares that it was ahead of the game and the umpire ran away." They played Leavenworth's Leaper team. After defeating the Leapers at Exposition Park, at Kansas City, by a score of 21 to 6, both clubs agreed to a return game at Leavenworth. *Lawrence Gazette* (July 11, 1893): "A return baseball game between the Kansas City Blues (colored) and the Lawrence Leapers will be played on the home grounds next Friday afternoon." *Kansas City Star* (July 15, 1893): "The Kansas City Blues (colored), defeated the Lawrence Leapers at Lawrence yesterday by a score of 7 to 1." *Springfield Republican* (June 12, 1894): "The Kansas City Blues defeated the Springfield Reds last Sunday by a score of 19 to 10, but the tables were turned yesterday when Springfield won by a score of 27 to 17. Both are colored base-ball clubs." By 1895, the team had developed another local rivalry. *Kansas City Times* (June 12, 1895): "The Times Hustlers defeated the original colored Kansas City Blues by a score of 31 to 11 yesterday."

SOURCES: "Base Ball Notes," *Kansas City (MO) Star*, May 28, 1892; "Base Ball Notes," *Kansas City Star*, Jul 26, 1892; "Sporting Notes," *Kansas City (MO) Times*, Jul 29, 1892 "Base Ball Notes," *Kansas City Star*, Jul 30, 1892; "Brief Bits of City News," *Kansas City Times*, Apr 11, 1893; "General Sporting Notes," *Kansas City Star*, May 13, 1893; "General Sporting Notes," *Kansas City Star*, May 18, 1893; "Amateur Base Ball Notes," *Kansas City Times*, May 22, 1893; "Amateur Base Ball Notes," *Kansas City Star*, May 31, 1893; "Amateur Base Ball Notes," *Kansas City Star*, Jun 2, 1893; "Amateur Base Ball Notes," *Kansas City Star*, Jun 16, 1893; "Amateur Base Ball Notes," *Kansas City Times*, Jun 19, 1893; "Amateur Base Ball Notes," *Kansas City Times*, Jun 26, 1893; "Amateur Base Ball Notes," *Kansas City Times*, Jul 10, 1893; "Base Ball Notes," *Kansas City Star*, Jul 10, 1893; "City Briefs," *Lawrence (KS) Gazette*, Jul 11, 1893; "Base Ball Notes," *Kansas City Star*, Jul 15, 1893; "Base Ball Notes," *Kansas City Star*, Jul 25, 1893; "Amateur Base Ball Notes," *Kansas City Star*, Aug 5, 1893; "Two Games Today," *Kansas City Times*, May 6, 1894; "Among the Amateurs," *Kansas City Times*, May 7, 1894; "Random Notes," *Springfield (MO) Republican*, Jun 12, 1894; "Lawrence Baseball Clubs," *Lawrence (KS) Weekly World*, Aug 9, 1894; "Times Hustlers in New Suits," *Kansas City Times*, Jun 12, 1895; "Amateur Base Ball," *Kansas City Times*, Jun 12, 1895; "Amateur Baseball," *Kansas City Times*, Jun 28, 1895.

Bradbury Base Ball Club (Kansas City, MO; 1890s–1900s). Owner(s): George Jones.

The Bradbury B.B.C. organized in the 1890s. The Bradburys, sponsored by the Bradbury Piano Company, played white and black aggregations. A local, black rivalry developed with the Union club. *Kansas City Journal* (May 11, 1898): "The Bradburys and the Unions, the two leading colored teams of Kansas City, met on Exposition Park yesterday afternoon, and the Bradbury's came out victors by a core of 6 to 1. The game was close enough from the start to be exciting, but the Bradburys or Grays, as the crowd called them, because of the uniforms they wore, secured a lead in the seventh inning, which the Unions, in blue suits formerly used by Manning's team, could not overcome." *Kansas City Journal* (June 11, 1899): "The Bradburys and Schmelzers met yesterday at Exposition Park, and when the clouds had rolled by, the scoreboard in the east end of the park showed that the Bradburys had taken their antagonists down the pike to the tune of 14 to 9. The feature of the game was the general work of the Brads. The Schmelzers also put up a strong game, and had it cinched until the eighth inning, when the Brads got on to Starup and batted out eight runs; of course, the Schmelzers made numerous errors."

SOURCES: "Baseball Notes," *Kansas City (MO) Journal*, May 8, 1898; "Won By the Bradburys," *Kansas City Journal*, May 11, 1898; "Unions and Bradburys to Play," *Kansas City Journal*, May 26, 1898; "Bradburys vs. Tigers," *Kansas City Journal*, May 28, 1898; "Baseball Notes," *Kansas City Journal*, May 29, 1898; "Bradburys and Times to Play," *Kansas City Journal*, Sep 26, 1898; "With the Amateur Players," *Kansas City Journal*, Aug 28, 1898; "Schmelzers vs. Bradburys," *Kansas City Journal*, Jun 11, 1899; "Notes of the Game," *Sedalia (MO) Democrat*, Jul 6, 1902.

Brown Stocking Base Ball Club (Kansas City, MO; 1870s–1890s)

The Brown Stocking B.B.C. organized in the 1870s, played black nines. *Lawrence Journal* (August 15, 1876): "A special from Kansas City last evening informs us of the victory of the Eagles over the Brown Stockings by a score of 30 to 20." A rivalry developed. *Lawrence Journal* (August 27, 1875): "The game today between the Kansas City Brown Stockings and the Topeka Westerns, resulted in favor of the Westerns by a score of 23 to 6. The Browns are the champions of western Missouri." *Kansas City Journal of Commerce* (August 27, 1876): "The Brown Stocking Base Ball Club (colored), of Kansas City, visited Lexington on Friday to play a match game with a club of Sedalia. On their return home yesterday morning they stopped off and played a match game with a colored club of this city. The score stood Independence, 12; Kansas City, 39." *Lexington Weekly Intelligencer* (September 2, 1876): "A game of base-ball was played near this city last Friday between the Sedalia Athletics and the Kansas City Browns. Kansas City was scooped, and the game resulted in 42 counts for the Athletics, while the Browns made 29. Both clubs are colored. The game was for a ball, which, we believe, was handed over to the victors…. These clubs will shortly play another game at Warrensburg." They reorganized in the 1880s. *Lawrence Journal* (August 3, 1886): "The Lawrence Eagles played the Kansas City Brown Stockings a game yesterday after resulting in a rather large victory for Kansas City—only 26 to 13 in favor of Kansas City." *Kansas City Star* (August 6, 1888): "The Kansas City Browns and the Wyandotte Black Stockings played a game of ball in Wyandotte yesterday. The score was 25 to 5 in favor of the Browns. Both organizations are colored." *Kansas City Star* (September 24, 1888): "The Kansas City Browns and the brick yards nine played a game at Harlem yesterday. The score was 8 to 4 in favor of the Browns. Pitchers, Smith and McClure."

SOURCES: "Jottings," *Kansas City (MO) Journal*, Jun 9, 1875; *Lawrence (KS) Journal*, Aug 27, 1875; *Kansas City Journal*, Aug 10, 1876; *Kansas City Journal*, Aug 15, 1876; *Kansas City Journal*, Aug 19, 1876; "Independence," *Kansas City Journal*, Aug 22, 1876; *Kansas City Journal*, Aug 24, 1876; *Kansas City Journal*, Aug 27, 1876; *Lexington (MO) Weekly Intelligencer*, Sep 2, 1876; "Shorts," *Lexington Weekly Intelligencer*, Sep 2, 1876; "Suburban Notes," *Kansas City Journal*, Aug 27, 1876; *Kansas City Journal*, May 15, 1877; Independence," *Kansas City Journal*, Aug 2, 1877; *Kansas City Journal*, Aug 1, 1878; *Kansas City Journal*, Aug 4, 1878; *Kansas City Journal*, Aug 8, 1878; *Kansas City Journal*, Aug 20, 1878; "Base Ball," *Lawrence (KS) Commonwealth*, Jul 30, 1879; "Colored Base Ball," *Kansas City Star*, Aug 21, 1881; "About the Kaw," *Star*, Sept. 18, 1882; "The City," *Kansas City (MO) Star*, Jul 30, 1883; "Late Locals," *Kansas City Star*, Aug 14, 1883; "The City," *Kansas City Star*, Aug 30, 1883; "Colored Base Ball Club," *Topeka (MO) Capital*, Jun 6, 1884; *Topeka Capital*, Jun 18, 1884; *Topeka Commonwealth*, Jun 18, 1884; "Base Ball," *Kansas City Journal*, Jul 31, 1886; *Kansas City Journal*, Aug 39, 1886; *Kansas City Journal*. Aug. 19, 1886; "Base Ball," *Kansas City (MO) Star*, Aug 6, 1888; "Base Ball," *Kansas City Star*, Sep 24, 1888; "Monticello," *Olathe (KS) Mirror*, Aug 23, 1888; "Rosedale," *Kansas City Star*, Aug 24, 1888; "Base Ball," *Kansas City Star*, Sep 24, 1888; "Base Ball Notes," *Kansas City Star*, June 22, 1891; "Base Ball Notes," *Kansas City Star*, July 8, 1891.

Colored Porters Base Ball Club (Kansas City, MO; 1890s)

The Colored Porters B.B.C. organized in the 1890s, played black teams. *Kansas City Times* (July 6, 1895): "The Times Hustlers will play two games Sunday at Fifteenth and Vine. The first game is with the I. X. L.'s and the second is with a nine composed of porters at different tailor shops." *Kansas City Star* (May 14, 1898): "The Kansas City Colored Porters will go to Holden Sunday morning to play the crack colored team of that town. The Porters will be weakened as James O'Brien, their crack pitcher, had a finger on his hand broke. 'Monk' Shea will pitch Sunday's game."

SOURCES: "Two More Victories in Night," *Kansas City (MO) Times*, Jul 6, 1895; "Amateur Base Ball Notes," *Kansas City (MO) Star*, May 14, 1898; "Amateur Base Ball Notes," *Kansas City Star*, May 15, 1898; "Amateur Base Ball Notes," *Kansas City Star*, May 26, 1898.

Fire Department No. 11 Base Ball Club (Kansas City, MO; 1890s). Owner(s): D. Gatewood and Frank Maupin.

The Fire Department No. 11 B.B.C. organized in the 1890s, played black nines. The team was nickname Maupin's No 11, after Frank Maupin, the star catcher. *Kansas City Star* (July 18, 1892): "There will be a ball game at Exposition Park Wednesday between the crack colored baseball team known as the Fire Department No. 11 and a picked nine." *Star* (July 21, 1892): "The Kansas City No. 11 ball club composed of local colored ball players yesterday defeated a picked nine with Frank Maupin its guiding spirit, by a score of 19 to 8. The local team put up a good game and in the eighth inning batted out 10 runs." *Star* (July 25, 1893): "The Kansas City No. 11 team, colored, say that they are willing to play the Blues, colored, at any time and place and for any amount that the Blues may name."

SOURCES: "Base Ball Notes," *Kansas City (MO) Star*, Jul 18, 1892; "Base Ball Notes," *Kansas City Star*, Jul 19, 1892; "Base Ball Notes," *Kansas City Star*, Jul 21, 1892; "General Sporting Notes," *Kansas City Star*, Apr 10, 1893; "General Sporting Notes," *Kansas City Star*, May 13, 1893; "Amateur Base Ball Notes," *Kansas City Star*, May 22, 1893; "Amateur Base Ball Notes," *Kansas City Star*, May 31, 1893; "Amateur Base Ball Notes," *Kansas City Star*, Jun 2, 1893; "Base Ball Notes," *Kansas City Star*, Jul 25, 1893.

Hector Base Ball Club (Kansas City, MO; 1880s)

The Hector B.B.C. organized in the 1880s, played black teams. *Kansas City Times* (August 5, 1885): "A very exciting and amusing game of baseball was played at League Park yesterday afternoon between the Hectors of Kansas City and the Novelties of Lawrence, Kansas. The game was won in the tenth inning by the local club by a score of 19 to 17. The Hectors announce that they are open to challenges from any of the colored clubs in this section." *Times* (August 15, 1885): "The Hectors and the Norvals, two colored clubs, played a match game of ball yesterday, resulting in a victory for the Hectors, by a score of 21 to 19. The feature of the game was the heavy batting of Hamilton of the Hectors." *Kansas City Star* (August 24, 1885): "The Lone Stars and Hectors, clubs composed of colored players, played a game of base-ball at Athletic Park yesterday. The game resulted in favor of the Lone Stars by a score of 14 to 7." *Kansas City Times* (August 23, 1885): "The Stars of West Kansas and Hectors will play a match game of base-ball at League Park this afternoon."

SOURCES: "Sporting Matters," *Kansas City (MO) Star*, Aug 24, 1884; "Base Ball Gossip," *Kansas City (MO) Times*, Aug 5, 1885; "Base Ball Notes," *Kansas City Times*, Aug 15, 1885; "Base Ball Notes," *Kansas City Times*, Aug 23, 1885.

IXL Base Ball Club (Kansas City, MO; 1890s). Organizer(s): Andrew Hardgraver and Bud Johnson; Perry Stephens.

The IXL B.B.C. organized in the 1890s. The I X L's played black teams. *Kansas City Star* (August 4, 1893): The IXLs is the name of a colored club just organized with Andrew Hardgraver as manager. They defeated the Olathe Blues by a score of 12 to 11." Feature of the

game was the pitching of Jackson, and the second base playing of Hardgraves." *Star* (June 12, 1894): "Perry Stevens has resigned the captaincy of the I X L's colored club and will sell the club uniforms at 565 Grand Avenue." *Star* (July 2, 1894): "The I X L Base Ball Club, colored, meets at 565 Grand Avenue at 7:00 o'clock tonight to make arrangements for a visit to Olathe July 4th to play the colored club of that place." *Star* (July 5, 1894): "The IXL's, colored, visited Olathe yesterday and defeated the rack nine of that place by a score of 19 to 13. Stevens's running catch and a triple play by Carson, Hardgraver and Kent were features of the game." *Star* (June 12, 1894): "The IXL team defeated the Olathe Blues Sunday by a score of 12 to 11. The features of the game were the pitching of Thomas and the second base playing of Hardgraver." *Star* (September 24, 1894): "The I X L colored team won two games yesterday. They won the morning game by a score of 17 to 7 and the evening 16 to 4." *Kansas City Times* (June 24, 1895): "The Times Hustlers played the I. X. L.'s yesterday at Fifteenth and Vine, and won by a score of 28 to 3."

SOURCES: "Amateur Base Ball Notes," *Kansas City (MO) Star*, Aug 4, 1893; "Amateur Base Ball Notes," *Kansas City Star*, Aug 8, 1893; "Amateur Base Ball Notes," *Kansas City Star*, Apr 16, 1894; "Amateur Base Ball Notes," *Kansas City Star*, Apr 23, 1894; "Amateur Base Ball Notes," *Kansas City Star*, Jun 12, 1894; "Amateur Base Ball Notes," *Kansas City Star*, Jun 26, 1894; "Amateur Base Ball Notes," *Kansas City Star*, Jun 27, 1894; "Amateur Base Ball Notes," *Kansas City Star*, Jul 2, 1894; "Amateur Base Ball Notes," *Kansas City Star*, Jul 5, 1894; "Amateur Base Ball Notes," *Kansas City Star*, Jul 9, 1894; "Amateur Base Ball Notes," *Kansas City Star*, Aug 27, 1894; "Amateur Base Ball Notes," *Kansas City Star*, Sep 13, 1894; "Amateur Base Ball Notes," *Kansas City Star*, Sep 24, 1894; "Amateur Base Ball Notes," *Kansas City Star*, Jun 22, 1894; "Amateur Base Ball Notes," *Kansas City Star*, May 27, 1895; "Times Hustlers Win," *Kansas City (MO) Times*, Jun 24, 1895; "Amateur Base Ball," *Kansas City Times*, Jul 2, 1895.

Junction Bootblack Base Ball Club (Kansas City, MO; 1890s)

The Junction Bootblack B.B.C. organized in the 1890s. *Kansas City Star* (May 14, 1898): "The Junction Bootblacks want a game Sunday afternoon with the Black Sports. The Junction Bootblacks have signed James and Noah O'Brien, Mooney Fisher, Bud Jackson and Joe Martinsen."

SOURCES: "Amateur Base Ball Notes," *Kansas City (MO) Star*, May 14, 1898; "Amateur Base Ball Notes," *Kansas City Star*, May 15, 1898.

Junction Hustler Base Ball Club (Kansas City, MO; 1890s). Owner(s): Toots Woodson, Henry Hewett and William L. Dunson.

The Junction Hustler B.B.C. organized in the 1890s, played black and white teams. *Kansas City Times* (May 20, 1895): "The Kansas City Times Hustler, a ball team composed entirely of colored newsboys who carry The Kansas City Times." They played white rivals in a much-anticipated contest. *Times* (May 20, 1895): "The Independence Stetsons were outplayed, out-batted, out-classed and finally wiped off the earth at Fifteenth and Vine streets by the Kansas City Times Hustlers." They challenged the Lone Stars, a black team for the local championship. *Kansas City Star* (June 17, 1895): "The Times Hustlers won a hard-fought game from the hitherto invincible Lone Star, at the corner of Fifteenth and Vine Streets yesterday afternoon. In the eleventh inning, the score stood 20 to 20 and the crowd was black in the face holding its breath. And then captain Toole called upon his men for a grand effort. They responded gallantly and captured the match by one score." Two weeks later the Lone Stars defeated the Hustlers by a score of 17 to 2. The Hustlers returned the favor, drubbing their opponents by a score of 31 to 13."

SOURCES: "Amateur Base Ball Notes," *Kansas City (MO) Times*, Jul 10, 1893; "Among The Amateurs," *Kansas City Times*, May 7, 1894;

"Amateur Base Ball Notes," *Kansas City (MO) Star*, Jul 3, 1894; "Manager Toots' Junction Hustlers," *Kansas City Times*, May 15, 1895; "Toots Men Won," *Kansas City Times*, May 20, 1895; "Future Professionals," *Kansas City Times*, Jun 15, 1895; "Amateur Baseball," *Kansas City Times*, Jul 1, 1895; "The Amateur Champions Yield One," *Kansas City Times*, Jul 9, 1895; "Amateur Base Ball," *Kansas City Times*, Aug 9, 1895; "Unions, 16; Hustlers, 14," Kansas City (MO). *Journal*, Jul 12, 1897; "Amateur Base Ball Notes," *Kansas City (MO) Star*, Aug 2, 1897; "Amateur Baseball Notes," *Kansas City Journal*, Mar 18, 1898; "Baseball Notes," *Kansas City Journal*, May 8, 1898; "Baseball Notes," *Kansas City Journal*, May 9, 1898; "They Are Champions No Longer," *Kansas City Journal*, May 27, 1898; "With the Amateur Players," *Kansas City Journal*, Jul 11, 1898; "Done By Lexington Tigers," *Kansas City Journal*, Jun 1, 1899.

Leaper Base Ball Club (Kansas City, MO; 1880s)

The Leaper B.B.C. organized in the 1880s, played black nines. *Kansas City Star* (June 4, 1883): "A match game was played between the Kansas City Leapers, the colored base-ball club of this city, and the Red Stockings at Sedalia on yesterday. There was a large attendance of colored people and much interest was manifested in the game from the opening to the finish." *Kansas City Times* (June 4, 1883): "There will be a game of baseball this afternoon at Athletic Park between the Kansas City Leapers and Leavenworth Leapers. William Zellner, the catcher, will don the mask for the home team." *Weekly Bazoo* (July 24, 1883): "On Wednesday the Sedalia Red Stockings defeated the Kansas City Leapers by a score of 16 to 12." *Star* (July 18,1883): "A match was played between the Kansas City Leapers of this city, and the Red Stockings at Sedalia on yesterday. There was a large attendance of colored people and much interest was manifested in the game from the opening to the finish. At the conclusion of nine innings the score stood 24 to 14 in favor of the Sedalia team." *St. Joseph Herald Gazette* (July 19,1884): "Flushed with two successive victories over the Sedalia Reds, and the Kansas City Pastime Base Ball Club, the crack colored organization of that city, arrived in St. Joseph yesterday afternoon, and during the afternoon met their colored brethren, the Eclipse nine, at the Exposition grounds, The St. Joseph lads proving anything but formidable rivals, the score at the end of nine innings standing 27 to16 in favor of the Kansas City nine." *Times* (August 19, 1884): "There will be a game of base-ball this afternoon at Athletic Park between the Kansas City Leapers and the Leavenworth Leapers. Both clubs are composed of colored men and lots of sport may be expected. W. Zellner, the crack catcher, will don the mask for the home team." They reorganized in 1889. *Times* (March 31, 1889): "The Leapers is the name of the crack base-ball team recently organized on the West Side. It is composed of colored men."

Sources: "Dusky Diamond," *Kansas City (MO) Star*, Jun 4, 1883; *Kansas City Star*, Jun 20, 1883; "Successful Coons," *Sedalia (MO) Weekly Bazoo*, Jul 24, 1883; "Colored Champions," *Kansas City (MO) Times*, Jul 16, 1884; "Defeat for *St. Joseph*," *St. Joseph (MO) Herald-Gazette*, Jul 19, 1884; "Short Stops," *St. Joseph (MO) Herald Gazette*, Jul 19, 1884; "Short Stops," *Kansas City (MO) Times*, Aug 19, 1884; "West Kansas City," *Kansas City Times*, Mar 31, 1889.

Lincoln High Base Ball Club (Kansas City, MO; 1890s)

The Lincoln High B.B.C. organized in the 1890s. The Lincoln High Schools club, named for the institution attended by its ball playing alumni, put a strong team in the field, competing against black and white clubs. *Kansas City Journal* (August 5, 1899): "The Lincoln High Schools played the strong Liberty Colts (white) at Liberty yesterday ad defeated them by a score of 7 to 1. The game was the best game seen on the Liberty grounds for years. The Colts were outplayed at every stage of the game. The battery work of the High Schools, aided by brilliant fielding and timely hitting, won the game. The pretty fielding of both teams called repeated applause from the spectators, and only for a costly error in the seventh inning the Colts would have been shut out. Pitcher McCampbell struck out eleven of the Liberty batsmen." The Moonlights played Lincoln High. *Journal* (August 14, 1899): "The Lincoln High Schools added one more game to its string of victories yesterday by defeating the Moonlights in a well-contested game. The High School outplayed the Moonlights at every stage, and played an up-hill and steady game, while the Moonlights failed to hit effectively, except in two innings."

Sources: "Puff from the Pipe," *Kansas City (MO) Journal*, Jun 23, 1899; "Lincoln High School Team," *Kansas City Journal*, Jul 21, 1899; "Amateur Baseball Notes," *Kansas City Journal*, Jul 26, 1899; "Amateur Baseball Notes," *Kansas City Journal*, Jul 30, 1899; "Amateur Base Ball Notes," *Kansas City Journal*, Aug 11, 1899; "Amateur Base Ball Notes," *Kansas City Journal*, Aug 13, 1899; "Amateur Base Ball Notes," *Kansas City Journal*, Aug 14, 1899; "Amateur Base Ball Notes," *Kansas City Journal*, Aug 19, 1899; "Amateur Base Ball Notes," *Kansas City Journal*, Aug 22, 1899; "Amateur Base Ball Notes," *Kansas City Journal*, Aug 25, 1899; "Amateur Base Ball," *Kansas City Journal*, Aug 27, 1899.

Lone Star Base Ball Club (Kansas City, MO; 1880s–1890s)

The Lone Star B.B.C. organized in the 1880s, played black teams. *Kansas City Star* (August 5, 1885): "The Pastimes of Kansas City were defeated at Merriam Park July 4 by the Lone Stars of Western Kansas City 8 to 3." *Star* (August 24, 1885): "The Lone Stars and the Hectors, clubs composed of colored players, played a game of base-ball at Athletic Park, yesterday. The game resulted in favor of the Lone Stars by a score of 14 to 7." They reorganized in the 1890s. *Kansas City Star* (August 4, 1894): "The Lone Stars will play the Swells at Fifteenth and Woodland Avenue tomorrow afternoon at 2:30 o'clock. The battery for the Lone Stars will be W. Smith and H. White." *Kansas City Times* (June 2, 1895): "The Times Hustlers' uniforms have come and they expect to put up a game for the name today against the best colored team in the city, the Lone Stars." *Kansas City Star* (June 17, 1895): "The Times Hustlers won a hard-fought game from the hitherto invincible Lone Star, at the corner of Fifteenth and Vine Streets yesterday afternoon. In the eleventh inning, the score stood 20 to 20 and the crowd was black in the face holding its breath. And then captain Toole called upon his men for a grand effort. They responded gallantly and captured the match by one score." Two weeks later the Lone Stars defeated the Hustlers by a score of 17 to 2. The Hustlers returned the favor, drubbing their opponents by a score of 31 to 13. *Kansas City Journal* (August 13, 1899): "Owing to their inability to arrange games with other 18 year-old teams, the Lone Stars have disbanded after winning every game played this season. McCampbell and Combs are playing with the Lincoln High Schools; Bruce and Wilkins with the Great Westerns; Wright and Ingram with the Kansas City Stars, and Williams, Price and Dale with the Wall's Laundry Blues."

Sources: *Topeka (KS) Capital*, Aug 1, 1885; "Topeka Browns Defeated," *Topeka Capital*, Aug 2, 1885; *Kansas City (MO) Star*, Aug 5, 1885; "The Colored Ball Tossers," *Kansas City (MO) Slur*, Aug 25, 1885; "Sporting Matters," *Kansas City Star*, Aug 24, 1885; "Amateur Base Ball," *Kansas City (MO) Times*, Jul 12, 1892; "Amateur Base Ball Notes," *Kansas City Star*, Jul 30, 1893; "Amateur Base Ball Notes," *Kansas City Star*, Jun 11, 1894; "Amateur Base Ball Notes," *Kansas City Star*, Jun 15, 1894; "Amateur Base Ball Notes," *Kansas City Star*, Jun 25, 1894; "Amateur Base Ball Notes," *Kansas City Star*, Aug 4, 1894; "Amateur Base Ball Notes," *Kansas City Star*, Aug 10, 1894; "Amateur Base Ball Notes," *Kansas City Star*, Aug 13, 1894; "Amateur

Base Ball Notes," *Kansas City Star*, Aug 14, 1894; "Amateur Base Ball Notes," *Kansas City Star*, Sep 13, 1894; "Future Professionals," *Kansas City Times*, Jun 15, 1895; "Amateur Base Ball Notes," *Kansas City Star*, Jun 28, 1894; "Amateur Base Ball," *Kansas City Times*, Jul 12, 1895; "News at Rosedale," *Kansas City Times*, Jul 23, 1895; "Amateur Base Ball Notes," *Kansas City Star*, Aug 8, 1896; "Amateur Base Ball Notes," *Kansas City Star*, Apr 22, 1897; "Amateur Baseball Notes," *Kansas City (MO) Journal*, Jul 16, 1899; "Amateur Baseball Notes," *Kansas City Journal*, Aug 4, 1899; "Amateur Baseball Notes," *Kansas City Journal*, Aug 13, 1899.

Maroon Base Ball Club (Kansas City, MO; 1880s–1890s). Organizer(s): O. C. Lear; J. E. Lovell.

The Maroon B.B.C. organized in the 1880s, played black nines. Kansas City and Lexington developed a rivalry. *Kansas City Times* (July 26, 1887): "The Black Socks club of Lexington came up yesterday with the intention of shutting out the Maroons, but that they had underestimated the crack colored organization of the west is shown by the score. They were beaten by the score of 14 to 3. Johnson, the Maroons' pitcher, used nothing but a drop ball but struck out seven men in succession and twelve during the game. The Lexingtons were outplayed at all points." *Leavenworth Advocate* (August 3, 1889): "The feature of the game was the pitching of Bud English, our twirler [Kansas City Maroons]; he striking out no less than 15 of the Kansas City boys." *Kansas City Journal* (May 31, 1897): "The Kansas City Maroons defeated the Sky Scrapers in a twelve-inning game yesterday by a score of 5 to 4 and would like games with out-of-town teams that have enclosed teams."

Sources: "The Maroons Win," *Kansas City (MO) Times*, Jul 26, 1887; "Base Ball To-Day," *Atchison (KS) Champion*, Sep 11, 1887; *Atchison (KS) Globe*, Sep 12, 1887; "Base Ball," *Springfield (MO) Republican*, Jul 4, 1888; "Local Mention," *Springfield Republican*, Jul 13, 1888; "Colored Ball Tossers," *Kansas City Times*, Jul 19, 1888; "Maroons, 14—Lexington, 3," *Kansas City Times*, Jul 24, 1888; *Leavenworth (KS) Advocate*, Aug 3, 1889; "Lexington vs. Kansas City," *Kansas City Times*, Jul 15, 1890; "Lexingtons, 8—Maroons, 7," *Kansas City Times*, Jul 16, 1890; "Colored Teams Play," *Kansas City Times*, Aug 28, 1890; "Maroons Have Reorganized," *Kansas City (MO) Journal*, Feb 25, 1897; "Amateur Baseball Notes," *Kansas City Journal*, May 31, 1897.

Moonlight Base Ball Club (Kansas City, MO; 1890s). Organizer(s): Frank Montgomery.

The Moonlight B.B.C. organized in the 1890s, played black and white teams. A rivalry developed with Kansas City's Lincoln Colored High School, an organization composed of alumni. *Kansas City Journal* (August 14, 1899): "The Lincoln High School added one more game to its string of victories yesterday by defeating the Moonlights in a well-contested game. The High School outplayed the Moonlights at every stage, and played an up-hill and steady game, while the Moonlights failed to hit effectively, except in two innings." They were formidable. *Kansas City Journal* (August 22, 1899): "The Moonlights won a double header Sunday by defeating the Argentine Tigers and Rose Bugs. The feature of the first game was the superb pitching of Alexander, holding them down to three hits. The feature of the second game was the pitching of Captain Fred Montgomery who shut the Rose Bugs out and held them down to one hit and struck out twelve men. The score was 19 to 0."

Sources: Amateur Base Ball Notes," *Kansas City (MO) Journal*, Aug 11, 1899; "Amateur Base Ball Notes," *Kansas City Journal*, Aug 13, 1899; "Amateur Base Ball Notes," *Kansas City Journal*, Aug 14, 1899; "Amateur Base Ball Notes," *Kansas City Journal*, Aug 19, 1899; "Amateur Base Ball Notes," *Kansas City Journal*, Aug 22, 1899; "Ama-teur Base Ball Notes," *Kansas City Journal*, Aug 25, 1899; "Amateur Base Ball," *Kansas City Journal*, Aug 27, 1899.

Novelty Base Ball Club (Kansas City, MO; 1880s)

The Novelty B.B.C. organized in the 1880s, played white and black teams. *Kansas City Times* (August 20, 1886): "The Kansas City Novels and Lawrence Eagles played a fine game of ball at the League Park yesterday afternoon. The game was the first one of a series for the championship of the west, both clubs being made up of colored amateur players. That Kansas City should win surprises nobody, as this town gets to the front on anything that comes under her notice, and the Novels did up the Eagles to the tune of 17 to 7." The great catcher, Frank Maupin, belonged to this team.

Sources: "Base Ball Briefs," *Kansas City (MO) Times*, Aug 19, 1886; "Amateur Games," *Kansas City Times*, Aug 20, 1886; "Base Ball Briefs," *Kansas City Times*, Aug 23, 1886; "Base Ball Briefs," *Kansas City Times*, Aug 24, 1886; "Base Ball," *Lawrence (KS) Journal*, Sep 3, 1886; *Lawrence Journal*, Sep 4, 1886; "Lawrence," *Kansas City Times*, Sep 16, 1886; "The Colored Club Wins," *Kansas City Times*, Sep 17, 1886; "Lawrence," *Kansas City Times*, Sep 30, 1886.

Pastime Base Ball Club (Kansas City, MO; 1880s)

The Pastime B.B.C. organized in the 1870s, played black teams. *Kansas City Times* (July 16, 1884): "A baseball game was played at Athletic Park yesterday between the Kansas City Pastimes and Sedalia Reds, both colored nines, resulting in a victory for the home team, 16 to 2. The game was witnessed by about 400 persons, and during the progress N. Jackson, catcher for the Sedalia team, and George Davis, third baseman for the same nine, had their fingers broken." *St. Joseph Herald Gazette* (July 19, 1884): "Flushed with two successive victories over the Sedalia Reds, and the Kansas City Pastime Base Ball Club, the crack colored organization of that city, arrived in St. Joseph yesterday afternoon, and during the afternoon met their colored brethren, the Eclipse nine, at the Exposition grounds, The St. Joseph lads proving anything but formidable rivals, the score at the end of nine innings standing 27 to 16 in favor of the Kansas City nine." They reorganized in 1885. *Kansas City Times* (May 6, 1885): "A communication from the Pastimes, a colored club, was received and filed." *Kansas City Star* (August 5, 1885): "The Pastimes of Kansas City were defeated at Mirriam Park July 4 by the Lone Stars of West Kansas City 8 to 3."

Sources: "Local Miscellany," *Kansas City (MO) Times*, Jun 1, 1884; "City Summary," *Kansas City Times*, Jun 2, 1884; "Colored Champions," *Kansas City Times*, Jul 16, 1884; "A Home Team That Wins," *Kansas City Times*, Jul 18, 1884; "Defeat for *St. Joseph*," *St. Joseph (MO) Herald-Gazette*, Jul 19, 1884; "The Commercial League," *Kansas City Times*, May 6, 1885; *Kansas City (MO) Star*, Aug 5, 1885.

Red Stocking Base Ball Club (Kansas City, MO; 1890s)

The Red Stocking B.B.C. organized in the 1890s, played white and black nines. They played against Springfield's Blues, a black team, in a two-game series at the latter's home field resulting in a split. *Springfield Democrat* (June 12, 1894): "The Springfield colored base-ball club were defeated by the Kansas City Reds Sunday but won today." *Springfield Leader* (June 13, 1894): "Yesterday afternoon the two aggregations came together again, and the home team knocked the opponents in to all sorts of cocked hat, chasing around the bases for 26 runs, while the men from Kaw smashed out 17."

Sources: "Base Ball Contests," *Springfield (MO) Democrat*, Apr 24, 1894; *Kansas City (MO) Star*, Jun 3, 1894; "Base Ball Contests," *Springfield Democrat*, Jun 3, 1894; "Base Ball Talk," *Springfield Democrat*, Jun 12, 1894; "Sport and Amusement," *Springfield (MO) Leader*, Jun 13, 1894.

Union Base Ball Club (Kansas City, MO; 1890s–1900s). Organizer(s): A. L. Dorsey and James Wear.

The Union B.B.C. organized in the 1890s, played white and black teams. *Kansas City Star* (June 21, 1896): "The Kansas City Unions colored defeated the Atchison Dragoons Thursday by a score of 11 to 7." In 1897, the Unions toured IL, IA, MO, TX, AR, LA, and the OK Territory. *Kansas City Journal* (June 24, 1897): "The Kansas City Unions defeated the Brookfield Quicksteps, Tuesday, by a score of 7 to 2. Batteries—Unions, Vaughn and Houston; Brookfield, Williams and Robinson." They faced another black team, at Mexico, MO. *Journal* (June 26, 1897): "The Kansas City Unions met the Mexico Grays Thursday at Mexico. The Grays are considered one of the strongest amateur teams in the state. Five successive errors in the first inning and a wild throw in the sixth gave Mexico the game. Batteries—Unions, Watts and Sayers; Grays, Hayes, Spurs and Jackson." *Journal* (June 27, 1897): "The Kansas City Unions defeated the Mexico, Missouri Grays, Friday, in the last game at Mexico by a score of 14 to 11." *Journal* (August 8, 1899): "The Kansas City Unions won two games from the Ottawa team." *Journal* (August 29, 1899): "The Kansas City Unions defeated the Paris colored team by a score of 10 to 8." *Journal* (May 11, 1898): "The Bradburys and the Unions, the two leading colored teams of Kansas City, met on Exposition Park yesterday afternoon, and the Bradbury's came out victors by as core of 6 to 1. The game was close enough from the start to be exciting, but the Bradburys or Grays, as the crowd called them, because of the uniforms they wore, secured a lead in the seventh inning, which the Unions, in blue suits formerly used by Manning's team, could not overcome." *Quincy Journal* (August 9, 1900): "The Quincy Unions and the Kansas City Unions, both colored teams, are playing a game of ball at Baldwin Park this afternoon." *Quincy Herald* (August 10, 1900): "The Kansas City Unions and the Quincy Unions, both colored, crossed bats at Baldwin Park yesterday afternoon, the former winning by a score of 14 to 13. The Kansas City team is a strong one and there is some talk of their playing the Reserves."

Sources: "Amateur Base Ball Notes," *Kansas City (MO) Star*, Jun 21, 1896; "Amateur Base Ball Notes," *Kansas City Star*, Jul 23, 1896; "Amateur Base Ball Notes," *Kansas City Star*, Jul 27, 1896; "Amateur Baseball Notes," *Kansas City (MO) Journal*, Jun 13, 1897; "Amateur Baseball Notes," *Kansas City Journal*, Jun 19, 1897; "Amateur Baseball Notes," *Kansas City Journal*, Jun 24, 1897; "Mexico Grays 7, K. C. Unions 5," *Kansas City Journal*, Jun 26, 1897; "K. C. Unions 14, Mexico Grays 13," *Kansas City Journal*, Jun 27, 1897; "Amateur Baseball Notes," *Kansas City Journal*, Feb 28, 1898; "Unions and Bradburys to Play Today," *Kansas City Journal*, Jul 9, 1898; "Amateur Base Ball Notes," *Kansas City Journal*, Jul 30, 1899; "Unions, 17–10; Ottawa, 5–3," *Kansas City Journal*, Aug 8, 1899; "Unions 9, Muscogee 1," *Kansas City Journal*, Aug 8, 1899; "Unions, 10; Paris, 8," *Kansas City Journal*, Aug 29, 1899; "Unions 9, Muscogee 1," *Kansas City Journal*, Aug 8, 1899; "Unions 7, Paris 1," *Kansas City Journal*, Aug 30, 1899; "Amateur Baseball Notes," *Kansas City Journal*, Sep 10, 1899; "Amateur Baseball Notes," *Kansas City Journal*, Sep 16, 1899; "Local and General News," *Quincy (IL) Journal*, Aug 9, 1900; "City Brevities," *Quincy (IL) Herald*, Aug 10, 1900.

Union Star Base Ball Club (Kansas City, MO; 1870s)

The Union Star B.B.C. organized in 1871, played black nines. Kansas City and Lawrence, KS developed a rivalry. *Lawrence Republican Journal* (July 6, 1871): "The Eagle club of this city [is] expecting a match game of base-ball with the Unions of Kansas City, and it is the request of the captain of the Eagles that they hold themselves in readiness to warm the Kansas City boys." *Republican Journal* (July 14, 1871) reported, "The Eagle Base Ball Club of this city made a visit to Kansas City yesterday, and engaged the Union club of that city in a friendly game of base-ball. The game was closely contested, and good playing was done on both sides. The Lawrence boys came out ahead, by a score of 31 to 7, which shows of itself the skill of the displayed."

Sources: "In the City," *Lawrence (KS) Republican Journal*, Jul 6, 1871; "Base Ball," *Lawrence Republican Journal*, Jul 14, 1871; "Base Ball Match," *Lawrence Republican Journal*, Aug 2, 1871; "Base Ball," *Kansas City (MO) Journal of Commerce*, Aug 8, 1871; "City Scrip," *Kansas City Journal of Commerce*, Aug 17, 1871; "The National Game," *Lawrence (KS) Kansas Tribune*, Aug 22, 1871.

White Stockings Union Base Ball Club (Kansas City, MO; 1870s–1880s)

The White Stockings Union B.B.C. organized in the 1870s, played black organizations. *Kansas City Journal and Commerce* (June 22, 1873): "A match game of ball came off between the Kaw Valley Club (colored) and the picked nine of the White Stockings Union of this city. The result terminated in favor of the Kaw Valleys." *Journal and Commerce* (July 12, 1876): "The White Stocking Base Ball Club of this city (colored), attempted to play the Blue Stockings Club of St. Louis, a colored club, yesterday afternoon at Eighteenth and Holmes Street. The score at the end of the ninth inning was St. Louis 20, Kansas City 2." They reorganized in the 1880s. *Kansas City Star* (August 12, 1889): "The Colored Stars defeated the Kansas City Whites at Amourdale yesterday, score 12 to 11."

Sources: "Jottings," *Kansas City (MO) Journal and Commerce*, Jun 22, 1873; "Jottings," *Kansas City Journal and Commerce*, Jun 3, 1875; "Jottings," *Kansas City Journal and Commerce*, Jun 9, 1875; "Jottings," *Kansas City Journal and Commerce*, Jul 12, 1876; "Base Ball Notes," *Kansas City (MO) Star*, Aug 12, 1889.

Wheeler Base Ball Club (Kirkwood, MO; 1870s)

The Wheeler B.B.C. organized in the 1870s, played black clubs. (The club adopted the name from the Rutherford B. Hayes and William A. Wheeler presidential ticket of 1876.). *St. Louis Globe-Democrat* (August 11, 1876): "The Kirkwood Wheelers surrendered to the Webster Blue Sox, yesterday, the score being 22 to 18. Both are colored organizations."

Sources: "Local Lines," *St. Louis (MO) Globe-Democrat*, Aug 11, 1876.

Black Stocking Base Ball Club (Lexington, MO; 1880s–1890s)

The Black Stocking B.B.C. organized in the 1880s, played black nines. Lexington and Kansas City developed a rivalry. *Kansas City Times* (August 19, 1887): "The Black Socks Club of Lexington came up yesterday with the intention of shutting out the Maroons, but that they had underestimated the crack colored organization of the west is shown by the score. They were beaten by the score of 14 to 3. Johnson, the Maroons' pitcher, used nothing but a drop ball but struck out seven men in succession and twelve during the game. The Lexingtons were outplayed at all points." *Kansas City Star* (July 16, 1890): "The Lexington Black Stockings defeated the Kansas City Maroons, at Exposition Park, yesterday by a score of 8 to 7."

Sources: "Kansas City, Kansas," *Kansas City (MO) Times*, Sep 9, 1886; "The Maroons Win Again," *Kansas City Times*, Aug 19, 1887; "Maroons, 14—Lexington, 3," *Kansas City Times*, Jul 24, 1888; "Lexington vs. Kansas City," *Kansas City Times*, Jul 14, 1890; "Lexington vs. Kansas City," *Kansas City Times*, Jul 15, 1890; "General Sporting Notes," *Kansas City (MO) Star*, Jul 16, 1890; "Colored Clubs Play," *Kansas City Times*, Aug. 24, 1890.

Tigers Base Ball Club (Lexington, MO; 1890s–1900s)

The Tigers B.B.C. organized in the 1890s, and formerly the Black Stockings, played black teams. *Kansas City Journal* (August 24, 1898):

"The Lexington Tigers defeated the Knobnoster Reds, at Lexington, by a score of 21 to 4. The features of the game were the pitching of Mady and the batting and base-running of George Smith, of the Tigers. The Bradburys will go to Lexington Friday to play the Tigers." *Journal* (June 1, 1899): "Toots Woodson and his aggregation of Times Hustlers went down to Lexington, Missouri, on Tuesday to play the Tigers and the aforementioned Tigers wiped the earth with them. It was a hot game, in which Tootsie got broiled until he looked like an overdone lobster. The feature of the game was the fielding of J. Lindsay and the hard hitting of Davis and Vaughn. The score was 13 to 8, and it is asserted that Toots didn't make a hit." *St. Joseph Gazette-Herald* (August 13, 1900): "A large crowd witnessed the game yesterday afternoon at the ball park between the Black Wonders of this city and the Tigers of Lexington, the two best teams in the colored interstate league. It was a walk away for the home team."

SOURCES: "Baseball Notes," *Kansas City (MO) Journal*, Apr 12, 1898; "Bradburys 7, Lexington, 5," *Kansas City Journal*, May 3, 1898; "Baseball Notes," *Kansas City Journal*, May 5, 1898; "Baseball Notes," *Kansas City Journal*, May 29, 1898; "With the Amateur Players," *Kansas City Journal*, Jul 11, 1898; "With the Amateurs," *Kansas City Journal*, Jul 12, 1898; "With the Amateur Players," *Kansas City Journal*, Aug 24, 1898; "Done by Lexington Tigers," *Kansas City Journal*, Jun 1, 1899; "Billiardmakers 5; Tigers 5," *Kansas City Journal*, Jun 6, 1899; "Puffs From the Pipe," *Kansas City Journal, Jun* 21, 1899; "Amateur Baseball Notes," *Kansas City Journal*, Jul 19, 1899; "Amateur Baseball Notes," *Kansas City Journal*, Jul 20, 1899; "A Challenge for the Bradburys," *Kansas City Journal*, Jul 26, 1899; "Black Wonders and Tigers," *St. Joseph (MO) Gazette-Herald*, Aug 12, 1900; "Black Wonders Win Victory," *St. Joseph Gazette-Herald*, Aug 13, 1900; "Wonders and Tigers," *St. Joseph Gazette-Herald*, Sep 16, 1900.

Athletics Base Ball Club (Sedalia, MO; 1870s–1900s)

The Athletics B.B.C. organized in the 1870s, if not earlier. The Athletics, a baseball organization of the Lincoln Institute (founded in 1866) challenged white and black nines. They challenged the Vampire nine, a white organization that adopted its moniker to express anti-black sentiments. They complained of government subsidies for black education, calling political opponents resurrectionists. When the Athletics challenged the Vampire club, they refused. *Democrat* (May 27, 1875): "When we fail to find a white club to play, we might notice your challenge for the purpose of lighting a fire. We are not willing to recognize the Civil Rights bill quite yet." The black club responded. *Democrat* (May 27, 1875): "The Athletic Base Ball Club will say in reply to the Vampires will burn the challenge as they see fit, but meet us on the base-ball ground any Saturday between this and the 11th of June, and we will show them a club that will burn their championship." *Democrat* (July 12, 1875): "This evening at the Fairgrounds, the Boonville colored club will play against the Sedalia colored club. No doubt large numbers of our citizens will go." When the Athletics reorganized, hey challenged the Kansas City Browns. *Lexington Weekly Intelligencer* (September 2, 1876): "A game of baseball was played near this city last Friday between the Sedalia Athletics and the Kansas City Browns. Kansas City was scooped, and the game resulted in 42 counts for the Athletics, while the Browns made 29. Both clubs are colored. The game was for a ball, which, we believe, was handed over to the victors.... These clubs will shortly play another game at Warrensburg."

SOURCES: "A Terrible Leak," *Sedalia (MO) Democrat*, Dec 23, 1871; "Base Bawl," *Sedalia Democrat*, May 27, 1875; "Boonville Items," *Sedalia Democrat*, Jul 12, 1875; "Independence," *Kansas City (MO) Journal of Commerce*, Aug 22, 1876; "Suburban Notes," *Kansas City Journal of Commerce*, Aug 27, 1876; "Shorts," *Lexington (MO) Weekly Intelligencer*, Sep 2, 1876; "Base Ball Gossip," *Kansas City (MO) Star*, May 29, 1900.

Red Stocking Base Ball Club (Sedalia, MO; 1880s). Organizer(s): B. Hampton and H. Reed.

The Red Stocking B.B.C. organized in 1882, played black teams. *Kansas City Star* (June 20, 1883): "A match game was played between the Kansas City Leapers, the colored base-ball club of this city, and the Red Stockings at Sedalia on yesterday. [A]t the conclusion of the nine innings the score stood 24 to 14 in favor of the Sedalia team. The return game will be played at Kansas City at an early date." In particular, they challenged the colored organizations of St. Louis, and the West End B.B.C. traveled to Sedalia for a two-game series. *St. Louis Globe-Democrat* (June 23, 1883): "The West End Base Ball Club, of St. Louis, played a second-match game in this city with the Red Stocking Club, of Sedalia. Until the eighth inning, the St. Louis Club was eight runs ahead. In these two innings, the Sedalia club made 9 runs and won the game. The score stood—Sedalia, 18; West End, 11." They challenged the Black Stockings, of St. Louis, managed by Henry Bridgewater. *Globe-Democrat* (July 5, 1883): "The Sedalia Reds (colored) would like to arrange a couple of games for August 3 and 5, in Sedalia, with the Black Sox or any other first class colored nine. George Davis, Secretary of the Club, says We think we have the best colored team west of the Mississippi." Sedalia and Kansas City developed a rivalry. *Kansas City Times* (July 16, 1884): "A baseball game was played at Athletic Park yesterday between the Kansas City Pastimes and Sedalia Reds, both colored nines, resulting in a victory for the home team, 16 to 2. The game was witnessed by about 400 persons, and during the progress N. Jackson, catcher for the Sedalia team, and George Davis, third baseman for the same nine, had their fingers broken."

SOURCES: "Ball and Bat," *Sedalia (MO) Weekly Bazoo*, Jun 13, 1882; "Bazoo, Buzz," *Sedalia Weekly Bazoo*, Jul 18, 1882; "Base Ball," *Kansas City (MO) Star*, Jun 20, 1883; "Diamond Chips," *St. Louis (MO) Republican*, Jun 23, 1883; "Diamond Dust," *St. Louis (MO) Globe-Democrat*, Jun 23, 1883; "Bazoo Buzz," *Sedalia Weekly Bazoo*, Jun 26, 1883; "Boss Base Ballists," *Sedalia (MO) Democrat*, Jun 29, 1883; "Sedalia Boys Defeat the West End Club," *St. Louis Globe-Democrat*, Jul 5, 1883; "Successful Coons," *Sedalia Weekly Bazoo*, Jul 24, 1883; "Laid Him Low," *Sedalia Weekly Bazoo*, Aug 21, 1883; "City Cullings," *Sedalia Weekly Bazoo*, Sep 4, 1883; "Colored Champions," *Kansas City (MO) Times*, Jul 16, 1884; "A Home Team That Wins," *Kansas City Times*, Jul 18, 1884; "The Colored Club," *Sedalia Weekly Bazoo*, Jun 16, 1885; *Springfield (MO) Leader*, Jul 22, 1889.

Shortridge-Robb Base Ball Club (Sedalia, MO; 1900s). Organizer(s): Scott Joplin and Henry Jackson.

The Shortridge-Robb B.B.C. organized in 1900s. The Ragtime composers, Scott Joplin and Henry Jackson, financed the team. *Sedalia Democrat* (July 17, 1900): "Messrs. Joplin and Jackson, colored, last night organized a base-ball club and named it Robb and Shortridge. The first game will be played here with a team from Kansas City on August 4." *Democrat* (July 18, 1900): "The Shortridge-Robb baseball club, colored, will play the J. W. Jenkins club, of Kansas City, on August 4th at Liberty Park."

SOURCES: "Ragtime Musicale," *Sedalia (MO) Democrat*, Jun 22, 1900; "Colored Base Ball Team," *Sedalia Democrat*, Jul 17, 1900; "Kansas City Coming," *Sedalia Democrat*, Jul 18, 1900.

White Stocking Base Ball Club (Shelbina, MO; 1870s)

The White Stocking B.B.C., of Springfield, MO, organized in the 1890s, played black teams. *Shelbina Democrat* (October 3, 1877): "The White Stocking (colored) Nine of Shelbina went out to

Granville on Saturday and played a game of base-ball with the Standaraounds, also colored, from Paris. Result: Stockings, 18, Standarounds, 5." *Shelbina Democrat* (May 29, 1878): "The colored base-ball club—don't know what they call themselves—of this place, went over to Paris one day last week, and defeated for the third time the colored club of that city, 13 to 8."

SOURCES: *Shelbina (MO) Democrat*, Oct 3, 1877; *Shelbina Democrat*, May 29, 1878.

Blue Stocking Base Ball Club (Springfield, MO; 1890s)

The Blue Stocking B.B.C. organized in the 1890s, played black aggregations. *Springfield Leader* (May 15, 1894): "The Springfield Blues and the Cabinets have been fighting a series of base-ball games, three in five for $200. The Blues and Cabinets are tied, having won two games each, and next Sunday will settle the agony. It is said that only one hit was made off Dean, the Cabinet pitcher, on Sunday and the umpire became rattled because the balls were tossed so swiftly." *Springfield Democrat* (June 3, 1894): "There will be a baseball contest between two colored teams, the Cabinets and the Blues at the fairgrounds at 3:30 p.m. The Springfield Blues and the Kansas City Reds will play three games, June 10, 11, 12."

SOURCES: "Play for $200," *Springfield (MO) Leader*, May 15, 1894; "Base Ball Contest," *Springfield (MO) Democrat*, Jun 3, 1894; "Base Ball Talk," *Springfield Democrat*, Jun 12, 1894; "Sport and Amusement," *Springfield Leader*, Jun 13, 1894; "Springfield Won Again," *Springfield (MO) Republican*, Jun 20, 1894; "A Crap Joint Raided," *Springfield Democrat*, Sep 2, 1894; "Those Crap Cases," *Springfield Democrat*, Sep 6, 1894.

C. A. Whites Base Ball Club (Springfield, MO; 1890s)

The C. A. Whites B.B.C. organized in the 1890s, played black nines. *Springfield Leader* (April 30, 1894): "The White Caps and the C. A. Whites, both colored teams, played a very strong game yesterday with [George] Kane and [James] Dean in trouble especially for the White Caps, and [Jack] Reeves and [N.] Jackson for the black Whites. The Caps won by a score of 5 to 3, the losing club making five errors and the winners none." *Springfield Democrat* (July 13, 1894): "The Springfield colored baseball club was defeated at Carthage Wednesday by the colored club of that town by as score of 17 to 13."

SOURCES: "They Played Ball," *Springfield (MO) Leader*, Apr 30, 1894; "They Played Ball," *Springfield (MO) Democrat*, Jul 13, 1894.

D. R. C. Base Ball Club (Springfield, MO; 1890s)

The D. R. C. B.B.C. organized in the 1890s. The "D. R. C.'s" played black nines. *Springfield Democrat* (June 18, 1895): "Tomorrow and Wednesday the Carthage Grays, a strong team of colored players, will meet the D. R. C. club of Springfield at the old fairgrounds." *Springfield Republican* (June 19, 1895): "The Springfield colored baseball club defeated the Carthage team at the old fairgrounds yesterday by a score of 31 to 17, and now claim the colored championship of the southwest." *Springfield Republican* (June 20, 1895): "The Springfield colored base-ball club defeated the Carthage team again yesterday. Quite a fair-sized audience witnessed, which was characterized by brilliant fumbles and numerous errors. The score was 26 to 21. The Carthage team is anxious for another game, which no doubt will be arranged soon, because the motto of the Springfield team is Carthago delendo est." *Springfield Leader* (August 3, 1895): "There will be a series of ball games today at Union Park, tomorrow and Monday between D.R.C.'s, the colored champions of Southwest Missouri, and a champion colored team from Fort Smith. John Reeves will be in the box for the D. R. C.'s tomorrow."

SOURCES: "Local Glances," *Springfield (MO) Democrat*, Jun 18, 1895; "Colored Baseball," *Springfield (MO) Republican*, Jun 19, 1895;

"Springfield Won Again," *Springfield Republican*, Jun 20, 1895; "Queen City Brevities," *Springfield Republican*, Jun 30, 1895; "Base Ball Today," *Springfield Republican*, Jul 28, 1895; "Base Ball Today," *Springfield Republican*, Aug 3, 1895; "Base Ball Today," *Springfield Republican*, Aug 7, 1895.

Lair's Cabinet Base Ball Club (Springfield, MO; 1890s).

Owner(s): John Lair.

The Cabinet B.B.C. organized in the 1890s, played black teams. John Lair's Cabinet nine was sponsored by Sim Cabinet's Saloon, an establishment located in Springfield's Patton Alley. *Springfield Leader* (May 15, 1894): "The Springfield Blues and the Cabinets have been fighting a series of base-ball games, three in five for $200. The Blues and Cabinets are tied, having won two games each, and next Sunday will settle the agony. It is said that only one hit was made off [James] Dean, the Cabinet pitcher, on Sunday and the umpire became rattled because the balls were tossed so swiftly." *Springfield Democrat* (June 3, 1894): "There will be a baseball contest between two colored teams, the Cabinets and the Blues at the fairgrounds at 3:30 p.m."

SOURCES: "Didn't Entice Him," *Springfield (MO) Democrat*, Apr 24, 1894; "They Played Ball," *Springfield (MO) Leader*, Apr 30, 1894; "Base Ball," *Springfield Leader*, May 12, 1894; "Play for $200," *Springfield Leader*, May 15, 1894; "Base Ball Contest," *Springfield Democrat*, Jun 3, 1894.

Red Stocking Base Ball Club (Springfield, MO; 1880s–1890s)

The Red Stocking B.B.C. organized in the 1880s, played black nines. *Kansas City Times* (July 19, 1888): "The Springfield Reds, a club which recently won two games from the Maroons, the colored cracks of this city, met defeat yesterday afternoon at the hands of their former victims, the score being 8 to 5. The game was played at League Park and was interesting throughout to the handful of spectators." *Kansas City Times* (July 20, 1888): "The colored ball players of this city and Springfield met again at League Park yesterday afternoon when the visitors turned the tables on the home team and won with hands down by a score of 13 to 7. The Maroons could nothing with Reeves' speedy delivery except in the sixth inning when by bunching a double, two singles, and a triple they earned four runs amid the wildest kind of excitement." They also contended with the Fort Smith black team. *Springfield Leader* (August 1, 1888): "The Springfield Reds will play a match game of base-ball today and tomorrow with the Fort Smith Black Stockings for the championship of the Southwest."

SOURCES: "Base Ball," *Springfield (MO) Republican*, Jul 4, 1888; "Base Ball," *Springfield (MO) Leader*, Jul 5, 1888; "Local Mention," *Springfield Republican*, Jul 13, 1888; "Colored Ball Tossers," *Kansas City (MO) Times*, Jul 19, 1888; "Reds 13—Maroons 7," *Kansas City Times*, Jul 20, 1888; "Base Ball Today," *Springfield Republican*, Aug 1, 1888; "Base Ball," *Springfield Republican*, Aug 3, 1888; *Springfield Leader*, Aug 3, 1888; "Memphis Route Notes," *Springfield Leader*, Jul 18, 1889; "Personal," *Springfield Leader*, Jul 22, 1889; "Local Mention," *Springfield Republican*, Jul 23, 1889.

White Caps Base Ball Club (Springfield, MO; 1890s)

The White Caps B.B.C. organized in the 1890s, played black nines. *Springfield Leader* (April 30, 1894): "The White Caps and the C. A. Whites, both colored teams, played a very strong game yesterday with [George] Kane and [James] Dean in trouble especially for the White Caps, and [Jack] Reeves and [N.] Jackson for the black Whites. The Caps won by a score of 5 to 3, the losing club making five errors and the winners none."

SOURCES: "They Played Ball," *Springfield (MO) Leader*, Apr 30, 1894.

Black Wonders Base Ball Club (St. Joseph, MO; 1890s–1900s). Organizer(s): John Gasaway; H. H. Walker and John W. Jackson ("Bud" Fowler).

The Black Wonders B.B.C. organized in the 1890s, played white and black organizations of MO, KS, and NE. *Atchison Champion* (July 31, 1895): The Black Wonders ball club of St. Joe will play a colored club of Atchison at Forest Park tomorrow afternoon." *Kansas City Journal* (June 26, 1899): "The Bradburys again defeated the St. Joseph Wonders Sunday by a score of 20 to 6." *St. Joseph Gazette-Herald* (June 9, 1898): "A ball game between the Black Wonders of St. Joseph and a local colored team attracted a large crowd. The St. Joseph team won by a score of 13 to 4." *Gazette-Herald* (August 13, 1900): "A large crowd witnessed the game yesterday afternoon at the ball park between the Black Wonders of this city and the Tigers of Lexington, the two best teams in the colored interstate league. It was a walk away for the home team." The Black Wonders fielded a team well into the 1900s.

Sources: "Atchison Affairs," *Atchison (KS) Globe*, May 28, 1895; "Emancipation Day," *Atchison (KS) Champion*, July 23, 1895; "The City Circuit," *Atchison Champion*, July 31, 1895; "Going After Atchison," *St. Joseph (MO) Gazette-Herald*, August 31, 1898; *St. Joseph Gazette-Herald*, June 9, 1899; "Bradburys 20; St. Joseph 6," *Kansas City (MO) Journal*, Jun 26, 1899; "A Colored League," *St. Joseph Gazette-Herald*, June 28, 1899; "Social and Personal," *Hiawatha (KS) World*, August 5, 1899; "A Colored League," *St. Joseph Gazette-Herald*, February 25, 1900; "Black Wonders and Tigers," *St. Joseph Gazette-Herald*, August 12, 1900; "Black Wonders Win Victory," *St. Joseph Gazette-Herald*, August 13, 1900; "Wonders and Tigers," *St. Joseph Gazette-Herald*, September 16, 1900; "Atchison Blues Won," *Atchison Champion*, July 23, 1912.

Eclipse Base Ball Club (St. Joseph, MO; 1880s). Organizer(s): Thomas O. Williams.

The Eclipse B.B.C. organized in the 1880s, played black nines of MO and KS. *Atchison Globe* (June 7, 1883): "The Black Stockings, colored base-ball club from Kansas City, passed through the city today for St. Joe, where they will play a match game today." *St. Joseph Gazette-Herald* (June 8, 1883): "The Eclipse Base Ball Club of this city, will go to Kansas City to meet the Black Stockings upon the diamond patch. These clubs are colored and lively tossers." A rivalry existed between Kansas City and St. Joseph, MO. *Gazette-Herald* (June 8, 1883): "Yesterday afternoon, at College Hill, the Black Stockings, of Kansas City, played the Eclipse nine of this city. The Kansas City nine was victorious, the score standing seven to two. The series consists of three games for the championship, and the return game will be played at Kansas City on the 20th. *Globe* (July 19, 1883): "A Colored Base-Ball Club from Leavenworth, the Blacks, went to St. Joe this morning to play a match game with the Mulattoes." *St. Joseph Herald Gazette* (July 19,1884): "Flushed with two successive victories over the Sedalia Reds, and the Kansas City Pastime Base Ball Club, the crack colored organization of that city, arrived in St. Joseph yesterday afternoon, and during the afternoon met their colored brethren, the Eclipse nine, at the Exposition grounds, The St. Joseph lads proving anything but formidable rivals, the score at the end of nine innings standing 27 to 16 in favor of the Kansas City nine."

Sources: "Emancipation Day," *St. Joseph (MO) Herald*, Aug 2, 1882; "Here and Near," *St. Joseph Herald*, Aug 6, 1882; "Mere Mention," *St. Joseph (MO) Gazette-Herald*, May 31, 1883; "The City," *Kansas City (MO) Star*, Jun 4, 1883; "A Base Ball Game," *St. Joseph Herald*, Jun 8, 1883; "Base Ball," *St. Joseph Gazette-Herald*, Jun 8, 1883; *Atchison (KS) Globe*, Jun 7, 1883; *Atchison Globe*, July 19, 1883; "Defeat for St. Joseph," *St. Joseph Herald-Gazette*, Jul 19, 1884.

Olympic Base Ball Club (St. Joseph, MO; 1870s)

The Olympic B.B.C. organized in the 1870s, played against black nines. *St. Joseph Morning Herald* (July 10, 1875): "Yesterday quite an interesting game was played on College Hill between the Olympics and the Stars. The Olympics were victorious with a score of 18 to 13." The Olympics also played the black club of Troy, MO. *Morning Herald* (July 29, 1875): "The Olympics (colored), of this city, played the Daisy Cutters (colored), of Troy yesterday, and beat them by the handsome score of 31 to 21. They are becoming as popular as our crack clubs of white boys."

Sources: "City Condensed," *St. Joseph (MO) Morning Herald*, July 10, 1875; "City Condensed," *St. Joseph Morning Herald*, July 18, 1875; "Base Ball," *St. Joseph Morning Herald*, Jul 29, 1875; "Gazettlets vs. Smokers," *St. Joseph Morning Herald*, August 10, 1875.

Pacific Base Ball Club (St. Joseph, MO; 1870s)

The Pacific B.B.C. organized in the 1870s, played against black nines. *St. Joseph Morning Herald* (May 20, 1875): "The Olympic and Pacific Base Ball Clubs, composed of colored men, had a lively contest yesterday, resulting in the defeat of the Pacifics by a score of 24 to 8."

Sources: "Olympic vs. Pacific," *St. Joseph (MO) Morning Herald*, May 20, 1876.

Star Base Ball Club (St. Joseph, MO; 1870s)

The Star B.B.C. organized in the 1870s, played against black nines. *St. Joseph Morning Herald* (July 29, 1875): "Yesterday quite an interesting game was played on College Hill between the Olympics and the Stars. The Olympics were victorious with a score of 18 to 13."

Sources: "City Condensed," *St. Joseph (MO) Morning Herald*, July 10, 1875; "City Condensed," *St. Joseph Morning Herald*, July 18, 1875; "Base Ball," *St. Joseph Morning Herald*, July 29, 1875.

Aetna Base Ball Club (St. Louis, MO; 1880s)

The Aetna B.B.C. organized in the 1880s. They played black nines. *St. Louis Chronicle* (September 9, 1882): "The Aetnas and Waverlys (both colored) will cross bats on the latter's grounds today. The Aetnas are managed by S. C. Mayo, and the team is as follows: Brown, Davis, Turner, Brooks, Grayso, Lee, Thomson, Massie and Anderson."

Sources: "Sporting News," *St. Louis (MO) Evening Chronicle*, Sep 9, 1882.

Akron Base Ball Club (St. Louis, MO; 1880s). Organizer(s): H. E. Bruckner.

The Akron B.B.C. organized in the 1880s, played black nines. *St. Louis Globe-Democrat* (June 25, 1888): "The Akrons (colored) defeated the Lindell Stars (white) at Compton Avenue Park by a score of 27 to 3, yesterday, and would like to hear from amateur nines." The Akrons played against the West Ends. *Globe-Democrat* (July 8, 1888): "The West End champion colored club of St. Louis, plays the Akrons, champion colored club of Missouri, at Compton Avenue Park, July 8. Game will be called at 3 p.m. and will be for a purse of $100."

Sources: "Diamond Dust," *St. Louis (MO) Globe-Democrat*, Jun 25, 1888; "Diamond Dust," *St. Louis Globe-Democrat*, Jul 4, 1888; "Diamond Dust," *St. Louis Globe-Democrat*, Jul 8, 1888.

Allegheny Base Ball Club (St. Louis, MO; 1870s)

The Allegheny B.B.C. organized in the 1870s, played black teams. *St. Louis Republican* (August 23, 1870): "A game of base-ball was played by the Sunset and Allegheny clubs, for a champion belt. Five innings were played and thee game lasted over three hour. The score stood Sunset 29, Allegheny 30. The latter consequently won the belt."

Sources: "Disturbance in a Dance Hall," *St. Louis (MO) Republican*, Aug 5, 1870 "Closed Celebration," *St. Louis (MO) Republican*, Aug 23, 1870.

Athletic Base Ball Club (St. Louis, MO; 1880s)

The Athletic B.B.C. organized in the 1880s, played black teams—among them, the Black Stockings, Eclipse, and Compton Browns. They also played LA teams. *St. Louis Republican* (July 17, 1884): "The Anchor Line colored club arrived from New Orleans last evening and cross bats at Compton Avenue Park at 3:30 p.m. with the Athletic colored club." *Republican* (July 20, 1884): "The Anchor Line Club of New Orleans, and the Athletics, of St. Louis, both colored, crossed bats yesterday at Compton Avenue Park in the presence of about 400 people. The Athletics won by a score of 17 to 16." The Athletics played against Henry Bridgewater's famed Black Stockings. *Republican* (August 18, 1884): "Never were two colored clubs paid a better compliment than the two which met on the Union Grounds yesterday. Their reception, in fact, was of a gigantic kind, fully 3,000 people gathering to do them honor. The work of the colored teams in the first two innings was a revelation to the crowd. [The Black Stockings eventually] took the sand out of the Athletics, and they failed to play ball afterwards. The play, however, seemed to please the spectators, and the work of both teams was often interrupted by peals of laughter intermingled with cheers." They played the Compton Browns. *St. Louis Post-Dispatch*: "The Athletics and Compton Browns, colored, will play their second game of three. The game will be called at 4 p. m."

SOURCES: "Diamond Chips," *St. Louis (MO) Republican*, Jun 8, 1884; "Diamond Chips," *St. Louis Republican*, Jun 9, 1884; "Sporting," *St. Louis Republican*, Jul 17, 1884; "Diamond Chips," *St. Louis Republican*, Jul 20, 1884; "Diamond Dust," *St. Louis Republican*, Aug 17, 1884; "Diamond Dust," *St. Louis Republican*, Aug 18, 1884; "Diamond Dust," *St. Louis (MO) Globe-Democrat*, Aug 28, 1884; "Black Sox, 19; Athletics, 12," *St. Louis Globe-Democrat*, Sep 1, 1884; "The Colored Championship," *St. Louis Republican*, Sep 1, 1884; "Diamond Dust," *St. Louis (MO) Post-Dispatch*, Sep 6, 1884.

Atlantic Base Ball Club (St. Louis, MO; 1870s)

The Atlantic B.B.C. organized in the 1870s, played black teams. The Atlantics played against the Franklins, losing by a score of 27 to 10. They defeated the Vinegar Hill nine, the score standing 18 to 17. They played the Black Stockings. *St. Louis Globe Democrat* (July 31, 1876): "A very interesting game of base-ball was played at Stock Park, last Sunday, for the State championship, between the Atlantics and Black Stockings, in which the former were defeated."

SOURCES: "Base Ball," *St. Louis (MO) Times*, Aug 16, 1875; "Short Stops," *St. Louis (MO) Globe-Democrat*, Aug 16, 1875; "Base Ball," *St. Louis Globe-Democrat*, Jul 31, 1876; "Local Lines," *St. Louis Globe-Democrat*, Aug 1, 1876; "Tips," *St. Louis Globe-Democrat*, Aug 7, 1876; "Amateur Base Ball Games Yesterday," *St. Louis (MO) Republican*, Sep 11, 1876.

Black Diamond Base Ball Club (St. Louis, MO; 1890s)

The Black Diamond B.B.C. organized in the 1890s, played black teams. In 1891, they played Denver's Black Champions for the championship, in CO. *Denver Rocky Mountain News* (May 15, 1891): "The Black Diamonds, of St. Louis, having fulfilled their engagements in Colorado Springs and Pueblo, have returned to fight out their championship game at the Broadway Athletic Park on Decoration Day, Saturday, May 30th, with the Black Champions of Colorado, who have been greatly strengthened by three great stars, Castone, Taylor and Bud Fowler, and will make it highly interesting for the Black Diamonds. That clever young pitcher, Overton, will pitch for the Denver team today." The Black Diamonds won the first and second games scores of 14 to 5, and 8 to 5; the Black Champions won the final contest.

SOURCES: "Between Shade and Shadow," *Denver (CO) Rocky Mountain News*, May 15, 1891; "On Sunday," *Denver Rocky Mountain News*, May 16, 1891; "Exciting Ball Game," *Denver Rocky Mountain News*, May 18, 1891; "On Sunday," *Denver Rocky Mountain News*, May 23, 1891; "Black Diamonds," *Denver Rocky Mountain News*, May 24, 1891; "Colored Stars in the City," *Denver Rocky Mountain News*, May 30, 1891; "Black Diamonds," *Denver Rocky Mountain News*, May 31, 1891; "Batting the Ball," *Denver Rocky Mountain News*, Jun 1, 1891; "Sport," *Indianapolis (IN) Freeman*, Jul 18, 1891; "Were Discharged," *Denver Rocky Mountain News*, Sep 3, 1891.

Black Stocking Base Ball Club (St. Louis, MO; 1870s–1900s). Organizer(s): Henry Bridgewater, Louis Helms and Charles H. Tyler; Henry Sanford; H. Lewis Canter; William Batice; Matthew Compton.

The Black Stocking B.B.C. organized in the 1870s. Between 1875 and 1900, the Black Stockings played white and black nines. In the late 1870s, they developed rivalries with the St. Louis Blue Stockings, and Chicago Uniques. In 1881, they received national attention when they played for the local championship. Under Harry Bridgewater's management, the Black Stockings opened the 1883 season against a local white nine composed of former professionals, semiprofessionals, and amateurs. They opened the season with an exhibition game against a local picked white nine, composed mostly of members of the Grand Avenues (reserves for the St. Louis Browns), easily defeating them at Sportsman's Park. The road tour included IL, MI, Upper Canada, and OH; it included a series against Rockford, IL's Red Stockings, a white organization. *Rockford Register* (June 20, 1883): "If the Rockfords allowed themselves to think for a moment that their colored friends from St. Louis could not play ball, they were certainly off base. The Black Stockings played beautifully, their fielding bringing down the pleased approbation of the spectators, among them there were many colored citizens. One of the St. Louis nine said he would have bet $100 that the Rockfords would not have seen third base if it had not been for the first error." In 1884, they played the Callender Minstrel Blues. The local Eclipse nine beat them five straight games for the black championship. In 1885, Bridgewater's team redeemed themselves, by defeating the Eclipse three straight games. The two teams briefly merged talent and toured the South, including LA. The Black Stockings also traveled to Chicago where they played the Gordons and Uniques. In 1886 and 1887, the St. Louis Lindell Stars and Euchres emerged as prominent local clubs. The Euchres were easily handled by Bridgewater's team. By 1888, the West Ends, had become the dominant black team in St. Louis. The Black Stockings, no longer owned by Bridgewater, declined as a local power. They continued to play regionally into the 1900s.

SOURCES: "Base Ball," *St. Louis (MO) Times*, Aug 31, 1876; "Local Ball Items," *St. Louis (MO) Republican*, May 20, 1876; "Enquirer Shrieks," *St. Louis Globe-Democrat*, Jul 8, 1876; "Topics," *St. Louis Times*, Aug 15, 1880; "Craps," *St. Louis (MO) Post-Dispatch*, Feb 21, 1881; "Base Ball," *St. Louis Post-Dispatch*, Aug 12, 1881; "Base Ball," *New York (NY) Clipper*, Aug 6, 1881; "Notes," *St. Louis Post-Dispatch*, Sep 8, 1882; "Base Ball Notes," *St. Louis (MO) Evening Chronicle*, Nov 11, 1882; "Base Ball Notes," *St. Louis Post-Dispatch*, Nov 11, 1882; "Diamond Dust," *St. Louis (MO) Globe-Democrat*, Nov 12, 1882; "Base Ball," *St. Louis (MO) Republican*, Nov 12, 1882; "Tip," *St. Louis Globe-Democrat*, Jan 23, 1883; "The Black Sox," *St. Louis Republican*, Apr 15, 1883; "The Sporting World," *Toronto (ONT/CAN) World*, Apr 20, 1883; "Sporting," *Topeka (KS) Daily Capital*, Apr 22, 1883; "The Black Stockings-Dayton Game To-Day," *Dayton (OH) Daily Democrat*, May 7, 1883; "The Colored League," *St. Louis Republican*, May 16, 1883; "Note," *Cincinnati (OH) Enquirer*, May 21, 1883; "The Coons Carry Off the Cake," *Rockford (IL) Register*, Jun 20, 1883;

"Colored Champions," *New York (NY) Times*, Jun 23, 1883; "BBC of St. Louis," *Little Rock (AR) Weekly Mansion*, Jul 28, 1883; "Victory for the Blacks," *St. Louis Republican*, Aug 29, 1883; "St. Louis, MO.," *Cleveland (OH) Gazette*, May 3, 1884; "St. Louis, MO.," *Cleveland Gazette*, May 10, 1884; "Sporting Sundries," *St. Louis Post-Dispatch*, Apr 25, 1884; "Diamond Chips," *St. Louis Republican*, May 21, 1884; "The Colored Clubs," *St. Louis Republican*, Jun 15, 1884; "Diamond Dust," *St. Louis Republican*, Aug 4, 1884; "The Colored Championship," *St. Louis Republican*, Sep 1, 1884; "The Colored Championship," *St. Louis Republican*, Sep 4, 1884; "Diamond Chips," *St. Louis Republican*, Oct 13, 1884; "Diamond Dust," *St. Louis Republican*, Apr 14, 1885; "Sporting," *St. Louis Republican*, Jun 8, 1885; "Around the Bases," *New Orleans (LA) Times-Picayune*, Jul 22, 1885; "Base Ball," *New Orleans Times-Picayune*, Jul 31, 1885; "Base Ball," *New Orleans Times-Picayune*, Aug 6, 1885; "A Colored Professional Team," *New Orleans Times-Picayune*, Aug 13, 1885; "The Colored Clubs," *New Orleans Times-Picayune*, Aug 23, 1885; "At Sportsman's Park," *St. Louis Republican*, Jun 6, 1886; "At Sportsman's Park," *St. Louis Republican*, Jun 18, 1886; "Diamond Dust," *St. Louis Globe-Democrat*, Apr 25, 1887; "Rakings," *New Orleans (LA) Weekly Pelican*, Jun 4, 1887; "Diamond Sparks," *St. Louis Post-Dispatch*, Jun 6, 1887; "Rakings," *New Orleans Weekly Pelican*, Jun 18, 1887; "Base Ball and Athletics," *St. Louis Globe-Democrat*, Jul 31, 1887; "Sporting," *St. Louis Globe-Democrat*, Aug 11, 1887; *Topeka Daily Capital*, Sep 7, 1887; "Diamond Dust," *St. Louis Globe-Democrat*, Apr 17, 1888; "Base Ball News," *Indianapolis (IN) Freeman*, Mar 30, 1889; "Base Ball Notes," *St. Louis Republican*, Apr 25, 1889; "Amateur Nines," *St. Louis Post-Dispatch*, Jul 7, 1890; "Among the Amateurs," *St. Louis Globe-Democrat*, Jul 8, 1890; "Base Ball Notes," *St. Louis Republican*, Apr 25, 1889; "Among the Amateurs," *St. Louis Post-Dispatch*, May 14, 1892; "Amateur Base Ball Notes," *St. Louis Post-Dispatch*, Sep 14, 1897; "Colored League of Ball Clubs," *St. Louis Post-Dispatch*, Sep 6, 1899.

Blue Stocking Base Ball Club (St. Louis, MO; 1870s–1880s). Organizer(s): James A. Johnson.

The Blue Stocking B.B.C. organized in 1875, played black and white teams. The Blues, formerly the Napoleon club, toured MO, KS and IL. An intense rivalry developed with Chicago. *St. Louis Globe-Democrat* (October 15, 1875): "The Blue Stockings, a colored organization of this city, started for Chicago on Friday last to play their return games with the Uniques, the champion colored club of that section of the country. They were to have played on Saturday, but rain interfered. On Monday, they met the Uniques and warmed them handsomely by a score of 12 to 8. On Wednesday, the St. Louisans against visited White Stocking Park and played against their Chicago rivals. The Uniques took the lead at the start, but, nothing daunted, the Blue Legs went to work to catch up. The Uniques, in nine innings, secured seventeen runs. When the Blues, with fourteen runs to their credit, got two men on bases in their half of the last inning, with nobody out, the first base man of the Chicago club hid the ball. Another was furnished and the umpire called 'play ball,' but the Chicago men, fearing defeat, refused to continue. The umpire was afraid to declare a forfeit, owing to the mob, who stoned the Blue Stocking omnibus as it left the grounds, severely hurting William Mitchell and William Pitts, two of the St. Louis nine. This outrageous conduct will not soon be forgotten by those who treated the Uniques so well when they played in this city." They developed a rivalry with Lawrence's Eagles. *Lawrence Republican Journal* (June 13, 1876): "A swarthy, sweaty, first-class assemblage witnessed the game of baseball yesterday between the Blue Stockings of St. Louis and the Eagles of Lawrence. The crowd was very decorous, though showing some enthusiasm at the several successes of the Eagles. The Blues will not go to Topeka, but will leave this morning for Louisville, Kentucky. They were entertained last evening in Miller's Hall. The call the Eagles the best amateur club they have met with west of St. Louis, and considering the fact that they have had no practice for eight consecutive months, we guess they are." They played white nines. *Globe-Democrat* (June 2, 1876): "A novel contest takes place at the Compton Avenue Park on Sunday next, when the Olives, a white organization, tests the strength of the colored Blue Stockings." *Globe-Democrat* (June 5, 1876): "About 500 enthusiast assembled at Compton Avenue Park, to witness the novel encounter between the colored Blue Stockings and their white rivals. The game was hotly contested throughout, and was a tie from the third to the ninth inning." In 1883, Springfield, IL's Excelsiors (a black team) defeated the Blues who, it appears, declined as a baseball power.

SOURCES: "Base Ball," *St. Louis (MO) Times*, Aug 31, 1875; "Base Ball," *St. Louis (MO) Republican*, Sep 9, 1875; "Local Gossip," *St. Louis (MO) Globe-Democrat*, Sep 13, 1875; "Base-Ball," *Chicago (IL) Inter-Ocean*, Oct 14, 1875; "Ball Talk," *St. Louis Globe-Democrat*, Oct 15, 1875; "Short Stops," *St. Louis Globe-Democrat*, Jun 2, 1876; "Shortstops," *St. Louis Globe-Democrat*, Jun 5, 1876; "Jottings," *Kansas City (MO) Journal*, Jun 12, 1876; "Blue Stockings vs. Eagles," *Lawrence (KS) Journal*, Jun 13, 1876; "Base Ball Match," *Lawrence (KS) Tribune*, Jul 13, 1876; "Base Ball," *St. Louis (MO) Post-Dispatch*, Aug 12, 1881; "Base-Ball," *Springfield (IL) Illinois State Register*, Sep 4, 1883.

Brown Stocking Base Ball Club (St. Louis, MO; 1860s–1870s). Organizer(s): Douglass Smith.

The Brown Stocking B.B.C. organized in 1869. The Browns were one of the earliest, if not the earliest, self-identified black professional organizations. *Utica Observer* (November 29, 1870): "The St. Louis Base Ball Club, composed of men with money, has undertaken to pay the traveling expenses of a strong nine of colored baseballists to travel through the Eastern States early in 1871. They desire the addresses of the secretaries of colored clubs throughout the States North." *New York Clipper* (April 8, 1871): "The Brown Stockings are looking for "colored professionals," a "good catcher and good left hand pitcher. A good salary will be given for the season." The Browns marched in St. Louis parade celebrating the ratification of the Fifteenth Amendment. By the mid–1870s, strong black teams challenged the Browns. In a match game of ball against the Franklins, the Brown Stockings were defeated by a score of 15 to 9. They also played the Franklin Juniors, composed of high school base-ballers.

SOURCES: "Amendment Jubilee," *St. Louis (MO) Missouri Republican*, Apr 12, 1870; "Base Ball," *Utica (NY) Observer*, Nov 29, 1870; "Base Ball," *New York (NY) Clipper*, Apr 8, 1871; "Miscellaneous," *St. Louis (MO) Times*, Sep 6, 1875; "Short Stops," *Globe-Democrat (St. Louis, MO)*, June 4, 1876; "Short Stops," *St. Louis Globe-Democrat*, June 5, 1876; "Short Stops," *St. Louis Globe-Democrat*, June 6, 1876.

Clipper Base Ball Club (St. Louis, MO; 1880s)

The Clipper B.B.C. organized in the 1880s, played black teams. *St. Louis Post-Dispatch* (September 27, 1884): "The Eclipse and Clipper (colored) Clubs will play their first game Sunday at Compton Avenue Park at 3:30 p.m. for $50 a side." *St. Louis Republican* (September 28, 1884): "The Eclipse, colored club, downed the Clippers at Compton Avenue Park yesterday by the long score of 22 to 2."

SOURCES: "Diamond Chips," *St. Louis (MO) Post-Dispatch*, Sep 27, 1884; "Diamond Chips," *St. Louis (MO) Republican*, Sep 28, 1884.

Colored Base Ball League (St. Louis, MO. Organizer(s): Henry Bridgewater; 1883).

In 1882, the baseballist "Bud" Fowler (Nee John W. Jackson) communicated with Henry Bridgewater about organizing a Colored Base

Ball League; Bridgewater managed St. Louis, MO's Black Stockings. Shuttling between New Orleans, LA and Richmond, VA, Fowler had shared their ideas with James Dudley, manager of Richmond's Black Swans. His dispatch, along with letters from Lynchburg, VA and Cincinnati, OH piqued Bridgewater's interest: he agreed to host a baseball convention. While New York City, Philadelphia, Cincinnati, Baltimore, Washington, D.C., Richmond, and St. Louis would attend, Bridgewater's goal was much more ambitious. Quietly, he planned to incorporate both eastern and western clubs. The St. Louis Colored Base Ball Convention would also be represented by CO clubs, including Denver, Leadville, CO Springs, Longmont, Fort Collins, Greeley, ID Springs and Lawson. A Louisville dispatch was sent to a Midwestern newspaper regarding the league's organization. *Cincinnati Enquirer* (February 25, 1883): "Please let us hear from the Colored Base Ball Association in your Sunday's issue, if they really have done anything; if not let us know. A great many read your paper on Sunday for the base-ball news it contains. If there is to be a Colored Base Ball Association and it you know the address of any of the projectors, please let us hear from you next Sunday. Yours truly, Louisville." The Colored League failed to materialize.

SOURCES: "Diamond Dust," *St. Louis (MO) Globe-Democrat,* Dec 10, 1882; "Notes," *Cincinnati (OH) Enquirer,* Feb 25, 1883; "Base Ball," *St. Louis Globe-Democrat,* Jan 27, 1883; "Base Ball," *St. Louis Globe-Democrat,* Feb 4, 1883; "In and Outdoor Sports," *Cleveland (OH) Plain Dealer,* Feb 6, 1883; "Commercial Nines," *New York (NY) Clipper,* Feb 10, 1883; "Diamond Dust," *Fort Wayne (IN) Gazette,* Feb 10, 1883; "Base Ball," *Cincinnati (OH) Gazette,* Apr 17, 1883; "Diamond Chips," *St. Louis (MO) Republican,* Apr 28, 1883; "Sporting," *St. Louis Republican,* Apr 28, 1883; "General Sporting News," *Topeka (KS) Capital,* May 2, 1883; "Diamonds," *Elgin (IL) Elgin Morning Frank,* May 10, 1883; "The Colored League," *St. Louis Republican,* May 16, 1883.

Compton Browns Base Ball Club (St. Louis, MO; 1880s)

The Compton Browns B.B.C. organized in the 1880s, played black teams. *St. Louis Post-Dispatch:* "The Athletics and Compton Browns, colored, will play their second game of three. The game will be called at 4 p. m." The Browns also played the Eclipse nine. *St. Louis Republican:* "The Eclipse Club, the colored champions of the United States, and the Compton Browns play the second game of their series of three at 4 p. m." *Republican:* "At Compton Avenue Park, the Eclipse downed the Compton Browns by a score of 17 to 12."

SOURCES: "Diamond Dust," *St. Louis (MO) Republican,* Aug 17, 1884; "Diamond Chips," *St. Louis Republican,* Aug 28, 1884; "Base Ball Briefs," *St. Louis Republican,* Sep 2, 1884; "Diamond Chips," *St. Louis Republican,* Sep 7, 1884.

Compton Reds Base Ball Club (St. Louis, MO; 1880s)

The Compton Reds B.B.C. organized in the 1880s, played black teams. *St. Louis Republican* (July 24, 1884): "The Eclipse and Compton Reds, colored clubs, will play their first game of the season, at Compton Avenue Park, Sunday afternoon at 4 o'clock." *Republican* (July 28, 1884): "The Eclipse scored another victory at the Compton Avenue Park, defeating the Compton Reds by a score of 8 to 1."

SOURCES: "Diamond Dust," *St. Louis (MO) Republican,* Jul 24, 1884; "Diamond Chips," *St. Louis Republican,* Jul 28, 1884.

Eclipse Base Ball Club (St. Louis, MO; 1880s). Organizer(s): Charles Brooks and W. L. Adams.

The Eclipse B.B.C. organized in the 1880s. Between 1883 and 1884, Charles Brooks and W. L. Adams managed the team. Crossing bats with both white and black nines, the Eclipse established a regional reputation. *St. Louis Republican* (July 1, 1884): "The Eclipse Club,

the colored champions of the United States, and the Compton Browns play the second game of their series of three at 4 p. m." *Republican* (July 17, 1884): "At Compton Avenue Park, the Eclipse downed the Compton Browns by a score of 17 to 12." *Republican* (August 24, 1884): "The Eclipse and Compton Reds, colored clubs, will play their first game of the season, at Compton Avenue Park, Sunday afternoon at 4 o'clock." *Republican* (August 25, 1884): "The Eclipse scored another victory at the Compton Avenue Park, defeating the Compton Reds by a score of 8 to 1." They challenged the Black Stockings for the local championship, and defeated them five times straight. In 1885, the reorganized with the battery of Acie and David Price. The Black Stockings promptly challenged them, defeating the Eclipse Club in three consecutive games. Bridgewater's club absorbed Eclipse players, and he formed a reserve team; the reserves traveled to LA, contesting the colored clubs of New Orleans. When the Eclipse reorganized in 1886, Joe Bailey, William Richardson, Steve Jones and Al Spencer form the nucleus. In the 1870s and early 1880s, Bailey and Richardson had played together for the Blue Stockings. Spencer had played with the Excelsiors of Springfield, IL, and St. Louis Black Stockings. By 1887, the Eclipse ceased to be a local power.

SOURCES: "Diamond Dust," *St. Louis (MO) Republican,* Apr 17, 1884; "Diamond Chips," *St. Louis Republican,* Jul 1, 1884; "Diamond Chips," *St. Louis Republican,* Jul 17, 1884; "Diamond Dust," *St. Louis (MO) Globe-Democrat,* Jul 28, 1884; "Local Brevities," *Springfield (IL) State Journal,* Aug 5, 1884; "Colored Excursionists," *Springfield State Journal,* Aug 5, 1884; "Local News," *Springfield State Journal,* Aug 19, 1884; "Diamond Dust," *St. Louis Republican,* Aug 24, 1884; "Diamond Chips," *St. Louis Republican,* Aug 25, 1884; "Diamond Chips," *St. Louis Republican,* Aug 28, 1884; "Diamond Chips," *St. Louis Republican,* Aug 30, 1884; "Base Ball Briefs," *St. Louis Republican,* Sep 2, 1884; "The Colored Championship," *St. Louis Republican,* Sep 5, 1884; "Diamond Chips," *St. Louis Republican,* Sep 12, 1884; "Diamond Dust," *St. Louis Republican,* Sep 13, 1884; "Diamond Chips," *St. Louis Republican,* Sep 14, 1884; "Diamond Chips," *St. Louis Republican,* Sep 15, 1884; "Diamond Chips," *St. Louis Republican,* Sep 23, 1884; "Diamond Chips," *St. Louis Republican,* Sep 27, 1884; "Diamond Dust," *St. Louis Republican,* Oct 4, 1884; "Diamond Dust," *St. Louis Republican,* Oct 5, 1884; "Diamond Chips," *St. Louis Republican,* Oct 6, 1884; "Diamond Dust," *St. Louis Republican,* Oct 12, 1884; "Diamond Chips," *St. Louis Republican,* Oct 13, 1884; "Diamond Dust," *St. Louis Republican,* Oct 19, 1884; "Diamond Dust," *St. Louis Republican,* Oct 20, 1884; "Amateur Base-Ball Brevities," *St. Louis (MO) Post-Dispatch,* May 30, 1885; "Diamond Dust," *St. Louis Globe-Democrat,* May 31, 1885; "Black Sox vs. Eclipse," *St. Louis Republican,* May 31, 1885; "Black Sox Victory," *St. Louis Republican,* Jun 1, 1885; "Diamond Chips," *St. Louis Republican,* Jun 8, 1885; "Base Ball," *New Orleans (LA) Times-Picayune,* Aug 5, 1885; "Diamond Notes," *New Orleans Times-Picayune,* Aug 11, 1885; "A Colored Professional Team," *New Orleans Daily Picayune,* Aug 13, 1885; "Base Ball," *New Orleans Times-Picayune.* August21, 1885; "The Colored Clubs," *New Orleans Times-Picayune,* Aug 23, 1885; "The Eclipse Team Defeats the Cohens," *New Orleans Times-Picayune,* Aug 24, 1885; "Around Home Bases," *New Orleans Times-Picayune,* Aug 27, 1885; "The Cohens Defeat the Visitors," *New Orleans Times-Picayune,* Aug 28, 1885; "The Amateurs," *St. Louis Republican,* Apr 19, 1886.

Euchre Base Ball Club (St. Louis, MO; 1880s–1890s). Owner(s): Henry Sanford and Charles Dixon.

The Euchre B.B.C. organized in the 1880s, played white and black teams. They had been members of the West Ends and Black Stockings' organizations. *St. Louis Sporting News* (June 14, 1886): "The Euchres defeated the Edwardsville Browns Sunday last by a score of

8 to 2." They played a match game against the St. Louis Amateurs, a white organization. *Sporting News* (June 18, 1887): "The St. Louis Anchors defeated the Euchres, the colored champions at Compton Avenue Park last Sunday by a score of 24 to 1. The Anchors are composed of some of the best amateur base-ball talent in the city." They reorganized in 1887. The Black Stockings challenged defeated the Euchres. *Globe Democrat* (July 31 1887): "The Black Socks, colored, defeated the Euchres, also colored, 18 to 7." *Globe Democrat* (August 1, 1887): "The Black Sox defeated the Euchres by a score of 20 to 7."

Sources: "Diamond Dust," *St. Louis (MO) Globe-Democrat*, Jun 6, 1886; "Caught on the Fly," *St. Louis (MO) Sporting News*, Jun 14, 1886; "Diamond Dust," *St. Louis Globe-Democrat*, Jul 16, 1886; "Diamond Dust," *St. Louis Globe-Democrat*, July 18, 1886; "Sporting," *St. Louis Globe-Democrat*, Jul 19, 1886; "Compton Avenue," *St. Louis (MO) Republican*, Aug 12, 1886; "Sporting," *St. Louis Globe-Democrat*, Sep 4, 1886; "Caught on the Fly," *St. Louis (MO) Sporting News*, Jun 18, 1887; "Diamond Dust," *St. Louis Globe-Democrat*, Jul 31 1887; "Diamond Dust," *St. Louis Globe-Democrat*, Aug 1, 1887; "Amateur Notes," *St. Louis Globe-Democrat*, Jun 2, 1891.

Favorite Base Ball Club (St. Louis, MO; 1890s). Organizer(s): Charles Renfro.

The Favorite B.B.C. organized in the 1890s, played black organizations. *St. Louis Post-Dispatch* (June 19, 1897): "The Mohawks, who for two years have been the champion colored team of St. Louis, will play the Favorites Colored Team at Forest Park next Sunday afternoon." *St. Louis Republic* (September 5, 1897): "The Favorites defeated the Mohawks Sunday at the old Sportsman's Park by a score of 16 to 10."

Sources: "Young Champions of the Diamond," *St. Louis (MO) Post-Dispatch*, May 10, 1896; "The Amateur Diamond," *St. Louis Post-Dispatch*, Jun 19, 1897; "Games For Sunday," *St. Louis Post-Dispatch*, Aug 21, 1897; "Amateur Base Ball Notes," *St. Louis Post-Dispatch*, Aug 29, 1897; "Future Champions," *St. Louis (MO) Republic*, Sep 5, 1897; "Amateur Base Ball Notes," *St. Louis Post-Dispatch*, Sep 14, 1897.

Franklin Base Ball Club (St. Louis, MO; 1870s)

The Franklin B.B.C. organized in the 1870s, played black teams. They defeated the Sure Beats, by a score of 9 to 4. In a match game of ball against the Laurels, of Decatur, IL, the Franklins won by a score of 12 to 11. A match game of ball was also played against the Black Stockings. The Franklins also played a series of games against the Brown Stockings.

Sources: "Base Ball," *St. Louis (MO) Times*, Aug 16, 1875; "Short Stops," *St. Louis (MO) Globe-Democrat*, Aug 16, 1875; "Amateur Games," *St. Louis (MO) Republican*, Aug 23, 1875; "Base Ball," *St. Louis Republican*, Jul 10, 1876; "Minor Games," *St. Louis Republican*, Jul 17, 1876; "Tips," *St. Louis Globe-Democrat*, Jul 17, 1876; "Tips," *St. Louis Globe-Democrat*, Jul 24, 1876; "Home Games," *St. Louis Republican*, Jul 26, 1876; "Stop Stops," *St. Louis Globe-Democrat*, Aug 9, 1876.

Franklin Junior Base Ball Club (St. Louis, MO; 1870s)

The Franklin Junior B.B.C. organized in the 1870s. The Franklin Juniors (high school students) played against black and white junior nines. They played against the Chicago Juniors, defeating them by a score of 18 to 14. The Franklin Juniors also played the senior organization, the Brown Stockings, defeating them by a score of 13 to 12.

Sources: "Base Ball," *St. Louis (MO) Republican*, Jul 17, 1876 "Tips," *St. Louis (MO) Globe-Democrat*, Jul 17, 1876.

Green Stocking ("Olives") Base Ball Club (St. Louis, MO; 1870s)

The Green Stocking B.B.C. organized in the 1870s, played black and white nines. *St. Louis Globe Democrat* (August 9, 1875): "Another colored club of this city is looming up as a candidate for honorable distinction in the National Pastime, and yesterday met a white organization called the Lyons. The colored boys call themselves the Green Sox. The game was closely contested, the white club winning by a score of 11 to 10, in six innings, when darkness settling in put a stop to further play. *St. Louis Times* (July 8, 1876): "The Olives and Blue Stockings—both colored—play at the Red's Park on Sunday. The latter soon start on a tour through the State and Kansas." They also played clubs outside of the city. *Globe-Democrat* (September 11, 1876): "The Green Sox, of this city, visited Mount Olive, Sunday, and played a fine game of base-ball. Seven innings were played, when darkness prevented further play."

Sources: "Short Stops," *St. Louis (MO) Globe-Democrat*, Aug 9, 1875; "Short Stops," *St. Louis Globe-Democrat*, Aug 16, 1875; "Base Ball," *St. Louis (MO) Republican*, Sep 13, 1875; "Minor Games," *St. Louis Republican*, Sep 27, 1875; "Short Stops," *St. Louis Globe-Democrat*, Jun 4, 1876; "The Colored Clubs," *St. Louis Globe Democrat*, Jun 14, 1876; "Local Lines," *St. Louis Globe-Democrat*, Jul 8, 1876; "Base Ball Notes," *St. Louis (MO) Times*, Jul 8, 1876; "Local Lines," *St. Louis Globe-Democrat*, Jul 9, 1876; "Minor Contests," *St. Louis Globe-Democrat*, Sep 4, 1876; "Minor Contests in and About the City," *St. Louis Globe-Democrat*, Sep 11, 1876.

Hartford Base Ball Club (St. Louis, MO; 1870s–1880s)

The Harford B.B.C. organized in the 1870s, played black teams. *Hartford Daily Courant* (August 7, 1875): "St. Louis has a Hartford nine, and so has Rochester—the [former] colored." *St. Louis Republican* (September 10, 1877): "Next Thursday the Black Stockings will play the Hartfords (colored Champions) at the Grand Avenue Park." They developed a rivalry with the Black Stockings. *Republican*: "Next Thursday the Black Stockings will play the Hartfords (colored champions) at the Grand Avenue Park." *St. Louis Globe Democrat* (August 1, 1877): "The Blue Stockings and Hartfords meet at Grant Avenue Park, this afternoon, to contend for the colored championship and a set of elk horns kindly presented to the boys by Superintendent Solari. Play will be called at 4 o'clock promptly." They played the Lindells, a nine composed of waiters of the Lindell Hotel. *Globe-Democrat* (August 28, 1881): "The Hartfords and Lindells will have a tilt for the colored championship."

Sources: "Base Ball," *Hartford (CT) Daily Courant*, Aug 7, 1875; "Outdoor Sports," *St. Louis (MO) Globe-Democrat*, Aug 14, 1876; "Diamond Dust," *St. Louis Globe-Democrat*, August 1, 1877; "Athletics," *St. Louis (MO) Republican*, Sep 10, 1877; "Base Ball Notes," *St. Louis Republican*, Sep 10, 1877; "Base Ball," *St. Louis (MO) Post-Dispatch*, Aug 26, 1881; "Base Ball," *St. Louis Republican*, Aug 27, 1881; "The Sport Today," *St. Louis Globe-Democrat*, Aug 28, 1881.

Independent Base Ball Club (St. Louis, MO; 1870s)

The Independent B.B.C. organized in the 1870s, played black nines. *St. Louis Times* (July 24, 1876): "The following amateur games were played yesterday in the various localities dedicated to the pursuit of willow-wielding and leather hunting: Black Sox 21; Independents, 19." *St. Louis Globe Democrat* (July 29, 1876): "At the Stocks' Park yesterday afternoon, the Black Stockings defeated the Independents—both strong colored clubs—by a score of 18 to 14. Al Pierce did not strive with the brilliancy of a Wright at short."

Sources: "Base Ball," *St. Louis (MO) Times*, Jul 24, 1876; "Base Ball Notes," *St. Louis Times*, Jul 29, 1876; "Base Ball Brevities," *St. Louis (MO) Globe-Democrat*, Jul 29, 1876

Lindell House Base Ball Club (St. Louis, MO; 1870s–1880s). Organizer(s): W. R. Smith.

The Lindell House B.B.C. organized in the 1870s, played black nines. The Lindells crossed bat with the Hartford and Black Stocking nines.

SOURCES: "Base Ball," *St. Louis (MO) Times*, Aug 31, 1875; "Minor Games," *St. Louis (MO) Republican*, Jul 3, 1876; "Base Ball," *St. Louis Republican*, Jul 10, 1876; "Base Ball," *St. Louis Republican*, Sep 4, 1876; "Minor Games," *St. Louis (MO) Globe-Democrat*, Sep 25, 1876; "Base Ball," *St. Louis Republican*, Aug 27, 1881; "Sporting," *St. Louis Globe-Democrat*, Apr 25, 1886; "At Sportsman's Park," *St. Louis Republican*, Jun 6, 1886; "Compton Avenue," *St. Louis Republican*, Aug 22, 1886; "Sporting," *St. Louis Republican*, Sep 4, 1886; "Diamond Dust," *St. Louis Globe-Democrat*, Jul 24, 1888.

Metropolitan Base Ball Club (St. Louis, MO; 1880s)

The Metropolitan B.B.C. organized in 1884, played black nines. *St. Louis Republican* (April 26, 1885): "The Eclipse club, the colored champions, and the Mets, also colored, play at Compton Avenue Park at 3 p.m. today.

SOURCES: "Base Ball," *St. Louis (MO) Globe-Democrat*, Apr 4, 1884; "Base Ball Briefly," *St. Louis (MO) Republican*, Apr 26, 1885.

Mohawk Base Ball Club (St. Louis, MO; 1880s–1890s). Organizer(s): E. Davis; James H. Miller.

The Mohawk B.B.C. organized in the 1880s, played white and black nines. *St. Louis Post-Dispatch* (July 29, 1889): "The West Ends and the Mohawks played the second game of their series of four games, and after a hard struggle the West Ends came out victorious." They split two games with the New Orleans Pinchbacks, a black organization visiting St. Louis, for the black championship of the West. *Post-Dispatch* (September 8, 1889): "The Mohawks defeated the Pinchbacks yesterday by a score of 10 to 6. These two clubs will decide their deciding game this morning." *St. Louis Globe-Democrat* (October 1, 1891): "The colored base-ball championship will be decided next Sunday afternoon at Compton Park between the Mohawks and the West Ends." The towns of St. Louis and Kansas City developed a black rivalry. *Kansas City Times* (August 25, 1890): "A yesterday afternoon a small but enthusiastic audience, composed mostly of colored people gathered at Exposition Park to witness a ball game between the St. Louis Mohawks and the Kansas City Club." *St. Louis Republic* (September 5, 1897): "The Favorites defeated the Mohawks Sunday at the old Sportsman's Park by a score of 16 to 10."

SOURCES: "Amateur Nines," *St. Louis (MO) Post-Dispatch*, Jul 29, 1889; "Pinchbacks vs. Mohawks," *St. Louis Post-Dispatch*, Sep 4, 1889; "Base Ball Briefs," *St. Louis Post-Dispatch*, Sep 6, 1889; "The Colored Championship," *St. Louis Post-Dispatch*, Sep 7, 1889; "The Colored Clubs," *St. Louis Post-Dispatch*, Sep 8, 1889; "Amateur Notes," *St. Louis (MO) Globe-Democrat*, May 24, 1890; "Amateur Nines," *St. Louis Post-Dispatch*, May 30, 1890; "Amateur Games," *Kansas City (MO) Times*, Aug 25, 1890; "Colored Teams to Play," *Kansas City Times*, Aug 25, 1890; "Sporting Notes," *Times*, Aug 27, 1890; "Amateur Notes," *St. Louis Globe-Democrat*, Oct 1, 1891; "The Amateur Diamond," *St. Louis Post-Dispatch*, Jun 19, 1897; "Mohawks vs. Sporting News," *St. Louis Post-Dispatch*, Jul 3, 1897; "Reserves vs. the Mohawks," *St. Louis Post-Dispatch*, Jul 18, 1897; "Saturday's Game at Sportsman's," *St. Louis Post-Dispatch*, Aug 12, 1897; "Games for Sunday," *St. Louis Post-Dispatch*, Aug 21, 1897; "Amateur Base Ball Notes," *St. Louis Post-Dispatch*, Aug 29, 1897; "Mohawks vs. 3 C's," *St. Louis Post-Dispatch*, May 28, 1898; "In the Local Parks," *St. Louis Post-Dispatch*, May 30, 1898; "Copper-Colored Coons Played Ball with Mohawks," *St. Louis (MO) Republic*, May 30, 1898.

Napoleon Base Ball Club (St. Louis, MO; 1870s)

Proprietor: James Johnson

The Napoleon B.B.C. organized in 1874, played black nines of MO and IL. The Napoleons developed a rivalry with Chicago's Uniques. *St. Louis Republican* (September 7, 1874): "The Napoleon (colored) base Ball Club of this city, left for Chicago yesterday evening to play the Unique club of that city for the championship of colored clubs." *Chicago Inter-Ocean* (September 11, 1874): "The game arranged for, between the Uniques, of this city, and Napoleons, of St. Louis, was not played yesterday, owing to the failure of the Napoleons to come on time. The game was, therefore, postponed until Saturday." The organization played into the late 1870s. *Springfield State Register* (June 8, 1879): "The Lowells will go to St. Louis to play three games with the Napoleon Cub, of that city."

SOURCES: "Base Ball Brevities," *St. Louis (MO) Globe*, Sep 6, 1874; "Sporting News," *Chicago (IL) Inter-Ocean*, Sep 6, 1874; "Local Brevities," *St. Louis (MO) Republican*, Sep 7, 1874; "Sporting News," *Chicago Inter-Ocean*, Sep 11, 1874; "Base Ball," *St. Louis (MO) Times*, Aug 31, 1875; "Base-Ball," *Chicago Inter-Ocean*, Oct 14, 1875; "Uniques of Chicago vs. St. Louis Blue Stockings," "Base Ball," *Chicago Daily Inter-Ocean*, Sep 11, 1874; "Base Ball," *Chicago Inter-Ocean*, Sep 12, 1874; "Springfield in Front Again," *Springfield (IL) State Register*, Jun 8, 1879; "General Gossip," *Springfield (IL) State Journal*, Jun 11, 1879.

Nine Star Base Ball Club (St. Louis, MO; 1880s). Organizer(s): Fred Godore and James Williams.

The Nine Star B.B.C. organized in the 1880s, played black nines. *St. Louis Republican* (April 12, 1885): "The Nine Stars is the name of a colored Base Ball Club organized during the past week. The club completed their organization by electing James Williams manager and Fred Godore president."

SOURCES: "Diamond Dust," *St. Louis (MO) Republican*, Apr 12, 1885.

No. 5 Base Ball Club (St. Louis, MO; 1890s)

The No. 5 B.B.C. organized in the 1890s. The nine played other black teams. *St. Louis Globe-Democrat* (June 15, 1890): "The great colored cracks, the West Ends, play the No. 5s, a strong colored club at Compton Avenue Park today, for $50 a side and gate receipts. The No. 5s have been practicing for this game hard all week."

SOURCES: "Among the Amateurs," *Globe-Democrat* (St. Louis, MO), June 15, 1890.

South End Base Ball Club (St. Louis, MO; 1890s)

The South End B.B.C. organized in the 1890s. The "South Ends" played black nines. *Globe-Democrat* (August 2, 1891): "Colored Base Ball circles will be agog with excitement today at Compton Park, as there is to be a championship game between South End and West End. The West Ends will have their star battery, [Jack] Reeves and [Edward] Garig, while Williams and Monroe will officiate for the South Ends." *Globe-Democrat* (August 4, 1891): "The West Ends polished off the South Ends at Compton Park Sunday by a score of 10 to 1. [Jack] Reeves of the West Ends kept the South Ends down to two hits."

SOURCES: "Amateur Notes," *St. Louis (MO) Globe-Democrat*, Aug 1, 1891; "Amateur Nines," *St. Louis (MO) Post-Dispatch*, Aug 8, 1891; "Amateur Notes," *St. Louis Globe-Democrat*, Aug 2, 1891; "Amateur Notes," *St. Louis Globe-Democrat*, Aug 4, 1891.

Sunset Base Ball Club (St. Louis, MO; 1870s–1890s)

The Sunset B.B.C. organized in the 1870s, played black teams. *St. Louis Republican* (August 23, 1870): "A game of base-ball was played by the Sunset and Allegheny clubs, for a champion belt. Five innings were played and thee game lasted over three hour. The score stood Sunset 29, Allegheny, 30. The latter consequently won the belt." *St.*

Louis Globe Democrat (August 29, 1875): "Quite a crowd was attracted to the Compton Avenue Park, yesterday afternoon, to witness the game between the Sunset and Blue Sox, two rival colored organizations. After a hot contest had been played, the former club succeeded in getting in seven runs in the eighth inning, and blacking their opponents in the ninth, won the game." The Sunsets played Chicago's Uniques. *Globe Democrat* (September 7, 1875): "The colored organizations, respectively of Chicago and St. Louis, gave a very creditable display of the beauties of the National game at the Grand Avenue Park, yesterday afternoon, in the presence of about 300 hundred spectators. The Chicago boys proved too much for their adversaries, the game finally resulting in their favor by a score of 16 to 9." *St. Louis Republican* (September 7, 1875): "The Chicago Uniques and the St. Louis Sunsets, both colored, played their second game yesterday at Grand Avenue Park. The Uniques won the game by a score of 5 to 9. The first game played on Sunday was won by the Sunsets in ten innings by a score of 26 to 9. Quite a large crowd of the dusky hued were present at both games." *St. Louis Times* (May 14, 1876): "The Sunsets and Blue Stockings, two of the most expert of local colored clubs, played yesterday at Grand Avenue Park. The players involuntarily adopted Spalding's different color business, ranging in line from the rich colored coffee color to the undiluted ebony. Much good and bad playing was done, but the Blues proved too much for the Sunsets."

SOURCES: "Closed Celebration," *St. Louis (MO) Republican*, Aug 23, 1870; "Local Gossip," *St. Louis (MO) Globe-Democrat*, Aug 29, 1875; "Base Ball," *St. Louis (MO) Times*, Aug 31, 1875; "Uniques vs. Sunsets," *St. Louis Globe-Democrat*, Sep 7, 1875; "Base Ball," *St. Louis (MO) Republican*, Sep 7, 1875; "Local Gossip," *St. Louis Globe-Democrat*, Sep 12, 1875; "The Colored Teams," *St. Louis Globe-Democrat*, Sep 13, 1875; "Short Stops," *St. Louis Times*, May 14, 1876; "The Amateur Day," *St. Louis Times*, May 15, 1876.

Tilden Base Ball Club (St. Louis, MO; 1870s)

The Tilden B.B.C. organized in 1877, played black nines. *Louisville Courier-Journal* (February 4, 1877): "St. Louis has a Tilden Base Ball Club composed of colored players."

SOURCES: "Gossip for the Gang," *St. Louis (MO) Globe-Democrat*, Feb 4, 1877; "League Lingo," *Louisville (KY) Courier-Journal*, Feb 11, 1877.

West End Base Ball Club (St. Louis, MO; 1880s–1890s). Owner(s): Harry H. Jones.

The West End B.B.C. organized in the 1880s, played black and white teams. In 1882, the Black Stockings and West Ends crossed bats. *St. Louis Globe-Democrat* (September 8, 1882): "There was an interesting game at Compton Avenue Park yesterday, between the Black Stockings and West Ends (colored clubs). It resulted in favor of the former—6 to 4." After the Black Socks, the West Ends are arguably the most successful 19th century St. Louis black team. They toured IL and MO. *Globe-Democrat* (June 26, 1883): "The West Ends defeated the Lightfoot nine at Du Quoin, Illinois, the score standing 18 to 2." *Globe-Democrat* (July 5, 1883): "The West End Base Ball Club, of St. Louis, played a second-match game in this city with the Red Stocking Club, of Sedalia. Until the eighth inning, the St. Louis Club was eight runs ahead. In these two innings, the Sedalia club made 9 runs and won the game. The score stood—Sedalia, 18; West End, 11." Reorganizing in 1888, the West Ends and New Orleans's Pinchback club battled for the black championship, playing in St. Louis and New Orleans. *Globe-Democrat* (August 26, 1888): "The New Orleans, backed by the colored ex-senator, Pinchback, of New Orleans, made their first appearance at Sportsman's Park yesterday, and defeated the West Ends, of St. Louis, the champion local club.

The Pinchbacks showed themselves to be a very clever team and outplayed the West Ends at every point. The battery work of Hopkins and Josephs was the best feature of the Pinchbacks. For the West Ends, Bracey, Jones, and pitcher Garig carried off the honors." When they traveled to the latter place in 1888, the West Ends made quite an impression, playing black clubs of New Orleans and Algiers. *New Orleans Times-Picayune* (October 22, 1888): "The St. Louis colored champions, the West Ends, made their first appearance on New Orleans grounds yesterday. The Pinchbacks, the crack colored local team, gave the visitors battle. There was a large crowd present and the game proved exciting enough to keep the people present shouting to the end. The West Ends are a fine fielding nine and run the bases like the white [St. Louis] Browns, who are not the world champions. They field tolerably well and throw like a shot. Tooley, the comical looking first baseman, who has to receive the hot shot, wears gloves on both hands, but he holds on to the ball. The star player yesterday was Bracey, who is an ungainly edition of Billy Kersands and even blacker. He moves clumsily, but gets there." On a return excursion trip to LA in 1889, the West Ends played the Blues, of Quincy IL. *Quincy Herald* (September 30, 1888): "The Quincy Blues will cross bats at Louisiana with the St. Louis West Ends, another colored nine." The West Ends continued the tradition—established by the Black Stockings—of inviting Louisville's black teams to St. Louis. *Globe-Democrat* (July 22, 1890): "There will be fun at Compton Avenue Park this afternoon. The Tonics, the champion colored club of Kentucky, will arrive by special train this morning and play the local colored champions, the West Ends. The Tonics are making a tour of the country, and go from here to Chicago. Play will begin at 2:30."

SOURCES: "Base Ball," *St. Louis (MO) Globe-Democrat*, Aug 26, 1882; "Diamond Dust," *St. Louis Globe-Democrat*, Aug 28, 1882; "Diamond Dust," *St. Louis Globe-Democrat*, Sep 8, 1882; "Sporting News," *St. Louis (MO) Evening Chronicle*, Sep 9, 1882; "Base Ball," *St. Louis (MO) Post-Dispatch*, Jun 1, 1883; "Diamond Chips," *St. Louis (MO) Republican*, Jun 21, 1883; "Base Ball," *St. Louis Republican*, June 24, 1883; "St. Louis Amateurs vs. West End," *St. Louis Globe-Democrat*, Jun 26, 1883; "Diamond Dust," *St. Louis Globe-Democrat*, Jul 4, 1883; "Sedalia Boys Defeat the West End Club," *St. Louis Globe-Democrat*, Jul 5, 1883; "Diamond Dust," *St. Louis Globe-Democrat*, Jul 7, 1883; "The Great Coon Game," *St. Louis (MO) Republic*, Aug 24, 1888; "New Orleans, 6; St. Louis, 1," *St. Louis (MO) Globe-Democrat*, August 26, 1888; "City News," *Quincy (IL) Journal*, Sep 29, 1888; "Base Ball," *Quincy (IL) Herald*, Sep 30, 1888; "Black Diamonds vs. West Ends," *Quincy (IL) Whig*, Sep 30, 1888; "Notes," *Quincy Journal*, Oct 1, 1888; "Black Browns," *New Orleans (LA) Times-Picayune*, Oct 22, 1888; "Notes," *Quincy Whig*, Oct 2, 1888; "Local Ball Games," *St. Louis Republic*, May 30, 1889; "The West Ends Win," *St. Louis Globe-Democrat*, Jun 15, 1889; "The River and Railroads," *Quincy (IL) Herald*, Jun 19, 1889; "West Ends Win," *St. Louis Republic*, Sep 1, 1889; "Today's Games," *St. Louis Republic*, Aug 31, 1889; "Among the Amateurs," *St. Louis Globe-Democrat*, Jul 22, 1890; "West Ends, 6; IXLs, 2," *St. Louis Globe-Democrat*, Aug 4, 1890; "Amateur Notes," *St. Louis Globe-Democrat*, Jun 9, 1891; "Future Champions," *St. Louis Republic*, Aug 1, 1891; "Future Champions," *St. Louis Republic*, Aug 1, 1891; "Amateur Notes," *St. Louis Globe Democrat*, Aug 2, 1891; "Future Champions," *St. Louis Republic*, May 14, 1892; "Future Champions," *St. Louis Republic*, Jun 19, 1892; "City Amateur League Games," *St. Louis Republic*, Jul 15, 1894; "Base Ball," *Edwardsville (IN) Intelligencer*, Aug 2, 1895; "With the Amateurs," *St. Louis Post-Dispatch*, May 20, 1899.

West End Butler (Coachmen) Base Ball Club (St. Louis, MO; 1890s–1900s)

The White Stocking B.B.C. organized in the 1890s, played against black and white aggregations. *St. Louis Post Dispatch* (May 20, 1899): "The Eads will cross bats with the West End Butlers, formerly the Mohawks at Forest Park Sunday fir $50 a side. The Butlers are the strongest colored team in St. Louis and a lively game is expected. The battery, William Wilkes and Biscuits will oppose the Eads."

SOURCES: "With the Amateurs," *St. Louis (MO) Post-Dispatch*, May 20, 1899; "Amateur Baseball Notes," *St. Louis (MO) Republic*, Sep 9, 1902; "Amateur Baseball Notes," *St. Louis Republic*, Apr 14, 1903.

White Stocking Base Ball Club (St. Louis, MO; 1870s)

The White Stocking B.B.C. organized in the 1870s, played against black teams. *St. Louis Globe-Democrat* (August 28, 1875): "Next Monday colored enthusiasts have a game at the Grand Avenue Park. The rival nines are designated White Stockings and Sunsets."

SOURCES: "Among the Amateurs," *St. Louis (MO) Globe-Democrat*, Aug 28, 1875; "Minor Games," *St. Louis (MO) Republican*, Jul 3, 1876.

Yellow Stocking Base Ball Club (St. Louis, MO; 1880s)

The Yellow Stocking B.B.C. organized in the 1880s, played black nines. *St. Louis Evening Chronicle* (June 17, 1881): "two colored clubs are going to play at the Reds Park on Sunday next. They call themselves the Black and Yellow Stockings."

SOURCES: "Sporting," *St. Louis (MO) Evening Chronicle*, Jun 17, 1881.

Daisy Clipper Base Ball Club (Troy, MO; 1870s)

The Daisy Clipper B.B.C. organized in the 1870s, played black nines. *Troy Kansas Chief* (August 5, 1875): "At Wathena, on Monday, the Daisy Clippers, of Troy, beat the Olympics, of St. Joes, by a score of 20 to 19, in a game of base-ball. Both clubs are composed of colored boys. The St. Joe club is reported to have resorted to the usual St. Joe tactics, and to have squealed when beaten." *St. Joseph Morning Herald* (August 10, 1875): "The Olympics (colored), of this city, played the Daisy Cutters (colored), of Troy yesterday, and beat them by the handsome score of 31 to 21. They are becoming as popular as our crack clubs of white boys." *Kansas Chief* (August 12, 1875): "On Monday, the Colored Base Ball Club, of St. Joe, came over and played the Troy Club (colored) a game. St. Joe won by three points, the score standing 24 to 21."

SOURCES: *Troy (MO) Weekly Kansas Chief*, Aug 5, 1875; "Gazettlets vs. Smokers," *St. Joseph (MO) Morning Herald*, Aug 10, 1875; *Troy Kansas Chief*, Aug 12, 1875.

Colored Base Ball Club (Union, MO; 18980s)

The Colored B.B.C. organized in the 1880s, played white and black teams. *Union Record* (May 1, 1884): "The Union Reserve Base Ball Club played and won a match with the colored boys last Saturday. They played for a Union League ball. On their last inning the gentlemen of color were even on the tally sheet, and as soon as the Reserves made another successful run, threw up the sponge and acknowledged a fair beat."

SOURCES: "Local and County News," *Union (MO) Union Record*, May 1, 1884.

Montana

Colored Base Ball Club (Anaconda, MT; 1890s)

The Colored B.B.C. organized in the 1890s. *Anaconda Standard* (June 20, 1898): "Yesterday was a fine baseball day, barring a rainstorm of about 30 minutes' duration, which began just when everybody in town was looking at a hot ball game. The Athletic field was soon converted into a sea of mud, and when the shower ceased the grounds were in no condition for a continuance of the game…. It was the same way up at Lake Park, where the Lone Stars (a junior nine) and the colored nine started to play a game of base-ball. They had reached the sixth inning when the rain interfered, with the score standing 11 to 2 in favor of the young boys."

SOURCES: "It Was Funny," *Anaconda (MT) Independent*, May 30, 1898; "Two Ball Games To-Day," *Anaconda (MT) Standard*, Jun 5, 1898; "Too Much Electricity," *Anaconda Standard*, Jun 20, 1898.

Hickory Tips (Butte, MT; 1890s). Organizer(s): George Rideout and William Johnson.

The Hickory Tips B.B.C. organized in the 1890, played black and white nines. *Anaconda Standard* (July 13, 1895): "The Hickory Tips are an aggregation of colored men, some of whom formerly played with the well-known nine, the Cuban Giants of Hoboken. They are the champions of their race of ball playing in the Northwest and will put up a strong game." *Standard* (July 15, 1895): "An exceedingly funning game of base-ball was played at the park yesterday between the Hickory Tips of Butte and the Anaconda Grays. The Hickory Tips are colored men and the team contains some very good players. The Grays won the game by a score of 22 to 14."

SOURCES: "Emancipation Day," *Anaconda (MT) Standard*, Sep 13, 1894; *Anaconda Standard*, Jun 26, 1895; "Base Ball Tomorrow," *Anaconda Standard*, Jul 13, 1895; "Was Quite Amusing," *Anaconda Standard*, Jul 15, 1895; "About the City," *Anaconda Standard*, Jul 27, 1895; "Slaughtered Them," *Anaconda Standard*, Jul 29, 1895.

Montanas (Helena, MT; 1890s). Organizer(s): James A. Mack.

The MT B.B.C. organized in the 1890s, played white and black teams. *Helena Independent* (May 29, 1889): "The Waverley Base Ball Club and the Montanas (colored) will cross bats at Seymour [Seymer] Park Thursday afternoon." The: "The Montanas defeated the North Pacific nine Sunday by a score of 9 to 3." *Independent* (July 2, 1889): "There will be a match game of base-ball at the Seymour Park today at 3 o'clock sharp between the Montanas and the Helena Reserves for fifty dollars."

SOURCES: "Reportorial Notes," *Helena (MT) Independent*, May 29, 1889; "Reportorial Notes," *Helena Independent*, Jul 2, 1889; "Reportorial Notes," *Helena Independent*, Jul 7, 1889.

Pastimes (Helena, MT; 1890s). Organizer(s): James A. Mack.

The Pastime B.B.C. organized in the 1890s, played white and black teams. *Helena Independent* (June 17, 1890): "Noticing the bluff of someone that he would bet $100 to $50 that there is not one baseball nine that can make one run in a game with the Athletics, the Pastime club, composed of colored men, do hereby offer to accept any such proposition, and they are ready with the money any time at the Eureka club rooms, in the Parchen block." *Independent* (July 27, 1890): "The Pastimes and Queen City teams will play this afternoon at Seymer [Seymour] Park Grounds. Game will be called at 2:30 pm." *Saint Paul Appeal* (August 20, 1890): "George Crawford [colored] of Great Falls, Montana, was in our city on a flying visit with a challenge to the Helena Pastimes Base Ball Club Sunday." The Pastimes belonged to a black athletic organization, the Eureka Club, which also had a boxing element.

SOURCES: "Helena, Montana," *Saint Paul (MN) Appeal*, Jun 14, 1890; "Base Ball and Football," *Helena Independent*, Jun 17, 1890; "Tips from the Bat," *Helena Independent*, Jul 6, 1890; "Another Game," *Helena Independent*, Jul 7, 1890; "Helena, Montana," *Saint Paul Appeal*, Jul 19, 1890; "Queen Citys vs. Pastimes," *Helena Independent*, Jul 20, 1890; "Tips from the Bat," *Helena (MT) Independent Record*, Jul 27, 1890; "Helena, Montana," *Saint Paul Appeal*, Aug 20, 1890.

Silver Leafs (Helena, MT; 1890s). Organizer(s): James A. Mack.

The Silver Leaf B.B.C. organized in the 1890s, played black and white teams. *Helena Independent* (April 17, 1891): "The Coliseum Base Ball team will open this season on Sunday with the colored ball nine of this city at Athletic Park. Players in the Coliseum team will appear in their theatrical costumes and their opponents will be arrayed in the handsome uniforms they wore last summer." The Silver Leaf –a sporting organization—was also a literary, educational, social, and mutual beneficial society.

SOURCES: "Play Ball," *Helena (MT) Independent*, Apr 17, 1891; "Base Ball Season Opened," *Helena Independent*, Apr 21, 1891; "Local Sporting Gossip," *Helena Independent*, Apr 30, 1891.

Union Base Ball Club (Helena, MT; 1890s)

The Union B.B.C. organized in the 1890s, played white and black aggregations. *Helena Independent* (May 1, 1899): "The first baseball game of the season was played at Fort Harrison yesterday by a team of Helena High School boys against one composed of colored soldiers at the fort. The game resulted in favor of the blue coats by a score of 16 to 6." *Independent* (May 7, 1899): "Today, the first good game of the season will be played, when the regulars play an exhibition game with the Unions, a colored team that defeated the Fort Harrison team a short time ago in a practice game. To make the game interesting, a battery [both colored players] will be furnished for the Unions out of a league team, Freeman catching for both and Condon pitching for the Unions and Ryan for the regulars." The colored soldiers of Fort Harrison organized a team that played against white and colored clubs, including Helena's Union B.B.C.

SOURCES: "Was an Extra Inning Game," *Helena (MT) Independent*, Apr 30, 1899; "Two Boys Won," *Helena Independent*, May 1, 1899; "Not Heavy Enough," *Helena Independent, May 7*, 1899; "Ball Game was a Fizzle," *Helena Independent*, May 8, 1899; "Ball Games Today," *Helena Independent*, Jul 7, 1899; "Unions Won the Game," *Helena Independent*, Jul 10, 1899; "Ball Game Sunday," *Helena Independent*, Oct 7, 1899.

Nebraska

Colored Giants Base Ball Club (Lincoln, NE; 1890s). Owner(s): George WA Castone.

The Colored Giants B.B.C. organized in the 1890s, played white and black teams. *Lincoln Capital City Courier* (May 24, 1890): "The Lincoln Giants met their first defeat Thursday at the hands of the Kearneys. One out of ten or more games played is a remarkably good gait, and Lincoln is represented by a remarkably good team." *Bee* (May 25, 1890): "The City Steams and Lincoln Giants play at the ball park this afternoon at 3:30 pm. The Lincoln Giants are a colored team, and the strongest professional team outside of Omaha in the state. A good game is assured, as the City Steams have out their strongest players, and are going to redeem themselves for their defeats in Lincoln." *Bee* (June 14, 1890): "The Lincoln Giants shut out the home team [Ulysses] in a great game of ball today, the former getting seven runs. [Jack] Reeves struck out eleven men…" *Bee* (June 19, 1890): "The Lincoln Giants today won their second game from Ulysses by a score of 4 to 3, fourteen innings. The feature of the game was the battery work of Castone and Maupin and the hitting of Carr, Taylor and Lewis." The aggregation reorganized in 1891. *Omaha World Herald* (July 25, 1891): "One of the largest crowds ever assembled on the Beatrice ball grounds was gathered there this afternoon to witness the second game between the Lincoln Giants and the Beatrice Club. The game throughout was noticeably free from the wran-

gling which distinguished yesterday's game. Each club was on its metal and played ball the best they knew how. The result was a splendid. Fairly won game by the home team from the strongest amateur team in the state."

SOURCES: "Additional Sporting News," *Omaha (NE) Bee*, Mar 30, 1890; *Omaha Bee*, May 24, 1890; *Lincoln (NE) Capital City Courier*, May 24, 1890; "The Game Today," *Omaha Bee*, May 25, 1890; "Gossip of the Game," *Omaha Bee*, Jun 7, 1890; "Shut Them Out," *Omaha Bee*, Jun 14, 1890; "Fourteen Inning Game," *Omaha Bee*, Jun 19, 1890; "A Game Sunday," *Omaha Bee*, Jun 18, 1890; "Lincoln vs. Genoa," *Omaha Bee*, Jun 22, 1890; "Amateur Game," *Omaha Bee*, Jul 23, 1890; "Gossip Among the Amateurs," *Omaha Bee*, Sep 1, 1890; "Here's a Chance," *Philadelphia (PA) Sporting Life*, Jan 30, 1891; "Gossip Among the Amateurs," *Omaha Bee*, Jan 11, 1891; "Base Ball Notes," *Lincoln (NE) News*, Jul 13, 1891; "Among the Amateurs," *Lincoln News*, Jul 17, 1891; "Ohiowa vs. Lincoln," *Omaha (NE) World Herald*, Jul 25, 1891; "Base Ball Notes," *Lincoln News*, Aug 12, 1891; "Base Ball Notes," *Lincoln News*, Aug 13, 1891; "The Band Played Ann Laurie," *Lincoln News*, Aug 14, 1891.

Cuban Giants Base Ball Club (Lincoln, NE; 1890s)

The Cuban Giants B.B.C. organized in the 1890s, played black and white teams. *Omaha World Herald* (May 14, 1899): "The Cuban Giants, a colored baseball aggregation from Lincoln, defeated the home team today by a score of 14 to 8." *Lincoln Nebraska State Journal* (June 27, 1899): "The Cuban Giants, a colored baseball aggregation from Lincoln and other places, met their Waterloo here today, being badly beaten by Crete by a score of 27 to 3. Two dusky pitchers were knocked out of the box and the home team was almost run to death."

SOURCES: "Cuban Giants Win," *Omaha (NE) World Herald*, May 14, 1899; "Cuban Giants Defeated," *Omaha (NE) Daily Bee*, May 16, 1899; "Two Games at Tecumseh," *Omaha Daily Bee*, May 19, 1899; "Cuban Giants Win and Lose," *Lincoln (NE) Nebraska State Journal*, Jun 25, 1899; "Giants Defeat Tecumseh," *Omaha Daily Bee*, June 25, 1899; "Giants Met Their Waterloo," *Lincoln (NE) State Journal*, Jun 27, 1899; "Sterling Defeats Cuban Giants," *Lincoln Nebraska State Journal*, Jul 5, 1899.

Kroner Silver Grays Base Ball Club (Lincoln, NE; 1890s). Organizer(s): Walter Alexander Plummer.

The Kroner Silver Grays B.B.C. organized in the 1890s, played black and white aggregations. *Omaha Daily Bee* (May 8, 1895): "Ten interesting innings of base-ball was played on the home grounds today between the Kroner Grays of Lincoln and the O. G. Blues of Blue Hill, resulting in a victory for the home team. The Kroner Grays are colored."

SOURCES: "Back From Kaw," *Lincoln (NE) Daily News*, Apr 15, 1895; "Blue Hall Wins Again," *Omaha (NE) Daily Bee*, May 9, 1895; "Grays Defeated at Wahoo," *Omaha Daily Bee*, May 10, 1895 "A Warm Game," *Lincoln Daily News*, May 22, 1895; "Wants to Get In," *Lincoln Daily News*, Jun 1, 1895; "Took in the Silver Grays," *Omaha Daily Bee*, Jun 22, 1895.

Beacon Hotel Base Ball Club (Omaha, NE; 1880s). Owner(s): Walter Alexander Plummer.

The Beacon Hotel B.B.C. organized in the 1880s. The team's chief organizer, Walter Alexander Plummer, had played baseball in New England, the East and Midwest. Plummer, once connected to the Cuban Giants, was well-respected as a talent scout by the sporting fraternity. The Beacons, composed of waiters, played black and white teams. *Omaha Bee* (April15, 1889): "The Omahas and the Beacons, the colored team, went out to the park yesterday to have a little fun with each other. They had it, and a crowd probably of one thousand people looked on with feelings of joy, regret, and remorse confusedly mingled. All three of the Omahas pitchers took a hand in the game, but Willis made the best showing of all, striking out no less than six, and not allowing Plummer's pounders a single hit. It should be explained that the colored team only embraced four of the Beacons' regular men."

SOURCES: "Plummer's Pounders," *Omaha (NE) Bee*, Mar 31, 1889; "Healthful Recreation," *Omaha Bee*, Apr 15, 1889; "Today's Ball Game," *Omaha (NE) Herald*, Apr 14, 1889; "They Are All Ball Players," *Omaha Herald*, Apr 15, 1889; "Crane Bros. 14, Beacons 6," *Omaha Bee*, May 6, 1889; "Local Nines Play Ball," *Omaha (NE) World-Herald*, Jun 2, 1889.

Evans Laundry Base Ball Club (Omaha, NE; 1890s). Owner(s): Richard Adams.

The Evans Laundry B.B.C. organized in the 1890s, played against white and black teams. *Omaha World Herald* (May 7, 1899): "A colored base-ball team has been organized here, with myself as manager, which I think will cut quite a swath on the western diamond this season. I have an aggregation of snappy players. My team will be known as the Evans Laundrys, and we will appreciate any mention you make of us in the best sporting paper in the country."

SOURCES: "Questions and Answers," *Omaha (NE) World Herald*, May 7, 1899.

Lafayette Hotel Base Ball Club (Omaha, NE; 1880s). Owner(s): Walter Alexander Plummer.

The Lafayette Hotel B.B.C. organized in the 1880s. The team's chief organizer, Walter Alexander Plummer, had played baseball in New England, the East and Midwest. Plummer, once connected to the Cuban Giants, was well-respected as a talent scout by the sporting fraternity. The Lafayettes, composed of waiters, played black and white teams. *Omaha Bee* (August 19, 1888): "The Lafayettes of Omaha played the North Bend Club on the home grounds today. The game was hotly-contested on both sides, resulting in a score of 7 to 4 in favor of the Lafayettes. Over 1200 people were present to witness the contest." *Council Bluffs Nonpariel* (July 20, 1888): "The ball game at Athletic Park yesterday afternoon between the Lafayettes of Omaha and the Council Bluffs, resulted in a victory for the former by a score of 6 to 5, the victors playing but eight innings and the home team nine." The aggregation reorganized in 1889. *Council Bluffs Nonpariel* (June 27, 1889): "The colored base-ball tournament opens on the 3rd and concludes on the 4th of July, under the auspices of the Boston Store nine of this city, and the Western Stars, of Omaha. Among the clubs expected to be present are the Kansas City Maroons, Leavenworth Leapers, All Stars of Lincoln, Black Stockings of St. Joe, Unknowns of Des Moines, Sioux City Sluggers, Brown Stockings of Atchison, Lafayettes of Omaha, and Eiseman's Pets of Council Bluffs."

SOURCES: "The Lafayettes," *Omaha (NE) Bee*, May 19, 1888; "Diamond Flashes," *Omaha Bee*, May 30, 1888; "Flashes From the Diamond," *Omaha Bee*, Jun 24, 1888; *Council Bluffs (IA) Nonpariel*, Jul 20, 1888; "Hardins vs. Lafayettes," *Omaha Bee*, Aug 19, 1888; "Lafayette 7, North Bend 4," *Omaha Bee*, Aug 23, 1888; "Hardins vs. Lafayettes," *Omaha Bee*, Aug 23, 1888; "Sporting Gossip," *Omaha Bee*, Jun 3, 1889; *Council Bluffs Nonpariel*, Jun 27, 1889; "Amateur Games," *Omaha Bee*, Jul 11, 1889; "The Lafayettes Beaten," *Lincoln (NE) Nebraska State Journal*, Jul 28, 1889; "Base Ball," *Lincoln Nebraska State Journal*, Jul 29, 1889; *Columbus (NE) Journal*, Jul 31, 1889; "Humphrey," *Columbus Journal*, Aug 7, 1889.

Pickwick Base Ball Club (Omaha, NE; 1880s)

The Pickwick B.B.C. organized in 1887, played black and white

nines. *Omaha Bee* (May 16, 1887): "The game was between the Lucas club, composed white players, and the Pickwicks, exclusively, colored. The colored troops fought nobly, but the machinations of the white forces, who had a superior knowledge of the new rules of the game, outdone them. The score was 20 to 15. The Pickwicks are regularly organized and have very presentable suits." *Bee* (August 5, 1887): "A large number of colored residents of this city went to Council Bluffs yesterday morning to celebrate Emancipation Day. There was speaking by several prominent persons, and a game of base-ball between the Pickwick Base Ball Club of this city, and the Manhattans [black] of Council Bluffs."

SOURCES: "Another Ball Game," *Omaha (NE) Bee*, May 16, 1887; "Sunday Sports," *Omaha Bee*, May 23, 1887; "A City Base Ball League," *Omaha Bee*, May 27, 1887; "Emancipation Day," *Omaha Bee*, Aug 5, 1887; "A Challenge to the Maynes," *Omaha Bee*, Aug 28, 1887.

Western Star Base Ball Club (Omaha, NE; 1880s)

The Western Star B.B.C. organized in the 1880s, played black and white nines. *Omaha Bee* (June 28, 1889): "The Boston Store nine [black] went to Waterloo, Nebraska, yesterday and defeated the Western Stars of Omaha, 9 to 0. They also defeated the Beacons of Omaha, 7 to 5." *Council Bluffs Nonpariel* (June 27, 1889): "The colored baseball tournament opens on the 3rd and concludes on the 4th of July, under the auspices of the Boston Store nine of this city, and the Western Stars, of Omaha. Among the clubs expected to be present are the Kansas City Maroons, Leavenworth Leapers, All Stars of Lincoln, Black Stockings of St. Joe, Unknowns of Des Moines, Sioux City Sluggers, Brown Stockings of Atchison, Lafayettes of Omaha, and Eiseman's Pets of Council Bluffs."

SOURCES: "Minor Mention," *Omaha (NE) Bee*, Jun 28, 1889; *Council Bluffs Nonpariel*, Jun 27, 1889 *Council Bluffs (IA) Nonpariel*, Jun 27, 1889.

Wilcox and Draper Base Ball Club (Omaha, NE; 1890s). Owner(s): Solly Barker.

The Wilcox and Draper B.B.C. organized in the 1890s. The Wilcox and Draper nine played black and white teams. *Omaha Bee* (July 1, 1895): "The Wilcox and Draper Shoe House Team won easily from the Omaha Business College Sunday. The college boys were unable to connect with Mr. Banks' curves, while Mr. Ryberg was dead easy for the colored giants. Solly has made a great find in Banks and Johnson of St. Joseph."

SOURCES: "Breezy Gusts from the Ball Field," *Omaha (NE) Daily Bee*, Apr 7, 1895; *Omaha Daily Bee*, Apr 17, 1895; "Wilcox & Draper Team Beaten by a Close Score at Dunlap," *Omaha Daily Bee*, May 26, 1895; "W. & D. Team Slaughtered," *Omaha Daily Bee*, Jun 2, 1895; "The Wilcox and Drapers Today," *Omaha Daily Bee*, Jun 30, 1895; "Games of the Lively Amateurs," *Omaha Daily Bee*, Jul 15, 1895; "Games of the Lively Amateurs," *Omaha Daily Bee*, Jul 21, 1895; "Chat with the Ball Cranks," *Omaha Daily Bee*, Aug 18, 1895.

New Jersey

Eclipse Base Ball Club (Atlantic City, NJ; 1880s–1890s)

The Eclipse B.B.C. organized in the 1880s. The Eclipse played white and black nines. *Washington Bee* (June 16, 1888): "The Eclipse Base Ball Club (colored) defeated the Neptune Club (white), by a score of 3 to 1. The Eclipse now holds the championship of Atlantic City. It was a hard fight and much interest was manifested by all present. There great features of the game were the pitching of Simkins and the catching of Mellix." *Philadelphia Inquirer* (June 29, 1895): "The Atlantic City Club badly defeated the colored Eclipse Club this afternoon. The game was called by mutual consent and the end of the sixth inning." *Norfolk Virginian* (August 29, 1895): "The Atlantic City team, colored, will meet the Red Stockings, of Norfolk, in a game today, the 29th, at League Park, Norfolk, at 4 o'clock p.m."

SOURCES: "Atlantic City, New Jersey Notes," *Washington (DC) Bee*, Jun 9, 1888; "Atlantic City, New Jersey Notes," *Washington Bee*, Jun 16, 1888; "Atlantic City, New Jersey Notes," *Washington Bee*, Jun 30, 1888; "Ten Innings at Atlantic City," *Philadelphia (PA) Inquirer*, Aug 29, 1890; "The Amateur Games," *Philadelphia Inquirer*, Aug 30, 1890; "Atlantic City's Big Score," *Philadelphia Inquirer*, Jun 29, 1895; "Atlantic City," *Norfolk (VA) Virginian*, Aug 29, 1895; "May's Landing Wins Two Games," *Philadelphia Inquirer*, May 31, 1899; "Pleasantville and Eclipse," *Philadelphia Inquirer*, Jun 25, 1899.

Mutual Base Ball Club (Atlantic City, NJ; 1880s)

The Mutual B.B.C. organized in the 1880s. The "Mutuals" played white and black nines. *Philadelphia Times* (September 20, 1882): "The Orions sustained their first defeat at the hands of a colored club Sept. 19 at Recreation Park, Philadelphia, PA, being then beaten by the Mutuals of Atlantic City, NJ, by a score of 10 to. 9." *Philadelphia Times* (September 20, 1882): "The Orions sustained their first defeat at the hands of a colored club Sept. 19 at Recreation Park, Philadelphia, PA, being then beaten by the Mutuals of Atlantic City, NJ, by a score of 10 to. 9." *Reading Times* (September 22, 1882): "This afternoon at 3 o'clock the Mutuals, of Atlantic City, N. J., known as the champion colored club of America, will play the Active [white] on the Active Grounds on Tuesday the Mutuals defeated the Orion (colored) club at Recreation Park by a score of 10 to 8." The team's core group later formed Princeton, NJ's Alpha club. A few of the players, the Simpson boys in particular, played for the Trenton Cuban Giants.

SOURCES: "Base Ball Notes," *Philadelphia (PA) Times*, Sep 20, 1882; *Reading (PA) Times*, Sep 22, 1882; *New York (NY) Clipper*, Sep 30, 1882; "New Jersey Notes," *New York (NY) Globe*, Jun 23, 1883; *New York Clipper*, Mar 29, 1884; "Down By The Seaside," *Harrisburg (PA) Journal*, Aug 2, 1884.

Shelburne Hotel Base Ball Club (Atlantic City, NJ; 1880s–1900s)

The Shelburne Hotel B.B.C. organized in the 1880s, if not earlier. The team, composed of waiters of Shelburne Hotel, played black and white teams. *Washington Bee* (May 19, 1888): "The Philadelphia Sunday Mercury has received a silver cup to be competed for by the Shelburne and Denales, which are the leading clubs in this city. Fine games will be played. They will be conducted respectively by Captain J. C. Miller of the Shelburnes and J. D. Southerwick of the Denales." *Washington Bee* (June 30, 1888): "The Shelburne Base Ball Club was defeated by the Eclipse Club, Monday last, for a bat and ball, by a score of 9 to 0." In the late 1890s, the Shelburnes belonged to the Hotel Base Ball League which included Shelburne, Isleworth, Traymore, Luray and Haddon Hall. They also played against other colored and white clubs not in their circuit. *Philadelphia Inquirer* (June 22, 1900): "Manager Meeteer arranged a game with the Shelburnes, colored champions, of this city. The home team found them an easy mark and played all around them to the tune of 18 to 1. The colored team used up three pitchers, but all were found easy."

SOURCES: "Atlantic City," *Washington (DC) Bee*, May 19, 1888; "Atlantic City," *Washington Bee*, Jun 9, 1888; "Atlantic City," *Washington Bee*, Jun 30, 1888; "Atlantic City Winds Handily," *Philadelphia (PA) Inquirer*, Jun 22, 1900; "Shelburne Babies Down Athletics," *Philadelphia Inquirer*, Jun 18, 1901; "A Popular Headwaiter," *Washington (DC) Colored American*, Jun 22, 1901.

Oriental Base Ball Club (Bergen, NJ; 1860s–1880s)

The Oriental B.B.C. organized in 1868, played black teams. *Jersey City Journal* (July 10, 1868): "A scrub game was yesterday afternoon played on the ground at the head of Pavenia Avenue between Oneida (colored) Club and of this city and the Orientals of Bergen. It is hard for us to tell which one won, as no score was kept. The superior batting of P. P. Lewis, and good fielding of Ben Cisco (both of the Oneidas) were the features of the game. Ball games were a feature of Emancipation Day celebrations, and the Orientals and Oneidas crossed bats. *Journal* (August 21, 1868): "The boys were on the Bergen field playing base-ball; the match being between the Oneidas of Jersey City and the Orientals of Bergen. We have never seen finer playing than that by the Orientals who decidedly distanced their opponents." The Keystones played against NY's Amicable club. *New York World* (September 30, 1871): "Though Mr. Green, their pitcher, created considerable amusement by his antics and quaint remarks, there was an amount of shrewdness and good generalship under his vein of comicality which stood his club in good stead. He did the largest portion of fielding himself, and he was supported behind the bat in a highly competent manner by Garrison. Walker, the second baseman of the Keystones, handled the ball, too." They reorganized in the 1880s, playing Brooklyn's Alpines. *Journal* (October 1, 1884): "No more interesting or exciting game than that of Monday has been played at the Rink during the season. The contestants were the two crack colored clubs, the Orientals of this city and Alpine of New York. The players were active, enthusiastic and excitable, and yells of admiration for some good playing, or denunciation for some one's failure, were blended with shouts of encouragement to runners all through the game. Somersaults, and hats thrown in the air, shouts and hand-shaking, characterized the conclusion of the game."

SOURCES: "Base Ball," *Jersey City (NJ) Journal*, Jul 9, 1868; "City Notes," *Jersey City Journal*, Jul 9, 1870; "Base Ball," *Jersey City Journal*, Jul 10, 1868; "Emancipation Anniversary," *Jersey City Journal*, Aug 21, 1868; "Base Ball," *Jersey City Journal*, Jul 19, 1870; "Base Ball," *Jersey City Journal*, Sep 21, 1870; "Base Ball," *Jersey City Journal*, Mar 20, 1871; "A Black Ball Game," *New York (NY) World*, Sep 30, 1871; "Base Ball," *Jersey City Journal*, Oct 2, 1871; "City Notes," *Jersey City Journal*, Apr 16, 1873; "Base Ball," *Jersey City Journal*, Jun 27, 1884; "Base Ball," *Jersey City Journal*, Jul 3, 1884; "Base Ball," *Jersey City Journal*, Aug 22, 1884; "Base Ball," *Jersey City Journal*, Oct 1, 1884; "Base Ball," *Jersey City Journal*, Oct 11, 1884.

Oneida Base Ball Club (Bergen, NJ; 1860s–1870s)

The Oneida B.B.C., of Jersey City, NJ, organized in the 1860s, played black nines. *Jersey City Journal* (July 10, 1868): "A scrub game was yesterday afternoon played on the ground at the head of Pavenia Avenue between Oneida (colored) Club and of this city and the Orientals of Bergen. It is hard for us to tell which one won, as no score was kept. The superior batting of P. P. Lewis, and good fielding of Ben Cisco (both of the Oneidas) were the features of the game." Ball games were a feature of Emancipation Day celebrations. *Journal* (August 21, 1868): "The boys were on the Bergen field playing base-ball; the match being between the Oneidas of Jersey City and the Orientals of Bergen. We have never seen finer playing than that by the Orientals who decidedly distanced their opponents." Ball games were a feature of Emancipation Day celebrations, and the Orientals and Oneidas crossed bats. *Journal* (May 2, 1876): "Yesterday afternoon, a game of base-ball was played at Claremont, between the Oneida and Quickstep Social Club. The game was very interesting and the playing on both sides was very fine, both parties being colored youths. The score was Oneidas, 55; Quicksteps, 26."

SOURCES: "City Notes," *Jersey City (NJ) Journal*, Dec 13, 1867;

"City Notes," *Jersey City Journal*, Dec 20, 1867; "City Notes," *Jersey City Journal*, Dec 20, 1867; "Base Ball," *Jersey City Journal*, Jun 6, 1868; "Base Ball," *Jersey City Journal*, Jul 10, 1868; "From Second Precinct," *Jersey City Journal*, Sep 19, 1870; "Base Ball," *Jersey City Journal*, May 2, 1876.

Black Stars Base Ball Club (Bloomfield, NJ; 1890s)

The Black Star B.B.C. organized in the 1890s. *New York Sun* (August 9, 1894): "A colored baseball team has been organized in Bloomfield, New Jersey, under the name of Black Stars. The team will play their first game on Saturday with the Black Diamonds, of Orange, New Jersey."

SOURCES: "Baseball Notes," *New York (NY) Sun*, Aug 9, 1894.

Ironside Base Ball Club (Bordentown, NJ; 1890s)

The Ironside B.B.C. organized in the 1890s, played black and white nines. *Trenton State Gazette* (March 22, 1898): "The following are the ball players at the Colored Industrial School at Ironsides: Whittow, Williams, Spriggs, C. Spriggs, Kersham, Morgan, Young, Taylor, Anderson." James M. Gregory taught at Bordentown, NJ's Colored Industrial School at Ironsides; here, the baseballist, who had managed Washington, DC's Howard University B.B.C., managed the Ironsides B.B.C.

SOURCES: "Bordentown Notes," *Trenton (NJ) State Gazette*, Mar 22, 1898.

Athletic Base Ball Club (Bridgeton, NJ; 1890s). Organizer(s): Ed Woodruff.

The Athletic B.B.C. organized in the 1890s. The "Athletics" played black and white teams. *Bridgeton Evening News* (August 22, 1894): "Captain Wells' Athletics, of this city, ran up against the colored Solar Tips, of Salem, at Tumbling Dam Park yesterday afternoon and went under by a score of 19 to 14, notwithstanding that the Athletics may eight runs in the second inning."

SOURCES: "Athletic Base Ball Nine," *Bridgeton (NJ) Evening News*, Mar 12, 1894; "Ball Game This Afternoon," *Bridgeton Evening News*, Mar 17, 1894; "Base Ball," *Bridgeton Evening News*, Mar 19, 1894; "Base Ball," *Bridgeton Evening News*, May 4, 1894; "Base Ball Pick-Ups," *Bridgeton Evening News*, Aug 17, 1894; "Base Ball," *Bridgeton Evening News*, Aug 22, 1894.

Colored Giants Base Ball Club (Bridgeton, NJ; 1890s). Organizer(s): P. Winder.

The Colored Giants B.B.C. organized in the 1890s, played black and white teams, the latter including the Bridgeton Reserve team. *Bridgeton Evening News* (July 16, 1897): The game between the Bridgeton Reserves and Colored Giants, which was to have been played at the park on Wednesday, had been postponed for a later date, and manager P. Winder, of the colored lads, will get a stronger club for that day. At the time for the game on Wednesday the rain and hail came down and it was a sight to see the people who were in attendance rush for the box office under the grandstand to keep from getting wet. After the rain was over and the sun came out the two clubs played a five-inning game in which the Reserves won by a score of 18 to 4."

SOURCES: "Bridgeton Reserves at the Park," *Bridgeton (NJ) Evening News*, Jul 13, 1897; "Reserves and Giants," *Bridgeton Evening News*, Jul 16, 1897; "Cake Walk Tonight," *Bridgeton Evening News*, Aug 5, 1897; "Greenwich Wins Both," *Bridgeton Evening News*, August 24, 1897.

Cumberland Hotel Base Ball Club (Bridgeton, NJ; 1880s–1890s). Organizer(s): Ed Woodruff.

The Cumberland Hotel B.B.C. organized in the 1880s, played black and white teams. *Bridgeton Evening News* (June 27, 1887): "At the

Fair Grounds last Saturday the game of base-ball between the Ferracute [white] and Cumberland teams made plenty of fun for the spectators. Some very fine plays were made on both sides, noticeable were Bonds and Hetzell's (both left field men) catching. Woodruff, catcher for the Cumberlands, having no mask on, caught a bad foul tip right in the face, making his nose bleed profusely and causing his cheek to swell out nearly twice its usual size. He is a plucky fellow, however, and went on catching after little delay." *Evening News* (July 6, 1894): "The Cumberland base-ball nine of this city, composed of colored players, went to Woodbury on the Fourth and defeated the colored nine of that city by a score of 14 to 9. The Cumberlands put up a good game and hit the ball hard."

SOURCES: "Home Notes," *Bridgeton (NJ) Evening News*, Aug 3, 1886; "News Notes," *Bridgeton Evening News*, May 26, 1887; "News Notes," *Bridgeton Evening News*, Jun 4, 1887; "The Dudes Succumb," *Bridgeton Evening News*, Jun 10, 1887; "The Colored Teams," *Bridgeton Evening News*, Jun 20, 1887; "Ferracutes Victorious," *Bridgeton Evening News*, Jun 27, 1887; "The Cumberlands Win," *Bridgeton Evening News*, Jun 8, 1894; "The Cumberlands Won," *Bridgeton Evening News*, Jul 6, 1894.

Fearless Base Ball Club (Bridgeton, NJ; 1890s). Organizer(s): Andrew K. Wells.

The Fearless B.B.C. organized in the 1890s, played black and white nines. *Bridgeton Evening News* (July 15, 1891): "New suits are being procured for the Fearless Base Ball Club, colored, of this city. Andrew K. Wells is the manager of the club and he is ready to hear from any good amateur nine." The first season was successful; by August, the organization had won fifteen games.

SOURCES: "Base Ball," *Bridgeton (NJ) Evening News*, Jul 16, 1891; *Bridgeton Evening News*, Aug 17, 1891; *Bridgeton Evening News*, Aug 15, 1891; "Base Ball," *Bridgeton Evening News*, Aug 17, 1891; *Bridgeton Evening News*, Jul 19, 1892.

Independent Base Ball Club (Bridgeton, NJ; 1890s)

The Independent B.B.C. organized in the 1890s, played black and white nines. *Bridgeton Evening News* (August 24, 1893): "The Independent Club will go to Salem next Saturday to play the colored nine of that place. Gross and Gould will do the battery work for the Independent."

SOURCES: "Too Short for a Head" *Bridgeton (NJ) Evening News*, Jul 28, 1893; "Will Play Salem," *Bridgeton Evening News*, Aug 24, 1893; "Base Ball," *Bridgeton Evening News*, Sep 25, 1893.

Pioneer Base Ball Club (Bridgeton, NJ; 1890s–1900s). Organizer(s): Andrew K. Wells.

The Pioneer B.B.C. organized in the 1890s, played black and white nines. *Bridgeton Evening News* (August 19, 1895): "An interesting game was played at Tumbling Dam Park Saturday afternoon between the Salem colored club and the colored Pioneer nine. Williams was not well and being a little unsteady he was hit pretty hard and had poor support in the field. The Pioneer were also a little weak in their batting." *Evening News* (April 27, 1896): "A game of base-ball was played on Saturday afternoon at the Slash grounds between the Pioneer Club (colored) and the Woolen Mill nine. It was their first game of the season and although the colored lads went on the field without any practice they easily proved themselves superior to their opponents, whom they defeated by a score of 16 to 8. Manager Wesley says that with a little practice he will have a winning team and stand ready to meet all comers. He would like to arrange a game for next Saturday with a good club."

SOURCES: "Will Play Their First Game," *Bridgeton (NJ) Evening News*, Jul 19, 1895; "Woolen Mill Beats the Colored Nine," *Bridgeton*

Evening News, Jul 23, 1895; "The Pioneer Won," *Bridgeton Evening News,* Jul 29, 1895; "Solar Tips, 12; Pioneer, 7," *Bridgeton Evening News,* Aug 19, 1895; "Base Ball Notes," *Philadelphia (PA) Times,* Aug 25, 1895; "Colored Players Won Easily," *Bridgeton Evening News,* Apr 27, 1896; "Victory for Ferracute," *Bridgeton Evening News,* May 12, 1896; "Will Play Ball," *Bridgeton Evening News,* May 15, 1896; *Bridgeton Evening News,* Aug 17, 1896; "Ariels Down Bridgeton's Colored Team," *Bridgeton Evening News,* Jul 5, 1900.

Cuban Giants Base Ball Club (Bridgewater, NJ; 1890s). Organizer(s): George Peterson.

The Cuban Giants B.B.C. organized in the 1890s, played white teams. *Bridgewater Courier-News* (May 24, 1894): "The Orientals of the East End will play the Cuban Giants on the Berkman Street grounds Saturday afternoon. The captain of the former is P. Melvin and of the latter, Lou Peterson." *Bridgewater Courier-News* (April 16, 1895): "The first game of ball for the season between the Orientals and Cuban Giants was played yesterday afternoon on the grounds at North Avenue and Richmond Street. The former won by the score of 27 to 13."

SOURCES: "By the Way," *Bridgewater (NJ) Courier-News,* May 24, 1894; "By the Way," *Bridgewater Courier-News,* Jul 2, 1894; "The Orientals Won the First Game," *Bridgewater Courier-News,* Apr 16, 1895; "The Centrals Win Again," *Bridgewater Courier-News,* Jun 17, 1895.

Fear Not Base Ball Club (Bridgewater, NJ; 1890s). Organizer(s): Benjamin Perkins and George Peterson.

The Fear Not B.B.C. organized in the 1890s, played black and white teams. *Bridgewater Courier-News* (May 18, 1896): "The recently organized colored base-ball team in the Fourth Ward, known as the Fear Nots, are open for engagements with any club, from the New York Giants down to the Piscataway Hustlers. The team is managed by Benjamin Perkins and George Peterson will do the twirling act, besides acting in the capacity of captain." *Courier-News* (June 18, 1896): "The West Ends and Fear Nots will play ball Saturday afternoon on LeGrande Avenue grounds."

SOURCES: "Notes from the Black Diamond," *Bridgewater (NJ) Courier-News,* May 18, 1896; "Here and There," *Bridgewater Courier-News,* Jun 18, 1896.

Gorham Base Ball Club (Bridgewater, NJ; 1890s). Organizer(s): George Peterson.

The Gorham B.B.C. organized in the 1890s, played white teams. *Bridgewater Courier-News* (July 13, 1893): "The Arlingtons played the Gorhams this morning and were defeated by a score of 22 to 11 in a very poorly played game. The Arlingtons had mostly substitute players. The Gorhams hit the ball very hard as the big score will tell." *Courier-News* (May 28, 1894): "The game of ball Saturday afternoon between the Gorhams and the Orientals resulted in a victory for the former with a score of 11 to 10. The Gorhams feel much elated over three successive victories and want to meet any of their size." *Courier-News* (August 21, 1896): "A game of ball was played on the Y.M.C.A. grounds yesterday afternoon, between the Gorhams and the famous Cranford crack ball team resulting in a victory for the Gorhams by a score of 13 to 10. The Cranfords put up a good game, but were not equal to their opponents."

SOURCES: "Pertinent Paragraphs," *Bridgewater (NJ) Courier-News,* May 27, 1892; "Base Ball Notes," *Bridgewater Courier-News,* Aug 20, 1892; "Another Decoration Day Ball Game," *Bridgewater Courier-News,* May 23, 1893; "Base Ball Chatter," *Bridgewater Courier-News,* Jul 13, 1893; "Pertinent Paragraphs," *Bridgewater Courier-News,* Jun 1, 1893; "Base Ball Notes," *Bridgewater Courier-News,* May 28, 1894; "Dust from the Diamond," *Bridgewater Courier-News,* Aug 21, 1896.

Octoroon Base Ball Club (Bridgewater, NJ; 1890s)

The Octoroon B.B.C. organized in the 1890s, played black and white teams. *Bridgewater Courier-News* (May 31, 1898): "The afternoon game furnished considerable amusement for the large crowd assembled to witness it. The Octoroons, of Orange, a colored team, faced the Crescents. The dusky ball tossers marched upon the diamond with an air of confidence that became as snows of yesteryear. When the smoke cleared away the Crescents had rolled up five runs by good stick work and bad fielding by their opponents, who made ten errors in the first two innings."

SOURCES: "Crescents Take Three Straight," *Bridgewater (NJ) Courier-News,* May 31, 1898.

Colored Base Ball Club (Camden, NJ; 1880s)

The Colored B.B.C. organized in the 1880s, played black teams. *Wilmington Morning News* (April 24, 1889): "This afternoon the Camden (NJ) nine will play the West Ends of this city at the Union Street grounds. Both teams consists of good colored players and a first class game may be expected. The game will be called at 3:30 o'clock and admission is 25 cents." *Morning News* (April 25, 1889): "The Camden, NJ., base-ball team defeated the West Ends of this city yesterday at the Union Street grounds by the following score: Camden, 19; West Ends, 14."

SOURCES: "Notes," *Wilmington (DE) Morning News,* Apr 24, 1889; "Local Base Ball," *Wilmington Morning News,* Apr 25, 1889.

Colored Giants Base Ball Club (Camden, NJ; 1890s)

The Colored Giants B.B.C. organized in the 1890s, played black and white nines. *Philadelphia Inquirer* (May 27, 1894): "The Colored Giants, of Camden, played the Mt. Holly team at this place today. It was a one-sided and uninteresting game, in which the Mt. Holly team came out ahead. The features were the battery work of Taylor and Lucas and the batting of E. Taylor."

SOURCES: "Base Ball Match," *Philadelphia (PA) Inquirer,* May 27, 1894; "T'was Easy for Camden," *Philadelphia Inquirer,* Aug 31, 1894; "Amateur Ball Scores," *Philadelphia Inquirer,* Jun 24, 1894; "Amateur Scores," *Philadelphia Inquirer,* Aug 9, 1894; "Camden Beats the Giants," *Philadelphia Inquirer,* Aug 26, 1894; "Other Games," *Philadelphia Inquirer,* Aug 27, 1894.

DeWitt Base Ball Club (Camden, NJ; 1870s)

The DeWitt B.B.C. organized in 1871, played against black teams. *New York Clipper* (July 8, 1871): "A match game for the championship of colored clubs was played on Wednesday, June 8th, on the Athletic Grounds, Philadelphia, between the Pythians of Philadelphia, and the De Witts, of Camden." *Clipper* (August 22, 1871): "The De Witt (colored), of Camden, NJ, defeated the Stantons, of Philadelphia, on April 10th; Score 51 to 16. They want to play any colored clubs in the country or any amateur or junior club, composed of white men, in the Quaker City."

SOURCES: "Base Ball," *New York (NY) Clipper,* Apr 22, 1871; "Pythian vs. De Witt," *New York Clipper,* Jul 8, 1871; "Base Ball," *New York Clipper,* Aug 22, 1871.

James Deegan Base Ball Club (Camden, NJ; 1880s)

The James Deegan B.B.C. organized in the 1880s, played black teams. *Philadelphia Times* (August 26, 1882): "At last the Orion (colored champions) have won a victory. At Camden yesterday, they beat the Deegan, of Camden, 12 to 10." *Wilmington Republican* (September 19, 1882): "The colored Our Boys of this city were defeated by the Deegan nine, of Camden, New Jersey, by the following score: Deegan, 17; Our Boys, 15."

SOURCES: "Base Ball Notes," *Philadelphia (PA) Times,* Aug 26, 1882; "Notes," *Wilmington (DE) Republican,* Sep 18, 1882; "Notes,"

Wilmington (DE) News Journal, Sep 19, 1882; "Base Ball," *Wilmington Republican*, Sep 19, 1882.

Resolute Base Ball Club (Camden, NJ; 1860s)

The Resolute B.B.C. organized in 1867. On October 10th, the Resolutes played against Philadelphia's Pythians at Camden, NJ, losing to the latter by a score of 50 to 6.

Sources: "Pythian Baseball Club; Scorecards" (Roll No. 8). *American Negro Historical Society Collection: Historical Society Microfilm Edition*.

Brilliant Star Base Ball Club (Elizabeth, NJ; 1870s)

The Brilliant Star B.B.C. organized in the 1870s, played against black nines. *Paterson Guardian* (July 19, 1872): "A match game of base-ball came off on the Broadway grounds between the Brilliant Star B. B. C., of Elizabeth New Jersey, and the Fear Not B. B. C., of this city. The nines of these clubs are composed of colored men, strong and sinewy. Indeed, there are considered the champion colored base-ballists of the State."

Sources: "Base Ball Match Between the Champion Colored Clubs," *Paterson (NJ) Guardian*, Jul 19, 1872.

Belmont Base Ball Club (Jersey City, NJ; 1890s)

The Belmont B.B.C. organized in the 1890s, played black and white teams. *Jersey City Journal* (June 12, 1897): "The Vigilant Field Club yesterday played the Belmonts, a team composed of colored players, whose knowledge of the game is shown by the score. The Vigilants were fortunate in bunching their hits in the opening innings, as it gave them the lead. The Belmonts batted hard in two innings only, the pitching of Meeker being very deceptive."

Sources: "They Are At It Again," *Jersey City (NJ) Journal*, Jun 12, 1897; "Around the Diamond," *Jersey City Journal*, Sep 8, 1897.

Colored Barbers Base Ball Club (Jersey City, NJ; 1880s). Organizer(s): Isaac Walker and Aaron N. Wheeler.

The Colored Barbers B.B.C. organized in the 1880s, if not earlier. They played the black barbers of Newark, NJ. *New York Freeman* (July 16, 1887): "The Jersey City Colored Barbers and invited guests proceeded to Newark on July 4 and played the colored barbers of that city a game of base-ball. At the end of the seventh inning, the score stood 27 to 9, in favor of Jersey City. Isaac Walker was manager and Aaron N. Wheeler captain of the Jersey City team. George Alames is manager and Charles Lewis captain of the Newark Nine."

Sources: "Jersey City Jottings," *New York (NY) Freeman*, Jul 16, 1887.

Hamilton Base Ball Club (Jersey City, NJ; 1890s). Organizer(s): Rufus Peterson.

The Hamilton B.B.C. organized in the 1890s, competed against white and black aggregations. *Jersey City Journal* (May 13, 1898): "The Hamilton Athletic Club of this city (colored) has placed a strong team in the field, and would like to hear from all amateur nines. Address Rufus Peterson, manager, 32 ? Bright Street."

Sources: "Games on the Diamond," *Jersey City (NJ) Journal*, May 13, 1898; "Games on the Diamond," *Jersey City Journal*, May 23, 1898; "Games on the Diamond," *Jersey City Journal*, May 27, 1898; "Games on the Diamond," *Jersey City Journal*, Jun 8, 1898.

Hudson Base Ball Club (Jersey City, NJ; 1880s)

The Hudson B.B.C., of New York, NY, organized in the 1880s. The Hudsons developed a rivalry with Brooklyn's Alpines. *Jersey City Journal* (May 18, 1886): "The newly organized colored base-ball club, the Hudsons, of this city, put on their new uniforms yesterday afternoon, and played their second game at Oakland Park, with their rivals,

the Alpines, of Brooklyn. The event was of great interest to the colored lovers of the game, and at times the excitement ran high among the fifty or more self-constituted umpires, who were deciding certain plays in advance of the real umpire. The home club out-played and out-batted their opponents, whom they beat badly." The Hudsons outplayed NY's Gorhams. *New York Freeman*: "The Hudson Base Ball Club went to Staten Island Tuesday to play the Gorhams. The latter was defeated by a score of 5 to 3." *Jersey City Journal* (May 27, 1886): "The Gorham nine, of New York, and the Hudsons, of this city, both composed of colored men, played a game of base-ball on the Grand Street ground, yesterday afternoon, and the Hudson nine won by a score of 19 to 4."

Sources: "Base Ball," *Jersey City (NJ) Journal*, Apr 30, 1886; "Colored Player at the Bat," *Jersey City Journal*, May 18, 1886; Jersey City Locals," *New York (NY) Freeman*, May 22, 1886; "Sporting Notes," *Jersey City Journal*, May 27, 1886.

Keystone Base Ball Club (Jersey City, NJ; 1870s–1890s). Organizer(s): DuBois Hallack.

The Keystone B.B.C. organized in 1870, played against the junior black clubs of NJ, PA, and NY. *Jersey City Journal* (September 21, 1870): "The Keystone and Oriental Clubs (colored folks) played a game yesterday which was won by the Keystone. Score: Keystone 31; Oriental 29." The following season, the Keystones played in various cities. The team traveled to Williamsburg, PA where they played the Quicksteps. They played against NY's Amicables. *Jersey City Journal* (September 30, 1871): "The Amicable Club of New York and the Keystone Club of New Jersey, both composed of colored citizens, played a game on the Union grounds," yesterday, Williamsburgh, in the presence of a crowd of spectators. The Keystones were evidently the better players. Walker, the second baseman of the Keystones, handled the ball with considerable skill. Of the NY players, Hoffman and Cartwright did good business." The organization also played Troy's Hannibal club.

Sources: "Base Ball," *Jersey City (NJ) Journal*, Sep 21, 1870; "Base Ball," *Jersey City Journal*, Mar 20, 1871; "City Notes," *Jersey City Journal*, Aug 23, 1871; "Base Ball," *Jersey City Journal*, Sep 28, 1871; "Base Ball," *Jersey City Journal*, Sep 30, 1871; "Base Ball," *Jersey City Journal*, Oct 2, 1871; "Keystone vs. Amicable," *New York (NY) Clipper*, Oct 14, 1871; "City Notes," *Jersey City Journal*, Oct 16, 1871; "City Notes," *Jersey City Journal*, Feb 6, 1872; "Entertainments to Come," *Jersey City Journal*, Feb 26, 1872; "Ball of the Keystone Club," *Jersey City Journal*, Feb 27, 1872; "Base Ball," *Jersey City Journal*, Jul 17, 1872; "The Keystone Base Ball Club," *Jersey City Journal*, Nov 27, 1872; "City Notes," *Jersey City Journal*, Apr 16, 1873; "Good Samaritans," *Jersey City Journal*, Jun 26, 1873; "Base Ball," *Jersey City Journal*, Jun 27, 1873; "The Keystone Social Club's Ball," *Jersey City Journal*, Mar 11, 1874; "Jersey City Items," *Freeman* (New York, NY), Dec 4, 1886; "Keystone Social Club," *Jersey City Journal*, Dec 16, 1886; "New Feature in Railroading," *New York (NY) Age*, Jul 12, 1890; "Jersey City Items," *New York Age*, Jan 31, 1891; "Jersey City Items," *New York Age*, Mar 7, 1891.

Liberty Base Ball Club (Jersey City, NJ; 1860s). Organizer(s): George Gale.

The Liberty B.B.C. organized in 1868. The "Liberty Club" was composed of barbers. *Jersey City Journal* (June 11, 1868): "The Liberty Club (colored players) of Jersey City, announce themselves as now open for the season. The following is the list of officers: George Gail, Isaac Walker, and Robert McClain."

Sources: "Base Ball," *Jersey City (NJ) Journal*, Jun 11, 1868.

Howland Hotel Base Ball Club (Long Branch, NJ; 1880s). Organizer(s): Frank P. Thompson and Rufus Peterson.

The Howland Hotel B.B.C. organized in the 1880s. The team, composed of waiters, played black nines. *New York Herald* (September 7, 1883): "The colored waiters, especially those who hail from Washington, have an especially fondness for the national game. Here, again, the two great hotels, at the west end of the beach are rivals. William H. Johnson, a lithe, active young mulatto, bosses the West End team, and Archie Reeves renders the same service for the Howland colored nine. A match game came off the other day between the nines, and $40 in consolidated tips was staked on the result. The West Enders captured the 'boodle' by a score of 5 to 4, and the yells of exultation that went up were so loud, long and continuous that a telephone message came to Howland's from the other end of the beach to know whether anybody was being murdered up there. Paris Archer, who pitched for the West Enders, was in the Cuban Giants, a colored nine who traveled through New England last season with considerable success."

SOURCES: "Base Ball," *New York (NY) Herald*, Sep 7, 1883; "Fishballs and Baseballs," *New York (NY) Herald*, Aug 7, 1887; "A Peacemaker Shot," *New York (NY) Times*, Aug 14, 1889.

Washington Hotel Base Ball Club (Long Branch, NJ; 1880s)

The Washington Hotel B.B.C. organized in the 1880s, played black nines. They often traveled to Pittsburgh. *Pittsburgh Post-Gazette* (June 29, 1882): "The J. A. White Club of the South Side played a game with the Washington colored club, resulting in a victory for the latter by the following score: Washingtons, 39; Whites, 9." *Pittsburgh Post-Gazette* (July 5, 1882): "The Mutual Club (colored), of this city, yesterday afternoon defeated the Washington (colored) Club of Washington, DC, by the following score at Union Park, in the presence of a good crowd of spectators. Mutual, 18; Washingtons, 12." *Pittsburgh Post-Gazette* (July 11, 1882): "The Washington Club defeated the Marker Rush Club by a score of 8 to 7 yesterday on the East Liberty Grounds. Both clubs are colored." They played Philadelphia's Orions for the blackball championship. *New York Herald* (September 13, 1882): "The Orions of Philadelphia and the Washingtons of Long Branch contested for the colored championship yesterday afternoon at the Polo Ground. There were about five hundred spectators present. The game was about equal to the average amateur playing. It was closely contested, however, and resulted in a well-earned victory for the Orions, who took the lead in the first inning and maintained it throughout, with the single exception of the sixth inning when the score was tied."

SOURCES: "Sporting Notes," *Pittsburgh (PA) Commercial Gazette*, Jun 29, 1882; "Sporting Events," *Pittsburgh Commercial Gazette*, Jul 5, 1882; "Cannon Balls," *Pittsburgh Commercial Gazette*, Jul 11, 1882; "Base Ball," *New York (NY) Truth*, Sep 10, 1882; "The Orions Win the Colored Championship," *New York (NY) Herald*, Sep 13, 1882; "Orion vs. Washington," *New York (NY) Clipper*, Sep 16, 1882.

West End Hotel Base Ball Club (Long Branch, NJ; 1870s–1880s). Organizer(s): William T. Green, George A. Smith and Anderson A. Marshall.

The West End B.B.C. composed of hotel waiters, played black and white nines. Some of the West End players were college baseballists. *New York Herald* (September 7, 1883): "The colored waiters, especially those who hail from Washington, have an especially fondness for the national game. Here, again, the two great hotels, at the west end of the beach are rivals. William H. Johnson, a lithe, active young mulatto, bosses the West End team, and Archie Reeves renders the same service for the Howland colored nine. A match game came off the other day between the nines, and $40 in consolidated tips was staked on the result. The west Enders captured the 'boodle' by a score of 5 to 4, and the yells of exultation that went up were so loud, long

and continuous that a telephone message came to Howland's from the other end of the beach to know whether anybody was being murdered up there. Paris Archer, who pitched for the West Enders, was in the Cuban Giants, a colored nine who traveled through New England last season with considerable success."

SOURCES: "Base Ball," *Washington (DC) Evening Star*, Jun 21, 1883; "Saratoga Gossip," *New York (NY) Globe*, Jul 7, 1883; "Base Ball Match," *New York Globe*, Jul 28, 1883; "New Jersey Summer Resorts," *New York Globe*, Aug 18, 1883; "Base Ball," *New York (NY) Herald*, Sep 7, 1883; "Ashbury Park and Ocean Grove," *New York (NY) Freeman*, Sep 8, 1883; "The West Ends Victorious," *New York (NY) Truth*, Sep 8, 1883; "Local Base Ball Matters," *Hartford (CT) Courant*, Sep 13, 1883; "Swinging the Ash," *Hartford Courant*, Sep 15, 1883; "Enough for an Omelet," *Hartford Courant*, Sep 18, 1883; "Fishballs and Baseballs," *New York Herald*, Aug 7, 1887.

Clinton Stars Base Ball Club (Newark, NJ; 1890s). Organizer(s): Joe Smith, E. Meyers and N. Johnson.

The Clinton Stars B.B.C. organized in the 1890s. *Newark Sunday Call* (July 23, 1893): "The Woodlands defeated the Clinton Stars, a crack colored club, of this city by a score of 8 to 6." *Newark Sunday Call* (May 5, 1895): "The Clinton Stars defeated the Mulberry Street Stars, by a score of 24 to 19."

SOURCES: "The Ball Tossers," *Newark (NJ) Sunday Call*, May 1, 1892; "How the Games Goes," *Newark Sunday Call*, Jun 26, 1892; "From Many Diamonds," *Newark Sunday Call*, Jun 18, 1893; "Diamond Dust," *Newark Sunday Call*, Jul 23, 1893; "The Diamond Field," *Newark Sunday Call*, May 5, 1895.

Colored Giants Base Ball Club (Newark, NJ; 1890s). Organizer(s): Benjamin M. Butler and Joseph Laveign.

The Colored Giants B.B.C. organized in the 1890s. *New York Press*: "B. M. Butler, manager of the late Gorhams and cakewalk organizer, has taken charge of Newark's Colored Giants, which are composed of some of the strongest ball tossers from all over the country." They played black and white teams. *Jersey City Journal*: "The prediction made last week in this column that the Colored Giants of Newark would make trouble for the Johnston Field Club in the game yesterday at Marion was verified. It was the second meeting of the series and the result gives no advantage. Johnston won the first game but the colored team had the pleasure of reversing the positions at the close of yesterday's contest. The element of luck that entered the game rested with the Giants. They succeeded in getting hits together and won out with a fast finish, which gave them nine runs in the last three innings."

SOURCES: "Base Ball Match," *Philadelphia (PA) Inquirer*, May 27, 1894; "T'was Easy for Camden," *Philadelphia Inquirer*, Aug 31, 1894; "Amateur Ball Scores," *Philadelphia Inquirer*, Jun 24, 1894; "Amateur Scores," *Philadelphia Inquirer*, Aug 9, 1894; "Camden Beats the Giants," *Philadelphia Inquirer*, Aug 26, 1894; "Other Games," *Philadelphia Inquirer*, Aug 27, 1894; "Notes of the Diamond," *New York (NY) Press*, Jul 29, 1897; "Base Hits," *New York (NY) Sun*, Jul 31, 1898; "Games on the Diamond," *Jersey City (NJ) Journal*, Aug 8, 1898; "Games on the Diamond," *Jersey City Journal*, Aug 22, 1898; "Notes of the Diamond," *New York Press*, Sep 28, 1898.

Cuban Giants Base Ball Club (Newark, NJ; 1890s–1900s)

The Cuban Giants B.B.C. organized in the 1890s. The "Jersey Cubans" played black and white aggregations. *Newark Sunday Call*: "The Newark Cuban Giants defeated the Johnston team of New Jersey last Monday afternoon, 23 to 3." *Jersey City Journal*: "The prediction made last week in this column that the Colored Giants of Newark would make trouble for the Johnston Field Club in the game yesterday at Marion was verified. It was the second meeting of the series and the result gives no advantage. Johnston won the first game but the colored team had the pleasure of reversing the positions at the close of yesterday's contest. The element of luck that entered the game rested with the Giants. They succeeded in getting hits together and won out with a fast finish, which gave them nine runs in the last three innings."

SOURCES: "On Many Diamonds, *Newark (NJ) Sunday Call*. August 8, 1897; "Tireless Ball Tossers, *Newark Sunday Call*. August 29, 1897.

Dusky Boys Base Ball Club (Newark, NJ; 1880s). Organizer(s): Frederick Nichols and David Prime.

The Dusky Boys Base Ball Club organized in the 1880s, played black teams. *New York Herald* (May 30, 1884): "The most amusing baseball match of the season was the contest which took place at the Polo Ground yesterday—between two colored clubs—the Alpines, of Brooklyn, and the Dusky Boys, from Newark, New Jersey. The crowd dubbed the players after some of the leading professionals, and it was great sport for the spectators to coach the colored boys. The Newark club took the lead from the start, as they knew more tricks than the unsophisticated representatives of Crow Hill. The Jersey men had one or two good batters, and the way they kept stuffing them in on their opponents was an outrage on the definition of the word 'cheating,' and would have put the best card stacker in the country to blush."

SOURCES: "Newark Notes," *New York (NY) Globe*, May 24, 1884; "Dusky Base-Ball Tossers," *New York (NY) World*, May 30, 1884; "Base Ball," *New York Herald*, May 30, 1884; "Two Colored Clubs Amuse a Small Crowd," *New York Herald*, May 30, 1884; "Base Ball," *Jersey City (NJ) Journal*, Oct 11, 1884; "An Ethiopian Draw Game," *New York Herald*, Oct 21, 1884; "Brooklyn," *New York Herald*, Oct 22, 1884.

Elwood Base Ball Club (Newark, NJ; 1890s). Organizer(s): Fred Heberle.

The Elwood B.B.C. organized in the 1890s, played white and black teams. *Newark Sunday Call* (July 25, 1897): "The employees of Stucky and Hecks have formed a baseball club, which played an interesting game with the Triton B.B.C. The Stucky and Hecks team is known as the Elwoods. The feature of the game was a double play by M. Meesel and C. Heberle." *Sunday Call* (August 1, 1897): "The Almas will cross bats with the Elwoods (colored champions), at Newark, on the former's grounds, foot of Thomas Street today." *Call* (August 8, 1897): "A nine made up of married men in the employ of Strieby and Heck played the tightest game yesterday with a tie at the wind-up with the Elwoods." *Sunday Call* (August 22, 1897): "The Almas will play the crack Elwoods (colored) on the former's grounds, foot of Thomas Street. As this will be the second game of the series a 'hot time' is expected. Game called at 2:30." *Sunday Call*: "The Almas will play the crack Elwoods (colored) on the former's grounds, foot of Thomas Street. As this will be the second game of the series a 'hot time' is expected. Game called at 2:30. *Sunday Call* (August 29, 1897): "The Almas defeated the Elwoods (colored) team last Sunday afternoon, 14 to 10. The Almas will play the Elwoods again this afternoon on the Almas grounds, foot of Thomas Street."

SOURCES: "On Muddy Diamonds," *Newark (NJ) Sunday Call*, Jul 25, 1897; "The Busy Baseballists," *Newark Sunday Call*, Aug 1, 1897; "On Many Diamonds," *Newark Sunday Call*, Aug 8, 1897; "The Ball Tossers," *Newark Sunday Call*, Aug 22, 1897; "Tireless Ball Players," *Newark Sunday Call*, Aug 29, 1897; "September Baseball," *Newark Sunday Call*, Sep 5, 1897; "Ball Tossers Still At It," *Newark Sunday Call*, Sep 12, 1897.

Hamilton Base Ball Club (Newark, NJ; 1860s)

The Hamilton B.B.C. organized in the 1860s, played black nines. *Newark Advertiser* (September 30, 1862): "Considerable excitement was created among the colored boys of this city yesterday by a baseball match between the Hamilton Club of this city and the Henson Club of Jamaica, Long Island, both composed of the descendants of Ham. The match was played on the grounds on Railroad Avenue, in the presence of a goodly number of the 'gentler sex,' and resulted in a favor of the Hensons." *Advertiser* (October 21, 1865): "An interesting match was played yesterday afternoon on the grounds on the Newark grounds between the Unknown Club of Long Island, and the Hamiltons of this city, both colored. The latter won the game by the score of 4 to 14."

SOURCES: *Newark (NJ) Advertiser*, Sep 30, 1862; "A New Sensation in Base Ball Circles—Sambo as a Ball Player and Dinah as an Emulator," *Brooklyn (NY) Eagle*, Oct 17, 1862; "Base Ball," *Newark Advertiser*, Oct 21, 1865.

Keystone Base Ball Club (Bridgeton, NJ; 1860s)

The Keystone B.B.C., of Newark, NJ, organized in the 1860s, played black nines. *Newark Advertiser* (July 13, 1865): "A match game of base-ball took place at East Newark, between the Monitors of East Newark, and the Keystones of Newark, which resulted in favor of the former, the score being 49 to 16." *Advertiser* (August 16, 1865): "A match game will be played on Friday, in this city, between two colored club—the Keystones, of Newark, and the Independent club, of New Brunswick, on the grounds at the foot of Chestnut street, commencing at half-past one o'clock." *Advertiser* (October 23, 1866): "A match game will be played on Friday, in this city, between two colored clubs, the Keystones of Newark, and the Independent club, of New Brunswick, at the grounds on the foot of Chestnut street, commencing at half-past one o'clock."

SOURCES: "Base Ball," *Newark (NJ) Advertiser*, Jul 8, 1865; "Local Matters," *Newark Advertiser*, Jul 8, 1865; "Local Matters," *Newark Advertiser*, Aug 16, 1865; *Newark Advertiser*, Aug 16, 1865; "Base Ball," *Newark Advertiser*, Oct 23, 1866.

Optimate Giants Base Ball Club (Newark, NJ; 1890s). Organizer(s): R. Oliver.

The Optimate Giants B.B.C. organized in the 1890s, played black and white nines. *Newark Sunday Call* (June 28, 1896): "The Optimate Giants challenge all uniformed clubs. Address R. Oliver, 65 Lincoln Park, Newark, New Jersey." *Sunday Call* (July 19, 1896): "The Little Giants and Optimate Giants, champion colored club of New Jersey, met on the Shooting Park grounds yesterday afternoon. The colored club took the lead in the first inning and held it till the eighth inning, when the Giants took a batting streak and hammered in six runs, making the score 10 to 10. In the last inning with two men out, the Giants scored the winning run."

SOURCES: "With The Ball Tossers," *Newark (NJ) Sunday Call*, Jun 28, 1896; "The Ball Tossers," *Newark Sunday Call*, Jul 19, 1896.

Metropolitans Base Ball Club (Newark, NJ; 1890s)

The Metropolitan B.B.C. organized in the 1890s, played black and white nines. *Newark Sunday Call* (July 11, 1897): "The Hudsons defeated the Metropolitans easily yesterday. In the second inning, Jacobius, who was playing third base for the Metropolitans, batted a ball which struck a spectator on the head. The injured boy was taken to the City Hospital and Jacobius was locked up. The game was resumed with Watson in Jacobius's place. The Mets has little heart for the contest after the accident."

SOURCES: "The Busy Baseballists," *Newark (NJ) Sunday Call*, Apr 1, 1897; "Hot Weather Baseball, *Newark Sunday Call*. July 11, 1897;

"On Many Diamonds, *Newark Sunday Call.* August 8, 1897; "Tireless Ball Tossers, *Newark Sunday Call.* August 29, 1897.

Mohawk Base Ball Club (Newark, NJ; 1890s)

The Mohawk Base Ball Club organized in the 1890s, played black and white teams. *Newark Sunday Call* (August 8, 1897): "The Mohawk Athletic Club defeated the Outer Edge Base Ball Club yesterday after an interesting game. The features were the batting of Henn and Winters of the Mohawks." *Sunday Call* (August 22, 1897): "The Almas and the Mohawks (Colored Giants) will meet on the Almas' grounds, foot of Thomas Street, this afternoon, and a very lively game is anticipated."

SOURCES: "The Busy Baseballists," *Newark (NJ) Sunday Call,* Aug 1, 1897; "On Many Diamonds," *Newark Sunday Call,* Aug 8, 1897; "With the Ball Tossers," *Newark Sunday Call,* Aug 22, 1897.

Cuban Giants Base Ball Club (New Brunswick, NJ; 1890s)

The Cuban Giants B.B.C., of Newark, NJ, organized in the 1890s., played black aggregations. *New Brunswick Times* (July 5, 1892): "The day was delightfully and pleasantly spent, the most marked feature being a game between the Cuban Giants of the Second Ward and the Quicksteps, of the Fifth Ward, in this city, which resulted in a victory for the Giants, by a score of 9 to 6." *Times* (July 7, 1894): "Two colored teams played a great game of base-ball on the lots of Remsen and Lee Avenues on July 4th. The contestants were the Brunswick Giants, of the Second Ward, and the Smuts of the Sixth Ward. The score stood 44 to 14 in favor of the Giants."

SOURCES: "Colored Ball Twirlers," *New Brunswick (NJ) Times, Jul 5, 1892; "Colored People's Day," *New Brunswick Times,* Aug 26, 1892. "Colored People's Day," *New Brunswick Times,* Aug 26, 1892; "Colored Base Ball," *New Brunswick Times,* Jul 7, 1894.

Only Boys Base Ball Club (New Brunswick, NJ; 1870s)

The Only Boys B.B.C. organized in the 1870s, played black nines. *New Brunswick Times* (July 19, 1877): "A match game of base-ball was played yesterday afternoon between the Only Boys, a colored club, and the Mutuals, a white club, both of this city, and resulted in a victory for the Only Boys, the score being nineteen to eleven at the end of the fifth inning. There were some very fine plays. The catching by Lee, the captain of the Only Boys was done in a style not to be sneezed at. The Only Boys are now ready to play any colored club in the State." *Times* (July 20, 1877): "The Only Boys and the Quicksteps (both colored clubs) of this city, crossed bats on the Livingston Avenue Grounds yesterday afternoon, the Only Boys waxing their opponents by a score of 39 to 34. They are now ready to play any colored club in the State."

SOURCES: "Base Ball," *New Brunswick (NJ) Times,* Jun 9, 1877; "The Dark Above the White," *New Brunswick Times,* Jul 19, 1877; "Base Ball," *New Brunswick Times,* Jul 20, 1877.

Quickstep Boys Base Ball Club (New Brunswick, NJ; 1880s)

The Quickstep B.B.C. organized in the 1870s, played black nines. *New Brunswick Times* (August 24, 1885): "A game of base-ball was played Saturday, between the Third Ward Quicksteps and the Young Eagles of the Sixth Ward. Score, 22 to 20, in favor of the Young Eagles." *Times* (September 4, 1888): "The day was delightfully and pleasantly spent, the most marked feature being a game between the Cuban Giants of the Second Ward and the Quicksteps, of the Fifth Ward, in this city, which resulted in a victory for the Giants, by a score of 9 to 6."

SOURCES: "News Notes," *New Brunswick (NJ) Times,* Jul 15, 1881; "Excelsiors vs. Quicksteps," *New Brunswick Times,* Jun 8, 1885; "Quicksteps vs. Eagles," *New Brunswick Times,* Aug 24, 1885; "City

Matters," *New Brunswick Times,* Sep 2, 1887; "City Matters," *New Brunswick Times,* Sep 3, 1887; "City and County News," *New Brunswick (NJ) Home News,* Sep 7, 1887; "Base Ball," *New Brunswick Times, Sep 4, 1888.

Golden Leaf Base Ball Club (Passaic, NJ; 1890s). Organizer(s): John H. Lavington.

The Golden Leaf B.B.C. organized in the 1890s, played black and white teams. *New York Sun* (June 20, 1897): "The Golden Leaf Baseball Club of Passaic, colored, would like to arrange games with uniformed clubs offering a guarantee; Brooklyn Colored Giants preferred. Address John H. Lavington, manager, 257 ? Chestnut Street, Passaic, New Jersey." *Paterson Evening News* (May 24, 1897): "About two hundred persons walked over the Red Hill yesterday and witnessed a fiercely contested game between two colored nines— the Golden Leaf A. C. of Passaic, and the Hackensack River Giants. The Passaic players were accompanied by their manager. The game resulted in a victory for the Golden Leafs by a score of 26 to 13."

SOURCES: "Getting Out of the Past," *Paterson (NJ) Evening News,* May 24, 1897; "Want to Play Games," *New York (NY) Sun,* Jun 20, 1897.

Jersey Cuban Base Ball Club (Passaic, NJ; 1890s–1900s). Organizer(s): H. B. Finch.

The Jersey Cuban B.B.C. organized in the 1890s. The Jersey Cubans, former Cuban Giants players, played black and white teams. *Jersey City Journal* (May 5, 1899): "The game on the Johnston Avenue grounds tomorrow afternoon between the Pacific Athletic Club [white] and the Jersey Cubans should draw the largest attendance of the season to the home of the P. A. C. The Cubans are a credit to the State and will prove the greatest rival of any colored team on the diamond to the Cuban Giants. They play good ball and present all the features that have made the original team so famous on the diamond. The Pacifics will play hard to win."

SOURCES: "Games on the Diamond," *Jersey City (NJ) Journal,* Aug 8, 1898; "Games on the Diamond," *Jersey City Journal,* Aug 15, 1898; "Games on the Diamond," *Jersey City Journal,* Aug 19, 1898; "Games on the Diamond," *Jersey City Journal,* Aug 22, 1898; "Games on the Diamond," *Jersey City Journal,* Sep 1, 1898; "Games on the Diamond," *Jersey City Journal,* Sep 3, 1898; "Games of Baseball," *Jersey City Journal,* May 5, 1899; "Games of Baseball," *Jersey City Journal,* May 8, 1899; "Baysides Defeat Cubans," *Jersey City Journal, Jul 6, 1899; "Amateur Baseball," *Paterson (NJ) Call,* May 12, 1900; "Hollywoods vs. Jersey Cubans," *Yonkers (NY) Statesman,* Jun 15, 1900; "Jersey Cubans Easily Beaten," *Yonkers Statesman,* June 18, 1900; *Port Chester (NY) Journal,* Jun 28, 1900; "Jersey Cubans Dead Easy," *Port Chester Journal,* Jul 5, 1900.

Colored Stars Base Ball Club (Paterson, NJ; 1890s). Organizer(s): James Green and John Mullen.

The Colored Stars B.B.C. organized in the 1890s, played against black and white organizations. *Paterson Evening News* (April 25, 1896): "The Young Colored Stars played the Young Golden Stars a game of baseball yesterday on the Overall grounds and beat them by a score of 21 to 8."

SOURCES: "Baseball," *Paterson (NJ) Call,* Apr 22, 1896; "Base Ball Today," *Paterson (NJ) Evening News,* Apr 23, 1896; "Other Games and Notes," *Paterson Evening News,* Apr 25, 1896; "Base Ball Today," *Paterson Evening News,* Apr 25, 1896.

Cuban Giants Base Ball Club (Paterson, NJ; 1880s–1890s)

The Cuban Giants B.B.C. organized in the 1890s, played black and white nines. *Paterson Evening News* (April 24, 1893): "The Quicksteps defeated the Paterson Cuban Giants, a colored team on Saturday afternoon on the Sandy Hill Grounds by a score of 8 to 7 before a large crowd of spectators." *Paterson Call* (June 18, 1894): "The Lafayette Stars played a game of baseball yesterday with the Paterson Cuban Giants, a local aggregation of colored players, and defeated them by a score of 14 to 5. Battery: Cuban Giants, J. Porter and N. Colman."

Sources: "Notes of Sport," *Paterson (NJ) Evening News*, Apr 24, 1893; "Other Games and Notes," *Paterson (NJ) Call*, Jun 18, 1894.

Fear Not Base Ball Club (Paterson, NJ; 1870s–1880s)

The Fear Not B.B.C. organized in the 1870s, played against black and white nines. *Paterson Guardian* (July 19, 1872): "A match game of base-ball came off on the Broadway grounds between the Brilliant Star B. B. C., of Elizabeth New Jersey, and the Fear Not B. B. C., of this city. The nines of these clubs are composed of colored men, strong and sinewy. Indeed, there are considered the champion colored base-ballists of the State." The Fearnots reorganized in the 1880s. *Guardian* (August 12, 1889): "Six-hundred spectators saw the Fearnots, Paterson's champion colored club, defeated the crack Haymakers on the Fifth Avenue Grounds yesterday afternoon. The game was full of interest from beginning to end…. In the last inning, when the score was 9 to 10 in favor of the Haymakers and the excitement was at a high pitch, the catcher allowed the ball to pass him while there was a runner at third, which tied the score, and as another runner reached third he threw the ball over the baserunner's head, which brought in the winning run, and the colored men left the field victorious. The fielding of both teams was excellent, as was also the work of the colored battery."

Sources: "Base Ball Match Between the Champion Colored Clubs," *Paterson (NJ) Guardian*, Jul 19, 1872; "Pick-Ups on the Ball Field," *Paterson Guardian*, Aug 12, 1889.

Young Rosebuds Base Ball Club (Paterson, NJ; 1880s–1890s)

The Young Rosebuds B.B.C. organized in the 1890s, played black and white aggregations.

Sources: "Base Ball Season Here," *Paterson (NJ) Evening News*, Mar 30, 1897.

Alpha Base Ball Club (Princeton, NJ; 1880s). Organizer(s): William K. Simpson.

The Alpha B.B.C. organized in the 1880s, played black and white teams. *New York Clipper* (March 29, 1884): "The Alpha Club, composed of colored players of Princeton, New Jersey, has recently been organized under the management of William K. Simpson. They will play their opening game April 12 with the Orion of Philadelphia. The pitcher is a pupil of John W. Ward's. Five of the Alpha's were members of the champion colored team of Atlantic City, New Jersey, in 1882. The Alphas would like to hear from all clubs with enclosed grounds."

Sources: "Games of a Colored Ball Nine," *New York (NY) Times*, Mar 27, 1884; "Base Ball," *New York (NY) Clipper*, Mar 29, 1884; "Holyoke Matters," *Springfield (MA) Republican*, Apr 13, 1884; "Base Ball Notes," *Boston (MA) Herald*, Apr 19, 1884; "Hampden County," *Springfield Republican*, April 25, 1884; "Other Games Played," *Boston Herald*, Jun 1, 1884; "Other Games Played," *Boston Herald*, Jun 15, 1884; "Briefly Mentioned," *Boston Herald*, Jun 22, 1884.

Colored Giants Base Ball Club (Princeton, NJ; 1890s–1900s)

The Colored Giants B.B.C. organized in the 1890s, played black and white teams. *Trenton Evening Times* (June 14, 1893): "Tomorrow on the Hill's Grove grounds the Trentons and the Princeton Giants begin a series of five games for $100 and the championship of the county. The Giants played several good games here last season, and as they are said to be stronger than ever they should be able to repeat

the operation." *Jersey City Journal* (May 22, 1900): "The largest crowd of the season at Dewey Park witnessed a rattling game yesterday afternoon between the Johnston Field Club and the Princeton Giants, the colored champions of New Jersey. The Johnstons won, but in order to do so they compelled to play the hardest kind of ball and gained the victory in the final inning during the greatest excitement. Cheering and throwing up of hats marked the hard-earned victory." They played the NY Cuban Giants. *Evening Times* (May 29, 1900): "The Cuban Giants and the Princeton Giants met yesterday afternoon at Association Field to decide the colored baseball championship of the State. The Cubans won by a score of 17 to 11 in a game that was as full of errors as an egg is of meat. The majority of the spectators were colored persons from Princeton, who gave their team all kinds of support."

Sources: "On the Green Diamond," *Trenton (NJ) Evening Times*, Jun 19, 1892; "Won By the C. H. Youngs," *Trenton Evening Times*, Jun 22, 1892; "Sporting News," *Trenton Evening Times*, Jun 14, 1893; "Base Ball Notes," *Trenton Evening Times*, Jun 16, 1893; "The Trenton Club's Movements," *Trenton Evening Times*, Jun 18, 1893; "Princeton Giants Defeated," *Trenton (NJ) True American*, Jun 28, 1893; "Trenton Against Princeton Giants," *Trenton Evening Times*, Jun 19, 1894; "Great Match," *Trenton Evening Times*, Jun 16, 1895; "The Herbert's Day Out," *Trenton Evening Times*, Jun 20, 1897; "The World of Sports," *Journal* (Trenton, NJ), May 22, 1900; "Diamond Dust," *Trenton Evening Times*, May 29, 1900; "Diamond Dust," *Trenton Evening Times*, May 31, 1900; "Barbeque Arrangements Have Been Made," *Trenton Evening Times*, Sep 10, 1900; "Lancaster Again Wins," *Philadelphia (PA) Inquirer*, Apr 26, 1896; "Crowds Prevent Cubans' Shutout," *Philadelphia Inquirer*, Aug 5, 1900.

Crescent Base Ball Club (Princeton, NJ; 1880s)

The Crescent B.B.C. organized in the 1880s, played black teams. *New York Herald* (September 8, 1883): "A game was played at the Polo grounds yesterday, between the West Ends, of Long Branch, and the Crescents, of Princeton, the crack colored clubs of New Jersey. It was rather amusing to see the Crescents go to pieces and pile up the errors while the West Ends were looking after their runs."

Sources: "Base Ball—Colored Championship," *Philadelphia (PA) Times*, Jun 27, 1883; "New Jersey Summer Resorts," *New York (NY) Globe*, Aug 18, 1883; "Base Ball," *New York (NY) Herald*, Sep 7, 1883; "Beaten in Philadelphia," *New York (NY) Times*, Sep 8, 1883; "Base Ball," *New York Herald*, Sep 8, 1883; "The West Ends Victorious," *New York (NY) Truth*, Sep 8, 1883; "Social Gossip," *New York (NY) Freeman*, Sep 15, 1883.

Metropolitan Base Ball Club (Princeton, NJ; 1880s). Organizer(s): Fred Nichols.

The Metropolitan B.B.C. organized in the 1880s, played black teams. *New York Globe* (September 8, 1883): "The Mets played their closing game of the season and defeated their opponents by a score fo 8 to 5. This base-ball club stands today the strongest club of color that we have, and if they hold together, they will surely hurt somebody." They reorganized, calling themselves the "celebrated Metropolitans." They visited Norfolk, VA and played black teams. *Norfolk Virginian-Pilot* (August 23, 1885): "The Orientals of Norfolk will play the Metropolitans at Gymnasium Park tomorrow at 4 pm. Both are colored clubs." *Norfolk Virginian-Pilot* (October 10, 1885): "There will be a match game of base-ball at the Gymnasium Park this afternoon, at 3 o'clock, between the Red Stockings, of Norfolk, and the Metropolitans. The Red Stockings have defeated almost every club in the Union, and they should draw a crowd today."

Sources: "New Jersey Summer Resorts," *New York (NY) Globe*, Jul 28, 1883; "Social Gossip," *New York Globe*, Aug 8, 1883; "New Jersey Summer Resorts," *New York Globe*, Aug 11, 1883; "Ashbury Park and Ocean Grove," *New York Globe*, Sep 8, 1883; "Social Gossip," *New York Globe*, Sep 8, 1883; "The National Game," *Norfolk (VA) Virginian-Pilot*, Aug 23, 1885; "Baseball," *Norfolk (VA) Virginian-Pilot*, Aug 23, 1885; "The National Game," *Norfolk Virginian-Pilot*, Oct 6, 1885.

Solar Tips Base Ball Club (Salem, NJ; 1890s)

The Solar Tips B.B.C. organized in the 1890s, played black aggregations. *Bridgeton Evening News* (August 22, 1894): "Captain Wells' Athletics, of this city, ran up against the colored Solar Tips, of Salem, at Tumbling Dam Park yesterday afternoon and went under by a score of 19 to 14, notwithstanding that the Athletics may eight runs in the second inning."

SOURCES: "Base Ball," *Bridgeton (NJ) Evening News*, Aug 22, 1894; "A Great Game," *Bridgeton Evening News*, August 14, 1895; "Solar Tips, 12; Pioneers, 7," *Bridgeton Evening News*, August 19, 1895.

African Greaser Base Ball Club (Trenton, NJ; 1880s)

The African Greaser B.B.C. organized in the 1880s. *Trenton Evening Times* (April 20, 1888): "The first nine of the African Greasers was organized last evening. They challenge any colored nine in the city, especially the second nine of the Cuban Giants." Some players substituted for injured/disgruntled players of Trenton's Cuban Giants.

SOURCES: "The African Greasers Organize," *Trenton (NJ) Times*, Apr 20, 1888; "Local Brevities," *Trenton Times*, Apr 21, 1888.

Capital City Base Ball Club (Trenton, NJ; 1890s)

The Capital City B.B.C. organized in the 1890s. *Trenton Times* (May 8, 1892): "The Capital City Club, composed of colored ball players, was organized yesterday as follows: H. Catto, Arthur Thomas, B. Martin, C. Johnston, N. Boardley, D. Henderson, Ben Brown, Ed Smith and W. Smith."

SOURCES: "Wins One," *Trenton (NJ) Times*, May 8, 1892; "Odds and Ends of Sport," *Trenton Evening Times*, Jun 12, 1892.

Colored Browns Base Ball Club (Trenton, NJ; 1880s). Organizer(s): William Simpson.

The Colored Browns B.B.C. organized in the 1880s. *Trenton Daily True American* (May 1, 1886): "The base-ball season in Trenton opened yesterday with a crushing defeat for the aspiring colored team that Manager Simpson has organized. The victors were the Jersey City Eastern League team. There was a good attendance in the early part of the game." The Browns were displaced by the Trenton Cuban Giants.

SOURCES: Trenton Defeats Princeton," *Trenton (NJ) True American*, May 1, 1886; "One for Long Island," *Trenton True American*, Jun 8, 1886.

Cuban Giants Base Ball Club (Trenton, NJ (Philadelphia, PA, and St. Augustine, FL); 1880s–1890s). Organizer(s): Frank P. Thompson and S. K. Govern; Walter Cook and M. D. Bright.

The Cuban Giants B.B.C. organized in 1885, played white and black teams. Before they arrived at Trenton in 1886, they were connected to Philadelphia and St. Augustine. *Baltimore Sun* (April 27, 1886): "The Cuban Giants, of St. Augustine, Florida, defeated, at Oriole Park yesterday, the Monumentals of this city, by the overwhelming score of 14 to 1. Both clubs are composed of colored men." *Baltimore American* (April 27, 1886): "Oriole Park yesterday afternoon was the scene of quite an amusing game of base-ball between the Cuban Giants, of the South, and the Monumental Club, of this city. The visitors had a very strong nine, and, besides being good fielder, batted with much ease and grace. They have had considerable experience on the diamond, and are all hotel waiters on holiday and

working their way to the various summer resorts. They started at St. Augustine, Florida, and had won five successive games before touching Baltimore. The Monumentals belong here, but were out of form, and got defeated. Some of the men, especially the catcher and first baseman on the latter nine were daisies, and would make Scott and Traffley (of the white Baltimore professional team) take a back seat." NY's Gorham club, organized in 1886, declared themselves rivals of the Cuban Giants. *Trenton True American* (August 14, 1886): "It was a contest for the colored championship of the United States. The Gorham club, of New York, was the only colored nine bold enough to dispute the Cuban Giants, and everybody expected they must possess some skill. They wanted to arrange for a series of three games, but Manager Cook declined this programme till they had shown what stuff they were made of. They showed it in a very short time yesterday, and the showing was not to their credit. The dusky visitors were startled by the Giants' style of driving the ball all over the lot, and their demoralization became so great that run getting for themselves was almost out of the question." These nines developed an intense rivalry. *New York Sun* (July 30, 1888): "About 1,800 persons saw the game between the Cuban Giants and Gorhams yesterday. Stovey was in the box for the Cubans, and the latter were not only unable to hit him but he struck out the side in the third, and two men in each inning but the sixth and ninth." The antics of the Cuban Giants included rattling their opponents. *New York Tribune* (September 19, 1888): "An interesting game between the two colored clubs, the Cuban Giants and Gorhams, was played at the Polo grounds yesterday. The game was stopped by darkness at the ending of the ninth inning, leaving each team with one run to its credit. Both Whyte and Stovey pitched in fine form, while the general fielding was excellent." *Bristol Herald* (August 14, 1890): "The colored gentlemen had voices with them like a steam calliope and their chops seemed to be the nearest thing to perceptual motion that one might conceive. Their favorite expression when heard away from the diamond sound decidedly flat. Boyd and his yelling of walking's getting better every day, he's sawing wood, let him walk a little, hold your horse old man, it looks like a pen to him, there's razors on the ball, and lot the noise, was about the funniest combination that has struck the town in sometime." The Cuban Giants returned to Port Chester where, after being drubbing by the local white aggregation, redeemed themselves. *Port Chester Journal* (September 11, 1890): "On Saturday afternoon, the Cuban Giants changed their tactics, and their coaching was not of the humorous style of their previous visit. They had a club before them that they could not trifle with, and that only hard-playing and luck could prevail against them."

SOURCES: "The Baseballists," *Williamsport (PA) Sun-Gazette*, Sep 22, 1885; "Around the Bases," *New York (NY) Herald*, Oct 6, 1885; "Gossip of the Diamond," *Baltimore (MD) American*, Apr 26, 1886; "Base-Ball in Baltimore," *Baltimore (MD) Sun*, Apr 27, 1886; "Colored Teams Playing Ball," *Baltimore American*, Apr 27, 1886; "Trenton Defeats Princeton," *Trenton (NJ) True American*, May 1, 1886; "Base Ball," *Trenton (NJ) Evening Times*, May 9, 1886; "Base Ball," *Trenton Evening Times*, May 9, 1886; "The Giants Triumph," *Trenton True American*, Aug 14, 1886; "Base Ball," *Trenton Evening Times*, Jul 15, 1886; "Sporting Notes," *Jersey City (NJ) Journal*, Jul 20, 1886; "Four to Two," *Trenton True American*, Jul 29, 1886; "The Giants Win a Game," *Wilkes-Barre (PA) Times-Leader*, Aug 28, 1886; "The Mets Puzzle the Cubans," *St. Louis (MO) Sporting News*, Apr 20, 1887; "The Cuban Giants," *Lowell (MA) Courier*, Sep 27, 1887; "Base Ball To-Morrow," *Trenton Evening Times*, Apr 3, 1888; "Base Ball," *Washington (DC) Evening Star*, Apr 19, 1888; "The Cuban Giants," *Trenton Evening Times*, Jun 17, 1888; "Miscellaneous Games," *New York (NY) Sun*, Jul 30, 1888; "New York Notes," *Washington (DC) Bee*, Aug 25,

1888; "The Sporting Chapter," *Buffalo (NY) Courier*, Sep 29, 1888; "The Cuban Giants," *Philadelphia (PA) Sporting Life*, Nov 7, 1888; "Base Ball," *Philadelphia Sporting Life*, Dec 19, 1888; "Among the Amateurs," *New York (NY) Press*, Jun 10, 1889; "Cuban Giants Tomorrow," *Meridian (CT) Journal*, Jul 28, 1889; "Coons as Kickers," *Bristol (CT) Herald*, Aug 14, 1890; "Victorious Coons," *Bristol Herald*, Aug 21, 1890; "Base Ball Galore," *Bristol Herald*, Aug 28, 1890; "A Great Game of Ball," *Port Chester (NY) Journal*, Sep 11, 1890.

Eureka Base Ball Club (Trenton, NJ; 1880s). Organizer(s): William Rodman.

The Eureka B.B.C. organized in the 1880s, played black and white clubs. *Trenton Evening Times* (July 30, 1885) reports "The Phoenix Base Ball Club, of Philadelphia, and the Eureka, of this city, are playing a match game on the Trenton grounds. Both teams are made up of colored men." *Evening Times* (August 2, 1885) reports "The Eureka Base Ball Club (colored) and the Police Gazette team (white) played a game yesterday afternoon on the Trenton ground, the Eureka being victorious. The score was 8 to 4."

SOURCES: "Brief Sporting Notes," *Trenton (NJ) Evening Times*, Jul 30, 1885; "Base Ball," *Trenton Evening Times*, Aug 2, 1885; "The Trenton Base Ball League," *Trenton Evening Times*, Aug 9, 1885; "Among the Sports," *Trenton Evening Times*, Aug 10, 1885; "Among the Sports," *Trenton Evening Times*, Aug 14, 1885; "Among the Sports," *Trenton Evening Times*, Aug 25, 1885.

Lincoln Junior Base Ball Club (Trenton, NJ; 1900s)

The Lincoln Junior B.B.C. organized in 1900, played black and white teams. *Trenton Evening Times* (May 8, 1900): "The Smashers A. C. baseball team, one of the strongest junior teams in the city, which defeated the Lincoln colored team, of this city, recently will play a return game at the Cadwalader Park Grounds. Should the colored lads win the coming game another game will be played on Saturday."

SOURCES: "Dust from the Diamond," *Trenton (NJ) Evening Times*, May 4, 1900; "Diamond Dust," *Trenton Evening Times*, May 8, 1900; "Dust from the Diamond," *Trenton Evening Times*, May 9, 1900.

National Hotel Base Ball Club (Trenton, NJ; 1870s)

The National Hotel B.B.C. organized in the 1870s. The National Hotel team, composed of waiters, played against similar organizations. *Trenton State Gazette* (July 14, 1877): "A game of base-ball played yesterday, between the waiters of the National Hotel and Trenton House, resulted in the latter being warmed."

SOURCES: "Base Ball," *Trenton (NJ) State Gazette*, Jul 14, 1877.

Orient Base Ball Club (Trenton, NJ; 1900s)

The Orient B.B.C. organized in the 1900s. The "Orients" played black nines. *Trenton Evening Times* (June 12, 1900): "The Orients defeated the Rough Riders on the Caldwalader Park diamond yesterday by a score of 12 to 8. Upton Johnson and carter were the stars for the Orients. Johnson made three doubles and a single."

SOURCES: "Dust from the Diamond," *Trenton (NJ) Evening Times*, May 9, 1900; "Diamond Dust," *Trenton Evening Times*, May 28, 1900; "Facts About the Orients," *Trenton Evening Times*, May 31, 1900; "Diamond Dust," *Trenton Evening Times*, Jun 9, 1900; "Dust from the Diamond," *Trenton Evening Times*, Jun 12, 1900; "Diamond Dust," *Trenton Evening Times*, Jul 25, 1900.

Polka Dot Base Ball Club (Trenton, NJ; 1880s). Organizer(s): D. Henderson, A. Bayard, W. S. Wickoff, William Johnson and S. Frost.

The Polka Dot B.B.C. organized in the 1870s. The "Polka Dots" Played black and white clubs. *Trenton State Gazette* (September 4, 1882): "Chase Watkins, while playing ball with the Polka Dots had his right thumb broken." They reorganized in 1883. *Trenton Evening Times* (June 3, 1883): "The Polka Dots and the American House nine had an interesting game on Tuesday which resulted in favor of the former, by a score of 16 to 12."

SOURCES: "Base Ball," *Trenton (NJ) Sentinel*, Apr 9, 1882; "Base Ball," *Trenton (NJ) State Gazette*, Sep 4, 1882; "Base Ball Events," *Trenton (NJ) Evening Times*, May 24, 1883; "Diamond Dots," *Trenton Evening Times*, May 27, 1883; *Trenton Evening Times*, May 31, 1883; "Base Ball," *Trenton Evening Times*, Jun 3, 1883; "Base Ball," *Trenton Evening Times*, Jun 1, 1883; Base Ball," *Trenton Evening Times*, Jul 22, 1883.

Trenton House Base Ball Club (Trenton, NJ; 1870s)

The Trenton House B.B.C. organized in the 1870s. The Trenton House team, composed of waiters, played against similar organizations. *Trenton State Gazette* (July 14, 1877): "A game of base-ball played yesterday, between the waiters of the National Hotel and Trenton House, resulted in the latter being warmed."

SOURCES: "Base Ball," *Trenton (NJ) State Gazette*, Jul 14, 1877.

Young Cuban Giants Base Ball Club (Trenton, NJ; 1880s). Organizer(s): George E. Green.

The Young Cuban Giants B.B.C. organized in the 1880s, played black and white teams. *Trenton Evening Times* (April 29, 1889): "The Little Cuban Giants are no slouches." *Evening Times* (June 2, 1889): "The Young Cuban Giants defeated the colored nine of Morrisville by a score of 5 to 2. Feeney did some good catching and Johnson played a good game also. They would like to hear from the Young America and the C. N. Heath nine." *Evening Times* (June 9, 1889): "Young Cuban Giants, 22; Normal Social Club 3. They also defeated a picked nine by the score of 11 to 3."

SOURCES: "Our Amateurs," *Trenton (NJ) Evening Times*, Apr 29, 1889; *Trenton Evening Times*, May 5, 1889; "Yesterday's Amateur Games," *Trenton Evening Times*, May 12, 1889; "The Amateur League," *Trenton Evening Times*, May 19, 1889; "Among the Amateurs," *Trenton Evening Times*, May 26, 1889; "Among the Amateurs," *Trenton Evening Times*, Jun 2, 1889; "Among the Amateurs," *Trenton Evening Times*, Jun 9, 1889.

New Mexico

Occidental Base Ball Club (Albuquerque, NM 1880s–1890s). Organizer(s): Joe Berry.

The Occidental B.B.C. organized in the 1880s, played black and white nines. In 1890, they joined NM's Colored League. *Santa Fe New Mexican* (March 26, 1889): "James Berry is a hard-nosed player, who hit the ball, stole bases, and fielded all challenges on the diamond." *Albuquerque Morning Democrat* (May 9, 1890): "The Occidental team, of Albuquerque, is to be reorganized for the season of 1890. There is talk that Joe Berry will be manager. It is said that Santa Fe, Las Vegas and Socorro will each have a colored club in the field this year." *Las Vegas Optic* (May 14, 1890): "The Occidentals are about organized at Albuquerque and will be ready in a few days to play any club in New Mexico." They regrouped in 1891. *Albuquerque Weekly Citizen* (July 4, 1891): "The Occidental Base Ball Club, colored boys, desires the Citizen to challenge for them any colored club in the Southwest for a game of base-ball."

SOURCES: "Base Ball Notes," *Santa Fe (NM) New Mexican*, Mar 12, 1889; "Round About Town," *Santa Fe New Mexican*, Mar 26, 1889; "Shamrocks vs. Occidentals," *Albuquerque (NM) Morning Democrat*. Apr. 23, 1889; "Local Laconics," *Albuquerque Morning Democrat*, Jul

3, 1889; "Local Laconics," *Albuquerque Morning Democrat*, Jul 3, 1889; Local Laconics," *Albuquerque Morning Democrat*, May 9, 1890; "The Territory," East Las Vegas (NM). *Optic*, May 14, 1890; "Base Ball Briefs," *Albuquerque Morning Democrat*, Mar 19, 1890; "The Territory," *East Las Vegas Optic*, May 14, 1890; "Local Laconics," *Albuquerque Morning Democrat*, Aug 26, 1890; *Albuquerque Morning Democrat*, Feb 2, 1890; *Albuquerque Morning Democrat*, Jul 2, 1891; *Albuquerque (NM) Weekly Citizen*, Jul 4, 1891.

New York

Athletic Base Ball Club (Albany, NY; 1860s)

The Athletic B.B.C. composed of young men, organized in 1868, following the Civil War. The Athletics played black nines. *Hudson Register* (September 4, 1868): "A base-ball match on the Hudson Grounds, was played yesterday between the Atlantics of this city, and a colored club of Albany, known as the Athletics. The game was called on the fourth inning, the score standing, 21 to 15 if the Atlantics." Among the local clubs, the Athletics played the Capital Citys and Mohicans. *Albany Argus* (September 15, 1868): "A match game of base-ball was played yesterday between the Athletics and Capital City clubs of Albany, on the grounds of the former, which resulted in favor of the Athletics by a score of 44 to 29." *Argus* (October 14, 1868): "The Athletics played the Mohicans yesterday, at the Parade Ground, and treated them to a waterloo defeat. The score standing: Athletics 36; Mohicans 20."

SOURCES: "Base Ball," *Hudson (NY) Evening Register*, Sep 4, 1868; "Base Ball," *Albany (NY) Argus*, Sep 15, 1868; "Base Ball," *Albany Argus*, Oct 14, 1868.

Capital City Base Ball Club (Albany, NY; 1880s)

The Capital City B.B.C. organized in the 1880s, played black nines. *Hudson Evening Register* (July 13, 1889): "A minstrel show was a funeral compared to this game. The game was the first of three for $100. The game was of great interest, as it could be conjectured what was coming next." *Evening Register* (August 16, 1889): "Charles Teabout, of the Capital Citys, deserves special for his beautiful backstop work, throwing to bases ad terrific batting. He made five runs out of six times at bat and a single and two triples, one of which ought to have been a homerun."

SOURCES: "Base Ball Matters," *Hudson (NY) Evening Register*, Jul 13, 1889; "Base Ball Notes," *Hudson Evening Register*, Jul 22, 1889; "Around the Bases," *Hudson Evening Register*, Jul 26, 1889; "Base Ball Matters," *Hudson Evening Register*, Aug 16, 1889; "Base Ball Matters," *Hudson Evening Register*, Sep 7, 1889.

Young Bachelor Base Ball Club (Albany, NY; 1860s–1870s). Organizer(s): James C. Matthews.

The Young Bachelor B.B.C. composed of young men, organized in 1865, playing black teams of NY, PA, NJ, MD, and WA. *Philadelphia Christian Recorder* (January 27, 1866): "I am pleased to say, the [ball] given on Thanksgiving evening, by the Bachelor Base Ball Club, at Bleeker Hall, was in every respect a success, and reflects great credit on the president, Mr. James C. Matthew, and his associates." They toured PA and NJ. *Albany Evening Journal* (September 27, 1866): "The Bachelor Base Ball Club will leave the city tonight on their annual tour of Newark (Keystones) and Philadelphia (National Excelsiors and Pythians)." The National Excelsiors traveled to Albany. *Albany Evening Times* (October 8, 1866): "There was great excitement among the colored population of our city, yesterday, on the occasion of the base-ball match at the Parade Ground, between the National Excelsiors, of Philadelphia, and the Bachelors of this

city. A large number of cable people of both sexes were present to witness it. The game was won by the Philadelphians." The Monitors, of Brooklyn, traveled to Albany to played them. *Albany Argus* (September 25, 1867): "Two clubs composed of American citizens of African descent, the Bachelors, of Albany, and the Monitors of Brooklyn, played a game here yesterday, resulting as follows: bachelors, 79, Monitors 35. The game drew a large concourse of colored folks." In 1868, Jamaica's Henson club defeated the Young Bachelors at Albany, by a score of 58 to 24. They split a series with Utica's Fearless nine. *Utica Observer* (October 29, 1868): "about thirty young colored men came up from Albany, New York to play with the young colored men of Utica." The Fearless were victorious. The organization reorganized in the late 1870s; the Saratoga Unions challenging them.

SOURCES: "Albany, NY," *Philadelphia (PA) Christian Recorder*, Jan 27, 1866; "Albany, NY," *Philadelphia Christian Recorder*, Jul 30, 1866; "City and Vicinity," *Albany (NY) Evening Journal*, Sep 27, 1866; "Base Ball Matches," *Syracuse (NY) Standard*, Oct 4, 1866; "Base Ball," *Albany Evening Journal*, Oct 5, 1866; "Base Ball," *Albany Evening Journal*, October 6, 1866; "Base Ball," *Albany (NY) Evening Times*, Oct 8, 1866; "Colored State Convention," *Albany Evening Journal*, Oct 16, 1866; "Colored State Convention," *Albany Evening Journal*, Oct 18, 1866; "Base Ball," *Newark (NJ) Advertiser*, Oct 23, 1866; "Base Ball," *Albany Evening Journal*, Jul 10, 1867; "Base Ball," *Albany (NY) Argus*, Sep 25, 1867; "State Items," *Syracuse Standard*, Oct 10, 1867; "Base Ball," *Utica (NY) Morning Herald*, Nov 2, 1867; "Base Ball," *Albany Argus*, Oct 9, 1867; "Base Ball," *Utica Morning Herald*, Oct 10, 1868; "Base Ball," *Utica (NY) Observer*, Oct 28, 1868; "Base Ball Extraordinary," *Utica Observer*, Oct 29, 1868; "Proceedings of the Colored State Convention," *Utica Morning Herald*, Jan 25, 1869; "Observations," *Utica Observer*, July 26, 1871; "Short Stops," *New York (NY) Clipper*, Jul 29, 1876; "Base Ball at Coxsackle," *Hudson (NY) Register*, Aug 17, 1876; "All Sorts," *Albany (NY) Morning Express*, Aug 19, 1876.

Eureka Base Ball Club (Auburn, NY; 1870s–1880s). Organizer(s): Isaac Mink.

The Eureka B.B.C. organized in the 1870s, competed against black teams. The Eurekas participated in a NY State's grand base-ball tournament. *Auburn News and Bulletin* (September 10, 1880): "The Eureka colored nine of this city, have entered a base-ball tournament at Geneva, Wednesday and Tuesday next week. The Eurekas, Captain Arthur Smith, are a good nine, having been in practice for two years. On the 17th, the day after the tournament, they will play the Fearless nine of Utica. The latter club is now on tour through the state and will attend the Geneva tournament. Auburn will expect to hear an honorable report from the Eureka, both from Geneva and at home." The Eurekas split the series. *Auburn Auburnian* (September 14, 1880): "At the colored base-ball tournament at Geneva yesterday the Fearless Club of Utica whitewashed the Eurekas of this city, 24 to 0." Following the tournament, the "Eurekas" made local news for failing to pay guest hotel expenses.

SOURCES: "Auburn's Colored Club," *Auburn (NY) News and Bulletin*, Sep 10, 1880; "Brief Mention," *Auburn (NY) Auburnian*, Sep 14, 1880; "Geneva Notes," *Rochester (NY) Union and Advertiser*, Sep 16, 1880; "Brief Mention," *Auburn Auburnian*, Sep 16, 1880; "Base Ballists in Limbo," *Auburn Auburnian*, Sep 27, 1880; "Another Jerry Rescue," *Auburn News and Bulletin*, Sep 27, 1880; "Vicinity Items," *Geneva (NY) Gazette*, Oct 1, 1880; "Auburn Matters," *Syracuse (NY) Evening Standard*, Oct 2, 1880; "Indignant Colored Men," *Auburn Auburnian*, Oct 1, 1880.

Keystone Athletic Base Ball Club (Babylon, NY (Philadelphia, PA and St. Augustine, FL); 1880s). Organizer(s): Frank P. Thompson.

The Keystone Athletic B.B.C. organized in 1884. The Keystone Athletics, composed of hotel waiters, first appeared in Philadelphia. They worked summers at Babylon's Argyle Hotel, and wintered at St. Augustine's San Marcos Hotel. The Keystone Athletics played white and black teams. *Palatka News* (April 28, 1885): "The waiters of the Hotel San Marco, at St. Augustine, left for the North … they intend playing match games of base-ball in Southern cities. They call themselves the Ancient City Athletics, and headwaiter Frank P. Thompson will act as umpire." *The Sporting Life* (April 29, 1885) notes: "The Athletic Base Ball Club, organized last summer at Babylon, Long Island, and managed by Mr. Frank P. Thompson, of that city, has, during the winter, been continued at St. Augustine, Florida. The members were waiters at the San Marco Hotel, and nearly all belong in Philadelphia." They played crack black clubs of Jacksonville, Savannah, Charleston, Richmond, WA, and Baltimore: "Monday last at Jacksonville, they defeated the local team by the close score of 26 to 18. Tuesday, they warmed the pets of Savannah 17 to 9." *Philadelphia Times* (June 2, 1885): "At Somerset Park yesterday the Somerset defeated the Keystone Athletic Club, composed of colored men." *Huntington Long Islander* (August 21, 1885): "A spirited game was played on the Argyle Grounds Tuesday afternoon between the Keystone Athletics, a club composed of the colored employees at the Argyle, and the Farmingdales, a white scrub club from Farmingdale. The cullud boys taught the white gents from Farmingdale how to play base-ball, winning by a score of 29 to 1."

SOURCES: *Palatka (FL) News*, Apr 28, 1885; "Colored Clubs at Union Park," *Baltimore (MD) American and Commercial Advertiser*, Apr 28, 1885 "Notes and Comments," *Philadelphia (PA) Sporting Life*, Apr 29, 1885; "Base Ball Notes," *Philadelphia (PA) Times*, May 19, 1885; "Base Ball Notes," *Philadelphia Times*, Jun 2, 1885; "Babylon," *Huntington (NY) Long Islander*, Aug 21, 1885.

Hotel Bennett Base Ball Club (Binghamton, NY; 1880s). Organizer(s): Charles S. Randall.

The Hotel Bennett B.B.C. organized in the 1880s, played black teams. *Owego Blade* (August 27, 1884): "There will be a base-ball match at Binghamton between the Parlor City and the waiters of Hotel Bennett." *Blade* (September 2, 1884): "Yesterday a game of base-ball was finally arranged between the Parlor City and the waiters employed at the Hotel Bennett. The contest took place on the old Crickets ground…. The Parlor City took the lead from the start and maintained it to the close, winning the contest by a score of 18 to 15. During the game, Fred Benson of Owego, catcher for the Parlor City club, had one of his fingers broken while catching behind the bat." *New York Freeman* (April 10, 1886): "A base-ball nine was organized last week, composed of waiters of Hotel Bennett and other young men. Charlie S. Randall was elected captain and manager. This club we believe has the heaviest first baseman of any club in the State. His weight is two-hundred and forty-two pounds. Their suits will be white flannel, blue trimmings." The nine developed a local rivalry with the Parlor City club, another black team. *Owego Blade* (August 7, 1886): "There will be a base-ball match at Binghamton between the Parlor City nine and the waiters of Hotel Bennett."

SOURCES: "Local Brevities," *Owego (NY) Blade*, Aug 27, 1884; "Local Brevities," *Owego Blade*, Sep 2, 1884; "Binghamton Notes," *New York (NY) Freeman*, Mar 13, 1886; "Binghamton Notes," *New York Freeman*, Apr 10, 1886; "Binghamton Notes," *New York Freeman*, Apr 24, 1886; "Binghamton Briefs," *New York Freeman*, May 29, 1886; "Yesterday's Score," *Owego Blade*, Aug 7, 1886; "Ithaca Inklings," *New York Freeman*, Aug 7, 1886; "Sporting Notes," *Geneva (NY) Gazette*, Sep 10, 1886.

Cuban Stars Base Ball Club (Binghamton, NY; 1890s)

The Cuban Stars B.B.C. organized in the 1890s, played black teams. *Elmira Gazette* (August 10, 1894): "The ball game between the two colored clubs at Driving Park yesterday was a success, as far as finances were concerned. The clubs were the Cuban Stars of Binghamton and the Casinos of this city. The Casinos played the best ball and 26 runs to a few of the visitors. E. Thompson was in the box for the Casinos and E. Daily, a one-armed man, and W. Dangerfield did the pitching for the visitors." *Elmira Morning Telegram* (August 10, 1894): "At the great emancipation game, played at Maple Avenue Park, Thursday, the [Cuban Stars] demonstrated that when they practice a little more they can catch the grand stand if it were pitched straight at them. One-armed Daley was in the box on the first half of the first inning, but there wasn't enough squares on the score card to score the runs the Casinos made off his pitching. The Elmiras pounded him until Captain Messer requested him to git in de game. As song and dance artist with an 'Uncle Tom's Cabin' company, the Cuban Stars would be a howling success, but they can't play ball with anything old but a female club."

SOURCES: "Emancipation Ball Game," *Elmira (NY) Morning Telegram*, Jul 29, 1894; "Colored Masons," *Elmira Daily Gazette and Free Press*, Aug 9, 1894; "Elmira Boys Win," *Elmira (NY) Gazette*, Aug 10, 1894; "Minor Locals," *Elmira Gazette*, September 8, 1894; "Elmira versus Casinos," *Elmira Morning Telegram*, Aug 10, 1894; *Morning Telegram*, Aug 11, 1894.

Parlor City Base Ball Club (Binghamton, NY; 1870s–1880s). Organizer(s): John Amos and Lyman Melvin.

The Parlor City B.B.C. organized in the 1870s, played black teams. *Montrose Democrat* (July 11, 1877): "A colored baseball club from Binghamton is expected to play the colored club of this place tomorrow." *Democrat* (July 11, 1877): "*Binghamton Times* says the Parlor City Base Ball Club, a team composed of young men, has been organized for this season with John Amos as captain. They will play their first game at Montrose on Thursday next, tomorrow, with the Valley Tiger Club of this place. A number of their friends expect to accompany them." *Democrat* (September 21, 1878): "A game of base-ball between the Parlor City nine, of Binghamton, and the Valley Tigers, of Montrose, on Thursday. Both clubs are colored. The Valley Tigers came out behind." The Parlor Citys played another PA nine. *Wilkes-Barre Record* (July 8, 1881): "The Olympic Base Ball Club [of Wilkes-Barre] played the Parlor City Club of Binghamton. The score was 7 to 7 in favor of the Olympics." *Owego Blade* (August 27, 1884): "There will be a base-ball match at Binghamton between the Parlor City nine and the waiters of Hotel Bennett." *Blade*: "There will be a base-ball match at Binghamton between the Parlor City and the waiters of Hotel Bennett." *Blade* (September 2, 1884): "Yesterday a game of base-ball was finally arranged between the Parlor City and the waiters employed at the Hotel Bennett. The contest took place on the old Crickets ground…. The Parlor City took the lead from the start and maintained it to the close, winning the contest by a score of 18 to 15. During the game, Fred Benson of Owego, catcher for the Parlor City club, had one of his fingers broken while catching behind the bat."

SOURCES: "Base Ball," *Utica (NY) Observer*, Oct 14, 1875; "Champion Games," *Utica (NY) Herald*, Sep 18, 1876; "Base Ball," *Utica Herald*, Sep 25, 1876; "Base Ball," *Syracuse (NY) Standard*, Sep 25, 1876; "Neighboring Counties," *Montrose (PA) Democrat*, Jul 11, 1877; "Happenings at Home," *Waverly (NY) Advocate*, Aug 7, 1878; "Town and County and Variety," *Montrose Democrat*, Sep 21, 1878; "Rah For the Parlor Citys," *Montrose Democrat*, Oct 18, 1878; "Local Brevities," *Wilkes-Barre (PA) Record*, Jul 8, 1881; "Local Brevities," *Owego (NY) Blade*, Aug 27, 1884; "Local Brevities," *Owego Blade*, Sep 2, 1884;

"Binghamton Notes," *New York (NY) Freeman*, Feb 20, 1886; "Binghamton Notes," *New York Freeman*, Apr 10, 1886; "Binghamton Notes," *New York Freeman*, Apr 24, 1886.

Alpine Base Ball Club (Brooklyn, NY; 1880s)

The Alpine B.B.C. organized in the 1880s, played white and black teams. *Jersey Journal* (October 1, 1884): "No more interesting or exciting game than that of Monday has been played at the Rink during the season. The contestants were the two crack colored clubs, the Orientals of this city and Alpine of New York. The players were active, enthusiastic and excitable, and yells of admiration for some good playing, or denunciation for some one's failure, were blended with shouts of encouragement to runners all through the game. Somersaults, am hats thrown in the air, shouts and handshaking, characterized the conclusion of the game." The Alpines also played Jersey City's Hudson nine. *Journal* (May 18, 1886): "The newly organized colored base-ball club, the Hudsons, of this city, put on their new uniforms yesterday afternoon, and played their second game at Oakland Park, with their rivals, the Alpines, of Brooklyn. The event was of great interest to the colored lovers of the game, and at times the excitement ran high among the fifty or more self-constituted umpires, who were deciding certain plays in advance of the real umpire. The home club out-played and out-batted their opponents, whom they beat badly." They developed a rivalry with Brooklyn's Remsens. *New York Herald* (May 27, 1885): "The match for the Colored Club championship of Brooklyn, which was played at Washington Park, proved to be not only very interesting to spectators, but the best played game of ball yet seen at the hands of colored nines in this city. The quick movements of the players, too, were noteworthy. The game was decidedly one of the most interesting outside games played at the Park this season." The Alpines played the Long Island Stars, a white team. *Long Island Star* (October 2, 1886): "The Stars defeated the colored Alpines on Saturday in a five inning game by a score of 9–8. The home team played very carelessly in the field, but slugged the ball in great shape. The Stars commenced the sixth inning and had five earned runs to their credit when the game was called back to the fifth inning on account of darkness. Hamlen twirled the sphere in splendid form holding the Sons of Ham down to three singles. His drop ball was a puzzle to the visitors."

Sources: "Base Ball," *New York (NY) Herald*, Sep 16, 1884; *New York (NY) Globe*, Sep 20, 1884; "Base Ball," *New York Herald*, Sep 29, 1884; "Base Ball," *Jersey City (NJ) Journal*, Jun 26, 1884; "Alpine vs. Orientals," *Jersey City Journal*, Oct 1, 1884; "When Greek Meets Greek," *New York Herald*, October 1, 1884; "Playing the National Game," *New York (NY) Tribune*, Oct 1, 1884; *New York Globe*, Oct 4, 1884; "Conquering Fielders," *New York Herald*, May 19, 1885; "A Dark Championship," *New York Herald*, May 26, 1885; "Winning the Colored Championship," *New York Herald*, May 27, 1885; "Brooklyn Briefs," *Philadelphia (PA) Sporting Life*, May 27, 1885; "The Colored Base Ball Match," *New York Herald*, May 27, 1885; "Notes and Comments," *Philadelphia Sporting Life*, Jun 3, 1885; "Base Ball Notes," *New York Herald*, Oct 7, 1885; "Base Ball Notes," *Jersey City Journal*, May 13, 1886; "Colored Players at the Bat," *Jersey City Journal*, May 18, 1886; "Jersey City Locals," *New York (NY) Freeman*, May 22, 1886; "Base Ball Notes," *New York Herald*, Aug 14, 1886; "What the Club is Doing," *Trenton (NJ) Evening Times*, Aug 24, 1886; "What the Club is Doing," *Trenton Evening Times*, Aug 26, 1886; "Amateur Games at the Park," *Brooklyn (NY) Eagle*, Sep 12, 1886; "Base Ball," *Long Island (NY) Star*, Oct 2, 1886.

Amateur Base Ball Club (Brooklyn, NY; 1890s)

The Amateur B.B.C. organized in the 1890s, played black and white nines. *Brooklyn Eagle* (June 24, 1896): "The Howard A. C. defeated the Amateurs, at the former's grounds, Halsey Street and Saratoga Avenue, last Saturday afternoon. The Amateurs played a plucky, uphill game, but were unfortunate in placing their hits, while the Howards not only smote the leather at opportune moments, but placed their hits out of the reach of the fielders." *Jersey City Journal* (August 17, 1896): "In a game Saturday on the Johnson Avenue Grounds, the Pacifics were defeated by the Amateurs, a crack colored team of Brooklyn, because of indifferent playing and careless base running. The game was interesting at times and until the last inning was in the Pacific's favor."

Sources: "Amateur Base Ball," *Brooklyn (NY) Eagle*, Jun 24, 1896; "Base Ball Tomorrow," *Jersey City (NJ) Journal*, Aug 15, 1896; "They Need a Shake-up," *Jersey City Journal*, Aug 17, 1896.

Colored Giants Base Ball Club (Brooklyn, NY; 1890s)

The Colored Giants B.B.C. organized in the 1890s, played black and white teams. *Putnam County Courier* (June 4, 1897): "The Brewster Base Ball Club won an easy victory over the Colored Giants, and in the first inning scored enough runs to win the game had they played ball." *Brooklyn Eagle* (September 6, 1897): "An interesting game was played between the Fraternal Colored Giants and the St. James sanctuary Union, in which the latter won by a score of 10 to 7."

Sources: Amateur Base Ball," *Brooklyn (NY) Eagle*, Apr 20, 1897; "Amateur Base Ball," *Brooklyn Eagle*, Apr 28, 1897; "Baseball Notes," *New York (NY) Sun*, May 13, 1897; "Baseball Notes," *New York Sun*, May 20, 1897; "Other Games," *New York Sun*, May 26, 1897; "Baseball Notes," *New York Sun*, Jul 5, 1897; "Other Games," *New York Sun*, Jul 5, 1897; "Brewster Nine Struck a Snag," *Carmel (NY) Putnam County Courier*, Jun 4, 1897; "Amateur Base Ball" *Brooklyn Eagle*, Sep 6, 1897.

Monitor Protective Union Base Ball Club (Brooklyn, NY; 1860s–1870s). Organizer(s): J. Hunter, Andrew Dosen, W. G. Brown and D. J. Brown.

The Monitor Protective Union B.B.C. organized in 1862, if not earlier. The Monitors played black teams of NY, NJ, PA, and RI. *Brooklyn Eagle* (October 17, 1862): "The dusky contestants engaged the game hugely, and to use a common phrase, they did the thing genteely. Dinah, all eyes, was there to applaud, and the game passed off satisfactorily. All appeared to have a jolly time, and the little Pickanninies laughed with the rest. It would have done Beecher, Greely, or any other of the luminaries of the radical wing of the Republican Party good to have been present." The Monitors and Uniques also played a match game. *New York Herald-Tribune* (October 4, 1867): "Base Ball is getting to be popular among colored folks, and many of them are skillful players. Yesterday the crack organizations of this vicinity, the Uniques and Monitors, both Brooklyn clubs, met in a contest for the championship on the Satellite grounds. The Monitors outplayed them at all points, but especially in batting, which, in the latter part of the match, they did in terrific style. A pretty even commencement lent the game interest, until the Monitors began to draw away from their opponents, who became demoralized, and their contest ceased, although play continued. The catchers on each side and the pitcher of the Monitors won the most credit for playing. Williams's pitching was especially efficient." D. J. Hunter, Andrew Dosen, D. J. Brown and W. G. Brown managed the club's affairs; their names appear in the 1867 Pythian archives. The Monitors traveled to Albany, where they played the Young Bachelors. *Albany Argus* (September 25, 1867): "Two clubs composed of American citizens of African descent, the Bachelors, of Albany, and the Monitors of Brooklyn, played a game here yesterday, resulting as follows: bachelors, 79, Monitors 35. The game drew a large concourse of colored folks." In 1870, the Monitors and Cambrias, of Providence, RI, played two games. *Providence Evening Press* (October 31, 1870): "The Cambria Base Ball Club, of this city played two matches in Brooklyn, NY, last week, one with the Monitors and the other with the Oceans. Result—once laid out their opponents, and once laid themselves."

Sources: "Pythian Baseball Club; Scorecards and Correspondence" (Roll No. 8). *American Negro Historical Society Collection: Historical Society Microfilm Edition*; "Base Ball," *Brooklyn (NY) Eagle*, Oct 17, 1862; "Negro Picnic at Morris Grove," *Brooklyn Eagle*, Aug 25, 1865; "Base Ball," *Albany (NY) Argus*, Sep 25, 1867; "The National Game," *New York (NY) Herald-Tribune*, Oct 4, 1867; "The Championship of Colored Clubs," *New York Herald-Tribune*, Oct 26, 1867; "Local News," *Providence (RI) Evening Press*, Oct 13, 1870; "Local News," *Providence Evening Press*, Oct 31, 1870.

Niantic Base Ball Club (Brooklyn, NY; 1890s). Organizer(s): D. L. Ross.

The Niantic B.B.C. organized in the 1890s, played black and white teams. *Newark Sunday Call* (May 17, 1896): "Five hundred spectators journeyed to the Jefferson Grounds yesterday to witness an interesting game between the Jefferson A. C. and the strong Niantic A. C., colored champions of New York. They were well repaid." *Brooklyn Eagle* (July 20, 1896): "In the game between the Howard Athletic Club and the Niantic Athletic Club, on Saturday last, at the former's grounds, Watkins of the Niantics made some very sensational plays, which were not accomplished, however, without an acrobatic performance accomplishing each play. The game was close until the sixth inning, when Bancroft of the Niantics lost control of the ball."

Sources: "Lots of Base Ball," *Newark (NJ) Sunday Call*, May 17, 1896; "This is the Last Day," *Jersey City (NJ) Journal*, Jun 1, 1896; *Brooklyn (NY) Eagle*, Jun 7, 1896; "Amateur Base Ball," *Brooklyn Eagle*, Jul 20, 1896.

Ocean ("Oceanic") Base Ball Club (Brooklyn, NY; 1870s)

The Ocean ("Oceanic") B.B.C. organized in the 1870s, played black teams. They developed a rivalry with Providence's Cambria club; the Oceans defeated the Cambrias by a score of 39 to 13. The latter travelled southwards, where they played Brooklyn's Oceans and Monitors. *Providence Evening Press* (October 31, 1870): "The Cambria Base Ball Club, of this city played two matches in Brooklyn, NY, last week, one with the Monitors and the other with the Oceans. Result—once laid out their opponents, and once laid themselves." In 1873, the Uniques and Oceans played for the championship: *New York Herald-Tribune* (August 12, 1873): "A match game was played on the Capitoline Grounds, yesterday, between the Uniques and Oceans, colored clubs. About 500 people were present. The batting of the Oceans was excellent, especially that of Bateman and Burns, the former making two home runs. On the other side Seymour excelled, making several fine hits." In 1875, Hempstead, NY hosted a black tournament for the Hempstead Mutuals, Brooklyn's Quicksteps and Oceans, and Henson's Lone Stars.

Sources: "Base Ball," *Jersey City (NJ) Journal*, Jul 7, 1870; "Local News," *Providence Evening Press*, Oct 31, 1870; "Base Ball," *Jersey City Journal*, Jul 19, 1870; "Amateur Games," *Brooklyn (NY) Eagle*, Jul 31, 1873; "Base Ball," *New York (NY) Herald-Tribune*, Aug 12, 1873; "Local News," *Providence (RI) Evening Press*, Oct 13, 1870; "Amateur Games," *Brooklyn Eagle*, Jul 31, 1873; "Base Ball," *New York Herald-Tribune*, Aug 12, 1873; "Base Ball," *Brooklyn Eagle, Nov 16, 1874*"Base Ball," *Brooklyn Eagle, Nov 16, 1874*; *Hempstead (NY) Queens County Sentinel*, Jul 22, 1875.

Athletic Base Ball Club (Williamsburgh (Brooklyn), NY; 1860s)

The Athletic B.B.C. organized in the 1870s, played against black nines. *Philadelphia Christian Recorder* (August 31, 1868): "The Athletic B.B.C. beat the Union Club of Brooklyn, August 19, by a score of 16 to

7; and the Mutual Club of New York, August 20, by a score of 18 to 16. The Athletic B.B.C. beat the Eckford Club, at Williamsburg, August 21, the score being—Athletics 23, Eckfords, 19. They have returned to Philadelphia. *Philadelphia Christian Recorder* (September 19, 1868): "The Athletic B.B.C. of this city (N.Y.), beat the Atlantic Club of Brooklyn last week, on the return game, by 37 to 13. As they had previously won the first game, they are now the champion colored club."

Sources: "States and Territories," *Philadelphia (PA) Christian Recorder*, Aug 31, 1868; "News of the Week," *Philadelphia Christian Recorder*, Sep 19, 1868.

Quickstep Base Ball Club (Brooklyn (Williamsburgh), NY; 1870s)

The Quickstep B.B.C. organized in the 1870s, played against black nines. Brooklyn's nines established long-standing rivals. *New York Herald-Tribune* (August 5, 1873): "The Uniques and Quicksteps, both colored, of Brooklyn, played a match game on the Capitoline grounds, yesterday, in the presence of a large number of spectators. The game was closely contested up to the end of the sixth inning, when the score stood 5 to 6 in the Uniques' favor. By good batting the latter scored fun runs in the seventh inning, and finally won the game by a score of 12 to 10." *Brooklyn Eagle* (November 11, 1874): "Tomorrow a match for the colored championship is to take place at the Park between the Quicksteps, of the Eastern District, and the Oceans of the Western, the Eckford and Atlantic clubs of the colored base-ball fraternity." *Brooklyn Eagle* (November 16, 1874): "The defeat of the Eastern District Quicksteps by the Oceans of the Western District by a score of 12 to 5, has been the topic of interest of late among the colored ball tossers of the city. The Oceans say they can do it again, but in this opinion the Quicksteps do not coincide. The match attracted a large crowd to the Park, and it was much enjoyed." *Brooklyn Argus-Union* (October 15, 1877): "The Quicksteps of the Eastern District defeated the Lone Stars, of Jamaica, at the capitol grounds, by a score of 15 to 13."

Sources: "Base Ball," *New York (NY) Herald-Tribune*, Aug 5, 1873; "The Amateur Arena," *Brooklyn (NY) Eagle*, Aug 5, 1873; "Base Ball," *Brooklyn Eagle*, Aug 20, 1873; "Keystone Social Club," *Jersey City (NJ) Journal*, Dec 26, 1873; "Base Ball," *Brooklyn Eagle, Nov 16, 1874*; "Keystone Social Club," *Jersey City (NJ) Journal*, Dec 26, 1873; ; "Base-Ball," *Brooklyn Eagle*, Nov 11, 1874; "Base Ball," *Brooklyn (NY) Argus-Union*, Oct 15, 1877.

Remsen Base Ball Club (Brooklyn, NY; 1880s). Organizer(s): Charles Williams and Fred Jackson; Fred Jackson, Frank B. Hoagland, C. Williams and Theodore W. Smith.

The Remsen B.B.C. organized in the 1880s, played against the black teams of NY and NJ. *New York Herald* (September 16, 1884): "the match for the Colored Club championship of Brooklyn, which was played at Washington Park, proved to be not only very interesting to spectators, but the best played game of ball yet seen at the hands of colored nines in this city. The quick movements of the players, too, were noteworthy. The game was decidedly one of the most interesting outside games played at the Park this season." They reorganized in 1885. *Brooklyn Eagle* (May 18, 1885): "The first game of baseball for the colored championship of Brooklyn will be played at Washington Park tomorrow, by the Alpine and Remsen Base Ball clubs." *Eagle* (May 20, 1885): "The contest at Washington Park for the colored championship of the metropolis, between the rural Alpine and Remsen teams resulted in the final success of the Alpines. The Alpines led up to the seventh inning by 7 to 6, but in the seventh the Remsens went to the front by 8 to 7. Then the former rallied at the bat and, being assisted by costly errors, they added eleven runs to their score on the last three innings and came in victors by 18 to 8."

SOURCES: "Base Ball," *New York (NY) Herald*, Sep 16, 1884; *New York (NY) Globe*, Sep 20, 1884; "Base Ball," *New York Herald*, Sep 29, 1884; *New York Globe*, Oct 4, 1884; "Playing the National Game," *New York Tribune, Oct 1, 1884*; "When Greek Meets Greek," *New York Herald*, Oct 1, 1884; "Sports and Pastimes," *Brooklyn (NY) Eagle*, Mar 8, 1885; "The Reporter's Note Book," *Brooklyn Eagle*, May 18, 1885; "Sports and Pastimes," *Brooklyn Eagle*, May 20, 1885; "Sports and Pastimes," *Brooklyn Eagle*, May 27, 1885; "The Colored Base Ball Match," *New York Herald*, May 27, 1885; "Brooklyn Briefs," *Philadelphia (PA) Sporting Life*, May 27, 1885.

Unique Base Ball Club (Brooklyn, NY; 1860s–1890s). Organizer(s): Ira P. Sayton; Benjamin M. Butler.

The Unique B.B.C. organized in the 1860s. New York City boasted several black baseball teams; among them, the Van Dekhens, Minervas, Oceans, Amitys, Eckfords, Atlantics, Unions, Athletics, and Uniques. The Uniques ranked among the strongest clubs. *New York Herald-Tribune* (October 26, 1867): "Base Ball is getting to be popular among colored folks, and many of them are skillful players. Yesterday the crack organizations of this vicinity, the Uniques and Monitors, both Brooklyn clubs, met in a contest for the championship on the Satellite grounds." Under the leadership of Ira P. Sayton, they played Philadelphia's National Excelsior and Pythian nines. They competed against Brooklyn's Ocean team for the championship. *Brooklyn Eagle* (July 31, 1873): "The batting of the Oceans was excellent, especially that of Bateman and Barnes, the former making two home runs. On the other side, Seymour excelled, making several fine hits." Under the former Gorham player and manager, the entertainment promoter Benjamin M. Butler, reorganized the Uniques in the 1890s. *New York Press* (May 25, 1896): "B. M. Butler, manager of the Uniques, formerly of Gorhams, has a number of open dates, and would like to hear from clubs having enclosed grounds."

SOURCES: "Pythian Baseball Club; Scorecards" (Roll No. 8). *American Negro Historical Society Collection: Historical Society Microfilm Edition*; "Emancipation Day," *Brooklyn (NY) Eagle*, Aug 3, 1867; "The Championship of Colored Clubs," *New York (NY) Herald-Tribune*, Oct 26, 1867; "Play Among Colored Folks," *New York (NY) Herald*, Oct 26, 1867; "The National Game," *New York Herald-Tribune*, Oct 4, 1867; "Outdoor Sports," *New York Herald-Tribune*, Jul 29, 1869; "Amateur Games," *Brooklyn Eagle*, Jul 31, 1873; "Summary of the News," *New York (NY) World*, Aug 1, 1873; "Base Ball," *New York Herald-Tribune*, Aug 5, 1873; "The Amateur Arena," *Brooklyn Eagle*, Aug 5, 1873; "Base Ball," *New York Herald-Tribune*, Aug 12, 1873; "Base Ball," *Brooklyn Eagle*, Aug 20, 1873; "Base Ball," *New York Herald-Tribune*, Aug 20, 1873; "Base Ball," *Brooklyn Eagle*, Nov 10, 1874; "Base Ball," *New York Herald-Tribune*, Sep 19, 1880; "City News and Gossip," *Brooklyn Eagle*, Jul 19, 1884; "Notes of the Diamond," *New York (NY) Press*, May 25, 1896.

Van Delken (Weldenken) Base Ball Club (Brooklyn (Williamsburg), NY; 1860s–1870s). Organizer(s): Joseph Trower.

The Van Delken B.B.C. organized in the 1860s, played against black nines. During Brooklyn's West India Emancipation Day Celebration, Williamsburg and Brooklyn contested for the colored championship. *Brooklyn Eagle*: "The [Emancipation Day] proceedings closed with a game of ball between sixteen young men of Brooklyn and sixteen of Williamsburg. The former were ahead when our reporter left, at 5 o'clock, at which time 2,000 tickets had been sold." The annual ball contest continued throughout the years. *Eagle*: "Then came the ball match for the champion ball and bat. The latter was carried away by the Van Delken Colored Base Ball Club, of Williamsburg, no claimants appearing to compete for the other."

SOURCES: "Emancipation Day," *New York (NY) Tribune*, Aug 1, 1862; "Negro Jubilee," *Brooklyn (NY) Eagle*, Aug 2, 1864; "Union Emancipation Jubilee," *Brooklyn Eagle*, Aug 3, 1864; "Negro Emancipation," *Brooklyn Eagle*, Aug 2, 1865; "Local Intelligence," *New York (NY) Evening Express*, Aug 2, 1866; "Emancipation Day," *Brooklyn Eagle*, Aug 2, 1866; "Emancipation Day," *Brooklyn Eagle*, Aug 3, 1867; "Williamsburgh," *New York Tribune*, Dec 28, 1867; "Anniversary of Negro Emancipation," *New York (NY) Herald-Tribune*, Aug 4, 1868; "Colored Mass Meeting in Williamsburg," *New York (NY) Evening Telegram*, Oct 21, 1868; "Emancipation Day," *Brooklyn Eagle*, Aug 3, 1869; "Postponed to No Purpose," *New York (NY) Sun*, Aug 7, 1877; "The Colored Voters," *Brooklyn Eagle*, Jun 25, 1884; "Only a Million Votes Lost," *New York (NY) Herald*, Aug 2, 1884; "Brooklyn News," *Newtown (NY) Register*, Jul 26, 1888.

"77" Base Ball Club (Buffalo, NY; 1890s)

The "77" B.B.C. organized in the 1890s. *Buffalo Express* (May 4, 1890): "The '77' Negro Baseball nine was organized in the city on Friday with the following players: E. Johnson, N. Cooper, A. Brown, W. Dallas, M. Landers, W. Story, W. Bright, W. Henderson, G. Dover. The club wishes to hear from any amateur nine in this part of the country."

SOURCES: "Among the Amateurs," *Buffalo (NY) Express*, May 4, 1890; "Just Behind the Bat," *Buffalo (NY) Commercial*, May 6, 1900.

Broezel House Base Ball Club (Buffalo, NY; 1890s)

The Broezel House B.B.C. organized in the 1890s, played similar black and white aggregations. *Buffalo Commercial* (June 8, 1893): "The Iroquois and Broezel House teams played an interesting game at the Front yesterday, the latter winning by 10 to 7." *Buffalo Commercial* (June 14, 1893): "The Fort Porter and Broezel Hotel nines played one of the most exciting games of the season at the Front yesterday afternoon, the former winning by a score of 8 to 7."

SOURCES: "Notes of Coming Men," *Buffalo (NY) Courier*, Jun 19, 1892; "Around the Bases," *Buffalo Courier*, Jun 20, 1892; "Around the Bases," *Buffalo Courier*, Jul 16, 1892; "Base Ball Brevities" *Buffalo (NY) Commercial*, Jun 8, 1893; "Baseball Notes," *Buffalo Express*, Jun 9, 1893; "Base Ball Brevities" *Buffalo Commercial*, Jun 14, 1893; "Sporting Briefs," *Buffalo (NY) Evening News*, Jul 18, 1893; "Amateur Ball Players," *Buffalo Courier*, Jul 7, 1894; "Amateur Ball Notes," *Buffalo Courier*, Aug 31, 1894; "Baseball Briefs," *Buffalo Evening News*, Jun 18, 1895; "Amateur Ball Tossers," *Buffalo Courier*, Jul 6, 1895.

City Hotel Base Ball Club (Buffalo, NY; 1880s). Organizer(s): R. W. Walker.

The City Hotel B.B.C. organized in the 1880s, played against black teams. *Buffalo Commercial* (August 12, 1884): "The Genesee and City Club nines (colored), having each won a game, the deciding match for superiority will be played at Olympic Park Thursday afternoon next. A small admission fee will be charged." *Buffalo Courier* (August 15, 1884): "The game between the Genesee and City (colored) base-ball clubs drew quite a large crowd to Olympic Park yesterday afternoon. The players from the Genesee proved themselves regular and true willow wielders and walked all over the City people, winning the game in seven innings. The score stood 14 to 9." They reorganized in 1885. *Buffalo Commercial* (May 13, 1885): "The nine from the Hotel Genesee defeated the City Club nine 16 to 15 yesterday." The waiters of Buffalo and Rochester developed a rivalry. *Rochester Democrat and Chronicle* (August 6, 1885): "A game of baseball will be played at the Union Street grounds this afternoon, between the Unexpecteds of this city and the Buffalo City's, of Buffalo, both colored teams, for a purse of $50."

SOURCES: "Brief Mention," *Buffalo (NY) Express*, Aug 9, 1884; "A

Wow and a Wumpus," *Buffalo (NY) Commercial*, Aug 12, 1884; "Sporting Matters," *Buffalo (NY) Evening Telegraph*, Aug 13, 1884; "Game Between Colored Amateurs," *Buffalo (NY) Courier*, Aug 15, 1884; "Brief Mention," *Buffalo Express*, Aug 21, 1884; "Sports of the Season," *Buffalo (NY) Evening News*, Apr 10, 1885; "Sporting Notes," *Buffalo Commercial*, Apr 10, 1885; "The World of Sports," *Buffalo Evening Telegraph*, Apr 11, 1885; "Town Talk," *Buffalo Commercial*, May 13, 1885; "Town Talk," *Buffalo Evening Telegraph*, May 13, 1885; "Sporting Matters," *Buffalo Evening Telegraph*, Jun 13, 1885; "Sporting News," *Buffalo Evening Telegraph*, Jul 30, 1885; "Base Ball Matters," *Rochester (NY) Democrat and Chronicle*, Aug 6, 1885; "Diamond Dust," *Rochester Democrat and Chronicle*, Aug 7, 1885.

Colored Stars Base Ball Club (Buffalo, NY; 1880s–1890s). Organizer(s): G. M. Butler and J. William Mitchell; W. Dowling.

The Colored Stars B.B.C. organized in the 1880s, played black and white nines. *Niagara Falls Gazette* (May 13, 1891): "The opening game of the season of the Buffalo and Buckhorn Island Base Ball League was contested on Buckhorn Island Sunday afternoon between the Buffalo Stars and Black Rocks. The event was not only a contest at baseball, but it was a game of chin for both sides had many opinions to express. In the first place the game was played under protest by the Black Rocks, owing to a man named Thompson playing with the Stars. It seems that the by-laws of the association provide that no player in any of the Buffalo clubs shall play with any other clubs of the league unless he has received a release from said club. It was claimed that Thompson was a member of the Casinos and had played two games with them. The score was 10 to 6 in favor of the Stars." *Batavia News* (July 24, 1889): "The worst defeat that the Batavia Wizards have administered to any nine yet this season they administered to the Stars, the nine of colored players from Buffalo, yesterday. For the Stars Sam Dallas, ex-mascot for the Buffalo International nine and second baseman for the old Buffalo newsboys' nine, played on second, putting up a great game and causing considerable amusement by his coaching. Daily, the Stars' one-armed pitcher, surprised the natives by making a two-base hit, but his work in the box was not remarkable."

SOURCES: "Sporting Notes," *Buffalo (NY) Express*, Jun 18, 1889; "The Colored Team Whitewashed," *Buffalo (NY) Courier*, Jun 20, 1889; Batavia (NY) News, Jul 20, 1889; "Colored Stars Badly Beaten," *Batavia News*, Jul 24, 1889; "Crandalls vs. Stars," *Buffalo Express*, June 20, 1889; "Over the Fence," *Buffalo Courier*, Jul 21, 1889; "Batavia, 21; Buffalo Stars, 4," *Buffalo (NY) News*, Jul 27, 1889; "Other Sporting News," *Buffalo (NY) Evening News*, Feb 11, 1890; "The Buffalo-Buck Horn Island League," *Buffalo Express*, May 10, 1891; "The Season Opened," *Niagara Falls (NY) Gazette*, May 13, 1891; "Colored Stars and almost Stars," *Buffalo Express*, Jun 7 1891; "Baseball Notes," *Buffalo Express*, Jun 12 1891; "Baseball Notes," *Buffalo Express*, Jun 13, 1891; "Base Hits," *Buffalo Express*, Jul 4, 1891; "Baseball Notes," *Buffalo Express*, Aug 13, 1891; "The Buffalo Stars Win," *Buffalo Evening News*, May 18, 1892.

Cuban Giants Base Ball Club (Buffalo, NY; 1890s–1900s). Organizer(s): Sam Bright and Oscar Bright.

The Cuban Giants B.B.C. organized in the 1890s, played black and white nines. *Buffalo Evening News* (May 22, 1899): "The Queens Citys played their second game of ball Sunday, with Harvey's Cuban Giants, and won by the score of 7 to 2." *Batavia News* (May 31, 1900): "The Batavia Baseball Club opened its season at Agricultural Park yesterday afternoon by defeating the Cuban Giants, a well-known Buffalo aggregation of colored players, by a score of 15 to 5. The game, which was an excellent one, was witnessed by about 850 people. The home team showed up in fine shape considering the short

time it has been organized. The visitors attributed their defeat, it is said, to the fact that their pitcher was in poor condition." *Buffalo Commercial* (June 25, 1900): "A scrappy game of baseball was witnessed by a very large crowd at Island Park yesterday. The 19th Centurys had the lead up to the fifth inning when Bufohl was taken with violent pains and was obliged to retire in the sixth inning. Knorr was substituted and held the Giants down in fine style. Hagen [of the Cuban Giants] was very effective at times and pitched a remarkably good game, having ten strike outs to his credit. The game was noted for its sharp playing at critical times, the features of the game were the sharp infielding of both teams."

SOURCES: "Amateur Baseball," *Buffalo (NY) Evening News*, May 22, 1899; "Oakdales, 14; Cuban Giants, 8," *Buffalo (NY) Express*, May 28, 1900; "Won Its First Game," *Batavia (NY) News*, May 31, 1900; "19th Centurys Won," *Buffalo (NY) Commercial*, June 25, 1900; "Amateur Baseball News," *Buffalo Commercial*, July 16, 1900.

Genesee Hotel Base Ball Club (Buffalo, NY; 1880s)

The Genesee Hotel B.B.C. organized in the 1880s. The team, composed of waiters, played black nines. *Buffalo Commercial* (August 12, 1884): "The Genesee and City Club nines (colored), having each won a game, the deciding match for superiority will be played at Olympic Park Thursday afternoon next. A small admission fee will be charged." *Buffalo Courier* (August 15, 1884): "The game between the Genesee and City (colored) base-ball clubs drew quite a large crowd to Olympic Park yesterday afternoon. The players from the Genesee proved themselves regular and true willow wielders and walked all over the City people, winning the game in seven innings. The score stood 14 to 9." They reorganized in 1885. *Commercial* (May 13, 1885): "The nine from the Hotel Genesee defeated the City Club nine 16 to 15 yesterday." The waiters of Buffalo and Rochester developed a rivalry. The Genesee Club participated in a black tournament at Lockport, NY, which included Niagara Falls Internationals, and Lockport's Dauntless and Home Club nines. *Lockport Journal* (August 13, 1884): "The baseball games on the fairgrounds between the colored clubs yesterday afternoon were quite exciting and some good playing was done between the Dauntless of this city, and the Genesee of Buffalo, the score standing 4 to 3 in favor of the Buffalo nine. The latter also defeated the Internationals of Niagara Falls by a score of 15 to 5."

SOURCES: "Brief Mention," *Buffalo (NY) Express*, Aug 9, 1884; "Our Colored Citizens," *Lockport (NY) Journal*, Aug 9, 1884; "The Ball Games Thursday," *Lockport Journal*, Aug 13, 1884; "Game Between Colored Amateurs," *Buffalo (NY) Courier*, Aug 15, 1884; "Brief Mention," *Buffalo Express*, Aug 21, 1884; "Sporting Matters," *Buffalo (NY) Evening Telegraph*, Sep 12, 1884; "Town Talk," *Buffalo (NY) Evening Telegraph*, May 13, 1885; "Town Talk," *Buffalo (NY) Commercial*, May 13, 1885; "Sporting Matters," *Buffalo Evening Telegraph*, Jun 13, 1885.

Invincible Base Ball Club. (Buffalo, NY, 1860s–1870s). Organizer(s): George Leggett and Frank Leonard.

The Invincible B.B.C. organized in the 1860s. The Invincible nine belonged to baseball's hotel-waiter subculture: they worked at Buffalo's Johnny Macs and the Tift house, and played black teams. *Buffalo Commercial* (August 6, 1869): "The Fearless club of Utica, and the Invincibles of this city, contested yesterday on the Sixth Street grounds, for the State championship among colored clubs. The game attracted quite a crowd of spectators. The Invincibles proved themselves decidedly vincible, as will be seen by the score of 88 to 18 runs in favor of the Utica boys." *Buffalo Courier and Republic* (October 20, 1868): "the colored people have caught the base-ball mania," adding the following: "The Lockport Excelsiors and Buffalo Invincibles (both colored troupes) met on the Perews grounds, and played a game which resulted in the Buffalo boys coming off victorious by considerable odds. The colored troops, we are assured by an eye witness, fought nobly." In 1869, the club was renamed Mutuals.

SOURCES: "Base Ball," *Buffalo (NY) Courier and Republic*, Oct 20, 1868; "Base Ball," *Buffalo Courier and Republic*, Jun 8, 1869; "The Base Ball Field," *New York (NY) Spirit of the Times*, Aug 1869; "Base Ball," *Buffalo (NY) Evening Telegraph*, Aug 3, 1869; "Base Ball," *Buffalo Courier and Republic*, Aug 4, 1869; "Base Ball," *Buffalo Courier and Republic*, Aug 6, 1869; "Base Ball," *Buffalo (NY) Commercial*, Aug 6, 1869; "Base Ball & c.," *Buffalo Evening Telegraph*, Aug 6, 1869; "Base Ball," *Buffalo Courier and Republic*, Aug 10, 1869; "Base Ball," *Washington (DC) Evening Star*, Aug 29, 1870.

Mutual Base Ball Club (Buffalo, NY; 1860s–1870s). Organizer(s): Frank Leonard, Thomas Clark, Thomas H. Wilson and George H. WA.

The Mutual B.B.C. organized in the 1869, played black teams. *Buffalo Express* (August 19, 1870): "A match game of ball will be played on the grounds at the corner of York and Sixth Streets, this week, Saturday afternoon, between the Mutual Base Ball Club, of Washington, D.C., and the Mutual Base Ball Club of Buffalo The members of both clubs are colored men."

SOURCES: "Base Ball," *Buffalo (NY) Express*, Oct 7, 1869; "Base Ball," *Buffalo (NY) Evening Post*, Oct 7, 1869; "Base Ball," *Buffalo (NY) Evening Telegraph*, Oct 7, 1869 "Base Ball Notes," *Buffalo Express*, Aug 19, 1870; "Base Ball," *Buffalo (NY) Courier*, Aug 24, 1870; "The Colored Base Ball Match," *Buffalo (NY) Evening Courier and Republic*, Aug 27, 1870.

Heavy Hitters Base Ball Club (Canajoharie, NY; 1860s—1880s)

The Heavy Hitters B.B.C. organized in 1865. The "Heavy Hitters" played against black clubs. In 1868, Schenectady's Excelsior nine and the Heavy Hitters crossed bats. *Schenectady Evening Star* (September 21, 1868): "The Heavy Hitters, a colored baseball club from Africa or some other place played a match game of baseball with a club belonging in Schenectady today on the flats. The Heavy Hitters were wictorius. De sclub from dis place feel werry badly satisfied. No further particulars." Between 1867 and 1871, they regularly played Utica's Fearless club. *Utica Observer* (September 27, 1868): "The Heavy Hitters knocked the Wide Awakes insensible in a base-ball match. Score, 17 to 5. The Wide Awakes received badges and bandages from the ladies, and by evening were in condition to unite with their friends in an ice cream festival held in Keller Hall." The team developed a rivalry with Little Falls. *Little Falls New Register* (July 28, 1887): "The Rocktons, of Little Falls, and Heavy Hitters, of Canajoharie, will soon play a match game of ball for $50. In the two games played Little Falls have been victorious. Both are colored nines."

SOURCES: *Schenectady (NY) Evening Star*, Sep 19, 1868; "Very Base Ball," *Schenectady Evening Star*, Sep 21, 1868; *Schenectady Evening Star*, Sep 26, 1868; "Base Ball," *Utica (NY) Observer*, Sep 27, 1868; "Base Ball Matters," *Utica (NY) Morning Herald*, Oct 1, 1868; "Base Ball," *Utica Observer*, Oct 1, 1868; "Black Ball," *Schenectady Evening Star*, Oct 5, 1868; "Events of the Week," *Utica (NY) Weekly Herald*, Sep 14, 1869; "Fearless and Heavy Hitters," *Utica Observer*, Sep 21, 1869; "Heavy Hitters vs. Fearless," *Utica Morning Herald*, Oct 1, 1869; "At Little Falls Yesterday," *Utica Observer*, May 25, 1870; *Gloversville (NY) Intelligencer*, Sep 19, 1875; "Local and General," *Fort Plain (NY) Mohawk Valley Register*, Jun 11, 1877; "Home News," *Little Falls (NY) Evening Times*, Jul 18, 1887; "Base Ball," *Little Falls Evening Times*, Jul 22, 1887; "Little Falls," *Newton (NY) Register*, Jul 28, 1887; "Little Falls," *Newton Register*, Jul 28, 1887; "Base Ball," *Utica Morning Herald*, May 18, 1889.

Hotel Kaaterskill Base Ball Club (Catskill, NY; 1880s–1890s). Organizer(s): John West.

The Hotel Kaaterskill B.B.C. organized in the 1880s, played white and black teams. *New York Age* (August 2, 1890): "Last week two baseball teams were organized under the names of Kaaterskill and Kaaterskill Reserves [white]. The former is composed entirely of whites and the latter of colored waiters. On Tuesday Captain Munsenheimer of the Kaaterskill and John West of the Kaaterskill reserve crossed bats and a decisive battle ensued, in which the colored team were defeated by a score of 9 to 9."

SOURCES: "Doings at Kaaterskill Peak," *New York (NY) Age*, Jul 13, 1890; "At Kaaterskill Peak," *New York Age*, Aug 2, 1890; "Hotel Kaaterskill," *Richmond (VA) Planet*, Aug 9, 1890; "The Field of Sport," *Indianapolis (IN) Freeman*, Aug 23, 1890; *New York (NY) Times*, Aug 21, 1892; "Waiters Won the Game," *New York (NY) World*, Aug 21, 1892.

Union Base Ball Club (Catskill, NY; 1860s–1870s)

The Union B.B.C. organized in the late 1860s, played against white and black nines. *Hudson Evening Register* (October 28, 1869): "The colored persuasion of Catskill having imbued with the same spirit as the 'white trash,' had a base-ball soiree at Catskill on Tuesday. Upon this occasion, they broke the friendly lance with the Independents of Ulster, and skunked them badly in five innings. The game stood Unions of Catskill 36, Independents of Kingston 7. Ex-senator [William V.] Fiero's darkey was captain of the Catskill nine, and pus on lots of airs over his victory." The club, of "Fiero's darkey," was composed of black waiters of the local resort hotels. Black and white inhabitants of Catskill and Cooperstown regularly organized joint dances and balls. By the 1870s, black clubs of Catskill and Hudson had developed a rivalry. *Evening Register* (July 17, 1874): "A return game of base-ball was played in this city, on Saturday, between the colored clubs, the Iron Sides, of Hudson, and the Unions, of Catskill. Games stood at its close Unions, 38; Iron Sides, 11. It was said to have been, by those present, a strong game." *Poughkeepsie Eagle* (August 9, 1876): "The Union Stars defeated the Resolutes [of Poughkeepsie] yesterday by a score of 20 to 5."

SOURCES: "Base Ball at Catskill," *Hudson (NY) Evening Register*, Oct 28, 1869; "Mokes on a Spree," *Hudson Evening Register*, Jul 17, 1874; "War of the Races at Catskill," *Hudson Evening Register*, Sep 7, 1874; "Base Ball Games," *Hudson Evening Register*, May 24, 1875; "Base Ball," *Poughkeepsie (NY) Eagle*, Aug 9, 1876.

Messenger Base Ball Club (Catskill, NY; 1870s)

The Messenger B.B.C. organized in the 1870s, played black teams. *Catskill Recorder* (October 8, 1875): "The Messengers of Catskill and the Reindeers of Coxsackle, both colored nines, played at the latter place Tuesday. Catskill won 28 to 25. They claim the championship of the river, having won all their games thus far."

SOURCES: "Horse Notes, Base Ball, Etc.," *Catskill (NY) Recorder*, Oct 8, 1875.

Lone Star Base Ball Club (Cold Springs, NY; 1870s–1880s)

The Lone Star B.B.C. organized in 1874, played black teams. The Lone Stars sparked interest regarding their town of origin. *Cold Springs Recorder* (June 22, 1874): "The Lone Star Club (colored) of Cold Springs, came to this city, this morning, to play the Butter Flies (colored) [Poughkeepsie]. The game is in progress in this p.m., on the P & E Grounds. A crowd is in attendance." *Cold Springs Recorder* (June 23, 1888): "In the [Poughkeepsie] *Press* of week before last, the darkey Lone Stars were said to be from Cold Spring, and we were upon the point of informing that paper that there had not been enough colored boys in town to make a nine, since the last century.

It now seems that the moaks hail from Newburgh, but *Press* says nothing about its former blunder. The Lone Stars, it seems, were composed of players from Newburgh and Cold Springs."

SOURCES: "Vicinity News," *Cold Springs (NY) Recorder*, Jun 22, 1874; "Base Ball," *Cold Springs Recorder*, Jun 9, 1888; "Base Ball," *Cold Springs Recorder*, Jun 23, 1888; "Nelsonville," *Cold Springs Recorder*, Jul 28, 1888.

Casino Base Ball Club (Elmira, NY; 1870s–1900s). Organizer(s): James E. Hazzard.

The Casino B.B.C. organized in the 1870s, played black and white teams. *Williamsport Bulletin and Gazette* (September 11, 1877): "The Lumber City Base Ball Club (colored), of Williamsport, champions of Pennsylvania, will play a game of ball with the Casinos (colored), of Elmira, for the championship, on Friday of this week at the Driving Park. The manager of this game is Mr. James E. Hazzard, of this city [Elmira], an acknowledged authority in base-ball, a great lover of the game, and himself a player of no diminutive qualifications. The admission to the grounds will be the usual. We predict a brilliant game, as there are 'no sticks' in the Lumber Club, while the Casinos can gyrate the festive diamond in a manner that is very suggestive of victory." *Gazette and Bulletin* (September 17, 1877): "The game of base–ball at Elmira on Friday last between the Lumber City Club, of Williamsport, and the Casinos, of Elmira, resulted in a victory for the Elmira Club by a score of eleven to six. The game at the commencement of the ninth inning was in favor of the Lumber Citys, and they would have no doubt won the game had it not been for their catcher, who it is claimed, sold them out." They participated in Emancipation Day celebrations, and the Casinos played Rochester's Douglass League nine. *Rochester Democrat Chronicle* (August 6, 1891): "At 4 o'clock this afternoon there will be a game of base-ball at Culver Park between the Elmira Casinos and a team from the Douglass League." They developed a rivalry with the Livingstons, a hotel waiters of Rochester, NY. *Elmira Telegram* (August 10, 1894): "The greatest ball game of the season will be played at the Fair Grounds next Tuesday, between the two colored clubs, Casinos, of Elmira, and Livingstons, of Rochester. The clubs were to have played on Emancipation Day and were both anxious for it, but the elements forbade, and the game was postponed. Go to see them if you want to see base-ball and hear coaching that is funnier than a minstrel show." They played Binghamton's Cuban Stars. *Elmira Gazette* (August 11, 1894): "The ball game between the two colored clubs at Driving Park yesterday was a success, as far as finances were concerned. The clubs were the Cuban Stars of Binghamton and the Casinos of this city. The Casinos played the best ball and 26 runs to a few of the visitors. E. Thompson was in the box for the Casinos and E. Daily, a one-armed man, and W. Dangerfield did the pitching for the visitors." The Casinos played against white nines. *Elmira Gazette* (September 8, 1894): "The Southport Stars yesterday defeated the Casinos at a game of ball by a score of ten to six. Stars battery was Conway and Harrington and the Casinos, Thompson and Strong."

SOURCES: "The Events of the Season," *Williamsport (PA) Gazette and Bulletin*, Sep 11, 1877; "The Great Combat Today," *Williamsport Gazette and Bulletin*, Sep 14, 1877; "The Great Contest," *Williamsport Gazette and Bulletin*, Sep 17, 1877; "A Challenge," *Williamsport Gazette and Bulletin*, Oct 13, 1877; "Livingstons vs. Casinos," *Elmira (NY) Telegram*, Aug 24, 1890; "Base Ball at Rochester," *New York (NY) Age*, Sep 27, 1890; "Emancipation Day," *Rochester (NY) Democrat and Chronicle*, Aug 6, 1891; "Minor Locals," *Elmira (NY) Gazette*, Jul 2, 1894; "Briefs," *Elmira Gazette*, Jul 12, 1894; "Successful Excursion," *Elmira Telegram*, Jul 22, 1894; "Elmira Boys Win," *Elmira Gazette*, Aug 10, 1894; "Elmira Versus Casinos," *Elmira Telegram*, Aug 10,

1894; *Elmira Telegram*, Aug 11, 1894; "Minor Locals," *Elmira Gazette*, Sep 8, 1894; "Minor and Locals," *Elmira Gazette*, May 16, 1895; *Elmira Gazette*, Jun 28, 1895; "Vicinity Department," *Elmira Gazette*, Jun 28, 1895.

Colored Base Ball Club (Flushing, NY; 1880s)

The Colored B.B.C. organized in the 1800s, played black nines. *Newton Register* (May 30, 1878): "The Colored Base Ball Club, of this village, play a match game with the Flushing Club, on the commons, this afternoon." *Flushing Times* (June 4, 1879): "In a match game between the colored base-ball tossers of Flushing and Newton, in which the Flushing boys were victorious by one run. During the game Jack martin, of the Newton club, was knocked senseless by a bat being thrown from the hands of the batter." *Register* (June 5, 1879): "In the afternoon a colored club from Flushing was matched against a club of colored players from this village [Newton] and returned home victory by one point. The game was very interesting, the principal excitement arising from the disputes that followed each other in quick succession, and the difficulty experienced by the umpire in satisfactory deciding the innumerable questions of judgment. Jack Martin received a knock down hit from a club in the hands of a careless batter and was carried off the field."

SOURCES: "Local," *Newton (NY) Newtown Register*, May 30, 1878; "Local," *Flushing (NY) Times*, Jun 4, 1879; "Local," *Newton Newtown Register*, Jun 5, 1879.

Bartholdi Base Ball Club (Flushing, NY; 1880s)

The Bartholdi B.B.C. organized in 1886. The Bartholdi nine played a benefit to raise funds in support of the Statue of Liberty project. *New York Freeman* (May 22, 1886): "About 150 persons gathered in Flushing, New York to witness the baseball game between the Flushing team and the Bartholdi Club, of New York, which resulted in a victory for the latter, the score being 12 to 10."

SOURCES: "Local Gossip," *New York (NY) Freeman*, Jan 23, 1886; "Local Gossip," *New York Freeman*, May 22, 1886.

Flushing Base Ball Club (Flushing, NY; 1880s)

The Flushing B.B.C. organized in the 1880s, played black nines. The Flushings played a benefit to raise funds in support of the Statue of Liberty project. *New York Freeman* (May 22, 1886): "About 150 persons gathered in Flushing, New York to witness the baseball game between the Flushing team and the Bartholdi Club, of New York, which resulted in a victory for the latter, the score being 12 to 10."

SOURCES: "Local Gossip," *New York (NY) Freeman*, Jan 23, 1886; "Local Gossip," *New York Freeman*, May 22, 1886.

Hunter Base Ball Club (Flushing, NY; 1850s–1860s)

The Hunter B.B.C. organized in the 1850s, played black teams. *Jamaica Long Island Farmer* (December 28, 1858): "This darkies in this village and Flushing determined not to be outdone by their white brethren, have recently organized a Club under the name of the Henson Base Ball Club of Jamaica and the Hunter Base Ball Club of Flushing. The first match between these two Clubs was played on Saturday last at Flushing and resulted in the defeat of the Henson Club by 15 runs. The return match will be played in this village on Saturday next, January 1st."

SOURCES: "Base Ball Match," *Jamaica (NY) Long Island Farmer*, Dec 28, 1858.

Colored Giants (Cuban) Base Ball Club (Geneva, NY; 1890s–1900s). Owner(s): F. J. Hardy.

The Colored Giants (Cuban) B.B.C. organized in the 1890s, played black and white teams. *Geneva Times* (June 15, 1895): "The Colored Giants, of Geneva, are in Syracuse today where they will cross bats with a nine composed of Onondaga Indians. The Geneva Club, under the management of F. J. Hardy is made up as follows: George Martin, John Rowe, Charles Granston, Bert Hazzard, H. F. Kenny, Avery Griger, W. Coleman, Frank Davis and Arthur Kinney." *Geneva Times* (May 24, 1900): "The Geneva Colored Athletic Association Base Ball Team had its first game yesterday at Pre-Emption Park with the Newark High School team. The match resulted in a score of 18 to 7 in favor of Newark. The colored population turned out I force to witness the game. The Geneva men deserve much credit for the manner in which they defended themselves. Derby, as a catcher, with a little training, will be a winner. Kinney was proved clever as an amateur pitcher. His delivery was speedy at times. The colored teams made several bad fumbles but with practice promise to eclipse the teams they play in the future."

SOURCES: "Home and Vicinity," *Geneva (NY) Times*, Aug 29, 1894; "City Briefs," *Geneva Times*, Jun 12, 1895; "City Briefs," *Geneva Times*, Jun 15, 1895; "Sport," *Geneva Times*, May 21, 1900; "Ball Game in Progress," *Geneva Times*, May 23, 1900; "Colored Men Defeated," *Geneva Times*, May 24, 1900; "Sport," *Geneva Times*, May 29, 1900; "Sport," *Geneva Times*, Jun 1, 1900; "Sport," *Geneva Times*, Jun 14, 1900; "News Condensed," *Geneva Times*, Jun 25, 1900; "News Condensed," *Geneva Times*, Jul 3, 1900; "News Condensed," *Geneva Times*, Aug 2, 1900.

Flies Base Ball Club (Geneva, NY; 1880s). Organizer(s): B. F. Cleggett, G. W. Allen and Henry Harden.

The Flies B.B.C. organized in the 1880s. The "Flies" played black nines. *Geneva Gazette* (August 20, 1880): "The plan already announced for a tournament of colored base-ball players in Geneva, will be carried into effect. B. F. Cleggett was made president; G. W. Allen, Treasurer; Henry Harden, Secretary; Henry Brown, Captain of the 'Flies,' Geneva nine." *Gazette* (September 17, 1880): "This sport, under the auspices of the colored people of Geneva, is still progressive at Pre-Emptive Park.... Second money prize, 430, was won by the Flies of Geneva, defeating the Stars and Auburns."

SOURCES: "Base Ball Tournament in Geneva," *Geneva (NY) Gazette*, Aug 20, 1880; "Grand Base Ball Tournament," *Geneva Gazette*, Sep 10, 1880; "Base Ball Tournament," *Geneva Gazette*, Sep 17, 1880.

None Such Base Ball Club (Geneva, NY; 1870s). Organizer(s): Harry Harden, Joseph Condol and Theodore Duffin.

The None Such B.B.C. organized in the 1870s. The nine played against white and black clubs. *Geneva Gazette* (September 10, 1880): "White vs. Black" or the "Resolute" against a nine composed of colored men, met for a friendly contest of base-ball on the cricket ground last Tuesday. From the first inning, it became apparent that the game was to be a one-sided affair—the Resolutes scoring therein 21 to 3 only for their opponents. The colored troops fought nobly up to the seventh innings, when they threw up the sponge, and consented the game be called—the score standing 73 to 15." They also played Utica's Fearless nine, a black club. *Geneva Gazette* (September 19, 1876): "Theodore Duffin [of the Geneva club] says the visitors were lightnin' in the game with a little of nitro glycerin in reserve for emergencies."

SOURCES: *Geneva (NY) Gazette*, Sep 4, 1876; "Local Affairs," *Geneva (NY) Courier*, Sep 12, 1876; "Local Affairs," *Geneva Courier*, Sep 13, 1876; "Vicinity Items," *Geneva Gazette*, Sep 15, 1876; "Colored Base Ballists," *Geneva Gazette*, Sep 20, 1876; "Vicinity Items," *Geneva Gazette*, Sep 22, 1876; "Base Ball," *Utica (NY) Morning Herald*, Sep 25, 1876.

Athletic Base Ball Club (Gloversville, NY; 1880s–1900s). Organizer(s): James E. Miller and W. H. Freeman.

The Athletic B.B.C. organized in the 1880s, played black teams. *Gloversville Leader* (August 3, 1892): "The colored Athletics of this city left this morning for Utica, where they will play the Fear baseball team of that city in a match game today." *Leader* (August 4, 1892): "The game of base-ball at Utica yesterday between the colored Athletics of this city and the Fearless team of Utica, resulted in a defeat for the local team by a score of 10 to 6." *Leader* (September 8, 1893): "The waiters of the Adirondack Hotel at Sacandaga Park, which comprises nearly all of the Athletics of this city, will meet the Northville team in a game of baseball Wednesday afternoon for a purse of $10." *Leader* (September 8, 1893): "The colored Athletics of this city went to Troy this morning to meet the Hannibals of that city on their diamond. They announced that a return game will be played here next Thursday."

SOURCES: "A Bird's Eye View," *Gloversville (NY) Leader*, Aug 6, 1889; "A Bird's Eye View," *Gloversville Leader*, Aug 23, 1889; "Local Record," *Gloversville Leader*, Jul 9, 1891; "Local Record," *Gloversville Leader*, Jul 10, 1891; "Local Record," *Gloversville Leader*, Jul 14, 1891; "Colored People's Picnic," *Gloversville Leader*, Jul 14, 1891; "Local Record," *Gloversville Leader*, Jul 11, 1891; "Local Record," *Gloversville Leader*, Aug 13, 1891; "Local Record," *Gloversville Leader*, May 16, 1892; "Local and Briefs," *Johnston (NY) Republican*, May 17, 1892; "Local Record," *Gloversville Leader*, May 31, 1892; "Local Record," *Gloversville Leader*, Jul 22, 1892; "Local Record," *Gloversville Leader*, Aug 3, 1892; "Local Record," *Gloversville Leader*, Aug 4, 1892; "Local Record," *Gloversville Leader*, Sep 8, 1893.

Fly Away Base Ball Club (Gloversville, NY; 1870s)

The Fly Away B.B.C. organized in the 1870, played black teams. *Gloversville Intelligencer* (July 9, 1871): "The Hannibals, of Troy, and the Flyaways of this village, (both colored clubs), played on a match game on the Union Fair Grounds, on Monday afternoon last, resulting in favor of the Hannibals, by a score of 39 to 34. Both clubs played splendidly." *Intelligencer* (July 20, 1871): "On Monday, two exciting games of ball were played on the Fair grounds. The first game was for a silver mounted bat, and was contested for by the Fly Aways of Gloversville, and the Wide Awakes, of this village (colored clubs). The Gloversville club flew away with the Wide Awakes b y a score of 21 to 18." They played Troy's Hannibal nine. *Troy Whig* (July 25, 1871): "The game played yesterday afternoon on the Haymakers' grounds between the Fly Aways of Gloversville and Hannibals of this city—both colored clubs attracted quite a good-sized audience, and furnished abundant entertainment for all who were present."

SOURCES: *Utica (NY) Observer*, Jul 22, 1870; "The Colored Championship," *New York (NY) Herald*, Jul 24, 1870; "Base Ball," *Troy (NY) Whig*, Jun 26, 1871; "Base Ball," *Troy Whig*, Jun 27, 1871; "Base Ball," *Troy (NY) Times*, Jul 18, 1871; "Base Ball," *Troy Times*, Jul 25, 1871; "Johnston and Vicinity," *Gloversville (NY) Intelligencer*, Jul 9, 1871; "Base Ball," *Gloversville Intelligencer*, Jul 20, 1871; *New York (NY) Spirit of the Times*, Aug 5, 1871.

Everett (Blue Stocking) Base Ball Club (Goshen, NY; 1880s). Organizer(s): Riley Mines and G. W. Jackson.

The Everett (Blue Stocking) B.B.C., of Port Jervis, NY, organized in the 1880s, played nines. Its rival was Port Jervis, NY. *Port Jervis Evening Gazette* (September 9, 1886): "A game of base-ball will be played on the Main Street grounds Thursday, September 9th, by two colored clubs, the Everetts of Goshen and Red Stockings of Port Jervis. Game called at 2:30 o'clock. An exciting game may be expected." *Evening Gazette* (September 10, 1886): "A closely contested game of base-ball was played on the Main Street grounds Thursday afternoon, between two colored clubs, the Everetts of Goshen, and Red Stockings of this village. The home club held the lead up to the eighth inning by a score of 8 to 6, but errors in the eighth and ninth innings gave five runs and the game to the Everetts." *Port Jervis Tri-States Union* (September 16, 1886): "The Red Stockings of Port Jervis and the Blue Stockings [Everetts] of Goshen, both colored, played a game on the Main Street grounds in this place Tuesday afternoon, it was sharply contested, and was won by the Goshen nine on a score of 13 to 11."

Sources: "Red Stockings Go to Goshen," *Port Jervis (NY) Evening Gazette*, Sep 25, 1885; "Paragraphs from Far and Near," *Port Jervis Evening Gazette*, Aug 25, 1886; "Paragraphs from Far and Near," *Port Jervis Evening Gazette*, Sep 9, 1886; "Base Ball By Colored Players," *Port Jervis Evening Gazette*, Sep 10, 1886; *Port Jervis (NY) Tri-States Union*, Sep 16, 1886; "Goshen," *Middletown (NY) Argus*, Aug 10, 1887.

Hemlock Base Ball Club (Goshen, NY; 1870s). Organizer(s): "Captain Sam" and Riley Mines.

The Hemlock B.B.C. organized in the 1870s, played black teams. *Middletown Argus* (July 20, 1877): "The Hemlock Base Ball Club of Goshen have accepted the challenge of the Lilies of this town [Middletown], Samuel Beasley, Captain, to play a colored match at the Orange Pleasure Ground tomorrow afternoon." *Middletown Press* (July 23, 1877): "A match game of base-ball between the colored clubs of Middletown and Goshen here on Saturday, the Water Lilies of the former place [Middletown] were victorious over the Hemlocks of the latter place by a score of 35 to 30."

Sources: "Base Ball," *Middletown (NY) Press*, Sep 23, 1876; "Local Notes," *Middletown (NY) Argus*, Jul 20, 1877; "Base Ball Notes," *Middletown Press*, Jul 23, 1877.

Orange County Cuban Base Ball Club (Goshen, NY; 1890s). Organizer(s): Bob Broadhead.

The Orange County Cuban B.B.C. organized in the 1890s. *Middleton Argus* (July 13, 1894): "Bobby Broadhead's delegation of dusky ball players went to Port Jervis, yesterday, and were defeated by the Port Jervisites by a score of 10 to 7. Captain Broadhead says they will play a return game here shortly, and predicts that then the results will be different." *Middleton Argus* (August 16, 1894): "The Orange County Cubans (colored) Base Ball Club will play a game of ball on the Driving Park Saturday, at 3pm, with the Montgomerys. This will be the attraction of the season, and the only cullahed ball players that ever played here."

Sources: "At the County Seat," *Middletown (NY) Argus*, Jul 13, 1894; "At the County Seat," *Middletown Argus*, Jul 13, 1894; "At the County Seat," *Middletown Argus*, Jul 21, 1894; "At the County Seat," *Middletown Argus*, Jul 30, 1894; "Emancipation Day Picnic," *Middletown Argus*, Aug 10, 1894; "Montgomery," *Middletown Argus*, Aug 16, 1894.

St. Elmo Hotel Base Ball Club (Goshen, NY; 1890s)

The St. Elmo Hotel B.B.C. organized in the 1890, if not earlier. The waiters played black teams. *Middleton Times* (August 1, 1892): "On Saturday last the Port Jervis Red Stockings, an aggregation of colored talent, came to Goshen to attempt to give Jim Green's club a severe drubbing on the baseball field." *Port Jervis Union* (August 1, 1892): "Saturday the Red Stockings of Port Jervis and the St. Elmos of Goshen played a match game at the latter place; Score St. Elmos; 9; Red Stockings, 8. This is the first of a series of three games to be played for $50."

Sources: "Goshen," *Middletown (NY) Times*, Jun 30, 1892; "Goshen," *Middletown Times*, Jul 28, 1892; "Goshen vs. Port Jervis," *Middletown Times*, Aug 1, 1892; "Base Ball," *Port Jervis (NY) Union*, Aug 1, 1892.

Colored Giants Base Ball Club (Greater New York, NY; 1890s)

The Colored Giants B.B.C. organized in the 1890s, played black and white clubs. *New York Herald* (August 24, 1891): "The newly organized Colored Giants made their first appearance at Atlantic Park, Long Island yesterday. Their opponents were the Nationals, of Brooklyn. The colored ball tossers could not play a little bit." The team's on-the-field performance, melding scientific play to the aesthetic theatrical style that enhanced the spectators' entertainment experience. *New York Sun* (May 21, 1898): "[The Colored Giants] kept up a continuous series of funny antics while at the bat which caused much laughter. One of their acts was to line up, five or six at a time, while one man at the bat as though they expected to tally runs by the score. However, the line-ups resulted harmlessly." *New York Press* (May 15, 1899): "B. M. Butler, manager of the Colored New Yorks, starts on his tour today up to Hudson in conjunction with the Chinese Giants and a Chinese band. They will play exhibition games in the following towns: Poughkeepsie, Hudson, Newburgh, Catskill and Yonkers." *Brooklyn Eagle* (May 21, 1899): "As exponents of how not to play the national game, the Chinese Giants are a thrilling success. It was funny for one inning only. In that time, the Colored New Yorks showed that they were simply having fun with the Mongolians and after the glamour of seeing a team of Celestials on the diamond had worn off, many of the spectators left the grounds."

Sources: "This Team is a Failure," *New York (NY) Herald*, Aug 24, 1891; "Base Ball Notes," *New York (NY) Sun*, May 21, 1898; "Games on the Diamond," *Jersey City (NJ) Journal*, Aug 22, 1898; "Among Local Ball Tossers," *New York (NY) Press*, May 15, 1899; "Colored New Yorks Win," *Brooklyn (NY) Eagle*, May 21, 1899.

Mutual Base Ball Club (Greenport, NY; 1870s)

The Mutual B.B.C. organized in the 1870s, played black clubs. *Southold Long Island Traveler* (March 5, 1874): "On Monday of last week, a colored base-ball club from Greenport went to Jamesport and played a game with a colored club of that place. The Greenporters beat by a score of 88 to 9, in eight innings, making 25 runs in the second inning. We are informed that on leaving all that could be seen of the Jamesport club were the whites of their eyes." *Long Island Traveler* (March 12, 1874): "The return game of base-ball between the Mutuals of this place and the Rising Stars of Northville (both colored0 was played in this village on Thursday. The Greenporters beat by a score of 51 to 4. The Stars rode into the village with flags flying. On taking the field they shone brightly, but when the contest ended they were obscured by a dark cloud, and the flag could be seen perceived as they drove home. *Long Island Traveler* (March 19, 1874): "The Irving Jr. Base Ball Club of Southold [white] played a match game of ball with the Mutual Club (colored) of Greenport, on Saturday, March 14th, and defeated them by a splendid score." They reorganized in 1876. *Sag Harbor Corrector* (June 13, 1876): "The Atlantics, of Sag Harbor, and Mutuals of Greenport, played their third trial game of Base-Ball on Monday, at the grounds on Bay Street. The game was well-played and resulted in a victory for the Atlantics, the score standing 7 to 4. Both clubs consist of colored Americans."

Sources: "Greenport," *Southold (NY) Long Island Traveler*, Mar 4, 1874; "Base Ball," *Southold Long Island Traveler*, Mar 12, 1874; "Greenport," *Southold Long Island Traveler*, Mar 19, 1874; "Base Ball," *Sag Harbor (NY) Corrector*, Jun 13, 1876

Colored Giants Base Ball Club (Harlem, NY; 1890s)

The Colored Giants B.B.C. organized in the 1890s, played black and white aggregations. *Carmel Putnam County Courier* (June 4, 1897): "The Brewster Base Ball Club won an easy victory over the Colored Giants of Harlem, on Saturday last, and in the first inning scored enough runs to win the game had they played ball. The colored pitchers were easy marks and their support was more than poor. They home team expected to have had a hard time to defeat the colored troupe, but were quite disappointed at the weak showing, as were the large gathering of spectators who attended the game." *Jersey City Journal* (June 11, 1897): "The Colored Giants, of Harlem, will introduce Styles and Boland, the well-known colored boxers, who are also clever ball players."

SOURCES: "Brewster News," *Carmel (NY) Putnam County Courier*, Jun 4, 1897; "A Rest for the Nines," *Jersey City (NJ) Journal*, Jun 10, 1897; "News of the Diamond," *Jersey City Journal*, Jun 11, 1897; "They Are At It Again," *Jersey City Journal*, Jun 12, 1897; "The Local Teams Won," *Jersey City Journal*, Jun 14, 1897.

Lone Star Base Ball Club (Harlem, NY; 1860s–1880s)

The Lone Star B.B.C. organized in 1860, played black nines. *Jamaica Farmer and Advertiser* (September 15, 1860): "The Henson Base Ball Club of this village will play a match game with the Lone Star Club of Harlem, on the grounds of the former in this village, on Wednesday (tomorrow)." By the late 1860s, the club had become a regular contender for the black championship of the State. The Williamsburg Uniques (later, the Brooklyn Uniques) played against the Lone Stars for the Colored Championship. *New York Clipper* (October 2, 1869): "The home and home games of the match between these crack colored clubs, the former [Unique] of Williamsburgh and the latter of Harlem came off at Ridgewood Park on September 23rd. The Uniques, who have held the championship for a number of seasons, were vanquished much to the surprise and disgust of their adherents. The Lone Stars talk of going Philadelphia to contend with the Pythians." *Clipper* (December 11, 1869): "The Lone Stars and Uniques (both colored), the former of Harlem and the latter of Brooklyn, played a sharp game for the championship, which had been held for a number of years by the Brooklynites. The score stood 8 to 6 in favor of the Lone Stars." *Brooklyn Eagle* (July 29, 1873): "Tomorrow there is to be a grand match at Capitoline grounds between the Ocean Club, of this city, and the Lone Star Club of Harlem, both champion clubs of their respective cities, composed of colored ball tossers of note." The organization participated as the only black team in Watertown's Base Ball Tournament. *Watertown Times* (September 10, 1873): "At 3:30 the Lone Stars of Harlem (a colored club) will play the Resolutes of Montpelier, Vermont." In 1875, the Lone Stars participated in a colored tournament at Hempstead, NY, involving Brooklyn's Quickstep, Brooklyn's Ocean, and Hempstead's Mutual organizations.

SOURCES: "Base Ball," *Jamaica (NY) Farmer and Advertiser*, Sep 15, 1860; "Unique vs. Lone Star," *New York (NY) Clipper*, Oct 2, 1869; "Base Ball," *New York Clipper*, Dec 11, 1869; "A Noteworthy Game," *Brooklyn (NY) Eagle*, Jul 29, 1873; "Amateur Games," *Brooklyn Eagle*, Jul 31, 1873; "Colored Champions," *New York (NY) World*, Jul 31, 1873; "A Noteworthy Game," *Brooklyn Eagle*, Jul 29, 1873; "Colored Champions," *New York World*, Jul 31, 1873; "The Amateur Arena," *Brooklyn Eagle*, Aug 5, 1873; "Tomorrow," *Watertown (NY) Times*, Sep 10, 1873; "Today," *Watertown Times*, Sep 11, 1873; "A Noteworthy Game," *Brooklyn Eagle*, Oct 18, 1877; "Base Ball," *Brooklyn (NY) Union and Argus*, Oct 18, 1877.

Mutual Base Ball Club (Hempstead, Long Island, NY; 1870s)

The Mutual B.B.C. organized in the 1870s, played black clubs. *Queens County Sentinel* (June 8, 1871): "A Base Ball Club, composed of gentlemen of color belonged to Jamaica, visited our village on Tuesday, and gave our fellow-citizens of African 'scent a specimen of their skill in the ball playing line. The score was 13 for the Jamaica Club and 8 for the Hempsteadites." The rivalry thrived into the 1870s. *Sentinel* (August 13, 1874): "The Mutuals of Hempstead, and the Hensons of Jamaica, play a game of ball on the old Enterprise grounds in this village on Saturday. Both clubs are composed of colored boys." *Sentinel* (August 20, 1874): "The game between the colored clubs

called for Saturday last was put off until Monday when the Jamaica Club [Lone Stars] visited this village and played a match with the Hempstead Club on the new Enterprise ground, beating the latter by three runs, the score standing 23 in favor of Jamaica to 20 for Hempstead."

SOURCES: *Hempstead (NY) Queens County Sentinel*, Jun 8, 1871; *Hempstead Queens County Sentinel*, Aug 13, 1874; *Hempstead Queens County Sentinel*, Aug 20, 1874; *Hempstead Queens County Sentinel*, Jul 22, 1875.

Brabender (Cuban Giant Juniors) Base Ball Club (Hudson, NY; 1880s–1890s). Organizer(s): Leander Deyo.

The Brabender B.B.C. organized in the 1880s, played black teams. *Hudson Evening Register* (July 22, 1889): "The Brabenders, a colored club of this city, will play the Trojans, a colored club of Troy, at Fountain Park grounds on Thursday. There will be a good game and more fun than was ever seen on a ball ground." *Evening Register* (August 16, 1889): "The Brabenders of this city (colored) and a colored club of Catskill are playing a game at Catskill village today." *Evening Register* (September 7, 1889): "A colored club calling itself the Brabenders made up in this city went to Riverside Park yesterday to play the Capital Citys (colored, of Albany, NY). The Albany Express calls them Cuban Giants, Jrs. Jackson and Deyo, of the Giants, made four hits apiece and did excellent work in the field."

SOURCES: "Base Ball Matters," *Hudson (NY) Evening Register*, Jul 13, 1889; "Base Ball Notes," *Hudson Evening Register*, Jul 22, 1889; "Around the Bases," *Hudson Evening Register*, Jul 26, 1889; "Base Ball Matters," *Hudson Evening Register*, Aug 16, 1889; "Base Ball Matters," *Hudson Evening Register*, Sep 7, 1889; "Base Ball Matters," *Hudson Evening Register*, Jun 19, 1890.

Iron Side Base Ball Club (Hudson, NY; 1870s)

The Iron Side B.B.C. organized in the 1870s, played against black nines. *Hudson Evening Register* (August 13, 1874): "A match game of base-ball was played on the Seminary Grounds, at Claverack, yesterday afternoon, between the Iron Sides and the Do-You-Ups of Hudson. The score stood 17 to 4, in favor of the Iron Sides. Both colored clubs." They reorganized in 1875. *Evening Register* (May 24, 1875): "A return game of base-ball was played in this city, on Saturday, between the colored clubs, the Iron Sides, of Hudson, and the Unions, of Catskill. Games stood at its close Unions, 38; Iron Sides, 11. It was said to have been, by those present, a strong game."

SOURCES: "Base Ball Games," *Hudson (NY) Evening Register*, Aug 13, 1874; "Base Ball Games," *Hudson Evening Register*, May 24, 1875.

Pioneer Base Ball Club (Hudson, NY; 1880s)

The Pioneer B.B.C. organized in the 1880s, played black clubs of NY and NJ. They developed a rivalry with Troy's Red Stockings. *Albany Evening Times* (June 1, 1889): "The Red Stockings of Troy and the Pioneers of Hudson, colored nines, played at the West Troy Grounds yesterday, and the Troy boys won, 15 to 8." *New York Age* (June 8, 1889): "About two hundred people attended the game of baseball on the West Troy ground Friday afternoon, between the Pioneers of this city and the Red Stockings of Hudson. Umpire Allen gave Troy the game, but the Hudson boys wanted to play it out. To satisfy them the Troy team played three more innings."

SOURCES: "Base Ball," *Albany (NY) Evening Times*, Jun 1, 1889; "Base Ball of Troy," *New York (NY) Age*, Jun 8, 1889; "Base Ball Matters," *Hudson (NY) Evening Gazette*, Sep 7, 1889.

Worth House Base Ball Club (Hudson, NY; 1880s–1890s)

The Worth House B.B.C. organized in the 1880s, if not earlier. The Worth House nine, composed of waiters, played similar organizations. *Hudson Evening Register* (July 13, 1889): "The game of base-ball played between the waiters of the Nelson House, this city, and the waiters of the Worth House, Hudson, played in the afternoon, showed that the Hudson boys were no match for the Poughkeepsians. The latter won the game by the score of 13 to 7. In the Nelson House nine R. Ross was the pitcher, Charles Treadway the catcher, and J. Rose, third base. In the Hudson nine Leandro Deyo was the pitcher, Mr. Hill the catcher, and Mr. Maw the third base man." *Rhinebeck Gazette* (September 29, 1889): "The game of base-ball played between the waiters of the Nelson House, Poughkeepsie and the waiters of the Worth House, Hudson, played in the afternoon, was won by the former by a score of 13 to 7."

SOURCES: "Base Ball Matters," *Hudson (NY) Evening Register*, Jul 13, 1889; "Base Ball Notes," *Hudson Evening Register*, July 22, 1889; "Around the Bases," *Hudson Evening Register*, July 26, 1889; "The County Fair," *Rhinebeck (NY) Gazette*, Sep 29, 1889.

Active Base Ball Club (Ithaca, NY; 1870s). Organizer(s): William H. Allen and William Benson.

The Active B.B.C. organized in the 1870s, played against black nines. *Utica Herald* (September 18, 1876): "The Fearless, of Utica, played the Actives, of Ithaca (both colored) at the latter place. The score published in the Ithaca papers is Fearless, 19; Actives, 20." The clubs split a season series. The Actives also participated in in a tournament, organized by Geneva's Flies, and consisting of Ithaca, Auburn, Geneva, and Utica.

SOURCES: "Base Ball," *Buffalo (NY) Evening Courier and Republic*, Aug 26, 1876; "Grand Base Ball Tournament," *Geneva (NY) Gazette*, Sep 10, 1876; "Local Affair," *Buffalo Courier*, Sep 13, 1876; "Vicinity Items," *Geneva Gazette*, Sep 15, 1876; "Base Ball Tournament," *Geneva Gazette*, Sep 17, 1876; "Champion Games," *Utica (NY) Herald*, Sep 18, 1876; "Base Ball," *Utica Herald*, Sep 25, 1876; "Base Ball," *Syracuse (NY) Standard*, Sep 25, 1876.

Colored Giants Base Ball Club (Ithaca, NY; 1890s–1900s)

The Colored Giants B.B.C. organized in the 1890s, played black and white teams. *Syracuse Standard* (August 1, 1897): "At the Driving Park a ball game between two colored teams, the Athens Browns of Athens, Pennsylvania, and the Ithaca Giants, will commence at 3:30 o'clock." *Ovid Independent* (August 25, 1900): "The manager of the Y.M.C.A. club went too Ithaca and engaged the Ithaca Giants, a fast club composed of gentlemen of color, to come up and amuse the home team for a little while, and done the job to the Queen's taste and no discount. The play was pretty from the start, and while many take little interest, or do not understand the game of baseball as she is played, they could not but be amused at the antics of the colored gentlemen from the university city, who kept the bleachers laughing at their droll remarks and fantastic capers on the diamond most of the time. The fielding of both teams was excellent, while the game itself was a pitchers' battle, each driving out the other in keeping down the score or,—keeping the batters from finding the ball."

SOURCES: "Negro's Emancipation Day," *Syracuse (NY) Standard*, August 1, 1897; "The Auburn Celebration," *Syracuse Standard*, Aug 6, 1897; "Ithaca's Colored Ball Players," *Ithaca (NY) Journal*, Aug 13, 1900; "Farmer," *Ovid (NY) Independent*, Aug 25, 1900; "Base Ball," *Farmer (NY) Review*, Aug 25, 1900; "Baseball Players Preparing for the Season," *Ithaca (NY) News*, May 3, 1902.

Forest City Base Ball Club (Ithaca, NY; 1880s). Organizer(s): Fred Stevens.

The Forest City B.B.C. organized in the 1880s, played black teams. *Ithaca Journal* (August 3, 1886): "The Forest Citys of this place will play the Wilkes-Barre, Pennsylvania, colored nine on the new grounds of the Susquehanna Hose Company at Owego, on Friday

next." *New York Freeman* (August 7, 1886): "Last Tuesday the Merry Makers of Geneva and the Forest City club played an exciting game of base-ball at the fairground. The home club won a decided victory, the score being 43 to 13." They defeated Auburn's black nine by a score of 27 to 7. In a rivalry with the Owego Imperials, the Forest Citys lost both home and away games. *Freeman* (August 18, 1886): "The Oswego baseball club again defeated the home team Monday afternoon in this city. It is evident from the first that the training and discipline of the Oswego nine were superior to ours."

SOURCES: "Sporting Matters," *Ithaca (NY) Journal*, Jun 13, 1884; "Sporting Notes," *Ithaca Journal*, Jul 23, 1886; "Sporting Notes," *Ithaca Journal*, Aug 3, 1886; "Local Record," *Owego (NY) Tioga County Record*, Aug 14, 1886; "Ithaca Inklings," *New York (NY) Freeman*, Aug 7, 1886; "Ithaca Inklings," *New York Freeman*, Aug 14, 1886; "Ithaca Inklings," *New York Freeman*, Aug 18, 1886; "Sporting Notes," *Geneva (NY) Gazette*, Sep 10, 1886; "Ithaca Inklings," *New York Freeman*, Jan 15, 1887.

Ithaca Hotel Base Ball Club (Ithaca, NY; 1890s)

The Ithaca Hotel B.B.C. organized in the 1890s, if not earlier. The hotel waiters played black teams. *Ithaca News* (May 25, 1899): "The colored waiters at the New Ithaca Hotel and Keystone Base Ball teams played a game of ball on their fairgrounds yesterday afternoon which resulted in the defeat of their Keystone team, in a score of 8 to 7. The batteries were Waiters, Gibbs, and Robinson; Keystones: Richard Jackson, Sharkey [Bert Clay], Eugene Smith and Walker."

SOURCES: "In Short," *Ithaca (NY) News*, Jul 16, 1897; "In Short," *Ithaca News*, Jul 21, 1897; "Keystones Defeated," *Ithaca News*, May 25, 1899.

Keystone Base Ball Club (Ithaca, NY; 1890s–1900s)

The Keystone B.B.C. organized in the 1890s, played black and white teams. *Ithaca Daily News*: "The colored waiters at the New Ithaca Hotel and Keystone Base Ball teams played a game of ball on their fairgrounds yesterday afternoon which resulted in the defeat of their Keystone team, in a score of 8 to 7. The batteries were Waiters, Gibbs, and Robinson; Keystones: Richard Jackson, Sharkey [Bert Clay], Eugene Smith and Walker."

SOURCES: *Rochester (NY) Democrat and Chronicle*, Aug 6, 1894; "Yates County," *Buffalo (NY) Evening News*, Aug 5, 1896; "In Short," *Ithaca (NY) News*, Jul 16, 1897; "In Short," *Ithaca News*, Jul 21, 1897; "Keystones Defeated," *Ithaca News*, May 25, 1899.

Henson Base Ball Club (Lone Star Base Ball Club) (Jamaica, NY (Long Island); 1850s–1890s). Owner(s): Robert Henson.

The Henson Lone Star B.B.C. one of the earliest black clubs in the East, organizing in the late–1850s. They played against black nines. *Jamaica Farmer and Advertiser* (December 28, 1858): "The Darkies in this village and Flushing determined not to be outdone by their white brethren, have recently organized a club under the name of the Henson Base Ball Club of Jamaica, and the Hunter Base Ball Club of Flushing. The first match between these two Clubs was played Saturday last at Flushing and resulted in the defeat of the Henson club by 15 runs. The return match will be played in this village on Saturday next, January 1st." The Unknowns played the Hensons. *New York Weekly Anglo-African* (November 15, 1859): "A match game was played between the Henson base Ball Club of Jamaica and the Unknown, of Weeksville, at Jamaica, Long Island, on Tuesday, November 15th, which resulted in another victory for the Henson." The Hensons played against the Harlem Lone Stars. *Jamaica Farmer and Advertiser* (September 15, 1860): "The Henson Base Ball Club of this village will play a match game with the Lone Star Club of Harlem, on the grounds of the former in this village, on Wednesday (tomorrow)." They played the Newark Hamiltons. *Newark Advertiser* (September 30, 1862): "Considerable excitement was created among the colored boys of this city yesterday by a base-ball match between the Hamilton Club of this city and the Henson Club of Jamaica, Long Island, both composed of the descendants of Ham. The match was played on the grounds on Railroad Avenue, in the presence of a goodly number of the gentler sex, and resulted in a favor of the Hensons." They played Young Bachelor club, of Albany. *Troy Whig* (1868): "Two colored clubs, the Bachelors, of Albany, and the Hensons of Jamaica, Long Island, contested a game for the championship, at the Parade grounds, Albany, yesterday. The Hensons were the victors, the score standing at the conclusion of the game 58 to 24. Quite a large number of Trojans witnessed the game." The reorganized Henson's Lone Stars played the Hempstead Mutuals. *Hempstead Queens County Sentinel* (June 8, 1871): "A Base Ball Club, composed of gentlemen of color belonged to Jamaica, visited our village on Tuesday, and gave our fellow-citizens of African 'scent a specimen of their skill in the ball playing line. The score was 13 for the Jamaica Club and 8 for the Hempsteadites." The rivalry thrived. *Queens County Sentinel* (August 13, 1874): "The Mutuals of Hempstead, and the Hensons of Jamaica, play a game of ball on the old Enterprise grounds in this village on Saturday. Both clubs are composed of colored boys." *Queens County Sentinel* (August 20, 1874): "The game between the colored clubs called for Saturday last was put off until Monday when the Jamaica Club [Lone Stars] visited this village and played a match with the Hempstead Club on the new Enterprise ground, beating the latter by three runs, the score standing 23 in favor of Jamaica to 20 for Hempstead." In 1875, Hempstead, NY's Mutuals, Jamaica's Henson's Lone Stars, and Brooklyn's Ocean and Quicksteps ball clubs played in a colored tournament hosted by Hempstead, NY. By 1877, the Lone Stars had developed rivalries with Brooklyn nines. *Brooklyn Union-Argus* (October 18, 1877): "The Quicksteps of the Eastern District defeated the Lone Stars of Jamaica, at the Capitoline Grounds, by a score of 15 to 12." In 1890, they played the Off Colored club, of Huntington, NY, crushing them by a score of 20 to 2. By 1892, the Lone Star club remained an organized competitor. *Brooklyn Eagle* (August 14, 1892): "The Young Men's League defeated the Lone Stars in a one-sided game yesterday," by a score of 21 to 8."

SOURCES: "Base Ball," *Jamaica (NY) Farmer and Advertiser*, Dec 28, 1858; *New York (NY) Weekly Anglo-African*, Nov 15, 1859; "Base Ball," *New York Weekly Anglo-African*, Dec 3, 1859; "Letter from Jamaica, Long Island," *New York Weekly Anglo-African*, Jan 21, 1860; "Base Ball," *Jamaica Farmer and Advertiser*, Sep 15, 1860; *Newark (NJ) Daily Advertiser*, Sep 30, 1862; "Emancipation Celebration," *New York (NY) Herald-Tribune*, Sep 4, 1867; "Base Ball," *Troy (NY) Whig.* 1868; "Base Ball Notes," *New York (NY) Herald*, Jul 12, 1869; "Notes," *New York (NY) Tribune*, Jul 12, 1869; "Base Ball," *New York (NY) Clipper*, Dec 11, 1869; *Hempstead (NY) Queens County Sentinel*, Jun 8, 1871; *Hempstead Queens County Sentinel*, Aug 13, 1874; *Hempstead Queens County Sentinel*, Aug 20, 1874; "Base Ball," *Brooklyn (NY) Union-Argus*, Oct 18, 1877; "Long Island," *Newton (NY) Register*, Aug 27, 1885; "Hempstead," *Babylon (NY) South Side Signal*, Aug 6, 1887; "Base Ball," *Hempstead Queens County Sentinel*, Jun 23, 1888; "Base Ball Notes," *Hempstead Queens County Sentinel*, Jun 24, 1888; "Celebrating Emancipation Day," *New York Herald-Tribune*, Aug 30, 1889; "Base Ball at Oyster Bay," *New York (NY) Age*, May 31, 1890; "Village Notes," *Huntington (NY) Long Islander*, Jun 14, 1890; "Amateur Base Ball," *Brooklyn (NY) Eagle*, Aug 14, 1892.

Acme Base Ball Club (Jamestown, NY; 1890s). Organizer(s): Harry Curtis.

The Acme B.B.C., of Jersey City, NJ, organized in the 1890s, played black and white nines. Manager Harry Curtis hyped the Acmes—adopting the name of his former white club. *Brooklyn Eagle* (April 22, 1898): "The Pacific A. C. will play the Acme Colored Giants on Sunday at the Former's grounds in New Jersey for the benefit of the Maine fund." *Buffalo Commercial* (June 1, 1898): "A ball game between the Celerons and Warren, Iron and Oil League, was a feature of Monday afternoon. It was close and well played. Celeron is represented this year by the Acme Colored Giants, who play a dashing and sensational game. They won by a score of 3 to 4." *Elmira Morning Telegram* (July 24, 1898): "The dusky galaxy of Senegambian ball tossers, who answer to the altitudinous title of the Acme Giants, have a twirler who is known as the Ebony Rusie. The backstop bears the title of the Rosewood McGuire, and the left fielder and captain stars himself as the Black Delehanty. One of the twirlers, who is the comedy light of the team, takes his title from Dad Clarke. The saffron Dad Clarke is his title. The prefix saffron was suggested by the colored of the wearer of the name, and is no reflection and Dad's—the original Dad's—nerves."

SOURCES: "Chipper Chambersburg," *Philadelphia (PA) Sporting Life*, Feb 12, 1898; "Celeron Base Ball Club," *Warren (PA) Evening Democrat*, Apr 7, 1898; "Local Sports," *Jamestown (NY) Evening Journal*, Apr 21, 1898; "Amateur Base Ball, *Brooklyn (NY) Eagle*. April 22, 1898; "Base Ball Game Today," *Scranton (PA) Tribune*, May 4, 1898; "News and Comment," *Philadelphia Sporting Life*, May 6, 1898; "Ridgway Loses First Game," *Philadelphia (PA) Inquirer*, May 10, 1898; "Neighborhood News," *Buffalo (NY) Commercial*, Jun 1, 1898; "Curtis Happy," *Philadelphia Sporting Life*, Jun 4, 1898; "Oil and Iron League," *Jamestown Evening Journal*, Jun 11, 1898; "Gossip of the Game," *Louisville (KY) Courier-Journal*, Jul 20, 1898; "Base Ball," *Elmira (NY) Telegram*, Jul 24, 1898.

Exile Base Ball Club (Johnstown, NY; 1880s)

The Exile B.B.C. organized in the 1880s, played black nines. *Johnstown Republican* (August 26, 1891): "The game of base-ball played on the fairground Tuesday between the Exiles, colored, of Johnstown, and the Athletics, colored, of the infant city [Gloversville], was quite spirited and well played, especially on the part of the Exiles, who by the way should change their name to something a little nearer home, as their fine playing showed plainly that Gloversville delegates wasn't in it at all, and before the game ended, the Athletics, like a certain lot of Gloversvillians, kicked because they couldn't win and no doubt ere this, they too, the Athletics called an indignation meeting. At the close of the eighth inning the game stood nine to the baby city representatives three…" *Republican* (August 23, 1892): "The two colored base-ball clubs, the Athletics of Gloversville and Exiles of this village, played a return game on the fairgrounds, Monday afternoon, in which the latter were done up, this time to the tune to 43 to 38."

SOURCES: "A Bird's Eye View," *Gloversville (NY) Leader*, Aug 6, 1889; "A Bird's Eye View," *Gloversville Leader*, Aug 23, 1889; "Local Record," *Gloversville Leader*, Jul 9, 1891; "Home Happenings," *Johnstown (NY) Republican*, Jun 10, 1891; "Home Happenings," *Johnstown Republican*, Jul 14, 1891; "Home Happenings," *Johnstown Republican*, Jul 21, 1891; "Base Ball," *Johnstown Republican*, Aug 20, 1891; "Base Ball Notes," *Johnstown (NY) Republican*, Aug 23, 1892.

Eureka Base Ball Club (Johnstown, NY; 1890s)

The Eureka B.B.C. organized in the 1890s, played black nines. *Johnstown Republican* (July 10, 1893): "There will be a game of base-ball on the fairgrounds tomorrow at 2:45 pm, between the colored teams, Eurekas of Johnstown and Athletics of Gloversville. Admission 25 cents." *Republican* (July 12, 1893): "The Athletics of Gloversville, defeated the Eurekas, of Johnstown, in a ball game on the fairgrounds yesterday afternoon by a score of 31 to 8."

SOURCES: "Items of Interest," *Johnstown (NY) Republican*, Jul 10, 1893; "Items of Interest," *Johnstown Republican*, Jul 12, 1893.

Flyaway Base Ball Club (Johnstown, NY; 1870s)

The Flyaway B.B.C. organized in the 1870s, played black nines. *Utica Observer* (September 20, 1871): "The Fearless Base Ball Club, of this city, the champion colored organization of colored men in the State, went to Ilion yesterday morning, to play the Flyaways of Johnstown, for a silver-mounted bat. The Utica boys were victorious, as usual. But seven innings were played, three of which were continued through a heavy rain storm. The score was 61 to 34, in favor of the Fearless."

SOURCES: "Base Ball," *Troy (NY) Whig*, June 26, 1871; "Base Ball," *Troy Whig*, June 27, 1871; "Base Ball," *Troy (NY) Times* (Troy, NY), July 18, 1871; "Base Ball," *Gloversville (NY) Intelligencer*, Jul 20, 1871; "Base Ball," *Utica (NY) Observer*, Sep 20, 1871.

Wide Awake Base Ball Club (Johnstown, NY; 1870s)

The Wide Awake B.B.C. organized in the 1870, played black nines. *Gloversville Intelligencer* (July 27, 1870): "On Monday, two exciting games of ball were played on the Fair grounds. The first game was for a silver mounted bat, and was contested for by the Fly Aways of Gloversville, and the Wide Awakes, of this village (colored clubs). The Gloversville club flew away with the Wide Awakes by a score of 21 to 18."

SOURCES: "The Colored Championship," *New York (NY) Herald*, Jul 24, 1870; "Ratification of the Fifteenth Amendment," *Gloversville (NY) Intelligencer*, Jul 27, 1870.

Kent House Base Ball Club (Lakewood/Jamestown, NY; 1880s–1890s). Organizer(s): A. C. Robinson.

The Kent House B.B.C., of Lakewood, NY, organized in the 1870s. The nine, composed of waiters, played black teams. *Cleveland Gazette* (August 1, 1885): "There was a highly interesting time at Lakewood on Saturday last. The waiters of the Lakeview House and Kent House indulged in a game of base-ball. The game results in a great victory for the Lake View House, the score being 7 to 5. The game was witnessed by everyone at Lakewood. There will be another match between the same people and at the same place on Saturday. None should fail to see it."

SOURCES: "Lakewood, NY," *Cleveland (OH) Gazette*, Aug 1, 1885; "Lakewood, NY," *Cleveland Gazette*, Aug 8, 1885; "Lakewood, NY," *Jamestown (NY) Evening Journal*, Aug 17, 1889; "Kent House Formally Opened," *Jamestown Evening Journal*, Jun 18, 1897.

Lakewood House Base Ball Club (Lakewood/Jamestown, NY; 1880s–1890s). Organizer(s): A. C. Robinson.

The Lakewood House B.B.C., of Lakewood, NY, organized in the 1870s. The nine, composed of waiters, played black teams. *Cleveland Gazette* (August 1, 1885): "There was a highly interesting time at Lakewood on Saturday last. The waiters of the Lakeview House and Kent House indulged in a game of base-ball. The game results in a great victory for the Lake View House, the score being 7 to 5. The game was witnessed by everyone at Lakewood. There will be another match between the same people and at the same place on Saturday. None should fail to see it."

SOURCES: "Lakewood, NY," *Cleveland (OH) Gazette*, Aug 1, 1885; "Lakewood, NY," *Cleveland Gazette*, Aug 8, 1885; "Lakewood, NY," *Jamestown (NY) Evening Journal*, Aug 17, 1889; "Kent House Formally Opened," *Jamestown Evening Journal*, Jun 18, 1897.

Excelsior Base Ball Club (Lockport, NY; 1860s–1870s). Organizer(s): Thomas Carroll.

The Excelsior B.B.C. organized in the 1860s. Thomas Carroll, a barber, at Lockport's American Hotel, organized and financed the team. *Lockport Daily Journal* (December 1, 1868): "Thomas Carroll, Fashionable Barber and Hair Dresser, would respectfully inform the Ladies and Gentlemen of Lockport and the country round about, that he has leased for a series of years, and fitted up in elegant style, the Front Rooms of the basement of Hosmers Block, for shaving and hair dressing. A Ladies' Hair Dresser will be employed, and a parlor fitted up in superb style." His Excelsior club played black nines: Albany's Bachelors, Rochester's Unexpecteds, Buffalo's Invincibles, Niagara Falls' Rapids, Pittsburgh's Rapids, Utica's Fearless and WA's Mutuals. *Lockport Journal* (July 30, 1868): "The colored people have caught the base-ball mania. The Lockport Excelsiors and Buffalo Invincibles (both colored troupes) met on the Perews grounds, and played a game which resulted in the Buffalo boys coming off victorious by considerable odds. The colored troops, we are assured by an eye witness, fought nobly."

SOURCES: "Base Ball," *Lockport (NY) Journal*, Oct 25, 1867; "The Twenty-Ninth Anniversary Celebration of the Colored People," *Lockport Journal*, Aug 4, 1868; *Davenport (IA) Gazette*, Aug 10, 1868; "Local Brevities," *Lockport Journal*, Jul 30, 1868; "Base Ball," *Buffalo (NY) Evening Courier and Republic*, Oct 20, 1868; "Base Ball," *Buffalo (NY) Courier*, Oct 31, 1868; *Lockport Journal*, Dec 1, 1868; "Games," *Cincinnati (OH) Commercial Tribune*, Aug 10, 1870; "For the Colored Championship," *Utica (NY) Observer*, Aug 24, 1870; "Base Ball," *Washington (DC) Evening Star*, Aug 29, 1870.

Rockton Base Ball Club (Little Falls, NY; 1880s)

The Rockton B.B.C. organized in 1887. The Rocktons played black and white nines. *Newton Register* (July 28, 1887): "The Rocktons, of Little Falls, and Heavy Hitters, of Canajoharie, will soon play a match game of ball for $50. In the two games played Little Falls has been victorious. Both are colored nines."

SOURCES: "Home News," *Little Falls (NY) Evening Times*, Jul 18, 1887; "Base Ball," *Little Falls Evening Times*, July 22, 1887; "Little Falls," *Newton (NY) Register*, Jul 28, 1887.

Athletic Base Ball Club (Middletown, NY; 1890s)

The Athletic B.B.C. organized in the 1890s, played black teams. *Middletown Times* (September 28, 1893): "Middletown colored baseball players calling themselves the Athletics will cross bats with a nine at Fishkill-on-the-Hudson on Thursday next. The club is made up of a strong nine and will give the club of that village a hustling time."

SOURCES: "Base Ball Notes" *Middletown (NY) Times-Press*, Aug 18, 1893; "A Colored Base Ball Club," *Middletown (NY) Times*, Sep 23, 1893; "Colored Base Ball Players at Fishkill," *Middletown Times*, Sep 28, 1893.

Haymaker Base Ball Club (Middletown, NY; 1880s). Organizer(s): Samuel Adams Beasley.

The Haymaker B.B.C. organized in the 1880s, played black nines. *Port Jervis Tri-States Union* (July 2, 1885): "During the afternoon a game of baseball was played between the Red Stockings, of this village, and the Haymakers, of Middletown, both clubs composed of colored players. The game was one-sided throughout and not very interesting. The Port Jervis boys were too hot for their Middletown adversaries and downed them by the score of 28 to 5."

SOURCES: "A Game Between Colored Clubs," *Port Jervis (NY) Evening Gazette*, Jun 20, 1885; "There Were 18 Colored Men," *Port Jervis Evening Gazette*, Jun 25, 1885; "The Masonic Picnic," *Port Jervis (NY) Tri-States Union*, Jul 2, 1885; "Colored Managers Quarrelling," *Port Jervis Evening Gazette*, Aug 15, 1885.

Light Hitters Base Ball Club (Middletown, NY; 1870s)

The Light Hitters B.B.C. organized in 1870, played black and white nines. *Port Jervis Gazette* (May 28, 1870): "The darkies didn't know whether they lived in Middletown, New York or elsewhere. They had come here anticipating an easy victory, but a-lack-a-day, victory was not for them! Adolphus George Washington Black was a superior hitter—right from the shoulder—he showed 'muckle' and considerable ivory and could bat any Delaware out of time. Theopholus Constantinople Blossom was not so much for his batting as his butting proclivities. Cream-colored Bartimeus Diogenes Aristedes Smithus was one of the best runners on the field...."

SOURCES: "Base Ball," *Port Jervis (NY) Evening Gazette*, May 28, 1870; "The Ball Match To-Morrow," *Port Jervis Evening Gazette*, May 31, 1870; "Base Ballists Than Usual," *Port Jervis Evening Gazette*, Jun 2, 1870.

Water Lilies Base Ball Club (Middletown, NY; 1870s). Organizer(s): Samuel Beasley.

The Water Lilies B.B.C. organized in the 1870s, played black teams. *Middletown Argus* (July 9, 1877): "An interesting game of base-ball came off on the old race course last Saturday before a large audience, between the Keystones of Chester and the Lilies of Middletown, both clubs being composed entirely of colored players. Billy Hasbrouck who acted as pitcher for the Lilies, made it quite warm for the opponents, sending in balls which were a little short of velocity of those projected by a cannon's mouth; but they were none too hot for Beasley the catcher, who received each one with his accustomed smile. Alex Gale, who held the responsible position of first base, was laid *hors du combat* in the early part of the game, catching a hot flyer which broke his finger at the joint. The two Bertholf brothers, who acted as pitcher and catcher on the side of the Keystones, showed their remarkable good play; in fact, had all their players been as proficient the game would have resulted differently. The score stood 32 to 14 in favor of the Lilies." *Argus* (July 20, 1877): "The Hemlock Base Ball Club of Goshen have accepted the challenge of the Lilies of this town [Middletown], Samuel Beasley, Captain, to play a colored match at the Orange Pleasure Ground tomorrow afternoon." *Middletown Press* (July 23, 1877): "A match game of base-ball between the colored clubs of Middletown and Goshen here on Saturday, the Water Lilies of the former place [Middletown] were victorious over the Hemlocks of the latter place by a score of 35 to 30."

SOURCES: "Base Ball," *Middletown (NY) Press*, Sep 23, 1876; "An Amusing Game," *Middletown (NY) Argus*, Jul 9, 1877; "Local Notes," *Middletown Argus*, Jul 20, 1877; "Base Ball Notes," *Middletown Press*, Jul 23, 1877; "Base Ball Notes," *Middletown Press*, Aug 3, 1877.

Colored Base Ball Club (Newburgh, NY; 1870s–1890s). Organizer(s): William King and William Johnson.

The Colored B.B.C. organized in the 1870s. Between the 1880s and 1890s, the nine was nicknamed Lone Stars (1874–1883), Live Oaks (1886), Fear Nothings (1887–1890), and Blues (1891). *Poughkeepsie Eagle* (October 11, 1874): "The Lone Stars of Newburgh and the Butterflies of Poughkeepsie play a game of base-ball in this city on Tuesday. The latter were victorious, the score standing at the close of the game 31 to 27." *Poughkeepsie Eagle* (July 22, 1875): "The Warm Springs Base Ball Club, (colored), of Fishkill Landing, hold a picnic at Dales' Grove.... The Warm Springs will play two games of baseball on that occasion with the Lone Stars of Newburgh, and the Fear Nothings, of Poughkeepsie. The West Chester Base Ball Club of Peekskill will also be present." *Newburgh Register* (July 10, 1886): "The Empires of Peekskill, and the Live Oaks of Newburgh will play on the Benkard grounds. Both clubs are composed of colored men." *Newburgh News* (June 13, 1887): "[William] Squirely King's famous Fearnothing ball club (colored) will play the Star club from Peekskill at the Benkard grounds tomorrow." *Newburgh News* (June 15, 1887): "The biggest ball game of the season was that played at the Washing-

ton Heights base-ball ground, between Captain Squirely King's Fearnothings of this city, and the Stars of Peekskill. The Fearnothings are made up of the cream of Newburgh's colored ball players, and the Stars are composed of dark-hued aristocrats from Peekskill." *New York Age* (September 5, 1891): "The baseball club of this city, under its captain, William Johnson, went to Poughkeepsie Tuesday to play a game with a nine [Grays] of that city. The Newburghers won by a score of 17 to 11. They will play another game on one of the county fair days in Poughkeepsie with the same team."

SOURCES: *Poughkeepsie (NY) Eagle*, Oct 11, 1873; *Poughkeepsie Eagle*, Oct 11, 1874; "Base Ball," *Poughkeepsie Eagle*, Jul 22, 1875; "Base Ball," *Poughkeepsie Eagle*, Aug 6, 1883; "Base Ball," *Poughkeepsie Eagle*, Aug 21, 1883; "A Tip to P. J. Coons," *Newburgh (NY) Register*, Mar 20, 1884; "The Red Stockings Defeated," *Port Jervis Evening Gazette*, Jul 21, 1885; "Boss Coon Club on Deck," *Port Jervis Evening Gazette*, May 18, 1886; "Baseball Boomlets," *Newburgh Register*, Jul 10, 1886; "Brief and Pointed," *Newburgh (NY) News*, Jun 13, 1887; "Great Ball Playing," *Newburgh News*, June 15, 1887; "The Coons at Play," *Newburgh Register*, Jul 21, 1888; "Base Ball," *Poughkeepsie (NY) Eagle*, Aug 26, 1890; "Bush Meeting at Newburgh," *New York (NY) Age*, Sep 6, 1890; "Newburgh Notes," *New York Age*, Sep 5, 1891.

Colored Base Ball Club (Newtown, NY; 1870s)

The Colored B.B.C. organized in the 1870s, played black nines. *Newton Register* (May 30, 1878): "The Colored Base Ball Club, of this village, play a match game with the Flushing Club, on the commons, this afternoon." *Flushing Times* (June 4, 1879): "In a match game between the colored base-ball tossers of Flushing and Newton, in which the Flushing boys were victorious by one run. During the game Jack martin, of the Newton club, was knocked senseless by a bat being thrown from the hands of the batter." *Register* (June 5, 1879): "In the afternoon a colored club from Flushing was matched against a club of colored players from this village [Newton] and returned home victory by one point. The game was very interesting, the principal excitement arising from the disputes that followed each other in quick succession, and the difficulty experienced by the umpire in satisfactory deciding the innumerable questions of judgment. Jack Martin received a knock down hit from a club in the hands of a careless batter and was carried off the field."

SOURCES: "Local," *Newton (NY) Newtown Register*, May 30, 1878; "Local," *Flushing (NY) Times*, Jun 4, 1879; "Local," *Newton Newtown Register*, Jun 5, 1879.

Alhambra Base Ball Club (New York, NY; 1890s)

The Alhambra B.B.C. organized in the 1890s. The club was composed of the members of the Alhambra Company and Jubilee Singers. *Australian Town and Country Journal* (July 9, 1892): "A baseball match between representatives of America and Australia was played on the Association Cricket Ground on Monday for the benefit of the unemployed, but the match did not create much public interest, as the attendance was very meager. The match, however, was very much enjoyed by the players, who entered into the contest with much interest. The Australian team was chosen of players from various Sidney baseball clubs. The Americans consisted of members of the Jubilee Singers and Alhambra Company. Five innings were played, the Australians eventually winning by five runs."

SOURCES: "Base Ball," Sydney (AUS) *Morning Herald*, Jul 5, 1892; "America vs. Australia," Sydney (NSW/AUS) *Town and Country Journal*, Jul 9, 1892.

Amicable Base Ball Club (New York, NY; 1870s)

The Amiable B.B.C. organized in the 1870s. The "Amiable club" played black nines. In 1871, they played against the Jersey City Keystones. *Jersey City Journal* (September 30, 1871): "The Amicable Club of New York and the Keystone Club of New Jersey, both composed of colored citizens, played a game on the Union Grounds," yesterday, Williamsburgh, in the presence of a crowd of spectators. The Keystones were evidently the better players. Walker, the second baseman of the Keystones, handled the ball with considerable skill. Of the NY players, Hoffman and Cartwright did good business."

The Amicables defeated the Royal Stars for the Colored Junior Championship of NY.

SOURCES: "Games of the Week," *Brooklyn (NY) Eagle,* Sep 3, 1871; "Sports and Pastimes," *Brooklyn Eagle,* Sep 23, 1871; "Base Ball," *Jersey City (NJ) Journal,* Sep 30, 1871; "Base Ball," *Jersey City Journal,* Oct 2, 1871; "Colored Junior Championship," *New York (NY) Evening Telegram,* Sep 20, 1871; "Keystone vs. Amicable," *New York (NY) Clipper,* Oct 14, 1871.

Arno Base Ball Club (New York, NY; 1880s)

The Arno B.B.C. organized in 1886. The "Arno Club" played black nines. *New York Globe* (May 26, 1883): "The first of a series of three games will be played on Decoration Day, May 30th, between the Arno and Acme Base Ball Clubs; of which William Aimes and W. Hallet Greene are captains respectively. The games are for the amateur championship and the silver tankard kindly offered by S. R. Smith, late of Philadelphia. The match is to be [played at the 118th Street and Sixth Avenue; the L Station between 116th Street and 8th Avenue. Umpire is George S. Smith."

SOURCES: "Local Gossip," *New York (NY) Globe,* May 26, 1883.

Callender Blue Stockings Base Ball Club (Georgia Minstrels) (New York City, NY. Organizer(s): Charles Callender and Charles B. Hicks; 1870s–1880s).

Baseball is entertainment. Athletically-inclined theatrical performers of (minstrels and, later, vaudevillians) formed baseball teams. While Williams & Walker Company (Bert Williams and George Walker), Ernest Hogan (the Rats B.B.C.) and Bill "Bojangles" Robinson organized colored baseball clubs in the 1900s, they followed a long-standing tradition in which colored minstrel troupes had formed competitive teams as early as the 1870s. The Callender Blues team of NY traveled with Callender's Minstrel Company (also called the GA Callender Minstrel Company). Charles Callender (white) owned the company, and Charles B. Hicks (black) served as business manager. Hicks, a performer in Callender's GA's Minstrel Company, had established himself as an able businessman in the late 1870s, taking a troupe called Hicks's GA Minstrel to Australia and New Zealand; his company had a baseball team that played against the St. Kilda B.B.C. (the oldest team in Australia). Similarly, Hicks introduced baseball to the new company: the Callender Blue Stockings played black and white teams. *Lowell Citizen and News* (August 10, 1877): "Callender's Georgia Minstrels were completely outdone yesterday afternoon by the colored nine, in their game with the Lowells." *St. Louis Post-Dispatch* (September 3, 1884): "Tomorrow (Thursday) afternoon, at Sportsman's Park, there will be one of the most amusing affairs of the week, this being the game of base-ball between Harry Bridgewater's St. Louis Black Sox, the champion colored club of the United States, and the Callender Minstrel team, which is composed of a number of excellent and clever base-ball tossers." Following the Black Stockings' victory over the Callender Blues, the St. Louis Sunday Call reported that Bridgewater's club wiped the earth with their opponents to the tune of All Coons Look Alike to Me. *Colorado Citizen* (October 9, 1884): "Callenders' Minstrels tackled a local colored base-ball club at Waco, and with ease knocked out the Central City Darkeys." The Callender Minstrels trumped them in a follow-up game. When not playing other teams, the Callenders—composed of

first and second nines—performed matches for spectators; the second nine was called Cuticura. The Callenders were considered professionals and the Cuticura, less professional.

SOURCES: "City and Vicinity," *Lowell (MA) Citizen and News,* Aug 10, 1877; "Base Ball," *New York (NY) Clipper,* Dec 30, 1882; "Are You Gwine to be Dar," *Helena (MT) Independent Record,* Jul 12, 1883; "Brief Items," *Helena Independent Record,* Jul 24, 1883; *Columbus (NE) Journal,* Aug 29, 1883; "The Black Sox-Callender Game," *St. Louis (MO) Post-Dispatch,* Sep 3, 1884; "Black Sox vs. Callender's Minstrels," *St. Louis (MO) Globe-Democrat,* Sep 4, 1884; "Callender's Minstrels vs. Black Socks," *St. Louis (MO) Republican,* Sep 4, 1884; "The City Yesterday," *Fort Scott (KS) Monitor,* Sep 13, 1884; "Waco Wirings," *Galveston (TX) News,* Sep 25, 1884; "Waco," *Galveston News,* Sep 26, 1884; "Base Ball," *Galveston News,* Sep 30, 1884; *Columbus (TX) Colorado Citizen,* Oct 9, 1884; *Indianapolis (IN) Freeman,* May 12, 1900; "Base Ball Notes," *Indianapolis Freeman,* Apr 27, 1907; "Our Actors as Baseball Players," *Indianapolis Freeman,* Apr 16, 1910; "In the Realm of Sport and Theatre," *New York (NY) Age,* May 3, 1928; "Elaborate Ceremonies Mark Opening," *New York Age,* Jul 18, 1931; "The Sports World," *New York Age,* Aug 7, 1931.

Cleveland Colossal Colored Minstrels Base Ball Club (New York, NY; 1890s). Organizer(s): W. S. Cleveland.

The Cleveland Colossal Colored Minstrels B.B.C. organized in the 1890s, played black and white teams. *Los Angeles Herald* (October 28, 1890): "Cleveland's minstrels and the grand opera house baseball nines will play next Friday at the new Temple Street Grounds. The Clevelands have some good ball talent in their club, and have won several games on their way to the coast."

SOURCES: "New Notes," *Los Angeles (CA) Herald,* Feb 21, 1890; "New Notes," *Los Angeles Herald,* Oct 27, 1890; "New Notes," *Los Angeles Herald,* Oct 28, 1890; "Base Ball," *Los Angeles Herald,* Oct 31, 1890; "New York City News," *New York (NY) Age,* Mar 7, 1891; "Cleveland's Colored Minstrels," *Worcester (MA) Daily Spy,* May 12, 1891.

Colored Union League Base Ball Club (New York, NY; 1900s). Owner(s): Mose Corbin.

The Colored Union League B.B.C. organized in the 1900s, played black and white aggregations. *New York Press* (March 15, 1900): "The Colored Union League Base Ball Club, organized for the season, composed of ex-Gorhams and ex-Cubans, would like to hear from all clubs within 200 miles of New York giving a guarantee."

SOURCES: "Among Local Ball Tossers," *New York (NY) Press,* Mar 15, 1900; "Among Local Ball Tossers," *New York Press,* Apr 22, 1900; "Among Local Ball Tossers," *New York Press,* May 5, 1900; "Among Local Ball Tossers," *New York Press,* Jun 20, 1900.

Genuine Cuban Giants Base Ball Club (New York, NY and Harrisburg, PA; 1890s–1900s). Organizer(s): John D. Bright.

After 1889, the history of the Cuban Giants gets complicated: dissenting players appropriate the moniker Cuban Giants, and they form other teams. Between 1888 and 1900, John D. Bright (white) owned/managed NJ's (and NY's) Cuban Giants. Following contractual disputes (and other issues), several players left his team after the 1889 season. *Philadelphia Sporting Life* (April 5, 1890): "Mr. Bright admits the loss of Selden, Thomas, Boyd, White, Malone, Frye and George Williams. Bright was left with Harrison and Grant. The famous Cuban Giants of '87, '88, and '89 will probably never again be seen in a team together." *Brooklyn Eagle* (April 7, 1890): "The colored champions—the Cuban Giants—have had a strike among their team, and now the present Cuban Giants have but two of last season's team on their payroll, namely Grant and Holmes, the other players having started a team in Harrisburg. Outside of these two the Cuban Giants are made up of played from the Gorhams, the latter club having all new players. Secession in the colored ranks is an anomaly." A list of men claiming to have played for the Cuban Giants is extensive. While name Cuban Giants had been appropriated by black teams throughout the country since 1888, it was the competitive Cuban X Giants that competed against the Genuine Cuban Giants. *Washington Evening Times* (May 23, 1896): "Owing to the fact that there is a club (colored) calling themselves the Cuban (X) Giants, and getting most terribly defeated everywhere, and when defeated, they send in their scores, calling themselves the Cuban Giants, thereby injuring the Genuine Cuban Giants' reputation and fooling the public at large. I [John D. Bright] am therefore compelled to take this means to notify you to look out for them fooling the various managers and public as well." *Bridgewater Courier-News* (September 6, 1898): "Seven hundred enthusiasts journey out to the Crescent Oval yesterday afternoon to see the ball game. They saw the Genuine Cuban Giants, and they saw the Riiverdales; and they said they saw a good game. The black Giants made fun for the crowd and everybody seemed to be pleased except Captain Bo. The Captain was angry because his men couldn't hit the ball. The trouble began at the start, when the Giants made two runs in each of the first three innings and that was more than enough to win." *Rochester Democrat and Chronicle* (July 21, 1900): "Moravia defeated the Genuine Cuban Giants here today in the hardest-fought game seen on the local grounds this season. The colored team looked like winners up to the eighth inning, when the home team fell onto Wilson for four singles, which, added to a base on balls, netted it three runs."

Sources: "The Cuban Giants," *Philadelphia (PA) Sporting Life*, Jan 8, 1890; "The Cuban Giants," *Philadelphia Sporting Life*, Apr 5, 1890; "The Mets Won," *Brooklyn (NY) Eagle*, Apr 7, 1890; "Plainville Base Ball," *Bristol (CT) Herald*, Aug 21, 1890; "A Great Game of Ball," *Port Chester (NY) Journal*, Sep 11, 1890; "Allertons, 18; Cuban Giants, 4," *New York (NY) Press*, Jun 15, 1891; "The Cuban Giants," *Philadelphia Sporting Life*, Dec 26, 1891; "Cuban Giants Reorganized," *Philadelphia (PA) Inquirer*, Feb 1, 1892; "Chat of the Diamond," *Philadelphia Inquirer*, May 12, 1892; "Camden Defeats Cuban Giants," *Philadelphia Inquirer*, May 27, 1892; "Cuban Giants Turn the Tables," *Philadelphia Inquirer*, Jul 7, 1892; "The Cuban Giants Defeat Meriden Professionals," *Meridian (CT) Weekly Republican*, Jul 7, 1892; "The Cuban Giants," *Philadelphia Sporting Life*, Nov 5, 1892; "The Cuban Giants," *Philadelphia Sporting Life*, Dec 31, 1892; "Base Ball Notes," *Middletown (NY) Times*, Jan 30, 1893; "Cuban Giants Win," *Trenton (NJ) True American*, Sep 12, 1893; "The Cuban Giants," *Philadelphia Sporting Life*, Feb 17, 1894; "Cuban Giants' Two Games," *Philadelphia (PA) Record*, Jul 5, 1894; "The Cuban Giants," *Philadelphia Sporting Life*, Feb 22, 1896; "The Only Cuban Giants," *Philadelphia Sporting Life*, Apr 4, 1896; "Genuine Cuban Giants," *Washington (DC) Evening Times*, May 23, 1896; "Bright's Idea," *Philadelphia Sporting Life*, Feb 27, 1897; "Gloversville Pleased," *Philadelphia Sporting Life*, Mar 6, 1897; "Minor Mention," *Philadelphia Sporting Life*, Apr 24, 1897; "Bright's Brief," *Philadelphia Sporting Life*, Apr 16, 1898; "The Cuban Giants," *Philadelphia Sporting Life*, Mar 19, 1898; "Bright's Bulletin," *Philadelphia Sporting Life*, Aug 13, 1898; "Riverdale Wins From Woodridge But Loses the Afternoon Game to the Cuban Giants," *Bridgewater (NJ) Courier-News*, Sep 6, 1898; "Games of Baseball," *Jersey City (NJ) Journal*, Aug 12, 1899; "Tomorrow's Ball Games," *Jersey City Journal*, Oct 7, 1899; "The Baseball World," *Jersey City Journal*, May 23, 1900; "Cuban Giants Made Pygmies Of," *Rochester (NY) Democrat and Chronicle*, Jul 21, 1900; "News of the Diamond," *Jersey City Journal*, Aug 23, 1900; "Games of Baseball," *Jersey City Journal*, Aug 25, 1900.

Jackson Base Ball Club (New York, NY; 1880s). Owner(s): John W. Jackson ("Bud Fowler").

The Jackson B.B.C. organized in the 1880s. The Jacksons, composed of Cuban Giant and Gorham players, toured CA. *Oakland Tribune* (April 21, 1888): "At Center Street Park tomorrow afternoon a game of baseball will be played between two nines of colored men, the Jacksons, lately from the East, and the Jamiesons of California. The game will be called at 2 pm." *Tribune* (April 23, 1888): "The audience at the Center Street Park yesterday afternoon was neither particularly large nor enthusiastic. The attraction at the grounds was a game of baseball between two nines of colored men named the Jacksons and the Jamiesons. The former team had a very easy victory. The players in both nines were attired in gaudy uniforms."

Sources: "The News," *St. Paul (MN) Western Appeal*, Aug 20, 1887; "Base Ball Notes," *Philadelphia (PA) Times*, Dec 19, 1887; "Sporting Notes," *Oakland (CA) Tribune*, Apr 21, 1888; "The Colored Clubs," *Oakland Tribune*, Apr 23, 1888.

Cuban X-Giants Base Ball Club (New York, NY; 1890s–1900s). Organizer(s): E. B. Lamar: Fred J. Mersheimer, William J. Davis and Frank Davis.

The Cuban X-Giants B.B.C. organized in 1896. The "Cuban X-Giants" played black and white teams. *Springfield Mercury* (March 26, 1896): "There is a rupture among the Cuban Giants ball team and two combinations will be in the field this season. They will be known as the Cuban Giants and the Cuban X-Giants. Williams and Grant are among Manager Bright's old team, while three of the Jacksons are members of the rival organization." *Utica Sunday Tribune* (August 7, 1898): "Yesterday afternoon about 600 people saw the Cuban X-Giants defeat the Ilions in a snappy, gingery game of ball by a score of 2 to 1. The Giants did not win until the ninth when second base was occupied with one out. Grant, for the visitors, was everywhere and did pretty work." *New York Morning Telegraph* (August 7, 1899): "Robinson, the man with the cannon-ball delivery, was too much for the West New York Field Club yesterday. The Jerseymen could not make hits when they wanted them and had to succumb to the Cuban X-Giants. It was a game in which fine fielding was plentiful, and Frank Grant carried off the honors. The victorious base play and hitting were up to League form." *Philadelphia Inquirer* (July 22, 1900): "After winning seventeen straight Atlantic City, in one of the greatest games of the season, were obliged to surrender to the Cuban X-Giants today. Selden pitched masterly ball and had the Atlantics guessing throughout the game."

Sources: "The National Game," *Springfield (NY) Mercury*, Mar 26, 1896; "A Cuban Victory," *New York (NY) World*, Jun 1, 1896; "On Diamond Fields," *New York (NY) Tribune*, Jul 6, 1896; "Cuban X-Giants Win," *New York Tribune*, Jul 13, 1896; "Ball Games in the West," *New York Tribune*, Aug 3, 1896; "Cuban X-Giants 12; Titusville, 9," *Cleveland (OH) Leader*, Sep 12, 1896; "Base Ball," *Brooklyn (NY) Standard Union*, Aug 30, 1897; "Asylums Badly Beaten," *Middletown (NY) Daily Argus*, Oct 1, 1897; "Cubans' Second Meeting," *New York World*, Oct 9, 1897; "Done Up By the Giants," *Greenville (PA) Record-Argus*, Jul 3, 1898; "Atlantic City Beaten," *Philadelphia (PA) Inquirer*, Jul 14, 1898; "The National Game," *Springfield Mercury*, Jul 22, 1898; "Base Ball," *New York Tribune*, Jul 25, 1898; "Cuban X-Giants Here Tomorrow," *Trenton (NJ) Evening Times*, Jul 28, 1898; "At Ilion," *Utica (NY) Sunday Tribune*, Aug 7, 1898; "Cuban X-Giants Victorious," *New York (NY) Morning Telegraph*, Aug 7, 1899; "Base Ball," *Springfield Mercury*, Aug 17, 1899; "Engages Two Havana Players," *NY Tribune*, Mar 18, 1900; "Nearby Ball Games," *Buffalo (NY) Evening News*, Jun 4, 1900; "Unions, 10; Cuban X-Giants, 5," *Chicago (IL) Tribune*, Jun 25, 1900; "Cuban X-Giants Bunched Hits," *Philadelphia Inquirer*, Jul 22, 1900.

Darktown Base Ball Club (New York, NY; 1900s)

The Darktown B.B.C. organized in the 1900s. *New York Press* (July 24, 1900): "On Staten Island the Polo Field Club took the Darktown Field Club into camp in a close and interesting game. The colored lads not only put up a fine game of ball, but they furnished a lot of amusement for the spectators."

SOURCES: "Polo F. C., 5; Darktown F. C., 2," *New York (NY) Press*, Jul 24, 1900; "Polo F. C., 14; Darktown F. C., 1," *New York Press*, Aug 6, 1900.

Gorham Base Ball Club (New York, NY; Newburgh, NY/New Haven, CT; Philadelphia and Harrisburg, PA; Newark, NJ; 1880s–1890s). Organizer(s): Benjamin M. Butler; Schnepper; Walter J. Pell and Ambrose Davis; Walter Jacobius.

The Gorham B.B.C., of New York, NY, organized in 1886, played black and white teams. The Gorhams boldly declared themselves rivals of the Trenton Cuban Giants. *Trenton True American* (August 14, 1886): "It was a contest for the colored championship of the United States. The Gorham club, of New York, was the only colored nine bold enough to dispute the Cuban Giants, and everybody expected they must possess some skill. They wanted to arrange for a series of three games, but Manager Cook declined this programme till they had shown what stuff they were made of. They showed it in a very short time yesterday, and the showing was not to their credit. The dusky visitors were startled by the Giants' style of driving the ball all over the lot, and their demoralization became so great that run getting for themselves was almost out of the question." The two teams developed an intense rivalry. *New York Sun*: "About 1,800 persons saw the game between the Cuban Giants and Gorhams yesterday. Stovey was in the box for the Cubans, and the latter were not only unable to hit him but he struck out the side in the third, and two men in each inning but the sixth and ninth." *New York Herald Tribune* (September 19, 1888): "An interesting game between the two colored clubs, the Cuban Giants and Gorhams, was played at the Polo grounds yesterday. The game was stopped by darkness at the ending of the ninth inning, leaving each team with one run to its credit. Both Whyte and Stovey pitched in fine form, while the general fielding was excellent." They also played white nines. *Herald-Tribune* (June 17, 1889): "Baseball generally loses caste when it becomes humorous and ridiculous, but yesterday's game at the Polo Grounds was so supremely wretched and out of the ordinary that the crowd really enjoyed the contest and laughed heartily through the burlesque. The contest was between the New York and Gorham nines, and the home club won by the modest score of 36 to 1. Yesterday the team [Gorhams] was weakened by the absence of its best players and the substitutes in made a terrible mess of it." *Lebanon News* (August 14, 1889): "About 1700 people witnessed the game between the Lebanon Grays and Gorhams yesterday afternoon at Penryn, and they saw a series of wrangles that were disgusting in the extreme. What occasioned the dispute was the fact that the fact had been lost five minutes, and another ball that had been produced in its place was not acceptable to the Gorhams." *New Haven Register* (April 20, 1892): "About 1,000 people witnessed the exhibition game of baseball between New Haven and the Gorhams of New York City at the Howard Avenue Grounds." *Boston Globe* (July 9, 1892): "The Burlingtons and Gorhams played an exciting game of ball today at Athletic Park. The visitors played a brilliant fielding game. The score was tied in the ninth, and a run in the Burlington half of the tenth gave the contest to the home boys." *Jersey City Journal* (June 1, 1896): "Saturday's game on Johnston Avenue ground drew a big holiday crowd, and the teams played good ball. The Pacific Athletic Club was opposed by the Gorhams, one of the best colored clubs in the vicinity.

They put up fast ball for the first five innings, but suffered a bad attack of the rattles in the sixth until the home players had scored seven runs. The pleasure of the contest was marred by the disturbance noted in another column, and the effect was more apparent in the Gorham's play than in the Pacifics, who were involved in the trouble, which looked serious at one."

SOURCES: "Base Ball," *Trenton (NJ) Evening Times*, May 9, 1886; "Trenton Beats Bridgeport," *New York (NY) Herald*, Aug 6, 1886; "Trenton Beats Bridgeport," *Trenton (NJ) True American*, Aug 12, 1886; "The Giants Triumph," *Trenton True American*, Aug 14, 1886; "Fun, Fast and Furious," *Pittsburgh (PA) Commercial Gazette*, May 7, 1887; "Colored League," *Louisville (KY) Courier-Journal*, May 9, 1887; "Colored League," *Louisville Courier-Journal*, May 10, 1887; "Colored League," *Louisville Courier-Journal*, May 11, 1887; "The Base Ball Field," *New York (NY) Age*, Sep 1, 1888; "Cuban Giants and Gorhams Tied," *New York (NY) Herald-Tribune*, Sep 19, 1888; "Now for a Step Higher," *New York Herald-Tribune*, Jun 17, 1889; "Giants Home Again," *New York Herald-Tribune*, Jul 8, 1889; "It Was a Fake," *Lebanon (PA) News*, Aug 14, 1889; "Notes from the Diamond," *Harrisburg (PA) Patriot*, Apr 18, 1890; "Cuban Giants, 11; Gorhams, 2," *Cleveland (OH) Gazette*, Oct 4, 1890; "Of Course the Gorhams Won," *New York Herald-Tribune*, Oct 12, 1891; "New Haven Victorious," *New Haven (CT) Register*, Apr 20, 1892; "Making Fun of the Gorhams," *New York Herald-Tribune*, May 2, 1892; "Won by the Gorhams," *Trenton Evening Times*, Jun 4, 1892; "Gorhams Receive a Trouncing," *Philadelphia (PA) Inquirer*, Jun 4, 1892; "Burlingtons 7; Gorhams 6," *Boston (MA) Globe*, Jul 9, 1892; "Other Games," *New York (NY) Sun*, Aug 7, 1893; "Base Ball," *Reading (NY) Times*, Jun 4, 1894; "The National Game," *Newark (NJ) Sunday Call*, Jul 1, 1894; "Among Young Men," *Mount Vernon (NY) Argus*, Jul 3, 1895; "Baseball Notes," *New York (NY) Sun*, Jul 14, 1896; "Amateur Baseball," *Brooklyn (NY) Eagle*, Sep 6, 1897.

Hicks-Georgia Minstrels Base Ball Club (New York, NY; 1870s). Organizer(s): Charles B. Hicks.

The Hicks-Georgia Minstrels B.B.C. organized in the 1870s. The aggregation played throughout the world. *Melbourne Argus* (June 21, 1879): "The deciding game between the St. Kilda Base Ball Club and Georgia Minstrels will be played on St. Kilda Cricket Ground, this afternoon, at 2 o'clock sharp. As each club has won a game, an exciting contest is expected." They played in the United States. *Cambridge City Tribune* (October 9, 1879): "Sprague's colored base-ball club challenged our boys for a game on last Saturday morning. They got it—the score standing at the end of the fifth inning 29 to 1 in favor of our boys."

SOURCES: "Hick's Georgia Minstrels," Hobart (TAS/AUS) *Mercury*, Apr 30, 1879; "Baseball," *St. Kilda (VIC/AUS) Telegraph*, Jun 7, 1879; "Arrived," *Melbourne (AUS) Argus*, Jun 21, 1879; "Base Ball," *Melbourne Argus*, June 21, 1879; "Hicks Georgia Minstrels," *Gippsland (VIC/AUS) Times*, Jul 30, 1879; *Gippsland Times*, Aug 1, 1879; *Cambridge (IN) Tribune*, Oct 9, 1879.

Hicks and Sawyers Minstrel Base Ball Club (New York, NY; 1880s). Organizer(s): Charles B. Hicks.

The Hicks and Sawyers Minstrel B.B.C. organized in the 1880s. The organization also played against black teams. *Montgomery Advertiser* (July 7, 1887): "The Georgia Minstrels play a match game of ball this afternoon with the Montgomery colored nine at Clisby's Park." They also played in Australia and New Zealand. *Brisbane Figaro and Punch* (November 8, 1888): "The Hicks-Sawyer Minstrels have among them several especially expert baseball players, and before leaving San Francisco for the Colonies they played a match game against a crack club." *Sydney Star* (March 6, 1889): "Some of the

Hicks-Sawyer Minstrels went practicing base-ball in the Gardens last Saturday afternoon. Those colored gents knew how to catch the ball. It was rather amusing to see the man with the club, and the wicket-keeper, if I might term him, immediately behind him with his face protected by a shield from the lightning deliveries of another colored gent [Irving Sayles], who was shying the ball as hard as he jolly well could."

SOURCES: "Hicks and Sawyer's Minstrels," *New York (NY) Freeman*, May 28, 1887; "At the Opera House," *Montgomery (AL) Advertiser*, Jul 7, 1887; "The Diamond," *San Francisco (CA) Alta*, Jul 28, 1888; "Sporting Echoes," Brisbane (QLD/AUS) *Figaro and Punch*, Nov 8, 1888; *Wellington (NZ) Evening Post*, Nov 8, 1888; "Base Ball in New Zealand," *New York (NY) Herald*, Dec 30, 1888; "Base Ball in Wellington," Sydney (AUS) *Star*, Mar 6, 1889; "Base Ball," *Adelaide (SA) Advertiser*, Apr 11, 1889; "Base Ball Match," Broken Hill (NSW/AUS) *Barrier Miner*, Apr 29, 1889.

Kersands Minstrel Base Ball Club (New York, NY; 1880s).
Organizer(s): Billy Kersands.

The Kersands Minstrel B.B.C. organized in the 1880s, played white and black teams. *Topeka Capital* (July 31, 1885): "The Brown Stocking Club will play the Kersands nine—the Burnt Cork Club—at the Fair Grounds Saturday afternoon at 4 o'clock." *Galveston News* (October 11, 1885): "This evening, at 3:30 o'clock, there will be a game of base-ball between the Kersands Minstrel nine and the Opera Glasses of Galveston."

SOURCES: "City Chat," *Topeka (KS) Capital*, Jul 31, 1885; "Stray Notes," *Galveston (TX) News*, Oct 11, 1885.

Metropolitan Hotel Base Ball Club (New York, NY; 1880s).
Organizer(s): Fred Nichols.

The Metropolitan Hotel B.B.C. organized in the 1880s, played black teams. *New York Globe* (September 8, 1883): "The Mets played their closing game of the season and defeated their opponents by a score of 8 to 5. This base-ball club stands today the strongest club of color that we have, and if they hold it together next season, they will surely hurt somebody." They challenged St. Louis's Black Stockings to a base-ball match.

SOURCES: "New Jersey Summer Resorts," *New York (NY) Globe*, Aug 11, 1883; "Social Gossip," *New York Globe*, Aug 18, 1883; "Ashbury Park and Ocean Grove," *New York Globe*, Sep 8, 1883; "Social Gossip," *New York Globe*, Sep 8, 1883.

National Police Gazette Base Ball Club (New York, NY; 1880s).
Organizer(s): P. L. Jacobs.

The National Police Gazette B.B.C. organized in 1884. *National Police Gazette* (June 14, 1884): "The Police Gazette Colored Base Ball Club, under the management of P. L. Jacobs, have started on a tour through the Eastern States, where they will give exhibitions and meet all local nines in the principal cities."

SOURCES: "Sporting News," *New York (NY) National Police Gazette*, Jun 14, 1884.

Sadie Thompson Base Ball Club (New York, NY; 1880s)
The Sadie Thompson B.B.C. organized in the 1880s. *New York Freeman* (March 5, 1887) reports; "Miss Sadie Thompson's baseball nine was irresistible with Misses Ann Jones as captain and first base; Annie Brown, pitcher; Florence Henderson, catcher; Maud Smith, second base; Eva Pearl, third base; Mary Gilford, right field; Rosa Stiles, shortstop; Grace White, left field and Nellie Brown, centre field. Their costume was blue flannel knee breeches, white jackets, blue caps, blue stockings and white shoes, and bat with ball."

SOURCES: "The Sporting Club's Masquerade," *New York (NY) Freeman*, Mar 5, 1887.

Williams and Walker Base Ball Club (New York, NY; 1900s).
Organizer(s): Bert Williams and Frank Mallory.

The Williams and Walker B.B.C. organized in the 1900s. Athletically-inclined theatrical performers (minstrels and, later, vaudevillians) formed baseball teams. While Williams & Walker Company (Bert Williams and George Walker [**Fig. 33**]) had organized its team around 1900, the company had followed a long tradition in which black troupes formed competitive teams. *Philadelphia Inquirer* (May 5, 1900): "There is great joy in the ranks of the Black Patti Troubadours owing to the great victories of their representatives. The first game was between the dark-complexioned gentlemen and attaches of the People's Theatre, while the second was for blood, between the members of the Williams and Walker's aggregation and Black Patti's pets. The first game was by far more interesting, requiring a full game for the decision." *Indianapolis Freeman* (May 12, 1900): "Now the Williams and Walker boys have organized a baseball team in which they are encouraged by the [Williams and Walker] girls, who wear their colors with much pride and never miss a game; always lending their presence as a mascot, cheering loudly as a boy, at a homerun or cry of foul ball if they think their side is being cheated."

SOURCES: "Hats Off to the Black Pattis," *Philadelphia (PA) Inquirer*, May 5, 1900; "Williams and Walker," *Indianapolis (IN) Freeman*, May 12, 1900.

Cataract House Base Ball Club (Niagara Falls, NY; 1860s–1880s). Organizer(s): J. C. Anderson and Richard W. Dangerfield.

The Cataract House B.B.C. organized in the 1860s. The team, composed of waiters, played black and white nines. In 1868, the Cataract House defeated the International House, both black organizations. The rivalry continued. In 1875, the Cataract Rapids defeated the

Figure 33. George Walker. In 1896, Bert Williams and George Walker made their New York debut. Walker has been credited as the performer who turned the strut into the cakewalk and made it famous. While introducing the cakewalk's high-stepping grace to legitimate theater, the comedy team also organized a baseball team. The team figured among other black theatrical clubs, including Ernest Hogan's vaudeville nine, which played games in Hawaii and Australia.

International Stars by a score of 56 to 9; the International Stars evened the series, vanquishing the Cataract nine by a score of 17 to 6. In 1878, the Cataracts defeated them by a score of 50 to 8. In 1881, the International Rainbows defeated the Cataract Cobwebs by a score of 12 to 8. *New York Freeman* (July 24, 1886): "The baseball craze among the waiters of the different hotels has somewhat subsided. The game that was to be played Aug. 10, Cataract vs. Buffalo, has been postponed. A quartet of young men serenaded the guests of the International. The singing was good and the applause great."

SOURCES: "Base Ball," *Niagara (NY) Gazette*, Jul 1, 1868; "The Twenty-Ninth Anniversary Celebration of the Colored People," *Lockport (NY) Journal*, Aug 4, 1868; "Brevities," *Niagara Gazette*, Aug 25, 1875; "Base Ball," *Niagara Gazette*, Aug 6, 1878; "Base Ball," *Niagara Gazette*, Aug 12, 1878; "Brevities," *Niagara Gazette*, Aug 28, 1878; "Brevities," *Niagara Gazette*, Aug 28, 1878; "Brevities," *Niagara Gazette*, May 14, 1879; "Base Ball," *Niagara Gazette*, Jun 15, 1883; "Base Ball," *Niagara Gazette*, Jun 20, 1883; "Brevities," *Niagara Gazette*, July 3, 1883; "Base Ball," *Niagara Gazette*, Jul 13, 1883; "Niagara Drippings," *New York (NY) Freeman*, Jul 24, 1886; "Niagara Drippings," *New York Freeman*, Aug 28, 1886; "Niagara Festivities," *New York Freeman*, Sep 9, 1886; "Niagara Drippings," *New York Freeman*, Sep 11, 1886.

International Base Ball Club (Niagara Falls, NY; 1860s–1900s). Organizer(s): John Murphy, Jr.; Richard Bennett.

The International House B.B.C. organized in the 1860s. Some lived in Niagara Falls; others came from around the country. In the 1860s, the majority of them came from Baltimore's famous Carrolltown Hotel, Baltimore. The International House attaches made time for baseball, the waiters playing black and white teams. In 1867, they called themselves the Rapids. They played WA's Mutuals, and suffered a crushing defeat. During the West Indies Emancipation Day festivities, the Internationals went to Lockport where they played the Excelsior club. With Frederick Douglass in attendance, the Niagara club won the game. By 1874, the Cataract Rapids had established a rivalry with the Stars, employees of the International Hotel. In 1875, the Rapids defeated them by a score of 56 to 9; the Stars evened the series, defeating the Cataract nine. In 1878, the Rapids crushed their opponents by a score of 50 to 8. In 1879, the Stars and Rapids briefly merged. In 1881, J. A. Jordan, of Syracuse, NY, had reorganized the Internationals, nicknaming them the Rainbows. They defeated the Cataract Cobwebs, by a score of 12 to 8. In 1883, they formed the Stalwarts and Independents, first and second nines. *Niagara Falls Gazette* (August 14, 1883): "Three innings of a very lively game of ball was played on the Ontario Street diamond yesterday afternoon. The contesting nines were from the dining room of the International Hotel, and styled the Stalwarts under W. B. Shiloh and the Independents under Captain T. Demery, with S. Burnette as umpire and Frank Cannon as scorer. Time was closed at the end of the third inning, when it stood Independents 18, Stalwarts 11." They played the waiters of the Spencer House, crushing them by the score of 20 to 8. In 1886, *New York Freeman* (July 24, 1886): "The Cataract boys have organized their famous Base Ball nine, with Mr. J. C. Anderson as manager, and Richard Dangerfield, captain. The boys of the International have also organized a club, and anticipate having some interesting games with the cataract boys, their old antagonists, Mr. Richard Bennett being captain." By 1893, the club was still going strong: in a doubleheader, Rochester, NY's Colored Athletics defeated the Internationals 24 to 6, and 11 to 2.

SOURCES: "Base Ball," *Niagara (NY) Gazette*, Jul 1, 1868; "The Twenty-Ninth Anniversary Celebration of the Colored People," *Lockport (NY) Daily Journal*, Aug 4, 1868; "Local and Vicinity," *Niagara Gazette*, Aug 17, 1870; "Brevities," *Niagara Gazette*, Aug 25, 1875; "Base Ball," *Niagara Gazette*, Aug 6, 1878; "Base Ball," *Niagara Gazette*, Aug 12, 1878; "Brevities," *Niagara Gazette*, Aug 28, 1878; "Brevities," *Niagara Gazette*, Aug 28, 1878; "Brevities," *Niagara Gazette*, May 14, 1879; "Banquet," *Niagara Gazette*, Jun 25, 1881; "Banquet," *Niagara Gazette*, Sep 10, 1881; "Brevities," *Niagara Gazette*, Aug 6, 1882; "Base Ball," *Niagara Gazette*, Jun 15, 1883; "Base Ball," *Niagara Gazette*, Jun 20, 1883; "Brevities," *Niagara Gazette*, Jul 3, 1883; "Base Ball," *Niagara Gazette*, Jul 13, 1883; "Brevities," *Niagara Gazette*, Jul 27, 1883; "Brevities," *Niagara Gazette*, Jul 29, 1883; "Brevities," *Niagara Gazette*, Jul 23, 1883; "An Interesting Game of Ball," *Niagara Gazette*, Aug 14, 1883; "From Niagara Falls," *New York (NY) Globe*, Jul 12, 1884; "Brevities," *Niagara Gazette*, Aug 21, 1885; "Niagara Drippings," *New York (NY) Freeman*, Jul 24, 1886; "Niagara Drippings," *New York Freeman*, Aug 28, 1886; "Niagara Festivities," *New York Freeman*, Sep 9, 1886; "Niagara Drippings," *New York Freeman*, Sep 11, 1886; "On the Diamond," *Niagara Gazette*, June 9, 1893.

Rising Star Base Ball Club (Northville, NY; 1870s)

The Rising Star B.B.C. organized in 1874, played black and white nines. *Long Island Southold Traveler* (March 12, 1874): "The return game of base-ball between the Mutuals and Rising Stars of Northville (both colored), was played in this village on Thursday. The Greenporters beat by a score of 51 to 4. The Stars rode into the village with flags flying. On taking the field they shone brightly, but when the contest was ended they were obscured by a dark cloud, and no flags could be perceived as they drove home."

SOURCES: "Greenport," *Southold (NY) Long Island Traveler*, Mar 12, 1874; "Mattituck," *Southold Long Island Traveler*, Mar 12, 1874; "Mattituck," *Southold Long Island Traveler*, Sep 9, 1874; "Mattituck," *Southold Long Island Traveler*, Dec 3, 1874; "Upper Aqueboque Record," *Babylon (NY) Signal*, Feb 26, 1876.

Eureka Base Ball Club (Nyack, NY; 1860s). Organizer(s): William Brown.

The Eureka B.B.C. organized in 1860s, played against black nines. They challenged Nyack's Adelphi nine for the black championship. *Rockland County Journal* (September 26, 1868): "On Saturday, a most remarkable game of base-ball was played between the Eurekas, the glorious sable champions of Piermont, and the 'Adelphis' of Nyack from Nyack. After the game was ended and which resulted favorably for the Eurekas by a score of 43 to 13, the ball which had been won was given up by the Adelphis."

SOURCES: "The Contest of the Races," *Nyack (NY) Rockland County Journal*, Nov 9, 1867; "The National Game," *Rockland County Journal*, Aug 29, 1868; "The National Game," *Rockland County Journal*, Sep 26, 1868.

Cuban Giants Base Ball Club (Olean, NY; 1900s)

The Cuban Giants B.B.C. organized in the 1900s, played white and black aggregations. *Rochester Democrat and Chronicle* (June 29, 1900): "The Albions defeated the Cuban Giants of Orleans on the Erie Street Grounds here today by a score of 13 to 7. The Cuban Giants of Orleans are a team composed entirely of colored players residing in Medina and Albion. Johnson at short played a fast game, accepting eight chances without an error. Allie Jones for the Giants led in batting and his work in right field was perfect."

SOURCES: "Base Ball," *Medina (NY) Register*, Jun 6, 1900; "Made a Strong Finish," *Rochester (NY) Democrat Chronicle*, Jun 29, 1900; "Batavia Juniors Won," *Batavia (NY) Daily News*, Sep 1, 1900.

Cottage Beach Hotel Base Ball Club (Ontario, NY; 1880s)

The Cottage Beach Hotel B.B.C. organized in the 1880s, played black and white clubs. *New York Freeman* (July 30, 1887): "The Cottage House Base Ball Nine played a match game with the Charlotte Stars (white), defeating them by a score of 8 to 1." *Freeman* (September 3, 1887): "One of the most exciting events which occurred last week was the base-ball match between the Cottage Hotel club (colored) and the Palmyras of Palmyra (white). As both teams had played and won games from the Othellos and Charlotte Stars great interest was taken in the match and quite a sum of money exchanged hands on the result. The result of 2 to 0 in favor of the Cottage club speaks for itself."

Sources: "Ontario Beach," *New York (NY) Freeman*, Sep 3, 1887; "Ontario Beach," *New York Freeman*, Jul 30, 1887; "Ontario Beach," *New York Freeman*, Aug 20, 1887; "Ontario Beach," *New York Freeman*, Aug 27, 1887; "Ontario Beach," *New York Freeman*, Sep 3, 1887.

Imperial Base Ball Club (Owego, NY; 1880s–1900s). Organizer(s): Charles King and Lyman Melvin.

The Imaperial B.B.C. organized in the 1880s, played black and white teams. An early rival was Ithaca's Forest Citys. *New York Freeman* (August 7, 1886): "Last Tuesday the Merry Makers of Geneva and the Forest City club played an exciting game of base-ball at the fairground. The home club won a decided victory, the score being 43 to 13." They defeated Auburn's black nine, by a score of 27 to 7. In a rivalry with the Forest Citys, the Owego Imperials split both home and away games. *New York Freeman* (September 4, 1886): "The Owego baseball club again defeated the home team Monday afternoon in this city. It is evident from the first that the training and discipline of the Owego nine were superior to ours."

Sources: "Ithaca Inklings," *New York (NY) Freeman*, Aug 7, 1886; "Ithaca Inklings," *New York Freeman*, August 14, 1886; "Ithaca Inklings," *New York Freeman*, Aug 18, 1886; "Ithaca Inklings," *New York Freeman*, Sep 4, 1886; "Sporting Notes," *Geneva (NY) Gazette*, Sep 10, 1886; "Oswego Occurrences," *New York Freeman*, Oct 16, 1886; "Ithaca Inklings," *New York Freeman*, Jan 15, 1887; "Colored Masons Will Convene," *Owego (NY) Record*, Jul 26, 1893; "Local Record," *Owego Record*, Jun 4, 1900; *Owego (NY) Tioga County Record*, Jun 7, 1900; *Owego Record*, Sep 6, 1900; *Owego Record*, Jun 27, 1901; *Owego Record*, Jun 26, 1901; "Our Colored Boys the Best," *Syracuse (NY) Journal*, Aug 29, 1901.

Lone Star Base Ball Club (Oyster Bay, Long Island, NY; 1880s–1890s). Organizer(s): Lance Conklin.

The Lone Star B.B.C. organized in the 1880s. The Lone Stars had great success during this period. *Huntington Long Islander* (August 28, 1885): "The Lone Star Base Ball Club are not satisfied with having defeated every club they have played this season but challenge any colored club on Long Island outside of Brooklyn. They are ready to play any day." *Newton Register* (September 22, 1887): "The Lone Star Base Ball Club [is] like Alexander the Great—weeping for more worlds to conquer. They have issued a challenged to any colored club in Queens and Suffolk Counties and cannot find a club that will accept their challenge. This being the case, they consider themselves champions of two counties." The Lone Stars developed a rivalry with the Lone Stars, of Jamaica, NY. *New York Age* (May 31, 1890): "There was an interesting game of base-ball played at Oyster Bay yesterday, on Saturday, between the Lone Stars of Jamaica and Lone Stars of Oyster Bay. The score was: Jamaica, 22; Oyster Bay, 14. There was great surprise at the defeat of the Oyster Bay, as they have not been defeated in 20 years."

Sources: "Oyster Bay," *Huntington (NY) Long Islander*, Aug 28, 1885; "Village Notes," *Huntington Long Islander*, Sep 11, 1885; "Oyster Bay," *Huntington Long Islander*, Aug 6, 1887; "Oyster Bay," *Huntington Long Islander*, Sep 17, 1887; "From Oyster Bay," *Newtown (NY) Register*, Sep 22, 1887; "Oyster Bay," *Huntington Long Islander*, Nov 5,

1887; "Oyster Bay," *Huntington Long Islander*, May 17, 1890; "Base Ball at Oyster Bay," *New York (NY) Age*, May 31, 1890; "Oyster Bay," *Huntington Long Islander*, Feb 22, 1890; "Oyster Bay," *Huntington Long Islander*, Jun 3, 1890; "Oyster Bay," *Huntington Long Islander*, Jun 7, 1890; "Oyster Bay," *Huntington Long Islander*, Apr 1, 1893; "Oyster Bay," *Huntington Long Islander*, Dec 15, 1894.

Peekskill ("Empires") Hotel Base Ball Club (Peekskill, NY; 1880s). Organizer(s): Aaron Briles and James L. Toliver.

The Peekskill ("Empires") Hotel B.B.C. organized in the 1880s. The team, composed of waiters (Empire Hotel of Syracuse), was organized by James L. Toliver and Aaron Briles. They developed a rivalry with Newburgh's black club. *Newburgh Register* (July 19, 1886): "The Empires of Peekskill, and the Live Oaks of Newburgh will play on the Benkard grounds. Both clubs are composed of colored men." *Cleveland Gazette* (August 7, 1886): "The Peekskill waiters have a baseball nine that is doing good work. They will play at Brooklyn next week. After they get home they will play any amateur nine in the State." *Newburgh News* (June 13, 1887): "[William] Squirely King's famous Fearnothing ball club (colored) will play the Star club from Peekskill at the Benkard grounds tomorrow." *Newburgh News* (June 15, 1887): "The biggest ball game of the season was that played at the Washington Heights base-ball ground, between Captain Squirely King's Fearnothings of this city, and the Stars of Peekskill. The Fearnothings are made up of the cream of Newburgh's colored ball players, and the Stars are composed of dark-hued aristocrats from Peekskill." They played white soldiers. *New York Sun* (July 13, 1887): "Yesterday the men of the Sixth Battery tried to beat the waiters at base-ball and got wolloped. Today the Forty-Seventh essayed the same tough job. They were beaten in four innings by 9 to 5. One of the [N]egroes was so delighted that he bounced up and down like a rubber ball on his head and heels."

Sources: "Baseball Boomlets," *Newburgh (NY) Register*, Jul 19, 1886; "The Coons at Play," *Newburgh Register*, Jul 21, 1886; "Syracuse Siftings," *New York (NY) Freeman*, Aug 14, 1886; "Syracuse, NY Siftings," *Cleveland (OH) Gazette*, Aug 7, 1886; "Brief and Pointed," *Newburgh (NY) News*, June 13, 1887; "Great Ball Playing," *Newburgh News*, June 15, 1887; "Doing Battalion Drill," *New York (NY) Times*, Jun 29, 1887; "Col. Gaylor Gets a Present," *New York (NY) Sun*, Jul 13, 1887.

Red Stocking Base Ball Club (Port Jervis, NY; 1880s–1890s). Organizer(s): John E. West; Robert Broadhead, Alex Taylor, Clarence Ray; John Westfall and Mark Brown.

The Red Stocking B.B.C. organized in 1885. The Reds played white and black nines. Its black rival was Middleton, NY. *Port Jervis Evening Gazette* (September 9, 1886): "A game of base-ball will be played on the Main Street grounds Thursday, September 9th, by two colored clubs, the Everetts of Goshen and Red Stockings of Port Jervis. Game called at 2:30 o'clock. An exciting game may be expected." *Port Jervis Tri-States Union* (September 16, 1886): "The Red Stockings of Port Jervis and the Blue Stockings [Everetts] of Goshen, both colored, played a game on the Main Street grounds in this place Tuesday afternoon, it was sharply contested, and was won by the Goshen nine on a score of 13 to 11." *Middleton Times* (July 28, 1892): "On Saturday last the Port Jervis Red Stockings, an aggregation of colored talent, came to Goshen to attempt to give Jim Green's club a severe drubbing on the baseball field." *Times* (August 1, 1892): "On Saturday this week the Port Jervis colored base-ball club will be taken to camp by the Goshen colored brethren. Bob Broadhead says they don't need to practice to 'slo' that Port Jervis crowd. Port Jervis players say Bob is a blower."

Sources: "There's a New Club in Town," *Port Jervis (NY) Evening*

Gazette, May 18, 1885; "Base Ball Notes," *Port Jervis (NY) Tri-States Union*, May 21, 1885; "Fun on the Ball Field," *Port Jervis Evening Gazette*, Jun 1, 1885; "A Game Between Colored Clubs," *Port Jervis Evening Gazette*, Jun 20, 1885; "The Paterson Excursion," *Port Jervis Evening Gazette*, Jun 25, 1885; "Base Ball," *Port Jervis Tri-States Union*, Jul 16, 1885; "Brief Mention," *Port Jervis Evening Gazette*, Jul 17, 1885; "The Red Stockings Defeated," *Port Jervis Evening Gazette*, Jul 21, 1885; "Red Stockings To Go To Goshen," *Port Jervis Evening Gazette*, Sep 25, 1885; "The Boss Coon Club," *Port Jervis Evening Gazette*, May 18, 1886; "Paragraphs from Far and Near," *Port Jervis Evening Gazette*, Sep 6, 1886; "Paragraph From Far and Near," *Port Jervis Evening Gazette*, Sep 6, 1886; "Base Ball by Colored Players," *Port Jervis Evening Gazette*, Sep 10, 1886; *Port Jervis Tri-States Union*, Sep 16, 1886; "Sport of the Diamond," *Port Jervis Evening Gazette*, May 15, 1889; "Goshen," *Middletown (NY) Times*, Jul 28, 1892; "Goshen vs. Port Jervis," *Port Jervis (NY) Times*, Aug 1, 1892.

Grays Base Ball Club (Poughkeepsie, NY; 1890s). Organizer(s): Garrett Deyo and Leander Deyo.

The Grays B.B.C. organized in the 1890s, played white and black nines. *Poughkeepsie Eagle* (May 28, 1890): "One of the closest games so far this season played Tuesday afternoon between the Poughkeepsie Grays, a nine of colored men, and the Review at the school grounds. There was good playing on both sides and some very hard hitting. Deyo, the pitcher for the Grays, made a clean hit over the trees into Eastman Park, one of the best hits ever made on the grounds. The Grays played a sharp game and batted well, but were unable to steal bases successfully...." *Eagle* (July 19, 1890): "There will be lots of fun on Warring's Base Ball Grounds when the Poughkeepsie Grays, the colored base-ball club of this city, will play with the Whiteports, a colored club, of Kingston. An admission fee of 15 cents will be charged to play necessary expenses."

Sources: "Base Ball," *Poughkeepsie (NY) Eagle*, May 19, 1890; "Base Ball," *Poughkeepsie Eagle*, May 28, 1890; "At Riverview," *Poughkeepsie Eagle*, May 31, 1890; "Base Ball Matters," *Hudson (NY) Evening Register*, Jun 19, 1890; "Rhinebeck Items," *Poughkeepsie Eagle*, Jul 1, 1890; "Sporting Matters," *Kingston (NY) Weekly Freeman and Journal*, Jul 3, 1890; "Fun today," *Poughkeepsie Eagle*, Jul 19, 1890; "Base Ball," *Poughkeepsie Eagle*, Jul 21, 1890; "Base Ball," *Poughkeepsie Eagle*, Aug 31, 1891.

Worth House (Independent) Base Ball Club (Poughkeepsie, NY; 1880s–1890s). Organizer(s): Garrett Deyo and Leander Deyo.

The Worth House (Independent) B.B.C. organized in the 1880s. The team, composed of hotel waiters, nicknamed themselves, the Independents. *Poughkeepsie Eagle* (August 6, 1883): "Quite a large assemblage of people gathered on the grounds of Professor Warring's Institute on Saturday afternoon to witness the game between the Lone Stars of Newburgh, and the Independents, of this city, both composed of colored men. The playing was very fine, especially on part of the Poughkeepsie club. Leander Deyo, first base, G. Deyo, pitcher, and B. Whitney, catcher, all of the Independents, played in a splendid manner throughout. Both teams wore neat and tasty uniforms, and presented a splendid appearance." They reorganized in 1884. *Eagle* (July 3, 1884): "A game of base-ball was played on Professor Warrings' grounds between the Independents (colored) and Volunteers, Friday afternoon. The Independents were victorious by a score of 12 to 10." *Hudson Evening Register* (September 25, 1889): "The game of base-ball played between the waiters of the Nelson House, this city, and the waiters of the Worth House, Hudson, played in the afternoon, showed that the Hudson boys were no match for the Poughkeepsians. The latter won the game by the score of 13 to 7. In the Nelson House nine R. Ross was the pitcher, Charles Tread-way the catcher, and J. Rose, third base. In the Hudson nine Leandro Deyo was the pitcher, Mr. Hill the catcher, and Mr. Maw the third base man." *Rhinebeck Gazette* (September 29, 1889): "The game of base-ball played between the waiters of the Nelson House, Poughkeepsie and the waiters of the Worth House, Hudson, played in the afternoon, was won by the former by a score of 13 to 7." They reorganized in 1891. *Poughkeepsie Eagle* (August 31, 1891): "A fine game of baseball was played on the Riverview grounds Saturday between the Atlantics and Independents, both teams being from this city. The Atlantics won by a score of 8 to 2. Rose and Deyo were the battery for the Independents."

Sources: "Base Ball—Newburgh Beaten," *Poughkeepsie (NY) Eagle*, Aug 4, 1883; "Base Ball," *Poughkeepsie Eagle*, Aug 6, 1883; "Colored Base Ball Club," *Poughkeepsie Eagle*, Aug 15, 1883; "Base Ball," *Poughkeepsie Eagle*, Aug 21, 1883; "Notes About Town," *Kingston (NY) Freeman*, Jun 11, 1884; "Base Ball," *Poughkeepsie Eagle*, Jul 3, 1884; "Base Ball," *Poughkeepsie Eagle*, Jul 5, 1884; "Base Ball," *Poughkeepsie Eagle*, Aug 9, 1886; "Base Ball Matters," *Hudson (NY) Evening Register*, Aug 12, 1886; "Base Ball—A Disappointment," *Poughkeepsie Eagle*, Sep 4, 1887; "Base Ball," *Poughkeepsie Eagle*, Sep 26, 1888; "Base Ball," *Poughkeepsie Eagle*, Sep 29, 1888; "Base Ball Matters," *Hudson (NY) Evening Register*, Sep 25, 1889; "The Base Ball Game," *Poughkeepsie Eagle*, Sep 26, 1889; "The County Fair," *Rhinebeck (NY) Gazette*, Sep 29, 1889 "Base Ball," *Poughkeepsie Eagle*, Aug 31, 1891.

Resolute Base Ball Club (Poughkeepsie, NY; 1870s). Organizer(s): Garrett Deyo and Leander Deyo.

The Resolute B.B.C. organized in the 1870s, played white and black teams. *Poughkeepsie Eagle* (November 1, 1874): "In a game between the Resolute and Atlantic clubs on Friday, the former were defeated. Score 55 to 13." *Eagle* (September 13, 1875): "There will be real enjoyment on the Eastman Park ball grounds this afternoon, being the match between the Resolutes of this city and the Lone Stars of Kingston, colored clubs. Both will play their best to win, and there will be lots of fun. An admittance of 15 cents will be charged to play expenses." *Poughkeepsie Eagle* (August 6, 1876): "The Monitors and Resolutes, colored base-ball clubs, played a game yesterday, resulting in favor of the Resolutes by a score of 33 to 11."

Sources: "The Ball and Bat," *Poughkeepsie (NY) Eagle*, Aug 4, 1874; "Base Ball," *Poughkeepsie Eagle*, Nov 1, 1874; "A Game of Ball," *Poughkeepsie Eagle*, May 31, 1875; "Base Ball," *Poughkeepsie Eagle*, Sep 13, 1875; "Base Ball," *Poughkeepsie Eagle*, Sep 22, 1875; "The Ball and the Bat," *Poughkeepsie Eagle*, Aug 4, 1876; "Base Ball," *Poughkeepsie Eagle*, Sep 29, 1876.

Earlington House Base Ball Club (Richfield Springs, NY; 1880s–1900s)

The Earlington Hotel B.B.C. organized in the 1880s, played white and black nines. A black rivalry with the Spring Hotel waiters developed. *Richfield Springs Mercury* (August 20, 1889): "The long talked of game of ball between representative nines from the Spring House and Hotel Earlington came off Monday afternoon. The clubs are both good as in former years as will be seen by the large scores, but the noise increased in proportion to the poor playing and the price of admission proved a good investment. Some remarkably good plays were made, notably the heavy batting of Gilliard, the battery work of Henry and Martin, whom the Earlingtons allege were brought here from Utica [Fearless Base Ball Club] for the occasion." The rivalry continued. *Richfield Springs Mercury* (August 14, 1890): "The most intensely exciting game of ball seen in Richfield in years was played at the Driving Park Friday afternoon between the Richfielders and the Earlington waiters. The score was about even throughout the game and the score was kept down to the average professional match."

Richfield Springs Mercury (September 8, 1891): "It was more beer than ball at the game Friday afternoon between the waiter nines, and it made ones' sides sore from laughing at the many ludicrous things done. The ball was batted for two or three baggers and home runs were numerous through wild throwing and poor catching. Noise! Well there was lots of it. Every player managed to get to third base hence none went dry. Only five innings were played, the score standing 22 to 20 in favor of the Earlingtons."

SOURCES: "Richfield Springs," *New York (NY) Freeman*, Aug 14, 1886; "Spring House Wins," *Richfield Springs (NY) Mercury*, Aug 22, 1889; *Richfield Springs Mercury*, Sep 5, 1889; "Local and Personal," *Richfield Springs Mercury*, Aug 7, 1890; "The Richfielders Win," *Richfield Springs Mercury*, Aug 14, 1890; "The Richfielders Win Again," *Richfield Springs Mercury*, Aug 21, 1890; "Town and Vicinity," *Richfield Springs Mercury*, Jul 30, 1891; "The Earlingtons Win," *Richfield Springs Mercury*, Aug 6, 1891; "Society," *Richfield Springs Mercury*, Sep 3, 1891; "Society," *Richfield Springs Mercury*, Sep 8, 1891; "Richfield, 6; Waiters, 1," *Richfield Springs Mercury*, Aug 13, 1891.

New American Hotel Base Ball Club (Richfield Springs, NY; 1880s–1890s)

The New American Hotel B.B.C. organized in the 1880s, played similar organizations. *Richfield Springs Mercury* (August 23, 1888): "The first regular match base-ball game took place at the Driving Park Tuesday afternoon, between the Richfield picked nine and the New American nine. The contest was brief, only five innings, which resulted in a score of 11 to 13 in favor of the New American nine. For the New Americans G. Booker was at his best, and proved a puzzle to the Richfields, and was well-backed by Smith. The other features were the fine fielding of [Francis] Cardozo and [Joseph] Savoy, and a remarkable catch by [G.] Goines." *Mercury* (August 23, 1888): "A brisk shower yesterday afternoon made the game of ball between the New Americans and Spring House nines look dubious, but it cleared away and the contest was begun. The grass was wet and the diamond muddy, and liberal doses of the mucky soil, was brought up town on the player's trousers. The game was as one-sided as the handle of a jug, and it will take a lively team to get away from the Americans. The feature of the game was a triple play on the first inning by [William T.] Smith, [Charles] Booker and [Francis] Cardoza."

SOURCES: "Summer Summary," *Richfield Springs (NY) Mercury*, Jul 19, 1888; "20 to 1," *Richfield Springs Mercury*, Aug 23, 1888; "Base Ball," *Richfield Springs Mercury*, Aug 8, 1892; "Base Ball," *Richfield Springs Mercury*, Aug 11, 1892.

Spring House Base Ball Club (Richfield Springs, NY; 1880s–1890s)

The Spring House B.B.C. organized in the 1880s, if not earlier. The club, composed of waiters, played black and white teams. *Richfield Springs Mercury* (August 23, 1888): "A brisk shower yesterday afternoon made the game of ball between the New Americans and Spring House nines look dubious, but it cleared away and the contest was begun. The grass was wet and the diamond muddy, and liberal doses of the mucky soil, was brought up town on the player's trousers. The game was as one-sided as the handle of a jug, and it will take a lively team to get away from the Americans. The feature of the game was a triple play on the first inning by [William T.] Smith, [Charles] Booker and [Francis] Cardoza." The Spring House regularly played the waiters of the Earlington Hotel. *Richfield Springs Mercury*: "It was more beer than ball at the game Friday afternoon between the waiter nines, and it made ones' sides sore from laughing at the many ludicrous things done. The ball was batted for two or three baggers and home runs were numerous through wild throwing and poor catching. Noise! Well there was lots of it. Every player managed to get to third

base hence none went dry. Only five innings were played, the score standing 22 to 20 in favor of the Earlingtons."

SOURCES: "Albany Notes," *New York (NY) Freeman*, Jun 26, 1886; "Richfield Springs," *New York Freeman*, Aug 28, 1886; "20 to 1," *Richfield Springs (NY) Mercury*, Aug 23, 1888; "Town and Vicinity," *Richfield Springs Mercury*, Jul 30, 1891; "The Earlingtons Win," *Richfield Springs Mercury*, Aug 6, 1891; "Society," *Richfield Springs Mercury*, Sep 3, 1891.

Colored Athletics Base Ball Club (Rochester, NY; 1890s). Organizer(s): Henry A. Williams.

The Colored Athletics B.B.C. organized in the 1890s, played white and black teams. *Niagara Falls Gazette* (June 9, 1893): "The Athletics and the International waiters played two games of baseball and in both the waiters were defeated. The battery for the winning team was McGill and Phillips and for the International boys Smith and Wesley. The first game was a very good one and some very creditable playing done, but in the last game wild throwing toward the end of the game was, as the Umpire said, Right in Order." *Rochester Democrat and Chronicle* (July 27, 1894): "The Colored Athletics beat the Powers Hotel Colored nine yesterday by a score of 27 to 5. The features of the game were the batting of John Rowe, Henry Thomas, Jack Gibbs, and a home run by George Gibbs." *Democrat and Chronicle* (September 9, 1894): "The Colored Athletics defeated the Pines [white] yesterday by a score of 10 to 6." *Democrat and Chronicle* (June 21, 1895): "The Genesees defeated the Colored Athletics at South Park grounds yesterday afternoon by a score of 22 to 12. Batteries: for the Genesees, Strowger and Ford; for the Athletics, Rowe and James."

SOURCES: "On the Diamond," *Niagara Falls (NY) Gazette*, Jun 9, 1893; "Told in a Line, or Two," *Niagara Falls Gazette*, Jun 29, 1893; "Amateur Ball," *Rochester (NY) Democrat and Chronicle*, Jun 20, 1894; "Amateur Ball," *Rochester Democrat and Chronicle*, Jul 27, 1894; "Amateur Ball," *Rochester Democrat and Chronicle*, Jun 20, 1894; "Amateur Ball," *Rochester Democrat Chronicle*, Sep 9, 1894; "Amateur Ball," *Rochester Democrat and Chronicle*, May 31, 1895; "Amateur Ball," *Rochester Democrat and Chronicle*, Jun 6, 1895; "Amateur Ball," *Rochester Democrat and Chronicle*, Jun 21, 1895; "Amateur Ball," *Rochester Democrat Chronicle*, Jun 17, 1896.

Dauntless Base Ball Club (Rochester, NY; 1880s). Organizer(s): J. J. Lawrence.

The Dauntless B.B.C. organized in the 1880s, played black teams. *Rochester Democrat and Chronicle* (August 27, 1886): "A ten inning game was played at the State Industrial Home yesterday between the Dauntless (colored) nine and the Excelsiors of the school, score being 8 to 8." *Cleveland Gazette* (September 4, 1886): "The game between the Dauntless and Excelsiors resulted in a tie. The prize, a beautiful bat, offered by Misses A. and E. Holmes to the gent who made the most home runs, was won by J. J. Lawrence, who made three."

SOURCES: "Stolen Bases," *Rochester (NY) Democrat and Chronicle*, Aug 27, 1886; "Rochester, NY," *Cleveland (OH) Gazette*, Aug 28, 1886; "Rochester, NY," *Cleveland Gazette*, Sep 4, 1886.

Douglass League (Rochester, NY; 1880s–1900s). Organizer(s): John W. Thompson; Thomas Platner and William Clark.

The Douglass League was a social club, with social/cultural/political interests. They organized a ball club that played black and white aggregations. The organization also hosted pleasant and profitable social and cultural entertainments. One event hosted a violin solo and address on the study of Henry W. Longfellow. John W. Thompson was a central figure of the organization. Thompson was a social reformer and member of the Colored Republican Party and a central figure in the socio-cultural life of black Rochester; in 1888, he served as President (which sponsored a ball club) and served as chairman for the monument committee dedicated to raising funds to build a testament to his friend, Frederick Douglass. He served as National Treasurer for the Afro-American Council. He rubbed shoulders with the periods literary and intellectual figures; among them Paul Lawrence Dunbar, Charles W. Chesnutt and W. E. B. DuBois. By 1891, the club's membership included the city's top black players; among them, Ed Matthews, J. Poindexter (of Williamsport, PA) and Fred Gilmore. The Douglass League celebrated the Emancipation Day celebration with a ball game. They had originally scheduled to play the Buffalo Colored Stars B.B.C. However, they backed out and the nine scheduled Elmira. *Rochester Democrat Chronicle* (August 6, 1891): "At 4 o'clock this afternoon there will be a game of base-ball at Culver Park between the Elmira Casinos and a team from the Douglass League." They played a Native American team. *Democrat and Chronicle* (July 4, 1895): "The game at Riverside Park will not be for any championship. It will perhaps be the most novel base-ball exhibition, it not the most scientific, as the contesting clubs are composed of members of the Douglass League of this city, while their adversaries come from the Onondaga reservation of Indians near Syracuse. Prizes are offered for good plays, and the Indians will coach their base runners in their native language. Game will be called at 3 o'clock." *Democrat and Chronicle* (July 8, 1897): "The team commonly known as Pony Moore's Stars defeated the Douglass League baseball team at South Park Tuesday afternoon in a very close and exciting contest by a score of 11 to 10."

SOURCES: "Rochester Ripples," *New York (NY) Age*, Nov 11, 1889; "Rochester Ripples," *New York Age*, November 30, 1889; "The League in Rochester," *New York Age*, Dec 21, 1889; "Rochester Ripples," *New York Age*, Feb 1, 1890; "On Emancipation Day," *Rochester (NY) Democrat and Chronicle*, Jun 24, 1891; "Rochester Ripples," *New York Age*, Sep 26, 1891; "Amateur Ball," *Rochester Democrat and Chronicle*, Jun 11, 1895; "Amateur Ball," *Rochester Democrat Chronicle*, Jun 14, 1895; "Amateur Ball," *Rochester Democrat Chronicle*, Jun 19, 1895; "Diamond Dots," *Rochester Democrat and Chronicle*, Jun 29, 1895; "Amateur Ball," *Rochester Democrat and Chronicle*, Jun 2, 1897; "Amateur Ball," *Rochester Democrat and Chronicle*, Jul 8, 1897.

Eureka Base Ball Club (Rochester, NY; 1870s). Organizer(s): Augustus Bloxsum, W. H. McDonald and Harry G. Johnson.

The Eureka B.B.C. organized in the 1870s, played against black nines. *Rochester Evening Express* (July 31, 1878): "The Eureka Base Ball Club was organized in this city July 17th, 1878; it is composed of colored men. They would like to hear from the Fearless of Utica, Pastimes of Syracuse, Casinos of Elmira, and all the other colored clubs in the State. All challenges to be sent to W. H. McDonald, secretary, No. 1118 West Main Street, Rochester." *Rochester Union and Advertiser* (September 18, 1878): "There will be a match game of base-ball on the Rochester grounds, Union Street, between the Eureka B. B. C. (colored) of this city, and the Pastime B. B. C., of Syracuse, (colored). Both are very fine clubs and a very interesting game may be looked for. Game to be called at 3 pm." *Syracuse Sunday Times* (September 29, 1878): "The Pastimes (colored), of this city, went to Rochester on Tuesday last, and laid out the Eurekas (colored0 of that place, by a score of 10 to 4."

SOURCES: "New York State News," *New York (NY) Evening Telegram*, Jun 29, 1876; "New York State News," *Rochester (NY) Evening Express*, Jul 31, 1878; "Local Matters," *Rochester (NY) Union and Advertiser*, Sep 18, 1878; "Sporting Events," *Chicago (IL) In-Ocean*, Aug 10, 1878; "Ball Notes," *Syracuse (NY) Standard*, Sep 24, 1878; "Notes," *Syracuse (NY) Sunday Times*, Sep 29, 1878.

Hartford Base Ball Club (Rochester, NY; 1870s). Organizer(s): H. WA, J. H. Wein and William Stewart.

The Hartford B.B.C. organized in the 1870s, played against black nines. *Rochester Democrat and Chronicle* (July 30, 1875): "The Hartford club (colored) played their first match game yesterday afternoon, with the Unexpected, Charles Bannister captain, and beat them by a score of 37 to 12. They then played a picked nine and won 33 to 6." The nine got into a dispute with a local white team over the use of the name. The Hartfords challenged them for name rights (in 1871, the Boston Resolutes had a similar dispute).

SOURCES: "Base Ball Notes," *Rochester (NY) Evening Express*, Jul 23, 1875; "The National Game," *Rochester (NY) Democrat and Chronicle*, Jul 27, 1875; "The National Game," *Rochester Democrat and Chronicle*, Jul 28, 1875; "Base Ball," *Rochester Democrat and Chronicle*, Jul 30, 1875; "Base Ball," *Rochester Democrat and Chronicle*, Aug 31, 1875; "Base Ball," *Rochester Democrat and Chronicle*, Sep 4, 1875.

Livingston Hotel Base Ball Club (Rochester, NY; 1880s–1890s). Organizer(s): Horace H. Hall.

The Livingston Hotel B.B.C. organized in the 1880s, if not earlier. The Livingstons played black and white nines. The black waiters of the Powers and Livingston hotels developed a rivalry. *Cleveland Gazette* (May 11, 1888): "a game of base-ball will be played between H. H. Hall's nine of Livingston [Hotel], and John W. Thompson's nine of the Powers Nine." *Rochester Democrat and Chronicle* (August 1, 1888): "A silver pitcher will be given to the victorious nine in the game at the Emancipation Day celebration at Maple Grove Thursday between the waiters of the Powers and Livingston. John W. Thompson is captain of the former nine and Horace H. Hall of the latter." *Democrat and Chronicle* (August 3, 1888): "A game of ball was played between nines from Powers Hotel and from the Livingston. The Livingstons won the game by a score of 19 to 14. The batteries were [John] Downes and [William] Brooks, [William H.] Phillips and [William H.] Stockton." They also played Elmira's famed Casino team. *Elmira Telegram* (August 24, 1890): "The greatest ball game of the season will be played at the Fair Grounds next Tuesday, between the two colored clubs, Casinos, of Elmira, and Livingstons, of Rochester. The clubs were to have played on Emancipation Day and were both anxious for it, but the elements forbade, and the game was postponed. Go to see them if you want to see base-ball and hear coaching that is funnier than a minstrel show." *Democrat and Chronicle* (June 25, 1890): "The Police nine [white] defeated the Livingston Hotel nine yesterday afternoon at Culver Park by a score of 10 to 5." They played against other black hotel teams. *Democrat and Chronicle* (August 23, 1890): "The Livingston Hotel nine will play the Powers Hotel nine at Culver Park, Tuesday afternoon, September 16th, at 3 o'clock." *Democrat and Chronicle* (July 27, 1894): "The Colored Athletics beat the Powers Hotel nine yesterday by a score of 27 to 5."

SOURCES: "Base Ball News," *Cleveland (OH) Gazette*, May 11, 1888; "Caught Between Bases," *Rochester (NY) Democrat and Chronicle*, Aug 1, 1888; "Emancipation Day," *Rochester Democrat and Chronicle*, Aug 1, 1888; "The Day They Celebrate," *Rochester Democrat and Chronicle*, Aug 3, 1888; New York (NY) "Rochester Ripples," *Age*, Jul 26, 1890; "The Amateurs," *Rochester Democrat and Chronicle*, Jun 25, 1890; "Notes," *Rochester Democrat and Chronicle*, Aug 23, 1890; "Livingstons vs. Casinos," *Elmira (NY) Telegram*, Aug 24, 1890; "Notes," *Rochester Democrat and Chronicle*, Sep 15, 1890; "Base Ball at Rochester," *New York Age*, Sep 27, 1890; "Amateur Ball," *Rochester Democrat and Chronicle*, Apr 26, 1894; "Amateur Ball," *Rochester Democrat and Chronicle*, Jul 27, 1894.

Powers Hotel (Flyaway) Base Ball Club (Rochester, NY; 1880s). Organizer(s): Andrew O. Dixon; John B. Hall and William Stockton; Thomas E. Platner.

The Powers Hotel (Flyaway) B.B.C. organized in the 1880s. Composed of waiters, they played black and white nines. *Rochester Democrat and Chronicle* (July 7, 1888): "A nine from the new Osburn House defeated the Powers Flyers yesterday by a score of 5 to 0. Only five innings were played. The Powers Flyaways were defeated by a club made up of Whitcomb House and Osborn House employees yesterday on the Monroe Avenue Grounds. The score stood 5 to 0. Battery for the Flyaways, John Downes and [A.] Brown. The Powers Hotel Dining Room Waiters will receive a challenge from any colored nine in the city. They will play at any time, having had due notice. The captain is John B. Hall, and the secretary is William H. Stockton." *Democrat and Chronicle* (July 15, 1888): "The Powers Base Ball Club, composed of dining room waiters of the Powers Hotel, defeated the Ermines [white] at Monroe Park yesterday by a score of 18 to 5, in a six-inning game. Battery: [William H.] Phillips and Scanlon." A rivalry developed with the black waiters of the Livingston Hotel. *Democrat and Chronicle* (August 1, 1888): "A silver pitcher will be given to the victorious nine in the game at the Emancipation Day celebration at Maple Grove Thursday between the waiters of the Powers and Livingston. John W. Thompson is captain of the former nine and Horace H. Hall of the latter." *Democrat and Chronicle* (August 3, 1888): "A game of ball was played between nines from Powers Hotel and from the Livingston. The Livingstons won the game by a score of 19 to 14. The batteries were [John] Downes and [William] Brooks, [William H.] Phillips and [William H.] Stockton."

SOURCES: "Base Ball News," *Cleveland (OH) Gazette*, May 11, 1888; "Touched Out," Rochester *(NY) Democrat and Chronicle*, Jun 23, 1888; "Fielder's Choice," *Rochester Democrat and Chronicle*, Jul 6, 1888; "Base Ball in Brief," *Rochester Democrat and Chronicle*, Jul 7, 1888; "Fielder's Choice," *Rochester Democrat and Chronicle*, Jul 15, 1888; "Struck Out," *Rochester Democrat and Chronicle*, Jul 20, 1888; "Caught Between Bases," *Rochester Democrat and Chronicle*, Aug 1, 1888; "Emancipation Day," *Rochester Democrat and Chronicle*, Aug 1, 1888; "The Day They Celebrate," *Rochester Democrat and Chronicle*, Aug 3, 1888.

Sumner Base Ball Club (Rochester, NY; 1870s). Organizer(s): Thomas Portland, J. H. Wein and Andrew Jackson.

The Sumner B.B.C. organized in the 1870s, played against white and black clubs. *Rochester Democrat and Chronicle* (September 4, 1875): "Thursday evening a colored club was organized under the title of the Sumner Base Ball Club. Yesterday they played a practice game with a picked nine on the Hunter Street grounds, which resulted in a victory for the Sumner club by a score of 32 to 27." *Democrat and Chronicle* (September 15, 1875): "The Sumner (colored) ball club played a game with the Unexpected, and defeated them by a score of 26 to 23."

SOURCES: "Base Ball," *Rochester (NY) Democrat and Chronicle*, Aug 31, 1875; "Base Ball," *Rochester Democrat and Chronicle*, Sep 4, 1875; "Base Ball," *Rochester Democrat and Chronicle*, Sep 15, 1875.

Unexpected Base Ball Club (Rochester, NY; 1860s–1880s). Owner(s): James B. Jenkins, Edwin H. Brown, William H. Bruce, Frank Stewart, Charles Redmond Douglass, Charles Bannister, Andrew O. Dixon.

The Unexpected B.B.C. organized in the 1860s, played black and white nines. Charles Bannister, William Stewart and Frank Stewart (along with Charles Redmond Douglass) helped to organize the team. Between 1866 and 1870, Frank Stewart—called a magnificent

player—caught for the team. *Rochester Evening Express* (August 2, 1869): "The Unexpected Club of this city will attend the Great Emancipation Celebration at Medina tomorrow and play for a prize silver cup valued at $25. Frank Stewart is the captain of the nine." In 1860s, they defeated prominent black nines, including Niagara Falls' Lincoln and Utica's Fearless nines. *Rochester Daily Union and Advertiser* (August 21, 1866): "The Unexpected (colored) Base Ball Club of this city yesterday played the Lincoln Club of Niagara Falls a match game of ball and succeeded in beating their opponent two to one. The playing of the Unexpected Club was said to be of the highest order." *Daily Union and Advertiser* (August 22, 1866): "The Unexpected Club of this city went to Niagara Falls yesterday and played a match game of ball with the Lincoln Club, of that place. Owing to the lateness of the hour only four innings were played, resulting in favor of the Unexpected Club by a score of 50 to 15." In the 1870s, led by Charles Bannister (probably Stewart's teammate), the Unexpecteds played white and black clubs. *Rochester Democrat and Chronicle* (July 30, 1875): "The Hartford club (colored) played their first match game yesterday afternoon, with the Unexpected, Charles Bannister captain, and beat them by a score of 37 to 12. They then played a picked nine and won 33 to 6." *Democrat and Chronicle* (September 15, 1875): "The Sumner (colored) ball club played a game with the Unexpected, and defeated them by a score of 26 to 23." *Democrat and Chronicle* (June 21, 1876): "The Colored club, the Unexpected, went down to Palmyra, and played with the Palmyra boys and were defeated by a score of 6 to 4." They reorganized in the 1880s. Andrew O. Dixon, of the Powers Hotel, assumed control of the club. *Democrat and Chronicle* (July 21, 1885): "The Unexpected Colored Base Ball Club, of Powers Hotel, has recently purchased new uniforms and is prepared to receive challenges." *Democrat and Chronicle* (July 29, 1885): "The Unexpected Base Ball Club, of Powers Hotel, defeated the Unknowns yesterday, by a score of 11 to 6." *Democrat and Chronicle* (May 23, 1886): "The Excelsiors of the House of Refuge [white], defeated the Unexpecteds, composed of Powers Hotel waiters, on the House of Refuge grounds yesterday by a score of 12 to 9." *New York Freeman* (August 21, 1886): "Rochester boasts of its colored base-ball club, as they are doing up all the other clubs they come in contact with."

SOURCES: "Base Ball at Niagara Falls," *Rochester (NY) Union and Advertiser*, Aug 21, 1866; "Base Ball at Niagara Falls," *Lockport (NY) Journal*, Aug 22, 1866; "Alerts and Protectives," *Rochester Union and Advertiser*, Aug 22, 1866; "Disbanding the Protectives," *Rochester Union and Advertiser*, Sep 6, 1866; "Ball Matches Yesterday," *Rochester Union and Advertiser*, Sep 11, 1866; "Common Council," *Rochester Union and Advertiser*, Oct 31, 1866; "Base Ball," *Rochester (NY) Evening Express*, Aug 2, 1869; "Base Ball," *Rochester (NY) Democrat and Chronicle*, Jul 30, 1875; "Base Ball," *Rochester Democrat and Chronicle*, Sep 15, 1875; "Base Ball," *Rochester Democrat and Chronicle*, Jun 21, 1876; "Emancipation Celebration," *Rochester Democrat and Chronicle*, Jun 16, 1885; "Emancipation Celebration," *Rochester Democrat and Chronicle*, Jun 21, 1885; "Diamond Dust," *Rochester Democrat and Chronicle*, July 29, 1885; "Diamond Dust," *Rochester Democrat and Chronicle*, Jul 30, 1885; "Base Ball Matters," *Rochester Democrat and Chronicle*, Aug 6, 1885; "Diamond Dust," *Rochester Democrat and Chronicle*, Aug 7, 1885; "Stolen Bases," *Rochester Democrat and Chronicle*, May 23, 1886; "Rochester Notes," *New York (NY) Freeman*, Aug 21, 1886.

Fearless Base Ball Club (Rome, NY; 1890s)

The Fearless B.B.C. organized in the 1890s, played black teams. *Rome Semi-Weekly Citizen* (May 31, 1890): "The Fearless Base Ball Club, of this city, and the Cuban Giants, of Oneida, played a match game at Riverside Park Monday. The Romans were victorious in a score of 32 to 7."

SOURCES: "The Local Diamond," *Rome (NY) Semi-Weekly Citizen*, May 31, 1890; "Base Ball," *Rome (NY) Sentinel*, Jul 15, 1890; "City Gab," *Rome Semi-Weekly Citizen*, Jul 16, 1890; "City Gab," *Rome Semi-Weekly Citizen*, Jul 18, 1890.

Vinnett Base Ball Club (Rome, NY; 1890s). Organizer(s): Frank Sears.

The Vinnett B.B.C. organized in 1890, played black and white teams. *Rome Roman Citizen* (May 10, 1890): "The Vinnet Base Ball Club is the name of a colored organization in this city. The players are Frank Sears, Will Wilson, Edward Wilson, Robert Wilson, Fred Jackson, Albert Freeman, Grant Jackson, Albert Wilson and Charles Sherman."

SOURCES: "The Local Diamond," *Rome (NY) Roman Citizen*, May 10, 1890; "The Local Diamond," *Rome (NY) Semi-Weekly Citizen*, May 31, 1890.

White Stockings Base Ball Club (Rome, NY; 1890s). Organizer(s): Frank Pell.

The White Stockings B.B.C., of Utica, NY, organized in the 1890s, played black and white teams. *Utica Union* (June 11, 1896): "The base-ball contest between the Fearless Juniors and the White Stockings at Riverside Park yesterday afternoon attracted quite a crowd. The Fearless team won by a score of 27 to 4. Batteries for Fearless; Jackson and Peresett; for White Stockings, Morris and Pell; managers, for Fearless, B. Pell; for White Stockings, Frank Pell; umpire: John Carter."

SOURCES: "Jottings," *Utica (NY) Daily Union*, Jun 11, 1896; "Local Base Ball," *Utica (NY) Journal*, Jul 26, 1896.

Frontenac Hotel Base Ball Club (Round Island, NY; 1890s)

The Frontenac Hotel B.B.C. organized in the 1880s, played black and white teams. The waiters, who all hailed from Philadelphia, claimed themselves champions of the river. *Watertown Times* (August 18, 1890): "A game of base-ball was played here yesterday afternoon between the colored waiters of the Thousand Island House and the college students. The score was 10 to 13 in favor of the former team."

SOURCES: "River Notes," *Watertown (NY) Times*, Aug 18, 1890; "Hibernians Picnic," *Syracuse (NY) Standard*, Jul 25, 1895; "Base Ball at the Bay," *Watertown Times*, Aug 24, 1895; "The River Resorts," *Syracuse Standard*, Jul 27, 1896; "The Islands," *Syracuse Standard*, Jul 11, 1897; "Frontenac," *Syracuse Standard*, Jul 15, 1897; "From the Island City," *Watertown (NY) Times*, Jul 17, 1897; "Notes From the Park," *Watertown Times*, Jul 19, 1897; "At the Islands," *Syracuse Standard*, Jul 26, 1897; "Weather Sets 'Em Planning," *Syracuse Standard*, Jul 29, 1897; "Events at the Islands," *Watertown Times*, Aug 5, 1897; "River Incidents," *Syracuse Standard*, Aug 13, 1897; "Isles Swept by a Gale," *Syracuse Standard*, August 14, 1897; "T. I. Park Notes," *Watertown Times*, Aug 13, 1897; "T. I. Park," *Watertown Times*, Aug 23, 1897; "At the Thousand Isles," *Watertown Times*, Aug 26, 1897.

Atlantic Base Ball Club (Sag Harbor, NY; 1870s)

The Atlantic B.B.C. organized in the 1870s, played against black and white nines. *New Clipper* (April 8, 1876): "They have a crack club in Sag Harbor, Long Island, which is ambitious of the championship honors of the colored nines of the Island, Where is the Williamsburg Unique Nine?" The Sag Harbor (NY) *Corrector* (June 13, 1876): "The Atlantics, of Sag Harbor, and Mutuals of Greenport, played their third trial game of Base-Ball on Monday, at the grounds on Bay Street. The game was well-played and resulted in a victory for the Atlantics, the score standing 7 to 4. Both clubs consist of col-

ored Americans." *Corrector* (June 20, 1876): "The Atlantic Base Ball Club (colored), of Sag Harbor, played a match game with the Exfords, of Southampton [white], on the 29th day of December 1875, Southampton. The score stood as follows: Atlantics, 3 innings, 22 runs; Exfords 4 innings, 7 runs. On the following Wednesday, the next game was played at Sag Harbor, with the following results: Atlantics 9 innings, 29 runs; Exfords, ditto, 15 runs."

SOURCES: *Sag Harbor (NY) Corrector*, Mar 11, 1876; "Base Ball Notes" *New York (NY) Clipper*, Apr 8, 1876; "Base Ball," *Sag Harbor Corrector*, Jun 13, 1876; "Fair Play," *Sag Harbor Corrector*, Jun 20, 1876.

Broughton House (Saratoga Springs, NY; 1880s–1890s). Owner(s): John C. Broughton.

John C. Broughton, a Brooklyn-based caterer, and saloonkeeper, opened the Broughton House. The summer resort, exclusively for blacks, had first class accommodations: *New York Globe* (August 11, 1883): "Its appointments are excellent. The addition contains single and double rooms, all light and airy and neatly furnished. The café and dining rooms are neat and comfortable. A new floor on the dancing platform would prove of great benefit to dancers." There was also a swing garden, bowling alley, croquet grounds, billiard room, barber shop and bar. Resort guests included ball players, musicians, and other cultural elites; having close connections with the waiters/base-ballists of the Clarendon hotel, athletes like Stanislau K. Govern (Washington, DC's Manhattans and Trenton, NJ's Cuban Giants), Frank Hart (Saratoga, NY's Leonatus Club, St. Louis, MO's Black Stockings and professional walker), and Henry Bridgewater (St. Louis Black Stockings). Its piazza and parlors would be filled with guests, entertained with singing, dancing and music.

SOURCES: "Saratoga Notes," *New York (NY) Globe*, Aug 11, 1883; "Saratoga Locals," *New York Globe*, Jul 19, 1884; "Troy Items," *New York Globe*, Aug 16, 1884; "Saratoga Locals," *New York Globe*, Sep 13, 1884; "Saratoga Springs Hotel," *Washington (DC) Bee*, Apr 17, 1886; "Saratoga Springs," *New York (NY) Freeman*, Jul 17, 1886; "Saratoga Springs," *New York Freeman*, Jun 25, 1887; "Some Race Doings," *Cleveland (OH) Gazette*, Oct 1, 1887; "Saratoga," *Washington Bee*, Sep 7, 1889; "Brooklyn Briefs," *New York (NY) Age*, Dec 6, 1890; "Brooklyn Briefs," *New York Age*, April 18, 1891; "Brooklyn Briefs," *New York Age*, May 2, 1891; "Obituary Notes," *New York (NY) Sun*, May 7, 1903; "Contests Broughton Will," *Brooklyn (NY) Eagle*, Mar 30, 1904.

Clarendon Base Ball Club (Saratoga Springs, NY; 1880s). Organizer(s): Stanislau K. Govern.

The Clarendon B.B.C. organized in the early 1880s. The Clarendons (predecessors of Washington, DC's Manhattan B.B.C.) competed with white and black hotel nines. *Saratoga Springs Saratogian* (July 20, 1882): "The Clarendons defeated the Grand Unions in a well contested game of base-ball Saturday afternoon on the South Broadway Grounds by a score of 11 to 2. The playing of Strather, Barker, Boyd, Buchanan and Wilson of the Clarendons, and Savoy and Smith of the Grand Unions was much enjoyed by hundreds of spectators. This is the eighth game won by the Clarendons this season without a single defeat." *New York Globe* (July 7, 1883): "The lovers of athletic sports, at the Clarendon, Congress, and Grand Union, have organized base-ball clubs. A practice game was played last Saturday, on South Broadway, between the Clarendon and Congress nines. The Clarendon nine proved their superiority by out-batting and out-fielding their opponents at every point. We suggest to the players that a stop board be erected behind the catcher ad the grass cut. This would involve a trifling expense. It is stated that Anderson Marshall will bring his nine [West Ends, of Long Branch] up later in the season to play the best team here. The team reorganized in 1884. *Saratogian* (August 14, 1884): "The Clarendons, of Saratoga, a colored club, will play next Saturday with T. Elixman Base Ball Club, and the Stars of Fort Edward the following week."

SOURCES: "Base Ball," *Saratoga (NY) Saratoga Springs Saratogan*, Jul 20, 1882; "Shorts," *Saratoga Springs Saratogian*, Aug 2, 1882; "Shorts," *Saratoga Springs Saratogian*, Aug 27, 1882; "Shorts," *Saratoga Springs Saratogian*, Aug 22, 1882; "Base Ball," *Saratoga Springs Saratogian*, Jul 17, 1882; "Shorts," *Saratoga Springs Saratogian*, Aug 12, 1882; "Shorts," *Saratoga Springs Saratogian*, Aug 30, 1882; "Shorts," *Saratoga Springs Saratogian*, Jun 16, 1883; "Shorts," *Saratoga Springs Saratogian*, Jul 4, 1883; "Saratoga Springs," *New York (NY) Globe*, Jul 7, 1883; "Base Ball," *Saratoga Springs Saratogian*, Jul 17, 1883; "Base Ball," *Saratoga Springs Saratogian*, Jul 18, 1883; "Pinafores Defeat the Clarendons," *Saratoga Springs Saratogian*, Jun 19, 1883; "Saratoga Letter," *New York Globe*, Jul 28, 1883; "From the Springs," *New York Globe*, Aug 4, 1883; "Base Ball," *Saratoga Springs Saratogan*, August 4, 1883; "Base Ball," *Saratoga Springs Saratogan*, August 6, 1883; "Saratoga Notes," *New York Globe*, Aug 11, 1883; "Base Ball," *Saratoga Springs Saratogan*, Aug 18, 1883; "Shorts," *Saratoga Springs Saratogan*, Aug 20, 1883; "Saratoga Gossip," *New York Globe*, Aug 25, 1883; "Saratoga Letter," *New York Globe*, Sep 1, 1883; "Corinth," *Saratoga Springs Saratogan*, Aug 14, 1884.

Davis Base Ball Club (Saratoga Springs, NY; 1880s)

The Davis B.B.C. organized in 1883. The team, named for Miss Vinton H. Davis, and composed of waiters, honored special guests visiting the resort. *Saratoga Springs Saratogian* (August 4, 1883): "The most pleasant and amusing game ever played in Saratoga was witnessed yesterday afternoon by about four hundred persons, the occasion being the first game between the Layton and Davis Base Ball Clubs. The arrival in Saratoga of Professor John Layton, the celebrated basso, and Miss H. Vinton Davis, the promising tragedienne, both of Washington, D.C. Messrs. William Browne, S. K. Govern and William Lazenberry organized the two clubs in their honor. The inaugural games proved to be quite interesting and satisfactory to all."

SOURCES: "Base Ball," *Saratoga Springs (NY) Saratogan*, Aug 4, 1883; "Base Ball," *Saratoga Springs Saratogan*, Aug 6, 1883; "Saratoga Notes," *New York (NY) Globe*, Aug 11, 1883; "Base Ball," *Saratoga Springs Saratogan*, Aug 18, 1883; "Shorts," *Saratoga Springs Saratogan*, August 20, 1883; "Saratoga Gossip," *New York Globe*, Aug 25, 1883.

Layton Base Ball Club (Saratoga Springs, NY; 1880s)

The Layton B.B.C. organized in 1884. The team, named for John Layton, and composed of waiters, honored special guests visiting the resort. *Saratoga Springs Saratogian* (August 4, 1883): "The most pleasant and amusing game ever played in Saratoga was witnessed yesterday afternoon by about four hundred persons, the occasion being the first game between the Layton and Davis Base Ball Clubs. The arrival in Saratoga of Professor John Layton, the celebrated basso, and Miss H. Vinton Davis, the promising tragedienne, both of Washington, D.C. Messrs. William Browne, S. K. Govern and William Lazenberry organized the two clubs in their honor. The inaugural games proved to be quite interesting and satisfactory to all."

SOURCES: "Base Ball," *Saratoga Springs (NY) Saratogan*, Aug 4, 1883; "Base Ball," *Saratoga Springs Saratogan*, Aug 6, 1883; "Saratoga Notes," *New York (NY) Globe*, Aug 11, 1883; "Base Ball," *Saratoga Springs Saratogan*, Aug 18, 1883; "Shorts," *Saratoga Springs Saratogan*, August 20, 1883; "Saratoga Gossip," *New York Globe*, Aug 25, 1883.

Leonatus (Leonidas) Base Ball Club (Saratoga Springs, NY; 1880s)

The Leonatus B.B.C. organized in 1883. The nine, composed of waiters, played similar organizations. *New York Globe* (August 11, 1883): "The challenge of the Leonatus Club is still open, none of the

other nines seeming to care to accept it, through a vague fear that the track boys will not give up the stakes if they lose." The Leonatus club played the Clarendons for the local black championship.

SOURCES: "From the Springs," *New York (NY) Globe*, Aug 4, 1883; "Saratoga Notes," *New York Globe*, Aug 11, 1883; "Saratoga Locals," *New York Globe*, Jul 5, 1884.

Pinafore Base Ball Club (Saratoga Springs, NY; 1880s). Organizer(s): William Lazenberry.

The Pinafore B.B.C., of Saratoga, NY, organized in 1883. The Pinafores were one of Saratoga's premiere black clubs. *Saratoga Springs Saratogian* (July 16, 1883): "The Pinafore Base Ball Club defeated the Clarendons on Saturday, after a hard and well-played game. Both clubs deserve credit for their good playing, making but a few errors. If the managers of the two clubs continue to keep the club in good training, the lovers of base-ball in Saratoga will be treated to some very fine games." *Saratogian* (July 18, 1883): "Managers William Lazenberry of the Pinafore and S. K. Govern of the Clarendon have made arrangements to play a series of games to take place on Wednesdays and Saturdays of each week during the season for the Championship of Saratoga and the Clarendon Hotel pennant for 1883, commencing today, the club winning the majority of the games to hold both for '84. The clubs are evenly matched and the anxiety of each to be victorious, with the discipline under which the managers keep the players will, no doubt, make the games between these clubs very interesting during the entire season." In the follow-up, the Clarendons won by a score of 3 to 2. In another contest, they played a tie game, 4 to 4. The Clarendons won the next contest by a score of 9 to 1. After losing a $50 wager and by their chief rival, the Pinafores, the Clarendons defeated the Pinafores for the fifteen dollar Silver Ball by a score or 5 to 1.

SOURCES: "Shorts," *Saratoga Springs (NY) Saratogian*, Jun 16, 1883; "Shorts," *Saratoga Springs Saratogian*, Jul 4, 1883; "Saratoga Springs," *New York (NY) Globe*, Jul 7, 1883; "Base Ball," *Saratoga Springs Saratogian*, Jul 17, 1883; "Base Ball," *Saratoga Springs Saratogan*, Jul 18, 1883; "Pinafores Defeat the Clarendons," *Saratoga Springs Saratogian*, Jun 19, 1883; "Saratoga Letter," *New York Globe*, Jul 28, 1883; "Base Ball," *Saratoga Daily Saratogian*, Aug 2, 1883; "From the Springs," *New York Globe*, Aug 4, 1883; "Base Ball," *Saratoga Springs Saratogan*, Aug 4, 1883; "Base Ball," *Saratoga Springs Saratogan*, Aug 6, 1883; "Saratoga Notes," *New York Globe*, Aug 11, 1883; "Base Ball," *Saratoga Springs Saratogan*, Aug 18, 1883; "Shorts," *Saratoga Springs Saratogan*, Aug 20, 1883; "Saratoga Gossip," *New York Globe*, Aug 25, 1883.

Union Base Ball Club (Saratoga Springs, NY; 1870s). Organizer(s): William Clemens, Frank Smith and Alex Brown.

The Union B.B.C. organized in 1870, played black and white clubs. Among the latter, the Unions played Saratoga's Hickory nine. *Saratoga Springs Saratogian* (May 19, 1870): "The Unions (colored) and Hickories contested a game of base-ball on the Loughberry Ground Thursday afternoon, resulting in a victory for the former 26 to 24. Some creditable playing was exhibited on both sides." They played a picked nine of black players from Troy's Hannibals, Gloversville's Flyaways and Schenectady's Colored Stars. *Saratogian* (June 8, 1872): "The Stars laid out a nice little game, hoping thereby to whitewash Saratoga's descendants of Ham. In making up the nine, they had secured aid of four Hannibals from Troy, three Julius Caesars from Gloversville, the remaining two being the only Stars in the game. Six innings were played." The Stars also played hotel nines, including the Grand Unions. They reorganized in 1874. *Saratogian* (September 14, 1874): "A base-ball game was played yesterday afternoon on the South Broadway Grounds, between the Unions, a Saratoga Club, and the Philadelphias, of the Grand Union. The result was a draw, each side scored 3. Frank Sanford made the best play of the Saratoga boys and B. Blanch did the same for the foreign club." The Philadelphias, composed of waiters, came from Philadelphia. *New York Clipper* (July 29, 1876): "At a meeting held July 19, 1876, the Union Base Ball Club (colored) of Saratoga, NY, was organized. The Unions have, it is said, has as fine an enclosed ground as there is in the State, and are ready to receive challenges from any colored club in the United States. They will share gate money liberally with visiting clubs, and give good accommodations. They are also prepared to receive propositions and make arrangements for games with all responsible clubs, as they oppose making an extended tour about the middle of September. All ball-tossers will please take notice, especially the Barbers, of Albany and Heavy Hitters of Johnston."

SOURCES: "Base Ball," *Saratoga Springs (NY) Saratogian*, May 19, 1870; "Base Ball," *Saratoga Springs Saratogian*, Jun 8, 1872; "Shorts," *Saratoga Springs Saratogian*, Oct 2, 1872; "Shorts," *Saratoga Springs Saratogian*, Jun 11, 1872; "Shorts," *Saratoga Springs Saratogian*, Oct 4, 1872; "Mutuals vs. Unions," *Saratoga Springs Saratogian*, Oct 7, 1872; "Shorts," *Saratoga Springs Saratogian*, Oct 11, 1872; "Shorts," *Saratoga Springs Saratogian*, Oct 14, 1872; "Locals," *Saratoga Springs Saratogian*, Sep 14, 1874; "Locals," *Saratoga Springs Saratogian*, Sep 18, 1874; "Shot Stops," *New York (NY) Clipper*, Jul 29, 1876.

United States Hotel Base Ball Club (Saratoga Springs, NY; 1870s–1890s). Organizer(s): Benjamin Franklin Boyd.

The United States Hotel B.B.C. organized in the 1870s, played similar organizations. *Saratoga Saratogian* (July 17, 1883): "The game was one-sided from start to finish, and Captain Jones, although a very fine player, will have to strengthen his nine before they can compete competitively with the Clarendons." *New York Tribune* (August 13, 1893): "Baseball contests between waiters representing some of the big caravansaries have attracted throngs to Woodlawn Oval two days this week. The Grand Unions and the United States faced each other Tuesday, and the Congress Hall and the Kensingtons met on the diamond Thursday. The waiters did the playing, while the guests from the hotel kept up at least a continuous applause, which at times became amazingly hilarious." Between 1894 and 1895, Benjamin Franklin Boyd, formerly of the original Cuban Giants, managed and captained the team.

SOURCES: "Base Ball," *Saratoga Springs (NY) Saratogian*, Jul 17, 1883; "Saratoga Springs," *New York (NY) Tribune*, July 23, 1893; "Saratoga at Its Best," *New York Tribune*, August 13, 1893; "Baseball Notes," *New York (NY) Sun*, July 23, 1894; "Baseball Notes," *New York Sun*, July 15, 1895.

Colored Base Ball Tournament (Schenectady, NY; 1870s)

Between 1870 and 1871, Schenectady, NY hosted two black baseball tournaments. In 1870, *New York Clipper* (August 20, 1870): "A colored tournament is to be held at Schenectady, New York, on the Alerts Grounds, August 22nd, to compete for the championship of the State. Four prizes are offered—a gold ball valued at $20; a silver ball valued at $20; and a gold and silver ball valued at $18 dollars. The Pastimes, of Schenectady; Baltimores of Troy; Heavy Hitters of Canajoharie; Fearless of Utica; Merry Nine of Geneva; the Wide Awakes of Johnston, and several other clubs whose names are unknown, are expected to enter." *Utica Observer* (August 23, 1870): "The tournament of colored base-ball clubs, which took place yesterday in Schenectady, passed off very quietly. The Hannibals of Troy won the first prize, a silver ball, and the Young Bachelors of Albany, the second prize. The Hannibals defeated the Flyaways of Johnston and the 'Pastimes' of Schenectady were defeated by the Bachelors." The Hannibals won the tournament. *Troy Whig* (August 23, 1870): "A base-ball tournament in which colored clubs were participants

took place at Schenectady yesterday. The Hannibal club of this city entered the list as competitors for the silver ball, which was one of the balls contended for. The Hannibals came off victorious by a score of 43 to 42 with an inning to spare." In 1871, another tournament occurred. *Brooklyn Eagle* (July 21, 1871): "The great event of the season is coming off at Schenectady on Monday next. The colored clubs of the State are to have a tournament in that ancient borough, and a splendid exhibition of the beauties of the National Game may be anticipated. The Hannibals of Troy intend to bring home the emblems of championship. Stand from under."

SOURCES: "On the Half Shell," *New York (NY) Clipper*, Aug 20, 1870; "Base Ball," *Troy (NY) Whig*, Aug 23, 1870; "New York State News," *Utica (NY) Morning Herald*. 1871; "Base Ball," *Troy Whig*, Jul 20, 1871; "Base Ball," *Brooklyn (NY) Eagle*, Jul 21, 1871; "Base Ball," *Troy Whig*, Jul 26, 1871.

Star Base Ball Club (Schenectady, NY; 1870s)

The Star B.B.C. organized in the 1870s. In 1870, the Stars played Saratoga's Union club. The team was composed of players from Troy's Hannibals, Gloversville's Flyaways, and the Stars. The Unions were too much. *Saratoga Springs Saratogian* (September 18, 1874): "The Stars laid out a nice little game, hoping thereby to whitewash Saratoga's descendants of Ham. In making up the nine, they had secured aid of four Hannibals from Troy, three Julius Caesars from Gloversville, the remaining two being the only Stars in the game. Six innings were played."

SOURCES: "Locals," *Saratoga Springs (NY) Saratogian*, Sep 14, 1874; "Locals," *Saratoga Springs Saratogian*, Sep 18, 1874.

Prospect House Base Ball Club (Shelter House, NY; 1880s). Organizer(s): George T. Tucker.

The Prospect House B.B.C. organized in the 1880s, played similar nines. *Brooklyn Eagle* (August 11, 1891): "The guests of the Prospect house, Shelter Island, are often engaged during the week watching the national game played on the grounds of the Prospect house, between the prospects, a nine composed of waiters of the house, and either clubs composed guests or visiting teams. So far, the Prospects have won every game but two they have played, and George T. Tucker, the headwaiter at the Prospect house, is more than pleased with the work his nine has done." *Brooklyn Eagle* (July 16, 1893): "The most interesting base-ball game of the week was played on Friday afternoon before an enthusiastic audience, which spread itself in true summer style over the grass over the hill overlooking the prospect grounds. The college team, much to the chagrin and disappointment of the waiters, won very easily. The latter were overconfident of their abilities and lost money on the result. No score was made by the waiters after the second inning."

SOURCES: "Sporting News from Shelter House," *Brooklyn (NY) Eagle*, Aug 11, 1891; "Two Novel Concepts at Long Island," *Brooklyn Eagle*, Jul 10, 1893; "Fun at Shelter island," *Brooklyn Eagle*, Jul 16, 1893.

Empire House Base Ball Club (Syracuse, NY; 1880s)

The Empire House B.B.C. organized in the 1880s, played against black teams. *Cleveland Gazette* (June 28, 1884): "The waiters of the Empire House have a base-ball nine and are ready for challenges from any hotel nine in the city." *Syracuse Herald* (August 21, 1886): The Leland Hotel nine defeated the Empire House waiters by a score of 14 to 7 on Friday afternoon at the Adams Street grounds. The batteries were Pessett and Stuart, and Cooper and Brown."

SOURCES: "Syracuse," *Cleveland (OH) Gazette*, Jun 28, 1884; "With the Amateurs," *Syracuse (NY) Herald*, May 26, 1889; "On the Diamond," *Syracuse (NY) Standard*, May 26, 1889.

Globe Hotel Base Ball Club (Syracuse, NY; 1880s–1900s). Organizer(s): William H. Franklin; William H. Franklin, Jr., and Fred Bennett.

The Globe Hotel B.B.C. organized in the 1880s, played black and white teams. *Cleveland Gazette* (October 3, 1885): "Last Monday the Globe Hotel Base Ball Club played a picked nine on the University Grounds and were too strong for their white opponents. The Globe boys demonstrated the fact that they can chase balls as well as plates. The score was: Globe boys, 12; Picked Nine, 7. Umpire: James Dixon."

SOURCES: "Syracuse Siftings," *Cleveland (OH) Gazette*, Oct 3, 1885; "Syracuse Siftings," *New York (NY) Freeman*, Aug 14, 1886; "In Baseball Circles," *Rochester (NY) Democrat and Chronicle*, Apr 16, 1897; "Our Colored Troops the Best," *Rochester Democrat and Chronicle*, Aug 29, 1901.

Pastime Base Ball Club (Syracuse, NY; 1870s–1890s). Organizer(s): J. J. Lawrence, James H. Allen, Jacob Francis and W. F. Meyers; William H. Franklin, J. H. Walters and George Ennols.

The Pastime B.B.C. organized in 1870. The Central Depot nine or "Pastimes," played black and white nines. *Syracuse Daily Journal* (October 7, 1875): "There will be an amateur game at Lakeside Park this afternoon, commencing at 3 o'clock, between the waiters at the Vanderbilt House and the Central Depot Dining Room." They established a rivalry with Utica's Fearless club. *Utica Morning Herald* (October 9, 1875): "The Fearless Base Ball Club, of this city, will play the Pastimes of Syracuse, in that city next Tuesday. The Fearless boys are the champion colored club of the State, and will probably bring brine into the eyes of its opponents." The organization formed the nucleus of Syracuse's Pastime B.B.C. *Syracuse Standard* (August 15, 1879): "Colored men of the Seventh and Eighth wards—mostly men who are employed at the Central Road depot dining rooms, some time ago organized a nine to be known as the Pastimes. They are to practice at Lake Park when the park is not otherwise engaged." *Syracuse Courier* (October 12, 1879): "The game was a good one and the few who witnessed it, had more than their money's worth. The Pastimes struggled manfully, and took their defeat in good spirit, trusting to better luck next time. The D. R. V. G.'s owe their victory to their hard hitting, which at times completely rattled their opponents." They played black and white clubs, the latter including the Central Citys. *Syracuse Standard* (May 5, 1880): "The Central Citys again defeated the Pastimes at Newell Park yesterday. But six innings were played, during which the batting of the Central Citys was heavy." The club reorganized in 1885. The press: "A meeting was held last night at William H. Franklin's for the organization of a base-ball team of colored men. William H. Franklin was elected president; J. H. Walters, treasurer; and George Ennols, secretary; Charles Jefferson was elected captain of the team, and Jacob Francis manager. A committee on by-laws was appointed. Messrs. Franklin, Donovan, and Francis were named as a committee to solicit subscriptions. The organization will take the name of 'Pastimes,' a colored club that played with great success in 1870."

SOURCES: "Base Ball Notes," *Syracuse (NY) Journal*, Oct 7, 1875; "City and County," *Utica (NY) Morning Herald*, Oct 9, 1875; "Base Ball," *Syracuse (NY) Standard*, Jun 3, 1876; "Base Ball," *Syracuse Journal*, Jul 12, 1879; "Base Ball Notes," *Syracuse Standard*, Aug 15, 1879; "Base Ball," *Syracuse (NY) Sunday Courier*, Oct 12, 1879; "Base Ball," *Syracuse Standard*, Mar 14, 1880; "Base Ball," *Syracuse Standard*, May 4, 1880; "A Hard Fight," *Syracuse Standard*, May 5, 1880; "Base Ball," *Utica (NY) Morning Herald*, Aug 10, 1880.

Wide Awake Base Ball Club (Syracuse, NY; 1880s)

The Wide Awake B.B.C. organized in the 1880s, played against white and black teams. *Syracuse Standard* (August 21, 1886): The

Syracuse Wide Awakes defeated the Hartford Wide Awakes by 2 to 1 in eleven innings. Tobin won the game by a home run."

SOURCES: "Sporting Notes," *Syracuse (NY) Journal*, Aug 20, 1886; "Sporting Notes," *Syracuse (NY) Standard*, Aug 21, 1886.

Centennial Base Ball Club (Troy, NY; 1870s)

The Centennial B.B.C. organized in the 1870s, played against black teams. *Hudson Register* (August 17, 1876): "A match game of baseball was played at Coxsackle Tuesday, between the Centennials of Troy, and the Bachelors of Albany, (both colored). Darkness came on at the close or the fourth inning. The game as far as played resulted in a victory for the Centennials, the score being 25 to 17."

SOURCES: "Base Ball at Coxsackle," *Hudson (NY) Register*, Aug 17, 1876; "All Sorts," *Albany (NY) Morning Express*, Aug 19, 1876.

Hannibal Base Ball Club (Troy, NY; 1860s–1890s)

The Hannibal B.B.C. organized in 1870, played white and black nines. In 1870, the Hannibals played one of the best teams in the Mid-Atlantic, the WA Mutuals, who defeated them twice at Troy, 60 to 13 and 40 to 39. That same year, the Hannibal nine participated in a black tournament at Schenectady. *Troy Whig* (August 23, 1870): "A base-ball tournament in which colored clubs were participants took place at Schenectady yesterday. The Hannibal club of this city entered the list as competitors for the silver ball, which was one of the balls contended for. The Hannibals came off victorious by a score of 43 to 42 with an inning to spare." *Gloversville Intelligencer* (July 20, 1871): "The Hannibals, of Troy, and the Flyaways of this village, (both colored clubs), played on a match game on the Union Fair Grounds, on Monday afternoon last, resulting in favor of the Hannibals, by a score of 39 to 34. Both clubs played splendidly." The Hannibals also challenged the local white nines, including the Haymakers and Putnams. In 1877, the organization again came to the forefront, defeating the Stars of Lansingburgh (white) by a score of 7 to 2. They reorganized in the 1890s. *Gloversville Leader* (September 8, 1893): "The colored Athletics of this city went to Troy this morning to meet the Hannibals of that city on their diamond. They announced that a return game will be played here next Thursday."

SOURCES: "Base Ball," *Troy (NY) Whig*, Aug 23, 1870; "Base Ball," *Troy Whig*, Aug 25, 1870; "Base Ball," *Troy Whig*, Aug 26, 1870; "Game Between Colored Clubs," *Troy (NY) Times*, Aug 23, 1870; "Base Ball," *Troy Times*, Aug 24, 1870; "Base Ball," *Troy Whig*, Sep 24, 1871; "Homespun," *Troy Whig*, Jun 21, 1871; "Base Ball," *Troy Whig*, Jun 27, 1871; "Base Ball," *Gloversville (NY) Intelligencer*, Jul 20, 1871; "Base Ball," *Troy Whig*, Jul 21, 1871; "Base Ball," *Brooklyn (NY) Eagle*, Jul 21, 1871; "Base Ball," *Troy Whig*, Jun 29, 1871; *New York (NY) Spirit of the Times*, Aug 5, 1871; "Sports and Pastimes," *Brooklyn Eagle*, Sep 23, 1871; *Albany (NY) Argus*, Sep 25, 1873; "Amusements," *Troy Times*, Aug 3, 1877; "Local Record," *Gloversville (NY) Leader*, Sep 8, 1893.

William Rich Base Ball Club (Troy, NY; 1860s). Organizer(s): William Rich.

The William Rich B.B.C. organized in the 1860s, played black nines. The William Rich nine was organized by tonsorial artist and community activist, William Rich. *Troy Press* (August 25, 1869): "At a practice game of the William Rich Base Ball Club on the Putnam Grounds Monday, the Colored Knights of the willow seemed at one time more ambitious in the line of breaking shins, than attending strictly to the legitimate requisitions of the game. The gorgeous uniform recently purchased by the club, left their treasury in such a state of numismatic emaciation that the purchase of the ball was a financial impossibility. A few members, however, 'pooled in,' purchase a ball, each one subscribing becoming a stockholder in the aforementioned spherical necessity, and the game commenced. A fine looking light colored citizen of Cohoes was present by special invitation, intending of course, to participate. A few members, however, jealous of Isaac's fairer hue, vociferously objected. He submitting gracefully, quietly purchased of a few stockholders a controlling interest in the ball and took his position in the field. Finally, a skyscraper coming his way was neatly hooked and securely bagged in the capacious pocket of the strategic Isaac. And now the fight began. One McCoy, of Waterford—a living argument that the [N]egro is a connecting link, and &c was deployed as skirmisher, but immediately went to the ground and doubled up, like a stale bologna, the inducement to the aforesaid position being the foot of the doughty Isaac [Baltimore]. Then the line of battle, led by Jim Schuyler, the African contortionist, like an avalanche came thundering down. The enemy, undismayed by the onset, 'went down' into his side pocket. The Schuylerites saw, turned, and ignominiously fled, leaving Isaac master of the field. He, the conqueror, withdrew his hand, took a chew of pigtail, smiled triumphantly, and returned to his own castle and his own country. Our colored troops fought nobly."

SOURCES: "Public Meeting," *Troy (NY) Whig*, Jul 19, 1836; "Meeting of Colored Citizens," *Troy (NY) Budget*, Mar 24, 1842; *Troy Whig*, Jun 12, 1844; "Grand Concert," *Troy Whig*. September 1844; "To the Citizens of Troy," *Troy Budget*, Nov 4, 1849; "Statement of Votes," *Troy Whig*, Nov 16, 1856; "Latest News Items," *Troy (NY) Times*, Aug 3, 1858; "New Items," *Batavia (NY) Herald*, Nov 12, 1859; "Examination of the William Rich School," *Troy Whig*, Feb 18, 1868; "Base Ball in a New Phase," *Troy (NY) Press*, Aug 25, 1869.

Baggs Hotel Base Ball Club (Utica, NY; 1870s– 1900s). Organizer(s): Frank Johnson.

The Baggs Hotel B.B.C. organized in the 1870s. Many of the players, who belonged to Utica's Fearless nine, played similar teams. *Utica Observer* (July 30, 1879): "The third and last game between the colored waiters of Bagg's Hotel and Butterfield House was played at Riverside Park yesterday. The feeling of rivalry ran high. The Bagg's Hotel boys obtained a fine lead early in the game, but at the end of the fifth ending the score stood 6 to 6. Howard, of the Butterfield nine made some of his celebrated slides, carrying with him everything on the base, including the baseman. Jackson, of the Bagg's hotel nine, caught well. Baker made a creditable record. Thompson stole second several times, and held some fly balls with professional skill. Anderson played well and little Moses Gray, the shortstop of the Butterfield team, was a favorite from beginning to end. When Moss kicked off his shoes, went in barefooted and scored his run, the applause was unanimous. Mr. Johnson made some fine stops and accurate throws to first. Samuel Freeman batted and stole bases like a first class salaried player. Howard made a two-base hit and came into the home plate literally on his ear." *Utica Morning Herald* (July 21, 1885): "Yesterday afternoon at Riverside a game was played by the Bagg's hotel and Butterfield waiters. The contest was characterized by numerous errors and heavy batting. Good playing was done by Langston, Johnson, F. Westerband, McDaniels, Dorsey and the Butterfield battery." *Utica Observer* (August 26, 1904): "There was a game of baseball between the waiters of Baggs Hotel and Butterfield and it created no end of interest. It resulted in a victory for the Butterfield waiters by a score of 14 to 8."

SOURCES: "Notes," *Utica (NY) Observer*, Jun 9, 1879; "Observations," *Utica (NY) Morning Herald*, Jun 14, 1879; "Base Ball," *Utica Observer*, Jul 2, 1879; "Observations," *Utica Observer*, Jul 2, 1879; "Observations," *Utica Morning Herald*, Jun 14, 1879; "Base Ball," *Utica Morning Herald*, Jul 20, 1885; "The Waiter's Game," *Utica Morning Herald*, Jul 21, 1885; "Pinafore in Utica," *Utica Observer*, Jul 30, 1879;

"Other Games and Gossip," *Utica Observer*, Jul 5, 1886; "Head Waiters' Picnic," *Utica (NY) Herald Dispatch*, Aug 10, 1904; "The Organizations," *Utica Observer*, Aug 26, 1904.

Butterfield House Base Ball Club (Utica, NY; 1870s–1900s)

The Butterfield House B.B.C. organized in the 1870s. Some players also belonged to Utica's Fearless nine. They played against Utica's Bagg's Hotel B.B.C. *Utica Observer* (July 30, 1879): "The third and last game between the colored waiters of Bagg's Hotel and Butterfield House was played at Riverside Park yesterday. The feeling of rivalry ran high. The Bagg's Hotel boys obtained a fine lead early in the game, but at the end of the fifth ending the score stood 6 to 6. Howard, of the Butterfield nine made some of his celebrated slides, carrying with him everything on the base, including the baseman. Jackson, of the Bagg's hotel nine, caught well. Baker made a creditable record. Thompson stole second several times, and held some fly balls with professional skill. Anderson played well and little Moses Gray, the shortstop of the Butterfield team, was a favorite from beginning to end. When Moss kicked off his shoes, went in barefooted and scored his run, the applause was unanimous. Mr. Johnson made some fine stops and accurate throws to first. Samuel Freeman batted and stole bases like a first-class salaried player. Howard made a two-base hit and came into the home plate literally on his ear." *Utica Morning Herald* (July 21, 1885): "Yesterday afternoon at Riverside a game was played by the Bagg's hotel and Butterfield waiters. The contest was characterized by numerous errors and heavy batting. Good playing was done by Langston, Johnson, F. Westerband, McDaniels, Dorsey and the Butterfield battery." *Utica Observer* (August 26, 1904): "There was a game of baseball between the waiters of Baggs Hotel and Butterfield and it created no end of interest. It resulted in a victory for the Butterfield waiters by a score of 14 to 8." In the 1890s, they played the Fearless nine. *Utica Sunday Journal* (July 26, 1896): "On the Mohawk Flats yesterday afternoon a game of base-ball was played between the Fearless and Butterfield House nines. The latter won 10 to 5."

SOURCES: "Notes," *Utica (NY) Observer*, Jun 9, 1879; "Observations," *Utica (NY) Morning Herald*, Jun 14, 1879; "Base Ball," *Utica Observer*, Jul 2, 1879; "Observations," *Utica Observer*, Jul 2, 1879; "Pinafore in Utica," *Utica Observer*, Jul 30, 1879; "Observations," *Utica Morning Herald*, Jun 14, 1879; "Base Ball," *Utica Morning Herald*, Jul 20, 1885; "The Waiter's Game," *Utica Morning Herald*, Jul 21, 1885; "Pinafore in Utica," *Utica Daily Observer*, Jul 30, 1879; "Other Games and Gossip," *Utica Observer*, Jul 5, 1886; "Local Base Ball," *Utica (NY) Journal*, Jul 26, 1896; "Amateur Ball Games," *Utica (NY) Union*, Jul 27, 1896; "Head Waiters' Picnic," *Utica (NY) Herald Dispatch*, Aug 10, 1904; "The Organizations," *Utica Observer*, Aug 26, 1904.

Empire Base Ball Club (Utica, NY; 1860–1870s)

The Empire B.B.C. organized in 1869, played white and black nines. *Utica Observer* (July 11, 1870): "Captain Jackson, of the Empires, says his club will shortly challenge the 'White Stockings,' to play 'mumble the peg' for a rubber toothing ring." *Observer* (July 14, 1870): "The train that carried the Veteran Zouaves to Richfield Springs took along a sprinkling of blue jacketed base-ball players. The nine sons of sunny Afric, who hid their tanned faces underneath the projected peaks of sky-blue skull caps, composed the Empire Club. They visited Richfield Springs to play the Union Club, of that place, and if successful, they had the promise of the veteran, Captain Jones, that they should receive a suitable prize. Play commenced near the American Hotel, in good season. Seven innings resulted in favor of the Empires by a score of 28 to 26. The first inning the prospect looked black enough for the lads in the sky blue regimentals. They got a bad 'goose egg.'" *Observer* (July 22, 1870): "Captain Jones, of the Veteran Zouaves, conducted a little presentation this morning.

On behalf of the Zoo-Zoos he gave Captain Jackson, of the Empire Base Ball Club, a gold-lined silver cup. Captain Jones was entirely overcome with grateful emotion, and he called upon pitcher Pell to make a speech for the Club. The crowded conditions of the column forbid that we should attempt to print Mr. Pell's eloquent remarks. Go 'way Fred Douglass."

SOURCES: "B.B.," *Utica (NY) Observer*, Jul 11, 1870; "The Empire Club at Richfield Springs," *Utica Observer*, Jul 14, 1870; "The Empire Prize," *Utica Observer*, Jul 22, 1870; *Utica Observer*, Aug 12, 1870.

Fearless ("Black Stockings") Base Ball Club (Utica, NY; 1860s–1900s). Organizer(s): Theodore Freeman, Charles H. Lewis and A. C. DeWitt; Arlington C. DeNike; Samuel Freeman; Richard E. Warmouth; James Pell; and John Titus.

The Fearless B.B.C. organized in 1866, is the oldest and longest-running black nine in North America. The Fearless club's legacy is illuminating. It witnessed the Reconstruction and post–Reconstruction eras; the Plessy vs. Ferguson Supreme Court decision of 1896 (Separate-But-Equal"); the post-bellum Gilded Age, and the Progressive era. Organized in the western part of NY, the Fearless players comprised generations of family members: the Freeman, Lippen, Van Alstine, Jackson, Denike, Henry, Moss, Sherman and Pell clans formed lasting bonds, some through marriage. During Reconstruction, the aggregation of homegrown talent played local and regional (both black and white) nines: among the black teams, the Albany Bachelors, Buffalo Invincibles, Troy Hannibals, Canajoharie Heavy Hitters, Syracuse Pastimes, Johnstown Wide Awakes, and WA Mutuals figured prominently. Between 1867 and 1868, however, the Bachelor and Fearless teams split two games. They challenged Buffalo's nine. *Buffalo Commercial* (August 6, 1869): "The Fearless club of Utica, and the Invincibles of this city, contested yesterday on the Sixth Street grounds, for the State championship among colored clubs. The game attracted quite a crowd of spectators. The Invincibles proved themselves decidedly vincible, as will be seen by the score of 88 to 18 runs in favor of the Utica boys." They reorganized in the 1870s. *Utica Observer* (September 20, 1871): "The Fearless Base Ball Club, of this city, the champion colored organization of colored men in the State, went to Ilion yesterday morning, to play the Flyaways of Johnstown, for a silver-mounted bat. The Utica boys were victorious, as usual. But seven innings were played, three of which were continued through a heavy rain storm. The score was 61 to 34, in favor of the Fearless." They developed a rivalry with a white team called Academys. *Utica Morning Herald* (September 18, 1878): "Yesterday afternoon, at Riverside Park, the Academys, played the Fearless club, a colored team. There were about three hundred people present. Many of these were colored spectators, the eastern end of the grandstand being nearly full of colored ladies, who took an intense interest in the game. The Fearless boys were a little rusty, and did not get down to work until their opponents had gained a heavy lead. Among other things they permitted the Academys to make two very simple double plays. With a little more discipline, the Fearless team can again show some of their old-time excellence." *Morning Herald* (August 10, 1880): "One of the largest crowds seen at Riverside this season was present, yesterday afternoon, to witness the first Oneida county championship game, postponed from Monday week, between the Mutuals and Fearless (colored). Those who attended expecting to see an exciting contest were not disappointed. The Fearless club was short three of its best men: otherwise they might have won." They reorganized in the 1890s, and 1900s. *Utica Sunday Tribune* (August 2, 1891): "To many of the spectators at the Active-Fearless game at Riverside yesterday afternoon it looked as if that much abused but highly necessary official, the umpire, was considerably at fault for the colored team's defeat. He was quite severe on them all through the contest, and was quite off in his judgment on balls and strikes when members of the Fearless were at bat. The game was a most clever exhibition on the part of both sides, several notably good plays being made. The Fearless put up an excellent fielding game. Henry pitched by far the best game of any twirler this season in the City League, allowing but two scratch hits and having twelve strikeouts. Gray caught him in good style and batted hard, making three of his team's six hits, two of them two baggers." They also played the Butterfield House waiters. *Utica Sunday Journal* (July 26, 1896): "On the Mohawk Flats yesterday afternoon a game of base-ball was played between the Fearless and Butterfield House nines. The latter won 10 to 5." The "Fearless" played organized ball well into the twentieth century. *Utica Herald-Dispatch*: "The visiting team yesterday was made up of the old colored Fearless club of Utica. The game was of a loose order, owing to the condition of the grounds. The home team swelled its batting averages by long drives and White had the visitors at his mercy, letting up in the last inning."

SOURCES: "Base Ball," *Utica (NY) Observer*, Oct 24, 1866; "Base Ball," *Utica (NY) Morning Herald*, Nov 3, 1867; "Base Ball Extraordinary," *Utica Observer*, Oct 29, 1868; "Base Ball," *Buffalo (NY) Commercial*, Aug 6, 1869; "Base-Ball Matters," *Cincinnati (OH) Commercial Tribune*, Aug 18, 1869; "Events of the Week," *Utica (NY) Weekly Herald*, Sep 14, 1869; "Fearless and Heavy Hitters," *Utica Observer*, Sep 21, 1869; "The Fearless Base-Ball Club," *Utica Observer*, May 4, 1870; "Grand Celebration of the Ratification of the Fifteenth Amendment," *Utica Observer*, Jun 17, 1870; "The Colored Championship," *New York (NY) Herald*, Jul 24, 1870; "Still Champions of the State," *Utica Observer*, Sep 20, 1871; "Base Ball," *Buffalo (NY) Evening Courier and Republic*, Aug 26, 1876; "Grand Base Ball Tournament," *Geneva (NY) Gazette*, Sep 10, 1876; "Local Affair," *Buffalo (NY) Courier*, Sep 13, 1876; "Vicinity Items," *Geneva Gazette*, Sep 15, 1876; "Base Ball Tournament," *Geneva Gazette*, Sep 17, 1876; "Colored Ballists," *Buffalo Courier*, Sep 20, 1876; "Vicinity Items," *Geneva Gazette*, Sep 22, 1876; "The Fearless Champions at Little Falls," *Utica Observer*, Jul 29, 1879; "Base-Ball," *Utica Morning Herald*, Sep 18, 1878; "Base-Ball," *Utica Morning Herald*, August 10, 1880; "Base-Ball," *Utica Morning Herald*, August 17, 1881; "No Run To Spare," *Syracuse (NY) Standard*, October 4, 1882; "Gone to Ithaca," *Utica Observer*, August 2, 1883; "The Local Diamond," *Rome (NY) Semi-Weekly Citizen*, May 31, 1890; "Local Sports Booming," *Utica (NY) Sunday Tribune*, Apr 19, 1891; "Local Sports Looks Up," *Utica Sunday Tribune*, May 3, 1891; "Local Sporting Notes," *Utica Sunday Tribune*, May 17, 1891; "Shamrocks vs. Fearless," *Utica (NY) Press*, May 28, 1891; "Sports Pressings," *Utica Press*, Jun 18, 1891; "The Honors Were Given," *Utica Sunday Tribune*, Jun 28, 1891; "Stopped by the Police," *Utica Press*, Jun 29, 1891; "Twenty-One Arrested," *Utica Observer*, Jun 29, 1891; "Events On Many Ball Fields," *Utica Press*, Jun 29, 1891; "The Colored Boys Win," *Utica Press*, Jul 16, 1891; "Sports Pressings," *Utica Daily Press*, Jul 30, 1891; A Great Amateur Game," *Utica Sunday Tribune*, Aug 2, 1891; "Acmes, 10; Fearless, 4," *Utica Daily Press*, Aug 6, 1891; "They Stood No Show," *Utica Press*, Sep 1, 1891; "Upward Go the Actives," *Utica Sunday Tribune*, Sep 13, 1891; "Local Base Ball," *Utica (NY) Journal*, Jul 26, 1896; "Jottings," *Utica (NY) Union*, Jun 11, 1896; "Local Ball Players Signed," *Utica Union*, May 6, 1897; "Local Base Ball," *Utica Union*, May 28, 1897; "Local Base Ball," *Utica Union*, Jun 5, 1897; "Colored Ball in Ilion," *Utica Union*, Jun 11, 1897; "Defeated at Ilion," *Utica Sunday Tribune*, May 22, 1898; "Base Ball Notes," *Utica Press*, Jul 3, 1898; "Base Ball Notes," *Utica Press*, Jul 9, 1898; "Forestpost, 18; Fearless, 8," *Utica Press*, Jul 10, 1898; "Base Ball Notes," *Utica (NY) Sentinel*, Mar 24, 1900; "Base Ball at Ilion," *Utica (NY) Herald-Dispatch*, May 21, 1900; "Base Ball League," *Utica Herald-Dispatch*, Mar 24,

1900; "Base Ball at Ilion," *Utica Herald*, May 21, 1900; "Other Games," *Syracuse (NY) Evening Telegram*, May 21, 1900; "Free Doin's Club Field Day," *Utica Herald-Dispatch*, Sept. 14, 1900.

Fearless Junior Base Ball Club (Utica, NY; 1870s)

The Fearless Junior B.B.C. organized in 1875, played against black and white nines. *Utica Morning Herald* (September 7, 1875): "The Fearless, Jr., Base Ball Club, composed of colored boys, played a match game with the White Stockings, of Corn Hill, white boys, yesterday, and beat their opponents by a score of 12 to 5. The Fearless boys are proud of their victory."

SOURCES: "Base Ball," *Utica (NY) Morning Herald*, Sep 7, 1875; "Home Matters," *Utica Morning Herald, Sep* 15, 1875.

Help Up Base Ball Club (Utica, NY; 1890s–1900s). Organizer(s): James Pell, Jr., Charles W. Titus and Mose Gray.

The Help Up B.B.C. organized in 1897, played black and white teams. *Utica Union* (May 6, 1897): "The Help-Ups, the champion colored base-ball team of Central New York, issue a challenge to any amateur team in the state." In 1900, they played against the Free Doin's B.B.C., a local colored nine. *Utica Sunday Journal* (September 16, 1900): "The Help-Ups, captained by Charles Washington, and the Free Doin's under the direction of E. R. Rich, were 'in.' It was a five-inning affair and the Free Doin's succeeded in downing their opponents to the tune of score of 14 to 1. Some brilliant plays were made and the game well worth witnessing."

SOURCES: "Local Ball Players Signed," *Utica (NY) Union*, May 6, 1897; "Local Base Ball," *Utica Union*, May 28, 1897; "Local Base Ball," *Utica Union*, Jun 5, 1897; "Colored Ball in Ilion," *Utica Union*, Jun 11, 1897; "Free Doin's Outing," *Utica (NY) Sunday Journal*, Sep 16, 1900.

Wide Awake Base Ball Club (Utica, NY; 1880s)

The Wide Awake B.B.C. organized in the 1880s, played black teams. *Utica Press* (September 9, 1887): "Those who witnessed the ball game at Riverside yesterday afternoon between the Fearless and Wide Awake Clubs, composed of local colored players received full returns for their money and time spent. The Fearless club had a walkover after the fourth inning, but they did not prevent the usual number of amusing plays and side splitting incidents."

SOURCES: "Too Easy for the Fearless Club," *Utica (NY) Press*, Sep 9, 1887.

Young Cuban Giants Base Ball Club (Utica, NY; 1890s–1900s)

The Young Cuban Giants B.B.C. organized in 1896, played black and white teams. *Utica Morning Herald* (September 5, 1896): "The Young Cuban Giants defeated the John Street Sluggers by a score of 42 to 8. The battery for the Cuban Giants was Sherman and Henry." *Utica Sunday Journal* (July 30, 1896): "The Young Cuban Giants defeated the Whitesboro Street Stars, by a score of 15 to 8. Battery for Giants: Green, Akehurst and Jackson. *Utica Press* (June 2, 1901): "The Young Help Up club Saturday defeated the Young Cuban Giants, score 3 to 0. Batteries, for Help Ups, Green and Freeman, for Cuban Giants, Glasby and Lyles."

SOURCES: "Brevities," *Utica (NY) Morning Herald*, Sep 5, 1896; "Local Ball Notes," *Utica (NY) Sunday Tribune*, May 10, 1896; "Base Ball Notes," *Utica (NY) Sunday Journal*, Jul 30, 1896; "Notes," *Utica (NY) Press*, May 24, 1899; "Base Ball Notes," *Utica Press*, Jun 22, 1899; "Base Ball Notes," *Utica Press*, Jun 30, 1896; "Base Ball Notes," *Utica Press*, Jul 20, 1899; "Base Ball Notes," *Utica Press*, May 21, 1900; "Base Ball Notes," *Utica Press*, Jun 2, 1901.

Woodruff House Base Ball Club (Watertown, NY; 1880s)

The Woodruff House B.B.C. organized in the 1880s. The ball club, composed of waiters, played black and white nines. *Watertown Times* (May 31, 1889): "The association Athletic grounds presented a very attractive appearance yesterday afternoon. All was in readiness for the visitors, who not only packed the ground stand, but lined the fences. Many were agreeably surprised that the association had been able to secure and fit up such complete grounds. An entertaining ball game was played between the Woodruff House nine and the Athletic club nine. The writers did themselves credit in sticking grittily at work till the end, and the club nine can be assured of patronage through the season. Some very pleasing work was done in all parts of the field and at the bat." The Woodruff House waiters belonged to Watertown's "colored society."

SOURCES: "Y.M.C.A.," *Watertown (NY) Times*, May 25, 1889; "Yesterday's Sports," *Watertown Times*, May 31, 1889.

Unknown Base Ball Club (Weeksville [Brooklyn], NY; 1850s–1860s). Owner(s): J. Nelson Edgar, John Poole, Jr., Silas Wright and Benjamin C. Poole.

The Unknown B.B.C. organized in the 1850s, played black nines. *Brooklyn Eagle* (August 7, 1858): "Abase-ball club was organized Monday 9th instant., under the title of the Unknown Base Ball Club, with the election of the following officers: Benjamin C. Poole, President, Silas Wright, Vice President, J. Nelson Edgar, Secretary, John Poole, Jr., Treasurer." *New York Weekly Anglo-African* (December 3, 1859): "A match game was played between the Henson base Ball Club of Jamaica and the Unknown, of Weeksville, at Jamaica, Long Island, on Tuesday, November 15th, which resulted in another victory for the Henson." *Weekly Anglo-African* (January 21, 1860): "By the combined efforts of Robert Henson and Joseph Henson, of the Henson Base Ball Club, a grand festival was given at Edwards' Hall.... That beautiful prize ball won and carried off in triumph by the Henson Base Ball Club, of Jamaica, in their late match with the Unknown, of Weeksville, Long Island, and for which they deserve a great deal of credit, the club being but lately organized." *Brooklyn Eagle* (October 17, 1862): "Our reporter found a match in progress between the Unknown and Monitor Clubs—both of African descent. Quite a large assemblage encircled the contestants, who were every one as black as an ace of spades. Among the assemblage, we noticed a number of old and well known players, who seemed to enjoy the game more heartily than if they had been the players themselves. The dusky contestants engaged the game hugely, and to use a common phrase, they did the thing genteely. Dinah, all eyes, was there to applaud, and the game passed off satisfactorily. All appeared to have a jolly time, and the little picaninnies laughed with the rest. It would have done Beecher, Greely, or any other of the luminaries of the radical wing of the Republican Party good to have been present."

SOURCES: "The News and Gossip," *Brooklyn (NY) Eagle*, Aug 7, 1858; "Base Ball," *New York (NY) Weekly Anglo-African*, Dec 3, 1859; "Letter From Jamaica, Long Island," *New York Weekly Anglo-African*, Jan 21, 1860; "Base Ball," *Brooklyn (NY) Eagle*, Oct 17, 1861; "A New Sensation in Base Ball Circles," *Brooklyn Eagle*, Oct 17, 1862.

North Carolina

Cuban Giants Base Ball Club (Asheville, NC; 1890s)

The Cuban Giants B.B.C. organized in the 1890s, played black teams. *Asheville Citizen* (September 15, 1891): "A hotly contested, though rather one-sided game of baseball was played yesterday afternoon, on the grounds of the Kenilworth Inn Company, between the Cuban Giants and the Kenilworth Inn team. It ended with the jug-handled score of 17 to 3, in favor of the Giants. The waiters of the Inn, of whom the Cuban Giants team are composed, are jubilant over their victory." They also played the local Black Diamonds. *Asheville*

Citizen (May 27, 1892): "The baseball game at the race course yesterday afternoon was witnessed by a considerable crowd. The Cuban Giants won the game from the Black Diamonds, the score being 7 to 5. There was some good playing." *Asheville Citizen* (June 15, 1892): "The Black Diamonds and Cuban Giants played ball yesterday. The score was 12 to 3 in favor of the Black Diamonds. The teams will play again tomorrow."

SOURCES: "A Great Game," *Asheville (NC) Citizen*, Sep 15, 1891; "Around Town," *Asheville Citizen*, May 25, 1892; "Around Town," *Asheville Citizen*, May 27, 1892; "Around Town," *Asheville Citizen*, Jun 2, 1892; "Around Town," *Asheville Citizen*, Jun 15, 1892.

Lone Stars (Asheville, NC; 1890s)

The Lone Star B.B.C. organized in the 1890s, played black teams. *Asheville Citizen* (July 20, 1893): "Greenville and Asheville met on the diamond again at Carrier's Track yesterday, the game between colored teams of these cities, however. The Greenville Independent Champions contested with the Lone Stars of Asheville and were defeated by the home team by a score of 13 to 12." *Asheville Citizen-Times* (May 26, 1894): "The Lone Stars and East Ends had a five-inning game at Allandale yesterday with score of 14 to 8 in favor of the latter."

SOURCES: *Asheville (NC) Citizen*, Jun 29, 1892; "Deserved Defeat," *Asheville Citizen*, Jul 20, 1893; "Around Town," *Asheville Citizen*, Jul 20, 1893; "Around Town," *Asheville Citizen*, Aug 14, 1893; *Asheville Citizen*, Aug 15, 1893; *Asheville Citizen*, Apr 9, 1894; "Around Town," *Asheville (NC) Citizen-Times*, May 26, 1894; *Asheville Citizen*, Jun 21, 1894; *Asheville Citizen*, June 27, 1894.

'76 Base Ball Club (Charlotte, NC; 1870s–1880s)

The '76 B.B.C. organized in the 1897s. The "'76 Club" played against black organizations. *Charlotte Observer* (July 2, 1876): "The members of the '76 Base Ball Club hereby challenge the members of the Recruit Club, to a match game, to be played Tuesday morning, the 4th inst., at 10 o'clock, on Carolina Park." *Observer* (June 28, 1876): "The '76 Base Ball Club (colored,) of this city has received no reply to their challenge to the Lone Star Club, of Concord to measures skill in the national game, at National Park, on the 4th. A club is expected to be here from Chester, S.C., to play them." They reorganized in 1884, playing the Biddle Memorial Institute. *Observer* (April 2, 1884): "A match game of baseball will be played this afternoon of 3:30 o'clock between the '76 club and the Biddle nine, both colored organizations that want the anticipated conflict duly announced." *Observer* (September 19, 1884): "Other towns in the State have gone nearly crazy on base-ball, but about Charlotte, the mania has been confined strictly to the colored population. Two colored clubs, the Lone Nine, of Concord, and the '76, of Charlotte will play a match game at the Fair Grounds this afternoon."

SOURCES: "Picnics of the Colored People," *Charlotte (NC) Observer*, Apr 19, 1876; "Local Ripples," *Charlotte Observer*, Jul 2, 1876; "Base Ball Challenge," *Charlotte Observer*, Jul 2, 1876; "Local Ripples," *Charlotte Observer*, Sep 11, 1883; "Local Ripples," *Charlotte Observer*, Sep 28, 1883; "Local Ripples," *Charlotte Observer*, Apr 2, 1884; "Local Ripples," *Charlotte Observer*, Sep 19, 1884.

Atlantic Base Ball Club (Charlotte, NC; 1880s)

The Atlantic B.B.C. organized in the 1880s, played against black teams. *Charlotte Observer* (April 29, 1882): "Yesterday afternoon, on the grounds of the Biddle Institute, a match game was played between the Atlantics and the nine of the Institute. The play was good on both sides, and the game vet closely contested, resulting in a victory for the Atlantics. The score was: Atlantics, 21; Biddle Institute, 20." *Observer* (April 20, 1882): "The captain of the Biddle Base Ball Club

(colored) is not willing to conceded the victory claimed by the Charlotte Atlantics (colored) and states that it was understood between the two captains that the match resulted in a tie." *Observer* (July 4, 1882): "The Atlantics and Concord base-ball nines, will have a battle with the ball and bat, at the Carolina Military Institute grounds this evening at 3 o'clock."

SOURCES: "Base Ball Match," *Charlotte (NC) Observer*, Apr 29, 1882; *Charlotte Observer*, Apr 30, 1882; "Home Briefs," *Charlotte Observer*, Jul 4, 1882; "Biddle University," *Charlotte Observer*, Sep 17, 1882; *Charlotte Observer*, Apr 2, 1884.

Biddle University Base Ball Club (Charlotte, NC; 1870s–1900s)

The Biddle University B.B.C. organized in the 1870s. Biddle University was the outgrowth of the Biddle Memorial Institute, which was founded in 1867. In 1883, the State Legislature renamed the institution Biddle University. They played against colored organizations. *Charlotte Observer* (April 29, 1882): "Yesterday afternoon, on the grounds of the Biddle Institute, a match game was played between the Atlantics and the nine of the Institute. The play was good on both sides, and the game vet closely contested, resulting in a victory for the Atlantics. The score was: Atlantics, 21; Biddle Institute, 20." *Observer* (April 2, 1884): "A match game of baseball will be played this afternoon between the '76 Club and the Biddle nine, both colored organizations that want the anticipated conflict duly announced." The Biddle Institute and Charlotte's Quicksteps developed a rivalry. *Observer* (April 16, 1895): "The Quicksteps downed the Biddle yesterday by a score of 11 to 9. The game was a good one." *Observer* (May 11, 1895): "Biddle colors are blue and yellow. The nine which was to do battle with the Quicksteps yesterday, marched into town about 3 o'clock to the sound of drum and fife, and with colors flying, and just as proudly it marched out again, with only the banner held higher than on the processional. They were victors of course. Everything was sixes and sevens, with the odd trump on the side of the Biddle." *Observer* (April 15, 1897): "There will be a game of baseball on Easter Monday between the Quicksteps and Biddle University. The clubs are pretty evenly matched, and a good game is expected. Pharr, the left-handed pitcher of the Quicksteps, will do the delivering for the University team."

SOURCES: "Base Ball Match," *Charlotte (NC) Observer*, Apr 29, 1882; *Charlotte Observer*, Apr 30, 1882; "Biddle University," *Charlotte Observer*, Sep 17, 1882; *Charlotte Observer*, Apr 2, 1884; "Biddle University, A Historical Sketch," *Charlotte Observer*, Jun 3, 1894; "The Freedman and the Fourth Today at the Park," *Charlotte Observer*, Jul 4, 1894; "Umpires Decisions," *Charlotte Observer*, Apr 11, 1895; "Colored Base Ball," *Charlotte Observer*, Apr 16, 1895; "Right Over the Plate," *Charlotte Observer*, May 10, 1895; "The Darktown Nines," *Charlotte Observer*, May 11, 1895; "Colored Baseball," *Charlotte Observer*, Jun 16, 1895; "No Muffs," *Charlotte Observer*, Mar 27, 1896; "Base Ball," *Charlotte Observer*, Apr 5, 1896; "Stevenson the Star," *Charlotte Observer*, Apr 7, 1896; "Eight to Seven," *Charlotte Observer*, Aug 5, 1896; "Easter Game—Cuban Giants Coming," *Charlotte Observer*, Apr 15, 1897; "The Base Ball Yesterday," *Charlotte Observer*, Jun 1, 1897; "Thar Now," *Charlotte Observer*, Apr 11, 1898.

Colored Grays Base Ball Club (Charlotte, NC; 1890s). Organizer(s): Gray Toole.

The Colored Grays B.B.C. organized in the 1890s, played black aggregations. The team, composed of barbers, belonged to the Queen City Club, an elite aristocratic organization. *Charlotte Observer* (August 8, 1893): "A new colored nine has been organized, named the Charlotte Grays. Gray Toole is manager, Tom Moore assistant manager and Charlie Taylor treasurer. There will be a game today between the Grays and Concord, tomorrow between the Grays and the Old Quicksteps." *Observer* (August 9, 1893): "The Charlotte Grays (colored) won a close game off Concord yesterday afternoon. Score 12 to 13. The Grays and Quicksteps play today." They reorganized briefly in 1894. *Observer* (July 5, 1894): "The Quicksteps and the Grays (colored) drew a good-sized crowd to the park yesterday afternoon. They are old enemies and went into the fight with a little more venom that discretion. The result was that they were several times on the verge of a strike out. It was a good game, one of the best, in fact, seen here this season. The game was the Quicksteps' by a score of 3 to 1." In 1894, the organization disbanded because the many scheduled games took too much time away from their barber profession.

SOURCES: "Brief Local Items," *Charlotte (NC) Observer*, Jun 29, 1892; "A Great Game of Ball," *Charlotte Observer*, Jun 22, 1892; "Arrested for Gambling," *Charlotte Observer*, Mar 11, 1893; "Baseball," *Charlotte Observer*, Aug 9, 1893; "Colored Twirlers," *Charlotte Observer*, Aug 10, 1893; "Local Ripples," *Charlotte Observer*, Oct 10, 1893; "In From Centerfield," *Charlotte Observer*, Mar 23, 1894; "Base Ball by Colored Players," *Charlotte Observer*, Mar 24, 1894; "Not Sacrifice Hits," *Charlotte Observer*, Apr 19, 1894; *Charlotte Observer*, May 6, 1894; "The Quicksteps Win," *Charlotte Observer*, May 6, 1894; "The Quicksteps Won," *Charlotte Observer*, Jul 5, 1894.

Fearless Giants (Neptune) Base Ball Club (Charlotte, NC; 1880s). Organizer(s): E. W. Butler, Richard North and John T. Hand.

The Fearless Giants (Neptune) B.B.C. organized in the 1880s. The Fearless, attaches of the Neptune Colored Fire Company, played black nines. *Charlotte Observer* (August 8, 1883): "The Neptune baseball club, composed of colored players, of this city, will play a match game in Wadesboro today, with the Wadesboro club." *Observer* (May 12, 1886): "Charlotte's colored baseball club, the Fearless, was badly worsted in a game with the Mutuals, at Wilmington yesterday." *Observer* (August 11, 1888): "The Fearless colored baseball club, of this city, seems to be invincible. They beat the Nationals two games in Raleigh this week, the first by a score of 7 to 1, and the second by a score of 7 to 3." They reorganized in 1889. *Observer* (May 29, 1889): "The Fearless Giants, colored, played the Blues yesterday. The score was 10 to 4 in favor of the Blues." The Fearless and Quickstep nines developed a local rivalry. *Observer* (July 5, 1889): "[The] game of base-ball at More's Park, between the Quicksteps and Fearless clubs, which was witnessed by an immense crowd, resulted in a victory for the Quicksteps, the score 7 to 5." *Observer* (June 25, 1889): "The Danville colored baseball club played the Charlotte colored nine yesterday. The score was 25 to 2 in favor of the Charlotte Club." *Observer* (August 6, 1889): "The Fearless Base Ball Club, colored, did up the Mutuals, the crack colored club, of Wilmington, Saturday last by a score of 11 to 9. [Bishop] Lomax pitched for Charlotte." *Observer*: "The colored Winston-Charlotte base-ball game yesterday resulted in a victory for Charlotte by a score of 5 to 3."

SOURCES: "Local Ripples," *Charlotte (NC) Observer* (August 8, 1883); "Local Ripples," *Charlotte Observer*, May 12, 1886; "Local Ripples," *Charlotte Observer*, May 13, 1886; *Charlotte Observer*, Jul 13, 1887; "Local Briefs," *Observer*, Aug 7, 1887; "Local Briefs," *Charlotte Observer*, Aug 17, 1887; "Minor Gleanings," *Charlotte Observer*, Aug 11, 1888; "Minor Gleanings," *Charlotte Observer*, Aug 12, 1888; "Base Ball," *Charlotte Observer*, May 12, 1889; "Brief Locals," *Charlotte Observer*, May 29, 1889; "Brief Locals," *Charlotte Observer*, Jun 4, 1889; "Brief Local Mention," *Charlotte Observer*, Jun 25, 1889; "The Day in Charlotte," *Charlotte Observer*, Jul 5, 1889; "Charlotte Downs Wilmington," *Wilmington (NC) Messenger*, Aug 4, 1889; "Two Fine Games of Ball by Colored Teams," *Wilmington Messenger*, Aug 6, 1889;

"Brief Local Items," *Charlotte Observer*, Aug 6, 1889; "Lively Locals," *Charlotte Observer*, Sep 19, 1889; "Pithy Locals," *Wilmington Messenger*, Jun 28, 1890; "The Fearless Won," *Charlotte Observer*, Sep 11, 1891.

Quickstep Base Ball Club (Charlotte, NC; 1890s–1900s). Organizer(s): George R. N. Taylor and Gray J. Toole; Walter A. Alexander; J. S. Coles; William Allen, L. D. Hayes and J. Rufus Williams; and A. Rives.

The Quickstep B.B.C. organized in the 1890s, played black teams. *Charlotte Observer* (July 5, 1889): "[The] game of base-ball at More's Park, between the Quicksteps and Fearless clubs, which was witnessed by an immense crowd, resulted in a victory for the Quicksteps, the score 7 to 5." *Wilmington Morning Star* (August 26, 1890): "A fine game of base-ball was played at the Seaside grounds yesterday afternoon between two colored clubs—The Quicksteps of Charlotte and the Fowlers of Wilmington. The first-name club won the game, with a score of 3 to 2." *Observer* (July 27, 1892): "The colored ball club of Richmond will arrive here this morning and give the Quicksteps a chance to retrieve their 'rep' and fortune. Charlotte has never felt that the Quicksteps never did their best on the Richmond diamond, for they have been invincible when and wherever they have played. The Richmond defeat was the only one ever chronicled against the Quicksteps. There is much conjecture on the game this afternoon, and Charlotte is banking on her men winning. The game will be on at 4:30. Mr. Lee Hand will umpire." *Observer* (July 19, 1895): "Excitement and interest increased as the day for the opening of the series approached. That day was yesterday. July 18, 1895—a day to be remembered in ball annals in Greensboro and Charlotte. One of the largest crowds ever seen at a ball game in Charlotte witnessed the contest yesterday. It was immense. The game was a good one, both teams playing a good steady game, interspersed with brilliant plays. The following is the score of the game, which is as near accurate as could be kept under the circumstances, as the Blue Shirts changed their batting order oftener than a dude changes his shirt, which made it a matter of impossibility to keep anything like a correct score of the game." Greensboro and Charlotte Quicksteps established a rivalry. *Observer* (July 16, 1896): "The Quicksteps and Greensboro High Points played a fine game of ball at Latta Park yesterday afternoon. The former won by a score of 4 to 1." In the second game, Cameal shut down the Quicksteps, defeating them by a score of 2 to 1. *Charlotte Observer* (May 12, 1898): "The game of ball yesterday between the Quicksteps and the Baltimore Blues resulted in a victory for the latter by a score of 9 to 7." They reorganized in 1898 and 1899. *Charlotte Observer* (September 15, 1899): "The Quicksteps are winning fresh laurels in South Carolina. They are beating Yorkville on Rock Hill soil." *Observer* (September 13, 1900): "The Quicksteps were altogether too strong for the Greensboro team, and showed their superiority for the third time yesterday by defeating the visitors by a score of 18 to 10, thus winning every contest in the series of three games."

SOURCES: "The Day in Charlotte," *Charlotte (NC) Observer*, Jul 5, 1889; "Base Ball," *Wilmington (NC) Morning Star*, Aug 26, 1890; "Brief Local Items," *Charlotte Observer*, Apr 27, 1892; "The Quicksteps Reorganize," *Charlotte Observer*, May 13, 1892; "Richmond vs. Charlotte," *Charlotte Observer*, Jul 27, 1892; "Brief Local Items," *Charlotte Observer*, Aug 7, 1892; "The Reidsville Excursionist," *Charlotte Observer*, Aug 13, 1892; *Charlotte Observer*, Sep 6, 1892; "Brief Local Items," *Charlotte Observer*, Sep 8, 1892; "To Celebrate," *Charlotte Observer*, Apr 30, 1893; "The Quicksteps Reorganize," *Charlotte Observer*, May 13, 1893; "A Big Game Tomorrow," *Charlotte (NC) News*, Jul 17, 1893; "Colored Twirlers," *Charlotte Observer*, Aug 10,

1893; "Base Ball," *Charlotte Observer*, Sep 15, 1893; "Quicksteps the Winners," *Charlotte Observer*, Jul 19, 1895; "The Quicksteps Meet Defeat," *Charlotte Observer*, Jul 17, 1896; "Colored Ball," *Charlotte Observer*, Jul 29, 1896; "A Race for the Pennant," *Charlotte Observer*, Aug 2, 1896; "Eight to Seven," *Charlotte Observer*, Aug 5, 1896; "Colored Ball," *Charlotte Observer*, Jul 16, 1896; "2 to 1," *Charlotte Observer*, Jul 16, 1896; "A Fight for Gold," *Charlotte Observer*, Sep 16, 1896; "Colored Ball," *Charlotte Observer*, May 16, 1897; "Minstrel Show on the Diamond," *Charlotte Observer*, Aug 26, 1897; "Atlanta Crack Team Will Play Here This Afternoon," *Charlotte Observer*, Sep 4, 1897; "Colored Ball," *Charlotte Observer*, Apr 7, 1898; "Thar, Now," *Charlotte Observer*, Apr 11, 1898; "Base Ball Today," *Charlotte Observer*, May 11, 1898; "The Blues Won," *Charlotte Observer*, May 12, 1898; "Colored Ball," *Charlotte Observer*, Jul 20, 1899; "Will Be Worth Seeing," *Charlotte Observer*, Aug 24, 1899; "A Switch Back," *Charlotte Observer*, Sep 15, 1899; "Quicksteps' Schedule," *Charlotte Observer*, Aug 18, 1900; "The Quicksteps Too Strong," *Charlotte Observer*, Sep 13, 1900.

Quickstep Junior Base Ball Club (Charlotte, NC; 1890s)

The Quickstep Junior B.B.C. organized in the 1890s, played black teams. *Charlotte Observer* (August 13,1892): "A game of ball was played at the park in the afternoon between the Young Quicksteps of Charlotte, and the North State Club of Reidsville. Eleven innings were played, the score standing at the end of 6 to 7 in favor of Charlotte. Jackson and Abernathy were the battery for the Young Quicksteps."

SOURCES: "Brief Local Items," *Charlotte (NC) Observer*, Apr 27, 1892; "The Quicksteps Reorganize," *Charlotte Observer*, May 13, 1892; "Richmond vs. Charlotte," *Charlotte Observer*, Jul 27, 1892; "Brief Local Items," *Charlotte Observer*, Aug 7, 1892; "The Reidsville Excursionist," *Charlotte Observer*, Aug 13, 1892; *Charlotte Observer*, Sep 6, 1892; "Brief Local Items," *Charlotte Observer*, Sep 8, 1892; "To Celebrate," *Charlotte Observer*, Apr 30, 1893; "Just Arrived," *Charlotte Observer*, Sep 10, 1897.

Hard Hitters Base Ball Club (Concord, NC; 1880s–1890s)

The Hard Hitters (Heavy Hitters) B.B.C. organized in the 1890s, played black teams. *Charlotte Observer* (September 4, 1885): "An interesting game of ball was played yesterday by Concord's colored teams, the Heavy Hitters, and the Lone Stars, which resulted in a score of 19 to 9 in favor of the Heavy Hitters." *Concord Standard* (May 29, 1893): "The Heavy Hitters and Big Mouth played a game of ball Saturday, the score was 25 to 9 in favor of Big Mouth." *Concord Times* (June 15, 1893): "Two match game of base-ball were played at the Fair Grounds yesterday evening by colored nines, the Heavy Hitters, of Concord, and the Quick Steps, of Charlotte. Concord was victorious in both games. The score of the first stood 4 to 3, and the latter 13 to 10." *Standard* (August 17, 1894): "The Heavy Hitters and the Blue Westerners, a visiting colored base-ball team, are to play ball at the fair Grounds this evening."

SOURCES: *Charlotte (NC) Observer*, Sep 4, 1885; "Snap Shot," *Concord (NC) Standard*, May 16, 1893; "Snap Shot," *Concord Standard*, May 29, 1893; "Local and Otherwise," *Concord (NC) Times*, Jun 15, 1893; *Concord Standard*, Aug 17, 1894; "A Batch of Local News," *Concord Standard*, Sep 24, 1895.

Lone Jack Base Ball Club (Concord, NC; 1880s)

The Lone Jack B.B.C. organized in the 1880s, played against black teams. *Concord Standard* (June 21, 1889): "The Lone Jack Base Ball Club challenges any colored base-ball club in North Carolina, for a game in Concord July 4, 1889. The Colored Base Ball Club here must be feeling themselves. They challenge the State for a game on the 4th

of July." *Concord Standard* (July 6, 1889): "There was considerable excitement on the baseball grounds in our town last Tuesday. The occasion was the meeting of the clubs of Salisbury and Concord for a match game of ball. They played a full game and the score stood: Concord, 23; Salisbury, 9. Mr. Charles Foil was the hero of the game, having placed the ball away in left field, thus bringing in three runs and himself for a home run. Mr. James Willeford also made a fine running catch." *Concord Times* (July 26, 1889): "Monday afternoon the Salisbury colored base-ball first nine played the Concord second. The game resulted in a victory for Salisbury, by a score of 12 to 13." The colored base-ball club of Charlotte played a game here yesterday evening with the Concord colored club."

SOURCES: "Short Locals," *Concord (NC) Standard*, Jun 21, 1889; "Short Locals," *Concord Standard*, Jul 5, 1889; "China Grove Items," *Concord Standard*, Jul 6, 1889; "Local and Otherwise," *Concord (NC) Times*, Jul 26, 1889; *Concord Times*, Aug 23, 1889.

Lone Star Base Ball Club (Concord, NC; 1870s–1890s)

The Lone Star B.B.C. organized in the 1870s, played black teams. *Charlotte Observer* (June 28, 1876): "The '76 Base Ball Club, colored, of this city, has challenged the Lone Star Club, colored, of Concord, to play a match game in this city on the 4th of July." *Wilmington Morning Star* (October 5, 1880): "[T]here was a match game of base-ball played between the Lone Star Club of Concord, and the National Pastime of Raleigh, resulting in a victory for the Concord Club." A rivalry developed. *Raleigh News & Observer* (October 1, 1880): "There was a match game of baseball played between the Lone Star Club of Concord, and the National Pastime Club of Raleigh, resulting in a victory for the Concord Club." *Charlotte Observer* (September 19, 1884): "A colored base-ball club from Concord came over yesterday and attacked the colored club of Charlotte. The score stood 13 for Concord and 11 for Charlotte." They reorganized in the 1890s. *Raleigh News & Observer* (August 31, 1897): "That game of base-ball yesterday between the Lone Stars, of Concord, and the Nationals of this city, both colored teams, was a one-sided affair. The Nationals had it all their own way from the very start, making three runs in the first inning and from two to eight each one thereafter, with innumerable hits. Manly pitched a fair game, and, as usual, was very effective at critical moments, though six hits, a two bagger and one three-bagger made off his delivery." *Concord Standard* (September 7, 1899): "Our base-ball season has closed and now the colored team has opened a series of games with the Charlotte Quicksteps. The played a game yesterday resulting in our Lone Stars being defeated by a score of 16 to 8." *Standard* (September 9, 1899): "Concord's colored base-ball team is also a winner on the diamond this year. Charlotte was defeated the last two days. The score of the last game was 9 to 10 in favor of Concord."

SOURCES: *Charlotte (NC) Observer*, Jun 28, 1876; "A Colored Fair," *Raleigh (NC) News and Observer*, Oct 1, 1880; *Wilmington (NC) Morning Star*, Oct 5, 1880; *Charlotte Observer*, Apr 19, 1881; "Local Ripples," *Charlotte Observer*, Sep 28, 1883; "Local Ripples," *Charlotte Observer*, Sep 19, 1884; *Concord (NC) Standard*, Jul 23, 1897; "Jack Winslow Happy Again," *Raleigh (NC) News and Observer*, Aug 31, 1897; "The Colored Teams Playing," *Concord (NC) Standard*, Sep 7, 1899; "Concord Out Ahead," *Concord Standard*, Sep 9, 1899.

Star Base Ball Club (Durham, NC; 1880s)

The Star B.B.C. organized in the 1880s, played black nines. *New Bern Journal* (September 11, 1884): "The colored nine from Durham played the colored Chapel Hill nine here Saturday. The score was 17 to 10 in favor of the Durham nine." *Raleigh News and Observer* (May 7, 1885): "Tomorrow afternoon, at the baseball park, the National club, of this city, plays a championship game, with the Star, of

Durham. The National was last season the crack colored club of the State."

SOURCES: "Chapel Hill Notes," *New Bern (NC) Journal*, Sep 11, 1884; "Observations," *Raleigh (NC) News and Observer*, May 7, 1885; "Observations," *Raleigh News and Observer*, May 8, 1885; "Observations," *Raleigh News and Observer*, Jul 17, 1885.

Teasers Base Ball Club (Fayetteville, NC; 1880s)

The Teasers B.B.C. organized in the 1880s, played black nines. *Wilmington Morning Star* (June 23, 1886): "There was a hotly contested game of base-ball played yesterday at Seaside Grounds between the Mutuals, of this city, and the Teasers, of Fayetteville, colored clubs. The game was won by the Mutuals with a score of 7 to 6. The visiting club won the favor of the spectators and the beginning of the game and held it until the close. They played well and promise to win today." *Morning Star* (June 24, 1886): "In the game of base-ball played yesterday between the Mutuals, of this city, and the Teasers, of Fayetteville, (both colored clubs), the home team beat the visitors, with the score of 8 to 5." *Smithfield Herald* (July 9, 1887): "The Colored Base Ball Clubs of this place and Fayetteville crossed bats on the 30th inst., which resulted in a victory for the home club, the score standing 19 to 17."

SOURCES: "Local Dots," *Wilmington (NC) Morning Star*, Jun 20, 1886; "Base Ball," *Wilmington Morning Star*, Jun 23, 1886; "Local Dots," *Wilmington Morning Star*, Jun 24, 1886; "Local News," *Smithfield (NC) Herald*, Jul 9, 1887.

Golden Leaf Base Ball Club (Fayetteville, NC; 1890s)

The Golden Leaf B.B.C. organized in the 1880s, played black nines. *Wilmington Morning Star* (May 31, 1893): "A game of base-ball was played yesterday afternoon at the old Seaside's Grounds by two colored clubs—the Gold Leaf, of Fayetteville, and the Hyacinth, of Wilmington. The score was Fayetteville 5; Wilmington, 13." *Fayetteville Weekly Observer* (July 6, 1893): "Quite a large number of colored people from Wilmington and Rocky Mount spent the 4th here. The game of ball between the colored teams of Rocky Mount and Fayetteville, played at the Fair Grounds, resulted in favor of the former team by a score of 12 to 10."

SOURCES: "Local Dots," *Wilmington (NC) Morning Star*, May 31, 1893; "Colored Teams Cross Bats," *Fayetteville (NC) Weekly Observer*, Jul 6, 1893.

Swiftfoot Base Ball Club (Fayetteville, NC; 1880s)

The Swiftfoot B.B.C. organized in the 1880s, played teams. *Wilmington Morning Star* (July 7, 1885): "By a telegram from Fayetteville, signed by Granderson and Torrance, we learn that at the match game of base-ball in that place on Saturday, between the Mutual Base Ball Club, of Wilmington, and the Swiftfoot Club, of Fayetteville, the score stood Mutuals 4 and Swiftfoots 1. Both clubs are colored." *Fayetteville Weekly Observer* (July 9, 1885): "Among the visitors were two colored Base Ball Clubs, one from Greensboro, the other from Wilmington, who played match games with the Fayetteville colored club. The Greensboro club played in the morning and proved too much for our club, the Wilmingtons in the afternoon."

SOURCES: "Local Dots," *Wilmington (NC) Morning Star*, Jul 7, 1885; "The Fourth," *Fayetteville (NC) Weekly Observer*, Jul 9, 1885.

Silver Leaf Base Ball Club (Goldsboro, NC; 1870s)

The Silver Leaf B.B.C. organized in the 1870s, played black clubs. *Wilmington Morning Star* (August 8, 1875): "We learn that the Goldsboro base Ball Club [Silver Leaf] challenged the Charles Sumner Club of this city for a match game to be played on Thursday, the 6th, which was accepted, but the former failing to put in an appearance the game was claimed by the latter, 9 runs to none. The Goldsboro

Club, we hear, is expected to be here next week." *Goldsboro Messenger* (September 4, 1879): "A party of colored excursionists from Wilmington arrived Monday and behaved in a very orderly manner. During their stay here, a game of base-ball was played between the Silver Leaf Club of this town and the Mutuals of Wilmington, the score resulting 36 for the Mutuals and 24 for the Silver Leaf."

SOURCES: "Colored Base Ballists," *Wilmington (NC) Morning Star*, Aug 8, 1875; *Goldsboro (NC) Messenger*, Sep 4, 1879.

Excelsior Base Ball Club (Goldsboro, NC; 1880s–1890s)

The Excelsior B.B.C. organized in the 1880s. The Excelsiors—nicknamed the "Two Johns"—played against black nines. *Wilmington Messenger* (June 30, 1889): "[A colored excursion] will bring down the crack colored base-ball team of Goldsboro, and an interesting game will be played between that club and a picked nine of Wilmington players. The game will take place at the Seaside Base Ball Grounds, and doubtless large crowds will attend. The clubs that will play are the Two Johns of Goldsboro and the Mutuals of Wilmington." *Messenger* (June 30, 1889): "The colored base-ball club of Goldsboro came to this yesterday, and played a game in the afternoon at the Seaside Base Ball Grounds with the Mutuals of this city. After some spirited playing, the Mutuals come out victors with a score of 7 to 4. These two clubs will play again this evening at 4:30pm, and tomorrow afternoon at the same hour." *Wilmington Morning Star* (August 8, 1889): "The match game of base-ball yesterday afternoon between the colored clubs of Wilmington and this city resulted in a victory for the latter by a score of 9 to 1." They reorganized in 1890s, playing New Bern's black nine. *New Bern Journal* (July 6, 1890): "The Button Baseball Club, colored, played the Goldsboro Club yesterday morning at the Fair Grounds, defeating them with the score three to one."

SOURCES: "Base Ball," *Wilmington (NC) Messenger*, Jun 26, 1889; *Wilmington (NC) Morning Star*, Jun 27, 1889; "Goldsboro vs. Wilmington," *Wilmington Messenger*, Jun 30, 1889; *Wilmington Morning Star*, Jun 30, 1889; "Colored Excursionists," *Wilmington Messenger*, Aug 13, 1889; *Wilmington Morning Star*, Aug 8, 1889; "Wilmington Downs Goldsboro," *Wilmington Messenger*, Aug 28, 1889; "The Mutuals Win Again," *Wilmington Messenger*, Aug 30, 1889; "The Fowlers Abroad," *Wilmington Messenger*, Oct 26, 1889; *New Bern (NC) Journal*, Jul 6, 1890.

Wayne Base Ball Club (Goldsboro, NC; 1880s)

The Wayne B.B.C. organized in the 1880s, played black teams. *Wilmington Review* (May 7, 1880): "A colored excursion party from Wilmington visited this town Monday. Their stay in town was exceedingly orderly. One of the features of their stay was a match game of base-ball between the Wilmington Red Stockings and Wayne Base Ball Club, which resulted in 23 for the Goldsboro boys and 34 for Wilmington."

SOURCES: "Briefs," *Goldsboro (NC) Messenger*, May 6, 1880; *Wilmington (NC) Review*, May 7, 1880.

Blue Shirt Base Ball Club (Greensboro, NC; 1880s–1900s)

The Blue Shirt B.B.C. organized in the 1880s, played black nines. *Greensboro North State* (July 7, 1887): "A match game of base-ball was played on the Fourth between the Long Branch and Blue Shirts Clubs, of this city, which resulted in a score of 22 to 3 in favor of the Blue Shirts." *Indianapolis Freeman*: "The Blue Shirts of Greensboro, North Carolina played the Black Swans of Danville, Virginia, Monday, July 10, at the Base Ball Park. Danville 24; Greensboro, 15." *Wilmington Messenger* (July 23, 1893): "There was a large crowd at Hilton Park yesterday afternoon to witness the game of ball between the Blue Shirts, of Greensboro, and the Black Stockings, of Wilmington, two colored teams. The Wilmington team won by a score of 10 to 2." They played Wilmington, NC's Black Stocking B.B.C. The developed a rivalry with Charlotte, NC Quickstep B.B.C. *Charlotte Observer* (July 21, 1895): "Excitement and interest increased as the day for the opening of the series approached. That day was yesterday. July 18, 1895—a day to be remembered in ball annals in Greensboro and Charlotte. One of the largest crowds ever seen at a ball game in Charlotte witnessed the contest yesterday. It was immense. The game was a good one, both teams playing a good steady game, interspersed with brilliant plays. The following is the score of the game, which is as near accurate as could be kept under the circumstances, as the Blue Shirts changed their batting order oftener than a dude changes his shirt, which made it a matter of impossibility to keep anything like a correct score of the game."

SOURCES: *Greensboro (NC) North State*, Jul 7, 1887; *Greensboro North State*, Jun 19, 1890; "Match Game of Base Ball," *Wilmington (NC) Messenger*, Aug 6, 1891; *Wilmington Messenger*, Aug 7, 1891; *Wilmington Messenger*, Jul 19, 1893; "A Creditable Excursion," *Indianapolis (IN) Freeman*, Jul 23, 1893; "Whiskey Men Dissatisfied," *Charlotte (NC) Observer*, May 4, 1894; *Wilmington Messenger*, Aug 8, 1894; "They Mean to Fight," *Charlotte Observer*, Jul 11, 1895; "Quicksteps the Winners," *Charlotte Observer*, Jul 19, 1895; "The Quicksteps Win Again," *Charlotte Observer*, Jul 20, 1895; "Won Three Straight Games," *Charlotte Observer*, Jul 21, 1895; "Local News," *Greensboro (NC) Patriot*, Jul 29, 1896; "A Race for the Pennant," *Charlotte Observer*, Aug 2, 1896; "A Tale of Two Cities," *Charlotte Observer*, Aug 7, 1896; *Greensboro Patriot*, Sep 5, 1900; "In the City," *Greensboro (NC) Telegram*, Sep 14, 1900.

Diamond Base Ball Club (Henderson, NC; 1880s). Organizer(s): H. Young, A. G. Perry, Eddie Hicks, L. P. Blackwell and W. H. Dunston.

The Diamond B.B.C. organized in the 1880s, played black clubs. *Raleigh News and Observer* (May 16, 1885): "The first game of baseball here, between the Raleigh Nationals and Henderson Diamonds, colored, resulted in a victory for the former 30 to 12." *Raleigh News and Observer* (June 4, 1885): "The National Baseball Club, colored, of this city, will play the Diamonds, of Henderson, at the latter place." *Henderson Gold Leaf*: "A communication handed to us reports that the Diamond Baseball Club, (colored) of Henderson, is being uniformed and will soon be prepared play any club in or out of state. The club will go to Norfolk and play the Red Stockings July 13th and 14th. There will be a match game here on the 4th also." *Gold Leaf* (May 10, 1888): "A match game of base-ball was played here Monday between the Diamonds and Lone Jacks, colored, which resulted in a score of 27 to 11 in favor of the latter." *Gold Leaf* (August 23, 1888): "A match game of baseball was played Monday afternoon between this place, the Diamonds, George W. Flood, captain, and the Lone Jacks, John Love, Captain, resulting in a score of 7 to in favor of the first named. There were only 5 of the Diamonds playing against 9 Nine Jacks."

SOURCES: "Observations," *Raleigh (NC) News and Observer*, Jun 27, 1884; "Observations," *Raleigh News and Observer*, Jun 29, 1884; "Observations," *Raleigh News and Observer*, May 16, 1885; "Observations," *Raleigh News and Observer*, Jun 5, 1885; "Spirits Turpentine," *Wilmington (NC) Morning Star*, Jun 13, 1885; "The Diamond Baseball Club," *Henderson (NC) Gold Leaf*, Jun 30, 1887; "Home Happenings," *Oxford (NC) Torchlight*, Jun 25, 1888; *Henderson Gold Leaf*, May 10, 1888; *Henderson Gold Leaf*, Aug 23, 1888; *Henderson (NC) News*, Aug 23, 1888.

Red Wasp Base Ball Club (Henderson, NC; 1880s)

The Red Wasp B.B.C. organized in the 1880s. The "Red Wasp" played black clubs. *Raleigh News and Observer* (August 5, 1884):

"This afternoon, the Red Wasp club, of Henderson, will play the Raleigh Nationals at the base-ball park."

SOURCES: "Observations," *Raleigh (NC) News and Observer*, Jun 27, 1884; "Observations," *Raleigh News and Observer*, Jun 29, 1884; "Observations," *Raleigh News and Observer*, Aug 5, 1884.

Lone Jack Base Ball Club (Henderson, NC; 1880s–1890s). Organizer(s): John Love.

The Lone Jack B.B.C. organized in the 1880s. The "Lone Jacks" played black clubs. *Henderson Gold Leaf* (May 10, 1888): "A match game of base-ball was played here Monday between the Diamonds and Lone Jacks, colored, which resulted in a score of 27 to 11 in favor of the latter." *Gold Leaf* (August 23, 1888): "A match game of baseball was played Monday afternoon between this place, the Diamonds, George W. Flood, captain, and the Lone Jacks, John Love, Captain, resulting in a score of 7 to in favor of the first named. There were only 5 of the Diamonds playing against 9 Nine Jacks." *Gold Leaf* (June 26, 1890): "The Lone Jack Colored Base Ball Club, of Henderson will go down on the excursion June 30th, and will play a match game with the Norfolk Club July 1st."

SOURCES: *Henderson (NC) Gold Leaf*, May 10, 1888; *Henderson Gold Leaf*, Aug 23, 1888; *Henderson (NC) News*, Aug 23, 1888; *Henderson Gold Leaf*, Jun 26, 1890.

Black Feet Base Ball Club (New Bern, NC; 1870s)

The Black Feet B.B.C. organized in the 1870s, played with black nines. *Raleigh Sentinel* (May 23, 1876): "A club of colored Newbern base-ballers are to arrive in this city tomorrow by the 11 am, train, to play a match game with the colored club here at 2 pm, at the Baptist Grove." *Raleigh Observer* (June 7, 1877): "Yesterday afternoon a match game of base-ball was played on the common in front of the colored deaf and dumb asylum between two colored clubs, the Black Feet of New Bern and the Pastimes of this city [Raleigh]. The game was an exciting one, and lasted about two hours and a half resulted in a victory for the Raleigh club by a score of 39 to 18. The batting was not as good as was expected, but the fielding, catching, and running of base was considerably above average." The series resumed at New Bern. *Newbernian* (August 11, 1877): "There was also a match game played between the Raleigh and Newbern base Ball Clubs, which resulted in a victory for the latter. We must be pardoned if we congratulate the Newbern club on the result, as they had to contend with foemen worthy of their steel."

SOURCES: *Raleigh (NC) Sentinel*, May 23, 1876; "The Match Game of Base Ball Game," *Raleigh (NC) Observer*, Jun 7, 1877; "Colored Odd Fellows," *New Bern (NC) Newbernian*, Jun 9, 1877; "The Colored Visitor," *New Bern Newbernian*, Aug 11, 1877.

Button Base Ball Club (New Bern, NC; 1880s–1900s)

The Button B.B.C. organized in the 1880s, played black teams. *New Bern Journal* (July 17, 1888): "A base-ball match between the Atlantic nine and Button nine (colored) yesterday resulted in a score of 15 for the Buttons and 6 for the Atlantics." *Journal* (July 7, 1889): "The Buttons and Wilson Baseball Clubs played a match game on the 4th and resulted in two to nothing in favor of the Buttons." *Journal* (July 6, 1890): "The Button Baseball Club, colored, played the Goldsboro club yesterday morning at the Fair Grounds, defeating them with the score three to one."

SOURCES: "Local News," *New Bern (NC) Journal*, Jul 7, 1888; "Local News," *New Bern Journal*, Jul 17, 1888; "Base Ball Match," *New Bern Journal*, Jul 20, 1888; "Excursion," *New Bern Journal*, Jul 24, 1888; "A Little Sunshine at Last," *New Bern Journal*, Jul 7, 1889; "Local News," *New Bern Journal*, Jul 7, 1889; "Local News," *New Bern Journal*, Jul 6, 1890; *New Bern Journal*, Mar 15, 1890; "Local News," *New Bern Jour-*

nal, Jul 6, 1890; *New Bern Journal,* Aug 29, 1890; "Premium List of the Colored Fair," *New Bern Journal,* Sep 11, 1890.

Excelsior Base Ball Club (New Bern, NC; 1890s). Organizer(s): Timothy Bow (Team President); T. H. Richardson (Team Secretary)

The Excelsior B.B.C. organized in the 1890s, played black nines. *New Bern Journal* (June 4, 1895): "The base-ball game at the Fair Grounds yesterday between the Black Stockings of Wilmington and the Excelsiors of New Berne resulted in a victory for Excelsiors. The score was 15 to 14 in favor of New Bern." *Journal* (June 16, 1896): "The Wilmington colored base-ball team downed the New Bern boys yesterday with the score: Wilmington Black Stockings, 10; New Bern Excelsiors, 3. Pharr did the twirling act for the Black Stockings, George Stamps handled the sphere in an admirable way for the Excelsiors. Marsh Mackey, captain of the Excelsiors was simply in a mood for catching. Stamps and Mackey make a strong battery and if the fielding had been as good as the battery work the score would be read differently."

SOURCES: *Wilmington (NC) Messenger,* May 27, 1890; "Local News," *Wilmington Messenger,* Jul 19, 1890; *Wilmington Messenger,* Jul 31, 1890; *New Bern (NC) Daily Journal,* Aug 13, 1893; *Wilmington Messenger,* Jun 21, 1894; *Wilmington Messenger,* Jun 22, 1894; *Wilmington Messenger,* May 24, 1895; "Excelsiors Won," *New Bern (NC) Journal,* Jun 4, 1895; "Excursion From New Bern," *Wilmington Messenger,* Jun 14, 1895; "A Poor Game," *Wilmington Messenger,* Jun 17, 1895; "Colored Base Ball Teams," *New Bern Daily Journal,* Jul 6, 1896; *Wilmington Messenger,* Jul 24, 1895; "News Adrift," *Wilmington Messenger,* Aug 14, 1895; "Base Ball," *New Bern Daily Journal,* Jun 16, 1896; "The Oriental Fair," *New Bern Daily Journal,* Aug 28, 1896; *New Bern Journal,* Sep 4, 1896; "Wilmington's Colored Ball Player's Victorious," *Wilmington Messenger,* May 19, 1897; *New Bern Daily Journal,* Aug 7, 1898.

Mutual Base Ball Club (New Bern, NC; 1890s)

The Mutual B.B.C. organized in the 1890s, played black teams. *New Bern Journal* (August 13, 1892): "Seven baseball clubs have held daily contests for the liberal premiums offered. The New Bern Mutuals played several games and won more contests than any other club, but they themselves were overcome at last and both prizes as stated go to clubs of other cities."

SOURCES: "Today's Fair Programme," *New Bern (NC) Journal,* Aug 10, 1892; "Colored Fair Notes," *New Bern Journal,* Aug 13, 1892; "Programme," *New Bern Journal,* Aug 13, 1893.

Stirrer Base Ball Club (New Bern, NC; 1890s)

The Stirrer B.B.C. organized in the 1890s, played black teams. *Wilmington Morning Star* (September 1, 1891): "At the colored Fair at New Bern the Mutual Base Ball Club of Wilmington won the first prize of $75; and the Stirrers of New Bern the second prize of $25."

SOURCES: "The Colored Fair," *New Bern (NC) Journal,* Aug 26, 1891; "Local News," *New Bern Journal,* Aug 30, 1891; *Wilmington (NC) Morning Star,* Sep 1, 1891.

Hyacinth Base Ball Club (Raleigh, NC; 1890s)

The Hyacinth B.B.C. organized in the 1890s, played black nines. *Wilmington Morning Star* (June 5, 1894): "There will be a game of ball on Monday afternoon at Carolina Beach between two colored clubs, the Black Stockings, Captain William Schenck, and the Hyacinths, Captain Alex Merrick." *Morning Star* (June 6, 1894): "The base-ball game played at Hilton Park yesterday afternoon between two colored teams, the Hyacinths, of Raleigh and the Black Stockings, of Wilmington, was one of much excitement and fun. The Raleigh team won with a score of 14 to 7. There was a large crowd out to witness the game and it was soon seen that Raleigh would win." *Wilmington Messenger* (June 6, 1894): "There will be a game of base-ball at the Hilton between the Hyacinths and Green Leaf clubs. Addison and Gause will be in the box for the Hyacinths, and Egerton and Walker for the Green Leaf's. A good game is guaranteed."

SOURCES: *Wilmington (NC) Messenger,* Jun 4, 1894; *Wilmington (NC) Morning Star,* Jun 5, 1894; "Base Ball at Hilton," *Wilmington Morning Star,* Jun 6, 1894; *Wilmington Messenger,* Jun 6, 1894; *Wilmington Messenger,* Aug 1, 1894.

National Base Ball Club (Raleigh, NC; 1870s–1890s). Organizer(s): John W. Winslow; Peter Cobb and Charles Cardwell.

The National B.B.C. organized in the 1870s, played against black nines. *Raleigh News and Observer* (July 4, 1882): "The National Base Ball Club, colored, will play a match game this afternoon with the Wake Forest Club, game to commence at 1:30 o'clock." *News and Observer* (May 20, 1884): "Yesterday afternoon, at the old fair grounds, there was an exciting match game of base-ball between the best colored clubs, the National and the Oriole. The former were the stronger at the bat, while their opponents' fielding was superior. The score stood National 23, Oriole 14. The former got the prize bat and ball." *Wilmington Morning Star* (September 23, 1885): "In the game between the Mutuals of this city, and the Nationals of Raleigh, (both colored clubs) which took place at the Seaside grounds yesterday afternoon, the Raleigh club was successful by one run; the score standing 6 to 7. The game was exciting and well played. Some hard hitting was done and the batteries of both clubs deserve special mention." *Morning Star* (July 24, 1886): "There was some good playing at the Seaside grounds yesterday in the game between the Mutuals of Wilmington and the Nationals of Raleigh. The pitcher of the latter club—Alonzo Ford—is said to have made the greatest hit of the season—knocking the ball fifty feet over the center field fence. The Nationals won the game with a score of 14 to 8." *News and Observer* (August 31, 1887): "A game of base-ball was played at the park yesterday by the Raleigh and Wilmington clubs, colored, resulting in the remarkable score of 42 to 11 in favor of Raleigh." *Louisburg Franklin Times* (May 27, 1892): "The game of base-ball between the colored clubs of Louisburg and Raleigh was very interesting and witnessed by a large number of both races. The Louisburg club is perhaps the best colored club in the State. The score stood 16 to 4 in favor of Louisburg." *Franklin Times* (August 11, 1893): "The result of the baseball game at Raleigh last Friday between the colored clubs of that city and Louisburg was 6 to 3 in favor of the latter." The Nationals traveled to VA. *Morning Star* (August 25, 1895): "The colored baseball team (Nationals) were defeated in Richmond yesterday by the Manhattan Giants of that city, by the score of 14 to 7. The Raleigh team claimed that the umpire did them." The Nationals developed a rivalry with Concord's Lone Star nine. *News & Observer* (August 31, 1897): "That game of base-ball yesterday between the Lone Stars, of Concord, and the Nationals of this city, both colored teams, was a one-sided affair. The Nationals had it all their own way from the very start, making three runs in the first inning and from two to eight each one thereafter, with innumerable hits. Manly pitched a fair game, and, as usual, was very effective at critical moments, though six hits, a two bagger and one three bagger made off his delivery."

SOURCES: "Observations," *Raleigh (NC) News and Observer,* Jul 4, 1882; "Observations," *Raleigh News and Observer,* May 6, 1884; "Observations," *Raleigh News and Observer,* Mar 16, 1884; "Observations," *Raleigh News and Observer,* Mar 18, 1884; "Observations," *Raleigh News and Observer,* March 20, 1884; "Observations," *Raleigh News and Observer,* May 6, 1884; "Observations," *Raleigh News and Observer,* May 16, 1884; "Observations," *Raleigh News and Observer,*

May 20, 1884; "Observations," *Raleigh News and Observer*, Jun 20, 1884; "Observations," *Raleigh News and Observer*, Jul 23, 1884; "Observations," *Raleigh News and Observer*, Aug 15, 1884; "Observations," *Raleigh News and Observer*, Aug 27, 1884; "Observations," *Raleigh News and Observer*, Aug 28, 1884; "Observations," *Raleigh News and Observer*, Sep 17, 1884; "Observations," *Raleigh News and Observer*, Mar 13, 1885; "Observations," *Raleigh News and Observer*, May 8, 1885; "Base Ball," *Wilmington (NC) Morning Star*, Sep 23, 1885; "Observations," *Raleigh News and Observer*, May 23, 1886; "Observations," *Raleigh News and Observer*, Jul 22, 1886; "Colored Base Ball," *Wilmington Morning Star*, Jul 24, 1886; "Observations," *Raleigh News and Observer*, Jul 25, 1886; "Observations," *Raleigh News and Observer*, Aug 31, 1887; "Multiple News Items," *Raleigh News and Observer*, Aug 19, 1890; "Observations," *Raleigh News and Observer*, August 21, 1890; "Pithy Locals," *Wilmington (NC) Messenger*, Aug 24, 1890; "Two Games of Ball Today," *Wilmington Messenger*, Aug 28, 1890; "Multiple News Items," *Raleigh News and Observer*, Mar 20, 1891; "Observations," *Louisburg (NC) Franklin Times*, May 27, 1892; *Louisburg Franklin Times*, Aug 11, 1893; "Raleigh News Budget," *Wilmington Morning Star*, Aug 25, 1895; "Wilmington Downs Raleigh," *Wilmington Messenger*, Aug 10, 1897; "Observations," *Raleigh News and Observer*, Aug 10, 1897; "Visitors from Wilmington," *Raleigh News and Observer*, Aug 10, 1897; "Jack Winslow Happy Again," *Raleigh News and Observer*, Aug 31, 1897.

Oriole Base (St. Augustine Normal School) Ball Club (Raleigh, NC; 1880s)

The Oriole B.B.C. organized in the 1880s. The Orioles, composed of students of St. Augustine Normal School, played black nines. *Raleigh News and Observer* (April 20, 1884): "An interesting and exciting game of baseball was played Saturday on the grounds, of St. Augustine School, between the Orioles (the school club) and a picked nine from Shaw University. On counting up the score stood 44 to 36 in favor of St. Augustine's boys." *Raleigh News and Observer* (May 20, 1884): "Yesterday afternoon, at the Old Fairgrounds, there was an exciting match game of baseball between the best colored clubs, the National and the Oriole. The former was stronger at the bat, while their opponents' fielding was superior. The score stood Nationals 23, Orioles 14. Th former got the prize bat and ball."

SOURCES: "Observations," *Raleigh (NC) News and Observer*, Apr 15, 1884; "Observations," *Raleigh News and Observer*, Apr 19, 1884; "Observations," *Raleigh News and Observer*, Apr 20, 1884; "Observations," *Raleigh News and Observer*, May 6, 1887; "Observations," *Raleigh News and Observer*, May 7, 1887; "Observations," *Raleigh News and Observer*, May 18, 1884; "Observations," *Raleigh News and Observer*, May 20, 1884.

Pastime Base Ball Club (Raleigh, NC; 1870s–1880s)

The National Pastime B.B.C. organized in the 1870s, played black teams. *Raleigh News* (April 29, 1874): "The base-ball fever has extended to the colored Market House loungers, who now spend the most of their valuable (?) time at the Old Baptist Grove." *Raleigh News* (May 23, 1876): "The New Bern Colored Base Ball Club plays a match game with the National Club, colored, of this city tomorrow evening at 2 o'clock at the Baptist Grove." *Raleigh Observer* (June 7, 1877): "Yesterday afternoon a match game of base-ball was played on the common in front of the colored deaf and dumb asylum between two colored clubs, the Black Feet of New Bern and the Pastimes of this city [Raleigh]. The game was an exciting one, and lasted about two hours and a half resulted in a victory for the Raleigh club by a score of 39 to 18. The batting was not as good as was expected, but the fielding, catching, and running of base was considerably above average." *Charlotte Observer* (July 17, 1878): "A base-ball match was

played in the afternoon, between the Recruits, of Charlotte, and the Pastimes, of Raleigh, the latter winning by a score of 19 to 7." The nine developed a rivalry with Concord's Lone Stars. *Wilmington Morning Star* (October 5, 1880): "At 10 o'clock there was match game of base-ball played between the Lone Star Club of Concord, and the National Pastime of Raleigh, resulting in a victory for the Concord Club." They played Charlotte's black clubs.

SOURCES: *Raleigh (NC) News*, Apr 29, 1874; *Raleigh News*, May 23, 1876; "Base Ball Challenge," *Charlotte (NC) Observer*, Jul 2, 1876; "The Match Game of Base Ball Game," *Raleigh (NC) Observer*, Jun 7, 1877; "Colored Odd Fellows," *New Bern (NC) Newbernian*, Jun 9, 1877; "Sporting Clubs," *Raleigh News*, Apr 19, 1878; "Local Briefs," *Raleigh Observer*, Apr 20, 1878; "Local Briefs," *Raleigh Observer*, Apr 23, 1878; "Spirits Turpentine," *Wilmington (NC) Morning Star*, Jun 21, 1978; "Colored Firemen," *Raleigh Observer*, Jul 5, 1878; "Local Briefs," *Raleigh Observer*, Jul 17, 1878; "Local Briefs," *Charlotte (NC) Observer*, Jul 17, 1878; "Gathering of the Colored People," *Raleigh Observer*, Jul 18, 1878; "Colored Base Ball," *Wilmington (NC) Review*, Sep 23, 1879; *Raleigh (NC) Evening Visitor*, May 31, 1880; *Wilmington Morning Star*, Oct 5, 1880.

Washingtonian Base Ball Club (Raleigh, NC; 1860s–1870s).

Organizer(s): George Stewart.

The Washingtonian B.B.C. organized in the 1860s, played against black nines. The Washingtonians developed a rivalry with Wilmington's Cape Fear Mutuals. *Raleigh Standard* (October 5, 1870): "There will be quite a party of colored people up from Wilmington, Nov. 2nd, to witness this Base Ball match for the championship among colored players of the State." *Raleigh Standard* (October 13, 1870): "All things have their seasons, but the game of base-ball, played by a score of half-grown [N]egro boys—all men—Nash Square, in the middle of a July day, is, we hardly think, just the thing. We would like to know how they earn a livelihood."

SOURCES: *Wilmington (NC) Morning Star*, Oct 5, 1870; *Wilmington Morning Star*, November 4, 1870; *Raleigh (NC) Standard*, Oct 13, 1870; *Wilmington (NC) Weekly Standard*, Oct 19, 1870; "Base Ball," *Raleigh (NC) Telegram*, Jul 18, 1871.

Athletic Base Ball Club (Rockingham, NC; 1870s)

The Athletic B.B.C. organized in the 1870s. *Rockingham Spirit of the South* (September 9, 1876): "The Athletic Base Ball Club (colored) of this town, played an interesting game with the O. K. Star Club (colored) of Wadesboro, on Saturday last. The Rockingham club came off victorious by a score of 85 to 47, the Wadesboro club surrendering the game in the eighth inning."

SOURCES: Local Ripples," *Rockingham (NC) Spirit of the South*, Sep 9, 1876.

Colored Base Ball Club (Still Creek, NC; 1890s)

The Colored B.B.C. organized in the 1890s, played black teams. *Newton Enterprise* (July 29, 1893): "A pretty fair game of ball occurred between the Corkers of Charlotte and the Steel Creek nine of the county. The home team won the game easily by a score of eight to one." *Charlotte Observer* (August 25, 1898): "The Dixie [N]egro baseball team, from Berryhill Township, beat the Steel Creek nine 16 to 4 at the park yesterday afternoon. P. W. Caruthers was captain of the Dixie boys and John Jones captain of the Steel Creek crowd."

SOURCES: "Today," *Charlotte (NC) Observer*, Jul 12, 1893; "A Trip to Seasboro," *Newton (NC) Enterprise*, Jul 29, 1893; "Colored Ball Game," *Charlotte (NC) Observer*, Aug 25, 1898.

Amateur Base Ball Club (Wilmington, NC; 1860s)

The Amateur B.B.C. organized in the 1860s. *Wilmington Post* (November 19, 1868): "The amateur game of Base Ball between members of the different Clubs in this city, (colored) came off at the corner of Sixth and Orange Streets on Monday at 3 P.M. Considering the time that has elapsed since any of the players were at the bat, the game was a very interesting one and elicited commendable remarks from the bystanders. The same players will play at the grounds on Monday next the 23d inst."

Sources: *Wilmington (NC) Post*, Nov 19, 1868.

Athletic Base Ball Club (Wilmington, NC; 1880s). Organizer(s): Monroe Byrd.

The Athletic B.B.C. organized in the 1890s, played black teams. *Wilmington Morning Star* (April 4, 1886): "The President of the Athletic Base Ball Club has accepted the challenge of the Mutual Base Ball Club, and will play a Match Game, on the 19th day of April. At the Sea Side Base Ball Grounds." They played against Raleigh's black nines. *Wilmington Morning Star* (May 26, 1886): "A private dispatch received in this city yesterday afternoon from Raleigh, says that in the game of base-ball played at that place between colored clubs— the Athletics of Wilmington and the Nationals of Raleigh, the former were a winner with the score of 12 to 9."

Sources: "Local Dots," *Wilmington (NC) Morning Star*, Jul 19, 1885; "Base Ball," *Wilmington Morning Star*, Jul 21, 1885; "Colored Base Ball," *Wilmington Morning Star*, Aug 19, 1885; "Play Ball—B. B.," *Wilmington Morning Star*, Apr 4, 1886; "Local Dots," *Wilmington Morning Star*, May 25, 1886; "Wilmington Beats Raleigh," *Wilmington Morning Star*, May 26, 1886; "The City," *Wilmington Morning Star*, Jul 22, 1886.

Black Stocking Base Ball Club (Wilmington, NC; 1890s–1900s). Organizer(s): William Schenck.

The Black Stocking B.B.C. organized in the 1890s, played black teams. *Wilmington Messenger* (August 4, 1894): "The Black Stockings, of Wilmington, and the Rough and Ready Base Ball Club of High Point, two good colored team, crossed bats yesterday afternoon at Hilton Park. The Wilmington team won by a score of 11 to 4. On Monday afternoon, the Black Stockings will play a game with the Blue Shirts, of Greensboro, which is said to be the finest colored teams in North Carolina." Prior to the 1895 season, the Black Stockings split a series with the Cuban Giants, losing 11 to 10 and winning 14 to 13. They played Norfolk, VA's Red Stocking B.B.C. *Wilmington Messenger* (August 21, 1895): "The Norfolk Red Stockings and Schenck's Black Stockings, two well-matched colored teams, played a fine game of ball at Hilton Park yesterday afternoon. The score was 6 to 3 in favor of Wilmington." Under the leadership of William Schenck, the Black Stockings became one of the best, clubs of NC. *Wilmington Messenger* (August 30, 1895): "The game of ball yesterday between Schenck's Black Stockings and Charlotte's crack club was played before the biggest crowd of the season, and resulted in a victory for the home team by the score of 13 to 9." *Charlotte Observer* (August 5, 1896): "The game of ball yesterday between the Quickstep and Wilmington clubs resulted in a score of 8 to 7 in favor of the home team. The game was a rattling good one—one of the best, in fact, ever seen on the Charlotte diamond." They developed a local rivalry with the Mutual club. *Wilmington Messenger* (July 16, 1897): "The Mutuals and Schenks' Black Stockings crossed bats at Hilton Park yesterday afternoon. The score was 20 to 11 in favor of the Black Stockings."

Sources: "Wilmington's Crack Colored Base Ball Team," *Wilmington (NC) Messenger*, Apr 29, 1890; *Wilmington Messenger*, Jun 10, 1894; *Wilmington (NC) Morning Star*, Jun 21, 1894; "The Game at Hilton Yesterday," *Wilmington Messenger*, Jul 20, 1894; "Base Ball at Hilton Park," *Wilmington Messenger*, Aug 4, 1894; *Wilmington Messenger*, Aug 23, 1894; *Wilmington Messenger*, Aug 27, 1894; *Wilmington*

Messenger, May 30, 1895; "Wilmington Downs Norfolk," *Wilmington Messenger*, Aug 21, 1895; "Base Ball," *Wilmington Morning Star*, May 3, 1895; *Wilmington Morning Star*, May 24, 1895; "Base Ball by Colored Men's Club," *Wilmington Morning Star*, Jun 25, 1895; "Wilmington Downs Norfolk," *Wilmington Messenger*, Aug 21, 1895; *Wilmington Messenger*, Aug 30, 1895; "Base Ball at Hilton Park," *Wilmington Messenger*, Sep 1, 1895; "Eight to Seven," *Charlotte (NC) Observer*, Aug 5, 1896; "Wilmington Won," *Charlotte Observer*, Aug 6, 1896; "Pithy Locals," *Wilmington Messenger*, July 16, 1897; *Wilmington Messenger*, Jul 21, 1897; *Wilmington Morning Star*, May 7, 1898; "Black Stockings Victory," *Morning Star*, Jun 21, 1898; *Wilmington Morning Star*, Aug 6, 1898; "Base Ball Today," *Wilmington Messenger*, Aug 30, 1900.

Blue Ridge Base Ball Club (Wilmington, NC; 1880s). Organizer(s): Amelia Bradley.

The Blue Bridge B.B.C. organized in 1885. The Blue Ridge female base-ball club played local black female nines (Muffins and Rough and Readys). *Wilmington Morning Star* (August 1, 1885): "A game of base-ball yesterday between the Wilmington Blue Ridge and the Muffin Clubs, won by the latter—18 to 0. Both colored clubs." *Wilmington Morning Star* (August 18, 1885): "A match game of base-ball is said to have taken place on Dickinson's Hill, yesterday afternoon, between two colored female clubs, the Blue Ridge and Rough and Ready, the score being 10 to 30 in favor of the latter." Amelia Bradley captained the winning base-ball nine, which lasted for two weeks. *Wilmington Star* (August 22, 1885): "We learn that the authorities have put a step to the colored female base-ball matches, which have been the attractions on Dickinson's Hill for a week or two."

Sources: *Wilmington (NC) Morning Star*, Aug 1, 1885; *Wilmington Morning Star*, Aug 18, 1885; *Wilmington Morning Star*, Aug 22, 1885; *Wilmington Morning Star*, Aug 19, 1885.

Colored Base Ball Club (Wilmington, NC; 1860s)

The Colored B.B.C. organized in the 1860s. The team, composed of various members of other nines, played exhibitions. *Wilmington Post* (November 19, 1868): "The amateur game of Base Ball between members of the different Clubs in this city, (colored) came off at the corner of Sixth and Orange Streets on Monday at 3 P.M. Considering the time that has elapsed since any of the players were at a 'the bat,' the game was a very interesting one and elicited commendable remarks from the bystanders. The same players will play at the grounds on Monday next the 23d inst."

Sources: *Wilmington (NC) Post*, Nov 19, 1868.

Fowler Base Ball Club (Wilmington, NC; 1880s–1890s). Organizer(s): Julius Murray.

The John Fowler B.B.C. organized in the 1880s. Named after the city's mayor, the Fowlers played black teams. *Wilmington Messenger* (August 20, 1889): "A game of ball played yesterday at the Seaside Grounds between the Fowler boys and the Ironside McCharmer, resulted in 9 to 7 in favor of the former." *Messenger* (August 23, 1889): "The Fowler Base Ball Club will leave tomorrow for Raleigh, to be present and play a series of games with other visiting clubs." *Wilmington Messenger* (July 16, 1890): "The game of ball between the Fowler nine, colored, of this city, and the Charlotte team [Quicksteps] yesterday resulted in a score of 5 to 4 for the latter club. There was some fine playing on both sides."

Sources: *Wilmington (NC) Messenger*, Aug 20, 1889; *Wilmington Messenger*, Aug 23, 1889; *Wilmington Messenger*, Aug 25, 1889; *Wilmington Messenger*, Aug 30, 1889; *Daily Messenger*, Sep 3, 1889; "Our Colored Ball Players," *Wilmington Messenger*, Sep 11, 1889; *Wilmington Messenger*, September 17, 1889; "Raleigh Downs Wilmington,"

Wilmington Messenger, Sep 18, 1889; "Good Ball in Prospect," *Wilmington Messenger*, Sep 22, 1889; *Wilmington Messenger*, Oct 20, 1889; "The Fowler Base Ball Club," *Wilmington Messenger*, Apr 6, 1890; *Wilmington Messenger*, May 8, 1890; "Base Ball," *Wilmington (NC) Morning Star*, May 27, 1890; *Wilmington Messenger*, Jun 20, 1890; "Going Off to Play Ball," *Wilmington Messenger, Jun 22, 1890*; "Gone After Scalps," *Wilmington Messenger, Jun 24, 1890*; "The Fowlers at Raleigh," *Wilmington Morning Star*, Jun 26, 1890; *Wilmington Messenger*, Jul 1, 1890; *Wilmington Messenger*, Jul 16, 1890; *Wilmington Messenger, Jul 27, 1890*; *Wilmington Messenger*, Aug 1, 1890; "An Exciting Game of Ball," *Wilmington Messenger*, Aug 2, 1890; "To Go To Winston," *Charlotte (NC) Observer*, Aug 9, 1900; *Wilmington Messenger*, Aug 17, 1890; "Quicksteps' Schedule," *Charlotte Observer*, Aug 18, 1900.

French Base Ball Club (Wilmington, NC; 1860s–1870s). Organizer(s): James Dry and Allan Evans.

The French B.B.C. organized in the 1860s, played against black nines. *Wilmington Morning Star* (May 10, 1868): "The George Z. French Base Ball Club (colored) intend having a match game tomorrow evening at 2 o'clock, at Camp Lamb, for a silver cup. The day following, they will have a select picnic at Porter's, on the plank road." *Wilmington Star* (May 23, 1869): "Tomorrow afternoon, at 3 ? o'clock, a game of base-ball will be played at the corner of Sixth, and Orange Streets. The clubs to participate in the pleasant amusement are the French Club, and the Amateur Nine, both colored."

SOURCES: "Base Ball Club," *Wilmington (NC) Post*, Aug 22, 1867; "Base Ball," *Post*, Oct 22, 1867; "Base Ball," *Wilmington Post*, Dec 31, 1867; "Base Ball," *Wilmington Post, Jan 4, 1868*; "Base Ball," *Wilmington (NC) Morning Star*, May 6, 1868; *Wilmington Morning Star*, May 10, 1868; *Wilmington Morning Star*, May 12, 1868; *Wilmington Morning Star*, Nov 19, 1868; "Base Ball," *Wilmington Morning Star*, May 6, 1869; "The George Z. French Base Ball Club," *Wilmington Post*, May 14, 1869; "Base Ball," *Wilmington Morning Star*, May 23, 1869; *Wilmington Morning Star*, Aug 26, 1870; *Wilmington Morning Star*, Oct 6, 1870.

Green Leaf Base Ball Club (Wilmington, NC; 1880s–1890s). Organizer(s): James Walker.

The Green Leaf B.B.C. organized in the 1890s, played black organizations. *Wilmington Messenger* (May 30, 1891): "Two colored clubs, the Green Leafs, Captain James Walker, and the Quickstep, Captain Willie Green, will play a game of ball at Seaside Baseball Grounds next Monday evening." They also played Raleigh, NC's Hyacinth B.B.C. *Wilmington Messenger* (August 1, 1894): "There will be a game of base-ball at the Hilton between the Hyacinths and Green Leaf clubs. Addison and Gause will be in the box for the Hyacinths, and Egerton and [James] Walker for the Green Leaf's. A good game is guaranteed."

SOURCES: "Colored Base Ball," *Wilmington (NC) Morning Star*, May 31, 1880; *Wilmington (NC) Messenger*, May 30, 1891; *Wilmington Messenger*, Jun 6, 1894; *Wilmington Messenger, Aug 1, 1894*.

Mutual Base Ball Club (Wilmington, NC; 1870s–1900s). Organizer(s): C. H. "Nat" Hayes.

The Mutual B.B.C. organized in 1870. The Mutuals, known as the Cape Fear Mutuals in the 1870s, played black nines. *Wilmington Morning Star* (September 10, 1870): "We learn that the first State match for the championship among the colored Base Ballists will be played on the Star Base Ball grounds, in Raleigh, November 2, 1870, between the Washingtons, of Raleigh, and the Cape Fear Mutuals, of Wilmington." Between 1872 and 1882, the Mutuals developed a reputation throughout the State. *Morning Star* (June 16, 1874): "The match game of base-ball yesterday afternoon between The Charles

Sumner and Cape Fear Mutual Base Ball Clubs, resulted in a victory for the latter. The Charles Sumner Cub scored 15 and the Cape Fear Mutuals 28." *Morning Star* (May 27, 1882): "The colored base-ball club known as the Wilmington Mutuals played a match game at the Athletic Club grounds with the Palmetto Club of Marion, South Carolina, the Wilmington club scoring 25 and the Marion club 12 runs." *Wilmington Review* (May 2, 1884): "There was a goodly number of visitors at the Athletics Grounds to witness a hotly contested game of base-ball between the Mutual and the Unknown nines. The former club was victorious in the score of 24 to 13 of the latter." *Morning Star* (July 7, 1885): "By a telegram from Fayetteville, signed by Granderson and Torrance, we learn that at the match game of baseball in that place on Saturday, between the Mutual Base Ball Club, of Wilmington, and the Swiftfoot Club, of Fayetteville, the score stood Mutuals 4 and Swiftfoots 1. Both clubs are colored." *Morning Star* (August 19 1886): "The Mutual Base Ball Club, colored, returned from Columbia, South Carolina, yesterday. They were winners in the two games played with the Rockaway club of that place, although the umpire was against them, as they allege." The Mutuals developed a rivalry with Charlotte's Quicksteps. *Charlotte Observer* (June 20, 1890): "Charlotte's colored baseball club has abandoned the blackberry fields around this section and for the past few days has been concentrating its energies in an attempt in effort to defeat the Mutuals, of Wilmington. The game was broken up in the fifth inning in a dispute over a foul ball." *Wilmington Messenger* (August 10, 1893): "The Mutual base-ball team, Wilmington's crack colored ball players, went up to Raleigh on the excursion yesterday morning and yesterday afternoon played a game with the Nationals, of Raleigh. The Wilmington team came off victorious with a score of 8 to 2."

SOURCES: *Wilmington (NC) Morning Star*, Sep 10, 1870; *Wilmington Morning Star*, Sep 25, 1870; *Wilmington Morning Star*, Oct 5, 1870; "Game of Ball," *Wilmington Morning Star*, Jun 16, 1874; "Local Dots," *Wilmington Morning Star*, Apr 30, 1879; *Wilmington Morning Star*, Mar 21, 1880; "Local Dots," *Wilmington Morning Star*, May 27, 1882; "Local Dots," *Wilmington Morning Star*, May 30, 1882; "Base Ball," *Wilmington (NC) Review*, May 2, 1884; *Wilmington Morning Star*, Jul 7, 1885; *Wilmington Morning Star*, Jul 21, 1885; *Wilmington Morning Star*, Jul 29, 1885; *Wilmington Morning Star*, Aug 10, 1885; *Wilmington Morning Star*, Sep 24, 1885; *Wilmington Morning Star*, Oct 6, 1885; "Local Dots," *Wilmington Morning Star*, Aug 19 1886; "Base Ball This Evening," *Wilmington (NC) Messenger*, Jul 26, 1889; "Two Fine Games of Ball by Colored Teams," *Wilmington Messenger*, Aug 6, 1889; "Our Colored Base Ball Players," *Wilmington Messenger*, Aug 16, 1889; *Wilmington Messenger*, Sep 3, 1889; "Wilmington! Champions," *Wilmington Messenger*, Sep 18, 1889; "Base Ball This Evening," *Wilmington Messenger*, Sep 19, 1889; "The Colored Baseballists in Wilmington," *Charlotte (NC) Observer*, Jun 20, 1890; "Pithy Locals," *Wilmington Messenger*, Aug 24, 1890; "Two Games of Ball Today," *Wilmington Messenger*, Aug 28, 1890; "Two Games of Ball Today," *Wilmington Messenger*, Aug 28, 1890; "Pithy Locals," *Wilmington Messenger*, Aug 15, 1893; "Our Colored Base Ball Players," *Wilmington Messenger*, Aug 16, 1893; "Wilmington vs. Newbern," *Wilmington Messenger*, Aug 18, 1893; "Marion vs. Wilmington," *Wilmington Messenger*, Aug 26, 1893; "Base Ball at Hilton Park," *Wilmington Messenger*, May 25, 1895; *Wilmington Morning Star*, May 26, 1897; "Wilmington Downs Raleigh," *Wilmington Messenger*, Aug 10, 1893; "Base Ball Today," *Wilmington Messenger*, Aug 31, 1900; "Pithy Locals," *Wilmington Messenger*, Sep 1, 1900.

Rough and Ready Base Ball Club (Wilmington, NC; 1880s)

The Rough and Ready B.B.C. organized in 1885. The Rough and Readys was female club that played female nines (Blue Ridge and

Muffins). *Wilmington Star* (August 1, 1885): "A game of base-ball yesterday between the Wilmington Blue Ridge and the Muffin Clubs, won by the latter—18 to 0. Both colored clubs." *Star* (August 18, 1885): "A match game of base-ball is said to have taken place on Dickinson's Hill, yesterday afternoon, between two colored female clubs, the Blue Ridge and Rough and Ready, the score being 10 to 30 in favor of the latter." Amelia Bradley captained the winning base-ball nine, which lasted for two weeks. *Star*: "We learn that the authorities have put a step to the colored female base-ball matches, which have been the attractions on Dickinson's Hill for a week or two." Following their victory, Bradley got into trouble. *Star* (August 22, 1885): "Amelia Bradley, said to be the captain of the base-ball nine that won the championship on Dickinson's Hill Monday afternoon, got tipsy and disorderly in her behavior while celebrating her victory, and was given the alternative of paying a fine of $10 or going below for thirty days."

SOURCES: *Wilmington (NC) Morning Star*, Aug 1, 1885; *Wilmington Morning Star*, Aug 18, 1885; *Wilmington Morning Star*, Aug 22, 1885; *Wilmington Morning Star*, Aug 19, 1885.

Scrapper Base Ball Club (Wilmington, NC; 1870s). Organizer(s): Alex Butler, Jr., and Benjamin Willis.

The Scrapper B.B.C. organized in the 1870s, played against black nines. *Wilmington Morning Star* (April 28, 1877): "Two colored base-ball clubs, the Scrap nine and the Select nine, will play a match game at Hilton on the 1st of May, commencing at 2 o'clock." *Morning Star* (August 9, 1877): "In the colored base-ball match, which came off at the corner of the Sixth and Orange Streets, yesterday between the Scrap Base Ball Club and the Unknown Nine, the latter were victorious by eight runs."

SOURCES: "Local Dots," *Wilmington (NC) Morning Star*, Apr 28, 1877; "Local Dots," *Wilmington Morning Star*, May 18, 1877; *Wilmington Morning Star*, Aug 3, 1877; "Colored Base Ball Club," *Wilmington Morning Star*, Aug 4, 1877; *Wilmington Morning Star*, Aug 5, 1877; "Colored Base Ball Match," *Wilmington Morning Star*, Aug 9, 1877.

Stonewall Jackson Base Ball Club (Wilmington, NC; 1870s). Organizer(s): Thomas Knight, William Harriss, Charles Howard and J. J. Neil.

The Stonewall Jackson B.B.C. organized in 1879. The Stonewall represented the reorganization of the Mutual and Red Stocking nines. *Wilmington Star* (April 30, 1879): "The Mutual and Red Stocking Base Ball Clubs were reorganized Wednesday under the name and style of the Stonewall Jackson Base Ball Club. The members of this club won the silver ball and bat in 1868. They say they are ready for a challenge from any club in the State." *Wilmington Star* (November 4, 1879): "The Stonewall and Oxford Base Ball Clubs (colored) propose to have a match game of base-ball at the Athletic Club Grounds, on Monday afternoon next, at 2 o'clock, sharp. The prizes to be played for consist of $25 and a basket of champagne."

SOURCES: *Wilmington (NC) Morning Star*, Apr 30, 1879; "Colored Base Ball," *Wilmington Morning Star*, Sep 26, 1879; "Base Ball," *Wilmington Morning Star*, Nov 1, 1879; "Base Ball," *Wilmington Morning Star*, Nov 4, 1879.

Unknown Base Ball Club (Wilmington, NC; 1870s–1880s). Organizer(s): Alex Robinson.

The Unknown B.B.C. organized in the 1870s, played black teams. *Wilmington Morning Star* (August 9, 1877): "In the colored base-ball match, which came off at the corner of the Sixth and Orange Streets, yesterday between the Scrap Base Ball Club and the Unknown Nine, the latter were victorious by eight runs." *Wilmington Review* (May 2,

1884): "There was a goodly number of visitors at the Athletics Grounds to witness a hotly contested game of base-ball between the Mutual and the Unknown nines. The former club was victorious in a score of 24 to 13 of the latter." *Morning Star* (August 19, 1884): "A base-ball match yesterday afternoon, between the Unknown and Mutual colored clubs, resulted in a victory for the Unknown, by a score of 17 to 16."

SOURCES: *Wilmington (NC) Morning Star*, Aug 3, 1877; "Colored Base Ball Club," *Wilmington Morning Star*, Aug 4, 1877; "Base Ball," *Wilmington (NC) Daily Review*, Aug 4, 1877; *Wilmington Morning Star*, Aug 5, 1877; "Base Ball," *Wilmington Daily Review*, Aug 8, 1877; "Colored Base Ball Match," *Wilmington Morning Star*, Aug 9, 1877; "Local News," *Wilmington Daily Review*, Apr 30, 1883; "Base Ball," *Wilmington Daily Review*, May 2, 1884; "Colored Base Ball Match," *Wilmington Morning Star*, Aug 14, 1884; "Local Dots," *Wilmington Morning Star*, Aug 19, 1884.

Ohio

Star Base Ball Club (Cadiz, OH; 1890s)

The Star B.B.C. organized in the 1880s, played black and white nines. *Cleveland Gazette* (July 12, 1884): "There was quite an interesting game of ball played at Harrisville by the colored Stars of Cadiz and the white club of Harrisville, June 28, resulting in favor of the Stars 10 to 1." *Gazette* (August 2, 1884): "The Stars, of Cadiz, played a match game of base-ball last Saturday, with a picked nine (white) which resulted in a score of 15 to 8 in favor of the Stars. The Stars play the Locust Grove next Saturday."

SOURCES: "Cadiz," *Cleveland (OH) Gazette*, Jul 12, 1884; "Local," *Cleveland Gazette*, Jul 19, 1884; "Cadiz Items," *Cleveland Gazette*, Aug 2, 1884; "Local Notes," *Cleveland Gazette*, Aug 30, 1884.

Dude Base Ball Club (Cambridge, OH; 1880s). Organizer(s): Andrew Wooster.

The Dude B.B.C. organized in the 1880s, played white and black nines. They defeated the Zanesville's black team by a score of 10 to 5. *Cambridge Jeffersonian* (July 5, 1883): "The Cambridge Blacks beat the Cambridge Whites in a base-ball game on Monday. Score, 48 to 28." Portsmouth's Independents (a strong nine) and the Dudes, split two games. Nearly one thousand spectators witnessed the match game between the Zanesville Standards and Cambridge Dudes, the former victors by a score of 24 to 15.

SOURCES: "County and Neighborhood," *Cambridge (OH) Jeffersonian*, Jul 5, 1883; "County and Neighborhood," *Cambridge Jeffersonian*, July 26, 1883; "County and Neighborhood," *Cambridge Jeffersonian*, Sep 27, 1883; "County and Neighborhood," *Cambridge Jeffersonian*, Jul 31, 1884; "Zanesville," *Cleveland (OH) Gazette*, Jul 19, 1884; "Zanesville," *Cleveland Gazette*, Jul 26, 1884; "Zanesville," *Cleveland Gazette*, Aug 2, 1884.

Live Oak Base Ball Club (Canton, OH; 1880s). Organizer(s): Harry Hall.

The Live Oak B.B.C. organized in the 1880s, played black and white teams. *Canton Repository* (June 3, 1889): "Harry Hall and his club of colored lads played a nine over which Dr. N. Lewis Myers asserts supremacy, yesterday afternoon. The score at the end of the fifth inning stood five to three in favor of the colored boys, and then Dr. Myers snuffing defeat and consequent humiliation in the air, by strategic kicking, brought the game to a close. Hall's throwing to the bases was a fine feature of the game." *Repository* (July 9, 1889): "For seven innings yesterday the club composed of Anglo-Saxons held their African opponents down to one base hit, although they had scored twice on errors. In the first half of the eighth with the score six to two in favor of the former, the colored brethren began to hit the ball and aided by several pretty rock errors of their adversaries slipped in six runs, and in the ninth they scored three times. When the game closed, the colored lads had won, by eleven to eight. Coleman for the Whites struck out eighteen men, and Fleming struck out thirteen."

SOURCES: "Massillon Matters," *Canton (OH) Repository*, May 28, 1889; "Massillon Matters," *Canton Repository*, May 30, 1889; "Massillon Matters," *Canton Repository*, Jun 3, 1889; "Massillon Matters," *Canton Repository*, Jul 9, 1889; "Massillon Matters," *Canton Repository*, Jul 20, 1889; "City Nine Wins," *Canton Repository*, Jul 23, 1889.

Active Base Ball Club (Cincinnati, OH; 1880s). Organizer(s): Charles Williams.

The Active B.B.C. organized in the 1880s, played black and white nines. *Sandusky Register* (August 25, 1885): "The Actives, of Cincinnati, Ohio's champion colored team, are giving clubs of the opposite color many tough tussles throughout the state." *Cincinnati Enquirer* (August 23, 1885): "The Active Base Ball Club, Champion colored club of Ohio, challenges any colored nine in the State of Ohio for the sum of $100 or $500 a side. Any deposit left with the sporting editor of the Enquirer will be covered." *Cleveland Gazette* (August 1, 1885): "Lots of crack base-ball teams in and about town, all clamoring for notoriety. The Actives of this city and the Eclipse of Walnut Hills, will cross bats at new Richmond next Sunday. Who says Charlie Williams and Jimmie O'Bannon do not form the finest battery in Ohio?" *Cincinnati Enquirer* (September 27, 1885): "There was a large crowd out at the Union Grounds yesterday afternoon to witness the contest between the Actives, the champion colored team of the State, and the Ohios (white). The game resulted in favor of the Ohios by a score of 26 to 10."

SOURCES: "Base Ball," *Cincinnati (OH) Commercial Tribune*, Feb 24, 1885; "Notes and Comments," *Philadelphia (PA) Sporting Life*, Apr 6, 1885; "Notes," *Cincinnati (OH) Enquirer*, Jun 21, 1885; "Base Ball," *Cleveland (OH) Gazette*, Aug 1, 1885; "Cincinnati," *Cleveland Gazette*, Aug 1, 1885; "Notes," *Cincinnati Enquirer*, Aug 23, 1885; "Notes," *Cincinnati Enquirer*, Aug 23, 1885; "Notes," *Sandusky (OH) Register*, Aug 25, 1885; "Struck with a Base Ball Bat," *Cincinnati Commercial Tribune*, Aug 31, 1885; "Today's Games," *Cincinnati Enquirer*, Sep 27, 1885.

Browns Base Ball Club (Cincinnati, OH; 1880s). Organizer(s): Horace McGee.

The Browns B.B.C. organized in the 1880s. The Browns planned to join the National Colored Base Ball League in 1887. Baseballist Horace McGee spearheaded those efforts (McGee and William Taylor operated a skating rink and saloon). In October of 1886, Walter S. Brown announced the league's formation; Cincinnati was not mentioned; in late November, the city was suggested as a possibility. By December 10, Cleveland took Cincinnati's place; on December 16, both cities had been announced. By late December, the "Queen City" was still doubtful. *Cleveland Gazette* (December 25, 1886): "Cleveland will probably be in the league and if not Columbus, Ohio entered as the original eighth club. Cleveland is preferred from the fact that they are next door neighbors to us [Pittsburg] and it will be a matter of great significance for the supremacy when the Cleveland and Pittsburg colored clubs come together." During this month, Cincinnati signed Kansas City's Frank Maupin, catcher, and announced that John Jackson ("Bud Fowler") would captain and manage the team. While discussions were being held as to where to hold the league's first convention, McGee offered Cincinnati. In February of 1887, the club's roster appeared along with the other league teams in sporting

journals, including Philadelphia's *Sporting Life*. They decided upon Baltimore, MD. During the convention, McGee was appointed to the National Colored Base Ball League's Board of Directors, and Cincinnati was admitted to the league. When Brown rolled out the schedule of games at the convention, however, Cincinnati was conspicuously absent. The league president would later add dates for Cincinnati and WA clubs, because they made good their bonds. As late as April, however, McGee was negotiating with the Cincinnati [Reds] management for the use of the Cincinnati Park. McGee engaged the following veteran players for the upcoming season included Hal Carroll, Sid Rogers, James Chapman, John Chapman, W. E. Owens, William Blackstone, John Austin, Ellsworth Downs, George Rankin and Lee Starks. Financial considerations forced McGee to withdraw Cincinnati from the Colored League.

SOURCES: "Advertisement," *Cleveland (OH) Gazette*, Apr 24, 1886; "A National League of Cullud Gemmen," *Quincy (IL) Journal*, Oct 2, 1886; "The Colored League," *St. Louis (MO) Globe-Democrat*, Nov 30, 1886; "The Colored League Formed," *Boston (MA) Globe*, Dec 10, 1886; *Lawrence (KS) Journal*, Dec 26, 1886; "Twin City News" *Cleveland Gazette*, Dec 25, 1886; "The Official Roster," *St. Louis (MO) Sporting News*, Jan 1, 1887; "Appeal of the Anarchists," *New York (NY) Freeman*, Jan 22, 1887; "Our Colored Citizens," *Cincinnati (OH) Commercial Tribune*, Jan 23, 1887; "National Colored League," *St. Louis Sporting News*, Jan 29, 1887; "The Ball League," *Cleveland Gazette*, Feb 12, 1887; "Notes and Comments," *Philadelphia (PA) Sporting Life*, Feb 16, 1887; "Sporting," *Auburn (NY) Bulletin*, Mar 1, 1887; "Sporting," Wheeling (WVA) *Register*, Mar 6, 1887; "The Colored League," *St. Paul (MN) Globe*, Mar 16, 1887; "Colored Base Ball Clubs," *New York (NY) Freeman*, Mar 26, 1887; "A Rink Smash-Up," *Cincinnati (OH) Post*, Apr 19, 1887.

Colored Zouaves Base Ball Club (Cincinnati, OH; 1880s). Organizer(s): Theodore Watkins.

The Colored Zouaves B.B.C. organized in 1883, played black teams. *Cincinnati Enquirer* (April 15, 1883): "Theodore Watkins, manager of the Colored Zouave Base Ball Club, of this city, desires the members of his nine to meet at the McAllister Hotel this evening to choose a delegate to represent the organization at the meeting of the colored clubs from different cities which will be held in St. Louis May 15th to organize a league." The Zouaves played Danville, KY's nine. *Stanford Interior Journal* (July 6, 1883): "A colored base-ball club came from Cincinnati on the 4th of July to play a match game with one of our clubs. The home niggers got away with them by a score of 24 to 23."

SOURCES: "Notes," *Cincinnati (OH) Enquirer*, Apr 15, 1883; "Base Ball," *Cincinnati (OH) Commercial Tribune*, Apr 17, 1883; "Boyle County," *Stanford (KY) Interior Journal*, Jul 6, 1883; "Base Ball," *Cleveland (OH) Gazette*, Sep 29, 1883.

Eels Base Ball Club (Cincinnati, OH; 1890s–1900s). Organizer(s): John H. Settles.

The Eels B.B.C. organized in the 1890s, played white and black teams. *Cincinnati Enquirer* (August 20, 1893): "The Eels, the crack colored nine, will play the Deltas on the Oakley grounds this afternoon." *Enquirer* (July 30, 1893): "At League Park this afternoon the Shamrocks play the Eels, the champion colored amateur team of Ohio. This is the first team a colored team will play at league Park since the Cuban Giants (colored) played the Red Stockings there. The Eels have a strong team, and will put up a good game." *Enquirer* (September 11, 1895): "The Colored Eels, of this city, would like to arrange a series of three games with any colored ball team in the state for the championship." *Enquirer* (August 24, 1897): "The game between the Eels and Locklands at Manhattan Park this afternoon promises to be hot stuff, as the Eels have not met with a defeat this season, and will have cut their strongest team. The Locklands have been strengthened considerably."

SOURCES: "In a Trance," *Cincinnati (OH) Enquirer*, Feb 28, 1892; "Buckeye Budget," *Indianapolis (IN) Freeman*, Sep 10, 1892; "Shamrocks vs. Eels," *Cincinnati Enquirer*, Jul 30, 1893; "Base Ball Notes," *Cincinnati Enquirer*, Aug 20, 1893; "Base Ball Gossip," *Cincinnati Enquirer*, Aug 20, 1893; *Cincinnati Enquirer*, Sep 11, 1895; "Hot Times," *Cincinnati Enquirer*, Aug 24, 1897; "Amateur Baseball," *Cincinnati Enquirer*, Jul 26, 1901.

Magnolia Base Ball Club (Cincinnati, OH; 1880s). Organizer(s): W. H. Reed.

The Magnolia B.B.C. organized in the 1880s, played black teams. *Cleveland Gazette* (August 1, 1885): "Lots of crack base-ball teams in and about town, all clamoring for notoriety. The Magnolias are coming to the front again and will play two games next Sunday with the Dexters and Spaldings."

SOURCES: "Cincinnati," *Cleveland (OH) Gazette*, Aug 1, 1885; "Notes," *Cincinnati (OH) Enquirer*, Aug 20, 1885.

Modoc Base Ball Club (Cincinnati, OH; 1870s)

The Modoc B.B.C. organized in the 1870s, played against white and black nines. The Modocs and the Independents played on the Riverside Grounds at Ironton. *Portsmouth Times* (July 30, 1870): "The colored folks have become demoralized too. The Modocs, of Cincinnati, came up to try the Independents of this city. The game came off on the Riverside grounds, in the presence of an enthusiastic crowd on Monday afternoon. The Portsmouth Chaps scooped the Cincinnati darkies by a score of 33 to 24." They played Cincinnati's Vigilants. *Cincinnati Times* (August 14, 1874): "Friday afternoon the Vigilance club (colored) met and defeated the Modocs (colored), on the Union Grounds, by a score of 20 to 12, in nine innings." *Cincinnati Star* (July 23, 1877): "The game of base-ball played between Mike O'Hearn's nine and the Modoc colored nine, resulted in a victory for the colored boys by a score of 25 to 7. Thomas Manley, the umpire, cheated Mike's nine."

SOURCES: "Base Ball Matters," *Cincinnati (OH) Commercial Tribune*, Jul 10, 1870; "Base Ball," *Portsmouth (OH) Times*, Jul 23, 1870; "Base Ball," *Portsmouth Times*, Jul 30, 1870; "Base Ball," *Cincinnati (OH) Times*, Aug 11, 1874; "Base Ball Notes," *Cincinnati Times*, Aug 14, 1874; "Base Ball," *Cincinnati (OH) Enquirer*, Aug 17, 1874; "Base Ball Matters," *Cincinnati (OH) Star*, Jul 23, 1877.

Runnymede Base Ball Club (Cincinnati, OH; 1870s)

The Runnymede B.B.C. organized in the 1870s, played against black and white teams. *Cincinnati Enquirer* (August 15, 1879): "B. F. Shott, the enterprising manager of the Cincinnati Stars, has arranged a game with the Runymede Base Ball Club, the champion colored nine of Ohio, for a game on the Star Ground."

SOURCES: *Cincinnati (OH) Enquirer*, Aug 15, 1879; "Base Ball," *Cincinnati (OH) Star*, Aug 18, 1879; "Base Ball," *Cincinnati Enquirer*, Aug 18, 1879.

Standard Base Ball Club (Cincinnati, OH; 1880s)

The Standard B.B.C. organized in the 1880s, played black teams. *Cincinnati Enquirer* (May 19, 1884): "The Standard Base Ball Club (colored), formerly Young Americans, has organized with the following players: A. Johnson, pitcher; J. Johnson, catcher; J. Coleman, left field; W. Reid, center field; J. Banks, right field; T. Adams, first base; E. Skinner, second base; H. Jones, third base; H. Glover; shortstop. Send all challenges to A. Johnson."

SOURCES: "Base Ball," *Cincinnati (OH) Enquirer*, May 19, 1884.

Vigilant ("Vigilance") Base Ball Club (Cincinnati, OH; 1870s). Organizer(s): William Copeland and George Turner.

The Vigilant B.B.C. dominated black baseball in the Queen City between 1871 and 1877. Organized March 1, 1871, the "Vigilants" had won by 1874, 165 games and lost none. They claimed the colored championship of the United States. William Copeland and George Turner managed the organization, which competed against black teams; among them, Cincinnati's Modocs, Indianapolis's Fair Plays, Covington's Actives, Louisville's Fair Players, and Frankfort's Athletics. The nine played at the Union grounds (in 1876, the Vigilants played at the newly-constructed Avenue grounds, north of the old ball park). They developed a rivalry with Covington's Actives. *Covington Ticket* (July 1, 1876): "The Actives of Covington and the Vigilants of Cincinnati, both colored clubs, play on the Star Grounds on Saturday afternoon, for the championship of Kentucky and Ohio, as far as colored clubs go." The Vigilants defeated the Actives by a score of 19 to 9. The Actives traveled to OH. *Cincinnati Times* (August 5, 1874): "The game between the Actives, of Covington, and the Vigilants, of Cincinnati, both colored clubs, which was played at the Cincinnati Base Ball Park, yesterday afternoon, resulted in favor of the latter by a score of 13 to 6."

SOURCES: "Base-Ball," *Cincinnati (OH) Times-Star*, Jul 11, 1874; "Base-Ball," *Times-Star*, July 16, 1874; *Cincinnati (OH) Commercial Tribune*, Jul 20, 1874; "Base-Ball," *Cincinnati (OH) Enquirer*, Jul 29, 1874; "Base-Ball," *Cincinnati (OH) Times*, Aug 5, 1874; "Base-Ball," *Cincinnati Enquirer*, Aug 8, 1874; "Base-Ball," *Cincinnati Times-Star*, Aug "Base-Ball Notes," *Cincinnati Times*, Aug 14, 1874; "Base-Ball Matters," *Cincinnati Times-Star*, Aug 27, 1874; "An Interesting Game of Base-Ball," *Louisville (KY) Courier-Journal*, Sep 16, 1874; "Dayton," *Commercial Tribune*, Sep 23, 1874; "Base-Ball," *Cincinnati (OH) Gazette*, Jul 30, 1875; "Base-Ball," *Cincinnati Enquirer*, Jul 30, 1875; *Covington (KY) Ticket*, Jun 27, 1876; *Covington Ticket*, Jul 1, 1876; "The League," *Cincinnati Enquirer*, Jul 16, 1876; "The League," *Cincinnati Enquirer*, Jul 20, 1876; "Base Ball Matters," *New York (NY) Clipper*, May 5, 1877; "Amateur Ball Games," *Indianapolis (IN) News*, Aug 28, 1877.

Western Union Base Ball Club (Cincinnati, OH; 1860s). Organizer(s): Peter H. Clark.

The Western Union B.B.C. organized in the 1860s, represented the reorganization of Cincinnati's Creole nine. The Creoles, light-complexioned men, worked as barbers. The Western Union played against a leading club of OH, Newton's Black Stockings. The Black Stockings were formidable: they defeated the Alerts (white) Club, by a score of 41 to 16, and they defeated the Temperance (white) Club, by a score of 47 to 16. Before more than 2000 spectators, they challenged the Western Unions, of Cincinnati (colored) for the championship. *New York Clipper* (August 28, 1869): "On the 12th the Independents, of Newton, and the Western Union club, of Porkopolis, both colored, played a match game for the championship of colored clubs of this country, in which the country boys cleaned out their city rivals to the tune of 38 to 26." They later walloped the Western Unions by a score of 68 to 20. Defeating white and colored nines, the Independents attained a degree of notoriety with colored society. They developed other rivals. *Cincinnati Commercial Tribune* (November 6, 1869): "The game between the rival colored clubs yesterday, on the Buckeye grounds, was called on time. Five innings were played, clean into the dark—resulting in favor of the Newton boys (seven brothers and two cousins)—the score standing 29 to 9."

SOURCES: "Base Ball Matters," *Cincinnati (OH) Commercial Tribune*, Jul 19, 1868; "Base Ball," *Cincinnati (OH) Enquirer*, Aug 11, 1869; "Base Ball Matters," *Cincinnati Commercial Tribune*, Aug 12, 1869; "Base Ball

Matters," *Cincinnati Commercial Tribune*, Sep 8, 1869; "Base Ball Matters," *Cincinnati Enquirer*, Aug 21, 1869; "Cincinnati Base Ball Items," *New York (NY) Clipper*, Aug 28, 1869; "The Black Stockings Victorious, 29 to 9," *Cincinnati Commercial Tribune*, Nov 6, 1869.

Blue Stocking Base Ball Club (Cleveland, OH; 1880s). Organizer(s): George Myers.

The Blue Stocking B.B.C. organized in 1883, played black organizations. They challenged Henry Bridgewater's St. Louis Black Stockings for the colored championship. *Cleveland Leader* (April 23, 1883): "The colored baseballists have organized a good, strong team, and, from what is known of their practice so far, they will make it exceedingly lively for any of the other colored teams in the country who wish to cross bats with them. The will lead the St. Louis Black Stockings on a merry race." *Leader* (May 10, 1883): "The colored boys of Cleveland yesterday met with the dusky blondes of St. Louis in the field, and the enemy captured the Cleveland lads that was remarkably wonderful to see. About 400 people witnessed the game at the League Park, mostly composed of the colored population, who went out to see how merrily our Cleveland colored ballists would do up the St. Louis nine. After the first inning, however, they did not have much confidence in the ability of the Cleveland boys to do it. Confidence in the home team was very strong when they opened up the game at bat and scored a run, and they thought how nice it would be if the St. Louis fellows retired without scoring, and then the Blue Stockings (the stockings were purple) would make a whole lot in the second, and when the game so easily, but it was not so nice, for the Black Stockings jumped in and walked on the canvas bags until they had scored four runs, all of them coming in on errors. There were many handsome black eyes watching the home team from the grand stand, and it is quite probable that our boys wanted to appear so fine before their fair admirers that in trying to outdo themselves they made some very grave errors, so the girls should let the boys down as light as possible in getting defeated, for they were in a measure slightly responsible for it."

SOURCES: "City and General," *Cleveland (OH) Plain Dealer*, Jan 8, 1883; "The Black Stockings Play Here," *Cleveland (OH) Leader*, Apr 23, 1883; "Sporting Matters," Cleveland (OH *Herald*, Apr 25, 1883; "In And Out-Door Sports," *Cleveland Plain Dealer*, May 10, 1883; "St. Louis Black Socks Gallantly Down the Cleveland Blues," *Cleveland Leader*, May 10, 1883; "Base Ball Notes," *Cleveland (OH) Gazette*, Jun 1, 1883; "A Game To-Day," *Cleveland Herald*, Jun 13, 1883; "Blue Stockings, 35—Clippers, 11," *Cleveland Herald*, Jun 14, 1883.

Crescent Base Ball Club (Cleveland, OH; 1870s)

The Crescent B.B.C. organized in the 1870s. The Crescents, originally members of the Twilight B. B. C., played black and white teams. *Cleveland Leader* (June 23, 1877): "The Crescents play the Twilights on the Case Commons.... A good game may be expected."

SOURCES: "In and About the City," *Cleveland (OH) Plain Dealer*, Jul 24, 1874; "Announcements," *Cleveland (OH) Leader*, Jun 23, 1877; "Local Brevities," *Cleveland (OH) Leader*, Jul 4, 1877; "In and About the City," *Cleveland Leader*, Jul 11, 1877; "Base Ball," *Cleveland Plain Dealer*, Jul 17, 1877.

Excelsior Base Ball Club (Cleveland, OH; 1880s–1890s). Organizer(s): Charles G. Starkey.

The Excelsior B.B.C. organized in the 1880s, played black and white teams. *Cleveland Plain Dealer* (September 5, 1886): "A fine game of ball was played yesterday at Brooklyn Park between the Lone Stars and Excelsiors before 500 people." *Cleveland Gazette* (April 23, 1887): "The Keystone Colored Base Ball Club, of Pittsburgh, Pennsylvania, play the Excelsiors [Cleveland] here May 2 or 3."

SOURCES: "Base Ball Notes," *Cleveland (OH) Plain Dealer*, Jun 5, 1885; "Base Ball Notes," *Plain Dealer*, August 17, 1886; *Cleveland (OH) Gazette*, Aug 21, 1886; "Base Ball Notes," *Cleveland (OH) Leader*, Aug 25, 1885; "Lone Stars 7, Excelsiors 3," *Cleveland Plain Dealer*, Sep 5, 1886; *Cleveland Gazette*, Apr 23, 1887; *Cleveland Gazette*, Apr 23, 1887; "Base Ball Notes," *Cleveland Plain Dealer*, May 1, 1887; "Base Ball Notes," *Cleveland Plain Dealer*, Jun 19, 1887.

Hollenden Hotel Base Ball Club (Cleveland, OH; 1890s). Organizer(s): William Hunley; Mart Johnston; Edward Turner.

The Hollenden Hotel B.B.C. organized in the 1880s, played white and black teams. *Cleveland Gazette* (June 13, 1891): "The Hollenden waiters' ball game with the East Cleveland Base Ball Club was a walkover for the former. Truly the star of the empire seems drifting westwards. Score: 14 to 7." They played similar hotel aggregations, including the Weddell House. *Gazette* (July 4, 1891): "The Hollenden and Weddell House Base Ball Clubs played a match game Tuesday afternoon, corner Wilson and Cedar Avenues. Score 25 to 4 in favor of the former. The Hollenden club challenges any colored ball club in the city." *Cleveland Plain Dealer* (June 10, 1895): "At Forest City Park two of the most hotly contested games ever played by amateurs were played yesterday afternoon. They were indeed battles royal. There were several questionable decisions on foul balls, which aroused the ire of the different clubs, but all in all the games were intensely interesting. First game: Hollenden 12, Main Stars 11. Second game: Hollendens 8, Old Stars 7." *Gazette* (July 7, 1898): "This club of young colts is open to meet any club in the city. We don't even bar Pat Tebeau's Indians. The players are supremely confident that they are going to do better work than they did in '97. They always do at this particular season of the year, and every last one of the baseball cranks is willing to give them all the encouragement in the world. It need not be repeated that it will take something more than words to satisfy the craving for good baseball in this particular latitude."

SOURCES: *Cleveland (OH) Gazette*, Jun 13, 1891; *Cleveland Gazette*, Jul 4, 1891; "Be Sure to Attend" *Cleveland Gazette*, Aug 29, 1891; *Cleveland Gazette*. Sept. 5, 1891; "Amateur Games," *Cleveland (OH) Plain Dealer*, Jun 10, 1895; "Main Stars, 12—Hollendens, 9," *Cleveland Plain Dealer*, Jul 5, 1895; "Amateur Notes," *Cleveland Plain Dealer*, May 14, 1896; "Amateur Notes," *Cleveland Plain Dealer*, May 8, 1896; "Amateur Notes," *Cleveland Plain Dealer*, May 18, 1896; "Amateur Notes," *Cleveland Plain Dealer*, May 24, 1896; "The Amateurs," *Cleveland Plain Dealer*, May 29, 1896; "Amateur Notes," *Cleveland Plain Dealer*, Jun 8, 1896; "Amateur Notes," *Cleveland Plain Dealer*, Jun 24, 1896; "Border City Personals," *Cleveland Gazette*, Jul 11, 1896; "Amateur Notes," *Cleveland Plain Dealer*, Apr 22, 1897; "Amateur Notes," *Cleveland Plain Dealer*, May 27, 1897; "Amateur Notes," *Cleveland Plain Dealer*, Aug 21, 1897; "Amateur Notes," *Cleveland Plain Dealer*, Jul 10, 1896; "Hollenden House Notes," *Cleveland Gazette*, Feb 26, 1898; "Hollenden House Calls," *Cleveland Gazette*, Jul 7, 1898; "Amateur Notes," *Cleveland Plain Dealer*, Jul 15, 1898.

Kennard House Base Ball Club (Cleveland, OH; 1880s–1900s). Organizer(s): M. Stevens; Sherman Larkins; John Fairfax.

The Kennard House B.B.C. organized in the 1880s. The Kennards, composed of waiters, played black and white teams. *Cleveland Plain Dealer* (June 6, 1894): "The Weddell House boys issue a challenge to any other hotel in the city for a match game of ball. Players to be selected from their own hotel for the championship of the city; the Hollendens or Kennards preferred. Answer all acceptances through this paper." They played the Cincinnati Pool Room boys, a white team. *Plain Dealer* (May 20, 1896): "The Cincinnati Pool Room defeated the Kennard House in a very exciting game on the old depot grounds yesterday afternoon, by a score of 12 to 11." *Plain Dealer*

(September 3, 1897): "The Kennard House would like to play the Weddell House team at any time suitable to the latter. The Kennards bat as follows: J. Smith, 3b, Charles Howard, cf, M. Stevens, 2b, W. Smith, p, J. Weaver, 1b, A. Kuehne, c, L. Jackson, rf, L. Hollenbeck, lf, K. Kuehne, ss." *Plain Dealer*: The Kennards will play the Weddells [colored hotel waiters] on the depot grounds Saturday afternoon."

Sources: "Amateur Notes," *Cleveland (OH) Plain Dealer*, Jun 6, 1894; "Amateur Notes," *Cleveland Plain Dealer*, May 20, 1896; "Amateur Notes," *Cleveland Plain Dealer*, Sep 3, 1897.

Keystone Base Ball Club (Cleveland, OH; 1890s–1900s). Organizer(s): William A. Johnson.

The Keystone B.B.C. organized in the 1890s, played black and white teams. *Cleveland Plain Dealer* (May 18, 1896): "The West Ends easily defeated the Keystones on the Brighton grounds yesterday afternoon in a one-sided game as the score will show. Talada had the Keystones at his mercy, they being able to make only four hits and he struck out twelve men." *Plain Dealer* (June 7, 1897): "The Keystones yesterday defeated the Defenders by a score of 15 to 7. The features of the game were the heavy batting of the Keystones and the battery work of Colwell and Turner, striking out sixteen men and allowing only three hits." *Cleveland Leader* (July 10, 1899): "The Keystones defeated the Woodland Grays on the plow works grounds yesterday in a hotly-contested game. The feature of the game was the battery work of Dixon and Nelson, Dixon striking out fourteen men. R. Colwell's home run in the ninth, with the score tied sand one man on base, won the game."

Sources: "Amateur Games," *Cleveland (OH) Plain Dealer*, May 18, 1896; "Amateur Games," *Cleveland Plain Dealer*, Jul 6, 1896; "Amateur Notes," *Cleveland Plain Dealer*. Apr. 22, 1897; "Amateur Notes," *Cleveland Plain Dealer*, May 27, 1897; "Amateur Notes," *Cleveland Plain Dealer*, Jun 7, 1897; "Amateur Notes," *Cleveland Plain Dealer*, Aug 21, 1897; "Amateur Notes," *Cleveland Plain Dealer*, Jul 15, 1898; "Amateur Notes," *Cleveland Plain Dealer*, Apr 29, 1899; "Amateur Notes," *Cleveland Plain Dealer*, Jun 19, 1899; "Woodland Grays Defeated," *Cleveland (OH) Leader*, Jul 10, 1899; "Amateur Notes," *Cleveland Plain Dealer*, Jul 17, 1899; "Amateur Notes," *Cleveland Plain Dealer*, Jul 22, 1899.

Maroon Base Ball Club (Cleveland, OH; 1880s–1890s). Organizer(s): Frank Doctor.

The Maroon B.B.C. organized in the 1880s, played bats with white and black teams. They established rivalry with one of Detroit's black clubs, the Plaindealers, meeting them in Detroit for a 4th of July doubleheader. *Detroit Plaindealer* (July 4, 1890): "Two games of ball played by the Maroons, of Cleveland, and the Plaindealers last Friday were full of interest. The morning game was closely contested, as both clubs seemed to be evenly matched, and after a great deal of hard work the Plaindealers won the first game in the eleventh inning, the score being a tie in the ninth and tenth innings. The afternoon game did not prove as exciting as the first. Both batteries, however, did some very effective work. Morning game: Maroons, 17; Plaindealers, 20. Afternoon game: Maroons, 5; Plaindealers, 22." The Maroons competed locally against the Maroons and a hotel nine, the Hollendens. *Cleveland Leader* (September 9, 1890): "The Wyandottes and Maroons will play for the colored championship this afternoon on the Dunham Avenue grounds." *Leader* (September 11, 1890): "Maroons defeated the Wyandottes yesterday afternoon for the colored championship, on the Dunham grounds. It was an easy victory for the Maroons." *Cleveland Gazette* (September 5, 1891): "The Hollendens defeated the Maroons at Forest City Park Tuesday by a score of 16 to 3." *Cleveland Plaindealer* (June 25, 1892): "The West Ends defeated the Maroons in a one-sided game yesterday afternoon."

Sources: "Mere Mention" *Detroit (MI) Plaindealer*, May 23, 1890; *Detroit Plaindealer*, July 4, 1890; *Cleveland (OH) Plain Dealer*, July 11, 1890; "Notes of the Amateurs," *Cleveland Plain Dealer*, Jul 27, 1890; "Notes of the Amateurs," *Cleveland Plain Dealer*, Aug 16, 1890; "Amateur Notes," *Cleveland (OH) Leader*, Aug 26, 1890; "Notes of the Amateurs," *Cleveland Plain Dealer*, Aug 29, 1890; *Cleveland Gazette*, Aug 30, 1890; *Cleveland Gazette*, Sep 6, 1890; "Among the Amateurs," *Cleveland Leader*, Sep 9, 1890; "Among the Amateurs," *Cleveland Leader*, Sep 11, 1890; "Notes of the Amateurs," *Cleveland Plain Dealer*, Sep 19, 1890; "Notes of the Amateurs," *Cleveland Plain Dealer*, Oct 12, 1890; "Notes of the Amateurs," *Cleveland Plain Dealer*, May 28, 1891; "Be Sure to Attend," *Cleveland Gazette*, Aug 29, 1891; *Cleveland Gazette*, Sep 5, 1891; *Cleveland Gazette*, Jun 25, 1892; "West Ends 13—Maroons 4" *Plaindealer*, Jun 25, 1892; "Notes of the Amateurs," *Plain Dealer*, Jul 23, 1893; *Cleveland Gazette*, Jul 30, 1892; *Cleveland Gazette*, Aug 6, 1892; "Competitive Drill," *Cleveland Plain Dealer*, Jun 20, 1893.

OK Hustlers Base Ball Club (Cleveland, OH; 1890s). Owner(s): William E. Smith.

The OK Hustler B.B.C. (nicknamed, Young Hustlers) organized in the mid–1890s. Managed William E. Smith, high school boys—George Sampson, Lewis Edward Turner, Albert Dennie, Ross Hunley, Charles S. Hackley, Roy Tucker, Paul Moody, Charles Stone, W. Scott Brown, O. Scott, Luther Nickens, Edward J. Turner, J. Early and J. H. Potter—represented the team. Some later played for major clubs; others played for the Cuban Giants. *Cleveland Gazette* (August 26, 1893): "The Hustlers (a base-ball club) intends to play with the Oberlins [colored] on Labor Day. Game [is] to be played at Oberlin." *Cleveland Leader* (September 6, 1893): "The Hustlers, of Cleveland, and the Oberlin Nonpariels played two game of ball here, Monday, in which the Cleveland boys outplayed the Oberlins at nearly every point. Score, first game, 17 to 13; second game, 14 to 9. These games finish the series with Cleveland in the lead." The young team developed quite a reputation. *Cleveland Plain Dealer* (April 29, 1894): "The Hollendens play the Hustlers at Glenview Park on Wednesday, Aug. 8, the first game of the series of five for the colored championship of Cleveland."

Sources: *Cleveland (OH) Gazette*, Aug 26, 1893; "O.K. Hustlers," *Cleveland Gazette*, Sep 2, 1893; "Won Two from Oberlin," *Cleveland (OH) Leader*, Sep 6, 1893; "Additional Sporting," *Cleveland (OH) Plain Dealer*, Apr 29, 1894; "Mrs. Annie Briscoe," *Cleveland Gazette*, June 2, 1894.

Olympic Base Ball Club (Cleveland, OH; 1870s). Organizer(s): George Starkey.

The Olympic B.B.C. organized in the 1870s. The Olympics, originally the Twilight B. B. C., played black and white teams. *Cleveland Herald* (July 20, 1874): "The Dorians, of Oberlin, and the Olympics, of Cleveland, both clubs colored, are to play a match game of baseball in this city on Thursday." *Cleveland Leader* (August 17, 1874): "The Dorian (colored) club of Oberlin came here yesterday and delivered up a ball to the Olympics (also colored) of this city, score Olympics 19; Dorians 9." *Cleveland Leader*: "The Olympics (colored) and the Brown Stockings (white) will play a game of baseball.... It will be a contest between the African and Caucasian races, and will, doubtless, excite some interest and amusement. We bet on Africa."

Sources: "City News," *Cleveland (OH) Herald*, Jul 20, 1874; "In and About the City," *Cleveland (OH) Plain Dealer*, Jul 24, 1874; "A Challenge Accepted," *Cleveland (OH) Leader*, Aug 24, 1874; "In and About the City," *Cleveland Plain Dealer*, Aug 13, 1875; "Local Brevities," *Cleveland Leader*, Aug 10, 1876; "Local Brevities," *Cleveland Leader*, May 30, 1877; "Base Ball," *Cleveland Plain Dealer*, Jul 17, 1877;

"Base Ball," *Cleveland Leader*, Aug 10, 1877; "Local Brevities," *Cleveland Leader*, Aug 11, 1877; "The White Caps Not Alert Enough," *Cleveland Leader*, Sep 5, 1878; "General Notes," *Cleveland Leader*, Jun 25, 1879; "In and Outdoor Sports," *Cleveland Plain Dealer*, Aug 29, 1879.

Owl Club (64 Public Square, 149 Champlain Street, Cleveland, OH; 1880s–1890s). Organizer(s): Charles G. Starkey and Charles Black.

In 1882, fifty young black men formed the Owl Club. The social and political organization rented rooms in the Northern OH Fair Building, taking possession of what had been gambling rooms (for Faro). Operated by gamblers Charles G. Starkey and Charles Black, the club became a crucial social outlet: it offered billiards, choice liquor brands, wines and cigars. It contained a tonsorial department and reading parlor. Its premises catered dinners and sponsored raffles. Its members were Owlets. It not only hosted billiardists and gamblers and other members of the colored sporting fraternity; it also served as the baseball headquarters for Cleveland's Southern Stars, Blue Stockings, and Unions. In the 1890s, the Hollenden B.B.C. formed the nucleus of the Owl Club.

SOURCES: "City and General," *Cleveland (OH) Plain Dealer*, Aug 1, 1882; "City and General," *Cleveland (OH) Leader*, Aug 24, 1882; "Billiards at the Owl Club," *Cleveland (OH) Gazette*, Sep 8, 1883; "Local Gossip," *Cleveland Gazette*, Nov 17, 1883; "Billiards at the Owl Club," *Cleveland Gazette*, September 8, 1883; "Local Gossip," *Cleveland Gazette*, November 17, 1883; "Our Man About Town," *Cleveland Gazette*, May 10, 1884; "Local Gossip," *Cleveland Gazette*, May 10, 1884; "No Title (Advertisement)," *Cleveland Gazette*, Sep 13, 1884; "The Owls in Court," *Cleveland Plain Dealer*, Mar 24, 1885; "Our Man About Town," *Cleveland Gazette*, Aug 15, 1885; "Our Man About Town," *Cleveland Gazette*, Dec 26, 1885; "Hollenden House," *Cleveland Gazette*, Feb 5, 1898; "Hollenden House Locals," *Cleveland Gazette*, Apr 2, 1898; "Hollenden House Locals," *Cleveland Gazette*, Apr 9, 1898; "Hollenden House Locals," *Cleveland Gazette*, Apr 30, 1898.

Phyllis Wheatley Lyceum (Cleveland, OH; 1890s)

The Phyllis Wheatley Lyceum was founded by several young baseballists. The founding literati included William E. Smith (President), George H. Ricks (Vice President), Charles S. Hackley (Recording Secretary), Luther Nickens (Corresponding Secretary), Walter H. Lawson (Treasurer), Paul Moody (Financial Director) and George Sampson (Chairman of the Standing Committee).

SOURCES: *Cleveland (OH) Gazette*, Jul 30, 1892; *Cleveland Gazette*, Mar 10, 1894.

Twilight Base Ball Club (Cleveland, OH; 1860s–1870s). Organizer(s): William Johnson.

The Twilight B.B.C. organized in the 1860s. The Twilights, composed of whitewashers, played against black nines. *Cleveland Plain Dealer*: "The new Twilight Base Ball Club (colored) is said to be a very strong one, and is thought to outrank any club in this part of the country. We believe they have a match on tapis with the Snow Drops of Springfield." The Springfield club's actual moniker was Foster. *Cleveland Herald* (August 31, 1867): "We are assured on good authority that a Manhood Club is organizing in Cleveland for the purpose of promoting the interests of base-ball among colored people, and that its first challenge will be sent to the Editors' reporters and compositors of the Plain dealer. We trust the match, if accepted, will not be postponed until late in the season." *Plain Dealer*: "Nine black white washers have challenged any nine of any other color, faith or persuasion, to play a game of base-ball. The challenge has been accepted by

the colored barbers, and it is supposed that the game will come off next Saturday. The proceeds are to be devoted to the purchase of uniforms for the Grant Boys in Blue." The Twilights later split into two clubs, the Crescents and Olympics.

SOURCES: "Base Ball and Our African Brother," *Cleveland (OH) Plain Dealer*, Aug 20, 1867; "Matters About Town," *Cleveland Plain Dealer*, Aug 21, 1867; "City Scraps," *Cleveland (OH) Herald*, Aug 22, 1867; "Another Match Probable," *Cleveland Herald*, Aug 31, 1867; "Another Muffin Match," *Cleveland Plain Dealer*, Aug 15, 1868; "Base Ball," *Cleveland Plain Dealer*, Jul 17, 1877.

Union Base Ball Club (Cleveland, OH; 1880s–1890s). Organizer(s): Charles H. Griffin.

The Union B.B.C. organized in the 1880s, played black and white teams. *Cleveland Gazette*: "The Unions defeated the Pittsburgh Stars Saturday, by a score of 10 to 4." *Gazette*: "The Union Base Ball Club were defeated for the first time since they organized, by a picked nine, consisting of the Weddell, Forest City, and Kennard House boys." *Cleveland Plain Dealer*: "The Unions would like to play the West Ends Sunday afternoon on the depot grounds. If satisfactory answer in Saturday morning's Plain Dealer, or call at No. 544 Central Avenue. The following players are requested to meet at No. 544 Central Avenue Saturday evening at 8 o'clock: Drayton, McPherson, Turner, Henderson, Ingraham, John Wilson, Adkins, Scott and Thompson. *Plain Dealer*: "The Unions would like to play the West Ends Sunday afternoon on the depot grounds. If satisfactory answer in Saturday morning's Plain Dealer, or call at No. 544 Central Avenue. *Plain Dealer*: "The Unions were defeated by the Anchors Sunday. They Unions played a good game and would have easily won but for the adverse decisions by the umpire. The Anchors' playing was good." *Plain Dealer*: "The Keystones yesterday defeated the Defenders by a score of 15 to 7. The features of the game were the heavy batting of the Keystones and the battery work of Colwell and Turner, striking out sixteen men and allowing only three hits."

SOURCES: *Cleveland (OH) Gazette*, Jul 16, 1884; "The Unions and Stars," *Cleveland (OH) Leader*, Aug 13, 1884; "Local Notes," *Cleveland Gazette*, Aug 30, 1884; *Cleveland Gazette*, May 2, 1885; *Cleveland Gazette*, Aug 25, 1885; "Amateur Notes," *Cleveland (OH) Plain Dealer*, Jun 29, 1896; "Amateur Notes," *Cleveland Plain Dealer*, Jul 6, 1896; "Amateur Notes," *Cleveland Plain Dealer*, Jul 18, 1896; "Amateur Notes," *Cleveland Plain Dealer*, Aug 8, 1896; "Amateur Notes," *Cleveland Plain Dealer*, Apr 22, 1897; "Amateur Notes," *Cleveland Plain Dealer*, May 27, 1897; "Amateur Notes," *Cleveland Plain Dealer*, Aug 21, 1897; "Amateur Notes," *Cleveland Plain Dealer*, Apr 21, 1899; "Amateur Notes," *Cleveland Plain Dealer*, May 17, 1899; "Amateur Notes," *Cleveland Plain Dealer*, Jul 22, 1899.

Weddell House Base Ball Club (Cleveland, OH; 1880s–1890s). Organizer(s): Palestine F. Turner.

The Weddell House B.B.C. organized in the 1880s, played black and white nines. *Cleveland Gazette* (June 20, 1891): "The Weddell House Base Ball Club will play anybody will come near enough. They were beaten by the Hollendens, however, 13 to 3, Monday." *Cleveland Leader* (June 23, 1889): "The Weddell house barbers play Gerling's barbers for the championship, on the afternoon of the Fourth of July, on Van Time's allotment. Game called at 4 o'clock pm, and everybody invited." *Cleveland Plain Dealer* (May 30, 1896): "The Weddell House boys issue a challenge to any other hotel in the city for a match game of ball. Players to be selected from their own hotel for the championship of the city; the Hollendens or Kennards preferred. Answer all acceptances through this paper."

SOURCES: "Notes of the Amateurs," *Cleveland (OH) Plaindealer*, Jul 3, 1889; "About Hotel Men," *Cleveland (OH) Gazette*, Jun 20, 1891;

"Amateur Notes," *Cleveland Plain Dealer*, May 15, 1894; "Amateur Notes," *Cleveland Plain Dealer*, Jun 6, 1894; "Among the Amateurs," *Cleveland (OH) Leader*, May 29, 1896; "The Amateurs," *Cleveland Plain Dealer*, May 30, 1896; "Among the Amateurs," *Cleveland Leader*, Jun 12, 1896; "Among the Amateurs," *Cleveland Leader*, Jul 3, 1896; "Among the Amateurs," *Cleveland Leader*, Aug 30, 1897; "Among the Amateurs," *Cleveland Leader*, Sep 4, 1897;

Windsor Southern Stars Base Ball Club (Cleveland, OH; 1880s). Organizer(s): William Wilson and Frank Doctor.

The Windsor Southern Stars B.B.C. organized in the 1880s. The Southern Stars, waiters and porters of the Windsor Club (white), played black and white nines. *Cleveland Leader* (August 19, 1882): "The Southern Stars defeated the Union by a score of 16 to 13 in eleven innings. Up to the sixth inning the game was exciting." In 1883, the team's core group formed the Blue Stockings, the championship club that played Henry Bridgewater's St. Louis Black Stockings.

Sources: "Base Ball," *Cleveland (OH) Leader*, Jul 4, 1882; "Miscellaneous Games," *Cleveland Leader*, Aug 19, 1882; "City and General," *Cleveland Leader*, Aug 24, 1882; "A Tour for the Kents," *Cleveland (OH) Herald*, Sep 1, 1882; "General Notes," *Cleveland Herald*, Sep 12, 1882; "The Colored Nine Get Left," *Cleveland Herald*, Sep 14, 1882; "The Windsor Club Waiter's Strike," *Cleveland Herald*, Sep 22, 1882; "Base Ball," *Cleveland Herald*, Oct 7, 1882.

Wyandotte Base Ball Club (Cleveland, OH; 1890s)

The Wyandotte B.B.C. organized in the 1890s, played black teams. *Cleveland Leader* (August 26, 1890): "The Maroons and Wyandottes will cross bats on the Mets' grounds today. This will be the Wyandotte's first game of the season." *Leader* (September 9, 1890): "The Wyandottes and Maroons will play for the colored championship this afternoon on the Dunham Avenue grounds." *Leader* (September 11, 1890): "Maroons defeated the Wyandottes yesterday afternoon for the colored championship, on the Dunham grounds. It was an easy victory for the Maroons."

Sources: "Amateur Notes," *Cleveland (OH) Leader*, Aug 26, 1890; "Among the Amateurs," *Cleveland Leader*, Sep 9, 1890; "Among the Amateurs," *Cleveland Leader*, Sep 11, 1890; "General Sporting Notes," *Cleveland (OH) Plain Dealer*, Oct 7, 1890.

"Z" Base Ball Club (Cleveland, OH; 1880s–1890s). Organizer(s): William Clifford and Charles Black.

The "Z" B.B.C. organized in the 1880s, played black and white nines. William Clifford and Charles Black organized and bankrolled the "Z" Club, which was a pleasure resort. The resort offered the choicest wines and cigars, pool, billiards, lunch, reading rooms, and tonsorial parlors; it hosted gambling activities attended by prominent and respected colored men. The club was comprised of former members of Cleveland's Blue Stockings, Clippers, and Unions. The Z Club was known as far as Upper Canada. In 1888, Black added a ticker to receive daily baseball coverage, and organized a baseball club called the Z Club. The aggregation played local contests and made road tours. They visited NY and played the Brooklyn Alpines. *Cleveland Gazette* (May 27, 1889): "The Woodlands [white] defeated the team from the Z Club Sunday afternoon on the Rubber's Grounds by a score of 22 to 12. The game was a very amusing and at times was a very exciting one. The funny coaching of the Z Club brought peals of laughter from the crowd which numbered nearly two thousand people. Both sides did some hard hitting and it was impossible for the fielders to get at any of the balls in the field, owing to the people." *Cleveland Plain Dealer* (September 16, 1889): "The Geneva Grays, a colored club form Geneva, were scarcely in the game with the Z Club yesterday afternoon. The batters of the local club early served the

oppositions' club's pitcher and batted the ball all over the lot. The Jackson brothers did superb work as the Z's battery and Fred Johnson's first base play was a feature of the game. The game was not close enough to be interesting, but the number of spectators who witnessed the contest was nearly as the usual present at Sunday's games at Beyerle Park."

Sources: *Cleveland (OH) Gazette*, Apr 17, 1886; "Z Club," *Cleveland Gazette*, Jun 19, 1886; *Cleveland Gazette*, Aug 14, 1886; *Cleveland Gazette*, Apr 23, 1887; "Wanted His Throat Cut," *Cleveland (OH) Plain Dealer*, May 7, 1887; *Cleveland Gazette*, Jul 2, 1887; "Z Club Fined," *Cleveland Plain Dealer*, Apr 26, 1889; "Bushwhacking the Z Club," *Cleveland Plain Dealer*, May 2, 1889; "Notes of the Amateurs," *Cleveland Plain Dealer*, May 26, 1889; "Base Ball Notes," *Cleveland Gazette*, Jun 1, 1889; "Local Amateur Games," *Cleveland (OH) Leader*, Jun 10, 1889; "Base Ball Notes," *Cleveland Gazette*, Jun 15, 1889; "The Ball Game," *Cleveland Gazette*, Sep 14, 1889; "Colored Gamblers," *Cleveland Plain Dealer*, Apr 25, 1889; "Brooklyn Items," *New York (NY) Age*, Jun 29, 1889; "The Ball Game," *Cleveland Gazette*, Sep 14, 1889; "Notes of the Amateurs," *Cleveland Plain Dealer*, Sep 15, 1889; "Zees, 20; Grays, 5," *Cleveland Plain Dealer*, Sep 16, 1889; "Notes of the Amateurs," *Cleveland Plain Dealer*, Apr 22, 1890; "Notes of the Amateurs," *Cleveland Plain Dealer*, Jul 11, 1890; "Notes of the Amateurs," *Cleveland Plain Dealer*, Jul 17, 1890; "Notes of the Amateurs," *Cleveland Plain Dealer*, Jul 25, 1890; "Notes of the Amateurs," *Cleveland Plain Dealer*, Jul 27, 1890; "Cleveland Shamrock 20; Z Club, 16," *Cleveland Plain Dealer*, Jul 28, 1890; "Notes of the Amateurs," *Cleveland Plain Dealer*, Aug 3, 1890; "Notes of the Amateurs," *Cleveland Plain Dealer*, Aug 6, 1890; "Notes of the Amateurs," *Cleveland Plain Dealer*, Aug 16, 1890; "About Men and Women," *Cleveland Gazette*, Sep 30, 1890; "Notes of the Amateurs," *Cleveland Plain Dealer*, Jun 4, 1891; "Incorporated," *Cleveland Plain Dealer*, Mar 21, 1894; "Z Club Raided," *Cleveland Plain Dealer*, Sep 23, 1896; "That Notorious Z Club," *Cleveland Gazette*, Nov 28, 1896; "Z Club Pulled," *Cleveland Plain Dealer*, Nov 2, 1897; "Z Club Raided," *Cleveland Plain Dealer*, Jul 28, 1900.

Zulu Base Ball Club (Cleveland, OH; 1870s)

The Zulu B.B.C. organized in the 1870s, played black and white teams. *Cleveland Leader* (August 28, 1879): "A game will be played this afternoon between the Red Stockings and the new colored nine, composed of some of the best colored players in town, as follows: C. Stanley, H. Smith, W. Wilson, J. Morris, E. Doctor, P. Henderson, W. Milligan, W. Brown, J. Bowler. Some good playing may be looked for." *Cleveland Leader*: "The Forest City House waiters defeated the Zulus yesterday afternoon, by a score of 11 to 8."

Sources: "General Notes," *Cleveland (OH) Leader*, Jul 25, 1879; "General Notes," *Cleveland Leader*. Aug 28, 1879; "In and Out-Door Sports," *Cleveland Leader*, Aug 29, 1879; "Turf and Field," *Kane (PA) Weekly Blade*, Sep 4, 1879.

All American Black Tourists Base Ball Club (Columbus, OH; 1890s–1900s). Organizer(s): John W. Jackson ("Bud" Fowler).

The All American Black Tourists B.B.C. organized in in the 1890s. The team was organized by John Jackson (aka Bud Fowler). The Black Tourists played against black and white aggregations. *Canton Repository* (May 7, 1900): "Drumm's aggregation of stickers defeated the Black Tourists in a fine exhibition of ball playing at Mahaffey Park Sunday afternoon. There were fully twelve hundred spectators at the game and they seemed well satisfied with the contest which was full of ginger and interesting. The local fans appreciated good sport. The Black Tourists are a sturdy lot of ball players and worked hard to win."

Sources: "Fowler's Fancy," *Philadelphia (PA) Sporting Life*, Feb 4, 1899; "News and Comment," *Philadelphia Sporting Life*, Jul 29, 1899;

"The Black Tourists," *Philadelphia Sporting Life*, Aug 12, 1899; "Base Ball Attraction," *Newton (KS) Kansan*, Aug 29, 1899; "Colored League of Ball Clubs," *St. Louis (MO) Post-Dispatch*, Sep 6, 1899; "All-American Black Tourists," *St. Louis Post-Dispatch*, Sep 30, 1899; "Tourists Go Down," *Cincinnati (OH) Enquirer*, May 7, 1900; "Tourists Go Down," *Canton (OH) Repository*, May 7, 1900; "Stopped By Rain," *Canton Repository*, May 9, 1900; "News and Comment," *Philadelphia Sporting Life*, Jun 9, 1900; "The City in Brief," *Marion (OH) Star*, Jul 25, 1900; "Big Game of the Season," *Marion Star*, July 27, 1900.

Mundane Base Ball Club (Fayette, OH; 1870s)

The Mundane B.B.C. organized in the 1870s, played black teams. *Wilmington Clinton Republican* (July 9, 1874): "In a base-ball match at Wilmington, Ohio, yesterday, between nines of color, the Mundanes of this place carried off the ball by a score of 39 to 15.—Fayette Herald."

Sources: *Wilmington (OH) Clinton Republican*, Jul 7, 1874.

Buckeye Base Ball Club (Gallipolis, OH; 1870s). Organizer(s): G. C. Casey.

The Buckeye B.B.C. organized in the 1870s. The Buckeyes played black organizations of OH and WV. They also challenged the township's local white nine (Pastimes). They played Ironton's Muffin club. *Gallipolis Journal* (August 11, 1870): "There will be a match game between the Buckeyes, of this place, and the Muffins, of Ironton, (colored) on the 4th of August, in this city." The Buckeyes defeated the Muffins by a score of 26 to 23; they also outlasted Middleton's Champions (black), by a score of 43 to 40. They reorganized in 1874, directing challenges to Portsmouth. *Portsmouth Times* (August 1, 1874): "The Buckeye Base Ball Club, colored, of Gallipolis, challenge any colored club in Lawrence or Scioto county." They also broadened the challenge. *Gallipolis Journal* (August 1, 1874): "[The Buckeyes challenge] any club of their own color in the counties of Meigs, Lawrence, Scioto, Wood, Mason, and Kanawha, West Virginia. *Gallipolis Journal* (August 6, 1874): "The Buckeyes of Gallipolis and the Silver Stars of Clendinen district, Mason County, West Virginia, both colored, played a match game on the grounds of the latter, Saturday, August 1st."

Sources: "Base Ball," *Gallipolis (OH) Journal*, Jul 28, 1870; "Base Ball," *Gallipolis Journal*, Aug 11, 1870; "Brevities," *Portsmouth (OH) Times*, Aug 1, 1874; "Brevities," *Gallipolis Journal*, Aug 1, 1874; "Base Ball," *Gallipolis Journal*, Aug 6, 1874; *Gallipolis Journal*, Aug 5, 1875.

Clipper Base Ball Club (Geneva, OH; 1880s). Organizer(s): E. C. Carmen.

The Clipper B.B.C. organized in the 1880s, played black teams. *Cleveland Gazette* (September 29, 1883): "The Clippers, of Geneva, played a match game against the Enterprise Machine Company at Base Ball Park. At the last half of the ninth inning, the score stood twenty-eight to ten in favor of the Enterprise. After which time, the Clippers went to work in earnest and made sixteen runs after two men had struck out, thus leaving the score twenty-six to twenty-eight in favor of the Enterprise. The Clippers say they are playing to catch the [Cleveland] Blue Sox but they won't bite." The Blue Stocking eventually did "bite" and "wiped the earth" with the Clippers.

Sources: "Base Ball Notes," *Cleveland (OH) Herald*, May 31, 1883; "A Game To-Day," *Cleveland Herald*, June 13, 1883; "Geneva," *Cleveland (OH) Gazette*. Oct. 13, 1883; "Base Ball," *Cleveland Gazette*, Oct 6, 1883; "The Ball Game," *Cleveland Gazette*, Sep 14, 1883; "Geneva," *Cleveland Gazette*, Sep 22, 1883; "Geneva, O.," *Cleveland Gazette*, Sep 29, 1883; *Cleveland Gazette*, Oct 27, 1883.

Grays Base Ball Club (Geneva, OH; 1880s). Organizer(s): Grant "Homerun" Johnson.

The Grays B.B.C. organized in the 1880s, played black teams. *Cleveland Plain Dealer* (September 15, 1889): "The Geneva Grays, a colored club form Geneva, were scarcely in the game with the Z Club yesterday afternoon. The batters of the local club early served the oppositions' club's pitcher and batted the ball all over the lot. The Jackson brothers did superb work as the Z's battery and Fred Johnson's first base play was a feature of the game. The game was not close enough to be interesting, but the number of spectators who witnessed the contest was nearly as the usual present at Sunday's games at Beyerle Park."

Sources: "Notes of the Amateurs," *Cleveland (OH) Plain Dealer*, Sep 15, 1889.

Warden Hotel Sureshot Base Ball Club (Granville, OH; 1890s)

The Warden Hotel Sureshot B.B.C. organized in the 1890s. *Newark Advocate* (June 3, 1897): "The Doty Horseshoes feel just as sure of winning the contest on the diamond as the Warden Sureshots are confident of pinning the Doty men's scalps to their belts." *Cleveland Gazette* (June 12, 1897): "The Hotel Warden and Doty Hotel waiters played a great game of baseball on the 4th. The Warden boys won in six innings: score 38 to 20. The features of the game were the superb fielding of Terry, Craig, Good and Toney, and the base stealing of Brown, who has played in professional games." *Advocate* (July 10, 1897): "The Doty House waiters went to Granville yesterday afternoon to play a ball game with the college town's colored tea and they returned this evening with Granville's scalp though they had to run the score up almost as high as the mercury to get it." *Granville Times* (July 15, 1897): "The base-ball game played here last Friday afternoon, at Denison University Athletic Park, between the colored waiters of the Hotel Doty, Newark and nine of Granville's colored baseball fans, did not attract a very large crowd of enthusiasts. Some very good plays were made by both teams. The game turned out to be a veritable slugging match…"

Sources: "Barrel of Fun," *Newark (OH) Advocate*, Jun 2, 1897; "The Struggle," *Newark Advocate*, Jun 3, 1897; "Warmed a Snake to Life," *Cleveland (OH) Gazette*, Jun 12, 1897; "Plenty of Runs," *Newark Advocate*, Jul 10, 1897; "Town talk," *Granville (OH) Times*, Jul 15, 1897.

King Killers Base Ball Club (Hillsboro, OH; 1890s). Organizer(s): Lewis Ellis.

The King Killers B.B.C. organized in the 1890s. Located in southern OH, Hillsboro, a small town, organized a baseball nine; among the club rivalries, WA Court House, PA. *Hillsboro News-Herald* (July 7, 1892): "The King Killers Kolored Ball Klub went to Washington C. H. on the fourth and defeated the club there by a score of 24 to 8." *News-Herald* (July 17, 1892): "The Killers Club is arranging for a series of games with the colored club of Chillicothe and will have them here probably the latter part of next week."

Sources: "Base Ball," *Hillsboro (OH) News-Herald*, Jun 23, 1892; "Mayor's Court," *Hillsboro News-Herald*, Jul 7, 1892; *Hillsboro News-Herald*, Jul 14, 1892; *Hillsboro News-Herald*, Jul 28, 1892.

Clipper Base Ball Club (Ironton, OH; 1880s). Organizer(s): T. A. Pogue.

The Clipper B.B.C. organized in the 1880s. The Clippers, composed of waiters and barbers, played black teams. *Cleveland Gazette* (August 16, 1884): "The Catlettsburg Base Ball Club and the Clippers, of our city, played a game, resulting, Clippers, 37, Catlettsburg. 13."

Sources: *Portsmouth (OH) Times*, May 31, 1884; "Ironton, OH," *Cleveland (OH) Gazette*, Jun 7, 1884; "Ironton, OH," *Cleveland Gazette*, Jul 12, 1884; "Ironton, OH," *Cleveland Gazette*, Aug 16, 1884; "Ironton,

OH," *Cleveland Gazette*, Oct 11, 1884; "Ironton, O., Doings," *Cleveland Gazette*, Jun 9, 1888; "Ironton, O., Chips," *Cleveland Gazette*, Jul 14, 1888; "Ohio News," *Cleveland Gazette*, Jul 20, 1889.

Muffers Base Ball Club (Ironton, OH; 1860s–1870s)

The Muffers B.B.C. organized in the 1860s, played against black nines of OH and KY. *Portsmouth Times* (July 31, 1869): "A game of base-ball will be played here next Tuesday, between the Independents of Portsmouth, and the Muffers of Ironton. Both Clubs are composed of colored boys." *Times* (July 23, 1870): "A game of base-ball was played on the Riverside Grounds last Thursday afternoon, between the Muffers, of Ironton, and the Forest City Club, of this city, both colored clubs; the former, a club of splendid training, and the latter an amateur club of only two weeks' practice. The game though rather loosely played by the Muffins in the third inning, and in the seventh by the Forest City, was closely contested, and was interesting to the bystanders, whose sympathies were of course with the home club, as they were the weaker party." *Gallipolis Journal* (July 28, 1870): "There will be a match game between the Buckeyes, of this place, and the Muffins, of Ironton, (colored) on the 4th of August, in this city." It was a well-contested game. *Gallipolis Journal* (August 11, 1870): "The game between the Buckeyes, of this place, and Muffins, of Ironton, (Colored), came off at this place on the 4th. The Buckeyes were victorious by a score of 26 to 23."

SOURCES: "Base Ball," *Portsmouth (OH) Times*, Jul 31, 1869; "Base Ball," *Portsmouth Times*, Jul 23, 1870; "Base Ball," *Gallipolis (OH) Journal*, Jul 28, 1870; "Base Ball," *Gallipolis Journal*, Aug 11, 1870; "Base Ball," *Portsmouth Times*, Aug 8, 1874.

Hottentot Base Ball Club (Lima, OH; 1890s)

The Hottentot B.B.C. organized in the 1890s, played black and white aggregations. *Lima Times Democrat* (May 27, 1897): "The base-ball season was given an informal opening here by a game at Faurot's Park yesterday afternoon. The contesting teams were the Hottentots, a team composed of local colored athletes, and a club made up chiefly of Marquette players, assisted by a few Indians from other city clubs. The Hottentots won by a score of 8 to 6. The Fountain brothers were the battery for the Hottentots." The club changed its name to Webster's Giants. *Lima News* (April 24, 1899): "The opening of the local base-ball season drew a large crowd to the park yesterday afternoon, and everyone who went was well repaid for the journey. The game was between the representative colored team of the city, the Webster Giants, and the Shamrocks. The fight was a bitter one, but in the eighth the Shamrocks batted out victory."

SOURCES: The Hottentots; Newly Organized," *Cleveland (OH) Gazette*, Apr 10, 1897; "A Narrow Escape," *Cleveland Gazette*, Apr 17, 1897; "Base Ball," *Lima (OH) Times-Democrat*, Apr 19, 1897; "Fine Players," *Cleveland Gazette*, May 8, 1897; "Hottentots Win," *Cleveland Gazette*, May 15, 1897; "Tales of the Town," *Lima Times-Democrat*, May 27, 1897; "Webster's Giants," *Cleveland Gazette*, May 29, 1897; "Personal Mention," *Cleveland Gazette*, Jun 26, 1897; "Tales of the Town," *Lima Times-Democrat*, Jul 2, 1897; "Tales of the Town," *Lima Times-Democrat*, Jul 8, 1897; "Notes," *Lima Times-Democrat*, Jul 29, 1897; "Notes," *Lima Times-Democrat*, Aug 9, 1897; "Shut Out," *Lima Times-Democrat*. Sept. 5, 1898; "A Great Game," *Lima (OH) Lima News*, Apr 24, 1899; "Defeated at Findlay," *Lima News*, May 11, 1899; "Crescents," *Lima News*, May 29, 1900; "Street Lounger," *Lima News*. Apr. 30, 1900; "Webster Giants," *Lima News*, Jun 4, 1900.

Black Diamond Base Ball Club (Newark, OH; 1890s). Organizer(s): Nathan Craig.

The Black Diamond B.B.C. organized in the 1890s, played black and white teams. *Cleveland Gazette* (April 5, 1890): "The B. D. Base Ball Club have organized: McConnell, Riggs, Toney, Beasley, Gates, Curry, Steward, Craig, Royall. All addresses to Nathan Craig, B & D Hotel."

SOURCES: "Buckeye Letters," *Cleveland (OH) Gazette*, Apr 5, 1890; "Newark's Items," *Detroit (MI) Plaindealer*, Apr 11, 1890.

Doty Hotel Horseshoe Base Ball Club (Newark, OH; 1880s–1890s)

The Doty Hotel Horseshoe B.B.C. organized in the 1880s. *Cleveland Gazette* (June 18, 1887): "A game of base-ball was played last Friday between the Tubbs House boys and the Doty House boys. The former were the winners; score, 8 to 2." *Newark Advocate* (June 3, 1897): "The Doty Horseshoes feel just as sure of winning the contest on the diamond as the Warden Sureshots are confident of pinning the Doty men's scalps to their belts." *Cleveland Gazette* (June 12, 1897): "The Hotel Warden and Doty Hotel waiters played a great game of baseball on the 4th. The Warden boys won in six innings: score 38 to 20. The features of the game were the superb fielding of Terry, Craig, Good and Toney, and the base stealing of Brown, who has played in professional games." *Advocate* (July 10, 1897): "The Doty House waiters went to Granville yesterday afternoon to play a ball game with the college town's colored tea and they returned this evening with Granville's scalp though they had to run the score up almost as high as the mercury to get it." *Granville Times* (July 15, 1897): "The base-ball game played here last Friday afternoon, at Denison University Athletic Park, between the colored waiters of the Hotel Doty, Newark and nine of Granville's colored base-ball fans, did not attract a very large crowd of enthusiasts. Some very good plays were made by both teams. The game turned out to be a veritable slugging match…"

SOURCES: "A Game of Base Ball," *Cleveland (OH) Gazette*, Jun 18, 1887; "Barrel of Fun," *Newark (OH) Advocate*, Jun 2, 1897; "The Struggle," *Newark Advocate*, Jun 3, 1897; "Warmed a Snake to Life," *Cleveland (OH) Gazette*, Jun 12, 1897; "Plenty of Runs," *Newark Advocate*, Jul 10, 1897; "Town talk," *Granville (OH) Times*, Jul 15, 1897.

Black Stockings Base Ball Club (Newton, OH; 1860s–1870s)

The Black Stockings B.B.C. organized in the 1860s. The Black Stockings were also called the Independents, Black Hawks, and Black Owls. They were formidable: they defeated the Alerts (white) Club, by a score of 41 to 16, and they defeated the Temperance (white) Club, by a score of 47 to 16. Before more than 2000 spectators, they defeated Cincinnati's Western Unions (black) for the championship. *New York Clipper* (August 28, 1869): "On the 12th the Independents, of Newton, and the Western Union club, of Porkopolis, both colored, played a match game for 'the championship of colored clubs' of this country, in which the country boys cleaned out their city rivals to the tune of 38 to 26." They also walloped them by a score of 68 to 20. *Cincinnati Commercial Tribune* (November 6, 1869): "The game between the rival colored clubs yesterday, on the Buckeye grounds, was called on time. Five innings were played, clean into the dark—resulting in favor of the Newton boys (seven brothers and two cousins)—the score standing 29 to 9." They reorganized in 1870. *Cleveland Leader* (May 14, 1870): "The colored base-ball club of Newton, Ohio, contemplate a challenge to all-first class club in the United States, with a view to the national championship."

SOURCES: "Base Ball," *Cincinnati (OH) Enquirer*, Aug 11, 1869; "Base Ball Matters," *Cincinnati (OH) Commercial Tribune*, Aug 12, 1869; "Base Ball Matters," *Cincinnati Commercial Tribune*, Sep 8, 1869; "Base Ball Matters," *Cincinnati Enquirer*, Aug 21, 1869; "Cincinnati Base Ball Items," *New York (NY) Clipper*, Aug 28, 1869; "The Black Stockings Victorious, 29 to 9," *Cincinnati Commercial Tribune*, Nov 6, 1869; "Base Ball," *Cleveland (OH) Leader*, May 14, 1870.

Browns Base Ball Club (Oberlin, OH; 1880s)

The Browns B.B.C. organized in the 1880s, played black teams. *Norwalk Reflector* (September 22, 1888): "The Norwalk Browns will play two games of Base Ball Monday, September 24th. In the morning at 9:30, with the Colored Stars of Sandusky. In the afternoon at 4 o'clock, with the Browns of Oberlin. The Oberlins are one of the strongest colored teams of the State."

Sources: "Base Ball," *Norwalk (OH) Reflector*, Sep 20, 1888; "Base Ball," *Norwalk Reflector*, Sep 22, 1888.

Dorian Base Ball Club (Oberlin, OH; 1870s)

The Dorian B.B.C. organized in the 1870s, played black and white teams. The Dorians also played against the famous Oberlin Resolutes, a white club, giving them all they could handle in a three game series leading up to a base-ball tournament. *Cleveland Leader* (July 6, 1874): "The Resolutes, who are recognized as the college nine have played many close and well contested games with the Dorian club composed of colored members, and considerable interest was manifested in the result of the game. Some fine playing was done on both sides and at the end of the ninth inning the game stood 24 to 10 in favor of the Resolutes." The Dorians and Cleveland's Olympics developed a rivalry. *Cleveland Plain Dealer* (July 24, 1874): "The Dorian (colored) club of Oberlin came here yesterday and delivered up a ball to the Olympics (also colored) of this city; score, Olympics, 19; Dorians, 9."

Sources: "Oberlin," *Cleveland (OH) Leader*, Jul 3, 1874; "At Oberlin," *Cleveland Leader*, Jul 6, 1874; "The City," *Cleveland Leader*, Jul 21, 1874; "In and About the City," *Cleveland (OH) Plain Dealer*, Jul 24, 1874; "Base Ball," *Cleveland Leader*, Jul 24, 1874; "Wellington," *Elyria (OH) Independent Democrat*, Jul 21, 1875.

Nonpariel Base Ball Club (Oberlin, OH; 1890s). Organizer(s): Edward "Inkdrop" Williams and Louis Brown.

The Nonpariel B.B.C. organized in the 1890s, played black teams. *Cleveland Gazette* (August 26, 1893): "The Hustlers (a base-ball club) intends to play with the Oberlins [colored] on Labor Day. Game [is] to be played at Oberlin." *Cleveland Leader* (September 6, 1893): "The Hustlers, of Cleveland, and the Oberlin Nonpariels played two game of ball here, Monday, in which the Cleveland boys outplayed the Oberlins at nearly every point. Score, first game, 17 to 13; second game, 14 to 9. These games finish the series with Cleveland in the lead." *Leader* (June 24, 1894): "The Hollendens, of Cleveland, and the Oberlin ball team played two games of ball here today, one in the forenoon and the other in the afternoon. The Oberlin boys were too much for the Cleveland men, and they were beaten in both games. The Oberlin boys now claim the championship over any colored team in the State."

Sources: *Cleveland (OH) Gazette*, Aug 5, 1893; *Cleveland Gazette*, Aug 26, 1893; "Won Two from Oberlin," *Cleveland (OH) Leader*, Sep 6, 1893; "William E. Smith's Locals," *Cleveland Gazette*, Sep 9, 1893; "Now Claim the Championship," *Cleveland Leader*, Jun 24, 1894.

Grays Base Ball Club (Oxford, OH; 1890s)

The Grays B.B.C. organized in the 1890s, played black teams. *Connersville Times* (June 20, 1894): "The Black Diamonds went to Oxford, Ohio, this afternoon, to beat the socks off the colored ball team of that classic village. The nine, composed of fellows named a few days ago, is managed by Tom Pierce and captained by George Bass." The series resumed at Connersville. *Connersville Times* (July 4, 1894): "The Oxford colored ball nine won the game with Connersville's Black Diamonds yesterday. There is always someone to blame, so the Connersville team lay their defeat at the hands of the umpire. The game was quite interesting, as was evidenced by the applause from the crowd present. The score stood 18 to 12." *Con-*

nersville News (July 14, 1897): "On Saturday, July 17th, the Grays, a colored ball team of Oxford, Ohio, and the Connersville Black Diamonds will engage in a game of ball at the ball park in this city. The stakes of the game, a watermelon and chicken, will be divided among the players of the winning team."

Sources: "Oxford," *Hamilton (OH) Democrat*, Jul 6, 1892; "Base Ball," *Hamilton Democrat*, May 28, 1894; *Connersville (IN) Examiner*, Jun 15, 1894; *Connersville (IN) Times*, Jun 20, 1894; "Whoop La; We'll Beat," *Connersville (IN) News*, Jun 29, 1894; "Oxford Wins," *Connersville Times*, Jul 4, 1894; "Oxford Wins," *Connersville News*, Jul 14, 1894; *Connersville News*, Jul 14, 1897.

Barbers Base Ball Club (Portsmouth, OH; 1890s)

The Barber B.B.C. organized in the 1890, if not earlier. *Portsmouth Times* (July 2, 1894): "The Manhattan Ball Club and the Barbers have made arrangements to play a game of ball at the old fairgrounds. The game will undoubtedly be an exciting one and the spectator can be assured of a huge time." *Portsmouth Times* (July 5, 1894): "The game of base-ball yesterday afternoon at the old fairgrounds, between the Manhattans and Barbers, resulted in favor of the former by a score of 25 to 10. 'Goose' Woods' coaching was a feature of the game."

Sources: "An Exciting Game," *Portsmouth (OH) Times*, May 12, 1894; "Manhattans vs. Barbers," *Portsmouth Times*, Jul 2, 1894; "The Manhattans Win," *Portsmouth Times*, Jul 5, 1894.

Drama Hotel Base Ball Club (Portsmouth, OH; 1890s)

The Drama Hotel B.B.C. organized in the 1890s. *Portsmouth Times* (June 30, 1896): "A game of Athletic Park between the barbers and hotel men is booked for next Monday at two o'clock. It will be a game for blood and money. Sherd Henderson and Jack Holliday will make up the barber battery and N. Haley and Jack Melvin the hotel boys battery. An admission fee of 10 cents will be charged."

Sources: "Base Ball Gossip," *Portsmouth (OH) Times*, Jun 30, 1896.

Independent (Forest City) Base Ball Club (Portsmouth, OH; 1860s–1880s)

The Independent (Forest City) B.B.C. organized in the 1860s, played black nines: Cincinnati's Modocs, Ripley's Chocolate Stockings, Ironton's Muffers, Greenup, KY's Wild Oats and Louisville's Mutuals. The Independents played a home and home series against Louisville's Mutuals. *New York Clipper* (August 2, 1867): "The Mutuals, of Louisville, Kentucky, and the Independents, of Portsmouth, Ohio played in the latter city July 24. Score being 11 to 10 in favor of the Mutes. Both nines are colored. They play again on July 25." They played against the Cincinnati Modocs on the Riverside Grounds at Ironton, OH. *Portsmouth Times* (July 31, 1869): "A game of base-ball will be played here next Tuesday, between the Independents of Portsmouth, and the Muffers of Ironton. Both Clubs are composed of colored boys." *Portsmouth Times* (July 30, 1870): "The colored folks have become demoralized too. The Modocs, of Cincinnati, came up to try the Independents of this city. The game came off on the Riverside grounds, in the presence of an enthusiastic crowd on Monday afternoon. The Portsmouth Chaps scooped the Cincinnati darkies by a score of 33 to 24." *Portsmouth Times* (August 8, 1874): "A game of base-ball was played on the Riverside Grounds last Thursday afternoon, between the Muffers, of Ironton, and the Forest City Club, of this city, both colored clubs; the former, a club of splendid training, and the latter an amateur club of only two weeks' practice. The game though rather loosely played by the Muffins in the third inning, and in the seventh by the Forest City, was closely contested, and was interesting to the bystanders, whose sympathies were of course with the home club, as they were the weaker party." They reorganized in the 1880s. The Independents played a two game series against Cambridge's Dude nine, an organization that claimed the black championship of eastern OH. They played Louisville's Mutuals and Chicago's Gordons. The Independents also played Maysville, KY's Maple Leaves nine.

SOURCES: "Base Hits Everywhere," *New York (NY) Clipper*, Aug 2, 1867; "Base Ball," *Portsmouth (OH) Times*, Jul 31, 1869; *Portsmouth Times*, Jul 31, 1869; "Base Ball," *Portsmouth Times*, Jul 23, 1870; "Base Ball," *Portsmouth Times*, Jul 30, 1870; "Base Ball," *Portsmouth Times*, Aug 8, 1874; *Portsmouth Times*, Aug 25, 1877; "Base Ball," *Portsmouth Times*, Aug 26, 1882; "Portsmouth," *Cleveland (OH) Gazette*, Apr 12, 1884; "Portsmouth," *Gazette*, May 10, 1884; "Local Department," *Portsmouth Times*, May 17, 1884; "Portsmouth," *Cleveland Gazette*, May 24, 1884; "Base Ball Notes," *Portsmouth Times*, Jun 21, 1884; *Portsmouth Times*, Jul 12, 1884; "Base Ball Notes Base Ball Notes," *Portsmouth Times*, Jul 26, 1884; "Portsmouth," *Cleveland Gazette*, Jul 26, 1884; "Zanesville," *Cleveland Gazette*, Aug 2, 1884; "Portsmouth," *Cleveland Gazette*, Aug 23, 1884.

Manhattan Base Ball Club (Portsmouth, OH; 1890s)

The Manhattan B.B.C. organized in the 1890s, played white and black teams. The Manhattans' rival was Ironton's Leaders. *Portsmouth Times* (May 12, 1894): "A game of baseball yesterday afternoon between the Manhattans, of this city, and a colored ball club from Ironton was witnessed by an exceptionally large crowd of spectators, a large percentage being white. In fact, there were more people present than the best games this summer has drawn. Those who came out to see a rioting, roistering, rollicking game were not disappointed."

SOURCES: "An Exciting Game," *Portsmouth (OH) Times*, May 12, 1894; "Manhattans vs. Barbers," *Portsmouth Times*, Jul 2, 1894; "The Manhattans Win," *Portsmouth Times*, Jul 5, 1894; "A Challenge," *Portsmouth Times*, Sep 10, 1894; "Base Ball Gossip," *Portsmouth Times*, Jun 30, 1896.

Athletic Base Ball Club (Springfield, OH; 1880s). Organizer(s): Frank Ford and Edward Gant.

The Athletic B.B.C. organized in the 1880s. The Athletics composed of waiters, played black and white teams. *Cleveland Gazette* (June 6, 1885): "The Springfield Base Ball Club played against the Richmond, Indiana boys last Thursday. The latter was defeated by a score of 24 to 8. The feature of the game was the skillful pitched of [Percy] Master Yates, who succeeded in striking out nineteen visitors. He was well-supported by Mr. Edward Gant."

SOURCES: *Richmond (IN) Item*, May 23, 1885; *Richmond Item*, May 27, 1885; "Our Colored Club," *Richmond Item*, May 29, 1885; *Richmond Item*, Jun 4, 1885; "The Champion City," *Cleveland (OH) Gazette*, Jun 6, 1885.

Arcade Hotel Base Ball Club (Springfield, OH; 1880s)

The Arcade Hotel B.B.C. organized in the 1880s, played black and white teams. *Cleveland Gazette* (April 17, 1886): "The boys of the Arcade and Lagonda House have organized their opposing base-ball clubs. The battery for the Arcade boys is Williams and Miller. Their first game, which takes place this coming Wednesday, is looked forward to with much interest." *Springfield Republic* (May 7, 1888): "The waiters of the St. James and Arcade Hotels crossed bats on the Center Street grounds Saturday. Clark and Hopkins were the battery for the St. James and Jackson and Farrell exchanged the ball for the Arcade. William Clay acted as umpire. Score: St. james 16, Arcade 7." *Republic* (May 10, 1888): "The St. James and Arcade teams played a match game Wednesday afternoon, the score standing 7 to 4 for the St. James boys." *Republic* (May 11, 1888): "Another interesting game of base-ball was played between the Arcade and St. James teams, which

resulted in a great victory for the Arcade club. The score stood 19 to 3 in favor of the latter club." *Republic* (July 13, 1888): "The Arcade team defeated the Dayton club in a game of base-ball played on Buck Creek grounds yesterday afternoon. The score was sixteen to one."

SOURCES: "Springfield News," *Cleveland (OH) Gazette*, Apr 17, 1886; "Base Ball Notes," *Springfield (OH) Republic*, May 7, 1888; "Base Ball," *Springfield Republic*, May 10, 1888; "Base Ball," *Springfield Republic*, May 11, 1888; "Local Brevities," *Springfield (OH) Republic*, Jul 10, 1888; "Local Brevities," *Springfield Republic*, Jul 13, 1888.

Ripper Base Ball Club (Springfield, OH; 1880s). Organizer(s): C. Stoffer, Robert T. Jackson, B. T. Fountain and J. H. Underwood.

The Ripper B.B.C. organized in the 1880s. The Rippers were composed of waiters of the Arcade and St. James Hotels. *Springfield Republic* (May 7, 1888): "The waiters of the St. James and Arcade Hotels crossed bats on the Center Street Grounds yesterday." *Springfield Republic* (May 11, 1888): "Another interesting game was played between the Arcade and St. James teams, which resulted in a great victory for the Arcade club. The score stood 19 to 3 in favor of the latter club." They played black and white nines. *Springfield Republic* (July 25, 1888): "The Urbana Base-Ball Club will cross bats with the Rippers tomorrow afternoon, at 3 o'clock, on the Buck Creek Grounds."

SOURCES: "Local Brevities," *Springfield (OH) Republic*, Jul 26, 1887; "Twenty to Nine," *Springfield Republic*, Aug 30, 1887; "About Town," *Springfield Republic*, Sep 6, 1887; "Base Ball Notes," *Springfield Republic*, May 7, 1888; "Base Ball," *Springfield Republic*, May 11, 1888; "Local Brevities," *Springfield Republic*, May 22, 1888; "Base Ball Notes," *Springfield Republic*, May 27, 1888; "The Rippers," *Springfield Republic*, Jul 17, 1888; "Local Brevities," *Springfield Republic*, Jul 25, 1888; "Local Brevities," *Springfield Republic*, Aug 10, 1888; "Base Hits," *Springfield Republic*, Aug 11, 1888.

Colored Champion Base Ball Club (Steubenville, OH; 1860s–1870s)

The Champion B.B.C. organized in in the 1860s. Steubenville and Wheeling, WV developed a rivalry. *Wheeling Intelligencer* (August 8, 1873): "A nine of a colored base-ball club of Steubenville, met a similar number of colored knights of the bat, belonging to this city, in a friendly game on the Island yesterday. The Steubevillians were too much for our home institution." In 1873, the Champions played against Wheeling's Idle Wild B.B.C. The Idlewilds met a crushing defeat, losing by a score of 70 to 13.

SOURCES: "Colored Base Ball," Wheeling (WVA) *Intelligencer*, Jul 13, 1869; "Base Ball," *Wheeling Intelligencer*, Aug 8, 1873.

North Side Base Ball Club (Steubenville, OH; 1890s). Organizer(s): Walter Howard and S.S. Clement.

The North Side B.B.C. organized in the 1890s. *Steubenville Herald* (August 6, 1897) writes: "The two colored ball clubs under the management of Walter Howard and S. S. Clement, will line up for tomorrow's centennial game. The North Sides will wear grey, while the South Sides will appear in white." Some fans later accused Clement, who umpired, of conspiracy to throw the game for the North Siders; the score standing 12 to 5 in favor of the North Enders (Sam's nine) after six innings."

SOURCES: "Colored Athletes," *Steubenville (OH) Herald*, Jul 28, 1897; "Play Ball," *Steubenville Herald*, August 6, 1897; "Conspiracy Charged," *Steubenville Herald*, Aug 7, 1897.

South Side Base Ball Club (Steubenville, OH; 1890s). Organizer(s): Walter Howard and S.S. Clement.

The South Side B.B.C. organized in the 1890s. *Steubenville Herald*

(August 6, 1897) writes: "The two colored ball clubs under the management of Walter Howard and S. S. Clement, will line up for tomorrow's centennial game. The North Sides will wear grey, while the South Sides will appear in white." Some fans later accused Clement, who umpired, of conspiracy to throw the game for the North Siders; the score standing 12 to 5 in favor of the North Enders (Sam's nine) after six innings."

SOURCES: "Colored Athletes," *Steubenville (OH) Herald*, Jul 28, 1897; "Play Ball," *Steubenville Herald*, Aug 6, 1897; "Conspiracy Charged," *Steubenville Herald*, Aug 7, 1897.

Buffalo Base Ball Club (Toledo, OH; 1890s–1900s). Organizer(s): H. Rex.

The Buffalo B.B.C. organized in 1896. The Buffaloes played black and white aggregations.

SOURCES: "Amateur Baseball," *Toledo (OH) Bee*, May 24, 1900; "Amateur Base Ball," *Toledo Bee*, May 29, 1900; "Amateur Base Ball," *Toledo Bee*, Jul 2, 1900; "Amateur Base Ball," *Toledo Bee*, Aug 10, 1900; "Amateur Baseball," *Toledo Bee*, Aug 16, 1900.

Athletic Base Ball Club (Urbana, OH; 1890s). Organizer(s): G. Andrews.

The Athletic B.B.C. organized in the 1890s, played black and white nines. *Detroit Plaindealer* (May 13, 1892): "A party of our young men met and organized a club of Base Ball players," the club of which bears the name 'Urbana Athletics.' G. Andrews manages the team while R. Chavers fill the office as captain. They are now ready to challenge any amateur nine in the State." *Plaindealer* (July 15, 1892): "The Mechanicsburg base-ball club was defeated by the Athletics of this city last Monday week."

SOURCES: "Urbana," *Detroit (MI) Plaindealer*, May 13, 1892; "Urbana," *Detroit Plaindealer*, Jul 15, 1892.

Half Moon Base Ball Club (Urbana, OH; 1860s)

The Half Moon B.B.C. organized in the 1860s. *Cincinnati Enquirer* (September 4, 1869): "The Half Moons, of this place, are the colored champions of Central Ohio. They have beaten the Springfield, Troy, Piqua, & c., and have not been excelled this season, Wednesday of last week they played with the Senecas, of Troy. Score: Half Moons, 50; Senecas, 42. We have here also a colored band, which is the champion colored band pf the state."

SOURCES: "From Urbana," *Cincinnati (OH) Enquirer*, Sep 4, 1869.

Eclipse Base Ball Club (Walnut Hills (Cincinnati), OH; 1880s). Organizer(s): Charlie Williams and James "Jimmie" O'Bannion.

The Eclipse B.B.C. organized in the 1880s. The Eclipse nine played white and black teams. *Cleveland Gazette* (July 24, 1884): "The chief feature or attraction of the day was a game of ball between the Eclipse of the Hill, and the Lockland club. The score was in favor of the former." *Cincinnati Enquirer* (August 4, 1884): "The Eclipse of Walnut Hills were defeated by the Warwicks of Cincinnati by a score of 15 to 14." *Gazette* (August 1, 1885): "The Actives, of this city, and the Eclipse, of Walnut Hills, will cross bats at New Richmond next Sunday. Who says Charlie Williams and Jimmie O'Bannion do not form the finest battery in Ohio? It is said that the Eclipse will go traveling. Maybe they will, after next Sunday's game."

SOURCES: "From the Queen City," *Cleveland (OH) Gazette*, Jul 24, 1884; "From the Queen City," *Cincinnati (OH) Enquirer*, Aug 4, 1884; "Cincinnati," *Cleveland Gazette*, Aug 1, 1885.

Nameless Base Ball Club (Wilmington, OH; 1870s)

The Nameless B.B.C. organized in the 1870s, played black teams. *Wilmington Clinton Republican* (September 7, 1876): "The Haymakers and Nameless, two colored clubs of this place, played on Monday

afternoon, and after five innings in two hours and a half, the Nameless threw up the sponge. Score 47 to 7. A good number of plays were made, principally among which was George Williams' of the Nameless, activity in running after balls in the left field."

SOURCES: "Base Ball," *Wilmington (OH) Clinton Republican*, Jul 2, 1868; "Base Ball," *Wilmington Clinton Republican*, Jul 23, 1868; *Wilmington Clinton Republican*, Oct 8, 1868.

Nameless Base Ball Club (Wilmington, OH; 1870s)

The Nameless B.B.C. organized in the 1870s, played black teams. *Wilmington Clinton Republican* (September 7, 1876): "The Haymakers and Nameless, two colored clubs of this place, played on Monday afternoon, and after five innings in two hours and a half, the Nameless threw up the sponge. Score 47 to 7. A good number of plays were made, principally among which was George Williams' of the Nameless, activity in running after balls in the left field."

SOURCES: "Base Ball," *Wilmington (OH) Clinton Republican*, Jul 2, 1868; "Base Ball," *Wilmington Clinton Republican*, Jul 23, 1868; *Wilmington Clinton Republican*, Oct 8, 1868.

Undine Base Ball Club (Wilmington, OH; 1860s)

The Undine B.B.C. organized in the 1860s, played black teams. *Wilmington Clinton Republican* (October 8, 1868): "The Undine Base Ball Club, (colored), paid a visit to our neighboring village, Harveysburg, and played a game with the Harveysburg Club and succeeded in defeating them by the handsome score of 74 to 37. This was the second game of the series, the first having been won by the latter, the score standing at the close, 56 to 35."

SOURCES: "Base Ball," *Wilmington (OH) Clinton Republican*, Jul 2, 1868; "Base Ball," *Wilmington Clinton Republican*, Jul 23, 1868; *Wilmington Clinton Republican*, Oct 8, 1868.

Rough and Ready Base Ball Club (Xenia, OH; 1880s)

The Rough and Ready B.B.C. organized in the 1880s, played white teams. *Xenia Gazette* (May 29, 1885): "The second nine of Antioch will play a colored nine from town in the woods." *Gazette* (April 20, 1886): "The High School team opened the season last Saturday by defeating the Rough and Ready's, the crack colored nine of the city, by a score of 22 to 11." *Gazette* (May 4, 1886): "The white High School nine and the colored High School nine, played a match game of ball in the Robert's Field yesterday afternoon, which resulted in a big victory for the colored boys. The score was 22 to 2. A return game will be played on Friday afternoon."

SOURCES: "Orphan's Home," *Xenia (OH) Gazette*, May 29, 1885; *Xenia Gazette*, Apr 20, 1886; *Xenia (OH) Gazette*, May 4, 1886; "Base Ball," *Xenia Gazette*, May 5, 1886.

Wilberforce University Base Ball Club (Xenia, OH; 1880s–1900s)

The Wilberforce University B.B.C. organized in the 1880s, if not earlier. The college baseballists played black and white teams. *Xenia Gazette* (June 26, 1883): "The game of base-ball between Wilberforce and Antioch resulted in a score of 25 to 31 in favor of Wilberforce." *Gazette* (June 1, 1886): "The game was played with great interest on both sides up to the sixth inning, when Hill, pitcher of the Nationals in trying to get over to first base, came into collision with Watkins, of the Wilberforce, who was running for the first, the result was Hill made a very graceful somersault. Hill was so disabled that it caused him to let down in his pitching. The Wilberforce began to bat him, making 12 runs in one inning. The return game will be played Monday on the Xenia grounds. The attendance was very large and no doubt it will be much larger next Monday." *Gazette* (Jun 8, 1886): "Once more the famous base-ball players of Wilberforce added another brilliant victory to their long list. The game was played on the Orphan House Grounds and was witnessed by quite a crowd in spite of the excessive heat. The game possessed many fine plays on both sides and some of the best batters ever seen in this locality. Wilberforce claims the championship of the county and feels if there exist any doubts to send challenges. While each of the Wilberforce club sustained his reputation as a ball player, Anderson, the pitcher did the best work of his life. He was ably supported by Arnett, in the absence of Wilson the regular catcher." *Gazette* (May 16, 1896): "A good game of ball was played at Wilberforce yesterday between the University team and Cedarville. The latter did not seem to hold out against their opponents at any stage of the game, and the score stood 12 to 1 in favor of Wilberforce, a couple of errors in the fifth inning being responsible for keeping the Cedarville boys from having goose eggs opposite their names. Bryant and Gilliam were the battery for Wilberforce."

SOURCES: "Xenia Local News," *Xenia (OH) Gazette*, Jun 14, 1883; *Xenia Gazette*, Jun 26, 1883; "Xenia Local News," *Xenia Gazette*, May 23, 1884; "Yellow Springs," *Springfield (OH) Republic*, May 14, 1885; *Xenia Gazette*, Jun 20, 1885; "Base Ball," *Xenia Gazette*, May 6, 1886; Base Ball," *Xenia Gazette*, May 15, 1886; "Base Ball," *Xenia Gazette*, May 28, 1886; "Nationals vs. Wilberforce," *Xenia Gazette*, Jun 1, 1886; "Wilberforce Sluggers," *Xenia Gazette*, Jun 8, 1886; *Xenia Gazette*, Jun 25, 1886; *Xenia Gazette*, Aug 6, 1886; "Base Ball Bat," *Xenia Gazette*, Apr 14, 1887; "Base Ball," *Xenia Gazette*, Apr 19, 1887; "Among Our Colored Citizens," *Xenia Gazette*, Jun 20, 1888; "A Wealthy Negro's End," *Indianapolis (IN) Freeman*, May 26, 1894; *Xenia Gazette*, May 16, 1896; "A Fine Game," *Xenia Gazette*, May 19, 1896; "Colored Items," *Xenia Gazette*, Jul 21, 1897; "Colored Items," *Xenia Gazette*, Jul 27, 1897; "Base Ball," *Gazette*, May 21, 1898; "Wilberforce a Winner," *Cleveland (OH) Leader*, May 31, 1898; "Heidelberg's Schedule," *Cleveland Leader*, Apr 18, 1899; *Xenia Gazette*, Jul 5, 1899; "College Boys," *Coshocton (OH) Gazette*, May 28, 1901.

Oklahoma

Black Jack Clippers Base Ball Club (Chadwick, OK Territory; 1890s)

The Black Jack Clippers B.B.C. organized in the 1890s. The Black Jacks played black and white aggregations. *Oklahoma City Times-Journal* (September 5, 1895): "The Black Jack Clippers will cross bats in this city with the Oklahoma Cyclones, Saturday evening at 3 o'clock. They are in better condition now than ever and declare they will wipe the early with our boys. All should turn out and witness a fine game." *Times-Journal* (September 30, 1895): "The best base-ball that has been played in the territory of Oklahoma territory this season was played Saturday evening at Chadwick, between the colored nine, better known as the Black Jack Clippers and Chadwick white nine. The Clippers were assisted by four of the Oklahoma Cyclone boys, while the Chadwick employed the Crooked Oak battery, shortstop and first baseman. Result of the game was 4 to 5 in favor of the Clipper club."

SOURCES: "Not Title," *Oklahoma City (OK) Times-Journal*, Sep 5, 1895; "A Good Game," *Oklahoma City Times-Journal*, Sep 30, 1895.

Blues Base Ball Club (Guthrie, OK Territory; 1895–1900s)

The Blues B.B.C. organized in the 1890s, played black teams. Guthrie organized a Colored League; it included the territorial towns of Guthrie, Vinita, OK City, El Reno, Hennessey, Chandler and Clifton. They played McKinney, TX's Clippers, a "professional negro baseball team." *Oklahoma State Capital* (June 18, 1900): "The ball team of McKinney, Texas played ball with the colored team of Guthrie

at island Park, yesterday afternoon and won by a score of 9 to 5. The two teams will play ball again next Sunday afternoon."

SOURCES: "Ball," *Oklahoma City (OK) Times-Journal*, Jun 15, 1895; "Ball," *Guthrie (OK) Leader*, Jul 15, 1897; *Oklahoma City Times-Journal*, Jul 17, 1900; *Guthrie Leader*, Jul 19, 1900; "Texas Ball Players," *Guthrie (OK) Oklahoma State Capital*, Jul 27, 1900.

Head Light Base Ball Club (El Reno, OK Territory; 1890s). Organizer(s): John Parris.

The Head Light B.B.C. organized in the 1890s, played black and white teams. *El Reno Herald* (July 11, 1895): "The El Reno Headlight colored baseball team respectfully challenge any team in the territory." The club participated in a Colored League, organized by Guthrie's colored organization, which included the "territorial towns" of Guthrie, Vinita, OK City, El Reno, Hennessey, Chandler and Clifton."

SOURCES: *Oklahoma City (OK) Times-Journal*, Jul 10, 1895; *El Reno (OK) Democrat*, July 11, 1895; *El Reno (OK) Herald*, Jul 11, 1895.

Sand Scratcher Base Ball Club (El Reno, OK Territory; 1890s). Organizer(s): John Parris.

The Sand Scratcher B.B.C. organized in the 1890s, played black aggregations. *Hennessey Kicker* (March 4, 1896): "John Parris says that the Sand Scratchers Base Ball Club will be organized and ready to open the season by the first of April. They have secured a new mascot to take the place of Mr. Blackburn, who has gone down into the nation to farm among the Indians. We will wager that Blackburn is captain of the Indian nine before the season closes. John says the S. S.'s are itching to get hold of the Hennessey nine."

SOURCES: *Hennessey (OK) Kicker*, Mar 3, 1896; "A Bit of Everything," *Hennessey Kicker*, May 28, 1896; *Hennessey Kicker*, Jul 2, 1896.

Cyclone Base Ball Club (OK City, OK Territory; 1890s)

The Cyclone B.B.C. organized in the 1890s, played black teams. Guthrie organized a Colored League, which included the territorial towns of Guthrie, Vinita, OK City, El Reno, Hennessey, Chandler and Clifton. *Oklahoma City Times-Journal* (June 20, 1895): "The Cyclones and Western League Ball Clubs (both colored) had a match game of ball yesterday, the score standing 28 to 7 in favor of the Cyclones. The Cyclones will cross bats with the Guthrie Blues on June 24th." *Times-Journal* (July 17, 1895): "The Oklahoma Cyclones will play the El Reno colored club in this city tomorrow at 3:30. A good game is expected." *Times-Journal* (July 19, 1895): "The game between El Reno and Oklahoma City colored clubs proved to be an interesting one. There are splendid players in both clubs, but we hear the battery of the home club mentioned as having done especially good playing."

SOURCES: "Base Ball," *Oklahoma City (OK) Times-Journal*, Jun 19, 1895; *Oklahoma City Times-Journal*, Jun 20, 1895; *Oklahoma City Times-Journal*, Jun 25, 1895; "Ball Game," *Oklahoma City Times-Journal*, Jul 17, 1895; "Match Ball Game," *Oklahoma City Times-Journal*, Jul 25, 1895; *Oklahoma City Times-Journal*, Sep 5, 1895.

Invincible Base Ball Club (OK City, OK Territory; 1890s). Organizer(s): Willis Tucker.

The Invincible B.B.C. organized in the 1890s. The "Invincibles" played black and white teams. Guthrie organized a Colored League, which included the territorial towns of Guthrie, Vinita, OK City, El Reno, Hennessey, Chandler and Clifton. *Oklahoma City Times-Journal* (July 12, 1895): "The Oklahoma Invincibles will play the colored baseball team of El Reno in this city, Friday afternoon. On Monday evening, July 15, the Guthrie Blues will cross bats with the Invincibles in this city also. It promises to be one of the best games every played in the territory. Nothing will be said that will mar the ladies' feelings."

SOURCES: *Oklahoma City (OK) Times-Journal.* Aug. 4, 1894; "Ball," *Oklahoma City Times-Journal,* Jun 15, 1895; *Oklahoma City Times-Journal,* Jun 25, 1895; *Oklahoma City Daily Times-Journal,* Jul 10, 1895; *El Reno (OK) Herald,* Jul 12, 1895; "The Colored Picnic," *Oklahoma City Times-Journal,* Jun 26, 1896.

Black Diamond Base Ball Club (Vinita, Indian Territory/OK; 1890s)

The Black Diamond B.B.C. organized in the 1890s, played black teams. The Black Diamonds played a two-game series against Kansas City's Union B.B.C. *Vinita Indian Chieftain* (August 10, 1899): "The Kansas City colored base-ball club beat the Vinita Black Diamonds Tuesday."

SOURCES: "Unions, 8; Vinita, 5," *Kansas City (MO) Journal,* Aug 10, 1899; Vinita (Indian Territory) *Indian Chieftain,* Aug 10, 1899; "Unions, 4; Vinita, 2," *Kansas City Journal,* Aug 12, 1899.

Pennsylvania

Mutual Base Ball Club (Allegheny, PA; 1880s). Organizer(s): George D. Sherrow.

The Mutual B.B.C. organized in the 1880s. The "Mutuals" played black teams. *Pittsburgh Commercial Gazette* (July 5, 1882): "The Mutual Club (colored), of this city yesterday afternoon defeated the Washington (colored) Club, of Washington, DC, by the following score at Union Park, in the presence of a god crowd of spectators. Mutual, 18; Washingtons, 12." *Commercial Gazette* (July 6, 1889): "The Mutual Base Ball Club (colored), formerly the Barber Base Ball Club, defeated the colored club of East … on Thursday by a score of 29 to 16."

SOURCES: "Sporting Notes," *Pittsburgh (PA) Commercial Gazette,* Jun 29, 1882; "Sporting Events," *Pittsburgh Commercial Gazette,* Jul 5, 1882; "Sporting Notes," *Pittsburgh Commercial Gazette,* Jul 6, 1889; "Sporting Notes," *Pittsburgh (PA) Dispatch,* Jul 11, 1889; "Sporting Notes," *Pittsburgh Commercial Gazette,* Jul 11, 1889.

Hotel Allen Base Ball Club (Allentown, PA; 1890s–1900s)

The Hotel Allenton B.B.C. organized in the 1890s, played white and black aggregations. *Allentown Morning Call* (August 23, 1895): "The Hotel Allen base-ball club defeated the strong amateur team, Reilly's 400, by a score of 8 to 3. The feature of the game was the fine pitching of Crampton, catching of Emery and the batting of Vaughn." The Black waiters of Bethlehem and Allentown developed a rivalry. *Allentown Leader* (March 30, 1897): "Two base-ball nines, composed of colored hotel waiters, played the first game of the season yesterday afternoon on the common between Lehigh Valley and Terminal stations." *Morning Call* (September 28, 1898): "The colored base-ball team known as the Wyandottes, of Bethlehem, will cross bats with their colored brethren of Allentown at Rittersville on Friday afternoon. R. Watson will be in the box for the Wyandottes and either White or Bradley will catch." *Leader* (October 14, 1898): "An interesting game of base-ball was played at Rittersville between colored nines from the Wyandotte Hotel, South Bethlehem, and the Hotel Allen, Allentown. The peanut chewers [Hotel Allen] were defeated by a score of 13 to 10." *Leader* (July 21, 1900): "At the Rittersville ball grounds the Bethlehem Cuban Giants defeated an Allentown team in a one-sided game. Score 14 to 5. Watson carried off the honors for the winners in the field and at the bat. Batteries: Bethlehem, Taylor and Watson; Allentown, Cranston and White. Umpire, Joe Yates."

SOURCES: "Reilly's 400 vs. Hotel Allen Waiters," *Allentown (PA) Morning Call,* Jun 15, 1895; "Reilly's 400 vs. Hotel Allen Waiters," *Allentown Morning Call,* Aug 8, 1895; "Hotel Allen vs. Reilly's 400," *Allentown Morning Call,* Aug 23, 1895; "Here, There, and Elsewhere," *Allentown (PA) Leader,* Mar 30, 1897; "Colored Men Play Ball," *Allentown Morning Call,* Sep 28, 1898; "Colored Base Ball," *Allentown Leader,* Oct 4, 1898; "Base Ball Notes," *Allentown Leader,* Jul 21, 1900.

Colored Base Ball Club (Altoona, PA; 1880s). Organizer(s): George Tillman.

The Colored B.B.C. organized in the 1880s, played black and white and nines. *Altoona Times* (June 18, 1884): "The colored club of this city will go to Hollidaysburg tomorrow to play the club of that place. Dhrew and Tillman will be the battery for the Altoona team." *Times* (June 20, 1884): "The game of ball played between the Hollidaysburg colored club and the Altoona colored club, yesterday, resulted in favor of the former by a score of 18 to 12." *Times* (July 3, 1884): "The Altoona colored club and the Hash Slingers at the Logan House will play a game of ball on the Pastime ground near McCauley's shops, on the fourth of July. Game to be called at half-past 3 o'clock sharp." *Times* (September 29, 1884): "The Logan House base-ball nine, colored, will play Gorge Tillman's nine on Tuesday at 3:30 p.m., instead of today as published. The game will be played on the Pastime grounds."

SOURCES: "Notes," *Altoona (PA) Times,* Jun 18, 1884; "Base Ball Briefs," *Altoona Times,* Jun 20, 1884; "Base Ball Briefs," *Altoona Times,* Jul 3, 1884; "Base Ball," *Altoona Times,* Sep 29, 1884.

Liberty Stars Base Ball Club (Altoona, PA; 1880s–1890s)

The Liberty Stars B.B.C. organized in the 1890s, played black and white and nines. *Altoona Tribune* (June 18, 1890): "The Liberty Stars, the colored base-ball club, of this city, will play the Hollidaysburg Champions Saturday next."

SOURCES: "Amateur Base Ball," *Altoona (PA) Tribune,* May 27, 1890; "With the Amateurs," *Altoona Tribune,* Jun 18, 1890; "With the Amateurs," *Altoona Tribune,* Jun 23, 1890.

Logan House Base Ball Club (Altoona, PA; 1880s–1890s). Organizer(s): Howard Lisle; Taylor Jones; William Deadford; Walter Williams.

The Logan House B.B.C. organized in the 1880s, played black and white and nines. *Altoona Times* (July 3, 1884): "The Altoona colored club and the Hash Slingers at the Logan House will play a game of ball on the Pastime ground near McCauley's shops, on the fourth of July. Game to be called at half-past 3 o'clock sharp." *Times* (September 29, 1884): "The Logan House base-ball nine, colored, will play Gorge Tillman's nine on Tuesday at 3:30 p.m., instead of today as published. The game will be played on the Pastime grounds." They reorganized in 1885. *Times* (May 28, 1885): "The Barbers' Base Ball Club, having walloped the waiters four times in succession, want to tackle the Browns, and have sent them a challenge." *Times* (June 2, 1885): "Yesterday the Logan House waiters were defeated by the Barbers by a score of 10 to 8. Howard Lisle, of the waiters nine, made a home run." *Altoona Tribune* (August 6, 1889): "A game of base-ball will be played this afternoon at Twenty-Fourth Street and Sixth Avenue, between the Logan House waiters and McIntosh's Combination. The waiters, under the management of Taylor Jones, have been greatly strengthened and a good game is looked for."

SOURCES: "Base Ball Briefs," *Altoona (PA) Times,* Jul 3, 1884; "Base Ball," *Altoona Times,* Sep 29, 1884; "Local Happenings," *Altoona Times,* May 28, 1885; "Base Ball Notes," *Altoona Times,* Jun 2, 1885; "Local Brevities," *Altoona (PA) Tribune,* Aug 1, 1889; "Local Brevities," *Altoona Tribune,* Aug 6, 1889; "Local Brevities," *Altoona Tribune,* Jun 19, 1891; "They Want an Answer," *Altoona Tribune,* Jun 20, 1891; "Tyrone Topics," *Altoona Tribune,* Jun 23, 1891; "Hollidaysburg's Happenings," *Altoona Tribune,* Jul 22, 1891.

Cross Cuts Base Ball Club (Altoona, PA; 1880s–1900s). Organizer(s): Taylor Jones; Charles Hall; G. W. Benson.

The Cross Cuts B.B.C. organized in the 1890s. The Cross Cuts, composed of Logan House waiters, played black and white nines. *Altoona Tribune* (August 6, 1889): "A game of base-ball will be played this afternoon at Twenty-Fourth Street and Sixth Avenue, between the Logan House waiters and McIntosh's Combination. The waiters, under the management of Taylor Jones, have been greatly strengthened and a good game is looked for." *Tribune* (June 30, 1891): "The Cross Cuts defeated the Do Nothings (formerly Samuel Lile's Combination) by a score of 19 to 7 last evening [Samuel Lile is Samuel Lyle, a Logan House waiter. His brother was Howard Lisle, another baseballist/waiter.]. *Tribune* (September 30, 1893): "The Cross Cuts accepted the challenge of the Liberty Stars [colored] for a game of ball on Saturday afternoon, September 30, on their grounds." The nine developed a rivalry with Bellwood's Defiance club, a white team. *Tribune* (July 31, 1895): "The Cross Cuts defeated the Bellwood Defiance on Monday by a score of 14 to 10. The game was well contested many brilliant plays being made. The eighteen year old boys felt very bad over the defeat. If these be boys, Bellwood is without a voter. The Cross Cuts also defeated Seely's combination by a score of 14 to 4."

SOURCES: "Local Brevities," *Altoona (PA) Tribune*, Aug 1, 1889; "Local Brevities," *Altoona Tribune*, Aug 6, 1889; "Grant Concert," *Altoona Tribune*, May 21, 1890; "Local Brevities," *Altoona Tribune*, Jun 16, 1891; "Tyrone Topics," *Altoona Tribune*, Jun 23, 1891; "Local Brevities," *Altoona Tribune*, Jun 30, 1891; "Hollidaysburg Happenings," *Altoona Tribune*, Jul 22, 1891; "Local Brevities," *Altoona Tribune*, Sep 30, 1893; "Notes," *Altoona Tribune*, Jul 31, 1895; "Miscellaneous Notes," *Altoona Tribune*, Aug 15, 1895; "Miscellaneous Notes," *Altoona Tribune*, Aug 20, 1895; "Local Brevities," *Altoona Tribune*, Aug 24, 1895; "Local Brevities," *Altoona Tribune*, Sep 24, 1895; "Local Brevities," *Altoona Tribune*, Mar 19, 1896; "Local Brevities," *Altoona Tribune*, May 22, 1897; "Here A Note," *Altoona Tribune*, Jun 9, 1897; "Bellwood Briefs," *Altoona Tribune*, Sep 27, 1897; "A Few Notes," *Altoona Tribune*, Jun 6, 1898; "Chat About Coming Stars of the Diamond," *Philadelphia (PA) Inquirer*, Sep 1, 1901.

Troublesome Base Ball Club (Altoona, PA; 1870s). Organizer(s): John Singleton.

The Troublesome B.B.C. organized in the 1870s. The Troublesomes, composed of barbers, played black nines. *Altoona Evening Mirror* (May 29, 1876): "John Singleton's colored nine (the Troublesome) will trouble the razor slingers at an early date." *Evening Mirror* (July 19, 1876): "The Troublesome Club, of Altoona, will play the Hummingbirds, of Hollidaysburg, on the Mountain City Grounds, Thursday afternoon, July 20. These clubs are composed of colored gentlemen." *Evening Mirror* (July 24, 1876): "The Humming Birds, of Hollidaysburg, walked away with our Razor Slingers to the tune of 35 to 16. The crowd in attendance, for some reason or other, went in over the fence."

SOURCES: "Base Ball Items," *Altoona (PA) Evening Mirror*, May 29, 1876; "Base Ball," *Altoona Evening Mirror*, Jul 19, 1876; "Base Ball Items," *Altoona Evening Mirror*, Jul 24, 1876.

Browns Base Ball Club (Athens, PA; 1890s)

The Browns B.B.C. organized in the 1890s, played black teams. *Syracuse Standard* (August 6, 1897): "At the fairgrounds those celebrators of athletic bent of mind saw an interesting game of ball between two colored teams, the Athens Brownies, of Athens, Pennsylvania and an Ithaca nine for a purse of $50. It was the jolliest collection of ball players that ever appeared on an Auburn diamond, and the coaching of both teams was an important team."

SOURCES: "Negro's Emancipation Day," *Syracuse (NY) Standard*, Aug 1, 1897; "The Auburn Celebration," *Syracuse Standard*, Aug 6, 1897.

Wyandotte Hotel Base Ball Club (Bethlehem, PA; 1890s–1900s)

The Wyandotte Hotel B.B.C. organized in the 1890s, played black aggregations. The waiters of Bethlehem and Allentown developed a rivalry. *Allentown Leader* (March 30, 1897): "Two base-ball nines, composed of colored hotel waiters, played the first game of the season yesterday afternoon on the common between Lehigh Valley and Terminal stations." *Allentown Morning Call* (September 28, 1898): "The colored base-ball team known as the Wyandottes, of Bethlehem, will cross bats with their colored brethren of Allentown at Rittersville on Friday afternoon. R. Watson will be in the box for the Wyandottes and either White or Bradley will catch." *Leader* (October 14, 1898): "An interesting game of base-ball was played at Rittersville between colored nines from the Wyandotte Hotel, South Bethlehem, and the Hotel Allen, Allentown. The peanut chewers [Hotel Allen] were defeated by a score of 13 to 10." In 1900, the organization changed its name. *Leader* (July 21, 1900): "At the Rittersville ball grounds the Bethlehem Cuban Giants defeated an Allentown team in a one-sided game. Score 14 to 5. Watson carried off the honors for the winners in the field and at the bat. Batteries: Bethlehem, Taylor and Watson; Allentown, Cranston and White. Umpire, Joe Yates."

SOURCES: "Reilly's 400 vs. Wyandotte," *Allentown (PA) Morning Call*, Jun 18, 1895; "Here, There, and Elsewhere," *Allentown (PA) Leader*, Mar 30, 1897; "Colored Men Play Ball," *Allentown Morning Call*, Sep 28, 1898; "Colored Base Ball," *Allentown Leader*, Oct 4, 1898; "Base Ball Notes," *Allentown Leader*, Jul 21, 1900.

Colored Base Ball Club (Blairsville, PA; 1890s). Organizer(s): Ambert Bell.

The Colored B.B.C. organized in the 1890s. *Indiana Progress* (October 3, 1894): "That old, old saying, 'When Greek meets Greek then comes the tug-of-war' was never more realistically illustrated in Indiana county than on Monday morning, when the colored baseball teams of Indiana and Blairsville came together for the first time this year. The game was played at Blairsville and Indiana won, the result of the magnificent game being 15 to 5." *Pittsburgh Press* (August 29, 1897): "The third of a series of games of baseball between Blairsville and Apollo teams will be played at Blairsville tomorrow. The two former games played by the teams caused a tie between them and the game tomorrow will determine the championship of Indiana and Armstrong counties, for which the two clubs are playing. Batteries for Apollo are G. Lee and Denny; Blairsville, T. Lee and McClellan. A hot contest is expected."

SOURCES: "Brought It Home Too," *Indiana (PA) Progress*, Oct 3, 1894; "Indiana Wins," *Indiana (PA) Gazette*, Oct 3, 1894; "Blairsville Defeated Again," *Indiana (PA) Messenger*, Oct 8, 1894; "African-American Notes," *Pittsburgh (PA) Press*, Aug 29, 1897.

Midnight Star Base Ball Club (Canonsburg, PA; 1890s–1900). Organizer(s): Granville McGrant and Samuel Wilson.

The Midnight Star B.B.C. organized in the 1890s. The Midnight Star nine, composed of barbers, played black and white teams. *Canonsburg Weekly Notes* (June 7, 1897): "The Junior Athletic club of Washington came down Saturday and played the Midnight Stars of Canonsburg, a junior nine. The Stars simply wiped up the ground with the Athletics, defeating them by a score of 32 to 6." *Weekly Notes* (August 28, 1897): "The Keystone Baseball club of Washington is playing the Midnight Star team at the East End grounds this afternoon. The Little Star Juniors, a colored baseball team of Washington, came down Friday and wiped up the earth with the Canonsburg Midnight Stars. Score 25 to 6 in favor of the Washington aggregation."

SOURCES: *Canonsburg (PA) Weekly Notes*, Jun 7, 1897; *Canonsburg Weekly Notes*, Jun 25, 1897; *Canonsburg Weekly Notes*, Aug 28, 1897; *Canonsburg Weekly Notes*, Sep 21, 1897; "Want to Play the Midnight Stars," *Canonsburg Weekly Notes*, Sep 22, 1897; "Sporting Notes," *Canonsburg Weekly Notes*, Sep 24, 1897; "In the Field Early," *Canonsburg (PA) Notes*, Feb 26, 1900; *Canonsburg Daily Notes*, June 29, 1900.

Wide Awake Base Ball Club (Canonsburg, PA; 1870s)

The Wide Awake B.B.C. organized in the 1870s, played black nines. *Washington Reporter* (August 25, 1875) states: "A game of base-ball was played at Canonsburg, on Thursday last, between the Independence Club, of Washington, and the Wide Awakes of Canonsburg, (both colored nines), the Washington club winning by a score of 31 to 8. Some fine playing was done on both sides, but Mac Anderson, the captain of the Independence club capped the climax by his fine batting; using only one hand to bat with which he made some very fine hits, and being asked why he did not use both hands, answered that he was afraid if he did that the ball would never be found."

SOURCES: "Base Ball," *Washington (PA) Reporter*, Aug 25, 1875.

Athletic Base Ball Club (Carlisle, PA; 1900s). Organizer(s): Gus Jordan.

The Athletic B.B.C. organized in the 1900s, played black aggregations. *Carlisle Evening Herald* (May 29, 1900): "Harrisburg Giants will play the Carlisle Colored Athletic club tomorrow at the Dickinson Athletic Park. Admission 15 cents. A good game may be expected." *Harrisburg Telegraph* (June 12, 1900): "Next Thursday, the colored Athletic Base Ball Club, of Carlisle, will play the Harrisburg Giants in this city. A return game will be played on the following Saturday at Carlisle."

SOURCES: "Base Ball," *Carlisle (PA) Evening Herald*, May 29, 1900; "Sport Potpourri," *Harrisburg (PA) Telegraph*, Jun 12, 1900.

Cross-Cut Base Ball Club (Carlisle, PA; 1880s–1890s). Organizer(s): Robert Jordan; Harry A. Young.

The Cross-Cut B.B.C. organized in the 1880s, played black aggregations. *Shippensburg Chronicle* (May 12, 1887): "The Cross-Cut Base Ball Club, of Carlisle, played the Shippensburg colored club last Friday and defeated them by a score of 42 to 19. It was a bad day for Shippensburg, but it must be remembered that this is a local option town, and if we get whipped it's our own fault." *Harrisburg Telegraph* (May 12, 1893): "The Harrisburg Cuban Giants were defeated by the Cross-Cuts, of Carlisle, Wednesday 6 to 4." *Carlisle Evening Herald* (May 15, 1891): "The Junior Cross-Cut team beat a picked nine last evening by a score of 31 to 22. The battery for the Cross-Cut was Young and Smith, and for the picked team Jackson and Smith. Both teams are colored." *Evening Herald* (May 18, 1891): "On Saturday evening there was a game of ball played between the Chain Makers and the Cross-Cut Juniors, both of Carlisle. Six innings were played and the result was a victory for the Cross-Cut." *Telegraph* (June 29, 1893): "Quite a crowd witnessed the Harrisburg Giants down the colored Cross-Cuts, of Carlisle, on the Sixth Street grounds yesterday by an overwhelming score. The Harrisburgers are in the lead for the series thus far."

SOURCES: "Local Miscellany," *Shippensburg (PA) Chronicle*, May 12, 1887; "Base Ball," *Carlisle (PA) Evening Herald*, May 15, 1891; *Carlisle Evening Herald*, May 18, 1891; "Bunted Balls," *Harrisburg (PA) Telegraph*, May 6, 1893; "Bunted Balls," *Harrisburg Telegraph*, May 12, 1893; "Ball and Bat," *Harrisburg (PA) Telegraph*, Jun 9, 1893; "Scraps," *Harrisburg Telegraph*, Jun 29, 1893; "Briefly Told," *Carlisle Evening Herald*, Apr 8, 1895; "Briefly Told," *Carlisle Evening Herald*, Jun 28, 1895.

Eclipse Base Ball Club (Carlisle, PA; 1890s). Organizer(s): Harry A. Young.

The Eclipse B.B.C. organized in the 1890s, played black aggregations. *Carlisle Evening Herald* (June 25, 1891): "This afternoon a team from this city is playing the Eclipse team from Carlisle." *Evening Herald* (August 8, 1891): "The Eclipse Base Ball team of this place today played a game with the Middletown club upon the latter's grounds. The Eclipse is a strong team and should return home victorious." *Evening Herald* (June 24, 1898): "The base-ball game between the Monarch and the Eclipse clubs has been postponed until next week. A. Jordan, Captain, Monarch; H. Young, Captain, Eclipse."

SOURCES: "Bat and Ball," *Carlisle (PA) Evening Herald*, Jun 25, 1891; "Brief Local Mention," *Carlisle (PA) Evening Herald*, Aug 8, 1891; "Ball and Bat," *Harrisburg (PA) Telegraph*, Jun 9, 1893; "Organized Another Base Ball Team," *Carlisle (PA) Evening Herald*, Apr 16, 1897; "Base Ball," *Carlisle Evening Herald*, Jun 24, 1898; "Baseball Tomorrow," *Carlisle Evening Herald*, Jul 21, 1898.

Excelsior Base Ball Club (Carlisle, PA; 1870s).

The Excelsior B.B.C. organized in the 1870s. The Excelsiors played against black organizations. *Harrisburg Telegraph* (June 26, 1875): "In a game of base-ball played at Carlisle yesterday between the Mystic Club of this city and the Excelsior of Carlisle, the former were victorious, the score standing 20 to 1." *Carlisle Weekly Herald* (September 16, 1875): "On Saturday afternoon two colored clubs of this place, the Excelsior and the Nonpariels, played a game of ball, the score standing 15 to 9, in favor of the first named."

SOURCES: *Harrisburg (PA) Telegraph*, Jun 16, 1875; "The City," *Harrisburg Telegraph*, Jun 26, 1875; *Carlisle (PA) Weekly Herald*, Sep 16, 1875.

High Boys Base Ball Club (Carlisle, PA; 1870s).

The High Boys B.B.C. organized in the 1870s, played against black organizations. *Harrisburg Telegraph* (September 26, 1875): "In a game of base-ball at Kanaga's woods, yesterday, between the High Boys of Carlisle, and the Tyroleans, of Harrisburg (both colored), the former club was defeated by a score of 3 to 42."

SOURCES: "The City," *Harrisburg (PA) Telegraph*, Sep 26, 1875.

Monarch Base Ball Club (Carlisle, PA; 1890s). Organizer(s): Samuel A. Jordan and R. J. Jordan; Charles Madison; Benjamin Jackson, Hall and Carrington.

The Monarch B.B.C. organized in the 1890s, played black nines. *Carlisle Evening Herald* (June 1, 1895): "The Monarchs defeated the Harrisburg Cuban Giants by a score of 14 to 7." *Evening Herald* (June 12, 1897): "The Pomeroy club which is considered amongst the strongest clubs of the Cumberland Valley will play the strongest club of Carlisle, known as the Monarchs on the Association grounds, Thursday, July 15, at 8 o'clock. Batteries for Pomeroy, Norris and Wells; Monarchs, Manning and Jordan."—Chambersburg Repository." *Evening Herald* (June 19, 1897): "The ball game on Thursday resulted in a victory for the Monarchs over the Chambersburg team. Score: 14 to 13." *Evening Herald* (June 30, 1898): "The Monarchs played the Waiters at the fairgrounds yesterday afternoon, and won by a score of 7 to 5. Lee was catcher for the Monarchs."

SOURCES: "Ball Team Organized," *Carlisle (PA) Evening Herald*, Apr 5, 1895; "County and Elsewhere," *Carlisle Evening Herald*, May 15, 1895; "Base Ball Manager Missed," *Harrisburg (PA) Independent*, May 30, 1895; "Base Ball," *Carlisle Evening Herald*, Jun 1, 1895; "Charles Madison Explains," *Harrisburg Independent*, Jun 1, 1895; "Briefly Told," *Carlisle Evening Herald*, Jun 19, 1897; "Around the Diamond," *Carlisle Evening Herald*, Jul 12, 1897; "Colored Base Ballists Playing," *Carlisle Evening Herald*, Jul 14, 1897; "Their Challenge,"

Carlisle Evening Herald, Jul 29, 1897; "A Challenge Made," *Carlisle Evening Herald,* Aug 3, 1897; "Base Ball Notes," *Carlisle Evening Herald,* Jun 30, 1898.

Olympic Base Ball Club (Carlisle, PA; 1880s)

The Olympic B.B.C. organized in the 1880s, played black teams. *Harrisburg State Journal* (May 24, 1884): "On Tuesday the Olympic Club, of Carlisle played a game with the Harrisburgs (Olympics) and were defeated after a long noisy disinteresting game. For the first few innings the Harrisburgs played an almost faultless game and at the beginning of the fourth inning the score stood 10 to 0 in their favor, this lead they allowed to be overcome by costly errors in the outfield, and from Johnson not having proper support behind the bat...."

Sources: *Harrisburg (PA) State Journal,* May 14, 1884; "Olympic vs. Olympic," *Harrisburg State Journal,* May 24, 1884; "Brief Locals," *Harrisburg State Journal,* May 31, 1884.

Our Boys Base Ball Club (Carlisle, PA; 1870s)

The Our Boys B.B.C. organized in the 1870s, played black teams. *Harrisburg Telegraph* (September 7, 1877): "The Our Boys nine of Carlisle and the Harley Club of your city will play a game of ball in this place on the 4th. These clubs are evenly matched." *Telegraph* (September 26, 1877): "The Carlisle Herald says the Harley Club of this city (Harrisburg) is afraid to measure bats with Our Boys of Carlisle." *Telegraph* (September 28, 1877): "The Harley Club of this city will play the Our Boys at Carlisle on Saturday." *Telegraph* (September 28, 1877): "The Harley Club of this city have defeated the Our Boys of Carlisle three times in match games, and they can do it again."

Sources: "Emancipation Celebration," *Carlisle (PA) Weekly Herald,* Aug 9, 1877; "From Carlisle," *Harrisburg (PA) Telegraph,* Sep 7, 1877; "Jottings," *Harrisburg Telegraph,* Sep 20, 1877; *Carlisle Weekly Herald,* Sep 20, 1877; "Jottings," *Harrisburg Telegraph,* Sep 26, 1877; *Carlisle Weekly Herald,* Sep 27, 1877; "Jottings," *Harrisburg Telegraph,* Sep 28, 1877; "City and Vicinity," *Harrisburg (PA) Patriot,* Oct 2, 1877; "Jottings," *Harrisburg Telegraph,* Oct 9, 1877;

Pastime Base Ball Club (Carlisle, PA; 1870s). Organizer(s): W. J. Hunter.

The Pastime B.B.C. organized in the 1870s, played black nines. *Harrisburg Telegraph* (July 16, 1875): "In a match game of base-ball, yesterday, the Mystic defeated the Tyrolean club by a score of 35 to 16." *Telegraph* (September 30, 1875): "A game of ball will be played on the Union Grounds, between the Pastimes, of Carlisle, and Mystics, of this city, on Friday." *Shippensburg News* (July 24, 1875): "The Napoleons of this place [Shippensburg, Pennsylvania], and the Pastimes of Carlisle, both colored base-ball clubs, had a match game of ball at the latter place, Thursday, in which the former were victorious by a score of 25 to 14." *Telegraph* (October 1, 1875): "The Mystics of this city and Pastimes of Carlisle are announced to play a game of base-ball on the Unions Grounds this afternoon. Both clubs are colored. Admission 15 and 25 cents."

Sources: "Entertainment," *Carlisle (PA) Weekly Herald,* Jul 13, 1871; "Items About Home," *Carlisle Weekly Herald,* Jul 20, 1871; "Items About Home," *Carlisle Weekly Herald,* Jul 22, 1871; "Entertainments," *Carlisle Weekly Herald,* May 14, 1874; "Match Game of Base Ball," *Carlisle Weekly Herald,* Jun 18, 1874; *Carlisle Weekly Herald,* Jul 2, 1874; "Base Ball Notes," *Carlisle Weekly Herald,* Sep 2, 1874; "Base Ball Match," *Carlisle Weekly Herald,* Sep 17, 1874; *Harrisburg (PA) Telegraph,* May 21, 1875; *Harrisburg Telegraph,* Jun 12, 1875; *Carlisle Weekly Herald,* Jun 24, 1875; *Harrisburg Telegraph,* Jul 16, 1875; "Home Digest," *Shippensburg (PA) News,* Jul 24, 1875; *Carlisle Weekly Herald,* Jul 29, 1875; "Tournament in Carlisle," *Carlisle Weekly Herald,* Jul 29, 1875; *Carlisle Weekly Herald,* Sep 16, 1875; "The City," *Harrisburg Telegraph,* Sep 30, 1875; "Miscellany," *Harrisburg (PA) Patriot,* Oct 1, 1875; "Our National Game," *Lebanon (PA) News,* Oct 27, 1875.

Shaw Base Ball Club (Carlisle, PA; 1860s)

The Shaw B.B.C. organized in the 1860s, played against black nines. *Harrisburg Telegraph* (September 26, 1866): "The Monrovias (colored) Base Ball Club of this city goes to Carlisle tomorrow, to play a game with the Shaw Club (also colored) of that place." *New York Clipper* (October 13, 1866): "Among the clubs of Pennsylvania are the Monrovia Club, of Harrisburg and the Shaw Club, of Carlisle, both composed of respectable colored men who propose playing a match for State Championship of the colored clubs this month. There are several clubs in this State, also composed of colored men, and they play a very good game."

Sources: "Base Ball," *Harrisburg (PA) Telegraph,* Sep 26, 1866; "Base Ball in Black," *New York (NY) Clipper,* Oct 13, 1866.

Alert Base Ball Club (Chambersburg, PA; 1880s). Organizer(s): William "Billy" Guy.

The Alert B.B.C. organized in the 1880s, played black teams. In 1884, they joined a Colored League. *Fort Wayne News* (January 11, 1884): "A Colored Base Ball League, with clubs at Baltimore [Mutuals and Haymakers], Harrisburg [Olympics], Pottsville, Washington and several other cities [Carlisle, Pennsylvania and Hagerstown, Maryland]." They established rivalries with the hotel waiters of Baltimore, the Mutuals and Haymaker nines. *Harrisburg State Journal* (June 14, 1884): "The Haymakers, of Baltimore, and the Alert, of our city, played a game of baseball on the day of the Baltimore excursion, which resulted in a victory for the home club. Score, 16 to 1." The Mutuals defeated the Alerts at Chambersburg, by a score of 9 to 1. Reorganizing in 1887, they played the Harrisburg Olympics. *Harrisburg Telegraph* (September 7, 1887): "Billy Guy's Alert Base Ball Club, of Chambersburg has received a challenge from the champion colored club of Harrisburg to play a game of ball on Wednesday, Sept. 14th. The challenge has been accepted and the game will be played at Norland Park. An interesting contest is expected."

Sources: "Local Lines," *Fort Wayne (IN) News,* Jan 11, 1884; "Chambersburg," *Harrisburg (PA) State Journal,* Jun 14, 1884; "Base Ball Notes," *Baltimore (MD) Sun,* Jun 24, 1884; "Chambersburg," *Harrisburg State Journal,* Jun 28, 1884; "Base Ball," *Harrisburg State Journal,* Jul 26, 1884; "Chambersburg Squibs," *Harrisburg State Journal,* Aug 23, 1884; "Chambersburg," *Harrisburg State Journal,* Sep 6, 1884; "Base Ball," *Baltimore Sun,* Jul 15, 1887; "Near-By-Notes," *Harrisburg (PA) Telegraph,* Sep 7, 1887; "Jottings," *Harrisburg Telegraph,* Sep 12, 1887.

Pomeroy Base Ball Club (Chambersburg, PA; 1890s)

The Pomeroy B.B.C. organized in the 1890s, played black nines. *Carlisle Evening Herald* (June 12, 1897): "The Pomeroy club which is considered amongst the strongest clubs of the Cumberland Valley will play the strongest club of Carlisle, known as the Monarchs on the Association grounds, Thursday, July 15, at 8 o'clock. Batteries for Pomeroy, Norris and Wells; Monarchs, Manning and Jordan."— Chambersburg Repository." *Evening Herald* (June 19, 1897): "The ball game on Thursday resulted in a victory for the Monarchs over the Chambersburg team. Score: 14 to 13."

Sources: "Briefly Told," *Carlisle (PA) Evening Herald,* May 21, 1897; "Around the Diamond," *Carlisle Evening Herald,* Jul 12, 1897; "Briefly Told," *Carlisle Evening Herald,* Jun 19, 1897.

Active Base Ball Club (Chester, PA; 1860s). Organizer(s): Abram Brown.

The Active B.B.C. organized in 1867, played black teams. In 1867, the Actives played against the Philadelphia Pythians. They also played a black nine of Wilmington, DE. *Wilmington Commercial* (September 17, 1867): "The first nine of the Lincoln B.B.C. (colored), of this city, go to West Chester on Monday, the 23rf, inst., to participate in a parade there on that day, and on Tuesday, the 24th, they play the first nine of the Active B.B.C. (colored) of that place."

SOURCES: "Base Ball," *Wilmington (DE) Commercial*, Sep 17, 1867; "Pythian Baseball Club; Scorecards" (Roll No. 8). *American Negro Historical Society Collection: Historical Society Microfilm Edition.*

Alert Base Ball Club (Chester, PA; 1860s–1880s). Organizer(s): Abram Brown, William L. Spriggs and William Price.

The Alert B.B.C. organized in the 1860s, played black teams. The Alerts had been formerly the Active nine. *Wilmington Evening Journal* (July 6, 1887): "The Our Boys of this city, and the Alerts of West Chester, both colored clubs, played a game in West Chester to a small assemblage. Wilmington defeated West Chester by a score of 24 to 23."

SOURCES: "Pythian Baseball Club; Scorecards" (Roll No. 8). *American Negro Historical Society Collection: Historical Society Microfilm Edition*; "The Our Boys Win," *Wilmington (DE) Evening Journal*, Jul 6, 1887.

Lincoln University Base Ball Club (Ashmun Club) (Chester (Oxford), PA; 1860s–1900s). Organizer(s): R. G. Thompson.

The Lincoln University B.B.C. organized in 1867, if not earlier (originally, the Ashmun Institute, the school was renamed Lincoln University in 1866. Ashmun Institute appears in the Philadelphia Pythian archives). In 1867, Lincoln University—challenged the Pythians and other black nines. R. G. Thompson, corresponding secretary for the Ashmun club, communicated with Charles McCullough, of the Pythians, regarding a match game. They also played Chester's Active club, another black nine. By 1884, the institution was playing Chester's Keystone, Wabash, Joseph Gallon, and Wilmington's black nines. *Lincoln University Alumni Magazine*: "The Alert and Enterprise Nines played one of the most interesting games of the season on Saturday, the 27th of September. During the week, the theme among the fraternity and their respective friends was which club would hold intact the University pennant. The farmers for miles around stopped work and wended their way towards the diamond field. The score stood at 8 to 2 in favor of the Alert. The feature of the game was the catching of Cummings and McLeon. The members of both nines would do credit to any League or Association nine." Lincoln University's long-standing base-ball tradition has been documented. Between 1877 and 1884, alumni included Charles P. Lee (Rochester's Dauntless Club), James Paynter (Long Branch's West End B.B.C.), John Curry (Long Branch's West End B.B.C.), Harry Sythe Cummings and James Raymond (Lord Baltimores). They played at Wilmington, DE. *Wilmington News Journal* (June 10, 1884): "This and tomorrow afternoons, the Wilmington and Lincoln University nines, both colored, play at the Front and Union Street grounds. They are considered strong amateur clubs." *Wilmington Republican* (June 11, 1884): "The Wilmington colored nine defeated the Lincoln University nine from Chester County yesterday on the Front and Union Street grounds by a score of 21 to 14. The game was very interesting. The same clubs will play again tomorrow." Regarding the 1892 season, *Indianapolis Freeman* (February 27, 1892): "The athletes met and organized a University baseball club, and under the leadership of Messrs. W. T. Richie, as manager, and N. L. Edwards, as captain. She unfurls her banner and champions her rivals in contest for victory." The ball club scheduled games with Howard University in 1897. *Washington Evening Star*: "The differences which have existed between the athletic associations of Howard and Lincoln University

of Chester, Pennsylvania, have been settled, and games are expected with them this season."

SOURCES: "Correspondence; 1867–1869," (Roll No. 8). *American Negro Historical Society Collection: Historical Society Microfilm Edition*; *Ashmun Institute and Lincoln University* Records, 1853–1875, Lincoln University; "South Chester Notes," *Chester (PA) Times*, Jan 4, 1882; "South Chester Items," *Chester Times*, May 2, 1882; "Festival," *Chester Times*, May 5, 1882; "South Chester Items," *Chester Times*, Jul 1, 1882; "South Chester Items," *Chester Times*, Jul 3, 1882; "South Chester Items," *Chester Times*, Jul 10, 1882; "South Chester Items," *Chester Times*, Aug 1, 1882; "South Chester Items," *Chester Times*, Aug 4, 1882; "In and About South Chester," *Chester Times*, Mar 25, 1884; "Notes," *Wilmington (DE) News Journal*, Jun 10, 1884; "Base Ball," *Wilmington (DE) Republican*, Jun 11, 1884; "Base Ball," *Alumni Magazine*. Philadelphia, PA. November 1884; *1883–1911 Minutes of the Lincoln University Faculty of Arts*. Lincoln University, PA; "Jupiter and Venus," *Indianapolis (IN) Freeman*, Feb 27, 1892; "Sketches from the Holy Land," *Indianapolis Freeman*, May 7, 1892; "Literaries in Full Blast," *Indianapolis Freeman*, Oct 21, 1893; "University Notes," *Washington (DC) Evening Star*, Mar 13, 1897.

Wabash Base Ball Club (Chester, PA; 1880s–1890s). Organizer(s): William Ruley.

The Wabash B.B.C. organized in the 1880s, played white and black teams. *Chester Times* (July 6, 1883): "The Wabash defeated the Gallon club yesterday at Houston Park by a score of 11 to 8. Both are colored clubs. W. Scott Fry was umpire." *Times* (July 7, 1883): "The Gallon nine are not satisfied with the result on Thursday and are of the opinion that they can yet beat the Wabash. They will soon be given another opportunity to do so as another game is being arranged between the two clubs to be arranged at an early date."

SOURCES: "In and About South Chester," *Chester (PA) Times*, Jun 12, 1883; "A Base Ball Dispute," *Chester Times*, Jun 15, 1883; "In and About South Chester," *Chester Times*, Jul 6, 1883; "South Chester Items," *Chester Times*, Jul 7, 1883; "Base Ball Notes," *Chester Times*, Jul 28, 1883; "Base Ball Notes," *Chester Times*, Aug 25, 1883; "Base Ball Notes," *Chester Times*, Aug 31, 1883; "The Wabash Defeated," *Chester Times*, Sep 1, 1883.

Giants Base Ball Club (Chester, PA; 1890s–1900s). Organizer(s): William H. Mack; William "Billy" Stewart.

The Giants B.B.C. organized in the 1890s, played white and black aggregations. *Chester Times* (July 13, 1899): "The Chester Giants won the first game of base-ball in the series of five with the McClure Giants, at Marcus Hook yesterday afternoon, by a score of 13 to 5. The game was an interesting one from start to finish, notwithstanding that the Chester boys had a walkover. The teams are composed of some of the best colored players in the county and yesterday's contest attracted a large number of spectators." *Times* (July 6, 1900): "The Chester Base-Ball Team and the Chester Giants, the latter composed of colored men from the lower end of the city, played a game of ball yesterday at Twelfth Street Park. The Chester won—it was a foregone conclusion—by the score of 15 to 8. It was an interesting game, not from the point of view of professional ball playing, nor yet of semi-professional kind, but from the funny man's standpoint."

SOURCES: "Sports of an All Sorts," *Chester (PA) Times*, Jul 8, 1899; "Sports of an All Sorts," *Chester Times*, Jul 13, 1899; "Chester Giants Defeated," *Chester Times*, Jun 21, 1900; "The Chester Club and the Chester Giants," *Chester Times*, Jul 6, 1900; "Strong Chester Giants Beaten," *Philadelphia (PA) Inquirer*, Jul 6, 1900; "Giants Were Easy," *Philadelphia Inquirer*, Aug 2, 1900; "Cake Walkers Meet Defeat," *Philadelphia Inquirer*, Aug 21, 1900.

J. Gallon Base Ball Club (Chester, PA; 1880s). Organizer(s): J. Gallon.

The J. Gallon B.B.C. organized in the 1880s, played white and black teams. *Chester Times* (July 6, 1883): "The Wabash defeated the Gallon club yesterday at Houston Park by a score of 11 to 8. Both are colored clubs. W. Scott Fry was umpire." *Times* (July 7, 1883): "The Gallon nine are not satisfied with the result on Thursday and are of the opinion that they can yet beat the Wabash. They will soon be given another opportunity to do so as another game is being arranged between the two clubs to be arranged at an early date." *Times* (August 19, 1886): "Quite a large and enthusiastic audience of both colored and white people gathered at Thurlow Park yesterday afternoon to witness a game of base-ball between the J. Gallen and Thurlow Reserves [white]. The Reserves expected an easy victory and made the remark that we will do them coons up before the games over, but according to the score the coons seem to have turned the tables. The batting of Pryor and Jackson of the J. Gallen and Witsell and Gross of the Reserves was among the features of the game while the fine playing of Driskett and Rothwell drew forth thunderous applause. The score resulted in 20 to 15 in favor of J. Gallen." They also played the Philadelphia Giants. *Philadelphia Record* (June 8, 1887): "The Philadelphia Giants (colored) played the Gallon Club (colored) at Cooper Park yesterday in the presence of 1000 people. The game was an interesting and exciting one, the Giants winning."

SOURCES: "In and About South Chester," *Chester (PA) Times*, Jul 6, 1883; "South Chester Items," *Chester Times*, Jul 7, 1883; "The Coons Defeat the Thurlow Reserves," *Chester Times*, Aug 19, 1886; "Colored Clubs to Play," *Chester Times*, Aug 21, 1886; "The Coons Defeat the Thurlow Reserves," *Chester Times*, Aug 19, 1886; "Colored Clubs at the Bat," *Chester Times*, Aug 24, 1886; "The 'Gallen' Wins," *Chester Times*, Sep 2, 1886; "Robinson and Gallen," *Chester Times*, Sep 14, 1886; "Gallen and Delaware," *Chester Times*, Oct 2, 1886; "Baseball at Thurlow," *Chester Times*, Oct 7, 1886; "Philadelphia Giant, 9; Gallon, 8," *Philadelphia (PA) Record*, Jun 8, 1887; "Delaware Doings," *New York (NY) Freeman*, Jul 9, 1887; "Delaware Doings," *New York Freeman*, Jul 23, 1887.

J. H. Hooper Base Ball Club (Chester, PA; 1890s). Organizer(s): John Blackman, William Purnsley and Charles Rothwell.

The J. H. Hooper B.B.C. organized in the 1880s, played black and white teams. *Philadelphia Inquirer* (July 1, 1894): "The Leiperville had arranged to play the Stafford of Philadelphia, but they didn't show up and the home club played against the strong, colored, Hooper team, of Chester, rain stopping the game in the sixth inning."

SOURCES: "Leiperville, 10; J. H. Hooper, 7," *Philadelphia (PA) Inquirer*, Jul 1, 1894; "Leiperville and J. H. Hooper," *Philadelphia (PA) Times*, Jul 1, 1894; "Other Games," *Philadelphia Inquirer*, Jul 2, 1894; "Sorad to Umpire," *Chester (PA) Times*, Oct 4, 1894; "Colored Clubs Play Ball," *Chester Times*, Oct 5, 1894; "The C. F. C. and Hoopers," *Chester Times*, Sep 12, 1895.

J. Robinson Base Ball Club (Chester, PA; 1880s). Organizer(s): J. Robinson.

The J. Robinson B.B.C. organized in the 1880s, played black teams. *Chester Times* (September 14, 1886): "The T. Robinson Base Ball Club, of North Chester, defeated the J. Gallen Club, of South Chester, in a well-played game of base-ball at Thurlow Park. This was the third game in a series of four won by the Robinson. The contest was a hot one throughout. Hinckson pitched in fine form, striking out eight of the Gallen batters, and was given fine support by Burton. Perrigan pitched for the Gallen, but was hit hard at times. He was supported in almost perfect style by Hackett. Ben Smith led the batting, having six hits for a total of 13 bases."

SOURCES: "Colored Talent at the Bat," *Chester (PA) Times*, Aug 3, 1886; "Colored Clubs to Play," *Times*, Aug 21, 1886; "Getting Off the Car," *Times*, Aug 24, 1886; "Colored Clubs at the Bat," *Evening Times*, Aug 24, 1886; "Robinson and Gallen," *Times*, Sep 14, 1886; "Base Ball Notes," *Times*, Sep 15, 1886.

Keystone Base Ball Club (Chester, PA; 1870s–1880s). Organizer(s): John Hackett and Isaac Rothwell.

The Keystone B.B.C. organized in the 1870s, played white and black teams. *Chester Times* (August 19, 1878): "A game of base-ball was played on Saturday afternoon between the Lightfoot of North Chester and Keystone of South Chester, on the grounds of the latter. Both clubs are colored, and some very good playing was done on both sides. The Keystone's thought the balls of their pitcher could not be struck by the Lightfoot, but the latter club took them by surprise when they knocked the balls all over the field. The game resulted in favor of the Lightfoot by a score of 16 to 10. The winning club was to get a ball, but the Keystone failed to produce it, which has adding nothing to their credit." The Keystones developed rivalries with black nines of Philadelphia, and Wilmington, DE. *Times* (August 1, 1882): "The Keystone base-ball club, of South Chester, will play the Our Boys club at Houston Park on Thursday. The game will be culled at 4 pm. The Our Boys club is from Wilmington, and are said to be good players. A good game is expected. Admission 10 cents." *Times* (October 11, 1882): "The Keystone Base Ball Club has reorganized with new and better players, and will play the Orion, the champion colored club of Philadelphia, at Houston Park."

SOURCES: "Base Ball," *Chester (PA) Times*, Jun 26, 1877; "Base Ball," *Chester Times*, Aug 19, 1878; "Base Ball," *Chester Times*, Oct 4, 1879; "Base Ball," *Chester Times*, Oct 6, 1879; "A Dangerous Man," *Chester Times*, Nov 26, 1880; "South Chester Notes," *Chester Times*, Jan 4, 1882; "Match Game," *Chester Times*, Apr 17, 1882; "South Chester Items," *Chester Times*, May 2, 1882; "Festival," *Chester Times*, May 5, 1882; "South Chester Items," *Chester Times*, Jul 1, 1882; "South Chester Items," *Chester Times*, Jul 3, 1882; "South Chester Items," *Chester Times*, Jul 10, 1882; "Base Ball Notes," *Chester Times*, Jul 28, 1883 "South Chester Items," *Chester Times*, Aug 1, 1882; "South Chester Items," *Chester Times*, Aug 4, 1882; "Base Ball," *Chester Times*, Oct 11, 1882; "South Chester Items," *Chester Times*, Oct 19, 1882; "Engineers at Work," *Chester Times*, Jun 8, 1883.

Wabash Base Ball Club (Chester, PA; 1880s–1890s). Organizer(s): William Ruley.

The Wabash B.B.C. organized in the 1880s. The Wabash club played against black and white nines. The Wabash and Gallon nines, developed a local black rivalry. Controversy surrounded the first scheduled match. *Chester Times* (June 15, 1883): "Judging by the heavy talk one would think that the Wabash baseball club did not know that the majority of the Gallon nine are over twenty years of age. The Wabash club first proposed to confine their game with clubs whose members are under twenty years of age, and it would no doubt be a good plan for them to stick to that proposition, for if they play the Gallon club it will be a cold day for them, and they certainly will get wiped out and left behind." The nine decisively defeated the J. Gallons. *Times* (June 28, 1883): "Two colored clubs, the Eclipse, of Philadelphia, and the Wabash, of this city, will play at Houston Park this afternoon." They played the Delawares, a strong white local club. They played the Ashcraft team, a local white club. *Times* (August 23, 1883): "Chester Park was invaded yesterday afternoon by the Ashcraft club and the Wabash colored club. Both teams were uniformed and determined to vanquish each other. The game was called at 4 o'clock in the presence of an audience made up principally of colored people. But, seven innings were played, owing to the manner in which the runs and errors wore being scored by each club. The colored team carried off the honors by a score of 29 to 25.

SOURCES: "Amateur Notes," *Philadelphia (PA) Sporting Life*, May 20, 1883; "In and About Chester," *Chester (PA) Times*, Jun 8, 1883; "In and About Chester," *Chester Times*, Jun 12, 1883; "Amateur Notes," *Philadelphia Sporting Life*, May 20, 1883; "In and About Chester," *Chester Times*, Jun 8, 1883; "In and About Chester," *Chester Times*, Jun 12, 1883; "A Base Ball Dispute," *Chester Times*, Jun 15, 1883; "In and About South Chester," *Chester Times*, Jul 6, 1883; "In and About South Chester," *Chester Times*, Jul 12, 1883; "In and About South Chester," *Chester Times*, Jul 21, 1883; "Base Ball Notes," *Chester Times*, Jul 28, 1883; "Base Ball Notes," *Chester Times*, Aug 1, 1883; "Base Ball Notes," *Chester Times*, Aug 23, 1883; "Base Ball Notes," *Chester Times*, Aug 25, 1883; "The Wabash Defeated," *Chester Times*, Sep 1, 1883; "Base Ball Notes," *Times*, September 18, 1883; "Big Sporting Carnival," *Chester Times*, Apr 27, 1885; "The Field of Sport," *Indianapolis (IN) Freeman*, Jan 17, 1891.

Douglass Base Ball Club (Columbia, PA; 1860s)

The Douglass B.B.C. organized in 1867. Named for civil rights activist, Frederick Douglass, the Douglass club competed against the white and black nines. They played against Harrisburg's Monrovia, Star, and Active black teams. In 1867, Tow Hill's black nine played Wrightsville's Anglo club, a white club. After five innings, the Douglasses stopped playing with the score tied at 22 to 22. They claimed they couldn't continue the game, on account of pressing obligations. *Columbia Spy* (July 13, 1867): "They themselves called the game drawn, and promised to play a return game upon our grounds, any time we should select." In a two-game series with the Monrovia club, they were thoroughly beaten. In game one, they lost by a score of 66 to 59. The Douglass fared no better in the second contest. *Harrisburg Telegraph* (June 30, 1868): "A game of base-ball was played at Columbia yesterday between the Monrovia Base Ball Club, of this city, and the Douglass Base Ball Club of that borough."

SOURCES: *Columbia (PA) Spy*, Jul 13, 1867; "Correction," *Columbia Spy*, July 13, 1867; "Base Ball," *Harrisburg (PA) Patriot*, Jun 26, 1868; "Base Ball Match," *Harrisburg (PA) Telegraph*, Jun 27, 1868; "The Base Ball Match," *Harrisburg (PA) Telegraph*, Jun 30, 1868; "Base Ball Match," *Harrisburg Telegraph*, Oct 7, 1868.

Sumner Base Ball Club (Columbia, PA; 1870s)

The Sumner B.B.C., of Harrisburg, PA, organized in the 1870s. The Sumner club played black nines. *Harrisburg Telegraph* (September 7, 1875): "The Olympic, of this city, and the Sumner Club, of Columbia, both colored, will play a match game of base-ball at the Union Grounds tomorrow afternoon. Game called at 3 o'clock." *Harrisburg Patriot* (September 11, 1875): "The Tyrolean Club, of this city, and the Sumner Club, of Columbia, played a game at the Union grounds, yesterday afternoon. The Tyroleans batted and fielded splendidly, notwithstanding, the bad condition of the grounds, after a smart shower about 3 pm. Up to the seventh inning the game stood 18 to 0 in favor of the Tyrolean Club, when by a little loose playing they allowed the Sumners to score one run. In the next inning, the Sumners were allowed another run, from courtesy it was plainly noticeable, the 'brown legs' playing in a very careless manner in the eighth inning. The Sumner Club is composed of a body of fine-looking men, who were dressed in neat and attractive uniform, but they were more than overmatched when they went into the field of the champion colored home club."

SOURCES: "Base Ball," *Harrisburg (PA) Telegraph*, Sep 7, 1875; "Base Ball," *Harrisburg Telegraph*, Sep 9, 1875; "Base Ball," *Harrisburg (PA) Patriot*, Sep 10, 1875; "Base Ball," *Harrisburg Patriot*, Sep 11, 1875; "Base Ball," *Harrisburg Patriot*, Sep 22, 1875.

Tigers Base Ball Club (Columbia, PA; 1880s)

The Tigers B.B.C. organized in the 1880s, played against black nines. *Lancaster Intelligencer* (August 31, 1888): "A well-contested game of ball was witnessed by a good-sized crowd on the Ironsides grounds yesterday between the Juniors, Lancaster's colored club, and the Columbias, also colored. The Juniors lost the game in the first inning by wild throwing to the bases, allowing Columbia to score seven runs, after which they steadied themselves and played a good uphill game, a runner being on third to tie the score when the last man fouled out in the ninth." They played against Harrisburg, PA's Olympic B.B.C. *Harrisburg Telegraph* (September 22, 1888): "The Olympics defeated the Tigers, of Columbia, in an interesting and amusing game on the Sixth Street Grounds yesterday. The final score was 14 to 12, and leaves the Harrisburg boys still champions."

SOURCES: "Base Ball," *Harrisburg (PA) Telegraph*, Aug 15, 1888; "Won Another Game," *Lancaster (PA) Intelligencer*, Aug 31, 1888; "Grass Cutters," *Harrisburg Telegraph*, Sep 21, 1888; "Newsy Base Ball Items," *Harrisburg Telegraph*, Sep 22, 1888.

Black Diamond Base Ball Club (Connellsville, PA; 1880s)

The Black Diamond B.B.C. organized in the 1880s, played black and white and nines. *Keystone Courier* (May 29, 1885): "A game of base-ball between white and colored lads took place, on Wednesday, in the Steel Works Ground. The J. E. Stillwagons downed Daddy Gordon's Black Diamonds, by a score of 19 1to 12."

SOURCES: "Base Ball," *Connellsville (PA) Keystone Courier*, May 29, 1885.

Keystone Stars Base Ball Club (Connellsville, PA; 1880s).

Organizer(s): Gillie Johnson.

The Keystone Stars B.B.C. organized in the 1880s, played white and black teams. *Connellsville Courier* (May 10, 1889): "The Keystone Stars Colored Base Ball Club was organized in New Haven. An effort will be made to have some of the best colored clubs in the State play here this season."

SOURCES: "Sporting Notes," *Connellsville (PA) Courier*, May 10, 1889; "Local Briefs," *Uniontown (PA) Evening Standard*, May 21, 1889; "Beat the Keystones 8 to 4," *Uniontown (PA) Evening News*, Jun 22, 1889; "Veteran's Reunion," *Uniontown Evening News*, May 21, 1893; "The Giants Win," *Uniontown Evening News*, Jul 7, 1893; "A Council Meeting," *Uniontown Evening News*, Jul 11, 1893; "Fined for Gambling," *Uniontown Evening News*, Jul 26, 1893 "An Exciting Base Ball Game," *Uniontown Evening News*, Jul 28, 1893.

Cuban Giants Base Ball Club (Frankford, PA; 1880s–1890s)

The Cuban Giants B.B.C. organized in the 1880s. The Cuban Giants played black and white nines. *Philadelphia Inquirer* (June 1, 1892): "The Oxford Club, of Frankford, defeated the Cuban Giants in a well-played game yesterday. Mellors pitched very effectively for Oxford, holding the Giants down to two hits." He served as part of the battery that included his brother, Charles, as pitcher. *Inquirer*: "The Norristown team defeated the Frankford colored team at Oak View Base Ball Park this afternoon." *Inquirer* (July 30, 1889): "The Somerset Club defeated the ambitiously named Cuban Giants of Frankford yesterday." *Inquirer* (July 2, 1893): "The Norristown team defeated the Frankford colored team at Oak View Base Ball Park this afternoon."

SOURCES: "A Somerset Victory," *Philadelphia (PA) Inquirer*, Jul 30, 1889; "General Sporting News," *Philadelphia Inquirer*, Feb 21, 1892; "Oxford Beats the Grants," *Philadelphia Inquirer*, Jun 1, 1892; "A Victory for Norristown," *Philadelphia Inquirer*, Jul 2, 1893.

Twilight Base Ball Club (Frankford, PA; 1880s)

The Twilight B.B.C. organized in the 1880s, played black and white nines. They played a two-game series, Charles Trusty (brother of

Shep Trusty) pitching both contests. While Trusty won the first game by a score of 4 to 2, he lost the second match. *Philadelphia Record* (June 12, 1887): "At Hartville Park yesterday the Hartville defeated the Twilight (colored) Club by the score of 24 to 11. Early in the season the Twilight Club defeated the Hartville in a five inning game."

SOURCES: "Twilight, 4; Hartville, 2," *Philadelphia (PA) Record*, Apr 24, 1887; "Hartville, 20; Twilight, 11," *Philadelphia Record*, Jun 12, 1887.

Colored Base Ball Club (Gettysburg, PA; 1890s)

The Colored B.B.C. organized in the 1890s, played black nines. *Westminster Democratic Advocate* (June 16, 1894): "The Westminster Grays (colored) defeated the Gettysburg team on Tuesday last by a score of 15 to 23. The heavy hitters for Westminster W. Adams, T. McClain and J. Ireland."

SOURCES: "Base Ball," *Westminster (MD) Democratic Advocate*, Jun 16, 1894.

Colored Sluggers Base Ball Club (Gettysburg, PA; 1890s)

The Colored Sluggers B.B.C. organized in the 1890s, played black and white nines. *Philadelphia Inquirer* (July 27, 1892): "The Gettysburg Seniors and the Colored Sluggers Clubs, of Gettysburg, played at Gettysburg, on July 23. Score: Gettysburg Seniors, 16; Colored Sluggers, 0. Batteries—Myers and Devan for the Colored Sluggers."

SOURCES: "Scores of the Amateurs," *Philadelphia (PA) Inquirer*, Jul 27, 1892.

Active Base Ball Club (Gettysburg, PA; 1860s–1870s)

The Active B.B.C., of Harrisburg, PA, organized in the 1860s, played black nines. *Harrisburg Telegraph* (July 31, 1869): "A match game of base-ball will be played on the grounds at West Portland and North Frederick Streets Grounds on Thursday, between the Star Base Ball Club of Harrisburg, and the Actives of this place. Both clubs are composed of colored gentlemen. The prize is a bat and ball. It will no doubt be an interesting game, as the Actives have lately achieved some honor, and the Star has the reputation of being the best club of the kind in this state. Actives be active." *Harrisburg Patriot* (August 12, 1875): "A lively game of two hours and a half's duration came off yesterday afternoon between the Tyrolean and Active nines (colored) of this city. The Tyroleans on this occasion wore a handsome uniform of white, trimmed with blue, with the letter T on their breasts. The Actives, a set of active, wide awake players, did some powerful batting and won the game easily. The fielding of the Tyroleans was decidedly careless, hence the great difference in the score which stood at the close of the game: Actives, 44; Tyroleans, 23." *Telegraph* (August 21, 1875): "In a game of base-ball between the Actives and Tyroleans (both colored), yesterday, the latter were victorious by a score of 37 to 18."

SOURCES: "Base Ball," *Harrisburg Telegraph*, Jul 31, 1869; "On the Fly," *Harrisburg (PA) Patriot*, Aug 12, 1875; "The City," *Harrisburg Telegraph*, Aug 21, 1875.

Apolia Base Ball Club (Harrisburg, PA; 1870s). Organizer(s): George Galbraith.

The Apolia B.B.C. organized in 1874. The "Apolias" included former members of Harrisburg's Monrovia club. *Harrisburg Telegraph* (June 9, 1874): "At a meeting a few nights ago the Apolia Base Ball Club (colored), of this city, elected the following officers for the present season. The club is prepared to receive challenges from any part of the State through the Treasurer, George Thomas." They played black and white clubs. *Telegraph* (July 14, 1874): "A match game of base-ball was played yesterday afternoon at Middletown, between the Apolia, of this city, and the Middletown Club. Richardson, of the Apolia Club, and Saunders, of the Middletown Club, played excellently.

SOURCES: "Another Base Ball Club," *Harrisburg (PA) Telegraph*, Jun 9, 1874; *Harrisburg Telegraph*, Jul 14, 1874.

Blue Stocking Base Ball Club (Harrisburg, PA; 1870s)

The Blue Stocking B.B.C. organized in the 1870s, played black nines. *Harrisburg Patriot* (March 12, 1879): The Blue Stockings also played against the colored clubs, of Carlisle, PA. *Harrisburg Telegraph* (August 12, 1879): "The Blue Stockings Base Ball Club, of this city, will play the Blue Mountain Boys, of Carlisle, at the latter place on September 4th." A rivalry developed. *Telegraph* (August 14, 1879): "The Blue Stockings and Excelsior Clubs, both colored, played a championship game of base-ball yesterday, on the North Street Grounds, the former winning by a score of 16 to 11."

SOURCES: *Harrisburg (PA) Patriot*, Mar 12, 1879; "Jottings," *Harrisburg (PA) Telegraph*, Aug 12, 1879; "Base-Ball Game Today," *Harrisburg Patriot*, Aug 13, 1879; "Jottings," *Harrisburg Telegraph*, Aug 14, 1879; "Jottings," *Harrisburg Telegraph*, Aug 30, 1879; "Miscellany," *Harrisburg Patriot*, Nov 28, 1879.

Charles Johnson Base Ball Club (Harrisburg, PA; 1880s)

The Charles Johnson B.B.C. organized in 1880, played black nines. *Harrisburg Patriot* (June 10, 1880): "The Charles Johnson Base Ball Club will play a match game with the Sibletown nine at the North Street Grounds this afternoon at three o'clock."

SOURCES: "New Base Ball Organization," *Harrisburg (PA) Patriot*, Jun 8, 1880; "City Siftings," *Harrisburg Patriot*, Jun 10, 1880; "City Siftings," *Harrisburg Patriot*, Jun 12, 1880.

Commonwealth Hotel Cyclone Base Ball Club (Harrisburg, PA; 1890s)

The Commonwealth Hotel Cyclone B.B.C. organized in the 1890s, played black and white teams. *Harrisburg Telegraph* (May 22, 1897): "The Lochiel Sluggers beat the Commonwealth Hotel men in a game of baseball by a score of 29 to 23. Battery: Grannison, Benner and Phillips." *Harrisburg Patriot* (May 28, 1897): "The Commonwealth Hotel Cyclones gained a victory over the Keystones yesterday afternoon on the South Cameron Street grounds in a slowly-played game."

SOURCES: "Coming Base Ball Game," *Harrisburg (PA) Patriot*, Jun 7, 1893; "Solar Tips Win," *Harrisburg Patriot*, Aug 5, 1893; "Cyclones Win the Game," *Harrisburg Patriot*, Apr 9, 1894; "The Second Game," *Harrisburg Patriot*, Apr 18, 1894; "Cyclones to Play at Lebanon," *Harrisburg Patriot*, Jun 28, 1894; "Base Ball," *Lebanon (PA) News*, Jul 5, 1894; "Saturday's Games," *Harrisburg Patriot*, Aug 27, 1894; *Lebanon News*, May 28, 1895; *Lebanon News*, May 30, 1895; "Cyclones Too Swift," *Harrisburg Patriot*, May 22, 1897; "Sporting Tidings," *Harrisburg (PA) Telegraph*, May 22, 1897; "Cyclones Play Ball," *Harrisburg Patriot*, May 28, 1897; "Ball Games Arranged," *Harrisburg Patriot*, Jun 4, 1897; *Lebanon News*, Aug 16, 1897; *Lebanon News*, Aug 23, 1897; "Base Ball," *Lebanon News*, July 25, 1900; "Steelton Slips," *Harrisburg Patriot*, Apr 17, 1897.

Cuban Giant Juniors Base Ball Club (Harrisburg, PA; 1880s–1890s). Organizer(s): Theodore Frye; George Strother; Benjamin Smith.

The Cuban Giant Juniors B.B.C. organized in the 1880s. Known also as the Colored Giants, they played black and white teams. *Harrisburg Telegraph* (June 22, 1893): "The Cuban Giants, Juniors, of this city, yesterday afternoon played an interesting game of ball with the Nationals, of Steelton, on the grounds of the latter. The features of the game were the exceptional fine fielding of H. Burrs and A. Lane and the batting of A. Baxter. Score, 10 to 10, game ending in the ninth inning." *Harrisburg Patriot* (August 5, 1893): "The Solar Tips played the Harrisburg Giants on the Sixth Street Grounds yesterday afternoon, winning with the utmost ease. As the first game between these two crack amateur clubs resulted 9 to 8 in favor of the Solar Tips, the Giants thought they were strictly in it and offered to play for $10 and the gate receipts." *Lebanon News* (August 31, 1900): "At Avon the Harrisburg Cuban Giants defeated the Lebanon Base Ball Club by a score of 8 to 5. A large crowd witnessed the game which was very exciting."

SOURCES: "Dropped Flies," *Harrisburg (PA) Telegraph*, May 3, 1889; "Splinters," *Harrisburg Telegraph*, Apr 14, 1890; "Grand Stand Chat," *Harrisburg Telegraph*, Jun 3, 1890; "Coming Base Ball Game," *Harrisburg (PA) Patriot*, Jun 7, 1893; "Hot Liners," *Harrisburg Telegraph*, Jun 22, 1893; "Williamsport Wins," *Harrisburg Telegraph*, Jul 17, 1893; "Bunted Balls," *Harrisburg Telegraph*, Jun 27, 1893; "Chat By the Wayside," *Harrisburg Telegraph*, Jul 22, 1893; "Gossip of the Diamond," *Harrisburg Telegraph*, Jul 24, 1893; "Solar Tips Win," *Harrisburg Patriot*, Aug 5, 1893; "Echoes of the Meeting," *Harrisburg Telegraph*, Apr 3, 1894; "Base Ball Briefs," *Harrisburg Telegraph*, Apr 30, 1894; "About Sports in General," *Harrisburg Telegraph*, May 30, 1895; "Charles Madison Explains," *Harrisburg Telegraph*, Jun 1, 1895; "Other Base Lines," *Harrisburg Telegraph*, May 29, 1900; "Lebanon Defeated," *Lebanon (PA) News*, Aug 31, 1900; "Tables Were Turned," *Lebanon News*, Sep 1, 1900.

Excelsior Base Ball Club (Harrisburg, PA; 1870s–1880s). Organizer(s): David Prime.

The Excelsior B.B.C. organized in the 1870s, played black nines. *Harrisburg Telegraph* (August 14, 1879): "The Blue Stockings and Excelsior Clubs, both colored, played a championship game of baseball yesterday, on the North Street Grounds, the former winning by a score of 16 to 11." *Telegraph* (September 18, 1879): "The Excelsior and Sibletown colored base-ball clubs will play a match next Monday on the North Street grounds fo $5 and the championship."

SOURCES: *Harrisburg (PA) Patriot*, Mar 12, 1879; "Jottings," *Harrisburg (PA) Telegraph*, Aug 12, 1879; "Base-Ball Game Today," *Harrisburg Patriot*, Aug 13, 1879; "Jottings," *Harrisburg Telegraph*, Aug 14, 1879; "Jottings," *Harrisburg Telegraph*, Aug 30, 1879; "Jottings," *Harrisburg Telegraph*, Sep 18, 1879; "Miscellany," *Harrisburg Patriot*, Nov 28, 1879; "The Ball and Bat," *Harrisburg Patriot*, Apr 5, 1880; "Little Locals," *Harrisburg Patriot*, May 21, 1880; "On the Diamond," *Harrisburg (PA) Independent*, May 31, 1880.

Geary Base Ball Club (Harrisburg, PA; 1870s)

The Geary B.B.C. organized in 1870, played black teams. In honor of the passage of the 15th Amendment, the nine was nicknamed for PA's Governor, John Geary, and the Colored Geary Council. *Harrisburg Telegraph* (July 25, 1870): "A game of baseball was played on Saturday between the Geary and Rough and Ready Clubs, both colored, which resulted in a victory for the former. The Geary is composed of boys, whose ages vary from twelve to seventeen years, while the other club are full of grown men."

SOURCES: "Base Ball Match," *Harrisburg (PA) Telegraph*, Jul 25, 1870.

Harley Base Ball Club (Harrisburg, PA; 1870s–1880s). Organizer(s): Charles W. Harley.

The Harley B.B.C. organized in the 1870s, played black nines. *Harrisburg Patriot* (June 15, 1877): "The Tyrolean and Olympic baseball clubs—two colored organizations known to have made good records during the existence of the old Expert and Harrisburg clubs—have reorganized for the season of 1877 under the title of the Harley Base Ball Club, as follows: William Pople, E. Earley, C. Myers, J. Allen, W. Jackson, William Shadney, David Brown, W. Rideout,

David Allen, and William Long. The club will be pleased to accept challenges from either white or colored base-ball clubs."

SOURCES: "Base Ball Matters," *Harrisburg (PA) Patriot*, Jun 15, 1877; "Jottings," *Harrisburg (PA) Telegraph*, Sep 7, 1877; "Jottings," *Harrisburg Telegraph*, Sep 20, 1877; "Jottings," *Harrisburg Telegraph*, Sep 21, 1877; "Jottings," *Harrisburg Telegraph*, Sep 26, 1877; "Miscellany," *Harrisburg Patriot*, Oct 2, 1877; "Jottings," *Harrisburg Telegraph*, Oct 9, 1877; "Jottings," *Harrisburg Telegraph*, Jun 7, 1878; "Base Ball Matters," *Harrisburg Patriot*, Aug 3, 1878; "The Ball and Bat," *Harrisburg Patriot*, Apr 5, 1880.

Marine Base Ball Club (Harrisburg, PA; 1890s). Organizer(s): Benjamin F. Smith.

The Marine B.B.C. organized in the 1890s, played black and white nines. *Harrisburg Patriot* (April 3, 1890): "The Solar Tips defeated the Marines by a score of 8 to 7." *Harrisburg Telegraph* (April 21, 1890): "The Solar Tips and Marine Club will cross bats at the Eleventh Street Grounds tomorrow afternoon at 3 o'clock." They also played the Fairview team. *Telegraph* (June 16, 1890): "The Marines, of your city, played against the home team on Saturday afternoon at this place. Score: 24 to 9 in favor of Fairview."

SOURCES: "Sporting Scintillations," *Harrisburg (PA) Telegraph*, Feb 28, 1890; "Sporting Sweepings," *Harrisburg Telegraph*, Mar 22, 1890; "The Game Today," *Harrisburg (PA) Patriot*, Apr 2, 1890; "Heard on the Beach," *Harrisburg (PA) Patriot*, Apr 3, 1890; "Base Ball Topics," *Harrisburg Telegraph*, Apr 21, 1890; "Grand Stand Chat," *Harrisburg Telegraph*, Jun 3, 1890; "Coming Base Ball Game," *Harrisburg Telegraph*, Jun 16, 1890; "Another Amateur Base Ball Directory," *Harrisburg Telegraph*, Jul 14, 1890; "Grand Stand Chat," *Harrisburg Telegraph*, Sep 2, 1890.

Monrovian Base Ball Club (Harrisburg, PA; 1860s–1870s)

The Monrovian B.B.C. formed in the 1866, played black and white nines. *Harrisburg Patriot* (June 20, 1867): "There are four negro base-ball clubs in Harrisburg." The Monrovias figured among them. In 1866, they played against the Shaw club. *Harrisburg Telegraph* (Sept. 26, 1866): "The Monrovias (colored) Base Ball Club of this city goes to Carlisle tomorrow, to play a game with the Shaw Club (also colored) of that place." In 1867, the Monrovias were defeated by the Philadelphia Pythians, by a score of 59–27. While the local black teams played against each other, the Monrovias played white nines as well. *Patriot* (June 21, 1867): "The Monrovia Base Ball Club, composed of indolent niggers—together with the 'Deacon,' went to Wrightsville on Tuesday, and played a match game with the Anglo (Heavy) Base Ball Club of the latter place. The day being an exceedingly warm one, it is said that the overheated nigs, &c, drank the town nearly dry, and the people considered it a God send when a sudden shower put an end to the game, and drove the coons from the place. It is also said that the air became very refreshing after the 'odor' had passed away." In 1868, the Monrovia club reorganized: they played the Independents, a black club of Williamsport, PA. In February, at the Freedman's Fair, the attendees expressed excitement over an upcoming contest between the Monrovia and Independent teams. The winner would receive a bats, bases, and balls. *Lycoming Gazette* (June 18, 1868): "A match game of base-ball will take place near the Herdic House between the First Nine of the Herdic House Club (colored), and the First Nine of the Monrovian Base Ball Club, of Harrisburg." The Monrovias competed locally against the black Stars and Actives. *Telegraph* (July 31, 1869): "A match game of base-ball will be played on the grounds at West Portland and North Frederick Streets Grounds on Thursday, between the Star Base Ball Club of Harrisburg, and the Actives of this place. Both clubs are composed of colored gentlemen. The prize is a bat and ball. It will no doubt be an interesting game, as the Actives have lately achieved some honor, and the Star has the reputation of being the best club of the kind in this state. Actives be active." The Stars and Monrovia rivalry was fierce. *Telegraph* (May 18, 1869): "A base-ball match came off yesterday between the Monrovia and Star Clubs of this city, which resulted in favor of the former. The score standing; Monrovia, 38; Star, 35. The Monrovia played at a disadvantage, being short of two men." The Stars later turned the tables. *Harrisburg Telegraph* (June 1, 1869): "A Match game was played between the Monrovia and Star Clubs yesterday afternoon, resulting in a victory for the latter, the score standing 23 to 29." They also played against the Active Club, colored, of Mechanicsburg, PA.

SOURCES: "Base Ball," *Harrisburg (PA) Telegraph*. Sept. 26, 1866; "A Heavy Base Ball Game," *Harrisburg (PA) Patriot*, Jun 20, 1867; "The National Game," *Harrisburg Patriot*, Jun 21, 1867; "Base Ball in Black," *New York (NY) Clipper*, Oct 13, 1867; "Going to Philadelphia," *Harrisburg Telegraph*, Oct 21, 1867; "Base Ball—The Pythian Club," *Philadelphia (PA) Inquirer*, Oct 22, 1867; "Base Ball," *Harrisburg Telegraph*, Oct 23, 1867; "The Freedman's Fair," *Harrisburg Telegraph*, Feb 28, 1868; *Williamsport (PA) Lycoming Gazette*, Jun 18, 1868; "Base Ball," *Harrisburg Patriot*, Jun 26, 1868; "Match Game," *Harrisburg Patriot*, Jun 29, 1868; "Base Ball," *Harrisburg Patriot*, Jun 30, 1868; *Williamsport Lycoming Gazette*, Aug 5, 1868; "Base Ball," *Williamsport Lycoming Gazette*, August 13, 1868; "Monrovia vs. Pythias," *Harrisburg Patriot*, October 10, 1868; "Tribute of Respect," *Harrisburg Patriot*. Jan. 27, 1869; *Harrisburg Telegraph*, May 18, 1869; "Base Ball," *Harrisburg Telegraph*, Jul 1, 1869; "Base Ball," *Harrisburg Telegraph*, Jul 31, 1869; "Base Ball Match," *Harrisburg Telegraph*, Aug 6, 1869; "Base Ball Match," *Harrisburg Telegraph*, Nov 4, 1870.

Mystic Base Ball Club (Harrisburg, PA; 1870s)

The Mystic B.B.C. organized in the 1870s, played black teams. The Mystics were formerly members of the Monrovia and Star nines. The Mystic, Tyrolean, and Olympic nines became local rivals. *Harrisburg Telegraph* (June 12, 1875): "In a return game of base-ball between the Mystic and Tyrolean clubs, colored, played on the North Street Grounds yesterday, the former was victorious by a score of 63 to 36." They also played against the black clubs of Mechanicsburg and Carlisle. *Telegraph* (June 26, 1876): "In a game of base-ball at Carlisle yesterday between the Mystic Club, of this city and the Excelsiors of Carlisle, the former was victorious, the score standing 20 to 1." *Harrisburg Patriot* (August 5, 1875): "Yesterday afternoon the Tyrolean and Mystic clubs (colored) played a six-inning game at Union grounds. The wet condition of the field made good play impossible. The Tyroleans (representing Verbeketown) defeated the Mystic, of the central portion of the city, by a score of 16 to 15." They reorganized in 1876. *Patriot* (May 19, 1876): "A game of base-ball was played between the Mystic and Tyrolean clubs (colored) at the North Street and Pennsylvania Avenue grounds yesterday afternoon, resulting in a score of 22 to 17 in favor of the Mystic."

SOURCES: *Harrisburg (PA) Telegraph*, Jul 14, 1874; *Harrisburg Telegraph*, May 21, 1875; "The City," *Harrisburg Telegraph*, Jun 12, 1875; "The City," *Harrisburg Telegraph*, Jun 26, 1875; "The City," *Harrisburg Telegraph*, Jul 1, 1875; "The City," *Harrisburg Telegraph*, Jul 16, 1875; "The City," *Harrisburg Telegraph*, Jul 22, 1875; "Base Ball," *Harrisburg (PA) Patriot*, Jul 28, 1875; "The Ball and the Bat," *Harrisburg Patriot*, Jul 30, 1875; "Base Ball," *Harrisburg Patriot*, Aug 3, 1875; "Field Spots," *Harrisburg Patriot*, Aug 5, 1875; "The City," *Harrisburg Telegraph*, Aug 5, 1875; "The City," *Harrisburg Telegraph*, Sep 30, 1875; "Miscellany," *Harrisburg Patriot*, May 19, 1876; "Miscellany," *Harrisburg Patriot*, Jun 7, 1876; "Base Ball Matters," *Harrisburg Patriot*, Jun 13, 1876; "Base Ball Matters," *Harrisburg Patriot*, Jun 14, 1876.

Old Reliable Club (Harrisburg, PA; 1870s–1880s)

The Old Reliable Club was founded at Harrisburg, PA in 1873. Black baseballists throughout PA belonged to this association that espoused Republican politics. It also actively promoted blackball throughout PA. Among the baseballists that belonged: David R. Chester, Aaron Still, Isaac Judah, F. C. Battis, George Galbraith, C. W. Harley, N. L. Butler, William Allen and William Furney.

SOURCES: "Colored Ball at Lancaster," *Philadelphia (PA) Times*, Apr 16, 1875; "The Old Reliable's Annual Meeting," *Philadelphia Times*, Apr 17, 1878; "The Inauguration," *Williamsport (PA) Gazette Bulletin*, Nov 26, 1878; "Inauguration Day," *Philadelphia Times*, Jan 21, 1879; "Colored Folks' Grand Ball," *Reading (PA) Eagle*, Apr 7, 1881; "The Old Reliable Club," *Philadelphia (PA) Inquirer*, Apr 7, 1882; "The Old Reliable Club of Pennsylvania," *Harrisburg (PA) State Journal*, Oct 15, 1884; "Solid Old Reliables," *Harrisburg (PA) Telegraph*, Oct 25, 1884; "Colored Men for Quay," *Philadelphia Times*, Oct 15, 1885; "Saloon Keeper Bettencourt Acquitted," *Philadelphia (PA) Inquirer*, Mar 22, 1888; "The Late Aaron Still," *Reading (PA) Times*, Jun 14, 1887; "Resolutions of Respect," *Harrisburg Telegraph*, Dec 13, 1889; "Laid to Rest," *Harrisburg Telegraph*, Dec 16, 1889.

Olympic Base Ball Club (Harrisburg, PA; 1870s–1890s). Organizer(s): N. Z. Butler, F. Battis, Thomas Christy, W. Hopkins, and John W. Simpson; Buck Burrs and Harry Sigler; Charles Johnson and Alderman John W. Simpson.

The Olympic B.B.C. organized in the 1870s, played black and later, white clubs. *Harrisburg Patriot* (September 15, 1875): "The friends of the Olympic and Tyrolean Base Ball Clubs are making arrangements for a grand match of base-ball for a purse of twenty-five dollars and the championship. Great rivalry exists between these clubs for superiority of playing. The Tyroleans have never been able to cope with the Olympic, although their games have been hotly contested. They have recently added several new players to their nine, which tends to increase their strength and they now feel able and willing to cope with the latter named club. The Olympics have been successful in every game they have played with several clubs in the central portion of the state, feel they are second to no club in the vicinity, and will contest the Tyroleans as soon as they arrangements for the game can be completed." In 1884, they played Carlisle's Olympic club. *Harrisburg State Journal* (May 24, 1884): "On Tuesday, the Olympic Club, of Carlisle played a game with the Harrisburgs and were defeated after a long noisy disinterested game. For the first few innings the Harrisburgs played a faultless game and at the beginning of the fourth inning the score stood 10 to 0 in their favor, this lead they allowed to be overcome by costly errors made by the outfield, and from Johnson not having proper support behind the bat. The Carlisle club contained quite a number of amateur acrobats or rather bats who knew little about acrobatics and they furnished amusements for the two or three hundred spectators during the game." The team also played the local white club. *Harrisburg Patriot* (July 29, 1884): "The game yesterday afternoon between the Nationals and the Olympic colored clubs proved to be close and exciting from the opening to the close. Rain fell at intervals and made it very unpleasant yet the game was played out. The majority of spectators, about two hundred in number, were colored people, who were greatly interested in their own boys. Thompson occupied the box for the Olympics and pitched a fine game. He was supported by Williams in good style. Throughout the umpiring was frightful and against the colored club. Had any fairness been shown they would have won the game. Another contest is expected to take place between the same clubs. It will draw a larger crowd to the grounds."

SOURCES: "Base Ball," *Harrisburg (PA) Patriot*, Sep 15, 1875; "Base

Ball," *Harrisburg Patriot*, Oct 13, 1875; "Harrisburg vs. Reading," *Harrisburg Patriot*, Oct 14, 1875; "Base Ball Matters," *Harrisburg Patriot*, Oct 26, 1875; "Base Ball Notes," *Harrisburg Patriot*, Apr 13, 1876; "Olympic Base Ball Club," *Harrisburg Patriot*, Apr 26, 1876; "Base Ball Matters," *Harrisburg Patriot*, Jul 23, 1876; "Base Ball," *Harrisburg Patriot*, Jul 27, 1876; "Base Ball Notes," *Harrisburg Patriot*, Jul 25, 1882; "National Game Notes," *Harrisburg Patriot*, Aug 22, 1882; "Base Ball Notes," *Harrisburg Patriot*, Sep 18, 1882; "Local Briefs," *Harrisburg Patriot*, Aug 13, 1882; "Base Ball Notes," *Harrisburg Patriot*, Aug 21, 1882; "Base Ball Notes," *Harrisburg Patriot*, Sep 2, 1882; "Jottings," *Harrisburg (PA) Telegraph*, Sep 5, 1882; "Local Briefs," *Harrisburg Patriot*, Sep 5, 1882; "The Mechanicsburg Champions(?)," *Harrisburg Telegraph*, Oct 19, 1882; "Olympic vs. Olympic," *Harrisburg (PA) State Journal*, May 24, 1884; "Brief Locals," *Harrisburg State Journal*, May 31, 1884; "Minor Locals," *Harrisburg Patriot*, Jul 25, 1884; "Gathered About Town," *Harrisburg Patriot*, Jul 26, 1884; "A Close Game," *Harrisburg Patriot*, Jul 29, 1884; "Olympics vs. Nationals," *Harrisburg Patriot*, Aug 2, 1884; "Local Briefs," *Harrisburg Patriot*, Sep 18, 1884; "The Olympics Defeated," *Harrisburg Patriot*, Sep 19, 1884; "Court Proceedings," *Harrisburg Patriot*, Apr 28, 1886; "Closing Session," *Harrisburg Telegraph*, May 20, 1886; "Yesterday's Police Record," *Harrisburg Patriot*, May 4, 1887; "Jottings," *Harrisburg Telegraph*, Sep 12, 1887; "In the Cumberland Valley," *Harrisburg Telegraph*, Sep 14, 1887; "Funeral of Lucy Potter," *Harrisburg Telegraph*, Feb 13, 1888; "Diamond Dots," *Harrisburg Telegraph*, Aug 15, 1888; "Hot Liners," *Harrisburg Telegraph*, Sep 22, 1888; "Sporting Scintillations," *Harrisburg Telegraph*, Feb 28, 1890; "Sporting Sweepings," *Harrisburg Telegraph*, Mar 22, 1890; "The Game Today," *Harrisburg Patriot*, Apr 2, 1890; "Base Ball Topics," *Harrisburg Telegraph*, Apr 21, 1890; "Grand Stand Chat," *Harrisburg Telegraph*, Jun 3, 1890; "Coming Base Ball Game," *Harrisburg Telegraph*, Jun 16, 1890.

Rough and Ready Base Ball Club (Harrisburg, PA; 1870s). Organizer(s): J. Edwards.

The Rough and Ready B.B.C. organized in 1870, played against black nines. The team included former members of Harrisburg's Monrovia and Star B.B.C.s. *Harrisburg Telegraph* (July 25, 1870): "A game of baseball was played on Saturday between the Geary and Rough and Ready Clubs, both colored, which resulted in a victory for the former. The Geary is composed of boys, whose ages vary from twelve to seventeen years, while the other club are full of grown men."

Sources: "Base Ball Match," *Harrisburg (PA) Telegraph*, Jul 25, 1870; "Base Ball Match," *Harrisburg Telegraph*, Nov 4, 1870,

Star Base Ball Club (Harrisburg, PA; 1860s–1870s). Organizer(s): Richard Snowden and James Butler.

The Star B.B.C. organized in the 1860s, competed against black nines. *Harrisburg Telegraph* (July 31, 1869): "A match game of baseball will be played on the grounds at West Portland and North Frederick Streets Grounds on Thursday, between the Star Base Ball Club of Harrisburg, and the Actives of this place. Both clubs are composed of colored gentlemen. The prize is a bat and ball. It will no doubt be an interesting game, as the Actives have lately achieved some honor, and the Star has the reputation of being the best club of the kind in this state. Actives be active." The Stars and Monrovias developed a rivalry. *Telegraph* (May 18, 1869): "A base-ball match came off yesterday between the Monrovia and Star Clubs of this city, which resulted in favor of the former. The score standing; Monrovia, 38; Star, 35. The Monrovia played at a disadvantage, being short of two men." Weeks later, the Stars turned the tables on their opponents. *Telegraph* (June 1, 1869): "A Match game was played between the Monrovia and Star Clubs yesterday afternoon, resulting in a victory for the latter, the score standing 23 to 29." They also played the "Actives" of Mechanicsburg.

Sources: *Harrisburg (PA) Telegraph*, May 18, 1869; "Base Ball," *Harrisburg Telegraph*, Jul 1, 1869; "Base Ball," *Harrisburg Telegraph*, Jul 31, 1869; "Base Ball Match," *Harrisburg Telegraph*, Aug 6, 1869; "Base Ball Match," *Harrisburg Telegraph*, Nov 4, 1870.

Tyrolean Base Ball Club (Harrisburg, PA; 1870s). Organizer(s): Thomas C. Christy.

The Tyrolean B.B.C. organized in 1875. The "Tyroleans" played black nines. *Harrisburg Telegraph* (June 12, 1875): "In a return game of base-ball between the Mystic and Tyrolean clubs, colored, played on the North Street Grounds yesterday, the former was victorious by a score of 63 to 36." The Tyroleans, a strong nine, played Mechanicsburg and Carlisle. *Telegraph* (July 26, 1875): "In a game of base-ball at Kanaga's woods, yesterday, between the High Boys of Carlisle, and the Tyroleans, of Harrisburg (both colored), the former club was defeated by a score of 3 to 42." Mechanicsburg fared no better. *Telegraph* (September 3, 1875): "The Tyrolean base Ball Club, of Harrisburg defeated the High Boys, of Mechanicsburg, yesterday, at that place, by a score of 55 to 8." The Olympics and Tyroleans developed a rivalry. *Harrisburg Patriot* (Sept. 15, 1875): "The friends of the Olympic and Tyrolean Base Ball Clubs are making arrangements for a grand match of base-ball for a purse of twenty-five dollars and the championship. Great rivalry exists between these clubs for superiority of playing. The Tyroleans have never been able to cope with the Olympic, although their games have been hotly contested. They have recently added several new players to their nine, which tends to increase their strength and they now feel able and willing to cope with the latter named club. The Olympics have been successful in every game they have played with several clubs in the central portion of the state, feel they are second to no club in the vicinity, and will contest the Tyroleans as soon as they arrangements for the game can be completed." Another rivalry developed with the Mystics. *Harrisburg Patriot* (August 5, 1875): "Yesterday afternoon the Tyrolean and Mystic clubs (colored) played a six-inning game at Union grounds. The wet condition of the field made good play impossible. The Tyroleans (representing Verbeketown) defeated the Mystic, of the central portion of the city, by a score of 16 to 15." They reorganized in 1876. *Patriot* (May 19, 1876): "A game of base-ball was played between the Mystic and Tyrolean clubs (colored) at the North Street and Pennsylvania Avenue grounds yesterday afternoon, resulting in a score of 22 to 17 in favor of the Mystic."

Sources: *Harrisburg (PA) Telegraph*, May 21, 1875 "The City," *Harrisburg Telegraph*, Jun 12, 1875; "The City," *Harrisburg Telegraph*, Jun 26, 1875; "The City," *Harrisburg Telegraph*, Jul 1, 1875; "The City," *Harrisburg Telegraph*, Jul 16, 1875; "The City," *Harrisburg Telegraph*, Jul 22, 1875; "Base Ball," *Harrisburg Patriot*, Aug 3, 1875; "Field Spots," *Harrisburg Patriot*, Aug 5, 1875; "The City," *Harrisburg Telegraph*, Aug 5, 1875; "The City," *Harrisburg Telegraph*, Aug 15, 1875; "Base Ball," *Harrisburg Telegraph*, Sep 3, 1875; "Base Ball," *Harrisburg (PA) Patriot*. Sept. 15, 1875; "The City," *Harrisburg Telegraph*, Sep 30, 1875; "Base Ball," *Harrisburg Patriot*. Oct. 13, 1875; "Harrisburg vs. Reading," *Harrisburg Patriot*, Oct 14, 1875; "Base Ball Matters," *Harrisburg Patriot*, Oct 26, 1875; "Base Ball Notes," *Harrisburg Patriot*. Apr. 13, 1876; "Olympic Base Ball Club," *Harrisburg Patriot*, Apr 26, 1876; "Miscellany," *Harrisburg Patriot*, May 19, 1876; "Miscellany," *Harrisburg Patriot*, Jun 7, 1876; "Base Ball Matters," *Harrisburg Patriot*, Jun 13, 1876; "Base Ball Matters," *Harrisburg Patriot*, Jun 14, 1876; "Base Ball Matters," *Harrisburg Patriot*, Jul 23, 1876; "Base Ball," *Harrisburg Patriot*, Jul 27, 1876; "Base Ball Matters," *Harrisburg Patriot*, Jul 15, 1877; "From Carlisle," *Harrisburg Telegraph*, Aug 3, 1877; "Base Ball Matters," *Harrisburg Patriot*, Aug 3, 1878.

Humming Birds Base Ball Club (Hollidaysburg, PA; 1870s)

The Humming Birds B.B.C. organized in the 1870s, played against black teams. *Altoona Evening Mirror* (July 19, 1876): "The Troublesome Club, of Altoona, will play the Hummingbirds, of Hollidaysburg, on the Mountain City Grounds. These clubs are composed of colored gentlemen." *Evening Mirror* (July 24, 1876): "The Humming Birds, of Hollidaysburg, walked away with our Razor Slingers to the tune of 35 to 16. The crowd in attendance, for some reason or other, went in over the fence."

SOURCES: "Base Ball," *Altoona (PA) Evening Mirror*, Jul 19, 1876; "Base Ball Items," *Altoona Evening Mirror*, Jul 24, 1876.

Phoenix Base Ball Club (Hollidaysburg, PA; 1860s–1870s)

The Phoenix B.B.C. organized in the 1870s, played white and black teams. *Huntingdon Journal and American* (July 14, 1869): "The principal feature of the [Fourth of July] exercises on Monday was a match game of baseball, in which the Ethiopian Club of Hollidaysburg played against the Timbuctoos of this place [Huntingdon], the latter being slightly better." *Huntingdon Journal and American* (July 14, 1869): "A game of baseball was played in that place, on Monday of last week, between a colored club from Hollidaysburg and the Timbuctoos of our town. The Hollidaysburghers carried off the blue ribbon by a score of 46 to 42." *Ebensburg Cambria Freeman* (July 15, 1869): "A Negro Base Ball Club went from Hollidaysburg to Huntingdon on the fifth and beat a Negro club of the latter place by a score of 46 to 42." *Ebensburg Cambria Freeman* (August 16, 1872): "A correspondent send us word that it was a scrub nine of white fellows, and not the Amateurs, that played the Phoenix (colored) club a game of base-ball in Johnston lately, and that the correct score was 44 to 45 in favor of the Phoenix." *Altoona Tribune* (September 26, 1872): "The members of the colored base-ball club of Johnstown, met with a signal defeat at the hands of the Phoenix club (colored) of Hollidaysburg, on Monday of last week."

SOURCES: "Local and Personal," *Huntingdon (PA) Journal and American*, Jul 14, 1869; "The Fourth," *Huntingdon Journal and American*, Jul 14, 1869; *Ebensburg (PA) Cambria Freeman*, Jul 15, 1869; "Memoranda," *Ebensburg (PA) Alleghenian*, Jul 22, 1869; "Suburban Intelligence," *Altoona (PA) Tribune*, Aug 15, 1872; "Haps and Mishaps Near and at Home," *Ebensburg Cambria Freeman*, Aug 16, 1872; "Suburban Intelligence," *Altoona Tribune*, Sep 26, 1872.

Colored Base Ball Club (IN, PA; 1890s)

The Colored B.B.C. organized in the 1890s. *Indiana Progress* (October 3, 1894): "That old, old saying, 'When Greek meets Greek then comes the tug-of-war' was never more realistically illustrated in Indiana county than on Monday morning, when the colored baseball teams of Indiana and Blairsville came together for the first time this year. The game was played at Blairsville and Indiana won, the result of the magnificent game being 15 to 5."

SOURCES: "Brought It Home Too," *Indiana (PA) Progress*, Oct 3, 1894; "Indiana Wins," *Indiana (PA) Gazette*, Oct 3, 1894; "Indiana 15; Blairsville 5," *Indiana (PA) Democrat*, Oct 4, 1894; "Blairsville Defeated Again," *Indiana (PA) Messenger*, Oct 8, 1894.

Active Junior Base Ball Club (Lancaster, PA; 1880s)

The Active Junior B.B.C. organized in the 1880s, played black nines. *Harrisburg Telegraph* (August 15, 1888): "On Wednesday, the Olympics of Harrisburg, played the Actives of Lancaster. The latter was downed by a score of 12 to 2." *Lancaster Intelligencer* (August 31, 1888): "A well-contested game of ball was witnessed by a good-sized crowd on the Ironsides grounds yesterday between the Juniors, Lancaster's colored club, and the Columbias, also colored. The Juniors lost the game in the first inning by wild throwing to the bases, allowing Columbia to score seven runs, after which they steadied themselves and played a good uphill game, a runner being on third to tie the score when the last man fouled out in the ninth." The Actives played a two-game series against Harrisburg's Olympics.

SOURCES: "Base Ball," *Harrisburg (PA) Telegraph*, Aug 3, 1888; "Diamond Dots," *Harrisburg Telegraph*, Aug 15, 1888; "Won Another Game," *Lancaster (PA) Intelligencer*, Aug 31, 1888.

Black Diamond Base Ball Club (Lancaster, PA; 1880s)

The Black Diamond B.B.C. organized in the 1880s, played black teams. *Lancaster Intelligencer* (August 5, 1885): "The Nameless colored club, of Mt. Joy, arrived in town this afternoon with two bats and a valise. They are playing the Black Diamond club at McGrann's park. The Lancaster coons want to run a white man in to catch for them, but the visitors are kicking about that, as they want no mixture of color." *Intelligencer* (June 25, 1886): "The Black Diamonds and Whackers, two colored ball clubs, played a game of ball on the Ironside grounds yesterday. The former won by 26 to 11." *Intelligencer* (July 2, 1886): "Yesterday afternoon, the Close Members and Black Diamonds, two colored ball clubs, played a game on the Ironsides Grounds. The former had Waters and Buch [Book] for their battery and the Diamonds had Jackson and Deen. The Close Members won by 9 to 5, and the game was not the worst seen here this year."

SOURCES: "The Last Game," *Lancaster (PA) Intelligencer*, Aug 5, 1885; "The Base Ball Field," *Lancaster Intelligencer*, Aug 6, 1885; *Marietta (PA) Register*, Aug 8, 1885; "Games on Thursday," *Lancaster Intelligencer*, Jun 25, 1886; "In Base Ball Circles," *Lancaster Intelligencer*, Jul 2, 1886.

Close Members Base Ball Club (Lancaster, PA; 1880s)

The Close Members B.B.C. organized in the 1880s, played black teams. *Lancaster Intelligencer* (July 2, 1886): "Yesterday afternoon, the Close Members and Black Diamonds, two colored ball clubs, played a game on the Ironsides Grounds. The former had Waters and Buch [Book] for their battery and the Diamonds had Jackson and Deen. The Close Members won by 9 to 5, and the game was not the worst seen here this year."

SOURCES: "In Base Ball Circles," *Lancaster (PA) Intelligencer*, Jul 2, 1886; "Interesting Base Ball News," *Lancaster Intelligencer*, Jul 16, 1886; "Among the Ball Players," *Lancaster Intelligencer*, Jul 19, 1886.

Giants Base Ball Club (Lancaster, PA; 1880s). Organizer(s): William Simpson and James Goodall.

The Giants B.B.C. organized in 1887, played white and black clubs. *Lancaster Intelligencer* (June 27, 1887): "On the Ironside Grounds yesterday afternoon the Bear Club of Columbia played their second game with the Lancaster Giants. This time the colored boys turned the tables upon their rivals and defeated them by outplaying them at every point of the game. The Giants presented Jackson, a new pitcher, and he did excellent work. It must be said of the Giants, that although they are colored, they are among the most gentlemanly lot of men that have ever played ball in Lancaster." The team disbanded in June.

SOURCES: "The Lancaster Giants," *Lancaster (PA) Intelligencer*, Jun 1, 1887; "The Latest Base Ball News," *Lancaster Intelligencer*, Jun 13, 1887; "Base Ball News," *Lancaster Intelligencer*, Jun 14, 1887; "Their First Game," *Lancaster Intelligencer*, Jun 16, 1887; "The Bears Beaten," *Lancaster Intelligencer*, Jun 24, 1887; "[Unintelligible]," *Lancaster Intelligencer*, Jun 27, 1887.

Cupola Base Ball Club (Lawrenceville, PA; 1880s–1890s). Organizer(s): C. D. Shelton.

The Cupola B.B.C. organized in the 1880s, played white and black teams. *Pittsburg Dispatch* (July 28, 1889): "The Keystones easily defeated the Cupolas, of Lawrenceville yesterday at Cycle Park. The attendance was large." *Pittsburg Press* (August 4, 1889): "The Cupolas, colored, of Lawrenceville, played two games yesterday, winning both. Score in the first game: Cupolas 26, Young Keystones 7; second game: Cupolas 35, White Oaks 14."

SOURCES: "Base Ball Notes," *Pittsburgh (PA) Dispatch*, Jul 27, 1889; "Easy for the Keystones," *Pittsburgh Dispatch*, Jul 28, 1889; "Amateur Atoms," *Pittsburgh (PA) Press*, Aug 4, 1889; ; "Twin City News," *Cleveland (OH) Gazette*, Jul 11, 1891.

Princeton Base Ball Club (Lock Haven, PA; 1870s)

The Princeton B.B.C. organized in the 1870s, played black nines. *Williamsport Gazette and Bulletin* (August 19, 1876): "Yesterday the Odd fellows, colored, held a picnic at Herdic Park. Among the festivities of the day was a game of base-ball between the Princetons, of Lock Haven, and the Enterprise of Williamsport. At the end of the game the score stood 18 to 19 in favor of the Enterprise."

SOURCES: "Dashes Here and There," *Williamsport (PA) Gazette and Bulletin*, Aug 16, 1876; "On the Way Down," *Williamsport Gazette and Bulletin*, Aug 17, 1876; *Williamsport Gazette and Bulletin*, Aug 19, 1876.

A. J. McClure Giants Base Ball Club (Marcus Hook, PA; 1890s–1900s). Organizer(s): James A. Fox.

The A. J. McClure Giants B.B.C. organized in the 1890s, white and black clubs. *Chester Times* (July 13, 1899): "The Chester Giants won the first game of base-ball in the series of five with the McClure Giants, at Marcus Hook yesterday afternoon, by a score of 13 to 5. The game was an interesting one from start to finish, notwithstanding that the Chester boys had a walkover. The teams are composed of some of the best colored players in the county and yesterday's contest attracted a large number of spectators."

SOURCES: "Colored Team at Hook," *Chester (PA) Times*, Jun 27, 1899; "Marcus Hook," *Chester Times*, Jul 7, 1899; "A Game at Hook Today," *Chester Times*, Jul 12, 1899; "Sports of All Sorts," *Chester (PA) Times*, Jul 13, 1899; "Two Coming Games," *Chester Times*, Jul 14, 1899; "Rival Ball Teams," *Chester Times*, Aug 29, 1899; "Yanigans vs. Giants," *Chester Times*, Aug 14, 1900; "McClure Giants Win," *Chester Times*, Sep 10, 1900.

Eureka Base Ball Club (Marietta, PA; 1880s). Organizer(s): Charles Brown.

The Eureka B.B.C. organized in the 1880s, played black nines. *Marietta Register* (May 31, 1884): "There is a colored club in this town, called Eureka, that will play any colored club in the county." *Marietta Register* (May 31, 1884): "The only genuine, first-class windy base-ball club in the country, is the Eureka, of this place, who have a bellows for a pitcher and an iron-clad backstop." *Register* (August 9, 1884): "A colored club from Columbia put the bug on the Eureka club of this place last Saturday, at the grounds above the station, to the tune of 30 to 10. Owing to the plenteous supply of apples the pitcher of the Eureka was unable to put in his double-acting, twisting curves. He is slowly recovering." *Register* (August 9, 1884): "A colored club from Columbia put the bug on the Eureka club of this place last Thursday, at the grounds above the station, to the tune of 30 to 10."

SOURCES: "Game of Ball," *Marietta (PA) Register*, Sep 29, 1883; "Base Ball Notes," *Marietta Register*, Oct 6, 1883; "Local Department," *Marietta (PA) Register*, May 31, 1884; "Base Ball Notes," *Marietta Register*, Aug 9, 1884; "Local Jottings," *Marietta Register*, Dec 6, 1884.

Active Base Ball Club (Mechanicsburg, PA; 1860s)

The Active B.B.C. organized in 1869. The "Actives" played against black organizations. *Harrisburg Telegraph* (August 6, 1869): "A match game was played yesterday between the Star Club, of this city and the Active of Mechanicsburg."

SOURCES: "Base Ball Match," *Harrisburg (PA) Telegraph*, Aug 6, 1869.

Colored Base Ball Club (Media, PA; 1880s–1890s)

The Colored B.B.C. organized in the 1880s, played against black teams. *Philadelphia Inquirer* (July 10, 1889): "The Crescent Club defeated the Media Club this afternoon by superior all-around work. The visitors could do nothing with Williams's delivery, while Lockwood was hit frequently and hard." *Inquirer* (July 11, 1890): "This afternoon the Media Club were defeated by the Crescents of this place by a score of 22 to 12. Both clubs are colored and the game was noted for its heavy batting and errors."

SOURCES: "Media Takes a Tumble," *Philadelphia (PA) Inquirer*, Jul 10, 1889; "The Crescents Defeat Media," *Philadelphia Inquirer*, Jul 11, 1890.

Colored Base Ball Club (Middleton, PA; 1870s)

The Colored B.B.C. organized in the 1870s, played black teams. *Harrisburg Telegraph* (July 14, 1874): "A match game of base-ball was played yesterday afternoon at Middleton between Apolia, of this city [Harrisburg], and the Middleton Club. Richardson, of the Apolia, and Saunders, of the Middleton Club, played excellently. Score: Apolia, 49; Middleton, 28."

SOURCES: *Harrisburg (PA) Telegraph*, Jul 14, 1874.

Midnight Star Base Ball Club (Monongahela, PA; 1890s). Organizer(s): Roy E. Sluby.

The Midnight Star B.B.C. organized in the 1890s, played white and black nines. *Monongahela Republican* (June 9, 1899): "The Midnight Stars played the baseball team of Elizabeth, Pa., on last Wednesday, scoring 18–19, in favor of the Monongahela boys." *Republican* (June 17, 1899): "A colored juvenile ball club from Monongahela, called the Midnight Stars, went to Elizabeth Wednesday of last week and played a picked nine of Elizabeth players. It took ten inning to decide the contest, and Elizabeth won by a score of 23 to 19. The Elizabeth boys will come to Monongahela and play a return game on Tuesday, June 20."

SOURCES: "Ball Club," *Monongahela (PA) Republican*, May 24, 1899; "Base Ball," *Monongahela Republican*, Jun 9, 1899; "Base Ball," *Monongahela Republican*, Jun 17, 1899.

Valley Tigers Base Ball Club (Montrose, PA; 1870s)

The Valley Tigers B.B.C. organized in the 1870s. The Valley Tigers played black teams. *Montrose Democrat* (July 11, 1877): "A colored baseball club from Binghamton is expected to play the colored club of this place tomorrow." *Democrat* (July 11, 1877): "*Binghamton Times* says the Parlor City Base Ball Club, a team composed of young men, has been organized for this season with John Amos as captain. They will play their first game at Montrose on Thursday next, tomorrow, with the Valley Tiger Club of this place. A number of their friends expect to accompany them." *Democrat* (September 21, 1878): "A game of base-ball between the Parlor City nine, of Binghamton, and the Valley tigers, of Montrose, on Thursday. Both clubs are colored. The Valley Tigers came out behind."

SOURCES: "Neighboring Counties," *Montrose (PA) Democrat*, Jul 11, 1877; "Happenings at Home," *Waverly (NY) Advocate*, Aug 7, 1878; "Town and County and Variety," *Montrose Democrat*, Sep 21, 1878; "Rah For the Parlor Citys," *Montrose Democrat*, Oct 18, 1878.

Nameless Base Ball Club (Mt. Joy, PA; 1880s)

The Nameless B.B.C. organized in the 1880s, played black teams. *Marietta Register* (September 29, 1883): "A colored nine from Mt. Joy made their first appearance of the season in this place Wednesday afternoon, where they played a game with a nine in town at the grounds west of the station. Marietta knocked three pitchers out of the box for the Mt. Joy, and wound up the game by a score of 29 to 13." *Lancaster Intelligencer* (August 5, 1885): "The Nameless colored club, of Mt. Joy, arrived in town this afternoon with two bats and a valise. They are playing the Black Diamond club at McGrann's park. The Lancaster coons want to run a white man in to catch for them, but the visitors are kicking about that, as they want no mixture of color." *Marietta Register* (August 8, 1885): "The Mt. Joy colored club secured the services of Charlie Brown [Marietta Eurekas], of this place, as pitcher the game at Lancaster on Wednesday. Archie was resplendent in a red, white and blue shirt, with a fine row of ivories, and a Mammoth cave pit in which to show them."

SOURCES: "Game of Ball," *Marietta (PA) Register*, Sep 29, 1883; "Base Ball Notes," *Marietta Register*, Oct 6, 1883; "The Last Game," *Lancaster (PA) Intelligencer*, Aug 5, 1885; "The Base Ball Field," *Lancaster Intelligencer*, Aug 6, 1885; *Marietta Register*, Aug 8, 1885.

Harrison and Reid Base Ball Club (New Castle, PA; 1890s)

The Harrison and Reid B.B.C. organized in the 1890s, played black teams. *New Castle News* (July 6, 1892): "a good game of ball was played yesterday afternoon between the Keystones, of Pittsburg and the Harrison and Reids of this city. The game was hotly contested from the first, but the Pittsburg team won the battle. The New Castle Club was organized but recently and have not had the advantage of much practice, which accounts for the low score on their side. Another game will soon be played, when the boys will be in better shape."

SOURCES: "Harrison and Reid Beaten," *Pittsburgh (PA) Dispatch*, Jul 1, 1892; "An Exciting Game," *New Castle (PA) News*, Jul 6, 1892.

Orion Base Ball Club (Norristown, PA; 1880s–1890s). Owner(s): Joseph Richardson and David Blackwell; Isaac Chase.

The Orion B.B.C. organized in the 1880s, black and white teams. *Norristown Register* (June 9, 1890): "The game on Saturday at Alert Park between the Alert and Orion Club was the most exciting played there this season.... The Alerts held the lead until the seventh inning, when the Orion made six runs on hits, aided by fielding errors. The Alerts took the lead again in the eighth and were tied by the Orion in the ninth." Black competition included Reading's Crescents. *Reading Times* (August 23, 1890): "Yesterday afternoon the colored baseball players of Norristown came to Reading to play the Crescent Club, also composed of colored players. The visitors at once took the lead, and the game at no time was in doubt. Howard and Newkirk for the Crescents did their work well, and on the part of the visitors the catching of Harry Fisher was of gilt-edge order, he accepting seventeen out of eighteen chances." *Philadelphia Times* (August 22, 1891): "The Orion local team, consisting of colored players, defeated the Jefferson Democratic Club, this afternoon at Oak View Park."

SOURCES: "A Somerset Victory," *Philadelphia (PA) Inquirer*, Jul 30, 1889; "Base Ball," *Norristown (PA) Register*, Jun 2, 1890; "Base Ball," *Norristown Register, Jun 9, 1890*; "Holiday Base Ball," *Norristown (PA) Weekly Herald*, Jul 7, 1890; "Games of the Amateurs," *Philadelphia Inquirer*, Jul 11, 1890; "Runs, Hits, Errors," *Reading (PA) Times*, Aug 22, 1890; "The Colored Clubs Play," *Reading Times*, Aug 23, 1890; "Orions, 8; Jefferson, 6," *Philadelphia (PA) Times*, Aug 22, 1891; "Norristown, 16; Orions, 7," *Philadelphia Times*, Aug 29, 1891.

Colored Base Ball Club (Pennlyn, PA; 1890s). Organizer(s): John J. Garrett.

The Colored B.B.C. organized in the 1890s. The aggregation played black and white teams.

SOURCES: "The Future Greats," *Philadelphia (PA) Inquirer*, Jul 28, 1897; "Norwood and Pennlyn," *Philadelphia Inquirer*, June 25, 1899; "Wyoming an Easy Winner," *Philadelphia Inquirer*, Sep 17, 1899.

Active Base Ball Club (Philadelphia, PA; 1870s)

The Active B.B.C. organized in the 1870s. The Actives played black teams. *Wilmington Commercial* (October 11, 1875): "A game between two colored clubs, the Delaware and the Active, (the latter from West Philadelphia), will be played at the Quickstep grounds, this afternoon."

SOURCES: "Base Ball," *Wilmington (DE) Commercial*, Oct 11, 1875.

Amos Scott Base Ball Club (Philadelphia, PA; 1880s)

The Amos Scott B.B.C. organized in the 1880s. The "Amos Scott Club," named for the prizefighter, "Amos Scott," played black and white clubs.

SOURCES: "Amos Scott Knocks Ben Bailey Down Eighteen Times in Four Rounds," *Philadelphia (PA) Times*, Mar 24, 1885; "Delaware Statutes," *New York (NY) Freeman*, May 14, 1887; "Pythians, 9; Scott Club, 6," *Philadelphia (PA) Record*, May 15, 1887; "Delaware Field Club and Amos Scott," *Philadelphia (PA) Inquirer*, May 19, 1887; "Local Base Ball," *Wilmington (DE) Morning News*, May 19, 1887; "The Week in Wilmington," *Philadelphia Times*, May 22, 1887; *Wilmington (DE) News Journal*, May 24, 1887; *Wilmington Morning News*, May 27, 1887; "Delaware Doings," *New York Freeman*, May 28, 1887; "News Notes," *Bridgeton (NJ) Evening News*. June 1887; "The Scotts Beaten," *Trenton (NJ) Evening Times*, Aug 25, 1887; "They Were All Gentlemen," *San Francisco (CA) Chronicle*, Jun 12, 1887.

Anchor Base Ball Club (Philadelphia, PA; 1890s)

The Anchor B.B.C. organized in the 1890s, played black and white clubs. *Philadelphia Inquirer* (August 2, 1896): "The Anchor Base Ball Club will play a game with the Germantown Club tomorrow at 3:30 P. M. at Wayne Junction."

SOURCES: *Philadelphia (PA) Inquirer*, Jun 2, 1896; "The Coming Greats," *Philadelphia Inquirer*, Aug 2, 1896; "Germantown 16; Anchor, 8," *Philadelphia Inquirer*, Aug 4, 1896.

Clover Base Ball Club (Philadelphia, PA; 1890s)

The Clover B.B.C. organized in the 1890s, played black and white nines. *Philadelphia Inquirer* (August 4, 1890): "The Star, Jr. and Clover Clubs, colored, played at East Park Saturday. The feature was the Clover's good batting. Batteries—Reed and Walker for the Star Jr., Club. Gardiner and Anderson for the Clover Club."

SOURCES: "Among the Amateurs," *Philadelphia (PA) Inquirer*, Aug 4, 1890.

Colored Institute Base Ball Club (Philadelphia, PA; 1890s)

The Colored Institute B.B.C. organized in the 1890s, played black and white nines. *Philadelphia Inquirer* (June 5, 1891): "The U. S. Grant Grammar School and Colored Institute Clubs played at Twenty-Ninth and South Streets June 3. The features were the fine playing of Harris, Barry and Manning and a one-handed stop of a hot-liner by Landen. Batteries—Manning, Harris and Anderson for U. S. Grant Club, Ray and Henson for the Colored Institute Club." *Philadelphia Inquirer* (June 10, 1894): "The St. Michael and the Institute for Colored Youth Clubs played at East Park yesterday. Score: St. Michael 36, I. C. Y. 29. Batteries—I. C. Y., C. Henson, Day, G. Henson."

SOURCES: "Scores of the Amateurs," *Philadelphia (PA) Inquirer*, Jun 5, 1891; "Amateur Ball Scores," *Philadelphia Inquirer*, Jun 10, 1894.

Cuban Giants, Jr. Base Ball Club (Philadelphia, PA; 1880s–1890s)

The Cuban Giants, Jr. B.B.C. organized in the 1880s. The Cuban Giants, Jr., played black teams. *Wilmington Evening Journal* (July 16, 1889): "The West End Base Ball Club will play the Cuban Giants, Jr., of Philadelphia, on Wednesday, at the Front and Union Street

Grounds. The Cuban Giants, Jr. are the champion colored club of Pennsylvania, and as the West End has signed three new players from Smyrna, a good game may be expected." *Wilmington Evening Journal* (July 18, 1889): "The West End Club of this city was defeated at the Union Street grounds yesterday afternoon by the Cuban Giants, Jr., of Philadelphia." *Philadelphia Inquirer* (August 23, 1892): "The Cuban Giants, Jr., and the Red Rose Clubs played at Frankford yesterday. The features were the pitching of Clemons, the batting of E. Barrett and the fielding of G. Barrett. The score—Cuban Giants, Jr., 44, Red Rose 9."

SOURCES: "City News in Brief," *Wilmington (DE) Evening Journal*, Jul 8, 1889; "Base Ball Notes," *Wilmington Evening Journal*, Jul 16, 1889; "Base Ball Notes," *Wilmington (DE) Morning News*, Jul 17, 1889; "Cuban Giants, Jr. vs. West End," *Wilmington Evening Journal*, Jul 18, 1889; "Scores of the Amateurs," *Philadelphia (PA) Inquirer*, Aug 23, 1892; "Two for East Greenville," *Philadelphia Inquirer*, Sep 3, 1893.

Diligent Cricket Club (Philadelphia, PA; 1850s–1860s). Organizer(s): George Augustes, Frank J. R. Jones and James H. Roberts.

The Diligent Cricket Club organized in the 1850s. *Philadelphia Times* (January 30, 1887): "Before the war the favorite game with the colored youths was cricket. Among the Diligents were George Augustes, Frank J. R. Jones, James H. Roberts, John Brown, Henry Jones, Thomas Swales and Jasper Johnson." Many of the club members later formed the Philadelphia Pythian, Brown, and National Excelsior B.B.C.s.

SOURCES: "Black Ball Players," *Philadelphia (PA) Times*, Jan 30, 1887.

Dolly Varden Base Ball Club (Philadelphia, PA; 1880s)

The Dolly Varden B.B.C. organized in 1883. The Dolly Vardens, a female professional club, played similar organizations. *Louisville Courier-Journal* (May 23, 1883): "If poor patient, melancholic Job could have seen the game of base-ball played yesterday at Lamokin Park, Pennsylvania, between the Dolly Varden and Captain Jinks Clubs, of South Winchester, he would have laughed heartily. The two clubs were composed exclusively of young colored women. Some of them were attired in ordinary female garb, but some were not. They ran like deer, threw the ball like a boy, with the right arm, and batted with lusty grace and freedom from restraint that was, to say the least, novel. The grounds were decidedly rural. On one side was a scrap of woods, on another the railroad, on the third a muddy brook, and, fronting the field, on the remaining side, there ran a row of dilapidated wooden shanties, upon the roofs of which, as well as on the adjacent fences, were perched as miscellaneous assemblage of colored folks as ever the sun looked down upon." They reorganized in 1884. *Chester Times* (May 3, 1884): "The female base-ball tossers will play at Chester Park on Monday. The game of last year was witnessed by a large number of people, and a crowd will probably attend on Monday."

SOURCES: "Miss Harris's Base-Ball Nine," *New York (NY) Times*, May 17, 1883; "Female Base Ballists," *Chester (PA) Times*, May 18, 1883; "Women at the Bat," *Louisville (KY) Courier-Journal*, May 23, 1883; "Base Ball," *Alden (IA) Times*, Jun 15, 1883; "A Novel Game of base Ball Between Teams of Colored Girls," *New Brunswick (NJ) Daily Times*, May 30, 1883; "Nine Dolly Vardins: Black Belles of Chester at the Bat," *Macon (GA) Telegraph*, May 22, 1883; "Sporting News," Guelph (ONT/CAN) *Daily Mercury*, May 22, 1883; "In and About South Chester," *Chester Times*, Mar 22, 1884; "Base Ball Notes," *Chester Times*, May 3, 1884.

Eldridge Base Ball Club (Philadelphia, PA; 1870s)

The Eldridge B.B.C. organized in the 1870s, played black nines. *Reading Eagle* (August 14, 1872): "The Excelsior Club (colored) of

this city played the Eldridge (also colored) of Philadelphia, on Monday last. The former were victorious by a score of 58 to 25"

SOURCES: "Sporting on Sunday," *Reading (PA) Daily Eagle*, Aug 14, 1872.

Giants Base Ball Club (Philadelphia, PA; 1880s–1900s). Organizer(s): Andrew Randolph and Isaac Rothwell; G. H. Hazzard.

The Giants B.B.C. organized in 1887, played black and white teams. *Philadelphia Record* (June 8, 1887): "The Philadelphia Giants (colored) played the Gallon Club (colored) at Cooper Park yesterday in the presence of 1000 people. The game was an interesting and exciting one, the Giants winning." *Philadelphia Inquirer* (June 10, 1894): "The Philadelphia Giants, the colored champions of Philadelphia, has organized for the coming season, and would like to hear from all clubs in and out of town giving a guarantee." They reorganized in the 1890s. *Inquirer* (May 3, 1895): "The Monarchs Base Ball Team yesterday defeated the Philadelphia Giants' team at the grounds of the Y.M.C.A. at Belmont and Elm Avenues. The game was the first on the grounds this season and brought out a crowded attendance." The organization continued to play in to the 20th century.

SOURCES: "Base Ball Notes," *Philadelphia (PA) Times*, Jun 7, 1887; "Philadelphia Giants, 9; Gallon, 8," *Philadelphia (PA) Record*, Jun 8, 1887; "Amateur Ball Scores," *Philadelphia (PA) Inquirer*, Jun 24, 1894; "Two Games at Millville," *Philadelphia Inquirer*, Jul 29, 1894; "Amateur Scores," *Philadelphia Inquirer*, Aug 9, 1894; "Camden Beats the Giants," *Philadelphia Inquirer*, Aug 26, 1894; "Other Games," *Philadelphia Inquirer*, Aug 27, 1894; "T'was Easy for Camden," *Philadelphia Inquirer*, Aug 31, 1894; "Amateur Base Ball," *Philadelphia Inquirer*, Mar 10, 1895; "Monarchs and Giants," *Philadelphia Inquirer*, May 3, 1895; "Chester and Giants," *Philadelphia Inquirer*, Jun 21, 1895; "Millville Boys with the Philadelphia Giants," *Philadelphia Inquirer*, Jun 30, 1895; "Richmond, 19; Philadelphia Giants," *Philadelphia Record*, Jul 3. 1898; "Wilmington A. A. and Giants Tie," *Philadelphia Inquirer*, Oct 11, 1902.

Jinks Base Ball Club (Philadelphia, PA; 1880s)

The Jinks B.B.C. organized in 1884. The Jinks, a female professional club, played similar organizations. *Louisville Courier-Journal* (May 23, 1883): "If poor patient, melancholic Job could have seen the game of base-ball played yesterday at Lamokin Park, Pennsylvania, between the Dolly Varden and Captain Jinks Clubs, of South Winchester, he would have laughed heartily. The two clubs were composed exclusively of young colored women. Some of them were attired in ordinary female garb, but some were not. They ran like deer, threw the ball like a boy, with the right arm, and batted with lusty grace and freedom from restraint that was, to say the least, novel. The grounds were decidedly rural. On one side was a scrap of woods, on another the railroad, on the third a muddy brook, and, fronting the field, on the remaining side, there ran a row of dilapidated wooden shanties, upon the roofs of which, as well as on the adjacent fences, were perched as miscellaneous assemblage of colored folks as ever the sun looked down upon." They reorganized in 1884. *Chester Times* (May 3, 1884): "The female base-ball tossers will play at Chester Park on Monday. The game of last year was witnessed by a large number of people, and a crowd will probably attend on Monday."

SOURCES: "Miss Harris's Base-Ball Nine," *New York (NY) Times*, May 17, 1883; "Female Base Ballists," *Chester (PA) Times*, May 18, 1883; "Women at the Bat," *Louisville (KY) Courier-Journal*, May 23, 1883; "Base Ball," *Alden (IA) Times*, Jun 15, 1883; "A Novel Game of base Ball Between Teams of Colored Girls," *New Brunswick (NJ) Daily Times*, May 30, 1883; "Nine Dolly Vardins: Black Belles of Chester at the Bat," *Macon (GA) Telegraph*, May 22, 1883; "Sporting News," Guelph (ONT/CAN) *Daily Mercury*, May 22, 1883; "In and About

South Chester," *Chester Times*, Mar 22, 1884; "Base Ball Notes," *Chester Times*, May 3, 1884.

Keystone Athletic Base Ball Club (Philadelphia, PA; 1880s). Organizer(s): Frank P. Thompson.

The Keystone Athletic B.B.C. organized in the 1880s. *Philadelphia Sporting Life* (April 29, 1885): "The Athletic Base Ball Club, organized last summer at Babylon, Long Island, and managed by Mr. Frank P. Thompson of that city, has, during the winter, been continued at St. Augustine, Florida. The members were waiters of the San Marco Hotel, and nearly all belong in Philadelphia. Their remarkable triumphs of last summer, have been repeated, during the winter, they having lost, we are told, but one game. They will open the summer season at Babylon in June." They played black and white nines of FL, NY, PA, MD, NJ, and NY. Frank P. Thompson scheduled a tour for his team from St. Augustine, FL back to Philadelphia. *Palatka News* (April 28, 1885): "The waiters of the Hotel San Marco, at St. Augustine, left for the North … they intend playing match games of baseball in Southern cities. They call themselves the Ancient City Athletics, and headwaiter Frank P. Thompson will act as umpire. They will open the summer season at Babylon, New York in June." They played black nines in Jacksonville, Savannah, Charleston, Richmond, WA, and Baltimore. Thompson alerted *The Sporting Life* to his team's activities. *Philadelphia Sporting Life* (April 29, 1885): "Monday last at Jacksonville, they defeated the local team by the close score of 26 to 18. Tuesday, they warmed the pets of Savannah 17 to 9." They traveled to Baltimore. *Baltimore American* (April 28, 1885): "The Athletics of Philadelphia and the Atlantics of Baltimore, two colored base-ball clubs, played a match game yesterday at Union Park. The result of the contest was a victory for the Atlantics, with a score of 19 to 3. There were about four hundred persons present to witness the game. They liberally applauded all the good plays." Prior to landing at Babylon, the ball club resided in Philadelphia where the Keystone Athletics played local talent and visiting team. *Philadelphia Times* (May 19, 1885): "At Somerset Park yesterday the Somerset defeated the Keystone Athletic Club, composed of colored men. The game was marked by sharp fielding." *Huntington Long Islander* (August 21, 1885): "A spirited game of base-ball was played on the Argyle grounds Tuesday afternoon between the Keystone Athletics, a club composed of the colored employees of the Argyle, and the Farmingdales, a white scrub club from Farmingdale. The cullud boys taught the white gents from Farmingdale how to play base-ball, winning by a score of 19 to 1."

Sources: "The Waiters' Summer," Philadelphia (PA). *Times*, Jun 8, 1884; "City Notes," *Palatka (FL) News*, Apr 28, 1885; "Base Ball," *Baltimore (MD) Sun*, Apr 28, 1885; "Colored Clubs at Union Park," *Baltimore (MD) American*, Apr 28, 1885; *Philadelphia (PA) Sporting Life*, Apr 29, 1885; "Base Ball Notes," *Philadelphia Times*, May 19, 1885; "Base Ball Notes," *Philadelphia Times*, Jun 2, 1885; "Notes and Comments," *Philadelphia Sporting Life*, Jul 1, 1885; "Babylon," *Huntington (NY) Long Islander*, Aug 21, 1885.

Leghorn Base Ball Club (Philadelphia, PA; 1880s). Organizer(s): William Payne and Oscar Jackson.

The Leghorn B.B.C. organized in the 1880s, played black organizations. *Philadelphia Inquirer* (January 11, 1888): "The application of the Leghorn (colored) Club was rejected to the Junior Amateur Base Ball League." *Philadelphia Inquirer* (February 3, 1889): "The West End Club, of Wilmington, would like to hear from the M. S. Quay and the Leghorns." *Wilmington Evening Journal*: "The West End defeated the Leghorns of Philadelphia at Union Park yesterday, by a score of 12 to 8."

Sources: "The Junior Amateurs," *Philadelphia (PA) Inquirer*, Jan 11, 1888; "Athletic B. B. Grounds, Wednesday, July 11," *Philadelphia Inquirer*, Jul 12, 1888; "Amateur Base Ball Day," *Philadelphia Inquirer*, Jun 24, 1888; "Amateur Scraps," *Philadelphia Inquirer*, Feb 3, 1889; "Base Ball Saturday," *Wilmington (DE) Evening Journal*, May 16, 1889; "Amateur Games," *Philadelphia Inquirer*, May 19, 1889; "West End Wins," *Wilmington (DE) Morning News*, May 24, 1889; "Base Ball Notes," *Wilmington Evening Journal*, May 24, 1889.

Lord Philadelphia Base Ball Club (Philadelphia, PA; 1890s–1900s)

The Lord Philadelphia B.B.C. organized in the 1890s. The former members of the Cuban X-Giants played black and white teams. *Philadelphia Record* (June 12, 1898): "The Tioga Club opened its season yesterday at broad and Jackson Streets, in a game with Lord Philadelphia. The latter were easily defeated by the score of 17 to 4." *Philadelphia Times* (September 4, 1898): "The Goshen and Court House Club wound up the season this afternoon by a game with the Lord Philadelphia Base Ball Club, colored, and defeated the latter easily, making twenty-four hits for a total of thirty-three bases."

Sources: "North Philadelphia, 23; Lord Philadelphia, 3," *Philadelphia (PA) Record*, May 22, 1898; "North Philadelphia Wins," *Philadelphia (PA) Inquirer*, May 22, 1898; "Sporting Notes," *Philadelphia (PA) Times*, Jun 10, 1898; "Sporting Notes," *Philadelphia Times*, Jun 11, 1898; "Tioga, 17; Lord Philadelphia, 4," *Philadelphia Record*, Jun 12, 1898; "The X-Ray's Won," *Philadelphia Times*, Jun 21, 1898; "Sporting Notes," *Philadelphia Times*, Jul 20, 1898; "Sporting Notes," *Philadelphia Times*, Aug 24, 1898; "Sporting Notes," *Philadelphia Times*, Aug 28, 1898; "A Heavy Hitting Game," *Philadelphia Times*, Sep 4, 1898; "Cape May Court House Wins," *Philadelphia Record*, Sep 4, 1898; "Scott A. A. Won Easily," *Philadelphia Inquirer*, May 28, 1902.

Manhattan Base Ball Club (Philadelphia, PA; 1880s). Organizer(s): Charles E. Lloyd and Cassius Govern.

The Manhattan B.B.C. organized in the 1880s. *Philadelphia Sporting Life* (June 17, 1885): "The Manhattan and Phoenix Clubs (colored), of this city, played an interesting game, the former winning by 19 to 15."

Sources: "Notes and Comments," *Philadelphia (PA) Sporting Life*, Jun 17, 1885; "Notes and Comments," *Philadelphia Sporting Life*, Jun 22, 1885; "Base Ball Today," *Philadelphia (PA) Times*, Jul 20, 1885; "Notes and Comments," *Philadelphia Sporting Life*, Nov 25, 1885.

Metamora Cricket Club (Philadelphia, PA; 1850s–1860s). Organizer(s): Henry Boyer, Jr., W. T. Jones and Andrew Jones.

The Metamora Cricket Club organized in the 1850s. *Philadelphia Times* (January 30, 1887): "Before the war the favorite game with the colored youths was cricket. Henry Boyer, Jr., W. T. Jones, Andrew Jones, Lumbard Nicken, Jacob R. Ballard, Martin and Joseph White, George B. Roberts, George Freeman and others called themselves the Metamora." Many of the club members later formed the Philadelphia Pythian, Brown, and National Excelsior B.B.C.s.

Sources: "Black Ball Players," *Philadelphia (PA) Times*, Jan 30, 1887.

National Excelsior Base Ball Club (Philadelphia, PA; 1860s–1870s). Owner(s): James Fields Needham, Edwin John, Daniel Holden and Francis Wood; George H. Wilson.

The National Excelsior B.B.C. organized in the 1860s, played black organizations. The Excelsior and Pythians nines were local rivals. *Philadelphia Evening Telegraph* (March 30, 1867): "There are two Base Ball Clubs, the Excelsior and Pythian, both of which are successful in operation, the former [Excelsior] having the reputation of being the best colored club in the country." The Excelsiors played against Bachelor club, of Albany, NY. *Albany Evening Journal* (September 27, 1866): "The Bachelor Base Ball Club will leave the city tonight on their annual tour of Newark (Keystones) and Philadelphia (National Excelsiors and Williams Club)." They traveled to Albany. *Albany Evening Times* (October 8, 1866): "There was great excitement among the colored population of our city, yesterday, on the occasion of the base-ball match at the Parade Ground, between the National Excelsiors, of Philadelphia, and the bachelors of this city. A large number of cable people of both sexes were present to witness it. The game was won by the Philadelphians." Several of the club's players joined the Pythians, including George Howard Wilson, Jessie Glascow, Joshua Adkins, Frank Jones, Henry Price, Harry J. Clark and Pliny L. Locke. In 1875, they traveled to Baltimore where the Atlantics met them at Newington Park. In 1879, the organization returned to Brooklyn where the players played the Unique Club.

SOURCES: "Advertisements," *Philadelphia (PA) Christian Recorder*, Feb 19, 1866; "Concert of the Excelsior Base Ball Club," *Philadelphia Christian Recorder*, Jun 1, 1866; "An Acknowledgment," *Philadelphia Christian Recorder*, Jun 23, 1866; "City and Vicinity," *Albany (NY) Evening Journal*, Sep 27, 1866; "Base Ball," *Utica (NY) Daily Standard*, Oct 5, 1866; "City and Vicinity," *Albany Evening Journal*, Sep 27, 1866; "Base Ball Matches," *Syracuse (NY) Daily Standard*, Oct 4, 1866; "Base Ball," *Albany Evening Journal*, Oct 5, 1866; "Base Ball," *Albany Evening Journal*, Oct 6, 1866; "Base Ball," *Albany (NY) Evening Times*, Oct 8, 1866; "Various Organizations of Colored People," *Philadelphia (PA) Evening Telegraph*, Mar 30, 1867; "Base Ball Matters," *Washington (DC) National Republican*, Sep 2, 1867; "The National Game," *New York (NY) Herald*, Oct 4, 1867; "State Items," *Syracuse Daily Standard*, Oct 10, 1867; "City Intelligence," *Philadelphia (PA) Inquirer*, Sep 13, 1870; "Base Ball," *Baltimore (MD) Herald*, Jul 15, 1875; "Base Ball," *New York (NY) Clipper*, Feb 21, 1880.

Olive Cricket Club (Philadelphia, PA; 1850s–1860s). Organizer(s): John R. Kennedy and Francis "Frank" Wood; Fielding Butler, James P. Clay, James H. Francis and William H. Swann.

The Olive Cricket Club organized in the 1850s. *Philadelphia Times* (January 30, 1887): "Before the war the favorite game with the colored youths was cricket. There were three clubs in the city, the Olive, Metamora, and Diligents." *New York Anglo-African* (October 29, 1859): "We, the first eleven of the Olive Cricket Club, do hereby challenge any other eighteen cricketeers of Philadelphia to play a game of cricket. All communications to be addressed to Francis Wood." Many of the club members later formed the Philadelphia Pythian, Brown, and National Excelsior B.B.C.s.

SOURCES: "Miscellaneous," *New York (NY) Anglo-African*, Oct 29, 1859; "Miscellaneous," *New York Anglo-African*, Nov 5, 1859; "Special Notices," *New York Anglo-African*, Feb 25, 1860; "Notice," *New York Anglo-African*, Jun 2, 1860; "Black Ball Players," *Philadelphia (PA) Times*, Jan 30, 1887.

Orion Base Ball Club (Philadelphia, PA; 1870s–1880s). Organizer(s): John S. Lang and Charles Jones; Julius Forbes.

The Orion B.B.C. organized in the 1870s, played black and white nines. *Philadelphia Times* (June 24, 1882): "The greatest novelty of the age and the first appearance in ten years of the famous champion colored club Orion." They played against the Long Branch Washingtons, hotel waiters, for the black championship. *New York Herald* (July 21, 1882): "The Orions of Philadelphia and the Washingtons of Long Branch contested for the colored championship yesterday afternoon at the Polo Ground. There were about five hundred spectators present. The game was about equal to the average amateur playing. It was closely contested, however, and resulted in a well-earned victory for the Orions, who took the lead in the first inning and maintained it throughout, with the single exception of the sixth inning when the

score was tied." They developed a rivalry with the Hartville club, a white organization. *The Philadelphia Sporting Life* (August 13, 1883): "At Hartville yesterday witnessed the game between the Orion colored club of Philadelphia and the Hartville. The colored boys out batted and out-fielded the Hartville everywhere, ending with a solid defeat for the Hartville's." *The Philadelphia Times* (August 3, 1884): "Seven hundred people witnessed the game between the Somerset and Orion (colored) Club, yesterday at Somerset Park. The score was Somerset, 13; Orion, 8." *The Philadelphia Times* (June 14, 1885): "The Orions, colored champions, defeated the Quaker City, with Lotz pitching, at the Athletic grounds on Friday. Score, 11 to 8." Several Orions played joined Philadelphia's Cuban Giants team in 1885. The Orions reorganized in the 1890s.

SOURCES: "Base Ball," *Trenton (NJ) Sentinel*, Jun 24, 1882; "Amusements," *Philadelphia (PA) Times*, Jul 16, 1882; "Notes," *Philadelphia Times*, Jul 19, 1882; "Ball and Bat," *Philadelphia Times*, Jul 20, 1882; "The Black Boys Badly Beaten," *New York (NY) Herald*, Jul 21, 1882; "An Amusing Base Ball Game," *New York (NY) Times*, Jul 21, 1882; "Saratoga Gossip," *New York (NY) Globe*, Jul 7, 1883; "The Actives vs. the Colored Champions of the World," *Reading (PA) Eagle*, Jul 28, 1882; "The Colored Club Defeated," *Philadelphia (PA) Press*, Aug 8, 1882; "The Colored Boys Knocked Out of Time," *New York Herald*, Sep 17, 1882; "Base Ball News," *New York Herald*, Sep 11, 1882; "The Orions Win the Colored Championship," *New York Herald*, Sep 13, 1882; "Base Ball," *New York (NY) Truth*, Sep 13, 1882; "South Chester Items," *Chester (PA) Times*, Oct 19, 1882; "Base Ball," *Washington (DC) Evening Star*, Jun 6, 1883; "In and About Chester," *Chester Times*, Jun 8, 1883; "In and About Chester," *Chester Times*, Jun 12, 1883; "Games Elsewhere," *Trenton (NJ) Evening Times*, Jun 24, 1883; "Black Superior to White," *Philadelphia (PA) Record*, Jul 8, 1883; "Base Ball," *Trenton Evening Times*, July 1, 1883; "Hartville Defeats the Colored Champions," *Record*, July 17, 1883; "Hartville Again Defeats the Orion," *Philadelphia Record*, Jul 20, 1883; *Bridgeton (NJ) Evening News*, Jul 21, 1883; "Base Ball," *Harrisburg (PA) Patriot*, Jul 30, 1883; "Sporting Notes," *Philadelphia Record*, Aug 1, 1883; *Bridgeton Evening News*, Aug 2, 1883; "From the Springs," *New York Globe*, Aug 4, 1883; "Saratoga Notes," *New York Globe*, Aug 11, 1883; "Miscellaneous," *Philadelphia (PA) Sporting Life*, Aug 13, 1883; "Orion Downs Hartville," *Philadelphia Record*, Aug 28, 1883; "The Wabash Defeated," *Chester Times*, Sep 1, 1883; "Orion Loses to August Flower," *Philadelphia Record*, Sep 4, 1883; "The Colored Championship," *New York Truth*, Sep 5, 1883; "Base Ball Notes," *Philadelphia Times*, Jun 15, 1884; "Base Ball Notes," *Philadelphia Times*, Aug 3, 1884; "Base Ball Notes," *Philadelphia Times*, Aug 26, 1884; "Base Ball Notes," *Philadelphia Times*, Sep 28, 1884; "Notes and Comments," *Philadelphia Sporting Life*, Jun 17, 1885; "Notes and Comments," *Philadelphia Sporting Life*, Jul 8, 1885; "Base Ball Notes," *Philadelphia Times*, Jul 12, 1885; "Notes and Comments," *Philadelphia Sporting Life*, Jul 12, 1885; "The Colored Curver," *Chester Times*, Jun 17, 1885; "A Victory for the Somersets," *Philadelphia Times*, Sep 1, 1885; "Base Ball Notes," *Chester Times*, Sep 25, 1885; "Games of the Amateurs," *Philadelphia Inquirer*, Jul 11, 1891; "Orions Whitewashed by Germantown," *Philadelphia Inquirer*, Aug 4, 1891; "Among the Amateurs," *Philadelphia Inquirer*, Aug 7, 1891; "The Colored Orions Win," *Philadelphia Inquirer*, Aug 22, 1891; "Colored Orions Again Defeated," *Philadelphia Inquirer*, Aug 29, 1891; "Chester, 55; Orions, 13," *Philadelphia (PA) Inquirer*, Aug 6, 1893.

Page Fence Giants Base Ball Club (Philadelphia, PA; 1890s)

The Page Fence B.B.C. organized in the 1890s, played black and white teams. *Philadelphia Inquirer* (September 17, 1899): "Wyoming easily defeated the Page Fence Giants, a colored team, in a heavy hitting game at Broadway and Jackson Streets, the features of which were the pitching of McSorley and the batting of Wyoming, in which Davis and Sharp excelled, while Severson fielded poorly, with the exception of Cummings."

SOURCES: "Wyoming an Easy Winner," *Philadelphia (PA) Inquirer*, Sep 17, 1899; "Wyoming's Walk Over," *Philadelphia Inquirer*, Sep 19, 1899.

Pythian Base Ball Club (Philadelphia, PA; 1860s–1880s). Organizer(s): James Whipper Purnell (1866–1869).

The Pythian B.B.C. organized in the 1860s, played white and black nines. The Pythians, organized by Octavius Catto, grew to over 70 members. *Philadelphia Evening Telegraph* (March 30, 1867): "There are two Base Ball Clubs, the Excelsior and Pythian, both of which are successful in operation, the former [Excelsior] having the reputation of being the best colored club in the country." The nine played white (Olympics and City Items) and black clubs of PA (Actives, National Excelsiors, and Monrovias), NJ (Blue Sky and Resolutes), MD (L'Ouvertures), Washington, D.C. (Mutuals and Alerts), NY (Uniques and Monitors), and IL (Uniques). *Philadelphia Inquirer* (September 20, 1871): "Yesterday afternoon a match game of baseball was played on the grounds at Twenty-fifth and Jefferson streets, between the Pythian Club, of this city, and the Unique, of Chicago. These clubs are colored organizations. The former is champion of the East and the latter champion of the West. Although the score was large the game was well played throughout. The fielding of the Unique was very good, as was the batting of the Pythian." The Pythians joined the National Colored Base Ball League. *Inquirer* (December 4, 1886): "The Pythian Club, of this city, has a large following, its stockholders are among the best colored people of the city. The club will have new grounds in West Philadelphia. Gilbert Ball is president and Herman Close manager. The players so far signed are as follows: James George Jackson, William Woods, Robert Still, Joseph Still, Charles P. Stinson, Walter James, John Vactor, York Hargett, C. H. Norwood, James O. Turner, James Aylor, John Stinson, Javan Emory, Gus Matthews and Norwood Turner." The team reorganized. *Philadelphia Record* (May 8, 1887): "The Pythian (Colored League) Club, of this city, has reorganized, and Gill Ball, John Brown and John Goodall are no longer connected to it. President Brown of the National Colored League has recognized the reorganized club, and Manager Still has reengaged all of the old players. The club played at Baltimore last Thursday and Friday under the new management, and will play championship games on the Athletic ball grounds in this city all week, meeting the Lord Baltimore Club on Monday and Tuesday, the Keystone, of Pittsburgh, on Wednesday and Thursday, and the Resolute, of Boston, on Friday and Saturday." In an exhibition contest, prior to the beginning of the league, the Pythians played the Scott nine, another black team. *Philadelphia Record* (May 14, 1887): "The Wilmington Club (colored) failed to show up in the city yesterday, so the Pythian Colored League Club played a picked nine styled the Scott team, and won by the score of 9 to 6." While the league collapsed that same year, the nine reorganized in 1888. *Philadelphia Times*: "The Pythian colored nine, who are matched to play the Cuban Giants for $1000 a side on July 15, will play the Frankford Club at Gloucester today."

SOURCES: "Pythian Baseball Club; Scorecards" (Roll No. 8). *American Negro Historical Society Collection: Historical Society Microfilm Edition*; "The Banneker Institute Celebration," *Philadelphia (PA) Inquirer*, Nov 16, 1860; "Proceedings," *Philadelphia (PA) Christian Recorder*, Aug 16, 1866; "City and Vicinity," *Albany (NY) Evening Journal*, Sep 27, 1866; "Base Ball Matches," *Syracuse (NY) Daily Standard*, Oct 4, 1866; "Base Ball," *Albany Evening Journal*, Oct 5, 1866; "Base Ball," *Albany Evening Journal*, Oct 6, 1866; "Various Organizations of Colored People," *Philadelphia (PA) Evening Telegraph*, Mar 30, 1867; "Base Ball Between Colored Clubs," *Washington (DC) National Republican*, Jul 9, 1867; "Base Ball Matters," *Washington National Republican*, Sep 2, 1867; *Charleston (SC) Courier*, May 27, 1868; "Removal of the Aldermen," *Charleston (SC) News*, May 27, 1868; "City Council," *Charleston News*, Jun 3, 1868; "Friendly Union Society," *Charleston News*, May 8, 1869; "Base Ball," *Philadelphia Inquirer*, Aug 14, 1871; "Base Ball," *Philadelphia Inquirer*, Sep 20, 1871; "Assassination," *Huntington (PA) Journal*, Oct 18, 1871; "Base Ball," *Washington National Republican*, Oct 18, 1879; "Colored League Representatives," *Philadelphia Inquirer*, Dec 1, 1886; "Colored Base Ball League," *Philadelphia (PA) Times*, Dec 4, 1886; "Black Ball Players," *Philadelphia Times*, Jan 30, 1887; "Colored Players," *Philadelphia Times*, Apr 3, 1887; "Pythian vs. University," *Philadelphia Times*, Apr 10, 1887; "Pythians and Wilkes-Barre," *Philadelphia Inquirer*, May 3, 1887; "Reorganization of the Pythian Club," *Philadelphia (PA) Record*, May 8, 1887; "Colored Men at Base Ball," *Philadelphia (PA) North American*, May 10, 1887; "Pythian 26; Lord Baltimore 6," *Philadelphia Record*, May 10, 1887; "Pythian 16; Lord Baltimore 9," *Philadelphia Record*, May 11, 1887; "Base Ball Pickups," *Philadelphia Record*, May 14, 1887; "The Colored League," *Philadelphia Inquirer*, Mar 14, 1887; "Pythian, 9; Scott, 6," *Record*, May 15, 1887; "The Colored Clubs," *Philadelphia Inquirer*, Mar 17, 1887; "Pythian 9; Gorham 8," *Philadelphia Record*, May 17, 1887; "Base Ball Notes," *Philadelphia Times*, Jul 4, 1888.

Williams Base Ball Club (Philadelphia, PA; 1870s). Organizer(s): John Cannon, Corbin Taylor, James Fields Needham and Jefferson Cavens.

The Williams B.B.C. organized in the 1870s, played black organizations. The Williams Club of the Seventh Ward, named after black politician Samuel Williams, was managed by former members of the Pythian Base Ball organization, including John Cannon, Corbin Taylor, James Fields Needham and Jefferson Cavens. *Washington National Republican* (August 26, 1875): "The Williams Club, of Philadelphia, vs. Manhattans, of Washington, DC, on Friday, August 27, 1875. The Williams Club are the Champions of the North, and the Manhattans are the champions of the South, a lively contest may be expected on the Olympic Grounds." *Philadelphia Times* (August 27, 1875): "In Washington, D.C., yesterday, the Williams Club, of Philadelphia, and the Alert, of Washington, both colored clubs, played, the Williams being on tour, and the Williams won by a score of 24 to 11." *Times* (August 31, 1875): "In Baltimore yesterday the Williams Club, of Philadelphia, defeated the Excelsior, of Baltimore, by 19 to 3. Both clubs are colored." *Wilmington News Journal* (August 18, 1876): "An interesting game of ball was played at the Adams Street grounds between the Independent nine of this city, and the Williams club, of Philadelphia. Both clubs played well and but few errors on either side were made. The Williams nine is considered one of the best clubs of Philadelphia, but notwithstanding, the Independents gave them considerable trouble. The score was 15 to 7 in favor of the visitors." Newspapers later reminisced about the team's exploits. *Times* (July 20, 1882): "In 187[5], the Williams Club, of this city, was considered the champion colored nine of the country and attracted large audiences. The Mutual, of Washington, a rival colored organization, visited this city in that year and played the Philadelphia nine. At the end of the third inning the score was 3 to nothing, in favor of the visitors, but towards the close the home nine did some terrific batting and won by a score of 17 to 6. The next day the Mutual played the Williams nine and the latter proved victorious, but the Washingtonians claimed that [William H.] Craver, the well-known player, who umpired, robbed them of the game."

SOURCES: "About Town," *Philadelphia (PA) Inquirer*, Aug 24, 1874; "Sports," *Brooklyn (NY) Daily Union*, Aug 27, 1874; "Sporting Notes," *Philadelphia (PA) Times*, Aug 27, 1874; "Amusements," *Washington (DC) National Republican*, Aug 26, 1875; "Sporting Corner," *Philadelphia Times*, Aug 27, 1875; "Base Ball Notes," *Philadelphia Times*, Aug 31, 1875; "The Ball Field," *Wilmington (DE) News Journal*, Aug 9, 1876; *Wilmington (DE) Commercial*, Aug 16, 1876; "The Ball Field," *Wilmington News Journal*, Aug 18, 1876; "Appeals to Voters," *Philadelphia Times*, Feb 17, 1877; "The Base Ball and Bat," *Philadelphia Times*, Jul 20, 1882.

Pinkney Giants Base Ball Club (Philadelphia, PA; 1890s–1900s)

The Pinkney Giants B.B.C. organized in the 1890s, played black and white and teams. *Philadelphia Inquirer* (August 16, 1896): "The G. C. and H. played two games this afternoon, meeting their first defeat this season, the Pinkney Giants, of Philadelphia, winning a game 8 to 7." *Inquirer* (June 3, 1897): "Bridgeton club were winners over the Pinkney Giants this afternoon."

SOURCES: *Philadelphia (PA) Inquirer*, Jun 2, 1896; "Pinkney Giants Were Easy," *Philadelphia Inquirer*, June 3, 1896; "The Coming Greats," *Philadelphia Inquirer*, Jul 21, 1896; "Young America, 15; Pinkney, 8," *Philadelphia Inquirer*, Jul 24, 1896; "Cape May Court House Wins," *Philadelphia Inquirer*, Jul 26, 1896; "The Coming Greats," *Inquirer*, Aug. 2, 1896; "Germantown 16; Anchor, 8," *Philadelphia Inquirer*, Aug 4, 1896; "The C. and C. H. Play Two Games," *Philadelphia Inquirer*, Aug 16, 1896; "Cape May C. H. and Pinkney Giants," *Philadelphia Inquirer*, Aug 23, 1896; "Clintons, 19; Pinkneys, 10," *Philadelphia Inquirer*, Sep 13, 1896; "Pinkney Giants, 11; Vineland, 10," *Philadelphia Inquirer*, Sep 27, 1896; "Amateur Base Ball Notes," *Philadelphia Inquirer*, Mar 14, 1897; "Wyoming and Giants," *Philadelphia Inquirer*, May 27, 1897; "Easy for Bridgeton," *Philadelphia Inquirer*, Jun 3, 1897; *Philadelphia Inquirer*, Jun 15, 1898; "Independence Wins Two Games," *Philadelphia Inquirer*, Jun 24, 1898; "Easy for North Philadelphia," *Philadelphia Inquirer*, Jul 14, 1898; "Vineland Wins an Interesting Game," *Philadelphia (PA) Times*, Jul 9, 1899; "Among the Amateurs," *Philadelphia Inquirer*, Jul 31, 1899; "Made Many Errors," *Philadelphia Inquirer*, Jun 22, 1900.

Acme Giants Base Ball Club (Pittsburgh, PA; 1890s). Organizer(s): Charles Jackson.

The Acme Giants B.B.C. organized in the 1890s, played black and white nines. *Canton Repository* (May 30, 1899): "A small crowd saw the Acme Giants of Pittsburg defeat the Cantons in an exciting game and close contest at Mahaffey Park, Tuesday afternoon. The Giants won the game by the score of 4 to 3, but the runs were secured as a result of costly errors. Frank Miller pitched for the Giants and has a pretzel delivery of a puzzling kind. He held the cantons down to four hits. Tuesday afternoon's contest will decide the championship series of three games."

SOURCES: "Base Ball Notes," *New York (NY) Sun*, Apr 20, 1899; "Giants at Homestead," *Pittsburgh (PA) Press*, May 9, 1899; "Our Boys Defeat Acme Giants," *Pittsburgh (PA) Post*, May 14, 1899; *Wheeling (WVA) Intelligencer*, Apr 29, 1899; "Defeated the Giants," *Pittsburgh (PA) Commercial Gazette*, May 11, 1899; "Acme Giants Defeated," *Pittsburgh Post*, May 14, 1899; "Canton Team on Tour," *Canton (OH) Repository*, May 21, 1899; "Dead Easy," *Canton Repository*, May 22, 1899; "Canton Lost," *Canton Repository*, May 30, 1899; "Canton Wins Two in Three," *Canton Repository*, May 31, 1899; "Other Saturday Games," *Pittsburgh Commercial Gazette*, Jun 5, 1899; "Acme Giants the Winners," *Pittsburgh Post*, Jun 18, 1899; "Acme Giants Get a Drubbing," *Pittsburgh Post*, Jun 23, 1899; "The Amateur Players," *Pittsburgh (PA) Post-Gazette*, Sep 14, 1899.

Browns Base Ball Club (Pittsburgh, PA; 1880s). Organizer(s): Walter S. Brown.

The Browns B.B.C. organized in the 1880s, played black nines. *Cleveland Gazette* (August 7, 1886): "The Pittsburgh Browns Base Ball Club defeated a picked nine, Aug. 2, score 7 to 6." A rivalry developed between WA and Pittsburg. *Pittsburgh Post-Gazette* (August 3, 1886): "The feature of the day was a game between the Pittsburgh Browns and a picked nine. Both teams were colored. The friends of each team had high hopes of victory for their side. Five innings were played when the score stood 7 to 6 in favor of the Browns." *Cleveland Gazette* (September 18, 1886): "The Pittsburg Browns, Base Ball Club, play the Washington Blues, of Washington DC, at Liberty Park, East End Saturday, September 18. This will be a great game as both clubs are evenly matched." The team participated in Emancipation Day festivities. *Pittsburgh Post* (July 4, 1887): "The Homestead club defeated the Pittsburgh Browns on Saturday by 12 to 11."

SOURCES: "Notes and Comments," *Philadelphia (PA) Sporting Life*, Mar 10, 1886; "Pittsburgh-Allegheny," Cleveland *(OH) Gazette*, Jul 17, 1886; "Colored People at Play," *Pittsburgh (PA) Post-Gazette*, Aug 3, 1886; "From the Twin Cities," *Cleveland Gazette*, Aug 7, 1886; "Notes," *Pittsburgh (PA) Post*, Sep 16, 1886; "Pittsburgh and Allegheny," *Cleveland Gazette*, Sep 18, 1886; "Base Ball Notes," *Pittsburgh Post*, Jul 4, 1887; "They Feel Aggrieved," *Cleveland Gazette*, Jun 9, 1888.

Cedar Rapids Base Ball Club (Pittsburgh, PA; 1870s). Organizer(s): B. S. Gray.

The Cedar Rapids B.B.C. organized in 1870, played white and black nines. *Pittsburgh Gazette* (May 23, 1870): "The Oceola (white) and the Rapid (colored) base-ball clubs play a game at Union Park next Saturday afternoon. The novelty of a game between white and colored base-ballists will no doubt attract a large crowd to witness it." *New York Clipper* (June 11, 1870): "The Oceolas, a white club, defeated the Rapids, colored, at Allegheny, Pennsylvania, on the 4th inst., by a tally of 10 to 6." The Rapids toured NY (Lockport, Buffalo, and Niagara Falls). Their won-lost record against black clubs, including the Lockport "Artics", Niagara "Blue Flies", Niagara "Shoe Flies", and Buffalo Clod Hoppers"—4 and 1.

SOURCES: "Base Ball," *New York (NY) Clipper*. Apr. 23, 1870; "Base Ball," *Pittsburgh (PA) Gazette*, May 23, 1870; "Base Ball Notes," *Pittsburgh (PA) Commercial*, May 23, 1870; "Oceola vs. Rapids," *Pittsburgh Commercial*, May 25, 1870; "City Matters," *Pittsburgh Commercial*, Jun 4, 1870; "On the Half Shell," *New York Clipper*, Jun 11, 1870; "Games," *Commercial Cincinnati (OH) Tribune*, Aug 10, 1870; "Base Ball," *Pittsburgh Gazette*, Sep 11, 1871.

Colored Barber Base Ball Club (Pittsburgh, PA; 1870s–1880s). Organizer(s): George D. Sherrow.

The Colored Barber B.B.C. organized in the 1880s, if not earlier. They played black and white nines. *Pittsburgh Post-Gazette* (June 29, 1877): "The barbers club (colored) challenge George Vollman's nine to play them a match the 4th of next month (July) for the championship." *Post-Gazette*: "The colored barbers, of this city, challenge the Allegheny white barbers to play them a match game on the next Wednesday afternoon." *Pittsburgh Commercial Gazette* (June 11, 1877): "The Colored Barbers challenge the German Barbers to play match game on Decoration Day." *Commercial Gazette* (July 5, 1882): "The Mutual Base Ball Club (colored), formerly the Barber Base Ball Club, defeated the colored club of East … on Thursday by a score of 29 to 16."

SOURCES: "General Notes," *Pittsburgh (PA) Post-Gazette*, Jun 11, 1877; "General Notes," *Pittsburgh Post-Gazette*, Jun 29, 1877; "Tips," *Pittsburgh (PA) Commercial Gazette*, Jun 22, 1881; "Sporting Notes,"

Pittsburgh Commercial Gazette, Jun 29, 1882; "Sporting Events," *Pittsburgh Commercial Gazette,* Jul 5, 1882.

Cuban Stars Base Ball Club (Pittsburgh, PA; 1890s). Organizer(s): W. T. Miller and E. Randall.

The Cuban Stars B.B.C. organized in the 1890s. The Cuban Stars played black and white teams. *Cleveland Gazette* (May 30, 1891): "The Cuban Stars B. B. C. will play two games at Phillipsburg, with a Tri-State league team. Battery in the morning Page and Stoner; afternoon Lee and Jones. Captain W. T. Miller expects to capture at least one game from these heavy hitters."

SOURCES: "The Coming Players," *Pittsburgh (PA) Dispatch,* May 24, 1891; "Each Received $15, 000," *Cleveland (OH) Gazette,* May 30, 1891.

Jolly 12 Base Ball Club (Pittsburgh, PA; 1890s). Organizer(s): W. T. Miller and Cyclone Pearce.

The Jolly 12 B.B.C. organized in the 1890s. *Cleveland Gazette* (April 3, 1893): "The Jolly twelve with their dark blue uniforms, dark stockings and belts made a fine appearance. Captain W. Miller and Cyclone Pearce were about the happiest persons on the grounds after the game. The boys in both teams played well say Frank Miller, the umpire. The score was 23 to 13 in favor of the Jolly 12 club." *Gazette* (June 17, 1893): There will be a championship game of baseball between the Jolly 12 and Y.M.S.C. for a handsome silk flag and banner, to be presented by the 'Gilt Edge' and 'Our Boys' clubs."

SOURCES: "Twin City Topics," *Cleveland (OH) Gazette,* Apr 3, 1893; "A Gala Day," *Cleveland Gazette,* Jun 17, 1893.

Keystone Base Ball Club (Pittsburgh, PA; 1880s–1900s). Organizer(s): Walter S. Brown, Milton Ricks, Charles H. Nelson, Charles H. O'Donnell, William Hauger and M. A. Spriggs; James Hackett, Thomas White, S. L. Morton and Walter S. Brown; William Stanard, J. W. Gatewood and Charles G. Armstrong; Thomas White and Jerry Thompson; Weldy W. Walker, William Stanard, Albert Douglass and David Markowitz; Ulysses Mosby; F. Tascoe and Thomas White; and William Stanard.

The Keystone B.B.C. organized in the 1880s. The Keystones played against white and black nines. In 1887, the joined the National Colored Base Ball League. *Pittsburgh Post* (May 18, 1887): "About 200 people witnessed the game [between the Lord Baltimores and Pittsburgh Keystones], which was exceedingly well-played on the part of the Keystones. Both sides made a few runs on passed balls and wild pitches, but that only raised the enthusiasm of the colored spectators." Following the league's collapse, the team took on an independent status. *Post* (October 27, 1887): "The Keystones beat the Cuban Giants yesterday in one of the first ball games that has been seen at Recreation Park for a long time. The score—3 to 2, shows that the playing was good. About 100 people were present. The fielding of the Keystones was excellent. The only made one fielding error. The fielding of the Giants was also good, but they failed to connect with [Frank] Miller, who pitched a great game." *Wheeling Register* (April 20, 1888): "The game of baseball yesterday between the home club and colored Keystones, of Pittsburgh, yesterday afternoon, on the home grounds, was full of fun and kicking. Pete Davis played in the Keystones yesterday. He broke a bat and made a base hit, and received a cheer every time he went to bat." In 1888, the Keystones competed against Trenton's Cuban Giants, NY's Gorhams, and Norfolk's Red Stockings in a colored championship tournament. *Cleveland Gazette* (June 2, 1888): "Mr. Weldy W. Walker, of Steubenville, Ohio, is making quite a success of the Keystone Base Ball Club. The club opened its season as an independent club, and has lost only one game in ten. The following well known men constitute the club: John

Brady, Charles Bell, Harvey Roy, Sol White, Thomas White, William Stanard, Henry Gant, Frank Miller, Ross Garrison, Charles Brown, James Mason, Albert Douglas, and Weldy Walker. The batteries are: Frank Miller and Weldy Walker, John Brady and Charles Bell, and Charles Brown and Harvey Roy." *New Castle News* (July 6, 1892): "a good game of ball was played yesterday afternoon between the Keystones, of Pittsburgh and the Harrison and Reids of this city. The game was hotly contested from the first, but the Pittsburg team won the battle. The New Castle Club was organized but recently and have not had the advantage of much practice, which accounts for the low score on their side. Another game will soon be played, when the boys will be in better shape." They also played against white teams. *Cleveland Leader* (July 6, 1888): "Today the Keystones put on their batting clothes, and pounded Beals, Beaver Fall's crack pitcher, all over the field, giving the outfielders plenty of exercise chasing the leather. Miller, of the Keystones, was very effective up to the eighth inning, when it was apparent he purposely eased up, allowing the visitors to make five runs." *Gazette* (May 7, 1892): "The Keystone Base Ball Club was defeated for the first time on last Saturday by the Homesteads. The game was witnessed by over 3,000 people. Robinson and Lyons, battery of the Keystones, acquitted themselves admirably. Score: 4 to 3." *Post* (July 8, 1895): "The Keystone colored club played at Homestead and won a victory over the team of that place, who thought the colored boys an easy mark. The game was replete with good plays." *Post* (September 3, 1896): "The Keystones locked horns with the home team this afternoon, and defeated them in a hot contest before a large crowd. The colored boys put up a very fast article of ball." *Pittsburgh Post* (June 20, 1897): "The hottest game of the season was played here today between locals and the Keystone colored club of Pittsburgh, the latter winning by a score of 9 to 8." *Post* (June 17, 1900): "The Keystone club, of Pittsburgh, defeated the Mars team here this afternoon in an exciting six-inning game by a score of 6 to 5."

SOURCES: "From the Twin Cities," *Cleveland (OH) Gazette,* Oct 2, 1886; "The Official Roster," *St. Louis (MO) Sporting News,* Jan 1, 1887; "The Colored League," Pittsburgh (PA *Commercial Gazette,* May 17, 1887; "The Colored League," *Pittsburgh Commercial Gazette,* May 18, 1887; "The Colored League," *Pittsburgh Commercial Gazette,* May 19, 1887; "The Colored League," *Pittsburgh Commercial Gazette,* May 21, 1887; *Wheeling (WVA) Register,* Sep 29, 1887; "Today's Game," *Wheeling Register,* Oct 1, 1887; "Yesterday's Game," *Wheeling Register,* Oct 2, 1887; "Beat the Cuban Giants," *Pittsburgh (PA) Post,* Oct 27, 1887; "Sporting Notes," *Pittsburgh Commercial Gazette,* Apr 10, 1888; "Sporting Notes," *Pittsburgh Commercial Gazette,* Apr 13, 1888; "Sporting Notes," *Pittsburgh Commercial Gazette,* Apr 20, 1888; "Twin City Topics," *Cleveland Gazette,* Jun 2, 1888; "Yesterday's Game," *Wheeling Register,* Apr 20, 1888; "Wheeling 16-Keystones 3," *Cleveland (OH) Plain Dealer,* Apr 20, 1888; "Sporting Notes," *Pittsburgh Commercial Gazette,* Apr 26, 1888; "The Colored League," *New York (NY) Sun,* May 29, 1888; "Sporting Notes," *Pittsburgh Commercial Gazette,* Apr 30, 1888; "The Colored League," *New York Sun,* May 29, 1888; "Sporting Notes," *Pittsburgh Commercial Gazette,* May 30, 1888; "Twin City Topics," *Cleveland Gazette,* Jun 2, 1888; "The Keystones' Tour," *Pittsburgh Commercial Gazette,* Jun 28, 1888; "The Keystones Ahead," *Cleveland (OH) Leader,* Jul 7, 1888; "Sporting Notes," *Pittsburgh Commercial Gazette,* Jun 18, 1888; "The Games at Steubenville," *Cleveland Leader,* Jul 1, 1888; "Our Boys Win," *Cleveland Leader,* Jul 6, 1888; "Our Boys Win Again," *Cleveland Leader,* Jul 7, 1888; "The Colored Ball Tournament," *Pittsburgh Commercial Gazette,* Aug 1, 1888; "Sporting Notes," *Pittsburgh Commercial Gazette,* May 23, 1889; "Colored Champions Beaten," *Pittsburgh Commercial Gazette,* Jun 20, 1889; "Sporting Notes," *Pittsburgh Commer-*

cial Gazette, Jun 29, 1889; "The Scotts Win," *Pittsburgh (PA) Dispatch*, Jul 2, 1889; "Sporting Notes," *Pittsburgh Commercial Gazette*, Jul 7, 1889; "Won a Good Game," *Pittsburgh Dispatch*, Jul 11, 1889; "Had an Easy Time," *Pittsburgh Commercial Gazette*, Jul 13, 1889; "A Fine Game," *Pittsburgh Dispatch*, Jun 16, 1889; "Very One-Sided," *Pittsburgh Dispatch*, Jul 21, 1889; "The Keystones Were Easy," *Pittsburgh Commercial Gazette*, Aug 3, 1889; "The Keystones Again," *Pittsburgh Dispatch*, Aug 25, 1889; "News and Comments," *Philadelphia Sporting Life*, Apr 4, 1892; "Zion Conference," *Cleveland Gazette*, May 7, 1892; "Harrison and Reid Beaten," *Pittsburgh Dispatch*, Jul 1, 1892; "An Exciting Game," *New Castle (PA) News*, Jul 6, 1892; "The Champion City," *Detroit (MI) Plaindealer*, Jul 15, 1892; "The Keystones in Salem," *New Brunswick (NJ) Daily News* (New Brunswick, NJ), July 18, 1892; "Base Ball," *Butler (PA) Citizen*, Aug 4, 1894; "Won By Sharon," *Cleveland Leader*, Aug 25, 1894; "Keystones Victorious," *Pittsburgh Post*, Jul 8, 1895; "Base Ball News," *Smethport (PA) McKean County Miner*, Jul 19, 1895; "Keystone Defeats Kensington," *Pittsburgh Post*, Sep 3, 1896; "To Be Played by Amateurs," *Pittsburgh (PA) Post*, May 15, 1897; "Hot Stuff at Evans City," *Pittsburgh Post*, Jun 20, 1897; "Keystones Got One Hit," *Pittsburgh Post*, Jun 12, 1898; "Keystones Get A Beating," *Pittsburgh Post*, Sep 4, 1898; "Famous Keystones Reorganized," *Pittsburgh Post*, Mar 15, 1900; "Keystone Win at Mars," *Pittsburgh Post*, Jun 17, 1900; "Keystone Team Defeated," *Pittsburgh Post*, Aug 12, 1900.

Stars Base Ball Club (Pittsburgh, PA; 1880s)

The Stars B.B.C. organized in the 1880s. The Pittsburgh Stars played black teams. *Cleveland Gazette* (August 30, 1884): "The Unions defeated the Pittsburgh Stars Saturday, by a score of 10 to 4."

SOURCES: "Local Notes," *Cleveland (OH) Gazette*, Aug 30, 1884.

Western Base Ball Club (Pittsburgh, PA; 1880s)

The Western B.B.C. organized in the 1880s. *New York Clipper* (February 10, 1883): "The Western Club, of Pittsburg, which claims to be the champion colored organization of Western Pennsylvania, will put the following team in the field next season: Keys, pitcher; Stoner, catcher; Butler, Henson and Anderson on the bases; Daisy, shortstop, Boyle, Stratton, and Askins in the outfield; Taper, change pitcher; Allen, change catcher; and Wilson and W. C. Lee, substitutes. The Westerns would like to hear from J. H. Dudley of Richmond, Virginia, in reference to the Colored League."

SOURCES: "Commercial Nines," *New York (NY) Clipper*, Feb 10, 1883.

Y.M.S.C. Base Ball Club (Pittsburgh, PA; 1890s)

The Y.M.S.C. B.B.C. organized in the 1890s. *Cleveland Gazette* (June 17, 1893): There will be a championship game of baseball between the Jolly 12 and Y.M.S.C. for a handsome silk flag and banner, to be presented by the 'Gilt Edge' and 'Our Boys' clubs."

SOURCES: "Twin City Topics," *Gazette* (Cleveland, OH), Apr. 3, 1893; "A Gala Day," *Gazette*, June 17, 1893.

Active Base Ball Club (Pottsville, PA; 1880s)

The Active B.B.C. organized in the 1880s, played teams. *Reading Eagle* (August 13, 1882): "The Crescents, Reading's colored baseball club, will visit Pottsville tomorrow and play a colored club of that place." *Harrisburg Telegraph* (August 21, 1882): "The Actives, Pottsville's colored club, will play the Crescents, Reading's colored organization, on the Active Grounds, in this city tomorrow, commencing at 3:30 pm." *Telegraph* (September 20, 1882): "The Olympics—colored—of this city, played the Actives at Pottsville on Saturday, darkness putting an end to the game when the score was 17 to 17." *Telegraph* (September 22, 1882): "The Harrisburg Olympics defeated the Pottsville Actives yesterday in this city by a score of 36 to 6. Both clubs are colored."

SOURCES: *Reading (PA) Eagle*, Aug 13, 1882; "Base Ball Notes," *Reading Eagle*. Aug. 21, 1882; "Base Hits," *Harrisburg (PA) Telegraph*, Sep 18, 1882; "Base Ball," *Harrisburg Telegraph*, Sep 20, 1882; "Base Ball Notes," *Harrisburg Telegraph*, Sep 22, 1882.

Goodwill Base Ball Club (Pottsville, PA; 1860s)

The Goodwill B.B.C., of Reading, PA, organized in the 1860s. *Reading Times* (September 30, 1882): "The match game between the Goodwill Club, of Pottsville, and the Harmony, of this city, (colored organizations), on Thursday last, resulted in a victory for the former by a score of 51 to 29."

SOURCES: "Base Ball," *Reading (PA) Times*, Sep 27, 1869; "Base Ball," *Reading Times*, Sep 30, 1869.

Cuban Giants, Jr. Base Ball Club (Pottstown, PA; 1890s)

The Cuban Giants Jrs. B.B.C. organized in the 1890s, played white and black organizations. *Philadelphia Times*: "East Greenville played all around the Cuban Giants, Jrs., of Pottstown, today, and won both games with ease."

SOURCES: "Two for East Greenville," *Philadelphia (PA) Inquirer*, Sep 3, 1893; "East Greenville and Cuban Giants, Jrs.," *Philadelphia (PA) Times*, Sep 3, 1893.

Atlantic Base Ball Club (Reading, PA; 1870s)

The Atlantic B.B.C. organized in the 1870s, played against black and white clubs. *Reading Times* (July 27, 1875): "The Archer and Atlantic Base Ball Clubs of this city, met yesterday afternoon, at Bridgeport, beyond Charles Evans cemetery, and indulged in a friendly game, the Archer winning by a score of 10 to 4." In 1875, the Atlantics reorganized as Reading's Lincoln B.B.C.

SOURCES: "Montgomery Items," *Reading (PA) Times*, Aug 21, 1874; "Colored Base Ball Club," *Reading Times*, Aug 31, 1874; "Ball and Bat," *Reading Times*, Jul 27, 1875.

Colored Base Ball Club (Reading, PA; 1880s)

The Colored B.B.C. organized in the 1880s. The waiters developed a rivalry with black barbers. *Reading Eagle* (June 19, 1882): "Following is the score of the game played in the 6th Street Hollow yesterday between two nines of colored gentlemen."

SOURCES: "Colored Men in the Ball Field," *Reading (PA) Eagle*, Jun 9, 1882; "Base Ball Notes," *Reading Eagle*, Jun 19, 1882; "Shoemakersville," *Reading (PA) Times*, Jul 18, 1882.

Colored Barbers Base Ball Club (Reading, PA; 1880s)

The Colored Barbers B.B.C. organized in the 1880s, if not earlier. The barber nine developed a local rivalry with the black waiters. *Reading Eagle* (June 9, 1882): "Following is the score of a game played in the 6th Street hollow yesterday, between two nines of colored gentlemen. Score—Waiters, 12; Barbers, 9." *Reading Eagle* (June 19, 1882): "Following is the score of the game played in the 6th Street Hollow yesterday between two nines of colored gentlemen."

SOURCES: "Colored Men in the Ball Field," *Reading (PA) Eagle*, Jun 9, 1882; "Shoemakersville," *Reading (PA) Times*, Jul 18, 1882; "Base Ball Notes," *Reading (PA) Eagle*, Jun 19, 1882.

Crescent Base Ball Club (Reading, PA; 1880s). Organizer(s): Henry C. Nelson and Charles H. Walker.

The Crescent B.B.C. organized in 1882, played black and white nines. They played a road-home series with Pottsville's Active club, a black organization. The Crescents won the home contest by a score of 17 to 16; they lost the away game by a score of 24 to 22, complaining that the umpire cheated them. They played against a hotel waiter team. Reading and Harrisburg developed a black rivalry. *Harrisburg Telegraph* (August 23, 1882): "The Reading Crescents defeated the Olympics of this city, yesterday 13 to 7." They played another black club, the "Princetons." *Reading Times* (July 17, 1883): "The Crescent and Princeton Clubs, both colored, of this city, played a game of ball on the Active Grounds yesterday afternoon at half-past three o'clock. It was noted for the one-sided condition of the score at the close of the game, which lasted two hours. The battery and the fielding of Harry C. Nelson are worthy of special mention, and the 'colored Carroll' added new laurels to his crescent." In 1890, the Crescents played one of Norristown's three black teams. *Times* (August 23, 1890): "Yesterday afternoon the colored base-ball layers of Norristown came to Reading to play the Crescent Club, also composed of colored players. The visitors at once took the lead, and the game at no time was in doubt. Howard and Newkirk for the Crescents did their work well, and on the part of the visitors the catching of Harry Fisher was of gilt-edge order, he accepting seventeen out of eighteen chances."

Sources: "Colored Men in the Ball Field," *Reading (PA) Eagle*, Jun 9, 1882; "Base Ball Notes," *Reading Eagle*, Jun 19, 1882; *Reading Eagle*, Aug 13, 1882; "Harrisburg vs. Reading," *Harrisburg (PA) Patriot*, Oct 14, 1875; "Local Briefs," *Harrisburg Patriot*, Aug 13, 1882; "The Colored Troops," *Reading (PA) Times*, Aug 16, 1882; "Base Ball Notes," *Harrisburg Patriot*, Aug 21, 1882; "Colored Players Playing Base Ball," *Reading Times*, Aug 23, 1882; "What a Pottsville Paper Says About the Colored Folks' Base Ball Game," *Reading Times*, Aug 24, 1882; "Base Ball Notes," *Harrisburg Patriot*, Sep 2, 1882; "Base Ball," *Reading Times*, Sep 5, 1882; "Jottings," *Harrisburg (PA) Telegraph*, Sep 5, 1882; "Local Briefs," *Harrisburg Patriot*, Sep 5, 1882; "Short Notes," *Reading Times*, Jun 22, 1883; "Local Base Ball Notes," *Reading Times*, Jul 17, 1883; "Base Ball Notes," *Reading Times*, Aug 9, 1883; "Reading Squibs," *Harrisburg (PA) State Journal*, Aug 2, 1884; "Reading Squibs," *Harrisburg State Journal*, Aug 16, 1884; "Reading Squibs," *Harrisburg State Journal*, Dec 27, 1884; "Runs, Hits, Errors," *Reading Times*, Aug 6, 1890; "Crescent vs. Icicle," *Reading Times*, Aug 13, 1890; "The Colored Clubs Play," *Reading Times*, Aug 23, 1890; "Base Ball Notes," *Reading Eagle*, Aug 7, 1891; "Other Games," *Reading Eagle*, Aug 8, 1891.

Cuban Giants Base Ball Club (Reading, PA; 1890s)

The Cuban Giants B.B.C. organized in 1890, played black teams. *Reading Eagle* (August 7, 1891): "The waiters and barbers played a 10 inning game, resulting 13 to 8 in favor of the waiters."

Sources: "Base Ball Notes," *Reading (PA) Eagle*, Aug 7, 1891; "Other Games," *Reading Eagle*, Aug 8, 1891; "Sixteenth Successive Victory," *Reading (PA) Times*, Aug 8, 1891; *Reading Eagle*, May 24, 1892.

Excelsior Base Ball Club (Reading, PA; 1870s). Organizer(s): William and Aaron Still.

The Excelsior B.B.C. organized in 1872. William and Aaron Still, of Philadelphia relocated to Reading, and formed Reading's Excelsior Cornet Band and Excelsior B.B.C. Through their connections, the Excelsiors scheduled matches against Philadelphia's black clubs. *Reading Eagle* (August 14, 1872): "The Excelsior Club, of this city, played the Eldridge (also colored) of Philadelphia on Monday last. The former club were victorious by a score of 58 to 25."

Sources: "Grand Concert and Ball," *Reading (PA) Eagle*, Mar 5, 1872; "Base Ball," *Reading Eagle*, Aug 14, 1872.

Harmony Base Ball Club (Reading, PA; 1870s)

The Harmony B.B.C. organized in the 1870s. William and Aaron Still, of Philadelphia relocated to Reading, and helped to form Reading's Harmony B.B.C. *Reading Times* (July 8, 1871): "The match game between the Goodwill Club, of Pottsville, and the Harmony, of this

city, (colored organizations), on Thursday last, resulted in a victory for the former by a score of 51 to 29."

Sources: "Base Ball," *Reading (PA) Times*, Jul 8, 1871; "Base Ball," *Reading Times*, Jul 11, 1871; "Base Ball," *Reading Times*, Sep 27, 1871.

Keystone Base Ball Club (Reading, PA; 1870s)

The Keystone B.B.C. organized in the 1870s, played black nines.

Sources: "The Ball Season," *Reading (PA) Times*, Mar 12, 1875; "A Stabbing Affray," *Reading Times*, Mar 15, 1875; "The Bat and Ball Here and Elsewhere," *Reading Times*, Mar 23, 1875; "Base Ball," *Reading Times*, Sep 18, 1875; "The Actives Again Defeated," *Reading Times*, Sep 20, 1875.

Lincoln Base Ball Club (Reading, PA; 1870s)

The Lincoln B.B.C. organized in 1875, played black nines. *Harrisburg Patriot* (October 14, 1875): "This unusual match was made up between the Olympics, of Harrisburg, and the Lincoln Club, of Reading. Both nines were fully uniformed, presenting a neat appearance, and for a while it appeared as if a first class eclipse had taken place. The Reading club was entirely eclipsed and had to give way and acknowledge the superiority of the visitors who are really a very fine club of amateur ball players. The antics of the players were at times laughable although their masterly style of handling the bat and ball was frequently applauded. A number of colored ladies were present who watched the game with considerable interest."

Sources: "Ball and Bat," *Reading (PA) Times*, Jul 27, 1875; "Late Local News," *Harrisburg (PA) Telegraph*, Oct 6, 1875; "Base Ball," *Reading Times*, Oct 9, 1875; "A Colored Tale of Two Cities," *Harrisburg Telegraph*, Oct 12, 1875; "Among the Colored Ball Tossers," *Harrisburg Telegraph*, Oct 13, 1875; "Harrisburg Again Victorious," *Harrisburg Telegraph*, Oct 14, 1875; "Harrisburg vs. Reading," *Harrisburg (PA) Patriot*, Oct 14, 1875.

Never Sink Base Ball Club (Reading, PA; 1900s)

The Never Sink B.B.C. organized in 1900, played black and white nines. *Reading Eagle* (August 19, 1900): "The Red Rose Juniors easily defeated the Neversink Base Ball team, composed of local colored players by a score of 17 to 4, on the grounds of Klapperthal, Saturday afternoon."

Sources: "Red Rose Club Wins," *Reading (PA) Eagle*, Aug 19, 1900.

Consumer Base Ball Club (Scranton, PA; 1890s)

The Consumer B.B.C. organized in the 1890s, played black and white teams. *Scranton Republican* (April 25, 1896): "A novel scheme for procuring uniforms has been adopted by the Consumers, an aggregation of colored players. The uniforms will be supplied by business concerns. Each uniform will display an advertisement of the concern which purchased it." They played the Evening Stars, a white aggregation. *Republican* (May 21, 1896): "The Consumers played a game with the Evening Stars, ten innings, the score being 4 to 2, in favor of the Consumers. This club played a game last week with the Irish Giants, playing eleven innings with a score of 5 to 4."

Sources: "Amateur Ball Notes," *Scranton (PA) Republican*, Apr 25, 1896; "Consumer's Ball Club," *Scranton Republican*, Apr 25, 1896; "Amateur Ball Notes," *Scranton (PA) Tribune*, May 8, 1896; "Amateur Base Ball," *Scranton Republican*, May 21, 1896; "Amateur Base Ball," *Scranton Republican*, Jun 9, 1896; "Amateur Base Ball," *Scranton Republican*, Jun 18, 1896.

Colored Giants Base Ball Club (Sharon Hill, PA; 1890s)

The Colored Giants B.B.C. organized in the 1890s, played black and white aggregations. *Philadelphia Inquirer* (July 26, 1899): "The All-Norwood team defeated the Colored Giants, of Sharon Hill, the champion colored team of Delaware County, today in a very exciting game at Norwood Park. This is the Colored Giants first defeat in two years."

SOURCES: "Richmond Won in a Walk," *Philadelphia (PA) Inquirer*, Jul 3, 1898; "Norwood's Great Victory," *Philadelphia Inquirer*, Jul 26, 1899.

Independent Base Ball Club (Shippensburg, PA; 1870s)

The Independent B.B.C. organized in the 1870s, played black nines. *Carlisle Weekly Herald* (September 17, 1874): "A return game of baseball was played between the Independents, of Shippensburg, and the Pastime, of Carlisle, in Cart's orchard, on Thursday last. The game at the close stood 25 for the Pastime, and 14 for the Independents. It is not yet decided upon where the game for the championship will be played." *Shippensburg News* (September 19, 1874): "A game of baseball, played last Saturday between the Excelsior (white) and the Independent (colored) clubs, of this place, resulted in a score of 96 for the former and 34 for the latter."

SOURCES: "Base Ball Match," *Carlisle (PA) Weekly Herald*, Sep 17, 1874; "Home Digest," *Shippensburg News*, Oct 3, 1874.

Napoleon Base Ball Club (Shippensburg, PA; 1870s)

The Napoleon B.B.C. organized in the 1870s, played black nines. *Carlisle Weekly Herald* (July 29, 1875): "On the mail train in the forenoon a large delegation of dashing young colored sports, rigged out in the latest styles, members of the Napoleon Base Ball Club, of Shippensburg, arrived in town. The game was called at eleven o'clock and concluded about one…" *Shippensburg News* (July 24, 1875): "The Napoleons of this place, and the Pastimes of Carlisle, both colored base-ball clubs, had a match game of ball at the latter place, Thursday, in which the former were victorious by a score of 25 to 14."

SOURCES: "Home Digest," *Shippensburg (PA) News*, Jul 24, 1875; "Tournament in Carlisle," *Carlisle (PA) Weekly Herald*, Jul 29, 1875.

Colored Female Base Ball Club (Steelton, PA; 1880s)

The Colored Female B.B.C. organized in the 1880s, played against black and white teams. *Harrisburg Telegraph* (May 18, 1889): "Steelton has a colored female base-ball club. Almost every afternoon match or scrub games are played by them on the grounds in Mummatown. The club is handsomely uniformed, and ready to accept challenges from any other female club in the country."

SOURCES: "Patience at Steelton," *Harrisburg (PA) Telegraph*, May 18, 1889.

Colts Base Ball Club (Steelton, PA; 1890s). Organizer(s): E. Duffums.

The Colts B.B.C. organized in the 1890s, played black aggregations. *Harrisburg Patriot* (April 17, 1897): "The Cyclones and Cyclone Jr., [Colts] crossed bats today in a game of ball with a score of 18 to 6 in favor of the Cyclones."

SOURCES: "Steelton Slips," *Harrisburg (PA) Patriot*, Apr 17, 1897; "Steelton Happenings," *Harrisburg Patriot*, May 7, 1897; "Steelton Happenings," *Harrisburg (PA) Independent*, May 7, 1897.

Cyclone Base Ball Club (Steelton, PA; 1890s–1900s). Organizer(s): Peter S. Blackwell.

The Cyclone B.B.C. organized in the 1890s, played black and white aggregations. *Harrisburg Patriot* (April 9, 1894): "The Cyclones defeated the Steelton base-ball team at the Gun club grounds on Saturday in the first game of the season. Five innings were played, the final score being 11 to 5. The same clubs will try it again on Saturday." *Patriot* (August 27, 1894): "The game between the Steelton A. A.'s and the Cyclones drew a large crowd to the gun club grounds. The

Cyclones won by eighteen to twelve. The batteries were Gibson and Porter and Jacobs and Pearce." *Patriot* (April 17, 1897): "The Cyclones and Cyclone Jr., crossed bats today in a game of ball with a score of 18 to 6 in favor of the Cyclones."

SOURCES: "Negro Enterprise," *Indianapolis (IN) Freeman*, Dec 12, 1892; "The Final Game," *Harrisburg (PA) Patriot*, Aug 24, 1893; "Blackwell Out for Legislature," *Harrisburg Patriot*, Jan 1, 1894; "Cuban Giants Play Here," *Harrisburg Patriot*, Apr 27, 1894; "Base Ball," *Lebanon (PA) News*, Jun 21, 1894; "Base Ball Club Organized," *Harrisburg Patriot*, Mar 17, 1894; "The Cyclones Beaten," *Harrisburg Patriot*, May 7, 1894; "P. R. R. Team to Play," *Harrisburg Patriot*, May 10, 1894; "The Game Postponed," *Harrisburg Patriot*, May 28, 1894; "A Wow And A Wumpus," *Harrisburg Patriot*, Aug 10, 1894; "The News of Steelton," *Harrisburg Patriot*, Aug 27, 1894; *Lebanon News*, May 28, 1895; *Lebanon News*, May 30, 1895; "The News of Steelton," *Harrisburg Patriot*, May 31, 1895; "Colored Giants to Play," *Harrisburg Patriot*, Sep 16, 1896; "Steelton Slips," *Harrisburg Patriot*, Apr 17, 1897; "Cyclones Play Ball," *Harrisburg Patriot*, May 28, 1897; "Game of Ball at York," *Harrisburg (PA) Independent*, May 29, 1900.

Eagles Base Ball Club (Steelton, PA; 1890s–1900s). Organizer(s): Roger Williams.

The Eagles B.B.C. organized in the 1890s, played black aggregations. *Harrisburg Patriot* (June 28, 1899): "A game of baseball will be one of the features of the celebration of the Fourth of July in the borough. The Steelton Eagles, a nine composed of colored players have arranged for a game with the colored team of York." *Harrisburg Independent* (May 7, 1900): "On Saturday afternoon, the Stars, of the Eastern section of the borough, and the Eagles, of the central part of town, crossed bats on the Cottage Hill grounds. The game was witnessed by a large crowd of people. The score resulted as follows: Eagles, 37; Stars, 23."

SOURCES: "The News of Steelton," *Harrisburg (PA) Patriot*, Jun 28, 1899; "Steelton Letter," *Harrisburg (PA) Independent*, Jun 30, 1899; "The News of Steelton," *Harrisburg Patriot*, Jul 3, 1899; "Steelton Letter," *Harrisburg Independent*, May 7, 1900.

Hard to Beat Base Ball Club (Stroudsburg, PA; 1870s)

The Hard to Beat B.B.C. organized in 1874, played white and black clubs. *Stroudsburg Jeffersonian* (September 17, 1874): "Quite an excellent game prevailed in our borough on last Saturday, growing out of a match game of base-ball contest, between the Hard to Beat and the Flyaways. The Hard to Beat are a fine body of colored lads. Come Davis you must play better than this, wake up them coons of yours and go for them again."

SOURCES: "Base Ball," *Stroudsburg (PA) Jeffersonian*, Sep 17, 1874.

Manhattan Base Ball Club (Uniontown, PA; 1900s). Organizer(s): Robert H. Spencer.

The Manhattan B.B.C. organized in the 1900s. *Pittsburgh Press* (January 21, 1900): "R. H. Spencer, of the Manhattan colored baseball club, of Uniontown, is trying hard to get together a first-class team for this season's play. He has already signed one good player from Ohio. Practice will begin about April 10."

SOURCES: "Afro-American," *Pittsburgh (PA) Press*, Jan 21, 1900.

C. H. Beall Cuban Giants Base Ball Club (Uniontown, PA; 1890s). Organizer(s): WC. H. Beall; Robert H. Spencer.

The C. H. Beall Cuban Giants B.B.C. organized in the 1890s. *Pittsburgh Post* (July 30, 1891): "The C. H. Ball Club of Uniontown, composed of colored players, defeated the [Mt. Pleasant] Blue Stockings (colored club) here today by a score of 20 to 3." *Uniontown Evening News* (July 7, 1893): "The Cuban Giants of this place [Uniontown] and a colored club from Connellsville crossed bats at Mountain View Park yesterday afternoon. The game was a great one from start to finish and resulted in a score of 13 to 8 in favor of the Giants. McClure and Bogus were the Uniontown battery and Johnson and Menafee the battery for the Connellsville team. The home team made 10 of their 13 runs in the first inning after which the battery of the visitors was changed. The features of the game were the first base playing of Col. Black and the all-around work of Johnson and Menafee. A limited and somewhat silent audience witnessed the game for a few innings." *Evening News* (September 1, 1893): "The Cuban Giants were defeated Wednesday at the hands of the Windsor's of Cumberland. The score was 6 to 1 in favor of Windsor." In 1895, the Cuban Giants joined a Colored Baseball League, composed of teams from Cumberland, MD and the PA towns of Johnston, Bedford, and Uniontown. *Cumberland Evening Times* (July 18, 1895): "The game of baseball played at Uniontown yesterday between the Windsors, of this city, and the Uniontown club, was won by the former, the score being: Windsors, 7; Uniontown 1." *Pittsburgh Post* (September 4, 1895): "There was an interesting game of base-ball played here this afternoon between the Uniontown Giants and the Windsors, of this city. The game resulted in a score of 4 to 3 in favor of the Uniontown club."

SOURCES: "Victorious Mt. Pleasant Team," *Pittsburgh (PA) Post*, Jul 30, 1891; "Two Out of Three," *Mt. Pleasant (PA) Journal*, Aug 4, 1891; "Our Colored Friends," *Mt. Pleasant Journal*, Aug 11, 1891; "Home Happenings," *Mt. Pleasant Journal*, Aug 18, 1891; "About Town," *Uniontown (PA) Evening News*, Jul 6, 1893; "The Giants Win," *Uniontown Evening News*, Jul 7, 1893; "People You May Know," *Uniontown Evening News*, Aug 21, 1893; "The Colored Club," *Uniontown Evening News*, Aug 22, 1893; "About Town," *Uniontown Evening News*, Aug 22, 1893; "About Town," *Uniontown Evening News*, Sep 1, 1893; "Colored Baseball League," *Pittsburgh (PA) Post*, Jul 12, 1895; "Will Play Ball at Uniontown," *Cumberland (MD) Times*, Jul 16, 1895; "The Windsor Boys Win," *Cumberland (MD) Evening Times*, Jul 18, 1895; "Uniontown Wins," *Pittsburgh Post*, Sep 4, 1895; "Colored Giants Win Again," *Pittsburgh Post*, Sep 5, 1895.

Lafayette Hotel Base Ball Club (Uniontown, PA; 1880s–1890s)

The Lafayette Hotel B.B.C. organized in the 1880s, played black and white aggregations. *Uniontown Evening Standard* (May 24, 1889): "The Lafayette colored club yesterday beat the Madison college nine by a score of 11 to 10." *Evening Standard* (May 16, 1891): "The Lafayette and West End Hotel colored ball teams played Thursday evening, the Lafayette sluggers winning a six inning game by a score of 4 to 6. Hunt and Boggus were the battery for the Lafayette's and Palmer and Black served in that capacity for the West End champions."

SOURCES: "Base Ball," *Uniontown (PA) Evening Standard*, May 24, 1889; "Local Brevities," *Uniontown Evening Standard*, May 16, 1891; "About Town," *Uniontown (PA) Evening News*, Jul 6, 1893.

Monarch Base Ball Club (Uniontown, PA; 1890s). Organizer(s): W. C. McCormick.

The Monarch B.B.C. organized in the 1890s. *Uniontown Evening Standard* (August 1, 1890): "W. C. McCormick's colored base-ball club of this place will play the Scottdale nine two games at Scottdale tomorrow at 10 o'clock and 3:30." *Pittsburgh Press* (August 3, 1890): "The colored Monarchs, of Uniontown, met a waterloo at the hands of the Scottdale club today. They played a good game at first, but soon went to pieces. The battery of Miller and Bassler were features. Neves and Bassler pitched well, and Battermore fielded well."

SOURCES: "Local Briefs," *Uniontown (PA) Evening Standard*, Aug 1, 1890; "Monarchs Downed," *Pittsburgh (PA) Press*, Aug 3, 1890.

West End Hotel Base Ball Club (Uniontown, PA; 1880s)

The West End Hotel B.B.C. organized in the 1880s. *Uniontown Evening Standard* (May 16, 1891): "The Lafayette and West End Hotel colored ball teams played Thursday evening, the Lafayette sluggers winning a six inning game by a score of 4 to 6. Hunt and Boggus were the battery for the Lafayette's and Palmer and Black served in that capacity for the West End champions."

SOURCES: "Base Ball," *Uniontown (PA) Evening Standard*, May 24, 1889; "Local Brevities," *Uniontown Evening Standard*, May 16, 1891.

Alert Base Ball Club (WA, PA; 1870s)

The Alert B.B.C. organized in the 1870, played against black nines. *Washington Reporter* (August 11, 1875): "Friday afternoon last a match game of Base Ball was played on the Fair Grounds between the Alert and Independent (both colored clubs) of this place. This game was to decide which should be the 'first nine,' and was to have been played on the 1st of August, but was postponed on account of rain."

SOURCES: "Game of Base Ball," *Washington (PA) Reporter*, Aug 11, 1875; "Local Items," *Washington Reporter*, Aug 11, 1875.

Dolly Varden Base Ball Club (WA, PA; 1870s)

The Dolly B.B.C. organized in the 1870s, played against black nines. *Washington Observer* (June 6, 1872): "The Dolly Varden B.B.C. (colored) meet eveningly to practice. We don't know who they are going to challenge, probably the club that wins next Saturday."

SOURCES: *Washington (PA) Observer*, Jun 6, 1872.

Independent Base Ball Club (WA, PA; 1870s). Organizer(s): Mac Anderson.

The Independent B.B.C. organized in the 1870s, played against black nines. *Washington Reporter* (July 21, 1875) states: "A game of base-ball was played at Canonsburg, on Thursday last, between the Independence Club, of Washington, and the Wide Awakes of Canonsburg, (both colored nines), the Washington club winning by a score of 31 to 8. Some fine playing was done on both sides, but Mac Anderson, the captain of the Independence club capped the climax by his fine batting; using only one hand to bat with which he made some very fine hits, and being asked why he did not use both hands, answered that he was afraid if he did that the ball would never be found." *Pittsburgh Post* (August 27, 1875) states: "A very lively game was played on the fairground at Greenburg Green County, yesterday, between two colored clubs, the Independents of Washington, Pa., and the Unions of Waynesburg, resulting in a clear victory for the Unions by a score of 21 to 15. This is the third game between the two clubs, and the third victory for the Unions."

SOURCES: "Base Ball," *Washington (PA) Reporter*, Jul 21, 1875; "Game of Base Ball," *Washington Reporter*, Aug 11, 1875; "Base Ball," *Washington Reporter*, Aug 25, 1875; "Base Ball Notes," *Pittsburgh (PA) Post*, Aug 27, 1875; "Base Ball," *Washington Reporter*, Sep 1, 1875; "Base Ball," *Washington Reporter*, Sep 8, 1875.

Union Base Ball Club (Waynesboro, PA; 1870s). Organizer(s): Mac Anderson and John Hammond.

The Union B.B.C. organized in the 1870s, played against black nines. *Pittsburgh Post* (August 27, 1875) states: "A very lively game was played on the fairground at Greenburg Green County, yesterday, between two colored clubs, the Independents of Washington, Pa., and the Unions of Waynesburg, resulting in a clear victory for the Unions by a score of 21 to 15. This is the third game between the two clubs, and the third victory for the Unions." *Wheeling Intelligencer* (July 11, 1878): "Peanut Scott's Red Stocking Base Ball Club [Wheeling, West Virginia] played a match game with a colored club at Waynesboro, Pennsylvania. The Waynesboro club, known as the Union Club, won by a score of 16 to 7. The game was called on the sixth inning on account of rain." *Wheeling Register* (August 21, 1878): "Any time yesterday a troop of saddle-colored gemmen of Waynesboro might be seen restlessly perambulating the streets, waiting impatiently waiting for the time when they might doff citizens' clothes and don blue pants and striped hose and appear at once demolishers of African hearts and baseball clubs. The Waynesboro pitching was too much for Wheeling, and many of Scott's team, including the veteran himself [Peanut Scott] could only blink at the sphere, as it went curving by, and after the ineffectual attempts to check its mad career, run frantically half way to first—and, came back."

SOURCES: "Base Ball," *Washington (PA) Reporter,* Jul 21, 1875; "Base Ball," *Washington Reporter,* Aug 25, 1875; "Base Ball Notes," *Pittsburgh (PA) Post,* Aug 27, 1875; "Local Brevities," *Washington (PA) Review and Examiner,* Sep 1, 1875; "Base Ball," *Washington Reporter,* Sep 8, 1875; "City Chips," Wheeling (WVA) *Register,* Jun 18, 1878; "Brief Mention," *Wheeling Register,* July 9, 1878; "City Chips," *Wheeling Register,* July 11, 1878; "Peanut Scott's Nine Defeated," Wheeling (WVA) *Intelligencer,* Jul 11, 1878; "City Chips," *Wheeling Register,* Aug 20, 1878; "The Waynesboro Club Victorious," *Wheeling Intelligencer,* Aug 21, 1878; "Black Diamond, Cut Diamond," *Wheeling Register,* Aug 21, 1878; "The Wheeling Mokes," *Wheeling Register,* Jul 17, 1879; "Base Ball," *Wheeling Register,* Aug 20, 1879; "Notes," *Wheeling Register,* Jul 15, 1879.

Crescent Base Ball Club (West Chester, PA; 1880s–1890s). Organizer(s): WA Henderson, Jacob Milby, Clifford Fry and James Edwards.

The Crescent B.B.C. organized in the 1880s, played against black teams. *Philadelphia Inquirer* (July 10, 1889): "The Crescent Club defeated the Media Club this afternoon by superior all-around work. The visitors could do nothing with Williams's delivery, while Lockwood was hit frequently and hard." *Inquirer* (July 11, 1890): "This afternoon the Media Club were defeated by the Crescents of this place by a score of 22 to 12. Both clubs are colored and the game was noted for its heavy batting and errors." *Inquirer* (September 11, 1890): "The Crescent Club, of this place, defeated the Orion, of Norristown, here in an interesting game today by a score of 9 to 7. The visitors were off at times in the field, but the local players won through timely hitting."

SOURCES: "Sporting Notes," *Wilmington (DE) Evening News,* Mar 15, 1889; "Notes," *Wilmington (DE) Morning News,* Apr 24, 1889; "Media Takes a Tumble," *Philadelphia (PA) Inquirer,* Jul 10, 1889; "The Crescents Defeat Media," *Philadelphia Inquirer,* Jul 11, 1890; "West Chester Defeats Norristown in a Very Exciting Game," *Philadelphia Inquirer,* Sep 11, 1890.

Black Diamond Base Ball Club (Wilkes-Barre, PA; 1890s). Owner(s): Abraham "Fatty" Moody and Charley Travers.

The Black Diamond B.B.C. organized in the 1890s, played white and black organizations. *Wilkes-Barre Times* (July 18, 1893): "At 2:45 yesterday the Black Diamond Base Ball Club went down to Market Street on its way to West Side Park. They were seated on one side of a large band wagon, while on the other side sat their guests, the Bloomsburg colored club, and the entire party making the air ring with jubilee melody. The game which followed demonstrated that the Bloomsburg club was not in it, their colored brethren of this city doing apparently as they pleased with them and when the game was called at the end of the seventh inning the score was 23 to 8 in favor of Wilkes-Barre." *Times* (August 10, 1893): "Moody's Black Diamonds are playing a return game with the Blue and Heddin's team at Bloomsburg today."

SOURCES: "Briefs," Wilkes-Barre *(PA) Times-Leader,* Jul 11, 1893; "Base Ball Notes," Wilkes-Barre *(PA) Times,* Jul 14, 1893; "Charley Traver's Black Diamond," Wilkes-Barre *(PA) News,* Jul 17, 1893; "Bre'r Moody's Gang Won," *Wilkes-Barre News,* Jul 18, 1893; "Today's Ball Game," *Wilkes-Barre Times,* Jul 18, 1893 "Ball Notes," *Wilkes-Barre Times-Leader,* Jul 18, 1893; "Base Ball Notes," *Wilkes-Barre Times,* Jul 23, 1893; "Passed Balls," *Wilkes-Barre Times,* Aug 10, 1893.

Olympic Base Ball Club (Wilkes-Barre, PA; 1870s–1880s). Organizer(s): J. Milford.

The Olympic B.B.C. organized in the 1870s, played white and black nines. *Wilkes-Barre Record* (August 10, 1877): "A match game was played between the Brewery Hill club and the Olympics. The playing was very good. The game ended with a score of 10 to 4 in favor of the Olympics, colored." *Record* (July 8, 1881): "The Olympic Base Ball Club of this city returned from their trip to New York State. They assert that they lost the game at Elmira, on account of the unfairness of the umpire. On Wednesday, they played the Parlor City Club of Binghamton. The score was 7 to 3 in favor of the Olympics."

SOURCES: "Base Ball," Wilkes-Barre *(PA) Daily Record of the Times,* Jul 20, 1876; "Base Ball Notes," *Wilkes-Barre Daily Record of the Times,* Aug 10, 1877; "Little Locals," Wilkes-Barre *(PA) Daily Union Leader,* Jun 27, 1881; "Little Locals," *Wilkes-Barre Daily Union Leader,* Jul 2, 1881; "Local Brevities," Wilkes-Barre *(PA) Record,* Jul 7, 1881; "Local Brevities," *Wilkes-Barre Record,* Jul 9, 1881; "Local Brevities," *Wilkes-Barre Record,* Aug 24, 1881;

Quickstep Base Ball Club (Wilkes-Barre, PA; 1870s). Organizer(s): William H. Thompson and William Lane.

The Quickstep B.B.C. organized in the 1870s, played white and black nines. *Wilkes-Barre Record of the Times* (July 3, 1877): "Two colored clubs, the Quicksteps of this city, and Red Skinners of Parsons, played a match game yesterday, the score standing eight to six in favor of the Quicks." *Record of the Times* (August 3, 1877): "In the game yesterday between the Stantons, white, and the Quicksteps, colored, on Stanton Hill grounds, eleven innings were played resulting in a score of 15 to 14 in favor of the Stantons."

SOURCES: "Base Ball," Wilkes-Barre *(PA) Daily Record of the Times,* May 1, 1875; "Base Ball," *Wilkes-Barre Daily Record of the Times,* May 7, 1875; "Base Ball," *Wilkes-Barre Daily Record of the Times,* Jul 20, 1876; "Base Ball," *Wilkes-Barre Daily Record of the Times,* Aug 8, 1876; "Base Ball," *Wilkes-Barre Daily Record of the Times,* Sep 6, 1876; "Local Brevities," *Wilkes-Barre Daily Record of the Times,* Jul 3, 1877; "Local Brevities," *Wilkes-Barre Daily Record of the Times,* Jul 21, 1877; "Base Ball Notes," *Wilkes-Barre Daily Record of the Times,* Aug 3, 1877; "Base Ball Notes," *Wilkes-Barre Daily Record of the Times,* Aug 30, 1877.

Enterprise Base Ball Club (Williamsport, PA; 1870s). Organizer(s): Enoch Emory.

The Enterprise B.B.C. organized in the 1870s. In 1876, Lock Haven's Princetons and Williamsport's Enterprise, both black nines, agreed to play. During their train ride to the Lumber City, a reporter captured the mood of the Princeton players. He recorded the team captain's colloquy on the ability of his men as baseballists. *Gazette and Bulletin* (August 17, 1876): "I want you darks to understand that if you let dem Williamsport niggers clip de tar off ob yer heels dat I'll knock ebery one of you out ob joint fore you lebbe da ground… de Lord help you all. You'll need it, if I goes fo' you." This scolding was hardly unusual: Javan Emory stylized similar colloquies designed to stiffen the spines of his players. *Gazette and Bulletin* (August 17, 1876): "Yesterday the Odd fellows, colored, held a picnic at Herdic Park. Among the festivities of the day was a game of base-ball between the Princetons, of Lock Haven, and the Enterprise of Williamsport.

At the end of the game the score stood 18 to 19 in favor of the Enterprise."

SOURCES: "Dashes Here and There," *Williamsport (PA) Gazette and Bulletin*, Aug 16, 1876; "On the Way Down," *Williamsport Gazette and Bulletin*, Aug 17, 1876; *Williamsport Gazette and Bulletin*, Aug 19, 1876.

Falling Star Base Ball Club (Williamsport, PA; 1890s)

The Falling Star B.B.C. organized in the 1890s, played black nines. The team was composed of black young ladies. The Harrisburg Telegraph (July 24, 1891): "A team composed of young colored girls in Williamsport is styled the Falling Stars. The other day they beat a team of colored boys by a score of 17 to 7."

SOURCES: "Hot Grounders," *Harrisburg (PA) Telegraph*, Jul 24, 1891.

Hepburn House Independent Base Ball Club (Williamsport, PA; 1860s–1880s). Organizer(s): Enoch Emory.

The Hepburn House Independent B.B.C. organized in the 1860s. The Independents, composed of waiters, developed a rivalry with Harrisburg's Monrovia nine. *Williamsport Lycoming Gazette* (June 18, 1868): "A match game of base-ball will take place near the Herdic House between the First Nine of the Herdic House Club (colored), and the First Nine of the Monrovian Base Ball Club, of Harrisburg." *Williamsport Gazette and Bulletin* (July 18, 1884): "A game of baseball was played Wednesday afternoon between the City Hotel waiters and the Hepburn House waiters, on the Newton Grounds, which resulted in a victory for the City Hotel waiters, by a score of 11 to 12. Thomson and Sims Emory constituted the battery for the City Hotel, and Mellicks and Alexandra for the Hepburn."

SOURCES: *Williamsport (PA) Lycoming Gazette*, Jun 18, 1868; "Base Ball," *Harrisburg (PA) Patriot*, Jun 26, 1868; "Match Game," *Harrisburg Patriot*, Jun 29, 1868; "Base Ball," *Harrisburg Patriot*, Jun 30, 1868; *Williamsport Lycoming Gazette*, August 5, 1868; "Base Ball," *Williamsport Lycoming Gazette*, Aug 13, 1868; "Game Between Hotel Waiters," *Williamsport Gazette and Bulletin*, Jul 14, 1884; "Between Hotel Waiters," *Williamsport Gazette and Bulletin*, Jul 18, 1884.

Kepford Base Ball Club (Williamsport, PA; 1890s). Organizer(s): Javan Isaac Emory & Kepford Soap Company.

The Kepford B.B.C. organized in 1890. The Williamsport's *Gazette and Bulletin* (July 28, 1891): "The Rubber Works Club, of the City League, donned their new uniforms yesterday and defeated the Kepford Soap Company Club, by a score of 11 to 4. It was a fine exhibition of ball up to the end of the sixth inning when the score stood 4 to 2 in favor of the Rubber Works. In the seventh and eighth innings Javan's team got rattled and allowed their opponents to score seven runs, while they were unable to score two."

SOURCES: "The Kepfords," *Williamsport (PA) Gazette and Bulletin*, May 25, 1891; *Williamsport Gazette and Bulletin*, Jul 1, 1891; "At Athletic Park," *Williamsport Daily Gazette and Bulletin*, Jul 9, 1891; *Williamsport Gazette and Bulletin*, Jul 28, 1891; "Brandons and Kepfords," *Williamsport Gazette and Bulletin*, Aug 7, 1891; "Tomorrow Afternoon," *Williamsport Gazette and Bulletin*, Aug 20, 1891.

Lumber City Base Ball Club (Williamsport, PA; 1870s–1900s). Organizer(s): Javan Emory; William Winston.

The Lumber City B.B.C. organized in the 1870s. A rivalry developed between Williamsport and Elmira, NY. *Williamsport Gazette and Bulletin* (August 14, 1877): "The game of base–ball at Elmira on Friday last between the Lumber City Club, of Williamsport, and the Casinos, of Elmira, resulted in a victory for the Elmira Club by a score of eleven to six. The game at the commencement of the ninth

inning was in favor of the Lumber Citys, and they would have no doubt won the game had it not been for their catcher, who it is claimed, sold them out." The team reorganized as the Lumber City Grays. *Gazette and Bulletin* (June 13, 1882): "Yesterday a number of young colored men, of this city, organized a new base-ball club, under the title of Williamsport Grays. The organization effected was as follows: President, William Winston; Secretary, J. H. Millford; Assistant Secretary, H. M. Boyd; Treasurer, H. M. Minor; Captain William H. Shadney; General Manager, W. T. Emory. The Nine: Javan T. Emory, catcher; William H. Shadney, pitcher; C. Braxton, shortstop; J. Forster, 1b; William T. Emory, 2b; Sims V. Emory, 3b; J. H. Millford, lf; W. Pleasant, cf; S. Benson, rf. In 1890, the team reorganized as the Lumber City Reds Base Ball Club. *Gazette and Bulletin* (June 26, 1890): "The Williamsport Reds is the name of a base-ball club in this city, composed entirely of colored players. It is said that they have been playing good ball this season. They claim that they have played twenty-one games, in which they have won twenty. They have played the Quicksteps, Old Oaks, and various other picked nines composed of good material. They will go to Lyons and Watkins, New York, where they will play the Athletics, on Emancipation Day." In 1892, the Lumber Citys reorganized as the Colts. They played Williamsport's Brandons, a white aggregation. *Daily Bulletin and Gazette* (August 10, 1893): "The college team and Javan Emory's Colts will hold forth at Athletic Park this afternoon. Javan is booked to do some silent coaching, which will be worth seeing. The Colts will put a new pitcher in the field, and expect to win with ease. The admission is ten cents and the grandstand free. Game called at 9 o'clock."

SOURCES: "Base Ball," *Williamsport (PA) Gazette and Bulletin*, Aug 14, 1877; "A Challenge," *Williamsport Gazette and Bulletin*, Oct 13, 1877; "A New Base Ball Nine," *Williamsport Gazette and Bulletin*, Jun 13, 1882; "Notes and Comments," *Philadelphia (PA) Gazette and Bulletin*, Feb 17, 1886; "Two Games," *Williamsport Gazette and Bulletin*, Jun 26, 1890; "The Kepfords," *Williamsport Gazette and Bulletin*, May 25, 1891; "At Athletic Park," *Williamsport Gazette and Bulletin*, Jul 9, 1891; *Williamsport Gazette and Bulletin*, Jul 28, 1891; "Tomorrow Afternoon," *Williamsport Gazette and Bulletin*, Aug 20, 1891; "General Sporting News," *Philadelphia (PA) Inquirer*, Feb 21, 1892; "Oxford Beats the Grants," *Philadelphia Inquirer*, Jun 1, 1892; "Around the Diamond," *Williamsport Gazette and Bulletin*, Aug 10, 1893; "A Regular Picnic," *Shenandoah (PA) Evening Herald*, Aug 21, 1893; "Base Ball Today," *Williamsport Gazette and Bulletin*, Apr 11, 1896.

Creedmoor Base Ball Club (Wrightsville, PA; 1870s). Organizer(s): William and Leonard Bear.

The Creedmoor B.B.C., of York, PA, organized in the 1870s, played white and black nines. They developed a rivalry with York's black club. *York Daily* (August 17, 1877): "Yesterday, a game of base-ball was played at Wrightsville, between the Alpha of York and Creedmoor of Wrightsville, resulting in favor of the Creedmoor, by a score of 82 to 6." *York Daily* (September 17, 1877): "Yesterday afternoon quite a crowd assembled on the Commons to witness the game of base-ball between the Creedmoor Base Ball Club of Wrightsville, and Alpha of York, both colored clubs. The game occupied 3 hours and ten minutes, and C. Warner acted as umpire. The game resulted in favor of the Creedmoor by a score of 59 to 12." In 1878, the team reorganized and renewed its rivalry with the York club. *York Daily*: "The Creedmoor Club, of Wrightsville, will play the Enterprise of York, a game of base-ball on the commons, this afternoon. The game will be called at 2 o'clock. Both clubs are colored." *York Daily* (September 16, 1878): "Yesterday afternoon a large number of persons assembled on the commons to witness the game of base-ball between

Creedmoor, of Wrightsville, and the Enterprise, of York, all colored. The game resulted in favor of the Creedmoors by a score of 42 to 24." The Creedmoors received a challenge from one of York's white nines. *York Daily* (October 6, 1877): "The Codorus B.B.C. will leave York this morning (in private conveyances) for Wrightsville, where they intend to play the Centennial and Creedmoor Base Ball Clubs of that place."

Sources: "Base Ball," *York (PA) Daily*, Aug 17, 1877; "Base Ball," *York Daily*, Sep 11, 1877; "Base Ball," *York Daily*, Sep 12, 1877; "Base Ball," *York Daily*, Sep 24, 1877; "Base Ball," *York Daily*, Sep 25, 1877; "Base Ball," *York Daily*, Oct 6, 1877; *York Daily*, Apr 2, 1878; "Base Ball This Afternoon," *York Daily*, Sep 16, 1878.

Alpha Base Ball Club (York, PA; 1870s)

The Alpha B.B.C. organized in the 1870s, played black nines. York and Wrightsville developed a black rivalry. *York Daily* (August 17, 1877): "Yesterday, a game of base-ball was played at Wrightsville, between the Alpha of York and Creedmoor of Wrightsville, resulting in favor of the Creedmoor, by a score of 82 to 6." *York Daily* (September 17, 1877): "Yesterday afternoon quite a crowd assembled on the Commons to witness the game of base-ball between the Creedmoor Base Ball Club of Wrightsville, and Alpha of York, both colored clubs. The game occupied 3 hours and ten minutes, and C. Warner acted as umpire. The game resulted in favor of the Creedmoor by a score of 59 to 12."

Sources: "Base Ball," *York (PA) Daily*, Aug 17, 1877; "Base Ball," *York Daily*, Sep 11, 1877; "Base Ball," *York Daily*, Sep 12, 1877; "Base Ball," *York Daily*, Sep 24, 1877; "Base Ball," *York Daily*, Sep 25, 1877.

Colored Cuban Giants Base Ball Club (York, PA; 1890s). Organizer(s): Charles Pinkney and George W. Bowles.

The Colored Cuban Giants B.B.C. organized in the 1890s, played black and white nines. *York Daily* (August 3, 1893): "The Keystone defeated the Cuban Giants by a score of 14 to 6." They played against a strong black club of Baltimore. *York Daily* (August 3, 1895): "The colored Cuban Junior Base Ball Club will leave York on the 12th of August for Baltimore and will play the Pioneer Base Ball Club of that city at Druid Park." *York Daily* (August 20, 1895): "The Colored Cuban Giants will play the York Grays team [white] on Monday afternoon at the Willow Park grounds." *York Daily* (August 23, 1895): "The Cuban Giants last evening defeated the Grays by a score of 5 to 4. They did it by heavy batting." They Cuban Giants and Grays developed a local rivalry. *York Daily* (August 27, 1895): "The Cuban Juniors defeated the Grays by a score of 11 to 10."

Sources: "Base Ball," *York (PA) Daily*, Jun 14, 1893; "Notes," *York Daily*. Aug. 3, 1893; "Base Ball," *York Daily*, Jun 7, 1895; "Base Ball Notes," *York Daily*, Jul 31, 1895; "Base Ball Notes," *York Daily*, Aug 8, 1895; "Notes," *York Daily*, Aug 19, 1895; "Base Ball Tomorrow," *York Daily*, Aug 20, 1895; "Base Ball," *York Daily*, Aug 23, 1895; "Brief Locals," *York Daily*, Aug 27, 1895.

Enterprise Base Ball Club (York, PA; 1870s). Organizer(s): J. W. Brown.

The Enterprise B.B.C. organized in 1876, played against black nines. *York Daily* (April 2, 1878): "A great event is in anticipation. Mr. Brown, of the Enterprise B.B.C. (formerly the Alpha nine) is on a visit to Wrightsville, it is reported, with a view to arrange with the Creedmoor B.B.C. a series of games, in the hope to wipeout the disgraceful defeats of the last season. Since their organization, the Enterprise claim to be strong indeed." Not strong enough. *York Daily* (September 17, 1878): "Yesterday afternoon a large number of persons assembled on the commons to witness the game of base-ball between Creedmoor, of Wrightsville, and the Enterprise, of York, all

colored. The game resulted in favor of the Creedmoors by a score of 42 to 24."

Sources: *York (PA) Daily*, Apr 2, 1878; "Base Ball This Afternoon," *York Daily*, Sep 16, 1878; "Base Ball," *York Daily*, Sep 17, 1878.

Hunter Base Ball Club (York, PA; 1880s). Organizer(s): Alexander Johnson.

The Hunter B.B.C. organized in 1876, played against white and black nines. They played a black club of Frederick, MD. *York Daily* (May 17, 1884): "More fun was developed in yesterday's game between the Hunters of York, and the Red Stockings of Frederick could not be well extracted from one game of base-ball. The audience yelled itself hoarse, and laughed until its sides ached; and more real rollicking fun is not often in return for an investment of twenty-five cents. In point of complexion the two teams were evenly matched, but on account of the difference in costuming they were designated by the audience as blondes and brunettes. *York Daily* (June 4, 1884): "A game of base-ball between the Anchor [white] and Hunter [colored] clubs on Saturday was well contested and resulted in a victory for the former by a score of 19 to 8." *York Daily* (August 21, 1885): "The Springgarden club of East York, defeated the Hunters, a colored club, of York, on Small's Field, to the tune of 19 to 9."

Sources: "Base Ball," *York (PA) Daily*, Apr 2, 1884; "Diamond Dots," *York Daily*, Apr 24, 1884; "Fun on the Diamond," *York Daily*, May 17, 1884; "Hunters vs. Anchors Today," *York Daily*, May 31, 1884; "Diamond Dots," *York Daily*, Jul 1, 1884; "Amusements," *York Daily*, Aug 24, 1884; "Base Ball," *York Daily*, Aug 21, 1885; "Today's Local Games," *York Daily*, May 8, 1886; "Brief Locals," *York Daily*, May 11, 1886; "Base Ball," *York (PA) Gazette*, Jul 28, 1887.

Monarch Base Ball Club (York, PA; 1890s). Organizer(s): James Monroe Kreiter, Jr.

The Monarch B.B.C. organized in the 1890s, played black and white aggregations. The former Cuban Giants' players belonged to the Interstate League. *Philadelphia Inquirer* (June 11, 1890): "The Monarchs were robbed of another game today by the rank decisions of the umpire, who not only aided the visitors in scoring eight runs but preventing them from a victory which was honestly won." *Harrisburg Telegraph* (July 31, 1890): "The Lebanon and the Dusky Monarchs from York played an exhibition game at Penryn Park yesterday in the presence of about 1,500 spectators. Daly and Whyte both pitched good ball, but Daly was wild at critical points of the game. The score was 2 to 0 in favor of the Monarchs." *Reading Times* (September 23, 1890): "James Monroe Kreiter, Jr., manager of the York Monarchs, arrived in this city last night after a tour through the western part of the State. This afternoon the Monarchs will play the Reading Club another game on the Marion Street Grounds. Manager Kreiter said that his club had attracted the largest audiences at base-ball games ever seen in the northern tier of counties, and whilst the Monarchs could not win at the games at Meadville, Erie, and Bradford, he was entirely satisfied with the results." *Reading Times* (July 29, 1890): "The York Club was again too much for the Hillsides in yesterday afternoon's contest, which attracted between 600 and 700 spectators at the home club's grounds."

Sources: "Altoona Snowed Under at York," *Philadelphia (PA) Inquirer*, May 10, 1890; "Interstate League," *Philadelphia Inquirer*, May 11, 1890; "The York Players at a Banquet," *Philadelphia Inquirer*, May 15, 1890; "A Rather One-Sided Game," *Philadelphia Inquirer*, May 21, 1890; "Interstate League," *Philadelphia Inquirer*, May 28, 1890; "Interstate League," *Philadelphia Inquirer*, Jun 3, 1890; "Altoona Shut Out at York," *Philadelphia Inquirer*, Jun 4, 1890; "Interstate League," *Philadelphia Inquirer*, Jun 11, 1890; "A Picnic for the Dusky Monarchs," *Philadelphia Inquirer*, Jun 12, 1890; "The Monarchs Win at Reading," *Philadelphia Inquirer*, Jun 24, 1890; "The York Club Will Survive," *Philadelphia Inquirer*, Jul 26, 1890; "Grand Stand Chat," *Harrisburg (PA) Telegraph*, Jul 31, 1890; "York 4; Harrisburg, 2," *Philadelphia Inquirer*, Aug 12, 1890; "Base Ball at Gloucester," *Philadelphia Inquirer*, Aug 18, 1890; "National Game Notes," *Reading (PA) Times*, Jul 2, 1890; "Base Ball Gossip," *Reading Times*, Jul 24, 1890; "The Nation's Game," *Reading Times*, Jul 29, 1890; "The Base Ball Season," *Reading Times*, Aug 11, 1890; "Played Finely in the Field," *Reading Times*, Aug 20, 1890; "Labor Day Base Ball," *Reading Times*, Sep 2, 1890; "Sporting Notes," *Reading Times*, Sep 8, 1890; "The York Monarchs Today," *Reading Times*, Sep 23, 1890; "Base Ball at Harrisburg," *Philadelphia Inquirer*, Oct 2, 1890.

Seminole Base Ball Club (York, PA; 1870s)

The Seminole B.B.C. organized in 1876, played white and black nines. *York Daily* (April 18, 1876): "Yesterday two base-ball clubs composed of young men, known as the Jack Rabbits and the Seminoles, played a game on the avenue, resulting in favor of the Seminoles by a score of 50 to 39." *York Daily* (May 2, 1876): "Yesterday afternoon, on the Avenue the Seminoles, colored club, played the Pick-me-ups composed of a picked nine of colored and white men, which resulted in favor of the former by a score of 19 to 18. Time of game two hours and 10 minutes."

SOURCES: *York (PA) Daily*, Apr 18, 1876; *York Daily*, May 2, 1876.

Rhode Island

Newport Base Ball Club (Newport, RI; 1890s)

Owner(s): George Seaforth

The Newport Colored B.B.C., of Providence, RI, organized in the 1890s. *New York Age* (May 24, 1890): "Our boys have organized a base-ball club called the Newports with the following officers: George Seaforth, President; Norman Wright, Vice-President; W. Phoenix, Secretary; H. Jones treasurer; S. Gaines, Manager.

SOURCES: "Notes from Newport," *New York (NY) Age*, May 24, 1890; "From Newport," *New York Age*, May 10, 1890.

Apollo Club (Providence, RI; 1870s–1890s).

The Apollo Club organized in 1875. By the 1880s, the club's membership included the city's top black baseballists; among them, Oran L. Skipworth, William Butler, George W. Brown, George Jackson, Henry Poindexter, William Walker, J. E. Johnson, J. H. Douglas and John Berry. The organization had some of the city's best musicians, including Brown and Jackson who gave parlor entertainments at the Newport and Narragansett Pier Hotels.

SOURCES: "The Apollo Ball," *New York (NY) Freeman*, Jan 16, 1886; "Providence People," *New York Freeman*, Jul 17, 1886; "Floating Trifles," *Providence (RI) Sunday Telegram*, Aug 31, 1886; "Apollo Club Entertainments," *New York Freeman*, Nov 13, 1886; "Providence People," *New York Freeman*, Jan 15, 1887; "Apollo Club Celebration," *New York Freeman*, May 30, 1891.

Cambria Base Ball Club (Providence, RI; 1870s)

The Cambria B.B.C. organized in 1870. Between 1870 and 1872, the "Cambrias" dominated local amateur base-ball. They played against white and black nines; among them, the Pioneers, Flying Boys, Keystones, Lone Stars, and Tack Drivers. *Providence Evening Press* (November 11, 1870): "The Cambria Base Ball Club played their last match on the Dexter Training Ground with the Pioneers of Providence, for the championship. The victory resulted in favor of the Cambria Club, after a hard struggle. Score: Cambria, 16; Pioneers, 13—nine innings." *Evening Press* (September 15, 1870): "An interest-

ing game of base-ball between Cambrias and Flying Boys, two club composed of colored members, took place in Dexter Training Ground yesterday afternoon, was witnessed by several hundred spectators. The victory was won by the Cambrias, the score standing 41 to 26." The Cambrias developed a black rivalry with Brooklyn's Ocean club; the Oceans came to Providence, and defeated them. The Cambrias later traveled to Brooklyn; they played the "Oceans" and "Monitors." *Evening Press* (September 18, 1871): "The Cambria Base Ball Club, of this city played two matches in Brooklyn, NY, last week, one with the Monitors and the other with the Oceans. Result—once laid out their opponents, and once laid themselves."

SOURCES: "Local News," *Providence (RI) Evening Press*, Sep 12, 1870; "Local News," *Providence Evening Press*, Sep 15, 1870; "Local News," *Providence Evening Press*, Oct 13, 1870; "Local News," *Providence Evening Press*, Oct 31, 1870; "The Pioneers," *Providence Evening Press*, Nov 11, 1870; "Local News," *Providence Evening Press*, Apr 26, 1871; "Local News," *Providence Evening Press*, Jul 28, 1871; "Base Ball," *Providence Evening Press*, Aug 8, 1871; "Local News," *Providence Evening Press*, Aug 10, 1871; "Local News," *Providence Evening Press*, Sep 2, 1871; "Local News," *Providence Evening Press*, Sep 18, 1871; "Local News," *Providence Evening Press*, May 24, 1872; "Local News," *Providence Evening Press*, Jun 27, 1872; "Local News," *Providence Evening Press*, Jul 18, 1872; "Local News," *Providence Evening Press*, Sep 11, 1872.

Grays Base Ball Club (Providence, RI; 1880s). Owner(s): Sidney S. Smith.

The Colored Grays organized in the 1880s, played white and black nines. *New York Freeman* (July 17, 1886): "A baseball nine, with Sidney S. Smith, captain, has organized and has purchased the suits of the Providence Grays, and assumed that name. They play weekly at the Messer ball grounds and deserve liberal patronage." They played against Olneyville's Athletics, a white team. *Sunday Telegram* (July 25, 1886): "The Providence Colored Grays defeated the Athletics, of Olneyville, on the Messer Street Grounds. Score: 17 to 9." Reorganizing in 1887, the Grays planned to play black teams throughout the country. They played four games against New London's Big Four B.B.C. They also played against Boston's Resolute B.B.C. *Boston Globe* (April 15, 1887): "Yesterday afternoon, the two colored ball nines representing Providence and the Hub, met at the Union Grounds for a contest of skill in handling the sphere, which ended entirely satisfactory for the Bostonian at least, as their opponents were obliged to leave for home a badly defeated club."

SOURCES: "Horsehoes, 3; Colored Grays, 2," *Providence (RI) Sunday Telegram*, Jul 4, 1886; "Notes from the Diamond," *Providence Sunday Telegram*, Jul 25, 1886; "Providence People," *New York (NY) Freeman* (New York, NY), July 17, 1886; "Providence Pencilings," *New York Freeman*, Jul 24, 1886; "Colored Grays, 17; Athletics, 9," *Providence Sunday Telegram*, Jul 25, 1886; "Base Ball Notes," *Providence Sunday Telegram*, Aug 1, 1886; "Providence Grays, 12; Aetnas, 10," *Providence Sunday Telegram*, Aug 8, 1886; "Providence Paragraphs," *New York Freeman*, Aug 21, 1886; "Rhode Island Celebration," *New York Freeman*, Aug 7, 1886; "Providence Paragraphs," *New York Freeman*, Aug 21, 1886; "Notes from the Diamond," *Providence Sunday Telegram*, Aug 29, 1886; "Providence Letter," *New York Freeman*, Apr 2, 1887; "Two Colored Nines," *Boston (MA) Globe*, Apr 15, 1887; "A Crack Base Ball Team," *New York Freeman*, Apr 16, 1887; "Providence People," *New York Freeman*, Apr 27, 1887.

Watch Hill House Base Ball Club (Watch Hill, RI; 1880s–1890s)

The Watch Hill House B.B.C. organized in the 1880s. *Springfield Republican* (June 24, 1888): "The team from Watch Hill House, of which McNaughton and Jennings were the battery, Williams was first base, Paige shortstop and Gates centerfield, has been invincible for several seasons. Guests bought the uniforms, paid for the trophies and in every way encouraged the nines of their respective hotels— all for the emolument and delectation of the boys." *North Adams Transcript* (June 28, 1895): "James Cary, the colored ball player, went to Watch Hill, Rhode Island, where he will work in a hotel and also play on the baseball team. He played with the Renfrews last year and is a good man on the diamond."

SOURCES: "Colored Nine 14, High Schools 1," *Springfield (MA) Republican*, Feb 25, 1888; "Springfield News and Comment," *Springfield Republican*, Jun 24, 1888; *North Adams (MA) Transcript*, Jun 28, 1895.

South Carolina

Dauntless Base Ball Club (Beaufort, SC; 1870s). Organizer(s): Robert Barnes.

The Dauntless B.B.C. organized in the 1870s. The "Dauntless" played black clubs. *Winnsboro Fairfield Herald* (September 8, 1875): "The Dauntless B.B.C., of Beaufort, SC, of which Congressman Robert Smalls (**Fig. 34**) is president, challenges any colored club South of WA for a match game." *Beaufort Tribune and Port Royal Commercial* (May 24, 1877): "The Dauntless Base Ball Club defeated the Olympics, by a score of 33 to 6."

SOURCES: *Beaufort (SC) Tribune*, June 9, 1875; "South Carolina," *Charleston (SC) News and Courier*, Sep 11, 1875; "Base Ball," *Charleston News and Courier*, Jun 9, 1875; "Base Ball," *Charleston News and Courier*, Sep 21, 1875; *Savannah (GA) Tribune*, Sep 22, 1875; *Savannah Tribune*, Oct 6, 1875; "Local Items," *Beaufort (SC) Tribune and Port Royal Commercial*, May 24, 1877; "Local Items," *Beaufort Tribune and Port Royal Commercial*, May 31, 1877; "Local Items," *Beaufort Tribune and Port Royal Commercial*, Jun 6, 1877; "Matters and Things Laconically Noted," *Savannah (GA) Morning News*, Aug 11, 1877; "Game of Base Ball," *Savannah Morning News*, Aug 25, 1877; *Beaufort (SC) Tribune and Port Royal Commercial*, Aug 30, 1877; "Base Ball Match," *Charleston News and Courier*, Oct 7, 1877.

Figure 34. Robert Smalls, 1879?1880. Smalls served as president of the Beaufort, South Carolina, Dauntless (1875-77) and Dictators (1880) ball clubs (Library of Congress).

Rising Sun Base Ball Club (Beaufort, SC; 1860s). Organizer(s): R. W. Butler.

The Rising Sun B.B.C. organized in the 1860s, played against black clubs. *Charleston News* (June 8, 1869): "The Rising Sun Base Ball Club regret to be compelled to inform their Charleston friends, and especially the Crescent Base Ball Club, that in account of the non-arrival of the steamer they were compelled to disappoint them in the match game to have been played in the 8th instant." The Rising Suns played against Charleston, SC's Crescent nine. *Charleston News* (June 25, 1869): "The Rising Sun Base Ball Club, of Beaufort, S.C., and the Crescent Club, of this city, both colored, will play a match game at the foot of Broad Street, this afternoon, at half past two o'clock."

SOURCES: "Reporters' Crumbs," *Charleston (SC) News*, Jun 8, 1869; "The Beaufort Base Ballists," *Charleston News*, Jun 25, 1869.

Arlington Base Ball Club (Charleston, SC; 1870s)

The Arlington B.B.C. organized in the 1870s, played against black teams. *Charleston News and Courier* (September 19, 1876): "The Arlingtons and Exacts played a game of base-ball on the Citadel Green, yesterday afternoon, the score resulting in 26 to 14 in favor of the Arlingtons." *News and Courier* (June 5, 1877): "A game of ball was played yesterday between the Arlington and Wild Rose, colored base-ball clubs, which resulted in favor of the Arlingtons, by a score of 24 to 9." They also played the Fultons. *News and Courier* (August 25, 1877): "A match game of base-ball will be played on the Citadel Green, commencing at half past 2 o'clock, between the Arlington and the Fulton Juniors."

SOURCES: "Talk About Town," *Charleston (SC) News and Courier*, Sep 19, 1876; "Colored Base Ball Club," *Charleston News and Courier*, Apr 25, 1877; "Base Ball," *Charleston News and Courier*, Jun 5, 1877; "The Bat and the Ball," *Charleston News and Courier*, Aug 25, 1877; "Odds and Ends," *Charleston News and Courier*, Sep 18, 1877.

Ashley Base Ball Club (Charleston, SC; 1860s). Organizer(s): C. H. Price; J. M. Matthews.

The Ashley B.B.C. organized in the 1860s. The Ashleys, composed of members of the Ashley Colored Fire Company, played against the black clubs. *Charleston News* (June 25, 1867): "Attend a special meeting for your club this evening, at seven o'clock, at 106 Coming-Street. Punctual attendance is required as business of importance is to be transcribed." *News* (July 29, 1868): "A match game of baseball was played in the Citadel Green yesterday afternoon before a large crowd of spectators, by the colored baseball clubs, Ashley and Mutual. The score stood Ashley, 27; Mutual, 12." They developed a rivalry. *News* (August 11, 1868): "The Colored Base Ballists seem to keep up the sport with much spirit. In a return game between the Mutual and Ashley clubs, played Monday afternoon, in Citadel Green, the latter won, the score standing twenty-two to twenty." They played the Crescent B.B.C. *News* (September 11, 1868): "A match game of base-ball was played on the Citadel Ground last evening, between the Ashley and Crescent (both colored). The Crescents won; the score being 26 to 24."

SOURCES: "Ashley Base Ball Club," *Charleston (SC) News*, Jun 25, 1867; "Base Ballists," *Charleston News*, Jul 29, 1868; "Base Ball," *Charleston News*, Aug. 11, 1868; "Colored Base Ball," *Charleston News*, Sep 11, 1868; "Base Ball," *Charleston News*, Sep 14, 1868; *Charleston News*, Sep 16, 1868; "Ashley Base Ball Club," *Charleston News*, Jan 19, 1869; "Ashley Fire Company," *Charleston News*, Feb 14, 1873.

Athletic Base Ball Club (Charleston, SC; 1880s)

The Athletic B.B.C., of Charleston, SC, organized in 18880s. They played against black nines. *Wilmington Morning Star* (July 1, 1885): "There was a large crowd on the Seaside Club grounds, yesterday afternoon, to witness a match game between the two colored clubs, the Mutuals of this city, and the Athletics, of Charleston, S.C. The visitors wore handsome blue uniforms and made a good appearance. Following is the score by innings, by which it will be seen that the home club were victors." *Morning Star* (July 21, 1885): "Two colored clubs—in striking uniforms—the Athletics and Mutuals—paraded the streets yesterday afternoon, with a band of music, and afterwards had a hotly contested game of baseball at Seaside grounds. The Athletics were largely the winners, as the following score will show." The Athletics competed in Charleston's Colored Base Ball League. *Charleston News and Courier* (July 4, 1887): "the Detroits, the champion colored club of Savannah, will play the Athletics, the champions of the local Colored League, at the Park tomorrow afternoon. The contest will be very interesting, as it is to settle the colored championship of the two States."

SOURCES: "Local Dots," *Wilmington (NC) Morning Star*, Jun 30, 1885; "Colored Base Ball Match," *Wilmington Morning Star*, Jul 1, 1885; "Base Ball," *Wilmington Morning Star*, Jul 21, 1885; "Ball and Bat," *Charleston (SC) News and Courier*, Mar 18, 1887; "Our Brothers in Black," *Charleston News and Courier*, Apr 18, 1887; "Our Brothers in Black," *Charleston News and Courier*, Apr 19, 1887; "The Colored League," *Charleston News and Courier*, Apr 20, 1887; "Base Ball Summary," *Charleston News and Courier*, Apr 21, 1887; "Base Ball Notes," *Charleston News and Courier*, Apr 21, 1887; "Nine to Nothing," *Charleston News and Courier*, Apr 23, 1887; "The Colored League," *Charleston News and Courier*, Apr 26, 1887; "In the Dusky Diamond," *Charleston News and Courier*, Apr 29, 1887; "In the Dusky Diamond," *Charleston News and Courier*, Apr 30, 1887; "Athletics Down Mascotts," *Charleston News and Courier*, May 3, 1887; "The Colored Ball Tossers," *Charleston News and Courier*, May 6, 1887; "Base Ball Notes," *Charleston News and Courier*, May 7, 1887; "Orientals and Mascotts," *Charleston News and Courier*, May 9, 1887; "The Fight for the Flag," *Charleston News and Courier*, May 9, 1887; "Base Ball Notes," *Charleston News and Courier*, Jul 4, 1887.

Catcher Base Ball Club (Charleston, SC; 1870s)

The Catcher B.B.C., of Charlotte, SC, organized in the 1870s. They played against black nines. *Charleston News and Courier* (October 3, 1877): "The Catchers Base Ball Club, at a recent meeting, elected the following players, Edward Myers, Peter Grant, W. McKinley, Robert Howard, H. C. Williams, C. C. Chaffee, S. McKinley, Edward Ryan, and Charles Brown."

SOURCES: "Base Ball," *Charleston (SC) News and Courier*, Oct 3, 1877; "Base Ball," *Charleston Daily News*, Oct 9, 1877.

Colored Base Ball League (Charleston, SC; 1880s). Organizer(s): Charles Nesbitt.

Colored Base Ball League organized in 1887. Its organizers were Charles Nesbitt (Team President), W. G. Friday (Director), M. H. Dingle (Director), R. C. Brown (Director), and M. C. McClennan (Director). Nesbitt, a Broad Street barber, was called "the baseball muskrat of Charleston." *Charleston News* (April 21, 1887): "[Fans] will see a fine game, and at the same time help the Charleston Club, which needs money sorely now to buy new pitchers. President Nesbitt has his teams in excellent condition, and some good playing will be seen this afternoon." He put a quality product on the field. *Charleston News* (April 21, 1887): "All of the league games are more than worth seeing than most people are aware of. The clubs are handsomely uniformed and composed mostly of good players, while President Nesbitt is careful to have everything conducted in an orderly manner and in strict accordance with regular playing rules." The league teams: Iolanthe, Mascotts, Orientals, Metropolitans, Athletics. Many of the players had tried out for Charleston's entry, the Fultons,

in the League of Southern Colored Base Ballists in 1886. Not all of the best local players were selected: one uniformed nine, the Resolutes, a strong local amateur club, soundly defeated the Fultons in a practice game. The league's strongest club, the Athletics, received challenges from other organizations to battle for the black championship of the South; Wilmington, NC's Mutual B.B.C., Savannah, GA's Detroit B.B.C., and Columbia, SC's Rockaway B.B.C. figuring prominently.

SOURCES: "All Around Town," *Charleston (SC) News and Courier*, Feb 8, 1887; "The Colored League," *Charleston News and Courier*, Feb 19, 1887; "Ball and Bat," *Charleston News and Courier*, Mar 18, 1887; "Our Brothers in Black," *Charleston News and Courier*, Apr 18, 1887; "Our Brothers in Black," *Charleston News and Courier*, Apr 19, 1887; "The Colored League," *Charleston News and Courier*, Apr 20, 1887; "Base Ball Summary," *Charleston News and Courier*, Apr 21, 1887; "Base Ball Notes," *Charleston News and Courier*, Apr 21, 1887; "Nine to Nothing," *Charleston News and Courier*, Apr 23, 1887; "The Colored League," *Charleston News and Courier*, Apr 26, 1887; "In the Dusky Diamond," *Charleston News and Courier*, Apr 29, 1887; "In the Dusky Diamond," *Charleston News and Courier*, Apr 30, 1887; "Athletics Down Mascotts," *Charleston News and Courier*, May 3, 1887; "The Colored Ball Tossers," *Charleston News and Courier*, May 6, 1887; "Base Ball Notes," *Charleston News and Courier*, May 7, 1887; "Orientals and Mascotts," *Charleston News and Courier*, May 9, 1887; "The Fight for the Flag," *Charleston News and Courier*, May 9, 1887; "Base Ball Notes," *Charleston News and Courier*, May 12, 1887; "Colored Base Ballists to the Front Again," *Charleston News and Courier*, Jun 7, 1887; "Colored Base Ballists to the Front Again," *Charleston News and Courier*, Jun 7, 1887; "Base Ball Notes," *Charleston News and Courier*, Jun 9, 1887; "Base Ball Notes," *Charleston News and Courier*, Jun 11, 1887; "Base Ball Notes," *Charleston News and Courier*, Jun 12, 1887; "Base Ball Notes," *Charleston News and Courier*, Jun 13, 1887; "Base Ball Notes," *Charleston News and Courier*, Jun 14, 1887; "Base Ball Notes," *Charleston News and Courier*, Jun 15, 1887; "Base Ball Notes," *Charleston News and Courier*, Jun 17, 1887; "Base Ball Notes," *Charleston News and Courier*, Jun 20, 1887; "Base Ball Notes," *Charleston News and Courier*, Jun 27, 1887; "Base Ball Notes," *Charleston News and Courier*, Jun 30, 1887; "Base Ball Notes," *Charleston News and Courier*, Jul 4, 1887; "Base Ball Notes," *Charleston News and Courier*, Jul 6, 1887.

Crescent Base Ball Club (Charleston, SC; 1860s–1870s). Organizer(s): Aaron McCoy, G. J. H. Graham, William Blakely and J. G. Kirk.

The Crescent B.B.C. organized in 1867, played against black nines. They played the Ashley club. *Charleston News* (June 25, 1867): "A match game of base-ball was played on the Citadel Ground last evening, between the Ashley and Crescent (both colored). The Crescents won; the score being 26 to 24." A rivalry developed with Beaufort, SC. *News* (July 29, 1868): "The Rising Sun Base Ball Club regret to be compelled to inform their Charleston friends, and especially the Crescent Base Ball Club, that in account of the non-arrival of the steamer they were compelled to disappoint them in the match game to have been played in the 8th instant." *News* (August 15, 1874): "The Rising Sun Base Ball Club, of Beaufort, S.C., and the Crescent Club, of this city, both colored, will play a match game at the foot of Broad Street, this afternoon, at half past two o'clock." *News* (August 8, 1869): "A match game of ball was played on Citadel Green last evening between the Ashley and Crescent Clubs (both colored). The Crescents won. The score being 24 to 22." *Charleston News and Courier* (August 15, 1874): "A match game of base-ball will be played on the Citadel Green this afternoon between the Crescent and Jersey Clubs, colored."

SOURCES: "Base Ball," *Charleston (SC) News*, Jun 25, 1867; "Base Ball," *Charleston News*, Jul 29, 1868; "Clubs and Stars," *Charleston News*, Feb 18, 1869; "Crumbs," *Charleston News*, Aug 8, 1869; "Base Ball," *Charleston News*, Aug 11, 1868; *New York (NY) Clipper*, Aug 29, 1868; "Good Advice," *Charleston News*, Sep 21, 1869; "Talk About Town," *Charleston (SC) News and Courier*, Jul 24, 1874; "Base Ball Notes," *Charleston News and Courier*, Aug 15, 1874; "Base Ball Notes," *Charleston News and Courier*, Aug 17, 1874.

Excelsior Base Ball Club (Charleston, SC; 1870s–1890s)

The Excelsior B.B.C. organized in the 1870s, played black nines. *Charleston News & Courier* (September 10, 1875): "The Excelsior and Planters Base Ball Clubs played a game at the Citadel Green yesterday afternoon, the former defeating the latter by 22 to 16. During the game a colored batter named John G. Miller was struck in the eye by a flying ball and was painfully hurt." They reorganized in 1890s, developing a rivalry with Wilmington's black teams. *Wilmington Messenger* (June 6, 1895): "The guarantee of $100 to get the Wilmington Black Stockings Base Ball Club here for three games next week has been secured, through the names of some of Charleston's most enterprising citizens. Correspondence has been opened with that club."

SOURCES: "Ball Tossers Captured," *Charleston (SC) News & Courier, Jul 28, 1875;* "A Sooty Scene," *Charleston News and Courier,* Sep 8, 1875; "Base Ball and Black Eye," *Charleston News and Courier,* Sep 10, 1875; "Excursion From Charleston," *Wilmington (NC) Messenger,* Jun 6, 1895; *Wilmington Messenger, Sep 7, 1895.*

Fear Not Base Ball Club (Charleston, SC; 1890s). Organizer(s): Frank W. Thorne.

The Fear Not B.B.C. organized in the 1890s, played black nines. *Charleston News and Courier* (August 15, 1891): "The colored population is having some great ball. Every afternoon this week, the Fear Nots and Mutuals have played at the Base Ball Park. The Fear Nots are the unquestioned champions of South Carolina and the Mutuals are boss ball tossers from Savannah, Georgia. The Charleston club has as its crack pitcher Shavers; Brown is the catcher. The chief battery for the Savannah club is Ralston, pitcher, and Mackay catcher." The rivalry persisted in the press. *Savannah Tribune* (June 25, 1892): "The Chatham Base Ball Club will leave tomorrow for Charleston where they will cross bats with the Fear Nots next week. On the following Sunday they will return accompanied by the Fear Nots and will play a series of games here next week. It will be remembered that these clubs kept up the base-ball spirit in the city last season when there were no league games." They developed an ongoing rivalry with Wilmington, NC's colored teams. *Wilmington Messenger* (June 6, 1895): "The guarantee of $100 to get the Wilmington Black Stockings Base Ball Club here for three games next week has been secured, through the names of some of Charleston's most enterprising citizens. Correspondence has been opened with that club."

SOURCES: "Some Good Black Base Ball," *Charleston (SC) News and Courier, Jul 5, 1890;* "Diamond Dots," *Charleston News and Courier,* Aug 12, 1891; "A Triumph for the Fear Nots," *Charleston News and Courier,* May 20, 1891; "A Day at Darlington," *Charleston News and Courier,* May 21, 1891; "A Possible Savannah Scalp," *Charleston News and Courier,* Jul 31, 1891; "Struggling for the Championship," *Charleston News and Courier,* Aug 15, 1891; "All Around Town," *Charleston News and Courier,* Jun 9, 1892; "Chathams the Champions," *Savannah (GA) Tribune,* Jun 25, 1892; "All Around Town," *Charleston News and Courier,* Apr 5, 1893; *Savannah Tribune,* May 27, 1893; "Excursion From Charleston," *Wilmington (NC) Messenger,* Jun 6, 1895; "Have You Heard This?," *Charleston (SC) Evening Post,* Jun 27, 1895.

Fulton Base Ball Club (Charleston, SC; 1870s–1880s)

The Fulton B.B.C. organized in the 1870s, played against black nines. *Charleston News and Courier* (October 5, 1876): "The Fulton Base Ball Club, colored, has gone into winter quarters and claims the championship over all the city and State clubs." *News and Courier* (September 4, 1877): "The Corrides and Fulton, colored, Base Ball Clubs, played a match game on the Citadel Green yesterday evening." They reorganized in the 1880s. *News and Courier* (September 18, 1877): "A match game of base-ball will be played on the Citadel Green, commencing at half-past 2 o'clock, between the Arlington and Fulton Juniors." In 1886, they joined the Southern League of Colored Base Ballists. *News and Courier* (June 20, 1886): "Those who expected to witness an interesting game of baseball between two of the best colored clubs in Charleston at the Base Ball Park were much disappointed in their expectations. The Fultons banked heavily on the pitcher, the phenomenal Babe Smith, who by the way was batted out the box about the middle of the game and his place supplied by a pitcher who was pounded all over the field. The Resolutes, which are only a picked nine recently organized for the purpose of playing the professional Fultons won the game by a score of 28 to 17." *Atlanta Constitution* (June 23, 1886): "The Atlanta Champions easily defeated the Fultons of Charleston yesterday, by a score of 12 to 6. Thompson and Maddox battery for the Champions."

SOURCES: "The Ball and Bat," *Charleston (SC) News and Courier,* Oct 5, 1876; "Base Ball," *Charleston News and Courier,* Sep 4, 1877; "Odds and Ends," *Charleston News and Courier,* Sep 18, 1877; "Black Diamonds," *Charleston News and Courier,* Jun 2, 1886; "The Colored Base Ball Players," *Charleston News and Courier,* Jun 3, 1886; "Our Brothers in Black," *Charleston News and Courier,* Jun 19, 1886; "Shut Out by the Umpire," *Charleston News and Courier,* Jun 20, 1886; "Diamond Dust," *Atlanta (GA) Constitution,* Jun 23, 1886.

Manhattan Base Ball Club (Charleston, SC; 1870s)

The Manhattan B.B.C. organized in the 1870s, played against black nines. *Charleston News and Courier* (September 12, 1877): "The Pacific and Manhattan (colored) Base Ball Clubs played a match game on the Citadel Green yesterday. The game was a close one at first but the Pacifics became demoralized in the last two innings and one of their players dropped out. The score stood: Manhattans, 24; Pacifics, 9."

SOURCES: "Odd and Ends," *Charleston (SC) News and Courier,* Aug 30, 1877; "Base Ball Match," *Charleston News and Courier,* Sep 6, 1877; "Ball and Bat," *Charleston News and Courier,* Sep 10, 1877; "Colored Base Ballists," *Charleston News and Courier,* Sep 12, 1877; "Base Ball Notes," *Charleston News and Courier,* Sep 12, 1877.

Mutual Base Ball Club (Charleston, SC; 1860s). Organizer(s): R. W. Matthews.

The Mutual B.B.C. organized in the 1860s, played against black teams. *Charleston News* (June 25, 1867): "Attend a special meeting for your club this evening, at seven o'clock, at 106 Coming-Street. Punctual attendance is required as business of importance is to be transcribed." *News* (July 29, 1868): "A match game of baseball was played in the Citadel Green yesterday afternoon before a large crowd of spectators, by the colored baseball clubs, Ashley and Mutual. The score stood Ashley, 27; Mutual, 12." A rivalry developed with the Ashleys. *News* (September 16, 1868): "The Colored Base Ballists seem to keep up the sport with much spirit. In a return game between the Mutual and Ashley clubs, played Monday afternoon, in Citadel Green, the latter won, the score standing twenty-two to twenty."

SOURCES: "Ashley Base Ball Club," *Charleston (SC) News*, Jun 25, 1867; "Base Ballists," *Charleston News*, Jul 29, 1868; "Base Ball," *Charleston News*, Aug 11, 1868; "Colored Base Ball," *Charleston News*, Sep 11, 1868; "Base Ball," *Charleston News*, Sep 14, 1868; *Charleston News*, Sep 16, 1868; "Ashley Base Ball Club," *Charleston News, Jan 19*, 1869.

Niagara Base Ball Club (Charleston, SC; 1870s)

The Niagara B.B.C. organized in the 1870s. The Niagaras, composed of members of the Niagara Colored Fire Company, played against black organizations. *Charleston News and Courier* (August 8, 1877): "The much discussed game of base-ball between the Niagara picked nine and the Charleston regular nine was played at the Citadel Green yesterday in the presence of a large crowd, colored, like the players. Both nines had a number of friends, who manifested a deep interest in the result. The playing was pretty good, and at some stages very exciting. But eight innings were played, when the score stood 21 to 18 in favor of the Niagaras, who were lustily cheered." *News and Courier* (August 9, 1877): "The second game of the series being played between the Niagaras and Charlestons will take place this afternoon, at the Citadel Green. Much interest is felt in the final result of the match."

SOURCES: "The Ball and Bat," *Charleston (SC) News and Courier*, Aug 2, 1877; "Match Game of Ball," *Charleston News and Courier*, Aug 8, 1877; "Niagaras vs. Charleston," *Charleston News and Courier*, Aug 9, 1877.

Oriental Base Ball Club (Charleston, SC; 1870s–1880s). Organizer(s): James Moore.

The Oriental B.B.C. organized in the 1870s, played against black nines. *Charleston News and Courier* (August 31, 1877): "The base-ball match which was expected to come off between a colored club from Columbia, and the Orientals of this city, yesterday, was prevented by the departure of most of the Columbia Club for home. A few of them remained, however, and with a well selected nine played a game with the Orientals, which resulted in a score of 22 to 8 in favor of the latter. The Red Wings, of this city, and the Dauntless of Beaufort, both colored, will play on the Citadel Green, this evening." The Orientals reorganized in the 1880s, joining Charleston's Colored Base Ball League.

SOURCES: "The Oriental Base Ball Club," *Charleston (SC) News and Courier*, Sep 22, 1877; "Colored Base Ball Clubs," *Charleston News and Courier*, Aug 31, 1877; "Ball and Bat," *Charleston News and Courier*, Sep 10, 1877; "Base Ball," *Charleston News and Courier*, Oct 9, 1877; "Base Ball," *Charleston News and Courier*, Oct 3, 1877; "Base Ball," *Charleston News and Courier*, Oct 9, 1877; "All Around Town," *Charleston News and Courier*, Feb 8, 1887; "The Colored League," *Charleston News and Courier*, Feb 19, 1887; "Ball and Bat," *Charleston News and Courier*, Mar 18, 1887; "Our Brothers in Black," *Charleston News and Courier*, Apr 18, 1887; "Our Brothers in Black," *Charleston News and Courier*, Apr 19, 1887; "The Colored League," *Charleston News and Courier*, Apr 20, 1887; "Base Ball Summary," *Charleston News and Courier*, Apr 21, 1887; "Base Ball Notes," *Charleston News and Courier*, Apr 21, 1887; "Nine to Nothing," *Charleston News and Courier*, Apr 23, 1887.

Pacific Base Ball Club (Charleston, SC; 1870s). Organizer(s): James Moore and William Gammon.

The Pacific B.B.C. organized in the 1870s, played black nines. *Charleston News and Courier* (August 31, 1877): "The Pacific Base Ball Club, colored, and a picked nine dubbed the Unknown, played a match on the Citadel Green yesterday, which resulted in a score of 14 to 14. A club which was expected from Beaufort did not come."

They played Charleston's Manhattans. *News and Courier* (September 6, 1877): "The playing of the Young Pacifics and Manhattans was in many instances remarkably good. The feature of the game was a beautiful running one hand catch by W. McKinley, shortstop, of the Pacifics in the left field. Gammon of the Pacifics also did well at the bat, making a clean score." Following their victory, there was a follow-up match. *News and Courier* (September 11, 1877): "The Pacific and Manhattan (colored) Base Ball Clubs played a match game on the Citadel Green yesterday. The game was a close one at first, but the Pacifics became demoralized in the last two innings, and one of their best players dropped out. The score stood: Manhattans 24; Pacifics 9."

SOURCES: "Short Stops," *New York (NY) Clipper*, Jul 17, 1875; "Talk About Town," *Charleston (SC) News and Courier*, Sep 21, 1875; "Odd and Ends," *Charleston (SC) News and Courier*, Aug 30, 1877; "Colored Base Ball Club," *Charleston News and Courier*, Aug 31, 1877; "Base Ball Match," *Charleston News and Courier*, Sep 6, 1877; "Base Ball on the Green," *Charleston News and Courier*, Sep 11, 1877; "Colored Base Ball Clubs," *Charleston News and Courier*, Sep 11, 1877.

Red Wing Base Ball Club (Charleston, SC; 1870s)

The Red Wing B.B.C., of Columbia, SC, organized in the 1870s, played against black nines. *Charleston News and Courier* (August 14, 1877): "The Charleston and Red Wing nines will play a match game at the Citadel Green this afternoon at 3 o'clock. These nines propose to play a series of three games for the city championship. *News and Courier* (October 3, 1877): "A game of ball was to have been played at the Citadel Green yesterday, between the Red Wings of this city and the Dauntless Club, of Beaufort. The Beaufort Club, not arriving, the Red Wings played the Orientals, the score standing 48 to 11 in favor of the latter."

SOURCES: "Base Ball," *Charleston (SC) News and Courier*, Aug 14, 1877; "Base Ball," *Charleston News and Courier*, Oct 2, 1877; "Base Ball," *Charleston News and Courier*, Oct 3, 1877.

Resolute Base Ball Club (Charleston, SC; 1870s–1890s)

The Resolute B.B.C., of Charleston, SC, organized in the 1870s, played black nines. *Charleston News and Courier* (June 2, 1886): "Those who expected to witness an interesting game of base-ball between two of the best colored clubs in Charleston at the Base Ball Park were much disappointed in their expectations. The Fultons banked heavily on their pitcher, the phenomenal Babe Smith, who by the way was batted out the box about the middle of the game and his place supplied by a pitcher who was pounded all over the field. The Resolutes, which are only a picked nine recently organized for the purpose of playing the professional Fultons won the game by a score of 28 to 17." They played Wilmington. *Wilmington Messenger* (May 29, 1891): "The Resolute Baseball Club colored ball players of Charleston, have challenged the Mutuals, the crack colored team of Wilmington. The Resolutes will come on the excursion from Charleston, which will have on Saturday, June 6th, and arrive here next day, June 8th, and the Mutuals have decided to cross bats with the Charlestonians on that day."

SOURCES: "Black Diamonds," *Charleston (SC) News and Courier*, Jun 2, 1886; "The Colored Base Ball Players," *Charleston News and Courier*, Jun 3, 1886; "Our Brothers in Black," *Charleston News and Courier*, Jun 19, 1886; "Shut Out by the Umpire," *Charleston News and Courier*, Jun 20, 1886; "To Cross Bats with Charleston," *Wilmington (NC) Messenger*, May 29, 1891; "The Excursion from Charleston," *Wilmington Messenger*, Jun 6, 1891.

Wild Rose Base Ball Club (Charleston, SC; 1870s)

The Wild Rose B.B.C. organized in the 1870s, played against black nines. *Charleston News and Courier* (June 5, 1877): "A game of ball was played yesterday between the Arlington and Wild Rose, colored base-ball clubs, which resulted in favor of the Arlingtons, by a score of 24 to 9." They also crossed with the Fultons. *Charleston News and Courier* (June 6, 1877): "The Wild Rose and Orange Blossom Base Ball Clubs, whose members are colored urchins, played a game at the Citadel Green yesterday, the score resulting 39 to 21, in favor of the Wild Rose."

SOURCES: "Base Ball," *Charleston (SC) News and Courier*, Jun 5, 1877; "Odds and Ends," *Charleston News and Courier*, Jun 6, 1877.

Allen University Base Ball Club (Columbia, SC; 1890s–1900s)

The Allen University B.B.C. organized in the 1890s. The aggregation played other black colleges, and independent clubs. *Charleston State* (April 20, 1895): "Yesterday afternoon, two colored baseball teams, the Howard School and Allen University, played a pretty game of ball at the park. The game was hotly contested throughout. There was a good attendance. The Howards won their second game from the Allens by a score of 7 to 5." *Columbia State* (May 11, 1895): "Yesterday afternoon the Allen University and Eastern Star baseball teams, colored, played a hotly contested game. Allen won by a score of 6 to 1." *State* (May 22, 1900): "The Howard baseball team again defeated the Allen team yesterday afternoon by a score of 6 to 12." *Columbia State* (May 27, 1895): "Today there is to be another colored baseball game at the baseball park between the Devils and the Allen University team. The sharpest rivalry exists between the two teams."

SOURCES: "Colored Baseball," *Columbia (SC) State*, Apr 11, 1895; "Colored Baseball," *Columbia State*, Apr 20, 1895; "Colored Ball Today," *Columbia State*, May 3, 1895; "Colored Baseball," *Columbia State*, May 11, 1895; "Colored Baseball," *Columbia State*, May 24, 1895; "Colored Baseball," *Columbia State*, May 27, 1895; "For the Colored Hospital," *Columbia State*, Jun 3, 1896; "Colored Baseball Game," *Columbia State*, May 4, 1900; "Allen Again Defeated," *Columbia State*, May 22, 1900.

Clipper Base Ball Club (Columbia, SC; 1890s)

The Clipper B.B.C. organized in the 1890s. *Columbia State* (June 24, 1891): "The Clippers, Columbia's crack colored base-ball club, is to go to Charleston tomorrow on the trip with the Capital City Guards, who are to make their visit on that day to the City by the Sea. They will wear new uniforms, consisting of blue striped caps, shirts of the same and black stockings and belts."

SOURCES: "Columbia's Colored Baseballists," *Columbia (SC) State*, Jun 24, 1891; "Baseball This Afternoon," *Columbia State*, Aug 10, 1891; "The Game Was A Tie," *Columbia State*, Aug 11, 1891; "Colored Base Ball," *Columbia State*, Aug 16, 1891; "Short Statements," *Columbia State*, Aug 18, 1891.

Howard University Base Ball Club (Columbia, SC; 1890s–1900s)

The Howard University B.B.C. organized in the 1890s, played black aggregations. *Charleston State* (April 20, 1895): "Yesterday afternoon, two colored baseball teams, the Howard School and Allen University, played a pretty game of ball at the park. The game was hotly contested throughout. There was a good attendance. The Howards won their second game from the Allens by a score of 7 to 5." *Charleston Evening Post* (April 11, 1900): "President Miller of the State Colored College and manager Wilkinson with a large number of teachers will be in the city Saturday with their strong baseball team. The team, which is regarded as the strongest among the colored schools of the State, will play a series of games next week with the Biddle, Bennett and Livingston college teams in North Carolina. They will cross bats with the Howards at the fairground." *Charleston Evening Post* (May 25, 1900): "The Howard, colored base-ball team,

defeated the Summerville team yesterday. The Howards were too much for their opponents. Jefferson and Williams pitched for the Howards: there were three base hits off Jefferson, not one off Williams. Howard's next game will be with Biddle University at Charlotte."

SOURCES: "Howards Victorious," *Columbia (SC) State*, Jul 21, 1894; *Columbia State*, Aug 10, 1894; "Good Game of Ball," *Columbia State*, Aug 16, 1894; "The Howards Win Again," *Columbia State*, Aug 31, 1894; "The Tables Turned," *Columbia State*, Sep 7, 1894; "Colored Baseball," *Columbia State*, Apr 20, 1895; "Colored Ball," *Charlotte (NC) Observer*, Jun 25, 1895; "Colored Baseball," *Columbia State*, Jul 31, 1895; "Each Won One," *Columbia State*, Aug 3, 1895; "For the Colored Hospital," *Columbia State*, Jun 3, 1896; "Short Statements," *Columbia State*, Jun 11, 1896; "Colored Baseball," *Columbia State*, Aug 30, 1896; "Baseball News," *Columbia (SC) Evening Post*, Apr 11, 1900; "Colored Base Ball Game," *Columbia State*, May 4, 1900; "News Notes," *Columbia Evening Post*, May 25, 1900; "Colored Baseball Today," *Columbia State*, Jun 11, 1900 "Howard vs. Savannah," *Columbia State*, Jul 1, 1900.

Manhattan Base Ball Club (Columbia, SC; 1870s)

The Manhattan B.B.C. organized in the 1870s. The "Manhattans" played against colored clubs, of SC. *Charleston News and Courier* (October 3, 1877): "The Oriental and Columbia, colored, base Ball Clubs will play a match game on the Citadel Green, this afternoon commencing at 2 o'clock."

SOURCES: "Base Ball," *Charleston (SC) News and Courier*, Oct 1, 1877; "Base Ball," *Charleston News and Courier*, Oct 2, 1877; "Base Ball," *Charleston News and Courier*, Oct 3, 1877.

Independent Champions (Greenville, SC; 1890s)

The Independent Champions B.B.C. organized in the 1890s, played black aggregations. *Asheville Daily Citizen* (July 20, 1893): "Greenville and Asheville met on the diamond again at Carrier's Track yesterday, the game between colored teams of these cities, however. The Greenville Independent Champions contested with the Lone Stars of Asheville and were defeated by the home team by a score of 13 to 12." *Asheville Citizen-Times* (July 21, 1893): "The Greenville Independent Champions and the second colored nine of Asheville played two games of baseball yesterday. The Greenvilles won both games, in the morning by a score of 16 to 6 and in the afternoon by 12 to 6."

SOURCES: *Asheville (NC) Citizen*, Jun 29, 1892; "Deserved Defeat," *Asheville Citizen*, Jul 20, 1893; "Around Town," *Asheville Citizen*, Jul 20, 1893; "Around Town," *Asheville (NC) Citizen-Times*, Jul 21, 1893; "Around Town," *Asheville Daily Citizen*, Aug 14, 1893; *Asheville Citizen*, Aug 15, 1893; *Asheville Citizen*, Apr 9, 1894; *Asheville Citizen*, Jun 21, 1894; *Asheville Citizen*, Jun 27, 1894.

Olympic Base Ball Club (Port Royal, SC; 1870s). Organizer(s): Arthur M. Hamilton and O. F. Duke.

The Olympic B.B.C., of Port Royal, SC, organized in the 1870s, played black nines. *Beaufort Tribune and Port Royal Commercial* (May 31, 1877): "The Dauntless Base Ball Club will go to Port Royal next Monday on the morning train to play a return game with the Olympics." *Tribune and Port Royal Commercial* (June 7, 1877): "The Dauntless Base Ball Club defeated the Olympics, by a score of 33 to 6."

SOURCES: "Local Items," *Beaufort (SC) Tribune and Port Royal Commercial*, Apr 26, 1877; "Local Items," *Beaufort Tribune and Port Royal Commercial*, May 24, 1877; "Local Items," *Beaufort Tribune and Port Royal Commercial*, May 31, 1877; "Local Items," *Beaufort Tribune and Port Royal Commercial*, Jun 7, 1877.

South Dakota

Plutonian Base Ball Club (Deadwood, SD; 1880s)

The Plutonian B.B.C. organized in 1881. The Plutonians, composed of soldiers, played white nines. *Deadwood Black Hill Weekly Pioneer* (April 23, 1881): "The match game of ball between the new Deadwood nine—Stars—and the colored club on the Ingleside grounds, resulted in favor of the Stars by a score of 27 to 7, in seven innings."

SOURCES: *Deadwood (SD) Times*, Apr 23, 1881; *Deadwood (SD) Black Hills Weekly Pioneer*, Apr 23, 1881.

Tennessee

Tigers Base Ball Club (Athens, TN; 1880s)

The Tigers B.B.C. organized in the 1880s, played against black teams. *Knoxville Journal and Tribune* (August 9, 1889): "A small crowd gathered at Beaman's Lake to witness the first game between Luck's Tigers of Athens and the Lone Stars, knew well how to use the willow dexterously. The Lone Stars held their own, winning by a score of 8 to 5."

SOURCES: "Another Base Ball Game," *Knoxville (TN) Journal and Tribune*, Aug 9, 1889; "The Lone Stars On Top Again," *Knoxville Journal and Tribune*, Aug 11, 1889.

A. W. Massengale Base Ball Club (Chattanooga, TN; 1880s). Organizer(s): A. W. Massengale.

The A. W. Massengale B.B.C. organized in the 1880s, played black teams. *Knoxville Chronicle* (July 4, 1885): "The A. W. Massengales, of Chattanooga, and the Lone Stars, of Knoxville, will play for the championship of East Tennessee today at 10 o'clock. The preliminary game yesterday afternoon between the Massengales, of Chattanooga, and the L. E. Paynes, of this city, both colored clubs, resulted in favor of the former by a score of 13 to 12. The game was in many respects a good one and showed considerable ball talent on both sides." *Chronicle* (July 5, 1885): "The Massengales, of Chattanooga, played the Lone Stars of this place yesterday, with the following score: Massengales, 18: Lone Stars, 9. The Lone Stars had better practice more and not smoke too many cigarettes."

SOURCES: "Base Ball," *Knoxville (TN) Chronicle*, Jul 4, 1885; "Base Ball," *Knoxville (TN) Chronicle*, Jul 5, 1885.

Olympic Base Ball Club (Chattanooga, TN; 1870s–1880s)

The Olympic B.B.C. organized in the 1870s, played against black nines. Following a bitter loss to Atlanta, GA's Colored Champions B.B.C., the Chattanoogans telegraphed *Atlanta Constitution*, saying that they beat them. It wasn't true. Atlanta players returning home discovered the deception and malice of its rivals. *Atlanta Constitution* (July 7, 1877): "So far as the comportment of the Atlanta colored club is concerned, we have nothing to indicate that it was not correct and gentlemanly. We hope that Chattanooga will give a better reception to others who may visit her city in the future." *Nashville Tennessean* (September 8, 1877): "The Chattanoogans came up to witness a match game of base-ball, to be played upon the Tan Yard grounds at 3:30 this afternoon, between the Olympics, of that city, and the Blue Clippers, of Nashville."

SOURCES: "Base Ball," *Atlanta (TN) Constitution*, Jul 7, 1877; "Colored Excursionists," *Nashville (TN) Tennessean*, Sep 8, 1877.

Champion Base Ball Club (Chattanooga, TN; 1880s). Organizer(s): Robert Smalls and S. G. Roberts.

The Champion B.B.C. organized in the 1880s, played black teams. *Memphis Appeal* (June 8, 1886): "The Chattanooga Champions (col-

ored) defeated the Eclipse (colored) Club of this city yesterday by a score of 11 to 10. The battery for the Eclipse were Pointer and Wood. Renfroe, the great Eclipse pitcher, did not play."

SOURCES: "Base Ball," *New Orleans (LA) Times-Democrats*, Jun 8, 1886; "Base Ball Notes," *Memphis (TN) Appeal*, Jun 8, 1886.

R. S. Smith Base Ball Club (Chattanooga, TN; 1880s)

The R. S. Smith B.B.C. organized in the 1880s, played black teams. *Nashville Tennessean* (July 3, 1882): "The Smith Base Ball Club of Chattanooga, arrived here this morning, and will play the A. K. Wards one day this week." *Nashville Tennessean* (July 6, 1882): "About three or 4000 people assembled on the Sulphur Spring Bottom yesterday afternoon to witness the match game of baseball played between the R. S. Smiths, of Chattanooga, and the A. K. Wards, of this city. A great deal of enthusiasm prevailed throughout the game. Score: Smiths 9, A. K. Wards 5."

SOURCES: "Base Ball," *Nashville (TN) Tennessean*, Jul 3, 1882; "Base Ball," *Nashville Tennessean*, Jul 6, 1882.

Tennessee Rangers Base Ball Club (Chattanooga, TN; 1870s–1880s). Owner(s): S. B. Du Boise.

The Tennessee Rangers B.B.C. organized in the 1870s, played black nines. *Memphis Appeal* (May 18, 1878): "The Tennessee Rangers, a crack colored base ball club of this city that has been defeating every club they have met this season, went down to Dalton yesterday, and played a game with the Wildcats of that place. A dispatch was received from Captain S. B. Du Boise says that the Chattanooga were victorious by a score of 25 to 8. The rangers expect to go up to East Tennessee soon, and teach the boys in that portion of the country also how to play ball." *Knoxville Chronicle* (August 24, 1880): "Yesterday the James A. Garfield Base Ball Club (colored), of Knoxville, played a match game of ball with the Tennessee Rangers (colored of this city). The Garfields were signally defeated, making only seven scores, while the Rangers scored thirty. Both clubs did good playing but the Chattanooga club is much better. Today the Smith's B.B.C., of this city [colored], W. C. Down, captain, will play the Garfields for a $20 purse. The Garfields desire to meet the Rangers or Smiths on their own grounds soon."

SOURCES: "Exchange Diamond Sparks," *Memphis (TN) Appeal*, May 18, 1878; "Base Ball," *Knoxville (TN) Chronicle*, Aug 24, 1880; "Base Ball Notes," *Knoxville Chronicle*, Aug 5, 1881.

Union Base Ball Club (Chattanooga, TN; 1900s). Owner(s): A. W. Massengale, John McCafferty, Thomas M. Henderson and Charles Brown.

The Union B.B.C. organized in the 1900s, played black aggregations. *Indianapolis Freeman* (July 28, 1900): "The Chattanooga Unions defeated the Florence Grays Monday afternoon July 16, Chattanooga defeated Florence 18 to 2. Quite a large crowd of both white and black attended." *Freeman* (August 11, 1900): "Base Ball was played between the Chattanooga Unions and the Atlanta Deppens, July 30 and 31 at Atlanta, Georgia. The boys met with great success financially and socially and say they had the best time they ever witnessed on a trip of that kind. We are proud to say the Chattanooga team beat the Atlanta team by a score of 16 to 9 on the 30th and 19 to 12 on the 31st." *Freeman* (August 25, 1900): "Chattanooga Unions played Knoxville Base Ball team Wednesday Aug. 8, on the Knoxville diamond the score being 8 to 3 in Chattanooga's favor. They challenge the Atlanta Deppens for two game Aug. 16 and 17."

SOURCES: "Chattanooga News," *Indianapolis (IN) Freeman*, Jul 28, 1900; "Interesting Items," *Indianapolis Freeman*, Aug 11, 1900; "Chattanooga News," *Indianapolis Freeman*, Aug 25, 1900.

White Stocking Base Ball Club (Chattanooga, TN; 1880s–1890s)

The White Stocking (Chattanooga Whites or Whitesides) B.B.C. organized in the 1880s, played black teams. *Knoxville Chronicle* (May 12, 1885): "There will be a match of base-ball between the I. E. Paynes of Knoxville, and the Whites of Chattanooga." *Huntsville Gazette* (July 17, 1886): "The Memphis Original Base Ball Club will cross bats with the Chattanooga Whites at the same time and place for a purse of $50.—Memphis Watchman." *Journal and Tribune* (August 29, 1889): "The Lone Stars, Knoxville's crack colored base-ball team, has returned from Chattanooga, where they cleaned up, defeated, and wiped out all the colored nines in that city. They defeated the Whitesides in two games and the J. J. Ivins in one game. The Lone Stars have won eight out of the nine games played this season."

SOURCES: "Colored Excursion," *Knoxville (TN) Chronicle*, May 12, 1885; "Notes and Sentiments," *Huntsville (AL) Gazette*, Jul 17, 1886; "Great Ball," *Knoxville (TN) Journal and Tribune*, Aug 22, 1889; "Victorious Lone Stars," *Knoxville Journal and Tribune*, Aug 29, 1889; "Crack Colored Teams," *Nashville (TN) Tennessean*, Aug 16, 1896; "Rock City Unions Win," *Nashville (TN) Tennessean*, Aug 18, 1896; "Three Straight Wins," *Nashville (TN) Tennessean*, Aug 20, 1896.

Blue Danube Base Ball Club (Clarksville, TN; 1870s)

The Blue Danube B.B.C. organized in the 1870s, played black nines. *Clarksville Weekly Chronicle* (August 28, 1875): "The Blue Danubes of this city defeated the Gray Eagles of Hopkinsville, in this city, last Thursday, by a core of 44 to 34.—Both clubs are colored."

SOURCES: "Base Ball," *Clarksville (TN) Weekly Chronicle*, Aug 28, 1875.

Queen City Base Ball Club (Clarksville, TN; 1890s)

The Queen City B.B.C. organized in the 1890s, played black nines. *Indianapolis Freeman* (September 9, 1893): "The Clarksville colored base-ball team played against the Rudolphtown last Saturday and the scores stood 5 to 3 in favor of the Clarksville boys." *Nashville Tennessean* (May 22, 1895): "The first game of base-ball in Clarksville this season was played between the colored clubs of Nashville and Clarksville resulting in a victory for Nashville. 9 to 6." *Hopkinsville Kentuckian* (May 24, 1895): "The first game of base-ball in Clarksville this season was played Monday between the colored clubs between Nashville and Clarksville, resulting in a victory for the Nashville Club. 9 to 6." *Evansville Courier and Press* (July 25, 1899): "The Majors of this city and the Queen Citys of Clarksville, Tennessee crossed bats yesterday afternoon. The Majors [of Evansville, Indiana] played an excellent game of ball and would have shut out the Queen City team had it not been for an error by Abe Jackson."

SOURCES: "The City of Bills," *Indianapolis (IN) Freeman*, Sep 9, 1893; "Handsomely Entertained," *Indianapolis Freeman*. September. 15, 1894; "General Sporting Notes," *Nashville Tennessean*, May 22, 1895; "Here and There," *Kentuckian* (Hopkinsville, KY), May 24, 1895; "Here and There," *Kentuckian*, June 7, 1895; "Here and There," *Kentuckian*, July 19, 1895; "Death of a Respected Citizen," *Indianapolis Freeman*, May 17, 1897; "General News," *Indianapolis Freeman*, Jun 10, 1899; "Base Ball," *Indianapolis Freeman*, Jul 8, 1899; "Interesting News," *Indianapolis Freeman*, Jul 15, 1899; "Among Colored Folks," *Courier and Press* (Evansville, IN), July 7, 1899; "Among Colored Folks," *Courier and Press*, July 14, 1899; "Among Colored Folks," *Courier and Press*, July 21, 1899; "Among Colored Folks," *Courier and Press*, July 25, 1899; "General News," *Indianapolis Freeman*, Aug 19, 1899; "Social Happenings," *Indianapolis Freeman*, Jul 19, 1900; "Sporting Notes," *Indianapolis Freeman*, Jul 23, 1900; "Sport," *Indianapolis Freeman*, Aug 18, 1900.

White Belts Base Ball Club (Clarksville, TN; 1880s)

The White Belts B.B.C. organized in the 1880s, played against black teams. *Nashville Tennessean* (August 20, 1884): "The game of base-ball between the Langstons, of this city, and the White Belts, of Clarksville, two colored clubs, was witnessed by several hundred colored persons, and about as many white men, who desired to see the sport."

SOURCES: "Base Ball," *Nashville (TN) Tennessean*, Aug 19, 1884; "Black Batters," *Nashville Tennessean*, Aug 20, 1884.

Blue Stocking Base Ball Club (Columbia, TN; 1870s)

The Blue Stocking B.B.C. organized in the 1870s, played black teams; among them, the Bethany Colored Apes (Colored Bengal Tigers), Bunker Hill Colored Flys, Elkton Colored Monks, and Pulaski's Colored Rifles B.B.C. *Pulaski Citizen* (July 6, 1876): "A match game of Base Ball took place on the grounds near Giles College Tuesday, June 27, between the Pulaski Rifles and the Columbia Blue Stockings, both colored clubs, in which the latter was again defeated, by a score of 36 to 24. This being the last game for the season, the Rifles have disbanded, carrying with them the trophy of victory,— the banner bearing the title Champion of Giles and Maury counties."

SOURCES: *Pulaski (TN) Citizen*, Jun 8, 1876; "Local News," *Pulaski Citizen*, June 29, 1876; "Base Ball," *Pulaski Citizen*, Jul 6, 1876; *Pulaski Citizen*, Sep 14, 1876.

Colored Base Ball Club (Columbia, TN; 1880s). Organizer(s): W. L. Miller.

The Colored B.B.C. organized in the 1880s, played black teams. *Nashville Tennessean* (July 14, 1885): "The Columbia Colored Base Ball Club, having defeated Franklin, Pulaski, and Fayetteville, hereby challenges any colored club of Nashville for a game on the 18th at Columbia."

SOURCES: *Pulaski (TN) Citizen*, Jun 25, 1885; *Pulaski Citizen*, Jul 2, 1885; "Nashville Challenged," *Nashville (TN) Tennessean*, Jul 14, 1885; *Pulaski Citizen*, Sep 24, 1885.

Bright Eagle Base Ball Club (Knoxville, TN; 1880s)

The Bright Eagle B.B.C. organized in the 1880s, played black teams. *Knoxville Journal and Tribune* (July 27, 1888): "Knoxville has only two colored base-ball clubs, and what the boys don't do in playing they make up in amusement for spectators. The clubs played all afternoon but only completed eight innings. The Carters got 38 and the Eagles 8 scores."

SOURCES: "Lively Ball Game," *Knoxville (TN) Journal and Tribune*, Jul 27, 1888; "The Colored People," *Knoxville Journal and Tribune*, May 26, 1888.

Carter Base Ball Club (Knoxville, TN; 1880s)

The Carter B.B.C. organized in the 1880s, played black teams. *Knoxville Journal and Tribune* (July 27, 1888): "There will be a game of base-ball at Fairmount Park, by the Carters, of Knoxville, and the Bristols." *Journal and Tribune* (May 26, 1888): "A game of base-ball at Fairmount Park, between Knoxville and Bristol colored nines, was to be played. The Bristol nine was victorious by a score of 18 to 15." *Journal and Tribune* (April 7, 1889): "Yesterday our little city was filled colored excursionists from Knoxville. They had a special train twelve coaches and all of them foiled to overflowing. They spent the day very pleasantly and returned home at 5:00 pm. The game of base-ball was decided in favor of Knoxville by a score of 25 to 18."

SOURCES: "Lively Ball Game," *Knoxville (TN) Journal and Tribune*, Jul 27, 1888; "The Colored People," *Knoxville Journal and Tribune*, May 26, 1888; "The Colored People," *Knoxville Journal and Tribune*, Apr 7, 1889.

James A. Garfield Base Ball Club (Knoxville, TN; 1880s). Owner(s): J. W. Hutson and Charley McNutt.

The James A. Garfield B.B.C. organized in the 1880s, played black teams. *Knoxville Chronicle* (August 10, 1880): "In a match game yesterday afternoon on the University grounds between the Crescents and the Garfields, two of our crack colored clubs, the former were victorious by a score of 17 to 7. The Crescents having won two out of three games are new champions and would be pleased to hear from any other colored club in East Tennessee." Rivalries developed with other nines in East TN. *Chronicle* (August 21, 1880): "The Garfield Base Ball Club (colored) of this city left on the early morning train this morning for Chattanooga, where they are to play a match game this afternoon with the Hancock Club (colored) of that place. The Garfield Club is composed of some crack ball tossers, the best our city affords. Their captain and manager are J. W. Hutson and Charley McNutt. We hope the boys may be successful in the match, and predict that the Hancocks will have to wake up to take the laurels." *Chronicle* (August 24, 1880): "Yesterday the James A. Garfield Base Ball Club (colored), of Knoxville, played a match game of ball with the Tennessee Rangers (colored of this city). The Garfields were signally defeated, making only seven scores, while the Rangers scored thirty. Both clubs did good playing but the Chattanooga club is much better. Today the Smith's B.B.C., of this city [colored], W. C. Down, captain, will play the Garfields for a $20 purse."

SOURCES: "Base Ball," *Knoxville (TN) Chronicle*, Aug 10, 1880; "Base Ball at Chattanooga," *Knoxville Chronicle*, Aug 21, 1880; "Base Ball," *Knoxville Chronicle*, Aug 24, 1880.

Lone Star Base Ball Club (Knoxville, TN; 1870s–1890s)

The Lone Star B.B.C. organized in the 1870s, played black teams. *Knoxville Chronicle* (July 16, 1879): "The Athletics and the Lone Stars, two colored base-ball clubs, of our city, will play a game at three o'clock this evening, on the Knoxville Grounds, near the terminus of the street car railway." *Chronicle* (July 17, 1879): "The game of base-ball between the Athletics and Lone Stars, the crack colored clubs of the place, was an interesting game, and attracted quite a crowd of spectators. The game resulted in a victory for the Lone Stars, by a score of 17 to 6." *Chronicle* (July 31, 1879): "The Independent Blues and the Lone Stars, also colored, will play a game on the same grounds tomorrow, Friday evening, commencing at 2:30." *Chronicle* (July 28, 1881): "The Rogersville Base Ball Club, as we learn from the Press and Times, again defeated the Lone Stars, in a match game last Saturday, by a score of 19 to 16 in eleven innings. At the end of the 9th and 10th innings the score was 16 to 16." *Chronicle* (July 5, 1885): "The Massengales, of Chattanooga, played the Lone Stars of this place yesterday, with the following score: Massengales, 18: Lone Stars, 9. The Lone Stars had better practice more and not smoke too many cigarettes." A rivalry developed with Chattanooga. *Journal and Tribune* (August 29, 1889): "The Lone Stars, Knoxville's crack colored base-ball team, has returned from Chattanooga, where they cleaned up, defeated, and wiped out all the colored nines in that city. They defeated the Whitesides in two games and the J. J. Ivins in one game. The Lone Stars have won eight out of the nine games played this season."

SOURCES: "Notice," *Knoxville (TN) Chronicle*, Mar 23, 1873; "Notice," *Knoxville Chronicle*, Mar 30, 1873; "Notice," *Knoxville Chronicle*, Apr 1, 1873; "Pencilettes," *Knoxville Chronicle*, Jul 16, 1879; "Base Ball Yesterday," *Knoxville Chronicle*, Jul 17, 1879; "Base Ball," *Knoxville Chronicle*, Jul 31, 1879; "Base Ball Notes," *Knoxville Chronicle*, Jun 5, 1881; "Pencilettes," *Knoxville Chronicle*, Jul 28, 1881; "Base Ball," *Knoxville Chronicle*, Jul 4, 1885; "Base Ball," *Knoxville Chronicle*, Jul 5, 1885; "The Colored People," *Knoxville (TN) Journal and Trib-une*, Jul 15, 1888; "The Colored People," *Knoxville Journal and Tribune*, Jul 21, 1888; "Lively Ball Game," *Knoxville Journal and Tribune*, Jul 27, 1888; "The Colored People," *Knoxville Journal and Tribune*, May 26, 1888; "The Colored People," *Knoxville Journal and Tribune*, Apr 7, 1889; "Another Base Ball Games," *Knoxville Journal and Tribune*, Aug 9, 1889; "The Lone Stars On Top Again," *Knoxville Journal and Tribune*, Aug 11, 1889; "Victorious Lone Stars," *Knoxville Journal and Tribune*, Aug 29, 1889; "The Stars Win," *Knoxville Journal and Tribune*, May 4, 1894.

National Reds Base Ball Club (Knoxville, TN; 1880s)

The National Reds B.B.C. organized in the 1880s, played black teams. *Knoxville Chronicle* (June 7, 1885): "The game yesterday afternoon between the National Reds of this city and the Clippers of Morristown, both colored clubs, resulted in favor fo the former in a score of 28…. The game was well played and another game may be looked forward to soon."

SOURCES: "Colored Excursion," *Knoxville (TN) Chronicle*, Jun 7, 1885.

Clifford Base Ball Club (Memphis, TN; 1890s–1900s)

The Clifford B.B.C. organized in the 1890s. The Cliffords played white and black nines. *Little Rock Gazette* (April 13, 1897): "An exciting game of baseball was played yesterday afternoon at West End Park between the Quapaws, of Little Rock, and the Memphis Cliffords, both crack colored clubs. The Memphis boys won by a score of 10 to 7." *Nashville Tennessean* (May 19, 1897): "The Rock City Unions, Nashville's crack colored team, turned the tables on the Memphis Cliffords, defeating them by a score of 15 to 10. The game was an exciting one from start to finish and was witnessed by about 500 enthusiastic spectators." *Chicago Inter-Ocean* (July 4, 1897): "The Chicago Unions defeated the Memphis Cliffords in the second game of the series yesterday. The Southerners put up a good fielding game, but could not win on account of the heavy batting of the Unions. Home-run hits were made by Harry Moore, Louis Reynolds, and two by Henry Hyde. Bell made a sensational catch of a high foul ball." *Little Rock Gazette* (April 26, 1900): "The Cliffords of Memphis defeated the Quapaws of Little Rock in an exciting game of baseball at West End Park, the score being 11 to 10. The colored populace was out in large force to see the game."

SOURCES: "Baseball," *Little Rock (AR) Gazette*, Apr 11, 1897; "Memphis Won," *Little Rock Gazette*, Apr 13, 1897; "At Atlanta," *Nashville (TN) Tennessean*, Apr 20, 1897; "For the Fans," *San Antonio (TX) Light*, Apr 25, 1897; "Will Play Ball," *Birmingham (AL) Age-Herald*, Apr 25, 1897; "Games This Week," *Birmingham Age-Herald*, May 2, 1897; "Base Ball," *Birmingham Age-Herald*, May 6, 1897; "Colored Southern League," *Nashville Tennessean*, May 12, 1897; "Turned the Tables," *Nashville Tennessean*, May 19, 1897; "Victory for Quapaw," *Little Rock Gazette*, May 26, 1897; "Base Ball Game at Memphis," *Galveston (TX) News*, Jun 10, 1897; "Cliffords Win," *Little Rock Gazette*, Jun 10, 1897; "Some Watermelon Slices," *Muskegon (MI) Chronicle*, Jul 2, 1897; "With the Amateurs," *Chicago (IL) Inter-Ocean*, Jul 4, 1897; "With the Amateurs," *Chicago Inter-Ocean*. Sept. 25, 1897; "Memphis vs. Quapaws," *Little Rock Gazette*, Apr 25, 1900; "Little Rock 17, Memphis 12," *Little Rock Gazette*, May 23, 1900.

Clipper Base Ball Club (Memphis, TN; 1870s)

The Clipper B.B.C. organized in the 1870s, played black teams. *Memphis Commercial Appeal* (October 7, 1876): "The Comus Base-Ball Club, of Little Rock, arrived in our city yesterday to play a match game with the Clippers of Memphis. As these are the champion base-ball clubs of the south, a large crowd might be anticipated at Central Park this afternoon to witness their only game."

SOURCES: "Base Ball," *Memphis (TN) Commercial Appeal*, Jun 15, 1875; "The Game Today," *Memphis Commercial Appeal*, Oct 7, 1876.

Colored Female Stars Base Ball Club (Memphis, TN; 1890s)

The Colored Female Stars B.B.C. organized in the 1890s. *Chicago Inter-Ocean* (June 9, 1895): "Farley, of the Edgars, is arranging games for colored girls who will be here about July 1 from the South." The black female athletes scheduled to play in against a black male club. *Inter-Ocean* (June 24, 1895): "The Chicago Unions will play at home July 4 this season, and have arranged to play the female colored club from Memphis, Tennessee." *Inter-Ocean* (July 4, 1895): "The Unions play a female colored team from Memphis today at the Union Park, Thirty-Seventh and Butler Streets."

SOURCES: "Amateur Baseball," *Inter-Ocean* (Chicago, IL), June 9, 1895; "Challenges and Announcements," *Inter-Ocean*, June 24, 1895; "Amateur Baseball," *Inter-Ocean*, July 3, 1895; "Amateur Baseball," *Inter-Ocean*, July 4, 1895.

Colored Rifles Base Ball Club (Pulaski, TN; 1870s)

The Colored Rifles B.B.C., of Pulaski, TN, organized in the 1870s, if not earlier. The "Colored Rifles" played against black organizations, including the Bethany Colored Apes (Colored Bengal Tigers), Bunker Hill Colored Flys, Elkton Colored Monks; the chief rival being Columbia, TN's Blue Stockings. *Pulaski Citizen* (July 6, 1876): "A match game of Base Ball took place on the grounds near Giles College Tuesday, June 27, between the Pulaski Rifles and the Columbia Blue Stockings, both colored clubs, in which the latter was again defeated, by a score of 36 to 24. This being the last game for the season, the Rifles have disbanded, carrying with them the trophy of victory,—the banner bearing the title 'Champion of Giles and Maury counties.'"

SOURCES: "Local News," *Pulaski (TN) Citizen*, Jun 1, 1875; "Local News," *Pulaski Citizen*, Jun 10, 1875; "Colored Base-Ballist," *Pulaski Citizen*, Jun 17, 1875; "Base Ball," *Pulaski Citizen*, Jul 22, 1875; *Pulaski Citizen*, Jun 8, 1876; "Local News," *Pulaski Citizen*, Jun 29, 1876; "Base Ball," *Pulaski Citizen*, Jul 6, 1876; *Pulaski Citizen*, Sep 14, 1876.

Eclipse Base Ball Club (Memphis, TN; 1880s–1880s). Organizer(s): Albert Harden; William James Renfroe.

The Eclipse B.B.C. organized in the 1880s. The Eclipse nine, self-proclaimed southern champions, played against black and white clubs. In 1886, the organization joined a black league. *New Orleans Picayune* (June 23, 1886): "The Southern Colored Base Ball League opened its games here yesterday. Judging from the first game, the colored clubs will furnish good sport, and the teams can play ball. The Unions, representing New Orleans, contested with the crack Eclipse team, of Memphis, at the New Orleans Base Ball Park, in presence of a large crowd. The Eclipse boys all fielded well and threw the ball like the best professionals. The only weak spot was Joiner at second base. Slotter, the first baseman, is great, and Pointer played a good game at third." The Eclipse played at least one whit team. *Memphis Appeal* (October 3, 1886): "A game of baseball will be played at Cycle Park between the Eclipse colored club and a white club captained by Bob Black." *Memphis Appeal* (June 5, 1887): "The Riverside and Eclipse clubs, both colored organizations, play at West Memphis today." *Memphis Appeal* (July 29, 1888): "The Eclipse, colored club, defeated the Athletics at Citizens' Park by a score of 17 to 8. [William James] Renfroe, manager of the home club, claims to have signed some of the best colored talent on the diamond, and promises to give Memphis good ball for the rest of the season. To this complexion, we have come at last."

SOURCES: "Local Paragraphs," *Memphis (TN) Appeal*, Aug 19, 1884; "Local Paragraphs," *Memphis Appeal*, Aug 24, 1884; "Colored

Baseball Players," *Atlanta (GA) Constitution*, Jun 10, 1886; "Around Home Bases," *New Orleans (LA) Times-Picayune*, Jun 16, 1886; "Baseball Notes," *Memphis Appeal*, Jun 17, 1886; "Baseball Notes," *Memphis Appeal*, Jul 4, 1886; "The Cohens Defeat the Memphis Team," *New Orleans Times-Picayune*, June 23, 1886; "Baseball Notes," *Memphis Appeal*, Jul 11, 1886; "Baseball Notes," *Memphis Appeal*, Jul 30, 1886; "The Unions Win at Memphis," *New Orleans Times-Picayune*, Aug 3, 1886; "The Colored Cracks," *Louisville (KY) Courier-Journal*, Aug 8, 1886; "City News," *Memphis Appeal*, Oct 3, 1886; "Diamond Dots," *Memphis Appeal*, Apr 13, 1887; "Diamond Dots," *Memphis Appeal*, Jun 5, 1887; "Diamond Dots," *Memphis Appeal*, Jul 14, 1888.

Eureka Base Ball Club (Memphis, TN; 1880s–1890s). Organizer(s): C. Thomas, J. H. Cummings, Levi Orr and Thomas F. Potter; Levi Orr; and Robert Higgins.

The Eureka B.B.C. organized in the 1880s, played against black nines. *Memphis Appeal* (May 20, 1884): "Between 900 and 1000 people witnessed the game at Olympic Park, between the Popular Lincks and Eurekas. The score was Lincks 11, Eurekas 5. Larry Chambers and Albert Hardin, of the Lincks, did fine work." *Memphis Appeal* (July 22, 1884): "The [Memphis] Rangers were defeated by the Eurekas at Olympic Park, by a score of 11 to 4." In 1886, the organization joined the League of Southern Colored Base Ballists. *Memphis Appeal* (July 15, 1886): "The Eclipse, of this city, play their first league game here today with the Eurekas, of Central Point. They also play tomorrow and give an exhibition game Sunday." *Memphis Appeal* (July 16, 1886): "The Eclipse of this city defeated the Eurekas by a score of 5 to 3. The game generally was very good, and the colored boys showed off in fine style, bot at the bat and on the diamond." *Weekly Pelican* (July 15, 1886): "The Eureka Base Ball Club, of Memphis, will arrive tonight from Memphis. They come for the purpose of playing the Pinchbacks for the colored championship of the South. The Eurekas are composed mostly of the discarded colored players of the International League, the said league having debarred colored players this season." *Nashville Tennessean* (June 20, 1894): "A good crowd witnessed the games yesterday at Athletic Park between the Eurekas, of Memphis, and the Rock Citys. Each won a game. Today's contest will determine the championship of the State."

SOURCES: "Local Paragraphs," *Memphis (TN) Appeal*, Apr 29, 1884; *Memphis Appeal*, May 20, 1884; "Local Paragraphs," *Memphis Appeal*, Jul 22, 1884; "Local Paragraphs," *Memphis Appeal*, Aug 24, 1884; "The Colored Picnic," *St. Louis (MO) Republican*, Sep 30, 1884; "Base Ball Notes," *Memphis Appeal*, Jul 11, 1886; "Baseball Notes," *Memphis Appeal*, Jul 15, 1886; "The Colored Cracks," *Louisville (KY) Courier-Journal*, Aug 8, 1886; *Memphis Appeal*, Feb 1, 1887; "Diamond Dots," *Memphis Appeal*, Apr 3, 1887; "Diamond Dots," *Memphis Appeal*, Apr 13, 1887; "Diamond Dots," *Memphis Appeal*, Apr 14, 1887; "Memphis and Pinchbacks," *New Orleans (LA) Weekly Pelican*, Jun 8, 1889; "Hits Outside the Diamond," *Nashville (TN) Tennessean*, Jun 14, 1894; "Hits Outside the Diamond," *Nashville Tennessean*, Jun 18, 1894; "Each Won a Game," *Nashville Tennessean*, Jun 20, 1894.

Peabody Hotel Base Ball Club (Memphis, TN; 1880s)

The Peabody Hotel B.B.C. organized in the 1880s, if not earlier. *Memphis Appeal* (May 1, 1884): "The colored waiters of the Peabody and Grayso have played a series of games, resulting as follows: First game, 20 to 19 in favor of Peabody; second game, 20 to 20; third game, 21 to 18 in favor of Grayso. Battery for Grayso is Astor and Henderson; for Peabody, Fleming and Smith."

SOURCES: "Baseball Notes," *Memphis (TN) Appeal*, May 1, 1884.

Popular Lincks Base Ball Club (Memphis, TN; 1880s). Organizer(s): Levi Orr.

The Popular Lincks B.B.C. organized in the 1880s. The Lincks played black nines of TN and KY. *Memphis Appeal* (June 18, 1883): "The Poplar Lincks and Remy Clarkes played a very close game yesterday, near Olympic Park, for $10 a side and the championship. The playing of William Pryor and Alf Horton is mentioned as having been exceedingly skillful." *Appeal* (July 8, 1884): "800 people at Olympic Park, witnessed the Rangers defeat the Lincks by a score of 14 to 7. The Lincks openly charge a traitor among the ranks." *Appeal* (August 5, 1884): "1000 spectators at Olympic Park witnessed the Poplar Links and Paducah Riversides; Links, 8; Riversides, 3." *Appeal* (August 24, 1884): "The Popular Lincks and Eurekas will cross bats at Olympic Park today. They are two of the best colored clubs of the city." *Appeal* (May 20, 1884): "Between 800 and 1000 people witnessed the game at Olympic Park, yesterday, between the Popular Lincks and Eurekas. The score was Lincks 11, Eurekas 5. Larry Chambers and Albert Hardin, of the Lincks, did fine work." They reorganized in 1886. *Appeal* (June 22, 1886): "In a match game of baseball between the Links and Caledoe, colored, Sunday, the former were victorious by a score of 14 to 13."

SOURCES: *Memphis (TN) Appeal, Jan 16, 1883*; "Base Ball," *Memphis Appeal*, Jun 18, 1883; "Local Paragraphs," *Memphis Appeal*, Mar 23, 1884; "Local Paragraphs," *Memphis Appeal*, Apr 15, 1884; "Local Paragraphs," *Memphis Appeal*, Apr 29, 1884; *Memphis Appeal*, May 20, 1884; "Local Paragraphs," *Memphis Appeal*, Jun 29, 1884; "Local Paragraphs," *Memphis Appeal*, Jul 6, 1884; "Local Paragraphs," *Memphis Appeal*, Jul 1, 1884; "Local Paragraphs," *Memphis Appeal*, Jul 8, 1884; "Special to the American," *Nashville (TN) Tennessean*, Aug 4, 1884; "Local Paragraphs," *Memphis Appeal*, August 5, 1884; "Local Paragraphs," *Memphis Appeal*, Aug 24, 1884; "Base Ball Notes," *Memphis Appeal*, Jun 22, 1886.

Reds Base Ball Club (Memphis, TN; 1890s)

The Reds B.B.C. organized in the 1890s, played black teams. *Little Rock Gazette* (August 27, 1896): "The Quapaw baseball club of this city won the second game of a three game series from the Memphis Reds at High Street Park yesterday afternoon by a score of 17 to 1. The Quapaw's battery was in fine form and it was to their excellent work that the game was won. The series with the Memphis club was very successful in a financial way, a large number of white admirers of the game attending."

SOURCES: "Quapaws Win Series," *Little Rock (AR) Gazette*, Aug 27, 1896.

Riverside Base Ball Club (Memphis, TN; 1880s)

The Riverside B.B.C. organized in the 1880s, played black teams. *Memphis Appeal* (June 5, 1887): "The Riverside and Eclipse clubs, colored organizations, play at West Memphis today."

SOURCES: "Local Paragraphs," *Memphis (TN) Appeal*, August 5, 1884.

Black Jacks Base Ball Club (Morristown, TN; 1870s)

The Black Jacks B.B.C. organized in the 1870s, played black teams. *Morristown Gazette* (June 21, 1876): "The Black Jacks of the South (colored base-ball club) went to Whitesburg last Saturday and beat the colored club there [by] 6 runs." *Gazette* (November 7, 1877): "A match game of base-ball was played between the Black Jacks of the South, the colored club of this place, and the colored club of White Pine, last Saturday, resulting in the defeat of the White Pine by 12 tallies."

SOURCES: *Morristown (TN) Gazette*, Jun 21, 1876; *Morristown Gazette*, Nov 7, 1877.

Gregg Base Ball Club (Morristown, TN; 1880s)

The Gregg B.B.C., of Morristown, organized in the 1880s, played black teams. *Morristown Gazette* (May 31, 1882): "The colored base-

ball club of Morristown [Greggs] goes to Rogersville, Tennessee, on the 8th proximo, to play a match game with the colored club [Spears] of that place. Thus far, the Morristown club wears the belt of the championship, having beat every nine that appeared in the field against them." *Gazette* (July 12, 1882): "A match game of base-ball was played in Morristown on the 4th instant., by the Spears Club (colored), of Rogersville, and the Gregg Club (colored), of this place, resulting in a defeat of the former. The game was hotly contested by both nines, and was witnessed by a number of our citizens, both white and black. The score, at the end of the ninth inning, stood: Spears 14, Greggs, 19." *Gazette* (June 25, 1884): "Our colored friends have arranged an interesting programme for the celebration of the Fourth of July at this place. In the afternoon, a match game of base-ball will be played between the Greggs of Morristown and the Johnsons of Knoxville."

SOURCES: "Local Notes and Other News," *Morristown (TN) Gazette*, May 31, 1882; "Local Notes and Other News," *Morristown Gazette*, Jul 12, 1882; "Local Notes and Other News," *Morristown Gazette*, Aug 23, 1882; "Local Notes and Other News," *Morristown Gazette*, Jun 25, 1884.

A. K. Ward Base Ball Club (Nashville, TN; 1880s). Organizer(s): D. Shannon Battle, B. W. Douglas and J. H. Stewart.

The A. K. Ward B.B.C. organized in the 1880s. The "A. K. Wards," formerly the F. W. Covington club, played black clubs of TN and AL. D. Shannon Battle, a former baseball waiter of Saratoga Springs, NY, captained the ball club. *Nashville Tennessean* (Jun 4, 1881): "The A. K. Wards defeated the West Nashvilles, in the Sulphur Spring Bottom, yesterday afternoon, by a score of 12 to 9. A large crowd witnessed the game." *Nashville Tennessean* (July 6, 1881): "The A. K. Wards and Rock City Blues will lock horns together on the Sulphur Spring grounds this afternoon." *Nashville Tennessean* (July 6, 1881): "The A. K. Wards beat the Rock Citys by a score of 12 to 8, yesterday." *Nashville Tennessean* (July 29, 1881): "The A. K. Ward Base Ball Club will shortly send a challenge to the Bowling Green Base Ball Club, offering to play for the championship at any time or any place." The A. K. Wards developed an intense rivalry with Huntsville's Red Stockings. *Nashville Tennessean* (August 9, 1881): "The A. K. Wards will leave this morning for Huntsville, Alabama, to play for the championship of the South and a prize of $200." *Memphis Appeal* (August 30, 1881): "The Huntsville Colored Base Ball Club took the cake from the crack colored nine from Nashville, Wednesday, in a game played in the first named city. The score stood 5 to 4. Time, one hour and forty minutes. Gate money: 49.80." The nine reorganized in 1882. *Nashville Tennessean* (April 22, 1882): "The A. K. Wards, the champions of last year, will play the Fisk University Club, this afternoon, on the University grounds." *Nashville Tennessean* (July 3, 1882): "The Smith Base Ball Club, of Chattanooga, arrived here this morning, and will play the A. K. Wards one day this week." *Nashville Tennessean* (July 6, 1882): "About three or 4000 people assembled on the Sulphur Spring Bottom yesterday afternoon to witness the match game of baseball played between the R. S. Smiths, of Chattanooga, and the A. K. Wards, of this city. A great deal of enthusiasm prevailed throughout the game. Score: Smiths 9, A. K. Wards 5."

SOURCES: "Ready for a Challenge," *Nashville Tennessean*, April 10, 1881; "Base Ball in the Sulphur Spring Bottom," *Nashville Tennessean*, May 31, 1881; "Base Ball in the Sulphur Spring Bottom," *Nashville Tennessean*, June 23, 1881; "A Match Game of Base Ball," *Nashville Tennessean*, June 24, 1881; "The Commercial Hotel," *Nashville Tennessean*, July 29, 1881; "Match for the Championship," *Nashville Tennessean*, August 9, 1881; "Huntsville vs Nashville," *Huntsville (AL) Gazette*, August 13, 1881; "The A. K. Wards," *Huntsville Gazette*,

August 20, 1881; "Local Paragraphs," *Memphis (TN) Appeal*, August 30, 1881; "A Base Ball Match," *Nashville Tennessean*, April 22, 1882; "Base Ball," *Nashville Tennessean*, July 3, 1882; "Base Ball," *Nashville Tennessean*, July 6, 1882.

Atlantic Base Ball Club (Nashville, TN; 1860s–1870s). Organizer(s): A. Alexander and William Martin.

The Atlantic B.B.C. organized in the 1860s. The "Atlantics" played for the local black championship. *Nashville Tennessean* (September 22, 1869): "The Atlantic Base Ball Club, colored, requests us to state that they will play the Lone Star club, colored, on the grounds near Fort Houston, fo the championship of the city." *Nashville Tennessean* (September 24, 1869): "The Atlantics and Lone Stars, both of Nashville, played for the Colored Championship; the Atlantics winning by a score of 30 to 29."

SOURCES: "A Challenge," *Nashville (TN) Tennessean*, Sep 22, 1869; "The Colored Championship," *Nashville Tennessean*, Sep 24, 1869.

Black Stocking Base Ball Club (Nashville, TN; 1880s–1890s)

The Black Stocking B.B.C. organized in the 1880s, played black teams. *Nashville Tennessean* (August 4, 1887): "The W. T. Linck Base Ball Club will play the Black Stockings today at the ball park this afternoon at 4 o'clock. This will be the first exhibition game between these popular colored clubs and some good ball playing is expected. The batteries—for the Lincks, Weaver and [Henry] Perkins; for the Black Stockings, [William] Moore and [Harrison] Waggoner." The aggregation reorganized in 1890. *Nashville Tennessean* (October 10, 1890): "The Rock City Greys and the Black Stockings will play a game of ball today at the Tanyard Bottoms."

SOURCES: "Sporting," *Nashville (TN) Tennessean*, Aug 4, 1887; "Limited Local Items," *Nashville Tennessean*, Oct 10, 1890.

Blue Clippers Base Ball Club (Nashville, TN; 1870s). Organizer(s): D. Shannon Battle and William M. Louis.

The Blue Clippers B.B.C. organized in the 1870s. The "Blue Clippers" played black clubs of TN. *Nashville Tennessean* (September 7, 1876): "A match game will be played in the Judge Spring Bottom, between the Odd Socks and the original Blue Clippers." *Nashville Tennessean* (September 8, 1877): "The Chattanoogans came up to witness a game of base-ball, to be played upon the tan yard grounds, between the Olympics, of that city, and the Blue Clippers, of Nashville." *Nashville Tennessean* (October 16, 1879): "The J. K. Tapps and the Blue Clippers will play a match gam of base-ball at the colored fair, this afternoon."

SOURCES: "All Over the City," *Nashville (TN) Tennessean*, Jul 6, 1875; "The Invincible Lincks," *Nashville Tennessean*, Aug 29, 1876; "Base Ball Gossip," *Nashville Tennessean*, Sep 7, 1876; "Colored Excursionists," *Nashville Tennessean*, Sep 8, 1877; "Base Ball Notes," *Nashville Tennessean*, Sep 9, 1877; "Base Ball at the Colored Fair," *Nashville Tennessean*, Oct 16, 1879.

Bosley Blues Base Ball Club (Nashville, TN; 1880s)

The Bosley Blues B.B.C. organized in the 1880s. *Nashville Tennessean* (September 4, 1884): "There will be a match game of baseball at the fairgrounds, this afternoon, between the Langstons and the Bosley Blues. An exciting game may be expected, as the two clubs are evenly matched. At their last game, the score stood 7 to 5 in favor of the Langstons. The Bosleys have been materially strengthened, and are confident of success. The Langstons have added to their team one of the best pitchers in the South." *Nashville Tennessean* (September 15, 1884): "The Langston Base Ball Club played the Bosley Blues at the fairgrounds yesterday to an audience of several hundred. These are the best two colored club in town. The Langstons beat the Bosleys by a score of 17 to 5."

SOURCES: "Base Ball," *Nashville (TN) Tennessean*, Sep 4, 1884; "Base Ball," *Nashville Tennessean*, Sep 15, 1884.

Brownlow's Black Boys Base Ball Club (Nashville, TN; 1860s)

The Brownlow's Black Boys B.B.C. organized in the 1860s. *Nashville Union and American*: "Sixteen Negroes, members of Brownlow's Black Boys Base Ball Club, for disorderly conduct on the Sabbath, were fined in the aggregate $128; and one white man, who gave them encouragement to continue in their sport, was mulched in $5 for his offensiveness."

SOURCES: "Recorder's Court," *Nashville (TN) Union and American*, Sep 18, 1866.

Centennial Giants Base Ball Club (Nashville, TN; 1890s–1900s)

The Centennial Giants B.B.C. organized in the 1890s, played black teams. The organization challenged the Iron Front team, of Bryan, TX. *Indianapolis Freeman* (July 18, 1891): "I have this day accepted the challenge of the Nashville Base Ball Club, for $250.00, aside the $150.00 forfeit to be made through their National Bank, requiring the same from us to be played on the 20th, and will meet them at New Orleans; please publish at once as we are anxious to meet the Giants; should we be successful The Freeman shall have a $20.oo gold piece. R. S. Lewis, captain of Iron Front Base Ball Club." *Nashville Tennessean* (May 24, 1896): "The Fisk team defeated the Nashville Giants in a game of base-ball on the Fisk university campus Thursday afternoon. So far the team has defeated everyone it has played."

SOURCES: "Sport," *Indianapolis (IN) Freeman*, Jul 18, 1891; "Fisk University," *Nashville (TN) Tennessean*, May 24, 1896; "Ball Players Fight," *Nashville (TN) American*, Sep 9, 1896; "All Turned Aloose," *Nashville Tennessean*, Sep 12, 1896.

Dalton Base Ball Club (Nashville, TN; 1890s)

The Dalton B.B.C. organized in the 1890s, played black aggregations. *Nashville Tennessean* (April 23, 1894): "The Rock City Unions and the Daltons will play at Athletic Park this afternoon, the game being called at 4 o'clock. The Rock City Unions are made up most of the members of the Rock City Grays and the Daltons are the crackerjacks of East Nashville." *Tennessean* (June 10, 1894): "Two colored clubs, the Daltons and the North Nashvilles, had engaged the park for tomorrow, but have postponed their games, and will play Tuesday and Wednesday." *Tennessean* (June 13, 1894): "The North Nashvilles and the Daltons, colored clubs. Played before a small audience at Athletic Park yesterday. The former won, 9 to 8. The same clubs play this afternoon, and a fine game is promised."

SOURCES: "Negro Clubs," *Nashville (TN) Tennessean*, Apr 23, 1894; "Will Meet Again," *Nashville (TN) Tennessean*, Jun 10, 1894; "Hits Outside the Diamond," *Nashville (TN) Tennessean*, Jun 13, 1894; "Ball Players Fight," *Nashville Tennessean*, Sep 9, 1896.

Excelsior Base Ball Club (Nashville, TN; 1860s)

The Excelsior B.B.C. organized in the 1860s, played black clubs. *Nashville Union and Dispatch* (December 21, 1866): "The colored young men of the city took the base-ball fever some time ago, and organized a club from the choicest material on hand, calling it the Excelsior. Having a high estimate of their skill in the National Game, the Excelsiors have challenged every other club in this city, but unfortunately without getting a response." *Nashville Tennessean* (February 9, 1868): "The Excelsior Base Ball Club (colored) announces its willingness to play against any club in Davidson County." *Nashville Union and American* (October 4, 1874): "The Atlantics defeated the Excelsiors in a match game of base-ball, by a score of 17 to 9."

SOURCES: "Local Jottings," *Nashville (TN) Union and Dispatch*, Dec 21, 1866; "Africa Against the Field," *Nashville (TN) Tennessean*,

Feb 9, 1868; "All Over the City," *Nashville Union and American,* Oct 4, 1874; "Over the City," *Nashville Union and American,* Aug 26, 1875.

Fisk University Base Ball Club (Nashville, TN; 1880s–1900s)

The Fisk University B.B.C. organized in the 1880s, played black colleges and independent teams. *Nashville Tennessean* (April 22, 1882): "The A. K. Wards, the champions of last year, will play the Fisk University Club, this afternoon, on the University grounds." In 1884, Central TN College defeated Fisk University, by a score of 24 to 16. *Nashville Tennessean* (April 19, 1884): "There will be a match game of base-ball this afternoon north of Jubilee Hall [Fisk campus." *Tennessean* (April 19, 1884): "There will be a match game of base-ball this evening on the grounds north of Jubilee Hall between the Fisk University club and the Belleview Blues. Both clubs will appear in uniform. Game called at 2 pm." *Tennessean* (April 29, 1894): "Athletics have revived among the students and base-ball games are of daily occurrence between the students of Roger Williams and Fisk universities. The first game was played on April 21st, and resulted in favor of the latter." *Tennessean* (May 6, 1899): "There will be a game of baseball this afternoon between the Fisk University nine and the Nashville Reds. Fisk has played three games this year so far and has not suffered a defeat. The Reds have a strong team, and an interesting game is expected." *Tennessean* (May 7, 1899): "The game of base-ball yesterday afternoon between the Nashville Reds and Fisk University was won by the latter by a score of 9 to 4." *Indianapolis Freeman* (October 17, 1896): "A game of base-ball was between Fisk University and Meharry Medical college teams on the Fisk campus on the 10th inst. The score was 13 to 3 in favor of Fisk." *Tennessean* (April 17, 1898): "About 350 spectators witnessed a well-played game between the Roger Williams and Fisk University teams yesterday afternoon on the Fisk campus. The teams were both in good trim and on account of the rivalry that exists between the ball tossers of the two schools there is always much interest attaching to their annual contests. The Roger Williams' team, although it has lost every series with the Fisk team for the last eight years, puts forth a stronger effort every year in order to win…. At the end of the game the score stood Fisk 18, Roger 7." *Tennessean* (April 18, 1899): "The Fisk and Rock City Unions played a game of baseball on the Fisk campus. The Fisk men showed their old-time alertness and skill, and they succeeded in piling up a score of 10 to 2 against the Unions."

SOURCES: "A Base Ball Match," *Nashville (TN) Tennessean,* Apr 22, 1882; "State Board of Education," *Nashville Tennessean,* Mar 18, 1884; *Nashville Tennessean, Apr 19, 1884;* "Base Ball," *Nashville Tennessean, Apr 19, 1884;* "Roger Williams University," *Nashville Tennessean,* April 29, 1894; "Amateur Games," *Nashville Tennessean,* April 28, 1895; "On Union Street," *Nashville Tennessean,* April 21, 1896; "Unions vs Hornets," *Nashville Tennessean,* June 22, 1896; "Fisk University," *Nashville Tennessean,* June 26, 1896; "Opening of Fisk University," *Indianapolis (IN) Freeman,* Oct 17, 1896; "General Sporting News," *Nashville Tennessean,* May 16, 1897; "Turned the Tables," *Nashville Tennessean,* May 19, 1897; "Athletics at Fisk," *Nashville Tennessean,* May 8, 1897; "Turned the Tables," *Nashville Tennessean,* May 19, 1897; "Fisk Won Easily," *Nashville Tennessean,* April 17, 1898; "Base Ball at Fisk," *Nashville Tennessean,* April 25, 1899; "Base Ball at Fisk," *Nashville Tennessean,* April 18, 1899; "Base Ball at Fisk," *Nashville Tennessean,* May 6, 1899; "Base Ball at Fisk," *Nashville Tennessean,* May 7, 1899; "Fisk Base Ball Team," *Nashville Tennessean,* May 1, 1900; "Base Ball at Fisk," *Nashville Tennessean,* May 2, 1900; "Fisk 19, Walden 5," *Nashville Tennessean,* May 5, 1901.

G. W. Foster Base Ball Club (Nashville, TN; 1870s–1880s)

The G. W. Foster B.B.C. organized in the 1870s, played black teams. *Nashville Tennessean.* (August 31, 1878): "A match game of base-ball will be played in the Tan Yard Bottom, Tuesday evening, between the G. W. Fosters and the West End Reds. The game will be called at 3 o'clock. The G. W. Fosters will play their championship game with the Blue Clippers, Thursday evening on the home grounds." *Tennessean* (September 4, 1878): "There was a large attendance on the Tan-yard grounds, yesterday, to witness the match game between the J. K. Tapps and the G. W. Fosters. The former won in handsome style by a score of 24 to 9."

SOURCES: "Base Ball," *Nashville (TN) Tennessean,* Aug 31, 1878; "Base Ball," *Nashville Tennessean,* Sep 4, 1878; "Base Ball," *Nashville Tennessean,* Jul 22, 1880.

Haymakers Base Ball Club (Nashville, TN; 1860s)

The Haymakers B.B.C. organized in the 1870s. *Nashville Tennessean* (September 15, 1871): "A match game of base-ball, between the Independents and Haymakers, resulted in favor of the former by a score of 44 to 33."

SOURCES: "Base Ball Match," *Nashville (TN) Union and American,* Aug 8, 1871; "The Colored People's Fair," *Nashville Union and American,* Sep 15, 1871; "The Colored Fair," *Nashville (TN) Tennessean,* Sep 15, 1871.

Independent Base Ball Club (Nashville, TN; 1870s). Organizer(s): Thomas Ewing.

The Independent B.B.C. organized in the 1870s. The Independents, organized by Thomas Ewing, a prominent barber, played black teams. Its local rivals were the Haymaker and Blue Clipper nines. *Nashville Tennessean* (September 15, 1871): "A match game of base-ball, between the Independents and Haymakers, resulted in favor of the former by a score of 44 to 33." *Tennessean:* "The Clippers and Independents had a match game, the former proving victorious. An unusually large crowd witnessed the contest, under the rays of a brilliant sun." *Tennessean:* "The Independents made it warm for the Clippers by a score of 25 to 17."

SOURCES: "Base Ball Match," *Nashville (TN) Banner,* Aug 8, 1871; "The Colored Fair," *Nashville (TN) Tennessean,* Sep 15, 1871; "The Colored People's Fair," *Nashville (TN) Union and American,* Sep 24, 1871; "Sidewalk Notes," *Nashville Banner,* Sep 3, 1874; "All Over the City," *Nashville Union and American,* Sep 24, 1874; "Base Ball," *Nashville (TN) Tennessean,* Jul 6, 1875; "All Over the City," *Nashville Banner,* Jul 6, 1875; "Base Ball Amateurs," *Nashville Banner,* Aug 6, 1875; "Base Ball," *Nashville Banner,* Aug 17 1875; "Sidewalk Notes," *Nashville Banner,* Aug 19, 1875.

Langston Base Ball Club (Nashville, TN; 1880s). Organizer(s): Ralph E. Langston.

The Langston B.B.C. organized in the 1880s. The Langstons, formerly the A. K. Wards nine, played black and white teams. *Washington Bee* (September 13, 1884): "The Langston Base Ball Club is the name of an association of young colored men at Nashville, Tennessee. They have named their club in honor of Ralph E. Langston. A game was played last week between the above-named club and one of the best clubs of white men at Nashville. The Langston club came out victorious." *Nashville Tennessean* (July 24, 1884): "There was an exciting game of base-ball played yesterday afternoon between the R. E. Langstons and the Belleview Blues in the Sulphur Spring Bottom, before a large crowd. The score stood: Langstons, 24; Belleview Blues, 12." *Tennessean* (August 20, 1884): "The game of base-ball between the Langstons, of this city, and the White Belts, of Clarksville, two colored clubs, was witnessed by several hundred colored persons, and about as many white men, who desired to see the sport. The game put up by the home club was first-class, and if they had not become somewhat excited at one time by the demonstration of applause of the crowd." *Tennessean* (September 27, 1884): "A match game of base-ball was played yesterday afternoon at the fairground between the Langstons, of this city, and the Huntsville, Alabama club, and was decided in favor of the former by a score of 15 to 10. The Langstons are the acknowledged champions of Tennessee, and the latter of their State, and the game was one of considerable interest. The colored base-ball lovers are much rejoiced over the result of the game."

SOURCES: "Base Ball," *Nashville (TN) Tennessean*, Aug 17, 1884; "Base Ball," *Nashville Tennessean*, Aug 19, 1884; "Black Batters," *Nashville Tennessean*, Aug 20, 1884; *Washington (DC) Bee*, Sep 13, 1884; "Base Ball," *Nashville Tennessean*, Sep 14, 1884; "Colored Players," *Nashville Tennessean*, Sep 27, 1884.

Lone Star Base Ball Club (Nashville, TN; 1860s)

The Lone Star B.B.C. organized in the 1860s, played for the local black championship. *Nashville Tennessean* (September 22, 1869): "The Atlantic Base Ball Club, colored, requests us to state that they will play the Lone Star Club, colored, on the grounds near Fort Houston, tomorrow, for the championship of the city." *Tennessean* (September 24, 1869): "The Atlantics and Lone Stars, both of Nashville, played for the Colored Championship; the Atlantics winning by a score of 30 to 29."

SOURCES: "A Challenge," *Nashville (TN) Tennessean*, Sep 22, 1869; "The Colored Championship," *Nashville Tennessean*, Sep 24, 1869.

Loves Base Ball Club (Nashville, TN; 1890s)

The Loves B.B.C. organized in the 1890s, played black aggregations. *Nashville Tennessean* (August 4, 1891): "Two colored base-ball clubs, the Loves and the South Nashville Reds, played a good game of ball yesterday afternoon. A large crowd was present and enjoyed the sport hugely. The game was close, hotly contested and exciting. It resulted in a score of 8 to 9 in favor of the Loves. They will probably play another game Thursday." *Tennessean* (August 20, 1891): "The last game of the season between colored clubs will be played at the Athletic Park this afternoon between the Loves and the South Nashville Reds. A good game is promised."

SOURCES: "Loves Victorious," *Nashville (TN) Tennessean*, Aug 4, 1891; "Base Ball Notes," *Nashville Tennessean*, Aug 18, 1891; "Last of the Season," *Nashville Tennessean*, Aug 20, 1891.

Meigs' School Greys Base Ball Club (Nashville, TN; 1880s)

The Meigs' School Greys B.B.C. organized in the 1880s, played black teams. *Nashville Tennessean* (August 17, 1884): "The colored people will have an excursion, Monday, to Chattanooga. The Meigs' School Greys Base Ball Club will play a game, and the Douglas Guards and Bell Rifles will drill against Atlanta, Rome, and Knoxville companies." *Tennessean* (June 24, 1886): "The Meigs' School Greys, of Nashville, defeated the Red Oaks, of this place [Evansville, Indiana], in a game of ball, by a score of 8 to 2. Stewart and Farrow ere the battery for Nashville." *Tennessean* (July 31, 1886): "The Slipaways had a walkover with the Meigs' School Greys yesterday, defeating them in fine style. Slipaways 12; Greys 5. Batteries—Bell and Smith, Stewart and Farrow." In 1887, this organization became the Nashville Greys.

SOURCES: "Excursion to Chattanooga," *Nashville (TN) Tennessean*, Aug 17, 1884; "The Amateurs," *Nashville Tennessean*, Jun 24, 1886; "Amateurs," *Nashville (TN) Tennessean*, Jul 31, 1886.

Pacific Coasts Base Ball Club (Nashville, TN; 1890s–1900s). Organizer(s): J. H. Stewart.

The Pacific Coasts B.B.C. organized in the 1890s, played black teams. *Nashville Tennessean* (August 11, 1891): "The Pacific Coasts and Rock City Grays, both colored, played a game of base-ball, which was witnessed by a large crowd, at the Athletic Park yesterday afternoon. And the colored troops fought nobly, but from the start to the finish the Pacifics had it all their own way." They played a second match. *Tennessean* (August 16, 1891): "[There was] a base-ball game between the two crack colored clubs, the Pacific Coasts and the Rock City Grays. The greatest interest prevailed throughout the game, and there was a display of the wildest enthusiasm when the score stood 10 to 10 at the end of the ninth inning. In the tenth the Pacifics sent two men across the plate, while the Grays only succeeded in getting one run. A prize of $30 in gold was awarded to the winners after the game." The Pacific Coasts reorganized in 1892, playing the Henderson, KY Dukes team. *Tennessean* (September 20, 1892): "For about an hour and a half yesterday afternoon the Pacific club, of this city, gave the Dukes, of Henderson, Kentucky, instructions as to how to play the national game of base-ball, and at the end of the exhibition the home club had twelve runs and the visitors six."

SOURCES: "Jerked Meat," *Indianapolis (IN) Freeman*, Jun 6, 1891; "A Great Game of Base Ball," *Indianapolis Freeman*, Jul 11, 1891; "Base Ball at Athletic Park," *Nashville (TN) Tennessean*, Jul 16, 1891; "Pacific Coasts and Grays," *Nashville Tennessean*, Aug 11, 1891; "Good Ball Game," *Nashville Tennessean*, Aug 16, 1891; "Base Ball Today," *Nashville Tennessean*, September 19, 1892; "The Pacifics Win," *Nashville Tennessean*, September 20, 1892.

Rock City Greys/Union Base Ball Club (Nashville, TN; 1880s–1900s). Organizer(s): A. H. Campbell; W. C. Ewing.

The Rock City Greys/Union B.B.C. organized in the 1880s. The Rock City Greys—later, the Nashville Unions—played black teams. This included an excursion match game at Bowling Green, KY. *Nashville Tennessean* (August 26, 1887): "A game of base-ball was played between the Rock City Greys and the Planets, of Bowling Green. Both clubs did some good playing, but it was evident from the start that the Grays were the favorite. The result was Greys 17 and Planets 8, the former receiving the prize of $25." *Tennessean* (September 2, 1887): "The Rock City Greys defeated the W. T. Lincks at the park yesterday. The Greys found out that the Lincks are not what they think they are on the field. Score, 12 to 5. Batteries—Greys, [William] Moore and [John] Trimble; Lincks, Weaver and Smith." *Nashville Tennessee Star* (November 25, 1887): "Rock City Greys B. B. C. reorganized last week and will fortnightly for purposes of keeping up the team. The Greys played several match games during the past season, coming out victors every time but one. The club will give a series of balls at Winters' Hall, beginning the 23rd instant." The nine played Louisville's black nines; in 1887, the played the Falls City. *Louisville Courier-Journal* (June 17, 1887): "The Fall Citys will not play in St. Louis, as expected, on June 19 and 20, the Sunday law putting a stop to Sunday playing, but will play Nashville's crack colored team here." *Tennessean* (October 10, 1890): "Th Rock City Greys and the Black Stockings will play a game of ball today at the Tanyard Bottoms." They developed a local rivalry. *Tennessean* (August 11, 1891): "The Pacific Coasts and Rock City Grays, both colored, played a game of base-ball, which was witnessed by a large crowd, at the Athletic Park yesterday afternoon. And the colored troops fought nobly, but from the start to the finish the Pacifics had it all their own way." They reorganized as the Rock City Unions in 1894. *Tennessean* (April 24, 1894): "The Rock City Unions and the Daltons will play at Athletic Park this afternoon, the game being called at 4 o'clock. The Rock City Unions are made up most of the members of the old Rock City Greys, and the Daltons are the cracker jacks of East Nashville." They played the Memphis Eurekas, Louisville Brotherhoods, Birmingham Unions. The Unions regularly visited Chicago, where they played the Chicago Unions and Columbia Giants. They also played white aggregations, including the College Hill Club of Decatur, IL. *Decatur Evening Republican* (July 21, 1899): "The Nashville Base Ball Club under the management of Nashville who were scheduled to play here failed to put in an appearance here and left Henderson under the cover of darkness for parts unknown. It has been since learned that Mr. Ewing dreaded coming here as he feared a defeat and shut-out of his club." *Evening Republican* (July 22, 1899): "The game between the members of the College Hill Base Ball team and a club of colored men from Nashville, Tennessee, yesterday, was witnessed by about 250 persons. It was the best game that has been seen in Decatur for a long time. The Nashville team, which is composed of colored men, won the game, the score being 6 to 4." In 1900, they met Louisville's Olympics. *Louisville Courier-Journal* (June 23, 1900): "At League Park today, the colored teams, Olympics, of this city, and Nashvilles, of Nashville, Tennessee, will play for a purse of $50. The game will be called at 3 o'clock. Both are crack teams and the chances are there will be a hot game." *Courier-Journal* (June 24, 1900): "At League Park today, the colored teams, Olympics, of this city, and Nashvilles, of Nashville, Tennessee, will play for a purse of $50. The game will be called at 3 o'clock. Both are crack teams and the chances are there will be a hot game."

SOURCES: "Notes of the Game," *Louisville (KY) Courier-Journal*, Jun 17, 1887; "Locals," *Hopkinsville (KY) Semi-Weekly South Kentuckian*, Aug 19, 1887; "G.O.O.F.," *Nashville (TN) Tennessean*, Aug 26, 1887; "Sporting," *Nashville Tennessean*, Sep 2, 1887; "Locals," *Nashville (TN) Tennessee Star*, Nov 25, 1887; "Locals," *Semi-Weekly South Kentuckian*, Jun 29, 1888; "Limited Local Items," *Nashville Tennessean*, Oct 10, 1890; "Pacific Coasts and Grays," *Nashville Tennessean*, Aug 11, 1891; "Negro Clubs," *Nashville Tennessean*, Apr 24, 1894; "Here and There," *Hopkinsville (KY) Kentuckian*, May 24, 1895; "Crack Colored Clubs," *Nashville Tennessean*, Jul 21, 1895; "Rock City Unions Win," *Nashville (TN) Tennessean*, Aug 18, 1896; "Turned the Tables," *Nashville Tennessean*, May 19, 1897; "Play Ball Today," *Nashville Tennessean*, Jun 7, 1897; "A Splendid Game," *Nashville Tennessean*, Jun 8, 1897; "With the Amateurs," *Chicago (IL) Inter-Ocean*, Jun 27, 1898; "Base Ball Today," *Nashville Tennessean*, Aug 18, 1898; "Unions and Reds," *Nashville Tennessean*, Jun 22, 1899; "Ball Game Today," *Decatur (IL) Evening Republican*, Jul 21, 1899; "Base Ball News," *Decatur Evening Republican*, Jul 22, 1899; "Cloudburst in Town," *Decatur (IL) Review*, Jul 22, 1899; "Giants Defeat Nashvilles," *Chicago (IL) Tribune*, Jul 24, 1899; "Nashville Won," *Chicago (IL) Evening Republican*, Aug 8, 1899; "Interesting Notes," *Indianapolis (IN) Freeman*, Sep 2, 1899; "Rock City Unions vs. Brotherhoods," *Louisville Courier-Journal*, Jun 23, 1900; "Amateur Ball Games," *Louisville Courier-Journal*, Jun 24, 1900; "Nashville Unions Win," *Nashville Tennessean*, Sep 19, 1900.

Roger Williams University Base Ball Club (Nashville, TN; 1880s–1900s)

The Roger Williams University B.B.C. organized in the 1890s, played black teams. In 1884, Central TN College defeated Roger Williams University, by a score of 24 to 17. *Nashville Tennessean* (April 20, 1894): "The Fisk University team will play the club from Roger Williams University on the Fisk University ground at 9 o'clock tomorrow morning." *Tennessean* (April 29, 1894): "Athletics have revived among the students and base-ball games are of daily occurrence between the students of Roger Williams and Fisk universities. The first game was played on April 21st, and resulted in favor of the latter." *Tennessean* (April 14, 1895): "The base-ball teams of Fisk University and Roger Williams University crossed bats yesterday afternoon on the former's grounds. The game resulted: Roger Williams 27, Fisk 11." *Tennessean* (April 28, 1895): "The Fisk University base-ball team

defeated the Roger Williams nine yesterday afternoon on the latter's grounds by a score of 26 to 23. The feature of the game was the heavy batting and base running of both nines." *Tennessean* (April 17, 1898): "About 350 spectators witnessed a well-played game between the Roger Williams and Fisk University teams yesterday afternoon on the Fisk campus. The teams were both in good trim and on account of the rivalry that exists between the ball tossers of the two schools there is always much interest attaching to their annual contests. The Roger Williams' team, although it has lost every series with the Fisk team for the last eight years, puts forth a stronger effort every year in order to win…. At the end of the game the score stood Fisk 18, Roger 7." *Tennessean* (April 15, 1900): "Roger Williams and Central University base-ball teams played a game yesterday afternoon on the Roger Williams' campus. The contest resulted in a score of 17 to 4 in favor of Roger Williams."

SOURCES: "State Board of Education," *Nashville (TN) Tennessean*, Mar 18, 1884; "Flashes from the Diamond," *Nashville Tennessean*, Apr 20, 1894; "Roger Williams University," *Nashville Tennessean*, Apr 29, 1894; "On Local Diamonds," *Nashville Tennessean*, Apr 29, 1894; *Nashville Tennessean*, Apr 14, 1895; "Amateur Games," *Nashville Tennessean*, Apr 28, 1895; "The Have One Each," *Nashville Tennessean*, May 3, 1896; "Fisk Won Easily," *Nashville Tennessean*, Apr 17, 1898.

Slipaway Base Ball Club (Nashville, TN; 1880s)

The Slipaway B.B.C. organized in the 1880s, played black teams. *Tennessean* (July 31, 1886): "The Slipaways had a walkover with the Meigs' School Greys yesterday, defeating them in fine style. Slipaways 12; Greys 5. Batteries—Bell and Smith, Stewart and Farrar." *Tennessean* (August 20, 1886): "The drill was proceeded by an amateur game of base-ball between the Slipaways and Fairfield nines of this city. The batteries of both clubs did good work up to the seventh inning, when the grounds were yielded to the drill."

SOURCES: "Amateurs," *Nashville (TN) Tennessean*, Jul 31, 1886; "Colored Troops," *Nashville Tennessean*, Aug 20, 1886.

South Nashville Reds Base Ball Club (Nashville, TN; 1880s–1890s)

The South Nashville Reds B.B.C. organized in the 1880s, played black aggregations. *Nashville Tennessean* (August 4, 1891): "Two colored base-ball clubs, the Loves and the South Nashville Reds, played a good game of ball yesterday afternoon. A large crowd was present and enjoyed the sport hugely. The game was close, hotly contested and exciting. It resulted in a score of 8 to 9 in favor of the Loves. They will probably play another game Thursday." *Tennessean* (August 20, 1891): "The last game of the season between colored clubs will be played at the Athletic Park this afternoon between the Loves and the South Nashville Reds. A good game is promised." *Tennessean* (May 6, 1899): "There will be a game of baseball this afternoon between the Fisk University nine and the Nashville Reds. Fisk has played three games this year so far and has not suffered a defeat. The Reds have a strong team, and an interesting game is expected." *Tennessean* (May 7, 1899): "The game of base-ball yesterday afternoon between the Nashville Reds and Fisk University was won by the latter by a score of 9 to 4."

SOURCES: "Loves Victorious," *Nashville (TN) Tennessean*, Aug 4, 1891; "Base Ball Notes," *Nashville Tennessean*, Aug 18, 1891; "Base Ball Game," *Nashville Tennessean*, Jul 11, 1892; "Last of the Season," *Nashville Tennessean*, Aug 20, 1891; "Amateur Games," *Nashville Tennessean*, May 8, 1895; "Base Ball at Fisk," *Nashville Tennessean*, May 6, 1899; "Base Ball at Fisk," *Nashville Tennessean*, May 7, 1899.

Squabbler Base Ball Club (Nashville, TN; 1890s). Organizer(s): John Clarke.

The Squabbler B.B.C. organized in the 1890s, played black aggregations. *Nashville Tennessean* (September 4, 1890): "John Clarke, manager of the Squabbler Base Ball Club, announces that his club accepts the challenge of the Salvators for a game tomorrow afternoon at 2:30 o'clock."

Sources: "Limited Local Items," *Nashville (TN) Tennessean,* Sep 4, 1890, *Nashville Tennessean,* Sep 28, 1890.

Union City Base Ball Club (Union City, TN; 1890s)

The Union City B.B.C. organized in the 1890s, played black and white aggregations. *Indianapolis Freeman* (June 19, 1897): "The Mayfield Base Ball Club played against the Union Citys Thursday and resulted in a victory for the Union City boys, 9 to 3. The battery for Union City was Rodgers and Shafer. The feature of the game was the pitching of Rodgers, striking out eleven men. Another was the batting of the Branford brothers, Sims and Thomas, and the first base work of Chambers. In the fourth inning Anderson of Mayfield ran into Holloman, the third baseman, and Holloman was badly hurt, and had to be carried off the grounds. It was an interesting game."

Sources: "A Prominent Couple Elopes," *Indianapolis (IN) Freeman,* Jun 19, 1897.

W. T. Linck Hotel Base Ball Club (Nashville, TN; 1870s–1880s)

The W. T. Linck Hotel B.B.C. organized in the 1880s, played black teams. *Nashville Tennessean* (August 29, 1887): "We the members of the original Blue Clippers B. B. C. do hereby challenge the members of the W. T. Linck B. B. C., to a match game to be played on your grounds, Friday, September 1, at 3 pm. William M. Louis, secretary." *Tennessean* (August 4, 1887): "The W. T. Linck Base Ball Club will play the Black Stockings today at the ball park this afternoon at 4 o'clock. This will be the first exhibition game between these popular colored clubs and some good ball playing is expected. The batteries—for the Lincks, Weaver and [Henry] Perkins; for the Black Stockings, [William] Moore and [Harrison] Waggoner." *Tennessean* (September 2, 1887): "The Rock City Greys defeated the W. T. Lincks at the park yesterday. The Greys found out that the Lincks are not what they think they are on the field. Score, 12 to 5. Batteries—Greys, [William] Moore and [John] Trimble; Lincks, Weaver and Smith." A KY team visited the Nashville nine. *Hopkinsville Semi-Weekly South Kentuckian* (September 16, 1887): "The Hard Hitters, colored base-ball club went over to Nashville Monday, and defeated the Lincks, of that city, by a score of 9 to 5."

Sources: "Sporting," *Nashville (TN) Tennessean,* Aug 4, 1887; "Over the City," *Nashville Tennessean,* Sep 2, 1887; "Sporting," *Nashville Tennessean,* Sep 2, 1887; "Here and There," *Hopkinsville (KY) Semi-Weekly South Kentuckian,* Aug 19, 1887; "Here and There," *Hopkinsville Semi-Weekly South Kentuckian,* Sep 16, 1887; "Sporting," *Hopkinsville Semi-Weekly South Kentuckian,* Sep 20, 1887.

Texas

Colored Base Ball Club (Abilene, TX; 1880s–1900s). Organizer(s): Clayte Perry.

The Colored B.B.C. organized in the 1880s, played black teams. *Albany News* (August 26, 1886): "The colored baseball nine of Abilene came over and played the Albany colored nine, or rather, we should say, a picked nine came over, for the pitcher, catcher, and first baseman were from Weatherford. The score stood 33 to 15 in favor of Abilene." A rivalry developed. *News* (September 9, 1886): "The colored base-ball nine of this place were challenged by the Abilene colored nine, and a match game was played at Abilene, in which the Albany nine came out winners by 48 to 17." *Abilene Reporter* (August 16, 1888): "About 500 people witnessed the game of ball near the stockpens yesterday evening between the Albany and Abilene colored nines, which resulted in a victory for the Albany team, the score standing 28 to 14." *News* (June 26, 1896): "The Albany colored base-ball club went to Abilene last Thursday and played a match game with the Abilene colored nine and scored a victory. The tally stood 33 to 26. The Abilene club will come over here and try to win back their laurels." *News* (July 17, 1896): "We learn that the colored baseball teams of Albany and Weatherford will cross bats in Albany, and there will be several games of ball during the two days following the first."

Sources: *Albany (TX) News,* Aug 26, 1886; *Albany News,* Sep 9, 1886; *Albany News,* Jun 23, 1887; "Local," *Abilene (TX) Reporter,* Aug 16, 1888; "Emancipation Day in Abilene," *Abilene Reporter,* Jun 26, 1896; *Albany News,* Jul 17, 1896; "Monday's News," *Abilene Reporter,* Aug 27, 1897.

Capitol Base Ball Club (Austin, TX; 1880s)

The Capitol B.B.C. organized in the 1880s. *Austin Weekly Stateman* (May 7, 1885): "A spirited game of baseball was played between the Austin Brown Stockings and Capitol Base Ball Club, two colored teams yesterday, the Capitols won by a score of 11 to 9." *Galveston News* (August 21, 1887): "There will be a game of base-ball this evening at Gulf City Park between the Galveston Flyaways and the Capitols of Austin, both colored clubs. A game will also be played at the park by the same clubs tomorrow evening." *News* (August 22, 1887): "The Capitol club of Austin and Flyaways of Galveston, two colored base-ball organizations, played a match game in this city yesterday, resulting in a victory for the Flyaways by a score of 12 to 8."

Sources: "Around Austin," *Austin (TX) Weekly Stateman,* May 7, 1885; "Flotsam and Jetsam," *Galveston (TX) News,* Aug 21, 1887; "Flotsam and Jetsam," *Galveston News,* Aug 22, 1887.

Colored Base Ball Club (Austin, TX; 1900s)

The Colored B.B.C. organized in 1900. *Galveston News* (July 29, 1900): "The Austin baseball club, the champions of the Lone Star State, will tackle the Galveston Fencibles at Beach Park, today and tomorrow, games at 4:30 pm. The Fencibles have strengthened considerably for the occasion and will endeavor to lower the champion's laurels."

Sources: "Austin vs. Galveston," *Galveston (TX) Daily News,* Jul 29, 1900.

Light Weight Base Ball Club (Austin, TX; 1880s–1890s)

The Light Weight B.B.C. organized in the 1880s, played black teams. *Dallas Weekly Herald* (July 5, 1883): "The colored base-ball club will play a match game here tomorrow." *The Austin Statesman* (July 5, 1883): "The Bastrop Base Ball Club came to Austin to play a match game with our colored club, the Light Weights. The rain and the mud prevented the game from being a success. The Bastrop club is composed of colored men and is said to play a skillful game. The Light Weights are heavy players too." *Austin Weekly Stateman* (July 12, 1883): "A company of colored base-ball players came to the city to contest the diamond field with the Light Weights, but a Negro has no more use for water on a patriotic occasion than a German, and the game was badly muddled." They reorganized in the 1890s. *San Antonio Light* (August 2, 1895): "The Austin Light Weights, a crack colored baseball team, arrived from Austin yesterday to play two games here with the Sunflowers, a local colored team. The first game will be played at the San Pedro Park this afternoon."

Sources: "San Antonio," *Galveston (TX) News,* Jun 20, 1883; "City Matters," *Austin (TX) Statesman,* Jul 5, 1883; "The State Capitol," *Dallas (TX) Weekly Herald,* Jul 5, 1883; "Austin vs. Galveston," *Austin (TX) Weekly Statesman,* Jul 12, 1883; "Colored Ball Game," *San Antonio (TX) Light,* Aug 2, 1895.

Red Stocking Base Ball Club (Austin, TX; 1880s–1890s)

The Red Stocking B.B.C., of Austin, TX, organized in the 1880s, played against black teams. *Galveston News* (June 11, 1894): "A large and well pleased audience gathered at Beach Park yesterday and witnessed a very exciting and well-played baseball game between two colored teams, Austin Red Stockings and Galveston Flyaways. This contest started promptly at 4:15 o'clock and from the time the first ball was pitched over the plate until Jones' line drive to left field brought Stafford in from second base, scoring the winning run, the interest never lagged. The Austin battery did splendid work and during the first three innings did not allow a Galveston man to reach first base. The throwing and general playing of Gordon, the Austin catcher, was very fine, while Jones and Brenham carried off the honors for the Flyaways. The teams are well-matched in playing strength and play good and interesting ball." *News* (August 3, 1895): "This afternoon at 5 o'clock and tomorrow afternoon at 4:30 the Austin Red Stockings, a crack colored club from the Capital City, will cross bats with the Galveston Flyaways at Beach Park. Austin's team is composed of some excellent colored ball tossers and their battery is said to be the best in the State." *Brenham Banner* (June 15, 1894): "At Stockbridge's pasture the Famous base-ball nine of this city played against the Red Stockings of Austin. The game was called with nearly a thousand spectators present.... They played a good game of ball but their umpire, was so manifestly partial in his decisions to the Brenham nine that it detracted from the interest in the game."

SOURCES: "Baseball at Beach Park," *Galveston (TX) News*, Sep 10, 1893; "Baseball at Beach Park," *Galveston News*, Sep 17, 1893; "Flyaways Winners," *Galveston News*, Sep 18, 1893; "Baseball at Beach Park," *Galveston News*, Oct 1, 1893; "Baseball at the Beach," *Galveston News*, Jun 11, 1894; "Ten to Thirteen," *Brenham (TX) Banner*, Jun 15, 1894; "Colored Teams to Play Today," *Galveston News*, Aug 3, 1895; *Brenham Banner*, Jul 10, 1896; *Brenham Banner*, Jul 25, 1896; *Brenham Banner*, Jul 28, 1896; "Base Ball Clubs," *Galveston News*, May 23, 1897; "Colored Clubs Matched," *Galveston News*, May 24, 1897; "Emancipation Celebration," *San Antonio (TX) Light*, Jun 18, 1897.

Yellow Jacket Base Ball Club (Austin, TX; 1900s)

The Yellow Jacket B.B.C. organized in 1900. *Galveston News*: "The Austin baseball club, the champions of the Lone Star State, will tackle the Galveston Fencibles at Beach Park, today and tomorrow, games at 4:30 pm. The Fencibles have strengthened considerably for the occasion and will endeavor to lower the champion's laurels."

SOURCES: "Austin vs. Galveston," *Galveston (TX) News*, Jul 29, 1900.

Colored Base Ball Club (Bastrop, TX; 1880s)

The Colored B.B.C. organized in the 1880s, played black teams. *The Austin Statesman* (July 5, 1883): "The Bastrop Base Ball Club came to Austin to play a match game with our colored club, the Light Weights. The rain and the mud prevented the game from being a success. The Bastrop club is composed of colored men and is said to play a skillful game. The Light Weights are heavy players too." *Austin Weekly Stateman* (July 12, 1883): "A company of colored base-ball players came to the city to contest the diamond field with the Light Weights, but a Negro has no more use for water on a patriotic occasion than a German, and the game was badly muddled." A rivalry developed. *Galveston News* August 24, 1884): "There was also a match between the colored clubs of Austin and Bastrop, with the following score: Austin 13, Bastrop 16."

SOURCES: "City Matters," *Austin (TX) Statesman*, Jul 5, 1883; "Austin vs. Galveston," *Austin (TX) Weekly Statesman, Jul 12, 1883; "Bastrop," *Galveston (TX) News*, Aug 24, 1884; "Sayers at Home," *Austin Weekly Statesman, Aug 28, 1884.

Crackerjacks Base Ball Club (Brenham, TX; 1890s–1900s). Organizer(s): John Tanner.

The Crackerjacks B.B.C. organized in the 1890s, played white and black teams. *Brenham Banner* (July 2, 1896): "A good crowd witnessed the match game of ball between the [Waco] Yellow Jackets and the Crackerjacks, two amateur colored nines. The game resulted in a victory for the Crackerjacks." *Banner* (August 5, 1896): "Crackerjacks is what the Galveston News calls the Brenham players in speaking of their victory over LaGrange. The press who suggested the name Invincibles now votes for Crackerjacks as a far more suitable name." *Banner* (April 10, 1897): "The Brenham Maroons and John Tanner's Crackerjacks crossed bats in a practice game." *Banner* (July 7, 1898): "The Brenham Crackerjacks and the Galveston Flyaways played a match game of ball at Stockbridge's Park in which Brenham was defeated by a score of 14 to 12." *Banner* (May 27, 1900): "The second game in the series between the Crackerjacks of Brenham and the Clippers of Cameron resulted in a victory for Cameron."

SOURCES: *Brenham (TX) Banner*, Jul 2, 1896; *Brenham Banner*, Aug 5, 1896; "Senators vs. Crackerjacks," *Brenham (TX) Banner*, Aug 23, 1896; "Navasota's Challenge," *Brenham Banner*, Apr 7, 1897; *Brenham Banner*, Apr 10, 1897; *Brenham Banner*, Jul 7, 1898; *Brenham Banner*, May 27, 1900;

Famous Base Ball Club (Brenham, TX; 1880s–1890s). Organizer(s): W. H. Browning, John Tanner, Ned Johnson and Henry Smith.

The Famous B.B.C. organized in the 1880s, played black teams. *Brenham Banner* (June 20, 1889): "Harrison's Famous Base Ball Club, of this place, defeated the Southern Clippers, of Hempstead, by a score of 11 to 4." After defeating the LaGrange nine on their home field, the Famous met their competitors at Brenham. *Banner* (June 15, 1894): "At Stockbridge's pasture the Famous base-ball nine of this city played against the Red Stockings of Austin. The game was called with nearly a thousand spectators present.... They played a good game of ball but their umpire, was so manifestly partial in his decisions to the Brenham nine that it detracted from the interest in the game." *Banner* (July 6, 1894): "The LaGrange baseball team will cross bats with the Famous Base Ball Club of Brenham today at Stockbridge's Grove. They have the support of Galveston and Austin and may be able to defeat the Famous, as Fox, the great Austin pitcher, will be in this game." *Banner* (August 14, 1894): "The Famous baseball nine of Brenham has at least met their Waterloo. For nine years, they have boasted victory with every team with which they have crossed bats, but a mixed team of Strikers defeat them at Stockbridge's Park with a score of 17 to 15, but it must be said to the credit of the Famous part of their own men were playing on the opposite side."

SOURCES: *Brenham (TX) Banner*, Jun 19, 1889; "The City," *Brenham Banner*, Jun 20, 1889; *Brenham Banner*, Aug 3, 1889; *Brenham Banner*, Aug 18, 1889; "Local News," *Brenham Banner*, May 1, 1892; "Local News," *Brenham Banner*, May 8, 1892; "Local News," *Brenham Banner*, May 29, 1892; *Brenham Banner*, May 31, 1892; "Local News," *Brenham Banner*, May 21, 1893; *Brenham Banner*, May 29 1894; "Local News," *Brenham Banner*, Jun 1, 1894; "Ten to Thirteen," *Brenham Banner*, Jun 15, 1894; "Local News," *Brenham Banner*, Jul 1, 1894; "LaGrange vs. Brenham," *Brenham Banner*, Jul 7, 1894; "Local News," *Brenham Banner*, Aug 12, 1894; "Local News," *Brenham Banner*, Aug 14, 1894; "Famous Reorganized," *Brenham Banner*, Jun 26, 1895; *Brenham Banner*, Jun 29, 1895; "Local News," *Brenham Banner*, Aug 11, 1895; "Famous Reorganized," *Brenham Banner*, Feb 27, 1896; "Local News," *Brenham Banner*, May 12, 1897; *Brenham Banner*, Jul 10, 1897.

Lone Star Base Ball Club (Brenham, TX; 1890s)

The Lone Star B.B.C. organized in the 1890s, played black aggregations. *Brenham Banner* (June 20, 1893): "In the match game of base-ball at the Fair Grounds between the Strikers and Lone Star nines, the game resulted in a score of 11 to 5 in favor of the Strikers."

SOURCES: *Brenham (TX) Banner*, May 22, 1890; "Local News," *Brenham Banner*, Jun 20, 1893.

Strikers Base Ball Club (Brenham, TX; 1890s)

The Strikers B.B.C. organized in the 1890s, played black teams. *Brenham Banner* (July 19, 1892): "The Strikers and True Blues, two local colored base-ball teams have arranged for a match game Sunday next at Camptown for $10 and the championship." *Banner* (June 21, 1896): "In the base-ball contest between the Strikers and [Waco] Yellow Jackets, the score stood 7 to 6 in favor of the Yellow Jackets."

SOURCES: "Local News," *Brenham (TX) Banner*, Jul 19, 1892; "Local News," *Brenham Banner*, May 26, 1895; "Local News," *Brenham Banner*, Jun 29, 1895; "Local News," *Brenham Banner*, Jun 30, 1895; "Local News," *Brenham Banner*, Aug 15, 1895; "Emancipation Celebration," *Brenham Banner*, Jun 21, 1896; "Hard Luck," *Brenham Banner*, Jul 22, 1896.

True Blues Base Ball Club (Brenham, TX; 1890s). Organizer(s): Henry Browning.

The True Blues B.B.C. organized in the 1890s, played black aggregations. *Brenham Banner* (July 19, 1892): "The Strikers and True Blues, two local colored base-ball teams have arranged for a match game Sunday next at Camptown for $10 and the championship."

SOURCES: "Local News," *Brenham (TX) Banner*, Jul 19, 1892.

Colored Base Ball Club (Bryan, TX; 1890s–1900s). Organizer(s): R. S. Lewis; J. C. Kernole.

The Colored B.B.C. organized in the 1890s. The nine, operating during the period under the nicknames, Stars, Iron Fronts, and Red Ants, played black aggregations. *Galveston News* (May 22, 1890): "The colored base-ball team of Bryan [Stars] today defeated a crack team from Hearne. Score 7 to 6. The Bryan colored team has not been defeated this season." *Indianapolis Freeman* (May 20, 1891): "The victorious Star Base Ball Team by a series of conquests is till Monarch of All It Surveys." *Freeman* (June 6, 1891): "The Bryan Stars defeated the Hempstead base-ball team with a score of 6 to 3." *Bryan Eagle* (August 15, 1895): "The Bryan Negro ball team fared better in Navasota than the pale face fans. They went down Friday evening and cleaned up the Navasota Negroes by a score of 9 to 7 in favor of Bryan." *Eagle* (May 29, 1901): "J. C. Kernole has taken the colored base-ball team to Palestine for a series of games. A tour of several towns will be made. The members of the team have a brilliant red uniform and are known as the Red Ants."

SOURCES: "Negro Ball at Bryan," *Galveston News*, May 22, 1890; "Monarch of All She Surveys," *Indianapolis (IN) Freeman*, May 20, 1891; "Monarch of All She Surveys," *Indianapolis Freeman*, Jun 6, 1891; "Fatally Stabbed," *Indianapolis Freeman*, Jun 13, 1891; "Sport," *Indianapolis Freeman*, Jul 18, 1891; *Bryan (TX) Eagle*, Aug 15, 1895; *Bryan Eagle*, Apr 27, 1898; "Monday-Tuesday," *Bryan Eagle*, Jun 8, 1899; "Saturday," *Bryan Eagle*, Jun 22, 1899; "Local News," *Bryan Eagle*, Jul 1, 1900; "Local News," *Bryan Eagle*, Jul 22, 1900; "Bryan Wins the Series," *Dallas (TX) Morning News*, Aug 1, 1900; *Bryan Eagle*, May 29, 1901; "The Red Ants Victorious," *Bryan Eagle*, May 30, 1901; "Local News," *Bryan Eagle*, Jun 13, 1901.

Athletic Base Ball Club (Dallas, TX; 1880s)

The Athletic B.B.C. organized in the 1880s, played black teams. *Dallas Herald* (September 12, 1884): "The Athletic colored club, of this city, played the Hard Hitters, the Fort Worth colored club, in that city Wednesday, and beat the by a score of 17 to 7."

SOURCES: "Chips," *Dallas (TX) Herald*, Sep 12, 1884.

Black Stocking Base Ball Club (Dallas, TX; 1880s–1890s). Organizer(s): Jasper Crutchfield; H. Armisted.

The Black Stocking B.B.C. organized in the 1880s. The *Dallas Morning News* (June 24, 1887): "The Dallas Black Stockings are a base-ball club made up for the most part of porters in the railroad offices of the city." The Black Stockings played black teams. *Galveston News* (May 21, 1884): "The Black Stocking Colored Base Ball Club went to Fort Worth today to play the Stars of that city to play a match game of ball for $30." That same year, the "Blacks" met Callender's Minstrel Blue Stocking B.B.C. *Dallas Herald* (September 22, 1884): "The game at the grounds yesterday afternoon between Callender's Minstrel Club and the Black Stockings of this city, both colored, was novel so to speak and rather entertaining. The game resulted in a score of 32 to 3 in favor of the Black Stockings." *Dallas Morning News* (June 21, 1886): "The colored base-ball clubs, the Black Stockings and Reds, played a very exciting game in Leftwick's brickyard. A great deal of batting and running and much hard work resulted in a score of 24 to 22 in favor of the Blacks." By 1887, Dallas and Galveston had developed a rivalry. *Morning News* (June 17, 1887): "The Black Stockings, the crack colored base-ball club of Dallas, with Captain H. Armisted at the head, will leave on Saturday for Galveston, where they will play the Tidal Waves and the Fly-a-Aways for the championship of the State and a purse of $100. *Galveston News* (June 21, 1887): "One of the most interesting things that occurred during the day was the match game of base-ball played between the Dallas Black Stockings and the Tidal Waves of Galveston, both colored clubs. After a sharp contest the Galveston Tidal Waves succeeded in defeating their opponents by a score of 12 to 3. The Dallas Black Stockings claim to be the best colored club in the state, and consequently the Tidal Waves feel elated over their victory." *News* (July 13, 1891): "On Twenty-ninth Street and Avenue P the two crack colored nines, the Black Stockings and the Flyaways, butted for supremacy, the latter winning by a score of 11 to 1." *Morning News* (August 26, 1894): "The Black Stockings and Santa Fe Blues, two colored teams, will play at the fairgrounds this evening for a $25 purse and the championship of Dallas. Both teams are very strong. The Black Stockings defeated the New Orleans team in that city by a score of 6 to 5, and the Blues lately defeated the Austin in Dallas by 11 to 7."

SOURCES: "Base Ball," *Dallas (TX) Weekly Herald*, Aug 30, 1883; "A Day at Dallas," *Fort Worth (TX) Gazette*, May 21, 1884; "Sparks from Dallas," *Galveston (TX) News*, May 21, 1884; "Colored Base Ball," *Dallas (TX) Herald*, Aug 3, 1884; "Colored Baseballists," *Dallas Weekly Herald*, August 28, 1884; "Localettes," *Fort Worth Gazette*, Sep 11, 1884; "Chips," *Dallas Herald*, Sep 12, 1884; "The Diamond," *Dallas Herald*, Sep 22, 1884; "Colored Base Ball," *Dallas (TX) Morning News*, Jun 21, 1886; "For the Championship," *Dallas Morning News*, Jun 17, 1887; "Dallas Dots," *Galveston News*, Jun 17, 1887; "Colored Celebrations," *Galveston News*, Jun 21, 1887; "Railroad News of the Day," *Dallas Morning News*, Jun 24, 1887; "The Colored Base Ball Players," *Dallas Herald*, Jun 24, 1887; "Local Notes," *Dallas Morning News*, Apr 7, 1888; "Local Notes," *Dallas Morning News*, Apr 7, 1888; "Amateur Games," *Dallas Morning News*, May 4, 1890; "Black Stockings vs. Fly Aways," *Dallas Morning News*, Jul 13, 1890; "Other Local Games," *Galveston News*, Jun 13, 1891; "Celebrated the Day," *Galveston News*, Jun 20, 1891; "Other Games To-Day," *Galveston News*, Jul 5, 1891; "Colored Base Ball," *Dallas Morning News*. *Dallas Morning News*, Jul 9, 1894; "Colored Base Ball," *Dallas Morning News*, Aug 26, 1894; "Base Ball," *Dallas Morning News*, Aug 27, 1894.

Brown Stocking Base Ball Club (Dallas, TX; 1880s–1890s). Organizer(s): Jasper Crutchfield.

The Brown Stocking B.B.C. organized in the 1880s. The Browns joined the TX Colored Base Ball League in 1888, and they play black nines. *Dallas Morning News* (May 27, 1888): "The second league game between the Dallas Browns and Fort Worth Blues, colored, was played at Fort Worth yesterday. At the end of the ninth inning the score stood 6 to 6. At the end of the tenth, 7 to 6 in favor of Dallas. The game is for $25 a side and two-thirds of the gate fee. The two clubs will play again today, and in the event the Fort Worth club wins the tie will be played off in Dallas." *Morning News* (May 28, 1888): "Yesterday afternoon the Fort Worth Blues and the Dallas Browns of the Colored State League played the first of the three league games today. The game was played at the East Dallas Colored Park, and was called at 3:30 o'clock, and, as usual, with Dallas, the Browns were successful. The game was hotly contested throughout and some good playing was done. The game for today, on account of the heavy and muddy condition of the ground has been postponed, says Jasper Crutchfield, the manager of the Dallas club." *Morning News* (July 22, 1894): "The crack colored team of Paris, Texas will play here tomorrow afternoon at the fairgrounds. They are on tour through the State. The Dallas team has been strengthened since their last game by signed Henderson Caldwell, Marshall's first baseman, and Will Bryan, Waco's crack pitcher." *Morning News* (June 1, 1897): "Two of the most interesting games of the season were those between the Dallas Browns, a colored team, and the Waxahachie Light Weights, a colored team, played at East End Park Friday and Saturday. The score in the first game stood 6 to 4 in favor of Dallas; the last game resulted in a score of 11 to 16 in favor of Dallas."

SOURCES: "Colored Base Ball League" *Galveston (TX) Daily News*, Mar 30, 1888; "The Colored Base-Ballists," *Galveston Daily News*, Apr 14, 1888; "Negotiating for a Cracker," *Fort Worth (TX) Gazette*, May 19, 1888; "The Colored League," *Dallas (TX) Morning News*, May 20, 1888; "Texas Colored League Game," *Dallas Morning News*, May 27, 1888; "Dallas and Fort Worth," *Dallas Morning News*, May 28, 1888; "Base Bits," *Dallas Morning News*, Jun 3, 1888; "Challenge Accepted," *Dallas Morning News*, Jun 17, 1888; "Colored Base Ball Game," *Dallas Morning News*, Jun 19, 1888; "Fly Aways Defeated," *Dallas Daily News*, Jul 30, 1888; "Local Base Ball," *Dallas Morning News*, Jun 6, 1894; "Local Base Ball," *Dallas Morning News*, Jul 22, 1894; "Dallas Got It Again," *Dallas Morning News*, Jun 1, 1896; "Local Base Ball Gossip," *Dallas Morning News*, Jul 26, 1896; "Browns Win Two Straight," *Dallas Morning News*, Jun 1, 1897; "Local Base Ball," *Dallas Morning News*, Jun 6, 1897; "Colored Base Ball," *Dallas Morning News*, Jun 19, 1897; "Dallas Lost All Three," *Dallas Morning News*, Jul 21, 1897; "Colored Ball Tossers," *Dallas Morning News*, Aug 1, 1897.

Clipper Base Ball Club (Dallas, TX; 1890s). Organizer(s): A. A. Hudson.

The Clipper B.B.C. organized in the 1890s. The Clippers played against colored organizations. *Dallas Morning News* (June 6, 1894): "The game announced to come off tomorrow between the Dallas and Waxahachie colored clubs has been declared off that all may turn out to the game between the Dallas Clippers and the Admirals for the benefit of Manager Leonard of the Dallas Clippers. Arrangements are about perfected for Tyler's battery Henry Harris and Ed Coats, to play here for the rest of the season."

SOURCES: "Local Base Ball," *Galveston (TX) News*, Jun 6, 1894; "Local Base Ball," *Galveston News*, Jul 28, 1894.

Santa Fe Blues Base Ball Club (Dallas, TX; 1890s)

The Santa Fe Blues B.B.C. organized in the 1890s, played black aggregations. *Dallas Morning News* (July 10, 1894): "The Marshall colored base-ball team played against the Dallas Black Stockings at the fair grounds and won by a sore of 11 to 5. Marshall has a strong team, having won 7 out of 12 games played in the State. The Santa Fe Blues will play them this evening at the fairgrounds." *Morning News* (July 10, 1894): "The Santa Fe Blues claim the score and Marshall Lightweights. The score was 14 to 12 in favor of the Marshall Lightweights."

SOURCES: "Colored Base Ball," *Dallas (TX) Morning News*, Jul 10, 1894; "The Field of Sport," *Dallas Morning News*, Jul 12, 1894; "Colored Base Ball," *Dallas Morning News*, Aug 26, 1894.

Quickstep Base Ball Club (Denton, TX; 1890s). Organizer(s): Tonsie Carey.

The Quickstep B.B.C. organized in the 1890s, played black nines. *Fort Worth Gazette* (June 14, 1894): "Tonsie Carey, captain of the colored base-ball team here, announces that he challenges any colored team in the state for a game of gate receipts. Any club accepting will address him at Denton." *Dallas Morning News* (June 23, 1899): "The Clippers, a Negro team from McKinney, defeated the colored team here, the Quicksteps, in a hotly contested game by a score of 7 to 6. The Quicksteps will play the Katy Flyers of Dallas Friday and the Denison Negro team on Saturday."

SOURCES: "Denton Dots," *Fort Worth (TX) Gazette*, June 14, 1894; "Denton," *Fort Worth Gazette*, August 30, 1894; "Challenges Everybody," *Fort Worth Gazette*, September 6, 1894; "Denton Dots," *Dallas (TX) Morning News*, June 23, 1899.

Light Weight Base Ball Club (also called Fort Worth Blues) (Fort Worth, TX; 1880s–1890s)

The Light Weight B.B.C. organized in the 1880s, played black teams. The Light Weight or Fort Worth Blues joined the Texas Colored League in 1888, and they played black teams. *Fort Worth Gazette* (May 18, 1888): "The colored base-ball club of Fort Worth will play two games with the Dallas Darktowns [Browns] on tomorrow and Sunday. *Dallas Morning News* (May 28, 1888): "The second league game between the Dallas Browns and Fort Worth Blues, colored, was played at Fort Worth yesterday. At the end of the ninth inning the score stood 6 to 6. At the end of the tenth, 7 to 6 in favor of Dallas. The game is for $25 a side and two-thirds of the gate fee. The two clubs will play again today, and in the event the Fort Worth club wins the tie will be played off in Dallas." *Dallas Morning News* (July 15, 1888): "The Sun Flowers of this city and Light Weights of Fort Worth, both colored, played a match game of ball at Fair Ground Park. Owing to the close score yesterday and the defeat of the Houston team, the game attracted quite a large crowd. The Houston team proved too strong for the Fort Worth crowd and won by a score of 7 to 0."

SOURCES: "Dallas Base Ball Notes," *Fort-Worth (TX) Gazette*, May 18, 1888; "Negotiating for a Cracker," *Fort-Worth Gazette*, May 19, 1888; "The Colored League," *Dallas (TX) Morning News*, May 20, 1888; "Texas Colored League," *Dallas Morning News*, May 27, 1888; "Dallas and Fort Worth," *Dallas Morning News*, May 28, 1888; "Base Ball Matters," *Galveston (TX) Evening Tribune*, Jun 9, 1888; "Colored League," *Galveston Evening Tribune*, Jun 15, 1888; "Game of Colored Base Ball," *Dallas Morning News*, Jun 22, 1888; "Sun Flowers vs. Light Weights," *Dallas (TX) Morning News*, Jul 15, 1888; "Localettes," *Fort-Worth Gazette*, Jun 5, 1891.

Star Hard Hitters Base Ball Club (Fort Worth, TX; 1880s)

The Star Hard Hitters B.B.C. organized in the 1880s, played against black teams. *Galveston News* (May 21, 1884): "The Black Stocking Colored Base Ball Club went to Fort Worth today to play the Stars of that city to play a match game of ball for $30." Fort Worth and

Dallas developed a rivalry. *Fort Worth Gazette* (May 21, 1884): "The most amusing game of base-ball ever played in Fort Worth was that between the Dallas [Athletics] and Fort Worth [Star Hard Hitters] colored clubs at the base-ball park yesterday afternoon. The Dallas won by a score of 17 to 78. The clubs play again this afternoon, the game commencing at 3 o'clock sharp." *Dallas Herald* (September 13, 1884): "The Athletic colored club, of this city, played the Hard Hitters, the Fort Worth colored club, in that city Wednesday, and beat them by a score of 17 to 7."

SOURCES: "Sparks From Dallas," *Galveston (TX) News*, May 21, 1884; "A Day at Dallas," *Fort Worth (TX) Gazette*, May 21, 1884; "Localettes," *Fort Worth Gazette*, Sep 10, 1884; "Chips," *Dallas (TX) Herald*, Sep 12, 1884; "Localettes," *Fort Worth Gazette*, Sep 13, 1884.

Young Strikers Base Ball Club (Fort Worth, TX; 1880s)

The Young Strikers B.B.C. organized in the 1880s, played black teams. *Fort Worth Gazette* (October 28, 1887): "In the afternoon the Fort Worth Colored Base Ball Club, the Young Strikers, undertook to play another game of ball with the Flyaways of Galveston, but were very badly defeated."

SOURCES: "The Base Ball Game," *Fort Worth (TX) Gazette*, Oct 27, 1887; "The Colored State Fair," *Fort Worth Gazette*, Oct 28, 1887.

Cuban Giants (Galveston, TX; 1880s)

The Cuban Giants B.B.C. organized in 1889, played black teams. *Galveston Evening Tribune* (March 22, 1889): "The colored boys in the east end have a base-ball nine which thus far has succeeded in vanquishing any team that has had the nerve to meet them on the diamond. The name of this invincible organization it the Cuban Giants, and for three seasons they have carried off the pennant. Next Sunday they will cross bats with a picked nine on avenue N and Fourteenth Streets." *Evening Tribune* (March 25, 1889): "The Cuban Giants defeated a picked nine yesterday by a score of 39 to 8."

SOURCES: "Giants at the Bat," *Galveston (TX) Evening Tribune*, Mar 22, 1889; "Coming and Going," *Galveston Evening Tribune*, Mar 25, 1889.

Fencible Base Ball Club (Galveston, TX; 1890s). Organizer(s): Henry Burrell.

The Fencible B.B.C. organized in the 1890s, played black nines. *Galveston News* (July 10, 1895): "The Galveston Fencible baseball club having defeated the Houston Hub Citys in Houston by a score of 5 to 0 for the championship of south Texas, will defend the title by playing on all comers, the Flyaways preferred." *News* (May 11, 1896): "The Fencibles of Galveston and the Pickwicks of Houston, colored teams, played an exciting game of ball at the park this afternoon in the presence of a large crowd of spectators. The score: Houston 17, Galveston 16." *News* (May 24, 1897): "The Fencibles (colored) baseball club of this city, under the management of Henry Burrell, arrived last night at 11:30 p.m. via the Missouri, Kansas, and Texas. The game between them and the Rose Buds, of Houston, ended with a score of 1 to 0 in the Fencibles' favor. Anderson and Taylor, battery for the Fencibles, did some clever work, while the work of the Houston battery was also good. The Fencibles are not only good ball tossers, but are also a team composed of some of the best vocal talent in the state. The team has four members that compose the famous Bailey Little Rock quartette club and last night at the Missouri, Kansas and Texas depot, while the victorious club was waiting for the arrival of the train some thirty minutes was passed in sweet vocal music that attracted a regular opera gathering."

SOURCES: "Amateur Base Ball," *Galveston (TX) News*, Jul 10, 1895; "The Flyaways Accept," *Galveston News*, Jul 30, 1895; "Base Ball," *Galveston News*, Aug 22, 1895; "Have Reorganized," *Galveston News*, Apr 26, 1896; "An Exciting Ball Incident," *Galveston News*, May 11, 1896; "Flyaways Won It," *Galveston News*, May 22, 1897; "Baseball Clubs," *Galveston News*, May 23, 1897; "The Fencibles Won," *Galveston News*, May 24, 1897.

Flyaway Base Ball Club (Galveston, TX; 1880s–1890s). Organizer(s): Henry James, C. Ransom, J. F. Ramsey and A. Runnels; Alexander Simpson.

The Flyaway B.B.C. organized in the 1880s, played black teams. *Fort Worth Gazette* (October 28, 1887): "In the afternoon the Fort Worth Colored Base Ball Club, the Young Strikers, undertook to play another game of ball with the Flyaways of Galveston, but were very badly defeated." They developed a rivalry with Houston. The Flyaways joined the Texas Colored League in 1888; they also traveled to LA, where they played the New Orleans Pinchbacks. *New Orleans Picayune* (July 15, 1888): "About 500 people witnessed the Galvestons defeat the Pinchbacks yesterday by a score of 10 to 3. Battery for the Galvestons, Runnels and Walker." They played the Houston Blues. *Galveston News* (August 6, 1889): "There was a game of baseball at the park this afternoon between two colored clubs, the Flyaways of Galveston and the Blues of this city. It attracted quite a crowd, mostly colored people, and proved highly entertaining from first to last. Many new feats were introduced, but without the scope of base-ball phraseology and will not be told here. The catchers played up right behind the bat all the time and the pitchers did some fine work. The umpire was a little off sometimes, but he equalized account pretty evenly. The game resulted in favor of Galveston, the score standing 18 to 17. Nobody could tell anything about the result of the game till the last player was caught out. They frequently made four runs after two were out." *News* (June 20, 1891): "The game of ball played between the Blackstockings and Flyaways was hotly contested and a case of see-saw all the way through. The fielding of both teams was excellent and the pitching of Reily for the Blacksox and Johnson for the Flyaways was quite effective." *News* (October 2, 1893): "The game of baseball between two colored clubs, Houston Brownstockings and Galveston Flyaways, which took place at Beach Park yesterday afternoon, was hotly contested and quite interesting. The Flyaways played hard and desperately, but were unfortunate in placing their hits when hits meant runs, leaving the bases full three times without scoring." *News* (June 22, 1894): "The Galveston Flyaways claim to be the colored champion baseball club of the state and are ready to defend their claim against all comers for any amount of money. Austin, Dallas, and Waco each have excellent colored baseball teams and there seems to be some question as to the right of the Flyaways to the championship title. In order to settle the question, manager Alex Simpson says his club is anxious to meet the Waco and Austin teams for three games each and that he has arranged for Dallas to play here next Saturday and Sunday, July 28 and 29." *News* (May 3, 1897): "Yesterday a fair crowd witnessed a game of baseball at Beach Park between the Galveston Flyaways and the Houston Rosebuds. The pitching of Chattanooga was very good. He struck out thirteen men and walker of the home team nine." *Brenham Banner* (July 7, 1898): "The Brenham Crackerjacks and the Galveston Flyaways played a match game of ball at Stockbridge's Park in which Brenham was defeated by a score of 14 to 12."

SOURCES: "The Base Ball Game," *Fort Worth (TX) Gazette*, Oct 27, 1887; "The Colored State Fair," *Gazette*, Oct 28, 1887; "Colored Base Ball League" *Galveston (TX) News*, Mar 30, 1888; "The Colored Base-Ballists," *Galveston News*, Apr 14, 1888; "The Colored League," *Dallas (TX) Morning News*, May 20, 1888; "Texas Colored League Game," *Dallas Morning News*, May 27, 1888; "Base Bits," *Dallas Morning News*, Jun 3, 1888; "Around Home Bases," *New Orleans (LA)*

Times-Picayune, Jul 15, 1888; "Fly Aways Defeated," *Galveston News*, Jul 30, 1888; "Black and White," *Galveston News*, Sep 17, 1888; "Flotsam and Jetsam," *Galveston News*, Mar 31, 1889; "Colored Base-Ballists," *Galveston News*, May 20, 1889; "Flyaways and Sluggers," *Galveston News*, May 1, 1890; "Amateur Games," *Galveston News*, May 4, 1890; "Black Stockings vs. Fly Aways," *Galveston News*, Jul 13, 1890; "Celebrated the Day," *Galveston News*, Jun 20, 1891; "Flyaways to the Front," *Galveston News*, Mar 27, 1893; "Baseball at Beach Park," *Galveston News*, Sep 10, 1893; "Baseball at the Beach," *Galveston News*, Jun 11, 1894; "Baseball at Beach Park," *Galveston News*, Jul 8, 1894; "To-Day," *Galveston News*, Aug 19, 1894; "Base Ball at Palestine," *Galveston News*, Aug 19, 1894; "Colored Teams to Play To-Day," *Galveston News*, Aug 3, 1895; "Flyaways Beat the Austins," *Galveston News*, Aug 5, 1895; "Baseball," *Galveston News*, Aug 22, 1895; "Flyaways vs. Little Rocks," *Galveston News*, Aug 28, 1895; "About the Flyaways," *Galveston News*, Sep 19, 1895; "Flyaways Won It," *Galveston News*, May 22, 1897; "Base Ball Clubs," *Galveston News*, May 23, 1897; *Brenham (TX) Banner*, Jul 7, 1898; "Puffs From the Pipe," *Kansas City (MO) Journal*, May 22, 1899; "Hot Time Over the Line," *Kansas City Journal*, May 28, 1899; "Colored Teams to Play," *Galveston News*, Sep 3, 1899.

Littlerock Base Ball Club (Houston, TX; 1890s)

The Littlerock B.B.C. organized in the 1890s, played black nines. *Galveston News* (August 3, 1893): "The Little Rock Baseball Club of the Fifth Ward will go to Galveston Sunday over the International and Great Northern road to play a game of ball at Beach Park with the Flyaways of the Island City." *Galveston News* (September 4, 1893): "The Galveston Flyaways defeated the Houston Littlerocks in yesterday's contest by fast and fortunate fielding and fine battery work by Jones and Williams. The Houston nine played hard but were never in the game after the third inning. The general playing of the Flyaways was perfect, not making an error during the entire game."

SOURCES: "Headlight Flashes," *Galveston (TX) News*, Aug 3, 1893; "Baseball at Beach Park," *Galveston News*, Aug 6, 1893; "Baseball at Beach Park," *Galveston News*, Aug 27, 1893; "Flyaways vs. Little Rocks," *Galveston News*, Aug 28, 1893; "Flyaways vs. Littlerocks," *Galveston News*, Sep 4, 1893.

Opera Glass Base Ball Club (Galveston, TX; 1880s). Organizer(s): W. Jackson and C. Hodge.

The Opera Glass B.B.C. organized in the 1880s, played black teams. *Galveston News* (August 12, 1883): "A colored club, sailing under the name of the Opera Glass Base-Ball Club, has challenged the Lorguettes [white] to meet them on the diamond field." *News* (October 1, 1883): "The Opera Glass and the White Wing Clubs, colored, resulted in a victory for the first named club, the score standing 16 to 9." Galveston and Houston continued their rivalry. *Galveston Evening Tribune* (July 27, 1885): "The game, yesterday afternoon, at the Beach Park, between the strong teams of colored baseballists, of Houston [Rosebuds] and Galveston [Opera Glass], was witnessed by quite a large assembly. In the seventh inning, W. Jackson and C. Hodge, both of the home team, were badly disabled. The game was won by the Houston club, by a score of 9 to 7." *News* (September 13, 1885): "The Rose Bud Base Ball Club, of [Houston], will play a match game with the Opera Glass Club, [of this city], both colored clubs, at Beach Park this afternoon. The Houston club is recognized as the champions of the state among colored clubs." The Opera Glass also a played minstrel nine. *News* (October 11, 1885): "This evening, at 3:30 o'clock, there will be a game of base-ball between the Kersands Minstrel nine and the Opera Glasses of Galveston."

SOURCES: "Base Ball," *Galveston (TX) News*, Aug 12, 1883; "Stray Notes," *Galveston News*, Aug 23, 1883; "Base Ball," *Galveston News*, Aug 26, 1883; "The City," *Galveston News*, Sep 10, 1883; "Base Ball,"

Galveston News, October 1, 1883; "Base Ball," *Galveston News*, Oct 11, 1883; "Special Notices," *Galveston News*, Jul 16, 1884; "Base Ball," *Galveston News*, Aug 12, 1885; *Galveston (TX) Evening Tribune*, Jun 26, 1885; "Base Ball," *Galveston Evening Tribune*, Jul 27, 1885; "Tribune Trifles," *Galveston Evening Tribune*, Aug 15, 1885; "Stray Notes," *Galveston News*, Sep 13, 1885; "Stray Notes," *Galveston News*, Oct 11, 1885.

Quickstep Base Ball Club (Galveston, TX; 1890s)

The Quickstep B.B.C. organized in the 1890s, played black aggregations. The Quicksteps challenged the Flyaways. *Galveston News* (July 23, 1894): "The game of base-ball at Beach Park yesterday between the Flyaways and Quicksteps, two local colored teams, was a challenging match from start to finish." After falling behind, the Flyaways rallied and won the contest by a score of 21 to 9.

SOURCES: "Baseball at Beach Park," *Galveston (TX) News*, Oct 1, 1893; "Detroit vs. Quicksteps," *Galveston News*, Apr 2, 1894; "Quickstep vs. Detroit," *Galveston News*, Apr 9, 1894; "Baseball at the Beach," *Galveston News*, Jun 24, 1894; "Baseball at the Beach," *Galveston News*, Jul 22, 1894; "Baseball Matters," *Galveston News*, Jul 23, 1894.

Texas Colored League (Galveston, TX; 1888). Organizer(s): Henry H. Swanston.

In 1888, Henry H. Swanston proposed the formation of the Texas Colored League. Organizers elected the following officers: President Henry H. Swanton, Galveston; Secretary W. P. Anderson, Waco; Treasurer J. F. Ramsey, Dallas. The Colored League embraced the following colored aggregations: Houston Sun Flowers, Dallas Browns, Fort Worth Light Weights, Austin Capitals, Waco Reds, and Galveston Flyaways.

SOURCES: "Colored Base Ball League" *Galveston (TX) News*, Mar 30, 1888; "The Colored Base-Ballists," *Galveston News*, Apr 14, 1888; "The Colored League," *Dallas (TX) Morning News*, May 20, 1888; "Texas Colored League Game," *Dallas Morning News*, May 27, 1888 "Base Bits," *Dallas Morning News*, Jun 3, 1888; "Flotsam and Jetsam," *Galveston News*, Jul 29, 1888 "Fly Aways Defeated," *Galveston News*, Jul 30, 1888.

White Wing Base Ball Club (Galveston, TX; 1880s)

The White Wing B.B.C. organized in the 1880s, played black teams. *Galveston News* (August 30, 1883): "The colored White Wing Base Ball Club, of Galveston, came up Sunday and played the colored Chicagoes, of this city, at the Fair Grounds for $100 a side. At the close of the game the score stood 31 to 19, in favor of the Houston club, and the $100 went to the Houston club's pocket." *News* (October 1, 1883): "The Opera Glass and the White Wing Clubs, colored, resulted in a victory for the first named club, the score standing 16 to 9."

SOURCES: "State Press," *Galveston (TX) News*, Aug 30, 1883; "Base Ball," *Galveston News*, Oct 1, 1883.

Black Diamond Base Ball Club (Hillsboro, TX; 1890s). Organizer(s): Dan Oliver; William Sanders.

The Black Diamond B.B.C. organized in the 1890s, played black nines. *Dallas Morning News* (June 12, 1897): "The Hillsboro Black Diamonds are now open for the season. We challenge any amateur nine in Dallas, Fort Worth, Waco, Houston, Brenham, Corsicana, or any nine that can play ball. Let us hear from you." Early in the season, they played the Dallas Browns. *Morning News* (June 29, 1897): "The Black Diamonds of this city and the Snowballs of Dallas [Browns], colored ball teams, are playing a series of games at Rice's park. The first game last evening stood 7 to 5 in favor of the Snowballs. The game this evening was won by the Snowballs, the game showing 7 to 3 in their favor."

SOURCES: "Colored Team's Challenge," *Dallas (TX) Morning News*, Jun 12, 1897; "A Challenge From Hillsboro," *Dallas Morning News*, Jun 15, 1897; "The Snowballs Won," *Morning News*, Jun 29, 1897; "Challenge," *Dallas Morning News*, Jul 11, 1897; "The Black Hawks Won," *Dallas Morning News*, Jul 11, 1897; "A Challenge Issued," *Dallas Morning News*, Aug 6, 1897.

Hornets Base Ball Club (Hillsboro, TX; 1890s). Organizer(s): Henry Bruce.

The Hornets B.B.C. organized in the 1890s. The Hornets played black aggregations.

SOURCES: "State and Territory Briefs," *Dallas (TX) Morning News*, Apr 16, 1898; "Challenges Colored Ball Teams," *Dallas Morning News*, Apr 30, 1898.

Mudcat Base Ball Club (Hillsboro, TX; 1890s). Organizer(s): Dan Oliver.

The Mudcat B.B.C. organized in the 1890s. The Mudcats played black aggregations.

SOURCES: "Challenge," *Dallas (TX) Morning News*, Jul 11, 1896.

Brown Stocking Base Ball Club (Houston, TX; 1890s)

The Brown Stocking B.B.C. organized in the 1890s, played black aggregations. *Galveston News* (September 3, 1893): "The Houston Brownstockings, a colored ball club from the Bayou City, composed of the pick of the disbanded Rosebud and Littlerock teams, will cross bats with the Galveston Flyaways, champion colored club of the State." Houston and Galveston continued its baseball rivalry. *Galveston News* (September 11, 1893): "Yesterday's game at Beach Park between the Galveston Flyaways and the Houston Brown Stockings, the crack colored teams of the state, resulted by a score of 7 to 6 in favor of the visiting club." *Galveston News* (September 18, 1893): "A game of baseball between the colored clubs—Houston Brown Stockings and Galveston Flyaways—which took place at Beach Park yesterday afternoon, was one of the most exciting and hotly contested games ever played on these historic grounds."

SOURCES: "Baseball at Beach Park," *Galveston (TX) Daily News*, Sep 3, 1893; "Baseball at Beach Park," *Galveston Daily News*, Sep 10, 1893; "Game at Beach Park," *Galveston Daily News*, Sep 11, 1893; "Baseball at Beach Park," *Galveston News*, Sep 17, 1893; "Flyaways Winners," *Galveston News*, Sep 18, 1893; "Flyaways Were Defeated," *Galveston News*, Oct 2, 1893.

Chicago Base Ball Club (Houston, TX; 1880s)

The Chicago B.B.C. organized in the 1880s, played black teams. *Galveston News* (August 23, 1883): "The Opera Glass Base-Ball Club (colored) goes to Houston to play the Chicagos of that city for $100 a side." *Galveston News* (August 30, 1883): "The colored White Wing Base Ball Club, of Galveston, came up Sunday and played the colored Chicagoes, of this city, at the Fair Grounds for $100 a side. At the close of the game the score stood 31 to 19, in favor of the Houston club, and the $100 went to the Houston club's pocket."

SOURCES: "Stray Notes," *Galveston (TX) News*, Aug 23, 1883; "Base Ball," *Galveston News*, Aug 26, 1883; "State Press," *Galveston News*, Aug 30, 1883; "The City," *Galveston News*, Sep 10, 1883; "Base Ball," *Galveston News*, Oct 1, 1883.

Creole Giants Base Ball Club (Houston, TX; 1890s). Organizer(s): A. A. Hudson.

The Creole Giants B.B.C. organized in the 1890s, played black aggregations. *Houston Post* (June 5, 1898): "There will be a baseball game at the League Park this afternoon between two colored teams of this city and Flyaways of Galveston. These are two crack colored teams of their respective cities, and as there is considerable rivalry between them a good game may be expected." *San Antonio Light* (June 20, 1898): "An interesting game of ball was played yesterday afternoon between two colored teams—the Alamo Grays, of San Antonio, and the Creole Giants, of Houston. The latter was strengthened by a number of San Antonio players, members of the Webster Colts, and won handily. The Houston pitcher was a puzzle mainly in that he had great speed. He struck out fifteen men."

SOURCES: "Baseball Today," *Houston (TX) Post*, Jun 5, 1898; "Base Ball," *San Antonio (TX) Light*, Jun 20, 1898.

Hub City Base Ball Club (Houston, TX; 1890s)

The Hub City B.B.C. organized in the 1890s, played black teams. *Galveston News* (July 10, 1895): "The Flyaways stopped over in Houston yesterday and played the Hub City Club, whom they defeated easily by a score of 21 to 1. The Flyaways knocked Nobles of the Hub City team out of the box in the fourth inning and would have shut them out had it not been for a costly error of one of the Flyway players."

SOURCES: "Colored Team to Play," *Galveston (TX) News*, Jun 23, 1895; "Amateur Base Ball," *Galveston News*, Jul 10, 1895; "The Flyaways Accept," *Galveston News*, Jul 30, 1895; "Took Everything in Sight," *Galveston News*, Aug 19, 1895; "Base Ball," *Galveston News*, Aug 22, 1895.

Rosebud Base Ball Club (Houston, TX; 1890s). Organizer(s): Charles Lane.

The Rosebud B.B.C. organized in the 1890s, played black teams. *Galveston News* (July 16, 1894): "Yesterday's game of base-ball between the two colored clubs, Houston Rosebuds and Galveston Flyaways, attracted a large and well-pleased audience, composed mainly of white patrons of the sport. The contest was interesting from the start and abounded in pretty plays, fine throws and heavy hitting. The Flyaways again outplayed their opponents and put up a splendid game." *Galveston News* (August 13, 1894): "Yesterday's game of baseball at Beach Park between the Galveston Flyaways and Houston Rosebuds was the most exciting game seen here in some time, it requiring ten innings to decide the question of supremacy, which resulted in favor of the visitors." *Galveston News* (September 10, 1894): "The first of a series of three Sunday games of base-ball between the colored clubs Houston Rosebuds and Galveston Flyaways was played before a good-sized audience at Beach Park yesterday afternoon. The contest was full of brilliant plays and heavy hitting and proved both interesting and exciting from start to finish. The umpiring of McBeth was without a blemish. He kept the players constantly on the move, and it is due to his excellent work that the game was played in the short time of one hour and thirty minutes."

SOURCES: "Fly Aways and Rosebuds," *Galveston (TX) News*, May 20, 1894; "Baseball at the Beach," *Galveston News*, Jun 24, 1894; "Baseball at the Beach," *Galveston News*, Jun 25, 1894; "Baseball at Beach Park," *Galveston News*, Jul 8, 1894; "The Rosebuds Defeated," *Galveston News*, Jul 9, 1894; "Rosebuds Again Defeated," *Galveston News*, Jul 16, 1894; "Sport of the Diamond," *Galveston News*, Aug 10, 1894; "Good Ball Playing," *Galveston News*, Aug 13, 1894; "Flyaways are Winners," *Galveston News*, Sep 10, 1894; "Close of the Season," *Galveston News*, Oct 1, 1894; "Flyaways Win Again," *Galveston News*, Oct 8, 1894.

Sun Flower Base Ball Club (also called the Houston Blues) (Houston, TX; 1880s)

The Sun Flower B.B.C. organized in the 1880s, played black teams. The Sun Flowers—nicknamed Houston Blues—joined the Texas Colored League in 1888, and they played black nines. *Galveston Evening Tribune* (May 11, 1888): "At Beach Park tomorrow the Sun

Flowers of Houston and the Fly Aways of Galveston will cross bats. These being the strongest teams in the State, a lively game is expected." *Galveston News* (May 14, 1888): "The Flyaways of Galveston and Sun Flowers of Houston, two of the leading clubs in the colored base-ball league, played a game yesterday at Beach Park, attracting quite an audience, the spectators embracing a great number of whit people. Both clubs play a strong game, the batting being particularly heavy. Up to the seventh or eighth inning the Sun Flowers of Houston had the game pretty much their own way. The Flyaways, however, came in strong on the homestretch, concluding the game by a score of 9 to 5 in favor." *Dallas Morning News* (July 15, 1888): "The Sun Flowers of this city and Light Weights of Fort Worth, both colored, played a match game of ball at Fair Ground Park. Owing to the close score yesterday and the defeat of the Houston team, the game attracted quite a large crowd. The Houston team proved too strong for the Fort Worth crowd and won by a score of 7 to 0." The Sun Flowers traveled to LA, where they played New Orleans's Union club. *New Orleans Times-Democrat* (July 16, 1888): "The visitors defeated the Unions last evening at the New Orleans Park before about 700 spectators, by a score of 18 to 8." The Union club secured the services of the Sun Flowers' pitcher, Mose Johnson, to play against St. Louis's West End nine.

SOURCES: "Flotsam and Jetsam," *Galveston (TX) News*, Apr 25, 1888; "Flotsam and Jetsam," *Galveston News*, Apr 30, 1888; "Colored Folks Picnic," *Galveston (TX) Evening Tribune*, May 10, 1888; "Base Ball Notes," *Galveston Evening Tribune*, May 11, 1888; "Colored Ball Tossers," *Galveston News*, May 14, 1888; "Personal," *Galveston News*, May 20, 1888; "The Bayou City Budget," *Galveston News*, Jul 11, 1888; "Sun Flowers vs. Light Weights," *Dallas (TX) Morning News*, Jul 15, 1888; "A Big Excursion From Texas," *New Orleans (LA) Times-Democrat*, Jul 15, 1888; "A Walk-Over for the Houston Blues," *New Orleans Times-Democrat*, Jul 16, 1888; "Flotsam and Jetsam," *Galveston News*, Jul 29, 1888; "Diamond Dots," *New Orleans Times-Democrat*, Sep 30, 1888; "The Colored Clubs," *New Orleans (LA) Picayune*, Oct 24, 1888; "The Colored Clubs," *New Orleans Picayune*, Oct 25, 1888.

Brown Stocking Base Ball Club (Huntsville, TX; 1890s)

The Brown Stocking B.B.C. organized in the 1890s, played black aggregations. *Galveston Daily News* (September 23, 1894): "The Huntsville Brown Stockings, and the Galveston Flyaways, two colored clubs, will meet for battle at Beach Park, this afternoon, commencing promptly at 4 o'clock. The Brown Stockings are made up of some of the best colored baseballists in the state and arrived in the city last night from Huntsville on the big colored excursion from that place."

SOURCES: "Baseball at the Beach," *Galveston (TX) News*, Sep 23, 1894.

Heavy Weight Base Ball Club (Marshall, TX; 1890s). Organizer(s): Charles Perry.

The Heavy Weight B.B.C. organized in the 1890s, played black teams of TX and LA. *Dallas Morning News* (June 30, 1893): "The Marshall colored base-ball team played against the Dallas Black Stockings at the fair grounds and won by a sore of 11 to 5. Marshall has a strong team, having won 7 out of 12 games played in the State. The Santa Fe Blues will play them this evening at the fairgrounds." *Dallas Morning News* (July 9, 1894): "The Santa Fe Blues claim the score and Marshall Lightweights. The score was 14 to 12 in favor of the Marshall Lightweights." *Shreveport Times* (April 24, 1895): "The Shreveport Blues and the Marshall Heavy Weights, colored clubs, played their second game with a score of 14 to 12 in favor of Shreveport." *New Orleans Times-Democrat* (August 10, 1894): "There was

a good game of base-ball at Sportsman's Park between the Baptiste club of this city and a club from Marshall, Texas. Both teams played well and the game ended in favor of the Baptistes by a score of 5 to 3. The same clubs will play today and tomorrow."

SOURCES: "At Marshall," *Dallas (TX) Morning News*, Jun 30, 1893; "Marshall vs. Shreveport," *Shreveport (LA) Times*, May 19, 1894; "Shreveport vs. Marshall," *Shreveport Times*, May 20, 1894; "Marshall Defeated," *Shreveport Times*, May 22, 1894; "Base Ball," *Marshall (TX) Messenger*, Jun 1, 1894; "Base Ball," *Shreveport Times*, Jun 5, 1894; "Colored Base Ball," *Dallas Morning News*, Jul 9, 1894; "The Field of Sport," *Dallas Morning News*, Jul 10, 1894; "Local Base Ball," *Dallas Morning News*, Jul 12, 1894; "Local Colored Base Ball," *Dallas Morning News*, Jul 17, 1894; "Marshall," *Fort Worth (TX) Gazette*, Jul 27, 1894; "Base Ball," *Marshall Messenger*, Jul 27, 1894; "Marshall vs. Longview," *Marshall Messenger*, Jul 27, 1894; "Colored Base Ball," *Dallas Morning News*, Jul 29, 1894; "Baptistes vs. Marshalls," *New Orleans (LA) Times-Democrat*, Aug 10, 1894; *Marshall Messenger*, Aug 17, 1894; "Base Ball," *Dallas Morning News*, Aug 27, 1894; "Base Ball at Marshall," *Shreveport (LA) Times*, Apr 24, 1895; "Shreveport vs. Marshall," *Shreveport Times*, Apr 25, 1895.

Pride Base Ball Club (Marshall, TX; 1880s)

The Pride B.B.C. organized in the 1880s, played black teams. *Dallas Morning News*: "There was a match game of base-ball this evening between the Marshall and home club, colored, which resulted in a victory for the home team, the score standing 35 to 12." *Shreveport Times*: "Two games will be played at Lakeside Park today between colored clubs. The second game will be called at 4:15 pm, when the champion Walkers of Shreveport and the Prides of Marshall, Texas will cross bats." *Shreveport Times*: "A colored team from Shreveport is playing Marshall. The first game, which was a pretty one, resulted in a victory for Shreveport by a score of 16 to 9."

SOURCES: "Colored Clubs," *Dallas (TX) Morning News*, Sep 16, 1888; "Base Ball," *Shreveport (LA) Times*, Aug 25, 1889; "Base Ball," *Shreveport Times*, Aug 27, 1889.

Clipper Base Ball Club (McKinney, TX; 1890s–1900s). Organizer(s): A. A. Hudson.

The Clipper B.B.C. organized in the 1890s, played black teams. In 1899, the Clippers toured OK, playing against several teams, including the Cyclones. *Oklahoma Leader* (July 17, 1900): "The professional negro baseball team from McKinney, Texas, is playing a series of good games here with the local team. The game yesterday was 9 to 4 in favor of the visitors. They play this evening and will play again tomorrow evening." The Cyclones won on a game-ending triple play. *Oklahoma State Capital* (July 27, 1900): "The ball team of McKinney, Texas played ball with the colored team of Guthrie at island Park, yesterday afternoon and won by a score of 9 to 5. The two teams will play ball again next Sunday afternoon."

SOURCES: "At Plano," *Dallas (TX) Morning News*, Jun 20, 1895; "Dallas Lost All Three," *Dallas Morning News*, Jul 21, 1897; "Plano Won From McKinney," *Dallas Morning News*, Jul 25, 1897; "Colored Ball Tossers," *Dallas Morning News*, Aug 1, 1897; *McKinney (TX) Democrat*, Jun 9, 1898; *McKinney Democrat*, Jun 16, 1898; "Clippers Were Winners," *Dallas Morning News*, Jun 23, 1899; "Sherman 6, McKinney 4," *Dallas Morning News*, May 7, 1900; *Oklahoma City (OK) Times-Journal*, Jul 17, 1900; *Guthrie (OK) Leader*, Jul 19, 1900; "Texas Ball Players," *Guthrie (OK) Oklahoma State Capital*, Jul 27, 1900.

Strikers Base Ball Club (Navasota, TX; 1890s)

The Strikers B.B.C. organized in the 1890s, played black teams. *Brenham Banner* (May 1, 1892): "The Famous colored base-ball nine leave this evening for Navasota to play a match game of ball with the club there." *Brenham Banner* (May 8, 1892): "Harrison's Famous and Navasota's Strikers, two colored base-ball nines, will cross bats in a match game near the old compress Sunday evening."

SOURCES: "Local News," *Brenham (TX) Banner*, May 1, 1892; "Local News," *Brenham Banner*, May 8, 1892; "Local News," *Brenham Banner*, May 24, 1892; "Local News," *Brenham Banner*, May 28, 1892; "Local News," *Brenham Banner*, May 29, 1892.

Alamo Grays Base Ball Club (San Antonio, TX; 1890s)

The Alamo Grays B.B.C. organized in the 1890s, played black aggregations. They developed a rivalry with the local Light Weight club. *San Antonio Light* (September 10, 1892): "The Alamo Grays and Matthews Light Weights will play ball at the latter's grounds tomorrow afternoon at 4 o'clock." They played against Waco's Yellow Jackets. *Light* (September 19, 1896): "An interesting game of baseball was played at San Pedro Park yesterday afternoon between the Waco Yellow Jackets, the champion colored team of North Texas, and the Alamo Grays, the crack local colored team. The Alamo Grays were defeated by a score of 2 to 1." They played the Webster Colts. *Light* (May 16, 1898): "A very interesting game of baseball was played at San Pedro Park, between two crack colored clubs of San Antonio, known as the Webster Colts and the Alamo Grays. Twelve innings were required to decide the game which was won by the Colts by a score of 7 to 4. It wasn't a pitchers' battle by any means, for both sides hit hard, and all that prevented them from scoring was sharp fielding."

SOURCES: *Indianapolis (IN) Freeman*, Aug 13, 1892; "Local News," *San Antonio (TX) Light*, Aug 26, 1892; "Light Flashes," *San Antonio Light*, Sep 10, 1892; "Waco Won," *San Antonio Light*, Sep 19, 1896; "Light Flashes," *San Antonio Light*, Sep 20, 1896; "Base Ball," *San Antonio Light*, May 15, 1898; "Colored Cracks," *San Antonio Light*, May 16, 1898; "Today's Ball Games," *San Antonio Light*, May 22, 1898; *San Antonio Light*, May 30, 1898; "Colored Celebration," *San Antonio Light*, Jun 12, 1898; *San Antonio Light*, Jun 20, 1898.

Rosebud Base Ball Club (San Antonio, TX; 1890s)

The Rosebud B.B.C. organized in the 1890s, played black teams. *San Antonio Light* (August 29, 1897): "The Rosebuds, one of San Antonio's crack colored baseball teams, and a colored team from Victoria, Texas, reputed as the Southwest Texas champions, engaged in a game of baseball at San Pedro Park yesterday afternoon. The Victorias were outclassed all around by the Rosebuds' superior work."

SOURCES: "Colored Base Ball," *San Antonio Light*, Aug 29, 1897; "The Rosebuds Won Again," *San Antonio Light*, Aug 30, 1897; "Light Rays," *San Antonio Light*, Jul 31, 1899; "Waco Yellow Jackets," *San Antonio Light*, Aug 12, 1899; "Rosebuds Were Easy," *San Antonio Light*, Aug 14, 1899.

Colored Base Ball Club (Sherman, TX; 1890s)

The Colored B.B.C. organized in the 1890s, played black nines. *Dallas Morning News* (June 21, 1899): "The game between Sherman and Fort Worth colored base-ball teams at Batsell's Park this afternoon resulted: Sherman 14, Fort Worth 7." The Sherman nine played a series against Kansas City's Unions, who were on a four State tour. *Morning News* (August 22, 1899): "In a game at Batsell's Park this afternoon between the colored teams of Kansas City and Sherman the score was 3 to 2 in favor of Sherman. In yesterday's game the score was 6 to 5 in favor of Sherman." The Shermans had talent. *Kansas City Journal* (August 23, 1899): "The Kansas City Unions defeated the Paris team by a score of 10 to 8. The feature of the game was the clean fielding of the Unions. Martin pitched great ball. Manager Dorsey has signed shortstop Collins, of Sherman, Texas."

SOURCES: "Denison Budget," *Dallas (TX) Morning News*, Jul 27, 1897; "Good Game of Ball," *Dallas Morning News*, Jun 14, 1899; "Dallas Boys Victors," *Dallas Morning News*, Jun 15, 1899; "Sherman Routed Fort Worth," *Dallas Morning News*, Jun 21, 1899; "Austin vs. Sherman," *Dallas Morning News*, Jun 28, 1899; "Sherman vs. Dallas," *Dallas Morning News*, Jul 13, 1899; "Dallas Defeated Sherman," *Dallas Morning News*, Jul 14, 1899; "Batsell's Park Game," *Dallas Morning News*, Aug 22, 1899; "Unions, 12–5; Sherman, 7–6," *Kansas City (MO) Journal*, Aug 23, 1899.

Athletic Base Ball Club (Tyler, TX; 1880s–1900s). Organizer(s): Ryan Stewart.

The Athletic B.B.C. organized in the 1880s. The Athletics played against black aggregations. *Galveston News* (August 3, 1883): "The Tyler Athletics and Palestine Blackstockings, colored nines, played a game of base-ball here today for a silver-mounted bat and ball. Palestine won by a score of 16 to 9." The team's star battery had played for the Dallas Browns. *Dallas Morning News* (August 5, 1894): "Harris and Coats, Tyler's crack battery, arrived last Friday and will be in the points today against Austin's great team." *Fort Worth Gazette* (August 24, 1894): "The colored base-ball team entered into a game of ball between the Jacksonville boys yesterday and the day before. The first day the Tyler boys wiped up the earth with them, by making thirty runs to ten. The next day it turned out 16 to 13 in favor of Tyler." *Dallas Morning News* (May 25, 1900): "A telegram from Ryan Stewart, manager of the Tyler colored ball teams, received this morning, states that the Tyler team defeated the Hot Springs team by a score of 9 to 7. Before returning the team will visit Little Rock, Pine Bluff and other Arkansas points."

SOURCES: "From Corsicana," *Waco (TX) Daily Examiner*, Aug 3, 1883; "Contest of Colored Clubs," *Galveston (TX) News*, Jul 17, 1888; "Mopped the Earth With Them," *Fort Worth (TX) Gazette*, Aug 24, 1894; "Local Base Ball," *Dallas (TX) Morning News*, Jul 28, 1894; "Colored Base Ball," *Dallas Morning News*, Jul 31, 1894; "Colored Base Ball," *Dallas Morning News*, Aug 5, 1894; "Today is Closing Day," *Dallas Morning News*, Jul 22, 1896; "Tyler vs. Waco," *Dallas Morning News*, Jun 25, 1899; "Tyler 9, Hot Springs 7," *Dallas Morning News*, May 25, 1900.

Central City Base Ball Club (Waco, TX; 1880s)

The Central City B.B.C. organized in the 1880s, played against black teams. *Colorado Citizen* (August 11, 1884): "Callenders' Minstrels tackled a local colored base-ball club at Waco, and with ease knocked out the Central City Darkeys." The Callender Minstrels trumped them in a follow-up game. They also played against local nines. *Waco Examiner* (May 12, 1885): "Walter Downs, captain of the Central City Base Ball Club has received a challenge from Alex Hayes, captain of the East Wacos, to play a match game on Saturday next. The challenge has been accepted." During one game, C. H. Gilber, of the Central Citys' players, encountered trouble. *Galveston News* (July 14, 1886): "C. H. Gilber, a colored baseballist, wanted in Falls County, is behind bars. As one of the picked nine of his club he came up to Waco to cross bats with the Conisal City Colored Club. The Fall City Club was in full uniform. As the game was called, Constable Jenkins spotted his man, composed himself on a seat, watched the contest to its finish, then quietly arrested the accused, and walked him to jail."

SOURCES: *Colorado (TX) Citizen*, Aug 11, 1884; "Waco Wirelets," *Fort Worth (T) Gazette*, Sep 26, 1884; "'Round About Town," *Waco (TX) Examiner*, May 12, 1885; "Round About Town," *Waco Examiner*, May 21, 1885; "Round About Town," *Waco Examiner*, Jul 8, 1885; "Waco," *Galveston (TX) News*, Jul 14, 1886.

East Waco Base Ball Club (Waco, TX; 1880s). Organizer(s): Alex Hayes.

The East Waco B.B.C. organized in the 1880s, played black nines. *Waco Examiner* (May 21, 1885): "Walter Downs, captain of the Central City Base Ball Club has received a challenge from Alex Hayes, captain of the East Wacos, to play a match game on Saturday next. The challenge has been accepted."

SOURCES: "Round About Town," *Waco (TX) Examiner*, May 21, 1885.

Yellow Jacket Base Ball Club (Waco, TX; 1890s–1900s)

The Yellow Jacket B.B.C. organized in the 1890s, played black aggregations. *Fort Worth Gazette* (June 29, 1891): "A game of baseball occurred yesterday at Riverside flats, between colored teams of Fort Worth and Waco, which was a walk-over for the local team, the Waco men finding it impossible to gauge Itson's curves and shoots, which were hardly touched. Waco's pitcher was on the other hand batted at will by the Fort Worth team, their work with stick netting eight runs, while Waco was not able to get a man across the plate." *San Antonio Light* (September 19, 1896): "An interesting game of baseball was played at San Pedro Park yesterday afternoon between the Waco Yellow Jackets, the champion colored team of North Texas, and the Alamo Grays, the crack local colored team. The Alamo Grays were defeated by a score of 2 to 1." *Light* (September 20, 1896): "The final game between the Waco Yellow Jackets and the San Antonio Rosebuds for the colored baseball championship of the state was played at San Pedro Park yesterday afternoon and resulted in an easy victory for the Yellow Jackets, the score being 11 to 3. The visitors presented the pitcher (Andrew "Rube" Foster), who proved himself invincible last Friday. Although his curves were not so delusive yesterday as on the previous occasion he succeeded in keeping the Rosebuds' hits scattered well enough to win the game." The team visited CO. *Denver Rocking Mountain News* (August 23, 1898): "The Waco Yellow Jackets, a baseball nine, are here today to play the Americans on the D.W.C. grounds, and they brought with them over 300 colored people for the South, who took advantage of a low rate over the Gulf Road. The Yellow Jackets have played forty-eight games and are likely to put up a stiff fight with the local players." The Yellow Jackets won the series.

SOURCES: "Going to Waco," *Fort Worth (TX) Gazette*, Jun 11, 1891; "Yesterday's Baseball Game," *Fort Worth Gazette*, Jun 29, 1891; "Local Notes," *Dallas (TX) Morning News*, May 31, 1896; "The Colored Players," *Galveston (TX) News*, Aug 31, 1896; "Waco Won," *San Antonio (TX) Light*, September 19, 1896; "Light Flashes," *San Antonio Light*, September 20, 1896; McKinney *(TX) Democrat*, Jun 16, 1898; "Amateur Base Ball," *Dallas Morning News*, Jun 26, 1898; *Denver (CO) Rocky Mountain News*, Aug 20, 1898; "Champion Cake Walkers of Texas," *Denver Rocky Mountain News*, Aug 23, 1898; "Yellow Jackets vs. Americans," *Denver (CO) Post*, Aug 23, 1898; "Yellow Jackets Won," *Denver Rocky Mountain News*, Aug 24, 1898; "In General," *Denver Rocky Mountain News*, Aug 25, 1898; "Tyler vs. Waco," *Dallas Morning News*, Jun 25 1899; "City Base Ball League," *Dallas Morning News*, Jul 9, 1899; "Traveling Salesman Killed," *Dallas Morning News*. September 1899; "Colored Baseball," *San Antonio (TX) Sunday Light*, Jun 3, 1900; "Briefly Related," *Little Rock (AR) Gazette*, Jun 13, 1900; "Local News," *Dallas Morning News*, Jul 29, 1900.

Light Weight Base Ball Club (Waxahachie, TX; 1890s). Organizer(s): Henry Nervis.

The Light Weight B.B.C. organized in the 1890s, played black teams. *Dallas Morning News* (June 9, 1891): "The Dallas colored baseball team arrived home last night from Waxahachie, where they yesterday defeated the crack colored team of that town, the score

standing Dallas 7, Waxahachie 3." *Dallas Morning News* (June 15, 1891): "The Dallas and Waxahachie colored baseball teams crossed bats at the fairgrounds yesterday evening. The score stood 10 to 11, in favor of Dallas. Twelve innings." *Dallas Morning News* (August 14, 1894): "The Waxahachie crack team will play the Dallas team next Sunday at the fairgrounds. Henry Nervis of Waxahachie, better known as Frenchie, is in the city making necessary arrangements." *Morning News* (June 1, 1897): "Two of the most interesting games of the season were those between the Dallas Browns, a colored team, and the Waxahachie Light Weights, a colored team, played at East End Park Friday and Saturday. The score in the first game stood 6 to 4 in favor of Dallas; the last game resulted in a score of 11 to 16 in favor of Dallas." *Dallas Morning News* (June 19, 1897): "At the fairgrounds baseball park today and Sunday the Waco and Waxahachie colored teams will play the Dallas Browns."

SOURCES: "Browns Win Two Straight," *Dallas (TX) Morning News*, Jun 9, 1891; "Sporting," *Dallas Morning News*, Jun 15, 1891; "Colored Base Ball," *Dallas Morning News*, Aug 14, 1894; "Browns Win Two Straight," *Dallas Morning News*, Jun 1, 1897; "Colored Base Ball," *Dallas Morning News*, Jun 19, 1897; "Colored Parade and Maifest," *Dallas Morning News*, Jun 1, 1899.

Red Stocking Base Ball Club (Waxahachie, TX; 1880s)

The Red Stocking B.B.C. organized in the 1880s, played black nines. *Dallas Herald* (August 26, 1884): "The first of two games to be played by the Dallas Black Stockings and the Waxahachie Red Stockings, was played yesterday afternoon on the base-ball grounds, resulting in a victory for the former club by a score of 35 to 7. The second and last game will be played this afternoon. The fielding was simply immense." *Dallas Weekly Herald* (August 28, 1884): "This afternoon and tomorrow at 3 o'clock there will be a contest between the Black Stockings, of Dallas, and the Red Stockings, of Waxahachie. Considerably interest is manifested by both black and white in this game, as both are considered crack clubs."

SOURCES: "Splinter," *Dallas (TX) Herald*, Aug 23, 1884; "Colored Base Ballists," *Dallas Herald*, Aug 26, 1884; "Colored Baseballists," *Dallas (TX) Weekly Herald*, Aug 28, 1884.

Black Hawk Base Ball Club (Whitney Hill, TX; 1890s)

The Black Hawk B.B.C. organized in the 1890s, played black nines. *Dallas Morning News* (May 24, 1897): "The Black Hawks of Whitney hereby challenge any amateur colored team in the state to play or Whitney or Hillsboro." *Dallas Morning News* (June 20, 1897): "Whitney's colored team, Black Hawks, and the Milford Crackerjacks crossed bats on the grounds of the former club at Whitney today. Score 23 to 3 in favor of the Black Hawks." *Dallas Morning News* (July 11, 1897): "Whitney's colored team, Black Hawks, took the glitter of Hillsboro's Black Diamonds in a score of 9 to 5 at the ball park at this place today."

SOURCES: "Black Hawks Want a Game," *Dallas (TX) Morning News*, May 24, 1897; "The Black Hawks Won," *Dallas Morning News*, Jun 20, 1897; "The Black Hawks Won," *Dallas Morning News*, Jul 11, 1897.

Utah

Fort Douglas Browns Base Ball Club (Salt Lake City, UT; 1890s).

The Fort Douglas Browns B.B.C. organized in the 1890s, played black and white aggregations. The Browns were composed of soldiers. *Salt Lake Herald* (June 21, 1897): "The Browns entered upon their last inning with great determination, and Wheeler took a two-base fall out of the first ball Harkness whirled in his direction. Countee delivered a large and luscious fly into centerfield, where Herbert, with a beautiful sprint gathered it in. Hughes sent a safe one into the field, and then Richards put a stiff to Lloyd at shortstop, who sent it to the first baseman too tardily, and there were three Browns hugging the bags. As Lovering went to bat there was great excitement. It was the critical point in the career of the Browns for that day. One, two, three balls went over the plate and the willow was too short each time for Lovering." *Herald* (August 29, 1898) reports, "Several hundred baseball enthusiasts journeyed to the fort with the expectation of witnessing a stiffly contested game. The Browns, since several of their crack players returned from the war, have gotten together again. They promised to put up a quality of ball that would knock large holes in the victorious front that the Short Lines had hitherto presented at the fort. When the game ended there were a good many disgusted soldiers at the fort who had hoped that the Browns would finish up better with their opponents. But the players themselves appeared to be in no wise discouraged. I haven't played ball all summer, said Harris, who has been spending the hot months pitching bullets at the Spaniards from the muzzle of a rifle. We'll get another chance at them and do better next time."

SOURCES: "Fort Douglas Wins," *Salt Lake City (UT) Herald*, May 24, 1897; "Soldiers are Defeated," *Salt Lake City Herald*, Jun 21, 1897; "Ft. Douglass Wins Game," *Salt Lake City Herald, Jul* 25, 1897; "Defeated the Browns," *Salt Lake City Herald, Aug* 15, 1898; "The Short Line Wins," *Salt Lake City Herald, Aug* 29, 1898; "Ball Game at the Fort Today," *Salt Lake City Herald, Sep* 11, 1898; "Browns and Short Line," *Salt Lake City Herald, Sep* 12, 1898; "Base Ball This Afternoon," *Salt Lake City Herald, Oct* 9, 1898; "Base Ball at the Fort," *Salt Lake City Herald, Oct* 10, 1898; "On the Diamond," *Salt Lake City Herald, Oct* 23, 1898; "The Elks Played in Luck," *Salt Lake City Herald, Oct* 24, 1898.

Santiago Base Ball Club (Salt Lake City, UT; 1890s).

The Santiago B.B.C. organized in the 1890s. The Santiagos, composed of men from Fort Douglas and Los Angeles, played white nines. *Salt Lake City Herald* (May 21, 1899): "At 3:30 this afternoon the Salt Lake Juniors and the 'Santiagos,' a team made up of the Fort Douglas men, will meet on the fort grounds. The game was hastily arranged, and has not received a very thorough announcement, but an interesting exhibition of the sport is promised."

SOURCES: "On the Diamond," *Salt Lake City (UT) Herald*, May 21, 1899.

Vermont

Cuban Juniors Base Ball Club (St. Albans, VT; 1890s)

The Cuban Juniors B.B.C. organized in the 1890s. The Cuban Juniors (also dubbed the Colored Stars) played black and white aggregations. *St. Albans Messenger* (July 5, 1893): "The game of baseball yesterday afternoon between the Central Vermont Athletic Club nine and a colored club was a decidedly jug-handled affair. The colored men played well but the Athletics got their eyes on the ball and pounded it terribly. *Messenger* (August 21, 1893): "The first of a series of games of balls between the Colored Stars and the Central Vermont Athletic Club team last Saturday afternoon resulted in a victory for the latter by a score of 10 to 1. The Stars made some very pretty plays, but the Athletics got their pitcher and knocked the ball into the sky at every attempt. The fielding of the Stars was equal, if not superior, to that of their opponents, but they could not hit Gould's pitching." In a six-game series, the Cuban Juniors won two games, lost three and tied one.

SOURCES: "Base Ball," *St. Albans (VT) Messenger,* Jul 5, 1893; "Town Affairs," *St. Albans Messenger,* Aug 7, 1893; "Town Affairs," *St. Albans Messenger,* Aug 21, 1893; "Town Affairs," *St. Albans Messenger,* Sep 1, 1893; "Town Affairs," *St. Albans Messenger,* Sep 4, 1893; "Town Affairs," *St. Albans Messenger,* Oct 3, 1893; "Town Affairs," *St. Albans Messenger,* Oct 10, 1893; "Town Affairs," *St. Albans Messenger,* Oct 13, 1893; "Town Affairs," *St. Albans Messenger,* Jul 30, 1894; "The Conductors' Picnic," *St. Albans Messenger,* Jul 30, 1894; "Town Affairs," *St. Albans Messenger,* Aug 23, 1894; "Town Affairs," *St. Albans Messenger,* Aug 24, 1894; "21 to 11," *St. Albans Messenger,* Aug 24, 1894.

Virginia

Monumental Base Ball Club (Alexandria, VA; 1860s)

The Monumental B.B.C. organized in the 1860s, played against black nines. *Alexandria Gazette* (September 27, 1867): "A match game of base-ball played yesterday, between the first nine of the Monumental, of this city, and the Blue Star, of Washington, colored, ended in favor of the former, by a score of 39 to 9." *Alexandria Gazette* (October 8, 1867): "It is announced in the Washington Republican that the Monumental Base Ball Club, (colored,) of Washington, on the 10th instant, to play the Monumental club, of this city, (colored,) for the championship of Virginia."

SOURCES: "Base Ball," *Alexandria (VA) Gazette,* Sep 27, 1867; "Games to be Played," *Washington (DC) National Republican,* Oct 2, 1867; "Base Ball," *Alexandria Gazette,* Oct 8, 1867.

Tecumseh Base Ball Club (Alexandria, VA; 1860s)

The Tecumseh B.B.C. organized in the 1860s, play black nines. *Washington Evening Star* (June 14, 1867): "A base-ball club, of Wyandotte, composed of colored men, all arrayed in the latest base-ball costume, arrive here this morning, in the eleven o'clock boat from Washington, and immediately proceeded to the grounds near the Catholic Cemetery, where they played a match game with the Tecumseh club, colored, of this city." *Washington Evening Star* (August 26, 1867): "The base-ball clubs, Mutual, of Washington, and Tecumseh, of Alexandria, came together in this place Thursday, the district boys laying out the others as cold as a wedge, the score being Mutuals 62, Tecumseh 7, at the close. We had intended to say nothing about the affair on account of the disastrous result, but the Washington boys paraded their victory, and let the cat out of the bag." *Alexandria Gazette* (September 27, 1867): "A match game was played yesterday afternoon, between the first nines of the Tecumseh, and Keystone Base Ball Clubs of this city, colored, ending in favor of the former, by a score of 63 to 25."

SOURCES: "Base Ball," *Washington (DC) National Republican,* Apr 15, 1867; "Base Ball," *Washington National Republican,* May 17, 1867; "Base Ball Match," *Washington National Republican,* Jun 12, 1867; "Alexandria Items," *Washington (DC) Evening Star,* Jun 14, 1867; "Base Ball," *Alexandria (VA) Gazette,* Jul 18, 1867; "In a Search of Pleasure," *Washington Evening Star,* Aug 18, 1867; "Base Ball Matters," *Washington National Republican,* Aug 23, 1867; "Base Ball," *Washington Evening Star,* Aug 26, 1867; "Base Ball," *Washington National Republican,* Sep 6, 1867; "Base Ball," *Washington Evening Star,* Sep 21, 1867; "Base Ball," *Washington National Republican,* Sep 21, 1869; "Base Ball," *Alexandria Gazette,* Sep 27, 1867; "Base Ball," *Washington Evening Star,* Sep 28, 1867; "Games to be Played," *Washington National Republican,* Oct 2, 1867; "Base Ball," *Washington National Republican,* Nov 30, 1867.

Giants Base Ball Club (Danville, VA; 1890s). Organizer(s): William Terry and Charles Gasney.

The Giants B.B.C. organized in the 1890s, played against black aggregations. *Richmond Planet* (July 3, 1897): "The Danville Giants of the fourth ward stand ready and do challenge any club that is organized in this city, in any city, town or hamlet adjacent thereto or any club in this state, or any state adjacent thereto."

SOURCES: "From Danville," *Richmond (VA) Planet*, Jul 3, 1897; "Grand Annual Excursion," *Richmond Planet*, Jul 13, 1897.

Hail Hitters Base Ball Club (Danville, VA; 1890s)

The Hail Hitters B.B.C. organized in the 1890s, played against black teams. *Winston-Salem Union Republican* (August 8, 1895): "The colored base-ball team at Danville, Virginia, wiped up the Winston coons by a score of 22 to 7." *Richmond Planet* (August 10, 1895): "On next Tuesday at West End Park the Hail Hitters will cross bats with the Manhattan Giants of this city. The contest promises to be exciting as both teams are practicing daily for the occasion. Our boys think that what they will do for them will be AP, but the other fellows aren't saying anything; but intend to show the Richmond boys are not in it. Let everyone go out and patronize the game and give the visitors a hearty welcome. Admission: 10 and 15 cents."

SOURCES: "Local News," *Winston-Salem (NC) Union Republican*, Aug 8, 1895; "Danville vs. Richmonds," *Richmond (VA) Planet*, Aug 10, 1895; "The Eclipse Wins Another Victory," *Richmond Planet*, Aug 22, 1896.

Virginia Reds Base Ball Club (Hot Springs, VA; 1890s)

The Virginia Reds B.B.C. organized in the 1890s, played black aggregations. *Richmond Planet* (August 31, 1895): "The boys from Staunton came on the early train Monday and the guests of both hotels were anxious to see the contest—indeed after seeing the boys from Staunton practice a little on the field our boys felt a little nervous, but when the hour came and a few hours played, the boys found they had a regular walkover. The first game resulted: Staunton 3, Virginia Reds 8; second: Staunton, 5; Virginia Reds, 17. While the Staunton boys were badly beaten and should have stayed at home to prepare themselves better before tackling such a team as the Virginia Reds."

SOURCES: "From Hot Springs," *Richmond (VA) Planet*, Aug 31, 1895; "From Hot Springs," *Richmond Planet*, Aug 29, 1896.

Lone Jacks Base Ball Club (Lynchburg, VA; 1880s–1890s)

The Lone Jack B.B.C. organized in the 1880s, played against black teams. *Washington National Republican* (August 13, 1883): "The colored club of this city, the Lone Jack, played with the Rosedales, of Amherst courthouse, and won by a score of 50 to 9. The Lone Jacks have been invincible in every battle they have ever played." *National Republican* (September 17, 1883): "The colored base-ball club of this city, the Lone Jacks, go to Danville on Monday, to play a match game with the colored club of that place. The club here is considered a very fine one." *Norfolk Pilot* (July 21, 1885): "The Lone Jacks, of Lynchburg, yesterday played the Orientals of, Norfolk, a seven-inning game of baseball at Gymnasium Park. The Lone Jacks won by as core of 24 to 15." *Pilot* (July 29, 1887): "The Lone Jacks defeated the Stonewalls [of Norfolk] by a score of 11 to 7 at DeBree's Park yesterday. Both are colored nines."

SOURCES: "A Challenge," *Washington (DC) Post*, Jul 23, 1883; "Lynchburg Notes," *Washington (DC) National Republican*, Aug 13, 1883; "Lynchburg Notes," *Washington National Republican*, Sep 17, 1883; "Base Ball by Colored Men," *Norfolk (VA) Pilot*, Jul 21, 1885; "Items in Brief," *Norfolk Pilot*, Jul 29, 1887; "From Danville," *Richmond (VA) Planet*, Sep 26, 1896.

Slides Base Ball Club (Lynchburg, VA; 1890s)

The Slides B.B.C. organized in the 1890s, played black teams. *Roanoke Times* (May 31, 1895): "About two hundred dusky rooters came up on a special train from Lynchburg to witness the game and about the same number of colored cranks from this city yelled themselves hoarse over the struggle. It resulted in a crushing defeat for the Hill City contingent, the score being 20 to 5. The visiting pitched had no terrors for the Roanoke batters, who pounded out twenty-two hits." *Roanoke Times* (July 3, 1897): "In the afternoon, the Lynchburg Slides played a game of ball with the Cuban Giants of Roanoke, the score standing 13 to 6 in favor of the latter."

SOURCES: "Home Colored Players Won Yesterday," *Roanoke (VA) Times*, Apr 4, 1894; "Another Roanoke Victory," *Roanoke Times*, May 31, 1895; "From Winston," *Richmond (VA) Planet*, Jul 3, 1897; *Roanoke Times*, Jul 11, 1897; "Excursion and Baseball," *Roanoke Times*, Jul 13, 1897.

Baltimore Athletic Base Ball Club (Norfolk, VA; 1890s). Organizer(s): Luke Eure.

The Baltimore Athletic B.B.C. organized in the 1890s, played black teams. *Norfolk Virginian-Pilot* (June 17, 1899): "The Baltimore Athletics, Suffolk's champion colored ball team, has reorganized under the management of Luke Eure. They are now ready to receive challenges from any colored team in Virginia. The faster the better. Any players looking for warm games should write the manager." *Virginia-Pilot* (June 21, 1899): "There was a right lively game of ball at Peanut Park this afternoon between colored teams. The Suffolks met the Baltimore Athletics and went to earth, 18 to 9. The feature of the game was hard-hitting. The Athletics hit harder and oftener. That's why the tally sheet gives them twice as many runs. Battery: Taylor and Watkins; Holloman and Johnson." *Virginian-Pilot* (July 5, 1899): "The Baltimore Athletics won two games today at Peanut Park. Their opponents were the Bostons. Morning game—Athletics, 14; Bostons, 3. Batteries: Boone and Overy; Holloman and Johnson. Umpire: Whitehurst. Afternoon game—Athletics, 22; Bostons, 2. Batteries: Taylor and King; Boone and Johnson. Umpire: Tate."

SOURCES: "Hard-Hitting Athletics," *Norfolk (VA) Virginian-Pilot*, Jun 17, 1899; "The Athletics Won," *Norfolk Virginian-Pilot*, Jun 21, 1899; "Ready for Challenges," *Norfolk Virginian-Pilot*, Jun 28, 1899; "Athletics Took Both," *Norfolk Virginian-Pilot*, Jul 5, 1899.

Brooklyn Base Ball Club (Norfolk, VA; 1870s)

The Brooklyn B.B.C. organized in the 1870s, played black teams. *Norfolk Virginian-Pilot* (September 8, 1875): "A match game of ball was played between the Brooklyn's and Red Wheels, colored. Brooklyn's, 51 and the Red Wheels… (?)" *Virginian-Pilot* (August 14, 1877): "There was a match game of base-ball played yesterday between the Brooklyns an Tramps. The score stood: Brooklyns, 13; Tramps, 9. The poor Tramps lost another ball and bat."

SOURCES: "Base Ball," *Norfolk (VA) Virginian-Pilot*, Sep 9, 1875; "Base Ball," *Norfolk Virginian-Pilot*, Aug 14, 1877.

Lancaster Base Ball Club (Norfolk, VA; 1890s). Organizer(s): James M. Harrison.

The Lancaster B.B.C. organized in the 1890s, played black teams. James M. Harrison captained the aggregation in 1891. The Lancasters played match games against the Suffolks and Portsmouth Water Lillies. *Norfolk Virginian* (July 25, 1895): "The game of ball played yesterday at League Park between the Lancasters, of Norfolk, and the Water Lillies, of Portsmouth, resulted in a victory for the Lancasters, the score being 12 to 5."

SOURCES: "In and About the City," *Norfolk (VA) Virginian*, Jun 27, 1893; "Local Brevities," *Norfolk Virginian*, Jun 28, 1895; "Suffolk Local," *Norfolk Virginian*, Jul 25, 1895; "Suffolk Local," *Norfolk Virginian*, Jul 28, 1895; "Suffolk Local," *Norfolk Virginian*, Jul 30, 1895;

"Unpublished History of Football and Baseball, 7," *Norfolk (VA) News Journal and Guide*, Feb 24, 1923.

Oriental Base Ball Club (Norfolk, VA; 1880s)

The Oriental B.B.C. organized in the 1880s, played black teams. *Norfolk Virginian-Pilot* (July 21, 1885): "The Lone Jacks, of Lynchburg, yesterday played the Orientals, of Norfolk, a seven-inning game of base-ball at Gymnasium Park. The Lone Jacks won by a score of 24 to 15." They also played the Princeton Metropolitans. *Norfolk Virginian-Pilot* (August 23, 1885): "The Orientals of Norfolk will play the Metropolitans at Gymnasium Park tomorrow at 4 pm. Both are colored clubs."

SOURCES: "Baseball by Colored Men," *Norfolk (VA) Virginian-Pilot*, Jul 21, 1885; "Baseball," *Norfolk Virginian-Pilot*, Aug 23, 1885.

Red Stocking Base Ball Club (Norfolk, VA; 1870s–1900s).

Organizer(s): M. Hicks and George White; Sidney Fentress and W. H. Baker; C. T. Brown.

The Red Stocking B.B.C. organized in the 1870s. By the mid–1880s, George White served as team captain (and later managed the team). The Red Stockings played black teams, and later, white organizations. Norfolk and Richmond had an established rivalry. *New York Globe* (June 16, 1883): "The Red Stockings met the Black Swans on Capitol Hill in good cheer, and defeated them for the championship of the State, scoring 16 runs to 10." *Norfolk Virginia-Pilot* (October 6, 1885): "There will be a match game of baseball at the Gymnasium Park this afternoon, at 3 o'clock, between the Red Stockings, of Norfolk, and the Metropolitans. The Red Stockings have defeated almost every club in the Unions, and they should draw a crowd today." The team's reputation grew. *New York Freeman* (August 21, 1886): "The Raleigh Base Ball Club accompanied the excursion and engaged the famous Red Stockings of this city. The game closed on Wednesday after playing ten innings, on account of darkness, at six for each club. Thursday was a walkover for the Norfolk nine, they having placed their champion battery upon the diamond. The game was won by a score of 25 to 1. The Red Stockings left with the excursionists for a return game in Raleigh." The Reds and Philadelphia Pythians played an exhibition match. *Philadelphia Record* (April 21, 1887): "The colored Pythian Base Ball Club met the Red Stockings of Norfolk, Virginia and were beaten." The Red Stockings joined a tournament that included Trenton's Cuban Giants, NY's Gorhams, and the Pittsburgh's Keystones. *New York Tribune* (August 27, 1888): "The Cuban Giants and the Red Sox teams play the final game of the colored championship series at the Long Island Grounds. The Cuban Giants outplayed their opponents at every point and won the game." The Red Stockings competed with black nines of Edenton, NC. *Norfolk Virginian* (July 30, 1895): "The Red Stockings, the champion colored ball team of this State, will play the Eclipse Club, of Edenton, the champions of North Carolina at League Park Wednesday at 1:00 p.m., for the championship of the State." *Norfolk Virginian* (May 23, 1897): "The Red Stockings and Athletics, two colored teams, will play for the championship of Virginia at League Park Monday afternoon." *Norfolk Virginian* (May 25, 1897): "At League Park yesterday an interesting game of base-ball was played by the renowned Red Stockings and the Athletics, both colored, local teams. Lewis was pitted against Dan McClellan. The former was knocked out of the box in the fourth inning and Stewart, of the Hygeia Giants, of Old Point, succeeded Lewis and held the colts down. The old vets (Red Stockings) were outplayed at every point, and only succeeded in tying the game in the fourth inning while dust was flying on the diamond similar to a storm in the Sahara." In 1899, they played and defeated NY's Shamrocks, a semi-professional white aggregation in a five-game series.

SOURCES: "Norfolk News," *New York (NY) Globe*, Jun 9, 1883; "Norfolk Letter," *New York Globe*, Jun 16, 1883; "Baseball," *Norfolk (VA) Pilot*, Jul 15, 1883; "Norfolk Letter," *New York Globe*, Mar 1, 1884; "Norfolk Correspondence," *New York Globe*, May 24, 1884; "Norfolk's New School," *New York Globe*, Aug 23, 1884; "Items in Brief," *Norfolk Virginian-Pilot*, Jun 18, 1885; "Colored Clubs Play," *Norfolk (VA) Virginian-Pilot*, Jul 28, 1885; "Boiled Down," *Norfolk Virginian-Pilot*, Aug 19, 1885; "The National Game," *Norfolk Virginian-Pilot*, Oct 6, 1885; "Norfolk Business Men," *New York (NY) Freeman*, Mar 27, 1886; "Local Intelligence," *Norfolk Virginian-Pilot*, May 12, 1886; "Amusements," *Richmond (VA) Dispatch*, May 19, 1886; "No Game Yesterday," *Richmond Dispatch*, May 20, 1886; "Norfolk News Budget," *New York (NY) Freeman*, Aug 21, 1886; "Norfolk's New School," *New York Freeman*, May 29, 1886; "Red Stockings, 10; Pythians, 9," *Philadelphia (PA) Record*, Apr 21, 1887; "Items in Brief," *Norfolk Virginian-Pilot*, Aug 31, 1887; "Items in Brief," *Norfolk Virginian-Pilot*, Sep 1, 1887; "Items in Brief," *Norfolk Virginian-Pilot*, Sep 23, 1887; "The Dark-Town Base-Ballists," *Richmond (VA) Times*, May 31, 1888; "Not Brooklyn's Day," *New York (NY) Herald-Tribune*, Aug 27, 1888; "Base Ball," *Richmond (VA) Planet*, Jun 30, 1894; "Newsiest Norfolk News," *Norfolk (VA) Virginian*, Mar 5, 1895; "Brevities," *Norfolk Virginian*, Apr 24, 1895; "In and About the City," *Norfolk Virginian*, Jul 30, 1895; "Local of the Readable Sort," *Norfolk Virginian*, Jul 31, 1895; "Edenton, N.C.," *Norfolk Virginian*, Aug 15, 1895; "Edenton, N.C.," *Norfolk Virginian*, Aug 21, 1895; "Atlantic City," *Norfolk Virginian*, Aug 29, 1895; "Notes and Comments," *Norfolk Virginian*, May 25, 1895; "Notes and Comments," *Norfolk Virginian*, May 23, 1897; "Notes and Comments," *Norfolk Virginian*, May 25, 1897; "Fight for Colored Championship," *Washington (DC) Post*, May 17, 1898; "Reds 13; Hygeia, 8," *Washington Post*, Jun 5, 1898; "The Red Stockings Reorganized," *Norfolk Virginia-Pilot*, Mar 4, 1899; "A Very Exciting Game," *Norfolk Virginia-Pilot*, Apr 6, 1899; "Hygeia's Defeat Red Stockings," *Washington Post*, May 3, 1899; "The Red Stockings Win," *Norfolk Virginia-Pilot*, May 31, 1899; "The Shamrocks Vanquished," *Norfolk Virginia-Pilot*, Jun 2, 1899; "Red Stockings Win," *Norfolk Virginia-Pilot*, Jul 25, 1899.

St. Clair Base Ball Club (Norfolk, VA; 1890s).

Organizer(s): James M. Harrison.

The St. Clair B.B.C. organized in the 1890s, played black teams. James M. Harrison captained the aggregation in 1891. *Norfolk Virginian* (June 27, 1893): "The St. Clair Baseball Club has been organized for the season of 1893 with the same players of last year, including James M. Harrison, who was captain of the Lancasters, of 1891."

The St. Claires played match games against the Mission College Grays, Quebecs, Barboursville Detroits, and Huntersville Soppers. *Norfolk Virginian* (July 6, 1893): "The St. Claire Club, and the Huntersville Soppers, two colored baseball clubs, had a game on the Fourth, resulting in a score of 11 to 7 in favor of the St. Claires."

SOURCES: "In and About the City," *Norfolk (VA) Virginian*, Jun 27, 1893; "Norfolk Local News," *Norfolk Virginian*, Jul 6, 1893; "Huntersville," *Norfolk Virginian*, Jul 13, 1893; "Norfolk Local News," *Norfolk Virginian*, Aug 31, 1893; "In and About the City," *Norfolk Virginian*, Sep 5, 1893; "Norfolk Local News," *Norfolk Virginian*, Sep 6, 1893; "Norfolk Local News," *Norfolk Virginian*, Sep 22, 1893.

Toledo Base Ball Club (Norfolk, VA; 1880s).

Organizer(s): Lewis H. Burnham.

The Toledo B.B.C. organized in the 1880s, played black teams. *Richmond Dispatch* (May 21, 1886): "The game of baseball played at Boschen's Park yesterday afternoon between the Toledos, of Norfolk, and Manhattans, of this city, was hotly contested, throughout—resulted in a tie—the score standing at the close of the contest 8 to 8. This was one of the finest games every played in this city between colored clubs." *Dispatch* (May 26, 1886): "The game of base-ball announced to take place at Boschen's Park yesterday afternoon, between the Toledos of Norfolk, and the Manhattans of this city, two colored clubs, was not played on account of rain. A game between the same clubs is announced for this afternoon and will come off if the weather will permit." *New York Freeman* (May 29, 1886): "Mr. Lewis H. Burnham returned from Richmond a few days ago, where he had gone in charge of the Toledo Base Ball Club of this city, to engage the champion club of the capital. The Richmond Dispatch says it was the best game played there by colored clubs. The return game will be played soon in this city."

SOURCES: "Advertisements," *Norfolk (VA) Pilot*, Mar 30, 1886; "Local Intelligence," *Norfolk Pilot*, May 12, 1886; "Amusements," *Richmond (VA) Dispatch*, May 19, 1886; "No Game Yesterday," *Richmond Dispatch*, May 20, 1886; "The Game a Tie," *Richmond Dispatch*, May 21, 1886; "Local Intelligence," *Norfolk Pilot*, May 22, 1886; "Norfolk's New School," *New York (NY) Freeman*, May 29, 1886.

Hygeia Hotel Base Ball Club (Old Point, VA; 1890s)

The Hygeia Hotel B.B.C. organized in the 1890s, if not earlier. The Hygeias played white and black aggregations. *Richmond Planet* (July 27, 1895): "The game of base-ball played by the Newmarkets [Market House] of Washington and the Hygeia Giants was a very exciting game and the Hygeias were the winning team. Long live the Hygeias." They played against the Cuban Giants. *Newport News Press* (April 7, 1898): "Yesterday afternoon the Cuban Giants and Hygeia colored base-ball teams again met at the Soldier's Home in an interesting game. The Giants suffered their first defeat, the score being 11 to 7 in favor of Hygeia." *Newport News Press* (April 7, 1898): "The East End Baseball Park this afternoon the crack white team of Washington, the Shamrocks, and the colored Hygeia hotel nine, of Old Point, will cross bats. A large crowd will doubtless attend the game."

SOURCES: "Manhattan Giants," *Richmond (VA) Planet*, Jul 13, 1895; "From Fortress Monroe," *Richmond Planet*, Jul 27, 1895; "From Old Point," *Richmond Planet*, Aug 10, 1895; "Personal and Briefs," *Richmond Planet*, Aug 24, 1895; "From Old Point and Hampton," *Richmond Planet*, Oct 5, 1895; "Eclipse Defeated," *Richmond Planet*, Sep 19, 1896; "Giants, 12; Hygeias, 4," *Newport News (VA) Press*, Apr 7, 1898; "The Giants Go Down," *Newport News Press*, Apr 9, 1898; "Played a Team of Waiters," *Washington (DC) Post*, Mar 23, 1899; "Hygeias Defeat Red Stockings," *Washington Post*, May 3, 1899 "Hygeias Defeat St. Clairs," *Washington Post*, Jul 14, 1899; "Hygeias vs. Shamrocks," *Newport News Press*, Jul 22, 1899; "Hygeias Won," *Newport News Press*, Jul 23, 1899.

Blue Stockings Base Ball Club (Petersburg, VA; 1870s–1880s)

The Blue Stockings B.B.C. organized in the 1870s, played against black organizations. *Petersburg Appeal* (August 5, 1878): "The first of a series of games of base-ball between the Blue Stockings and the Star Lights, of Pocahontas, two colored clubs of this city, was played Saturday afternoon. Both clubs appeared in uniform, and the game resulted as follows: the Starlights, of Pocahontas 9; the Blue Stockings 13." *Appeal* (September 9, 1878): "A match game was played Saturday afternoon between the Petersburg Blue Stockings and First Ward Blue Caps. The result was in favor of the Blue Caps by a score of 11 to 9." *Appeal* (July 8, 1881): "A match game of base-ball was played Saturday, between two colored clubs, the Blue Stockings and Early Yorks, which resulted in a victory for the former by the following score: Blue Stockings, 11; Early Yorks, 8."

SOURCES: "Base Ball," *Petersburg (VA) Appeal*, Sep 9, 1878; "Base Ball Game," *Petersburg Appeal*, Jun 25, 1878; "Base Ball," *Petersburg Appeal*, Jul 19, 1880; "Base Ball," *Petersburg Appeal*, Aug 17, 1880; "Base Ball," *Petersburg Appeal*, Jul 8, 1881.

Fifth Ward Independent Base Ball Club (Petersburg, VA; 1870s)

The Fifth Ward Independent B.B.C. organized in the 1870s played against black organizations. *Petersburg Appeal* (June 25, 1878): "A game of base-ball was played yesterday afternoon between the Fifth Ward Independent Base Ball Club, and the Starlight, of Pocahontas. The score resulted at the end of the ninth innings, in 17 runs for the former and 5 for the latter." *Petersburg Appeal* (August 26, 1878): "A match game of base-ball was played Saturday evening between the Star Light of Pocahontas and Fifth Ward for the championship, which resulted in a victory for the Fifth Ward by a score of 10 to 8." *Appeal* (September 23, 1878): "A match game of base-ball was played Saturday afternoon between the Blue Caps, of Blanford, and the Fifth Ward Club, colored, by a score of 20 to 5."

SOURCES: "Base Ball," *Petersburg (VA) Appeal*, May 22, 1878; "Base Ball Game," *Petersburg Appeal*, Jun 25, 1878; "Base Ball," *Petersburg Appeal*, Jul 15, 1878; "Game of Base Ball," *Petersburg Appeal*, Aug 19, 1878; "A Match Game of Base Ball," *Petersburg Appeal*, Aug 26, 1878; "A Match Game of Base Ball," *Petersburg Appeal*, Sep 16, 1878; "Match Game of Base Ball," *Petersburg Appeal*, Sep 17, 1878; *Petersburg Appeal*, Sep 21, 1878; "Base Ball," *Petersburg Appeal*, Sep 23, 1878; "Local," *Weldon (NC) Roanoke News*, Jul 31, 1879.

Granite League Base Ball Club (Petersburg, VA; 1890s)

The Granite League B.B.C. organized in the 1890s, played black aggregations. *Richmond Planet* (Aug. 15, 1896): "We learned that there was one of the closest and most exciting games ever witnessed in West End Park between the Granite Leagues of Petersburg, who for three years had successfully met and defeated every team they came in contact with, and the Eclipse of Richmond. The game was called at 4:30 P.M. The Petersburgs led off and scored five runs before they were retired. The Eclipse failed to make a run until the fifth inning and then they were retired with six runs, having tied the score. Price pitched the greatest game of his life, only one man got his base on balls, and only two more runs were scored for Petersburg."

SOURCES: "The Petersburgs Eclipsed," *Richmond (VA) Planet*, Jun 20, 1896; "The Eclipse Victorious," *Richmond Planet*, Aug 15, 1896.

Blue Jackets Base Ball Club (Pocahontas, VA; 1890s)

The Blue Jackets B.B.C., of St. Petersburg, VA organized in the 1870s, played against black nines. *Indianapolis Freeman* (July 18, 1891): "The Black Jackets, a base-ball team of Pocahontas, Virginia, challenges any club in the state. The boys are all crack twirlers and heavy hitters and intend to make it warm for all competitors."

SOURCES: "Sport," *Indianapolis (IN) Freeman*, Jul 18, 1891.

Silver Kings Base Ball Club (Pocahontas, WV; 1890s)

The Silver Kings B.B.C. organized in the 1890s, played black organizations. *Bluefield Telegraph* (June 2, 1896): "The colored teams of Pocahontas and Elkhorn will hold forth at Bluefield Park this afternoon at the usual hour." *Telegraph* (June 6, 1896): "The Silver Kings, of Pocahontas, and Wild West of Elkhorn, colored base-ball teams, will play a match game at the park grounds Saturday morning at 10 a.m."

SOURCES: "In and About the City," Bluefield (WVA) *Telegraph*, Jun 2, 1896; "On the Base Ball Field," *Bluefield Telegraph*, Jun 6, 1896.

Star Light Base Ball Club (Pocahontas, VA; 1870s–1880s)

The Star Light B.B.C. organized in the 1870s, played against black nines. *Petersburg Appeal*: "A match game of base-ball was played Saturday evening between the Star Light of Pocahontas and Fifth Ward for the championship, which resulted in a victory for the Fifth Ward by a score of 10 to 8." The Star Lights and Blue Stockings developed a rivalry. *Petersburg Appeal* (August 5, 1878): "The first of a series of games of base-ball between the Blue Stockings and the Star Lights, of Pocahontas, two colored clubs of this city, was played Saturday afternoon. Both clubs appeared in uniform, and the game resulted as follows: the Starlights, of Pocahontas 9; the Blue Stockings 13."

SOURCES: "Base Ball," *Petersburg (VA) Appeal*, May 22, 1878; "Base Ball Game," *Petersburg Appeal*, Jun 25, 1878; "Base Ball," *Petersburg Appeal*, Jul 15, 1878; "A Match Game of Base Ball," *Petersburg Appeal*, Aug 5, 1878; "Game of Base Ball," *Petersburg Appeal*, Aug 19, 1878; "A Match Game of Base Ball," *Petersburg Appeal*, Aug 26, 1878; "A Match Game of Base Ball," *Petersburg Appeal*, Sep 16, 1878; "Match Game of Base Ball," *Petersburg Appeal*, Sep 17, 1878; *Petersburg Appeal*, Sep 21, 1878; "Base Ball," *Petersburg Appeal*, Sep 23, 1878; "Base Ball," *Appeal*, July 19, 1880; "Base Ball," *Petersburg Appeal*, Aug 17, 1880.

Black Swan Base Ball Club (Richmond, VA; 1880s). Organizer(s): James Dudley, J. Richard Harrison and John W. Jackson ("Bud" Fowler).

The Black Swan B.B.C. organized in the 1880s. The Black Swans played against black organizations. *Richmond Dispatch*: "The Swan and Peabody Base-Ball Clubs (colored) will play the first of a series of games Monday evening at 3:30 o'clock, at Richmond Base-Ball Park, head of Clay Street." *Dispatch*: "The second game of the series between the Swan and Peabody Clubs will take place today at half past 3 o'clock at Richmond Base-Ball Park, top of Clay Street. Score last game, 10 to 8 in favor of Swan Club." *Dispatch*: "The Peabody Base-Ball Club defeated Swan Club in the odd game, and are now the colored champions of Richmond." *Dispatch* (May 22, 1881): "There will be a match-game of base-ball between the Richmond Blues and Richmond Swans Base Ball Clubs Monday evening at Richmond Base Ball Park." The Black Swans also played against Petersburg's Blue Stocking and Stonewall teams. Challenging the Baltimore's Lord Hannibals, an organization claiming the black championship of MD, the Black Swans defeated them by a score of 11 to 1. They agreed to join a Colored League in 1882, which included NY, Philadelphia, Cincinnati, Baltimore, Washington, D.C., and St. Louis. The league failed to materialize. The Swans and WA Manhattans developed a rivalry. *Washington Bee* (April 26, 1883): "The game between the Manhattans and Richmond Swans was a tie, after eleven innings. The second game between the Swans and Manhattan resulted in a victory for the latter by a score of 23 to 9." *Dispatch* (May 31, 1883): "An interesting and well-contested game of base-ball was played yesterday, between the Manhattans, of Washington, DC, and the Richmond Swans, of Richmond, at Base-Ball Park. Both clubs are colored. The game resulted in a tie, the score standing 13 to 13."

SOURCES: "Hannibal Base Ball Club, of Baltimore vs. Swan, of Richmond," *Richmond (VA) Dispatch*, Jul 15, 1880; "Base Ball," *Richmond Dispatch*, Jul 19, 1880; "Brief Items," *Richmond Dispatch*, Sep 5, 1880; "Base Ball," *Richmond Dispatch*, Sep 11, 1880; "Brief Items," *Richmond Dispatch*, Sep 12, 1880; "Personal," *Richmond Dispatch*, Sep 22, 1880; "Brief Items," *Richmond Dispatch*, Oct 8, 1880; "Base Ball," *Richmond Dispatch*, May 22, 1881; "Base Ball," *Richmond Dispatch*, Jul 10, 1881; "Colored Base Ball," *Washington (DC) National Republican*, Apr 23, 1883; "Base Ball Games in this City and Elsewhere Today," *Washington National Republican*, Apr 26, 1883; "Base Ball Notes, *Washington (DC) Evening Critic*. April 26, 1883; "Defeated in Their First Game," *Washington (DC) Post*, Apr 27, 1883; "Base Ball," *Washington National Republican*, Apr 27, 1883; "Base Ball," *Washington Post*, Apr 28, 1883; "Local Matters," *Richmond Dispatch*, May 31, 1883; "Locals," *Washington (DC) Bee*, Jun 9, 1883.

Eclipse Base Ball Club (Richmond, VA; 1890s). Organizer(s): T. H. Jackson.

The Eclipse B.B.C. organized in the 1890s. The Eclipse nine, nick-

named Gray Jackets, played black aggregations: Portsmouth Giants, Richmond Manhattan Giants, Norfolk Red Stockings, Danville Hall Hitters, Petersburg Slides, and Roanoke Cuban Giants. *Richmond Planet* (June 27, 1896): "The Eclipse means to eclipse every team in the state this season and stand ready at all times to play any and all respectable clubs." *Richmond Planet* (September 18, 1897): "The Eclipse Base Ball Club is still winning. A few weeks ago, they shut out that strong club, the Winston Giants, 12 to 0, and the same week they repeated the dose, white-washing the crack team of Manchester, Virginia."

SOURCES: "Base Ball," *Richmond (VA) Planet*, Jul 20, 1895; "Notes From the Diamond," *Richmond Planet*, Jun 13, 1896; "Petersburgs Eclipsed," *Richmond Planet*, Jun 20, 1896; "Base Ball Gossip," *Richmond Planet*, Jul 25, 1896; "The Roanokes-Eclipse," *Richmond Planet*, Jun 27, 1896; "Eclipse to go to Norfolk," *Richmond Planet*, Jul 4, 1896; "Base Ball Gossip," *Richmond Planet*, Jul 25, 1896; "The Eclipse Victorious," *Richmond Planet*, Aug 15, 1896; "Eclipse Again Victorious," *Richmond Planet*, Aug 22, 1896; "Still Another Victory," *Richmond Planet*, Aug 29, 1896; "Eclipse Defeated," *Richmond Planet*, Sep 19, 1896; "Base Ball Season Opens," *Richmond Planet*, May 15, 1897; "Base Ball," *Richmond Planet*, Sep 18, 1897.

Manhattan Giants Base Ball Club (Richmond, VA; 1880s–1890s)

The Manhattan Giants B.B.C. organized in the 1880s, played black and white teams. *New York Freeman* (May 29, 1886): "Mr. Lewis H. Burnham returned from Richmond a few days ago, where he had gone in charge of the Toledo Base Ball Club of this city, to engage the champion club of the capital. The Richmond Dispatch says it was the best game played there by colored clubs. The return game will be played soon in this city." *Richmond Times* (July 16, 1892): "Richmond was again triumphant at Island Park yesterday afternoon, for the Manhattan Giants wiped the field up with the Baltimores [Orioles] to the tune of twelve to six. Both are colored teams." *Richmond Planet* (August 10, 1895): "On next Tuesday at West End Park the Hail Hitters will cross bats with the Manhattan Giants of this city. The contest promises to be exciting as both teams are practicing daily for the occasion. Our boys think that what they will do for them will be AP, but the other fellows aren't saying anything; but intend to show the Richmond boys are not in it. Let everyone go out and patronize the game and give the visitors a hearty welcome. Admission: 10 and 15 cents." *Wilmington Weekly Star* (August 30, 1895): "The colored base-ball team (Nationals) were defeated in Richmond yesterday by the Manhattan Giants of that city, by a score of 14 to 7. The Raleigh team claim that the umpire did them."

SOURCES: "Personal Points," *Richmond (VA) Dispatch*, May 9, 1886; "Norfolk's New School," *New York (NY) Freeman*, May 29, 1886; "Base Ball," *Richmond (VA) Planet*, Jun 12, 1886; "Base Ball," *Richmond Planet*, Jun 7, 1890; "Base Ball," *Richmond Planet*, Jun 5, 1892; "Th Manhattans and Baltimores," *Richmond (VA) Times*, July 15, 1892; "Colored Carnival," *Richmond Dispatch*, Aug 4, 1891; "Manhattan Giants and Cyclone Base Ball Club," *Richmond Dispatch*, Aug 16, 1891; "Base Ball," *Norfolk (VA) Virginian-Pilot*, Aug 23, 1891; "To Play With Negroes," *Richmond Dispatch*, Aug 7, 1892; "Blackballing," *Richmond Dispatch*, Jul 14, 1892; "Race Gleanings," *Indianapolis (IN) Freeman*, Aug 27, 1892; "Colored Ball Players," *Norfolk (VA) Virginian-Pilot*, Jun 6, 1894; "Attention, Sir Knight," *Richmond Planet*, Jul 28, 1894; "Charlottesville Letter," *Richmond Planet*, Aug 18, 1894; "Richmond Rooters 'Cycle Club," *Richmond Planet*, Jun 1, 1895; "Personals and Briefs," *Richmond Planet*, Jun 22, 1895; *Richmond Planet*, Jun 22, 1895; "Manhattan Giants," *Richmond Planet*, Jul 13, 1895; "Base Ball," *Richmond Planet*, Jul 20, 1895; "Base Ball," *Richmond*

Planet, Aug 10, 1895; *Wilmington (NC) Weekly Star*, Aug 30, 1895; "Around Town," *Asheville (NC) Citizen*, Jun 15, 1896; "Affairs in General," *Norfolk Virginian-Pilot*, Jun 1, 1897 "Every Day Small Chat," *Norfolk Virginian-Pilot*, Jun 1, 1897.

Red Stocking Base Ball Club (Richmond, VA; 1890s)

The Red Stocking B.B.C. organized in the 1890s. *Richmond Planet* (July 21, 1894): "Last Thursday night a meeting was held in the rooms of the Lion Athletic Club, North 3rd to reorganize the Red Stockings Base Ball team. Vice President George E. Taylor called the meeting to order and the following players were elected: Eugene Russell, Robert Davis, James Jasper, J. Birchett, H. Taylor, J. Quarles, C. Poindexter, M. Payne, Lee Dudley, W. Johnson, C. Birchett. We are ready to meet any team."

SOURCES: "Base Ball," *Richmond (VA) Planet*, Jul 21, 1894.

Cuban Giants Base Ball Club (Roanoke, VA; 1890s)

The Cuban Giants B.B.C. organized in the 1890s, played black teams. *Richmond Planet* (June 27, 1896): "The Roanoke team, (colored), whose base-ball record has been unparalleled for four years came to Richmond with the expressed intention of winning austerity over our boys. Like the great Napoleon, at whose name the nations of Europe trembled and whose brilliant victories and exalted eminence served only to make his downfall greater, so it was with the Roanokes..." *Salem Times-Register* (July 10, 1896): "The Bad Eye Base Ball Club, of Vinegar Hill, defeated the Cuban Giants, of Roanoke, to the tune of 5 to 4." *Roanoke Times* (July 13, 1897): "About two hundred dusky rooters came up on a special train from Lynchburg to witness the game and about the same number of colored cranks from this city yelled themselves hoarse over the struggle. It resulted in a crushing defeat for the Hill City contingent, the score being 20 to 5. The visiting pitched had no terrors for the Roanoke batters, who pounded out twenty-two hits."

SOURCES: "Another Roanoke Victory," *Roanoke (VA) Times*, May 31, 1895; "Among Our Colored Friends," *Salem Times-Register*, Apr 3, 1896; "All About in Spots and Places," *Salem (VA) Times-Register*, Apr 24, 1896; "Personal Happenings," *Salem Times-Register*, Jun 26, 1896; "Salem News," *Roanoke Times*, Jun 27, 1896; "The Roanokes-Eclipse," *Richmond (VA) Planet*, Jun 27, 1896; "Among Our Colored Friends," *Salem Times-Register*, Apr 16, 1897; "Washington Victorious," *Roanoke Times*, Jun 4, 1897; "Two Games Today," *Roanoke Times*, Jun 5, 1897; "With Our Colored Friends," *Salem Times-Register*, Jul 2, 1897; "Personal Happenings," *Salem Times-Register*, Jul 10, 1897; "Baseball," *Roanoke Times*, Jul 11, 1897 "Excursion and Baseball," *Roanoke Times*, Jul 13, 1897; "Colored Baseball," *Roanoke Times*, Jul 30, 1897; "Local News," *Salem Times-Register*, Aug 20, 1897.

Athletic Base Ball Club (Staunton, VA; 1890s)

The Athletic B.B.C. organized in the 1890s, played against black teams. *Richmond Planet* (August 31, 1895): "The boys from Staunton came on the early train Monday and the guests of both hotels were anxious to see the contest—indeed after seeing the boys from Staunton practice a little on the field our boys felt a little nervous, but when the hour came and a few hours played, the boys found they had a regular walkover. The first game resulted: Staunton 3, Virginia Reds 8; second: Staunton, 5; Virginia Reds, 17. While the Staunton boys were badly beaten and should have stayed at home to prepare themselves better before tackling such a team as the Virginia Reds." *Planet* (May 22, 1897): "The Union Grays defeated the Staunton Athletics Monday. The game was interesting from start to finish, and ended in a victory for the Grays by a score of 8 to 0. Union Grays: Carr and Rogell. Athletics: Burke and Parris." *Planet* (June 19, 1897): "The Union Grays defeated the Athletics Monday in a handsome

game by a score of 17 to 7. Union Grays: Captain Garrison and Jones. Athletics: Hester and Gordon."

SOURCES: "From Hot Springs," *Planet* (Richmond, VA), *Planet*, Aug. 31, 1895; "From Staunton," *Planet*, May 22, 1897; "Staunton Letters," *Planet*, June 19, 1897.

Washington

Blues Base Ball Club (Tacoma, WA; 1890s). Organizer(s): Bob Monroe.

The Blues B.B.C. organized in the 1890s, played black aggregations. *Tacoma News*: "The attraction of the afternoon is a baseball game which begins at 2 o'clock this afternoon. Two teams composed of Tacoma and Seattle colored men are battling for supremacy. Big Bob Monroe has charge of the local men and another big man is watching points for the visitors. Perry Payne is captain and first baseman of the Tacoma nine."

SOURCES: "Ginger's Predicament," *Tacoma (WA) News*, May 26, 1891; "Colored Folks Happy," *Tacoma News*, Aug 1, 1893; "We Kids Has Struck," *Tacoma News*, Aug 2, 1893.

Washington, D.C. (District of Columbia)

Alert Base Ball Club (Washington, D.C.; 1860s–1870s). Organizer(s): George F. T. Cook, R. A. Burton, John Thomas Johnson, John A. Gray, John H. Brooks.

The Alert B.B.C. organized in the 1860s. *Washington National Republican* (February 8, 1866): "A meeting of this association [Alert Base Ball Club] will be held at Davis' Hotel on Friday evening, February 9, at 7 o'clock. Punctual attendance is required to transact business of importance. George F. T. Cook, President." The Alerts played black and white organizations. *National Republican* (June 12, 1867): "Yesterday, the Monumental and Alert Base Ball Clubs (colored) played a match game just in the rear of the State Department, which resulted in the Monumentals scoring 33 to 20 for the Alerts." *Washington Evening Star* (August 4, 1869): "A match game of base-ball was played yesterday afternoon on Kalorama heights, between the Alert Base Ball Club, of this city, and the Howard University Club, which resulted in a victory for the College nine by a score of 28 to 25." *Evening Star* (September 14, 1871): "The Unique [of Chicago] and Alert Base Ball Clubs had another game yesterday afternoon on the National grounds, resulting Alerts 34, Uniques 19." The Uniques had defeated them the day before, by a score of 21 to 18. *National Republican* (January 26, 1872): "The old Alert Base Ball Club, so well and favorably known among ballists of this city, have reorganized by the election of the following gentlemen to serve one year: F. T. Cook, John H. Brooks, Edward Savoy, Joseph T. Mason, Robert Robinson, William W. Grimes, Benjamin Freeman, Sandy Bruce, W. Dent, Robert Talliferro, M. Washington, and Joseph Cook. Negotiations have been entered into with some of our most expert players, and there is scarcely any doubt but what the Alerts will give a good account of themselves the coming ball season." The Alerts and Mutuals, both black nines, became local rivals. *National Republican* (September 26, 1873): "The game between the Alert and Mutual clubs, on the Olympic grounds, was close and exciting. The Mutuals, as will be seen here, won the game, and have thus closed the series in three straight games." The Alerts played a white team. *National Republican* (September 20, 1873): "Yesterday afternoon, pursuant to advertisement in the Republican of that morning, the Alerts (colored) played their first match game with the Washingtons, (white), on the

Olympic Grounds. The game was a one-sided affair, the Alerts not being able to put in a score until the seventh inning, when by a streak of luck they managed to tally two runs. In the eighth inning, the colored boys put in a streak of good batting, which, aided by the poor playing of the whites, resulted in adding six to the two already obtained, each side was skunked in the ninth inning, the game resulting 16 to 8 in favor of the Washingtons."

Sources: "Alert B. B. C.," *Washington (DC) National Republican*, Feb 8, 1866; "Local Department," *Washington National Republican*, Apr 17, 1867; "Base Ball Match," *Washington National Republican*, Jun 12, 1867; "Base Ball Between Colored Clubs," *Washington National Republican*, Jul 9, 1867; "Base Ball," *Washington (DC) Evening Star*, Aug 4, 1869; "Base Ball," *Washington National Republican*, Sep 21, 1869; "Independence Day," *Washington Evening Star*, Jul 5, 1870; "Condensed Locals," *Washington Evening Star*, Sep 12, 1871; "Condensed Locals," *Washington Evening Star*, Sep 14, 1871; "Base Ball," *Washington National Republican*, Jan 22, 1872; "The Alert Base Ball Club," *Washington Evening Star, Jan 26, 1872*; "Base Ball," *Washington National Republican*, Sep 10, 1873; "Alerts vs. Washingtons," *Washington National Republican*, Sep 20, 1873; "Base Ball Matters," *Washington National Republican*, Mar 3, 1876; "Alert Base Ball Club," *Washington National Republican*, Sep 1, 1875; "Alert Base Ball Club," *Washington National Republican*, Sep 2, 1875; "The Alert Base Ball Club," *Washington National Republican*, Apr 4, 1878; "The Ball Grounds," *Washington National Republican*, Aug 2, 1879; "Sports of the Field," *Washington National Republican*, Aug 8, 1879; "Sports of the Field," *Washington National Republican*, Aug 20, 1879.

Athletic Base Ball Club (Washington, D.C.; 1860s). Organizer(s): Dave Garrett and Samuel Lewis.

The Athletic B.B.C. organized in the 1860s, played against black teams. *Evening Star* (August 8, 1867): "There was a game of base-ball played between the Athletics and Old Dominion, in which the score stood 54 to 27 in favor of the former club. Home runs for the Athletics: 9; Old Dominion: 2." *Washington Evening Star* (August 8, 1867): "There was a match game of base-ball played on Tuesday, between the Athletics and Good Will Base Ball Clubs, of this city, in which the score stood in favor of the Athletics, 56 to 11." *Evening Star* (September 9, 1867): "There was a very interesting game of ball played on Friday, between the junior clubs (colored) of this city, known as the Athletics and Monumentals, in which the former were victorious by a score of 39 to 27. This is the first defeat the Monumentals have sustained this since their organization."

Sources: "Base Ball," *Washington (DC) Evening Union*, Jun 15, 1867; "Base Ball," *Washington (DC) Evening Star*, Jul 3, 1867; "Presentation to a Base Ballists," *Washington (DC) National Republican*, Jul 29, 1867; "Base Ball," *Washington Evening Star*, Aug 8, 1867; "Base Ball," *Washington Evening Star*, Aug 8, 1867; "Base Ball Matters," *Washington National Republican*, Aug 21, 1867; "Base Ball Matters," *Washington National Republican*, Aug 23, 1867; "Base Ball Matters," *Washington National Republican*, Sep 2, 1867; "Base Ball," *Washington National Republican*, Sep 9, 1867; "Games To be Played," *Washington National Republican*, Oct 2, 1867.

Atlantic Base Ball Club (Washington, D.C.; 1860s–1880s)

The Atlantic B.B.C. organized in the 1860s, played against black teams. *Washington National Republican* (August 23, 1867) reports, "A match game of base-ball was played between the Atlantics and Monumental clubs (colored), by which the Monumentals came off victorious. We cannot refrain from speaking of the playing of Landrick, Waters, and Brooks of the Monumental, and Campbell and Skill of the Atlantics." *New York Clipper* (September 9, 1882): "The deciding game for thee colored championship of Baltimore and

Washington was played September 1 at Newington Park, in the former city. The contestants were the Mansfields of Baltimore and the Atlantics of Washington, the former winning by a score of 18 to 14. About three thousand people, mostly colored, witnessed the game."

Sources: "Base Ball Matters," *Washington (DC) National Republican*, Aug 23, 1867; *New York (NY) Clipper*, Sep 9, 1882.

Awkward Base Ball Club (Washington, D.C.; 1860s)

The Awkward B.B.C. organized in the 1860s. The Awkwards played black organizations. *National Republican*: "A match game of base-ball was played yesterday between the first nines of the Monumental and Awkward Base Ball Clubs."

Sources: "Base Ball," *Washington (DC) National Republican*, Sep 6, 1867.

Blue Star Base Ball Club (Washington, D.C.; 1860s)

The Blue Star B.B.C. organized in the 1860s, played against black teams. *Alexandria Gazette* (September 27, 1867): "A match game of base-ball played yesterday, between the first nine of the Monumental, of this city, and the Blue Star, of Washington, colored, ended in favor of the former, by a score of 39 to 9." *Alexandria Gazette* (October 8, 1867): "It is announced in the Washington Republican that the Monumental Base Ball Club, (colored,) of Washington, on the 10th instant, to play the Monumental club, of this city, (colored,) for the championship of Virginia."

Sources: "Base Ball," *Alexandria (VA) Gazette*, Sep 27, 1867; "Base Ball," *Alexandria Gazette*, Oct 8, 1867.

Blue Stocking Base Ball Club (Washington, D.C.; 1880s)

The Blue Stocking B.B.C. organized in the 1880s, played against black teams. *Cleveland Gazette* (September 18, 1886): "There is considerable rivalry between the Pittsburg fellows and those from Washington in Athletic sports." The WA boys often came out in front. *Washington Bee* (July 16, 1887): "The baseball game between the Pittsburgs and Washingtons was very interesting. Gilbert Joy and Berry were the battery for the Washingtons [Blues], and the Pittsburgs were defeated by a score of 12 to 8."

Sources: "Notes," *Pittsburgh (PA) Post*, Sep 16, 1886; "Pittsburg and Allegheny," *Cleveland (OH) Gazette*, Sep 18, 1886; "Cresson Springs, PA," *Washington (DC) Bee*, Jul 16, 1887; "Locals," *Washington Bee*, Aug 10, 1889.

Calathumpian Base Ball Club (Washington, D.C.; 1860s)

The Calathumpian B.B.C. organized in the 1860s. played black teams. *Washington Evening Star* (August 18, 1868): "The Calathumpian Base Ball Club landed from the ferry boat at half-past 1 o'clock yesterday, and armed with the instruments used in the noble game, and preceded by a drum corps of three, marched up King Street, in full glory reflected. In search of pleasure, which they found in the open space between the canal basin, the river and cotton factory. On this historical spot, they encountered the second nine of the Rising Sun Club whom they demolished after a spirited contest of two hours and sixteen minutes. Score 26 to 102."

Sources: "In Search of Pleasure," *Washington (DC) Evening Star*, Aug 18, 1868.

Capital City Base Ball Club (Washington, D.C.; 1890s–1900s)

The Capital City B.B.C. organized in the 1890s, played black aggregations. They developed local rivalry with the Empires. *Washington Times* (July 3, 1897): "The Capital Citys met and soundly trounced the Empires yesterday at National Park. Coleman was in the box for the victors, and his work was next to that of a wizard, and only four runs were scored by the Empires while the Capital Citys made eighteen." They developed a local rivalry with the Spartas. *Washington*

Times (September 16, 1897): "There will be a game of baseball at the National Park this afternoon between the Sparta and Capital City teams, which promises a good contest. Both of these aggregations are composed of colored players, and they number among their ranks come of the best amateurs in the District game and will be called at 4:15." They played white teams. *Washington Evening Star* (August 26, 1898): "The Shamrocks, the champions of the District, defeated the Capital City team, colored champions of the District, yesterday at National Park by a score of 11 to 8 in a well-played game." *Evening Star* (September 4, 1900): "The contest between the Easterns and Capital City was replete with brilliant plays throughout, the weakness of the latter's pitcher in the eighth inning allowing the former to score three runs and cinch the game. Stanley, the ex-Senator, did the twirling for the Easterns, and he had his colored opponents at his mercy throughout, the tallies being made by them in the first inning through loose playing. Both teams are to be commended for the manner in which they accepted the decisions of the umpires, not a kick being made throughout the game."

SOURCES: "The City at a Glance" WA (DC) *Evening Star*. May 23, 1896; "The Capital City Club," WA (DC) *Bee*. August 15, 1896; "Capital Citys Won," WA (DC) *Times*. September 10, 1896; "With the Amateur," *Washington Times*. September 12, 1896; "With the Amateur," *Washington Evening Times*. September 15, 1896; "The Capital City Club," *Washington Bee*. October 24, 1896; "Takoma Park," *Washington Evening Star*. August 27, 1896; "A Game at National Park," *Washington Evening Times*. July 1, 1897; "Empires Soundly Trounced," *Washington Evening Times*. July 3, 1897; "Colts vs. Capital Citys," *Washington Times*. July 11, 1897; "Capital Citys 14, Colts 7," WA (DC) *Post*. July 16, 1897; "Emancipation Day at Frederick, MD," *Washington Bee*. August 14, 1897; "A Hot Game Tomorrow," *Washington Evening Star*. August 17, 1897; "Atlantics Are Still Winning," WA (DC) *Morning Times*. September 4, 1897; "Amateurs to Play," *Washington Times*. September 16, 1897; "Capital City Team Won," *Washington Times*. September 17, 1897; "Capital City Club Open House," WA (DC) *Colored American*. March 12, 1898; "Capital Citys vs. Sparta," *Washington Times*. August 7, 1898; "Undefeated Champions," *Washington Evening Star*. August 26, 1898; "The Capital City's Smoker," *Washington Colored American*. October 1, 1898; "Capital City Club Closes," *Washington Colored American*. May 20, 1899; "Easterns vs. Capital City," *Washington Times*. August 13, 1900; "Eastern Athletic Club," *Washington Times*. September 2, 1900; "Eastern Athletic Club," *Washington Times*. September 9, 1900.

Country Base Ball Club (Washington, D.C.; 1860s)

The Country B.B.C. organized in the 1860s, played against black teams. *Washington Evening Star* (October 1, 1867): "A match game between these colored clubs [Alert and Country] took place on Thursday afternoon, on the grounds in the rear of the State Department, with the following result: Alert; 38; Country, 15." *Evening Star* (August 10, 1868): "This afternoon, a match game of base-ball is in progress between the Country and Pythian clubs." *Washington National Republican* (July 22, 1869): "A match game between the Country and the Mutual base-ball clubs will be played on the grounds of the Howard University Club on Friday commencing at 3:30 pm." *Evening Star* (October 26, 1869): "A match game of base-ball between two colored clubs, the Country and Mutuals, will take place on the grounds of the National club tomorrow."

SOURCES: "Base Ball," *Washington (DC) Evening Star*, Oct 1, 1867; "Colored Picnic," *Washington Evening Star*, August 10, 1868; "Base Ball Match," *Washington (DC) National Republican*, Jul 22, 1869; *Washington Evening Star*, October 26, 1869.

Douglass Base Ball Club (Washington, D.C.; 1870s–1890s).

Organizer(s): Charles Boyd, D. W. Downing, L. Thomas, E. Brown, L. H. Richardson, S. Lincoln and J. Green.

The Douglass B.B.C. organized in the 1870s. The team moniker honored civil rights activist Frederick H. Douglass. The Douglass nine played white and black nines. *Washington Critic* (September 1, 1876): "The Keystone and Douglass Base Ball Clubs, (colored), played a match game of base-ball on the Olympic Grounds yesterday, which was won by the former by a score of 10 to 9." They joined Colored League of WA in 1880, which included the Keystones, Manhattans, Uniques, and Mutuals. *Washington National Republican* (July 29, 1880): "The Douglass and Manhattan clubs came together yesterday afternoon in a contest for the league championship. As these are the two strongest clubs in the organization, there was a fair attendance to witness the match." They also played the Eagle club. *National Republican* (August 12, 1880): "The game yesterday afternoon between the Douglasses and Eagles was won by the former. The Eagles played well up to the seventh inning, then, by a series of errors, they allowed their opponents to make three runs and in the next innings four more. They out-batted the Douglasses, but seemed in their usual bad luck. Carroll caught a good game, but is not up to all the points and plays too slow." In 1880 the Douglass nine defeated the Orions for the championship. The Douglass and Orion developed a rivalry. *Philadelphia Times* (June 23, 1883): "The first game of baseball for the colored championship of the United States since 1880 was played at Recreation Park yesterday between the Douglass nine, of Washington, D.C., and the Orions, of this city. The Douglass club had won the championship in 1888 but had not played outside of Washington since. The Orions were cowed in the first part of the game, but regained confidence toward the close, when they played a really brilliant game. The audience numbered about seven hundred." *Washington Evening Star* (September 12, 1891): "The Douglass Base Ball Club (colored Champions), colored champions of the District, will play the Mount Pleasant and Brown Base Ball Club, colored, tomorrow evening at the National Park on Tuesday, September 15." *Evening Star* (August 13, 1889): "The Douglass team defeated the Never Sweats yesterday 25 to 9." *Evening Star* (September 23, 1891): "The Douglass Club (colored Champions) will play the Market House B. B.C. tomorrow evening at the National baseball grounds." They organization reorganized as the Douglass Stars B.B.C. *Washington Morning Times* (September 4, 1897): "The Atlantics defeated the Douglass Stars, the crack colored team, by the scores of 10 to 2 and 27 to 9."

SOURCES: "In Brief," *Critic* (Washington, D.C.), Sept. 1, 1876; "Sports of the Field," *National Republican* (Washington, D.C.), Aug. 20, 1879; "Local," *People's Advocate* (Washington, D.C.), Sept. 27, 1879; "The Colored Nines," *National Republican*, July 8, 1880; "The Colored Champions," *National Republican*, July 14, 1880; "The Colored League," *National Republican*, July 22, 1880; "Base-Ball," *National Republican*, July 27, 1880; "Another Scalp for the Douglass Club," *National Republican*, August 12, 1880; "The 'Conjur' Under First Base," *National Republican*, August 17, 1880; "Sports of the Field," *National Republican*, Aug. 20, 1880; "District Brevities," *National Republican*, May 9, 1881; "A New Base Ball Nine," *Williamsport (PA) Gazette and Bulletin*, Jun 13, 1882; "Colored Champions," *New York (NY) Times*, Jun 23, 1883; "Notes and Comments," *Philadelphia (PA) Sporting Life*, Jan 23, 1884; "Shortstop Did It," *Washington Evening Star*, Aug 18, 1888; "Notes of the Diamond," *Washington Evening Star*, Jun 1, 1889; "Base Ball Notes," *Washington Evening Star*, Jun 29, 1889; "Daisy Cutters," *Washington Evening Star*, Aug 3, 1889; "Within the Ring," *Washington Evening Star*, Aug 13, 1889; "Balls and Strikes," *Washington Evening Star*, Aug 24, 1889; "Short Stops," *Washington Evening Star*, Sep 24, 1889; "Finishing Touches," *Washington Evening*

Star, Oct 5, 1889; "Notes," *Washington Evening Star*, Sep 12, 1891; "Notes," *Washington Evening Star*, Sep 23, 1891; "In and Outdoor Sports," *Washington Evening Star*, Apr 11, 1892; "Amateur Base Ball," *Washington Evening Star*, Jun 28, 1892; "Atlantics Are Still Winning," *Morning Times* (Washington, D.C.), September 4, 1897.

Eagle Base Ball Club (Washington, D.C.; 1870s–1880s)

The Eagle B.B.C. organized in the 1870s, played white and black nines. *Washington Post* (September 11, 1878): "There was a well-contested game of ball between the Eagles and Uniques (colored) yesterday at Eagles Park. Nine innings were played resulting in a victory for the Eagles by a score of five to four." They joined the Colored League of WA in 1880, which included the Keystones Douglass, Manhattan, Unique, and Mutual nines. *Washington National Republican* (August 12, 1880): "The game yesterday afternoon between the Douglasses and Eagles was won by the former. The Eagles played well up to the seventh inning, then, by a series of errors, they allowed their opponents to make three runs and in the next innings four more. They out-batted the Douglasses, but seemed in their usual bad luck. Carroll caught a good game, but is not up to all the points and plays too slow." They also played against local white amateur nines, of the city.

SOURCES: "In Brief," *Washington (DC) Critic*, Sep 1, 1876; "Base Ball," *Washington (DC) National Republican*, Oct 20, 1877; "In Brief," *Washington (DC) Critic-Record*, May 21, 1878; "Muscular Matinees," *Washington (DC) Post*, Jul 8, 1878; "Sports and Pastimes," *Washington Post*, Aug 27, 1878; "Games and Recreations," *Washington National Republican*, Aug 28, 1878; "The Two Great Games," *Washington Post*, Sep 3, 1878; "Catchers and Pushers," *Washington Post*, Sep 11, 1878; "Base Ball," *Washington National Republican*, Mar 11, 1879; "The Ball Grounds," *Washington National Republican*, Aug 8, 1879; "The Uniques and Eagles," *Washington National Republican*, Jul 9, 1880; "The Colored Champions," *Washington National Republican*, Jul 14, 1880; "The Eagles and Manhattans," *Washington National Republican*, Aug 3, 1880.

Eastern Star Base Ball Club (Washington, D.C.; 1890s)

The Eastern Star B.B.C. organized in the 1890s. *Washington Times* (May 8, 1897): "The Eastern Stars defeated the Young Models by a score of 19 to 16. The game was called at 2:15 pm on their grounds, between M Street and Trinidad Avenue. Henry Kane pitched for the Stars. The Stars used three different pitchers, none of whom were effective."

SOURCES: "Future Champions," *Washington (DC) Times*, Apr 18, 1897; "Amateur Ball Players," *Washington (DC) Evening Times*, May 8, 1897.

Empire Base Ball Club (Washington, D.C.; 1890s)

The Empire B.B.C. organized in the 1890s, played white and black aggregations. The Empires and Capital Citys developed a rivalry. *Washington Times* (July 3, 1897): "The Capital Citys met and soundly trounced the Empires yesterday at National Park. Coleman was in the box for the victors, and his work was next to that of a wizard, and only four runs were scored by the Empires while the Capital Citys made eighteen." They played the Neversweats, another black team. *Washington Evening Times* (June 7, 1897): "The Empires defeated the Neversweats in a well-played game of ball yesterday at National Park for the championship of the district, by a score of 13 to 6."

SOURCES: "Amateur Baseball," *Washington (DC) Evening Times*, May 19, 1897; "Amateur Baseball," *Evening Times*, May 21, 1897; "Serious Fight After A Base Ball Match," *Washington (DC) Evening Star*, May 29, 1887; "The Empires Successful," *Washington Evening Times*, Jun 7, 1897; "A Game at National Park," *Washington Evening Times*, Jul 1, 1897; "Empires Soundly Trounced," *Washington Evening Times*, Jul 3, 1897.

Excelsior Base Ball Club (Washington, D.C.; 1870s)

The Excelsior B.B.C. organized in the 1870s. *Washington People's Advocate* (September 27, 1879): "In a prospective base-ball match between a 'Married' and 'Single' nine, made up of past, present and future base-ballists of our city, which is expected to come off on the grounds of the National Base Ball Club, on Thursday afternoon."

SOURCES: "The Ball Grounds," *Washington (DC) National Republican*, Aug 2, 1879; "Local," *Washington (DC) People's Advocate*, Sep 27, 1879; "Local," *Washington People's Advocate*, Oct 11, 1879.

Good Will Base Ball Club (Washington, D.C.; 1860s)

The Good Will B.B.C. organized in the 1860s, played against black nines. *Washington Evening Star* (August 8, 1867): "There was a match game of base-ball played on Tuesday, between the Athletics and Good Will Base Ball Clubs, of this city, in which the score stood in favor of the Athletics, 56 to 11."

SOURCES: "Base Ball," *Washington (DC) Evening Star*, Aug 8, 1867.

Howard University Base Ball Club (Washington, D.C.; 1860s–1900s). Organizer(s): Furman Shadd, James Gregory Robert A. Caskie, William G. Sears and James Howard; Ed Morrison and R. C. Kelly; Charles DeReef.

The Howard University B.B.C. organized in the 1860s, played white and black teams. *Washington Evening Star* (August 4, 1869): "A match game of base-ball was played yesterday afternoon on Kalorama heights, between the Alert Base Ball Club, of this city, and the Howard University Club, which resulted in a victory for the College nine by a score of 28 to 25." *Washington National Republican* (May 24, 1876): "A very interesting game of base-ball was played between the Mutual and Howard University Base Ball Clubs yesterday, which resulted in a score of 15 to 17, in favor of Howard University Base Ball Club." *New York Globe* (May 24, 1884): "The Eureka Base Ball Club of this city (Alexandria, Virginia), are to play a championship game with the Howard University nine at an early date." In 1886, the Colored Base Ball Association formed; it included Howard University, the Junior Assembly, and Lincoln Colored High School. *Washington Bee* (June 5, 1886): "The Junior Assembly defeated the High School Wednesday, by a score of 11 to 6. The Assembly tied the Howard University for first place in the League." *Evening Star* (May 17, 1896): "The YMCA team, of Fairfax Virginia, was beaten Saturday afternoon by Howard University, 19 to 6." Scouting reports described him as "as strong hitter and good base runner." *Evening Star* (March 13, 1897): "The prospects of the Howard University team this season are bright. While the team has lost considerable by the graduation of old players, some of the new material is expected to equal if not excel that which has gone. A number of the old team are still in the game, and will serve to steady the younger players. They played the Capital Citys, a local black organization. *Evening Star* (May 16, 1898): "The Howard University and the Capital City Base Ball Clubs will meet in a match game Tuesday at the university."

SOURCES: "Base Ball," *Washington (DC) Evening Star*, Aug 4, 1869; *Washington (DC) National Republican*, May 24, 1876; "The Howard University," *Washington National Republican*, Mar 26, 1879; "F. J. Shadd," *New Orleans (LA) Louisianan*. Oct. 11, 1879; "Out-Door Amusements," *Washington (DC) Post*, May 11, 1884; "Alexandria Doings," *New York (NY) Globe*, May 24, 1884; "The Ball Players," *Washington Evening Star*, May 3, 1886; "The Small Things of the Day, *Washington National Republican*. May 3, 1886; "Not At All Cast Down," *Washington Post*, May 9, 1886; "Local," *Washington (DC) Bee*, Jun 5, 1886; "The Field Sport," *Indianapolis (IN) Freeman*, May 24, 1890; "Howard University in Football," *Washington Post*, Nov 17, 1894; "Howard University," *Washington Evening Star*, Apr 23, 1896; "They Play on the Lots," *Washington Evening Star*, Apr 27, 1896; "College Base Ball," *Washington Evening Star*, May 4, 1896; "Howard University 19, YMCA 6," *Washington Post*, May 17, 1896; "Howard University," *Washington Evening Star, Jan 9, 1897*; "University Notes," *Washington Evening Star*, Mar 13, 1897; "Howard University," *Washington Evening Star*, Mar 27, 1897; "Colored High School Won," *Washington (DC) Times*, Apr 25, 1897; "At Howard University," *Washington Evening Star*, Mar 19, 1898; "University Athletics," *Washington Evening Star*, Apr 30, 1898; "College Athletics," *Washington Evening Star*, May 16, 1898; "Base Ball for Season 1900," *Washington (DC) Colored American*, Apr 14, 1900.

Ideal Base Ball Club (Washington, D.C.; 1890s)

The Ideal B.B.C. organized in 1896, played white and black aggregations. *Washington Times* (August 17, 1896): "The Shamrocks, the champions of the District Amateur League, will cross bats at National Park Monday at 4:30 o'clock with the Ideals (colored), a team picked from the Market House Club, and the strongest amateurs around the city."

SOURCES: "Shamrocks and Ideals," *Washington (DC) Evening Star*, Aug 15, 1896; "Shamrocks vs. Ideals," *Washington (DC) Times*, Aug 17, 1896.

Junior Alert Base Ball Club (Washington, D.C.; 1870s)

The Junior B.B.C. organized in 1875. *National Republican* (September 1, 1875): "The regular meeting of the Alert Base Ball Club was held at the residence of Mr. Robert Davidge, 1028 Nineteenth Street. The minutes of the previous meeting were read and approved, after which applications for membership were presented from the following junior players, with the request, that they be empowered to play as Junior Alerts, viz: Harry Johnson, Jr., Jacob Strather, Jerome Osborn, Charles Mason, Ed Mason, Frederick Moore, Wilson Carey, Alexander Shippen, and John Parker. The applications were received, and upon motion of Sandy Bruce, the request was granted."

SOURCES: "Alert Base Ball Club," *Washington (DC) National Republican*, Sep 1, 1875.

Junior Assembly Base Ball Club (Washington, D.C.; 1880s)

The Junior Assembly B.B.C. organized in the 1880s, played black teams. The formation of the Colored Base Ball Association included Howard University, the Junior Assembly, Lincoln School, and High School. *Washington Evening Star* (May 3, 1886): "Clubs representing Howard University, the High School, Lincoln School, and the Junior Assembly have formed a base-ball association, to be known as the District school association. The officers are W. Handy Johnson, president; James Usher, secretary, and James Shamwell, treasurer. A schedule of games has been arranged." *Washington Bee* (June 5, 1886): "The Junior Assembly defeated the High School Wednesday, by a score of 11 to 6. The Assembly tied the Howard University for first place in the League."

SOURCES: "The Ball Players," *Washington (DC) Evening Star*, May 3, 1886; "The Small Things of the Day," *Washington (DC) National Republican*, May 3, 1886; "Not At All Cast Down," *Washington (DC) Post*, May 9, 1886; "Local," *Washington (DC) Bee*, Jun 5, 1886.

Keystone Base Ball Club (Washington, D.C.; 1870s–1880s).

Organizer(s): D. C. Grant, J. Lacy, A. J. Brooks and C. S. Burley.

The Keystone B.B.C. organized in the 1870s. The Keystones played white and black organizations. *Washington Post* (August 28, 1878): "Yesterday afternoon the Keystone met the Manhattan on the National Grounds, in presence of a large number of spectators, and won another victory by a score of 17 to 9. The game was a very exciting one, especially by the heavy hitting of the Keystone club." They joined the Colored League of WA in 1880, which included the Eagle, Douglass, Manhattan, Unique, and Mutual nines. *Washington National Republican* (July 17, 1880): "The game between the Keystones and Uniques of the colored league in the National Grounds yesterday afternoon was witnessed by a goodly number of spectators. It was not had work for the Keystones to win, because they played better and showed superior discipline." The Keystone nine reorganized in 1881. *Washington Critic* (August 2, 1881): "A game of base-ball was played on the National Grounds, yesterday, between the Keystone club of this city, and the Brooklyn of Portsmouth, Virginia, which resulted in a victory for the home club by a score of 18 to 12."

SOURCES: "In Brief," *Washington (DC) Critic-Record*, May 21, 1878; "Muscular Matinees," *Washington (DC) Post*, Jul 8, 1878; "Games and Recreation," *Washington Post*, Aug 28, 1878; "Games and Recreations," *Washington (DC) National Republican*, Aug 28, 1878; "The Two Great Games," *Washington Post*, Sep 3, 1878; "Base Ball," *Washington National Republican*, Oct 4, 1878; "Base Ball," *Washington National Republican*, Mar 11, 1879; "The Colored League," *Washington National Republican*, Jul 17, 1880; "The Colored League," *Washington National Republican*, Jul 22, 1880; "Pertinent Paragraphs," *Washington (DC) Critic*, Aug 2, 1881.

Manhattan Base Ball Club (Washington, D.C.; 1870s–1880s).

Organizer(s): James Briscoe and James Thomas Tolliver; Stanislau K. Govern.

The Manhattan B.B.C. organized in the 1870s, played white and black organizations. *Washington National Republican* (May 20, 1872): "The Manhattan Base Ball Club will play the Howard University Base Ball Club, on the university grounds, Friday, May 24. As both clubs are composed of first-class players, it is supposed that the game will be quite interesting." *Washington National Republican* (August 24, 1872): "The Olympic Grounds yesterday were the scene of a very interesting game of base-ball between the Monumental and Manhattan clubs. Both are well known in this city. The game resulted in a victory for the Monumental by a score of 29 to 23." The Manhattans also roundly defeated the Mutual nine, by a score of 37 to 13. They played the WA Nationals, a white organization. *Washington Post* (September 28, 1878): "The Nationals [white] have arranged a game with the Manhattan club, which will no doubt be very interesting and well attended. The latter club is composed of colored men, and has played some really very fine games during the past season. The pitcher [Gaines] is a phenomenon in his way, and his delivery is said to be very peculiar and effective." They joined the Colored League of WA in 1880, which included the Eagle, Douglass, Keystone, Unique, and Mutual nines. *Washington Sunday Herald* (August 15, 1880): "On Friday the Manhattans defeated the Douglass in a ten-inning contest, the score being 10 to 3, the Manhattans making seven runs in the tenth-inning." They played the Richmond Black Swans, managed by Bud Fowler. *Washington Bee* (June 9, 1883): "The Manhattan Base Ball Club returned from their southern trip a few days ago. It is reported that the game between the Manhattan and Richmond Swans was a tie, after eleven innings. The game with the Peabody was interesting, score being, Manhattan, 9, Peabody, 3. The second game between the Swans and Manhattan resulted in a victory for the latter by a score of 23 to 9. Mr. [Arthur] Thomas, it is said, was pronounced the best catcher who has ever been in Richmond." Between 1881 and 1884, the players worked as waiters at Saratoga Springs' Clarendon Hotel; they played for the Clarendon club. Its chief local rival for colored baseball supremacy was the Douglass Club. Among the local white teams, the Manhattans played the Nationals. In 1883, the team, managed by Stanislau K. Govern, Charles Jones (former player for the Philadelphia Orions) and John F. Lang (a white barber, promoter, and gambler) declared professional status.

SOURCES: "Base Ball," *Washington (DC) National Republican*, May 20, 1872; "Base Ball," *Washington National Republican*, Jul 27, 1872; "City Small Talk," *Washington National Republican*, Aug 24, 1872; "City Small Talk," *Washington National Republican*, Sep 17, 1872; "Local Miscellany," *Washington National Republican*, Jul 11, 1874; "Base Ball," *Washington National Republican*, Oct 23, 1877; "In Brief," *Washington (DC) Critic-Record*, Jul 23, 1878; "Getting the Hang of It," *Washington (DC) Post*, Sep 28, 1878; "Base Ball," *Washington National Republican*, Oct 4, 1878; "Base Ball," *Washington National Republican*, Oct 5, 1878; "Fighting for the Championship," *Washington National Republican*, Jul 10, 1880; "Base Ball," *Washington (DC) Sunday Herald*, Aug 15, 1880; "Base-Ball," *Washington National Republican*, May 20, 1882; "Base-Ball," *Washington National Republican*, Jul 10, 1882; "Local Items," *Washington National Republican*, Apr 25, 1883; "The Diamond Field," *Washington National Republican*, Apr 26, 1883; "Locals," *Washington (DC) Bee*, May 5, 1883; "Picnic," *Washington Bee*, May 12, 1883; "Locals," *Washington Bee*, Jun 9, 1883; "Saratoga Gossip," *New York (NY) Globe*, Jul 7, 1883; "Saratoga Letter," *New York Globe*, Jul 28, 1883; "From the Springs," *New York Globe*, Aug 4, 1883; "Saratoga Notes," *New York Globe*, Aug 11, 1883.

Market House Base Ball Club (Washington, D.C.; 1880s–1900s). Organizer(s): Lafayette Jefferson.

The Market House B.B.C. organized in the 1880s, played white and black aggregations. *Washington Evening Star* (September 23, 1891): "The Douglass Club (colored Champions) will play the Market House B. B. C. tomorrow evening at the National baseball grounds." *Washington Bee* (July 14, 1894): "The Market House Baseball Club defeated the Richmond House team by a score of 12 to 7, on Tuesday." *Washington Morning Times* (July 18, 1895): "Over 900 people saw the Washington Market House peacefully lay the Washington Stars to sleep in a hotly contested game at Washington Park yesterday afternoon. The exhibition was an unusually interesting one, especially in the eighth inning, when the East Washington boys mustered up courage enough to go in and tie the score. The Market House aggregation scored in their half of the eighth, and when their opponents took their stand at the plate in the ninth the excitement was intense. The Market House people distinguished themselves as by far the best colored team in the District. They all knew their business and the result was that they played the game with snap and beauty, both in the field and with the stick."

SOURCES: "Notes," *Washington (DC) Evening Star*, Sep 23, 1891; "Sporting Notes," *Washington (DC) Bee*, Jul 14, 1894; "Stars Twinkled No More," *Washington (DC) Morning Times*, Jul 18, 1895; "Amusements," *Washington Morning Times*, Sep 7, 1895; "Market House Boys Win Again," *Washington Morning Times*, Sep 11, 1895; "Market House Team Ran Against Some Professionals," *Washington Morning Times*, Oct 8, 1895; "Won by the Nationals," *Washington Evening Star*, Aug 15, 1895; "A Game at National Park," *Washington (DC) Evening Times*, Jul 1, 1897; "Empires Soundly Trounced," *Washington Evening Times*, Jul 3, 1897; "Shamrocks vs. Ideals," *Washington Morning Times*, Aug 17, 1896; "Atlantics Are Still Winning," *Washington Morning Times*, Sep 4, 1897; "Will Play the Shamrocks," *Washington Evening Star*, Aug 20, 1898; "Shamrocks Victorious," *Washington (DC) Times*, Sep 6, 1898; "Amateur Baseball," *Washington Morning Times*, May 21, 1899; "Two Games on Decoration Day," *Washington Evening Times*, May 29, 1900; "Stronger at the Bat," *Washington Times*, May 31, 1900.

Metropolitan Base Ball Club (Washington, D.C.; 1870s). Organizer(s): R. H. Robinson, Nathan Addison and Robert Brown.

The Metropolitan B.B.C. organized in 1870. *Washington Evening Star* (August 10, 1870): "A number of young colored men assembled yesterday evening in Gallant Hall and organized a club to be known as the Metropolitan Base Ball Club. The club resolved to purchase a twenty-five pennant, to be held by the champion colored club of the district. All clubs in the district desiring to wrest this pennant from the Metropolitans will send along their challenges. The corresponding secretary will be obliged if the several clubs in the district will furnish him with a list of officers, places of meeting, and etc."

SOURCES: "New Base Ball Club," *Washington (DC) Evening Star*, Aug 10, 1870; "Metropolitan Club," *Washington (DC) National Republican*, April 7, 1871.

Monumental Base Ball Club (Washington, D.C.; 1860s–1870s). Organizer(s): H. C. Galloway.

The Monumental B.B.C. organized in the 1860s. In 1867, the Monumentals, played over 30 games against black nines. *Washington National Republican* (October 2, 1867): "The Monumental Base Ball club, of this city, colored, will visit Alexandria on the 10th of October, to play the Monumental club, of that city, colored, for the championship of Virginia, in which Mr. H. C. Galloway, of the Athletics of this city, has kindly volunteered his service to play left field for the Monumental boys. The Monumental boys of this city (Washington, DC), have sustained but one defeat out of twenty-eight games. Good enough." The Monumental boys opened the 1867 season with a victory over the Island Light nine, 21 to 5. They defeated Alexandria's Old Dominion nine, winning by a score of 41 to 36. They defeated WA's Alerts, 33 to 20; WA's Atlantics, 44 to 21, and crushed WA's Awkwards, 20–1. At season's end, they defeated a picked nine (composed of players from the Alerts and Athletics), 28 to 18. The Monumentals and Manhattans developed a rivalry. *National Republican* (August 24, 1872): "The Olympic grounds yesterday were the scene of a very interesting game of base-ball between the Monumental and Manhattan clubs, both well known in this city. The game resulted in a victory for the Monumental by a score of 29 to 23." They played Baltimore teams. *National Republican* (September 4, 1873): "A match game was played between the Excelsior club, of Baltimore, and the Monumental, of this city. The score stood: Monumental, 27; Excelsior, 14."

SOURCES: "Base Ball," *Washington (DC) National Republican*, Apr 15, 1867; "Base Ball," *Washington National Republican*, May 17, 1867; "Base Ball," *Washington National Republican*, Jun 12, 1867; "Base Ball," *Washington (DC) Evening Union*, Jun 15, 1867; "Base Ball," *The National Republican*, Sept. 6, 1867; "Base Ball," *Washington (DC) Evening Star*, Sep 9, 1867; "Games to be Played," *Washington National Republican*, Sep 12, 1867; "Games to be Played," *Washington National Republican*, Oct 2, 1867; "City Small Talk," *Washington National Republican*, Aug 24, 1872; "City Small Talk," *Washington National Republican*, Sep 17, 1872; "Base Ball," *Washington National Republican*, Mar 14, 1873; "Base Ball," *Washington National Republican*, Sep 3, 1873; "Excelsior vs. Monumental," *Washington National Republican*, Sep 3, 1873; "Excelsior vs. Monumental," *Washington National Republican*, Sep 4, 1873; "Base Ball," *Washington National Republican*, Oct 3, 1877; "Base Ball," *Washington National Republican*, Oct 19, 1877.

Mutual Base Ball Club (Washington, D.C.; 1860s–1880s). Organizer(s): T. R. Hawkins, Henry F. Grant, A. I. Augusta, Louis A. Bell, Dr. A. W. Tucker, Dr. Charles B. Purvis, George D. Johnson; Charles R. Douglass, Charles R. Douglass, George D. Johnson, John W. Bell, Charles F. Bruce, James Harry Smith, Thomas H. Wheeler, Calvin T. S. Brent, Robert A. Gray, R. H. Nugent, Charles F. Bruce, A. Smith (Thomas H. Barlow) and James W. Bell (Beall).

The Mutual B.B.C. organized in 1865, played against white and black teams. *Washington National Republican* (July 22, 1867): "On Saturday, the Mutual (colored) B. B. Club, of this city, played a match game of ball, in Philadelphia, with the Pythian club of that city. The

Mutual won by a score of 44 to 43." The rivalry continued into the 1870s. They played a local white nine. *New York Clipper* (October 23, 1869): "On the 12th inst., the Olympics, of Washington, D. C., accepted the invitation of the Mutual club (colored) to play a friendly game of ball. The Olympics were short four of their nine on account of the elections, and had but two men in their regular positions. Their play was of the muffin kind, dropping no less than from fly balls. The Mutuals fielded well and batted heavily, but lost the game by not played steadily." In 1870, the Mutual successful road tour went as far north as Niagara Falls. A local rivalry between the Mutuals and Alerts that began in the 1860s, also continued. *National Republican* (September 9, 1875): "Among the many amateur base-ball clubs in this city, there are two ell-known colored organizations, viz., the Alert and Mutual. These two clubs have maintained an organization since 1865. For a year or two the Alert held the championship over all their adversaries, but of late years the Mutuals, by making but few changes in their nine, have, at the close of each season, held the championship in their own hands." The Mutuals played a prominent Chicago nine in 1871. *Washington Evening Star* (September 13, 1871): "The Mutuals defeated the Uniques of Chicago, on the Olympic grounds, by a score of 34 to 11." They regularly scheduled games in New England, playing white and black teams. *Boston Advertiser* (August 19, 1871): "The game yesterday at the Boston grounds, between the Resolutes, the nominal junior champions of the State, and the Mutuals of Washington (both colored), proved to be a very poor display of skill. Both nines seemed to vie with each other in muffing indiscriminately every fly offered, while the umpire [Octavius Catto, of the Pythians] seemed to known but little of the game. The Resolutes took the lead at the beginning, and retained it to the end of the game." *Lowell Citizen and News* (September 14, 1875): "The game on the Fair Grounds yesterday between the Lowells and Mutuals attracted quite a concourse of spectators, and resulted in a victory for the colored boys." They arranged exhibitions with black university teams. *Washington National Republican* (May 24, 1876): "A very interesting game of baseball was played between the Mutual and Howard University Base Ball clubs yesterday, which resulted in a score of 15 to 17, in favor of the Howard University Base Ball Club. In the late–1870s, the organization developed strong rivalries with local black teams. *Washington National Republican* (August 30, 1879): "The Uniques and Mutuals met again yesterday on the National grounds and played a good game of ball, which resulted in favor of the former by a score of 11 to 6." They joined the Colored League of WA in 1880, which included the Eagle, Douglass, Keystone, Unique, and Manhattan nines.

SOURCES: "Washington Colored B. B. Club Wins," *Washington (DC) National Republican*, Jul 22, 1867; "Match Game," *Washington National Republican*, Aug 22, 1867; "Base-Ball Matters," *Washington National Republican*, Aug 23, 1867; "Base-Ball," *Washington National Republican*, Aug 24, 1867; "Base-Ball," *Washington National Republican*, Oct 13, 1869; "Base Ball," *Washington (DC) Evening Star*, Aug 7, 1870; "Notes," *New York (NY) Herald-Tribune*, Aug 26, 1870; "Local News," *Washington Evening Star*, Jul 7, 1870; "Base-Ball," *Philadelphia (PA) Inquirer*, Aug 12, 1871; "Base-Ball," *Philadelphia Inquirer*, Aug 14, 1871; "Base-Ball," *Philadelphia (PA) Public Ledger*, Aug 14, 1871; "Base-Ball," *Boston (MA) Advertiser*, Aug 19, 1871; "Base-Ball," *Philadelphia (PA) Press*, Aug 25, 1871; "Local News," *Washington Evening Star*, Sep 13, 1871; "Base-Ball," *Washington National Republican*, Sep 10, 1873; "Base-Ball," *Washington National Republican*, Sep 26, 1873; "Base-Ball Notes," *St. Louis (MO) Globe-Democrat*, Apr 12, 1875; "Base-Ball Gossip," *Boston Advertiser*, Jul 7, 1875; "Other Games," *Boston Advertiser*, Sep 13, 1875; "Other Games," *Boston (MA) Journal*, Sep 13, 1875; "Base Ball," *Lowell (MA) Citizen and News*, Sep 14, 1875; "Base-Ball Gossip," *Boston (MA) Post*, Sep 15, 1875; "Base-

Ball," *Washington National Republican*, May 24, 1876; "Base-Ball Matters," *Washington National Republican*, Aug 23, 1876; "Other Games," *Boston Advertiser, Aug 11, 1877*; "Base Ball," *Lowell (MA) Citizen and News*, Aug 11, 1877; "News of the Day," *Lowell Citizen and News*, Aug 18, 1877; *Brooklyn (NY) Eagle*, Aug 27, 1877; "The Diamond Field," *Washington National Republican*, Aug 1, 1879; *Washington National Republican*, Apr 28, 1880; "Sports of the Field," *Washington National Republican*, Aug 20, 1879; "Base Ball Between Colored Clubs," *Washington National Republican*, Jul 9, 1867; "Base Ball—Pythians vs. Mutuals," *Philadelphia Press*, Aug 14, 1871; "Base Ball," *Philadelphia Inquirer*, Aug 14, 1871; "Homespun," *Troy (NY) Whig*, Aug 15, 1871; "Base Ball," *Boston Advertiser*, Aug 19, 1871; "Base Ball," *Washington National Republican*, Sep 10, 1873; "Base Ball," *Washington National Republican*, Sep 26, 1873; "Base Ball," *Washington National Republican*, Mar 23, 1876; "Sports of the Field," *Washington National Republican*, Aug 8, 1879; "Base Ball," *Washington National Republican*, Aug 27, 1879; "Out-Door-Sports," *Washington National Republican*, Aug 30, 1879; "Base Ball," *Washington National Republican*, Apr 28, 1880.

Neversweat Base Ball Club (Washington, D.C.; 1880s–1890s)

The Neversweat B.B.C. organized in the 1890s, played white and black aggregations. *Washington Evening Star* (August 13, 1889): "The Douglass team defeated the Never Sweats yesterday 25 to 9." *Evening Star* (August 22, 1889): "The Post newsboys will play the Neversweats, colored, Saturday at 4:30 p.m. at Capitol Park."

Evening Star (May 28, 1892): "The Neversweats (colored) and the Primrose teams will cross bats Monday morning at Capitol Park. The Neversweats are a strong team, having several of the old Cuban Giants." *Evening Star* (May 21, 1897): "The Empires defeated the Neversweats in a well-played game of ball yesterday at National Park for the championship of the District, by a score of 13 to 6."

SOURCES: "Local Notes," *Washington (DC) Evening Star*, Jul 8, 1889; "Notes," *Washington Evening Star*, Jul 23, 1889; "Notes of the Ball Field," *Washington Evening Star*, Jul 25, 1889; "Daisy Cutters," *Washington Evening Star*, Aug 3, 1889; "They Say," *Washington (DC) Bee*, Aug 10, 1889; "Within the Ring," *Washington Evening Star*, Aug 13, 1889; "Grounders," *Washington Evening Star*, Aug 22, 1889; "Finishing Touches," *Washington Evening Star*, Oct 5, 1889; "Amateur Base Ball," *Washington Evening Star*, May 28, 1892; "Emancipation Echoes," *Frederick (MD) News*, Aug 12, 1892; "Amateur Baseball," *Washington Evening Star*, May 19, 1897; Amateur Baseball," *Washington Evening Star*, May 21, 1897.

Quill Driver Base Ball Club (Washington, D.C.; 1880s)

The Quill Driver B.B.C. organized in the 1880s. The Quill Drivers, employees of the federal government, played black teams. *Washington Bee* (June 13, 1885): "Saturday evening our reporter, with a full stomach of boarding house mosaic mixture, wended his way slowly across the green grassy fields in search of wild flowers to put in his best girl's hair on Saturday, when his ears were seduced by a terrific yell from the captain of the Quill Driver's Base Ball Club to his left field to throw the ball home, in order to put out Harry Smith, the dandy pitcher of the Birch-Wielder's Base Ball Club, who had just struck the ball for one base. The Quill Drivers were uniformed in red caps and stockings, white shirts and blue pants. The Birch-Wielders were dressed in a delicate green cap and stocking, blue shirts and yellow pants and the way they were made to hunt leather was a shame."

SOURCES: "A Great Game of Ball," *Washington (DC) Bee*, Jun 13, 1885; "They Say," *Washington Bee*, Jun 20, 1885.

Richmond House Base Ball Club (Washington, D.C.; 1890s). Organizer(s): William H. Brooker.

The Richmond House B.B.C. organized in the 1890s, if not earlier. The ball club, composed of waiters, played against similar colored clubs, including the Market House Club. *Washington Bee* (August 18, 1894): "The Richmond House played the Ramsdell of Northeast Washington. The score was 19 to 6 in favor of Richmond. On Emancipation Day at Frederick the Richmond played the Royal Blue of Baltimore, Maryland. 19 to 0 in favor of Richmond." They played against the Market House team. *Washington Bee* (July 14, 1894): "The Market House Baseball Club defeated the Richmond House team by a score of 12 to 7, on Tuesday." *Washington Bee* (August 31, 1895): "Mr. William H. Brooker is an up-to-date man. He is now manager of the Richmond House Base Ball Club, one of the best crack teams in the city. Mr. Brooker will escort his team to Hampton, Virginia, where they will play a club there. There will be a large crowd that will go to Hampton with the boys. Mr. Brooker is an up-to-date sport, who always makes it pleasant for the boys when you go with him."

SOURCES: "Sporting Notes," *Washington (DC) Bee*, Jul 14, 1894; "Locals," *Washington Bee*, Aug 10, 1894; "Locals," *Washington Bee*, Aug 18, 1894; "Locals," *Washington Bee*, Aug 31, 1895.

Sparta Base Ball Club (Washington, D.C.; 1870s–1890s) Organizer(s): James D. Kennedy

The Sparta B.B.C. organized in 1878. In 1880, the high society organization renovated its club house, and elected James H. Smith, a prominent lawyer (who also had pitched for WA's Mutual team). Former president, James D. Kennedy, had pitched for New Orleans' Pickwick club. Sparta club members were baseballists: they played black and white nines. *Washington Evening Star* (July 25, 1893): "The Spartans have defeated the Market House nine by 17 to 4." Its rival was the Capital Citys. *Washington Times* (September 16, 1897): "There will be a game of baseball at the National Park this afternoon between the Sparta and Capital City teams, which promises a good contest. Both of these aggregations are composed of colored players, and they number among their ranks come of the best amateurs in the District game and will be called at 4:15." *Washington Times* (September 17, 1897): "The ebony-hued ball team known as the Capital City nine administered a drubbing to their equally dusky opponents, the Spartas at National Park, yesterday afternoon. Ragged playing at critical moments was accountable for the defeat of the latter. The features of the game were the fielding of Payne and Curry of the Capital Citys and of Washington and Jefferson of the Spartas. Henson's pitching, with good support, would have won the game for the Spartas."

SOURCES: "Local," *Washington (DC) People's Advocate*, Nov 8, 1879; "Sparta Club," *Washington (DC) Bee*, Jan 17, 1880; "Sparta Club," *Washington (DC) National Republican*, Jan 26, 1880; "A Bon-ton Colored Club," *Washington (DC) Post*, May 16, 1881; "The Sparta Reception," *Washington Bee*, Feb 10, 1883; "The Sparta Club," *Washington Bee*, Jun 18, 1883; "The Sparta Picnic," *Washington Bee*, Jun 23, 1883; "Trustee James H. Smith Complimented," *Washington Bee*, Aug 11, 1883; "The Sparta Opening," *Washington Bee*, Oct 11, 1884; "Local Briefs," *Washington (DC) Critic-Record*, Jan 7, 1885; "The Ball Players," *Washington (DC) Evening Star*, May 3, 1886; "Not At All Cast Down," *Washington Post*, May 9, 1886; "Amateur Base Ball," *Washington Evening Star*, Jul 25, 1893; "South Carolina Sufferers," *Washington Evening Star*, Sep 25, 1893; "Amateurs to Play," *Washington (DC) Times*, Sep 16, 1897; "Capital City Team Won," *Washington Morning Times*, Sep 17, 1897; "Capital City Team Won," *Washington Morning Times*, Sep 17, 1897; "Capital Citys vs. Sparta," *Washington Morning Times*, Aug 7, 1898.

Unique Base Ball Club (Washington, D.C.; 1870s–1880s). Organizer(s): J. Lacy, Charles WA and L. Thomas.

The Unique B.B.C. organized in the 1870s, played black and white teams. *Washington Post* (September 11, 1878): "There was a well-contested game of ball between the Eagles and Uniques (colored) yesterday at Eagles Park. Nine innings were played resulting in a victory for the Eagles by a score of five to four." *Washington National Republican* (September 13, 1878): "The Keystone and Unique, both colored clubs, played a game yesterday afternoon on the National Grounds in the presence of a large and enthusiastic audience. The contest was first class and the 'Second Warders' came out ahead by a score of 6 to 1." *Washington Post* (October 11, 1878): "The Nationals [white] put the Uniques through a course of sprouts, scoring 13 to their opponents' 0. The colored boys got but one hits off Lynch." They joined the WA Colored League in 1880, which included the Keystone, Douglass, Manhattan, and Mutual nines.

SOURCES: "Sports and Pastimes," *Washington (DC) Post*, Aug 27, 1878; "Fall Diversions," *Washington Post*, Sep 5, 1878; "Catchers and Pushers," *Washington Post*, Sep 11, 1878; "Base Ball," *Washington (DC) National Republican*, Sep 17, 1878; "For Charity's Sake," *Washington Post*, Sep 18, 1878; "Autumnal Recreations," *Washington Post*, Sep 20, 1878; "The Men at the Bat," *Washington Post*, Sep 24, 1878; "The Diamond Field," *Washington National Republican*, Sep 24, 1878; "Getting the Hang of It," *Washington Post*, Sep 28, 1878; "Base Ball," *Washington National Republican*, Sep 30, 1878; "Base Ball and Chess," *The Post*, Oct. 1, 1878; "Base Ball," *National Republican*, Oct. 1, 1878; "Base Ball," *Washington Post*, Oct 11, 1878; "The Bat and Ball," *Washington National Republican*, Aug 7, 1879; "Sports of the Field," *Washington National Republican*, Aug 8, 1879; "Outdoor Sports," *Washington National Republican*, Aug 28, 1879; "Base Ball," *Washington National Republican*, Aug 29, 1879; "Out-of-Door Sports," *Washington National Republican*, Aug 30, 1879; "The Uniques and Eagles," *Washington National Republican*, Jul 9, 1880; "The Colored Champions," *Washington National Republican*, Jul 14, 1880; "The Eagles and Manhattans," *Washington National Republican*, Aug 3, 1880.

Whacker Base Ball Club (Washington, D.C.; 1880s). Organizer(s): Oran Skipworth.

The Whacker B.B.C. organized in the 1880s, played against black teams. *Critic* (July 7, 1882): "A game was played between two colored nines, one from this city [Alexandria, Virginia], and the other, the Whackers, from Washington, DC, resulting in a victory for the latter, by a score of 14 to 3." *Critic* (July 17, 1882): "The Douglass' will play their first game today, having as opponents a new team called the Whackers. The game will take place on the grounds at Ninth and S streets." The WA (DC) *Critic* (June 19, 1883): "The Whackers and the Washington Base Ball clubs played a game yesterday which resulted in a tie of 16 to 16—a very bad game. You must do better next time boys." *Critic* (June 29, 1883): "The Whackers and the Washingtons played a game of baseball yesterday, and the Whackers defeated the Washingtons by a score of 11 to 10."

SOURCES: "Base Ball," *Alexandria (VA) Gazette*, Jul 7, 1882; "West Washington," *Washington (DC) Critic*, Jul 7, 1882; "Pertinent Paragraphs," *Washington Critic*, Jul 17, 1883 "Laconic Locals," *Washington Critic*, Jun 19, 1883; "Notes About Town," *Washington Critic*, Jun 29, 1883; "West Washington," *Washington Critic*, Jul 7, 1883.

West Virginia

Black Feet ("Black Stockings") Base Ball Club (Bellaire, WV; 1870s)

The Black Feet B.B.C. organized in the 1870s, played black teams. The towns of Bellaire and Wheeling had a rivalry. The Bellaire nine was composed of barbers. *Wheeling Register* (August 14, 1874): "The

Idlewild Base Ball Club, of this city, composed exclusively of colored youths, will play a colored club in Bellaire, called the Black Feet, a match game tomorrow afternoon. These clubs played a game some weeks ago, in which the Idlewilds were victorious." *Register* (August 18, 1874): "The colored boys of Wheeling did some very good batting, especially Jack, the long-legged barber of the Island, but the Black Feet excelled in catches, the little pitcher of Bellaire taking more than all others of both sides." *Register* (August 18, 1874): "The game of base-ball between those colored individuals yesterday proved bad for the reputation of the Bellaire Darks, and we advise them to keep dark hereafter; 62 to 37 in favor of the Wheeling chaps was the result."

SOURCES: "Base Ball," Wheeling (WVA) *Intelligencer*, Aug 1, 1874; "Neighborhood News," *Wheeling Register*, Aug 3, 1874; *Wheeling Register*, Aug 4, 1874; *Wheeling Register*, Aug 7, 1874; "Base Ball," *Wheeling Register*, Aug 18, 1874; "Neighborhood News," *Wheeling Register*, Aug 18, 1874; *Wheeling Register*, Sep 11, 1874; "Bellaire Locals," *Wheeling Intelligencer*, Jul 28, 1875.

Colored Base Ball Club (Bluefield, WV; 1890s)

The Colored B.B.C. organized in the 1890s, played black nines. *Bluefield Telegraph* (July 6, 1897): "The Bluefield and Elkhorn colored teams played two games of baseball here yesterday. The first developed in a score of 35 to 21 in favor of Bluefield and the second in a score of 17 to 1 in favor of Elkhorn. Glass and Johnson were the Bluefield's battery and Warick and Anthony were in the points for Elkhorn. The features of the game were the fielding of Warick."

SOURCES: "In the City and Coal Field," Bluefield (WVA) *Telegraph*, Jul 6, 1897.

Wild West Base Ball Club (Elkhorn, WV; 1890s)

The Wild West B.B.C. organized in the 1890s, played black teams. *Bluefield Telegraph* (June 2, 1896): "The colored teams of Pocahontas and Elkhorn will hold forth at Bluefield Park this afternoon at the usual hour." *Telegraph* (June 6, 1896): "The Silver Kings, of Pocahontas, and Wild West of Elkhorn, colored baseball teams, will play a match game at the park grounds Saturday morning at 10 a.m." *Telegraph* (July 6, 1897): "The Bluefield and Elkhorn colored teams played two games of baseball here yesterday. The first developed in a score of 35 to 21 in favor of Bluefield and the second in a score of 17 to 1 in favor of Elkhorn. Glass and Johnson were the Bluefield's battery and Warick and Anthony were in the points for Elkhorn. The features of the game were the fielding of Warick."

SOURCES: "In and About the City," Bluefield (WVA) *Telegraph*, Jun 2, 1896; "On the Base Ball Field," *Bluefield Telegraph*, Jun 6, 1896; "In the City and Coal Field," *Bluefield Telegraph*, Jul 6, 1897.

Ordinary Base Ball Club (Sulphur Springs, WV; 1900s).

The Ordinary B.B.C. organized in the 1900s. *Colored American* (August 4, 1900): "A game of baseball was played here last Friday between the Ordinary or Old Reserves and the Dining Room boys resulting in a score of 5 to 1 for the Ordinary team of which Mr. Louis Tolliver is captain and Mr. John Pryor manager; Mr. Andrew Jackson is manager of the Dining room team. The batteries were as follows: for the Ordinary, John Pryor and Samuel Webb; for the dining room, Stuart Grant and Brazil Jackson. The Ordinary team is successful in winning all games played and stand ready to meet all comers."

SOURCES: "At White Sulphur Springs," *Washington (DC) Colored American*, Aug 4, 1900; "White Sulphur Letter," *Washington Colored American*, Aug 18, 1900.

Active Base Ball Club (Wheeling, WV; 1880s). Organizer(s): Joshua Couch ("Peanut Scott").

The Active B.B.C. organized in the 1880s, played black nines. *Wheeling Intelligencer* (August 25, 1882): "The Actives (colored) and Buckeyes played a game of base-ball on the Island yesterday, the Actives defeating their opponents by a score of 16 to 14." *Intelligencer* (August 29, 1882): "The Actives (colored) played the Roughs and Readys yesterday on the Island and defeated them by a score of 24 to 11." *Intelligencer* (August 30, 1882): "The Actives, a colored base-ball club, of Wheeling, have issues a challenge to the colored people of Bellaire to play them a match game, and it is probably that a nine will be found to play them." *Intelligencer* (September 15, 1882): "Our colored base-ball club, the Actives, did it up brown for the Sun Flowers, of Bellaire, yesterday, defeating them by a score of 12 to 8."

SOURCES: "Local Observations," Wheeling (WVA) *Intelligencer*, Aug 25, 1882; "City Brevities," *Wheeling Intelligencer*, Aug 30, 1882; "City Shorts," *Wheeling Intelligencer*, Aug 29, 1882; "City Brevities," *Wheeling Intelligencer*, Sep 15, 1882.

Expert Base Ball Club (Wheeling, WV; 1890s). Organizer(s): H. C. Richards.

The Expert B.B.C. organized in 1896. Composed of Pittsburgh and Steubenville, OH players, the Experts played white teams. *Wheeling Register* (May 10, 1896): "The H. C. Richards Experts would like to swipe the Jepson Stars next Saturday afternoon at the Central house glass works." *Register* (August 5, 1896): "Snow, the crack colored coacher of Pittsburgh, will be down Saturday to play with the H. C. Richards team in the game with the J. C. Hennings, at the Island Park." *Register* (August 9, 1896): "A fair-sized crowd witnessed the game at Island Park yesterday between the Hennings and H. C. Richards colored team. It was a close and very pretty contest for nine innings, and the spectators were treated to an exhibition of scrappy ball. The game resulted in a victory for the Hennings, by a score of 6 to 5."

SOURCES: "Amateur Notes," Wheeling (WVA) *Register*, Apr 30, 1896; "Amateur Notes," *Wheeling Register*, May 10, 1896; "Amateur Notes," *Wheeling Register*, Aug 4, 1896; "Amateur Notes," *Wheeling Register*, Aug 5, 1896; "The Hennings Won," *Wheeling Register*, Aug 9, 1896; "Great Game on the Island," *Wheeling Register*, Sep 4, 1896; "Amateur Notes," *Wheeling Register*, Sep 6, 1896.

Idlewild Base Ball Club (Wheeling, WV; 1870s–1880s). Organizer(s): Joshua Couch ("Peanut Scott").

The Idlewild B.B.C. organized in 1873. The Idlewild played black organizations, including the Champions, of Steubenville; the Champion nine included Weldy and Moses Fleetwood Walker. *Wheeling Intelligencer* (August 8, 1873): "A large number of the lady and gentlemen friends of the Champions came along, and they, with many of our own people, retired to the Fair Grounds, at two o'clock, to see the game. It was apparent from the first that the Idles were nowhere. The Champions could have discounted them, and played on their hands and knees, and then have beaten them." Bellaire and Wheeling developed a rivalry. *Intelligencer* (August 1, 1874): "The Idlewild Base Ball Club, composed of a number of cullud gemmen in this city, will go down to Bellaire on Monday to play a match game with a club of the same complexion down there." *Wheeling Register* (August 14, 1874): "The Idlewild Base Ball Club, of this city, composed exclusively of colored youths, will play a colored club in Bellaire, called the Black Feet, a match game tomorrow afternoon. These clubs played a game some weeks ago, in which the Idlewilds were victorious." *Register* (August 18, 1874): "The colored boys of Wheeling did some very good batting, especially Jack, the long-legged barber of the Island, but the Black Feet excelled in catches, the little pitcher of Bellaire taking more than all others of both sides." *Register* (August 18, 1874): "The game of base-ball between those colored individuals yesterday proved bad for the reputation of the Bellaire Darks, and we advise them to keep dark hereafter; 62 to 37 in favor of the Wheeling chaps was the result."

SOURCES: "Base Ball," Wheeling (WVA) *Intelligencer*, Aug 8, 1873; "Base Ball," *Wheeling Intelligencer*, Aug 1, 1874; "Neighborhood News," Wheeling (WVA) *Register*, Aug 3, 1874; *Wheeling Register*, Aug 4, 1874; *Wheeling Register*, Aug 7, 1874; "Base Ball," *Wheeling Register*, Aug 18, 1874; "Neighborhood News," *Wheeling Register*, Aug 18, 1874; *Wheeling Register*, Sep 11, 1874; "Wanted: A Base Ball Boom," *Wheeling Intelligencer*, Jul 20, 1882.

Keystone Base Ball Club (Wheeling, WV; 1890s)

The Keystone B.B.C. organized in the 1890s, played black and white teams. *Wheeling Register* (July 4, 1890): "The Keystone colored base-ball club played a picked nine on Tunnel Green yesterday afternoon. Score 13 to 5 in favor of Keystone. Batteries: Taber [Taper] and Johnson; picked nine Gray and McClellan." *Register* (July 9, 1890): "The Keystones and Pink Garters play a match game at Island Ball Park Thursday, July 10." *Register* (July 11, 1890): "The Pink Garters and the Keystones, colored champions of the State, will play this afternoon on the base-ball park." *Register*: "The Keystones and a picked name played a match game on the Tunnel Green."

SOURCES: "Base Ball Notes," Wheeling (WVA) *Register*, Jun 22, 1890; "Base Ball Notes," *Wheeling Register*, Jun 22, 1890; "Diamond Dust," *Wheeling Register*, Jul 4, 1890; "Base Ball Notes," *Wheeling Register*, Jul 6, 1890; "Base Ball Notes," *Wheeling Register*, Jul 9, 1890; "Base Ball Notes," *Wheeling Register*, Jul 11, 1890.

Quickstep Base Ball Club (Wheeling, WV; 1870s–1890s). Organizer(s): Peanut Scott.

The Quickstep B.B.C. organized in the 1870s, played white and black teams. *Wheeling Register* (June 3, 1875): "A colored base-ball club of this city, known as the Quicksteps, went to Washington, Pa., to play a game with the Lightning Nine, a club of same complexion in that place. Quite a large crowd was in attendance. The Quicksteps were victorious by a score of 37 to 35." *Register* (July 26, 1875): "There will be a grand game of base-ball at the Fair Grounds this afternoon. It will between two colored clubs, the Quicksteps of this city, and the Bellaire club. The game will be called at 2 o'clock, and as the nines are pretty evenly matched, it will be a close and exciting game. There is more fun watching our colored brethren play base-ball than the white boys. Go and see them." *Register* (July 26, 1890): "The Colored Quicksteps would like to hear from the White Oaks for any price from $1 up. Address William Morris, 1103 Eoff Street." *Register*: "The Quicksteps defeated the Pink Garters, on the Peninsula Grounds, by a score of 18 to 12, yesterday. Battery for the Quicksteps: McGee and Scott."

SOURCES: "Colored Base Ball," Wheeling (WVA) *Register*, Jun 3, 1875; "Other Games," *Wheeling Register*, May 5, 1889; "The Amateurs," *Wheeling Register*, May 31, 1889; "Mansfield Defeated," *Wheeling Register*, Jun 1, 1889; *Wheeling Register*, Jun 29, 1889; "Base Ball Notes," *Wheeling Register*. Apr. 21, 1890; "Base Ball," *Wheeling Register*, Jul 26, 1890.

Red Stocking Base Ball Club (Wheeling, WV; 1870s). Organizer(s): John Couch ("Peanut Scott").

The Red Stocking B.B.C. organized in the 1870s. *Wheeling Intelligencer* (July 11, 1878): "Peanut Scott's Red Stocking Base Ball Club played a match game with a colored club at Waynesboro, Pennsylvania. The Waynesboro club, known as the Union Club, won by a score of 16 to 7. The game was called on the sixth inning on account of rain." *Wheeling Register* (August 21, 1878): "Any time yesterday a troop of saddle-colored gemmen of Waynesboro might be seen restlessly perambulating the streets, waiting impatiently waiting for the time when they might doff citizens' clothes and don blue pants and striped hose and appear at once demolishers of African hearts and baseball clubs. The Waynesboro pitching was too much for Wheeling, and many of Scott's team, including the veteran himself [Peanut Scott] could only blink at the sphere, as it went curving by, and after the ineffectual attempts to check its mad career, run frantically half way to first—and, came back."

SOURCES: "Colored Base Ball Clubs," *Pittsburgh (PA) Post-Gazette*, Jul 10, 1878; "City Chips," Wheeling (WVA) *Register*, Jul 11, 1878; "Peanut Scott's Nine Defeated," Wheeling (WVA) *Intelligencer*, Jul 11, 1878; "City Chips," *Wheeling Register*, Aug 20, 1878; The Waynesboro Club Victorious," *Wheeling Intelligencer*, Aug 21, 1878; "Black Diamond, Cut Diamond," *Wheeling Register*, Aug 21, 1878; "Police Court," *Wheeling Intelligencer*, Nov 18, 1878; "Notes," *Wheeling Register*, Jul 15, 1879; "The Wheeling Mokes," *Wheeling Register*, Jul 17, 1879; "Base Ball," *Wheeling Register*. 20, 1879.

Turkish Bath Base Ball Club (Wheeling, WV; 1890s)

The Turkish Bath B.B.C. organized in the 1890s. The nine played other black aggregations. *Wheeling Register* (April 22, 1894): "The Clippers defeated the Colored Turkish Bath Club on the Tunnel Green yesterday by a score of 21 to 8. Batteries for Clippers, Wilson and Richards, and for Turkish Bath, Franklin and Jackson." *Register* (May 5, 1894): "The Turkish Bath club defeated the Moonlight club by a score of 20 to 12. T.C.B. would like to hear from the Hod Carriers." *Register* (May 12, 1894): "The Hess and Lemons defeated the Turkish Bath at the Old Fair Grounds yesterday by a score of 38 to 13."

SOURCES: "Local Base Ball," Wheeling (WVA) *Register*, Apr 22, 1894; "Local Base Ball," *Wheeling Register*, May 5, 1894; "Local Base Ball," *Wheeling Register*, May 12, 1894.

Wisconsin

Atlantic Base Ball Club (Beloit, WI; 1870s). Organizer(s): Rush Hopson.

The Atlantic B.B.C., of Rockford, IL, organized in 1870, played against black nines. *Rockford Register* (August 20, 1870): "The Atlantics, of Beloit, will play the Rockfords next Thursday on the Fairgrounds." *New York Tribune* (August 26, 1870): "The Forest City nine of Rockford are to play the Atlantics, of Beloit—a colored club—today."

SOURCES: "Notings," *Rockford (IL) Weekly Gazette*, Jun 30, 1870; "The Colored Clubs," *Rockford Weekly Gazette*, Aug 6, 1870; "The National Game," *Rockford (IL) Register*, Aug 20, 1870; "Base Ball From A Colored Point Of View," *Chicago (IL) Tribune*, Aug 24, 1870; "Notes," *New York (NY) Herald*, Aug 26, 1870; "Out Door Sports," *New York (NY) Tribune*, Aug 26, 1870.

National Base Ball Club (Beloit, WI; 1870s–1880s). Organizer(s): Rush Hopson.

The National B.B.C. organized in the 1870s, played against black nines. Beloit and Rockford developed a rivalry. *Rockford Weekly Gazette*: "The colored folks of Rockford and Beloit, are going to have a gala here in Rockford, upon which occasion a game of base-ball will be played between the White Stockings of Rockford (colored) and the Base Ball Club of Beloit (colored), at the Fair Grounds." *Madison State Journal* (August 28, 1877): "The Beloit colored nine and the Rockford (IL) colored nine played a match game of ball, at the fairgrounds, Saturday, which was rather a novelty. Between two hundred and three hundred ladies and gentlemen were on the ground. The game was well played up until the sixth inning, the game standing 20 to 13 in favor of Beloit. At the close of the seventh inning the Rockford threw up the sponge in favor of the Beloits, the score standing, Beloit 34, Rockford, 16." *Chicago Inter-Ocean* (September 19, 1877): "The [National], of Beloit, Wisconsin, and the [Clippers], of Rockford, two colored clubs, had a game Monday afternoon on the Rockford Grounds, which resulted in favor of the Wisconsin team by a score of 11 to 1. The Wisconsin club played an excellent game in the field and equally well at the bat."

SOURCES: "Local Jottings," *Rockford (WI) Weekly Gazette*, Aug 17, 1876; *Rockford Weekly Gazette*, Aug 18, 1876; "Beloit vs. Rockford," *Rockford Weekly Gazette*, Aug 31, 1876; *Rockford Weekly Gazette*, Sep 1, 1876; "Beloit Items," *Madison (WI) State Journal*, Aug 28, 1877; *Rockford Weekly Gazette*, Sep 6, 1877; *Rockford Weekly Gazette*, Sep 8, 1877; "Local Items," *Rockford (IL) Journal*, Sep 15, 1877; "Cullud Clubs," *Chicago (IL) Inter-Ocean*, September 19, 1877; *Rockford Weekly Gazette*, Sep 21, 1877; "Rush Hopson," *Rockford Weekly Gazette*, Aug 30, 1882.

Boston Dip Base Ball Club (Milwaukee, WI; 1890s). Organizer(s): Randall Phillips.

The Boston Dip B.B.C. organized in the 1890s. The Boston Dips, composed of hotel waiters, played similar organizations. In 1892, *Milwaukee Sentinel* (June 2, 1892): "A large crowd witnessed the colored athletic games at Athletic Park Sunday afternoon. The ball game was close and exciting. It was won by the Boston Dips. The score: Boston Dips, 9; Milwaukee Reds, 8." *Milwaukee Sentinel* (July 11, 1893): "Captained by Napoleon Brody, the Milwaukee Reds yesterday defeated the Boston Dips in a game of Base-Ball, at National Park by a score of 8 to 7. Both clubs are made up of colored players."

SOURCES: "Amateur Items," *Milwaukee (WI) Journal*, Jun 2, 1892; "Colored Team to Play Here," *Milwaukee Journal*, Jul 16, 1892; "A New Summer Diversion," *Milwaukee Journal*, Jul 20, 1892; "A Novelty in Athletics," *Milwaukee Journal*, Jul 23, 1892; "Colored Nines to Play," *Milwaukee Journal*, Jul 24, 1892; "Colored Athletes," *Milwaukee (WI) Sentinel*, Jul 25, 1892; "Napoleon Brody's Team Won," *Milwaukee Sentinel*, Jul 11, 1893.

Klondike Base Ball Club (Milwaukee, WI; 1890s)

The Klondike B.B.C. organized in the 1890s. The Klondikes, participants in Milwaukee's Amateur Baseball League, played white aggregations. *Milwaukee Sentinel* (June 12, 1897): "The Klondike Baseball Club defeated the Fourth Ward Badger Boys yesterday at National park by a score of 14 to 12. The Klondikes have reorganized with the following players George Byron, John Ellis, Will Simmons, Frank Watkins, C. Morgan, Simon Epps, Walter Vine, William Hawkins, Al Lawrence and Harry MacAllister." The Klondikes reorganized for the 1898 season, and they again participated in the City League. *Milwaukee Sentinel* (June 16, 1897): "The Klondikes were defeated by the City Halls yesterday. 12 to 8."

SOURCES: "City League Games," *Milwaukee (WI) Sentinel*, June 12, 1897; "City League Games To-Day," *Milwaukee Sentinel, Jun* 16, 1897; "Among the Amateurs," *Milwaukee Sentinel*, May 6, 1898; "Among the Amateurs," *Milwaukee Sentinel*, May 9, 1898; "Among the Amateurs," *Milwaukee Sentinel*, May 30, 1898; "Two City League Games Today," Milwaukee *Sentinel*, Jun 19, 1898.

Plankinton Hotel Base Ball Club (Milwaukee, WI; 1890s). Organizer(s): Nelson Broady.

The Plankinton Hotel B.B.C. organized in the 1890s, if not earlier. The nine, composed of waiters, nicknamed the Milwaukee Reds, played similar nines. *Milwaukee Sentinel* (June 2, 1892): "A large crowd witnessed the colored athletic games at Athletic Park Sunday afternoon. The ball game was close and exciting. It was won by the Boston Dips. The score: Boston Dips, 9; Milwaukee Reds, 8." *Milwaukee Sentinel* (July 11, 1893): "Captained by Napoleon Broady, the Milwaukee Reds yesterday defeated the Boston Dips in a game of Base-Ball, at National Park by a score of 8 to 7. Both clubs are made up of colored players."

SOURCES: "A Colored Nine," *Milwaukee (WI) Sentinel*, May 8, 1890; "Base Ball Notes," *Milwaukee Sentinel*, May 8, 1890; "Milwaukee, Wisconsin News," *Cleveland (OH) Gazette*, May 17, 1890; "Base Ball Notes," *Milwaukee Sentinel*, Jun 8, 1890; "Milwaukee, Wisconsin, Locals," *Cleveland Gazette*, Jun 14, 1890; "Amateur Base Ball Notes," *Milwaukee Sentinel*, Jun 26, 1890; "Among Amateur Ball Players," *Milwaukee Sentinel*, Jun 30, 1890; "General Sporting Small Talk," *Milwaukee Sentinel*, Jul 3, 1890; "Among Amateur Players," *Milwaukee Sentinel*, Jun 30, 1892; "Milwaukee," *Detroit (MI) Plaindealer*, Jul 1, 1892; "Colored Team To Play Here," *Milwaukee (WI) Journal*, Jul 16, 1892; "Cream Citys Won It," *Milwaukee Sentinel*, Jul 17, 1892; "The Colored Ball Teams," *Milwaukee Journal*, Jul 23, 1892; "Colored Athletes," *Milwaukee Journal*, Jul 25, 1892; "Napoleon Broady's Team Won," *Milwaukee Sentinel*, Jul 11, 1893.

Underwood House Base Ball Club (Milwaukee, WI; 1880s–1890s). Organizer(s): B. F. Underwood.

The Underwood House B.B.C. organized in the 1880s, played black teams. *Cleveland Gazette* (May 14, 1887): "The Rounders were defeated by the Underwood Base Ball Club; score 9 to 0. Rush and Fields did effective work. The Underwoods also defeated the Arlington Heights by a score of 10 to 5. The feature of the game was Elliott and Fields' double play."

SOURCES: "Milwaukee, Wisconsin," *Cleveland (OH) Gazette*, Sep 25, 1886; "Cream City News," *Cleveland Gazette*, May 14, 1887; "Cream City News," *Cleveland Gazette*, Jun 18, 1887; "Cream City News," *Cleveland Gazette*, Aug 18, 1887; "Fine Base Ball Club," *Cleveland Gazette*, May 18, 1889; "Milwaukee, Wisconsin News," *Cleveland Gazette*, Feb 16, 1890; "Milwaukee, Wisconsin News," *Cleveland Gazette*, May 3, 1890; "A Colored Nine," *Milwaukee (WI) Sentinel*, May 8, 1890; "Base Ball Notes," *Milwaukee Sentinel*, May 8, 1890; "Milwaukee, Wisconsin News," *Cleveland Gazette*, May 17, 1890; "Base Ball Notes," *Milwaukee Sentinel*, Jun 8, 1890; "Amateur Base Ball Notes," *Milwaukee Sentinel*, Jun 26, 1890; "Among Amateur Ball Players," *Milwaukee Sentinel*, Jun 30, 1890; "Milwaukee, Wisconsin News," *Cleveland Gazette*, May 17, 1890; "General Sporting Small Talk," *Milwaukee Sentinel*, Jul 3, 1890.

Club Rosters, 1858–1900

The rosters in this section are organized first by year, then by state, and finally by city or town. This arrangement has the advantage of showing how black baseball grew, or in some instances contracted, from season to season and place to place. The individuals listed include all known players, managers, owners, and even scorers associated with the clubs.

1858

New York

Hensons (Jamaica, NY)

William Johnson, c
Robert Henson, p
John Van Wyck, 2b
Hanke, 1b
George Anthony, 3b
J. Anthony, rf
Ferris, ss
Elias Wilmore, cf
Jacob Hewlett, lf
William Austin, Team Scorer

1859

New York

Hensons (Jamaica, NY)

William Johnson, c
Robert Henson, p
John Van Wyck, 2b
Hanke, 1b
George Anthony, 3b
James Anthony, rf
Ferris, ss
Elias Wilmore, cf
Jacob Hewlett, lf
William Austin, Team Scorer

Unknowns (Weeksville, NY)

John Poole, p
H. Smith, c
J. Smith, ss
Ricks, 1b
Joseph Thompson, 3b
Albert Thompson, rf
V. Thompson, lf
C. W. Anderson, 2b
Charles Johnson, lf
William Johnson, c

Durant, rf / p
Jacob T. Baker, ss

1860

New York

Hensons (Jamaica, NY)

William Johnson, c
Robert Henson, p
John Van Wyck, 2b
Hanke, 1b
George Anthony, 3b
Joseph Anthony, rf
Ferris, ss
Elias Wilmore, cf
Jacob Hewlett, lf
William Austin, Team Scorer

1862

New York

Monitors (Brooklyn, NY)

Edward Dudley, 1b
W. Cook, rf
Williams, ss
William Marshall, 3b
George Abrams, p
W. G. Brown, c
Charles Cook, lf
Orater, 2b
James Abrams, cf
Jones, Team Scorer

Unknowns (Weeksville, NY)

John Poole, 3b
V. Thompson, lf
Thomas Wright, 2b
Joseph Thompson, p
J. Smith, cf
William Johnson, c
Albert Thompson, 1b

Durant, rf
David V. W. Harvey, ss
Jacob T. Baker, ss / Team Scorer

1866

New York

Fearless (Utica, NY)

Samuel Freeman, ss
Peter Tonssant, cf
Charles Peterson, p
Arlington Denike, 1b
John E. Lippin, 2b
Thomas Lippin, 3b
Robert Van Alstine, rf
T. Denor, lf
Nathan Green, lf
Caesar Jackson, c
Sarralt Logan, 2b / lf
Thomas Johnson
Peter Freeman
J. H. Freeman
Albert Freeman
C. W. Anderson
Reuben R. Lippin
Joseph Gordon
Peter Feeler
Charles Hedges
Samuel Dove
Wallace W. Denike, Secretary
Charles H. Lewis, Vice President
Theodore Freeman, President

Pennsylvania

Monrovians (Harrisburg, PA)

Horatio Burton, c
David M. Robinson, c
William Lane, 2b
George W. Sanders, cf
Joseph G. Pople, ss
William Gray, p

Daniel R. Chester, 3b
D. Burton, lf
J. Williams, rf
D. Lane, 1b
F. W. Harris
John Chilton, lf / c
George W. Scott, cf
Alexander T. Harris
John Recy
John Fayettes
George Galbraith

National Excelsiors (Philadelphia, PA)

Frank Jones, 3b
Henry Price, 2b / lf
Harry J. Clark, 2b / p
Pliny L. Locke, cf
George Howard Wilson, cf
Thomas J. Irons, rf / cf
Thomas Wheeler, p
Joseph Brister, rf
James Bracy, ss
Edward Thomas
William Stout
Joseph Rogers
James H. Francis, President / 2b
Francis Wood, Vice-President
James Fields Needham, Rec. Sec.
Edwin John, Cor. Secretary
Daniel Holden, Treasurer
Frisby Stevens, Director
George R. Scott, Director
John Bruce, Director / c

Pythian (Philadelphia, PA)

John Cannon, p
James Sparrow, ss
John Graham, c / lf
Jefferson Cavens, 1b
R. R. Calbert, 1b
Spencer Hanley, c /cf
Joshua Adkins, 3b
Andrew J. Jones, 3b
Raymond J. Burr
William Morris, rf
James H. Francis, 2b
Francis Wood
Charles Thomas
Octavius Catto, 2b / Manager
William Walker
Frederick Walker
R. J. Barr
John L. Webster
William Taylor
George Howard Wilson
Jacob C. White, Secretary
James Whipper Purnell, President

1867

Illinois

Dexter Star (Springfield, IL)

Charles Parker, President / rf
Moses McCloud, Vice President / ss
Henry Dyer, Treasurer / p
Alfred Dyer, 1b / Captain
Richard Dyer, c
Dennis Williams, 2b
George Jenkins, lf
Napoleon Whitfield, / cf
George Williams, rf

New Jersey

Resolutes (Camden, NJ)

Charles Davis, c
John S. Dutton, p
William T. Emory, 2b
John H. Williams
Freeman Gould, ss
Alexander T. Harris, cf
James Dutton, ss
John G. Kelsh, 1b
R. J. Marshall, rf
Alfred Rich, 3b
John T. Streets, rf
Aldnige Rowen, Manager
Thomas Frisbee, lf / President

New York

Monitors (Brooklyn, NY)

Isaac Heady, lf
H. Brown, c
James Williams, p
F. W. Hicks, 1b
Samuel Anderson, 2b
Lewis, ss
Fred Jackson, 2b
Cornelius Henry, cf
Samuel Jackson, rf
W. G. Brown, Secretary
D. J. Hunter, Corr. Secretary
Andrew Dosen, Manager

Fearless (Utica, NY)

Samuel Freeman, ss
Peter Tonssant, c / cf
Charles Peterson, p / 2b
Arlington Denike, 1b / Captain
John Lippin, 2b
Thomas Lippin, 3b
Robert Van Alstine, rf
T. Denor, lf
Nathan R. Green, lf
Caesar Jackson, c
Sarralt Logan, 2b / lf
Peter Feeler
Samuel Dove

Reuben R. Lippin
Thomas Johnson
P. Freeman
J. H. Freeman
Albert Freeman
Charles Hedges
C. W. Anderson
Joseph Gordon
James H. Washington
G. S. Thompson
W. W. Denike, Secretary
Charles H. Lewis, Vice President
Theodore Freeman, President

Uniques (Williamsburg, Brooklyn, NY)

Morse, cf / 3b
James Furman (Fairman), p
Hardy Mobley, c
L. Peterson, 1b
C. W. Anderson, 2b / ss
Bowman, 3b
D. J. Mobley, ss
Farmer, lf
William Prince, rf
Kennard, cf
William Bunce, lf
Peter T. Jewell, rf
James Davis, 2b
R. H. Miner, lf
Ira P. Sayton, Manager

North Carolina

George Z. French (Wilmington, NC)

First Nine

Robert H. Brown, p / Secretary
J. H. Brown, c / Treasurer
James A. King, 1b / Corr. Secretary
George Mabson, 3b
William Kellogg, 2b
McCoy, ss
William H. Nash, rf
James Merrick, lf
A. H. Galloway, cf
James Hostler, 3b
Jackson, rf
E. McBride, lf

Second Nine (Mutuals)

Joseph Green, c
Edgar Miller, p
James Dry, 1b / Vice President
Brown, 2b
Charles Mallette, 3b
William Sullivan, ss
Joseph Wingate, rf
Francis Payne, cf
Mark Johnson, lf
Reed, ss
Lewis, 1b

George M. Arnold, c
Allan Evans, President

Pennsylvania

Monrovians (Harrisburg, PA)

Horatio Burton, c
David M. Robinson, c
William Lane, 2b
George W. Saunders, p / cf
Joseph G. Pople, ss
William Gray, p
Daniel R. Chester, 3b
David Burton, lf
J. Williams, rf
David Lane, 1b
John Chilton, lf / c
George Scott, cf
James G. Thompson, c
Isaac Taylor, Sr., Director
John Fayettes, Director
Charles H. Cann, Director
G. W. Higgins, Director
Jacob C. Christie, Director
Charles H. Vance, Director
Frank W. Harris, Team Scorer
Alexander T. Harris, Secretary
John Recy, Secretary
George Galbraith, Secretary / Scorer

National Excelsiors (Philadelphia, PA)

Frank Jones, 3b
Henry Price, 2b / lf
James H. Francis, 2b
Joshua Adkins, ss / c
George Scott, c
E. R. Hutchinson, lf
Harry J. Clark, 2b / p
Thomas J. Irons, rf / cf
Thomas Wheeler, p
Joseph Brister, rf
James Bracy, ss
Jessie Glascow, 2b / 1b
George H. Wilson, Corr. Secretary

Pythians (Philadelphia, PA)

John Cannon, p
George Brown, p
James Sparrow, ss
John Graham, c / lf
Jefferson Cavens, 1b
Spencer Hanley, c /cf
Joshua Adkins, 3b / c
Andrew J. Jones, 3b
Raymond J. Burr
William Morris, rf / cf
James Jenkins, cf
Francis J. R .Jones, lf
Pliny L. Locke, cf
James H. Francis
Francis Wood

R. R. Calbert, 1b
George Howard Wilson, lf
William Walker, cf
Frederick Walker, rf
F. Anderson, 3b
William Taylor
William H. Minton, Team Scorer
Charles Thomas, Substitute
Octavius Catto, 2b / Manager
Jacob C. White ("Jake"), Scorer / Secretary
William C. Bolivar, Asst. Secretary
James W. Purnell, President

Actives (West Chester, PA)

William L. Spriggs, cf
Pitison, 2b
Abram Brown, 1b
William C. Price, c
Cusimingo, lf
Nathaniel Tyndale, ss
Henry Smith, cf
Ross Proctor, rf
Jonathan Bell, 3b

Virginia

Tecumseh (Alexandria, VA)

J. Barnes, c
S. Thompson, p
J. Davis, ss
Robert Webster, 1b
John Lane, 2b
C. Copler, 3b
F. Hopper, lf
A. Burton, cf
E. Seaton, rf
Robert S. Mitchell
C. Seaton, Scorer

Lone Stars (Alexandria, VA)

Robert B. Hopkins
John Seaton
Erastus Green
William Miller
Traverse B. Pinn
Charles Seales
Lewis Hurley
James Thompson
E. E. White
Edgar Beckley
Lafayette Windsor
Amos Payne

Washington, DC

Alerts (Washington, DC)

Robert Green, 1b
Edward L. Savoy, rf
Frank Stewart, lf
Robert Webster, 3b
Charles R. Douglass, 2b
Warner H. A. Wormley, cf

Robert E. Taliaferro, c
John Henson, p
Thomas Barlow (A. Smith), ss
William H. Miller, Scorer
James E. Carter, p / Secretary
Samuel James Datcher, Secretary
James Green, Assist. Secretary
Louis Bell, Corr. Secretary
George F. T. Cook, p / President

Athletics (Washington, DC)

J. Jefferson, 2b
George Garrett, rf
William Triplett, cf
Thomas Gray, lf
George Dunmore, 3b / Captain
John H. Brooks, c
James Triplett, 1b
Taylor Triplett, ss
Benjamin Butler, c
John Lane, 2b
John Henson, p
H. Dorsey, rf
Randolph Bowie, cf
H. C. Galloway, lf
George Park Costin
L. Butler, c
Samuel N. Adams, Scorer
Dave Garrett, Team President

Atlantics (Washington, DC)

George Briscoe, c
John Clinton, p
William Campbell, 1b
S. Coleman, 2b
Skill, ss
Millekin, rf
Sandy Hawkins, lf
John Keys, 3b
George Fairfax, cf

Awkward (Washington, DC)

James Curtis, c
Joseph Jackson, p
Robert F. Waters, 1b
R. Jackson, rf
Thomas Sorrell, lf
Delaney, ss
K. Brown, cf
John H. Lawson, 2b
Harrison, 3b

Monumental (Washington, DC)

H. C. Galloway, lf / Manager
James Triplett, 1b
John H. Brooks, c / 1b
S. Thompson, 2b
George E. Landrick, ss / p
Robert Waters, p
R. H. Miner, 3b / rf
Elliott, rf / cf

J. Nelson, cf
George Johnson, ss / rf / lf
Hamilton D. Cole, 3b
James W. Gibbs, lf
Whitney, rf
Taylor, ss
L. Thomas, 3b
L. Washington, 2b
Lewis Davis, cf
Lomack, cf / lf
Gurden Snowden, 2b
Henry C. Bolden, 3b
John Lane, 2b
George Stanard, Scorer
William Talbott, Scorer

Mutuals (Washington, DC)

James Harry Smith, c
H. Brown, 1b
William H. Harris, 3b
Horace W. Parke, 2b
J. H. W. Burley, p
Thomas Gray, lf
David A. Fisher, cf
Thomas Barlow, rf
Richard Matthews, p
James Whiggs, ss
George Anderson, 2b
Daniel C. Chew
T. R. Hawkins
Henry F. Grant
A. I. Augusta
Dr. A. W. Tucker
Dr. Charles B. Purvis
George D. Johnson, Secretary
James Carter, Scorer / Assistant Secretary

Picked Nine (Washington, DC)

Harry Johnson, ss
Taylor, 2b
S. Thompson, 1b
William M. Williams, p
Charles Parke, rf
Berckson, 3b
Horace W. Park, lf
George Tucker, cf
K. Brown, c

1868

Kansas

Unions (Lawrence, KS)

Lindsey, 2b
E. Matthews, p
R. Berry, c
William Harris, 1b
James Gross, rf
David Kinsey, lf
Wilson, cf

Hunter, 3b
James Barker, ss / Captain

Independents (Leavenworth, KS)

Tilman, c
Field, p
Green, 1b
Rice, 2b
J. Smith, 3b
Young, ss
A. Smith, rf
Perkins, lf
Robinson, cf

New Jersey

Orientals (Bergen, NJ)

John Mitchell, c
Anthony Jackson, p
Dubois H. Hallack, ss
A. Johnston, 1b
J. Brown, 2b
John Hamilton, 3b
David Green, lf
W. Johnston, cf
James Johnson, rf

Liberty Club (Jersey City, NJ)

Isaac Walker, President
Robert L. McClain, Secretary
George Gale, Captain

Oneidas (Jersey City, NJ)

Samuel Jackson
Peter P. Lewis
Benjamin Cisco
George B. Feeks
Anthony Jackson
Percy Benham
George Walker
Adam Thompson
Charles Schenck
John Williams
Rodney Simon
William Cisco
Arthur Jackson
J. W. Green

New York

Invincibles (Buffalo, NY)

Charles P. Lee, p
Edward Simpson, c
Edward Crosby, 1b
Richard Kinney, 2b
Charles H. Butler, 3b
Albert D. Thompson, lf / Treasurer
D. Jackson, cf / Director
James H. Washington, rf
George Leggett, President
Frank A. Leonard, Vice President

Thomas A. Wilson, Secretary
C. Williams, Director
William Bartlett, Director
A. Briggs, Director

Heavy Hitters (Canajoharie, NY)

Thomas Miller, lf
Brumley Hoke, p
Rans Jackson, 3b
A. Cunningham, cf
T. Harris, c
W. Mosby, rf
John Miller, ss
Charles Walrod, 1b
William Jackson, 3b
Spencer Clausen, rf
A. Hamilton, cf
Emory Skinner, 1b / c
J. Hoke, Team Scorer

Cataract House (Niagara, NY)

Edwin Jeffrey, c
William Gray, p
John Murphy, Jr., ss
Manly, 1b
Elison, 2b
A. D. Taylor, 3b
Brown, lf
William Reynolds, cf
George Cole, rf
Stoway, Scorer

International House (Niagara, NY)

Johnson, ss
Joseph Gordon, 3b
G. Smith, lf
Williams, 1b
H. Hawkins, c
Sartee, rf
F. Shaw, cf
Samuel Francis, 2b
Steward, p
A. Wells, Scorer

Fearless (Utica, NY)

Samuel Freeman, ss
Peter Tonssant, c / cf
Charles Peterson, p / 2b
Arlington Denike, 1b / Captain
John Lippin, 2b
Thomas Lippin, 3b
Robert Van Alstine, rf
George Tucker, cf / ss
T. Denor, lf
Nathan R. Green, lf
Sarralt Logan, 2b / lf
Peter Feeler
Samuel Dove
Reuben R. Lippin
Thomas Johnson

Peter Freeman
J. H. Freeman
Albert Freeman
Charles Hedges
C. W. Anderson
Joseph Gordon
James H. Washington
G. S. Thompson
Charles H. Lewis, Vice President
Theodore Freeman, President

North Carolina

Amateurs (Wilmington, NC)

J. P. Howe, p
Ezekiel Chadwick, rf
Harris, lf
Moore, 3b
Martin, ss
Gyer, cf
H. P. Howe, 2b
Mackey, 1b
McCoy, c

Colored Nine (Wilmington, NC)

William Howe, 2b
George Arnold, p
Davis, 1b
Solomon Wash, c
Charles Mallette, rf
Johnson, 3b
Richard Stove, cf
Lewis, lf
Jackson, ss

George Z. French (Wilmington, NC)

First Nine

Allen Evans, President
Robert H. Brown, p / Secretary
J. H. Brown, c / Treasurer
James A. King, 1b / Corr. Secretary
George Mabson, 3b
William Kellogg, 2b
McCoy, ss
William H. Nash, rf
James Merrick, lf
A. H. Carraway, cf
James Hostler, 3b
W. H. Bradley, lf
James Hostler, c
Jackson, rf
E. McBride, lf

Second Nine (Mutuals)

Joseph Green, c
Edgar Miller, p
James Dry, 1b / Vice President
Brown, 2b
Charles Mallette, 3b
William Sullivan, ss

Joseph Wingate, rf
Francis Payne, cf
Mark Johnson, lf
Hezekiah Reed, ss
Lewis, 1b
Edgar Miller 2b
George M. Arnold, c
Allan Evans, President

Ohio

Creoles (Cincinnati, OH)

J. A. Washington, p
William "Bill" Smith, c
Jameson, rf
Caleb Calloway, lf
Myers, cf
Kooner, 3b
Jonathan Tosspot, 1b
Alexander Morris, 2b
Fountain Lewis, ss
W. W. Watson, p
Lewis P. Brooks, rf / p
Michael Clark
Elliott Clark
Wilson Bates
Henry Hunster
John Dixon

Pennsylvania

Douglass (Columbia, PA)

William Jones, c
George Cisco, p
William Kelley, 1b / 2b
Walters, ss
William Jackson, 2b
William Reynolds, cf
James Moore, lf
Michael Moore, ss
Laurell, ss
Abram Martin, rf
Neth Jordan, rf
Simon Malson, 3b
T. Stafford, Team Scorer

Monrovians (Harrisburg, PA)

David M. Robinson, c
Ed Roberson, 1b
D. Burton, ss
George W. Saunders, p
Daniel R. Chester, 1b
Joseph Pople, ss
William Lane, 2b
D. Lane, 3b
John Chilton, lf / c
George W. Scott, cf
Horatio Burton, rf / c
J. Williams, 3b
Samuel A. Burton, rf / 3b
David Burton, 3b / lf

Samuel W. Pople, ss
William Gray
Isaac Taylor
Alex Dennee
John Fayettes
George Galbraith, Team Scorer
Alexander T. Harris
F. W. Harris, Team Scorer

Pythians (Philadelphia, PA)

First Nine

John Cannon, p
John Graham, c / lf
Jefferson Cavens, 1b
Francis L. R. Jones
Spencer Hanley, c /cf
James Sparrow, c / ss
Joshua Adkins, 3b
William Walker, cf
Octavius Valentine Catto, 2b / Manager
A. J. Harris, Team Scorer
Charles Thomas, Team President

Second Nine

Raymond J. Burr
Andrew J. Jones
Frederick Walker, lf
Richard E. D. Vennings
David Knight
Charles W. Thomas
Etienne C. Vidal, rf
Augustus Hazzard
James Ash
James Whipper Purnell, Captain

Third Nine

Joseph Minton
Jacob C. White, Sr.
Horatio Francis
Edman M. Burrell
William H. Minton
Henry Boyer
Thomas Charnook
Morris Brown, Jr.
Horace Owens
Thaddeus Manning
Jacob R. Ballard, Captain

Fourth Nine

Robert M. Adger
William C. Bolivar
Beverly D. May
Joseph S. White
Cyrus B. Miller
Julius Boisden
Cobin Taylor
Woley Baseone
William Chain
Tom Morris
Henry Lee
Charles Selsey

Herdic House Independents
(Williamsport, PA)

Samuel Cain, c
Perry Summers, cf
Isaac L. Hamilton, 1b
William T. Emory, ss
Alexander Offord, 3b
Richard Mitchell, rf
W. Hamilton, p
Charles Johnson, lf
Thomas Lans, 3b
C. H. Nichols
Charles E. Lloyd, Scorer
Enoch Emory, Manager

South Carolina

Ashleys (Charleston, SC)

Thomas S. Dennison
James Bruce
James M. Matthews
Leander Gibbs
Benjamin Martin
W. M. G. Strong
James F. Harrison
G. M. Simons
Larry S. Dennison
Prince Smalls
A .T. Deas
M. Richardson
R. E .Savage
J. B. Spencer
James Lee
G. W. Green
Julius Jacobs
R. Middleton
J. G. Brown
C. Mills
R. W. Matthews
John Patrick
Edward Jennings
E. C. Tucker

Washington, DC

Alerts (Washington, DC)

Robert Green, 1b
Edward L. Savoy, rf
Frank Stewart, lf
Robert Webster, 3b
Charles R. Douglass, 2b
Warner H. A. Wormley, cf
Robert E. Taliaferro, c
John Henson, p
Thomas Barlow (A. Smith), ss
Louis A. Bell
William H. Miller, Scorer

Mutuals (Washington, DC)

James Harry Smith, c
H. Brown, 1b
William H. Harris, 3b

Horace W. Parke, 2b
J. H. W. Burley, p
R. Gray, lf
David A. Fisher, cf
Thomas Barlow (A. Smith), rf
Richard Matthews, p
James Whiggs, ss
George Anderson, 2b

1869

Illinois

Dexter Star (Springfield, IL)

Charles Parker, President / rf
Moses McCloud, Vice President / ss
Henry Dyer, Treasurer / p
Alfred Dyer, 1b / Captain
Richard Dyer, c
Dennis Williams, 2b
George Jenkins, lf
Napoleon Whitfield, / cf
George Williams, rf
Charles Morgan, Scorer

New Jersey

Oriental (Bergen, NJ)

John Mitchell, c
Anthony Jackson, p
Dubois H. Hallack, ss
A. Johnston, 1b
J. Brown, 2b
John Hamilton, 3b
David Green, lf
W. Johnston, cf
James Johnson, rf

Oneidas (Jersey City, NJ)

Samuel Jackson
Peter P. Lewis
Benjamin Cisco
George B. Feeks
Anthony Jackson
Percy Benham
George Walker
Adam Thompson
Charles Schenck
John Williams

New York

Unique (Brooklyn, NY)

Bowman, 1b
James Furman, 3b
Heady Mobley, 3b
George Banks, lf
Skidmore, rf
Ward, p
Binghorn, cf
Raymond, 2b
D. Mobley, c

Invincibles (Buffalo, NY)

Charles P. Lee, p
Edward Simpson, c
Dean Wilson, ss
Edward Crosby, 1b
Richard Kinney, 2b
Charles H. Butler, 3b
Albert D. Thompson, lf / Treasurer
D. Jackson, cf / Director
James H. Washington, rf
George A. Leggett, President
Frank A. Leonard, Vice President
Thomas A. Wilson, Secretary
C. Williams, Director
William Bartlett, Director
A. Briggs, Director

Heavy Hitters
(Canajoharie, NY)

Thomas Miller, lf
Brumley Hoke, p
R. Jackson, 3b
A. Cunningham, cf
T. Harris, c
W. Mosby, rf
John Miller, ss
Charles Walrod, 1b / p
W. Jackson, 3b
Spencer Clausen, rf
A. Hamilton, cf
Emory Skinner, 1b
J. Hoke, 2b / Team Scorer

Lone Star (Harlem, NY)

James Williams, ss
R. Williams, 2b
A. Nichols, c
Jacob T. Baker, cf
James Miller, 1b
Charles Williams, lf
Murphy, rf
M. Williams, 3b
James Stephenson, p

Fearless Black Stockings
(Utica, NY)

Samuel Freeman, ss
Peter Tonssant, c / cf
Charles Peterson, p / 2b
Arlington Denike, 1b
John Lippin, 2b
Thomas Lippin, 3b
Robert Van Alstine, rf
George Tucker, cf / ss
T. Denor, lf
Nathan R. Green, lf
Sarralt Logan, 2b / lf
H. C. Falling, Team Scorer
Peter Feeler
Reuben R. Lippin
Samuel Dove
Thomas Johnson

P. Freeman
J. H. Freeman
Albert Freeman
Charles Hedges
C. W. Anderson
Joseph Gordon
James H. Washington
G. S. Thompson
Charles H. Lewis, Vice President
Theodore Freeman, President

George Z. French
(Wilmington, NC)

First Nine

Robert H. Brown, p / Secretary
J. H. Brown, c / Treasurer
James A. King, 1b / Corr. Secretary
George Mabson, 3b
William Kellogg, 2b
McCoy, ss
William H. Nash, rf
James Merrick, lf
A. H. Galloway, cf
James Hostler, 3b
Jackson, rf
E. McBride, lf

Second Nine (Mutuals)

Joseph Green, c
Edgar Miller, p
James Dry, 1b / Vice President
J. H. Brown, 2b
Charles Mallett, 3b
William Sullivan, ss
Joseph Wingate, rf
Francis Payne, cf
Mark Johnson, lf
Reed, ss
Lewis, 1b
George M. Arnold, c/Secretary
Allan Evans, President

Ohio

Western Unions (Cincinnati, OH)

J. A. Washington, p
William "Bill" Smith, c
Jameson, rf
Caleb Calloway, lf
Myers, cf
Kooner, 3b
Jonathan Tosspot, 1b
Alexander Morris, 2b
Fountain Lewis, ss
W. W. Watson, p
Lewis P. Brooks, rf / p
Elliott Clark
Michael Clark
Wilson Bates
Henry Hunster
John Dixon
Peter H. Clark, President

Black Stockings (Newton, OH)

R. Wadkins, cf
W. Mills, rf
U. Grant, lf
R. Wadkins, ss
M. Wadkins, 1b
C. Wadkins, 2b
Samuel Mills, 3b
W. Greigs, p
G. Wadkins, c
Matt Dively, Scorer

Pennsylvania

Monrovians (Harrisburg, PA)

David M. Robinson, c
Ed Roberson, 1b
George W. Saunders, p
Daniel R. Chester, 1b
Joseph Pople, ss
William Lane, 2b
D. Lane, 3b
John Chilton, lf / c
George Scott, cf
Thomas Scott, 3b
Horatio Burton, rf / c
J. Williams, 3b
Samuel A. Burton, rf / 3b
D. Burton, ss / 3b / lf
Samuel W. Pople, ss
William Gray
Alexander T. Harris
Alex W. Dennee
George Galbraith Team Secretary / Team Scorer

Stars (Harrisburg, PA)

Charles H. Brown, c
George W. Saunders, p
William Butler, ss
William Gray, 1b
Isaac Taylor, 2b
George Scott, 3b
J. Edwards, lf
William Dorsey, cf
William Stewart, rf
James Butler, President
Richard Snowden, Vice President

Actives (Mechanicsburg, PA)

William H. Johnson, c
Thomas Williams, p
Scipio Smith, ss
Edward Gordon, 1b
Clines, 2b
John Bowls, 3b
Charles Price, lf
Robert Claton, rf
Slamter, cf

Pythians (Philadelphia, PA)

John Cannon, p
Octavius Valentine Catto, 2b

H. J. Clark, c
George Waters, 3b
James Sparrow, ss
R. R. Calbert, 1b
Joshua Adkins, lf
Spencer Hanley, cf
William Walker, rf
Jefferson Cavens, 1b

Washington, DC

Alerts (Washington, DC)

H. C. Bolden, lf / c
Gurden Snowden, ss
Warren Dent, 2b
James H. Washington, c
J. Nelson, p
Randolph Bowie, cf
P. Nelson, rf
S. Thompson, 3b / Scorer
Joseph Bland, 1b
George H. Richardson, lf
Charles R. Douglass, p / rf
James Whiggs, 3b
George Johnson, Scorer

Mutuals (Washington, DC)

John Tyler, 2b
James Harry Smith, p
K. Brown, c
James Whiggs, 3b
Horace W. Parke, lf
George Garrett, cf
Josiah H. Settle, lf
Jacobs, ss
Thomas Barlow (A. Smith), rf
H. Brown, 1b
Charles F. Bruce, Scorer

1870

Illinois

Blue Stockings (Chicago, IL)

Robert Johnson, 2b
Zacharias Daniels, ss
George Brown, c
William P. Johnson, p / 2b
Henry Hampton, lf
Charles Wing, p
Henry Smith, cf
Frank Adams, rf
T. Brown, 3b
Carter, 1b
William Berry, rf / Team Scorer
Henry P. Hall, manager

Hunters (Chicago, IL)

John Sanders, 1b / p
Simon Johnson, lf
Thomas Hamilton, 3b / 2b
John Tyler, lf
T. Marshall, c

J. Briddle, lf
George Gray, rf
Charles Deveney, rf / ss
John E. Shaw, cf / Captain
Henry Beauford

Rapids (Chicago, IL)

S. Taylor, rf / lf / cf
John Simms, rf
Giles Powell, 3b
Benjamin Cleary, 2b
R. Moody, p / 1b
H. Coombs, cf
William Speed, p
Carey Jackson, 3b / ss
J. Cole, rf
E. Brown, c
J. Moor

Pink Stockings (Rockford, IL)

Reuben Armstrong, lf
Joseph Graham, 1b
John Williams, rf
Henry C. Winn, 2b
Wright, 2b
Manuel Abraham, cf
Newton Pender, 3b
Kingman, p
Thomas, c

Dexter Star (Springfield, IL)

Charles Parker, President / rf
Moses McCloud, Vice President / ss
Henry Dyer, Treasurer / p
Alfred Dyer, 1b / Captain
Richard Dyer, c
Dennis Williams, 2b
George Jenkins, lf
Napoleon Whitfield, / cf
George Williams, rf
Charles Morgan, Scorer

Kansas

Rock Creek Valleys (Clinton, KS)

Peterson, 3b / p
Dunn, 2b
W. Smith, c
Dillard, 1b / c
Bennett, cf /ss / Captain
Winfrey, p / 2b
Watkins, rf / cf
Smith, lf / 3b
Gregg, ss
McGee, lf
L. King, c
C. King, p
Thompson, 2b
Hill, rf
Dent, c

Eagles (Lawrence, KS)

E. Matthews, p
Frank Thomas, c
Anthony Porter, 1b/2b
J. Burnside, rf
James Gross, 3b
R. Berry, cf
J. Jenkins, lf
Phil Smith, 2b/ ss
James Hoyt, ss
James Barker, 2b
T. W. Young, 1b
Harvey Pilcher, 2b
George Wilson, cf
Harribal Lett, rf
William Harris, 1b
Harrison Banks, cf
David Kinsey, lf
Thomas Berry, Secretary
T. J. Banks, President

Friendship (Ottawa, KS)

Bell, c
Harris, p
Sear, 1b
Clark, 2b
Wright, 3b
Gross, 3b
Phillips, rf
Ransom, cf
Ewing, lf

Kentucky

Starlights (Covington, KY)

Isaac Black, President
William J. Hamilton, Secretary
George W. Durgin, Treasurer
Fred A. Williams, Captain
R. D. Cross
C. W. Bell
J. H. Nixon
Howard Haggard
John Thomas
William Page
Charles Morgan
William Coleman

Massachusetts

Resolutes (Boston, MA)

Banfield, ss
A. Churchill, 2b
William H. Cruckendle, cf / ss
M. T. Gregory, p
Paul Humphrey, 1b
Emanuel Molineaux, 3b
D. E. Sheppard, lf
William Taylor, c
James Taylor, rf
William Lee, cf
Peter Latimer, cf
William H. Walker, cf

H. B. Chapman, cf
Frank Johnson, 2b
Benjamin Lancaster, 2b

New Jersey

Oriental (Bergen, NJ)

John Mitchell, c
Anthony Jackson, p
Dubois H. Hallack, ss
A. Johnston, 1b
J. Brown, 2b
John Hamilton, 3b
David J. Green, lf
W. Johnston, cf
James Johnson, rf

Keystone (Jersey City, NJ)

Percy F. Benham, cf / Captain
Edward Wales, rf / p
Thomas E. Rias, lf
Isaiah Sampson, ss
Charles Benham, 3b
Garrison, c
Charles Wanzer, 1b / Vice President
Joseph C. Rias, Secretary
George Abrams, rf Corresponding
    Secretary
George Gale, Treasurer
H. Pigerman, Director
William Sampson, ss /Director
George Walker, 2b / Director
DuBois Hallack, President

New York

Oceanic (Brooklyn, NY)

P. Stevens
George W. Batum
Samuel Corneilson
L. Jackson
H. Brown, c
James Williams, p
J. Coburn
S. Barnes
John Coleman

Invincibles (Buffalo, NY)

Charles P. Lee, p
Edward Simpson, c
Dean Wilson, ss
Edward Crosby, 1b
Richard Kinney, 2b
Charles H. Butler, 3b
D. Jackson, cf /
James H. Washington, rf
Thomas A. Wilson, Secretary
Albert D. Thompson, lf / Treasurer
Frank A. Leonard, Vice President
George A. Leggett, President
C. Williams, Director
William Bartlett, Director
A. Briggs, Director

Fly Aways (Gloversville, NY)

Charles Walrod, 2b
T. Harris, cf
Brumley Hoke, p
A. Cunningham, 3b
George Moore, lf
Charles Jackson, ss
John Miller, rf
W. Jackson, c
H. Smith, 1b

Wide Awakes (Johnston, NY)

Charles Walrod, 1b / p
Brumley Hoke, ss
Charles Leggins, 2b
Ricks, c
Frank Stewart, cf / c
A. McKinney, lf
Arthur Smith, 3b
Samuel Winnie, rf
Rans Jackson, p
William Frank, cf / ss

Original Georgia Minstrels (New York, NY)

A. L. Smith
G. W. Smith
Bob Height
George W. Danforth
Aaron Banks
C. M. Marshall
J. E. Johnson
Len Johnson
Charles Crusoe
C. Arlington
John W. Wilson
George A. Skillings
William D. Porter
J. Manning
Charles B. Hicks, Manager

Hannibals (Troy, NY)

George Edward Harden, 3b
Eric Young, 2b
La Tona, p
Hall, ss
Charles Oliver, 1b
T. Demery, rf / p
John Harden, c
Henry Oliver, cf
M. Snowden, lf

Unions (Saratoga Springs, NY)

Alex Brown, President/ Treasurer
D. Henry Granger, Vice President
John M. Van Dyke, Secretary
Frank Smith, Captain William Clemens
Edward Anthony
Phillip Alexandie
Frank Sanford
Charles Peterson

Fearless (Utica, NY)

Samuel Freeman, ss
Peter Tonssant, c
Charles Peterson, p
Arlington C. Denike, 1b / Captain
John Lippin, 2b
Thomas Lippin, 3b
Joshua Atkins, rf
Fred Jackson, rf
Harry Moss,
James Pell, cf
Galway, lf
Sarralt Logan, 2b / lf
Thomas J. Thompson, Team Scorer

Empires (Utica, NY)

Charles Jackson, c / Captain
George Baker, 1b
George Edward Harden, 2b
John Jacobs, 3b
Eli Atkins, cf
William "Will" Jackson, rf
Ed Husbands, lf
Walter Sherman, ss
Frank Pell, p

Light Hitters (Middletown, NY)

Samuel Hasbrook, c
John B. Ellis, p
Gray, ss / c
W. Hasbrook, 1b
Theodore Jarvis, 2b
Samuel Jackson, 3b / c
Lewis Warfield, cf
Milton Jarvis, cf
Charles E. Waterford, rf

North Carolina

Cape Fear Mutuals (Wilmington, NC)

First Nine

Henry Nash, c
Frank Thomas, p
William Barker, L. B.
Charles Matthews, 2b
Maclison Branch, 3b
George L. Stewart, ss
Hilliard Hill, lf
Jackson Winslow, cf / Captain
George Joiner, rf
George L. Stewart, President

Second Nine

McKeller
Edgar Miller
Robinson
Robert H. Brown
J. H. Brown
Edward Davis
"Unknown"
Tobias Kelley

Ohio

Muffers (Ironton, OH)

Jackson Page, c
George Tolliver, cf
John Evans, p
William Pogue, ss
Calvin, 2b
Walter Gray, lf
Charles Scott, ss
Lawson, 1b
French Pogue, 3b / Captain
V. O. Harvey, cf

Black Stockings (Newton, OH)

R. Wadkins, cf
W. Mills, rf
U. Grant, lf
R. Wadkins, ss
M. Wadkins, 1b
C. Wadkins, 2b
S. Mills, 3b
W. Greigs, p
G. Wadkins, c
Matt Dively, Scorer

Independents (Portsmouth, OH)

Wilson Minor
Joseph J. Minor
Lloyd Henson
Henry Baker
Frank Johnson
J. H. Scott
Lilly Ross
Frank White
Henry Holliday
Charles Peen

Pennsylvania

Geary (Harrisburg, PA)

T. Spriggs, c
E. Brown, p
J. Cook, 1b
James Murray, ss
W. Wallace, 2b
T. Stewart, 3b
J. Paton, lf
D. Brown, cf
C. Jones, rf

Monrovians (Harrisburg, PA)

David M. Robinson, c
Ed Roberson, 1b
George W. Sanders, p
Daniel R. Chester, 1b
Joseph Pople, ss
William Lane, 2b
D. Lane, 3b
John Chilton, lf / c
Thomas Scott, cf
George R. Scott, 3b
Horatio Burton, rf / c

J. Williams, 3b
Samuel A. Burton, rf / 3b
D. Burton, ss / 3b / lf
Samuel W. Pople, ss
Alex W. Dennee

Rough and Ready (Harrisburg, PA)

Coleman, c
H. Jackson, p
J. Miller, 1b
James Barton, ss
J .Smith, 2b
J. Edwards, 3b
S. Burles, lf
A. Coleman, cf
W. Faucet, rf

Stars (Harrisburg, PA)

Charles H. Brown, c
George Saunders, p
William Butler, ss
William Gray, 1b
Isaac Taylor, 2b
George R. Scott, 3b
Edwards, lf
William Dorsey, cf
William Stewart, rf
James Butler, President
Richard Snowden, Vice President

Cedar Rapids (Pittsburgh, PA)

B. S. Gray, President
Charles H. Davis, Secretary
Milton Winn, Treasurer
Judson Taylor, Captain

Washington, DC

Metropolitans (Washington, DC)

R. H. Robinson, President
R. R. Brown, Vice President
M. L. Robinson, Recording Secretary
G. W. Smith, Corresponding Secretary
Arthur E. Payne, Treasurer
Nathaniel Addison, Director
Charles Johnson, Director
J. R. Brooks, Director
Joseph Bland, Director
C. H. Addison, Director

Alerts (Washington, DC)

Henry C. Bolden, lf / c
Gurden Snowden, ss
Warren Dent, 2b
Charles Washington, c
J. Nelson, p
Randolph Bowie, cf
P. Nelson, rf
S. Thompson, 3b
Joseph Bland, 1b
George H. Richardson, lf

James Whiggs, 3b
George F. Cook

Mutuals (Washington, DC)

John Tyler, c
James Harry Smith, p
K. Brown, 2b
Horace Park, 1b
Josiah Settle, cf
Jordan, ss
Thomas Barlow, 3b
Charles R. Douglass, rf / Team President
David Fisher, lf

1871

Illinois

Blue Stockings (Chicago, IL)

Charles Wing, p
Zacharias Daniels, ss
Henry Smith, cf
Frank Adams, c
T. Brown, 1b
J. Briddle, lf
Benjamin Cleary, 2b
Thomas Hamilton, 3b
Skinner, rf

Dexter Star (Springfield, IL)

Moses McCloud, President / ss
Napoleon Whitfield, Vice President / lf
Dennis Williams, Secretary / 2b
Henry Dyer, Asst. Secretary / p
Richard Dyer, Treas. / Captain / c
Alfred Dyer, 1b
Morrison Wilson, 3b
William Eusaw (Hansaw), cf
Charles Landers, rf
F. Willis. lf
D. Enson, rf
J. Johnson, c

Home Boys (Jacksonville, IL)

S. Harrison
W. Burghardt
T. Roundtree
F. Rogers
J. Harrison
J .Wagner
H. Johnson
W. Kenchler
H. Brown

Uniques (Chicago, IL)

George Brown, Captain / c / 2b
William P. Johnson, p
Henry Hampton, ss
John Sanders, 1b
Samuel Johnson, lf
Robert Johnson, 3b

Thomas Hamilton, 3b / 2b
Zacharias Daniels, 2b
John E. Shaw, cf
John Simms, rf
William D. Berry, rf
John Tyler, lf
T. Marshall, 1b
Samuel Gray, rf
S. Taylor, rf / lf / Scorer

Kansas

Rock Creek Valleys (Clinton, KS)

Peterson, p/3b
Davis, 3b
W. Smith, c
Dillard, 1b
Bennett, cf /ss/Captain
Watkins, rf/cf
Smith, lf/3b
McGee, lf
King, c/2b

Eagles (Lawrence, KS)

E. Matthews, p
F. Thomas, c
A. Porter, 1b
J. Burnside, rf
James Gross, 3b
R. Berry, cf
J. Jenkins, lf
Phil Smith, 2b
James Hoyt, ss
James Barker, 2b
Thomas Berry, Secretary
T. W. Young, Captain
John R. Kenzie, lf / Scorer

Maryland

Alerts (Baltimore, MD)

Higgins, lf
West, 1b
George Wilson, 3b
Sparks, cf
Hazacilhurste, c
Thomas, rf
Chipman, p
Snow, 2b
Markham, ss

Enterprise (Baltimore, MD)

Woods, c
Mills, ss
Cross, 3b
Cooke, 2b
Spillman, p
Olivier, lf
Jones, cf
Shipley, 1b
Woodsworth, rf

Massachusetts

Resolutes (Boston, MA)

William H. Cruckendle, ss
Emanuel D. Molineaux, 3b
M. T. Gregory, p
Paul Humphrey, 1b
A. Churchill, 2b
William Taylor, c
H. B. Chapman, cf
William Warren, rf
Charles H. Robbins, lf
D. E. Sheppard, lf
Paul Molineaux, rf
Richard Joshua, rf / lf
William H. Walker, cf
George Tompkins, rf
John B. Bailey, Scorer

Missouri

Union Stars (Kansas City, MO)

A. Rice, p
J. Fustor, c
G. White, 1b
C. Walker, rf
L. Lewis, 3b
Mutchmore, cf
Bass, lf
Littleton, rf
C. Green, cf
J. Ellington, lf
J. Montgomery, 2b
E. Russ, ss
Lewis, lf
C. Watson, Scorer

New Jersey

DeWitts (Camden, NJ)

H. J. Clark, p
Lockmann, 2b
George Howard Wilson, lf
Beverly D. May, 3b
James Sparrow, ss
John G. Kelsh, c
Richard Mitchell, cf
Polk (Poke), 1b
Walter Quinn, rf

Keystone (Jersey City, NJ)

Percy F. Benham, cf / Captain
Edward Wales, rf
Thomas E. Rias, lf
Isaiah Sampson, ss
David J. Green, p
Charles Benham, 3b
Garrison, c
Charles Wanzer, 1b / Vice President
Joseph C. Rias, Secretary
George Abrams, Corresponding Secretary
George Gale, Treasurer
H. Pigerman, Director

W. Sampson, Director
George Walker, 2b / Director
DuBois Hallack, President

New York

Fly Aways (Gloversville, NY)

Charles Walrod, 2b
T. Harris, cf
Brumley Hoke, p
A. Cunningham, 3b
George Moore, lf
Charles Jackson, ss
John Miller, rf
W. Jackson, c
H. Smith, 1b

Amicable (New York, NY)

Lymon Babcock, 1b
Thomas T. Hoffman, p
George Mitchell, 3b
John Murray, ss
A. Hamilton, cf
Frank Vanderpoel, lf
George Pratt, rf
William Cartwright, 2b
Thomas Ringgold, c

Hannibals (Troy, NY)

George Edward Harden, c
H. Gifford, 2b
B. Blanch, p
Frank Chew, ss
Charles Oliver, 1b
T. Barlett, rf
Richard Vanchoick, 3b
John Harden, cf
M. Snowden, lf
Eric Young, 2b
La Tona, p
Hall, ss
T. Demery, rf / p

Fearless (Utica, NY)

Samuel Freeman, ss
Peter Tonssant, c
Charles Peterson, p
Arlington Denike, 1b / Captain
John Lippin, 2b
Thomas Lippin, 3b
Joshua Adkins, rf
Fred Jackson, rf
Harry Moss, c / 2b
James Pell, cf
Galway, lf
Sarralt Logan, 2b / lf

Pennsylvania

Pythians (Philadelphia, PA)

John Cannon, 3b
Spencer Hanley, 1b
Octavius V. Catto, ss

Henry Price, 2b / lf
James Sparrow, rf
George Teamer, rf
Frank Jones, 2b
H. J. Clark, 3b
John Graham, lf
Pliny L. Locke, cf
Joshua Adkins, c
Daniel Neal, rf
James Glascow, 1b
George Brown, p
Dr. M. Brown, Scorer

Washington, DC

Alerts (Washington, DC)

H. C. Bolden, lf / c
George Snowden, ss
Warren Dent, 2b
Charles Washington, c
J. Nelson, p
Randolph Bowie, cf
P. Nelson, rf
S. Thompson, 3b
Joseph Bland, 1b
George H. Richardson, lf
James Whiggs, 3b

Mutuals (Washington, DC)

Josiah Thomas Settle, lf
Horace W. Parke, 1b
J. Tyler, c
Thomas Barlow, 3b
Jordan, 2b / ss
J. W. Bell, cf / 3b
George Brown, ss / 2b
Charles E. Douglass, p / rf
William H. Harris, rf
Jerome Thomas, cf
James Harry Smith, p
David A. Fisher, lf

1872

Illinois

Dexter Star (Springfield, IL)

Moses McCloud, President / ss
Napoleon Whitfield, Vice President / lf
Dennis Williams, Secretary / 2b
Henry Dyer, Asst. Secretary / p
Richard Dyer, Treas. / Captain / c
Alfred Dyer, 1b
Morrison Wilson, 3b
William Eusaw, cf
Charles Landers, rf

Magnolias (Alton, IL)

Barter, c
Williams, p
Moore, ss
Kendall, 1b
Worden, 2b

Draper, 3b
Johnson, lf
Hall, cf
Allen, rf
H. Burnap, Scorer

Uniques (Chicago, IL)

George Brown, Captain
William P. Johnson, p / 2b
Henry Hampton, ss
John Sanders, 1b
Robert Johnson, 3b
John E. Shaw, cf
George Overland, rf
John Simms, rf
John Tyler, lf
Zacharias Daniels, 2b

Massachusetts

Albions (Boston, MA)

William H. Walker, c
Lewis H. Prattis, ss
Charles Leggett, lf
T. Milton, p
William Godwin, 2b
A. Churchill, 3b
Charles Reed, cf
Howard L. Smith, 1b
William I. Powell, rf

Resolutes (Boston, MA)

William H. Cruckendle, ss
Emanuel D. Molineaux, 3b
M. T. Gregory, p
Paul Humphrey, 1b
A. Churchill, 2b
William Taylor, c
William Warren, rf
D. E. Sheppard, lf
Paul Molineaux, rf
William H. Walker, cf
H. B. Chapman, cf / President
James Taylor, Vice President
C. Waller, Secretary
Joseph F. Delyons, Treasurer
Lawlor, Director
Prince, Director
Richard Joshua, Director
Charles H. Robbins, Director
George Tompkins, Director

Fearless (Utica, NY)

Samuel Freeman, ss
Peter Tonssant, c
Charles Peterson, p
Arlington Denike, 1b / Captain
John Lippen, 2b
Thomas Lippen, 3b
Joshua Adkins, rf
Fred Jackson, rf
Harry Moss,
James Pell, cf

Galway, lf
Sarralt Logan, 2b / lf

Washington, DC

Alerts (Washington, DC)

George F. T. Cook, President
John H. Brooks, Vice President
Edward Savoy, Treasurer Joseph T. Mason
Corresponding Secretary
Robert Robinson, Recording Secretary
William M. Grimes, Captain
Sandy Bruce, Director
Warren Dent, Director
Robert E. Talliaferro, Director
M. Washington, Director
Joseph T. Cook, Director
Benjamin Freeman, Scorer

Manhattan (Washington, DC)

George Briscoe, ss
D. W. Downing, rf
Henry C. Bolden, 2b
George H. Richardson, 1b
Charles Bolden, 3b
James Talbott (Talbert), c
John Grinnell, cf
Robert W. White, lf
James Thomas Tolliver, p

Mutuals (Washington, DC)

John Tyler, c
William Winston, ss / 1b
K. Brown, 2b
R. R. Calbert, 1b / 2b
Charles R. Douglass, rf
James Harry Smith, p
David A. Fisher, cf
J. W. Bell, 3b
Pliny L. Locke, lf / ss
Thomas Barlow (A. Smith), lf

1873

Illinois

Uniques (Chicago, IL)

George Brown, 2b / c
William P. Johnson, p / 2b
Henry Hampton, ss
Thomas Watkins, 1b
Giles Powell, 3b
Charles Deveney, rf
John E. Shaw, cf
John Tyler, lf
Zacharias Daniels, 2b
William W. Fisher, p / 2b

Kansas

Eagles (Lawrence, KS)

E. Matthews
James Gross

R. Berry
Anthony Porter
Charles Johnson
James Miller
Frank Thomas
Harvey Pilcher
Harrison Banks
Smith
W. H. Barker
James Barker, captain
Elijah Matthews, President

Union Stars (Leavenworth, KS)

John Leury
Smith
C. Green
Harry Cragg
L. Woods
L. Lewis
Fletcher
D. A. Jones
John Parris
Montgomery
Bass
Fristo
Clay
Gauthin
Henry Holmes, Scorer

Massachusetts

Albion (Boston, MA)

William H. Walker, President / Captain / c
Howard L. Smith, Secretary / 1b
William I. Powell, Treasurer / rf
L. H. Prattis, ss
Charles Leggett, lf
T. Milton, p
William Godwin, 2b
A. Churchill, 3b
Charles Reed, cf

New Jersey

Oriental (Bergen, NJ)

A. Johnston, 1b / President
Dubois H. Halleck, ss / Vice President
Anthony Jackson, lf / Secretary
John Mitchell, c / Treasurer
Anthony Jackson, p
J. Brown, 2b
John Hamilton, 3b
David Green, lf
W. Johnston, cf
James Johnson, rf

Keystones (Jersey City, NJ)

F. Butler
Isaiah Sampson
A. E. Jordan
Isaac A. Walker

Robert L. McClain
Percy F. Benham, President
Thomas E. Rias, Vice President
David Green, Business Manager
George Abrams, Recording Secretary
Walter Quinn, Financial Secretary
George Gale, Treasurer

Unions (Jersey City, NJ)

Mark Laws
Samuel Jackson
Charles Brown
Augustus Freeman
Arthur Jackson
Peter P. Lewis
Simon S. Rodney
Henry Dernings
Arthur Townsend
James W. Green
William Cisco

New York

Quicksteps (Brooklyn, NY)

George Banks
T. Boherson
L. Peterson
J. Walker
J. Merritt
Hopson
Gainor
Morse
Wood

Oceans (Brooklyn, NY)

P. Stevens
John Coleman
George Batum
W. Brown
G. Robbins
Samuel Corneilson
David V. W. Harvey
S. Barnes
H. Leferro
S. Bateman

Colored Nine (Geneva, NY)

Benjamin Cleggett
John Bland
Christopher Gillam
William H. Holland
William Gibson
William Kinney
Fred Wells
Henry H. Brown
Theodore Duffin
Glenn Brown
Charles Gates
Henry Beach

Lone Stars (Harlem, NY)

James Williams, ss
H. Stevenson, cf

John Williams, 2b
James Miller, 1b
R. Williams, 3b
A. Nichols, c
C. Williams, lf
J. Stevenson, p
Howard Williams, rf

Fearless (Utica, NY)

Samuel Freeman, ss
Peter Tonssant, c
Charles Peterson, p
Arlington Denike, 1b / Captain
John Lippin, 2b
Thomas Lippin, 3b
Joshua Adkins, rf
Fred Jackson, rf
Harry Moss,
James Pell, cf
Sarralt Logan, 2b / lf

Ohio

Champions (Steubenville, OH)

Weldy Walker, c
Oscar McPherson, p
Robert Payne, ss
Frank Morris, 1b
James T. McPherson, 2b
Moses F. Walker, 3b
Merriman, rf
Melvin J. Harris, cf
Lewis N. Norman, lf

West Virginia

Idle Wilds (Wheeling, WVA)

Osborne Gray, c
Alexander, p
David Grant, ss
Hardgraves, 1b
David Luker, 2b
Gardner, 3b
Joshua Couch, lf
Howard Newby, cf
Jones, rf

Washington, DC

Alerts (Washington, DC)

Robert E. Talliaferro, ss
Amos W. Jenkins, c
Benjamin Lancaster, 2b
Horace W. Parke, 3b / 1b
Charles H. Whitlow, 1b / cf
Richard Davidge, rf / 3b
William C. Chase, p
Joseph T. Cook, lf
Josiah Thomas Settle, cf / 3b
Walter H. Harris, cf
Jerome Thomas, 3b
Warren Dent, 2b
J. Davis, ss

Mutuals (Washington, DC)

J. Tyler, c
William Winston, ss / 1b
K. Brown, 2b
R. R. Calbert, 1b / 2b
Charles R. Douglass, rf
James Harry Smith, p
David A. Fisher, cf
J. W. Bell, 3b
Pliny L. Locke, lf / ss
Thomas Barlow (A. Smith), lf

Picked Nine (Washington, DC)

John Tyler, 1b
James Talbott (Talbert), ss
Josiah T. Settle, 3b
George Johnson, 2b
Amos W. Jenkins, rf
William C. Chase, p
William E. Winston, lf
Horace W. Parke, cf
Samuel Brooks, c

Manhattan (Washington, DC)

George Briscoe, ss
D. W. Downing, rf
Charles Bolden, 2b
George H. Richardson, 1b
Henry C. Bolden, 3b
James Talbott (Talbert), c
John Grinnell, cf
Robert W. White, lf
James Thomas Tolliver, p

1874

Georgia

Mutuals (Macon, GA)

W. G. Perkins, Captain
J. N. Blackshear, President
Thomas Lockett, Vice-President
D. E. Tucker, Secretary

Illinois

Quicksteps (Cairo, IL)

Frank Robertson
Samuel Smith
Henry Hayes
Albert Stein
Richard Coleman
Reuben Smith
Elias Coleman
Walter Matthews
William Lane
Ed Frazier

Unique Ten (Chicago, IL)

George Brown, Captain / c
William P. Johnson, p / 2b
Henry Hampton, ss
Giles Powell, 3b

Thomas Watkins, 1b
John E. Shaw, cf
Charles Deveney, rf
Samuel Brown, 2b
R. Johnson, lf
Vertner Johnson, lf
Zacharias Daniels, 2b
William H. Fisher, p / 2b
William Berry, Manager

Kansas

Colored Nine (Wichita Valley, KS)

A. M. Thornton, 2b
Spencer Thomas, 1b
W. H. Barker, rf
Johnson, ss
James Hoyt, c
Ewing, p
Tom Adams, cf
Dennis A. Jones, lf
James Miller, 3b

Kentucky

Globes (Louisville, KY)

Croghan, 1b
James Morton, 3b / 2b
Lucien Wagner, 2b
Daniel E. Brown, cf
Henry Hayden, p
Frank Garrett, ss
William Letcher, lf
George Burks, c
Jacob Rooney, rf
Logan McElroy, rf
William Hays, lf

Maryland

Orientals (Baltimore, MD)

Brown, ss
John Simms, c
Cyrus Wilson, 1b
William Wright, 3b
Williams, rf
Risley, lf
Smith, 2b
Louis Barnie, cf
Howard, p

Atlantics (Baltimore, MD)

George Williams, p
William Berryman, 1b
George Wilson, 2b
Joseph Deaver, ss
Solomon Paine, 3b
Daniel Coats, lf
John W. Groom, cf
Charles Sheridan, rf
William Briscoe, c

Michigan

Victims (Battle Creek, MI)

Sam Bassett, lf
Charley Lock, rf
William Ward, 2b
Dick Collins, ss / Assistant Director
Ike Silence, cf / Director
Charley Tyler, p / Captain
John Gaines, c / Secretary
Charley Artson, ss / Treasurer
John Colvin, 3b / Vice President
Martin Snodgrass, 1b / President

Missouri

Napoleons (St. Louis, MO)

J. Joiner, 1b
George Taylor, 2b
Joseph Bailey, 3b
William Richardson, p
Phil Smith, c
Henry Day, ss
William A. Pitts, lf
Webb, cf
George Turner, rf

New Jersey

Keystones (Jersey City, NJ)

Thomas E. Rias
F. Butler
David Green
George Gale
W. Quinn
Isaiah Sampson
A. E. Jordan
Isaac A. Walker
R. L. McClain
Percy F. Benham

New York

Mutuals (Hempstead, NY)

Abram Willard, ss
Henry Johnson, p
Edward Hicks, c
James DuBois, 1b
Silas Willard, cf
George Thompson, 2b
John H. Townsend, 3b
S. Townsend, rf
Isaiah Stevenson, lf

Henson's Lone Stars (Jamaica, NY)

John White, ss
Elias Wilmore, p
W. H. Jackson, 1b
Jones, 2b
W. Davis, 3b
Benjamin Hicks, lf
William Johnson, rf

Charles Johnson, c
Stephen ("Sam") White, cf

Rising Stars (Northville, NY)

J. Thomas, c
W. Rix, p
G. Richter, 1b
E. Brown, 2b
J. Garvey, 3b
G. Smith, ss
G. Casley, lf
J. Hamilton, cf
G. Kerwin, rf

Stars (Schenectady, NY)

Theodore Brown
Moses Brown
William Childers
Joseph Prince
Samuel Hegeman
Anthony Schulyler
M. Snowden
Charles Oliver
T. Harris
H. Smith

Fearless (Utica, NY)

Samuel Freeman, ss
Peter Tonssant, c
Charles Peterson, p
Arlington Denike, 1b / Captain
John Lippin, 2b
Thomas Lippin, 3b
Joshua Adkins, rf
Fred Jackson, rf
Harry Moss,
James Pell, cf
Sarralt Logan, 2b / lf

Ohio

Muffers (Ironton, OH)

Jackson Page, c
Tolliver, cf
John Evans, p
W. Pogue, ss
Thomas Calvert, 2b
Gray, lf
Charles Scott, ss
Lawson, 1b
F. Pogue, 3b / Captain
V. O. Harvey, cf

Forest City (Portsmouth, OH)

Wilson Minor, 1b
Joseph J. Minor, p
John T. Rose, 2b
Miller, cf
James Stephenson, ss
Lloyd Henson, c
Henry Baker, rf / Captain

Erastus Wilson, lf
Harry Melvin, substitute
Frank Johnson, 3b

Pennsylvania

Pastimes (Carlisle, PA)

Benjamin Smith, p
Isaac Stewart,
T. Smith, 1b
Andrew Jackson, 2b
C. Smith, 3b
J. Cook, ss
W. J. Hunter, lf
Franklin P. Thompson, rss
Charles Andrews, cf
William Johnson, rf

Apolia (Harrisburg, PA)

L. Earley, cf / Captain
James Murray, c
John Black, p
William Long, ss
Arthur Jackson, 1b
W. Wallace, 2b
Richardson, 3b
Isaac Taylor, lb
William Jackson, rf
George Galbraith, President
Henry Lee, Vice President
Joseph Pople, Secretary
George Thomas, Treasurer

Colored Nine (Middletown, PA)

James A. Shultz, c
Reuben Banks, p
Thomas Cuff, ss
David Thompson, 2b
Spofford, 1b
John E. Shultz, rf
Charles Loyd, cf
Lanaus, 3b
Samuel Brown, rf

Atlantics (Reading, PA)

William Foos, 3b
John Smith, lf
Edward Malson, cf
George Temple, rf
Levi Wilson, 1b
Joseph Dobbins, 2b
William Carter, ss
James Malson, p
Tilghman Cornish, Captain, c

Hard to Beat (Stroudsburg, PA)

James W. Huff, c
Charles Adams, 1b
Theodore Ray, 2b
Quakau, 3b
William Ray, lf

Moses Washington, ss
Stephen Adams, cf
Robert Smith, rf
Arthur Davis, p

South Carolina

Crescents (Charleston, SC)

Aaron McCoy, President
G. J. H. Graham, Vice President
W. L. Blakely, Secretary / cf
J. G. Kirk, Treasurer / ss
L. G. Bivin, Team Scorer
Peter Grant, Captain / c
G. W. Kennedy, p
H. Fortune Fishburne, 1b
J. Davis, 2b
B. Savage, 3b
J. J. Young, rf

West Virginia

Idle Wilds (Wheeling, WVA)

Osborne Gray, c
Alexander, p
John Sawyer, ss
Gardner, 3b
Tilton, rf
Manly, p
David Luker, 2b
Adam Johnson, cf
Hardgraves, 1b
Joshua Couch, lf

Black Feet (Bellaire, WVA)

Manniette
Young White
John Kirk
David Wooten
James McPherson
George Ransom
William Seaton
Jacob Capito
Turner
Frank Jackson

Washington, DC

Manhattan (Washington, DC)

George Briscoe, ss
D. W. Downing, rf
Bowden, 2b
George H. Richardson, 1b
H. C. Bolden, 3b
James Talbott (Talbert), c
John Grinnell, cf
Robert W. White, lf
James Thomas Tolliver, p

Mutuals (Washington, DC)

John Tyler, c
William Winston, ss / 1b
K. Brown, 2b

R. R. Calbert, 1b / 2b
Charles R. Douglass, rf
James Harry Smith, p
David A. Fisher, cf
J. W. Bell, 3b
Pliny L. Locke, lf / ss
Thomas Barlow (A. Smith), lf

1875

Illinois

Lake Citys (Chicago, IL)

Henry P. Hall, President
H. Beauford, Manager
William D. Berry, Manager

Pytheus (Chicago, IL)

E. Brown, c
William Speed, p
W. Johnson, ss
R. Moody, 1b
D. Brown, 2b / Captain
H. Coombs, cf
Carey Jackson, 3b
J. Cole, rf
J. Moor, Substitute
A. Smith, Secretary

Uniques (Chicago, IL)

Giles Powell, 3b
George Overland, rf
George Brown, lf / c
Charles Deveney, p
Henry Wilson, 2b
John E. Shaw, cf
William Dyson, c
Samuel Brown, 1b
Henry Hampton, ss
George Ecoton, ss
Henry P. Hall, President

Iowa

Clippers (Burlington, IA)

Alonzo B. Golden, p
James Morse, 1b
George Sidner, cf
Thomas Foster, ss
Louis, 2b
Washington Green, 3b
Housely, rf
Pete Palmer, lf
James Canterberry, c

Kansas

Wide Awakes (Atchison, KS)

Henry Hubanks, c
Charles Smith, p
William Woodyard, 2b
Harry McGee, 3b
Henry Pendleton, ss
Richard Schleckman, cf

John Taylor, lf
William Spriggs, rf
George Reed, 1b / Captain

Stars (Fort Scott, KS)

Frank E. Eagleson
William Eagleson
Helson Eagleson
David Berry
Adam H. Pigeon
Henry Hawkins
John B. Loving
Billy W. Walker
David Gordon
Al M. Thornton
James Eagleson

Daisy Clippers (Troy, KS)

Hubert, c
Showls, rf
Mason, lf
Fonts, 1b
Henry Carter, p
Henry Hubanks, ss
Henry Miller, 2b
J. E. Carter, 3b
Charles Ewing, cf

Kentucky

Actives (Covington, KY)

Smith Williams, ss
Ford, p
Burrell Lumpkin, c
James Ross, 1b
John Delaney, 2b
Charles Gray, 3b
John Neal, cf
Robert Page, rf
William Page, lf
William Coleman, director
Charles Morgan, director
Julius Miller, director

Athletics (Frankfort, KY)

H. Dozier, ss
J. B. Merrett, p
James Woolfalk, c
Smith, 2b
William Dickerson, lf
C. Maguire, cf
Robert Tyler, 1b
William Woolfalk, rf
Booker, 3b

Brown Stockings (Louisville, KY)

William Jones, c
William Bullitt, p
William H. Gibson, ss
Albert White, 1b
Horace MacCauley, 2b
Calvin Curry, 3b

Henry Reed, lf
John Pembleton, cf
E. Helm, rf

Fair Play (Louisville, KY)

William Jones, c
John Bell, p / c
William Woods, 3b / ss / c
Logan McElroy, 1b
Tommy Adams, 2b / cf
Henry Payne, 3b
Nelson Tarrance, lf
James Thomas, cf
W. Pratt Ennis, 2b
Carlton Frey, rf
William H. Gibson, 2b
Robert Armstrong, 3b / lf

Globes (Louisville, KY)

Croghan, 1b
James Morton, 3b / 2b
Lucien Wagner, 2b
Daniel E. Brown, cf
Henry Hayden, p
Frank Garrett, ss
William Hays, lf
William Letcher, lf
George Burks, c
Rooney, rf
James Ferguson, 2b
Logan McElroy, rf
Thomas Callamels, c
Horace MacCauley, lf
Charles W. Hines, rf
W. Morgan, Scorer

Massachusetts

Albions (Boston, MA)

Albert Saunders, 3b
Edward Smith, 1b
Andrew Randolph, c
George Tompkins, cf
W. F. Simpson, ss / p
Meldon, 2b
Singleton, rf
Charles H. Robbins, ss
Charles Reed, lf

Missouri

Blue Stockings (St. Louis, MO)

Phil Smith, c
William "Bill" Richardson, 3b
T. C. Richardson, cf
George Taylor, 2b
Henry Day, ss
William Collins, p
William A. Pitts, rf
Robert Sharp, 1b
Douglas Grant, cf / p
Casey, lf
Peter Hayes, 1b
Andrew Goodall, 2b

Joseph Bailey, 1b / cf
Green, rf
George Jones, rf
George Lillie, 1b
William Mitchell
James A. Johnson, Manager

Sunsets (St. Louis, MO)

Albert Pierce, c
Wilson, cf
Logan, 3b
Reuben Henderson, 2b
Turner Anderson, p
Samuel "Sam" Rice, 2b
Lewis, 1b
Hershfield, ss
Williams, rf
Thomas Marshall, lf
Slaughter, cf
Emile Hayden, rf / p
William Pierce, lf
Charles Brooks, 1b
Frank Spear(s), c

White Stockings (St. Louis, MO)

Henry Day, ss
B. Campbell, rf
George Turner, c
John Johnson, lf
John Matthews, 2b
Henry Campbell, lf
Humphries, 3b
Henry Lawrence, p
Sullivan, cf

New York

Mutuals (Hempstead, NY)

Abram Willard, ss
Henry Johnson, p
Edward Hicks, c
James DuBois, 1b
Silas Willard, cf
George Thompson, 2b
John H. Townsend, 3b
S. Townsend, rf
Isaiah Stevenson, lf

Henson's Lone Stars (Jamaica, NY)

John White, ss
Elias Wilmore, p
Jackson, 1b
Jones, 2b
W. Davis, 3b
Benjamin Hicks, lf
William Johnson, rf
Charles Johnson, c
Stephen ("Sam") White, cf

Pastimes (Syracuse, NY)

Al Lawrence, 1b
W. P. Myers, 3b

J. A. Mason, ss
H. M. Mitchell, rf
N. J. Jones, 2b
T. Owens, cf
J. A. Jordan, c
J. Tripp, lf
S. P. Jordan, p

Fearless (Utica, NY)

B. Blanch, 1b / p
Arlington Denike, 1b
Samuel Freeman, ss / p
Henry Harden, cf
Arthur Jackson, p / rf
Samuel "Sam" Jackson, rf
Pliny Locke, lf
James Pell, 3b
Charles Peterson, ss
Thomas Lippin, 3b
Sarralt Logan, lf
Galway, 2b
Theodore H. Freeman, Jr., cf
Robert Van Alstine, rf
Theodore Freeman, President

Ohio

Vigilants (Cincinnati, OH)

James Ferguson, 2b
Phillip B. Ferguson, lf
Andrew J. DeHart, cf
Samuel Lewis, ss
John "Phas" Flowers, 3b
Hooks, rf
Hiram Carroll, p
William Brown, c
Morris Handy, 1b
Archie Lewis
S. Newcomb
William Copeland, President
George W. Turner, VP
William H. Jones, Secretary
Sedrick Saunders, Treasurer

Pennsylvania

Mystic (Harrisburg, PA)

John E. Price, c
Harry J. Clark, p
Robert Verner, 1b
Isaac Taylor, 2b
Henry Lee, 3b
George W. Scott, ss
C. Myers, lf
Plater, cf
William Stewart, rf

Olympics (Harrisburg, PA)

Charles H. Brown, 2b
William Shadney, p / Captain
Horace Murray, rf
David Allen, c
T. Brown, c

W. Rideout, ss
S. Burles, p
Arthur Jackson, 1b
James Murray, 3b / Captain
Edward Earley, ss
William Jackson, rf
George Jackson, cf
George McMullen, cf
R. Humphrey, 3b
Thomas C. Christy, Manager

Tyroleans (Harrisburg, PA)

C. Jones, c
J. Allen, p
Thomas Scott, 1b
William Long, 2b
R. Carter, 3b
W. Carney, ss
J. Wilson, lf
E. Carr, cf
David Prime, rf
Joseph Pople, 3b
James Murray, c
Dangerfield Garner, Secretary

Lincolns (Reading, PA)

Tilghman Cornish, c
James Malsen, p
Levi Nelson, 1b
Henry C. Nelson, 2b
B. Addison, ss
W. Gross, 3b
Solomon B. Seidel, lf
Charles H. Walker, cf
John Smith, rf

South Carolina

Excelsiors (Charleston, SC)

Abram Owens
George Butler
Henry Holmes
David Carwheel
Edward Brown
James Boon
Barrett Gourdin
Joseph Abrams
Charles Smith

Tennessee

Colored Rifles (Pulaski, TN)

James Rose
Thomas Thompson
Joseph Walker
George Burch
Robert Boyd
Thomas Drish
Billy Batte
Lewis Meredith
Willis Upshaw
Robert Rhodes

Washington, DC

Alerts (Washington, DC)

George F. T. Cook
Henry Nichols
Thomas L. Watson
Joseph T. Cook
Harry Johnson
William H. Bruce
William D. Campbell
Shermonte Lewis
Benjamin L. Freeman
Sandy Bruce Jr.
Horace W. Parke
Richard Davidge
Charles Davis
Edward L. Savoy
Lemuel Matthews
Edward Augustine Savoy
George Alexander
John W. Curry
Jerome A. Johnson
William Grymes, President
William D. Kelly, Secretary

Junior Alerts (Washington, DC)

Harry Johnson, Jr.
Jacob C. Strather
Jerome Osborn
Charles Mason
James "Ed" Mason
Frederick Moore
Wilson Carey
Alexander Shippin
John Parker

Mutuals (Washington, DC)

Charles H. Washington, p
James Thomas Tolliver, c
Lottie, 1b
George Anderson, 2b
Henry Brooks, 3b
James Talbot, ss
David A. Fisher, cf
Benjamin Boyd, rf / 2b
R. R. Calbert, lf
Charles F. Bruce, Scorer

1876

California

Logans (Oakland, CA)

J. Montague, p
H. Tanner, 1b
John H. Scott, c
Edward A. Clark, 3b
McHiner, rf
N. S. Purnell, ss
J. Martell, 3b

J. Robinson, lf
John R. Widener, rf / Captain

Palace Hotel (San Francisco, CA)

Moses K. Brown, p
Isaac Pierson, 1b
Abraham Strather, c
Joseph Carroll, 3b
James Henry Vodery, cf
Cole, ss
Horace Perkins, 2b
A. Anderson, p / rf
J. C. Smith, lf / Captain Joseph Fletcher,
Secretary

Illinois

Brown Stockings (Springfield, IL)

William Lyles, President
William Lee, Secretary
C. Naylor, Captain
H. Curtis
L. Morgan
H. Jimmerson
W. Rite
C. Lyman
J. Woods
W. Hansaw

Uniques (Chicago, IL)

George Overland, rf
George Brown, 2b
Charles Deveney, lf
Vertner Johnson, p
Giles Powell, ss
William Dyson, 2b
John Tyler, c
John E. Shaw, cf
Samuel Brown, 1b
Benjamin Beatty

Indiana

Colored Barbers (Indianapolis, IN)

William Fletcher, c
Thomas White, 1b
Albert J. Farley, p
G. A. Smith, 2b
Isaac Johnson, 3b / f
Robert A. Brown, rf
Mallory, ss
E. Felder, lf
William Dixon, cf
C. Lanier, 1b
D. Dunlap, ss
J. Dixon, 3b
W. H. Bibbs, Substitute
C. Brown, Substitute

Hotel Bates (Indianapolis, IN)

J. Frye, p
G. W. Hilliard, rf

Sam Henderson, 3b
A. Waters, cf
Lou Sanders. ss
Tom Marshall, 2b
C. W. Murray, 1b
Cal White, lf
S. Sanders, Captain
R. P. Brown, Manager

Slow Boys (Logansport, IN)

James Waldron, c
John Turner, p
Horace Turner, ss
John Parker, 1b
Charles Parker, 2b
Dan Johnson, 3b
James Brooks, cf
C. Moss, 2b
Rolla House, rf
Reuben Buckner, lf
Perry Watson, lf

Kansas

Olympics (Fort Scott, KS)

H. B. Denniston
I. A. Anthony, c
Robinson, ss
Charlie Mortimer, p
J. L. Wareham, 1b
P. Bryant, cf
Needles, rf
Marsden, p
Charles J. Feist, 2b
W. H. Beard, 3b
William Patterson, Secretary/Scorer

Eagles (Lawrence, KS)

Elijah Matthews, ss
A. Miller, lf
Thomas Berry, c
Thomas Gross, rf
Anthony Porter, 1b
George Berry, p
Frank Thomas, 3b
G. Matthews, 2b
George Barker, cf
Jessie Matthews
Spencer Thomas, 3b
George A. Stebbins
James Gross, President / Captain
William Gray, Vice President
James H. Holmes, Secretary
Charles A. Johnson, Secretary
Nashville Walker, Director

Red Stockings (Lawrence, KS)

Frank Hunter, President
Henry Holmes, Secretary
C. H. Stewart, Treasurer
Luke Berry, Captain

Kentucky

Actives (Covington, KY)

Smith Williams, ss
Ford, p
Robert Burrell, c
James Ross, 1b
John Delaney, 2b
Charles Gray, 3b
John Neal, cf
Robert Page, rf
William Page, lf
John Page, rf
Charles Britton
William Coleman, director
Charles Morgan, director
Julius Miller, Director

Athletics (Frankfort, KY)

H. Dozier, ss
J. B. Merrett, p
James Woolfolk, c
Smith, 2b
Dickerson, lf
C. Maguire, cf
Robert Tyler, 1b
William Woolfolk, rf
Booker, 3b

Fair Plays (Louisville, KY)

Nelson Tarrance, 1b
Robert Armstrong, 3b
Lucien Wagner, lf
Logan McElroy, ss
Tommy Adams, cf
William H. Gibson, c
William "Billy" Woods, rf
W. P. Ennis, 2b
John Bell, p

Globes (Louisville, KY)

Croghan, 1b
William Jones, 2b
William Bullitt, 3b
Daniel E. Brown, cf
Frank Garrett, ss
George Burks, c
William Hays, lf
Robert Tyler, rf
E. Helm, cf
Henry Hayden, p

Louisiana

Excelsiors (Donaldsonville, LA)

James Ray, President
Joseph Lacroix, Vice President
Charles W. Kling, Secretary
Numa Brand, Corresponding Secretary
Oscar Vedal, Captain

Pickwicks
(New Orleans, LA)

Edward M. Cohen, President
Joe Johnson, Vice President
O. F. Boisseau, Secretary
Stephen Ternoir, Asst. Secretary
Richard Nixon, Treasurer
Walter L. Cohen, Captain

Massachusetts

Albions (Boston, MA)

Albert Saunders, 3b
Edward Smith, 1b
Andrew Randolph, c
George Tompkins, cf
W. F. Simpson, ss / p
Meldon, 2b
Singleton, rf
Charles H. Robbins, ss
Charles Reed, lf

Minnesota

Unions (Minneapolis, MN)

George W. Williams
Richard Jackson
Lewis Mason
W. J. Gardner
James W. Cunningham
Cheatum
William P. Johnson
Abraham Myrick
David Williams
Thomas Williams
George Todd
E. H. Hamilton
William Berry

Blue Stars (St. Paul, MN)

W. M. Johnson
C. Allen
Harry J. Edwards
James C. Murray
Matthew Bailey
F. Gill
W. Gill
W. Perkins
Thomas Combs
William F. Johnson
William Barnes
James Combs

Missouri

Sunsets (St. Louis, MO)

Albert Pierce, ss
M. Wilson, cf
Reuben Henderson, 3b
Turner Anderson, p
Samuel "Sam" Rice, 2b
Emile Hayden, rf / p
William Pierce, lf

Charles G. Brooks, 1b
Frank Spear(s), c

Blue Stockings
(St. Louis, MO)

William Collins, rf / cf
Ned Harris, rf
Phil Smith, c
James Tilley, 1b
Henry Campbell, 2b
George Jones, rf
Frank Spear(s), c
Joseph Bailey, 3b / c
William A. Pitts, lf
William Brown, 2b
George Taylor, ss / 2b
William Dyson, c / 2b
Douglas Grant, p
Jim Bailey, 3b
Henry Day, ss
William Richardson, 3b
Robert Sharp, 1b
James A. Johnson, Manager

New York

Nonesuch (Geneva, NY)

Benjamin F. Cleggett
George W. Allen
Henry Harden
Henry W. Brown
Charles Condol
Glenn Brown
Harry Moore
Henry Beach
John Bland
Christopher Gillam

Actives (Ithaca, NY)

William H. Allen, c
William Benson, 1b
James Blackman, cf
William H. Guinn, 2b
Lyman Melvin, ss
Henry Moore, rf
Edward M. Newton, 3b
Samuel Smith, lf
Peter Tonssant, p

Rising Stars (Northville, NY)

J. Thomas, c
W. Rix, p
G. Richter, 1b
E. Brown, 2b
J. Garvey, 3b
G. Smith, ss
G. Casley, lf
J. Hamilton, cf
G. Kerwin, rf

Unions (Saratoga Springs, NY)

Alex Brown
John M. Van Dyke

D. Henry Granger
Charles Peterson
Frank Sanford
William Clemens, President
Edward Anthony, Secretary
Phillip Alexandie, Treasurer
Frank Smith, Captain

Unexpected (Rochester, NY)

B. Jackson, 1b / captain
Harry G. Johnson, 2b
Samuel Francis, 3b
Charles Moore, ss
John Downes, p
William Stewart, c
A. Yorks, lf
C. White, cf
Dennis Gibbs, rf / p
Arthur L. Smith, cf
R. Murry, 2b

Central Depot
(Syracuse, NY)

Al Lawrence, 1b
W. P. Myers, 3b
J. A. Mason, ss
H. M. Mitchell, rf
N. J. Jones, 2b
T. Owens, cf
John A. Jordan, c
J. Tripp, lf
S. P. Jordan, p

Pastimes (Syracuse, NY)

Al Lawrence, 1b
W. P. Myers, 3b
A. M. Mason, ss
H. M. Mitchell, rf
N. J. Jones, 2b
T. Owens, cf
J. A. Jordan, c
J. Tripp, lf
S. P. Jordan, p

Fearless (Utica, NY)

B. Blanch, 1b / p
Arlington Denike, 1b
Samuel Freeman, ss / p
Henry Harden, cf
Arthur Jackson, p / rf
Samuel "Sam" Jackson, rf
Pliny Locke, lf
James Pell, 3b
Charles Peterson, ss
Thomas Lippin, 3b
Sarralt Logan, lf
Galway, 2b
Theodore H. Freeman, Jr., cf
Robert Van Alstine, rf
A. C. DeWitt, Secretary
Theodore Freeman, President

Ohio

Vigilants (Cincinnati, OH)

James Ferguson, 2b
Phillip B. Ferguson, lf
Andrew J. DeHart, cf
Samuel Lewis, ss
John "Phas" Flowers, 3b
Hooks, rf
Hiram Carroll, p
William Brown, c
Morris Handy, 1b
Brooks, rf
William Copeland, President
George W. Turner, VP
William H. Jones, Secretary
Sedrick Saunders, Treasurer

North Carolina

Pastimes (Raleigh, NC)

R. Millikin, ss
L. M. Nash, p
N. G. Millikin, 3b
G. W. Gross, rf
H. Blake, lf
A. Jordan, 1b
M. Hawkins, 2b
F. B. Curtis, c
William Hawkins, cf

Pennsylvania

Olympics (Harrisburg, PA)

G. McMullen, 1b
Armor Wilson, 2b
James Murray, 3b / Captain
James Barton, cf
S. Burrs, p
Edward Early, ss
David Allen, c
H. Miller, lf
B. Boone, rf
William Shadney, p
Charles W. Harley, Scorer
J .W. Simpson, President
W. Hopkins, Treasurer
N .Z. Butler, Director
F. Battis, Director
Thomas Christy, Director

Tyroleans (Harrisburg, PA)*

D. Brown, 2b
William Shadney, p / Captain
Horace Murray, rf
David Allen, c
T. Brown, c
W. Rideout, ss
Arthur Jackson, 1b
James Murray, 3b / Captain
S. Burrs, p
James Barton, lf
Edward Early, ss

William Jackson, rf
George Jackson, cf
George McMullen, cf
R. Humphrey, 3b
J. Stewart, 2b / Scorer
Thomas C. Christy, Manager
*Olympics and Tyroleans
briefly merged

Enterprise (Williamsport, PA)

Javan Isaac Emory, c / cf
Charles Davis, rf
Alexander Davage, p
William T. Emory, 2b
John Butler, 1b
Benjamin Taylor, lf
F. Lee, 3b
Suller, rf
J. W. Fairfax, ss
Javan D. Emory, 3b / lf
Alexander Offord, ss

Tennessee

Blue Stockings (Columbia, TN)

Brown
Kennedy
English
William McCrady
Rhymes
Green
Allison
Miller
Jesse Saunders
Loer Mack

Colored Rifles (Pulaski, TN)

Rose
H. H. Thompson
Walker
Burch
Boyd
Thomas Drish
Batte
Meredith
Upshaw
Robert Rhodes

Washington, DC

Mutual (Washington, DC)

James W. Bell, President
Charles F. Bruce, Secretary
David A. Fisher ("Davy"), Treasurer /
    Team Captain
Thomas H. Barlow (A. Smith), Captain /
    Vice President
Ed Montague, Director
Pliny L. Locke, Director
G. Bruce, Director

Uniques (Washington, DC)

William Carroll, c
Jesse Roy, p

J. Chatham (Cheatham), 1b
Rufus Savoy, 2b
Hamilton D. Cole, 3b
Abraham Hall, ss
B. Willis, lf
F. Jackson, cf
Samuel Brooks, rf
John Wesley Brent, lf

1877

Illinois

Brown Stockings (Springfield, IL)

William Lyles, President
William Lee, Secretary
C. Naylor, Captain
H. Curtis
L. Morgan
H. Jimmerson
W. Rite
C. Lyman
J. Woods
W. Hansaw

Lone Star (Springfield, IL)

Moses McCloud, President / ss
Dennis Williams, Secretary / 2b
R. Wright, c
D. Minare, p
Charles Morgan, 1b
Al Williams, 3b
Henry Courtney, cf
W. Grubbs, lf
J. Stevens, rf

Indiana

Carthagenians (Indianapolis, IN)

John Hines, p
George Goins, 2b
Val Moss, 1b / Captain
William Walden, ss
Dan Well, 3b
Dan Williams, c
Cambridge Peters, cf
George Bartlett, lf
William Fletcher, rf / c

Colored Barbers (Indianapolis, IN)

William Fletcher, c
Thomas White, 1b
Albert J. Farley, p
G. A. Smith, 2b
Isaac Johnson, 3b / f
Robert A. Brown, rf
Mallory, ss
E. Felder, lf
William Dixon, cf
C. Lanier, 1b
D. Dunlap, ss
J. Dixon, 3b

William A. Bibbs, lf
C. Brown, Substitute

Exchange Hotel
(Indianapolis, IN)

George Hilliard, 3b
George Thomas, 2b
Ceil Saunders, ss
William A. Bibbs, lf
Cousins, p
E. M. Scott, rf
William Shelton, cf
John Stewart (Stuart), c
Leslie Mack, 1b
C. W. Murray, 1b
J. Louis, c
S. Henderson, 3b
R. Rusk, 3b
E. Thuston, lf
E. Frayler, cf
B. Davis, p
J. Woods, rf
Jesse Ringgold, Substitute

Optics (Logansport, IN)

James Waldron, c
John Turner, p
Horace Turner, ss
John Parker, 1b
Charles Parker, 2b
Dan Johnson, 3b
William Johnson, rf
James Brooks, cf
Frank Brooks, cf
C. Moss, 2b
Rolla House, rf
Perry Watson, lf
Howe, rf
Reuben Buckner, lf

Kansas

Eagles (Lawrence, KS)

James Miller, President
Thomas Berry, Captain / c
James Hoyt, Secretary / Manager
James Gross, Treasurer / rf
E. Matthews, ss
A. Miller, lf
Anthony Porter, 1b
George Berry, p
F. Thomas, 3b
George Matthews, 2b
George Barker, cf

Missouri

Tildens (St. Louis, MO)

Henry Spiers, c
Turner Anderson, p
William Pierce, 1b
Samuel Rice, 2b / Captain
Reuben Henderson, 3b
Henry Campbell, ss

William "Billy" Cool, lf
Robert "Bob" Collins, cf
Charles Jackson, rf

New Jersey

Nationals (Trenton, NJ)

Henry Johnson
William Cruzen
Isaac Sanderson
William Rodman
James Seruby
William Phillips
Henry Rice
Matt Hall
Joseph Huff

Trenton House (Trenton, NJ)

John Sanderson
Robert Seruby
Case
Charles Scudder
Charles "Charley" Wright
William Perrine
J. Lowery
L. Lowery
William Johnson

New York

Casinos (Elmira, NY)

Benton Thomas, c
W. Shorts, rf
Rowles, ss
Caesar, rf
C. B. Lee, 3b
Ed Matthews, p
Wood, 2b
William Condol, lf
T. Milton, cf
H. H. Stevens, Scorer
James E. Hazzard, Manager

Hick's Georgia Minstrels
(New York, NY)

O. T. Jackson
J. R. Matlock
J. W. Mills
William Sanders
T. Brown
Sam Keenan
J. Morton
C. J. Jackson
George Harris
Frank Hewitt
T. Ellis

Fearless (Utica, NY)

B. Blanch, 1b / p
Arlington Denike, 1b
Samuel Freeman, ss / p
Henry Harden, cf
Arthur Jackson, p / rf

Samuel Jackson, rf
Pliny Locke, lf
James Pell, 3b
Charles Peterson, ss
Thomas Lippin, 3b
Sarralt Logan, lf
Galway, 2b
Theodore H. Freeman, Jr., cf
Robert Van Alstine, rf
Theodore Freeman, President

North Carolina

Recruits (Charlotte, NC)

Gray J. Toole
W. H. Robinson
J. C. North
Abram North
Jeffrey Sumner
Samuel Mosely
Alex Webb
A. C. Munroe
William Kelley
Alex Harris
H. C. Hutchinson
Rufus Hyde
Yank Norwood

Black Feet
(New Bern, NC)

James T. Lewis, lf
Lewis Randolph, 2b
L. Bryant, lf
B. F. Pool, p
C. Haywood, 3b
B. Williams, 1b
William Jackson, cf
M. Dewy, ss
Joseph Fenderson, rf

Pastimes (Raleigh, NC)

R. Millikin, ss
L. M. Nash, p
N. G. Millikin, 3b
G. W. Gross, rf
H. Blake, lf
A. Jordan, 1b
M. Hawkins, 2b
F. B. Curtis, c
William Hawkins, cf

Unknowns
(Wilmington, NC)

Alex Robinson, Captain
J. Johnson, catcher
Thomas Byrd, 1b
C. Parker, 2b
J. Hall, 3b
W. T. Finch, ss
J. Hayes, lf
C. Smith, cf
C. Howard, rf

Scraps (Wilmington, NC)

James E. Starkey, c
Alex B. Butler, Jr. p / President
Benjamin Willis, 1b / Secretary
James Proctor, 2b / Moderator
James Winfield, 3b
John W. Mosely, ss
Charles Norwood, rf
Joshua Davis, cf
Edgar C. Robinson, lf

Pennsylvania

Harley (Harrisburg, PA)

L. Earley, ss
C. Myers, cf
J. Allen, 3b
William Jackson, 1b
William Shadney, p
David Brown, c
William Long, rf
William Pople, lf / Corresponding
    Secretary
Charles W. Harley, 2b / Manager

Lumber City (Williamsport, PA)

Javan Isaac Emory, c / cf
Charles Davis, rf
Alexander Davage, p
William T. Emory, 2b
John Butler, 1b
Benjamin Taylor, lf
F. Lee, 3b
David Allen, c
Bager, cf
Suller, rf
J. W. Fairfax, ss
Javan D. Emory, 3b / lf
Alexander Offord, ss

Creedmoor (Wrightsville, PA)

William Jamison, c
J. C. McPeak, p
Leonard Bear, ss
J. Jamison, 1b
Benjamin Hollis, 2b
J. T. Harris, 3b
Butler, rf
Daniel Rice, cf
William A. Bear, lf / Captain

Alphas (York, PA)

W. Gross, c
A. Mason, p
Gus A. Burton, ss
George Joice, 1b
C. Mead, 2b
J. W. Brown, 3b
A. Kenny, rf
J. G. M. Brown, cf
W. Gooden, lf

Ohio

Clippers (Ironton, OH)

James Friese
Peter Housen
Fielding Housen
W. E. Robinson
William Harvey
V. Viney
William F. Clark
Henry Woodson
Samuel Bryant
William Bryant
R. G. Mortimer, Jr.

Independents (Portsmouth, OH)

Wilson Minor
Joseph J. Minor
Lloyd Henson
Henry Baker
Frank Johnson
J. H. Scott
Lilly Ross
Frank White
Henry Holliday
Charles Peen

Louisiana

Pickwick (New Orleans, LA)

Edward M. Cohen, ss / President
Joe Johnson, rf / Vice President
O. F. Boisseau, rf
Stephen Ternoir, Secretary
Richard Nixon, Treasurer
L. J. Reeves, Vice President
Walter Lewis Cohen, 1b / Captain
James Duncan Kennedy, p
E. Denis, c
L. Deaufeauchard, 2b
P. Landry, 3b
Joseph G. Thomas, lf
James Cohen, cf

North Carolina

Scraps (Wilmington, NC)

Alex Butler, Jr., President/p
Benjamin Willis, Secretary/1b
James Proctor, 2b
James E. Starkey, c
James Winfield, 3b
John Mosely, ss
Charles Norwood, rf
Joshua Davis, cf
Edgar C. Robinson, lf

Unknowns (Wilmington, NC)

Alex Robinson, p / Captain
Joshua Johnson, c
Thomas Byrd, 1b/Secretary
Charles Parker, 2b

J. Hall, 3b
W. T. Finch, ss
James Hayes, lf
C. Smith, cf
Charles W. Howard, rf
W. F. Tucker
Shepherd Smith
James Hall

South Carolina

Arlingtons (Charleston, SC)

J. Nathan, President
J. Wilson, Vice President
J. Smith, p / Captain
E. Porter, c
G. Galliard, 1b
Henry Carroll, cf
W. Owens, rf
G. Bead, lf
G. Smith, 3b
William Simmons, ss

Catchers (Charleston, SC)

Edward Myers, p
Peter Grant, c
W. McKinley, ss
Robert Howard, 1b
H .C. Williams, 2b / Captain
C. C .Chaffee, 3b
S. McKinley, rf
Edward Ryan, cf
Charles Brown, lf

Manhattans (Charleston, SC)

J. Davis, ss / President
H. Jackson, p / Vice Pres.
R. Brown, c
J. Thompson, 1b
D. Fields, 2b
G. Dean, 3b
F. Small, lf
J. Smith, cf
J. Manigault, rf
T. B. Wilson, Captain

Orientals (Charleston, SC)

James Moore, President
F. Weston, Vice President
William Gammon, Secretary
Peter Grant, Treasurer / 3b
John Williams, c
William Jones, p
W. McKinley, ss / Captain
Andrew Wilson, 1b
P. Dennis, 2b
Andrew Brown, lf / cf
G. Bellinger, cf / rf
R. Brown, rf

Young Pacifics (Charleston, SC)

James Moore, President
F. Weston, Vice President

William Gammon, Secretary
Peter Grant, Treasurer / 3b
J. R. Williams, c
William Jones, p
W. McKinley, ss / Captain
A. Wickles, 1b
Primus P. Dennis, 2b
A. Brown, lf
G. Bellinger, cf
R. Brown, rf

Manhattans (Columbia, SC)

E. D. Bevel, p / Captain
E. Robinson, c
George Moore, ss
Henry D. Nash, 1b
R. Holmes, 2b
A. W. Cooke, 3b
J. King, lf
J. Allen, rf
H. Sightler, cf

Washington, DC

Mutuals (Washington, DC)

James Talbott (Talbert), 2b
George Anderson, c / lf / 3b
Lottie, 1b
Henry Brooks, ss
Benjamin Boyd, cf
George H. Richardson, 3b / lf
James H. Washington, p / 2b
Bryde, cf
Smith, rf
James T. Tolliver, lf / c
Thomas T. Barlow (A. Smith), rf

Uniques (Washington, DC)

William Carroll, c
Jesse Roy, p
J. Chitham (Cheatham), 1b
Rufus Savoy, 2b
J. William Cole, 3b
Abraham Hall, ss
B. Willis, lf
F. Jackson, cf
Samuel Brooks, rf
John Wesley Brent, lf

1878

Illinois

Uniques (Chicago, IL)

Henry Johnson, p / 2b
Giles Powell, c / 3b
Henry Hampton, ss
Carey Jackson, 3b
D. Brown, 2b
Thomas Watkins, 1b
George Overland, lf / ss
Benjamin Cleary, rf
Ed Harden, 1b / c / lf

James Tilley, cf
Samuel Brown, 1b
William Berry, Manager

Kansas

Eagles (Lawrence, KS)

James Miller, lf
Thomas Berry, c
James W. Hoyt
E. Matthews, ss
Spencer Thomas, 3b
George Berry, p
Perry Polk, 2b
Israel Allen, rf
Frank Hunter, cf

Osage Champions (Burlingame, KS)

James Shannon, First Nine / Captain
Levi Ford, Second Nine / Captain
Henry Austin, Secretary
Willis Williams, Treasurer

Louisiana

Pickwick (New Orleans, LA)

Edward M. Cohen, ss / President
L. J. Reeves, Vice President
S. Ternoir, Secretary / Treasurer
Walter Lewis Cohen, 1b / Captain
James Duncan Kennedy, p
E. Denis, c
L. Deaufeauchard, 2b
P. Landry, 3b
Joseph G. Thomas, lf
James Cohen, cf
O. F. Boisseau, rf

Massachusetts

Resolutes (Boston, MA)

William H. Walker, President
James DeWitt, Vice President
William H. Cruckendle, Secretary
John B. Bailey, Treasurer

Michigan

Eckfords (Battle Creek, MI)

F. Corbin, p
Martin Snodgrass, 1b
Charles Tyler, 2b
Ed Chavers, 3b
V. Hackley, ss
Will Scott, lf
Charles Locke, rf
Charles Artson, cf / Treasurer
John Gaines, c / Captain

New York

Eurekas (Auburn NY)

Arthur Smith, Captain
Fred Williams

Henry James
Henry Smith
Alonzo Dale
James Warren
Edward Williams
Harry Gordon
Benton Thomas
Isaac Mink, Manager

Georgia Minstrels (New York, NY)

Charles A. Crusoe
C. M. Marshall
Buffalo
Taylor Brown
Austin
Andrew Jackson
Hosea Easton
James W. Mills
O. Jackco
Charles B. Hicks, Manager

Eurekas (Rochester, NY)

Benjamin Jackson, 1b / Captain
Harry G. Johnson, 2b
Samuel Francis, 3b
Charles Moore, ss
John Downes, p
William Stewart, c
A. Yorks, lf
C. White, cf
Dennis Gibbs, rf
Arthur L. Smith, Substitute
R. Murry, Substitute
A. Higgins, Substitute
B. Spicer, Substitute

Fearless (Utica, NY)

Walter Pell, 3b
Abram Teabout, 1b
Charles Peterson, 2b
Glenn Brown, rf / p
J. Jackson, p
Thomas Lippin, lf
William Jackson, c
Charles Teabout, cf
Theodore Freeman, ss

Recruits (Charlotte, NC)

Gray J. Toole
W. H. Robinson
J. C. North
Abram North
Jeffrey Sumner
Samuel Mosely
Alex Webb
William Kelley
Alex Harris
H. C. Hutchinson
Rufus Hyde
Yank Norwood

Pennsylvania

Harleys (Harrisburg, PA)

D. Brown, 2b
W. Ridock, cf
David Allen, c
W. Jackson, lf
L. Earley, ss
William Shadney, p
James Murray, 3b
S. Burrs, rf
A. Jackson, 1b
George R. Scott, Manager
James A. Howard, Secretary, Secretary
Charles W. Harley, President

Creedmoor (Wrightsville, PA)

William Jamison, c
J. C. McPeak, p
Leonard Bear, ss
F. Reed, 1b
Benjamin Hollis, 2b
J. T. Harris, 3b
Levi Barton, rf
Daniel Rice, cf
John Vonne, Substitute
William A. Bear, lf / Captain

Enterprise (York, PA)

W. Gross, c
A. Mason, p
Gus A. Burton, ss
George Joice, 1b
C. Mead, 2b
J. W. Brown, 3b
A. Kenny, rf
J. G. M. Brown, cf
W. Gooden, lf

Virginia

Fifth Ward (Petersburg, VA)

Valentine, 2b
Branch, c
Ross, rf
Thompson, 3b
Wilkins, 1b
Hill, cf
Harris, lf
Jaime, p
J. Thompson, ss

Star Lights (Pocahontas, VA)

Wilkins, p
Jones, c
Powell, 3b
Howard, ss
Hunter, cf
Williams, 1b
Coleman, rf
Shelby, lf
B. Jones, 2b
N. N. Durphy, Scorer

Washington, DC

Alerts (Washington, DC)

Henry Johnson, President
Archibald "Archie" Lewis, Vice President
William C. Chase, Secretary
James L. Matthews, Treasurer
Horace Parke, Director / Captain
Edward L. Savoy, Director
George F. T. Cook, Director
P. Lewis, Director
Richard Davidge, Director
Jerome A. Johnson, Scorer

Keystones (Washington, DC)

Warren Dent, rf
P. Nelson, c
Charles Shorter, p
John Tyler, 2b
Sims Emory, 1b
James Washington, 3b / c
Jerome Thomas, cf
Preston Brooks, p / lf
Lottie, 1b
Smith, 1b
Alexander Gordon, ss
Wayman Brooks, cf
Charles Patton, Team Captain
Henry Brooks, ss /Board of Directors
C. S. Burley, President
A. J. Brooks, Vice President

Manhattan Reds (Washington, DC)

Benjamin Boyd, 2b
Phil Smoot, rf / 1b
James Talbott (Talbert), ss
James Thomas Tolliver, c
George H. Richardson, 1b
John Wesley Brent, 3b
Robert C. Gaines, p
Alexander Gordon, lf
William Carroll, cf
Harry Johnson, cf
Arthur Thomas, c / cf
J. Nelson, rf
Henry Schools, ss
Charles Davis, p

Mutuals (Washington, DC)

James H. Smith, President
C. T. S. Brent, Vice President
Charles Bruce, Treasurer / Secretary
William Grymes, Board of Directors
Thomas S. Brooks, Board of Directors
Thomas Barlow, Captain
John W. Bell
David Fisher

Uniques (Washington, DC)

William Carroll, c
Jesse Roy, p
J. Chitham (Cheatham), 1b

Rufus Savoy, 2b
Hamilton D. Cole, 3b
Abraham Hall, ss
B. Willis, lf
F. Jackson, cf
Javan Emory, c
Samuel Brooks, rf
John Wesley Brent, lf
L. Thomas, Treasurer
J. Lacy, Board of Directors
Charles Washington, Board of Directors

1879

Florida

Athletics (Jacksonville, FL)

Garvin, 1b
Hall, c
Coleman, 2b
Bryant, lf
Green, rf
Pierce, ss
Jackson, cf
Hodges, 3b
Brown, p
Thomas Baxter, Captain

Georgia

Chathams (Savannah, GA)

Richard Block, p
A. C. Lewis, 2b
John Dillon, 3b
Warrick Quarterman, 1b
Frank P. Thompson, rf / c
Thomas A. Simmons, c
Mordecai, ss
John Morrell, lf
Boifeulette, cf

Illinois

Uniques (Chicago, IL)

Benjamin Cleary, p
Samuel Brown, 1b
John Shaw, 2b / cf
Robert P. Jackson, c
Henry Hampton, ss / 3b
Giles Powell, 3b / c
D. Brown, 2b
Thomas Watkins, 1b
George Overland, lf
Carey Jackson, 3b / p
Devinney Davis, rf
James Tilley, cf / 1b
F. C. Bryant, rf
Edward Hardin, lf / 1b
Harry J. Edwards, 3b
Clakeworn, cf / 1b
William Johnson, p
William Berry, Manager

Acmes (Springfield, IL)

A. Knight, President
W. F. Knight, Secretary / 3b
J. Smith, c
H. Jimmerson, p
Ben Black, ss
William Lyles, 1b
C. Craig, 1b
J. Jackson, lf
A. Turner, cf
George McKinney, rf
Marlon McKinney, Scorer

Indiana

Colored Barbers (Indianapolis, IN)

Eugene Jones
John Hines
Albert J. Farley
William Walden
William Floyd
Jeff Dickinson
Thomas Marshall,
William Fletcher
Thomas White

Colored Waiters (Indianapolis, IN)

John Lewis
Beck Davis
John Pernell
Jesse H. Ringgold
Ceil Saunders
Joe Johnson
John Stewart
Amos Jones
John Fisher

Kansas

Colored Nine (Fort Scott, KS)

Ed Brown, 1b
Perry, rf
Parker, ss
Curran, 2b
Nick Myers, lf
I. A. Anthony, c
Vese W. Bowman, 2b / Captain
J. L. Wareham, 3b

Olympics (Fort Scott, KS)

H. B. Denniston, 3b
Charles Chapman, ss
Ed Brown, p / Captain
Charles Brown, c
Charles Walters, lf
W. H. Beard, cf
I. A. Anthony, rf / 3b
H. C. Loucks, 2b
Vese W. Bowman, 2b
J. L. Wareham, 1b
S. M. Jackson, c

Saunders, ss
William Patterson, Secretary/Scorer

Colored Nine (Mill Creek, KS)

Bigger, c
N. Blair, p
Frary, 1b
Thompson, 2b
Dwyer, 3b
E. Blair, ss
Harvey, lf
L. Blair, rf

Nameless (Parsons, KS)

J. R. Lemist, ss
F. F. Wiggins, p
W. J. Britt, 2b
H. T. Lemist, rf
M. F. Koehler, cf/rf
McCarter, lf/cf
G. W. Ragland, 1b
G. Chapman, c
G. T. Willett, 3b
W. C. Bradley, lf
A. S. Stevens, Scorer
J. F. Shaughnessy, Substitute
S. W. Woodruff, Substitute

Louisiana

Pickwicks (New Orleans, LA)

E. Denis
L. Deaufeauchard, rf
O. F. Boisseau, cf
Jules Caufield, ss
P. Langry, 3b
R. Brooks, 2b
Walter Lewis Cohen, 1b / Captain
P. G. Collins, c
John Kennedy, p
Stephen Ternoir, Secretary / Treasurer
A. Roudez, Vice President
Edward Cohen, lf / President

Massachusetts

Resolutes (Boston, MA)

W. F. Simpson, President
A. D. White, Secretary
John B. Bailey, Treasurer

New York

Eurekas (Auburn NY)

Arthur Smith, Captain
Fred Williams
Henry James
Henry Smith
Alonzo Dale
James Warren
Edward Williams
Harry Gordon
Benton Thomas
Isaac Mink, manager

Hick's Georgia Minstrels (New York, NY)

O. T. Jackson
J. R. Matlock
James W. Mills
William Sanders
T. Brown
Sam Keenan
J. Morton
C. J. Jackson
George Harris
Frank Hewitt
T. Ellis

Central Depot (Syracuse, NY)

Al Lawrence, 1b
W. P. Myers, 3b
J. A. Mason, ss
H. M. Mitchell, rf
N. J. Jones, 2b
T. Owens, cf
John A. Jordan, c
J. Tripp, lf
S. P. Jordan, p

Pastimes (Syracuse, NY)

William H. Franklin, President
James H. Allen, Vice President
Henry H. Waters, Manager
Jacob B. Francis, cf / Secretary / Treasurer
Augustus Jordan, Team Captain
Al Lawrence, 1b / c
Edward Wilson, ss / c
Phillip Jordan, lf
John A. Jordan, 2b
John Downes, p
N. J. Jones, lf
W. P. Myers, 3b
Clinton Peters, c
H. M. Mitchell, cf
J. Tripp, rf
D. Tyler, lf
Wadsworth, 2b

Vanderbilt House (Syracuse, NY)

Aaron Briles, p
Augustus Jordan, c
Nobles, 1b
Charles Jefferson, ss
Jones, rf
Ed Wilson, 2b
Wilbur Jackson, lf
J. Randolph Robinson, cf
James H. Allen, 3b

Bagg's Hotel (Utica, NY)

Albert Jackson, c
Samuel Freeman, p
Richard H. Carter, 1b
W. C. Anderson, 2b
Joseph Johnson, ss

John W. Thompson, 3b / 2b
William Carter, 3b
Henry Willis, lf
Andrew Campbell, cf
Samuel Jackson, rf / c
Brown, lf
Albert Wilson, cf
R. Hollenbeck, lf

*Butterfield House
(Utica, NY)*

Watson Potter, p
George Howard, lf / p
Brown, cf
William Pell, rf
James Pell, 1b
Boller, 2b
Frazier, 3b
Moses Gray, ss
Richard Wallace Sherman, p
Rans Jackson, c

Fearless (Utica, NY)

Samuel "Sam" Freeman, ss
Peter Tonssant, c
Charles Peterson, p
Arlington C. DeNike, 1b
John Lippin, 2b
Thomas Lippin, 3b
George Atkins, rf
Charles Pell, cf
Shepard Moss, lf
Jacob T. Baker, ss

North Carolina

*Stonewall Jacksons
(Wilmington, NC)*

William H. Nash, Captain
J. J. Neil, President
Charles Howard, Vice President
Thomas Knight, Secretary
William Harriss, Treasurer

Ohio

*Runymedes
(Cincinnati, OH)*

Robinson, rf / p
G. O'Bannion, 2b / c
C. O'Bannion, ss
James Chapman, 3b
Thompson, cf
James O'Bannion, 1b
Downs, lf
Robert Burrell, c / rf
Butler Horner, c / rf

Zulus (Cleveland, OH)

Charles Stanley, c
Henry C. Smith, p
William Wilson, ss
James H. Morris, 1b
Ed Doctor, 2b

Powhattan Henderson, 3b
Walter L. Milligan, lf
W. Brown, cf
J. Bowler, rf

Pennsylvania

Harley (Harrisburg, PA)

Edward Earley, ss
C. Myers, cf
J. Allen, 3b
William Jackson, 1b
William Shadney, p
D. Brown, c
William Long, rf
S. Burrs, p
William Pople, lf
Sims Emory, c
C. W. Harley, 2b / Manager

Virginia

Fifth Ward (Petersburg, VA)

James Valentine, 2b
Clem Branch, c
Sumerfield Ross, rf
Oster Thompson, 3b
John Wilkins, 1b
Charles Hill, cf
Richard Harris, lf
Jaime, p
James Thompson, ss

Washington, DC

Douglass (Washington, DC)

William Brown, p
William Braxton, ss
William Carroll, 3b
James Talbott (Talbert), 2b
Charles Boyd, rf
R. W. White, 1b
D. W. Downing, lf
J. Pinckney, c
Alexander Gordon, cf

Excelsiors (Washington, DC)

Holly Parke, c
James Myers, p
Charles Whitlow, 1b
Harry Johnson, Jr., 2b
Benjamin Simms, 3b
Steve Wall, ss
Dick Thompkins, rf
Ralph Langston, lf
George T. F. Cook, cf
James Harry Smith, c
Fred Douglass, Jr., p
George Richardson, 1b
Thomas Barlow, 2b
Richard Davidge, 3b
Shermonte Lewis, ss
Jerome "Jere" Johnson, lf

Judd Malvin, rf
Christopher Fleetwood, cf

*Howard University
(Washington, D.C.)*

Furman J. Shadd, President
James Howard, Vice President
Robert A. Caskie, Secretary
William G. Sears, Treasurer
Prof. James M. Gregory, Manager
L. O. Posey, Asst. Manager
Matthew Lewis, Captain

Mutuals (Washington, DC)

Benjamin Holmes, 3b
P. Nelson, lf
Peter Richmond, c / 3b
William Barker, 2b / cf
Louis Smith, p
Frank Bell, rf
W. H. Dade, ss / 2b
John H. Lawson, 1b
V. Ralph, c
James Carter, p / rf
Thomas Welch, lf
William Grymes, President
S. H. Burnett, Vice President
C. F. Bruce, Secretary / Treasurer
George F. Coakley, Director
Charles H. Whitlow, Director
T. L. Brooks, Director

Uniques (Washington, DC)

J. William Cole, 3b
Abraham Hall, ss
Jacob C. Strather, rf
Charles Jones, cf
Rufus Savoy, 2b
James Thomas Tolliver, c
J. Chatham (Chitham), 1b
Charles Proctor, 1f
Jesse Roy, p
Javan Emory, c

1880

Connecticut

Colored Nine (Bristol, CT)

Joseph Brown
Charles Davis
Halsey Bradford
Eugene Wall
John Crump
Theodore Crump
James Sims
William Barker
John Hunt
James Davis
Stephen Tuno
Shadrach Elliott
Isaac Washington, Manager

Georgia

Chathams (Savannah, GA)

Block, p
J. B. Lewis, 2b
John Dillon, 3b
Warrick Quarterman, 1b
Frank P. Thompson, rf / c
Thomas A. Simmons, c
Mordecai, ss
W. H. Morrell, lf
Boifeulette, cf

Illinois

Uniques (Chicago, IL)

Benjamin Cleary, p
John Shaw, 2b / cf
Henry Hampton, ss / 3b
Giles Powell, 3b / c
D. Brown, 2b
Thomas Watkins, 1b
George Overland, lf / rf / ss
Carey Jackson, 3b / p
F. C. Bryant, rf
Edward Hardin, lf
Harry J. Edwards, 3b
Clakeworn, cf / 1b
Samuel Brown, 1b
Irvin Hardy, 1b
William P. Johnson, p
William Berry, Manager

Kansas

Nameless (Parsons, KS)

J. R. Lemist, ss
F. F. Wiggins, p
W. J. Britt, 2b
H. T. Lemist, rf
M. F. Koehler, cf/rf
McCarter, lf/cf
G. W. Ragland, 1b
G. Chapman, c
G. T. Willett, 3b
W. C. Bradley, lf
A. S. Stevens, Scorer

Louisiana

Aetnas (New Orleans, LA)

Alex Redon, c
Henry Bolden, 1b
Robert Brooks, 2b
R. Toney, 3b
William Johnson, ss
James Griffin, lf
George Thomas, cf
Alfred Phillips, rf
Joseph Mitchell, p / Captain
Augustus Williams, Steward
James Henri Burch, Manager
A. V. Woods, Treasurer

Robert Gould, Corresponding
  Secretary
John Pursloe, Secretary
George Walker, Vice President
A. S. Perkins, President

Orleans (New Orleans, LA)

Walter L. Cohen, 2b
E. Denis, c
Joseph Delmar, ss
James Cohen, lf
Ernest Fondal, 1b
Rafael, rf
James D. Kennedy, p
P. F. Collins, cf
John E. Oliver, 3b

New York

Eurekas (Auburn NY)

Arthur Smith, Captain
Fred Williams
Henry James
Henry Smith
Alonzo Dale
James Warren
Edward Williams
Harry Gordon
Benton Thomas
Isaac Mink, manager

Flies (Geneva, NY)

Benjamin F. Cleggett, President
George W. Allen, Treasurer
Henry Harden, Secretary
Henry W. Brown, Captain
William Kenney
Garrett Kenney
George Cortright
William Condol
Burt Brown
Glenn Brown

Pastimes (Syracuse, NY)

Al Lawrence, 1b / 3b / 2b
J. A. Mason, 2b / 1b
W. P. Myers, 3b / Team Captain
Phillip Jordan, lf / ss
John H. Jordan, ss
Arthur Jackson, c
Samuel "Rans" Jackson, ss / lf / cf
Edward N. Powell, p / rf
John Downes, p
J. Tripp, cf
H. M. Mitchell, rf
Edward Thompson, rf / p
Edward Wilson, c
Jacob Francis, cf / lf / Secretary / Treasurer
William H. Franklin, Manager

Fearless (Utica, NY)

J. Lawrence, 2b / p
James Pell, 1b

Augustus Jordan, lf
James H. Washington, cf
William Jackson, rf / 3b
Samuel Jackson, c
Frank Pell, cf
Thomas Carter, rf
Joseph Johnson, 2b
Arthur Jackson, c
Samuel Freeman, p / 2b
Charles Sherman, 3b / rf
Jacob T. Baker, ss

North Carolina

National Pastimes (Raleigh, NC)

R. Millikin, ss
L. M. Nash, p
G. W. Gross, rf
H. Blake, lf
A. Jordan, 1b
M. Hawkins, 2b
F. B. Curtis, c
William Hawkins, cf
D. W. Nash, Captain
N. G. Millikin, 3b / Secretary
W. H. Sumner, Vice President
A. Foy, President

Pennsylvania

Charles Johnsons (Harrisburg, PA)

John Fry, ss
Charles Spottwood, 3b
Thomas Wilson, c
Armor Wilson, rf
Ethan Thomas, 1b
William Williams, 2b
John Black, rf
Horace Murray, cf
William Long, lf
Wilson Carney, p
Charles Johnson, Manager
Dangerfield S. Garner, Secretary
Clarence Johnson, President

Tennessee

Garfields (Knoxville, TN)

Jake Henry, c
H. Ramsey, p
C. Amos, Captain / 1b
J. W. Hutson, Captain
Richard Henry, 2b
W. Atkins, 3b
John Banks, ss
Los. Magby, lf
J. Koss, cf
Robert Hazen, rf
Charley McNutt, Manager

Washington, DC

Douglass (Washington, DC)

S. Pinckney, c

Charles Boyd, rf / 1b
William Braxton, ss
James Talbott (Talbert), 2b
Harry Johnson, cf
D.W. Downing, cf
William Brown, p / 3b
Benjamin Holmes, 3b
R. W. White, 1b / rf
William Carroll, cf / c
Alexander Gordon, lf
Richmond Robinson, cf
Robert Hayes, cf
Benjamin Lancaster, ss
R. L. Gaines, p

Eagles (Washington, DC)

J. W. Bell, lf
Rufus Savoy, 2b
Benjamin Lancaster, ss
Jesse Roy, 1b
Warren Dent, 3b
Ralph Parrot, c / lf
J. Chatham (Cheatham), cf
Harry C. Johnson, c / 1b
William Carroll, rf
Robert W. White, 2b
W. F. Ferguson, lf
Robert Hayes, cf
Richmond Robinson, 3b / c
Ralph Langston, 2b
William Barker, c / lf
Alfred Pope, 1b
George Coakley, cf
William Holmes, p
Hurbet, lf
William Carter, p
James Carter, p

Keystone (Washington, DC)

P. Nelson, c / lf
James Brooks, 2b
Preston Brooks, p / lf / 3b
Charles Washington, 3b / cf
Henry Brooks, ss
Thomas Barlow (A. Smith), 1b
John Tyler, 2b / p
Matthew Emory, lb
R. W. White, rf / lf
F. Jackson, cf
Ridgeley, cf
Jerome Thomas, rf
Peter Richmond, 3b / c

Manhattans (Washington, DC)

Richmond Robinson, ss
William Hattan, p
Henry Schools, c / 3b / cf
James Thomas Tolliver, c
R. W. White, lf / rf
J. Washington, 1b / rf
S. Alexander, 2b
Jerome Thomas, cf

William Sheppard, 3b
William Brown, rf
Robert Hayes, lf / rf / 3b
Ralph Parrot, c
W. H. Dade, rf
Follun, c

Mutuals (Washington, DC)

Benjamin Holmes, 3b
P. Nelson, cf
Richmond Robinson, 2b
Barker, lf
James Harry Smith, p
J. Carter, rf
V. Ralph, c
W. H. Dade, ss
Thomas H. Barlow, 1b / Captain
Simon A. Burnette, President
Charles R. Douglass, Vice President
Lawson Brooks, Secretary / Treasurer
Harry Ormett, Director
William W. Grymes, Director
Charles F. Bruce, Director
Charles H. Whitlow, Director

Sparta (Washington, DC)

Christopher A. Fleetwood
James H. Smith
Harry Johnson, Jr.
J. L. Brooks
Shermonte Lewis
James Duncan Kennedy
Thomas Barlow
E. A. Savoy
William Harris
John C. Nalle
C. B. Governs

Uniques (Washington, DC)

J. Chitham (Cheatham), 1b
Charles Proctor, lf
Jesse Roy, p
Fred Jackson, cf
Abraham Hall, ss
Rufus Savoy, 2b
Rawlings, rf
William Carroll, c
J. William Cole, 3b
Jacob C. Strather, lf
Charles Jones, cf
Wells, rf

1881

Illinois

Browns (Springfield, IL)

George McKinney, 3b
Walter Oglesby, 2b
Thomas Brown, 1b
Alfred Williams, c
Valentine Allen, p
William Joiner, ss

John Spencer, lf
Jordan Murray, cf
Barney Cline, rf

Indiana

Colored Nine (Fort Wayne, IN)

Will Cooper
Martin Bulgar
Charles Brackenridge
Louis T. Bourie
Harry Bossler
William H. Coombs
John Olds
A. H. Carrier
T. G. Hedekin
Joseph Momer
Oliver Patterson

Kansas

White Stockings (Lyndon, KS)

C. Barrett, c
W. Miller, p
H. Whitman, 1b
Kingslery, 2b
L. Whitman, 3b
H. Rogers, ss
H. Richards, lf
W. Olcott, cf
R. Miller, rf

Louisiana

A. J. Dumonts (Algiers, LA)

E. Fondal, ss
Charles H. Jackson, p
Joseph Delmar, 2b
Joseph Kyle, 3b
John Hunter, 1b
Albert Harvey, lf
P. Thomas, cf
Edward Williams, rf
T. Walker, c

Frank Williams (Algiers, LA)

J. W. Bibb, President
E. Beattie, Vice President
J. Victor Alexander, Captain
W. Ferguson, Treasurer
H. J. Carter, Secretary
E. Platard, Steward
J. Fonchey, Sergeant-At-Arms

Pacifics (New Orleans, LA)

W. Labarosiere, President
Edgar Blandin, c
F. Lavinge, 1b
E. Native, 2b
E. Despicas, 3b
Dan Mitchell, rf
R. Rouseves, lf
J. Mare, cf
F. Gaspard, ss

Pickwicks (New Orleans, LA)

Edward Williams, ss
William J. Turner, 2b
James Duncan Kennedy, p
Al "Ed" Robinson, rf
Walter L. Cohen, 1b / Captain
Edward Francis, c
Edward M. Cohen, cf / President
Jules Caufield, 3b
O. F. Boisseau, lf
James Madison Vance, Manager
Willis Vermuille, Honorary President
A. Alix, Treasurer
C. W. Vance, Recording Secretary
Richard Nixon, Corresponding Secretary

New York

Fearless (Utica, NY)

James Pell, 1b
Charles Moore, lf / ss
James H. Washington, 2b
William Jackson, lf
Samuel Freeman, ss / p
Samuel Jackson, c / cf
George Howard, 1b / 3b
William Rans Jackson, 2b / lf
Frank Bell, cf
J. Lawrence, p
Frank Anderson, rf
W. Drumm, lf / p
J. Dever, ss
Alonzo Raymore, rf
Thomas Carter, rf
Arthur Jackson, lf
Joseph Johnson, 2b

Washington, DC

Spartas (Washington, DC)

M. Bruce
L. Brown
Joseph Savoy
John Hyman
S. Gray
William Syphax
John Gibson
William Curry
E. Rowe
William Welch

1882

Georgia

Champions (Atlanta, GA)

Robert Shields
Aleck Dawson
Thomas Green
Mack Gordon
Clarence Hurd
Thomas Ham
William Pope

Ed Walton
James Davis
William Crockett
Emanuel Gay

Young Americans (Macon, GA)

C. V. Fambro, 3b
Alfred Laney, cf
W. O. Coleman, ss
Joe Johnson, c
E. E. Palmer, ss
Sam Carlos, 1b
Lee Dukes, p
Gus Rafeel, 2b
Jerry Battle, rf

Illinois

Adelaides (Elgin, IL)

Granville N. Hackley, 1b / Team Captain
Watts, c
Buckner, p
Edward Newsome, ss
Smith, 2b
Aaron White, 3b
Benjamin Hyde, rf / 3b
Joseph Garret, cf / ss
James Oates, lf
B. Middleton, 2b
George Middleton, rf/ c
Robert "Bob" Garret, p
George Taylor, 1b
Walker Pride, cf
W. J. Christie, Manager

Blue Stockings (Elgin, IL)

Henry Oates, c
Robert "Bob" Garret, p
Eddie Newsome, ss
Granville N. Hackley, 1b / c / Captain
Benjamin Hyde, 2b
Aaron White, 3b
James Oates, lf
Joseph Garret, cf
Frank Suggs, rf

Browns (Springfield, IL)

George McKinney, 3b
Walter Oglesby, 2b
Thomas Brown, 1b
Alfred Williams, c
Valentine Allen, p
William Joiner, ss
John Spencer, lf
Jordan Murray, cf
Barney Cline, rf

Indiana

Clippers (Paris, IN)

P. Thomas, p
Williams, c
J. Timos, ss
Dawson, 1b

Duncan, 2b
Miller, 3b
West, lf
Kelly, cf
Miller, rf

Browns (Terra Haute, IN)

Charles Clark, p
Nathan Tate, c
James H. Newsome, ss
Carter, 1b
Cauthorn, 2b
Harry Clark, 3b
Pope, lf
Malone, cf
Howard, rf

Kansas

Liberties (Fort Scott, KS)

Henry Curtis, c
Andy Giles, p
Lewis Webber, 1b
Frank Hawkins, 2b
Henry Hawkins, 3b
Dan Myers, ss
Nick Myers, lf
Henry Campbell, cf
Bud Langton, rf

Westerns (Fort Scott, KS)

Alfred Bradford, c
Curt Tyler, p
Nathan Barker, 1b
Oscar Red, 2b
Jasper Camp, 3b
Tom Duval, ss
Harrison Woodley, lf
Will Harris, cf
Stokes Fredwell, rf
F. White, Captain

Louisiana

Pickwick (New Orleans, LA)

Edward Williams, ss
William J. Turner, 2b
John "Bud" Fowler, p
Al "Ed" Robinson, rf
Walter L. Cohen, 1b
Edward Francis, c
Edward M. Cohen, cf / 2b
Jules Caufield, 3b
O. F. Boisseau, lf

Unions (New Orleans, LA)

R. W. B. Gould
James Griffin, p
A. Spall, rf
E. Denis, 2b
J. S. Walker, cf
O. P. Sullivan, p
Charles Ogden, lf
James Recasner, 3b

George J. Irvine, ss
Peen Johnson, c
William J. Turner,1b / Captain
Joseph Mitchell, Manager
C. J. Frost, Corresponding Secretary
H. L. Bradley, Secretary
A. Walba, Treasurer
M. Kellum, Vice President
M. C. Oliver, President

New Jersey

Mutuals (Atlantic City, NJ)

Edward Davis
Cornelius Hoagland
Edward Simpson
Hebert Simpson
Benjamin Davis
Fred Nichols
P. Gobton
C. Galleger
Ed Scudder
W. Hegeman
W. L. Underwood

Deegans (Camden, NJ)

Jackson, c
Sullivan, c
Robinson, 3b
Benson, lf
Wilson, rf
Reed, 1b
Slivin, p
Derry, 2b
G. W. Gardner, cf / Captain
W. O. Castor, Manager
J. H. Garner, Secretary
C. E. Williams, ss / p / President

Washingtons (Long Branch, NJ)

Harry S. Cummings, 2b
Wilson Carey, c
Joseph Myers, cf
James H. Paynter, 1b
Abraham Hall, p
Oscar Jackson, lf
Joseph H. Wilson, lf
Phil Smoot, ss
John Stewart, rf
Anderson Marshall, 3b
Clarence Page, rf
William Dennis, cf / 2b
Aaron Russell, lf
Jacobs, c

New York

Callender Blues (New York, NY)

P. Adams, p
C. Waters, c
Charles Williams, 1b
Frank Girard, 2b

George Freeman, ss
Al Smith, 3b
Wolf, rf
Lewis L. Brown, cf
Burrell Hawkins, lf

Clarendons (Saratoga Springs, NY)

William P. Hatton, p
William Brown, p / 2b
Robert Brown, rf
Benjamin Boyd, 3b / cf / rf
McKnight, 2b
James Washington, 1b / rf
Jacob C. Strather, rf
Benjamin Holmes, 3b / c
James Talbott (Talbert), ss
William Braxton, ss
William H. Barker, cf / 2b
John H. Lawson, 2b
Samuel Alexander, 2b
Mumford, 1b
C. Wilson, lf / cf
Andrew Marshall, 3b / ss
Louis Buchanan, lf / cf
S. K. Govern, p / Manager

Fearless (Utica, NY)

Frank J. Williams, ss
Phillip Jordan, cf
James Pell, 1b
Samuel Freeman, 2b
William Jackson, 3b
Jacob Francis, lf
Charles Jefferson, rf
Arthur Jackson, p
Samuel Jackson, c

Ohio

Southern Stars (Cleveland, OH)

Henry C. Smith, p / c
Charles Stanley, c / 1b
Frank Doctor, 1b / 3b
William Wilson, 2b
Oswald (Osworth), 3b
Williams, ss
Edward Huston, rf
Jones, cf
Walter L. Milligan, lf
William Clifford, rf / p
Willis B. Ross, cf
John Cook, p
Zimmer, ss
Kerver, rf

Missouri

Aetnas (St. Louis, MO)

S. C. Mayo
D. Brown, c
William Davis, p
Scott Turner, ss
Charles Brooks, 1b

E. Gray, 3b
P. Lee, ss
Charlie Thompson, lf
Massie, cf
Turner Anderson, rf

Black Stockings (St. Louis, MO)

William Davis, p
John "Bud" Fowler, 2b / p
Caesar Bracey, cf
Lewis Canter, ss
William Sutton, lf
Ed Rogers, 1b
Phil Smith, c
Charles Gardner, rf
Sylvester Chauvin, 3b
Henry Bridgewater, Manager

Pennsylvania

Mutuals (Allegheny, PA)

Will Taper, 1b
John Chilton, 3b
B. C. Makins, ss
Milford Wilson, 3b
Sam Griffin, c
J. Kess, p
William Robinson, rf
C. H. Lowry, lf
Charles Catlin, rf
George Sherrow, Manager

Keystones (Chester, PA)

John Hackett, c
Henry Sterling, p
John Hart, 1b
R. Smith, 2b
W. Harris, 3b
Isaac Rothwell, ss / 2b
W. Reiley, rf
Alexander Sheppard, cf
E. Watson, lf
David Perrigan, 3b
G. Perrigan, p
Benjamin Driskett, 1b
Warner Pryor, ss
Aaron Fields, cf

Ladomus Juniors (Chester, PA)

Monroe, c
McCallum, p
Ross, 1b
Stoever, 2b
John Hinkson, 3b
Wallace, ss
Birtwell, lf
Walter Hinkson, rf
L. Smith, rf
W. Ladomus, Manager

Olympics (Harrisburg, PA)

Henry Puller, c / rf
Sandy Burrs, lf

Steven Burrs, 2b / rf
Clarence Williams, c / 2b
George McMullan, 3b / ss
D. Halley, cf
D. Williams, 2b
J. Kelley, lf
James Barton, Captain
Buck Burr, Manager
Harry Sigler, Secretary

Orions (Philadelphia, PA)

George Williams, 2b
Daniel McDonald, c
Clarence Williams, c
James George Jackson, lf
Julius Forbes, ss/1b
George Fisher, rf
William Fisher, 2b
Charles Fisher, cf
D. Thompson, 1b
Walter Orr, 3b
Charles Jones, cf
Charles Davis, lf
Sims Emory, c
J. Williams, p
William Harris, ss / 1b
William Frisby, p
Edward Harris, rf
William Payne, c
William Bowers, cf
J. Hall, ss / rf
E. Hall, 2b
Abraham Harrison, ss / p
William James, c / p / 2b
John Johnson, 1b
John Taper (Taber), rf
William Carter, lf
John S. Lang, Manager

Colored Waiters (Reading, PA)

H. Kline, c
A. Hughes, p
C. Robinson, 1b
David Gibson, 2b
J. Brown, 3b
J. Blackburn, ss
Solomon B. Seidel, lf
S. Underwood, cf
David Fry, rf

Crescents (Reading, PA)

Henry C. Nelson, p
Charles H. Walker, c
Howard Bower, p / rf
C. Gibson, cf
William Jackson, 1b
P. Clark, 2b
Benjamin F. Smith, ss
Charles Seidel, 3b
J. Johnson, rf
E. Lloyd, lf
George Dorsey, Jr.

Lumber City Grays (Williamsport, PA)

Javan Emory, c
William H. Shadney, p
Charles Braxton, ss
J. Forster, 1b
Sims V. Emory, 3b
J. H. Millford, lf / Secretary
W. Pleasant, cf
S. Benson, rf
William T. Emory, 2b / General Manager
H. M. Minor, Team Captain
Arthur Winston, President
Sylvester Pleasant, Vice President
H. M. Boyd, Treasurer

Hunters (York, PA)

Ben Rhodes, c
Samuel Green, p
Charles Rhodes, ss / p
James Briscoe, 1b
Perry Wineberry, 2b
George Mason, 3b
William Lewis, rf
James Anderson, lf
Gus A. Burton, cf
S. Johns, Substitute
A. Mason, Substitute
F. Humphries, Substitute
A. Kenny, Substitute
Alex Johnson, Manager

Washington, DC

Manhattans (Washington, DC)

Richmond Robinson, ss
William Hattan, p
Henry Schools, c / 3b / cf
James Thomas Tolliver, c
Robert W. White, lf / rf
James Washington, 1b / rf
Samuel Alexander, 2b
Jerome Thomas, cf
William Sheppard, 3b
William Brown, rf
Robert Hayes, lf / rf / 3b
Ralph Parrot, c
W. H. Dade, rf

Douglass (Washington, DC)

Robert Brown, c
William Braxton, ss
James Talbott (Talbert), 2b
D.W. Downing, lf
William Brown, p
Jesse Brown, 3b
Charles Boyd, rf
McCartney, 1b
Harry C. Johnson, cf
E. C. Allen, p

1883

Alabama

Red Stockings (Huntsville, AL)

Percy Ware
William Hereford, Captain
Joseph Nemore
Benjamin Cooper
James "Jim" Binford
Charles "Charlie" Scott
William "Bill" Teal
Charles Brickell
Henry Fearn
Tommy J. Brandon

Connecticut

Wallace Club (Ansonia, CT)

Guy Day, ss
Brooks, lf
William Roberson, p
Fitch, c
Magruder, 3b
Ferguson, 2b
Charles Bell, ss
Dixon, cf
Camp, rf

Georgia

Lightfoot (Columbus, GA)

John A. Howard, Captain
Lee Reedy (Reader)
Jerry Key
Tom Jones
Jack Preer
John Griffin
John Thomas
Major Parks
West Sturgis

Metropolitans (Columbus, GA)

John A. Howard
Lee Reedy (Reader)
West Sturgis
Sam Hawkins
Jake Parker
William Bass, p
Jerry Key
John Thomas
Jack Preer, c
Charles Parks, Captain
William H. Harris, Manager

Stars (Columbus, GA)

Charles Parks, Captain
Augusta L. Tucker
Joe McDuffee
William Bass
Sam Hawkins
Squire Simpson
B. Kelly

Jake Parker
Henry Micken

Illinois

Senegambians (Aurora, IL)

Adams, c
Washington, lf
Benjamin Butler, ss
Smith, 2b
Willis "Chub" Artist, p
Meredy, rf
William Lucas, 3b
Pierce, 1b
Edwards, cf

Garden Citys (Chicago, IL)

S. Walker, p
William Albert Jones, c
S. Herndon, 2b
L. Robinson, cf
James Houck, ss
Wilbur F. Lewis, rf
L. Bell, 1b
William Brown, 3b
William Henderson, lf

Adelaides (Elgin, IL)

Aaron White, c / 3b
Benjamin Hyde, 3b / lf
Joseph Garret, ss
Augustus Hall, lf/c
George Middleton, 2b
Robert Garret, p
George Taylor, 1b
Walker Pride, cf
Benjamin Middleton, rf
Watts, c
W. J. Christie, Manager
Augustus Hall, President
Ed Newsome, Secretary / Treasurer

Pearly Blues (Peoria, IL)

Williams, cf
William Hellems, lf
Washington, c
Hanley, ss
A. Turner, 3b
Thomas Cheek, 1b
McCoy, rf
William Lyons, 2b
Charles Spears, p

Black Diamonds (Springfield, IL)

Frank Brandon, 2b
S. V. Casey, p
Sanders, ss
Benjamin Black, 3b
William Hudson, lf
William Renfro, 1b
Al Williams, cf
William Sappington, c
Ed Wormley, rf

Excelsiors (Springfield, IL)

Walter Oglesby, 2b
Al Williams, p
John Spencer, ss
Barney Clem, 3b
William Joiner, lf
F. Willis, 1b
William Parker, cf
William Sappington, c
Thomas Mann, rf
Qualls, Manager

Indiana

Logan Blues (Logansport, IN)

Charles Brooks, c
Sheridan Tutt, p
Henry Ashworth, ss
Frank Turner, 1b / captain
James "Jim" Allen, 3b
Frank Carter, 2b
Joshua Dent, lf
George Allen, rf
James "Jim" Carter, cf

Kansas

Lone Stars (Atchison, KS)

Ed Stewart, c
Ed Mack, p
Henry Irving, 1b
Harry "Ham" Evans, 2b
Thompson, rf
John Finley, ss
Fred Gleason, cf
Walt Booker, lf
Sam Phips, 3b
William Lewis
A. Williams, Manager
T. Lewis, Manager
A. McSpiatten, Scorer

Modocs (Topeka, KS)

John B. Jones, c/Captain
John H. Wash, p
Orrin Giles, ss
William H. Blythe, 1b
Harry Franklin, 2b
Lacy Woods, 3b
James Welch, p
Aleck Mackamore, lf
Henry Essex, cf
Harry McVeigh, rf
Scott "Doc" Smith, rf
William Roberts, cf
George Ware, Scorer
Wesley Brown, Umpire
William D. Donnell, Manager

Kentucky

Colored Nine (Hartford, KY)

Walker Kahn, 2b

Luke Barrett, 3b
Anderson Phipps, ss
Loyd Jackson, lf
Wes Bacon, cf
Sam Jackson, rf
Crit Taylor. P
Sam Moseley, c
S. W. Jackson, Scorer
Judson Phipps, 1b / Captain

Blue Stockings (Louisville, KY)

Alonzo Kieger, cf
James Armstrong, 2b / p
Clarence Manuel, cf / c
Lafayette Condon, p
Frank Garret, ss
William Woolfolk, cf
W. Jessie, ss
James Thomas, 1b
Fred Mayfield, c / cf
Moses Clark, 2b
George Burks, lf
Nelson Tarrance, 3b
Lucien Wagner, c

Massachusetts

Vendomes (Boston, MA)

John Saunders, cf
W. T. Gassaway, c
T. J. Gassaway, 2b
Marshall Thompson, lf
William Whitaker, p / 2b
Andrew C. Randolph, rf
Sam Harris, 3b
George W. Greene, ss
Richmond Robinson, 1b

Missouri

Black Stockings (Kansas City, MO)

Phil Hingston
H. Dale
W. Hammet
J. S. Buford
Dan White
James Miller
Spencer Mormon
Isaac Henderson
Samuel Thomas, Captain

Red Stockings (Sedalia, MO)

Charles Martin, 1b
H. Watson, p
N. Jackson, c
J. Staley, 3b
J. Williams, ss
J. Millor, cf
H. Patterson, rf
George Davis, lf / Manager
A. B. Stanford, 2b / Captain

Eclipse (St. Joseph, MO)

W. C. Cathrell
H. Ward
A. Love
H. Whitten
J. Cooper
Thomas Jackson
R. Wilson
J. Minor
Thomas O. Williams, Captain

Black Stockings (St. Louis, MO)

Joseph Harris, c
William Davis, p / 2b / c
Caesar Bracey, 3b / rf
Phil Smith, cf
David E. Gordon, cf / p
Isaac Carter, 2b / 3b / lf
Lewis Canter, ss
William Sutton, lf
Alonzo Keiger, rf
Ed Rogers, 1b
Richmond Robinson, lf
William Smith, 3b / 2b
Sylvester Chauvin, 3b / lf
Charles Gardner, rf
Ben Johnson, p / lf
William Coons, rf
Jimmie Dukes, p
John Howard, lf / p
Harry Johnson, 3b
Ross, ss / 3b / c / p
George Burks, lf
Clarence Manuel, cf
Alonzo Kieger,
Henry Bridgewater, Manager
Charles H. Tyler, President
Louis Helms, Director

West Ends (St. Louis, MO)

Charles Thompson, lf
Ned Harris, rf
N. Costello, c
E. Clay, 2b
A. Costello, ss
Caesar Bracey, ss
Ben Buchanan, cf
Steve Jones, p
Frank Cabell, 3b
Frank Brown, Manager

Young Buffalos (St. Louis, MO)

A. Lewis, c
P. Harris, p
W. Wallace, 1b
A. Bailey, 2b
E. Thompson, 3b
H. Alexander, ss
D. Brown, lf
L. Muerson, cf

W. Studson, rf
William Hudson, Manager

New Jersey

West Ends (Long Branch, NJ)

Joseph H. Wilson, lf
Wilson N. Carey, 2b
James H. Paynter, 1b
Arthur Thomas, c
Phil Smoot, 3b
Benjamin Simms, ss / rf
Robert Brown, cf
Benjamin Holmes, 3b
William H. Brown, p
Joseph Myers, cf
John Curry, rf
Abraham Hall, p
Joseph Middleton, rf
J. Willard, 3b
George A. Smith, Manager
William T. Green, Treasurer
Anderson A. Marshall, Manager

W. T. Greenes (Long Branch, NJ)

Joseph H. Wilson, lf
Wilson Carey, 2b
James H. Paynter, 1b
Arthur Thomas, c
Phil Smoot, rf
Benjamin Holmes, p / 3b
Robert Brown, 3b / p
William H. Brown, cf
Benjamin Simms, ss

Alpha (Princeton, NJ)

Peter Richmond, c
Edward Simpson, p
Herbert Simpson, 1b
George Furman, 2b
Benjamin Davis, ss
James Simpson, 3b
William Long, lf
Cornelius Hoagland, Captain / cf
Edward Davis, rf / p
William E. Simpson, Manager

Crescents (Princeton, NJ)

W. Hegeman, ss
Eugene Scudder, p
Benjamin Davis, 2b
Herbert Simpson, 1b
James Simpson, 3b
John Meade, c
Goldstein, cf
C. Galleger, lf
Edward Davis, rf

Metropolitans (Princeton, NJ)

P. Gobton, Captain / cf
Eugene Scudder, p

Peter Richmond, 1b
Herbert Simpson, 2b
Benjamin Davis, 3b
James Simpson, ss
W. Hegeman, lf
C. Galleger, c
Edward Davis, rf
Samuel Scudder, c
Louis Smith, lf
Fred Nichols, Manager

Polka Dot (Trenton, NJ)

D. Henderson, Captain
S. Frost, Captain
Horace Willard
William Johnson, Manager / Treasurer
W. S. Wickoff, President
A. Byaid, Secretary

New York

Eagles (Brooklyn, NY)

William Harris, c
C. Cummings, 3b
Wellen Grayson, 2b
Charles Kingsland, 1b
Charles Leslie, ss
Archie Reeves, lf
Benjamin Holmes, cf
Gasby, rf
Charles Johnson, p / Captain

International Independents (Niagara Falls, NY)

Robert Wilson, 1b / c
Wiley, cf / c
Wayman, ss
Charles Moore, c
J. C. Barnes, 2b
W. B. Shiloh, 3b
Joseph Johnson, rf
Pitman, lf
Sims Emery, p
Samuel Burnette

Callender Blues (New York, NY)

P. Adams, p
C. Waters, c
Charles Williams, 1b
Frank Girard, 2b
George Freeman, ss
Al Smith, 3b
Wolf, rf
Lewis L. Brown, cf
Burrell Hawkins, lf
John Rice, President

Clarendons (Saratoga Springs, NY)

William P. Hatton, p
William Brown, p / 2b
Robert Brown, rf

Benjamin Boyd, 3b / cf / rf
James Washington, 1b / rf
Jacob C. Strather, rf
Samuel Alexander, 2b
Benjamin Holmes, 3b
James Talbott (Talbert), ss
William Braxton, ss
Clayton Young, rf
Louis Buchanan, cf
John H. Lawson, 2b
Al Hackley, c / cf / p
H. L. Whitney, 3b
Joe Stewart, ss
McKnight, 2b
Mumford, 1b
S. K, Govern, p / Manager

Davis (Saratoga Springs, NY)

William Lazenberry, p
R. Watkins, v
J. C. Anderson, 1b
William Sanders, 2b
T. Cooke, ss
William Gray, 3b
W. Manning, rf
J. Gates, cf
E. A. Butler, lf

Laytons (Saratoga Springs, NY)

William Brown, 1b
Hamilton D. Cole, c
S. K. Govern, p
John H. Lawson, 2b
W. Miner, 3b
N. Wallace, ss
James Talbert, cf
S. Asher, rf
B. Monroe, lf

United States Hotel (Saratoga Springs, NY)

Samuel Gibson
Robert Johnson
William Stanard
Edward Stanard
George Ham Cole
Durham Jackson
Christian Fields
Leonard Wilkins
J. F. Brown
James Reed

Fearless (Utica, NY)

Samuel Freeman, ss / Captain
J. Lawrence, 3b
R. Jackson, 2b
Charles Moore, rf
Charles Teabout, lf
Jacob Francis, cf / lf
Samuel Jackson, c
James Pell, 1b
Arthur Jackson, p

D. Jordan, cf
Williams, ss
Charles Jefferson, rf
Charles Peterson, Substitute

North Carolina

Neptunes (Charlotte, NC)

John T. Smith
P. C. Hall
Mack Taylor
J. C. Worth
Pemberton Jones
Sandy Thompson
William Hall
M. Shepard
William Kelly
Thomas Cornelius
W. H. Robinson
D. A. Leercraft

Ohio

Zouaves (Cincinnati, OH)

James Chapman, 1b
Theodore Watkins, 2b / Captain
Isaac Campbell, 3b
Elsworth Downs, ss
Hiram Carroll, p
William Brown, c
John "Phas" Flowers, lf
John Campbell, cf
Melvin Payne, lf

Blue Stockings (Cleveland, OH)

William Wilson, ss
Charles Stanley, c
William Sabb, rf / 2b / Secretary
James Morris
Henry C. Smith, p
Samuel "Sam" Smith, cf
James H. Morris, cf
Edward Wilson, 2b / rf
C. A. Tripp, 2b
Walter L. Milligan, lf
Edward Doctor, 1b
B. Powhattan Henderson, rf
W. Goodwin, rf
Sam Jackson, 3b
William B. Morris, Substitute
George Myers, Team President / Manager

Clippers (Geneva, OH)

G. N. Robinson, ss
J. Grant Johnson, 3b
T. H. Gardner, 1b
John Johnson, cf / Manager
C. W. Washington, lf
J. Rogers, rf
J. Bowder, rf
Oscar Carmen, 2b / Captain
E. C. Carmen, p

Pennsylvania

Dolly Varden (Chester, PA)

Cord Patten, Captain / p
Mollie Johnson, 1b
Sallie Johnson, 2b
Ella Thompson, c
Ella Johnson, cf
Rhoda Showell, lf
Agnes Hollingsworth, rf
Lizzie Waters, 3b

J. Gallon (Chester, PA)

John Hackett, c
James Perrigan, p
John Hart, 1b
Henry Sterling, 2b
David Perrigan, 3b
Abraham Fields, cf
Warner Pryor, rf
William Cotman, lf
Alexander Sheppard, ss
Joseph Gallen, Captain

Jinks (Chester, PA)

Fannie Watts, Captain
Martha Mustard
Anna Maria Jones
Hanna Kates
Rose Feely
Maria Thompson
Susie Corbitt
Jennie Pepper
Philopena Morris

Thornton (Chester, PA)

W. Reily, c
F. Scanlan, p
J. Black, 1b
Wood, 2b
B. F. Ganister, ss
John Brown, 3b
Trainor, lf
E. Evans, rf

Wabash (Chester, PA)

Henry Reed, p
William Purnsley, c
Benjamin Driskett, 1b
Aaron Fields, 2b
A. Ferrell, ss
David Perrigan, 3b
George Savin, rf
I. Sommers, cf
A. Jones, lf / p
George Williams, p
Daniel McDonald, c
F. Scanlan, p
B. F. Ganister, ss
W. Reily, c / rf
Isaac Rothwell, c
William Ruley, Manager

Orions (Philadelphia, PA)

George Williams, 2b / p / c
Daniel McDonald, 2b / 3b
Sheppard Trusty, p / c
William "Bill" Harris, ss
William Fisher, 2b / cf
George Fisher, lf
E. Hall, 3b / c
J. Hall, ss / rf
William Payne, c
John Johnson, 1b / cf / 3b
Oscar Jackson, lf
Walter Orr, rf
William Curry, 2b
William Bowers, cf
William E. Carter, cf
Eugene Scudder, c
William D. Kelley, cf
Moses Lewis, ss
William Long, 3b
Julius Forbes, 1b / Manager

Westerns (Pittsburgh, PA)

Spencer Keys, p
David Stoner, c
C. Butler, 3b
Henson, 2b
John W. Anderson, 1b
John Daisy, ss
B. Boyle, lf
Ed Stratton, cf
John W. Askins, rf
Scott Taper, p
Lewis Allen, c
Milford Wilson, cf / 1b
W. C. Lee, Manager

Crescents (Reading, PA)

H. Swoyer, p
A. Hughes, c
Tilghman Cornish, ss
C. Robinson, 1b
Henry Bower, 3b / p
George Brown, 3b
Henry C. Nelson, lf
Ed Means, cf
Charles Gibson, rf

Lumber Citys (Williamsport, PA)

Javan Emory, 2b / c / p
Charles Braxton, lf
Clarence Williams, c / 2b
Sims Emory, 1b / c
George W. Stovey, p / 1b
Samuel Davage, 1b
David Green, cf
William Shadney, p
Dell, rf

Tennessee

Poplar Lincks (Memphis, TN)

George Wormeley

William Pryor
Elias Carr
Neely Houston
Eph Pruden
Robert Suddon
William Downey
Eddie Coswell
David Shaw
Levi Orr, Manager

Virginia

Swans (Richmond, VA)

J. Blakey, cf
A. Christian, lf
Thomas Carter, rf
William Harris, c / 1b
George Brown, 1b / 3b
William P. Gray, ss
Simon Epps, 3b
F. Mormon, 2b
John "Bud" Fowler, p
Arthur Thomas, c
Anthony Richardson
James Archer
Henry Marshall
Moses Lewis, c
Carter, rf
J. Richard Harrison, 2b / Secretary
James H. Dudley, Manager

Washington, DC

Douglass (Washington, DC)

Robert Brown, c
William Braxton, ss
James Talbott (Talbert), 2b
William Brown, p
George Brown, 3b
Charles Boyd, rf / Manager
McCartney, 1b
Harry Johnson, cf
Samuel Alexander, 2b
Samuel Anderson, rf
James H. Washington, 1b
D. W. Downing, lf / Manager

Manhattans (Washington, DC)

William P. Hatton, p
William Frisby, p
William Brown, Captain / p
Robert Brown, rf
Arthur Thomas, c
George R. Williams, c
Benjamin Boyd, cf
James H. Washington, ss
Jacob C. Strather, rf
William Jackson, 1b
Samuel Alexander, 3b
Benjamin Holmes, 2b
James Talbott (Talbert), ss
Samuel Anderson, lf / cf

William Braxton, ss
J. S. Tusby, p
George R. Williams, c
William Barton, cf
B. Boyle, rf
Charles Jones, Manager
John Gans, Manager
Stanislau K. Govern, Manager
John Lang, Manager

1884

Delaware

Unknown Boys (Wilmington, DE)

E. Grooms, c
E. Reed, p
William Boulden, ss
W. Naudian, 1b
J. Daker, 2b
E. Viney, 3b
G. Dutton, cf
J. Buck, rf
G. Hastings, lf

Illinois

Sunsets (Aurora, IL)

Benjamin Butler
Adams
Robert "Bob" Garret, ss
Watts, c
Willis "Chub" Artist
Smith, 2b
Mason
Buckner, p
William Lucas, 3b
Gus Demary, Manager

Gordons (Chicago, IL)

William Davis, p / 3b / cf / 2b
Joseph Campbell, p / cf
Grant Campbell, lf
D. Brown, 2b
Wilbur F. Lewis, 1b
James Houke, 1b
T. Walker, cf
William Albert Jones, lf / c
Alexander Plummer, 1b
William Turner, 3b / ss
William Brown, p / 2b
John C. Nelson, 2b / cf
Rufus Savoy, 2b / cf
William H. Curd, ss
George Wallace, 2b / 3b
Tobins Herndon, 2b
William Sutliffe, p
William C. Holmes, p / rf
Carel, ss
Smith, c / ss
Joseph Harris, c / Manager
William H. M. Fisher, President

Henry Johnson, Vice President
Jackson Gordon, Secretary
Daniel Scott, Treasurer
Harry Teenan Jones, Director

Unknowns (Chicago, IL)

William Holmes, p
James Lewis, c
C. Williams, ss
E. Davage, 2b
Ed Hardin, 3b
William Brown, lf
G. Sivens, cf
Albert Hackley, rf
George M. Crisup, 2b
Alexander Plummer, 1b
William Albert Jones, c / Manager

Stars (Decatur, IL)

Robert Stewart, c
Peck Miller, p
William Holland, p
A.Y. Hester, ss
Solomon Chadore, 1b
Jack Breyles, 2b
Eli Brown, 2b
Lewis Page, rf
Louis Stewart, lf
Charles Brown, cf / Captain
Houston Singleton, Manager

Adelaides (Elgin, IL)

Aaron White, c / 3b
Benjamin Hyde, 3b / lf
Joseph Garret, ss
Augustus Hall, lf/c
George Middleton, 2b
Robert "Bob" Garret, p
George Taylor, 1b
Walker Pride, cf
Benjamin Middleton, rf
Watts, c
W. J. Christie, Manager
Augustus Hall, President
Ed Newsome, Secretary / Treasurer

Busters (Rockford, IL)

Phil Reed
James Reed
John Baxter
Henry Harris
James Carlin
Edgar Cornish
Charles Ferguson
Pete McGrath
George O'Brien
Watts
Benjamin Davis, Manager / p

Black Diamonds (Springfield, IL)

William Renfro, 1b
Frank Brandon, 2b / p

S. V. Casey, p
Sanders, ss
Benjamin Black, 3b
William Hudson, lf
Al Williams, cf
Will Sappington, c
Harry Hodges, 2b
Oscar Yates, 3b
Ed Wormley, rf
F. Willis, cf
W. H. Hogan, Manager
F. Hicklin, Secretary
George W. Birdsong, Treasurer

Excelsiors (Springfield, IL)

Walter Oglesby, 2b
Alfred Williams, p
John Spencer, ss
Barney Clem, 3b
J. Joiner, lf
B. Willis, 1b
William Parker, cf
Smith, c
Thomas Mann, rf / p

Kansas

Lone Stars (Atchison, KS)

Ed Stewart, c
Ed Mack, p
Henry Irving, 1b
Harry "Ham" Evans, 2b
Thompson, rf
John Finley, ss
Fred Gleason, cf
Walt Booker, lf
Sam Phips, 3b
William Lewis
A. Williams, Manager
T. Lewis, Manager
A. McSpiatten (McSpadden), Scorer

Liberties (Fort Scott, KS)

Henry Curtis, c
Andy Giles, p
Lewis Webber, 1b
Frank Hawkins, 2b
Henry Hawkins, 3b
Dan Myers, ss
Nick Myers, lf
Henry Campbell, cf
Bud Langton, rf
Colonel Jordan, Manager

Westerns (Fort Scott, KS)

Al Bradford, c
Curt Tyler, p
Nathan Barber, 1b
Oscar Red, 2b
Jasper Camp, 3b
Tom Duval, ss
Harrison Woodly, lf

Will Harris, cf
Stokes Fredwell, rf

Leapers (Leavenworth, KS)

Crawford, 1b
William Montgomery, 2b
David Gray, 3b
Parker, ss
James Mayo, lf / Manager
Burns, cf
J. Walters, rf
Wayne, c
Fred Hedge, p

Modocs (Topeka, KS)

John B. Jones, c/Captain
John H. Wash, p
Orrin Giles, ss
William H. Blythe, 1b
Harry Franklin, 2b
Lacy Woods, 3b
Aleck Mackamore, lf
Henry Essex, cf
Harry McVeigh, rf
Scott "Doc" Smith, rf
James Welch, p
William Roberts, cf
George Ware, Scorer
Wesley Brown, Umpire
W. D. Donnell, Manager

Kentucky

Athletics (Frankfort, KY)

Sam Robinson
Henry Robinson
John Delaney
Daniel Brown
Robert Brown
Charles Higdon
Bowen Dotson
Albert Scoggins
S. J. Johnson, Secretary
James W. Woolfolk, Manger
Robert Hampton, Manager
Wyatt Bailey, Manager
Preston Scott, Manager

Mutuals (Louisville, KY)

James Armstrong, 3b
B. Frank Garret, ss / Captain
Lafayette Condon, p / 2b
John M. Pierson, c / Assistant Captain
Robert Armstrong, rf
William Brooks, 2b
Alonzo Kieger, rf
Lucien Wagner, cf
James Turner
James Morton, 2b
James Thomas, 1b
James Smith, p
Priest, ss

James Rattle, 2b
Henry Payne, p / 1b
William Jackson, cf / 1b
Clarence Manuel, c
John W. Fowler, 2b / Manager

Louisiana

A. J. Dumonts (Algiers, LA)

Albert Harvey, p
Houma Walker, c
James Obaire, 1b
Joseph Delmar, 2b
Joseph G. Thomas, 3b
Jules Caufield, ss
William Gibson, lf
Al "Ed" Robinson, cf
Francis Joseph, rf

Aetnas (New Orleans, LA)

J. H. Burnside
A. V. Woods
A. L. Perkins
J. D. Macon
Joseph Mitchell
H. L. Baptiste
J. Griffin
John E. Oliver
R. Phillips
D. Lancy
H. Baldwin

Reds (New Orleans, LA)

H. Thompson, c
W. Dunn, p
J. Dunn, 1b
H. Dumas, 2b
J. Panther, 3b
S. Morris, ss
P. James, lf
G. Lonia, rf
F. Ward, cf

Unions (New Orleans, LA)

James Arnold, p
William Johnson, c
George Irwin, 2b
William Davis, 3b
Randolph Landry, 1b
John Anderson, cf
James Recasner, ss
Charles Spott, lf
Edmond Blanche, rf
Lawrence Scott, Manager

Maryland

Atlantics (Baltimore, MD)

H. A. Mitchell, 1b
George Burrell, p / c
Frank Call, 3b
Frank Thomas Dorsey, 2b
William Gray, of

James Harris, of
Joseph Harris, c
Joe Johnson, p / c
Henry Proctor, p / c
James Payne, lf
Charles Slaughter, lf
L. Washington, ss
Solomon Williams, of
John Stewart, p

Red Stockings (Frederick, MD)

Pean Robinson, c
Dave Robinson, p / Captain
William Boose, ss
James James, 1b
James Staunton, 2b
Weaver Dean, 3b
Griffin Burck, lf
Robert Palm, cf
Adam Robinson, rf

Massachusetts

Hub Citys (Boston, MA)

John L. Ruffin, Chairman
J. D. Powell, Jr., Secretary
William H. Walker
David Drummond
Charles B. Churchill
Charles R. Williams
Howard L. Smith
Charles Chapman
Robert Carter
Morrill, Manager
Charles Wedeu, Scorer

Memorials (Cambridge, MA)

Nichols, p
Benjamin Allen, c
Edward Smith, 1b / c
Phillips, 2b
Seaman, 3b
Baker, ss
LeMoyne, lf
Crocker, lf
Lovering, rf

Minnesota

Barber Merchants (St. Paul, MN)

Lloyd Wheeler, c / rf
Shaffer, p
E. Lewis, ss / cf / c
Austin, 2b
W. Barnes, 1b
Benjamin Underwood, 3b
James H. Smith, lf / rf / 3b
Brown, rf
Will Howard, cf
Fisher, 1b
George B. Williams, 2b
Cogmire, 3b
Herman, ss

A. D. Adams, 2b
Hayes, rf
Milton Fogg, ss / ss
A. H. Grooms, cf

Hall's Barbers (St. Paul, MN)

George Peterson, c
Will Howard, p
William Waddell, ss
O. C. Hall, 1b
Scott, 2b
Benjamin Underwood, 3b
Carpenter, rf
Hudson, lf
Andrew Cotton, cf
O. C. Hall, Manager

Metropolitans (St. Paul, MN)

A. Lewis, c
Henry Lawrence, p
Louis De Lyon, ss
Besey, 2b
W. C. Coleman, 1b
John Coleman, 3b
William W. McCoy, lf
Davis, rf / cf
C. Allen, cf / ss
William Berry, 2b
Garling, rf
John H. Graham, 3b

Missouri

Red Stockings (Sedalia, MO)

Charles Martin, 1b
H. Watson, p
N. Jackson, c
J. Staley, 3b
J. Williams, ss
J. Millor, cf
H. Patterson, rf
George Davis, lf / 3b
A. B. Stanford, 2b / Captain
B. Hampton, Manager
H. Reed, Manager

Athletics (St. Louis, MO)

Samuel Rice, cf
James Woods, 2b
Ben Watkins, 3b
Al Spencer, lf
M. W. Samuels, c
Edward Samuels, p
Turner Anderson, 1b
William Ambrose, rf
Harry Johnson, ss

Black Stockings (St. Louis, MO)

Ed Rodgers, 1b
Benjamin Johnson, p
Sholt Johnson, c / 3b
Henry Lawrence, 2b / c
Lewis Canter, ss

Sylvester Chauvin, 3b / rf
William Sutton, cf
David E. Gordon, c / p
Charles Gardner, lf
Caesar Bracey, rf
S.Y.C. Stewart, ss
Harry Johnson, ss
M. W. Samuels, 2b
S. Samuels, c
Steve Jones, 2b
Hope, c
Henry Bridgewater, Manager

Buffalos (St. Louis, MO)

A. Lewis, c
P. Harris, p
C. Thompson, p
W. Wallace, 1b
A. Hall, 2b
E. Thompson, 3b
J. Alexander, ss
D. Brown, rf
A. Bailey, cf
William Hudson, Jr., lf
C. Churchill, Substitute

Cardinals (St. Louis, MO)

Paul Chauvin, p
B. Leger, c
James Brooks, 1b
H. Brown, 2b
G. Fields, 3b
William Collins, ss
John Johnson, lf
J. Thomas, cf
C. Mann, rf
L. Paul, Substitute

Eclipse (St. Louis, MO)

Joseph Bailey, c
Scott Turner, 1b
Sam Wills, 2b
Wallace Long, 3b
Ed Barber, ss
Matt Long, rf
E. F. Godare, lf
Charles M. Washington, cf
William Griswold, p
Charles Brooks, Manager
W. R. Adams, Secretary

Lime Kiln (St. Louis, MO)

John Mullen, Captain / ss
Gus Cumbers, cf
Emmanuel Lemon, lf
Charles Emory, rf
Thomas R. Chatman, 1b
Solomon James, 2b / c
Henry Shaw, 2b
Ned Harris, p
Jeff Clay, c
Ike Poll, Substitute

Harry Smith, Substitute
Dave Chandler, Manager

Metropolitans (St. Louis, MO)

George Fuqua, 1b
H. Buchanan, 2b
H. Dickson, 3b
S. Nash, ss
J. Velar, lf
W. Cable, cf
A. Martin, rf
Acie Price, p
T. Iverson, Substitute
David Price, c / Manager

Sumners (St. Louis, MO)

Spence Y. C. Stewart, ss
T. C. Richardson, cf
William Roberson, c
Scott Turner, 2b
D. Anderson, p
William Jackson, 1b
John Mullen, rf
M. Seymour, lf
F. Gibbs, 3b
Charles Emory, Substitute
Henry Shaw, 2b

New Jersey

Orientals (Bergen, NJ)

Charles Matthews, cf
Forton, rf
H. Jackson, 3b
Benjamin "Kid" Brown, ss
Robert "Bob" Jackson, c
Young Benjamin, 2b
Weds, lf
Edward Wales, p
Evans Washington, 1b

Dusky Boys (Newark, NJ)

Richard Vanlew, 2b
John Good, p
Eugene Scudder, cf
Edward De Groat, 1b
George Brown, c
John Meade, ss
Paul S. Jackson, 2b
Smith, cf
William Prince, rf
Frederick Nichols, Manager
David Prime, Manager

Alpha (Princeton, NJ)

Peter Richmond, c
Edward Simpson, p / rf
Herbert Simpson, 1b
George Furman, 2b
Benjamin Davis, ss
James Simpson, 3b
William Long, lf

Edward Davis, rf / p
Cornelius Hoagland, Captain / cf

New York

Alpines (Brooklyn, NY)

Frank Harris, ss / p
Frederic W. Putnam, cf
John H. Nelson, p / rf
N. Johnson, 1b
Roberts, lf
A. Johnson, cf
Sherman Porter, rf / 2b
Charles Johnson, 3b
Howard Havens, c / 1b
Richard Potter, 1b
Theodore Jarvis, c
Haywood, c
Edward DeMund, lf / 2b
Edmund A. Salomon, Manager

Remsens (Brooklyn, NY)

W. Hancock, cf
H. Lafavre, lf
Andrew Jackson, 3b
W.R. Hill, ss
Henry Payne, rf
Alfred Jupiter, c
George W. Batum, 2b
Oscar R. Smith, p
John Oliver, 1b
F. B. Hoagland, Secretary
C. Williams, Manager

City Club (Buffalo, NY)

Albert Thompson, 2b
Samuel Johnson, lf
A. Jackson, p
N. J. Jones, 1b
J. Tripp, 2b
Caesar Jackson, c
D. Tyler, ss
G. Smith, cf
George Giles, rf

Genesee Hotel (Buffalo, NY)

Edward N. Powell, c
John Downes, p
J. C. Barnes, 1b
Mack, 2b
W. P. Myers, 3b
B. F. Palmer, p / rf
Spark, ss
Dan Boohrie, rf / Captain
Steptoe, cf
J. B. Robinson, lf

Callender Blues (New York, NY)

P. Adams, p
C. Waters, c
Charles Williams, 1b
Frank Girard, 2b
George Freeman, ss

Al Smith, 3b
Wolf, rf
Lewis L. Brown, cf
Burrell Hawkins, lf
John Rice, President

Police Gazette (New York, NY)

H. Carter, c
A. Tobias, p
B. Smith, ss
Harry Woodson, 1b
Sam Bea, 2b
H. Shaw, 3b
A. Smith, lf
George Howard, rf
P. L. Jacobs, cf / Manager

Clarendon (Saratoga Springs, NY)

William Barker, c
William P. Hattan, p
L. Howard, 1b
Mumford, 2b
Chris Jones, 3b
Joe Stewart, ss
Louis H. Buchanan, cf
Hunter, rf
S. P. Buchanan, lf
Nathaniel Johnson, Substitute

Leonidas (Saratoga Springs, NY)

T. J. Gassaway, c
George Williams, p
Richmond Robinson, 1b
Frank Anderson, 2b
E. Richards, 3b
Julius Booker, cf
B. Monroe, rf
Charles Jones, lf
Frank H. Hart, ss
Frederic W. Putnam, cf

Fearless (Utica, NY)

Samuel Freeman, ss / Captain
J. Lawrence, 3b
R. Jackson, 2b
C. Moore, rf
Charles Teabout, lf
Jacob Francis, cf
Samuel Jackson, c
James Pell, 1b
Arthur Jackson, p
D. Jordan, Substitute
Charles Peterson, 1b

Ohio

Stars (Cadiz, OH)

James Smith
J. Williams
J. Puling
Theodore Mason
R. Smith

J. Brown
A. Brooks
John Smith
R. Williams

Standards (Cincinnati, OH)

A. Johnson, p
J. E. Johnson, c
J. Coleman, lf
W. Reid, cf
J. Banks, rf
Tommy Adams, 1b
E. Skinner, 2b
H. Jones, 3b
H. Glover, ss

Capital Citys (Columbus, OH)

Ed Tuplett, 1b
Robert Allen, p
A. Williams, 2b
T. Henderson, ss
T. Reynells, lf
J. Draper, rf
A. Huston, p / cf
J. Walls, c
S. Jacobs, 3b
Herman Wilson, Manager

Independents (Portsmouth, OH)

J. H. Scott, Treasurer / Captain / p
Willis Scott, c
Thomas Parks, ss
Ned Davis, 1b
J. T. Scott, 2b
Aaron Thomas, 3b
Henry Holliday, lf
Charles Scott, cf
Rodney Starks, rf
Charles Peen, President
Abe Clark, Secretary
Henry Baker, Director
Lilly Ross, Director
Frank White, Manager
John Fox, Scorer

Pennsylvania

Olympics (Carlisle, PA)

Robert "Gus" Jordan, c
Henry Moore, p
Bud Moore, ss
Samuel Lane, 1b
Thomas Jefferson, 2b
David Lane, 3b
Taylor Smith, lf / p
Charles Bell, cf
Benjamin Moore, rf

Alerts (Chambersburg, PA)

Frank Brooks, c / Manager
Richard Brown, 3b

William Guy, 1b / c
George Jenkins, ss
Isaac Scott, p / c
Curry Taylor, lf
Jacob Allen, cf
John Fisher, p / 2b
George Stevens, rf

Dolly Varden (Chester, PA)

Cord Patten, Captain / p
Mollie Johnson, 1b
Sallie Johnson, 2b
Ella Thompson, c
Ella Johnson, cf
Rhoda Showell, lf
Agnes Hollingsworth, rf
Lizzie Waters, 3b
Jennie Pepper, ss

J. Gallon (Chester, PA)

John Hackett, p
James Perrigan, c
John Hart, 1b
Henry Sterling, 2b
David Perrigan, 3b
Abraham Fields, rf / cf
Warner Pryor, rf
William Cotman, lf
Alexander Sheppard, ss
Joseph Gallon, Manager

Jinks (Chester, PA)

Fannie Watts, Captain
Martha Mustard
Anna Maria Jones
Hanna Kates
Rose Feely
Maria Thompson
Susie Corbitt
Ella Harris
Philopena Morris

Olympics (Harrisburg, PA)

William Barton, lf
Harry Fiatz, 2b
Theodore Fry, rf
Edward Cunningham, 3b
James Phillips, ss
William S. Long, 1b / Captain
Harry Porter, cf
Nathan Cooper, c
William S. Johnson, p
R. Henry Herbert, 1b
Thomas Matthews, 3b
Thompson Herbert, 1b
Clarence Williams, c
William Lee
Charles Johnson, Manager

Alerts—Lincoln University (Oxford, PA)

Harry Sythe Cummings, c
F. Daniels, p

Franklin A. Denison, 1b
H. Banks, 2b
James B. Raymond, 3b
Roberts, ss
Walter Brooks, rf
John Wright, lf
Thomas D. Campbell, cf

Enterprise—Lincoln University (Oxford, PA)

Fletcher R. McLeon, c
William C. Green, p
John H. Blake, 1b
Cadd O'Kelly, 2b
William G. Hepbern, 3b
Isaiah R. Reed, ss
John A. Whitted, rf
Coyden H. Uggams, lf
Thomas H. Lee, cf

Mutuals (Philadelphia, PA)

John Butler
James Sisco
C. Cooper
A. Fisher
F. Fisher
William Fisher
Edward "Ed" Harris
D. Jones
A. Mitchell

Orions (Philadelphia, PA)

George Williams, 2b / p
Clarence Williams, c
D. McDonald, 2b / 3b
Sheppard Trusty, p
William Harris, ss
Abraham Hall, 3b/c
William Payne, c
Harry Johnson, cf / 3b
William Carter, cf
Oscar Jackson, lf / p
Trundle, rf
Eugene Scudder, c
Julius Forbes, 1b / Manager

Lumber Citys (Williamsport, PA)

Javan Emory, 2b / c / p
Charles Braxton, lf
Clarence Williams, c / 2b
Sims Emory, 1b / c
George W. Stovey, p / 1b
Samuel Davage, 1b
David Green, cf
Ethan Thomas
William Shadney, p /Team Secretary
Dell, rf

Tennessee

Eclipse (Memphis, TN)

Edward Hardin, p / c
William James Renfro, p / 2b

Matt Pointer, 1b
Smith, 2b / ss
Sam Pointer, 3b
William Joyner, ss / p
E. Ward, rf / c
Shorter, lf / 1b
Robert Higgins, p / lf
R. F. Newman, rf

Poplar Lincks (Memphis, TN)

George Wormeley
William Pryor
Elias Carr
Neely Houston
Eph Pruden
Alfred "Alf" Horton
William Downey
Eddie Coswell
Larry Chambers, p
David Shaw
Albert Hardin, c
Levi Orr, Manager

Texas

Black Stockings (Dallas, TX)

A. Guinn
A. Weathers
J. Lucas
L. Gilbert
C. Lee
Charles White
John T. White
J. Griffin
H. Boyd
William Pool
Joseph Crutchfield, Manager

Washington, DC

Douglass (Washington, DC)

Robert Brown, c
William Braxton, ss
James (Talbert) Tolbert, 2b
D. W. Downing, lf
William Brown, p
R. C. Gaines, 3b
John Brown, rf
McCartney, 1b
Harry Johnson, cf

Howard University (Washington, DC)

John H. Lawson, c
P. R. Stewart, p
James L. Usher, Captain/ 1b
A. D. Wood, 2b
William Handy Johnson, 3b
Joseph Savoy, ss
Harry B. Lewis, lf
Robert C. Gaines, cf
Lincoln Cole, rf
S. J. McFarland, Manager
R. L. Morris, Manager

1885

Arkansas

Cadets (Little Rock, AR)

Elison, c
Godold, cf
Giles, ss
Henderson, lf
James Williams, rf
James Rollins, 3b
Blair, 2b
Andrews, 1b
Wilson, p

Reds (Little Rock, AR)

Alfred Jennings, 2b
Andrew Bolden, c
Jones, 1b
Taylor, 3b
Jones, p
Morris Hill, rf
C. H. Wallace, ss
Yorick Jennings, cf
Henry Lewis, lf

Connecticut

Blues (Hartford, CT)

Eugene Randall, Captain / c
George Brown, p
Harvey Okray, ss
R. A. Marshall, 1b
John Johnson, 2b
C. Rheddick, 3b
John A. Stokes, rf
A. H. Miner, cf
W. H. Blake, lf
Eli Williams, p

Illinois

Brown Stockings (Alton, IL)

James Brooks, cf / Captain
William Bevenue, 1b / Treasurer
Allen Bibb, 2b
Thomas Mayo, 3b
Lee Jackson, ss
Hatcher, rf
James Brooks, lf
Al Williams, p
William Baker, Manager / c

Acmes (Chicago, IL)

William Albert "Al" Jones
John C. Nelson
Henry C. Blue
Charles W. Spear
Grant Campbell
Charles W. Scott
William Hutchinson
Wilbur F. Lewis
James Houck

Richard C. Hubbard, 1b / Captain / Manager
A. Campbell, President
Albert Garrett, Vice-President
C. Pope, Secretary
Henry Green, Director
R. Smally, Director
A. Brown, Director
S. Harris

Gordons (Chicago, IL)

Grant F. Campbell, lf
Joseph Campbell, p
Charles W. Scott, cf / p / 2b
John C. Nelson, rf
James Lewis, p / lf
William Albert Jones, c
Richard Hubbard, 1b
Charles W. Spear, ss
George M. Crisup, 3b
Andrew Porter, 3b / cf
Charles M. Washington, rf
William Holmes, cf
James Houck, 1b
George Wallace, 2b
Al "Ed" Robinson, lf
H. M. Fisher, President
H. Johnson, Vice President
Jackson Gordon, Secretary
Daniel Scott, Treasurer
Harry Teenan Jones, Director

Black Diamonds (Decatur, IL)

Peter Williams, c
Ed Phoenix, p
Isham Page, ss
Henry B. Langford, 1b
Dick Carter, 2b
Alfred Langford, 3b
Bill Short, cf
John Caldwell, rf
William Lucas, lf

Pearly Blues (Peoria, IL)

Williams, cf
William Hellems, lf
Washington, c
Hanley, ss
A. Turner, 3b
Thomas Cheek, 1b
McCoy, rf
William Lyons, 2b
Charles Spears, p

Reds (Springfield, IL)

Walter Oglesby, 2b
Charles Parker, cf
William Renfroe, 1b
Ben Black, c
John Spencer, ss
Alfred Williams, p
William Joiner, lf
William Sappington, rf

George McKinney, 3b
Marlon McKinney, Scorer

Indiana

Spaulding Blues (Logansport, IN)

Charles Brooks, c
Sheridan Tutt, p
Henry Ashworth, ss
Frank Turner, 1b / captain
James "Jim" Allen, 3b
Frank Carter, 3b
Joshua Dent, lf
George Allen, rf
James "Jim" Carter, cf

Waynes (Richmond, IN)

William Trevan, lf
Sparks, rf
Mills,
J. N. Croker, ss
Thompson, 2b
Moore, 1b
Moses Gee, cf
Powell, 3b
Johnson, p
Will Hunter, Manager

Iowa

Olympics (Dubuque, IA)

Lou Christopher, cf
Will Love, lf
John Greene, 3b
Charles Greene, 2b
Sterling Greene, 1b
John Morgan, ss
James Dunnigan, c / rf
William Morgan, c / Captain
Richard Sheppard, Manager

Kansas

Lone Stars (Atchison, KS)

Ed Stewart, c
Ed Mack, p
Henry Irving, 1b
Harry "Ham" Evans, 2b
Thompson, rf
John Finley, ss
Fred Gleason, cf
Walt Booker, lf
Sam Phips, 3b
William Lewis
A. Williams, Manager
T. Lewis, Manager
A. McSpiatten (McSpadden), Scorer

Browns (Topeka, KS)

John Jones, c / Captain
Aleck Mackamore, p / ss
Henry Essex, ss / p
A. Richardson, 1b

Harry Franklin, 2b
Lacy Woods, 3b
George Hightower, rf
Orrin Giles, cf
William H. Blythe, lf / ss
Alf Withers, ss
William Dorcas Lincoln, ss
J. F. Richardson, Scorer
Eugene McVey, Scorer
Henry Dillard, Manager
W. D. Donnell, Manager

Kill Me Quicks (Wichita, KS)

W. P. Bettes, p / Captain
C. C. Tyler, c
L. W. Lawless, 1b
A. W. Thomas, 2b
Rufus Johnson, 3b
Tom Duval, ss
Sam Hayden, rf
George Huff, lf
Billy May, cf

Blue Stockings (Wichita, KS)

J. E. Bramden, cf / Captain
Thomas P. Rhoades, c
Abe Rideout, p
George Silvers, 1b
Tom Otis, 2b
Sam Jones, 3b
Steven Jewett, ss
Will Perry, lf
Billy Punch, rf

Kentucky

Athletics (Frankfort, KY)

Sam Robinson
Henry Robinson
John Delaney
Daniel Brown
Robert Brown
Charles Higdon
Bowen Dotson
Albert Scoggins
S. J. Johnson, Manager / Secretary
James W. Woolfolk, Manger
Robert Hampton, Manager

Black Stockings (Louisville, KY)

Gus Brooks, 2b
Moses Clark, ss
H. Glover, cf
W. F. Peyton, 1b
John Kinkeide, lf / p
Joshua Slaughter, c
Samuel Nelson, rf
Walker, 3b
Arthur Anderson, p / lf
J. Vaughn, 1b
Napoleon Ricks, s

Fall Citys (Louisville, KY)

Lafayette Condon, c / Manager
Patterson, 3b
Nelson Tarrance, p
Samuel Snowden, ss
Samuel Trabue, 2b
George Tarrance, 1b
M. Yancey, rf
L. Stevison, cf
William Thompson, lf
Wyatt Beatty, Jr., Manager
Preston Scott, Manager

Louisiana

A. J. Dumonts (Algiers, LA)

Albert Harvey, p / lf
Joseph Walker, c / cf
James Obaire, 1b
Joseph Delmar, 2b
William Turner, 1b
Joseph Recasner, 2b
George Irvin, ss
P. Thomas, 3b
William Davis, 3b
Joe Louis, ss / lf
Houma Walker, c
John Hunter, rf
John Louis, lf / p
Francis "Frank" Joseph, rf

James Lewis Juniors (New Orleans, LA)

Bernard Johnson, Captain / ss
George Francois, c
James Lewis, 1b
A. Henderson, p
William Smith, 2b
M. Clark, 3b
F. Williams, lf
Henry Williams, rf
H. Adolphus, cf
Isaac Jackson, President
G. Moore, Vice President
Theodore Rouseves, Secretary
Joseph Hill, Treasurer

Unions (New Orleans, LA)

James Arnold, p
C. Moise, c
William Turner, 1b
G. Jerom, 2b
Joseph Recasner, 3b
Joseph Pean Johnson, ss / c
T. Walker, lf
William Davis, rf
O. Sullivan, cf / rf
J. J. Astier, rf
John Spall, cf
George Irvin, rf
Al "Ed" Robinson, lf

James Tilley, cf
Lawrence Scott, Manager

W.L. Cohens (New Orleans, LA)

John Jones, p / rf
Edward Williams, c / ss
William Turner, 1b
Joseph Delmar, 2b
Jules Caufield, 3b
Francis Gaspard, ss
Dan Mitchell, lf / cf
Joseph Gaspard, cf / lf / p
Francis Joseph, rf /3b
Joseph J. Astier, rf
James Obaire, 1b
Al "Ed" Robinson, lf
David Price, c
Acie "Asa" Price, p / rf
William H. Hall, lf / p
Richard Nixon, Team Scorer
Walter L. Cohen, rf / Manager

Maryland

Atlantics (Baltimore, MD)

Joseph Harris, c
William Slaughter, p
George Burrell, 2b
H. Proctor, 1b
L. Washington, 1b
C. Gray, ss
Joseph Stewart, 3b
Thomas Dorsey, lf
James Payne, rf

Massachusetts

Franklins (Boston, MA)

Charles R. Williams, lf
Delaney, 1b
J. Smith, 3b
William H. Selden, p
D. Kelley, 2b
C. Kelley, 3b
George A. Sharkey, ss
Linuel, cf
Bursten, rf
Edward C. Smith, c

Resolutes (Boston, MA)

Robert Brown, lf
Purdham/Puritan, 1b
William H. Selden, 3b
Frank Johnson, ss / 3b
William Holmes, c
Charles R. Williams, 2b / ss
John "Bud" Fowler, 2b
Charles Posey, rf / cf
Albert Sanders, cf
D. A. Wesley, lf / rf
Charles H. Robbins, lf

Minnesota

Hotel St. Louis (Minneapolis, MN)

Fields, p
Carter, c
Thomas Marshall, 1b
E. Harrison, 2b
O. C. Hall, cf
L. Perry, rf
W. Clark, lf
Henry Lewis Canter
J. Taylor, 3b / Captain

Lafayette Bell Boys (St. Paul, MN)

H. Dellmore, p
J. Nichols, c
White, ss
Feeny, cf
E. F. Comstock, lf
Joseph Dellmore, 2b
Welch, 1b
William C. McCoy, 3b
Andy, rf

Lafayette Waiters (St. Paul, MN)

Albert Roberts, p / 3b / rf
William C. Brown, c
F. Herndon, 1b
Alexander Plummer, 2b
James Tilley, cf
J. A. Mason, 2b
Frank Doctor, ss
William Wilson, lf
D. Bennett, cf
S. Deas, rf
Finch, cf
Nilson, c
Zack Dean, ss
T. W. Bennett, lf
Andrew Labwo, 2b

Lake Park (St. Paul, MN)

Louis De Lyon, manager
W. C. Coleman, p
Charles Tyler, c
William W. Freeman, 3b
Ellis Matthews, 2b
Phil Jackson, ss / rf
William Walker, 1b
H. Huffman, cf
Frank Sillsby, rf
Robertson, 2b
H. Huffman, lf / cf
John H. Graham, ss
William Truman, c
Andrew Jackson, c / p

Missouri

Red Stockings (Sedalia, MO)

Charles Martain, 1b
Henry Watson, p

N. Jackson, c
J. Staley, 3b
J. Williams, ss
J. Millor, cf
Henry Patterson, rf
George Davis, lf
Ab Stanford, 2b / Captain
B. Hampton, Manager
H. Reed, Manager

Black Stockings
(St. Louis, MO)

Joseph Harris, c
Sholt Johnson, c
Ben Watkins, c
Ed Rodgers, 1b
Benjamin Johnson, 2b
Harry Watkins, 3b
Lewis Canter, ss
Sylvester Chauvin, Captain / lf
W. Sutton, cf
David E. Gordon, rf
Charles Gardner, lf / rf
William Davis, p
Harry Woodson, rf
Harry Johnson, ss
M. W. Samuels, 2b
James Robinson, rf
Al Spencer, rf
Sullen, 1f
Henry Bridgewater, Manager / President

Eclipse (St. Louis, MO)

David Price, c
Asa "Acie" Price, p
William Griswold, 1b
E. Buchanan, 2b
William Roberson, 2b
Ben Watkins, 3b
William Garrett, lf
Spence Y.C. Stewart, ss / Captain
John Matthews, lf
Steve Jones, cf / 1b
Joseph Bailey, rf / c
Caesar Bracey, 3b
Ben Black, Substitute
Thomas C. Richardson, rf / Secretary
Charles Richardson, Manager

Hartfields (St. Louis, MO)

B. Thompson, p
M. Samuels, c
S. Samuels, 1b
S. Rice, 2b
H. Rollinson, 3b
A. Hedgmen, lf
James Woods, cf
Henry Sanford, rf
C. W. Roberson, Manager

Nine Stars (St. Louis, MO)

David Smyth, c
Charles Franklin, p

Moses Johnson, 1b / c
Payton Williams, 3b
Edward Barber, ss
Matt Long, rf
Wallace Long, lf
John Robertson, cf
Joseph Johnson, Substitute
William Jones, Substitute
John Davis, rf / ss
Henry Alexander, 2b / Captain
James Williams, Manager
Fred Godare, President

New Jersey

Eureka (Trenton, NJ)

John H. Wash, p
Richard C. Coleman, c
Walter Seruby, lf / ss / rf
Frank Hunt, 1b
William Dennis, 2b / cf
Dayton Blackwell
Matt Hall
John Shennie
Henry Catto, ss
John Walsey
Harry Rodman
Miles Bilgas
William Rodman, Manager

New York

Argyle Hotel (Babylon, NY)

Benjamin Boyd, cf / 2b
John Milton Dabney, rf / lf
Guy Day, 2b
William Eggleston, ss
Frank Harris, p
Abraham Harrison, ss
Benjamin Holmes, 3b
Robert Martin, p
Charles Nichols, lf / rf
George Parego, p
Andrew Randolph, 1b
Sheppard Trusty, p
George Williams, 2b / 1b
John F. Lang, Manager
Frank P. Thompson, Manager

Alpines (Brooklyn, NY)

Frank Harris, p
John H. Nelson, p
Ellsworth, c
Howard Havens, c
Edward DeMund, 1b
Theodore Jarvis, 2b
Charles Johnson, 3b
A. Johnson, ss
Arthur Jackson, lf
Frederic W. Putnam, cf
Sherman Porter, rf
H. H. Johnson, Manager

Remsens (Brooklyn, NY)

W. Hancock, cf
H. Lafavre, lf
John Coleman, lf
George Douglas, cf
L. Peterson, 1b
W. R. Hill, ss
Henry Payne, rf
Alfred Jupiter, c
George W. Batum, 2b
James Williams, c
Henry Smith, of
Oscar H. Smith, p / rf
John Oliver, 1b / 3b / p
W. L. Bolden, c
Fred Jackson, Secretary / Treasurer
C. Williams, Manager
Theodore Smith, manager

City Club (Buffalo, NY)

J. Powell, p
R. Tripp, 3b
Charles Rowe, c
J. Day, 1b
Charles Mack, 3b
R. Tripp, 3b
S. Sparks, ss
C. Forrester, lf
G. Jones, cf
R. G. Walker, rf / Manager

Genesee Hotel (Buffalo, NY)

Edward N. Powell, c
John Downes, p
J. C. Barnes, 1b
Mack, 2b
F. Myers, 3b
B. F. Palmer, p / rf
Spark, ss
Dan Boohrie, rf / Team Captain
Steptoe, cf
J. B. Robinson, lf

Kent House
(Lakewood, NY)

T. Riley, c
Stephen Boyd, p
Barr, 1b
William Barton, 2b
T. Mines, lf
Rise, 3b
Andrew L. Smith, rf
Chank, cf
C. Davis, ss

Lake View (Lakewood, NY)

William H. Wilson, p
William D. Clifford, c
Edward Wilson, 1b
George Snowden, 2b
George Moody, 3b
R. Williams, ss

John Brock, cf
A. Lett, rf
John McKee, lf

Cuban Giants (New York, NY)

Sheppard Trusty, p / 1b / c
George Williams, c
Ed Harris, ss
Benjamin Boyd, 2b / cf
Benjamin Holmes, 3b
George Parego, 1b / p
Clarence Williams, cf / c /p
George Samuel Jackson, lf / p
William T. Whyte, rf
William Shadney, p / c / rf
James Payne, rf / c / 1b
John Oliver, cf
John Lang, Manager

Kersands Minstrel (New York, NY)

P. Adams, p
C. Waters, c
Charles Williams, 1b
Frank Girard, 2b
George Freeman, ss
Al Smith, 3b
Wolf, rf
Lewis L. Brown, cf
Burrell Hawkins, lf
Billy Kersands, President

Cataract House (Niagara Falls, NY)

Wesley Smith, p
Richard W. Dangerfield, p
C. H. Uggams, c
W. Andross, 1b
A. Spriggs, 2b
Ulysses S. Polk, 3b
Edward Johnson, ss
A. Brown, rf
John King, cf
John Ballard, lf
A. B. Green, ss
J. C. Anderson, Manager

Internationals (Niagara Falls, NY)

Horace H. Hall, 3b
Henry Ball, c
John Downes, p / ss
George Gibbs, 3b / ss
B. F. Palmer, p
T. Demery, 3b / rf
Joseph Seeling, 2b
Richard Bennett, 1b / rf
William Tyrell, 2b
E. Hill, cf

Lone Star (Oyster Bay, NY)

J. H. Saco
Lance Conklin

Richard Potter
Frank Potter
John Specks
Benjamin Specks
William Lott
James Stephenson
William Denton

Red Stockings (Port Jervis, NY)

J. Westfall, 3b
Robert Broadhead, lf
J. Smith, cc / ss
G. Freeman, 2b / rf
C. Brinson, f
R. Lewis, 1b
S. Brown, cc / ss
A. Taylor, p / rf
C. Ray, p / 2b

Unexpected (Rochester, NY)

W. Wharton
Charles Lee
Paris Lindsay
William H. Stewart
George Morris
A. Jackson
Robert Epps
R. H. Stevens
W. H. McDonald
John W. Thompson
R. R. Thompson
Andrew O. Dixon, Manager

Globe Hotel (Syracuse, NY)

C. Davis, p
William Sims, c
S. Davis, 1b
Johnson, 2b
Holland, ss
James Ennols, 3b
William H. Franklin, lf
Watson, cf
Frank J. Williams, rf

Palestine (Syracuse, NY)

Arthur Jackson, c
Charles F. Jefferson, Captain
J. W. Anderson
Tom H. Clark
Aaron Briles
William H. Thomas
Charles Shorter
H. A. Williams
N. J. Jones
C. F. Chapman
J. Tucker
William Pine
A. T. Bentley
R. Robinson
C. H. Smith
G. W. Washington

Samuel Jackson
Theodore Duffin
Henry Harden
Charles Peterson
M. Frank
James J. Tolliver, Manager

Pastimes (Syracuse, NY)

Samuel Jackson, ss
Jason Thomas, p
S. Donovan, c
Samuel Freeman
Robert Jackson, c
Arthur W. Collins, cf
E. N. Powell, p
George Vandermark, p / lf
Robert Jordan
George Williams, c
Al Lawrence, 1b
J. A. Mason, 2b
W. P. Myers, 3b
Daniel Page
Murdock, cf
Jacob Francis, Manager
William H. Franklin, President
John Dining, Vice President
John H. Walters, Treasurer
George Ennols, Secretary

Bagg's Hotel (Utica, NY)

Frank Anderson, 3b / ss / p
Ashbury Dale, cf
J. B. Robinson, lf
L. R. Ridley, c / 3b
Isaiah Lisle, ss / 2b
Fitzhugh, rf / 2b
L. Washington, 3b / p
Joseph Johnson, 2b / ss / c

Butterfield House (Utica, NY)

James Lee, 3b
Adams, lf
Fred Westerband, 3b
D. McDaniel, 1b / p
E. D. Lancaster, ss
William Henry, c
William Westerband, p / 1b
John Dining, rf
Arthur Buckingham, cf

North Carolina

Nationals (Raleigh, NC)

J. W. Winslow, President
Solomon Christmas, V.P.
George Rogers, Secretary
Thomas Taylor, Treasurer
William Williams, Captain
Wilson Warren, Asst. Captain

Hanovers (Wilmington, NC)

George D. Riley, Captain, c

Hewitt, p
Dixon, 1b
Ellis, 2b
Charles Burnett, 3b
Moore, ss
John Lane, lf
Howell, cf
Alexander Davis, rf

Ohio

Capital Citys
(Columbus, OH)

Ed Tuplett, 1b
Robert Allen, p
A. Williams, 2b
T. Henderson, ss
T. Reynells, lf
J. Draper, rf
A. Huston, p / cf
J. Walls, c
S. Jacobs, 3b
Herman Wilson, Manager

Lumber Citys
(Williamsport, PA)

Javan Emory, 2b / c / p
Charles Braxton, lf
Clarence Williams, c / 2b
Sims Emory, 1b / c
George W. Stovey, p / 1b
Alexander Davage, 1b
D. Green, cf
Mellicks, ss / p
Dell, rf

Athletics (Philadelphia, PA)

Guy Day, c
James Hackett, 2b
George Parego, 1b
Alfred Sharp, cf
George A. Smith, ss
William Whitaker, 3b / p
Henry Johnson, lf
Robert Martin, rf
Frank P. Thompson, Manager

Manhattans
(Philadelphia, PA)

John Butler
W. Butler
E. Fisher
A. Fisher
A. Hunter
F. Lee
J. Sisco, Captain
W. Tennant
William Ruby
C. Benson
George Waters
Charles E. Lloyd, Manager
Cassius Govern, Manager

Washington, DC

Birch Wielders
(Washington, DC)

Clarence Coleman, c
Oran L. Skipworth, p
Sam Williams, ss
Charles R. Douglas, 1b
Tom Upshaw, 2b
Charlie Beale, 3b
W. R. Davis, lf
L. Pulies, cf
Wallace McCary, rf

Quill Drivers
(Washington, DC)

John H. Lawson, c
James Harry Smith, p
Joseph Savoy, ss
James "Jim" Usher, 1b
Harry Peters, 2b
Loraine Peters, 3b
Ulysses Black, rf
John Nalle, cf
Harry Lewis, lf

1886

Canada

Black Stockings (Indiantown, New Brunswick, Canada)

Charley Hector, c
James Hector, p
Joe Hector, 1b
Ozzie Hector, 3b
G. Hector, rf
W. H. Burt, 2b
Ira Stewart, ss
Charlie Morrison, cf
Sam Dingee, lf

Resolutes (St. John, New Brunswick, Canada)

Nelse Breen, p / 3b
John Blizzard, p / c
E. Washington, ss
C. Sparrow, 2b
Bill Diamond, 3b / rf
George Watts, lf / rf
Alex Johnston, cf
Jack Cupee, cf
Robert Washington, 1b / Captain

Alabama

Saucy Boys (Mobile, AL)

Johnson, p
Carter, c
Bernard, ss
Crawford, 1b
Randolph, 2b
Lewis, 3b

Conway, rf
Wilder, lf
Powell, Captain

Thompsons (Mobile, AL)

Herman, 2b
Seymour, 1b
Crimins, 3b
Thompson, cf
Jackson, rf
Moulton, lf
Williamson, ss
Taylor, c
Caldwell, p
Francis, ss

Connecticut

Athletics (New London, CT)

Calvin V. Wheeler, p
Luke Weeks, c
John Bell, 3b
William H. Jordon, 2b
Alfred Wheeler, ss
Charles Warren, rf
James Talbott, cf
John Dickenson, lf
George Johnson, 1b / Captain
Albert Stewart, Captain / 1b
DuBois Hallack, President
Charles Benham, Vice President
George Mitchell, Secretary
Richard Dawson, Treasurer / Manager

Georgia

Champions (Atlanta, GA)

Freeman Coachman, ss
William M. Hughes, 3b / c
John Thompson, p / Captain
Thomas E. Cox, rf / cf
Hill, 1b / c
James Roberts, 3b / c
Mansell, lf
Maddox, cf
Pullin, 1b
Adams, rf
George Green, c
Robert Brown, p
E. D. Mitchell, p / Manager

Augusta Hotel
(Augusta, GA)

Willie Tutt, 1b
Douglas Green, 2b
Dennis Walker, 2b
Lloyd Tutt, ss
Willie Jordan, p
Willie Evans, c
C. H. Wayright, cf
Vince Chavious, rf
Wade Wideman, lf

Globe Hotel (Augusta, GA)

Ed Marshall, p
Robert Allen, c
S. Red, 1b
Nelson Red, 2b
Ed Jordan, 3b
William Little, cf
Robert Hart, lf
Thomas Ellis, rf
John Willis, ss

Illinois

Brown Stockings (Alton, IL)

James Brooks, cf / Captain
Charles Giles, p
Ed Ryder, rf
William Bevenue, 1b
William Drew, 2b
John Williams, p
Tom Mayo, 3b
Lee Jackson, ss
Phillip Tonie, lf
William Baker, c / Manager

Gordons (Chicago, IL)

Grant Campbell, ss
Eugene Caldwell, c
William Hutchinson, 2b / ss
John C. Nelson, rf
William Holmes, 1b
Joseph Campbell, p
James Houke, 3b
Joseph Adams, cf
Charles W. Scott, c
Albert "Al" Garret, cf / Captain
William H. Henderson, ss
William Albert Jones, lf / Manager
H. M. Fisher, President
H. Johnson, Vice President
Jackson Gordon, Secretary
Daniel Scott, Treasurer
Harry Teenan Jones, Director

Uniques (Chicago, IL)

T. Watkins, 1b
George Overland, lf
George M. Crisup, c
Richard Hubbard, 2b
Frank Spear, ss
Vertner Johnson, cf
Louis Reynolds, 3b
F. C. Lipscomb, c
Henry C. Blue, c / rf
James Lewis, p
William Sutliffe, p / Manager

Experts (Decatur, IL)

William Love, Captain
Henry Langford, Assistant
Lewis Page, Treasurer
Benjamin Bristow, Secretary
Robert Stewart

Indiana

Browns (Crawfordsville, IN)

Frank Smith, p
Jim Bowman, c
Jesse Case, 1b
Henry Nettle, 2b
Luther Munroe, 3b
Henry Humphrey, ss
Willie Jordan, rf
James "Jimmy" Smith, lf
Jim Ross, cf
Huff Robinson, c
Mose Vanderbilt, c

Kansas

Westerns (Fort Scott, KS)

Lawlers
Nathan Barker
John Bowlegs
Reed
Collier
Oscar Red
George Baylor
Will Reeder
Tole

Eagles (Lawrence, KS)

Squire Anderson, ss
John Seymour, p
Harry Polk, ss / 3b
Charles Johnson, 1b
Albert Gregg, 2b
James Holmes, 3b
Charles Frey, cf
S. Berry, rf
George Berry, lf
George Moore, c
John "Bud" Fowler, p / 2b
Frank Maupin, c
George W. Castone, p
Demore, cf
Wilson, cf
Parker, rf
William M. Fry, Captain
James W. Hoyt, Team Captain/Manager

Western Clippers (Topeka, KS)

Willie Newman, c
Edward Harris, p
Fred Adams, 1b
Fred Marshall, 2b
Charles Dennie, ss
Will Scott, 3b
John May, lf
Will Roger, cf
Fred Moore, rf
Charles Charles, Manager
B. F. Hatcher, Manager
William Hallum, Manager

Kentucky

Claytons (Clayton, KY)

T. Bess, 2b
Morris, c
R. Long, rf
George Lemiline, 3b
J. Long, cf
M. Bess, 1b
Edwards, p
McCluskey, ss
P. Bess, lf
Clifford, 1b

Athletics (Frankfort, KY)

Sam Robinson, p
Moses Clark, cf
James Edward Thomas, c
L. Daniels, 1b / p
James Woolfolk, 2b
Harry Robinson, 3b / lf
John Delaney, ss / 3b
James Veney, rf
Robert Brown, ss
William Woolfolk, cf
Smith, p
Charles Higdon

Sailor Boys (Hopkinsville, KY)

James Henry Glass
Edward Glass
William Glass
William Gray
William Guild
Dan Marshall
Marcus L. Young
H. H. McCallen
Lewis Gladdfish

Black Stockings (Louisville, KY)

William Brooks, 2b
Moses Clark, ss / c
H. Glover, cf
W. F. Peyton, 1b
John Kincade, lf / p
Joshua Slaughter, c
Samuel Nelson, rf
Walker, 3b
Arthur Anderson, p / lf
J. Vaughn, 1b
Napoleon Ricks, s
Daniel Brown, 1b
Haines, 3b
Brackenridge, ss
Braxton, cf

Fall Citys (Louisville, KY)

LaFayette Condon, p
Fred Mayfield, c
Samuel Trabue, 1b
William Thompson, 2b / c
W. Jessie, 3b
Frank Garrett, ss / Captain

Alonzo Kieger, rf
James Armstrong, lf
Harry Gillespie, cf
James Combs, 1b
John Kinkeide, p
James Smith, p / 2b
James Thomas, 1b
William S. Purnsley
Al Prater, c
Patterson
James Archer
Ben Shipley, Manager
C. H. Ennis, Manager

Old Honestys (Louisville, KY)

Tom Young, lf
William Woods, c
James Thomas, rf
Branon, 1b
Priest, ss
Joseph Burdine, cf
Beehel, 2b
Vincanse (Vincian), 3b
Tom Williams, p
Samuel Snowden, 2b
M. Yancy, cf

Sterlings (Louisville, KY)

Nelson Tarrance,
James Combs, lf
Johnson, p
Samuel Snowden, 2b
James Thomas, 1b
Charles Gray, cf
Harry Payne, cf
George Tarrance, ss
R. Long, c

Louisiana

Unions (New Orleans, LA)

R. Bruce Johnson, ss / c
William J. Turner
J. P. Brown, rf
George Irvin
George Ogden
T. Walker, lf
Joseph Walker, rf
James Arnold, cf
John "Bud" Fowler, p
Joseph Recasner, 2b
C. Moise, c
James Tilley, cf
James Obaire, 1b
George William Hopkins, 3b / p
Lawrence Scott, Manager

W.L. Cohens (New Orleans, LA)

Edward Williams, c / ss
Dan Mitchell, rf
J. J. Astier
Joseph Delmar, 2b

Jules Caufield, 3b
Francis Gaspard, ss
Frank Joseph
James Obaire, 1b
Acie Price, p
Joseph Ferrand, lf
John Jones, p
Joseph Recasner, 2b
George Irvin, ss
Al "Ed" Robinson, lf
C. Moise, lf
T. Walker, rf
William Turner
Walter L. Cohen, cf / Manager

R. E. Lees (Shreveport, LA)

William Patterson
Hoyer
McFarland
Frank Haughton
Conley
Channel
Skinner
Cook
Johnson

Maryland

Boot Blacks (Frederick, MD)

John Mills, c
William Brown, p
C. Staunton, ss
A. Baton, 1b
C. Harris. 2b
I. Sommer, 3b
A. Porter, rf
Lee Whiting, lf
Joseph Zedricks, cf

Massachusetts

Resolutes (Boston, MA)

Charles R. Williams, 1b / c
Joseph R. Harris, 2b
William H. Selden, p
Winslow Tyrrell, 3b
Benjamin Holmes, ss
Edward Smith, c / rf
Dan Penno, 2b
L. O. Posey, cf / rf
Joseph H. Wilson, lf
Brown, cf
Taylor, ss
Waller, 3b
Wilson, 1b
Alfred Jupiter, p / lf
Alexander A. Selden, Manager

Michigan

Colored Nine (Battle Creek, MI)

Harris, 1b
C. W. Dorsey, p / 3b

Gaines, c
Henderson, p / 2b
Dailey, lf
Alexander Valentine, rf
G. Tyler, ss
C. Tyler, 2b
Cook, cf / 2b

Colored Nine (Grand Rapids, MI)

James Jones
Charles Pinkney
George Williams
James Price
Will Matthews
Morris Tucker
Charles Conway
George Walker
Elijah Walker, Manager

Colored Nine (Kalamazoo, MI)

Jones, c
Bryce, p
Dave Morgan, 1b
L. G. Phillips, 2b
S. C. Phillips, 2b
John Morgan, ss
Van Dusen, lf
J. W. Phillips, cf
Benjamin Bolden, rf
A. Hoyt, p / rf
Perry Williams,
L. Moss, c
Tom Bolden, rf

Mississippi

F. O'Neal (Vicksburg, MS)

Battie Sanders, c
Ernest Jones, 1b
Frank Johnson, p
Mitchell Gordon, 2b
Sam Ellis, ss
John Ellis, 3b
West Nettles, ss
Charles Mitchell, cf
Mitchell Gordon, lf
Ellick McCarroll, rf

J. M. Doyle (Vicksburg, MS)

N. Reed, c
B. Moore, p
Frank Johnston, ss
H. Minor, 1b
D. Brown, 3b
S. Smith, lf
A. Adams, cf
R. Bellinger, rf
E. Whitlock, 2b / Captain

Vicksburgs (Vicksburg, MS)

Gordon
Johnson

Jordan
Jones
Nettles
Mitchell
J. Ellis
Mener
S. Ellis

Missouri

Novels (Kansas City, MO)

Frank Maupin, c
H. Johnson, p
Washington, ss
William Burt, 1b
Joseph Hicks, 2b
Loews Maupin, 3b
H. Burt, cf
Chouteau, rf
William Dayton, lf

Black Stockings (St. Louis, MO)

M. W. Samuels, 2b
Al Spencer, rf
Charles Gardner, p
Steve Jones, 1b
Spence Y. C. Stewart, rf
William Jones, c
Spimots, cf
William Sutton, cf
David E. Gordon, p
Lewis Canter, ss
James Robinson, 2b
Sholt Johnson, c
H. Rollinson, rf
Curtin, ss
Henry Bridgewater, Manager

Crescents (St. Louis, MO)

J. Johnson, c
Charles Franklin, p
W. Henderson, 1b
Smyth, 2b
Williams, 3b
Fred Godare, lf
Andrews, ss
Reynolds, cf
Mace Johnson, rf

Eclipse (St. Louis, MO)

Gant, p
Gossit, p
Solomon James, c
Steve Jones, 1b
James Robinson, 2b
Joseph Bailey, 3b / Captain
S. Y. C. Stewart, ss
Thomas C. Richardson, rf
Al Spencer, cf
Charles Emory, cf
John Mullen, ss

Euchres (St. Louis, MO)

Charles Franklin, p
J. Collins, c
P. Lee, lf
Sholt Johnson, c / 2b
Steve Jones, 1b
E. Clay, 2b
Ben Watkins, 3b
Reid, ss
C. McElhaney, lf
Caesar Bracey, cf
Ned Harris, rf
S. Y. C. Stewart, ss
Joseph Bailey, cf
Henry Sanford, Manager

Lindell Stars (St. Louis, MO)

David Price, c
N. Costello, c
Frank Cabell, p
Robert Martin, p
A. Costello, 1b
Ben Buchanan, 2b
Caesar Bracey, 3b
W. Cable, ss
G. Fuqua, cf
John Matthews, lf
J. Velar, lf
H. Dickson, rf
J. Stubbs, rf
W. Battise, Substitute
W. R. Smith, Substitute / Manager
W. J. Floyd, President

West Ends (St. Louis, MO)

David Price, c
Ed Garig, c
David Garig, p
James Brooks, 1b
Mace Johnson, 2b
Caesar Bracey, 3b
C. McElhaney, lf
F. First, cf
William Jackson, rf
H. H. Jones, ss / Manager

New Jersey

Cumberland Hotel (Bridgeton, NJ)

Ed Woodruff, c
Taylor, ss / 1b
Jeremiah Tudas, cf
Andrew K. Wells, 2b
Ed Wilkinson, 1b / ss / Captain
John Long, p / 3b
Samuel Bond, lf
Robinson, rf
Morgan, 3b / p
Elstery, cf
Riley, rf
John Wesley Harris, p

Hudsons (Jersey City, NJ)

George Jackson, rf / p / Captain / Vice President
Benjamin "Kid" Brown, cf
Willis Hendricks, lf
Evans Washington, 2b
George Mitchell, 1b / President
Frank Nelson, c
Robert Jackson, ss / c / Secretary
Edward Wales, p
Robert Thompson, 3b / Sergeant-at-arms

Keystones (Jersey City, NJ)

John Lapruce
John Casey
Willis Henderson
George Coase
Arthur Lane
Benjamin Butler
Albert Gale, President
W. Russell, Vice President
Charles Benham, Secretary
George McClain, Treasurer

Browns (Trenton, NJ)

Richmond Robinson, rf
Herbert Simpson, 1b
Andrew Randolph, lf
Eugene Scudder, c
William H. Brown, p
William Conover, 3b
Edward Davis, lf / 2b
Benjamin Davis, 2b
William Coats, ss
James Simpson, cf
John Vactor, p
Ben Boyd, 2b
Ben Holmes, 3b
George Parego, p
Arthur Thomas, c
William E. Simpson, Manager

Cuban Giants (Trenton, NJ)

Richmond Robinson, rf
Frank Harris, ss
Benjamin Boyd, ss
Abe Harrison, ss
Ben Holmes, 3b
George W. Stovey, p
John M. Dabney, 1b / lf
Sheppard Trusty, p
George Parego, p / rf
Arthur Thomas, c
John "Jack" Frye, 1b / 2b
George Jackson, p / cf
Julius Forbes, 1b
Andrew Randolph, 1b
Sims Emory, c
William T. Whyte, p / lf
William Brown, p / cf
Harry Johnson, cf / 2b
J. Oscar Curry, p

William Shadney, rf / p
Paris Archer, p
William S. Purnsley, c

New York

Alpines (Brooklyn, NY)

Stolb, ss
John H. Nelson, p
Oscar Jackson, c
Arthur Jackson, lf
Edward Simpson, rf
George Evans, 2b
Charles Johnson, 3b
Roberts, cf
S. Nelson, 1b
H. H. Johnson, manager

Flushings (Flushing, NY)

William S. Ames, c
Albert Graham, ss
Robert Treadwell, rf
W. Hicks, 3b
Andrew O. Dixon, 1b
Lynn, 2b
Theodore, p
James S. Grant, lf
B. Hicks, cf

Forest Citys (Ithaca, NY)

L. Stewart, 1b
William H. Allen, p
John Thompson, c
R. Robbins, 2b
John Allen, 3b
William Woodson, rf
James Collins, lf
Fred Carlisle, cf
Charles Moore, ss
Fred Stevens, Manager

Gorhams (New York, NY)

Ambrose Davis, rf / 3b
Pete Fisher, c
Garner, 3b
C. H. Hamilton, 2b
Harry Johnson, cf / p
William Patterson, lf
Richmond Robinson, 1b
Phil Smoot, ss
M. White, p
William Peterson, p / 3b
Samuel Sheppard, c / ss
Harland, c
B. B. H. Smith, 3b / p
Jones, 2b
Jackson, ss
Barrett, lf
Harry Pryor, cf
Holcomb, rf
William T. Whyte, p
Benjamin M. Butler, Manager

Bartholdi Club (New York, NY)

Frank Harris, p / 1b
I. W. Bolden, c
George Derrickson, lf
Dandridge, ss
D. A. Agys, cf
A. Johnson, 2b
Benjamin Jackson, p
William H. Topp, rf
Charles Bell, 3b

Cataract (Niagara, NY)

Richard W. Dangerfield, p
C. H. Uggams, c
W. Andross, 1b
A. Spriggs, 2b
Ulysses S. Polk, 3b
G. L. Lane, ss
A. Brown, rf
John King, cf
R. L. Tankerd, lf
A. B. Green
J. C. Anderson, Manager

International (Niagara, NY)

Henry H. Ball
Joseph Seelig
Horace Hall
Richard Bennett
John Ballard
E. A. Butler
T. Demery
Wesley Smith
J. A. Mason

Imperials (Oswego, NY)

Charles King, 1b
William Cheeks, p
John Williams, c
Frank Benson, ss
William Benson, 2b
Charles Williams, 3b
Bert Williams, lf
Ed Scott, cf
L. White, rf

Unexpected (Rochester, NY)

W. Wharton
Charles Lee
Paris Lindsay
W. H. Stewart
George Morris
A. Jackson
Robert Epps
R. H. Stevens
W. H. McDonald
R. R. Thompson
Andrew Dixon, Manager

Colored Giants (Syracuse, NY)

George Williams, 3b
Samuel Freeman, 1b

W. Bentley, 2b
V. Ralph, ss
G. Van Smark, lf
Arthur H. Collins, cf
Burns Whitney, c
E. N. Powell, p
George Banks, 2b
B. Collins, rf

Wide Awakes (Syracuse, NY)

Arthur W. Collins, c
E. N. Powell, p
F. Jackson, rf
George Van Smark, lf
William N. Freeman, 1b
George Williams, 3b
V. Ralph, ss
W. Bentley, cf
William Tobin, p
Aaron Prime, 1b
Hughes, c
Robert Jordan, 1b / 2b / Captain
James J. Tolliver, Manager
Frank J. Williams, Secretary

Bagg's Hotel (Utica, NY)

L. R. Ridley, c
D. McDaniel, p
M. H. Dorsey, 1b
S. S. Staples, 2b / 3b
Charles Peterson, ss
Joseph Johnson, 2b / 3b
D. Tyler, rf
L. Washington, cf
J. Reeves, lf

Butterfield House (Utica, NY)

James Lee, 3b
James Pell, 1b
E. D. Lancaster, ss
William Henry, c
Peter Henry, p
Fred Westerband, lf
William Westerband, 2b
Charles Peterson, ss
Ashbury Dale, cf

Fearless (Utica, NY)

Samuel Freeman, ss
James Pell, 1b
E. D. Lancaster, 3b
John L. Jacobs, rf / 3b
Samuel Jackson, c
William Freeman, 3b
Jacob Francis, cf
William Westerband, rf
F. Hence, 3b
Peter Henry, lf / c
Mose Gray, lf / c
Charles Moore, lf
T. Harris, rf
Richard E. Warmouth, Manager

North Carolina

Athletics (Wilmington, NC)

Monroe Byrd, President
A. Merrimon, Manager
L. Connor, Captain

Ohio

Capital Citys (Columbus, OH)

Ed Tuplett, 1b
Robert Allen, p
A. Williams, 2b
T. Henderson, ss
T. Reynells, lf
J. Draper, rf
A. Huston, p / cf
J. Walls, c
S. Jacobs, 3b
Herman Wilson, Manager

Excelsiors (Cleveland, OH)

Preston Lucas, c / 2b
Charles Griffin, p
Jess Sanford, ss
Fred Johnson, 1b
John Jackson, 2b / c
Weldy Walker, 3b
Samuel "Sam" Smith, lf
Clark Britton, cf
McMillan, cf
John Brown, ss
William H. Wilson, cf
J. Montgomery, rf
George Alexander, 3b
Foster Vaughn, Substitute
George Starkey, Manager

Pennsylvania

J. Gallon (Chester, PA)

John Hackett, p / c /rf
John Butler, c
S. Hinckson, 1b
H. Smith, 2b
B. Smith, 3b
Isaac Rothwell, ss / 2b
Louis Smith, lf
Aaron Fields, cf
William A. Farrell, rf
Warner Pryor, ss / c
Benjamin Driskett, lf
A. Perrigan, ss / c
D. Perrigan, 3b
J. Perrigan, p
Jackson
William Ruley, Manager

J. Robinson (Chester, PA)

L. South, lf
H. South, 1b
J. Smith, 2b
Walter Hinckson, rf

E. Smith, ss
G. Burton, 2b
Ben Smith, 2b
J. Burton, c
J. Dougherty, cf
John Hinckson, p
John Robinson, Manager

Manhattan (Philadelphia, PA)

John Butler
W. Butler
E. Fisher
A. Fisher
A. Hunter
F. Lee
J. Sisco, Captain
W. Tenant
William Ruby
C. Benson
George Waters
C. E. Lloyd, Manager

Browns (Pittsburgh, PA)

David Allen, c
J. B. Allen
Thomas Astor
David Stoner
George Groves
James Gray
Howard P. Bowers
B. Hatfield
Frank Miller, p
J. Kess
William Standard
Charles Catlin
George W. Cain

Lumber City Reds (Williamsport, PA)

George W. Stovey, p
George Jackson, p
Clarence Williams, c
William Shadney, c
Sims Emery, 1b
Williams, 2b
Alexander Davage, 3b
Javan Emory, ss
Daring, Substitute
A. Green, cf / lf / p
Melix, rf
Charles Braxton, ss
William E. Winston, Substitute

Rhode Island

Grays (Providence, RI)

Dan Penno, p / ss
George Vessells, c
Abraham Henry, 1b
Winfield Wickes, 2b
George Johnson, ss
George W. Brown, 3b

Henderson Poindexter, of
L. Penno, 1b
S. Hellum, of
R. Waite, of
Lewis Howard, p
Sidney Smith, Captain
W. Elsey
F. Turner
Frank H. Butler
E. Richard Jones, Manager

Hawthornes (Providence, RI)

George H. Jones
Benjamin Ringgold
William H. Young
D. R. Jones
S. Coleman
Frank J. LaPene
W. Solomon
W. Elsey
W. Posells
R. Talbot
Lewis Howard
J. D. Edgeworth

South Carolina

Fultons (Charleston, SC)

B. White, 1b / cf
Thaddeus Small, 2b
Gus Holmes, 3b
Joseph Dereef, lf
Sam Washington, cf
George Washington, rf
William Brown, c
B. B. H. Smith, p / lf
James Smith, cf / c
James Coles, sub
Steve Jones, ss
Nathan H. Williams, lf / ss / c Captain
Primus P. Dennis, 3b / p
Campbell, p
James Williams, c
Edward Ryan, rf
James Roberts, 2b
J. J. Young, Manager
T. L. Grant, Chairman
L. R. Clark, Secretary
H. E. Myers, Treasurer

Resolutes (Charleston, SC)

W. Jones, 3b
J. Pinckney, cf
C. Robertson, 2b
P. C. Grant, ss / Captain
Campbell, lf
C. Johnston, rf
James Williams, c
James Cuthbert, 1b
Primus P. Dennis, p
Thaddeus Small, 2b

Tennessee

Eclipse (Memphis, TN)

Albert Harden, p / c
William James Renfro, p / c / 2b
Matt Pointer, 1b
Smith, 2b / ss
Sam Pointer, 3b
William Joyner, ss / p
E. Ward, rf / lf / cf / c
L. Daniels, cf
James Shorter, lf / 1b / cf
Robert Higgins, lf
R. F. Newman, rf
James Williams, p

Eurekas (Memphis, TN)

Robert Higgins
William Cole
William Pryor
J. Davis
J. McGowan
S. Jackson
William Downey
Eddie Coswell
Elias Carr
James Williams
R. Bowden
William Pointer
J. H. Cummings, Manager
C. Thomas, Secretary
Levi Orr, Manager

Washington, DC

Assembly (Washington, DC)

Joseph Savoy, 2b
W. H. Johnson, c
G. W. Simmons, 3b
Whitlow, ss
Francis Cardozo., lf
William Syphax, rf
George Cardozo, p
S. J. McFarland, 1b / President
Eugene Silence, cf / Secretary
Archie L. Marshall, Cor. Sec.
William Myers, Treasurer
Ulysses Black, rf / sergeant-at-arms

Blues (Washington, DC)

Gilbert Joy, p
Benjamin Berry, c
Ed Lee, 3b
Jason Joy, lf
Julius Forbes, 1b
William Neale, cf
Robinson, ss
William H. Harrison, 2b
Charles Morgan, lf

Howard University (Washington, DC)

P. H. Lumpkins, 3b

Edwards, c
Ambler, 2b
Robert L. Gaines, p
R. A. Henderson, rf
Robert H. Terrell, cf
Harry Lewis, ss
Thomas Howard Diggs, lf
James H. Usher, 1b / Secretary
James Shamwell, Treasurer
William Handy Johnson, President

Spartas (Washington, DC)

Cornelius Clark, c
Lincoln Cole, p
John W. McIntosh, 1b
T. H. Clark, 2b
William D. Wilkinson, 3b
William Smith, ss
Harry Lewis, Captain / lf
Garrie Booker, cf
John W. T. Smith, rf

1887

Connecticut

Athletics (New London, CT)

Calvin V. Wheeler, p
William H. Purdy, p
Luke Weeks, c
John Bell, 3b
William H. Jordon, 2b
Alfred Wheeler, ss
Charles Warren, rf
James Talbott, cf
John Dickenson, lf
George Johnson, 1b / Captain
Albert Stewart, Captain / 1b
DuBois Hallack, President
Charles Benham, Vice President
George Mitchell, Secretary
Richard Dawson, Treasurer / Manager

Delaware

Grays (Wilmington, DE)

George Jefferson, 2b
Charles Backus, 1b
James Wright, p
James Berry, 3b
Samuel Brown, cf
Lewis Boyer, ss
Spencer Anderson, rf
Empson Williams, lf
Jacob Chippey, c / Captain

Wilmingtons (Wilmington, DE)

Alex Wortenberry, c
Alonzo Ward, p
Charles Lambert, 1b
Alfred Grinnage, 2b
William Gales, 3b
Horace Berry, ss

Peter Spicer, lf
James Chippey, cf
William Maxfield, rf
Henry Berry, Captain / Treasurer
W. H. Trusty, Manager
Edward L. States, Manager

Illinois

Gordons (Chicago, IL)

Grant F. Campbell, 1b
Joseph Campbell, p
Eugene Caldwell, 3b / c
John C. Nelson, rf
Joseph Adams, cf
William Hutchinson, 2b / c
William Turner, ss
Charles Walker, lf
Lloyd Wheeler, p / 3b
Randall Phillips, p
H. M. Fisher, President
H. Johnson, Vice President
Jackson Gordon, Secretary
Daniel Scott, Treasurer
Harry Teenan Jones, Director

Unions (Chicago, IL)

Grant Campbell, lf
Joseph Campbell, p
Darby Cottman, 3b
Albert Hackley, lf
Orange W. Fox, rf
William Stitt Peters, c / 1b
Charles Scott, 2b / ss
Frank C. Leland, cf
William Albert Jones, c / Manager

Uniques (Chicago, IL)

T. Watkins, 1b
George Overland, lf
Richard Hubbard, 2b
Frank Spears, ss
Vertner Johnson, cf
Louis Reynolds, 3b
F. C. Lipscomb, c
Henry C. Blue, c
James Lewis, p
George M. Crisup, President
William Sutliffe, Manager

Indiana

Black Stockings (Lafayette, IN)

Charles Smith, p
James Smith, lf
Sam Grant, c
Dave Banister, 1b
Bill Robinson, 2b
Dave Brown, 3b
James McDonald, rf
Thomas Wilson, lf
Joe Cranshaw, cf / p
Daniel Gwinn, ss

Hustlers (Crawfordsville, IN)

Frank Smith, p
Jim Bowman, c
Jesse Case, 1b
Henry Nettle, 2b
Luther Munroe, 3b
Henry Humphrey, ss
Willie Jordan, rf
James Smith, lf
Jim Ross, cf
Huff Robinson, c

Iowa

Colored Nine
(Cedar Rapids, IA)

James H. Bowlin
Louis Tyler
William Walker
Ed Thompson
John Curtis
Allen
George Ingleman
Seward
Brown

Kansas

Lone Stars (Atchison, KS)

Henry Irving, 1b
Disick, rf
Edward Stewart, c
Walter Booker, cf
Harry Evans, 2b
William Lewis, 3b
John Finley, lf
A. McSpiatten, lf
Ed Mack, p

Eagles (Lawrence, KS)

Squire Anderson. p / c
S. Berry, rf
John Seymour, p
Harry Polk, ss / 3b
C. Anderson, lf
Barlow, 2b
S. Harvey, ss
Israel Allen, p / rf
W. H. Barker, cf

Leapers
(Leavenworth, KS)

George Smith, rf
David Mozee, 1b
George Moore, 2b
William Jackson, 3b / p
David Gray, p
L. Moore, ss
Rowdy, cf
Henry Johnson, c / p
George Robinson, lf
Dennis Jones, Jr, Manager

Kentucky

Fall Citys (Louisville, KY)

Frank Garrett, Captain / ss
William Purnsley, c
James Thomas, 1b
Alonzo Kieger, rf
Fred Mayfield, lf/c
William Woods, ss
J. Armstrong, 1b
James Combs, 1b / p
Napoleon Ricks, ss
John Kinkeide, p
Al Prater, c
Timothy Masterson, Jr., p
Fred Harper, Substitute
James Tilley, Substitute
Charles W. Hines, Manager
William B. Franklin, Manager
Lafayette Condon, p / Manager
William Thompson, c / Manager
G. W. Garrett, Board of Directors /
    President

Tom Bordens (Louisville, KY)

Charles Whitcer, ss
W. King, 1b
Jesse Palmer, 2b
L. Smith, 3b
A. Jackson, lf
S. Washington, cf
J. Helms, rf
B. Taylor, p
G. Boyle, c

Louisiana

Acid Iron Earth (Algiers, LA)

August Lewis, President
H. H. Tyler, Secretary
Benjamin Yates, Treasurer
Robert Washby, Manager
George Mills, Steward
Houma Walker, Captain
Albert Harvey, Assistant Captain

Indomitable Sluggers
(Lafourche, LA)

Peter Alexander, p
Edmund Belcher, c
Albert Page, 1b
C. Morris, 2b
John Vining, 3b
Warren Page, rf
Robert Billups, cf
Eugene Knox, lf
Camille Smith, ss / Captain
John Purnell, Manager

Calanthe (New Orleans, LA)

N. Jefferson, c
Lewis M. Spriggins, p

James Lewis, 1b
N. C. Mitchell, 2b
H. S. Baptiste, 3b
S. I. Brown, ss
H. C. Wallace, rf
J. A. Richards, cf
C. B. Wilson, lf

Camelias (New Orleans, LA)

J. N. Spotts, c / Secretary
R. Wiggins, Captain / p
J. Vaughn, 1b
Michael Lavinge, 2b / President
E. Vandange, lf / Vice President
S. L. Johnson, rf
A. C. Williams, cf
G. Hill, 3b / Treasurer
A. Taylor, ss
E. Whirley, Steward

Can't Get Away
(New Orleans, LA)

M. Doleman, c
Joubert Lewis, p
W. Rittenberg, 1b
J. Boyd, 2b
Fred Lopez, 3b
Louis Williams, ss
E.W. Ford, rf
J.H. Fuller, cf
A.J. Mayfield, lf

E. Knox Club
(New Iberia, LA)

Bud Thomas
Edward Dauphin
William Williams
Harry Scott
H. Burns
L. Richard
M. Perry
Joseph Crosieŕ
Eugene Knox, Manager
Rudolphe Dezauche, Manager

F. A. Johnson
(New Orleans, LA)

Theo L. Harris
Henry Gant
William Smith
A. C. Williams
M. Walker
Joe Walker, Captain
Jack Hill
William Perry
Abe Johnson
Allen Mickey, Scorer
H. Grigsbey, President
W. L. Ford, Vice President
F. A. Johnson, Manager
D. Noble, Jr., Manager

Frederick Douglass
(New Orleans, LA)

J. P. Brown
Henry S. Baptisté
R. S. Scott
E. W. Ford
N. C. Mitchell
W. T. Richards
Joseph A. Landry
William Wittenburg
J. N. Kinchen
Louis Williams
W. R. Harris
William H. Wilson
James Collins
Charles Merritt
Lewis M. Spriggins

Geddes (New Orleans, LA)

J. Dorsey
W. H. Whaley
B. Sheppard
William Thompson
E. G. Romar
T. O. Alcorn
Emile Fox
F. F. Sullivan
P. Dasp
R. Hamilton, President
A. V. Woods, Vice President
George D. Geddes, Jr., Secretary
George D. Geddes, Treasurer
C. M. Montgomery. Manager

H. A. Hills
(New Orleans, LA)

William H. Whaley, President / p
S. L. Johnson, Vice President / c
George V. Watts, Secretary / lf
Emile Fox, Treasurer / 1b
W. G. Burris, Warden / 3b
Ernest Banduit, 2b
Frame Woods, ss
John Woods, ss
John Allen, rf
Alfred Gueringer, cf

H. T. Hastings
(New Orleans, LA)

B. Sheppard
L. Gallery
E. Garrett
Henry Hastings
J. Phillips
F. H. Bodley
G. Tillman
P. H. Smith

Lang (New Orleans, LA)

Joseph Matthews, Captain
Henry Johnson
J. Douglass
J. Goodridge

N. Green
George Stuttney
A. Davis
Albert Felix
Henry Anderson

Pickwicks (New Orleans, LA)

Robert Brooks, 1b
Edward C. Williams, c / Captain
William J. Turner, 2b
Joseph Delmar, 2b
Francis Joseph, lf
John Murray, ss
Dan Mitchell
Jules H. Caufield, 3b
William Davis, 2b
Joseph Kyle
Joseph J. Astier
George W. Hopkins, p
Acie Price, 1b
Joseph Ferrand, rf
Wilson H. Williams, 3b
Frank Sylvester, Hon. President / Board Director
J. F. Jalliot, President
Charles H. Jackson, Vice President
Joseph Wilkins, Treasurer
Homer A. Plessy, Board Director
E. Stykes, Board Director
H. Stackhouse, Board Director

R. E. Foremans
(New Orleans, LA)

Abraham Johnson, Captain
P. Gray
R. Gray
H. Lowe
J. N. Kinchen
Edward Meyers
H. Lewis
J. B. Robertson
A. Lewis
William P. Brown
Robert Wiggins
Charles Daniels, Sergeant-at-arms
Morris Antoine, Team Scorer
H. Harris, Steward
John E. Oliver, President
Joseph Brown, Vice President
William Garrick, Financial Secretary
A. Cleveland, Recording Secretary
P. F. Collins, Treasurer
R. E. Foreman, Manager

Straight University
(New Orleans, LA)

Lamark, p
Braxton, c
N. Hawkins, 1b
Smith, 2b
Wakefield, 3b
Parend, ss

John Johnson, lf
Cove, cf
B. Butler, rf
Charles Gaudet, rf
Charles Medley
Paul Trevigne, Jr.
A. Boisdore
Joseph Fondal
A. Ray
William Stevens
W. Montreuil
L. Dezazant
William Joublanc

Southerns (New Orleans, LA)
Southern University

William R. Pinchback, p
W. H. Whaley, c
A. C. Williams, lf
Emile Fox, 1b
John Brown, 2b
Joseph Burns, 3b
Joseph Moore, ss
John Allen, cf
Charles Gaudet, rf
John White
William Henry
Joseph Walker
Charles Lee, Captain

Unions (New Orleans, LA)

Victor Griffin, p
Honer, p
Paul Bryant, c
Lawrence Scott, 1b
James Recasner, 2b
Henry Anderson, 3b
James Brennan, ss
J. S. Walker, lf
Brown, cf
John Brady, rf
James Arnold, p
C. Moise, c
George Hopkins, p

William Wilson
(New Orleans, LA)

Clovis Coca, Captain
Joubert Lewis, Assistant Captain
William Pinchback, Secretary
Alfred Gueringer
Octave Thomas
William Cayon
Charles Gintz
Victor Griffin, p / rf
Walter Lee
E. Whirley
Michael Lavigne
William H. Wilson, Manager / Treasurer

Hudsons (Shreveport, LA)

William Patterson
J. McMillan, rf

D. A. Smith, 1b
Frank Haughton
B. Johnson
N. Hawkins, cf
R. Bennett, p
Horton, 2b
L. T. Garduet
B. Battle
J. Chalmers
A. A. Hudson, Manager

Maryland

Lord Baltimores (MD)

Harry S. Cummings, p
William P. Gray, 2b / c
Fletcher McLeon, c
Joseph Stewart, p
Frank T. Dorsey, 2b / ss
Raymond, 1b
Jerome Thomas, 3b / 2b
John R. Simms, cf / 3b
James Brooks, 2b / c
A. C. Crain
J. H. Hordy
Harry Proctor, ss
James Payne, cf
Wilson, 1b
J. B. Weyman
Thomas Pinder, 2b
George Haywood, 3b / c
J. R. Young
George Cole
James Harris
Joseph R. Harris, rf
George D. Press
R. H. Prout
Charles Dandridge
D. D. Dickson
W. T. Lewis
Jesse J. Callis, Manager
P. Johnson Tarrer, Asst. Manager
William H. Malone, 3b / p
William Standard, cf

Mutuals (South Baltimore, MD)

Thomas Pinder, 2b
Fields, 1b
J. Coleman, ss
M. Lucas, cf
Wilson, p / 1b / c
Perry, 3b
George Hayward, lf
William Matthews, c
J. Matthews, rf

Massachusetts

Resolutes (Boston, MA)

Charles B. Churchill, cf
L. O. Posey, lf

Samuel Alexander, 2b
William Holmes, 3b
David Allen, c
D. A. Wesley, rf
Jones, 1b
Joseph Palmer, p
William H. Cruckendle, ss

Resolutes (Boston, MA)

William H. Selden, p
Edward C. Smith, c
Richard Davis, c
Peter Leon Lewis, ss
Dan Penno, p / 2b / ss
George Waters, rf / 3b
Andrew Randolph, rf
Louis Howard, cf
William Whitaker, ss
Charles R. Williams, 2b
James W. Horn
George Mullen
Robert Brown, lf / rf
Benjamin Cross, 1b
William Walker, 3b
Tiersile, cf
Harry C. Taylor, p / lf / Secretary
J. W. Noon, Asst. Manager
Marshall Thompson, lf / Manager
Alexander A. Selden, Manager
R. S. Church, Manager

Vendomes (Boston, MA)

John Saunders, cf
William Selden, p
Edward Smith, c
T. J. Gassaway, 2b
Marshall Thompson, lf
William Whitaker, ss
Andrew Randolph, rf
Frank Johnson, 3b
Louis Howard, cf

Puritans (Worcester, MA)

Fred R. Gimby, Manager
Benjamin Walker, captain
E. Stewart
W. Bostic
H. Jackson
Jackson Scott
F. Fuller
J. Wilson
E. Brooks
J. Smith
S. Dyer

Minnesota

Black Diamond (Minneapolis., MN)

Henry Ogden, President
George Bloom, Manager
John Samuels, Captain

Mascotts (Minnetonka, MN)

William McElroy, c
John W. Estelle, p
F. R. Lanier, 1b / Captain
H. Tompkins, 2b
A. Covington, ss
Frank Darnell, lf
Edward Sadler, rf
John Lewis, p
D. Redlight, Substitute
M. Boyd, Substitute
A. Cathorn, Substitute
Harry J. Edwards, 3b / Manager
Emile Mehl, Mascot
Maxy Harris, Director
I. E. Greau, Director
F. W. Harvie, Director
H. J. Hennett, Director
Frank Waldron, Director

Quicksteps (St. Paul, MN)

Leo E. Green, c / lf
William Springer, rf
James Duke, p
T. H. Long, c
Robert Lewis, p / cf / c
Billy Knox, 1b
B. Hill, 2b
Frank Golden, 3b / c
Billy Watters, ss
Charles Burch, rf
Henry W. Fairfax, ss
William H. Brown, c
Charles A. Lett, 2b
C. Wilkins, 3b
H. F. Newton, lf
A. Laboo, cf
Frank Waldron, lf / c / Treasurer
Frank McBeth, cf / p / Captain
Maxy Harris, Substitute
William Gibson, Substitute
Dave Pope, Substitute
Dennis Pickens, Substitute
Andrew A. Cotton, Substitute
W. D. Carter, Manager
Ed Smith, President / Manager

Missouri

OK's (Independence, MO)

Alec Haynes
Scott
Jones
Sallie
Samuels
Syles Olden
Meadows
Todd
Chin

Maroons (Kansas City, MO)

Doe "Doc" Payne, 1b
Walter Zellner, rf

Frank Maupin, c
H. Burt, cf
Joseph Hicks, cf
Loews Maupin, 3b
James Lincoln, ss
Lewis, ss
Johnson, p / rf
Tate, ss
George W. Castone, p / rf
O. Lear, Manager

Black Stockings (St. Louis, MO)

Frank Cabell, p
David Price, c
John Robinson, 3b / cf
Al Spencer, 1b
David E. Gordon, p / rf
Sholt Johnson, 2b / c
Steve Jones, 3b
Charles H. Brady, rf
William Garrett, ss
Harry B. Gaus, 2b
Lewis Canter, ss / Manager

Sumner (St. Louis, MO)

Joe Bailey, c
Colgrove, c
Crane, p
Kennedy, p
Offly, 1b
Powers, 2b
Venneman, 3b
Tutt, ss
William Sutliffe, rf
Mace A. Johnson, cf / Manager
Patterson, lf

Nebraska

Pickwicks (Omaha, NE)

A. J. King, p
William Dyson, c
Louis Catlett, 1b
George Hughbanks, 2b
Harry Hughbanks, 3b
Albert Green, ss
C. A. Dishman, rf
Hugh Hughbanks, cf
George Smith, lf

New Jersey

Cumberland (Bridgeton, NJ)

Woodruff, c
Taylor, ss / 1b
Jeremiah Tudas, cf
Andrew K. Wells, 2b
Ed Wilkinson, 1b / ss / Captain
John Long, p / 3b
Samuel Bond, lf
Robinson, rf
Morgan, 3b / p
Elstery, cf

Riley, rf
John Wesley Harris
Charlie Taft, Manager

Cuban Giants (Trenton, NJ)

Benjamin Boyd, ss
Abraham Harrison, ss
Ben Holmes, 3b
Sheppard Trusty, p / rf
George Parego, p / rf
Arthur Thomas, c
John Frye, 1b / 2b
William T. Whyte, p
Clarence Williams, rf
George Williams, 2b
Oscar Curry, p
William Bird, cf
Ebens Washington
William "Bill" Johnston, rf
Joe Johnson, c / p
Frank Miller, rf
William H. Selden, lf
Alfred Jupiter, p
William Malone, lf / p
Norman Van Dyke, rf
Clarence Sampson, ss
B. Boyle, cf

New York

Hunkidoris (Johnston, NY)

Theodore Pell, 3b
Joseph Johnson, p
Charles Jackson, c
James Pell, 1b
Spencer Clauson, 2b
Thomas Henry, ss
Charles Moore, lf
David Green, cf
Fred Westerband, rf

Sadie Thompsons (New York, NY)

Annie Jones, 1b/Captain
Annie Brown, p
Florence Henderson, c
Maud Smith, 2b
Eva Pearl, 3b
Mary Gilford, rf
Rosa Stiles, ss
Grace White, lf
Nellie Brown, cf

Gorham (New York, NY)

Samuel Jackson, c
B. B. H. Smith, cf
Andrew Jackson, 3b
Robert Jackson, 1b / c
John Nelson, p
M. White, p / c
Phil Smoot, ss / 1b
Richmond Robinson, 1b
Samuel Sheppard, ss

Lewis Allen, c
David Allen, c / lf
Peter Fisher, c
George Evans, 2b / c
Ambrose Davis, rf
John Evans, 1b / 2b
Joseph Palmer, p
Holsombe, rf
B. Willis, lf / 2b
Hamilton, 2b
Thomas Ray
John Eyre
Benjamin Butler, Manager

Cottage House (Ontario, NY)

Henry Mitchell, President
A. Harris, Vice President
H. H. Hall, cf / Manager / Treasurer
Henry B. Ball, c / Secretary
Frank Johnson
C. A. Wilkes, 3b
J. Williams
E. Hill
S. Hall
D. Olmstead
D. Jackson
A. Pryor
C. Taylor
A. D. Taylor
C. Douge
C. Rowell

Colored Nine (Peekskill, NY)

V. Ralph, p
Arthur Collins, c
Williams, 1b
Jordan, 2b
Gorman, 3b
E. N. Powell, ss
Crown, lf
Bins, cf
B. Collins, rf

Fearless (Utica, NY)

Samuel Freeman, ss
James Pell, 1b
E. D. Lancaster, 3b
John L. Jacobs, rf / 3b
Samuel Jackson, c
W. Freeman, 3b
Jacob Francis, cf
William Westerband, rf
F. Hence, 3b
Peter Henry, lf / c
Moses Gray, lf / c
Charles Moore, lf
Ed Harris, rf
Patterson, 2b
Richard E. Warmouth, Manager

Wide Awakes (Utica, NY)

Peter Henry, p
Moses Gray, c

William Westerband, lf
L. Washington, 2b
Theodore Pell, ss / 3b
Thomas Henry, ss
Aaron Prime, 1b
Louis R. Ridley, 3b / cf
Jacob Francis, cf

North Carolina

Diamonds (Henderson, NC)

H. Young, President
A. G. Berry, 1st Vice-President
E. Hicks, 2nd Vice-President / rf
L. B. Blackwell, 3rd Vice-President
W. H. Dunston, 4th Vice-President
W. H. Walton, 5th Vice-President
G. W. Floyd, p / Captain
Richard Foster, c
Junius Hawkins, 1b
C. W. Peace, 2b / Business Manager
M. Mayfield, 3b
Isaac Curtis, ss
A. Albright, lf
J. F. Satterwhite, cf / Business Manager

Ohio

Browns (Cincinnati, OH)

Hal Carroll
Sidney Rogers
W. E. Owens
Ellsworth Downs
James Chapman
John Chapman
William Blackstone
John Austin
George Rankin
George Matthews
Lee Starks

Excelsior (Cleveland, OH)

Preston Lucas, rf
Charles Griffin, p
Fred Johnson, 1b
John Jackson, c
James Jackson, ss
Clark Britton, cf
Frank Henderson, 3b
Foster Vaughn, 2b
Edward Turner, lf
George Starkey, Manager

Rippers (Springfield, OH)

H. S. Brown, Captain / p
W. Jackson, 1b / p
C. Jackson, c
Charles Wyatt, lf
J. Espy, c / lf
W. Espy, 2b / c / lf
Samuel Williams, p
Chan Miller, c
Clark, p

Percy Yates, p
Ulysses Hopkins, c
John Russell, 3b
Thomas Farrell, cf
Pinn, ss
B. T. Fountain, Manager
C. Stoffer, rf / Secretary
Robert T. Jackson, 2b / Treasurer
J. H. Underwood, President

Pennsylvania

J. Gallon (Chester, PA)

John Hackett, p / c / rf
S. Hinckson, 1b
Isaac Rothwell, ss / 2b
Louis Smith, lf
Aaron Fields, cf
Warner Pryor, ss / c / lf
A. Perrigan, ss / c
D. Perrigan, 3b
G. Perrigan, p
J. Parego, ss
D. Parego, 3b
George Parego, p
Henry Sterling, 2b
William Ruley, Manager

Twilight (Frankford, PA)

V. Gibbs, 1b
D. Thompson, ss
Charles Rothwell, 3b
Jobe Trusty, c
D. Holly, cf
Alfred Jenkins, rf
Charles Trusty, p
Albert Rothwell, lf / p
Isaac Rothwell, 2b / rf
Kennedy, 2b
Brinkley, rf
MacKenzie, ss
Stein, lf
Abraham Harrison, c / 2b

Giants (Lancaster, PA)

Julius Forbes, 1b
Andrew Randolph, 3b
James G. Jackson, 1b / p
John Vactor, p
Henry Catto, p
Alonzo Hall, 2b
James Simpson, cf
Harry Johnson, 1b / 2b
Eddie Day, c
Norwood Turner, 3b
William Bowers, lf
William Long, lf / rf
William Conover, 2b
Eugene Scudder, c
William E. Simpson, Manager
James Goodall, President
Benjamin Driskett, lf / rf

Giants (Philadelphia, PA)

Frank Robinson, p
Julius Forbes, 3b
Peter Fisher, 2b / cf
John Butler, c
Isaac Rothwell, s / 2b
William D. Kelly, lf
Brooks, rf
Andrew Randolph, 1b
Charles Trusty, cf / ss

Pythians (Philadelphia, PA)

Sims Emery, 1b / 2b
John Vactor, p / ss
C. H. Norwood, Substitute
William Bowers, rf
William Wood, ss / p
George Jackson, p / c
Julius Forbes, 3b / 1b
William Payne, lf / c / cf
Eugene Scudder, c
Charles Stinson, Substitute
John Stinson, Substitute
James Aylor, cf
William Malone, cf / p / 3b
William Still, 1b
J. L. Jarvin, 2b
Joe Still, Substitute
William Walter James, c
Javan Emery, 3b / rf
J. O. Turner, cf / c
Norwood Turner
Gus Matthews
York Hargett, 3b
E. Hall, 2b
William Simpson, lf
Robert Still, Director
Stanislau K. Govern, Manager
Herman Close, Manager
James L. Goodall, Manager
Robert G. Still, Manager
Gilbert A. Ball, President
C. W. Aylor, President
C. J. Perry, Treasurer
C. Howard Johnson, Secretary
George Hilton, Director
Isaac Judah, Director

Scotts (Philadelphia, PA)

John Butler, c
James Dorsey Robinson, p
Henry Brooks, ss
Peter Fisher, 1b
Isaac Rothwell, 2b
Isaac Chase, 3b / rf
William D. Kelley, lf
John Johnson, cf
George Waters, rf / 3b
John Johnson, cf

Keystones (Pittsburgh, PA)

Samuel Jackson, c
James Lindsey, rf
Solomon White, 2b
Harvey Roy, lf
Henry Gant, 3b
William Walker, c / of
William H. Wilson, ss
Charles Griffin, p / rf
Benjamin Cross, rf / p
Arthur Cross
William Stanard, cf
Al Card, 3b
David Grant, 3b
James Malson, p
Frank Miller, p
James Green, rf / p
Charles Thornton, p
George Zimmerman, c
William H. Brown, 1b
Lewis Allen, lf / 1b
John Brady, lf
Thomas White, 2b / 3b
J. Phillip Jordan
James Jackson, p
William Saunders, of
Charles Brown, p
Albert Douglass, ss / 3b / p
William Lyons, c
D. Thompson, ss
Harry Puller, c
M. R. Ross, lf
John Hart, c / 1b
B. Hatfield, ss
Peter Davis, 2b
Henry Byars, 2b
John Gaines, 2b
Horatio Burton
Alonzo Hall
Walter Martin
William Grimm
Arthur Winston
William Jones
William Newman
William Smallwood
William Truman
James Lindsey
William S. Brown, Manager
Charles H. O'Donnell, Management
William Hauger, Vice President
M. A. Spriggs, President
Milton Ricks, Management
Charles H. Nelson, Management

Rhode Island

Grays (Providence, RI)

Dan Penno, p / ss
George B. Vessels, c
Abraham Henry, 2b
Oran L. Skipworth, cf
W. Wickes, 2b

George Johnson, 3b
George W. Brown, p
Henderson Poindexter, lf
L. Penno, 1b
S. Hellum
R. Waite, rf
Hooper, p
E. Richard Jones, Manager

Tennessee

Eurekas (Memphis, TX)

Robert Higgins, p
William Cole, c
William Pryor
J. Davis
J. McGowan
S. Jackson
J. Williams
R. Bowden
William Pointer
J. H. Cummins, Manager
C. Thomas, Secretary
Levy Orr, Team President

*Rock City Greys
(Nashville, TX)*

William T. Smith, c
Moses Cain, c
William Moore, p / rf
William Coffey, p / rf
William Cain, p
R. B. Weakley, 1b
P. L. Nichols, 2b
Henry Hyde, 3b
Tom Taylor, ss
John Trimble, lf
W. C. Ewing, cf
A. H. Campbell, Manager

Texas

Young Strikers (Fort Worth, TX)

White, c
Henderson Caldwell, p
Wimms, 1b
Frank Gilbert, 2b
Greer, 3b
Beckham, ss
Best, rf
Burts, cf
Adams, lf

Flyaways (Galveston, TX)

Joseph Walker, c
A. Runnels, p
Williamson, 1b
Wiley, 2b
George Upps, 3b
Jackson, ss
Bud Walker, rf
F. Bryant, cf
William Conway, lf

Virginia

Red Stockings (Norfolk, VA)

Edwards, 3b
Sidney Fentriss, p
William Johnson, ss
William Parker, cf
George White, 1b
Massey, 2b
Isaac McCoy, c
Webb, lf
Augustus Taylor, rf

Washington, DC

Blues (Washington, DC)

Gilbert Joy, p
Benjamin Berry, c
Ed Lee, 3b
Jason Joy, lf
Julius Forbes, 1b
William Neale, cf
Robert Robinson, ss
William H. Harrison, 2b
Charles Morgan, lf
Jerome Thomas, ss
John Chase, 1b / Manager

*Capital Citys
(Washington, D C)*

R. W. White
Nathan H. Williams
Joseph Williams
E. J. Williams
J. G. Loving
Eddie Perry
Robert Holland
Solomon "Sol" White
Jesse F. Binga
Fred Mayfield
Jerome Thomas
Thomas Pinder
George Lettlers
Frank C. Leland
Joseph H. Wilson, 1b
Nelson M. Williams, Manager

Wisconsin

*Underwoods
(Milwaukee, WI)*

Walter E. Sparks, p
F. D. Fields, c / Secretary
C. W. Dorsey, ss
Benjamin F. Underwood, 2b / Captain
Frank J. Chapman, lf
J. C. Croft, 3b
R. Rand, p / cf
S. W. Geron, rf
W. A. Adkins, Substitute
T. Ducat, Substitute
Thomas W. Elliott, 1b / p / Manager

1888

California

Quicksteps (Los Angeles, CA)

William Griffin, c / 1b
Detrick, p
E. Hancock, 1b
William Nettles, 2b
Hammond, 3b
Joseph Grant, ss
L. Hamilton, rf
Pennington, 2b
George Fuller, lf

Young Strikers (Los Angeles, CA)

William Griffin, 1b
William Nettles, lf
L. Hamilton, cf
Young, c / p
George Fuller, 2b
E. Hancock, rf
William Hamilton, ss
Hammond, 3b
Detrick, p / Manager

Connecticut

Colored Nine (New Haven, CT)

Lowry, c
Swan, p
Charles Hawley, 1b
Coston, 3b
Jackson, ss
Archie Williamson, rf
John Bell, lf
Robinson, cf
Louis Howard, 2b

Gorhams (New Haven, Connecticut)

Fred (Nat) Collins, Captain
Arthur Jackson, 3b
Oscar Jackson, lf
Robert "Bob" Jackson, c
John Nelson, p
John Foster
John Vactor, rf
William Bell, p / rf
Charles Bell, ss / p
Ed Chamberlain, 1b
William Gray, c
Sheppard Trusty, p
George Stout, rf / p
George Evans, 2b
Holcombe, Substitute
William Henderson, Substitute
Solomon White, 2b
Ben Butler, Manager
Schnepper, Manager

Georgia

Athletics (Macon, GA)

Joe Johnson
Frank Barner
Felix Corbin
William Jordan, Captain
C. P. Stubbs
C. H. Wallace
Squire Simpson
William Lewis
George Ellins
Alex Carrol
James Hickson
Frank Brooks
Robert H. Hart, Treasurer
John T. White, Manager

Illinois

Reds (Bloomington, IL)

Charlie A. Grace, p / rf
William Watson, c /cf
Charlie Smith, ss
Henry Ross, 1b
Stewart Hamilton, 3b
Thomas Miller, lf
William Wise, cf / c
Charlie Mitchell, rf / p
Clinton L. Hill, 2b / Captain
Matthew Hamilton, Manager / Secretary

Brockway & Milan (Chicago, IL)

William H. Lee, President
M. Black, Secretary
M. Pearse, Treasurer
M. Modley, Captain

Unions (Chicago, IL)

Grant Campbell, cf
William T. Smith, rf
William Freeman, 3b
William Peterson, 1b
Albert Hackley, cf / lf
R. Lee, ss / lf
Albert E. Robinson, 3b
William Stitt Peters, 1b
Frank Scott, 2b / ss
Joseph Campbell, p
William A. Jones, c / Manager
E. M. Russell, Board
Granville N. Hackley, 1b / Board
J. R. Van Pelt, Board

Kansas

Lone Stars (Atchison, KS)

Henry Irving, 1b
Disick, rf
Edward Stewart, c
Walter Booker, cf
Harry Evans, 2b

William Lewis, 3b
John Finley, lf
A. McSpiatten, lf
Ed Mack, p

Athletics (Hutchinson, KS)

Thaddeus Stevens, c
H. B. "Babe" Owens, p
Black, 1b
Crow, 2b
Hawk, 3b
Granville Sanders, ss
Brown, cf
William Miller, lf
Charlie Bean, rf

Leapers (Leavenworth, KS)

Robert Dobbs, c
Gabe Johnson, c
T. Davis, ss
William English, p
William Jackson, 2b / p
Smart, cf
James Mayo, 1b
Turner, 3b
J. Moore, lf
Parker, rf
Joseph Creesey, c

Duffers (Olathe, KS)

W. R. Moten, c
John Guthery, p
Robert Miller, 1b
Walter Rollins, 2b
John Jenkins, 3b
James Bentley, ss
Abe Miller, lf
R. B. Moten, cf
Ed Roberts, rf

Colored Nine (Weston, KS)

O. L. Boyd
C. Colman
John Rolston
Abe Weston
William Rickman
Charles Fox
James McClain
A. J. Tandy
W. A. Brown
Mike Vance

Colored Nine (Weston, KS)

Abe Weston
John Rawson
Charles Fox
Charles Goldman
Ulysses Rickman
George Venice
John McClain

Frank House
Henry Underwood

Kentucky

Colored Nine (Shelbyville, KY)

William Orphan, c
James Prentis, p
John Clairbourn, ss
John Williams, 2b
Dave Massie, 1b / Manager
George Fortune, 3b
James Bloomer, rf
Buck Robinson, cf
Harry Payne, lf

Louisiana

Browns (Algiers, LA)

Johnson, p
James Stocks, c
James Obaire, 1b
Albert Harvey, 2b
Joubert Lewis, 3b
William Henry, ss
Goodman, lf
James Lewis, cf
William H. Hall, rf

Pinchbacks (New Orleans, LA)

Edward Williams, c / ss
James J. Ross, c / cf
Joseph Ferrand, lf
William J. Turner, 1b
Francis Joseph, ss / cf
John Murray, 2b
Ed Garig, c
Cameal, rf
A. Defauchard, 2b
Acie Price, ss
James Brennan, p
Paul Bryant, c
George W. Hopkins, p
John, rf / c
Walter L. Cohen, Manager

Unions (New Orleans, LA)

J. G. Griffin, p
William Bryant, c
Lawrence Scott, 1b
James Recasner, 2b
Henry Anderson, 3b
James Brennan, ss
J. S. Walker, lf
Brown, cf
John Brady, rf
James Stocks, c

Hudsons (Shreveport, LA)

R. Bennett, p
William Bailey, 3b
Williams, c
N. Hawkins, cf
D. A. Smith, 1b

William Patterson, ss
McMillan, rf
Channel, lf
Horton, 2b
A. A. Hudson, Manager

Massachusetts

Franklins (Cambridge, MA)

C. Kelley, ss
D. Kelley, 1b
William Clark, 2b
Dolan, cf
George Sharkey, 2b
Linnell, lf / p / rf
McCarter, p
O'Brien, rf
J. Smith, 3b
Mulverhill, 3b
Burke, rf / p
William Clark, c
Toomey. rf

Resolutes (Boston, MA)

Richard E. Walker, 2b
Richard Davis, ss / 2b
Benjamin Cross, 1b
Joseph Palmer, p
Samuel Alexander, rf
Joseph H. Wilson, cf
Joseph Carrington, 3b
Alfred Jupiter, lf
William T. Green, c / ss
H. F. Hicks, Secretary
Marshall Thompson, Manager

Resolute Junior (Boston, MA)

H. H. Ash
C. Page
Henry Carter
George Williams
C. Wilson
Hodges
Gray
Long
Timberlake
Moses Hipkins
E. C. Bryant, Manager

Michigan

Central City (Jackson, MI)

Fred Harper, p
Ed Thomas, c
Robert Thurman, 1b
Jordan Green, 2b
Elijah Stewart, 3b / Captain
John Wesley, ss
Robertson, lf
William Carter, rf
W. Bucks, lf
D. Coleman, ss
R. A. Madison, cf / Secretary

Taylor Carter, President
Frank M. Thurman, Treasurer

Missouri

Maroons (Kansas City, MO)

Frank Maupin, c
William Castone, p
Joseph Hicks, 2b
William Burt, cf
James Lincoln, ss
Doc Payne, 1b
Loews Maupin, 3b
Tate, lf
William Bird, cf
Leonard, ss / cf
Walter Zellner, rf
H. Johnson, p
John Reeves, p
C. Lear, Manager

Black Stockings (Lexington, MO)

Gideon, p
Thirkies, lf
Heywood, 1b
James Lindsey, 2b / c
Frank Lindsey, c
L. Brown, cf
R. Smith, rf
W. Johnson, ss
B. Alexander, rf
James Bullock, p

Reds (Springfield, MO)

E. Clayton, c
John Reeves, p
Massey, 2b
James Dean, cf
Farries, ss
Starks, 1b / rf
Cain, 3b
Farlee (Fairer), lf
J. Moore, rf
Andrew Love, 1b

Black Stockings (St. Louis, MO)

D. Hyames, p
Charles Franklin, p
Al Spencer, c
E. Butler, c
James Brooks, 1b
William Robinson, 2b
Lewis Canter, 3b
Spence Y. C. Stewart, ss
G. Williams, lf
Harry B. Gaus, 2b
E. Gray, cf
Robert Hyde, rf
David E. Gordon, rf
Henry Sanford, lf / rf

West Ends (St. Louis, MO)

Dan Garig, p
Ed Garig, c
James Brooks, 1b
Sholt Johnson, 2b / c
Caesar Bracey, 3b
C. McElhaney, lf
F. First, cf
William Jackson, rf
David Price, c
William Macklin, p
"Stump" Tooley, 1b
W. J. Anderson, lf
Hyatt, rf
H. H. Jones, ss / Manager

Nebraska

Lafayette (Omaha, NE)

George Smith, p
George Hughbanks, 2b
Parker, c
O'Neal, c
Harry Hughbanks, ss
William Lewis, 3b
Louis Catlett, lf
A. J. King, rf / p
William L. King, cf / c
Alexander Plummer, 1b / Manager

New Jersey

*African Greasers
(Trenton, NJ)*

James Seruby, 1b / Captain
Thomas Brown, ss
P. McCauley, p / Manager
P. Bruthers, c
Allen Crippin, 2b
F. Allan, 3b
D. Thompson, lf
C. Thompson, rf
William Rodman, cf

Cuban Giants (Trenton, NJ)

George Williams, 2b / 3b
Clarence Williams, c
Arthur Thomas, rf / c
Abraham Harrison, ss
John Frye, 1b
Ben Boyd, cf / 2b
William H. Selden, lf
Benjamin Holmes, 3b
George Washington Stovey, p / lf
George Parego, cf / p / lf
William T. Whyte, p
William Malone, lf / p
Walter Seruby, lf
Julius Forbes, 1b / rf
Harry Pryor
Andrew Randolph, 1b / lf / cf
George Jackson, p

Harry Johnson, cf / 2b
Henry Catto, ss
David Allen, 1b / c
John Milton Dabney, lf
William Payne, rf / c
Thomas Browne, ss
Fred Holloman, 3b
O. Sullivan, rf / c
S. K. Govern, Manger

Frye's Nine (Trenton, NJ)

Clarence Williams, c
Abraham Harrison, ss
Benjamin Boyd, 2b
William Malone, 3b
George Parego, p
George Jackson, lf
Walter Seruby, cf
Andrew Randolph, rf
William Johnston, 2b
Arthur Thomas, c
George W. Stovey, p
William Whyte, lf
John Frye, 1b / Manager

New York

*Harrison and Morton
(Buffalo, NY)*

E.N. Powell, p
L. L. Kunes, c
J. Eckerson, 1b
Al Jackson, 3b
W. Alexander, 3b
G. Smith, lf
William Bright, cf
John Dallas, rf
William Merritt Landers, ss / Manager

*Lone Stars
(Cold Springs, NY)*

C. Brown, ss
W. Brown, c
J. Brooks, lf
John Foster, 1b
Blakely, 2b
W. Brown, rf
Buckman, p
McHravey, 3b
J. Barton, cf

*Hicks-Sawyer Minstrels
(New York, NY)*

John Connors, c
Irving Sayles, p
William H. Speed, 1b / Captain
Jack Evans, 2b / 3b
Dick Johnson, 3b / ss
Harry Thomas, 2b
George Connors, ss
Charles Washington, lf / 2b
Hosea Easton, rf
William H. Downes, cf

E. Connors, rf
Horace Copeland, 1b
Charles B. Hicks, Manager

Jacksons (New York, NY)

Frank Grant
Arthur Thomas
Chambers
Robert Jackson
Shep Trusty
John Nelson
Dave Jackson
Ambrose Davis
Jack "Bud Fowler" Jackson, Manager

*Powers Hotel
(Rochester, NY)*

Nathan Wye, 1b
John Rowe, p / Captain
Walter Brooks, c
John Downes, ss
W. H. Stockton, 3b / Secretary
William Jackson, 2b
J. Smith, rf
Charles P. Lee, p
Horace H. Hall, rf
Joseph B. Hall, cf
George Gibbs, lf
William H. Phillips, p / c
Andrew Dixon, Manager
John W. Thompson, President

*New Americans
(Richfield Springs, NY)*

F. Booker, 2b
G. Goines, 3b
F. Cardoza, 1b
G. Booker, p
J. Stewart, rf
N. Mitchell, lf
G. Burke, ss
W. T. Smith, c
M. Curry, cf

*Spring House
(Richfield Springs, NY)*

George W. Martin, ss
Joseph Leggett, p
John Rider, 1b
M. Bulware, c
Charles Wright, 3b
John Pollard, rf
A. Gilliard, lf
W. Bowen, 2b
Frank Kennedy, cf

Fearless (Utica, NY)

Samuel Freeman, ss
James Pell, 1b
John L. Jacobs, rf / 3b
S. Jackson, c
William Freeman, 3b
Jacob Francis, cf

W. Westerband, rf
F. Hence, 3b
Peter Henry, lf / c
Mose Gray, lf / c
Charles Moore, lf
Richard E. Warmouth, Manager

North Carolina

Maple Leafs (Wilmington, NC)

Mingo Cochran
John Forbes
Willie Freeman
Isaiah Lillinhost
Dan Tucker
Jerry Baker
Ed Crawford
Alonzo Ford, p
Thomas Terrell, c

Mutuals (Wilmington, NC)

William Nash
Gus Nixon
Albert Nixon
Frank Gause
John Hawkins
Joseph Hawkins
David Hawkins
Joseph Hawkins
James Freeman
Elijah Freeman
Neal Hayes, Manager

Ohio

Rippers (Springfield, OH)

H. S. Brown, Captain / p
W. Jackson, 1b / p
C. Jackson, c
Samuel Williams, p
Thomas Farrell, cf
Pinn, ss
Charles Wyatt, lf
John Russell, 3b
Chan Miller, c
Clark, p
Percy Yates, p
Ulysses Hopkins, c
Robert Jackson, 2b / Treasurer
C. Stoffer, rf / Secretary
B. T. Fountain, Manager
J. H. Underwood, President

Pennsylvania

Nonpareils (Philadelphia, PA)

Joseph King, President
Charles Akers, Treasurer
Edmund Royal, Manager

*Colored Barbers
(Pittsburgh, PA)*

James W. Gray, 1b
Charles Catlin, 2b / Captain

William Truman, 3b
H. Matthews, ss
B. Burke, lf
C. Brooks, cf
H. W. Jones, rf
G. Lee, p
David Stoner, c
Arthur Gross, 2b
George D. Sherrow, Manager

Keystones (Pittsburgh, PA)

John Brady, p
Charles Bell, c
Harvey Roy, c
Thomas Ray, c
Solomon White, 2b
Thomas White, 3b
Henry Gant, ss
Ross Garrison, ss
Frank Miller, p
Charles Brown, p
James Malson, p
Javan (Levanti) Emory, c
Jacobs, c
Weldy W. Walker, c / Manager
William Stanard, cf / rf / Manager
Albert Douglass, p / ss / Manager

Standards (Pittsburgh, PA)

John Brady, 3b / ss
Charles Bell, rf / cf / lf
Harvey Roy, rf
Solomon "Sol" White, 2b
Thomas White, 3b
William Stanard, cf
Henry Gant, 1b
Ross Garrison, ss
Charles Brown, p
James Mason, p,
Albert Douglass, p / 1b
Frank Miller, p
Weldy Walker, c / Manager

Tennessee

Bright Eagles (Knoxville, TN)

John Ross
R. Wallace
Pleas Burke
Sterling Stewart
John Massengill
Alexander Copeland
John Singleton
Henry Clay
Eph Daniels

Carters (Knoxville, TN)

Alexander Franklin, Captain
J. McCorkle
Will Lones
Markam Mitchell
Alfred Patton
John Lane

Charles Smith
Dick Boyd
Joe Carter, Manager

Eurekas (Memphis, TX)

William Cole, c
William Pryor
J. Davis
J. McGowan
S. Jackson, 2b
J. Williams
R. Bowden
William Pointer
Robert Higgins, p / Manager

*Rock City Greys
(Nashville, TX)*

William T. Smith, c
Moses Cain, c
William Moore, p / rf
William Coffey, p / rf
William Cain, p
R. B. Weakley, 1b
P. L. Nichols, 2b
Henry Hyde, 3b
Tom Taylor, ss
John Trimble, lf
W. C. Ewing, cf
A. H. Campbell, Manager

Texas

Black Stockings (Dallas, TX)

John Ward, c / ss
Malone, rf / p
Clarkson, 1b
Clark, ss / c
D. Smith, 3b
Mansfield, 2b
Edwards, lf
Coffee, cf
Kelly, rf / p

Browns (Dallas, TX)

Stephens, c
Frank Gilbert, ss / 2b
H. Lee, p / 1b
A. Stone, cf
Joseph Julius, 3b / rf
D. Smith, 2b
Milligan, rf
John W. Simon, lf
Simonson, c
J. F. Ramsey
Jasper Crutchfield, Manager / lf

Forneys (Forney, TX)

Butler, p
Ervin, c
Yates, 1b
Mayfield, 2b
Cox, cf
Reeves, lf

Boles, ss
Ridgell, lf
Peers, rf
Spence, 3b
Towne, 2b
Dunham, 3b

Blues (Fort Worth)

Wimms, c
Anderson Alexander, ss
William Fulbright, c
Walter Paris, p
Adams, p / lf
Beckham, p
Edwards, 1b
Terry, cf
George Guinn, 3b / c
Joe Thompson, 2b / 1b
Peate (Pete), rf / ss
F. Lee, 3b
Milligan, rf
William Snow, lf
Brockman, 1b
Greer, 2b

Fly Ways (Galveston, TX)

Jackson, ss
Joseph Walker, 2b
C. J. Williams, c
George Upps, 1b
A. Runnels, cf
Frank Coleman, p
William Conway, lf
Mose Johnson, 3b
D. Stafford, rf
Henry Swanston, Manager

Rhode Island

Grays (Providence, RI)

Dan Penno, p
George Vessell, p / c
Abraham Henry, 1b / 2b
Winfield Wickes, 2b
George Johnson, ss
James Johnson, cf
George W. Brown, 3b / ss
Henderson Poindexter, of
Walter Hazard, 3b
R. Waite, of
Louis Howard, p
James Buvard, rf
W. Elsey
R. Talbot
J. D. Edgeworth
F. Turner
Frank H. Butler
E. R. Jones, Manager

Hawthornes (Providence, RI)

Louis Howard, p
W. Solomon, c
W. Elsey, if

W. Posells, if
R. Talbot, if
Lewis Howard, if
J. D. Edgeworth, of
F. Turner, of
F. H. Butler, of

Virginia

Red Stockings (Norfolk, VA)

Sidney Fentriss, c / Captain
Augustus Taylor, 2b
Henry Ruffin, 3b
Cyrene Fisher, p
Dan McClennan, 1b
Moore, 1b
"Bub" Baker, cf
Wertham, rf
William Johnson, ss
James Knox, 3b
George Fentriss
George Elliott

Washington, DC

Blues (Washington, DC)

Gilbert Joy, p
Benjamin Berry, c
Ed Lee, 3b
Jason Joy, lf
Julius Forbes, 1b
William Neale, cf
Robert Robinson, ss
William H. Harrison, 2b
Charles Morgan, lf
Jerome Thomas, ss

1889

California

Enterprise (San Francisco, CA)

W. H. Honey, ss / Captain
C. Lancaster, p
B. Lancaster, c
J. Gladman, 1b
W. Morton, 2b
A. Dennis, 3b
M. Watson, lf
J. Brown, rf
H. Carter, cf
T. Smith, Substitute

Union Stars (San Francisco, CA)

W. H. Honey, ss / Captain
C. Lancaster, p
B. Lancaster, c
J. Gladman, 1b
W. Morton, 2b
A. Dennis, 3b
M. Watson, lf
J. Brown, rf

H. Carter, cf
T. Smith, Substitute

Connecticut

Elm City (New Haven, CT)

William H. Dyer, President
Clarence Page, Treasurer
George Stevens, secretary
James Roston, Manager

Delaware

West Ends (Wilmington, DE)

Spencer Anderson, c / rf
James Berry, cf / p
Alonzo Ward, 2b
Peter Spicer, lf
Spencer Greenwood, 3b
Charles Backus, 1b
Nathan Hanley, c
Thomas G. Kane, ss / 1b
James Chippey, ss
Lewis Boyer, 3b
Donahes, p
George Jefferson, 2b
Williams, lf
Thomas H. Gibson, cf
Virgil Wright, rf
James Wright, p
Jake Hefferon, 1b
J. Wilson, 2b
Edward States, Manager

Illinois

Reds (Bloomington, IL)

Charles A. Grace, p / rf
William Watson, c / cf
Charles Smith, ss
Henry Ross, 1b
Stewart Hamilton, 3b
Thomas Miller, lf
William Wise, cf / c
Charles Mitchell, rf / p
Clinton L. Hill, Captain / 2b
Matthew Hamilton, Manager

Athletics (Chicago, IL)

A. Cotman, c / rf
Lee Stark, rf /c
Wilbur Lewis, p
G. Gleaves, ss
Charles Weekly, 1b
George Hankins, 1b
Theo Hubbard, 3b
Link Brown, lf
William V. Freeman, cf
S. J. Chadwick, Manager

Australian Giants (Chicago, IL)

Lee Starks, 2b / c
Robert Foote, c

Frank C. Leland, ss / 1b
George Gleaves, cf
William Freeman, 3b
Darby Cottman, rf / p
T. Landers, lf
William L. Dunson, 1b
M. A. Arnold, ss
C. Cary, c
James O'Bannion, c
Orange W. Fox, Manager

Black Stockings (Chicago, IL)

Edward Dunson, c
Frank Butler, p
Hurley, ss
Walter G. Prime, rf
William L. Dunson, 1b
William Woodson, lf
F. Ross, p
William Braxton, 1b
Edward Prime, cf
George Foster, p / Manager

Gordons (Chicago, IL)

W. Warren, p
William Petit, c
M. Starbuck, 1b
A. Conner, 2b
Stearns, 3b
F. Starbuck, ss
Hueting, cf
William Coates, rf
Nick Williams, lf / p
F. Graham, Manager

Jolly Boys (Chicago, IL)

William Payne, c
M. Stewart, c
George Mead, p
William Walton, p
Joe Scott, 1b
Phil Reidy, 3b
John Scott, cf
E. Hayes, cf
E. Fersdorf, lf
E. Ward, lf
William Smith, rf
William Basey, cf
George B. Smitt, 2b / ss / Manager

Models (Chicago, IL)

Joe Johnson, c / p
George Mead, p
John H. Howard, 1b / c
William Payne, 2b / c
Frank Ramsay, 3b
Darby Cottman, c
Wesley Parker, lf / c / ss
Henry Ross, cf / 1b
Dinney Davis, rf / ss
J. Woods, p

Clarence Coleman, c
Nick Williams, ss / lf
Arthur Anderson, p / Captain
Willis Jones, c
William White, cf
William Holmes, p
Sam Hanley, 1b
John Cranshaw, rf
W. Young, 2b
Billy May, cf
W. Warren, 3b / p / ss
Charles Thompson, cf
H. Baxter, lf
Mud, p
William Holman
Robert P. Jackson, Manager
William Johnson, President

Resolutes (Chicago, IL)

Lee Starks, 2b / c
Robert P. Jackson, c / 2b
Joseph Wickliffe, 1b
William Renfroe, p / rf
Harry Walker, 3b
William Stitt Peters, c
George Gleaves, cf
James Smith, p
D. Coleman, p
William Freeman, 3b
Darby Cottman, rf / p
Longmeres, lf / cf
Robert Ward, lf
M. A. Arnold, ss
C. Cary, c
James O'Bannion, c
William White, 2b
Layden (Lauden), O., rf
William L. Duncan, 1b
Frank Leland, ss / 1b / Manager
Orange W. Fox, Manager
Ed Brown, lf / President

Rhodes Boys (Chicago, IL)

Robert Hull, p
Walter G. Prime, c
William Stewart, c
Wilson, 1b
William Walton, 2b
Fowler, 3b
Willis Jones, lf
John A. Mayer, cf / p
Victor Griffin, p
Hagg, c
Woodruff, c
Harvey Chappell, lf
B. Ward, lf / rf
Morton Towles, 3b
William Turner, 3b
R. Rhodes, ss / Manager

Uniques (Chicago, IL)

William Kelly, p

Conway, c
Cleadon, 1b
Joseph "Joe" Case, 2b
E. Schenk, 3b
William Rowland, ss
Edward O'Brien, cf
Martin Jeffers, lf
O. Layden (Lauden), rf

Unions (Chicago, IL)

Grant F. Campbell, cf
Arthur Anderson, p
William T. Smith, rf
William Freeman, 3b
William S. Peterson, 1b
A. Lee, ss / lf
Joseph Campbell, p
William Baskins, cf
Marshall Coffey, 2b
Frank C. Leland, cf
James Smith, p
William Ramsay, rf
William Stitt Peters, 1b
J. Arthur, cf
George Holbert, cf
William Hawkins, rf
E. Ward, rf
William A. Jones, c / Manager
Robert R. Jackson, rf / c / Manager
Albert Hackley, cf / President

Indiana

Sheldon Blues (Evansville, IN)

Abe Jackson
Mason McKinney
George D. Simpson
George Beverly
Sanford Wharton
J. N. Robinson
Alexander Caldwell
John Gardner
Loveland
Hollingsworth, c
Charles Johnson, p
Matthew Wright, Manager

Black Stockings (Indianapolis, IN)

William Craven
James Anderson
George Thomas
John Barbour
Elzy Hart
George White
Bud Banks
William "Bud" Cook
Moses Allen
William Shelton
Noah Moore

Kansas

Colored Nine
(Coffeyville, KS)

Phillip Bassett
John H. B. Wilson
W. D. Driver
Wash Waterhouse
Sam Bledsoe
Henry Bledsoe
Charles Crouch
Jack Crouch
Scott Smith

Athletics (Hutchinson, KS)

Thaddeus Stevens, c
H. B. "Babe" Owens, p
Black, 1b
Crow, 2b
Hawk, 3b
Granville Sanders, ss
Brown, cf
William Miller, lf
Charlie Bean, rf

Browns (Leavenworth, KS)

George Moore
"Gabe" Johnson
Jesse Hughes
Henry Robinson
Alex Johnson
Lewis Johnson
William Richardson
A. Richardson
George Walker
Harry Young
William Harris, Captain
Alley Jones, Manager

Colored Champions
(Wichita, KS)

Syl Anderson, p
Brent Anderson, c
William Green, ss
Charles Anderson, 1b
Artie White, 3b
William Able, lf
Ozie Cunningham, p
Benis, cf
William Able, rf
Lake Anderson, 2b / Manager
George W. Robinson, Manager

Louisiana

Pinchbacks (New Orleans, LA)

George W. Hopkins, p / President
James Arnold, rf
Victor Griffith, p
Edward Williams, c / Captain
James Brennan, p
Paul Bryant, c
William J. Turner, 1b / Secretary

William H. Hall, 1b
John Brady, c
James J. Ross, cf
Gaspard Joseph, 2b
John Murray, 3b / Vice President
Acie Price, ss
J. W. Douglass, ss
Joseph Ferrand, lf
Jules Caufield, cf
A. Defauchard, rf
Walter L. Cohen, Manager

Unions
(New Orleans, LA)

Victor Griffith, p
Joseph "Pean" Johnson, c
W. Scott, 1b
Joseph Recasner, 2b
John Brady, 3b / rf
J. W. Douglas, ss
William Brown, lf / cf
James Simpson, cf
T. Williams, rf
C. Moise, sub
James Brennan, ss
T. Walker, lf
Joseph H. Fuller, Manager

Massachusetts

Franklins (Boston, MA)

Frank Battles, p
Currier, c
Gage, 1b
Sheppard, 2b
Dill, 3b
Folsom, lf
Black, rf
Wilson, cf
A. W. Bright, ss / Manager

Seasides (Boston, MA)
Formerly the Resolutes

William Tyrrell
M. Hill
Horace Gray
Daniel Walker
Alexander Banks
E. C. Bryant
William C. Holmes
E. Richardson
Benjamin Cross
Alfred Davis
Percy Bond
Benjamin F. Allen
Guy Alexander
W. Lomax
William Jones
Charles Posey
C. Wilson
W. Palmer
Theodore E. Roberts, Manager

Michigan

Unions (Detroit, MI)

George Rice, p
E. Lith, 1b
C. Miller, 2b
P. Beasley, ss
Harry Moore, 3b
Charles Griffin, lf
Jesse Cook, cf / p
S. Parker, rf
Deibel, p
Fred Slaughter, c / Manager

Missouri

Maroons (Kansas City, MO)

Frank Maupin, c
William Castone, p
Hicks, 2b
H. Burt, cf
James Lincoln, ss
Doc Payne, 1b
Loews Maupin, 3b
Tate, lf
Walter Zellner, rf
H. Johnson, p
John "Jack" Reeves, p
C. Lear, Manager

Black Stockings (St. Louis, MO)

Frank Cabell, p
John Robinson, p
Dave Price, c
Sholt Johnson, c
Steve Jones, 1b
Spence Y. C. Stewart, 2b
Lewis Canter, ss / Manager
William Garrett, lf
Al Spencer, cf
David E. Gordon, rf
Caesar Bracey, 3b
William Batice, President

West Ends (St. Louis, MO)

Edward Garig, c
F. First, ss
James Brooks, lf
"Stump" Tooley, 1b
H. H. Jones, 2b / Manager
William Macklin, p
William Garig, 3b
Jefferson Johnson, rf
Young, cf
C. McElhaney, 3b
W. Anderson, lf
Caesar Bracey, cf
Hyatt, rf

Montana

Montanas (Helena, MT)

Ed Mack, c
Jesse C. Binga, p

William Summerville, 2b
John Robinson, 1b
Charles Robinson, 3b
M. Boyd, ss
Miles York, lf
E. G .Cole, cf
Ed Johnson, rf

Nebraska

Beacons (Omaha, NE)

William Perno, p
Andrew Love, ss
Harry Evans, c
William Lewis, lf
A. J. King, p
Eddie Carr, rf
John Finley, 2b
Louis Catlett, 3b
Albert Green, 3b
Alexander Plummer, 1b / Manager
Harvey Rennicks, cf

New Jersey

Cuban Giants (Trenton, NJ)

Ben Boyd, ss
Abe Harrison, ss
Ben Holmes, 3b
George Stovey, p
William T. Whyte, p
Arthur Thomas, Captain / c
John Frye, 1b / Captain
Frank Grant, 2b / Assistant Captain
Harry Catto, rf / c
Clarence Williams, rf / c
George Williams, 2b
William H. Selden, lf
George W. Stovey, p / lf
William Malone, lf / p
William Murphy, p
Fred Holloman, 3b
Harry Johnson, lf / cf
William F. Whyte, p / 1b
Stanislau K. Govern, Manager
John M.D. Bright, Team President and
  Treasurer

*Young Cuban Giants
(Trenton, NJ)*

F. Fisher, p / Captain
Alfred Inguard, c
A. Jackson, 1b
A. Wright, 2b
J. Conner, 3b
Elmer Johnson, ss / 3b
John Inguard, rf / p
George Frost, cf
Fred Myers, c
Edward Feeney, c
Little, 3b / lf
George E. Green, Manager

New Mexico

Occidentals (Albuquerque, NM)

Henry Madison
Joseph Berry
Hank Thomas
Henry Johnson
Thomas Robinson
A. R. Cassels
H. Knox
W. W. Tate
Nick Carper
C. Pulliam
T. S. Wade
William Earikson

New York

Capital Citys (Albany, NY)

Charles Teabout, c
William Thompson, 1b
Bishop, rf
Jones, 3b
Wilson, lf
Edward Ellick, ss
George Van Valkenburgh, p
Charles Lett, 2b
Chester, cf

*Brabenders/Cuban Giants Jrs.
(Hudson, NY)*

Moore, 3b
Leander Deyo, c
Lord, cf
Jackson, ss / p
J. Marshall Smith, lf
Prince, 1b
George Morris, rf
Clark, 2b

All Americans (New York, NY)

Nat Collins, c / 1b
George Washington Stovey, p
Benjamin Holmes, 1b / 3b
Abraham Harrison, ss
William Malone, 3b / p
Frank Grant, 2b / Captain
Jacob C. Fagan, lf
E. Schenk, cf
William Peterson, 1b / rf
Fisher, rf

*Hicks-Sawyer Minstrels
(New York, NY)*

John Connors, c
Irving Sayles, p
William H. Speed, 1b / Captain
Jack Evans, 2b / 3b
Dick Johnson, 3b / ss
Harry Thomas, 2b
George Connors, ss
Charles Washington, lf / 2b
Hosea Easton, rf

William H. Downes, cf
E. Connors, rf
Horace Copeland, 1b
Charles B. Hicks, Manager

*Earlington Hotel
(Richfield Springs, NY)*

Frazier, p
Frank Anderson, c
A. Coleman, 1b
A. D. Taylor, 3b
Henry Harris, 2b
L. Burrell, cf
Cody Johnson, lf
L. White, rf
Moses Gray, ss

*Spring House
(Richfield Springs, NY)*

Frank Kennedy, c
Joseph Leggett, 1b
George Martin, ss
William Kenney, cf
Ewell, p
Swan, 3b
C. A. Wilkes, 2b
Monahan, lf
A. Gilliard, lf
Peter Henry, ss
Frederick Fuller, rf

Pioneers (Troy, NY)

John Chew, p / 2b
S. Thompson, 1b
Edward Ellick, c / 2b
J. C. Lodge, lf
Austin Costello Gordon
William Kelly, cf
William Archer, rf
Johnny Graham, 3b
George Van Valkenburg, lf
Carasol, c / 2b

*Woodruff House
(Watertown, NY)*

Phipps, rf
Arthur Thomas, c / 1b
J. W. Anderson, 1b / c
Lee, lf
T. Booker, cf
R. Hall, 2b
Julius Booker, ss
Joe Stuart, 3b
Harris, p

North Carolina

Fearless (Charlotte, NC)

E. W. Butler, Manager
Richard North, Captain
John T. Hand, Secretary
James D. Coles
Thad Tate

Thomas Moore
Milus Thompson
Wellington Lomax
Nathan White
Mack Taylor
Alfred Dixon
William Jones

Diamonds (Henderson, NC)

H. Young, President
A. G. Perry, 1st V.P.
Eddie Hicks, 2nd V.P.
L. P. Blackwell, 3rd V.P.
W. H. Dunston, 4th V.P.
George W. Floyd, p / Captain
Richard Foster, c
Junius Hawkins, 1b
C. W. Peace, 2b / Business Manager
M. Mayfield, 3b
Isaac Curtis, ss
A. Albright, lf
J. F. Satterwhite, cf / Business Manager

Dread Naughts (Wilmington, NC)

Thomas Knights
M. Nichols
Emanuel Nichols
J. C. Simpson
L. Gause
George Murray
Louis Larkins
Peter Flowers
John Barry
John Smith
Henry Moore
John Lee
R. Peden
William Groom

Fowlers (Wilmington, NC)

Charlie Burnett, p
Ed Larkins, c
John Fields, c
Dave Hawkins, 1b
Edmund Jones, 2b
Frank T. Manly, 3b
George Evans, rf
James Freeman, lf / p
Robert Ellerbe, ss
Charles Wortham, p / c / lf
William H. Cutlar, cf / Secretary
Julius A. Murray, Manager
Arrie Bryant, Manager
Alexander L. Manly, cf / President

Mutuals (Wilmington, NC)

Grant Torrence, c / Captain
Ed Conner, p / ss
Henry Lane, rf
John Holmes, 2b
John Lee, lf / p
Charles Wortham, p / c

John Mallett, lf
Joseph Sampson, 3b / ss
Frank Gause, c / 1b
William H. Mitchell, ss

Ohio

Gerlings (Cleveland, OH)

Isaac, c
Markay, p
Clarence Williams, ss
Polls, 1b
Frank Henderson, 2b
Temple, 3b
Shirley Moore, rf
John Brown, cf
Frank Ellison, lf
Thomas Branson, Substitute

Weddells (Cleveland, OH)

Edward Williams, lf
Clarence R. Gordon, p
Joseph Winters, 1b
James Joyce, rf
Arms, 3b
James Benson, 2b
William Harrison, c
Fred Johnson, cf
Warren J. Cossey, ss

Z Club (Cleveland, OH)

W. Nelson, c
James Jackson, p
Joseph Jackson, c
Frank Johnson, 1b
Charles Griffin, 2b / p / 3b
James Lindsay, 3b / lf
William H. Wilson, ss / Captain
John Jackson, lf
Charles Howard, 1b
William Standard, cf
David Wyatt, c
William Sabb, 2b
Robert Gross, rf
O. Hall, Substitute
Foster Vaughn, rf / p
Beckett, cf
Henry Cummings, rf / p
Charles Black, Manager / Treasurer
Frank Doctor, Secretary

Clippers (Geneva, OH)

Grant Perkins, c
John Hamilton, p
R. Miller, 1b
O. C. Cameron, 2b
R. Holland, 3b
S. Mitchell, ss
Clarence Gordon, lf
C. Cameron, cf
John Grant Johnson, rf
C. Adams, Substitute

Grays (Geneva, OH)

Grant Perkins, c
John Hamilton, p
R. Miller, 1b
O. C. Cameron, 2b
R. Holland, 3b
S. Mitchell, ss
Clarence Gordon, lf
C. Cameron, cf
John Grant Johnson, rf
C. Adams, Substitute

Pennsylvania

Mutuals (Allegheny, PA)

James W. Gray, 1b
William Truman, 3b
H. Matthews, ss
B. Burke, lf
C. Brooks, cf
H. W. Jones, rf
G. Lee, p
David Stoner, c
H. Hill, ss
George Catlin, lf
William N. Robinson, p
Arthur Gross, 2b
George Gill, c
Charles Catlin, 2b / Captain
George D. Sherrow, Manager

Keystone Stars (Connellsville, PA)

Albert Jenkins, c
William Johnston, p
Barker, 1b
Harry B. Gaus, 2b
Wallis Clifford Gordon, 3b
B. Wright, ss
John Askins, lf
Shepperson, cf
James Taylor, rf
Gillie Johnson, Manager
Thomas White, Manager

Cuban Giants (Frankford, PA)

Charles Rothwell, ss
J. Tuner, c
William Brooks, 1b
Albert Rothwell, lf
George Rothwell, 3b / lf
Sims Emory, 2b
V. Gibbs, cf / 1b
Shep Trusty, p
Cornelius Hoagland, cf
Norwood Turner, c
Fred Hogan, cf
W. Frisby, p
James O. Turner, 3b
Isaac Rothwell, ss
F. Lee, rf

Colored Nine (Gastown, PA)

David Allen, 1b
Solomon White, 2b
Frank Grant, 3b
Ross Garrison, ss
Thomas Ray, lf
John Brady, rf
Charles Bell, lf
Frank Miller, p
Albert Douglass, p
Moses F. Walker, c
Lewis Allen, c
Thomas White, Manager
Charles Molten, C / Manager

Cuban Giant Juniors (Harrisburg, PA)

B. Smith, c
G. Williams, p
A. Reed, 1b
Al Baxter, 2b
C. Jones, ss
Alfred Burrs, lf
D. Saunders, 3b
J. Jones, cf
William Pinkney, rf
James Murphy
S. Coles
Hyle Lucas
James Thompson

Cupolas (Lawrenceville, PA)

R. "Willie" Washington, ss
H. C. Jones, ss
Edward Jackson, lf
H. Poindexter, 2b
A. J. Sellers, cf
Henry Gant, p
Irwins, lf
C. D. Shelton, c
Young, rf

Colored Barbers (Pittsburgh, PA)

G. Lee, p
George Gill, c
Charles Butler, 1b
Arthur Gross, 2b
H. Hill, ss
Charles Catlin, 3b
George Catlin, lf
William N. Robinson, cf
G. Wright, rf
George D. Sherrow, Manager

Gorhams (Philadelphia/Eastonia, PA)

Arthur Jackson, 3b
Frank Bell, cf
Solomon White, 2b
Javan Emory, cf / rf / c
Ross Garrison, ss / c

Oscar Jackson, lf
Frank Miller, rf / p
George Stovey, p
Nathan Fred Collins, c / 1b
Edward Chamberlain, 1b
Abraham Harrison, ss
Jesse Brown, 2b / ss
George Evans, 2b
Charles H. Nelson, lf / p
William Bell, ss
Mumford, rf
Thomas White, 2b
Brayton, rf
Thomas C. Schenk, rf Coffins, lf
Walter J. Pell, Manager Ambrose Davis, rf / Manager

Keystones (Pittsburgh, PA)

Harvey Roy, cf
Jerry Thompson, c / ss
James Green, 2b / p
Benjamin Gross, lf
Horace Gray, ss
Henry Gant, 2b
R. "Willie" Washington, lf
Walter Countee, rf / p
Albert Douglass, p
Chase Lyons, ss
Charles McClure, p
William Stanard, rf
Thomas Allen, lf / 1b
Edward Jackson, c / rf
James McKeever, 3b / 2b
Henry Puller, c
M. R. Ross, lf
Charles Bell, ss
James Hackett, Manager
Thomas White, 3b / Manager
S. L. Morton, Manager
Walter S. Brown, Manager

Crescents (Reading, PA)

Charles H. Walker, c
Thomas C. Boston, lf
C. W. Prince, lf / cf
Jefferson Hunter, cf / 3b
E. J. Richardson, 2b
J. W. Brown, 1b
Benjamin F. Smith, 2b / rf
Harry C. Nelson, ss
C. Gibson, lf
Frank L. Terry, lf / cf / 3b
C. Robinson, 1b
Eddie Day, 2b

Wyoming House (Scranton, PA)

Johnson, cf
W. Russell, p
Robert Treadwell, ss
Pitts, rf
Marshall, 1b
Allen, c

Fred Neumis, lf / p
Sam Smith, 2b
Hawley, 3b
Rose
Robinson, Substitute

Tennessee

Tigers (Athens, TN)

J. T. Logan, p / rf
J. B. Branner, c
Gibson, p / rf
Smith, c
Lovern, 2b
Logan, p / rf
Sherman, 1b
Sam Cleague, lf / 2b
C. McGhee, ss / 3b
Jones, cf

Lone Stars (Knoxville, TN)

Claude Dederick, p / 1b
McGaughey, c / 3b
G. W. Turner, ss
P. E. Jones, 1b / 3b / p
George Evans, rf
Joe Carter, cf
Craigmiles, rf
Sam Cleague, 2b
McEwen, c
Montgomery, lf
Staples
Morris, p

Eurekas (Memphis, TN)

Robert "Bob" Higgins, p
Pryor, c
Bright, 1b
Sam Pointer, 2b
Rayfield, 3b
Williams, ss
Lee, lf
Davis, cf
O'Neal, rf

Texas

Cuban Giants (Galveston, TX)

James Blair, 1b
Charles Mills, 2b
Benjamin Bryant, ss
George Lemons, p
Charles Bee, c
Zach Day, rf
Willie Williams, lf
Dan Hunter, cf
James Simmons, 3b
George Chandler, Substitute

Fly Aways (Galveston, TX)

C. J. Williams, c
Frank Coleman, p
George Upps, 1b

Robert Nelson, 2b
D. Stafford, 3b
A. Runnels, ss
William Conway, lf
Joseph Walker, cf
Frank McBeth, rf
W. L. Jones, p
Henry James, President
C. Ransom, Vice-President
W. P. Anderson, Secretary
J. P. Ramsey, Treasurer

Washington, DC

Blues (Washington, DC)

Gilbert Joy, p
Benjamin Berry, c
Ed Lee, 3b
Jason Joy, lf
Julius Forbes, 1b
William Neale, cf
Robert Robinson, ss
William H. Harrison, 2b
Charles Morgan, lf

1890

California

Colored Nine (Pasadena, CA)

H. Boone, President
William Prince, Treasurer
Hanson Turner, Secretary
F. M. Prince
Jason Wilson

*Lightweights
(Los Angeles, CA)*

James M. Alexander, ss
M. Jones, cf
William Nettles, c
E. D. Johnson, p / Captain
William Griffin, 1b
W. F. Woodyard, lf
A. Harper, 2b
William Prince, rf
L. Peppers, 3b
Lucius Alexander, ss
Hill, rf
Boggs, 2b

Colorado

*Stillman Giants
(Colorado Springs, CO)*

M. Hackley, p
Degn (?), c
A. Reed, 1b
George Hackley, 2b
G. Johnson, 3b
Grant, ss
Bafen, lf
Coltier, cf

Thomas Carter, rf
T. J. Manley, Manager

*Black Champions
(Denver, CO)*

Joseph Smith, c
Grant Overton, p
Overton, 3b
George Taylor, 1b
Smith, 2b
Porter, ss
Billy May, cf
Ewing, rf
Carmichael, cf
Knight, 1b

Connecticut

*Crocker House
(New London, CT)*

James H. Reed, President
C. Wheeler, Vice President
J. Burton, Secretary
Frank Blue, Treasurer
Alfred Wheeler
D. A. Wesley
W. B. Butler
W. E. James
Charles Teabout
J. A. Sorrel
R. C. Morse
J. Rankin
J. T. Hamilton
Oliver Williams

Athletics (New Haven, CT)

Allen D. Lohman
George Smith
W. Pierce
John Ross
Charles Simmons
George Williams
William Hall
Walter Miller
James Roston
W. Russell
Wilson
George L. Bush
Charles H. Johnson
Louis A. Fenderson

Florida

Onwards (Pensacola, FL)

Charles Shelback, Captain / ss
W. O'Brien
Sebastian "Pons" Barrios, p
George Wells
Harry Adams
Ben McIntosh
D. Fullwood
L. Charles
Theodore Pons

Harry Williams, cf
A. Shelback
John Boyle, Manager / Director
George Broadie, Director
William Caldwell, Director
A. Soto, Director

*Ponce De Leon
(St. Augustine, FL)*

Frank Miller, p
B. Whitaker, p
Thomas Gee, c
S. Epps, c
Emmett Dabney, 1b
Thomas Paige, 2b / p
Benjamin Holmes, 3b
William Eggleston, ss
Austin Costello Gordon, lf
Jackson, cf
Samuel Gee, rf
Woodward, 2b
Hovington, rf
Brew, cf
Stanislau K. Govern, Manager

*Alaczars
(St. Augustine, FL)*

Benjamin Smoot, 1b
Henry Stewart, ss
W. Goens, c
Jefferson Price, p / rf
Young Benjamin, 2b
William Shadney, p
Charles Booker, rf
P. Gray, 3b
Thomas H. Diggs, lf / c
Whitfield, Manager

*Cordovas
(St. Augustine, FL)*

Benjamin Smoot, 2b
Henry Stewart
Drew
Hawkins
W. Goens, c
William H. Eggleston, ss
James Chapelle, 2b
Robert Jones, 3b / ss / cf
Harry Pryor
Albert Lewis, ss / rf

*Ponce de Leon
(St. Augustine, FL)*

John Milton Dabney, 1b
C. Paige, 2b / c
James Chappelle, 2b
Woodward, 3b
Drew, cf / ss
Thomas Gee, c / 1b
Arthur Collins, cf / lf
William Shadney, p
John Thomas, rf

Georgia

Nine Brothers (Augusta, GA)

Augustus Preston
Jack Jossie
Reuben Jenkins
Isaac Jenkins
John Jenkins
Charles Attaway
Ryal Ware
George Taylor
John Gould
Henry Watts
Mose Ellis
Jim Jackson

Illinois

Artics (Chicago, IL)

Darby Cottman, p / 3b
Lee Starks, c
P. Lee, ss / lf
Grant Campbell, lf
Arthur Anderson, p / rf
William Peterson, 1b
Wesley Parker, 3b
Andrew Porter, p / cf
Joe Johnson, rf / 2b / p / c
Dinney Davis, 2b / c
William Ferguson, c
Hasting Brown, c
C. Newell, 1b
Bishop, 3b
Eddy, ss
Samuel Gray, cf
Burkard, lf
Leonard, rf
Pompey Spears
Sam Hanley
Charley Thompson, lf
John Howard
James Thompson
Lincoln, 2b
Whitman, Substitute
Robert P. Jackson, Manager

Fistics (Chicago, IL)

Johnny Cranshaw, c / rf
Lee Starks, c / 2b
Arthur Anderson, p
William Ferguson, 3b
Dinney Davis, 2b / ss
William Stitt Peters, 1b
Charles "Charley" Thompson
Pompey Spears
Carey Jackson
Sam Hanley
William "Will" Banks
Robert R. Jackson, Manager

Garretts (Chicago, IL)

C. Thompson
B. Jackson

G. Cheatham
S. French
S. Barber
Frank Spears, President
H. Warfield
W. Blue
R. Harris
C. McGowan
George Grant
J. Beasley
J. Blackburn
C. Bennett, Secretary
A. Garrett, Treasurer
Charles Spears, President

Gordons (Chicago, IL)

E. Connor, p
Nick Williams, c / p / lf
P. Gill, p
Gates, rf
William Coats, c
Henry Moore, 2b / rf
R. F. Newman, c / rf
M. Starbuck, 1b
A. Connor, 2b
Sells, c
Frank Hankforth, p
F. Starbuck, ss
Hogan, p
Firanan, c
W. Warren, p
William Pettit, c
Stearns, 3b
Hueding, cf
C. J. Sullivan, Manager
F. Sullivan, Manager

Lake Browns (Chicago, IL)

C. Newell, c
Samuel Gray, p
Burkard, 1b
William Hawkins, 2b
Nick Williams, ss
Conaidine, lf
Marshall, rf
McGinnis, cf
W. C. Brown, 3b / Captain / Manager

Lincolns (Chicago, IL)

Joseph Friend, p
Kurz, c
Connell, 1b
Ebert, 2b
Wesley Parker, ss
F. Hollis, lf
J. Hollis, lf
Kirby, cf
Adams, rf

Models (Chicago, IL)

Arthur Anderson, p
J. Woods, p
Clarence Coleman, c

Darby Cottman, 3b / p
John H. Howard, 1b
William Payne, 2b
Frank Ramsay, 3b
Nick Williams, cf
Wesley Parker, lf / cf / c / ss
H. Ross, cf / 1b
George Mead, p / Manager
Robert Jackson, Manager

Rhodes Boys (Chicago, IL)

Robert Hull, p
C. Stewart, c
Wilson, 1b
William Walton, 2b
Fowler, 3b
Willis Jones, lf
John A. Mayer, cf / p
William Turner, 3b
Harvey Chappell, lf
B. Ward, lf / rf
R. Rhodes, ss / Manager

South Ends (Chicago, IL)

Edward Prime, p / 3b
Walter G. Prime, lf
D. McGovern, c
William Harvey
Dinney Davis, 2b
John A. Mayer, p / cf
Robert Hull, c / p
Hurley, ss
Major, p
William L. Dunson, 1b
W. Walton, 2b
E. Ward, rf / c
Harvey Chappell, p
William Turner, Manager

South End Juniors (Chicago, IL)

D. Bell, c
Ed James, p
Morris Lewis, ss / captain
Charles Parker, 1b
John Johnson, 2b
William James, 3b
Benjamin Sharp, cf
Byron Reed, lf
Sam Kelly, rf

Unions (Chicago, IL)

William H. Baskins, 2b
Peter Burns, c
Grant F. Campbell, lf
Joseph Campbell, p
Darby Cottman, 3b
Albert Hackley, lf
George "Senator" William Hopkins, p
William Albert "Abe" Jones, c
F. King, ss
William T. Smith, p
William James Renfro, p

Marshall Coffey, 2b
Wesley Parker, cf
William Stitt Peters, 1b
George Franklin, p
Bolivar
Bastain
A. Practor
W. H. Blake
William Ferguson, c / 2b
R. Shields, 3b
L. Spears, ss
A. Campbell, lf
George Hurlburt
Frank Leland, 1b / Manager
Abraham "Abe" Jones, President
Frank L. Scott, ss / 3b / Vice President
H. Travis Elby, Vice President
Harry Teenan Jones, Treasurer

Uniques (Chicago, IL)

Joe Green, c
John Johnson, p
Dick Hubbard, 1b
William Payne, 2b
Frank Ramsey, 3b
Wesley Parker, ss
Andrew Porter, rf
William Johnson, cf
Thomas
William Waffle
Robert Jackson, Manager

Kansas

Browns
(Leavenworth, KS)

George Moore
"Gabe" Johnson
Jesse Hughes
Henry Robinson
Alex Johnson
Lewis Johnson
William Richardson
A. Richardson
George Walker
Harry Young
John Clark, Captain
Robert Brooks, Secretary
William Harris, Manager

Colored Nine
(Parsons, KS)

Calvin Williams, c
William Montgomery, p
Nelson Loveless, 1b
Joe Eckels, 2b
Pete Kinney, 3b
Oliver Flynn, ss
Higgins, lf
John Hood, cf
William Cullen, rf

Matthewson House
(Parsons, KS)

Charles "Sliden" Walker, c
Steve Jefferson, p
Bill Washington, 1b
Robert Kelley, 2b
Jones, 3b
Monroe Watt, ss
Moses Pierson, lf
Albert Helm, cf
Leonard Mason, rf

Maryland

Pioneer (Baltimore, MD)

J. Blake, 1b
P. W. Jenkins, 2b
J. Ringold, ss
Carroll, lf
P. Savoy, cf
E. Carroll, rf
Savoy, p
Wilson, p
Rennolds, c
Jenkins, c
P. Pinder, 3b / Manager

Massachusetts

Resolute Jrs. (Boston, MA)

Richardson, c
J. Pickney, p
Morris, 1b
Henry Carter, 2b
George Williams, ss
Selden, 3b
C. Wilson, cf
Horace Gray, rf
Brown, lf
H. F. Hicks, Manager

Michigan

Plaindealer (Detroit, MI)

Walter Stovers, c
Charles Piper, c
Lomas Cook, p
William Webb, ss
Manfred Hill, 1b / 2b / c
William Gailey, 2b / rf
Charles Webb, 2b / ss
Robert Pelham, Jr., rf
Warren Richardson, cf
Walter Johnson, lf
Joseph Ferguson, lf
William Smith, cf
Milton Johnson, rf
Madrill, c
Frank Griggs, 3b
Tom Morton, 1b
R. Harrison, cf
Henry Wise, p
Daniel Mills, lf

Marchell, c
David Lowe, lf
Thomas W. Stewart, p / Manager

Unions (Detroit, MI)

George Rice, p
Harry Moore, cf
Edward Smith, 3b
E. Hill, 1b
William Gailey, p
H. Carter, p
S. Evans, 3b
C. Miller, 2b
Deibel, p
Fred Slaughter, Captain / c

Minnesota

Ryan Hotel (St. Paul, MN)

Morris Porter
Robert Lewis
W. Rowland
M. Parker
James Todde
Walter Parker
J. Shamwicke
Herbert Howdem
Lincoln Leonard
S. W. Light
A. Yedell
H. Willard
Robert Charles
Jesse James
J. W. Scott
Moses Davis, President

Missouri

Maroons
(Kansas City, MO)

Frank Maupin, c / 3b
B. Adams, c
William Dayton, 1b
Joseph Hicks, ss
H. Burt, cf
Doc Payne, 2b
Lewis Hamilton, lf
H. Johnson, p
John "Jack" Reeves, p / rf
C. Lear, Manager

Black Stockings
(St. Louis, MO)

William Campbell, c
James "Horn Foot" Sweeney, 1b / Captain
W. J. Willyatt, 3b
C. McElhaney, 2b
J. Wheeler, cf
L. Higgins, lf
T. Landers, rf
A. Spross, ss
David Price, c
James White, p / Manager

Clippers (St. Louis, MO)

A. Covington, p
Joseph Bailey, c
Mace Johnson, 1b
W. Robinson, 2b
G. Williams, 3b
S. Y. C. Stewart, Captain / ss
Al Spencer, lf
J. Johnson, cf
Butler, rf
William Holland, ss / p
Simpson, sub
James Savignac, Manager

Mohawks (St. Louis, MO)

James Williams, 1b
F. First, 3b
Ed Garig, 2b
Wilson, lf
James Woods, cf / c
D. Hyames, rf
Smith, p
David Garig, p
Edward Samuels, p
Whitley, c
L. Sexton, p
William Murphy, c
James H. Miller, Manager

West Ends (St. Louis, MO)

Steve Jones, 3b
Ed Garig, c
Fischer, ss / p
James Brooks, 1b
Hicks, cf
Young, lf
"Stump" Tooley, 2b
David Price, cf
William Macklin, p
C. H. Thompson, Secretary
H. H. Jones, Manager

Montana

Pastimes (Helena, MT)

John Robertson, 1b
James Vass, 3b
James A. Mack, p
Al Marshall, c
Ed Mack, c / rf
James Talbert, 2b
Leslie Triplett, rf
Davis, ss
Frank Burns, cf
Will Foshe, lf

Nebraska

Giants (Lincoln, NE)

Frank Maupin, c
Joe "Kid" Miller, p
James Hightower, 1b
George Hightower, 2b

John W. Patterson, 3b / cf / 1b / 2b
Jesse Brown, ss / 2b
George Hughbanks, cf / lf
George Taylor, lf / c / 1b
Eddie Carr, rf
William Newman, c / 1b
James Lincoln, ss / 2b
Hugh Hughbanks, 2b
John "Jack" Reeves, p / 2b
James Bullock, p / of
William Jackson, c
Bud English, p
George William Castone, p / Manager
William "Blackest" Lewis, Manager / lf / cf

Lafayettes (Lincoln, NE)

George William Castone, p
Frank Maupin, c
George Taylor, lf
Jesse Brown, ss / cf
James Hightower, 1b
George Hubanks, 2b
H. Hubanks, cf / ss
John W. Patterson, 3b
Bud English, p
Joe Miller, p
Ed Carr, p / rf
William Jackson, c
Jack Reeves, p
Newman, cf
William Lewis, Manager

New Jersey

Eclipse (Atlantic City, NJ)

William "Gus" Brooks, 3b
Patton, c
Eisberg, 1b
J. Paul, 2b
Jacob Trusty, p
W. H. White, lf
Hensbury, cf
Clifford Toney, ss
D. Jones, rf / p

Cuban Giants (Trenton, NJ)

George W. Stovey, p / Assistant Captain
Clark, c
Frank Grant, c / Captain
Andrew Jackson, 3b
Abraham Harrison, ss
Frank Miller, p
Ross Garrison, ss
Benjamin Holmes, lf
Solomon White, 2b
J. H. Dickerson, cf
H. C. Bolden, 3b
J. Buck, p / rf
Smith, rf
Edward DeMund, ss
William Douglass, p
J. M. Murray, cf
Willie Mouton, c

Edward Chamberlain, 1b
Oscar Jackson, 2b
S. Cook
J. R. Young, rf
D. Thompson, cf / 1b
John Jackson, lf
Charles Fisher, lf / rf / 1b
Alfred Jupiter, p
William Woods, 3b
Frank Holland, p
John Nelson, lf
Winslow Terrell, ss
Conway, c
John Vactor, p
James Knox, 3b
George E. Green, rf / p
John D. Bright, Manager

New Mexico

Occidentals (Albuquerque, NM)

Henry Madison
Joseph Berry
Hank Thomas
Henry Johnson
Thomas Robinson
A. R. Cassels
H. Knox
W. W. Tate
Nick Carper
C. Pulliam
T. S. Wade

New York

"77" (Buffalo, NY)

E. Johnson, p
N. Cooper, c
A. Brown, 1b
William Dallas, 2b
M. Landers, ss
William H. Story, 3b
William Bright, lf
William Henderson, cf
George Dover, rf

Kaaterskill (Catskill, NY)

Isaiah Jackson
William Miller
Horace Brown
Washington Bean
Daniel Fleming
Charles Craig
Alexander McDaniel
Thomas A. Calaman
Andrew Edwards
Lloyd Brown
John West, Captain

Brabenders/Cuban Giants Jrs. (Hudson, NY)

Moore, 3b
Leander Deyo, c

Lord, cf
Jackson, ss / p
J. Marshall Smith, lf
Prince, 1b
George Morris, rf
Clark, 2b

Colored Nine (Newburgh, NY)

George Lewis, c
William Johnson, p / Captain
James Arnold, 1b
William Lane, 2b
Henry Reed, 3b
William King, ss
George Hasbrouck, cf
Frederick Schoolmaker, lf
Edward Alsdorf, rf

Cleveland Minstrels (New York, NY)

Billy McClain, p
Eddie Brewer, c
Charles Carey, 1b
Dan Palmer, 2b
James Wilson, 3b
McGowan, ss
E. W. Pickett, lf
Tom Williams, cf
Harry S. Eaton, rf
R. Moody, 1b
Irving "Doc" Sayles, p

Colored Nine (New York, NY)

Oscar Jackson, c
George W. Stovey, lf
Ulysses Grant, 2b
John Nelson, ss / p
Nathaniel Collins, 1b / c
Frank Holland, 2b
Jacob Fagen, p / ss
Taylor, cf
John Dean, rf

Earlingtons (Richfield Springs, NY)

Jones, ss
Charles Wells, 1b
George Banks, c
Billings, rf
Allen, cf
Spencer, lf
Ed Matthews, p
James H. Luke, 2b
N. Mitchell, 3b

Lime Kiln (Rochester, NY)

Charles B. Lee
Gilbert W. Wright
Wilson Brooks
William H. Allen
J. Hogan
F. Myers
Charles Wilson

L. Cocheron
O. Dennis, Manager

Livingston Hotel (Rochester, NY)

J. Barnes, 3b
A. Coleman, lf
Charles Wells, 1b
William H. Allen, p
D. B. Armstead, cf
W. Brooks, c
Fred Hogan, rf
J. Poindexter, ss
John Rowe, c
Ed Matthews, Mascot

Powers (Rochester, NY)

Charles P. Lee, 1b / cf
C. J. Caldwell, 2b
William Jackson, p
John Downes, 3b
Oliver Dennis, rf
Charles B. Lee, cf
Charles Wilson, cf
Clarence Wilson, lf
R. H. Thompson, ss
W. H. Stockton, c / Mascot

Fearless, Jr. (Rome, NY)

Robert Wilson, 1b / Captain
Fred Jackson, 2b
Charles Sherman, 3b
Edward Wilson, p
Willie Wilson, c
William Bradley, ss
Albert Wilson, cf
Louis Hall, rf
W. "Gussie" Freeman, lf
Charles W. Vulgen, Manager

Vinnet (Rome, NY)

Frank Sears, 3b / Captain
William Wilson, c
Edward Wilson, p
Fred Jackson, 1b
Robert Wilson, 2b
Albert Freeman, ss
Grant Jackson, lf
Albert Wilson, cf
Charles Sherman, rf

Fearless (Utica, NY)

Theodore Pell, ss / Captain
Moses Gray, c / p
G. Cooper, p / 1b
Floyd Peresett, c / 1b
Robert Moss, lf / Field Captain
Walter Pell, rf
Will Pell, 2b
J. L. Smith, 3b
Robert Jackson, p / 3b
John Titus, 3b / rf
George Beach, p / lf

Adam Henry, 2b / rf
Jacob Francis, cf
Wilbur Jackson, lf
James Pell, Asst. Manager
Richard E. Warmouth, Manager

North Carolina

Fowlers (Wilmington, NC)

Charlie Burnett, p
Ed Larkins, c
Dave Hawkins, 1b
Edmund Jones, 2b
Frank Manly, 3b
George Evans, rf
William Cutlar, cf
Alexander Manly, cf
James Freeman, lf
Ed Conner, ss
Robert Ellerbe, ss
Alexander Sauls, c
Clayton McLaurin, p
William Mitchell, rf
A. F. Murray
John Richards
Charles Burnett, c
Julius A. Murray, Manager

Mutuals (Wilmington, NC)

William Schenck, c
Charles Burnett, p
William Henry Lane, ss
Frank Ganse, lf
William Mitchell, rf
William Cutlar, cf
David Hawkins, 1b
Henry Sampson, 2b
Edmund Jones, rf
C. H. "Nat" Hayes, Manager

Nationals (Raleigh, NC)

Alonzer Ford, p
Thomas Terrell, c
Dan Pugh, ss
G. Taylor, rf
James Jones, cf
N. Sledge, 1b
M. C. Jones, 2b
Robert Smith, 3b
R. F. O'Kelly, lf / Manager

Ohio

Maroons (Cleveland, OH)

James Brooks, 1b
William H. Wilson, 3b
Clarence Williams, lf / 3b
John Jackson, c / p
Charles Griffin, 2b / lf
Harry Fairfax, p
William Cisco, rf
Warren J. Cossey, cf / p
Mart Johnston, 1b
James Lindsey, cf

William Carroll, c
Albert Dennie, p
John Mitchell, p2b
W. Brooks, 3b
William Cisco, cf / rf
Wilkinson, cf
U. Brooks,
A. J. Sellers, cf / lf
Sinkey, 3b
Meedrent, Substitute
Harry Tolbert (Talbert), Substitute
Clarence R. Gordon, ss / Manager

Z Club (Cleveland, OH)

William H. Wilson, ss
James Brooks, 1b
John Jackson, lf
Frank Johnson, c / 1b
Charles Griffin, 2b
A. Praiter, 3b
Walter Brooks, rf
James Lindsey, cf
James Jackson, p
William Saab, cf
Charles "Doc" Howard, 1b
Alberts, Substitute

Black Diamonds (Newark, OH)

William Riggs, 2b
Howard Curry, lf
G. Beasley, 1b
Theodore Taylor, rf
Clifford Toney, 3b
B. Craig, cf
Nathan Gates, c / Manager
M. Cobins, p
Charles Royal, ss
McConnell, cf
Melvin Stewart, p

Oregon

Newports (Portland, OR)

Billy Wilds, p
Galiway, c
June Dennis, ss
Wilson, 1b
Cochrane, 2b
A. Dennis, 3b
Severs, lf
Tracy Drake, cf
J. Brown, c / rf

Pennsylvania

Logan House (Altoona, PA)

Charles J. Durham
Walter Williams
William Bolyer
Harry Morgan
Samuel Lyles
W. T. Shorter

R. M. Hughes
J. Cantlin
William Deadford
J. L. Thomas
J. A. Little
Harry Smith

Cuban Giants (Frankford, PA)

Charles Rothwell, ss
George Rothwell, p
Norwood Turner, c
Sims Emery, 2b
Charles Trusty, rf
V. Gibbs, 1b
Kelsh, 3b
A. Rothwell, lf
Cornelius Hoagland, cf

Cuban Giant Juniors (Harrisburg, PA)

B. Smith, c
G. Williams, p
A. Reed, 1b
Al Baxter, 2b
C. Jones, ss
Alfred Burrs, lf
D. Saunders, 3b
J. Jones, cf
William Pinkney, rf
James Murphy
J. Coles
Hyle Lucas
James Thompson

Gorhams (Harrisburg, PA)

William Barton, 1b
Charles Bell, ss
C. Murray, cf
N. Evans, 2b
William Conover, c
John Vactor, p
Charles Nelson, p
Frank Miller, p
Ed Woods, 3b
Oscar Jackson, 2b / c
Andrew Jackson, 3b
Henry Gant, 1b
Ed Chamberlain, 1b
Moses F. Walker, c
George W. Stovey, p / rf
Peter "Yeoman" Fisher, rf
Fred (Nat) Collins, cf
William Freeman, lf
William Thompson, c / lf
J. Buck, rf
H. Poindexter, p
J. H. Dickinson, lf
Wool, ss
Shaerey, lf
George E. Green, p / rf
George Peters, p / 1b

Ambrose Davis, rf / Manager
James Farrington, Manager

Marines (Harrisburg, PA)

George Barton, c / Captain
James Williams, c / rf
James Jackson, p
Robert Lee, p
Thomas Matthews, ss
William Williams, 1b
James Carey, 2b
William T. Dixon, 3b
George Grant, lf
Charles Potter, cf
William Strothers, Manager

Unions (New Castle, PA)

Fred Bland, 1b
Gus Coleman, 2b
Albert Lewis, 3b
Pere Jefferson, ss
Tom Brown, cf
Joe Williams, lf
Tom Williams, rf
William Chapman, c / Captain
John W. Benerley, c / Treasurer
Leroy Richardson, p
Frank Lawson, Manager

Orions (Norristown, PA)

David Blackwell, cf
J. Fisher, lf
Richardson, rf
Isaac Chase, p
B. Fisher, 3b
John Wilmer, 2b
Robert Parker, ss
Howard Smith, 1b
Harry Fisher, c

Colored Monarchs (York, PA)

Robert Jackson, Captain
T. Bell, cf / rf
Alfred Jupiter, p / lf
John Nelson, p
Benjamin Holmes, 1b
Winslow Tyrrell, cf
William Jackson, c
P. Grant, c / rf
Frank Miller, p
George L. Williams, Captain / 3b
Solomon White, 2b
George Washington Stovey, lf
Arthur Thomas, c
Benjamin Boyd, cf
Ross Garrison, ss
Frank Grant, 2b
Harry Catto, p / lf
Sheppard Trusty, p
William H. Selden, p
Abe Harrison, ss
William H. Malone, p / 1b

William Woods, ss
John Goode, rf / p
Edward Chamberlin, 1b
Charles Davis, p
Miguel Gonzales, of
S. Cook
William Bird, 2b
Thomas Schenck, rf
Peter Fisher, lf
Henry Gant, Manager
John Monroe Kreiter, Manager

Crescents (Reading, PA)

Charles H. Walker, c
Samuel Newkirk, c
H. Swoyer, p
Thomas C. Boston, lf / 3b
C. W. Prince, lf / cf
E. J. Richardson, 2b / cf
Harry C. Nelson, ss
Howard Bower, 2b / p
Charles Gibson, lf
C.W. Prince, rf
W. Butler, rf
C .Robinson, 1b
E. Lewis, lf
Eddie Day, 2b / p

Lumber City (Williamsport, PA)

Sheldon, p
Arthur Winston, p
Jones, ss
Javan Emory, c / 1b
Wiley, 2b
Hutchison, 3b
Stewart, lf
A. Green, cf
Johnson, rf

Texas

Black Stockings (Dallas, TX)

Nichols, c
A. Runnels, p
Peachery, 1b
Simms, 2b
Thomas, 3b
James Blair, ss
Moore, rf
William Bryant, cf
W. P. Anderson, lf
Calvin, Substitute

Sluggers (Galveston, TX)

Nichols, c
Green, p
Samuel Anderson, 1b
Slus, 2b
Thomas, 3b
William Bryant, ss
F. Ford, lf

Weston, cf
James Blair, rf

Fly Aways (Galveston, TX)

C. J. Williams, c
Frank Coleman, p
George Upps, 1b
Robert Nelson, 2b
D. Stafford, 3b
A. Runnels, ss
William Conway, lf
Joseph Walker, cf
C. D. MacBeth, rf
W. L. Jones, p

Rhode Island

Newports (Newport, RI)

George O. Seaforth, President
Norman Wright, Vice President
W. Phoenix, Secretary
H. Jones, Treasurer
S. Gaines, Manager

Virginia

Red Stockings (Norfolk, VA)

Sidney Fentriss, c / Captain
Augustus Taylor, 2b
Ruffin, 3b
Cyrene Fisher, p
Dan "Devil" McClennan, 1b
Moore, 1b
"Bub" Baker, cf
Wertham, rf
William Johnson, ss
James Knox, 3b

Rouses (Rouse Point, VA)

John Milton Dabney, 1b
Thomas Gee, c
William H. Eggleston, p
Miles Page, 2b
S. Epps, 3b
A. Morton, ss
O. Gordon, lf
T. Hatchet, cf
Samuel Gee, rf

West Virginia

Keystones (Wheeling, WVA)

Harvey Roy, cf
William Green, 2b
M. Scott, c
Chase Lyons, ss
Johnson, c
Scott Taper, p
Walter Countee, rf / p
Arthur Gross, lf
John "Jack" Dean, 1b
Pete Davis, 3b

Pearly Williams, p
Johnson, c

Washington, DC

Colored Nine (Washington, DC)

Cole, cf
Francis Cardozo, rf
James A. Payne, 3b
John H. Lawson, 2b
Gant, c
Devoe, c
Robert Ford, lf
George Betters, ss
Simms, 1b
Hughes, p

Wisconsin

Reds (Milwaukee, WI)

William "Billy" Johnson, 1b
Benjamin "Ben" Underwood, 2b
Napoleon Broady, 3b
William Lyons, rf / ss
Frank J. Chapman, cf
Bud Demley, lf
Randall Phillips, c
Burt Hutchinson, p
Spencer Butler, ss
James Hightower, ss / 2b
J. B. "Bud" Alden, rf
A. Thirrl, lf
James Blaine, Manager

1891

California

Lightweights (Los Angeles, CA)

James M. Alexander, ss
M. Jones, cf
William Nettles, c
E. D. Johnson, p / Captain
William Griffin, 1b
W. F. Woodyard, lf
A. Harper, 2b
William Prince, rf
L. Peppers, 3b
Lucius Alexander, ss
Hill, rf
Boggs, 2b

Colorado

Black Champions (Denver, CO)

Joseph Smith, c
Grant "Black Ace" Overton, p
Overton, 3b
George Taylor, 1b
Smith, 2b
John "Bud" Fowler, 3b
Porter, ss
William Castone, lf

Billy May, cf
Ewing, rf
Carmichael, cf
Knight, 1b

Connecticut

Colored Nine
(New London, CT)

James N. Reed, President
C. Wheeler, Vice President
J. Burton, Secretary
M. Blue, Treasurer

Cuban Giants (Ansonia, CT)

George Williams, ss
Frank Grant, 2b
John H. Frye, 1b
Abraham Harrison, ss
Benjamin Boyd, cf
C. Jackson, 3b
Henry Gant, 3b
Robert "Bob" Jackson, p
John Nelson, p
Winslow Tyrell, ss
Clarence Williams, 3b
Peter Fisher, lf / ss / cf
William Douglass, rf / cf / p / 3b
Benjamin Brown, lf / 3b
William Jackson, rf / lf
William Davis, rf
William Woods, 3b
William Barton, c
Henry Catto, cf / 2b
Nat Collins, c
Andrew Jackson, 3b
Ed Chamberlain, 1b / rf
Joby Trusty, 3b
John M. Watkins, cf
Dan Penno, lf
William T. Whyte, 1b / p
N. Freeman, cf
Solomon "Sol" White, 2b
Charles Bell, ss / rf / 2b
George W. Stovey, p
Sheppard Trusty, p / 1b / rf
George Evans, lf / rf
Garnet, 3b
G. Fisher, lf
Lovill (Lorill), 2b
William Jackson, c
James Dorsey Robinson, p
Ortho Stanton, rf / c
James Malson, rf / p
C. Page, rf
Eddie Day, rf
Russell, rf
Fagan, 2b / 1b / rf
J. D. Baker, rf / cf
S. Cook, rf
Dickerson, rf
E. K. Myers, Co-owner
John D. Bright, Manager

Florida

Alaczars (St. Augustine, FL)

Thomas Gee, c
William Miller, p
John Nelson, ss
Quinly, rf
Ed Davis, 1b
William Singleton, 3b
William Whitaker, cf
James Chapelle, 2b
C. Cummings, lf

Indiana

Colored Nine (Bloomington, IN)

William Bass, p / Captain
Frank Jones, c
Hase Gann, 1b
George Campbell, 2b / Secretary
John Curry, 3b / Treasurer
Newt White, ss
William Foster, ss
Cliff Estell, cf
John Dunham, rf

Illinois

Auditorium Hotel
(Chicago, IL)

Lee Stark, c
John Johnson, p / c
Arthur Anderson, p / rf
Joe Green, c
James Thompson, p / 3b
David Lawrence, lf
Shepherd Ware, rf / p
Andrew Porter, c / cf / rf
Oscar Curry, c
Clinton Hill, 2b
S. Cochran, 2b
John Mayer, ss
A. Hilberts, cf
W. Roberts
James Renfroe, p
C. Stewart, c / 2b
William Gubbins, ss
Morton Towles, 2b
Fisher, p
Massey, c
Scipio Spinks, p / Manager / Captain

Colored Nine (Chicago, IL)

L. Martin, Captain
George Harmon
Joe Garritt
William "Billy" Spicer
George Porter
Thomas Pitman
Al Grant
Sam Davis
J. E. Shelley

Models (Chicago, IL)

George Stamps, 1b
Tom Hayden, 2b
Willie Foley, 1b
James Byrnes, ss
Tony Roche, rf
Clarke O'Brien, cf
William "Willie" Finley, cf
Frank "Bud" English, p
William "Willie" Turner, c / Manager

Unions (Chicago, IL)

William Baskins, 2b
Peter Burns, c
Grant F. Campbell, cf
William Peterson, 1b / c
Joseph Campbell, p
Darby Cottman, 3b
Albert Hackley, rf
George Hopkins, p
William Albert Jones, c
William Smith, p / cf
A. L. King, 2b
E. King, ss
William Ferguson, c
James Smith, p
Wesley Parker, lf
C. L. Hunt, Manager
William Stitt Peters, 1b / Manager
Travis H. Elby, Financial Secretary
T. T. Farley, Secretary

Union Reserves (Chicago, IL)

E. Taylor, 3b
James Smith, rf
Wilson, cf
Butler, lf
J. Taylor, 1b
Jesse Collier, ss
Fisher, 2b
Albert Jones, c
Oglesby, p

Union Juniors (Chicago, IL)

George Gordon, c
H. H. Ash, p / Captain
Eugene James, 2b
B. Reed, 3b
William James, ss
Benjamin Sharp, rf
W. Fugley, cf
W. J. Green, lf
George Green, Substitute
W. Bell, Substitute
Charles Parker, 1b / Manager
John Duncan, Manager

Uniques (Chicago, IL)

Richard Hubbard, 2b / 1b
Arthur Anderson, p, cf
John Johnson, p / c
Charles "Charlie" Green, c

Lee Starks, c / 2b
Frank Ramsey, 3b / Captain
Dinney Davis, 2b / ss / lf / cf
Andrew Porter, p / cf / rf
James Thomas, 1b
Joe Green, c
William Payne, 2b
Wesley Parker, ss
William Johnson, cf
Thomas, Substitute
William Waffle
Osgeen, c
Robert P. Jackson, c / Manager

South Branch Terrors
(Chicago, IL)

J. Milligan, p
B. Raven, ss
J. Conroy, c
L. Thomas, 1b
Sam Edwards, 2b
B. Merrick, 3b
Hastings V. Brown, ss
W. Scott, rf
W. Sherwood, 2b
L. Thomas, cf
G. Shively, lf
J. Gallagher, cf
Henry Wilson, Substitute
William "Bill" Hennessey, Substitute
C. A. Wall, Substitute
H. Raven, Manager

Thomsons *(Chicago, IL)*

Arthur Anderson, p
Hall, p / c
Lee Starks, c
George Weir, p / c
Shepard "Kid" Ware, c
Phil Reidy, lf
William Hutchinson, rf
Newton, 2b
Staples, 1b
Devinney Davis, rf
William Johnson, lf
John Johnson, rf
P. Thomson, 2b
Watkins
Hara
David R. Lawrence, 3b / Captain
James L. Thomson, ss / Manager

Young Oaks *(Chicago, IL)*

R. Cupler, c
J. Williams, p
A. Conner, 1b
F. Starbuck, 2b
William Warren, 3b
W. Barton, ss
E. Coats, rf
R. France, cf
C. Hoyle, lf

L. Wills, Substitute
William Coats, Substitute

Clippers *(Rockford, IL)*

Lifa Berch, p
Herbert Tucker, lf / ss
John Baxter, c
Scott, cf / c
Frank "Deacon" Ferguson, 1b
Aaron White, rf
J. Reddrick, 2b
Charles "Cully" Ferguson, 3b
F. Anderson, p
Henry Harris, 3b

Florida

Ponce de Leon
(St. Augustine, FL)

Frank Miller, p
William Whitaker, p / rf
T. Gee, 1b / c
C. Paige, 2b / p
Benjamin Holmes, 3b
William H. Eggleston, ss
O. Gordon, lf
Jackson, cf
S. Gee, rf
Nathan T. Hovington, rf
Drew, cf
Woodward, 2b
John Milton Dabney, 1b
Simon Epps, c
S. K. Govern, Manager

Alcazars
(St. Augustine, FL)

T. Gee, c
W. Miller, p
John Nelson, ss
Sam V. Quinly, rf
Ed Davis, 1b
William Singleton, 3b
William Whitaker, cf
James Chappelle, 2b
C. Cummings, lf

Kansas

Leapers *(Lawrence, KS)*

Jess Harper, c
J. N. Clark, p
George Walker, 1b
Tom Gross, 2b
Charles Frey, ss
Perry Polk, 3b
Richard Bivens, lf
Nelson, cf
Warfield, rf
George Ellis
Charles Anderson
William H. Barker, Manager

Colored Nine
(Leavenworth, KS)

Frank Green
Ulysses Green
Frank O'Banion
Henry Thomas
John Trusty
Thomas Collins
John Teal
Windsor Coleman
David Grey
Dave Stewart, Captain
Arthur Todd, Manager

Black Diamond Kings
(Topeka, KS)

Mote Ware, p / Captain
Willis McCoy, c
H. Lewis, 1b
Julius Lowery, lf
George Ware, cf
Tom Pullin, 3b
George Wellington Gross, 2b
Tom Gross, ss
Henry Edwards, rf

Maryland

Pioneer *(Baltimore, MD)*

J. Blake, 1b
P. W. Jenkins, 2b
J. Ringold, ss
Carroll, lf
P. Savoy, cf
E. Carroll, rf
Savoy, p
Wilson, p
Rennolds, c
Jenkins, c
P. Pinder, 3b / Manager

Massachusetts

Resolutes *(Boston, MA)*

George Parego, rf
William Jones, 2b
Thomas Gee, c / ss
Alfred Davis, ss / c
C. Wilson, lf
William Henderson, 1b
Joseph Palmer, cf / p
William Holmes, 3b
Alfred Jupiter, p / cf
George Williams, c
Theodore Roberts, cf / rf
Hannihan, 3b
Thomas Brown, p
H. Jackson, c
Benjamin Gross, rf
Matthews, c
Charles Posey, p
Charles Roosa, 2b / c

Padmore, ss
Norris, lf
McSear, 3b
Bibby, 2b / p
Willis, c
William N. Freeman, cf
Carrington, c / 2b / 3b

Resolute Reserves
(Boston, MA)

A. Caskins, c
Robert M. Rooker, p
C. Reddick, 1b
T. Whiting, ss
W. Carter, 2b
P. Marshall, 3b
J. Neal, lf
T. Watson, cf / 3b
N. Whiting, rf
Hilk, p
Lewis, c
Bicker, 2b
J. D. Gordon, ss
Jones, cf
Tucker, cf
Albert DeLeon, Manager

Missouri

Black Diamonds
(St. Louis, MO)

James White, c
Weathers, p
Townsend, 1b
Gus Cumbers, 2b
James Williams, 3b
Burley, ss
Tom Bacon, lf
William Henderson, cf
Charles Franklin, rf

Euchres (St. Louis, MO)

Walter Scott
James Williams, 2b
Ford
James White, p
Thompson
Leslie
Ned Harris, rf / cf
Shelton
Davis
C. Dixon, manager

North Ends
(St. Louis, MO)

H. Mines, p
M .Wilson, c
A. Miner, 1b
James Williams, 2b
Sam Cheulain, ss
H. Brown, 3b
A. Reed, cf
H. Pearker, lf

C. Jackson, sub
W. Bibb, sub
Paul Chauvin, rf / Manager

West Ends (St. Louis, MO)

John Reeves, p
Ed Garig, c
Madison
James Brooks, 1b
C. McElhaney, lf
Fisher, p
F. First, p / cf
Steve Jones, ss
L. Sexton, c
Beeries, p
Sholt Johnson, c / 2b
H. H. Jones, Manager

Montana

Silver Leafs (Butte, MT)

James Williams, p
James Houck, 1b
James Wesley, 2b
Henry McFarland, ss
Davis, 3b
William Allen, lf
Sam Horne, cf
Waters, p
Ed Mack, c
James Mack, rf / Manager

Nebraska

Giants (Lincoln, NE)

Frank Maupin, c
Charles Miller, p / 3b
James Hightower, 1b / ss
George Hughbanks, cf / 2b
George Taylor, lf / 1b
William Lincoln, ss / 2b
Eddie Carr, cf / c
Harry Banks, p / 2b
James Bullock, p / of
Broadus, lf
James Dean, of
Robert Dobbs, c
Harding, p / of
John Patterson, 3b / 2b
Smith, of
George William Castone, p / c / Manager
George Timpson, of

New Jersey

Fearless (Bridgeton, NJ)

Morgan
William Edwards,
Robinson
Austin
Cox
Samuel Bond,
Oscar Tudas
John Long

John Wesley, Captain
Andrew K. Wells, Manager

New Mexico

Occidentals
(Albuquerque, NM)

Henry Madison
Joseph Berry
Hank Thomas
Henry Johnson
Thomas Robinson
A. R. Cassels
Carter
James Bell
Will Earikson
C. Crockett
C. Vincent

New York

Colored Stars (Buffalo, NY)

W. Merritt Landers, Captain
Edwin D. Thompson
William Abranders
John Dallas
William Dallas
John Pride
Theodore Ashby
W. Buch
E. Grnas
J. B. Robinson
William H. Story
John Rose
A. Brown
William Harris
A. L. Crawford
Lincoln Strong
Edward Brooks
John Rowe
George Peters
Gross
G. M. Butler, Manager
J. William Mitchell, Judiciary Committee
William Henderson, Umpire

Colored Giants
(Long Island, NY)

Edward DeMund, 1b
Holiday, ss
Rudd, 2b / lf
Jacent, 2b
O'Dell, p / 3b
Dickson, c
William Bunce, lf / p
Anderson, rf
Williams, cf

Douglass League
(Rochester, NY)

John Rowe, c
J. H. Jackson, p
R. Eggleston, 1b
William H. Allen, ss

E. Poindexter, 2b
Charles P. Lee, 3b
William Wilson, rf
Harry Smith, lf
J. P. Mills, cf
John H. Thompson
William H. Stockton, c / 3b
Oliver Dennis, c / rf
Ed Matthews, President / p
J. Poindexter, Manager
Fred Gilmore, Secretary

Earlington Hotel
(Richfield Springs, NY)

H. Smith, 1b
M. Smith, 3b
Mathers, 2b
Edward N. Powell, p
William Stewart, c
Field, ss
Frank Kennedy, cf
Van Holden, lf
Bryant, rf

Spring House
(Richfield Springs, NY)

Mears, 3b
Collins, lf
Walter F. Wilson, rf
Joseph Leggett, p / ss
Hayden, 2b
Albert Teabout, ss / p
Mitchell, cf
Bolden, c
Abram L. Myers, 1b

Prospect House
(Shelter Island, NY)

G. Giles, p
John Watkins, c
W. Hughes, ss
R. Hughes, 1b
George Waters, 2b
C. Cuffy, 3b
George Elliot, lf / Captain
Samuel Johnson, cf
George Reese, rf
George T. Tucker, Manager

Fearless *(Utica, NY)*

Nathan R. Green, 2b
William Pell, rf / 1b
Harry Moss, lf
Theodore Pell, ss
Bert Pell, 1b
Floyd Peresett, cf / c
Jared Peresett, 3b
Charles P. Morse, p
Henry Waples, 3b
Jacob Francis, cf
Peter Henry, p
Moses Gray, c
David Denike, 2b

John Titus, 3b / rf
Pete Pell, ss
Theodore Pell, ss
Lee Adam Pell, 2b / rf
V. Ralph, 2b
Wolten, rf
G. Cooper, p
Jason Thomas, cf
Vondhelm, 3b
Fred Cheaney, 3b
Edward Wilson, p / 3b
Wimple, 3b
Richard Moss, lf / Captain

North Carolina

Nationals *(Raleigh, NC)*

Peter Cobb, Vice President
James Jones, Secretary
Daniel Pugh, Captain
Junius Hawkins
Charlie Wortham
Edmon Jones
M. C. Jones
Nathan Sledge
Alonzer Ford
James H. Jones
Thomas Terrell
F. O'Kelly, manager

Ohio

Maroons *(Cleveland, OH)*

John Jackson, p
Charles "Charlie" Griffin, 2b
William Wilson, ss
Albert Dennie, p
James Lindsey, rf
David Wyatt, c
S. John "Jack" Dean, 3b
Consens, cf
R. Johnson, c
Frank Johnson, 1b
William Grimn, 2b
James Jackson, lf
John Mitchell
Edward "Inkspot" Williams, p / 3b

Lincoln *(Newark, OH)*

Tom Brown, p
William Walker, 1b
Nathan "Nate" Gates, 2b
Jesse Cook, 3b
Melvin Stewart, ss
William Lindsay, cf
Clifford Tony, lf
Homer Murphy, rf
Charles Royal, c / Manager

Pennsylvania

Logan House *(Altoona, PA)*

Charles J. Durham
Walter Williams

William Bolyer
Harry Morgan
Samuel Lyles
W. T. Shorter
R. M. Hughes
J. Cantlin
William Deadford
J. L. Thomas
J. A. Little
Harry Smith

Gorhams
(Harrisburg, PA)

George Williams, 1b
Thomas White, 2b
Clarence Williams, c
Arthur Thomas, rf
Frank Grant, ss
Frank Miller, p / rf
Arthur Thomas, c
V. Jackson, lf
Solomon White, 2b
William Selden, lf
Oscar Jackson, cf
Andrew Jackson, 3b
Nathan Fred Collins, ss
N. Freeman, lf
William Barton, c
George Evans, 2b
William Peterson, 1b
James Williams, c / 1b
William Malone, rf
William Thomas
E. Jackson, c
Henry Gant, ss
George W. Stovey, p
Benjamin Holmes, 3b
Poindexter, p
Smith, cf
Winters, rf
Leon, lf
Burton, c
J. H. Dickerson, rf
S. K. Govern, Manager
Ambrose Davis, rf / Manager
James Farrington, Manager

Orions
(Norristown, PA)

George Rothwell, p
Javan Emery, 3b
Tucker, ss / rf
A. J. Sellers, cf
V. Gibbs, lf
Norwood Turner, 1b
Edward Smith, c
Wilson Brooks, c
Frank Robinson, p
Isaac Chase, p / c
Harry Fisher, c
Richardson, p

Pearls
(Philadelphia, PA)

Payne C. Hargett, 2b
John Merriman, lf
George Jackson, 1b
P. Dunlap, 1b / rf
Donnelly, cf
Miller, 3b
J. Jackson, p / ss
William Carney, rf
York Hargett, Manager, c

Colored Waiters
(Reading, PA)

George Brown, p
Charles H. Walker, c
Thomas C. Boston, 1b
E. J. Richardson, 2b
James Whiten, 3b
Harris, ss
Harry C. Nelson, rf
Jefferson Hunter, cf
C. W. Prince, lf

Kepfords (Williamsport, PA)

A. Green, 3b
William Thompson, ss / p
Frank Battles, c
R. Farr, cf
E. Watson, lf / cf / ss
Joseph P. Mellix, p
Steward (Stuart), rf
Haywood
J. D. Baker, lf
Wagner, p
Hutchinson, 3b
Sims Emery, 1b
Javan S. Emery, 2b / Manager

South Carolina

Colored Nine
(Abbeville, SC)

Sam Baker
Spencer Watt
Dennis Harris
Richard Grant
Willie Jones
Lee Rapley
Gussie Romans
James Hodges
Florence Kennedy

Rough and Readys
(Anderson, SC)

Alex B. Johnson
Jess Williams
Joe Brown
Toney Hunter
Walter Johnson
John Payton
John Butler

Barbus Frazer
William Oliver
Jonas Edwards

Colored Nine
(Cokesbury, SC)

Quincey Wilson
Jell Keys
Petter Reeder
Nathan Wilson
Elijah Washington
Foster Murphy
Ben Adams
James Dickson
Alex Shaw

Clippers (Columbia, SC)

M. Crawford, 2b
H. Clifton, ss
H. Mitchell, c / Captain
J. Davies, 1b
S. Johnson, p
W. Prior, 3b
T. Williams, cf
E. Brown, lf
James Roberts, rf
B. Walls, Substitute
M. Hudson, Scorer

Tennessee

Lone Stars (Knoxville, TN)

P. McEwen, captain / c
V. Cheatham, p
J. Lane, 2b
G. Evans, rf
S. Howard, lf
L. Halleck, cf
M. Mitchell, 1b
M. Turner, 2b
F. Staples, 3b
C. Lacey, Substitute
John McKinney, Substitute
Walter Yardley, Scorer
Charles Giles, Manager / President

Lookouts (Knoxville, TN)

A. Gillespie
Alfred Patton
John Singleton
C. McGhee
J. Ghant
R. Reddy
C. Burrough
William B. Barnes, Treasurer
J. W. Massengill, Captain
Longmeres, Manager
R. Wallace, Secretary

Texas

Blues (Fort Worth, TX)

Wimms, c
Frank Itson, p

Brockman, 1b
William Fulbright, c
Greer, 2b
Adams, cf
Beckham, 3b / c
Johnson, 3b
John Carter, 3b /rf
Smith, ss
Pratt, lf
Adams, cf
Young, ss
Gibson, cf
Gibson, rf

Blues (Houston, TX)

Dan, p
Gettle, c
Sidney, 1b
Parker, 2b
Kay, 3b
Nickerson, ss
Dewanitie, rf
Wright, cf
Walker, lf

Yellow Jackets (Waco, TX)

Silas Solomon, c
Warner, p
Robert Snow, 1b / 2b
Wells, 3b
W. Giles, 1b / lf
Goodman, lf
Jack Hankins, ss
Johnson, cf
Pomey, rf
Drake, c
Riley Wiggins, cf
Alexander Ahart, 3b
Lafayette Graves, ss
Ritchie, rf

1892

Canada

Colored Nine (St. John,
New Brunswick/Canada)

George Hope, p
Duke Ritchie, c
James Hector, 1b
Bunt Wilson, 2b
John Blizzard, 3b / Captain
Robert McKenzie, ss
Joseph Hector, lf
George Watts, rf
James Cookson, cf

Truros (Victoria,
Nova Scotia/Canada)

Douglas Parris, p
W. E. Mintus, 1b
C. Parris, 2b
Bert Prevost, 3b

Billy Parris, ss
Hugh Parris, lf
Bill Byers, rf
Henry Parris, cf
E. H. Borden, c / Captain

Arizona

Fort Huachuca (Huachuca, AZ)

Anderson, ss
James, p / 3b
Barrett, c
Jenrey, 3b / p
Steed, 2b
Smith, rf
Baker, lf
Brown, cf
Whiting, 1b

Arkansas

Clippers (Newport, AR)

Willie Owens, 2b
James Spencer, p
James Woods, 1b
Thomas, 3b
Colton, cf
Norwood, lf / p
Slaughter, p
James, c
R. Edgar, ss / Manager

California

Colored Nine (Oakland, CA)

Marshall, 3b
P. Walker, lf
H. Sanderson, ss
Horace M. Wilds, c
Oscar Lee, cf / 1b
E. Williams, 1b
D. Thompson, 2b
C. Reiley, rf
W. Burne, 3b
W. Powell, cf
William Townsend, p

*Lotus Club
(San Francisco, CA)*

J. F. Summers, rf / 2b / cf
W. Derrick, 2b / rf / lf
W. E. Dennis, 3b
J. Derrick, p
J. Sands, lf / rf
J. Jordan, c
D. W. McDonald, cf / ss
W. G. Maddox, rf
William H. Dillard, 1b
J. V. Campbell, 2b / ss / p

*Vaudevillians
(San Francisco, CA)*

Irving Sayles
Edward Conners

O. McAdoo
E. McAdoo
R. H. Collins
R. Johnson
R. Allen
William H. Downes
George Conners

Georgia

*Cuban Giants
(Thomasville, GA)*

Billy Reid
Charles Sharp
Wash Jackson
Sam Banion
Abe Brown
James Bracewell
William Gray
John Sapp
Robert Ross
Sam Dixon

Illinois

Harlems (Chicago, IL)

Edward Huston, c
Edward Sadler, p
Otis B. Duncan, 1b
George Foster, 2b
David Lane, 3b / c
Baker, ss
Harry Moore, lf
Walter G. Prime, cf
Cookey, rf
Wince Delorney, cf
J. Matthews, rf
Hughston, lf
Dinney Davis, c / 2b / rf

Stars (Chicago, IL)

James Reynolds, p
Marriner, c
William C. Holmes, 1b
Richards, 2b
Marshall, ss
Grant Campbell, 3b
Lowe, lf
W. C. Hurley, cf
Boone, rf
William Hennessy, p
William Murphy, c

Unions (Chicago, IL)

Peter Burns, c
Gus Brooks, 2b
Grant F. Campbell, cf
Joseph Campbell, p
Darby Cottman, 3b / 2b
E. King, rf / ss
Albert Hackley, rf / ss
George Hopkins, p
William Smith, p / cf
Wesley Parker, lf / cf

James Smith, ss / p
Joseph Friend, p
Robert Foote, c / 2b
William Stitt Peters, 1b / Manager
Travis H. Elby, Financial Secretary
William Albert Jones, Team President

Uniques (Chicago, IL)

William James Renfro, p / 2b / rf
William Harvey
Vines, p / rf
William Ferguson, c / rf
Lee Starks, c / 2b
John Johnson, p / c
Earl Nash
William Ramsey, 3b
Dinney Davis, 2b / c
Andrew Porter, c / cf / 3b

Browns (Decatur, IL)

Bunt Fields, c
John Hawkins, p
Cook Long, cf
Clayton Holland, 2b
Harry Robinson, lf
Will Buchanan, ss
Charles Fields, 1b
George Hopper, lf
Dick Thorp, 3b

Kansas

Stars (Leavenworth, KS)

William "Bud" English, p
Ellsworth, c
James Mayo, 1b
Phillips, 2b
B. Vaughn, 3b
H. English, ss
William Miller, lf
Johnson, cf
Williams, rf

Browns (Topeka, KS)

William Cannon, p / 3b
George Wallace, p / rf
A. Richardson, 1b
Frank Buffkin, c
Granville Sanders, ss
Riley Slaughter, 2b
Charlie Williams, p
Parcells, 3b
Johnson, cf
Willis McCoy, c
James Booker, Manager

*Colored Champions
(Wichita, KS)*

Syl Anderson, p
Brent Anderson, c
William Green, ss
Charles Anderson, 1b
Artis White, 3b

Robert Able, lf
L. Thomas, p
A. W. Thomas, 2b
Benis, cf / ss
Frank Able, rf / 3b
Robert Carr, p / rf
Lake Anderson, 2b / Manager
George W. Robinson, Manager

Kentucky
Colored Nine (Melrose, KY)

A. Roberts
T. McQuinney
William Taylor
W. White
D. Allen
John Weaver
L. Williams
D. Logan
Charles Anderson

Maryland
Pioneer (Baltimore, MD)

J. Blake, 1b
P. W. Jenkens, 2b
J. Ringold, ss
Samuel Carroll, lf
Thomas Savoy, cf
Edward Carroll, rf
Henry Savoy, p
Wilson, p
Reynolds, c
Jenkens, c
P. Pinder, 3b / Manager

Massachusetts
Resolute Reserves (Boston, MA)

A. Caskins, c
C. Reddick, 1b
T. Whiting, ss
W. Carter, 2b
P. Marshall, 3b
J. Neal, lf
T. Watson, cf / 3b
N. Whiting, rf
Hilk, p
Bicker, 2b
Tucker, cf
Robert M. Rooker, p
J. D. Gordon, ss / Manager

Missouri
No. 11 (Kansas City, MO)

Henry Robinson, p
Frank Maupin, c
Peter Greenberry, 1b
Hale, 2b
Pearson, 3b
Eddie Carr, rf
James Lincoln, ss

Dover, lf
Hall, cf
Joco Payne, rf
Dudley Gatewood, Manager

Stars (Kansas City, MO)

H. Johnson, p
Brethic, c
Peter Greensberry, 1b
A. Johnson, 2b
W. Burt, 3b
James Lincoln, ss
Pierson, lf
W. Smith, cf
Reedy, rf
Hall, c

Red Onions (St. Louis, MO)

John Perkins, c
Bud Thornton, p
John Branch, 1b
William Palmer, 2b
Bud Brooks, 3b
Walter Scott, ss
William Pullmum, lf
Robert, cf
William Webster, rf
Topsy Tursley, Manager

New Jersey
Cuban Giants (Hoboken, NJ)

John Frye, 1b
William Tyrell, 3b
Abe Harrison, ss
Benjamin Boyd, cf
William Whyte, p
William Malone, p
John Nelson, p
Albert Douglass, p
William Selden, p
William Jackson, c
Robert Jackson, c
Frank Grant
Dan Penno, lf
George Stovey, p
Bell, lf
J. M. Bright, Manager

Capital City (Trenton, NJ)

Henry Catto, p
Arthur Thomas, c
B. Martin, 1b
C. Johnston, 2b
N. Boardley, 3b
D. Henderson, ss
Benjamin Brown, rf / c
Ed Smith, lf
W. Smith, cf

Colored Giants (Princeton, NJ)

Henry Simpson, 1b
Peter Richmond, 2b

William Scudder, c
A. Miller, lf
James Simpson, cf
E. Freeman, ss
Jesse Hoagland, 3b
Joseph James, p
R. Washington, rf
J. Scudder, ss

New York
*Hotel Kaaterskill
(Kaaterskill, NY)*

C. E. Robinson
Young Benjamin
W. James
Henry Drayton
D. B. Williams
Henry Cummings
George Chapman
Richard Rogers
A. Morton

*Colored Champions
(Lake Champlain, NY)*

Andrew Jackson, 3b
William Eggleston, ss
Solomon "Sol" White, 2b
Frank Miller, cf / lf
William Malone, p / lf
Winslow Tyrell, c
C. Page, 1b
Henry Catto, cf / p
George Parego, rf

*Spring House
(Richfield Springs, NY)*

Joseph Leggett, 1b
Henderson, cf
Pidgeon, p
Burbage, cf
Pollard, 2b
Anderson, ss
Booker, 3b
Smith, lf
Brown, c

Alhambra (New York, NY)

Irving Sayles, lf
E. Conners, rf
O. M. McAdoo, 3b
R. H. Collins, c
E. McAdoo, 2b
Richard "Dick" Johnson, ss
R. Allen, p
William H. Downes, cf
George Conners, ss
John Conners, c / 1b

North Carolina
Quicksteps (Charlotte, NC)

George Stevenson, c
Freeman Bell, 2b

John Brown, lf
Tom Hall, ss
James, 1b
James Diamond, rf
Wellington Lomax, cf
J. S. Harris, p
Charles Robinson, 3b

Grays (Charlotte, NC)

Gray Toole
Milas Thompson
Jerry Gaffney
John Hand
E. W. Butler
Julius Holt
Cicero Mosley
George Alexander
Walter Moore
Henry Hayes
Henry Bird
Tom Moore
Commodore Moore

Ohio

King Killers (Hillsboro, OH)

Lewis "Lew" Ellis, c / Captain
Tom Kittrell, p
Ed Trimble, 1b
Hurd Day, 2b
Dick Delaney, 3b
Lud Sneed, ss
Emanuel M. Hudson, lf
William Hurley, cf
Stewart Kittrell, rf
Tom Settles, Substitute
Will Good, Substitute

Maroons (Cleveland, OH)

John Jackson, p
William Wilson, ss
James Lindsey, 2b
David Wyatt, 3b
Hull, cf
Charles "Doc" Howard, lf
Frank Johnson, 1b
James Jackson, c
R. Holland, rf

Colored Nine (Newark, OH)

Nathan Gates, 2b
Jesse Cook, lf
Frank Ransom, p
Benjamin Thornton, 1b
Oliver "Ollie" Collins, c
P. Poindexter, cf
F. Cole, 3b
Fred Berry, rf
Charles Royal, ss
Waite, Substitute
Lumpkin, Substitute
I. S. Coles, Manager

A. E. Stars (Zanesville, OH)

T. M. Tate, 1b
Frank Forney, 2b
Richard Cary, ss
G. W. Johnson, 3b
Gilbert Turner, lf
P. Colston, cf
John F. Guy, rf
Edward Heater, p / Captain
John Jackson, c / Manager
J. H. Hargraves, Substitute
J. C. McNabb, Substitute

Pennsylvania

Gorhams (Farmington, PA)

Frank Grant, 2b
George Williams, c / 1b
Clarence Williams, c
Arthur Thomas, ss
William Selden, p / ss
Robert Jackson, c
William Malone, rf
Oscar Jackson, cf / lf
Andrew Jackson, 2b / 3b
Solomon White, 2b
George Barton, of
Henry Gant, rf
Ed Chamberlin, 1b
George Stovey, p / c / cf
Benjamin Davis, 2b
Frank Miller, p
Benjamin Holmes, 1b
Winslow Tyrrell, c / 2b
William Eggleston, ss
Albert Douglass, ss
William Peterson, rf
Harry Catto, cf
William Brown, 2b / lf
William Page, rf
W. A .Farrell, ss
John Oliver, lf
William Norman, cf
James Malson, cf / p
Thompson, c
Peter Fisher, rf / c
William Woods, 3b
William Freeman, lf
Thomas C. Schenk, lf
Caulbert Sparrow, cf
William Norman, ss
Peterson, lf / rf
Smith, rf / lf
Patterson, cf
I. Bolden, 2b
Sam Bolden, 3b
J. Buck, rf
Charles Bell, lf / ss
Ambrose Davis, Manager
William Primrose, Manager

Colored Giants (Harrisburg, PA)

Oscar Potter, lf
James Barton, 1b
Burns, rf
T. Brown, cf
James Williams, ss / cf / rf
John W. Porter, c
Robert Jordan, c
Alexander Harris, 2b
J. James, 3b
A. Jackson, p
Al Baxter, rf / p
Willis Wise, p
John Burris, p
Isaac B. Taylor, ss
Theodore Frye, Secretary

Harrison and Reids (New Castle, PA)

John Beverly, c
J. Williams, p
Sylvester Page, 1b
Fred Bland, 2b
T. Scott, 3b
J. Chinn, ss
Albert Lewis, rf
D. Warden, cf
C. Robinson, lf
J. Loving, p

Young Cuban Giants (Philadelphia, PA)

Charles Rothwell, ss
George Rothwell, cf
V. Gibbs, rf
Norwood Turner, 1b
Albert Rothwell, 3b
Joseph Trusty, c
Delaney, lf
Charles Trusty, p
Sims Emery, 2b

Keystones (Pittsburg, PA)

Frank Miller, lf / 2b
Henry Gant, 3b
Solomon "Sol" White, 2b
Ross Garrison, ss
James Carter, rf / p
Ray Wilson, cf / c / 1b
William Stanard, lf
William Robinson, p / cf
William C. Lyons, c / rf
B. Lyons, lf
Charles Howard, cf / c
Benjamin Gross, p
Wilson Williams, ss / 3b
Thomas Jackson, lf / 3b
Clarence Williams, c
James Lindsey, cf
Harvey Roy, cf / lf
Thomas Ray, cf

John Nelson, c
George Groves, p
M. Millar, p
R. Cargo, c
C. Paige
William Shadney, p
Gaul, 3b
Yarborough, lf
Charles G. Armstrong, Manager
J. W. Gatewood, Secretary

Colored Barbers (Reading, PA)

Harry Lewis, c
Henry Bower, p
J. Brown, 1b
B. F. Smith, 2b
Jones, 3b
Henry C. Nelson, ss
Thomas C. Boston, lf
Jasina, rf
Frank L. Terry, cf

Colored Waiters (Reading, PA)

Charles H. Walker, c
George Brown, p
J. A. Augusta, 1b
E. J. Richardson, 2b
Prigg, 3b
James Whiten, rf
George Stevens, lf
Gutrich, ss
William Jackson, cf

Cuban Giants (York, PA)

George Williams, Captain / 2b
Henry Gant, rf
Andrew Jackson, 3b
Frank Grant, 3b
George Parego, lf
William Barton, lf
George Washington Stovey, cf
Solomon "Sol" White, 2b
Abe Harrison, ss
John H. Frye, 1b
William H. Malone, p
William Douglass, p
Robert Jackson, c
William Jackson, c
Edward Chamberlin, c / 1b
Divia Hargett, rf
Charles Nelson
James Roberson
Dan Penno, lf / p
William T. Whyte, rf
Benjamin Brown, 2b / lf
Alfred Jenkins, Captain / 1b
J. Mora
Rudolph, lf
John Payne, c
Norwood Turner, c
A. Russell, rf

Pyre
Gifford, 1b / c
York Hargett, 1b / Treasurer / Secretary
William D. Davis, Manager
George Williams, Vice-President

Lumber City Colts (Williamsport, PA)

J. D. Baker, ss / p
Jones, 1b
Snowden, cf / rf
Frank Battles, c / 2b
W. Alexandria, lf
E. Watson, ss
Henson, 3b
John H. Bell, p / cf
James Reed, rf / p / ss
Javan I. Emery, 2b / c Preteile, c
Charles Anderson, Manager

Quicksteps (Charlotte, NC)

George Stevenson, c
Bell, 2b
John Brown, lf
Tom Hall, rf
James, 1b
James Daniels, Captain / ss
Wellington Lomax, cf
John Harris, p
Horace Robinson, 3b
Gray J. Toole, ss / Manager

Virginia

Red Stockings (Norfolk, VA)

Sidney Fentriss, c / Captain
Augustus Taylor, 2b
Ruffin, 3b
Cyrene Fisher, p
Dan McClennan, 1b
Moore, 1b
"Bub" Baker, cf
Wertham, rf
William Johnson, ss
James Knox, 3b

Washington, DC

Douglass (Washington, DC)

L. Thomas, President
E. Brown, Vice President
L. H. Richardson, Treasurer
J. Green, Manager
S. Lincoln, Secretary

Wisconsin

Boston Dips (Milwaukee, WI)

Randall Phillips, p
Burt Hutchinson, c
William Hawkins, 1b
T. D. Ellis, 2b
Wilson Black, 3b
John White, ss

Fred Watson, lf
Berry, cf
Hoyt, rf

Reds (Milwaukee, WI)

F. J. Chapman, p / cf
Harrison, c
Thomas W. Elliott, 3b / 1b
J. B. "Bud" Alden, 2b / Captain
Napoleon Broady, 1b / ss
W. Adkins, rf
J. Jackson, cf
B. Adkins, lf
William "Will" Simmons, p
Daintyfield, c
Hoppley, 3b
John White, c
R. Rand, ss
Johnson, c
Demley, rf
Ellis, ss
Payne, p
Sunday, lf

1893

Arkansas

Browns (Newport, AR)

George Green, President
William Owens, 2b / Secretary
Robert E. Edgar, ss / Manager / Treasurer
J. Morris Spencer, p / Business Manager
James Woods, 1b
Thomas, 3b
Colton, cf
Norwood, lf / p
Slaughter, p
James, c

California

Lotus Club (San Francisco, CA)

D. Yeary, p
George Davis, c
B. Williams, 1b
J. Reed, 2b
F. Johnson, 3b
Gill Buford, ss
D. Grant, rf
W. Alexander, cf
F. Worden, lf

Georgia

Nine Brothers (Augusta, GA)

Augustus Preston
Jack Jossie
Reuben Jenkins
Isaac Jenkins
John Jenkins
Charles Attaway
Ryal Ware

George Taylor
John Gould
Henry Watts
Mose Ellis
Jim Jackson

Blues (Savannah, GA)

Washington, c
Govern, p
McNeil, 1b
G. W. Gary, 2b / Captain
C. Zackery, 3b
Logan, ss
White, lf
Lark, cf
Mulligan, rf
Morrison, Substitute

Forest Citys (Savannah, GA)

Black, c
Telfair, p
T. A. Milledge, 1b / Captain
Williams, 2b
Carr, 3b
Hernandez, ss
Miller, lf
Taylor, cf
Gadsen, rf

Illinois

Eclipse (Bloomington, IL)

Isaac Witherspoon, c
Robert McCrary, p
Jack Thomas, 1b
Robert Watson, 2b
A. Watkins, 3b
Archie Hayden, ss
Dan Carroll, lf
Will Watson, cf
James Hicks, rf

Clippers (Chicago, IL)

William James Renfroe, 2b / Manager
James Smith, 3b
Solomon "Sol" White, 2b
William Waller, cf
Lee Starks, c
B. Ward, lf / cf
F. Lewis, rf
E. King, ss
Walter Vines, p
William Wallace, 1b
Frank Scott, ss
R. F. Newman, p
E. Ward, cf
James Thompson, rf
James Rayfield, lf
Ed Bowen, Manager

Chicago Unions (Chicago, IL)

Gus Brooks, rf
George Hopkins, p

Joseph Campbell, lf
Peter Burns, c
Albert Hackley, 3b
Frank Scott, ss
L. Sexton, 2b / c
Marshall Coffey, 2b
George Franklin, rf / p
Harp
Charles Walker, 1b
Coleman, p
William Joyner, rf
John Johnson, p / c
Robert P. Jackson, ss
Charles Grant, 2b
Fowler, 3b
William Stitt Peters, 1b / Manager
Al Donegan, President

Goodwins (Chicago, IL)

Scipio Spinks, p / Manager
F. First, p
William Hawkins, 1b
William James Renfroe, 2b
William Smith, 3b
Robert Jackson, 3b / ss
William "Billy" Holland, lf
Gus Brooks, cf
Charles Griffin, rf
Hastings V. Brown, lf
Lee Starks, rf
L. Sexton, c

Black Diamonds (Springfield, IL)

Payton, c
Sanders, p
Casey, ss
Ferguson, cf
Walter Casey
Cook, cf
Pollard, rf
Booth, lf
Burton, rf
Grey, 1b
Williams, 2b
T. Bowman, 3b
C. Maxwell, ss
Frank Lewis, cf
Koll, lf

Kansas

Browns (Hutchinson, KS)

J. W. Francis, c
T. W. Kirk, p
J. Walters, 1b
S. Tom Owens, 2b
F. Graves, 3b
W. Kens, lf
S. Kirk, cf
Harris, p
Bradley, c / rf
James Monroe, c / rf

Benjamin Moore, rf
Thaddeus Stevens, ss
Benjamin K. Holley, p

Clippers (Hutchinson, KS)

James Lincoln, c
Charles Moppins, p
Walters, 1b
S. Tom Owens, 2b
W. Owens, 3b
W. Roberson, lf
J. W. France, lf
Thaddeus Stevens, cf
John Price, rf

Boston Athletics (Wichita, KS)

H. Shears, c / lf
Syl Anderson, p
Burrell Anderson, c
Lake Anderson, 1b
Charles Anderson, 2b / ss
G. McCullen, lf
L. Woods, 3b
Fuller, ss
Frank Able, 3b
William Jones, 2b
J. Thomer, cf
Charles Johnson, rf
John Hudson, lf / rf
Brent Anderson, cf
Robert Able, rf / 3b
F. Gardenshire, ss
William Green, 2b
R. B. Johnson, lf

Maryland

Trotters (Frederick, MD)

O. Stanton, c
William Lee, rf
James Dorsey Robinson, p
J. Stanton, lf
Benjamin Cole, 3b
Bruce Tonsil, ss
Hall, 2b
Mitchell, 1b
Smith, cf
James Thomas Tolliver, Manager

Massachusetts

Monarchs (Boston, MA)

William H. Selden, p
James Cary, c
George Stevens, 1b
Thomas White, 2b
Winslow Tyrrell, 3b
Alfred Davis, ss / 2b
William Malone, lf
James D. Robinson, p / rf
Charles Bell, ss

Joseph Palmer, lf
Frivell, 3b
Brown, rf
Williams, 1b
Alfred Jupiter, cf / Manager

Resolute Reserves (Boston, MA)

A. Caskins, c
C. Reddick, 1b
T. Whiting, ss
W. Carter, 2b
P. Marshall, 3b
J. Neal, lf
T. Watson, cf / 3b
N. Whiting, rf
Hilk, p
Bicker, 2b
Tucker, cf
Robert M. Rooker, p / Manager

Michigan

News Boys (Detroit, MI)

R. Colwell, c
G. Hall, p
A. Colwell, 1b
T. Lawson, 2b
C. Miller, 3b
Charles Gorman, ss
A. Gorman, lf
F. Selwood, cf
L. Rappenport, rf

Missouri

Bay Pets (Kansas City, MO)

Walter Carter, p
Charles Smith, c
William Jackson, 1b
Loots, 2b
Coulter, 3b
J. Payne, ss
George Martin, lf / p
Williams, cf
B. Moore, rf

Blues (Kansas City, MO)

Reed, p
Arthur Greer, c
James Lindsay, c
Henry Robinson, 2b
Robert P. Searcy, ss
Hollis, lf
F. Woodson, cf
Sam Christian, c
Jack Jameson, rf / p
A. L. Thomas, 1b / Secretary
F. Woodson, Secretary
J. Fields, Manager

No. 11 (Kansas City, MO)

Henry Robinson, p
Frank Maupin, c

Peter Greenberry, 1b
Hale, 2b
Pearson, 3b
Eddie Carr, rf
James Lincoln, ss
Dover, lf
Hall, cf
Joco Payne, rf
Dudley Gatewood, Manager

New Jersey

Eclipse (Atlantic City, NJ)

William Brooks, 3b
Patton, c
Eisberg, 1b
Paul, 2b
Trusty, p
White, lf
Hensbury, cf
William J. Toney, ss
Jones, rf

Clinton Stars (Newark, NJ)

H. Galvin
C. Charmers
G. Cole
C. Oliver
C. Stone
G. Phillips
G. Hickock
H. Johnson
J. Finnerson
Joe Smith, Jr., Captain
E. Myers, Secretary
N. Johnson, Manager

Colored Giants (Princeton, NJ)

Henry Simpson, 1b
Peter Richmond, 2b
William Scudder, c
A. Miller, lf
James Simpson, cf
E. Freeman, ss
Jesse Hoagland, 3b
Joseph James, p
R. Washington, rf
J. Scudder, ss

New York

Cuban Giants (Long Island, NY)

Andrew Jackson, 3b
Arthur Thomas, c
Oscar Jackson, cf
Clarence Williams, c
Frank Grant, 2b
Abe Harrison, ss / lf
George W. Stovey, p / 2b
William Jackson, 1b / c
John Nelson, rf
Dan Penno, rf / 1b

Henry Catto, lf / p / rf
Frank Miller, rf / p
James Malson, rf
Solomon White, 2b
George William Castone, p
John Patterson, lf
James Dorsey Robinson, p
William Johnston, lf
George Foster, p

Athletics (Middletown, NY)

Fred Brum, c
George Smith, p
Cody Johnson, 1b
Alexander "Alex" Gale, 2b
Jamesy Miller, ss
James Van Houten, 3b
Frederick Beasley, lf
Alfred Sharp, cf
John Bull, rf
George Sharp, Substitute

Gorhams (New York, NY)

Dan Penno, cf
George Stovey, p / 1b
Albert Douglass, ss
Shank, 3b
Ben Brown, 2b
F. Lee, lf
Booker, rf
Joseph Winters, c / rf / 1b
J. Andrews, p

Colored Giants (New York, NY)

Oscar Jackson, c
Andrew Jackson, 3b
Frank Grant, ss
George W. Stovey, lf
John Nelson, p
Ben Boyd, cf
David Penno, ss / lf
William T. Whyte, 1b
Gwyn, rf

Prospect House (Shelton Heights, NY)

Bromfield
George Reese
Sampson
Monde
Slowe
Poindexter
W. B. Butler
Samuel Johnson
Cutler
George Tucker, manager

North Carolina

Grays (Charlotte, NC)

Milas Thompson
Jerry Gaffney
John T. Hand

E. W. Butler
Julius Holt
Cicero Mosley
George Alexander
Walter Moore
Henry Hayes
Henry Bird
John Daniel
Guss Abernathy
George Stevenson
Commodore Moore
Charlie Taylor, Secretary
Tom Moore, Assistant Manager
Gray J. Toole, Manager

Quicksteps (Charlotte, NC)

George Stevenson, c
John Brown, lf
John Daniels, rf
John Harris, p / 2b
Guss Abernathy, 1b
Walter Slade, ss
Edward "Toad" Torrence,
James Diamonds, ss / Captain
Horace Robinson, 3b
George R. N. Taylor, 2b / Secretary
Gray J. Toole, p / Manager

Ohio

O.K. Hustlers (Cleveland, OH)

George M. Sampson, Captain / 3b
Lewis Edward Turner, p / rf
Albert Dennie, p
Ross Hunley, c / rf
Charles S. Hackley, 2b
Roy Tucker, 1b
Paul Moody, ss
Charles H. Stone, cf
W. Scott Brown, lf
William E. Smith, Manager

Colored Nine (Newark, OH)

R. J. Benson, Manager
Charles Royal, Captain / ss
Nathan Gates, 2b
Charles Carter, 3b
B. Thornton, c / p
O. Collins, c
Jesse Cook, 1b
W. Stewart, 2b
H. Jones, cf
W. Terry, rf
T. Simpkins, lf

Pennsylvania

Cuban Giants (Frankford, PA)

Jobe Trusty, c
D. Halley, rf
Frank Storkey, 1b
Charles Rothwell, ss
Charles Trusty, p

Albert Rothwell, 3b
Delaney, lf
Davis, cf
George Rothwell, 2b

Colored Giants (Harrisburg, PA)

Oscar Potter, lf
James Barton, 1b
Burns, rf
T. Brown, cf
James Williams, ss / cf / rf
John W. Porter, c
Robert Jordan, c
Alexander Harris, 2b
J. James, 3b
A. Jackson, p
Al Baxter, rf / p
Willis Wise, p
John Burris, p
Isaac B. Taylor, ss
Theodore Frye, Secretary

Cuban Giant Juniors (Harrisburg, PA)

B. Smith, c
G. Williams, p
A. Reed, 1b
Al Baxter, 2b
C. Jones, ss
Alfred Burrs, lf
D. Saunders, 3b
J. Jones, cf
William Pinkney, rf
James Murphy,
J. Coles
Hyle Lucas
James Thompson

Jolly 12 (Pittsburg, PA)

J. Thornton, c
George Pearce, p
W. Miller, ss
A. Russell, 1b
George Elliott, 2b
C. Jackson, 3b
C. Webster, lf
John Roseman, cf
Joe Highgrates, rf

Keystones (Pittsburg, PA)

J. Staunton, c
James Robinson, p
Ray Wilson, 1b
Frank Miller, 2b
Ross Garrison, ss
Henry "Crow Wing" Gant, 3b
Thomas Jackson, rf
Charles Lyons, cf
John "Doe" Howard, lf
Joseph Allen, Substitute

YMSC (Pittsburg, PA)

Hanson, c
William Page, p
George Gross, 1b
J. Proctor, 2b
C. Hankley, ss
E. Randalls, 3b
J. Taper, lf
John Tyler, cf
H. Hill, cf
W. Talliferro, rf

Cuban Giants, Jrs (Pottstown, PA)

Jackson, c
Johnson, p
Phillips, 1b
Black, 2b
Lud, 3b
Buster, ss
Wilson, rf
Howard, cf
Gutrich, lf
Lacey, cf

Colts (Williamsport, PA)

Javan Emory, 2b
D. Battles, c
Jasina, 1b
Snowden, cf
E. Watson, ss
J. D. Baker, 3b
Henson, rf
W. Alexanderia, lf / 3b
William H. Reed, p / rf
Jones, 1b
Bell, p
"Smut" Moore

Colored Monarchs (York, PA)

William Chambers, cf
John Lee, rf
George Green, lf
John Joice, 3b
Marshall Brown, 2b
George Woodward, 1b
Sylvester Page, p
Punch Howard, ss
Charles Rhodes, c
Frank Robinson, c / Captain
James Washington, Manager

Cuban Giants (York, PA)

Charles Pickney, c
James Furness, 1b
Bob Thompson, 2b
George Anderson, p
Burt Devinney, ss
George Falbow, rf
George Moody, 3b
Richard Lee, cf
Davis, c
James Washington, Manager

Texas

Fly Aways *(Galveston, TX)*

Frank Coleman, p / ss
J. Coleman, cf
Williams, c / 1b
George Upps, 1b
Joseph Walker, 2b
D. Stafford, 3b
A. Runnels, ss
Bud Walker, lf
Charles D. McBeth, cf / lf
King, cf / rf
J.M. Davis, rf
Ed Riley, p
James, rf
W. L. Jones, p / ss / c

Brown Stockings *(Houston, TX)*

William H. Nobles, p
Early, p
Byrd, c
Stevens, 1b / c
Walcott, 2b
Singleton, 3b
Ellis Nickerson, ss
Anderson Alexander, lf
Wheat, cf / p
Joe Thompson, rf

Littlerocks *(Houston, TX)*

Wade Hamilton, p
Nookless, c
Charles Mills, 1b
Riddley, 2b
Busby, 3b
Diamond, ss
Riddell, lf
Sledge, cf
Wheat, rf
Pipkin, Substtitue

Rosebuds *(Houston, TX)*

William H. Noble, p
Hardy, c
Harris, 1b
Dillard, 2b
Ellis Nickerson, 3b
Richard Cuney, lf
Brenham, ss
Casey, lf / c
Fritz, cf / lf
Sidney, rf
Willis, cf
Simms, rf
Griffin, sub

Washington

Athletics *(Tacoma, WA)*

Perry Payne, 1b / Captain
Fred "Ginger" Conna, p
Silas Bievens, 1b
M. J. Hawkins, 3b

Cyrus Wilkins "Professor" Wilks, 2b
Fred Ross, ss
Eli Harris, lf
Thomas Devan, rf
Gill Buford, cf
A. C. Moore, 2b
Tom Williams, ss
John Warner, rf
Henry Johnson, cf
Ernest De Leon, lf
Robert "Big Bob" Monroe, Manager

1894

Arizona

Colored Barbers *(Phoenix, AZ)*

F. Gardner, c
T. Johnson, p
Waiter, 1b
Gorden, 2b
Perry Polk, 3b
Ed Thomas, ss
Polecks, cf
J. W. Bolton, rf
Hinks, lf
Fred Shirley, Manager

California

Browns *(Los Angeles, CA)*

Lucius Alexander, c / 2b
W. Griffin, p / ss
Sandy Gardner, 1b
William Carroll, 2b / p
William Nettles, ss / c
William "Billie" Stewart, 3b
Henry Grant, lf
W. F. Woodyard, cf
Benjamin Perkins, 2b
Emery, rf
G. Johnson, 3b

Georgia

Young Experts *(Savannah, GA)*

Dan O'Neil
Son James
Homer Styles, p
Buber McIntosh
Edward Hopkins
Henry Nesbitt, c
Adolphus Williams, c / p
Alonza Henderson
Johnnie Slay
Loly Graham, c
Robbie Coapley, p
Simmons, p

Vigilants *(Thomasville, GA)*

Billy Reid
Charles Sharp

Wash Jackson
Sam Banion
Abe Brown
James Bracewell
William Gray
John Sapp
Robert Ross
Sam Dixon

Illinois

Boycotts *(Chicago, IL)*

Tyler Crittenden
Harry Hutchinson
James "Jimmie" Mason
Meritt Dowling
Willis Miller
Joe Dowling
Marcellus Echols
Leroy Christy
Joe Smith

Chicago Unions *(Chicago, IL)*

Frank Butler, 3b
Michael Moore, 2b / rf
William Joyner, rf / 1b
Willis Jones, c
Frank Scott, rf / cf
Arthur Anderson, rf
William "Handsome Willie" Stitt Peters, 1b / 2b
Albert Hackley, ss
Marshall Coffey, 2b
Louis Smith, lf
Gus Brooks, 2b
Peter Burns, c / p
Robert P. Jackson, ss / 2b / cf
William J. Holland, ss / p
Joseph "Kit" Friend, p
George W. Hopkins, p
William T. Smith, c
Joseph Campbell, 3b
Lamont, p
Farley, c
Ward, 3b
Fisher, ss
D. Bell, 2b
Saller, Substitute

Eclipse *(Chicago, IL)*

Isaac P. Rivers, p
George Scott, c
Caleb Minton, p
R. Lee, c
Henry Ross, 1b
Moses Clark, 2b
Hayman, 3b
William Hutchinson, ss
Fair, rf
Clarence Outland, cf
F. Ross, lf
William James Renfroe, p

O'Haughn, sub
Ed Bowen, Manager

Emergencies (Chicago, IL)

Julius N. Avendorph, 3b
Charles M. Washington, 2b
William Brown, 1b
William Smith, ss
Richard B. Harrison, lf
Benjamin Simpson, rf
Dr. George Hall, cf
Albert Hackley, p
Lee Starks, c
David R. Lawrence, rf
A. Smith, 2b
E. L. Burnett, Substitute

Jackson Parks (Chicago, IL)

Joseph Campbell, ss
Bert T. French, 2b
Royce, cf
Wesley Parker, 3b
Boughton, 1b
G. Frederickson, p
E. O' Connor, c
Kerns, lf
Hurt, rf

Tourgees (Chicago, IL)

Albert H. Roberts, 3b
Jesse Binga, 2b
Harry Teenan Jones, 1b
Dr. A. M. Curtis, ss
Dr. P. D. Garnett
Lloyd Wheeler, rf
Robert Shaw, cf
Arthur Anderson, p / rf
William Albert Jones, c
Scipio Spinks, p
H. Gee, 2b
Midget, cf
Franklin A. Denison, Substitute

Ward's Unions (Chicago, IL)

Peter Burns, c
John H. Howland, p
Harry Joyner, 1b
Robert Jackson, 2b
Fisher, ss / p
Gus Brooks, cf
Joseph Campbell, rf
George Foster, ss
Frank Butler, rf
William Stitt Peters, 1b
Schmidt, p
Ben Black, c / p
George Foster, p
R. Ward, 3b / Manager

Colored Nine (Spokane Falls, IL)

Thomas Stephens, c / Manager
Sol Brown, p

Charles Farmer, 1b
Elijah Douglas, 3b
C. Maxwell, ss
Frank Lewis, lf
E. Kirby, cf
D. Thorpe, rf
G. Hall, rf
A. E. Douglas, Team Captain

Indiana

Black Diamonds
(Connersville, IN)

Charles Rodgers, p
Tom Rice, p
Charles Rice, 3b
George Bass, c
Tom Pierce, 1b
J. Patton, 3b
Louis Bryant, 2b / ss
T. Israel, rf
F. Bryant, cf
Henry Patton, rf
H. Norman, lf
Ed "Rastus" Thurman, ss
Frank Pierce, Manager

Colored Barbers
(Connersville, IN)

F. Cappel, c
Tom Rice, p
Zebulon Hart, ss
George Bass, 1b
Tom Pierce, 2b
Jim Ferguson, 3b
Frank Bass, cf / 1b
H. Eddy, lf
C. Massey, rf
F. Bryant, ss
C. Rice, 3b
Charles Rodgers, c
J. Patton, rf
Henry Patton, lf

Black Diamonds
(Fort Wayne, IN)

George Wilson, 1b
Web Jones, 2b / c
Ed Black, Captain / ss
Henry Greene, 3b / p
Robert "Bob" Hill, c
William Warfield, p
Ed Jones, lf
William Goodall, rf
John Jones, cf
Dan Wallace, Water Boy
William Dorsey, Bat Carrier

Skyscraper (Indianapolis, IN)

Parker, p / 3b
Herrman, ss
Williams, 2b
Smith, rf

Taylor, rf
Conley, p / lf
Johnson, c
E. DeHarney, 1b / Manager

Browns (Logansport, IN)

Charles W. Hill, 3b / Secretary
Harry Gilmore, 1b
William Ratliff, c
George Chatman, p / Captain
George C. Hill, cf
Charles Parker, lf
James A. Carter, 2b
James C. Hill, rf
Willard Butler, c
Gernie Winslow, rf / 3b / Manager

Colored Nine (Rushville, IN)

House, c
Brown, p
Frank Carter, ss
Lumeny, 1b
Stewart, 2b
Piney, 3b
James Melton, lf
Cosby, cf
Geiger, rf

Iowa

Sons of Enterprise
(Cedar Rapids, IA)

O. B. Claire
W. H. Lavell
G. W. Kidd
R. Browdie
Joe Ross
Henry Davis
Cos Murphy
William Hollands
C. H. Bird
Albert Glusby
John Oliphant

Kansas

Eastern Stars (Coffeyville, KS)

Hugh Hicks, c
C. Taylor, p
Will Haddock, rf
Alex McAmore, 2b
W. Rucker, 3b
George Hicks, ss
George Hardrack, rf
Al Jefferson, cf
C. Moss, 3b

Browns (Hutchinson, KS)

J. W. France, c
W. Kirk, p
J. Walthew, 1b
S. Tom Owens, 2b
Frank Graves, 3b
W. Kens, lf

S. Kirk, cf
Harris, p
Bradley, c / rf
James Monroe, c / rf
John Price, p
James King, c
Benjamin Moore, rf
Thaddeus Stevens, ss
Benjamin K. Holley, p

Models (Leavenworth, KS)

Smith, c
English, p
Baker, ss
Green, 1b
Barton, 2b
Williams, 3b
Davis, lf
Fields, rf
Furd, cf
John Kellum, manager

Topeka Locals (Topeka, KS)

Epp Love, rf
Ed Stewart, 3b
George McAdoo, p
E. Slaughter, 2b
H. Edmunds, lf
George Richardson, ss
John Ewing, 1b
Will Lincoln, cf
Thomas McAdoo, c
Walter Brown, p

Rounders (Topeka, KS)

Tilford Davis, p
Fred Davis, c
John Matthews, 1b
S. H. Thompson, 2b
Sam Branch, 3b
Lige Davis, ss
G. W. Wood, rf
I. F. Bradley, cf
B. S. Smith, lf
F. F. Davis, Substitute

Boston Athletics (Wichita, KS)

Brent Anderson, c
Lake Anderson, 1b / 2b
Charles Anderson, 2b / 1b
Reed Anderson, ss / p
Fuller, 3b
L. Woods, ss
Robert Able, rf / c
Frank Able, 3b
Ed Hobson, lf
Syl Anderson, p
F. Gardenshire, ss
C. Henderson, 1b
B. Henderson, c
Sam Harden, 3b
Frank Ray, c

J. Hudson, rf
Jack Taylor, p
R. H. Johnson, lf
William Green, p / rf
"Kid" Donovan, p / ss
Hawkins, cf
S. Forrow, c
H. Shears, cf / Captain
W. A. Betts, Manager

Cary Hotel (Wichita, KS)

F. Craig, ss
B. Hopkins, c
S. Forris, p
R. Woods, 1b
G. Smith, 2b
Joe Bradford, 3b
William Woods, rf
B. Hickerson, cf
B. Dannal, lf
J. D. Mason, Manager

Louisiana

Allens (Carrollton, LA)

W. Brown, 2b
Robert Brooks, p
James Simpson, rf
Joubert Lewis, rf / c
Jeff Lewis, p
J. B. Robertson, 1b
John Brady, c / 3b
Madison, ss
Peter Lucien, cf
Colbert, 3b / p
John Johnson, lf
Davidson, 1b

Granites (Shreveport, LA)

James Rogers, p
William Rip (Rio), c
Chandler, 1b
Demple (Dennis), 2b
McCoy, 3b
Smith, ss
Martin, lf
Ellis Nickerson, cf
Sanders, rf

Maryland

Lord Baltimores (Baltimore, MD)

Randall, rf
Fleet, cf
Jones, 1b
Galloway, 2b
Gray, c
J. R. Harris, lf
Howard, ss / p
Tydings, 3b
Hayward, 3b
Sanders, p

Trotters (Frederick, MD)

O. Staunton, c
William Lee, rf
James Dorsey Robinson
John Staunton, lf
Benjamin Cole, 3b
Bruce Tonsil, ss
Hall, 2b
Mitchell, 1b
Smith, cf
J. Thomas Tolliver, Manager

Missouri

Trents (Kansas City, MO)

W. Roberts
T. Gideon
Andrew Hardgraves
S. Carson
F. Bryant
F. Lee
J. Pinn
H. Trent

Nebraska

Colored Nine (Omaha, NE)

George Taylor, 1b
George Hughbanks, 2b
Frank Maupin, rf
Danger Talbot, cf
William Lewis, lf
Charles South, c
Vasco Graham, p
Joe "Kid" Miller, ss
Jim Hall

Midway (Omaha, NE)

Joe "Kid" Miller
Vasco Graham
George Taylor
Charles South
Douglas
McAdow
Jordan
Robertson
Dorcas
Hawley

New Jersey

Black Stars (Bloomfield, NJ)

Jones, 1b
John Oliver, 2b
Strother, 3b
George Stout, rf
Irving, lf
H. Thompson, c
J. Barnes, ss
Schuyler, cf
Newman, p

Athletics (Bridgeton, NJ)

Ed Wilkinson, c
John Wesley, p
John Long, 3b
Frank Gould, 1b
Andrew Pierce, lf
Wilbert Gross, ss
Howard Gross, c
Oscar Brown, cf
Fred Berry, rf / 3b
John Humphries, c
Isaac Saxton, c
Samuel Bond, cf
Herbert Morgan, cf
Charles Lewis, 3b
William Edwards, 1b / Captain
Andrew Wells, 2b / Captain
Joseph Tillman, 2b / Manager

Colored Giants (Camden, NJ)

Henry Vallie, lf
Edward C. Gunby, cf
Joseph Trusty, p
Ed Chamberlain, 3b
Ruffen, 1b
Isaac Rothwell, ss
Edward Lodine, rf
Jones, c
William "Gus" Brooks, 2b

New York

Cuban Stars (Binghamton, NY)

Charley Snyder, rf
Charles Hummel, c
Charles Teabout, 2b
Butch Lee, lf
William Cheeks, ss
Caesar Jackson, 3b
W. Dangerfield, cf
E. Daily, p / rf
J. Lewis, p / rf
Joseph Messer, 1b / Captain

Casinos (Elmira, NY)

William H. Condol, rf
James "Jim" Armstrong, cf
Edwin Thompson, p
Lincoln Strong, c
George W. Stovey, p / 1b
W. Thompson, ss
W. Cheeks, 3b
D. Gareck, lf
John Rowe, 2b / c

Colored Giants (Geneva, NY)

George Martin, p
John Rowe, 1b
Charles Granston, 2b
Bert Hazzard, 3b
Herman F. Kinney, ss

John Cartwright, lf
Avery Griger, cf
W. Coleman, rf
Frank Davis, c
Arthur Kinney, p
F. Hardy, Manager

Cuban Giants (New York, NY)

John Patterson, lf
William Jackson, c
Solomon "Sol" White, 2b
Frank Grant, ss
Andrew Jackson, 3b
Oscar Jackson, 2b / cf
Winslow Tyrrell, lf
John Nelson, rf / 2b
William H. Selden, p
George Washington Stovey, rf
James Williams, 1b
Dan Penno, p
A. S. Wright, 2b
Johnson, lf
Sneeden, cf
Henry Catto, lf
James Mason, p
John D. Bright, Manager

Gorhams (New York, NY)

Dan Penno, lf
Edward DeMund, 1b
Boyd, ss / cf
J. Andrews, p
William Douglas, 2b
Schenck, cf / 3b
Ed Wilkinson, c
John M. Watkins, c / lf
Alfred Jenkins, c
Sam Bolden, 3b
Hugh McWinters, rf / p
Albert Spriggs, 3b
Frank Anderson, p
James Moorman, Manager

Cuban Giants (Port Jervis, NY)

William Brooks, 2b
Keefe, cf
B'son, 3b
Frank Miller, p / ss
E. Baker, p / ss
West, lf
A. Baker, rf
F. Myers, c
Brown, 1b

Livingstons (Rochester, NY)

Albert Thomas, 1b / Captain
George Gibbs, p
Henry Thomas, 2b
Charles Wells, 3b
Jack Gibbs, ss
Fred Cheaney, c
Henry McDurphy, cf

Thomas James, lf
Ben Jackson, rf
Henry Williams, Manager

Athletics (Rochester, NY)

Albert Thomas, 3b
George Gibbs, 1b
Henry Thomas, ss
John "Jack" Gibbs, ss
Thomas James, lf / c
Fred Cheaney, lf
John Rowe, p
Benjamin Earles, rf
Simon Gibbs, cf
John Thomas, Substitute

United States Hotel (Saratoga Springs, NY)

R. Phillips, p
Clarence Page, c
George Baker, 1b
Benjamin F. Boyd, 2b
Benjamin Holmes, 3b
Sam Bolden, ss
Joshua Rogers, lf
Louis Buchannan, cf
William Harmon, rf
Van Rannins, p

Fearless (Utica, NY)

Henry "Harry" Waples, 3b
William "Bill" Pell, 1b
Theodore Pell, ss
P. Henry, ss / p
Harry Moss, lf
Moses Gray, c
William Pell, rf
Charles W. Titus, cf
Edward Wilson, p / c
James Pell, rf

North Carolina

Grays (Charlotte, NC)

Milas Thompson
Jerry Gaffney
John Hand
E. W. Butler
Julius Holt
Cicero Mosley
George Alexander
Walter Moore
Henry Hayes
Henry Bird
John Daniel
Guss Abernathy
C. Robertson
George Stevenson
Commodore Moore
Charlie Taylor, Secretary
Tom Moore, Assistant Manager
Gray Toole, Manager

Blue Shirts
(Greensboro, NC)

Campbell, p / 2b
Gillmore, c / lf
W. Nelson, cf
King, lf / p
Donald, 3b / c
C. Walls, 2b / c
D. Carsey, c / 1b / ss
James C. Banks, rf,
B. Carsey, ss
Lewis Cameron, p

Mutuals
(Wilmington, NC)

John Lee, President
W. H. Lane, Vice President
Henry Sampson, Rec. Secretary
William H. Mitchell, Financial Secretary
J. E. Malette, Cor. Secretary
Thomas Moore, Treasurer
Grant C. Torrence, Captain
Fred T. Gause, Asst. Captain
C. Hayes, Manager
William H. Harris, Asst. Manager

Ohio

Hollendens (Cleveland, OH)

W. O. Bowers, 1b
P. Poindexter, 2b
John "Jack" Dean, rf / ss
Al Dennie, lf
G. Baker
James Jackson, p
P. Weir
M. D. Johnston
N. M. Craig
W. P. Merchant
John Jackson, c
Edward Wilson, ss
Alexander Frye, 3b / c
John Mitchell
Pinkney, cf / c
Thompson, p
Bundy, 2b
Adam, cf
Emerson, rf
Manning, 3b
Brown, c
Douglas, lf
Lewis Edward Turner
Edward Williams, p

Kennard House
(Cleveland, OH)

George Washington, c
John Morris, 1b
John Johnson, ss
Andrew Talbert, 2b
Benjamin Taylor, 3b
Good, cf

Stephen Boyd, rf / p
Cooper, lf / p
John Oldwein, p / rf

McKinleys (Cleveland, OH)

Charles Griffin, 2b
Pettemore, 3b
I. Sommers, p
William Lindsay, lf
S. Mitchell, cf
O. Hall, c
Walter Brooks, rf
Bigben, 1b
William Craig, ss
William H. Cole, c

O. K. Hustlers (Cleveland, OH)

O. Scott, p / ss
George Sampson, 3b
Edward Turner, c
Luther Nickens, 1b
Charles H. Stone, lf
Charles Hackley, 2b
E. J. Turner, p
J. Early, rf
J. H. Potter, c

The Leaders (Ironton, OH)

L. Moore, 1b
Mac Black, 2b
Ed Goodwine, cf
William Douglass, p
Sam Kibby, ss
William Page, lf
John Evans, c
John Walker, 3b
William Cormutte, 1b

Grays (Oxford, OH)

F. Reed, c
G. Tyner, p
H. Williams, ss
C. Bredenburg, 1b
J. Reed, 2b
H. Rowe, 3b
R. Dohemar, lf
J. Marshall, rf
S. Perk, cf

Colored Barbers
(Portsmouth, OH)

Wilson W. Minor, c
Sheridan Henson, p
Louis S. Minor, ss
Charles E. Minor, 1b
M. Friese, 2b
M. Beckam, 3b
J. Jackson, lf
Ed Washington, cf
James Weaver, rf
Dan Bell, 2b
Robert Gross, 2b

Colored Nine
(Portsmouth, OH)

Adolphous Parker, 3b
Sam Scott, 1b
William Woods, ss
Oliver Davis, lf
Joe Dill, cf
Arthur Welsh, 2b
Dan Bell, 2b
Isaac Foley, cf
Robert Gross, 2b
John "Jack" Holliday, c
Sheridan Henson, p / rf
William Henson, cf

Manhattans
(Portsmouth, OH)

Adolphous Parker, p / 2b
John Potley, lf
William Woods, ss
Sam Scott, 1b
William Henson, cf
Louis S. Minor, lf
Tom Parker, 3b
Arthur Welch, 2b
John "Jack" Holliday, c
Sheridan Henson, 2b / p

Pennsylvania

Colored Nine (Blairsville, PA)

Skinner, c
Lee, p
McClellan, 1b
Jackson, 2b
Newman, 3b
Stratter, ss
William Johnston, lf / p
Harris, cf
Jackson, lf

J. H. Hooper (Chester, PA)

J. Pridgeon, p
Charles Rothwell, 2b
William Purnsley, 1b
George Dorsey, lf
J. C. Kingman, c
C. Daniels. 3b
Tilson, rf
George Brown, cf
E. Larnee, ss

Giants (Harrisburg, PA)

George Barton, 2b / Captain
Jordan, c
James Murray, ss / c
Wilson, 1b
Porter, 3b
Potter, 1b
William Williams, cf / c
Harris, rf
H. Burrs, p

George Williams, p
George Potter, Secretary
George Strother, Manager

Colored Nine (Indiana, PA)

Tasker, ss
Lewis, cf
Ambert Bell, 2b / Captain
George Sutherland, p
Bert "Tramp" Horner, c
Charles Taylor, c
W. Sutherland, 1b
Harry McClurken, 3b
Jennings, lf
James Washington, rf

Giants (Philadelphia, PA)

Charles Rothwell, ss
Frank Storkey, 1b
George Rothwell, p
William Brooks, 3b / c
Roy Hughes, 2b
Albert Rothwell, c / 3b
Charles Trusty, cf
F. Myers, rf
Thomas, p
Governs, c
William Tennant, lf

Cyclones (Steelton, PA)

Oscar Potter, lf
Stewart, 3b
Ray Wilson, rf
John W. Porter, c / Captain
Alexander Harris, 2b
Willis Wise, p / ss
Bro'n'ss, cf
Thomas Jefferson, 2b
Hamilton Gibson, p / cf
Peter S. Blackwell, Manager
T. Kent, Assistant Manager
Louis Poston, President
Charles Brown, Treasurer

Colored Barbers (Washington, PA)

Isaac E. Asbury
William Bolden
James Carroll
Thornton Viney
George Johnson
Reuben Baker, Jr.
William Gross
Harry Garrett
Jerry J. Thomas
Harry Hughes, Manager

Texas

Red Stockings (Austin, TX)

Nat Shackelford, ss
Holmes, 1b
Joe Thompson, 3b

John Ward, 2b
Frank Itson, p
Samuel Allen, c
Gordon, c
W. Franklin, p
J. Franklin, cf
Mose Johnson, lf
Mackie, rf

Clippers (Dallas, TX)

Henry Harris, p
Ed Coats, c
Best, 1b
Henderson Caldwell, 2b
Davis, 3b
Hardin, ss
Kearby, lf
Wesley, cf
Berry, rf
A. A. Hudson, Manager

Detroits (Houston, TX)

A. Campbell, p
Henry Burrell, c
George Jones, 1b
Milton Turner, 2b
B. Taylor, 3b
James Blair, ss
F. Bryant, lf
H. Fields, cf
H. Hollis, rf
Henry Vincent, rf
William Simmons, ss / p
Brenham, 3b / 1b
H. Lee, Substitute

Quicksteps (Houston, TX)

J. Brice, p
R. Nichols, c
G. Ellis, 1b / 2b
C. Cage, 2b / 3b
Henry Vincent, 3b
William Simmons, ss
J. Wilson, lf
S. Wilson, p / cf
William Bailey, rf
Samuel Anderson, p
Morris, rf
W. Bailey, 1b
J. Hubbard, cf
Charles Mills, 1b

Rosebuds (Houston, TX)

William H. Noble, p
Anderson Washington, c / rf
Simms, 1b
Brenham, 2b
Dillard, 3b
Nixon, ss
Miller, lf
Wheat, rf / p
Wright, 3b

Hicks, 2b
Ellis Nickerson, ss
Kelly, 2b / 3b
Borders, lf
Canhle, cf
Dorbey, 1b
Brown, rf
Stephens, c / lf
Charles Lane, Secretary

Fly Aways (Galveston, TX)

Fox, p
C. J. Williams, c / 1b
Goodman, p / rf
A. Campbell, 1b / c
George Upps, 2b / lf
W.L. Jones, 3b / p
James Blair, ss / cf
Joseph Walker, lf
E. Coleman, cf
William H. Noble, p
Abraham Coleman, 1b / rf
William Bailey, 3b / lf / rf
Brenham, ss
C. Cage, rf
Walter Paris, 2b / lf
Johnny Jones, 3b
Johnson, 3b
Bauswell, 2b
Walter Downs, 2b
R. Craig, rf
Alexander Simpson, Manager

Brown Stockings (Huntsville, TX)

Houston, p
Bolden, c
George Jones, 1b
Herndon, 2b
Morrow, 3b
R. Bolden, ss
Nat Shackelford, lf
Cole, cf
June, rf

Brown Stockings (Palestine, TX)

B. Miller, c
J. Brotton, p
George, 1b
J. Miller, 2b
W. Hoffen, 3b
"Happy Jack," ss
Mose Johnson, rf
Williams, lf
Parker, cf

Yellow Jackets (Waco, TX)

Mose Johnson, 3b / 2b
Joseph "Joe' Booker, lf
Duval, c

Hooker 1b
John Carter, cf
L. Graves, ss
David, c
Joseph Hicks, 1b / 3b
Goodman, p/ rf/cf
Mason, p
Irving, c
William Bryant, rf / p
Clarence Carter, cf/c
Lafayette O. Graves, ss
C. McClelland, 2b
Drake, c/rf
William M. Spencer, Team Promoter

Virginia

Red Stockings
(Norfolk, VA)

Dan McClennan, c
Smith, c
Thomas Wright, p
James Lewis, p
William H. Harrison, p
William Parker, 3b
Wash Stewart, ss
Cyrene Fisher, 2b
Hill, lf
Moseley, cf
Hodges, rf
George White, 1b / Manager

Eclipse (Richmond, VA)

James Chapelle, cf
C. Smith, ss
B. Wright, 3b
E. Robinson, c
W. Smith, 1b
J. Butler, rf
J. Christian, lf
C. Moore, 2b
W. Lightfoot, p
T. Christian, p
C. P. Robinson, Manager

Cracker Jacks
(Richmond, VA)

George Reese, Captain
Robert Nelson
Jack Nelson
Thomas Hall
Sam Hall
Sonnie Robinson
Eddie Thompson
Robert Weaver
John Freeland
George Chiles

Red Stockings
(Richmond, VA)

Eugene Russell
Robert Davis
James Jasper

J. Birchett
H. Taylor
J. Quarles
C. Poindexter
M. Payne
Lee Dudley
W. Johnson
C. Birchett
George E. Taylor, VP

Roasters (Richmond, VA)

John White, Captain
Sam Hope
Thad Mayo
Joe Richardson
Dick Davis
Pete Austin
L. Bradley
P. Washington
Lawrence Tinsley
Willie White

Washington, DC

Howard University
(Washington, DC)

Ed Morrison, Captain / c
W. G. Avant
F. W. Avant, 1b
George Brewer
W. O. Bundy, lf
R.L. Jones
J. C. Holmes
C. M. Butler
Joseph Rapier, c
R. C. Kelly, Manager

Market House
(Washington, DC)

Newton, 3b
Smith, cf
Louis Phillips, p / c / 3b
Lafayette Jefferson, 1b / Manager
A. Atkinson, 2b / lf
George Betters, ss
Devereaux, c / 3b
William Carter, rf
Lany Wade, lf / p
Charles S. Payne, 2b / 3b

Richmond House
(Washington, DC)

Nared Williams, ss / captain
William Coats, c
Joe Filmore, c
Charles Patton, 1b
Lewis Johnson, lf
L. Perry, rf
Willie Joyce, 2b
James Young, 3b
Matt Patton, cf
William H. Brooker, Manager

1895

California

Colored Nine
(Los Angeles, CA)

William "Will" Brown, p
A. Harper, 1b
Joe Whitesides, c
George Fuller, 2b
J. Blackburn, 3b
Benjamin Perkins, ss
Gus Williams, rf
Charles Woods, cf
Joe Grant, lf
William Griffin, p
E. Hancock, Captain / Manager

Trilbys
(Los Angeles, CA)

William Carroll, c / ss / Captain
William McLaughlin, ss
Lucius Alexander, rf
Robert Shaw, p
William Nettles, cf / 3b
William Griffin, 3b / p
E. Gardner, 1b
William Stewart, ss
F. White, 2b
G. Henry, c
Bragg, rf
S. Gardner, 1b
George Fuller, cf
Dunning, ss
Emery, rf
Smith, ss / cf
Henry Harris, Manager

Assemblys
(San Francisco, CA)

June Dennis, ss
Oscar Lee, 1b
S. Cohen, cf
Horace Wilds, c
Meadows, 2b
A. Sanderson, rf
J. Burns, 3b
H. Sanderson, lf
B. Martin, p

OKs
(San Francisco, CA)

George Vassals (Vessels), lf
Joshua Slaughter, 3b
F. Butler, cf
George Marshall, ss
W. Peck, 1b
S. Baker, p
R. Reed, c
B. White, 2b
N. Coger, rf

Georgia

Heavyweights (Macon, GA)

J. A. Rollins, c
W. Smith, p
A. G. Terrell, 1b
T. B. Irwin, 2b
Kirk Bayne, ss
William H. Harris, ss
J. D. Wilder, rf
Mose Green, cf
G. W. Jordan, lf
J. Brown, Substitute
J. F. Mitchell, Substitute
F. H. Waver, Team Scorer

Lightweights (Macon, GA)

D. Demerest, c
N. Appling, p
J. Hall, 1b
C. Long, 3b
Morris "Huff" Hill, ss
W. Moore, 3b
James Weaver, cf
Sam Weaver, rf
F. Carter, cf
R. Ross, lf
Squire Simpson, ss
T. Peresley, Substitute
W. Brazell, Team Scorer

Telegraph (Macon, GA)

T. B. Irwin, c / Manager
W. L. Hill, p
J. A. Rollins, 1b
Joe Vann, 2b
Joe Gilbert, ss
C. W. Morgan, 3b
H. T. Burney, lf
W. H. Phillips, cf
S. J. Carrol, cf
A. J. Carrol, rf
Ragged Pit, Utility

Vigilants (Thomasville, GA)

Billy Reid
Charles Sharp
Wash Jackson
Sam Banion
Abe Brown
James Bracewell
John Sapp
Robert Ross
Sam Dixon

Illinois

Avondales (Chicago, IL)

James Thompson, 3b
Henry Wulff, 1b / Captain
Duffy, 2b
John A. Mayer, ss / p
Sells, rf

P. Thompson, lf
Arthur Anderson, p / rf
J. Sweeney, p
Tress, c / 2b
Phil Reidy, cf
Elliott, c
Robert Shields, 2b
Andrew "Andy" Porter, c / Manager

Clippers (Chicago, IL)

Eugene Somerville, p
Arthur Anderson, p
William Fergusson, c
Lee Starks, c
James Smith, c / p / 3b
William James, c
Charles Green, cf
Henry Webster, rf
William Waffle, ss
Bruce West, 1b
Noah Stone, lf
David Bradley, 2b
Shirl Emerson, rf
John Johnson, p
George Scott, Manager
Tom Moore, Mascot

Dearborns (Chicago, IL)

N. Blackshear
William Thompson, rf
Louis Hoffman, p
Lawrence C. Hoffman, c
Charles Morgan, p
J. Lynch, p
Jesse Collier, ss
William McLaughlin, ss
F. C. Curtain
A. Laughlin
F. Daly, c
M. Fleming, p / c
Robert Foote, c
M. Sullivan

Delawares (Chicago, IL)

Frank Hamilton, Captain / 1b
William C. Holmes, 2b
Fred Barrett, 3b
Louis Hudson, ss
Harry Walker, cf
Arthur Kennedy, lf
Dave Stevenson, rf
Charles Hutchinson, p
Charles Ryan, c
Louis Kelton, sub
John A. Mayer, Manager

Giants (Chicago, IL)

George Weir, p
Robert Jackson, c
Grant F. Campbell, 2b / Manager
Ward, 3b
Fisher, ss
Edward Wilson, lf

George Foster, cf / p
Joseph Campbell, rf
George "Senator" Hopkins, p / 2b
Frank C. Leland, 1b / Manager

St. Thomas (Chicago, IL)

Solomon Taylor, p
Joseph H. Wilson, c
F. Montgomery, 2b
J. A. Wilson, p
Houseman, 3b
Phelan, ss
Dick Sheppard, lf
Harry Wallace, rf
James Gleans, p
William Smith, p
Orange W. Fox, p
John J. Fitzgerald, cf / Manager

Warrens (Chicago, IL)

Wilcox, 1b
Darrow, 2b
Phillips, ss
Smith, 3b
Condon, rf
Berry, c
D. Glendon, p
White, c
Clements, p
S. Taylor, p
H. V. Brown, p
McGraw, lf
McDonald, cf
Kelly, p
Wheat
William Cobden, Manager

Unions (Chicago, IL)

Grant F. Campbell, lf
Joseph Campbell, p
William J. Holland, p / ss
George Williams "Senator" Hopkins, 2b / p
Frank Scott, ss / cf
William Joyner, ss
F. First, p / cf / 3b
Peter Burns, c
Marshall Coffey, 2b
Harry Hyde, 3b
Harry Moore, 2b
Frank Butler, lf
Albert Hackley, cf
Robert Foote, c
William T. Smith, p / 2b
Fisher, 3b / ss / 2b / 1b
A. Smith, 2b
Jessie Collier, ss
Gus Brooks, rf / cf
Sells, 3b
Hedge, cf
Bryant, lf
Troots, c
George Green, rf

Bert Jones, rf
William Harvey, 3b
William "Handsome Willie" Stitt Peters,
c / 1b / Manager

Colored Nine (Decatur, IL)

Stanton Fields, p
Clayton Holland, ss
Charles Brown, 3b
Harry Moore, 2b
William Burnell, 1b
Charles Love, c
Charles Fields, cf
Cook Long, lf
William Winston, rf
Alford Langston, Substitute
Carrie Burnell, Substitute
Howard Lewis, Substitute

Black Diamonds (Springfield, IL)

W. Parks, c
Eugene Blakeman, 1b / 2b / p
Frank Brandon, 2b
Payton, 3b
Sanders, ss
Davis, rf
Ferguson, cf
Henry, lf
Dixon, c
James Brumnell, p
Harry Hodge, c

Hussars (Edwardsville, IL)

James Berry
Joseph Brown
Nathan West
Will Williams
Joseph Knox
Urgent Childers
Frank Jones
Charles Bradley
Arthur Samuels

Indiana

Studebakers (Connersville, IN)

Charles Rodgers, p
George Bass, c
Tom Pierce, 1b
Lou Patton, 2b
J. Patton, 3b
Lewis Bryant, ss
T. Israel, rf
E. Bryant, cf
H. Norman, lf
Rastus Thurman, ss
R. Demos, cf

Black Diamonds (Fort Wayne, IN)

C. Brown, lf / p
John Rhodes, 1b / Captain

Edward Jones, 2b
Fred Jones, 3b
Henry Green, ss / p
Moses Molton, c
Harry Brown, c
Albert Bray, p
Robert "Bob" Hill, rf
George Parker, cf
Will Archer, Substitute

Herculean (Indianapolis, IN)

Paul Floyd, rf
Daniel McAfee, lf
Sam Cook, ss
George Adams, 2b
Elzie Dehorney, 2b
Charles Lane
Walter Cline
Charles Taylor, p
Alfred White, p
Irvin Hardy, 1b / Captain
William Cook, cf /Captain
Robert Foote, c
Louis Hoffman, p
Maurice White, Manager

Skyscraper (Indianapolis, IN)

Parker, p / 3b
Herrman, ss
E. DeHarney, 1b / Manager
Williams, 2b
Smith, rf
Taylor, rf
Conley, p / lf
Johnson, c

Iowa

Bystanders (Des Moines, IA)

Ed Wallace, ss / Captain
L. Washington, 3b
C. Wilson, lf
John McClain, 2b
A. Perguson, cf
W. Taylor, rf
G. Perguson, 1b
William E. Fine, c
J. Adamson, p

Unions (Mondamin, IA)

Johnson, 3b
Taylor, 1b
Williams, 2b
Watkins, rf
Mills, lf
H. Watkins, ss / Manager
Young, cf
Hess, p
Cary, c / Captain
Cypril, Secretary

Kansas

Clippers (Atchison, KS)

Robert Carr, p
William Gibson, p
Joe Lewis
Charles Porter
John Price
Doe "Bud" Payne
Ward Johnson
Walter Booker
William Generals
Henry Whitney
William Miller
Jones, p

Browns (Hutchinson, KS)

J. W. France, c
W. Kirk, p
J. Walters, 1b / c
S. Tom Owens, 2b
Frank Graves, 3b
W. Kens, lf
S. Kirk, cf
Benjamin Moore, rf
Harris, p
Bradley, c
Thaddeus Stevens, ss
Benjamin K. Holley, p

Browns (Osage City, KS)

John Witt
Samuel Lyons
Isaac Talley
Harrison McCombs
John Davis
Albert Jefferson
Harry O'Dair
Albert Orendorff
Isaac Hibbs
Clark Austin

Kentucky

East End (Maysville, KY)

Watt Whaley, p
William Gray, c
Alexander, 1b
Slater, 2b
Johnson, 3b
Humphrey, ss
Munday, rf
Alexander Gordon, cf / 3b
Washington, lf

West End (Maysville, KY)

Anderson Haley, p
John Green, c
Albert Lewis, p / 1b
Charles Randolph, 2b
Isaac McAllister, 3b
Gibbs, ss
Wheatley, rf / p

John Dimmitt, cf
Clayton, lf

Louisiana

Allens (Carrollton, LA)

William Brown, 2b
Robert Brooks, p
James Simpson, rf
Joubert Lewis, rf / c
J. B. Robertson, 1b
John Brady, c / 3b
Madison, ss
Peter Lucien, cf
Colbert, 3b / p
John Johnson, lf
Davidson, 1b

Cohens (New Orleans, LA)

Joseph Ferrand, p
N. Ross, 2b
Joubert Lewis, c
W. Scott, 1b
Murray, ss
Peter Lucien, rf
Millen, 3b
N. Green, cf
Robert Brooks, p
Colbert, p
Caillioux, c
W. L. Cohen, Manager

Michigan

Page Fence Giants (Adrian, MI)

Ed "Gus" Brooks, cf
J. Grant Johnson, ss
Peter Burns, c
George Taylor, 1b / ss
William Malone, rf
Solomon White, 2b
James Lincoln, 3b / rf
George W. Hopkins, p / lf
Vasco "Roscoe" Graham, c
William J. Holland, p / 3b / rf
Frank Maupin, rf
Frank Nelson, rf / cf
Frank Van Dyke, p / rf
George Miller, p / rf
James Chavous, p / lf
William Wendell Gaskins, p
Barnes, c
William Malone, cf / p
J. W. Patterson, 3b / Manager
Edward Kelley, c
Robert "Bob" Higgins, p
George Taylor, 1b
Fred Patterson, 3b
Tom Kelley, rf
John "Bud" Fowler, 2b / Manager

Powers Giants (Adrian, MI)

Scott Green
Adelbert Green

Frank Waters
George Grassman
James Bird
Allie Johnson
Sumner Lewis
Fred Clayton
Walter Stone
Silver Butler
William Snyder

Unions (Kalamazoo, MI)

Charles W. Williams, c
John Oglesby, p
Henry Rose, 1b
William Cousins, 2b
William Stewart, 3b
Robert Hackley, ss
Foster Myers, lf
Benjamin Bolden, cf
Stephen T. Boyd, rf

Minnesota

St. Peters (St. Paul, MN)

J. P. Banks, c
Charles R. Williams, p
W. F. Williams, 1b
Frederick L. McGhee, 2b
J. C. Clark, 3b
H. Ward, ss
R. E. Anderson, lf
Jesse Henry, cf
Andrew Combs, rf

Strike Outs (St. Paul, MN)

S .E. Hardy, c
James H. Loomis, p
W. J. Garner, 1b
J. Talbert, 2b
P. T. Green, 3b
R. C. Howard, ss
Ed Lee, lf
P. F. Johnson, lf
L. Liverpool, rf

Missouri

Republics (Dresden, MO)

K. C. Lee, c
F. W. Campbell, p
R. J. Bentley, 1b
C. W. Kemp, 2b / Captain
A. R. Clark, 3b
E. Church, lf
L. Pearson, rf
F. R. Satterwhite, cf
W. A. Satterwhite, ss / Umpire
L. Wood, Substitute

Hustlers (Kansas City, MO)

F. Emery, p
C. Caulder, 1b / ss
H. Buchanan, 2b

A. Roberson, ss / 2b
L. Davenport, 3b / lf
J. Garnet, rf / 3b
B. Pollard, 3b
J. Coleman, cf
W. Burt, lf
F. Stevens, cf
C. Radley, 1b
William Carter, p
L. Roberts, 1b
J. Moore, rf
William Jackson, 3b
John Campbell, Assistant Captain
F. Woodson, p
T. C. Woodson, c / Captain
James Davenport, Manager

Silver Stars (Kansas City, MO)

J. McClure, p
B. Manuel, 1b
C. McClelland, c
W. Curtis, 2b
E. Hobson, ss
C. Dates, 3b
L. Brown, rf
W. Sparks, lf
W. Johnson, cf

Montana

Hickory Tips (Butte, MT)

Marion Cooper, p
Al C. Porter, p / 3b
Davis, c/rf
Dave Henderson, 1b
Dan Williams, lf
Harry Parker, ss
Sam Lewis, c
Joseph Humphrey, 2b
George Rideout, cf/Secretary
William Johnson, Manager

Nebraska

Wilcox & Drapers (Omaha, NE)

Dangerfield Talbot, c
Vasco Graham, c / ss
Joe Johnson, p / c
Charles Miller, p
David Lewis, 1b
Lewis, 2b
George Hughbanks, 2b
William Halle, 3b / p
George Wood, ss
George Taylor, 1b
Burley (Burleigh), ss
Walter Paris, lf
Banner Keene, cf / 3b
Thompson, rf / 2b
W. Smith, rf / p
James Hall
H. Banks, p

J. T. Logan, rf
Ford, c
F. Ward, 2b
Solly Barker, Manager

New Jersey

Eclipse (Atlantic City, NJ)

Mellicks, p
Clark, c
Brown, p
Elstery, cf
Andrew Paul, rf
Jackson, 3b
A. Jones, c
Moore, 2b
Glenn, ss
Fitzgerald, 1b
J. Paul, lf
C. Parker Gorden, Manager

Pioneer (Bridgeton, NJ)

Eugene Williams, p
Wilbert Gross, c
William Edwards, 1b / 2b
William Porter, 2b
Phillip Winder, ss
Paul Saxton, c
Fred Berry, 3b
Oscar Brown, rf
Samuel Bond, cf
Claude Beam, lf

Colored Giants (Princeton, NJ)

Henry Simpson, 1b
Peter Richmond, 2b
William Scudder, c
A. Miller, lf
James Simpson, cf
E. Freeman, ss
Jesse Hoagland, 3b
Joseph James, p
R. Washington, rf
J. Scudder, ss

New York

Casinos (Elmira, NY)

William Condol, rf
James "Jim" Armstrong, cf
Edwin Thompson, p
L. Strong, c
George W. Stovey, p / 1b
W. Thompson, ss
William Cheeks, 3b
D. Gareck, lf
John Rowe, 2b / c
Butch Lee,

Spring House (Richfield Springs, NY)

Watkins, 2b
Chadwell, ss

Frank Williams, 1b / Captain
Cody Johnson, lf
Jackson, cf
Yarborough, rf
McLendon, c
Paine, p
Nathan, 3B

Colored Giants (Geneva, NY)

George Martin, p
John Rowe, 1b / c
Charles Granston, 2b
Bert Hazzard, 3b
Herman F. Kinney, ss
John Cartwright, lf
Avery Griger, cf
W. Coleman, rf
Frank Davis, c
Arthur Kinney, p
F. Hardy, Manager

Cuban Giants (Long Island, NY)

Oscar Jackson, cf
John W. Patterson, 3b
Arthur Jackson, rf
Frank Grant, 2b
Harry Moore, ss
Clarence Williams, c
William H. Selden, p
Richmond Robinson, lf
John Nelson, 1b
Frank Bell, rf
James Robinson, p / lf
Windsor W. Tyrrell, ss
George Stevenson, 2b / c
Frank Pell, cf
John M. D. Bright, Manager

Athletics (Rochester, NY)

Albert Thomas, 3b
George Gibbs, 1b
Henry Thomas, ss / c
John "Jack" Gibbs, ss
Thomas James, lf
Fred Cheaney, lf
Thomas James, c
John Rowe, p
Henry Thomas, ss
Benjamin Earles, rf
Simon Gibbs, cf
John Thomas, Substitute

United States Hotel (Saratoga Springs, NY)

Randall Phillips, p
William Diggs, c
Baker, 1b
J. Dean, ss
D. Dowens, lf
H. Furgerson, cf
William Harmon, rf
Van Rannins, p

Benjamin Holmes, 1b / Captain
Benjamin F. Boyd, 2b / Manager

North Carolina

Barbers (Charlotte, NC)

John Hand
E. W. Butler
J. H. Moppen
Walter Alexander
Robert Pugh
T. O. Moore
Charles E. Webb
John McCall
William Nelson
Henry Gaither
Commodore Moore
George C. Theus, Captain
Thaddeus L. Tate, Manager

Bufords (Charlotte, NC)

Thomas Sloan
John Toole
Walter Smith
James Danmons
Richard Graham
William Simmons
George Owens
Rufus Welham
Edward Torrence, Substitute
W. T. Waltar, Substitute
Rhey Streeter, Substitute
Pleas Johnson, Manager
William Johnson, Captain

Quicksteps (Charlotte, NC)

T. Hall, ss
C. Robertson, c
Rufus Williams, cf
John Harris, p / 2b / rf / Captain
John Brown, 1b / lf
George Stevenson, 2b / c / 1b
Edward Torrence, 3b
White, lf / rf
John Pharr, rf / p
James Daniels, p
Guss Abernathy, rf
Walter A. Alexander, Manager

Blue Shirts (Greensboro, NC)

Campbell, p / 2b
Gillmore, c / lf
W. Nelson, cf
King, lf / p
Donald, 3b / c
C. Walls, 2b / c
D. Carsey, c / 1b / ss
James C. Banks, rf,
B. Carsey, ss
Lewis Cameron, p

Black Stockings
(Wilmington, NC)

John Gause, cf / c
James "Son" Addison, p
William Albert McRae, ss
James "Monk" Phillips, ss
Ed "Cooley" Evans, 2b / rf
William Barnett, 2b
Charles Burnett, c / rf
William Mosely, lf
Thomas James, cf
H. Schenk, p
William Schenk, 3b / 1b /Captain /
  Manager

Mutuals *(Wilmington, NC)*

Grant Torrence, c / Captain
Ed Conner, p
John Holmes, 2b
Charles Wortham, p / c
John Mallett, lf
Joseph Sampson, 3b / ss
John Lee, lf / p / President
William Henry Lane, rf / Vice President
William H. Mitchell, ss / Financial
  Secretary
Thomas Moore, Treasurer
John E. Mallett, Corr. Secretary
Henry Sampson, Secretary
C. Hayes, Manager
Frank Gause, c / 1b / Asst. Captain

Ohio

H.A.C. *(Cleveland, OH)*

Lem Archer, lf
Pettemore, ss
John "Jack" Dean, 2b / rf
Jere L. Brown, 1b
William H. Cole, rf / lf / Manager
William Smith, 3b
Edward Turner, p
J. Earley, c
James W. Rawles, lf / p
John Jackson, p / c
James Brooks, 1b / 3b
R. B. Kelly, c / ss
William Craig, cf
Ed "Inkspot" Williams, p
Adams, lf / 1b
McPherson, rf
Zimmer, ss
Miller, cf
C. H. Stump, 3b
Goodman, p
William Lyons (Lines), 2b

Hollendens *(Cleveland, OH)*

William Pittman, ss
Edward Turner, rf
John Jackson, rf / p
P. Poindexter, 2b
Edward Williams, 3b

Charlie Griffin, 1b
Al Dennie, lf
Alexander Frye, c
Charles Stone, cf / lf
J. Earley, c
James Jackson, c
Storie, cf
Yates, ss
Sherman Larkin, cf
Benjamin F. Taylor, ss
George Stout, cf
Samuel Wiggins, rf
Frank Johnson, Substitute
William Hunley, Manager

Manhattans
(Portsmouth, OH)

John Potley, lf
William Woods, ss
Sam Scott, 1b
William Henson, cf
Louis S. Minor, lf
Tom Parker, 3b
Arthur Welch, 2b
John "Jack" Holliday, c
Sheridan Henson, 2b / p

Oklahoma

Invincibles
(Oklahoma City, OK)

Wade, p
Rogans, c
J. Cook, 1b
T. Cook, 2b
R .Williams, 3b
Jackson, ss
Leath, cf
J. Rogans, lf
William Fulbright, c / rf
William Tucker, Manager

Pennsylvania

Giants *(Philadelphia, PA)*

Roy Hughes, 2b / Captain
Charles Rothwell, ss
Albert Rothwell, 3b
George Rothwell, lf
Frank Storkey, 1b
Wesley Lopman, cf
Charles Trusty, p
Wilson Williams, c
John "Jack" Vactor, p / rf
Wilson Brooks, 2b / c
Ruffin, c
G. H. Hazzard, manager

Cuban Giants *(York, PA)*

Charles Pickney, c / lf
Lewis Johnson, p
James Finney, ss
Charles Rhodes, c

William Mills, ss
Clayton Cannon, 2b
Robert Dorsey, 3b
Edward Harr, lf
James Henderson, cf
Lorenzo Butler, rf
Samuel King, p / Umpire
George Anderson, 1b / Captain
George W. Bowles, Manager

Tennessee

Colored Female Stars
(Memphis, TN)

Mrs. Moore, p
Fannie Turner, c
Maud Winter, 1b
Grace Howard, 2b
May Parker, 3b
Annie Ford, ss
Mrs. Hownes, rf
Jennie Butler, cf
Mrs. Crawford, lf

Texas

Red Stockings *(Austin, TX)*

Gordon, p / c
Joseph Fuller, c
J. M. Davis, 1b
Brown, 2b
Bradley, 3b
Joe Thompson, ss
Holmes, lf
Underwood, 3b
Davis, 2b
Walker, p
Lott, ss
Carpenter, cf
John Ward, Captain / cf
W. L. Jones, p

Fly Aways *(Galveston, TX)*

Abraham Walker, p / lf
William Bryant, p
Frank Itson, 1b
W. Campbell, c
Rison (?), 1b
W.L. Jones, p
D. Stafford, 3b / 2b
Bluford, 3b
Johnny Jones, 3b
James Blair, ss
Gray, ss
C. J. Williams, lf
Joseph Walker, cf / c
Frank Coleman, rf
Bud Walker, cf
George Upps, Manager

Reds *(Galveston, TX)*

J. M. Davis, c
W. Franklin, p

Jackson, 1b
Brenham, 2b
Alec Quander, 3b
William H. Nobles, ss
Goodman, lf
Andrew "Rube" Foster, cf
J. Franklin, rf

Fencibles (Houston, TX)

Burles, c
William H. Nobles, p
George Jones, 1b
C. Cage, 2b
Milton Turner, 3b
James Blair, ss
William Bailey, lf
William Bryant, cf
Calvert, rf

Hub Citys (Houston, TX)

Brenham, 1b
William H. Noble, 2b
Wheat, rf
Harris, 3b
P. Bailey, lf
William Bailey, cf
B. Miller, c
J. Miller, p
J. M. Davis, ss
Dillard, Substitute

Virginia

Red Stockings (Norfolk, VA)

Dan McClennan, c
Smith, c
Thomas Wright, p
James Lewis, p
James M. Harrison, p
William Parker, 3b
Wash Stewart, ss
William Johnson, 2b
Hill, lf
Moseley, cf
Hodges, rf
Louie, c
George White, 1b / Manager

Virginia Reds (Hot Springs, VA)

Waverly Peters, c
T. J. Jackson, p
B. P. Scott, 1b
J. B. Jackson, 2b
U. Jones, 3b
Robert Possey, rf
George Thomas, ss
W. Sherman, lf
Edward Anderson, cf

Manhattan Giants (Richmond, VA)

Buck Johnson
Willie Hunter

A. R. Smith
Benjamin Bowler
Timothy Freeman
Richard Williams
Chris Draper
James Johnson
Albert Jenkins
Buck Spottswood, Manager

Colored Nine (Roanoke, VA)

Stewart, cf / c
Walls, ss
Anderson, p
"Bub" Baker, 2b
Goodson, cf
Brooks, lf
Sheverly, rf
Douley, c
Edwards, 3b

Colored Nine (Staunton, VA)

James Stribbling, c
Edward Shelton, p
R. M. Braxton, 1b
William Braxton, 2b
Luther Jennings, 3b
Morris Jackson, ss
Thomas Payne, rf
William Johnson, cf
George Lacy, lf

Washington, DC

Market House (Washington, DC)

William Newton, 3b
Smith, cf
Devereaux, c
Richard Phillips, p
George Betters, ss
Lany Wade, 2b / lf
E. A. Atkinson, 3b / c
J Atkinson, 2b
William Carter, rf / p
Lawson, lf
Charles S. Payne, 2b / 3b
Thomas Howard Diggs, lf / c
Lafayette Jefferson, 1b / Manager

Mohawks (Washington, DC)

William Newman
L. Thompson
R. Jones
F. Ruffin
W. Barbour
William Newton
T. Clark
J. Monday
S. Johnson
W. Shields
R. Armfield
William H. Whaley

Carey
P. Marshall
Washington
King
Brooks
Charles
John Campbell
Fenwick
Magruder
John Wallace, Manager

Richmond House (Washington, DC)

Nared Williams, ss / captain
William Coats, c
Joe Filmore, c
Charles Paton, 1b
Lewis Johnson, lf
L. Perry, rf
Willie Joyce, 2b
James Young, 3b
Matt Patton, cf
William H. Brooker, Manager

1896

Arkansas

Arlingtons (Hot Springs, AR)

Fertiller, p / rf
Henry Lewis, c
Davis, cf
Childs, p / lf
Hardy, 3b
Murphy, c
John Patillo, p / cf
Huff, cf / 3b
Fields, p / 2b
Rowell, ss / c
Arthur Greer, p / c

Quapaws (Little Rock, AR)

R. Butler, 2b
B. Butler, ss
McClure, 3b
Richardson, 1b
Keaton, p
W Crawford, c
Reed, lf
F. Crawford, rf
Prince, cf
Goodwin, p
Houston, c
James Williams, p

California

McKinley Guard (Los Angeles, CA)

S. B. Carr, 2b
N. Clark, cf

Hance Turner, ss
W. R. Dent, 1b
William Griffin, 2b
F. Ford, rf
W. G. Seagraves, lf
William Carroll, c
Boston, p
Robert Shaw, c
Mattoon, p
Foster, c

Trilbys (Los Angeles, CA)

Robert Shaw, p
Lucius Alexander, c / cf
S. Gardner, rf
Lige Walker, 3b
Joseph Marrione, ss / 2b
Benjamin Perkins, 2b
William Carroll, c / ss
W. Anderson, lf
James Mason, p
W. Griffin, p
William Nettles, 1b
Anthony, ss
John Majors, rf
Edward Nichols, 2b
William Prince, 3b
S. B. Carr, ss
N. Clark, rf
W. G. Seagraves, lf
W. R. Dent, cf
Cane, 2b
James Holmes, Manager

Stars (Pasadena, CA)

William Griffin, c
W. G. Seagraves, p
W. R. Dent, 1b
William Prince, 3b
G. Clark, ss
N. Clark, rf
F. Ford, cf
S. B. Carr, 2b
W. Boynton, lf

Colorado

Clippers
(Colorado Springs, CO)

George Motley, c
James West, p
James Carter, ss
Lige Walker, 1b
J. M. Booker, 2b
R. Moore, 3b
Fred Slaughter, cf
Fred Reed, rf
William Dean, p
Ed Stewart, c
J. G. Whitesell, c
Vendible, lf
William Dean, p

Giants
(Colorado Springs, CO)

Fred Reed, c
James West, p
George Motley, 1b
Booker, 2b / Captain
John Davis, 3b
James Carter, ss
Fred Slaughter, lf
Charles West, cf
Vendible, rf

Picked Nine
(Colorado Springs, CO)

John Watson, c
George Hackley, p
Williams, 1b
Comicker, 2b
Albert Largent, 3b
William Nelson, ss
W. J. Morris, lf
George Hackley, cf
Henry Grant, rf

Connecticut

Elm City
(New Haven, CT)

L. A. Fenderson, c
R. Wright, c
Charles Maxwell, c
George Jefferson, p / cf / Captain
Daniel Hurd, p / cf / rf
G. A. Stevens, 1b
W. Jefferson, 2b
F. Breckenridge, ss
W. Brown, 3b
J. Wilson, lf
James H. Allen, President
George Jefferson, Secretary
Kendrick Williams, Treasurer
John W. Murphy, Manager

Georgia

Vigilants (Thomasville, GA)

Billy Reid
Charles Sharp
Wash Jackson
Sam Banion
Abe Brown
James Bracewell
William Gray
John Sapp
Robert Ross
Sam Dixon

Illinois

Avondales (Chicago, IL)

James Thompson, 3b
Robert Shields, ss / 2b
John A. Meyer, p / lf / rf

Hasting V. Brown, c / rf
Hering, 2b / rf
Arthur Anderson, rf / p / lf
John Johnson, c / ss
Nicholson, 1b
Henry Wulff, c
Fred Hollis, 2b
Wisdom, cf
James Johnson, ss
Hume, p
Wilson, lf
Roderick, cf
McFarland, 1b
P. Thompson, cf / rf

Bar Boys (Chicago, IL)

Bruce West, p
William James, c
Boughton, 1b
George Foster, 2b
David Bradley, 3b
Stratten, ss
Charles "Charlie" Green, rf
William Malone, cf
J. Dehoney, lf / 3b
Joe Robertson, Manager

Crystals (Chicago, IL)

Richard Sheppard, p / cf
Joseph H. Wilson, c
Orange W. Fox, p / 3b / rf
Al Bob, 2b / p
George Wallace, 1b / 2b
R. Wilson, 2b / lf
Houseman, 3b
F. Montgomery, ss
Guy Hicks, Manager

Emergencies (Chicago, IL)

James Renfroe, p
F. Lewis, c
Franklin A. Denison, 1b
Frank B. Waring
David Bradley, ss
William T. Smith, sub
Julius N. Avendorph, Captain / 3b
David R. Lawrence, lf
Louis Smith, cf
Charles Washington, rf
Albert Hackley, 2b
William Albert Jones, c
Richard B. Harrison, 1b
Jessie Collier, ss / c
Bert Anderson, cf
Taylor, c
William T. "Big Boy" Smith, Substitute

Favorites (Chicago, IL)

Benjamin F. Sharp, p
D. Sharp, c
Toots Woodson, 1b
George Scott, 2b
William Hutchinson, 3b

Clarence Outland, ss
F. Lewis, rf
Wesley Parker, cf
M. Mitchell, lf
Chadwell, Manager

Letter Carriers
(Chicago, IL)

Orange W. Fox, c
Colwell, p
Peter Burns, 1b
Westberry, 2b
George Banks, 3b
Elliott, ss
William A. Sherill, rf
B. J. Yantis, cf
Combs, lf
N. Blackshear, Substitute
William Turner, Substitute

Lone Stars (Chicago, IL)

Bruce West, 1b
McNeal, rf / p
David Bradley, 2b
W. Mitchell, 3b / c
J. Mitchell, lf
Sides, cf
George Evans, ss / c
William James, c
Little, p
Charles "Chick" Green, p
Louis Smith, c

Oaklands (Chicago, IL)

James A. Carter, 2b
Frank Collier, 1b
Cook, ss
Chester, 3b
Solomon Taylor, p / c
Clement, lf
Kidd, p
Glass, rf
McAllister, cf

Oakleys (Chicago, IL)

Scotty, p
R. Lee, c / Captain
F. Lewis, 1b / c
B. Simpson, ss / lf
George Andrews, 3b / Captain
F. Washington, lf / 3b
T. Chilton, cf
Henry "Teenan" Jones, rf / p
J. Storrs, 1b
Charles Spears, ss
H. Baxter, lf
D. McGowan, cf
Joseph Adams, rf
F. King, 3b
C. Outland, p
F. Lewis, c
N. Peters, 1b / 3b
Charles Gardner, Substitute

F. Washington, Substitute
Bert T. French, 2b

Scottys (Chicago, IL)

R. Lee, p
F. Lewis, 1b
William Lancaster King, 2b
B. Simpson, ss
George Andrews, Captain / 3b
Charles M. Washington, lf
T. Chilton, cf
J. N. Jones, rf
George Scott, p / Manager

Tybells (Chicago, IL)

Condon, p / 3b
C. L. Hunt, lf
Dickinson, ss
Woods, 1b
E. King, 2b
F. White, rf
Harry Robinson, 3b / p
J. Taylor, cf
Pierce, c

Unions (Chicago, IL)

Albert Hackley, lf / cf / rf
Ed Woods, p / rf / c
Robert Foote, c / 1b / 3b
George W. Hopkins, p
Harry Hyde, 3b / 1b
S. Taylor, p
J. Taylor, c
Bert Jones, p
J. Woods, p / 3b
William Horn, p
Willis Jones, cf / rf / lf
David Wyatt, ss
Harry Buckner, p
Harry Moore, p / 1b / 2b
William Joyner, ss / lf
William T. Smith, 3b /p / rf / ss
Frank Butler, lf / p
George Foster, c / p
Charles Morgan, p
A. J. King, rf
Wordes, rf
P. D. Arnett, 1b
Lamar, lf
Fort, c
Moon, p
Schmidt, rf / p
William James
William "Bill" Gaynor
L. H. Bradley, Assistant Manager
William "Handsome Willie" Stitt Peters,
  1b / c / Manager

Union Reserves (Chicago, IL)

E. Taylor, 3b
William C. Smith, rf
Ed Wilson, cf
Frank Butler, lf

J. Taylor, 1b
Jessie Collier, ss
Fisher, 2b
Willis Jones, c
John Oglesby, p

Warrens (Chicago, IL)

Glendon, c / p
King, lf
Warrens, p
Sullivan, p
Hangdon, 1b
Barry, 2b
Carder, ss
Riley, 1b
O'Connell, 3b
McGraw, rf
Kelly, cf / rf
Lange, cf
Benjamin F. Sharp, lf
A. Lee, p
Pettebone, c
William Cobden, Manager

Hussars (Edwardsville, IL)

Charles Bradley
James Berry
Joseph Brown
Nathan Ward
Ernest Williams
Will Williams
Joseph Knox
Urgent Childers
Frank Jones
Arthur Samuels

Colored Nine (Rockford, IL)

Frank Ferguson, p
Charles Ferguson, c
William Holmes, 1b
Ed Lee, 2b
John Reddrick, 3b
Herbert "Sode" Tucker, ss
Fred Lewis, rf
M. Powell, cf
Chandler Baxter, lf

Nelson House (Rockford, IL)

S. Towser, p
W. Rogers, c
Walter Holloway, 1b
W. Emmeke, 2b
G. Brown, ss
Boston Powell, rf
J. Clark, cf
Robert "Bob" Miller, lf
William Harris, 3b

Black Diamonds
(Springfield, IL)

W. Parks, c
Eugene Blakeman, p
Sanders, ss

Henry Hodge, 1b
Frank Brandon, 2b
Payton, 3b
Ferguson, lf
Henry, rf
Davis, cf

Indiana

Silver Sprays (Connersville, IN)

F. Bryant, c
F. Jordon, p
Tom Rice, ss
George Bass, 1b
Tom Pierce, 2b
R. Demos, cf
B. Rice, rf
H. Norman, 3b
William Pierce, lf

Colored Nine (Jeffersonville, IN)

Ike Booker
Ed Booker
Dan Carter
James Parker
Joe Miller
Bert Campbell
W. O. Morgan
James Ferguson
Zeke Ray

London Creole Giants (Muncie, IN)

Harry Hyde, 3b
William Stewart, ss
Marshall Coffey, 2b
Jasper Dustan, 1b
William Daily, cf
Harry Satterfield, lf
Moses Cain, c
William Jackson, p
Sheppard Ware, p
Harry Buckner, p
Haywood Rose, c
Hart, p
Elwood DeMoss, rf
John Fowler, 2b / Manager

Reds (West Baden, IN)

Eugene Morton, c
Tom Morton, rf / p
Andy Dickson, ss
J. Tisdal, 1b
Lum Beacham, cf
Jonah Hardin, 2b
James Johnson, 3b
J. Gordon, lf
Henry Brown, p

Iowa

Colored Giants (Sioux City, IA)

Dangerfield Talbot, c

John South, cf
Walter Paris, p
Duval, ss
Williams, 3b
Charles Grant, rf
Louis Minor, lf
Johnson, 1b
Gray, 2b
Lew Hall, Manager

Kansas

Clippers (Coffeyville, KS)

Walter Brown, p
Alexander H. Scipio, c
Walter Carter, 2b
Horace Bledsoe, 1b
George Walker, 3b
Isaiah Donnelly, lf
John White, ss
James Roberts, cf
George W. Martin, rf
Lee Roan, Manager

Clippers (Atchison, KS)

Robert Carr
Joe Lewis
Charles Porter
John Price
Doe "Bud" Paine
Ward Johnson
Walter Booker
William Generals
Henry Whitney
Will Miller
William Gibson
Bert Jones

Rattlers (Wichita, KS)

Brent Anderson
Lake Anderson
Reed Anderson, ss / p
Syl Anderson, p
Charles Anderson, 1b
Robert Able, c
Frank Able, ss / c
H. Shears, lf / captain
Sam Harden, 3b
Frank Ray, c
William Green, ss / rf
Lacy Wood, 2b
Hawkins, cf
Holton, lf / p
Charley Strawn, p
Smith, c
George W. Robinson, Manager
William Betts, Manager

Kentucky

Brotherhoods (Louisville, KY)

W. H. Lee, lf
Elzy Hart, 2b

Napoleon Ricks, ss
Thomas O'Neal, cf
Moses Allen, 1b
Haywood Rose, c
Talbert, 3b
John Bowman, rf
Ward, p
Jackson, p
Marshall, p
Brown, 1b
Tom Means, rf
A. W. Stewart, Manager

Red Oaks (Louisville, KY)

Moses Clark, c
Marshall, p
Jesse Palmer, lf
Wallace, ss
Daniel Brown, 1b
Henry Clay, cf
H. C. "Dickey" Dickens, rf
Pierce, 3b
Evans, 2b

Louisiana

Allens (Carrollton, LA)

W. Brown, 2b
Robert Brooks, p
Joubert Lewis, rf / c
James Simpson, rf
J. B. Robertson, 1b
John Brady, ss
Joseph Ferrand, 1b / lf
Peter Lucien, cf
N. Ross, 2b
John Johnson, lf
Davidson, 1b
Davidson, 1b
Madison, ss
Colbert, 3b / p / rf
Gaspard Joseph, rf
Cottar, Substitute

Michigan

Page Fence Giants (Adrian, MI)

Grant Johnson, ss
William "Will" Binga, 3b
Peter Burns, c
George Taylor, 1b
Vasco Graham, rf
Charles Grant, 2b
George Wilson, lf
Fred Van Dyke, cf
William J. Holland, p
James Chavous, p / rf
Frank Miller, p / ss / c
Jackson, cf
Frank Waters, p / cf
Barnes, c

Missouri

Maroons (Kansas City, MO)

A. Brear
S. Bradley
Frank Maupin
James Monroe
S. Harris
John "Jack" Reeves
S. Searcey
B. Vaughn
Walter Sparks

Unions (Kansas City, MO)

William Smith, p
Sam Christian, c
S. Colbert, 1b
Peter Greenbury, 2b
Sawyers (Sayres), 3b
R. Smith, ss
Sublette, lf
B. Vaughn, cf
Long, rf

New Jersey

Pioneers (Bridgeton, NJ)

Claude Beam, lf
Nathan Gould, 2b
Frank Gould, ss
John Long, 3b
Andrew Pierce, cf
Eugene Williams, p
Oscar Brown, 1b
William Willis, lf
Howard Gross, c / ss
Wilbert Gross, c
Johns, rf
John Wesley Harris, p / Manager

Colored Nine (Trenton, NJ)

Titus
Tobolt
Vandegrift
Bennett
Baker
McGowan
Hunt
Stratton
Brooks, p
Burk, p

New York

Amateurs (Brooklyn, NY)

A. Purnell, c
W. Purnell, p
Chism, 1b
J. Buck, 2b
Little, 3b
Gilbert, rf
Johnston, cf
Williams, lf

Sands, ss
Charles Beale, 3b
Smith, ss

Niantic (Brooklyn, NY

D. L. Ross, lf
Bancroft, ss
John M. Watkins, c
John Paterson, lf
Miran, ss
Henderson, rf
Miller, cf
E. Schenk, 3b
McMann, 1b
Hultz, 2b
Stokes, 3b
Sam Bolden, ss
William Norman, p
Joseph Gaston, ss
Hugh McWinters, rf
Benjamin Brown, 1b

Cuban Giants (Geneva, NY)

George Martin, p
John Rowe, 1b / c
Charles Granston, 2b
Bert Hazzard, 3b
Herman F. Kinney, ss
John Cartwright, lf
Avery Griger, cf
W. Coleman, rf
Frank Davis, c
Arthur Kinney, p
F. Hardy, Manager

Cuban Giants (Long Island, NY)

Henry Gant, 2b
William Jackson, rf
Thomas White, 3b
John W. Patterson, 3b
Sheppard Trusty, cf
Abraham Harrison, ss
Frank Miller, p
Louis Smith, 1b
Solomon "Sol" White, 2b
George W. Stovey, p
William Selden, p
Bernard Jackson, lf
Andrew Jackson, c
Oscar Jackson, cf
Winslow Tyrrell, rf
Robert Jordan, c / 1b / lf
Taylor Smith, p / 1b
William Cole, c / p
William James, rf / p
Alexander Banks, 1b
Ray Wilson, 1b
Benjamin Brown, rf
Pearly Williams, c
William Williams, rf
James "Jim" Taylor, lf

Frank (Henson) Hinson, p
Jobe Trusty, p
Frank Grant, 3b
Can Moore
Whiton, ss
James D. Robinson, 1b
John Howard, ss / p
Lamar, c
Frustead, lf
William Farrell, ss

Gorhams (New York, NY)

Dan Penno, lf
Edward DeMund, 1b
Sam Bolan, ss
E. Schenck, 3b
Harry Styles, 2b / 3b
Alfred "Mundy" Jenkins, c
Craft, rf
William "Billy" Norman, p
William Singleton, p
M. Grady, c
Beckett, ss
Washington, 2b
Burgess, rf / p
Bancroft, p
William Freeman, rf
Richards, c
Joseph Gaston, ss
Henry Moore, cf
Benjamin Brown, cf / Manager

Cuban X-Giants (New York, NY)

N. Jackson, ss
Solomon White, 2b
Oscar Jackson, lf
Andrew Jackson, 3b
Robert Jackson, c / 1b
Clarence Williams, c
George Barton, rf
Ray Wilson, 1b
William H. Selden, p
Frank Hinson, p
Frank Miller, rf / p
John Nelson, p / ss / 2b
Dan Penno, 2b
George W. Stovey, p
William Williams, c / lf
J. W. Wilson, c / rf
Winslow Tyrrell, p / ss
Henry Catto, p
Ed Jackson, rf
John Milton Dabney, p / rf
Alexander Banks, p / cf
William Tennant, ss
William James, rf
Stanislau K. Govern, Manager

Uniques (Staten Island, NY)

Edward Demund, 1b
Washington, 2b

Henry Moore, 3b
Gaston, ss
Burgess, cf / p
Beckett, lf
Andrew Randolph, rf
Bancroft, p
Richards, c
Smith, Substitute

Fearless (Utica, NY)

Frank Peresett, c
Charles Walter Titus, p / Manager
J. W. Anderson, 1b / c
Edward Cleghorn, 2b
Henry Moss, 3b
Walter Pell, ss
Slavin, lf
Jackson, cf
William McIntyre, rf
Moses Gray, c
Kingsley, p

Butterfield House (Utica, NY)

Kinsella, c
McMullen, p
Curtis, p
James Pell, 2b
O'Brien, 3b
Frank Pell, lf
David Van Alstine, cf
Peter Henry, rf / c
Theodore Pell, ss

North Carolina

Quicksteps (Charlotte, NC)

John Brown, 1b / lf
Julius Holt, c
C. Robertson, 2b / c
John Pharr, 3b
Rufus Williams, ss / p
White, lf / cf
Edward Torrence, cf
John Harris, rf / Captain
Charles Wortham, 1b
T. Hall, ss
Toole Gray, 2b
O. Hall, rf
L. D. Hayes, Secretary
J. S. Coles, Manager

Black Stockings (Wilmington, NC)

John Phillips, ss
George Stevenson, 2b
John Gause, c
William McRae, ss / Treasurer
William "Black Cat" McQueen, cf
William Moseley, lf
John Pharr, rf
Campbell, p

Fred Love, 1b
James Addison, p
George Simmons, rf / Secretary
Thomas James, cf
James Walker, lf / rf
William Schenk, 3b / Captain / Manager

Blue Shirts (Greensboro, NC)

Campbell, p / 2b
Gillmore, c / lf
W. Nelson, cf
Morehead, rf
Wright, 3b
D. Carsey, c / 1b / ss
J. Carsey, 2b
H. Nelson, lf
B. Carsey, ss / 1b
Lewis Cameron, p

Ohio

H.A.C. (Cleveland, OH)

John "Jack" Dean, 2b
William Lyons (Lines), cf
Zimmer, ss
William Craig, rf
J. Sherman Larkin, lf
William H. Wilson, 3b
David Wyatt, c
R. B. Kelly, 1b
Edward Turner, p
C. H. Stump, p

Hollendens (Cleveland, OH)

J. Moss, p / 1b
K. L. Nelson, c
Thomas Wallace Fleming, p
Moxley
Al Dennie, lf
P. Poindexter, 2b
John "Jack" Dean, rf
Ed "Inkspot" Williams, p
H. Cole, lf / rf
William Pittman, lf / cf
J. Earley, c / 1b
John Jackson, p
James Jackson, c
Storie, cf
Alexander Frye, c
Charles "Charlie" Griffin, 1b
Taylor, ss
Edward Turner, 3b / Manager

Kennards (Cleveland, OH)

James Weaver, 3b
A. Kuehne, c
M. Stevens, 1b / 2b
B. Smith, p
J. Smith, 2b
F. Kuehne, ss
William Graves, rf

Charles Howard, cf
Robert Davis, lf
L. Jackson, rf
R. Hollenbeck, lf
T. Riley, c
William Smith, p

Keystones (Cleveland, OH)

James Gaines, lf / cf
William Gales, cf / 3b
R. B. Kelley, 1b
Robert Davis, ss / lf
John "Jack" Dean, 2b / lf
Thomas Smith, cf / p / rf
Fred Wilson, 3b / ss
William Craig, rf / cf
Connel, c
John Jackson, p
Wallace, 2b
J. Moss, 1b
William H. Cole, c
Ed "Inkspot" Williams, 3b
Jack Pleasant, rf
Hutchins, 2b / 3b
William A. Colwell, c
Goodman, 3b
William Lyons, cf / rf
Zimmer, ss
Allen, rf
W. Arthur Goines, rf / 2b
Clarence R. Gordon, 3b
J. Thomas, p
David Wyatt, lf / rf / cf
C. H. Stump, p
Willie Carroll, c
Nokes
Pierson, 2b
Brodie, lf
William A. Johnson, Manager

Unions (Cleveland, OH)

Frank Henderson, p / c
Horace Gibbs
M. Scott
John Redman
Powell, p
C. H. Stump
S. McPherson
H. McPherson
George H. Ricks
Curtiss
Kuth
Haffa
Moyer
Charles McAfee
George Dunn
Walworth Drayton
F. J. Sellers, p

West Ends (Cleveland, OH)

Goodman, 3b
W. Lyons (Lines), cf

W. Craig, 2b
Zimmer, ss / 2b
William H. Cole, c
David Wyatt, lf
C. H. Stump, p
R. B. Kelly, 1b
Allen, rf
Thomas, p

Colored Barbers
(East Liverpool, OH)

Charles Howard, p/1b
James Brown, c
Elmer Good, 2b
John Henderson, c
Pete Lyons, p
John Bell, ss
Francis Prior, 1b
George Johnson, 3b
P. S. Smith, lf
Walter Allen, cf
Alexander Vaughn, rf
"Foggy" Miller, p
William H. Miller, c

Keystones (Piqua, OH)

Willie White
Joseph McKnight
G. Moss
M. Brown
B. Williams
Albert Bailey
Lon Smith
John Clay
Fred Wilson
W. A. Johnson, Manager

Pennsylvania

Cross Cuts (Altoona, PA)

Howard Gordon, 3b
William Love, 2b
Samuel Lyles, 1b
Luke Moore, c
Charles Knox, lf
George W. Benson, ss
J. W. Alexander, p
Charles Holmes, cf
Taylor Jones, lf
John Cox, Substitute
Gassett, Substitute
Charles Hall, Manager

Anchor (Philadelphia, PA)

Ransome, 1b
Aaron Carmile, lf
Minners, p
William A. Farrell, c
Alfred Jenkins, 2b
William Banks, ss
Thomas G. Kane, rf
W. Shorts, cf
A. J. Sellers, 3b

Giants (Pinkney, PA)

Alfred "Mundy" Jenkins, c
Fred Myers, c
Gus Matthews, lf / 2b
Wilson Brooks, c
W. Shorts, rf
Courtney, ss
Edward Lodine, 3b
C. Murray, rf
Paul Harris, 2b
William Adams, cf
W. Butler, p
J. Vincent, cf
Mattson, lf
Brown, 1b
William Jackson, c
Coleman, 1b / p

Consumers (Scranton, PA)

George Brown, p
D. Norton, ss
Sam Smith, 1b
Fred Stevenson, 2b
Fred Neumis, 3b / Captain
William Jones, ss
George Pierce, rf
Frank Williams, cf
Charles E. Simpson, p
D. Battles, p / c / 2b
Austin, Substitute
Robert "Boo" Payne, Manager

Flurory's Cuban Giants
(Williamsport, PA)

Javan Isaac Emory, c
D. Battles, p
Sims Emory, 1b
Henson, 2b
Baker, 3b
E. Watson, ss
George W. Stovey, lf
William H. Reed, cf
Johnson, rf
Joseph Allison, c

Monarchs (York, PA)

Charles Rhodes, c
George Bolden, p
Clayton Cannon, 2b
Robert Dorsey, 3b
William Mills, ss
Charles Pickney, rf / c
James Finney, lf
Harry Harris, cf
Lincoln Harris, cf
John Joice, 3b

Texas

Tigers (Dallas, TX)

Davis, 2b
George Weathers, p

Simeon Weathers, 3b
Williams, 1b
Cecil, cf
John W. Simon, lf / p
Tyler, ss
Pitman, rf
Bowe, c
Scott, 3b
Wheeler, p
Williams, lf
J. G. Griffin, Manager

Fencibles (Galveston, TX)

Henry Burrell, c
D. Taylor, c
William H. Nobles, p
C. Cage, p
George Jones, 1b
William Simmons, 2b
Milton Turner, 3b
James Blair, ss
William Bailey, lf
William Bryant, cf
Charles Mills, rf

Fly Aways (Galveston, TX)

C. J. Williams, c
William Bryant, p
Joseph Walker, 1b
Abraham Coleman, rf
E. Coleman, 2b
James Blair, 3b
Nat Shackelford, ss
M. Walker, lf
Robert Hennessey, rf
Clarence Carter, cf
Johnny Jones, 3b

Alamo Grays
(San Antonio, TX)

Lee Mitchell, 3b
Wiley Haywood, ss
H. Fred Poulin, 2b
Early, p / rf
Frank Itson, 1b
B. Miller, lf / p
William Bird, cf
Anderson Washington, c
Bradford Norman, lf
Ed Patterson, cf / p
Rube Tucker, 2b / p

Yellow Jackets (Waco, TX)

Duval, c
Travis Irving, p
Willis, 1b
McClennan, 2b
Smith, 3b
Gray, ss
Henderson Caldwell, lf
Clarence Carter, rf
Mason, cf / p

Virginia

Red Stockings
(Norfolk, VA)

Dan McClennan, c
Smith, c
Thomas Wright, p
James Lewis, p
James H. Harrison, p
William Parker, 3b
Wash Stewart, ss
William Johnson, 2b
Hill, lf
"Snide" Moseley, cf
Hodges, rf
George White, 1b / Manager

Hygeia Giants
(Old Point, VA)

Matthews, ss
Lyles, cf
Tarleton, 3b
Brown, rf
Cooper, 1b
Maven, p
Rogers, 2b
Martin, lf
Sutton, c

Granite Leagues
(Petersburg, VA)

Cranley, cf
Jackson, ss
Hill, 3b / c
Lewis, 1b
Lynch, lf
Parham, p
Thomas, rf
Johnson, 2b
Hastings, c / 3b

Eclipse Gray Jackets
(Richmond, VA)

Woody, 1b
Miles Page, 2b
Moses Robinson, c
Jeff "Kid" Price, p
Hickman Price, lf
James H. Lee, ss
William H. Harrison, 3b
W. Lightfoot, lf / p
John Morton, 2b
Timothy Freeman, 3b
John White, 1b
Pagey Morris, rf
Moses Robinson, c
C. P. Robinson, cf / Captain
Thomas H. Jackson, rf / Manager

Colored Nine (Roanoke, VA)

Stewart, cf
B. Walls, ss
Anderson, p

"Bub" Baker, 2b
Goodson, cf
Brooks, lf
Sheverly, rf
Douley, c
Edwards, 3b

West Virginia

H. C. Richards (Wheeling, WVA)

Bryant, c
Howard Newby, p
Arthur Branson, 1b
Davis, 2b
William Monroe, ss
Elsworth Branson, p
Louis Jackson, 3b
John Sawyer, lf
Harvey Roy, cf
M. Scott, lf
George Johnson, c / cf
William Cunningham, s
Ernie Branson, Substitute

Experts (Wheeling, WVA)

Bryant, c
Howard Newby, p
Arthur Branson, 1b
Davis, 2b
William Monroe, ss
Elsworth Branson, p
Louis Jackson, 3b
John Sawyer, lf
Harvey Roy, cf
M. Scott, lf
George Johnson, c
William Cunningham, ss

Washington, DC

Howard University
(Washington, DC)

Ed Morrison, Captain / c
F. W. Avant, 1b
R. Hughes, 2b
C. M. Butler, ss
B. S. Jackson, rf
C. I. Smith, cf
W. O. Bundy, lf
George Garner, p
W. W. West, p
J. W. Enos, p
Joseph Rapier, c
W. E. Carter, Substitute
Prof. C. C. Cook, Substitute

Ideals (Washington, DC)

John F. Henson, p
Benjamin Moore, p
A. Atkinson, c
Howard Diggs, c
Lafayette Jefferson, 1b
Walter Countee, 2b

William Newton, 3b
William Bird, ss
Moses Hipkins, lf
Cox, cf
Joseph Anderson, rf / 3b

Market House (Washington, DC)

William Newton, 3b
John F. Henson, p
Benjamin Moore, p
Moses Hipkins, lf
Louis Phillips, p
E. A. Atkinson, 2b / lf
George Betters, ss
Charles S. Payne, 2b / 3b
Joseph Anderson, cf
Countee, 2b
Tom Wade, lf / p
Lafayette Jefferson, 1b / Manager

Pat Smiths (Washington, DC)

W. Haley, c
G. Monday, p
Harry Wallace, 1b
Joseph Campbell, 2b
John Wallace, ss / Secretary
U. Mason, 3b
P. Carter, rf
H. Mason, cf
Shorty Frank, lf

1897

Arizona

Colored Nine (Phoenix, AZ)

W. J. Anderson, Manager
Perry Polk, Captain
Ed Thomas, Secretary
J. W. Bolton, Treasurer

Arkansas

Arlingtons (Hot Springs, AR)

Fertiller, p / rf
Henry Lewis, c
Davis, cf
Childs, p / lf
Hardy, 3b
Murphy, c
John Patillo, p / rf
Huff, cf
Rowell, c / ss
Fields, p / 2b / 3b
Arthur Greer, p / c
Spencer, p
Williams, c
Jackson, p

Quapaws (Little Rock, AR)

R. Butler, 2b
B. Butler, ss
McClure, 3b

Richardson, 1b
Keaton, p
W Crawford, c
Reed, lf
F. Crawford, rf
Prince, cf
Goodwin, p / c
Houston, c / p
D. Stafford, c
Robinson, p / rf
John Stoball, p / rf
James Williams, p

California

Trilbys (Los Angeles, CA)

Robert Shaw, p
Lucius Alexander, c / cf / p / 2b / 3b / Manager
Lige Walker, 3b
A. Anderson, lf
William Nettles, 1b
Harry Brown, ss / rf
Henry Grant, rf
F. White, 1b
Benjamin Perkins, 2b / 3b
William Carroll, c / ss
E. Johnson, p / rf
G. Johnson, lf / cf / 3b
John Majors, 3b / p
E. D. Johnson, rf / p
R. Moore, p / cf
E. Gardner, rf
Maxwell, rf / 2b
James Bullock, lf / rf
Joseph Marrione, ss / 2b / 3b
Paul A. Brothers, ss
Bankhead, 3b

Colorado

Clippers (Colorado Springs, CO)

Vendible, lf
George Motley, c
John Watson, rf
James Carter, ss
R. Moore, 3b
J. M. Booker, 2b / Captain
T. Carter, cf
James West, 1b / c
Fred Slaughter, p

Pastimes (Colorado Springs, CO)

John H. Wash, c
Fred Slaughter, p
George Motley, 1b
Booker, 2b
James Carter, ss
R. Moore, 3b
Vendible, lf
Thomas Carter, cf
John Watson, rf / c

Connecticut

Gorhams (Waterbury, CT)

Dan Penno, p
John M. Watkins, c
Sam Bolan, ss
John W. Patterson, 1b
Hugh McWinters, cf
George Schenck, 2b
Jones, 3b
J. Buck, lf
Jones, rf
Ross Garrison, rf

Georgia

Fats (Macon, GA)

Hubbard Lanier, c
J. D. Wilder, p
Will Harris, 2b
Mose Green, 3b
Kirk Bayne, ss
Gus Terrell, lf
Morris Hill, cf
T. B. Irwin, rf
W. A. Smith, Substitute
Thomas Jackson, Substitute
James A. Rollins, Captain

Leans (Macon, GA)

Jeff Clemons, p
William Demerest, c
Frank Disroon, 1b
William Melton, 2b
F. C. Jackson, rf
R. L. Ross, ss
George Hamilton, 3b
James Waver, cf
J. T. Mitchell, lf
W. O. Coleman, Substitute
N. C. Appling, Manager

Illinois

Clippers (Chicago, IL)

Bruce West, 3b
Charles Green, c / rf
James Smith, p / 3b
David Bradley, 2b / 3b / ss
Frank Butler, lf / p
P. D. Arnett, cf / lf
Harry Buckner, ss
Mansfield, p / 3b
Robert Shaw, 1b
John Oglesby, p / rf / 2b
William "Billy" Holland, p
William S. Peters, 1b / rf / 3b / c
N. Peters, 1b / 3b
Frank Griggs, 2b / ss / lf
Spruce, rf
Robert Foote, c
George Foster, 2b
Robert "Bob" Ward, c

Jesse Collier, ss
Bert Jones, 1b
Little, cf
Peter Cobb, rf / p
Crooks, rf
Jackson, p

Emergencies (Chicago, IL)

Charles M. Washington
Albert Hackley
Jessie Collier, c
David R. Lawrence
William J. Renfroe, p / rf
James Smith, 2b
Joe Shoecraft, ss
Frank B. Waring
Franklin M. Denison
George Taylor, 1b / rf
Louis Anderson, p / c / lf
Harry C. Jackson, 3b
Julius N. Avendorph, 3b / Manager

Flippers (Chicago, IL)

Bruce West, 3b
Charles "Charlie" Green, rf
William Smith, 2b
Robert Shaw, p
David Bradley, ss
Frank Butler, lf
George Evans, c
Benjamin "Benny" F. Sharp, 1b
Harry Buckner, 3b / ss
William Eugene James, c
P. D. Arnett, cf / Manager

Orientals (Chicago, IL)

Scales, p
Morgan, c
Spruce, 1b
Smith, p
Frank Griggs, ss
George Foster, 1b
David Bradley, 2b / ss
Harry Buckner, 3b
Charles Green, lf / rf
Frank Butler, cf / lf
M. Mitchell, rf / lf
Robert P. Jackson, ss
William James, c
Robert Shaw, p

Unions (Chicago, IL)

Robert Shaw, p
Robert Foote, c / p / lf
Louis Reynolds, 1b
Harry Moore, 2b / lf / p
Harry Hyde, 3b
Willis Jones, lf / rf / c
William C. Smith, cf
Bert Jones, p / rf
George W. Hopkins, p / 2b
William J. Holland, ss
P. D. Arnett, rf

Harry Buckner, p
Charles E. Williams, 2b / ss
Ed Woods, p
William Carroll, c / 1b
Robert Jackson, c / 1b
H. Jackson, p
William T. Smith, c
William "Bill" Joyner, rf
Frank C. Leland, Secretary

Indiana

Governor Street High School
(Evansville, IN)

Matt Mitchell
Frank Grey
James Sheldon
Lige Sorden
Clarence Jones
William Gordon
J. N. Robinson
Benjamin Goodwin
Edwin Killdrew

Colored Nine
(Gibsonville, IN)

Armstead B. Brown, c
David G. Brown, p
W. W. Allen, 1b
John L. Clemons, 2b
Samuel Willis, 3b
John Thornton, Captain / ss
F. Crondup, lf
Will Jackson, cf
Ed Brooks, rf
Pud English, Substitute
Earnest Allen, Substitute
Aaron Clay, Substitute
Richard, Manager
Kelley, Manager

Colored Nine
(Jeffersonville, IN)

Albert Boarman, c
Robert Boarman, p
Charles Webb, 1b
James Woodforth, 2b
Evans Morrison, ss / Manager
Sam Willis, 3b
Joe Strange, lf / Manager
Willie Smith, cf
Burl Hayden, rf
Willie Talkoner, Substitute
Robert Bowman, Captain

Up-To-Dates
(Logansport, IN)

William Henry Harrison Childs, cf
Harry "Battle Axe" Brown, ss
Harry Gilmore, p
Keene, rf
George Hill, 3b
James A. Carter, 2b

Matthew Carter, 1b
George Parker, 1b
A. Winslow, lf
Charles S. Jones, c / Manager

Reds (West Baden, IN)

John Hardin, ss
J. Johnson, lf
Jonah Hardin, 2b
Alexander, cf
Eugene King, c
Stevenson, 1b
Briscoe, 3b
J. J. "Strat" Dupee, rf
George Wilson, p

Kansas

Athletics (Abilene, KS)

Lake Anderson
Charlie Anderson
Syl Anderson
Henry Shears
Fred Hutton
Burrell Anderson
Fred Dunavin
William Woods
Strong

Clippers (Coffeyville, KS)

W. D. Driver, c
James Roberts, p
Sam Bledsoe, 1b
Walter Carter, 2b
Horace Bledsoe, 3b
John White, ss
Isaiah Donnelly, rf
Hayes Jones, cf
Lemuel Martin, rf
Alexander H. Scipio, c
Lee Roan, Manager

Kentucky

Brotherhood
(Louisville, KY)

Moses Clark, c
Haywood Rose, c / 2b
John Bowman, p
Masterson, p
Daniel Brown, 1b
Lee Halton (Holton), 2b
Napoleon Ricks, ss
Marshall, p
Tom Means, 3b
Webb, 3b
W. H. Lee, ss/lf
Ward, cf
Wallace, rf
Dey, lf
Moses Allen, cf
George Talbott, rf
A. W. Stewart, Manager

Olymps (Louisville, KY)

I. English, lf
William Kelly, cf
S. Ballard, rf
W. Gordon, 3b
A. Smith, 2b
G. Barrett, 1b
J. Murphy, ss / Captain
J. Rilmer, c
T. Williams, c
B. Mason, p
B. Taylor, p
A. Ross, p
R. Hill, ss
O. T. Adams, Manager

Louisiana

Allens (Carrollton, LA)

Robert Brooks, p
Joubert Lewis, rf / c
J. B. Robertson, 1b
John Brady, ss
Joseph Ferrand, 1b / lf
Peter Lucien, cf
N. Ross, 2b
Davidson, 1b
Madison, ss
Colbert, 3b / p / rf
Gaspard Joseph, rf
Cottar, Substitute

Dan Kings
(New Orleans, LA)

Francis Joseph, p
Joe Louis, c
N. Ross, 1b
L. Ross, 2b
Otto Vinne, 3b
Arron "Kid" Wiley, ss
Cribbons, rf
John Calaborn (Claiborne), cf
Alfred Tarker (Parker), lf

Maryland

Cliftons (Annapolis, MD)

H. E. Spriggs, c
J. Stephaney, p
J. Pomter, 1b
W. Addison, 2b
H. Hill, ss
J. C. Darnell, 3b
J. Miller, lf
George Collins, cf
Thomas Gray, rf
Samuel Davage, Captain
Wallace Parker, Manager

Cuban Giants
(Baltimore, MD)

Tilghman, rf
Lewis, 2b

Charles Calder, 3b
Henry Savoy, cf
Ed Chamberlain, 1b
William Farrell, c
P. Pinder, ss
Harry Buckner, p
Robert Pinder, lf

Pennsylvanias
(Baltimore, MD)

Tilghman, lf
Lewis, 2b
Charles Calder, 3b
Henry Savoy, cf
Ed Chamberlain, 1b / ss
Farrell, c / 1b
Robert Pinder, ss
Harry Buckner, p
Joshua Rogers, rf / cf
Reynolds, c
Thomas, rf
William T. Jordan, Manager

Michigan

Page Fence Giants
(Adrian, MI)

William "Billy" Holland, lf
John W. Patterson, 3b
J. Grant Johnson, ss / Captain
George Taylor, 1b
Peter Burns, c
William Binga, cf
Charles Grant, 2b
Robert Shaw, p
Joe Miller, rf / p
George Wilson, p
Ed Woods, cf
Sherman Barton, cf
William Johnson, Jr., lf
A .S. Parsons, Manager

Minnesota

Douglass (St. Paul, MN)

A. M. Lee, p
C. H. Miller, c
Willie Williams, 1b
George Bailey, 2b
Harp Franklin, 3b
Andrew Combs, ss
R. Farr, lf
John Kelley, cf
Willie Greene, rf
Hall, p / c
John Howard, p
C. M. Tibbs, Manager

Missouri

Maroons (Kansas City, MO)

A. Brear
S. Bradley

Frank Maupin
James Monroe
S. Harris
John "Jack" Reeves
S. Searcey
B. Vaughn
Walter Sparks

Colored Nine (Macon, MO)

Billy Mason, rf
Kid Higbee, cf
Bunch Smith, lf
Bert Barbour, 2b
William Oliver, 3b
Parks, ss
Rutherford Brothers, c
Bobbie Enix, p
Tiger Gray, p
E. T. Barbour, Team Captain
William Allen, 1b / Manager

New Jersey

Colored Giants
(Bridgeton, NJ)

Fields, 3b / cf
Lee, 2b
Clarence Wright, lf
Cass, ss
Samuel Bond, cf / rf
Williams, p / lf
Wilbert Gross, c / ss / p
Oscar Brown, lb
Morton, lf / p
Paul Saxton, 2b / c
Fred Berry, rf
T. Pierce, 3b
P. Winder, Manager

Belmont (Jersey City, NJ)

William Freeman, c
R. McGraw, p / lf / 3b
Johnson, p / lf / ss
King. 1b
W. Bell, ss / p
W. McCoy, 3b
Ponder, lf / 3b
John M. Watkins, 2b
Lewis, cf

Colored Giants (Newark, NJ)

Norwood Turner, ss
Valentino, p
William Freeman, 3b
John Meade, 1b
Gustavus Ray, c / rf
Paul Harris, 2b
Albert Maize, ss
W. Bell, p
Riker, lf
William Jackson, cf
R. McGraw, rf
Sam Bolden, rf / c

Walter McCoy, 2b / lf
Charles Beal, c / lf
Van Doran, rf
James Moorman, cf / p
Andrew Watson, 2b / c / Captain
Joseph Laveign, Manager

Cuban Giants (Newark, NJ)

Norwood Turner, ss
William Freeman, 3b
William Jackson, 1b / c
Gustavus Ray, c / rf
W. Bell, lf / c
Sam Bolden, rf / c
Walter McCoy, 2b
Charles Beal, c / lf
James Moorman, cf / p

Metropolitans (Newark, NJ)

Conlon, cf
Turnbull, 2b
Kay, rf
William Kelley, 1b
Goodrich, lf
Thomas, c
Donald, ss
Watson, 3b
James Moorman, p
Jacobus, rf

Colored Giants
(Princeton, NJ)

Henry Simpson, 1b
Peter Richmond, 2b
William Scudder, c
A. Miller, lf
James Simpson, cf
E. Freeman, ss
Jesse Hoagland, 3b
Joseph James, p
R. Washington, rf
J. Scudder, ss

New York

Colored Giants (Brooklyn, NY)

M. R. Ross, 3b
Hugh McWinters, lf
Hutchins, ss
Williams, rf
Bryant, cf / p
Patterson, 1b
Sam Bolan, 2b
John Watkins, c
Christopher, p / rf
J. Buck, cf / p
Brown, p
Stewart, p
Fagan, c

Genuine Cuban Giants
(Johnston, NY)

Frank Grant, ss
Ross Garrison, ss

William Malone, 2b
Frank Miller, rf / p / 1b
W. Robinson, p
Solomon "Sol" White, 2b
Abraham Harrison, rf / ss
William Barton, p
Ross Jordan, c
William Jackson, c / cf
John Howard, 3b
Alfred Jupiter, p
William Jones, lf
Eddie Day, c / p
William Gailey, cf
Louis Smith, lf
William H. Cole, p / c
Beckett, rf
Edgerton, ss
Tom Wade, cf / 2b
Smart, ss
Benjamin Brown, rf
Joe Stuart, ss
Robert Shaw, p
Robert Wilson, c
Richard Phillips, p
Clarence Sampson, lf
William Moulton, 1b
Mechez, p
Gordon, c
G. Grant, ss
Perrin, rf
James, p
James Manning, p
Thomas C. Schenk, cf / 3b
Edward DeMund, 1b
John Mickey, p / rf
Pete Hill, 3b
Pickett, p
William Frank, Assistant Manager

Cuban-X Giants
(New York, NY)

William Jackson, ss / cf
Clarence Williams, c
Oscar Jackson, rf
Raymond Wilson, rf / 1b
Andrew Jackson, 3b
William Barton, 2b / p / rf
Robert Jackson, rf
William Kelley, ss
William Selden, p / lf
George W. Stovey, p
Winslow Tyrrell, ss / p
John Nelson, p
Solomon "Sol" White, 2b
William Williams, c / lf
Sully James, 2b
Lamar, cf

Douglass
(Rochester, NY)

Fred Gilmore, Manager
Albert Thomas, Treasurer

Henry Thomas, Secretary
John Rowe, Team Captain

Help Up *(Utica, NY)*

Walter Pell, ss
Peter Henry, p
Charles Lippin, c
Martin, 3b
Albert Jackson, 2b
T. Henry, 1b
Harry Moss, lf
Charles W. Titus, cf
James DeNike, p / rf
Roscoe Anderson
Floyd Peresett, c
Brietenstein, p
Mose Gray, c / Manager

North Carolina

Mutuals *(Wilmington, NC)*

Fred T. Gause, c
Sam Addison, p
William Schenck, 1b / c
Betts, 3b
John Phillips, ss
William McQueen, rf
Thaddeus Tate, cf
James Walker, lf
George Stevenson, 2b / Captain
John W. Lee, Manager

Quicksteps *(Charlotte, NC)*

John Brown, 1b
Robertson, 2b
Holt, c
John Pharr, rf
Edward Torrence, cf
White, lf
James Daniels, p
John Harris, Captain
J. R. Williams, Secretary
Rufus Williams, ss / Manager / Team
    Captain
J. D. Coles, Manager
Allen, 3b / Manager
L. D. Hayes, Secretary

Ohio

Hollendens *(Cleveland, OH)*

John Jackson, p / c / rf
J. Earley, c / 1b
Al Dennie, lf
Walworth Drayton
John "Jack" Dean
Campbell
Smith, p
Thompson, p
Randolph, 1b
S. McPherson, c / rf
David Wyatt, cf
William Pittman, ss

Ed "Inkspot" Williams, 3b
Edward Turner, p
H. Turner, rf
Frank Henderson,
K. L. Nelson, 2b / c
George Sampson, 1b

Kennards *(Cleveland, OH)*

Jack Pleasant, 2b
J. Smith, ss
William Ferguson, c
William E. Smith, 3b
Keeney, 1b
John Brown, cf
Cuddy, lf
Wright, rf
Earson, p
Cooper, Substitute
John B. Hunter, Substitute

Keystones *(Cleveland, OH)*

William M. Craig, lf / c
Ashbury Larkin, rf
A. Colwell, c
Harry Hart, lf
William H. Cole, c
Ben Randolph, 1b
Thomas Queen, lf
J. Thomas, p
Cary White, 2b / lf / ss
J. Early, 1b / c
Robert Colwell, 3b / p
J. Moss, 2b / 1b
W. Porter, 2b
Weems, p
Edward "Inkspot" Williams, 3b / p
McPherson, lf
John Jackson, 2b
Dammon, p
J. Andrews
C. Wocton
William Pittman
Edward Turner, 3b / p

Horseshoes *(Newark, OH)*

Robert Brown, 1b
James "Jim" Taylor, 2b
James Hogan, 3b
Bert Craig, cf
Cliff Toney, rf
William Terry, lf
Burt "U.S." Craig, p
Oliver Collins, c
Robert Davis, ss
Ross Johnson
Mose Price, c / 2b
Harry Toney, ss
Frank Ransom, lf
Fred Herman
Robert "Bob" Murphy
Ben Thornton

Sureshots (Newark, OH)

James Fouse, 1b
Fred Hessenaur, 2b
William Gray, 3b
C. B. Swan, cf
Peter Good, rf
Nat Goines, lf
Harry Toney, p
Mose Price, c
Robert "Bob" Lee, ss

Northside (Steubenville, OH)

William Burdy, 1b
Edward Bolden, 2b
Andrew Guy, 3b / 1b
George Bolden, rf / lf
George Scott, cf
William Scott, ss / Captain
Charles Linden, c
Samuel Burke, p
Joseph McCullough, lf / 2b
William Green, c / ss / 2b
John Redman, rf
George Meyers, Substitute
N. McCullough, Substitute
Charles Porter, Substitute
Stanley Howard, Substitute
Samuel S. Clement, Manager

Southside (Steubenville, OH)

Louis Fletcher, ss
Lorenzo Howard, rf / lf
Harry Bowman, 3b
Robert Fletcher, cf
Samuel Thomas, 2b
Melvin Christian, lf
Rufus Gilliam, c
J. M. Ford, Captain / 1b
John Cowans, p
Garfield Christian, ss
Harry Fletcher, rf
Thomas Ferris, Substitute
Carter Smith, Substitute
Bud Woods, Substitute
Mark Ford, Manager

Pennsylvania

Midnight Stars (Canonsburg, PA)

Granville McGant, c / Secretary
Samuel Wilson, pitcher
Lee Wheeler, ss
John Robinson, 1b
George Sherrow, 2b
John Robinson, 1b
William Walter James, rf
Thomas Brown, cf
Hugh L. Hickey, ss
Charles Skinner, lf

James Kennedy, p
Robert Brown, Substitute
Roy E. Sluby, 3b / Manager

Cuban Giants (Harrisburg, PA)

William Banks, p / Captain
Barnetts, c
Jones, ss
Clarence Williams, 1b
A. Baxter, 2b
A. Reed, 3b
Wilson, lf
William Pickney, cf
Brown, rf
Benjamin Smith, Manager

Marines (Harrisburg, PA)

William Banks, p / Captain
Barnetts, c
Horace Murray, c
Jones, ss
Clarence Williams, 1b
A. Baxter, 2b
A. Reed, 3b
Wilson, lf
William Pickney, cf
Brown, rf
Benjamin Smith, Manager

Tennessee

Cliffords (Memphis, TN)

Johnson, cf
Jackson, 2b
A. J. King, 1b
Robert Higgins, ss
Charles M. Washington, rf
Mansfield, 3b
Miller, p
Frank Bell, c
Robert "Bob" Ward, lf / cf
John Oliver, c
Peter Cobb, p
Allen, cf
Sam Pointer, lf
James Tierney, ss

Texas

Fencibles (Galveston, TX)

Samuel Anderson, p
D. Taylor, c / p
George Jones, 1b / rf
Henry Vincent, 2b / 1b
Milton Turner, 3b
William Simmons, ss
William Bailey, lf
Charles Mills, rf / cf
Henry Burrell, cf / 2b / Manager
W. H. Noble, Assistant Manager
Jesse De Bruhl, Assistant Manager

Fly Aways (Galveston, TX)

A. Campbell, c
William Bryant, p
H. Lee, 1b
George Upps, 2b
Abraham Coleman, 3b
James Blair, ss
P. Coleman, lf
Bud Walker, cf
Robert Hennessey, 1b
C. J. Williams, rf
Ransome, cf

Rosebuds (Houston, TX)

Samuel Anderson, p
D. Taylor, c
George Jones, 1b
Henry Vincent, 2b
Milton Turner, 3b
William Simms, ss
William Bailey, lf
Johnny Jones, 3b
Thes Fletcher, rf
Charles Mills, rf
Ramsey "Chattanooga", p
Henry Burrell, cf / Manager
James Hickey, Manager

Utah

Browns (Salt Lake City, UT)

Adams, lf
Reid, 2b
Thomas Countee, ss / 3b
Loving, 1b
Armstrong, 3b / lf
Corbin, cf / 3b
Hollems, rf
Wheeler, c / rf
Harris, cf
Jackson, rf / c
Hughes, ss
Richards, p

City Team (Salt Lake City, UT)

M. E. Mulvey, c / Captain
John Allen, p
R. P. Morris, 1b
B. T. Lloyd, 2b
E. M. LeProhon, 3b
J. J. Stuart, ss
George Olson, cf
Jack May, rf
W. A. McKay, lf

Monarch (Salt Lake City, UT)

Ford, c / Captain
Howell, p
Fred Reed, 2b
Alloy Jackson

Thomas, ss
Mitchell, 3b
Townsend, rf
Henderson, cf
Thurmond, rf
Hall, p
Flowers, lf
Horace Wilds, c
Charles Hill, Captain
J. J. Bamberger, Manager
A. H. Grice, Asst. Manager

Virginia

Red Stockings (Norfolk, VA)

"Bub" Walker
George White
William Parker
George Wright
Walter Cason
Amos Cason
Wash Stewart
Ed Dobsey
Sidney Fentriss
Cyrene Fisher
Dan McClennan
Isaac McCoy
"Snide" Moseley
Tom Wright

Eclipse (Richmond, VA)

John Milton Dabney, 1b
John Morton, 2b
Thomas Jefferson, 3b
Albert Jenkins, ss
James H. Harrison, lf
James H. Lee, ss / cf
Pagey Morris, rf
Hiram Crutchfield, c
Moses Robinson, c
Hickson Price, p
Jefferson Price, p
James Robinson, rf
W. Lightfoot, p
William H. Harrison, c

Washington, DC

Capital Citys (Washington, DC)

Johnson, 1b
Wallace Coleman, p / ss
James A. Payne, p / 2b
William Curry, c / cf
William Carter, rf
James Crawford, c
Charles Jones, 2b
William Wilkinson, p
Eugene Russell, lf
Henry Hines, c
Thomas Howard Diggs, c
Logan, 2b / p
Charles S. Payne, 2b / 3b
Joe Scott, rf / p

Benjamin Moore, c
James Washington, cf
Joseph Anderson, 3b
Hoffman, 1b
Andrews, 3b
Marshall, lf
Taylor, cf
I. L. Henson, Manager

Eastern Stars (Washington, DC)

Henry Kane, p
Benjamin Moore, c
Percy Ball, 1b
Joseph Hardruff, 2b
William Hill, 3b
Newton Hammer, ss
Arthur Mullen, rf
John Fyers, lf

Empires (Washington, DC)

John H. Campbell, p
J. Washington, c
Casey, 1b
Robert Ford, 2b
Johnson, ss
Benjamin Simms, 3b
L. Daniels, rf
King, cf
Taylor, lf
Jones, 1b
William E. Tilghman, c
Euel
William Coats
Dixon
J. H. Allen, Manager

English Colts (Washington, DC)

J. F. Henson, p
J. Washington, c
Crown, 1b
Robert Ford, 2b
James Young, 3b
John H. Dickerson, ss
A. W. Dangerfield, lf
Charles Delever, cf
Taylor, rf
George Johnson, Manager

Howard University (Washington, DC)

B. S. Jackson, 3b
F. W. Avant, 1b
I. Finley, 2b
C. M. Butler, ss
Joseph Rapier, c
D. O. W. Holmes, cf
G. W. Garner, rf
W. O. Bundy, lf
W. W. West, p
J. M. Enos, p

Edward C. Allen, p
Nibbs, p

Market House (Washington, DC)

William Carter, rf
Frank Settlers. 2b
Lafayette Jefferson, 1b
C. I. Smith, cf
S. Coleman, c
George Betters, ss
Arthur Anderson, 3b
W. Dangerfield, lf
R. A. Henderson, p

Neversweats (Washington, DC)

Louis Philips, p / 3b
Frank Settlers, p / 3b
Henry "Harry" Gant, c
Henry Hines, c
Benjamin Simms, 1b
L. Brown, 2b
George Betters, ss
H. C. Childs, rf
M. Lucas, cf
William E. Carter, lf
Willie Joyce
Brooks
James Young, p / rf
Captain Henderson, Manager

Spartans (Washington, DC)

Henry Mason, lf / Captain
Patrick, 2b
A. J. Booker, p
L. Brown, p
William E. Tilghman, c
T. Jefferson, 1b
William "Billy" Smith, 2b
Francis Cardozo, ss
J. Washington, 3b
Wade, lf
William R. Pinchback, cf
B. Butler, rf

Wisconsin

Klondikes (Milwaukee, WI)

George Bryon, ss / Captain
John Ellis, rf
William Simmons, c
Fred Watkins, 2b
Charles Morgan, 3b
Simon Epps, 1b
Walter Vines, p
William Hawkins, p / lf
Al Lawrence, cf
John White, c
Harry MacAllister, Substitute

1898

Alabama

Colored Nine (Eufala, AL)

James Grimes, 1b
Charles Fisher, 2b
James Fisher, 3b
Rich Hayward, p
Judson Davis, c
Charles Haywood, ss
Abb Scott, lf
E. B. Moore, cf
Joseph Oliver, rf

California

Colored Nine (Bakersfield, CA)

E. Pinckney, c
Walter Bodyston, p
J. Price, 1b / c
H. Houston, 2b
A. Houston, 3b / ss
John Pinckney, ss / 1b
W. Winters, lf / rf
F. White, cf
B. Russell, rf
H. Simpson, ss
G. Vessell, cf / lf
Peter W. Pinckney, Substitute

Trilbys (Los Angeles, CA)

Robert Shaw, p / 2b
William Carroll, c / ss
Maxwell, cf / c / 2b
Lucius Alexander, 1b / cf
G. Johnson, rf / cf
William Nettles, 3b
Harry Brown, ss
W. Anderson, lf
John Majors, p / 1b
W. Griffin, 1b
Joseph Marrione, 2b / 3b
Porter, 3b
Lige Walker, rf
Paul A. Brothers, ss
Riley, c
James Bullock, p / rf
Henry Harris, Manager
Alhuga, Manager

Stars (Pasadena, CA)

Lucius Alexander, c
Harry Brown, p
Benjamin Perkins, 1b
S. B. Carr, 2b
T. Torfur, 3b
J. Moden, ss
Walter Bodyston, lf
W. C. Dent, cf
G. Henry, rf

Colorado

Americans (Denver, CO)

Alec Thompson, p
L. Martin, c
Lige Walker, 2b
W. R. Euker, rf
W. Stean, 1b
A. George, 3b
Frank Kempton, ss
Andrew "Andy" Snell, lf
Ashford, cf
James Carter, 2b
R. Hill, Manager
George Montgomery, Manager

Illinois

Clippers (Chicago, IL)

Alexander Gordon, c
John Oglesby, p
N. Peters, 1b
Frank Griggs, 2b
Jesse Collier, ss
James Smith, 3b
Frank Butler, lf
P. D. Arnett, lf
Charles Green, rf

Chicago Unions (Chicago, IL)

Harry Moore, p
Harry Buckner, p
William Holland, p
William T. Smith, c
Robert P. Jackson, c
George Hopkins, 2b
Clarence Carter, 3b
Alexander Gordon, 3b
Grant Johnson, ss
Willis Jones, lf
Bert Jones, p / rf
Robert Foote, c
Harry Hyde, 3b
David Wyatt, ss
William C. Smith, cf
William Joyner, rf
Alfred Jupiter, p
Louis Reynolds, rf
George "Chick" Green, p / 3b / ss
Harlan, p
Frank C. Leland, Secretary

Columbia Giants (Chicago, IL)

Charles Grant, 2b
George Johnson, ss
Edward Wilson, p
George Taylor, 1b
William Binga, 3b
John Johnson, c / 1b
Peter Burns, rf
Joe "Kid" Miller, rf / p

Louis Reynolds, rf
Harry Buckner, p
Bert Jones, p / rf
George Wilson, p
Sherman Barton, c
Charles H. Washington, Financial Manager
John W. Patterson, 1b / Manager

Records (Springfield, IL)

W. Parks, c
Oscar Henry, c
Forrest Cooper, c
Robert Blake, p
William Sanders, ss
Elijah Douglas, ss
Frank Brandon, 2b
Harry Payton, 3b
Carl Ferguson, lf
William Pollard, cf
John Davis, rf
Harry Dell Hodges, 1b / Captain
Fred Wright, Manager

Indiana

West Sides (Evansville, IN)

Matt Mitchell
Frank Grey
James Sheldon
Lige Sorden
Clarence Jones
William Gordon
J. N. Robinson
Benjamin Goodwin
Edwin Killdrew

Iowa

Giants (Sioux City, IA)

Danger, c
South, cf
Paris, p
Duvall, ss
Williams, 3b
Grant, rf
Minor, lf
Johnson, 1b
Gray, 2b
Lew Hall, Manager

Kentucky

Black Hill Stars (Louisville, KY)

Fields, p
Larance, c
Carnell, ss
Burns, 1b
D. Walton, 2b
Jonson, 3b
Gibson, lf
B. Gates, cf
W. Walton, rf

Brotherhood
(Louisville, KY)

Prendergast, c
Bowerman, p
Ross, p / ss
C. Murphy, lf
Evans, 1b
D. Holton, 2b
B. Allen, 3b
Washington Nesby, 1b
L. Halton, cf
Garrett, rf
Timothy Masterson, p

Diamond Joe
(Louisville, KY)

C. Thomas, c
Thomas Higgins, ss
N. Hines, 1b
Charles Anderson, 2b
E. Hines, 3b / Captain
L. Simmon, lf
A. Reif, cf
C. Graham, rf
Charles Helm, p
John Weaver, Manager

Old Imps (Louisville, KY)

Bud Watson, p
Jesse Palmer, c
E. Hill, ss
J. Murphy, 1b / ss / Captain
Garnett, 2b
William Kelly, 3b / cf
William Gordon, 3b
I. English, lf
Tom Williams, cf
Burns, rf
A. Smith, 2b
G. Barrett, 1b

University (Louisville, KY)

Haywood Rose, c
Jackson, p
George Hudspeth, 1b
Ed Clark, 2b
Charles Oglesby, 3b
Henderson, ss
Lewis, lf
Ellis F. D. Trimbo, cf
Wadkins, rf

Louisiana
Allens (Carrollton, LA)

Robert Brooks, p
Joubert Lewis, rf / c
J. B. Robertson, 1b
John Brady, ss
Joseph Ferrand, 1b / lf
Peter Lucien, cf
N. Ross, 2b
Davidson, 1b

Madison, ss
Colbert, 3b / p / rf
Gaspard Joseph, rf
Cottar, Substitute

Maryland
Blues (Baltimore, MD)

H. Hill, ss
William E. Farrell, c
Thomas Savoy, cf
E. Duval, p
Jacob C. Fagan, p
S. Pendull, c
Leon Ritterson, 1b
E. Gross, lf
Samuel Bolden, 2b
H. Dennis, rf
Charles Calder, 3b
William T. Jordan, Manager

Detroits
(Baltimore, MD)

Frank Madden, c
Douglas Camel, p
Levi Fisher, p
Louis Downs, 1b
George Hill, 2b
Charles "Buck" Washington, ss
Jack Norris, 3b
William Smith, lf
Harry Moody, cf / Captain
Benjamin Cole, rf
Joshua Rogers, lf
Edward Thomas, Substitute
Walter Williams, Manager

Massachusetts
Atlantics (Boston, MA)

Eastern, cf
Rodie, lf
Paine, c
Moody, lf
Johnson, ss
George Allen, p
Minor, 3b
Benjamin Allen, 2b
Wilkins, rf

Cuban X-Giants
(North Adams, MA)

Solomon White, 2b
Andrew Jackson, 3b
Clarence Williams, c / 1b
Frank Grant, ss
Robert Jordan, 1b / c
Ross Garrison, cf
James D. Robinson, lf / rf
William Selden, rf / p
John Nelson, p / lf
John Howard, rf / p

Michigan
Page Fence Giants
(Adrian, MI)

John W. Patterson, 3b
William Johnson, Jr.,
William Binga, c / 3b
Sherman Barton, 3b / p
Peter Burns, c
George Taylor, 1b
George Wilson, p / cf
Charles Grant, 2b
J. Grant Johnson, ss

Stars (Kalamazoo, MI)

David Perry, c
H. Bolden, p
Bert Hackley, cf
Robert Hackley, cf
Lester Bolden, 2b
Elmer Bolden, lf
C. Outland, rf
Foster Myers, 2b
George Tillman, 1b

Missouri
Bradburys
(Kansas City, MO)

Sam Hanley, c
D. Allen, p
Peter Greenbury, 1b
R. Smith, 2b
Patterson, 3b / cf
S. Colbert, ss
J. Vaughn, lf / p
Greer, cf
Walter Booker, lf
Hooper, rf / 3b
David Wyatt, lf
Guss Abernathy, rf
L. Brown, lf
H. Franklin, rf
Hollingsworth, p
George Jones, manager

Colored Porters
(Kansas City, MO)

Al Rhodie
Noah O'Brien
James O'Brien
Jerry Costigan
"Nig" Jarboe
Willace Jarboe
"Money" Fisher
Tim Shea
"Speck" Buford
John Wise
Charles Smith

Unions (Kansas City, MO)

Sawyers (Sayres), c
Joe Miller, p

Hollingsworth, p / lf
William Lewis, 1b
David Wyatt, 2b
Bright, 3b
William Jackson, ss
Reedy, cf
Long, rf
W. Johnson, p
John Lindsey, c
James Lindsey, 3b
Walter Lindsey, rf

Times Hustlers
(Kansas City, MO)

Frank Maupin, c
Frank Montgomery, p
T. C. Woodson, 1b
Jack Reeves, 2b
William Harris, 3b
Ross Bradley, ss
F. Emory (Emery), lf
Sterman, lf
Lake Anderson, rf
Franklin, rf
George Jones, Manager

Tigers (Lexington, MO)

Frank Lindsey, c
James Lindsey, p
Joseph Hicks, 1b
John Lindsey, 2b
S. Lindsey, 3b
Mady, ss / p
E. Hayden, lf
Gates, cf
S. Hayden, rf
Walter Lindsey, 2b
Coates, rf
Green, p
George Smith, lf / p
H. Hayden, cf
Charles Joiner, Manager

Montana

Colored Nine (Anaconda, MT)

A. Bass, p
Sam Freeman, c
Lash Homer, 1b
H. Stroup, 2b
John Taylor, 3b
James Parnell, ss
Dave Stroter, rf
A. R. Ridley, lf
W. M. Lytle, cf
Adrich, p

Nebraska

Colored Giants (Omaha, NE)

Vasco Graham, c
Eddie Carr, p
Charles South, 1b

Dorcas Lincoln, 2b
Paris, 3b
Danger Talbot, ss
Ross, lf
Townsend, cf
Scott, rf

New Jersey

Ironsides (Bordentown, NJ)

Whittow, lf
Williams, c
Spriggs, 1b
C. Spriggs, ss
Kersham, 2b
Morgan, p
Young, 2b
Taylor, rf
Anders, cf

Hamiltons (Jersey City, NJ)

F. Smith, 1b
C. Gaynor, 2b
H. Thompson, 3b
W. McCoy, p
Joseph H. Rias, ss
W. Parker, rf / 1b
J. Redfield, 2b
W. Norris, 3b
J. Ruis, ss
E. Perry, lf
C. Gurdeen, rf
E. Perry
C. Henry, cf, lf
Rufus Peterson, rf / Manager

Cuban-X Giants
(Hoboken, NJ)

William Jackson, ss / cf
Clarence Williams, c
Oscar Jackson, rf
Fred "Biddy" Wilson, lf / rf
Andrew Jackson, 3b
Robert P. Jackson, rf
William Selden, p / rf
Winslow Tyrrell, ss
John Nelson, p
Ray Watson, 1b
Solomon White, 2b
Robert Jordan, rf / c
Frank Grant, 2b
Ross Garrison, ss / cf
D. S. Howard, lf
Abraham Harrison, ss
James Robinson, p
Partland, c
E. B. Lamar, Manager

Colored Giants
(Newark, NJ)

N. Freeman, 3b
Andrew Watson, rf
Norwood Turner, ss

W. McCoy, lf / cf
John Meade, 1b
Booker, 2b
James Moorman, cf
Sam Boland, c
Charlie Beale, p
Charles Bell, p
Abe Harrison, 2b
W. Harrison, rf
B. Burke, Manager

Colored Giants
(Pennington, NJ)

J. Smith, c
George Jennings, p
A. Smith, 1b
N. Smith, rf
A. Smith, ss
Lewis Boyer, 3b
Pierson, 2b
Walter Seruby, cf
J. Smith, lf

New York

Colored Giants
(Greater NY, NY)

Benjamin Brown, lf / 2b
William Jackson, p / c / rf
Louis Smith, 1b
Dan Penno, 3b
John McCreary Watkins, rf
John Patterson, lf
Hugh McWinters, cf
Sam Bolan, ss
William Carter, p
Frank Miller, p
Jackson, lf
Stewart, ss

Acme Colored Giants
(Jamestown, NY)

Frank Blue, 1b
Al Baxter, 2b / rf
George Edsall, lf
William Booker, 2b
Eddie Day, ss
Ed Wilson, p / 1b
William Kelly, 3b
John Mickey, p
John Southall, c
Oda Jones, cf
Walter Williams, p
Clarence Wright, 1b
William "Doc" Payne, cf
Thomas White, rf
James Lindsey, c
Alfred Jupiter, p
Fred Collins
David Wyatt
James Carter, p
Harry Curtis, Manager

Genuine Cuban Giants
(New York, NY)

William Jackson, lf / c
Oscar Jackson, 1b
Dan Penno, 2b / cf
Joseph Trusty, ss / p / c
John Mickey, cf
E. Schenk, 3b
John Oliver, c / rf
Ed Chamberlain, 1b / c
John Jackson ("Bud" Fowler), 2b
Charles Carter, p
Anthony, rf
F. Lee, cf / 3b
William Carter, p
Frank Bell, ss / p
William H. Cole, p / c
DuMund, 1b
Sam Bolan, 3b
James Johnson, rf / c
Charles Walter Titus, rf
Taylor Smith, p / rf
Price, cf
Banes, cf
Soffel, ss
Healy, cf
Razor, cf
Beckett, rf
Tom Wade, cf / 3b
Martin, rf / cf
David Drummond, lf
J. Buck, rf / p
John McCreary Watkins, 1b

Fearless (Utica, NY)

Bond, p
Wilbur B. Jackson, rf
Samuel Jackson, c / ss
Peter Henry, p
R. Robbins, lf
Avery Griger, 3b
Henry Moss, cf
Roscoe Anderson, 2b
Charles W. Titus, 1b / President
John L. Jacobs, lf / Vice President
Charles Lippen, c / Treasurer
Fred Jackson, rf / Secretary

Ohio

Hollenden (Cleveland, OH)

Harry Bronson, p
P. Poindexter, c
Lewis Kinney, 1b
A. Bernard, 2b
W. Burke, ss
B. Dooley, 3b
Henry Smith, rf
Joseph Stanley, cf
Shirley Moore, lf
Ed Poindexter, Water boy

Keystones (Cleveland, OH)

W. Craig, rf
William Colwell, c
Al Dennie, lf
J. Moss, 1b
J. Earley, c
George Sampson, 3b
Charles Gorman, ss
G. Weems, cf
Wiese, 3b
M. McGinty, p
E. Turner, ss
J. Andrews, p / c
A. Colwell, 3b
John Jackson, cf
Ed Williams, p / 3b
W. Arthur Goines, rf
Thomas, p

Unions (Cleveland, OH)

Woding
John Morris
Charles McAfee
McPherson
Jones
Edward Turner
Al Thompson
Warfield
Frank Henderson
M. Scott
Ed "Inkspot" Williams
William Turner

Wilberforce University
(Xenia, OH)

Wright, ss
W. H. Reid, lf
Benjamin W. Arnett, 3b
William Anderson, 2b
Jackson, c
Collins, p
Simpson, 1b
James Gaines, lf
William Wallace, cf
Rufus Gilliam, c

Pennsylvania

Douglass (Philadelphia, PA)

R. Horwar, 1b
W. Thornton, ss
C. Cummings, 2b
Jones, 3b
William "Kid" Whittington, lf
J. Green, rf
J. Johnson, cf
P. Williams, c
E. Gordy, p
Pearly Williams, Captain

Giants (Philadelphia, PA)

Junor, ss
Davis, 3b

Bouts, 1b
George Rothwell, p
Jobe Trusty, c
Lang, cf
Delaney, rf
Charles Trusty, 2b
Dutton, lf

Lord Philadelphia
(Philadelphia, PA)

Vallie, cf
Peter Davis, 3b
Charles Green, rf / p
William Toner, lf
Fowler, ss / lf / 3b
Clarence Grant, c
Tumney, 2b
Roy Hughes, 1b / ss / 2b
J. Johnson, p
Charles Scott, c / p
Edward C. Gunby, 2b
Frank Storkey, cf
Edward Lodine, 3b / rf
D. Halley, 1b
Spencer, rf
John Freeland, 1b / p
Fred Myers, c / 3b
Ed Hall, 3b / c
John Butler, ss
William Tenant, lf
Wheeler, p
Chick, p

Tennessee

Fisk University (Nashville, TN)

George Bryant, p
Sam Neely, c
H. Gillam, 1b
S. H. Dudley, 2b / captain
JA Stewart, 3b
L. E. Gideon, ss
M. McQuitty, rf
A. Gillam, cf
A. P. Harris, lf

Rock City Unions
(Rock City, TN)

William Monroe, 3b
Harry Satterfield, rf
William "Lightning Bill" Stewart, ss
Heistand, c
Moses Cain, 1b
Jasper Dunstan, cf
Marshall Coffey, 2b
William Ramsey, p
Hurt, lf
W. C. Ewing, Manager

Texas

Fly Aways (Galveston, TX)

A. Campbell, c
W. L. Jones, p

C. J. Williams, 1b
Robert Hennessey, 2b / p
Abraham Coleman, 3b
James Blair, lf
Frank Coleman, ss
Bud Walker, cf
Joseph Walker, rf
George Upps, p / 2b
J. Walsh, c

Creole Giants (Houston, TX)

Addison, p
Frank Itson, 1b
J. Miller, 2b
Foley, 3b
Mitchell, ss
Sheppard, lf
L. Booker, cf
Early, rf / p
Alec Quander, 3b
Dillard, 2b
Allen Washington, c
Ramsey "Chattanooga", p
Brucker, lf
Chaney, rf
Dailey, cf
Tom Anderson, c / Manager

Rosebuds (Houston, TX)

Anderson Washington, c
Ramsey "Chattanooga", p
Frank Itson, 1b
Johnny Jones, 3b
Dillard, 2b
Thes Fletcher, rf
Alec Quander (?), 3b
Miller, ss
Brucker, lf
Dailey, cf
Chaney, rf

Alamo Grays (San Antonio, TX)

William Patterson, p / cf
Thes Fletcher, cf
C. J. Williams, c
Wiley Haywood, ss
Green, 1b
Foley, 2b
Bradford Norman, lf
"Kid" Morris, rf
Shooks, p
Ashford, 3b
Houston, p

Colts (San Antonio, TX)

William Jahn, lf
C. Mitchell, 3b
Goodman, 1b
Wood, 2b / p
Jones, ss
Anderson Washington, rf
H. Fields, cf
B. Miller, c

Yellow Jackets (Waco, TX)

Travis "Trave" Irvin, p
Mose Johnson, 3b
L. Graves, ss
H. Evans, c
D. Smith, 2b
John Carter, lf
Joe Booker, rf
A. Campbell, 1b
T. Denham, p
R. Craig, cf
Cameron, 1b
Sam Claybourne, Manager
M. J. Riche, Manager

Utah

Browns (Salt Lake City, UT)

Ford, c
Crandall, c
Williams, p
Hall, p
Fuller, 1b / 3b
Palmer, ss
Mitchell, 1b / 2b
N. Harris, 2b / p / ss
H. Clark, 3b / rf
Cylans, 3b
Flander, 3b
Jones, cf / lf
Smith, rf
U. Harris, lf
Jackson, ss / c
Hollems, 3b / 1b
Willis, 2b
K. Harris, p
Tansey Reid, 2b
Howell, lf
Campbell, cf / lf / c
Armstrong, cf
Lewis, 1b

Virginia

Lancasters (Norfolk, VA)

Cornelius Hayes, p / lf
James Harrison, p
William Bailey
John Johnson, c
J. Woodhouse, c
Ed Nottingham, c
William "Duck" Davis
George Lynier
John Lynier
Miles Page
Gus Johnson
Phillip Scott
Caulbert Sparrow
Sam "Crook" Keeling
Otis Harrison
Bob Wilson
Alton Harrison

William Ford
Arthur Quetrell

Red Stockings (Norfolk, VA)

"Bub" Walker
George White
William Parker
George Wright
Walter Cason
Amos Cason
Wash Stewart
Ed Dobsey
Sidney Fentriss
Cyrene Fisher
Dan McClennan
Isaac McCoy
"Snide" Moseley
Tom Wright

West Virginia

Adelphi House (Huntington, WVA)

Barnet, c
Seals, p
Elsie Brooks, ss
William Carter, 1b
Brown, 2b
Johnson, 3b
Sidney, lf
Goble, rf
Booker, cf

Florentine House (Huntington, WVA)

Morris, c
Price, p
Kendall, ss
Finley, 1b
Whirl, 2b
Jackson, 3b
Taylor, lf
John McKeever, rf
White, cf

Washington, DC

Capital Citys (Washington, DC)

H. Smith, 1b
B. Betters, 2b
S. Payne, 3b
T. Dickerson, ss
S. Coleman, c
D. Wilkins, p
B. Carter, rf
W. Curry, cf
W. Wade, lf
W. Moore, Substitute
H. Hines, Substitute
Grayson, c

Howard University
(Washington, DC)

W. O. Bundy, 1b
G. L. Baton, 2b
C. J. Ridgeley, 3b
J. McCoy, ss
B. S. Jackson, c
C. A. Oliver, p
R. E. Smalls, rf
D. O. W. Holmes, cf
P. W. Mosley, lf
J. W. Fox, Substitute
T. W. Turned, Substitute
J. M. Enos, Substitute

Market House
(Washington, DC)

Anderson, 3b
A. Atkinson, 2b
Louis Phillips, p
Frank Settlers, cf
Lafayette Jefferson, 1b
George Betters, ss
Robert Ford, lf
William E. Tilghman, c
William Bird, rf
William Diggs, cf
John F. Henson, p

Wisconsin

Klondikes (Milwaukee, WI)

George Bryon, p / Captain
John White, c
Al Lawrence, 1b
William "Will" Simmons, 2b
Fred Watkins, 3b
F. Taylor, 3b
J. Ellis, lf
C. Kincaid, cf
William Hawkins, cf
W. Harris, ss
Walter Vines, p
A. Bowman, lf
C. Morgan, rf
J. Tate, rf
William "Billy" Simmons, p / 2b
Simon Epps, 3b / c /1b
Alex Price, Manager

1899

Alabama

Colored Nine (Eufala, AL)

James Grimes, 1b
Charles Fisher, 2b
James Fisher, 3b
Rich Hayward, p
Judson Davis, c
Charles Haywood, ss
Abb Scott, lf

E. B. Moore, cf
Joseph Oliver, rf
Bailey, cf

Arizona

Bullys (Phoenix, AZ)

Robert Stevens, c
Theodore Thomas, p
Adolphus Cretil, 1b
G. W. Caldwell, 2b
Perry Polk, 3b
R. S. Stearns, ss / Captain
Frank Turner, rf
Al Williams, cf
Otto Williams, lf
Fred Gardner, c
Richard "Jeff" Briscoe, c

California

Coast Giants (San Diego, CA)

Jackson, p / lf
J. Wilson, c
Hamilton, 1b
Hunter, 2b
Marshall, 3b
Saunders, ss / p / Captain
Bullock, lf / ss
Wilson, rf
John Price, cf / rf
Hughes, 2b
Townsend, 3b
Al Williams, rf

Trilbys (Los Angeles, CA)

Harry Brown, ss
William Carroll, ss / 2b / p
R. Moore, c / cf
E. Johnson, p / rf
W. Anderson, lf
S. Gardner, 1b / p
John Majors, 3b
A. Anderson, lf / rf
Scott, cf
Perry Polk, 1b / 3b
Fred Slaughter, c / p
Lucian Alexander, cf
E. Whiteside, 3b
F. Washington, lf / 1b
A. Robinson, lf
Harry Edwards, 1b
James Bullock, p / 1b
Turbin, 2b
G. Henry, rf
White, p
Gascon (Gaskins), 2b
Sommers, cf / 1b
Henry Harris, Manager

Colorado

Pastimes (Colorado Springs, CO)

John Watson, c

Benjamin Holley, p
Fred Reed, 1b / c
Thomas Carter, 3b
James Carter, ss
George Motley, lf
George Hackley, cf
Raymond Streeter, rf
Elliott, Substitute
Arrey, Substitute
Booker, 2b / Manager

Georgia

IPC (Savannah, GA)

R. Brown, c
M. W. Bryan, p
John Moore, 1b
Edward Williams, 2b
James Sanders, 3b
A. T. Johnson, ss
J. T. Meyers, lf
James Coston, cf
S. A .King, rf
Willie Allen, Substitute

YMSC (Savannah, GA)

Jones, p
Gleton, 1b
C. H. Sheftal, 2b
A. Butler, 3b
W. L. Garey, ss
Joseph Ford, lf
John Giles, cf
F. Cuyler, rf
R. Boifeullet, c

Illinois

Columbia Giants
(Chicago, IL)

Charles Grant, 2b
George Johnson, ss / 1b
Harry Buckner, rf
George Wilson, p
Joe Miller, p
Peter Burns, c
Sherman Barton, cf
Solomon "Sol" White, ss
William Binga, 3b
Al Garrett, cf
Frank Miller, p
Charles Morgan, 1b / rf
E. Smith, cf
Louis Reynolds, lf
John W. Patterson, lf / Manager
Julius N. Avendorph, President
W. R. Cowan, Vice-President
D. P. French, Club Member
C. M. Washington, Club Member
Anderson Brodie, Club Member
P. R. Miller, Club Member
G. Hardingrand, Club Member

Emergencies (Chicago, IL)

Eugene Renfroe, p
Lee Starks, c
R. B. Harrison, 1b
Will Phillips, 2b
William Smith, ss
Julius N. Avendorph, Captain / 3b
Payton Taylor, lf
Joe Shoecraft, cf
Wellen Grayson, rf
Albert Hackley, 2b
Claude Alexander, Substitute

Unions (Chicago, IL)

William Monroe, ss / lf
Willis Jones, lf
William J. "Billy" Holland, cf / p
George Hopkins, p / 2b
William Joyner, rf
Harry Hyde, 3b
Harry Buckner, p / Captain
Bert Jones, p
William Horn, p
William Smith, p
Ed Woods, p
David Wyatt, ss
Harry Moore, rf
Louis Reynolds, 1b
Robert P. Jackson, c
Clarence Carter, 3b
Robert Footes, rf / p
Bert Wakefield, 1b / 2b
Thomas Ham, p / rf
James Woods
Frank Busby, c
Warner, c
William Peters, Manager

Clippers (Rockford, IL)

Charles Ferguson, c
Frank Ferguson, p
Herbert "Sode" Tucker, ss
William Holmes, 1b
Reeves, 3b
Williams, 2b
Fred Lewis, rf
Chandler Baxter, lf
William "Will" Harris, cf
Leo Miller, c

Indiana

Gold Dollars (Evansville, IN)

H. Tyson, c
Robert Sandefur, p
J. Shelby, 1b
H. Daniels, 2b
Horace Hayhurst, 3b
J. J. Beecher, ss
W. Johnson, rf
Samuel Howard, rf / p
Abe Jackson, c

James Gibson, p
John Mosley, 2b
H. Tate, Substitute
Burton Slaughter, cf
E. White, Substitute
Browder, Substitute
Clarence McFarland, lf / Manager

Majors (Evansville, IN)

George Williams, p
William Brown, lf / Captain
Fred Roberts, 1b / 3b
James Webb, c
John Mosley, 2b
Matt Mitchell, 3b
Samuel Howard, rf
Burton Slaughter, cf
Abe Jackson, c
P. Gipsy, p
William Polk, rf
Henry Elkins, rf
James Nance, cf
Harry Bluford, rf / cf
John Simpson, 2b / c
Frank Clenna, 1b
Jessie Posey, p
William Reed, ss
Joseph Tut, 3b
William Pope, rf
Jessie Multon, p
Frank Hosey, 3b
James Gibson, p
P. Williams, c
Joseph Gibson
Dock Walker
George Amos
Joseph Wesley
John Roberts, Manager
Ernest Tidrington, c / Manager
Echolas K. Watson, 1b / 2b / Manager
George Blakey, Manager
"Scrap" Allen, Manager

Kansas

Sure Shots (Coffeyville, KS)

Alfred Shobe, lf / Treasurer
Will Jones, rf
D. W. Garrett, cf / Captain
Sterling Owens, ss
Jake Jones, 1b / p
Billie Erving, 2b
Charlie Walters, 3b
James Roberts, p / Manager
John White, c
Sanford Jones, p
Hayes Jones, c
George Wallace, c

Blues (Osage, KS)

Henry Benford, Team Captain / c
Emery Jefferson, p
G. D. Hanks, ss

F. Harding, 1b
C. Douglas, 2b
A. Jefferson, 3b
J. Tilford, rf
F. Tyler, lf
V. Lyons, cf
T. Colman, Substitute
J. S. Hanks, Manager

Kentucky

Heavy Hitters (Lexington, KY)

Bennie Williams
Turner, p
Henry Guthrie
James Dancer
Dave "Squirrel" Davis, p
Maniel Simpson, c
Henry Jones
Sanford Murray
Archie Cowan
Wash Farra

Black Hill Stars (Louisville, KY)

Fields, p
William Larance, c
Carnell, ss
Burns, 1b
D. Walton, 2b
Jonson, 3b
Gibson, lf
B. Gates, cf
W. Walton, rf

Brotherhoods (Louisville, KY)

C. Helms, p
Dallas Carter, p
Henry Clay, p
Daniel Brown, 1b
Prendergast, 2b
Ross, ss / p
George Talbott, 3b
Anderson, c
Toots, c
Haywood Rose, c
E. Hines, ss
N. Hines, 1b
Robert Foots, 1b
Bowling, 2b
Hart, 2b
Moses Allen, 3b
John Taylor, lf / p
Thomas O'Neal, cf
Tom Williams, rf
Barrett Grant, cf
W. Lee, rf / lf
Samuel Gibbs, Manager

Old Imps (Louisville, KY)

Bud Watson, p
Jesse Palmer, c
R. Hill, ss

J. Murphy, 1b
Frank Garrett, 2b
William Kelly, 3b
I. English, lf
Tom Williams, cf
Burns, rf
A. Smith, p
John Welch, c

Roses (Louisville, KY)

Anderson, c
Wilson, p
Tom Means, p
Charles Helm, p
George Talbott, ss
Daniel Brown, 1b
Elzy Hart, 2b
George White, 3b
W. H. Lee, lf
Lee Halton (Holton), cf
Washington Nesby, rf
John Taylor, 1b / p
Bowling, 2b
Charles Oglesby, ss
Dallas Carter, p
Moses Allen, 3b
A. Reily, lf
Sims, rf
Barrett Grant, cf
Haywood Rose, c

Grays (Paducah, KY)

George E. Marshall, President
James Arrington, Vice President
J. W. Moore, Treasurer
Benjamin Boyd, Manager

Louisiana

Allens (Carrollton, LA)

Robert Brooks, p
Joubert Lewis, rf / c
J. B. Robertson, 1b
John Brady, ss
Joseph Ferrand, 1b / lf
Peter Lucien, cf
N. Ross, 2b
Davidson, 1b
Madison, ss
Colbert, 3b / p / rf
Gaspard Joseph, rf
Cottar, Substitute

Maryland

Colored Giants (Baltimore, MD)

Reynolds, 2b / ss / c
Wilson, 3b
Henry Hill, lf / 1b
Hopper, ss
Joshua Rogers, lf
Thomas Savoy, cf

Eddie Day, ss / p
Jenkens, 1b / c
John McClennan, p
Charles Washington, rf
S. Pinder, c
John Pharr, p
E. Duvall, p / 1b
William T. Jordan, Manager

Colored Nine (Rockville, MD)

W. Smith
J. Harris
J. Thomas, Jr.
H. Oflet
R. Smith
A. Ross
N. Smith

Michigan

Bootblacks (Kalamazoo, MI)

Charles Johnson, p
William Hackley, 3b
Arthur Hackley, ss
M. Casey, 2b
Bert Henley, cf
Willie Christman, rf
Sharer, c
Hawley, lf
Franklin, c
Bert Hackley, 1b
J. Hackley, Manager

Colored Stars (Kalamazoo, MI)

William Stewart, Captain / Manager
Bert Hackley
James Bell
Foster Myers
George Tillman
Lester Bowlin
David Perry
Elmore Bowlin
Clarence Outland
Walter Jackson
Robert Hackley
W. M. McCollough
William Hackley
L. L. Gilbert
Byrd

Missouri

Bradburys (Kansas City, MO)

P. Greenbury, 1b
R. Smith, 2b
S. Colbert, 3b
McKnight, ss
Sterman, lf
Long, cf
Patterson, rf
D. Allen, p
J. Vaughn, p

W. Smith, p
D. Allen, p
Hooper, 3b
Wyatt, lf
Abernathy, rf / p
Hollingsworth, lf
F. Emory (Emery), c
Frank Lindsey, c
Frank Maupin, c
H. Franklin, rf
Walt Booker,
L. Brown, cf / rf
Louis Lee, c
Sam Hanley, c / 1b
George Jones, Manager

Lincoln High (Kansas City, MO)

Thomas McCampbell, p
E. McCampbell, 1b
A. Pullam, 2b
F. James, 3b
James A. "Kid" Combs, ss
Robert Ricketts, lf
A. Gillham, cf
John Haynes, rf
Horace Conway, ss / lf
Jack Hubbard, Captain
Louis Little, Manager
William Houston, c / Manager

Lone Stars (Kansas City, MO)

Thomas McCampbell, p
James A. "Kid" Combs, ss
Bruce
Wilkins
Wright
Munroe Ingram
Williams
Price
Dale

Moonlights (Kansas City, MO)

T. Davis, ss
W. Pace, 1b
J. Passaul, 2b
Lou Lee, c
W. Redmond, cf
F. Ward, rf
W. Smith, lf
J. Parrant, cf
J. Leneer, 1b
B. Alexander, p
Henry Robertson, rf / c
A. Ewing, lf
W. Johnson, lf / p
Enyard, lf
Rectman
Milligan, Substitute
King, Substitute
Frank Montgomery, p / 3b / Captain

Star (Kansas City, MO)

McCrary
Campbell
F. James
W. Curtis
Maddox
Logan
Lewis Hamilton
Thatcher
Basker
Flogan

Times (Kansas City, MO)

John "Jack" Reeves, 2b / p
William Lincoln, ss
Frank Maupin, c
J. Montgomery, 3b
Frank Montgomery, p
Ransom, rf
W. Redmond, lf
Williams, cf
F. Emery, 3b
W. Pace, ss
Sprangles
Ed Hixon
Whaley
A. L. Dorsey
Hollingsworth, p
J. Parrant, cf
William L. Dunson, Manager
"Toots" Woodson, President

Unions (Kansas City, MO)

Watts, 1b
Rose, 2b
Cure, 3b
Bright, ss
Sayers, rf
Long, cf
West, lf
T. Lewis, c
Jones, p
Anders, c
Frank Montgomery, p
R. Martin, p
Andrews, c
Andrews, Substitute
James Wear, Secretary
A. L. Dorsey, Manager

Tigers (Lexington, MO)

James Hollingsworth, p / lf
Mady, p
James Lindsey, p
Frank Lindsey, c
George Smith, p / rf
Sam Hanley, c
Walter Lindsey, rf
John Lindsey, 2b
E. Hayden, cf
Davis
B. Vaughn

Albert Williams, Manager
Thomas Boldridge, Manager

Blues (Sedalia, MO)

John Abbott, p
John Williams, c
Homer Phillips, 1b
Lee Pierman, 2b / Captain
Anderson Wright, 3b
Will Travis, ss
J. Shackelford, lf
Charles Smith, cf
Jerry Nelson, rf
Dr. J. M. Harris, Director
George Davis, Director
Daily Steele, Director
Ed Hodges, Director

Montana

Colored Nine
(Fort Harrison, MT)

H. Smith, c
J. Smith, 2b
Robinson, 3b
Holmes, p
Emerson, p / ss
Monroe, 1b / cf
Goodwin, cf
Johnson, lf
Piner, rf
Waters, ss
Taylor, 3b
Simpson, c
Jackson, 2b
Motem, rf

Unions (Helena, MT)

R. C. Howard, ss
Lash Homer, 1b
Irwin, 2b
Palmer, 3b
Lewis, lf
Mason, cf
Baker, rf
Sam Freeman, c
Wesley, c
Howell, 3b
Reed, cf
Alexander, lf
Cooper, Substitute

Nebraska

Evans Laundrys (Lincoln, NE)

James Hall, 3b / Captain
Danger Talbot, lf
Jess Harper, c
Pot Thomas, rf
Chick Berry, 2b
Mose O'Bannion, cf
Arthur McAllister, 3b
Charles Davis, 1b

James Woods, c
George Richardson, ss
Charles Frye, p
Richard Adams, Manager

New Jersey

Jersey Cubans (Passaic, NJ)

Andrew Watson, 3b
W. McCoy, 1b / ss
John Jones, cf / lf
Augustus Ray, ss
Frank Holland, rf
A. Tobias, 2b
Turner, 2b
McGraw, lf / 1b
Pete Hill, p
Gustavus Ray, ss
John Garcia, c
W. Miller, c
John Oliver, cf
Hewlett, cf
T. Bell, p / rf
James Collins, ss / 3b
Fred Wilson, rf / p
O'Brien, rf
Dumont, 1b

Colored Giants
(Trenton, NJ)

Upton Johnson, p
Abraham "Abe" Harrison
Harry Catto, ss / 1b
F. Washington, p / rf
R. Washington, 1b
C. Murray, 3b
J. Dixon, lf
W. Van Sickels, cf
William Williams, 2b

New York

Stars (Buffalo, NY)

John Rowe, c
Tom S. Rodgers, cf
William Bright, 1b
O. Bright, 2b
Theodore Pell, ss
Saunders, 3b
J. Bright, lf
Smith, cf
Frank Gibbs, rf

Giants (Ithaca, NY)

Napoleon Jackson, p / Captain
Bert Clay, p
Richard Jackson, c
Bert Washington, 1b
Thomas Lewis, 3b
Eugene Smith, ss
Ern Russell, cf
John Wise, rf
J. W. Jackson, Team Manager

Acme Giants (New York, NY)

Walter Booker, 2b
Brown, c
Edward Demund, 1b
John Watkins, 3b
McCary, ss
Charlie Beale, lf
Bell, rf
Sam Bolan, cf
Frank Miller, p

Colored New Yorks (New York, NY)

Edward Demund, 1b
John M. Watkins, c
Bancroft, p
J. Blake, 2b
J. Buck, ss
Harry Styles, 3b
Pope, lf
Albert Douglass, cf
M. R. Ross, rf

Cuban Giants (New York, NY)

Edward Smith, c / 2b / p
Clarence Sampson, lf
Frank Pell, ss
Drew, 3b
Benjamin Brown, 2b
John Watkins, 1b / lf / c
James Manning, p / ss / cf
Charles W. Titus, cf / 1b
Charles Griffin, rf
William Carter, p
William Gailey, rf
William Cole, p / c
Robert Jordan, cf / lf
Al Baxter, ss
Vasco Graham, 2b / c
Dan Penno, cf
William Henderson, p / rf
E. B. Lamar, Manager

Cuban X-Giants (New York, NY)

William Jackson, lf
Solomon White, 2b
Frank Grant, ss
Andrew Jackson, 3b
Robert "Gus" Jordan, rf
Clarence Williams, c
Joseph H. Wilson, lf
John Nelson, cf / p
D. S. Howard, lf
William H. Selden, rf
Henry Catto, rf
James Robinson, p
William Henderson, p / rf
John Jones
William Williams, c / lf
Fred J. Mersheimer, President / Manager
William J. Davis, Treasurer

Frank Davis, Secretary
E. B. Lamar, Manager

Fearless (Utica, NY)

Charles W. Titus, 1b / Manager
Charles Lippen, c
Wilbur B. Jackson, rf
Samuel Jackson, ss
Arlington DeNike, 2b
Walter Pell,
Peter Henry, p
R. Robbins, lf
Avery Griger, 3b
Henry Moss, cf
Roscoe Anderson, 2b
John Titus, rf / 3b
Charles Henry

Ohio

Keystones (Cleveland, OH)

McPherson, 2b
Fred Wilson, lf
K. L. Nelson, c
Frank Henderson, 1b / p / cf / c
Edward Turner, p / ss / c
Harry Hart, rf
William Gales, 3b
William Turner, ss / 3b
W. Craig, cf / rf
A. Colwell, cf / 2b
W. Pittman, lf / cf / rf
Marshall, ss / lf
Al Dennie, lf
W. Arthur Goines, 2b
Ashbury Larkin, c
Thomas, p
John Jackson, c / p
Robert Colwell, 1b / cf
George Green, p
Ford, 2b
Clarence Wilson, lf
Dixon, p
M. Scott, p

Unions (Cleveland, OH)

John Wilson
S. McPherson
Frank Henderson
Edward Turner
C. Wilson
Horace Gibbs
Thompson
John Ingraham
Lewis Adkins
Walworth Drayton
M. Scott

Black Tourists (Findlay, OH)

Porter, p
James Lindsay, p
Redmond, p
Kossoch, c

Mack,
Heistand, 1b
Fowler, 2b
Meyers, ss
Richards, 3b / ss
Bissell, lf
Keller, cf
Sackett, 3b
Spiesman, c
Wagner, p
Huling, rf
Ball, p
Coffman, p
A. S. Peal, Manager

Pennsylvania

Midnight Stars (Monongahela, PA)

Parker Brooks
Steve Batch
Emmitt McPherson
George Catlin
Will Griffey
Brint Jones
Perry Simmons
Elliot Young
Hugh L. Hickey
Charles Skinner
Roy E. Sluby

Acme Giants (Philadelphia, PA)

Payne, rf
Jackson, 3b
Henry Gant, 1b
Wilson, p
Jones, lf
Miller, 2b
William Chase Lyons, c
Barks, ss
T. Jackson, cf

Dewey A. A. (Philadelphia, PA)

Watson, c
Coles, 1b
Shorter, 2b
A. Jones, p
Hamilton, ss
E. Lewis, p
King, c
R. Fisher, rf
William Purnell, lf
Morris, cf
Bowie, Substitute
Dennis, Substitute
L. W. Canon, 3b / Manager
William Thomas, Manager

Page Fence Giants (Philadelphia, PA)

L. Thomas, ss
Cook, 1b

C. Cummings, cf
E. Thomas, 2b
D'on, 3b / rf
Willis, rf / 3b
Eugene Thomas, c
Hyson, lf / p
Askew, p

Colored Nine (Pennlyn, PA)

Alfred Jenkins, lf
Harvey Roy, 2b
John Butler, ss
Farrell, c
Lyle, cf
John J. Garrett, rf
Rankins, 1b
Wheeler, p
Fred Storkey, 3b
Freeland, p

Acme Giants (Pittsburg, PA)

James Payne, rf / 3b
Frank Miller, rf / p
Henry Gant, 1b
Ross Garrison, 2b
Ray Wilson, p
Jackson, p / ss / cf
Jones, lf
Southall, c
Mickey, p
Washington, 2b
T. Jackson, cf
William Lyons, c
Alexander Banks, p
Clinton E. Smith, Manager

Colored Giants (Sharon Hill, PA)

Groves, c
A. Mitchell, 2b
D. Jones, 1b
Shrees, ss
Charles E. Simpson, p
David Wilson, 3b
Frederick Hopkins, rf
Copple, lf
Walter Cork, cf

Cuban Giants (York, PA)

Hendrickson, cf
Samuel King, 3b
Lewis Johnson, c / p
Charles Pinkney, lf
William Mills, ss
Lincoln Harris, rf
James Manning, p
Bert Devinney, 2b
George Bolden, p
George Hill, p
Edgar Waters, c
Benjamin Rhodes, p / ss / c
James Pallad, Manager

Tennessee

Nashvilles (Nashville, TN)

Satterfield, 2b
William Stewart, ss / 3b
Guffin, cf
Hurt, 1b
Jasper Dunston, lf
Moses Cain, c
Jones, 3b
James Bailey, cf
Grant F. Campbell, rf
Sheppard Ware, p
Brown, p
Bunn, lf
W. C. Ewing, Manager

Queen City Grays (Clarksville, TN)

Budd Johnson, 1b
Thomas Mason, 2b
John Drain, 3b
Robert Lewis, lf
Charles Warfield, rf
Willie Warfield, ss
James Drain, c
James Gill, p
William Wisdom, cf
W. L. Johnson, Manager

Texas

Fly Aways (Galveston, TX)

Abraham Campbell, c
Bud Walker, p
S. Williams, 1b
J. Jones, 2b
D. Stafford, 3b
C. Mitchell, ss
E. Woods, lf
Joe Booker, cf
Frank Coleman, rf
W. Piggy, p

Yellow Jackets (Waco, TX)

Mose Johnson, 3b
L. Graves, ss
John Carter, lf
Smith, 2b
Bolden, rf
Alexander Hayes, c
Willie, cf
Duval, 1b
Andrew Foster, p

Rosebuds (San Antonio, TX)

J. Jones, ss
Foley, cf / 2b
White, cf
Green, 1b
Gatewood, rf
Anderson Washington, 2b / c / Captain

Solomon Chew, p
Mathis, c
Mose Johnson, 3b
Jackson, lf
Fletcher, rf

Utah

Browns (Salt Lake City, UT)

Jackson, c
Jones, p
James Bullock, 1b
Turner, 2b
Simmons, 3b
J. W. Francis, ss
Johnson, rf
Frederick, cf
N. Clark, lf

Santiagos (Salt Lake City, UT)

Jackson, c
Williams, p
James Bullock, 1b
Mitchell, 2b
Brown, 3b
J. W. Francis, 3b
Smith, lf
N. Clark, cf
William Griffin, rf

Virginia

Hygeia Giants (Newport, VA)

White, c
Hill, ss
John Butts, 3b
R. Hill, lf
Matthews, cf
"Ham" Williams, rf / p
Mann, p
Hamilton, 3b
Isaac "Ike" McCoy, c
Deveaux, c

Red Stockings (Norfolk, VA)

William Parker, 1b/Captain
Dan McClennan, c
Charles Jones, c
James "Wet Ball" Lewis, c
Daniel "Devil" McClennan, p
Caleb Minton, p
Daniel Terry, p
Charles Olds, 3b
Willie James, ss
Wash Stewart, 2b
William Johnson, cf
Thomas Wright, lf
John Burton, rf
William Bailey, c
Isaac McCoy, c
C. T. Brown, Manager

St. Clair (Norfolk, VA)

"Brist" Smith, c
Mills, cf
James Beckett, 3b
John Butts, 2b
William "Billy" Parker, rf
Alton Harrison, lf
Ed Nottingham, lf
Craig, ss
James M. Harrison, p

Washington, DC

Capital City (Washington, DC)

H. Smith, 1b / p
J. Atkinson, 2b
S. Payne, 3b
S. Coleman, c
James A. Payne, ss
George Betters, cf
Magruder, rf
Water, lf
William Wilkinson, p
Arthur Anderson, p

Congress Hall (Washington, DC)

J. Sawyer
O. Griffin
Madger
J. Reed
A. Brown
S. Allen
V. Charles
M. Seuner
T. Taylor

Market House (Washington, DC)

William E. Tilghman, c
Wallace Coleman,
H. Brown, p
Lafayette Jefferson, 1b
J. Atkinson 2b
John H. Dickerson, ss
James A. Payne, 3b
George Betters, lf
William Bird, cf

Old Has Beens (Washington, DC)

G. W. Simmons
William Savoy
E. C. Allen, p
S. A. Tyler
Lafayette Jefferson
Wilfred "Will" Carter
T. Griffin
J. W. Brooks

Stockton Hotel (Washington, DC)

W. Taylor
A. Buck

L. Scott
Lewis Thomas, Captain
S. Scott
Maddock
C. Brooks
W. S. Taylor, Manager
H. Price, Secretary

1900

Alabama

Colored Nine (Eufala, AL)

J. Davis
William Johnson
Robert Grimes
Q. Johnson
Charles Fisher
R. Haywood
P. Haywood
A. Woolingham
Clifford Jordan

California

Trilbys (Los Angeles, CA)

Harry Brown, ss
William Carroll, ss / 2b / p
R. Moore, c / cf
E. Johnson, p / rf
W. Anderson, lf
S. Gardner, 1b / p
M. Majors, 3b
A. Anderson, lf / rf
William Nettles, rf / 3b
Fred Slaughter, c / p
Lucian Alexander, cf
E. Whiteside, 3b
F. Washington, lf
A. Robinson, lf
Edwards, 1b
Joseph Marrione, 3b
Robertson, rf
Andrews, lf
Wilson, c
Jackson, 1b
R. E. Simpson, Manager

Coast Giants (San Diego, CA)

Jackson, p / lf
J. Wilson, c
Hamilton, 1b
Hunter, 2b
Marshall, 3b
Saunders, ss / p
James Bullock, lf / ss
Wilson, rf
J. Price, cf / rf
Hughes, 2b
Townsend, 3b
Al Williams, rf

Colorado

Pastimes (Colorado Springs, CO)

P. Carter, c
Benjamin Holly, p
Ratliff, 1b
Raymond Streeter, 2b
Motley, 3b
J. Carter, ss
Elliott, lf
George Hackley, cf
Davidson, rf

Lipton Tea's (Denver, CO)

A. Snell, c
Benjamin Holly, p
R. Holly, p
Porter, 1b
Emerson, 2b
Taylor, 3b
Goodrich, ss
Allen, lf
Hennerson, cf
Banks, rf
Williams, c
McWilliams, lf
McAdow, cf
Anderson, rf
McAleer, 3b
Dorsey, c
Moore, 3b
McAllister, lf

Florida

Colored Nine (Ocala, FL)

Ike E. Tompkins, President
W. A. Parker, Manager
Vannie Simms, Captain
W. H. Williams, Secretary

Georgia

Clark University (Atlanta, GA)

S. Dilworth, p
J. Bowland, c
M. M. Calloway, p
Charles L. Taylor, 3b
William M. Gordon, Captain / 2b
Clifton Barlow, lf
Lyndon Hill, 1b
Emmett Lester, rf
Edward L. Gordon, cf
Willie Crogman, ss
Willie Hall, Substitute
E. L. W. Prather, Manager
William Long, Team President

Illinois

Chicago Unions (Chicago, IL)

Grant Johnson, ss
Harry Moore, cf

Bert Wakefield, 1b
Harry Hyde, 3b
Richardson, 2b
Willis Jones, lf
Bert Jones, p
Mitchell, c
Munroe Ingram, p
William Joyner
Means, rf
Harlan, cf / p
Morgan, rf
William Horn, p
William Stitt Peters, Manager

Clippers (Chicago, IL)

Charles Green
James Smith
P. D. Arnett
John Oglesby
William Stitt Peters
N. Peters
Tony Hopkins
Lallar
Jackson

Columbia Giants (Chicago, IL)

George Wilson
Sol White
Charles Grant
Joe Miller
William Binga
George Johnson
Pete Burns
Sherman Barton
Harry Buckner
William Holland
J. W. Patterson

Emergencies (Chicago, IL)

Eugene Renfroe, p
Lee Starks, c
R. B. Harrison, 1b
William Phillips, 2b
William Smith, ss
Julius N. Avendorph, Captain / 3b
Payton Taylor, lf
Joe Shoecraft, cf
Wellen Grayson, rf
Albert Hackley, 2b
Claude Alexander, Substitute

Unions (Danville, IL)

Matt Mitchell, c
Fred Roberts, ss
W. M. Brown, lf
W. M. West, 2b
John Taulkner, cf
Louis Minor, rf
Thomas Radford, 1b
C. Jackson, c
Abe Jackson, p
Robert Jackson
J. L. Tisdell, Substitute

T. Jackson, Substitute
William Webster, Manager

Unions (Decatur, IL)

Harry Moore, c
Stanford Fields, p
Albert Phoenix, 1b
Cass Jacobs, 2b
George Isabel, 3b
Gene Graves, ss
Frank Phoenix, cf
Clayton Holland, rf
Willis Page, lf
Alabama Blossom, Substitute
John Whitted, Manager

Eagles (Jacksonville, IL)

George Smith, c
H. Woods, p
G. Woods
T. Butler
F. Muse
A. Smith
J. Russel
West
Walters

Clippers (Rockford, IL)

Charles Ferguson, c
Frank Ferguson, p
Herbert "Sode" Tucker, ss
William Holmes, 1b
Reeves, 3b
Williams, 2b
Fred Lewis, rf
Chandler Baxter, lf
William "Will" Harris, cf

Indiana

Cyclones (Evansville, IN)

C. Jones, c
G. Williams, p
C. Robertson, 1b
I. Wyatt, 2b
C. Ward, 3b
Sheridan Goins, ss
G. Shanks, rf
F. Henderson, lf
G. Todd, cf
Bluefoot, c
W. Suggs, Substitute
George Smith, Manager

Delmonicos (Evansville, IN)

H. Tyson, c
Robert Sandefur, p
J. Shelby, 1b
H. Daniels, 2b
I. Wyatt, rf
M. Johnson, 3b
C. McFarland, lf / Manager
George Williams, p

J. R. Beecher, ss
H. Hayhurst, 2b
C. Ward, 3b
Burton Slaughter, lf
J. D. Miller, President

Harling Clippers (Evansville, IN)

George Carthy, rf
Burton Slaughter, cf
Seven Simms, lf
Ed Curry, 1b
Joe Snyder, 2b / Captain
Monk Osburn, ss
Robert Sandefur, p
James Willett, c
Henry Newton, p
Ernest Tidrington, c
George Williams, p
George Snyder, lf
Tim Mack, Manager
William Woods, President

Logan Giants (Logansport, IN)

John Calicott, c
Fred Gilmore, 1b
Charles S. Jones, 3b / Manager
George Parker, lf / Manager
George Hill, 2b / Captain
Harry Brown, ss
Foster, rf
Payton, cf
Stone, p
John Turner, Substitute
Thomas, Substitute

Kansas

Black Diamonds (Chanute, KS)

Arthur Dawson, ss / 3b
John Dawson, rf
Romp Rager, p / 1b
Frank Fields, c
Walter Peterson, c
William Washington, p
Lewis McCullough, 2b
Jerry Campbell, rf
Tom Tisdell, cf

Rattlers (Wichita, KS)

Wallace, 2b
B. Ross, ss / c
Collins, c / ss
Lawton, cf
Vernon, p / 1b / 3b
Whittier, 3b / 2b
A. Lowe, 1b
Frank Kennedy, lf / cf
Burl Anderson, rf
Bufford, p
Kendall, p
Fanlas, cf
Frank Gardenshire, 3b
Syl Anderson, Captain

Kentucky

Heavy Hitters (Lexington, KY)

Bennie Williams
Turner, p
Guthrie
James Dancer
Dave "Squirrel" Davis, p
Simpson, c
Henry Jones
Sanford Murray
Archie Cowan
Wash Farra

Brotherhoods (Louisville, KY)

W. H. Lee, lf
George White, 3b
Washington Nesby, cf
Jesse Palmer, ss
Elzy Hart, 2b
Williams, 1b
Ward, rf
Moses Clark, c
Ross, p
Marshall, p

Old Olymps (Louisville, KY)

S. Ballard, c
John Taylor, p
Carr, 1b
Haywood Rose, 2b / c
Moses Allen, 3b
Daniel Heins, ss
I. English, lf
Jesse Palmer, rf
W. H. Lee, lf
George White, 3b
Washington Nesby, cf
Elzy Hart, 2b
Ward, rf
Moses Clark, c
A. Ross, p
Marshall, p
Tom Williams, 1b
Joseph Burdine, cf
Barrett Grant, cf / Captain

L.O. 4 (Paducah, KY)

Andrew Boyd, c
Ollie Catlewt, p
William "Bill" Hall, 1b
Andrew Williams, 2b
H. M. Fowler, 3b / Captain
C. Robinson, ss
John Catlewt, lf
Henry Morse, rf
Wallace Strickland, cf
Tom Robinson, Manager

R.R. (Paducah, KY)

Louis "Lou" Matthews
Philbert Pasen

Edward "Eddie" Wood
James Kimbell
Pete Travis
Sid Henderson
Lord Vinegar
Ernest Jefferson
Lee Mitchell

Maryland

Giants (Baltimore, MD)

George Ackwood, ss
Wilson, 2b
Savoy, cf
Henry Hill, 1b
Church, 3b
E. Duvall, p
Robert Pinder, c
Charles Washington, rf / p
Reynolds lf
James Green, c
Charles Davis, ss
Evans, c
Brown, p
William T. Jordan, manager

Missouri

Colored Nine (Desoto, MO)

George Bozier
Arthur Ewing, 1b
R. Blake, 2b
N. Wilson, 3b
Gus Tracey, ss
H. H. Mitchell, rf
H. C. Mitchell, lf
G. Rogers, cf
Benjamin "Ben" DeBose, c
Walter Jennings, p
William L. Smith, Manager

Unions (Kansas City, MO)

Watts, 1b
Rose, 2b
Cure, 3b
Bright, ss
Sayers, rf / c
Long, cf
West, lf
T. Lewis, c
Frank Montgomery, p
R. Martin, p
Andrews, Substitute
Andrews, Substitute
A. L. Dorsey, Manager

Tigers (Lexington, MO)

Hollingsworth, p / lf
Madey, p
James Lindsey, p
Frank Lindsey, c
George Smith, p / rf
Hanley, c
Walter Lindsey, rf

John Lindsey, 2b
E. Hayden, cf
Albert Williams, Manager

New Jersey

Shelburne (Atlantic City, NJ)

Small, lf / p
T. Gates, cf
Scott, c / 1b
Jackson, ss
Washington, 2b
Courtney, 3b / p
E. A. Atkinson, c
Benter, rf
Oliver, p / 2b

Jersey Cubans (Passaic, NJ)

Stokes, cf
Turner, 2b / ss
Watson, rf / 2b
Harrison, 1b
William Braxton, ss
W. Miller, 1b / rf
Pete Hill, 3b
John Daniels, p / ss
W. Harrison, lf
Miller, rf
Clarence Henry, cf
Martin, 2b
J. Finch, rf
Edward Demunde, lf
Jacco, c
J. Buck, lf / 1b
H. B. Finch, Manager

Browns (Pennington, NJ)

Joseph Smith, c
Jennings, p / ss
Ashby Seruby, 1b
A. Smith, 2b
P. Smith, 3b / p
J. Smith, ss / rf
Downes, rf / 2b
S. Seruby, cf
Net Smith, rf
Fred Boyer, c / 2b / Team Manager

Giants (Princeton, NJ)

William Scudder, c
R. Washington, 1b
Buss, 2b
Joseph James, 3b
Jacob Scudder, ss / lf
Henry Johnson, lf
F. Washington, p
J. Brown, rf
W. Williams, 2b / 1b
Upton Johnson, p
S. "Cy" James, p
G. Redding, ss
E. Freeman, 1b
J. Mitchell, c

Peter Richmond, 2b
A. Miller, p / c
L. Yates, lf
Cowen, rf
A. Jackson, rf
Black, cf
Winslow Tyrrell, 1b
George A. Smith, ss
Frederickson, lf
J. Thompson, 2b
Madison, c
Fullerton, p
Stone, p
Jesse Hoagland, 3b

Cuban X-Giants Juniors
(Trenton, NJ)

James, c
Dayton Blackwell, p
Little, lf
George Frost, 1b
Morris Ganges, 2b
T. Pierce, 3b
Jones, ss
Douglass, cf
Miller, cf
S. Johnson, Manager

Orients (Trenton, NJ)

Arthur Griffin, c
William Carter, p
E. Kinney, 1b
J. Vincent, 2b
Upton Johnson, ss
S. Kinney, cf
Thomas, lf / Captain
William Edwards, rf
J. Brown, Substitute
George Frost, Substitute
Major, Substitute

Lincoln Juniors (Trenton, NJ)

James, c
Blackwell, p
George Frost, 1b
Morris Ganges, 2b
Little, 3b
Josephs, ss
Thomas, lf / Team Captain
A. Miller, cf
Douglass, rf

Rough Riders (Trenton, NJ)

George Johnson, c
C. Taylor, p
R. Washington, 1b
Upton Johnson, 2b
Abe Harris, ss
W. Dutch, 3b
W. Brown, rf
H. Harris, cf
J. Thomas, lf

New Mexico
San Juans
(Fort Wingate, NM)

Prather, c
Clarke, p
Pumphrey, 1b
Corbit, 2b
Lyons, 3b
Reed, ss
Nelson, lf
Golden, cf / p
Sanders, rf
Middleton
Harris
Wheeler
Cumby
Murray
Jenon Anderson, Manager

New York
Darktown Field Club
(Brooklyn, NY)

Hill, cf
Scott, rf
Johnson, ss
Heywood, lf
Williams, 1b
Chapman, 2b
Roberts, c
Stone, p
Bruce, 3b
Drake, c
Spencer, p
Martin

Cuban Giants (Buffalo, NY)

Hanley, c
Frank Barchel, p
Robert Slattery, 1b
O. Bright, 2b
John Bright, cf
William Bright. rf
Tom S. Rodgers, 3b
Theodore Pell, ss
William Schuyler, cf
Ollie Johnson
B. Smith, lf

Giants (Geneva, NY)

Charles Rice, Captain
Theodore Derby, c
Arthur Kinney, p
Albert Hazzard, 1b
Harry Johnson, 2b
William Rowe, 3b
William Schuyler, ss
Harry Terry, lf
Herman Kinney, cf
Henry Harden, rf
John Rowe, cf
A. Benney, p

Charles Johnson, Substitute
Latimer, Manager

Giants (Ithaca, NY)

Napoleon Jackson, p / Captain
Bert Clay, p
Richard Jackson, c
Bert Washington, 1b
Thomas Lewis, 3b
Eugene Smith, ss
Ern Russell, cf
John Wise, rf
J. W. Jackson, Team Manager

Black Patti Troubadours
(New York, NY)

William Cook, 1b
James Bland, 2b / cf
George Holt, c
Leslie Triplett, 3b / ss
Judson Hicks, rf / 2b
Forster, ss
Rich, lf
Augustus Hall, cf / 3b
Anthony D. Byrd, p
James Escort Lightfoot, lf

Cuban X-Giants
(New York, NY)

William Galloway, 3b
Williams, c
W. Wilson, 1b / c
C. McClellan, rf / c
John Nelson, 2b / ss
Alfred Jupiter, rf
William Stewart, ss
James D. Robinson, p
William Jackson, lf
James, cf / ss
Munn, rf
Parker, 1b
E. B. Lamar, Manager

Genuine Cuban Giants
(New York, NY)

Ed Chamberlain, 1b
Parker, 1b
Pete Hill, 3b
Ulysses "Frank" Grant, 2b
William T. Smith, c
D. Thompson, cf
William Thompson, c
Bell, ss / p / lf
Benjamin Brown, cf
John Watkins, rf / c
R. Brown, p
William "Bill" Williams, p
J. Buck, 1b
Greene, p / cf / ss
John Nelson, cf
Butte, 2b
Wilkins, c
Edward French, cf

Thomas James, cf / ss
John Mickey, p
Munn, rf
Clarence Sampson, rf
William Kelly, lf / c
Norwood Turner, rf
William Galloway, 3b
Ray Wilson, cf / p
John Porter, 1b / c
William Bailey, c
Wiley, c

Williams & Walker
(New York, NY)

Ed "Black Carl" Johnson, ss
Clarence, p
William H. Chappelle, 2b
William C. Elkins, rf
Charles Davis, c
Robert N. Thompson, 3b
Allen McDonald, 1b
Blackmon, lf
George Harris, cf
Bert A. Williams, Manager

Cuban Giants (Olean, NY)

Allic Berry, p
A. Johnson, lf
R. Johnson, ss / c
J. Carter, 1b
Allie Jones, rf
R. Berry, 2b / ss
W. Cone, 3b
William Schuyler, cf
Charles Berry, c / 2b

Imperials (Oswego, NY)

H. Williams, cf
G. Cheeks, 1b
F. Dennis, lf
R. Williams, 3b
Frank T. Pell, 2b
Percy Whitman, c
W. Hill, ss
Charles Williams, p
G. Jones, rf

St. Marks (Syracuse, NY)

David Titus, p
J. Shepherd, c
J. Murdock, 1b
J. Talbot, 2b
Wilbur Jackson, 3b
J. B. Robinson, ss
Fred Bennett, cf
Ed Joiner, lf
Mose Gray, rf / c
B. Smith, 2b

Fearless (Utica, NY)

Charles Henry, 1b
Avery Griger, p / c
Peter Pell, ss

Roscoe A. Anderson, 3b
Fred Jackson, rf
Charles Walter Titus, cf
R. Robbins, lf
Peter Henry, c / p
D. DeNike, 2b
John Titus, rf / 3b

Free Doin's (Utica, NY)

Edward R. Rich, 3b / Captain
Floyd Peresett, c / Manager
James DeNike, p
George Johnson, 1b
David DeNike, 2b
William Johnson, rf
D. Right, lf
E. Clarke, cf
George W. Martin, ss

Help-Ups (Utica, NY)

C. Sherman, c
R. Robbins, p
F. Henry, 1b / c
Angle, 2b
Right, 3b
Louis Hall, rf
Peterson, cf
Nick Lavender, p
Roscoe Anderson, lf
James Rose, p

North Carolina
Quicksteps (Charlotte, NC)

John Daniels, p
John Brown, 1b
Charles Wortham, 2b
Robeson, ss
J. S. Coles, 3b
Julius Holt, c
Williams, p
White, lf
Ed Torrence, cf
James Diamonds, rf
Frank Simmons, ss
Burrell Washington
J. Rufus Williams, p
A. Rives, Manager

Mutuals (Wilmington, NC)

Grant Torrence, Treasurer
George Williams, Secretary
Henry Johnson, Captain

Southside Barbers
(Wilmington, NC)

James McKathern, c / Captain
H. Clinton, p
P. Chesnut, 1b
Ed Guion, 2b
Charles Crawley, 3b
Sam Johnson, ss
James Yates, lf

Bruce Walker, cf
E. Jenkins, rf
Fred Merrion, Substitute
David Jacobs, Manager

Yarborough and Murrays
(Wilmington, NC)

Julius Murray, p
Yarborough, c
Harris, 1b
F. Fennell, 2b
George Peamon, 3b
John Joyner, ss
Simmons, lf
L. D. Richardson, cf
Joseph P. Sampson, rf
Albert McRae, p

Ohio
Keystones (Cleveland, OH)

William Turner, 3b
E. Turner, rf / p
William Albert Colwell, 1b
W. Pittman, ss
Frank Henderson, c / 1b
W. E. McPherson, lf
John Jackson, c
J. Smith, p
W. Nelson, 3b / c
Hittman, ss
Fred Wilson, 3b
R. H. Shaw, 2b
Gray, p
J. Early, cf
Williams, ss
Albert Dennie, lf
Robeson, cf

Unions (Cleveland, OH)

Shaw, 2b
William Turner, 3b
William A. Colwell, 1b
W. Pittman, ss
Frank Henderson, c
McPherson, lf
John Jackson, cf
J. Smith, p
W. Nelson, 1b / c
Gray, p
Edward Turner, rf

Black Tourists (Columbus, OH)

James Chavous, 3b
Bud Fowler, 2b
B. Harris, c
Wilbur Randolph, cf / p
Cary White, ss
William Robison, 1b
Thomas Allen, rf
William Jones, lf
William Lyons, p
A. S. Peal, Manager

Oklahoma

Blues (Guthrie, OK)

R .Owens
Gray
McDonald
Riddley
K. Hayes
H. Fields
Alexander Hayes
Henry
Jordan

Pennsylvania

Midnight Stars (Canonsburg, PA)

Granville McGant, c / Asst. Manager
Samuel Wilson, pitcher / Manager
Shirley Sluby, rf / Captain
John Robinson, 1b
Charlie Robinson, 2b
Earl Catlin, 3b
Louis Henderson, ss
C. Brown, cf
Wesley Dungee, cf
James Kennedy, lf
W. Griffin, Mascot

C. J. C. (Canonsburg, PA)

Robert Price, c
Edward Williams, p / Captain
B. Catlin, ss
G. Jones, 1b
H. Donaldson, 2b
A. Williams, 3b
G. Worstell, lf
C. Campbell, cf
A. Smith, rf

Giants (Chester, PA)

Bergen, cf
Johnson, ss
Sock, 3b
Jones, 2b
Barnes, 1b
Mack, 1b
Mastin, 1b / rf
J. Green, rf
David Lawrence, lf
J. Perrigan, 2b
Blackson, 3b
Callender, 3b
Green, cf
Smallwood, lf
Bland, rf
Roberts, 2b
Sevry, c
Lock, c
Gordy, p
Spencer, p
William "Billy" Stewart, Manager

Cuban Giants (Harrisburg, PA)

John "Jack" Potter, lf
Al Baxter, c / 3b
William Banks, p / ss
James Barton, 2b
George Williams, 1b
N. Williams, 3b
Thomas James, ss / p
Robert "Bob" Jordan, c / cf
William R. Williams, rf
Horace Murray, 1b
Ray Wilson, c / p / cf
Isaac B. Taylor, cf
James Murphy, cf
James Manning, p
Doen, 3b
Henry Moore, ss

Non Pariels (Lock Haven, PA)

Frank Henson, p
Orrin Patterson, c
Elmer Burgess, 1b
George Grimes, 2b
Ellery Washington, 3b
William Mitchell, ss
Charles Brown, rf
Creighton Roberts, lf
Charles Howard, cf
William Mitchell, Captain

Never Sinks (Reading, PA)

Fisher, ss
Smith, 3b
Hutch, cf
Allen, cf
Ino, 1b
Warrick, p
Nugent, c
Robinson, lf
Carroll, rf
Tucker, rf

Cuban Giants Jr. (York, PA)

James Hendrickson, c / 1b
Charles H. Pinkney, lf / c
Clayton Cannon, rf
White, 2b
Hall, 3b
George Bolden, p
Devon, c
William Mills, ss
S. John, c / lf

Tennessee

Unions (Chattanooga, TN)

Charlie Dewberry, p
Moses Cain, c
A. W. Massingale, Manager
Thomas M. Henderson, Secretary
John McCafferty, President
Charles Brown, Vice President

Colored Nine (Jackson, TN)

Bob Scott, Captain / p
J. Jones, c
B. Robertson, 3b
J. Smith, lf
M. Windon, lf
W. Holoway, cf
M. Anderson, rf
P. Brown, rf
A. Duke, ss
G. Johnson, 1b
B. E. Rogers, 1b
S. Ellis, 2b
W. Smith, p
James Lee, p
Bud Richerson, President
June Scott. Manager

Rock City Unions (Nashville, TN)

N. Fhy, c
S. Fhy, p
Denross, 1b
P. L. Nichols, 2b
Johnson, 3b
King, ss
Harry Saithow (Southpaw), lf
Collins, cf
McKinney, rf
Washington, 2b
Frank Bell, Captain
W. C. Ewing, Manager

Colored Nine (Austin, TX)

Phillips, c
McCratle, p
M. Dodson, 1b
Jefferson, 2b
Burdett, 3b
Lott, ss
Lewis, lf
Jones, cf
C. Dodson, rf

Fencibles (Galveston, TX)

Lewis, c
Miller, p
Jones, 1b
Coleman, 2b
James Blair, 3b
Simmons, ss
Mills, lf
Anderson, cf
Bailey, rf

Rosebuds (Houston, TX)

Knockless, c
Hamilton, p
Mays, 1b
Bird, 2b
W. Busby, 3b
E. Busby, ss

White, lf
Venson, cf
Jackson, rf

Clippers
(McKinney, TX)

Braddix
Rector
Cook
Baker
C. Henderson
Ward Johnson
Clarence Carter
Abraham
Rice

Washington, DC

Capital Citys
(Washington, DC)

Harry Smith, 1b
A. Atkinson, 2b
S. Payne, 3b / ss
S. Coleman, c
Burke, rf / lf
Arthur Anderson, p / 3b
Henry Hines, rf / c / 1b
C. I. Smith, cf
George Betters, cf
Magruder, rf
Waters, lf
William D. Wilkinson, p

Arthur Anderson, p
Samuel Jones, Substitute

Holmes House
(Washington, DC)

James Robinson, 3b
Green, 2b
M. Wilkinson, 1b
William Byrd, ss
J. Wilkinson, lf
James Crawford, cf / c
B. S. Jackson, rf
S. Coleman, c
John F. Henson, p
Long, p

Directory:
Managers, Promoters
and Other Contacts, 1867–1900

Without league schedules to rely on, early black baseball teams, like later barnstorming clubs, relied heavily on the work of managers, presidents, secretaries, and others to seek out (often within the newspapers) potential competition and coordinate dates and travel plans. The list below, organized by year, includes the name and position of each team's primary contact and the address at which he could be reached by those hoping to engage his team.

1867

Gus P. Rivers, President—El Dorado
No. 1 South Charles Street
Baltimore, MD

George D. Johnson, Secretary—Mutuals
Freedmen's Bureau
Washington, DC

Samuel J. Hatcher, Secretary—Alerts
Sparks and Simms Building
Corner of New York and 111th Street
Washington, DC

Louis A. Bell, corresponding Secretary—Alerts
Sparks and Simms Building
Corner of New York and 111th Street
Washington, DC

Samuel Freeman, Manager—Fearless
No. 5 Main Street
Utica, NY

Ira P. Sayton, Secretary—Uniques
19 Fourth Street
Brooklyn, NY

D. J. Hunter, Assistant Secretary—Monitors
67 & 71 Broadway Street
Brooklyn, NY

W. G. Brown, Secretary—Monitors
187 Navy Street
Brooklyn, NY

Andrew Dosen, Manager—Monitors
44 DeKalb Street
Brooklyn, NY

Jacob C. White, Secretary—Pythians
713 Lombard Street
Philadelphia, PA

Henry Bascom, Assistant Secretary—Pythians
120 South 10th Street
Philadelphia, PA

William C. Bolivar, Corresponding Secretary—Pythians
906 Rodman Street
Philadelphia, PA

George H. Wilson, Secretary—Excelsiors
713 Lombard Street (Broad and Lombard)
Philadelphia, PA

George Galbraith, Secretary—Monrovias
"Rooms of the Monrovia Club"
Harrisburg, PA

Abram Brown, Secretary—Alerts
West Chester, PA

1868

Abram Brown, Secretary—Alerts
West Chester, PA

1869

Charles R. Douglass, Secretary—Mutuals
Third Auditor's Office
Washington, DC

R. G. Thompson, Secretary—Ashmun Club
Lincoln University
Lincoln University, PA

Charles McCullough, Secretary—Pythians
718 Lombard Street
Philadelphia, PA

Abram Brown, Secretary—Actives
West Chester, PA

1870

R. H. Robinson, President—Metropolitans
1236 Tenth Street NW
Washington, DC

Charles R. Douglas, Secretary—Mutuals
Third Auditor's Office
Washington, DC

William P. Johnson, Secretary—Blue Stockings
228–230 South Clark Street
Chicago, IL

Douglass Smith, manager—Brown Stockings
109 North 5th Street
St. Louis, MO

DuBois H. Hallack, Secretary—Keystones
256 Newark Avenue
Bergen Point, NJ

Charles McCullough, Secretary—Pythians
756 South Eighth Street
Philadelphia, PA

1871

Charles R. Douglass, manager—Mutuals
Third Auditor's Office
Washington, DC

William D. Berry, manager—Uniques
No. 77 Clark Street
Chicago, IL

James Taylor, manager, Resolutes
7 Alston Street
Boston, MA

Douglass Smith, Secretary—Brown Stockings
108 North 6th Street
St. Louis, MO

1872

William Grymes, Team President—Alerts
No. 1028 Nineteenth Street
Washington, DC

Charles R. Douglass, Manager—Mutuals
Third Auditor's Office
Washington, DC

James Taylor, Manager, Resolutes
7 Alston Street
Boston, MA

DuBois H. Hallack, Secretary—Keystones
253 Newark Avenue
Bergen Point, NJ

William D. Berry, Manager—Uniques
No. 77 Clark Street
Chicago, IL

1874

William D. Berry, Team Manager—Unique Ten
No. 328 South Clark Street
Chicago, IL

1875

Charles R. Douglass, Team Captain—Mutuals
1116 F Street
Washington, DC

Chicago, IL E. Brown, Manager—Pytheus
537 South Clark Street
Chicago, IL

Henry P. Hall, Manager—Uniques
No. 328 South Clark Street
Chicago, IL

James A. Johnson, Manager—Blue Stockings
615 Washington Avenue
St. Louis, MO

Benjamin F. Cleggett, Team President—Nonesuch
No. 8 Seneca Street
Geneva, NY

Dangerfield S. Garner, secretary—Tyroleans
122 Cowden Street
Harrisburg, PA

1876

William Davidge, Team President—Alerts
No. 1026 Nineteenth Street
Washington, DC

Charles J. Hardy, Team Secretary—Lord Hannibals
254 Hamburg Street
Baltimore, MD

William Matthews, Team Secretary—Mansfields
No. 47 Forest Street
Baltimore, MD

Joseph Lucas, Team Secretary—Pioneers
No. 12 Boyd Street
Baltimore, MD

Benjamin F. Cleggett, President—Nonesuch
No. 8 Seneca Street
Geneva, NY

Edward Anthony, Team Secretary—Unions
Saratoga Springs, NY

A. C. DeWitt, Corresponding Secretary—Fearless
No. 58 Charlotte Street
Utica, NY

1877

C. W. Harley, Team President—Harleys
517 East State Street
Harrisburg, PA

James A. Howard, Team Secretary—Harleys
605 South Street
Harrisburg, PA

C. W. Harley, Team Secretary—Olympics
517 East State Street
Harrisburg, PA

Samuel Brown, Secretary—Uniques
418 South Clark Street
Chicago, IL

Leslie Mack, Manager—Fairplays
66 North Pennsylvania
Indianapolis, IN

Sam Lewis, Team Manager—Vigilants
No. 211 West 7th Street
Cincinnati, OH

1878

C. W. Harley, Team President—Harleys
517 East State Street
Harrisburg, PA

James A. Howard, Team Secretary—Harleys
605 South Street
Harrisburg, PA

1879

William D. Berry, manager—Uniques
No. 328 South Clark Street
Chicago, IL

A. D. White, secretary—Resolutes
22 Porter Street
Boston, MA

Aaron Briles, manager—Colored Nine
Vanderbilt House
Syracuse, NY

Henry H. Waters, manager—Pastimes
Globe Hotel
Syracuse, NY

C. W. Harley, Team President—Harleys
517 East State Street
Harrisburg, PA

James A. Howard, Team Secretary—Harleys
605 South Street
Harrisburg, PA

1880

William D. Berry, Manager—Uniques
No. 328 South Clark Street
Chicago, IL

Horace H. Hall, Manager—Internationals
International Hotel
Niagara, NY

1881

Horace H. Hall, Manager—Internationals
International Hotel
Niagara, NY

J. A. Jordan, Secretary—Internationals
International Hotel
Niagara, NY

C. W. Harley, Team President—Harleys
517 East State Street
Harrisburg, PA

James A. Howard, Team Secretary—Harleys
605 South Street
Harrisburg, PA

Charles Jones, manager—Orions
1215 Wood Street
Philadelphia, PA

1882

Walter Price, manager—Elm City
83 Eaton Street
New Haven, CT

W. J. Christie, manager—Adelaides
Hall Brothers Tonsorial Palace
Elgin, IL

Henry Bridgewater, manager—Black Stockings
725 North Eleventh Street
St. Louis, MO

John Dolan, manager (white)—Black Stockings
No. 111 South Tenth Street
St. Louis, MO

Frank Doctor, secretary—Southern Stars
Windsor Club
Bank Street
Cleveland, OH

C. W. Harley, secretary—Olympics
517 East State Street
Harrisburg, PA

Harry S. Sigler, secretary—Olympics
Williams Street and Basins Avenue
Harrisburg, PA

George Sherrow, manager—Mutuals
No. 51 Eleventh Street
Pittsburgh, PA

George Sherrow, manager—Mutuals
1215 Wood Street
Pittsburgh, PA

John Jones, manager—Orions
1215 Wood Street
Philadelphia, PA

John Lang, manager—Orions
308 Race Street
James Hotel
Philadelphia, PA

Robert G. Still, manager—Pythians
244 South Twelfth Street
Philadelphia, PA

J. C. Harrison, manager—Swans
Richmond, VA

1883

George S. Coutee, secretary—Black Stockings
Denver City Post Office
Denver, CO

Charles Boyd, manager—Douglass Club
2206 Eleventh Street
Washington, DC

D. W. Downing, manager—Douglass Club
2206 Eleventh Street
Washington, DC

W. J. Christie, manager—Adelaides
Hall Brothers Tonsorial Palace
Elgin, IL

George Davis, secretary—Reds
K & T Railroad
Sedalia, MO

Henry Bridgewater, manager—Black Stockings
725 North Eleventh Street
St. Louis, MO

Frank Brown, secretary—West Ends
2628 Morgan Street
St. Louis, MO

William Hudson, manager—Young Buffalos
1530 Orange Street
St. Louis, MO

Wilson N. Cary, manager—West Ends
West End Hotel
Long Branch, NJ

William Johnson, manager—Polka Dots
35 West Hanover Street
Trenton, NJ

Frank Seton, manager—Colored Seniors
New York, NY

George Myers, manager—Blue Stockings
Weddell House—Barber Shop
Cleveland, OH

John Brown, secretary—Thorntons
Northeast Corner of Tenth and Columbia Avenue
Chester, PA

Julius "Jack" Forbes, manager—Orions
717 North Sixteenth Street
Philadelphia, PA

D. W. Downing, manager—Douglass Club
137 Washington Street
Pittsburgh, PA

W. C. Lee, manager—Westerns
Peon Street and Sixth Avenue
Pittsburgh, PA

Javan I. Emory, manager—Lumber Citys
99 Gilman Street
Williamsport, PA

R. D. White, manager—Lone Jack Base Ball Club
223 Twelfth Street
Lynchburg, VA

John Fowler, manager—Black Swans
123 South Eighth Street
Richmond, VA

1884

Joseph Harris, manager—Gordons
103 East Harrison Street
Chicago, IL

William Sutliffe, manager—Gordons
103 East Harrison Street
Chicago, IL

William Albert "Al" Jones, manager—Unknowns
7 East Polk Street
Chicago, IL

W. H. Hogan, manager—Black Diamonds
912 East Washington Street
Springfield, IL

Lafayette Condon, manager—Fall Citys
No. 1725 Columbia Street
Louisville, KY

Henry Bridgewater, manager—Black Stockings
725 North Eleventh Street
St. Louis, MO

E. Thompson, manager—Buffalos
1421 Orange Street
St. Louis, MO

Charles H. Brady, secretary—Eclipse
1927 Charles Street
St. Louis, MO

William H. Griswold, manager—Eclipse
1717 Jackson Street
St. Louis, MO

David Price, manager—Metropolitans
2319 Papin Street
St. Louis, MO

S. Steward, manager—Sumner
115 Elliott Avenue
St. Louis, MO

George Davis, secretary—Reds
K & T Railroad
Sedalia, MO

Edmund Saloman, Manager—Alpines
1421 Dean Street
Brooklyn, NY

H. Z. Zimmer, manager—Alpines
513 Chestnut Street
Brooklyn, NY

Dan Boohrie, Secretary/Captain—Genesees
Genesee Hotel
Buffalo, NY

Morris Edward Wilson, Manager/Captain—Lone Stars
114 East 119th Street
New York, NY

Cassius Govern, Manager—Manhattans
Washington, DC
New York, NY

P. L. Jacobs, Manager—Police Gazette Colored Club
Police Gazette Office
New York, NY

W. H. Reed, manager—Magnolias
74 Longworth Street
Cincinnati, OH

A. Johnson, manager—Standards
257 ½ John Street
Cincinnati, OH

Charles H. Griffin, manager—Unions
31 Maple Street
Cleveland, OH

Herman Wilson, manager—Capital Citys
Exchange Hotel
Columbus, OH

Frank Ford, manager—Athletics
33 South Market Street
Springfield, OH

Javan Emory, manager—Lumber Citys
Anderson and Shield's Barber Shop
99 Gilmer Street
Williamsport, PA

1885

Samuel Jefferson, manager—Clippers
Washington, DC

Andrew M. Porter, secretary—Acme
2938 State Street
Chicago, IL

Lafayette Condon, manager—Falls Citys
1725 Columbia St.
Louisville, KY

Walter Louis Cohen, manager—W. L. Cohens
233 Bienville St.
New Orleans, LA

Alexander A. Selden, manager—Resolutes
116 Elliot Street
Boston, MA

W. C. Ward, manager—Bay States
No. 19 Kendall Street
Boston, MA

Henry Bridgewater, manager—Black Stockings
725 North Eleventh St.
St. Louis, MO

Thomas Richardson, secretary—Eclipse
829 North Eighth Street
St. Louis, MO

B. Hampton, manager—Reds
Sedalia, MO

T. Carroll Johnston, manager—Crescent
248 East Hanover St.
Princeton, NJ

H. H. Johnson, manager—Alpines
1450 Bergen Street
Brooklyn, NY

F. B. Hoagland, secretary—Remsens
31 Chapel St.
Brooklyn, NY

H. H. Johnson, manager—Remsens
318 Fulton Street
Brooklyn, NY

H. Kiffe, secretary—Remsens
318 Fulton Street
Brooklyn, NY

Theo W. Smith, manager—Remsens
No. 219 Bridge Street
Brooklyn, NY

Charles Williams, manager—Actives
307 John Street
Cincinnati, OH

W. H. Reed, manager—Magnolias
74 Longworth Street
Cincinnati, OH

Charles Griffin, manager—Unions
1464 Garden St.
Cleveland, OH

John Lang, manager—Lang's Colored Giants
No. 332 York Avenue
Philadelphia, PA

C. E. Lloyd, manager—Manhattans
307 Walnut Street
Philadelphia, PA

1886

John W. Jones, Team President—League of Southern Colored Base Ballists
Lock Box 298
Jacksonville, FL

K. W. Riley, manager—Lone Stars
449 West Sixty-Second Street
Chicago, IL

William C. Sutcliffe, manager—Uniques
No 261 State St.
Chicago, IL

C. H. Ennis, manager—Falls Citys
No. 616 Tenth Street
Louisville, KY

Walter Louis Cohen, manager—W. L. Cohens
233 Bienville Street
New Orleans, LA

Alexander A. Selden, manager—Boston
107 Cambridge
Boston, MA

Benjamin F. Allen, manager—Seasides
2 Park Street
Boston, MA

T. W. Scott, manager—Bay State
865 Washington St.
Boston, MA

Alexander A. Selden, manager—Resolutes
107 Cambridge Street
Boston, MA

H. F. Hicks, manager—Resolutes
145 Chambers Street
Boston, MA

Jesse C. Binga, manager—Colored Nine
54 Cadillac Square
Detroit, MI

William Malone, secretary—West Ends
No. 65 Bronson Street
Detroit, MI

Henry Bridgewater, manager—Black Stockings
725 North Eleventh Street
St. Louis, MO

Henry Sanford, manager—Euchres
No. 1627 Gay Street
St. Louis, MO

W. R. Smith, manager—Lindells
2318 Papin Street
St. Louis, MO

John J. Young, manager—Fultons
98 Smith Street
Charleston, NC

Richard Dawson, manager—Hudsons
450 Henderson Street
Jersey City, NJ

Stanislau K. Govern, manager—Cuban Giants
No. 4 Polk's Building
Trenton, NJ

James Thomas Tolliver, manager—Wide Awakes
No. 78 Madison
Syracuse, NY

Frank J. Williams, secretary—Wide Awakes
No. 78 Madison
Syracuse, NY

Andrew Dixon, manager—Dauntless
Powers Hotel
Rochester, NY

Benjamin Butler, manager—Gorhams
23 Cornelia Street
New York, NY

A. Johnson, manager—Standard BBC
267 ½ John Street
Cincinnati, OH

Charles C. Starkey, manager—Excelsiors
No. 57 Michigan Street
Cleveland, OH

Javan Emory, manager—Lumber City Reds
Anderson and Shield's Barber Shop
99 Gilmer Street
Williamsport, PA

E. Richard Jones, manager—Colored Grays
Naragansett Hotel
7 Jackson Court
Providence, RI

1887

Jacob Chippey, manager—Delawares
1110 Tatnall Street
Wilmington, DE

Theodore H. Gray, manager—Flyaways
810 Tatnall Street
Wilmington, DE

Sterling and Jones, manager—Golden Cross
219 West 11th Street
8th and Tatnall Street
Wilmington, DE

E. L. States, manager—Wilmingtons
233 West Eighth Street
Wilmington, DE

William Sutcliff, manager—Uniques
Room 906, Insurance Exec Building
Chicago, IL

Charles W. Hines, Sr., manager—Falls Citys
1729 Clay St.
Louisville, KY

D. Noble, Jr., manager—Browns
258 Chartres Street
New Orleans, LA

J. J. Arnold, manager—Iolathes
No. 121 James Street
New Orleans, LA

Joseph Jailliot, manager—Pelicans
No. 258 Canal Street
New Orleans, LA

Walter Louis Cohen, manager—Pickwicks
233 Bienville St.
New Orleans, LA

William J. Turner & Joseph Jalliot, managers—Pickwicks
No. 258 Canal St.
New Orleans, LA

R. E. Foreman, manager—R. E. Foremans
686 Dryades Street
New Orleans, LA

William J. Turner, manager—Unions
No. 258 Canal St.
New Orleans, LA

T. W. Scott, manager—Bay States
865 Washington Street
Cambridge, MA

George A. Sharkey, manager—Franklins
123 Elm Street
Cambridgeport, MA

Marshall Thompson, manager—Resolutes
c/o The Globe
Boston, MA

D. Marsh, manager—Seaside Juniors
92 Union Street
Boston, MA

L. T. Roberts, manager—Seasides
1045 Washington Street
Boston, MA

William D. Carter, manager—Quicksteps
Minnesota Club
Corner of 4th and Cedar
St. Paul, MN

H. E. Bruckner, manager—Akrons
1619 Wash Street
St. Louis, MO

Lewis Canter, manager—Black Stockings
1724 Webster Ave.
St. Louis, MO

Mace A. Jefferson, manager—Sumner B.B.C.
Jefferson Barracks
St. Louis, MO

Stanislau K. Govern, field manager—Cuban Giants
No. 173 Broad Street
Trenton, NJ

J. M. Bright, business manager—Cuban Giants
153 Prince Street
New York, NY

J. M. Bright, business manager—Cuban Giants
No. 160 West Houston Street
New York, NY

John M. Bright, manager—Cuban Giants
200 Spring Street
New York, NY

Charles C. Starkey, manager—Excelsiors
No. 57 Michigan Street
Cleveland, OH

William Simpson, manager—Giants
428 South Thirteenth Street
Lancaster, PA

Stanislau K. Govern, manager—Cuban Giants
New Hotel Lafayette
Philadelphia, PA

Robert G. Still, manager—Pythians
244 South Twelfth Street
Philadelphia, PA

Walter S. Brown, president—National Colored Baseball League
515 Smithfield Street
Pittsburgh, PA

D. Richard Jones, manager—Colored Grays
Naragansett Hotel
7 Jackson Court
Providence, RI

1888

Joe Green, manager—Cuban Giants No. 2
Lock Box 401
Chicago, IL

C. Newell, manager—West Side Browns
No. 57 North Aun Street
Chicago, IL

Walter Louis Cohen, manager—P.B.S. Pinchbacks
233 Bienville Street
New Orleans, LA

H. F. Hechs, manager—Resolutes
145 Chambers Street
Boston, MA

Marshall Thompson, manager—Resolutes
145 Chambers Street
Boston, MA

Marshall Thompson, manager—Seasides
92 Union Street
Boston, MA

Charles Campbell, secretary—Ashlands (white)
78 Waltham Street
Boston, MA

T. W. Scott, manager—Bay State
865 Washington St.
Boston, MA

E. C. Bryant and Henry Carter, manager—Resolute Juniors
7 Sears Place
Boston, MA

C. Miller, manager—Grays
383 Washington Street
Cambridge, MA

E. C. Bryant, manager—Resolute Juniors
40 Plymouth Street
Cambridgeport, MA

Henry Ogden, President—Little Diamonds
311 Washington Avenue
St. Paul, MN

John Samuels, Team Captain—Little Diamonds
256 6th Avenue S.
St. Paul, MN

H. E. Bruckner, manager—Akrons
1619 Wash Street
St. Louis, MO

Henry Sanford, manager—Black Stockings
1216 North Fifteenth Street
St. Louis, MO

William R. Smith, manager—Lindells
2318 Papin Street
St. Louis, MO

Arthur Jackson, manager—F.O.B.
Englewood, NJ

P. McCauley, manager—African Greasers
West Hanover Street
Trenton, NJ

Stanislau K. Govern, manager—Cuban Giants
Trenton, NJ

Robert Maner, secretary—Young Cuban Giants
No. 6 Decatur Street
Trenton, NJ

M. Landers, manager—Harrison and Morton
No. 67 Clinton Street
Buffalo, NY

Jacob Feggans, manager—Lone Stars
267 West 124th Street
Harlem, NY

Morris Wilson, secretary—Lone Stars
125 East 125th Street
Harlem, NY

Benjamin M. Butler, manager—Gorhams
137½ Bleecker Street
New York, NY

Ward Mack, manager—Monitors
187 East One Hundred and Seventeenth Street
New York, NY

Edmund Royal, manager—Nonpareils
629 Lombard Street
Philadelphia, PA

Walter S. Brown, president—Keystones
Central Hotel
Pittsburgh, PA

D. Richard Jones, manager—Colored Grays
Naragansett Hotel
7 Jackson Court
Providence, RI

Henry Swanson, manager—Fly Aways
175 Center Street
Galveston, TX

1889

D. L. Ross, manager—Stonington B.B.C.
Stonington, CT

R. Rhodes, manager—Rhodes Boys
2817 State St.
Chicago, IL

Orange W. Fox, manager—Australian Giants
No. 464 State Street
Chicago, IL

Edward Prime, manager—Black Stockings
No. 1920 Clark Street
Chicago, IL

Robert Jackson, manager—Chicago Unions
464 S. State Street
Chicago, IL

William Albert Jones, manager—Chicago Unions
464 S. State Street
Chicago, IL

P. Gill, manager—Gordons
No. 4062 Lake Avenue
Chicago, IL

F. Graham, Manager—Gordons
No. 17 Bryant Avenue
Chicago, IL

Robert Jackson, manager—Models
2127 ½ Clark St.
Chicago, IL

Orange W. Fox, manager—Resolutes (formerly, the Australian Giants)
No. 462 State Street
Chicago, IL

Frank C. Leland, manager—Resolutes (formerly, the Australian Giants)
No. 464 State Street
Chicago, IL

S. J. Chadwick, manager—South End Athletics
No. 168 South Wabash Ave.
Chicago, IL

W. Sammons, manager—Unknowns
No. 34 Newberry Avenue
Chicago, IL

John Leonard, manager—Young Acmes
No. 235 West Harrison Street
Chicago, IL

Eric Elder Cooper, manager—Black Stockings
155 Indiana Avenue / Freeman Building
Indianapolis, IN

Walter L. Cohen, manager—Pinchbacks
13 Canal Street
New Orleans, LA

H. F. Hicks, manager—Elliotts
1 Pemberton Square
Boston, MA

A. W. Bright, manager—Franklins
65 Franklin Street
Boston, MA

Marshall Thompson, manager—Resolutes
c/o The Globe
Boston, MA

Pinder, manager—Pioneer Club
820 Parrish Street
Baltimore, MD

Henry Gregory, manager—Afro-American B.B.C.
210 Champlain St.
Detroit, MI

Lorne Neville, secretary—Unions
378 Champlain Street
Detroit, MI

Fred Slaughter, manager—Unions
Room 4
Merrill Block
Detroit, MI

Fred Slaughter, manager—Unknowns
878 Champlain Street
Detroit, MI

Lewis Canter, manager—Black Stockings
1724 Webster Ave.
St. Louis, MO

George E. Green, manager—Young Cuban Giants
No. 9 Taylor Alley
Trenton, NJ

William Freeman, manager—Beavers
228 Sullivan Street
New York, NY

John M. D. Bright, manager—Cuban Giants
153 Prince Street
New York, NY

Benjamin Brown, manager—Gorhams
450 Sixth Avenue
New York, NY

Benjamin Butler, manager—Gorhams
No. 137½ Bleeker Street
New York, NY

Charles Black, manager—Z Club
No. 64 Public Square
Cleveland, OH

George D. Sherrow, manager—Colored Barbers
118 Wylie Avenue
Pittsburg, PA

Walter S. Brown, president—Keystones
Central Hotel
Pittsburgh, PA

George Sherrow, manager—Mutuals
118 Wylie Avenue
Pittsburgh, PA

W. B. Moore, manager—Colored Nine
Box E 6
Corsicana, TX

1890

E. D. Johnson, secretary—Lightweights
Hollenbeck Hotel
Los Angeles, CA

M. L. Hackley, manager—Stillman Giants
222 ½ South Tejon St.
Colorado Springs, CO

Robert Jackson, manager—Artics
No. 2834 Butterfield Street
Chicago, IL

Charles Jones, manager—Capitals
No. 516 Wells St.
Chicago, IL

Frank C. Leland, manager—Chicago Unions
No. 468 State St.
Chicago, IL

W. Ball, manager—Clippers
424 State Street
Chicago, IL

H. Smith, manager—"Colored Nine"
No. 158 Harrison St.
Chicago, IL

Robert Jackson, manager—Fistics
No. 2629 Butterfield Street
Chicago, IL

R. Harris, manager—Garretts
807 Austin Avenue
Chicago, IL

C. Spear, secretary—Garretts
215 Ferdinand Street
Chicago, IL

P. Gill, manager—Gordons
No. 4062 Lake Avenue
Chicago, IL

Andrew "Andy" Porter, manager—Gordons
No. 2008 Milwaukee Ave.
Chicago, IL

J. J. Powers, manager—Hard Times
No. 163 Canalport Avenue
Chicago, IL

W. C. Brown, manager—Lake Browns
370 West Lake Street
Chicago, IL

Ed Smith, manager—Model Juniors
2723 Dearborn Avenue
Chicago, IL

George Mead, manager—Models
No 2974 Dearborn St.
Chicago, IL

R. Rhodes, manager—Rhodes Boys
2817 State St.
Chicago, IL

William Turner, manager—South Ends Athletics
202 Twenty-Sixth St.
Chicago, IL

Morris Lewis, manager—South Ends Juniors
2970 Butterfield St.
Chicago, IL

Robert Jackson, manager—Unions
No. 2834 Butterfield Street
Chicago, IL

William Harris, manager—Browns
Advocate Publishing Corporation.
Leavenworth, KS

P. Pinder, manager—Pioneer Club
820 Parrish Street
Baltimore, MD

Fred Slaughter, manager—Unions
378 Champlain Street
Detroit, MI

J. White, manager—Black Stockings
215 South Twenty-First St.
St. Louis, MO

James Savignac, manager—Clippers
21 South Eighth St.
St. Louis, MO

James H. Miller, manager—Mohawks
3004 Market Street
St. Louis, MO

L. Hull, manager—Rose Buds
2733 Wash St.
St. Louis, MO

H. H. Jones, manager—West Ends
2576 Warren St.
St. Louis, MO

John J. Young, manager—Fultons
444 King St.
Charleston, NC

John J. Young, manager—Fultons
98 Smith St.
Charleston, NC

M. Landers, manager—"77"
No. 16 Vine Street
Buffalo, NY

Stanislau K. Govern, manager—Ponce De Leons
Hotel Champlain
Clinton County, NY

Ambrose Davis, manager—Gorhams
137½ Bleeker Street
New York, NY

Benjamin M. Butler, manager—Gorhams
137½ Bleeker Street
New York, NY

H. Goggins, manager—International Baseball Club
International Hotel
Niagara, NY

Charles W. Vulgem, manager—Fearless
Vulgem & Freeman Barber Shop
112 North Washington Street
Rome, NY

William Strothers, manager—Marines
1318 William Street
Harrisburg, PA

John C. Shehan, manager—Black Beauties
532 Walnut Street
Philadelphia, PA

Henry Irving Ziegler, manager—Black Beauties
Corinthian Club
Broad and South Penn Square
Philadelphia, PA

George Groves, manager—Boyd Hill Stars
13 Shingle Street
Pittsburgh, PA

Javan Emory, manager—Lumber City Reds
610 Erie Avenue
Park Hotel
Williamsport, PA

Sim V. Emory, secretary—Lumber City Reds
610 Erie Avenue
Park Hotel
Williamsport, PA

James Blaine, manager—Milwaukee Reds
Boot Blacking Department
Kirby House
Milwaukee, WI

William Morris, manager—Quick Steps
1103 Eoft Street
Wheeling, WV

1891

E. D. Johnson, captain—Lightweights
Hollenbeck hotel
Los Angeles, CA

George Foster, manager—Black Stockings
9 Polk Street
Chicago, IL

George Foster, manager—Black Stockings
9 and 11 Polk Street
Chicago, IL

William Murphy, manager—Browns
32 Walter St.
Chicago, IL

William Harvey, manager—Chicago Unions
2816 S. Dearborn Street
Chicago, IL

Al Jones, manager—Chicago Unions
2642 State Street
Chicago, IL

H. C. Cumberland, manager—East Ends
No. 464 West Polk Street
Chicago, IL

Frank Hanford, secretary—Gordons
4323 School Street
Chicago, IL

John O'Neil, manager—Gordons
4142 Wentworth Avenue
Chicago, IL

C. J. Sullivan, manager—Gordons
1968 West Twelfth Street
Chicago, IL

William A. Jones, manager—Hard Times
2642 State Street
Chicago, IL

D. H. McCarthy, manager—Independents
997 South Ashland Avenue
Chicago, IL

Joe Altmann, manager—Jolly Boys
104th Thirty-Forth Street
Chicago, IL

Walter Pigott, manager—Models
309 West Harrison Street
Chicago, IL

Ed Stewart, manager—Mutuals
Chicago Stamping Works, Harrison and Peoria
Chicago, IL

H. Raven, manager—South Branch Terrors
635 Fairfield Avenue
Chicago, IL

James L. Thomson, manager—Thomsons
No. 151 Dearborn Street
Chicago, IL

Walter Pigott, manager—Times
309 West Harrison Street
Chicago, IL

T. T. Farley, Secretary—Unions
No. 121 Wabash Avenue
Chicago, IL

Dick Hubbard, secretary—Uniques
Battery "D"
Chicago, IL

Richard "Dick" Hubbard, manager—Uniques
Battery "D"
Chicago, IL

Robert. P. Jackson, manager—Uniques
3729 Cottage Grove Ave.
Chicago, IL

H. H. Ash, Secretary—Union Juniors
162 Dearborn Street
Chicago, IL

John Duncan, manager—Union Juniors
Auditorium Theatre
Chicago, IL

William Harvey, secretary—Union Juniors
No. 2816 Dearborn Street
Chicago, IL

Charles Parker, manager—Union Juniors
105 LaSalle Street
Chicago, IL

James Smith, manager—Unique Juniors
2724 Dearborn Avenue
Chicago, IL

Albert De Leon, manager—Resolute Reserves
P. O. Box 9
Boston, MA

A. Gaskins, secretary—Resolute Reserves
14 Grove Street
Boston, MA

J. D. Gordon, manager—Resolute Reserves
P. O. Box 3662
Boston, MA

Theodore E. Roberts, manager—Resolutes
29 Union St.
Boston, MA

P. Pinder, manager—Pioneer Club
820 Parrish Street
Baltimore, MD

J. Johnson, manager—Browns
42 Charles Street
Detroit, MI

Charles Dixon, manager—Euchres
1422 North Eleventh Street
St. Louis, MO

J. Miller, manager—Mohawks
3004 Market Street
St. Louis, MO

Paul Chauvin, manager—North Ends
1101 North Eleventh Street
St. Louis, MO

Topsy Turley, manager—Red Onions
No 710 North Eleventh Street
St. Louis, MO

James Davis & James Tany, manager—South Ends
No. 1319 Morgan Street
St. Louis, MO

H. H. Jones, manager—West Ends
Mary Institute
27th and Locust Streets
St. Louis, MO

William Castone, manager—Giants
Tremont House
Lincoln, NE

Andrew Wells, manager—Fearless
Bridgeton, NJ

G. Harris, manager—Alpines
40 West Twenty-Sixth Street
New York, NY

J. M. Bright, manager—Cuban Giants
153 Prince Street
New York, NY

William Primrose, manager—Gorhams
153 Prince Street
New York, NY

James Pell, Jr., secretary—Fearless
40 Pearl Street
Utica, NY

Charles W. Titus, manager—Fearless
14 Post Street
Utica, NY

Mart Johnston, manager—Hollendens
No. 43 Forest Street
Cleveland, OH

William Wilson, manager—Maroons
No. 449 Sterling Avenue
Cleveland, OH

William H. Cole, manager—West Ends
No. 122 Oregon Street
Cleveland, OH

Charles Black, manager—Z Club
No. 64 Public Square
Cleveland, OH

Alonzo Smith, manager—Colored Base Ball Club
70 Seventh Avenue
Beaver Falls, PA

1892

S. Lincoln, secretary—Douglass Club
101 Q Street Northwest
Washington, DC

William Stitt Peters, manager—Chicago Unions
No. 199 South Clark Street
Chicago, IL

L. T. Brown, manager—Rattlers
No. 355 North Market Street
Wichita, KS

G. W. Saffell, manager—People's Enterprise
Frankfort, KY

J. D. Gordon, secretary—Resolute Reserves
Box 3662
Boston, MA

H. F. Hicks, manager—Resolute Reserves
20 ½ Howard Street
Boston, MA

P. Pinder, manager—Pioneer Club
820 Parrish Street
Baltimore, MD

Charles Bushong, manager—Actives
276 W. Sixth Street
Detroit, MI

Topsy Turley, manager—Red Onions
No. 710 North Eleventh Street
St. Louis, MO

Thomas Elliott, manager—Colored Nine
No. 11 Fire Station
1290 Independence Avenue
Kansas City, MO

Arthur Thomas, manager—Capital Citys
29 Barnes Street
Trenton, NJ

W. H. Freer, President—Athletics
No. 4 Parkhurst Block
Gloversville, NY

John M. Bright, manager—Cuban Giants
153 Prince Street
New York, NY

W. D. Davis, manager—Cuban Giants
No. 436 North Eighteenth Street
New York, NY

A. Davis, manager—Gorhams
137 ½ Bleecker Street
New York, NY

Louis Todd, manager—Condors
No 100 Chapple Street
Walnut Hills, OH

Charles G. Armstrong, Manager—Keystones
20 Wylie Avenue
Pittsburgh, PA

W. N. Broady, manager—Red Stockings
Plankinton House
Milwaukee, WI

Louis Jackson, secretary—Keystone Juniors
1024 Market Street
Wheeling, WV

1893

William S. Peters, Manager—Chicago Unions
No. 199 South Clark Street
Chicago, IL

Scipio Spinks, manager—Clippers
No. 3844 Dearborn Street
Chicago, IL

James Edward Bowen, Manager—Eclipse
No. 96 Dearborn St. / No. 96 Fenton St.
Chicago, IL

Dick Hubbard, manager—Uniques
Battery D
Chicago, IL

J. Callahan, manager—African Ramblers
50 Saxon St.
Boston, MA

Alfred Jupiter, manager—Colored Monarchs
1931 Washington Street; 5 Burlington Street
Boston, MA

W. Hawkins, manager—Glendons
11 Dartmouth Place
Boston, MA

William Griffin, manager—Red Stockings
Bolton St.
Boston, MA

R. M. Booker, manager—Resolute Reserves
6 Beacon Street
Boston, MA

F. Woodson, manager—Blues
566 Oak St.
Kansas City, MO

J. N. Clak, Secretary—Colored Nine
313 East 18th Street
Kansas City, MO

D. Gatewood, Manager—Fire Department No. 11
Engine House No. 11
Kansas City, MO

Joco Fields, secretary—Junction Hustlers
1612 ½ East 18th Street
Kansas City, MO

Joco Fields, secretary—Junior Blues
313 East 18th Street
Kansas City, MO

J. Payne, secretary—Junior Blues
707 Central Street
Kansas City, MO

I. W. Clark, secretary—Maroons
314 East 18th Street
Kansas City, MO

N. Johnson, manager—Clinton Stars
Corner of Clinton Avenue and Clinton Place
Irvington, NJ

E. Myers, secretary—Clinton Stars
Hawthorne Avenue
Irvington, NJ

Joe Smith, Jr., Team Captain—Clinton Stars
29 West Parker Street
Irvington, NJ

Dean Wilson, manager—Dean Wilsons
No. 79 Virginia Street
Buffalo, NY

H. Goggin, secretary—Internationals
International Hotel
Niagara Falls, NY

Benjamin F. Holmes, manager—Colored Nine
United States Hotel
Saratoga Springs, NY

John H. Settles, manager—Eels
413 West Fifth Street
Cincinnati, OH

Charles Pickney, secretary—Cuban Giants
116 South Park Avenue
York, PA

Frank Robinson, secretary—Colored Monarchs
126 East King Street
York, PA

1894

Frank Shirley, manager—Colored Barbers
Shirley's Barber Shop
Phoenix, AZ

J. M. Alexander, manager—Browns
171 North Spring Street
Los Angeles, CA

Lafayette Jefferson, manager—Market House
400 Center Market
Washington, DC

J. Betters, manager—Young Colts
1846 Thirteenth Street Northwest
Washington, DC

Tyler Crittenden, manager—Boycotts
2784 Armour Ave
Chicago, IL

William Stitt Peters, manager—Chicago Unions
No. 199 South Clark Street
Chicago, IL

William James Renfro, manager—Goodwins
2531 Armour Avenue
Chicago, IL

Charles Morgan, manager—Harlems
462 State St.
Chicago, IL

Robert Ward, manager—Ward's Unions
No. 464 State Street
Chicago, IL

Bud Wood and Wince Delorney, manager—Woods Base Ball Club
No. 464 State St.
Chicago, IL

Henry Robinson, secretary—Colored Nine
Denison Hotel
Indianapolis, IN

Charles Hill, secretary—Brownies
312 Pearl Street
Logansport, IN

P. Greenbury, manager—Blues
825 Independence Avenue
Kansas City, MO

Perry Stevens, Manager—IXLs
565 Grand Avenue
Kansas City, MO

James Moorman, manager—N. Y. Gorhams
27 Bergen Street
Newark, NJ

George Gibbs, secretary—Livingstons
No. 65 Silver Street
Rochester, NY

Albert Thomas, co-secretary—Livingstons
Livingston Hotel
Rochester, NY

Henry Williams, manager—Livingstons
Livingston Hotel
Rochester, NY

Benjamin F. Holmes, manager—Colored Nine
United States Hotel
Saratoga Springs, NY

James Pell, Jr., secretary—Fearless
40 Pearl Street
Utica, NY

Charles W. Titus, manager—Fearless
14 Post Street
Utica, NY

Richard W. Harris, manager—Logans
Circleville, OH

Edward J. Turner, manager—Euclids
No. 30 Quebec Street
Cleveland, OH

Edward J. Turner, manager—OK Hustlers
No. 30 Quebec Street
Cleveland, OH

Edward J. Turner, manager—West Ends
No. 30 Quebec Street
Cleveland, OH

John Jackson (Bud Fowler), manager—Giants
H22 North Main Street
Findlay, OH

John W. Lewis, manager—Morrisvilles
Box 114
Morrisville, PA

George Hazzard, manager—Giants
No. 720 Lombard Street
Philadelphia, PA

George Potter, secretary—Giants
326 Colder Street
Harrisburg, PA

George Pierce, Manager—Delmonicos
Bellefonte Street, East End
Pittsburgh, PA

Thomas White, Manager—Keystones
20 Wylie Avenue
Pittsburgh, PA

C. P. Robinson, manager—Eclipse Gray Jackets
3013 M. Street
Richmond, VA

1895

Lafayette Jefferson, manager—Market House
400 Center Market
Washington, DC

William Newman, manager—Mohawks
Fourteenth and D Streets Northwest
Washington, DC

J. Phillips, manager—Neversweats
No. 1255 Four-and-a-half Street Southwest
Washington, DC

John Howard (non-manager—colored ballplayer's address)
2730 Armour Ave.
Chicago, IL

George Scott, manager—Clippers
No. 2942 Armour Avenue
Chicago, IL

James Smith, manager—Clippers
No. 339 Twenty-Seventh Street
Chicago, IL

Grant Campbell, secretary—Chicago Giants
2023 Clark Street
Chicago, IL

Frank C. Leland, manager—Chicago Giants
No. 1205 State Street
Chicago, IL

William S. Peters, manager—Chicago Unions
No. 199 South Clark Street
Chicago, IL

C. J. Sullivan, manager—Gordons
1968 W. Twelfth Street
Chicago, IL

Louis Hoffman, manager—Dearborns
3603 Dearborn Street
Chicago, IL

John Mayer, manager—Delawares
1633 Michigan Avenue
Chicago, IL

Nick Williams, manager—Models
No. 3 East Lake Street.
Chicago, IL

H. R. Emerson, manager—Oakleys
No. 409 Marquette Building
Chicago, IL

T. T. Farley, manager—Unions
No. 121 Wabash Avenue
Chicago, IL

William Cobden, manager—Warrens
No. 1047 West Madison Street
No. 1014 West Madison Street
Chicago, IL

John Rhodes, manager—Black Diamonds
292 East Wayne Street
Fort Wayne, IN

Henry Robinson, secretary—Colored Nine
Denison Hotel
Indianapolis, IN

Maurice White, manager—Herculean
98 West Washington Street
Indianapolis, IN

M. F. White, secretary—Herculeans
78 West Washington Street
Indianapolis, IN

Walter A. Alexander, manager—Quicksteps
29 North Tryon St.
Charlotte, NC

George Stevenson, captain—Quicksteps
No. 8 East Trade Street
Charlotte, NC

F. Johnson, manager—Colored Nine
29 Garfield Avenue
Bordentown, NJ

William Clark, manager—Douglass
Powers Hotel
Rochester, NY

R. M. Attwell, manager—Niantics
571 Putnam Avenue
Brooklyn, NY

Ambrose Davis, manager—Gorhams
461 Sixth Avenue
New York, NY

John H. Settles, manager—Eels
413 West Fifth Street
Cincinnati, OH

William H. Cole, manager—Hollenden Athletic Club
No. 122 Oregon Street
Cleveland, OH

George Hazzard, manager—Giants
No. 720 Lombard Street
Philadelphia, PA

T. B. Jones, manager—Phalanx
Charlottesville, VA

W. F. Walker, secretary—Phalanx
Charlottesville, VA

Buck Spottswood, manager—Manhattan Giants
North 17th Street
Richmond, VA

1896

Lafayette Jefferson, manager—Market House
400 Center Market
Washington, DC

John Wallace, manager—Mohawks
72 Canal Street Southwest
Washington, DC

John Wallace, manager—Pat Smiths
72 Canal Street, SN
Washington, DC
Al Hackley (business address)
36th Street between State and Dearborn Streets
Chicago, IL

Andrew Porter, manager—Avondales
2598 Milwaukee Avenue
Chicago, IL

Frank C. Leland, manager—Chicago Unions
No. 1206 State Street
Chicago, IL

William Stitt Peters, manager—Chicago Unions
No. 1175 North Forty-Fourth Street
Chicago, IL

M. Mitchell, manager—Clippers (formerly the Lone Stars)
No. 563 State Street Flat 14
Chicago, IL

George Scott, manager—Clippers
2942 Armour Avenue
Chicago, IL

Julius N. Avendorph, manager—Emergencies
No. 1410 Champlain Building
Chicago, IL

P. D. Arnett, manager—Flippers
No. 717 37th Street
Chicago, IL

William Stitt Peters, manager—Fosters (17 year-old club)
No. 1175 North Forty-Fourth Street
Chicago, IL

Frank C. Leland, manager—Giants
No. 1265 State Street
Chicago, IL

E. Davis, manager—Mohawks
3119 Wash Street
Chicago, IL

William Coats, manager—Oakley Juniors
No. 85 Miller Street
Chicago, IL

William Cobden, manager—Warrens
No. 1258 Monroe Street
Chicago, IL

Walter Carter, secretary—Clippers
Coffeyville, KS

John H. B. Wilson, secretary—Black Diamonds
Little Sunbeam
Chetopa, KS

H. F. Hicks, manager—Resolute Reserves
20 ½ Howard Street
Boston, MA

C. C. Patterson, Manager—Portland B.B.C.
Rockville, MD

R. Oliver, Manager—Optimate Giants
65 Lincoln Park
Newark, NJ

John M. Bright, manager—Cuban Giants
130 Varick Street
New York, NY

E. B. Lamar, manager—Cuban X-Giants
134th Street and Anne's Avenue
New York, NY

Benjamin "Kid" Brown, Manager—Gorhams
450 Sixth Avenue
New York, NY

Benjamin M. Butler, manager—Uniques
189 Bleecker Street
New York, NY

John H. Settles, manager—Eels
413 West Fifth Street
Cincinnati, OH

Jason M. Tilley, manager—Hollendens
No. 91 Sheriff Street
Cleveland, OH

Edward Turner, manager—Hollendens
No. 152 Brownell Street
Cleveland, OH

Robert Colwell, manager—Keystones
No. 91 Sheriff Street
Cleveland, OH

John Joice, secretary—Colored Monarchs
118 South Duke Street
York, PA

John Joice, manager—Cuban Giants
118 South Duke Street
York, PA

W. B. Moore, manager—Colored Nine
Box E 6
Corsicana, TX

George D. Johnson, manager—Chamberlains
Chamberlain Hotel
Old Pointe Comfort, VA

Thomas H. Jackson, manager—Eclipse
809 North Jackson 30th Street
Richmond, VA

Willie Bowles, manager—Imperials
731 North 2nd Street
Richmond, VA

1897

Julius N. Avendorph, manager—Emergencies
No 125 Dearborn Street
Chicago, IL

P. D. Arnett, manager—Flippers
No 717 37th Street
Chicago, IL

William Cook, manager—East End Stars
1729 East Jackson Street
Springfield, IL

A. W. Stewart, manager—Brotherhood
519 W. Broadway
Louisville, KY

George W. Allen, manager—Atlantics
352 Washington Street
Boston, MA

William A. Walker, manager—Resolute Reserves
Saville's Hotel
Boston, MA

Bob Rooker, manager—Resolute Reserves
c/o Barney Gray
78 Phillips
Boston, MA

William A. Walker, manager—Resolutes
Saville's Hotel
Boston, MA

J. H. Dixon, manager—Franklins
872 Broadway.
South Boston, MA

William T. Jordan, Manager—Pennsylvanias
709 Pennsylvania Avenue
Baltimore, MD

J. E. Lowell, manager—Maroons
617 East Fifteenth Street
Kansas City, MO

Lewis H. Cameron, manager—Colored Nine
Fayetteville, NC

William Lincoln, manager—Colored Nine
1006 Capital Avenue
Omaha, NE

Theodore Green, Captain—Colored Giants
93 Bank Street
Newark, NJ

Fred Heberle, Captain—Elwoods
35 Railroad Avenue, c/o Stuckey & Heck
Newark, NJ

Joseph Laveign, Manager—Colored Giants
154 Market Street
Newark, NJ

M. M. Laveign, Secretary—Colored Giants
154 Market Street
Newark, NJ

Bert Rolinson, Captain—Mohawk Colored Giants
208 Broome Street
Newark, NJ

John H. Savington, manager—Golden Leaf
257 ½ Chestnut Street
Passaic, NJ

George Stout, Captain—Rowans
11 Beaver Street
Trenton, NJ

M. R. Ross, manager—Colored Field Club
604 Franklin Avenue
Brooklyn, NY

Benjamin M. Butler, manager—Colored Giants
No. 125 MacDougal Street
New York, NY

Ambrose Davis, manager—Gorhams
450 Sixth Avenue
New York, NY

M. D. Bright, manager—Cuban Giants
448 West Broadway
New York, NY

E. B. Lamar, manager—Cuban X-Giants
1792 Bathgate Avenue
New York, NY

F. Gilmore, manager—Douglass
No. 123 West Main Street
Rochester, NY

James Pell, Jr., assistant manager—Help-Ups
18 Post Avenue
Utica, NY

Charles W. Titus, manager—Help-Ups
18 Post Avenue
Utica, NY

John H. Settles, manager—Eels
413 West Fifth Street
Cincinnati, OH

Richard W. Harris, manager—Logans
Circleville, OH

William H. Cole, manager—Keystones
No. 91 Sheriff Street
Cleveland, OH

Jason M. Lilly, manager—Keystones
No. 91 Sheriff Street
Cleveland, OH

Edward J. Williams, manager—Oberlins
No. 29 East Vine Street
Oberlin, OH

G. W. Benson, manager—Cross Cuts
1414 Tenth Avenue
Altoona, PA

William Banks, manager—Cuban Giants
450 Hay Street
Harrisburg, PA

Benjamin Smith, manager—Cuban Giants
1314 Marion Street
Harrisburg, PA

Benjamin Smith, manager—Marines (formerly Cuban Giants)
1314 Marion Street
Harrisburg, PA

John J. Garrett, manager—Pennlyn Giants
619 Chestnut Street
Pennlyn, PA

William Adams, secretary—Pinkney Giants
1230 Kater Street
Philadelphia, PA

T. H. Jackson, manager—Eclipse
809 North 30th Street
Richmond, VA

C. P. Robinson, assistant manager—Eclipse
809 North 30th Street
Richmond, VA

Willie Bowles, manager—Imperials
731 North 2nd Street
Richmond, VA

Alex Price, manager—Klondikes
192 Third Street
Milwaukee, WI

1898

William Carroll, manager—Trilbys
118 San Pedro Street
Los Angeles, CA

Frank Griggs, manager—Clippers
No 464 State Street
Chicago, IL

Frank Butler, manager—Exiles
Cloud Court and State Street
Chicago, IL

Fred Wright, manager—Records
226 ½ South Fifth Street
Springfield, IL

John Weaver, manager—Diamond Joe's
423 East Madison Street
Louisville, KY

O. T. Adams, Manager—Olymps
525 Brook Street
Louisville, KY

George W. Allen, manager—Atlantics
352 Washington Street
Boston, MA

W. T. Johnson, manager—Atlantics
16 Piedmont
Boston, MA

Fletcher McGuire, manager—J. D. Dillworths
Sears Building
Boston, MA

Walter Williams, manager—Colored Blues
709 Pennsylvania Avenue
Baltimore, MD

William T. Jordan, manager—Detroits
510 St. Paul Baltimore Street
Baltimore, MD

J. W. Stevens, manager—Page Fence Giants
Adrian, MI

A. C. Vernon, manager—Blues
369 North Lexington Street
Harrisonville, MO

Charles Joiner, manager—Tigers
Lexington, MO

James O'Brien, manager—Black Selects
1619 Washington Street
Kansas City, MO

George Jones, manager—Bradburys
1000 Walnut Street
Kansas City, MO

George Jones, manager—Bradburys
1500 Walnut Street
Kansas City, MO

James O'Brien, manager—Colored Porters
151 Walnut Street
Kansas City, MO

Frank Montgomery, manager—Moonlights
100 West Ninth Street
Kansas City, MO

Henry Hewett, manager—Times Hustlers
15 West Sixth Street
Kansas City, MO

Harry Curtis, manager—Acme Colored Giants
Box 11
Hawthorne, NJ

Rufus Peterson, manager—Hamiltons
33 ½ Bright Street
Jersey City, NJ

B. Burke, manager—Colored Giants
49 Hickory Street
Orange, NJ

H. B. French, manager—Jersey Cubans
19 State Street
Passaic, NJ

Harry Curtis, manager—Acme Colored Giants
84 Cortland Street
New York, NY

Harry Curtis, manager—Acme Colored Giants
98 Duane Street
New York, NY

E. B. Lamar, manager—Cuban X-Giants
N. E. Corner 134th Street and St Anne's Avenue
New York, NY

John L. Jacobs, manager—Nonpareil Athletics
22 Seneca Street
Utica, NY

Charles W. Titus, assistant manager—Nonpareil Athletics
22 Seneca Street
Utica, NY

John H. Settles, manager—Eels
413 West Fifth Street
Cincinnati, OH

Pearly Williams, manager—Douglass
1309 Lombard Street
Philadelphia, PA

Alex Price, manager—Klondikes
102 Third Street
Milwaukee, WI

1899

Frank Shirley, manager—Bullys
Shirley's Barber Shop
Phoenix, AZ

J. M. Booker, manager—Pastimes
Alamo Hotel
Colorado Springs, CO

Percy McCloud, manager—Black Diamonds
Mason Street (between 15th and 16th streets)
Springfield, IL

Samuel Gibbs, manager—Brotherhood
Louisville, KY

O. T. Adams, manager—Olymps
525 Brook Street
Louisville, KY

B. F. Tate, manager—Riversides
Sanborn House
Boston, MA

Walter Smith, manager—Atlantics
Sidney Street
Lowell, MA

Joseph A. Ivy, manager—Riversides
4 Middletown Street
Malden, MA

William T. Jordan, manager—Colored Giants
709 Pennsylvania Avenue
Baltimore, MD

George Jones, manager—Bradburys
1000 Walnut Street
Kansas City, MO

William Houston, manager—Lincoln High
c/o The Journal Sporting Editor
Kansas City, MO

Erville Moppins, manager—Moonlight Juniors
559 Harrison
Kansas City, MO

Frank Montgomery, manager—Moonlights
Dental Parlors (upstairs)
900 Main Street
Kansas City, MO

Frank Montgomery, manager—Moonlights
Bunker Building
100 West Ninth Street
Kansas City, MO

A. L. Dorsey, Manager—Unions
1816 East Eighth Street
Kansas City, MO

James Wear, Secretary—Unions
1009 East Twelfth Street
Kansas City, MO

"Toots" Woodson, manager—Times
Sixth and Walnut Streets
Kansas City, MO

Richard Adams, manager—Evans Laundrys
824 P Street
Lincoln, NE

Walter Jacobus, manager—Gorhams
1214 Park Avenue
Rutherford, NJ

H. B. French, manager—Jersey Cubans
19 State Street
Passaic, NJ

L. Howard, Manager—Alpines
79th Fourth Place
Brooklyn, NY

John H. Settles, manager—Eels
413 West Fifth Street
Cincinnati, OH

William H. Mack, manager—Chester Giants
909 Fillmore Street
Chester, PA

Clinton E. Smith, Manager—Acme Giants
No. 630
Homestead, PA

Clinton E. Smith, Manager—Cuban Giants
No. 630
Homestead, PA

L. W. Canon, Manager—Dewey Athletic Association
1008 S. Bouvier Street
Philadelphia, PA

W. L. Johnson, manager—Queen City Grays
Clarksville, TN

C. T. Brown, manager—Red Stockings
697 Church Street
Norfolk, VA

1900

Frank Shirley, manager—Braves
Shirley's Barber Shop
Phoenix, AZ

L. H. King, manager—Clark University
South Atlanta, GA

William Brown, manager—Clippers
2836 State Street
Chicago, IL

O. T. Adams, manager—Olymps
525 Brook Street
Louisville, KY

G. W. Allen, manager—Winsors
312 Washington Street
Boston, MA

Joseph A. Ivy, manager—Riversides
4 Middletown Street
Malden, MA

William T. Jordan, manager—Colored Giants
709 Pennsylvania Avenue
Baltimore, MD

A. L. Dorsey, manager—Unions
1816 East Eighth Street
Kansas City, MO

William Keeble, manager—Athletic Club
907 East Market Street
Greensboro, NC

Gus Turner, Manager—Manhattan Cuban Giants
8 Hill Street
Orange, NJ

H. B. French, manager—Jersey Cubans
19 State Street
Passaic, NJ

William Tobin, manager—Widewakes
No. 8 117 Oneida Street
Syracuse, NJ

George Frost, secretary—Cuban X-Giants, Jrs.
No. 8 Belvidere Street
Trenton, NJ

George Frost, manager—Orient
No. 322 Calhoun Street
Trenton, NJ

Thomas, secretary—Orient
No. 322 Calhoun Street
Trenton, NJ

Oscar Bright, manager—Cuban Giants
No. 167 Elm Street
Buffalo, NY

George A. Smith, manager—Y. M. S. C.
No. 140 Lincoln Street
Flushing, NY

Leander Webb, manager—Centrals
No. 162 South Ninth Avenue
Mount Vernon, NY

Mosses Corbin, manager—Colored Union League
Nos. 158 and 160 Twenty-Ninth Street
New York, NY

E. B. Lamar, Jr., manager—Cuban X-Giants
766 East 176th Street
New York, NY

J. M. Bright, manager—Genuine Cuban Giants
Empire Flats
Hancock Street
New York, NY

J. M. Bright, manager—Genuine Cuban Giants
174 West Houston Street
New York, NY

Benjamin M. Butler, manager—Newark Colored Giants
No. 125 Macdougal Street
New York, NY

John Titus, manager—Colored Giants
11 Broadway
Utica, NY

John H. Settles, manager—Eels
413 West Fifth Street
Cincinnati, OH

William Turner, manager—Keystones
No. 450 Erie Street
Cleveland, OH

A. S. Peal, manager—All-American Black Tourists
78 North Third Street
Columbus, OH

Jack Potter, secretary—Cuban Giants
328 Calder Street
Harrisburg, PA

W. S. Hunt, manager—Cliffords
275 Main Street
Memphis, TN